Fodor's

NEW YORK STATE
FIRST EDITION

Where to Stay and Eat
for All Budgets

Must-See Sights
and Local Secrets

Ratings You Can Trust

Fodor's Travel Publications   New York, Toronto, London, Sydney, Auckland
www.fodors.com

FODOR'S NEW YORK STATE
Editor: Chris Swiac

Editorial Production: Tom Holton

Editorial Contributors: Gary Allen, Lynne Arany, Karen Bjornland, Doug Blackburn, Heather Buchanan, Mary Bulkot, Collin Campbell, Mary Catt, Andrew Collins, Marianne Comfort, Kathie Connelly, Tania Garcia de Rosier, John J. Donohue, Ruth Fantasia, Erica Freudenberger, Joanne Furio, Melisse Gelula, Bob Goepfert, Gwendolen Groocock, Ann Hammerle, Breath A. V. Hand, Melissa Hantman, Elise Harris, Richard Haubert, Steve Hopkins, Jan Hughes, Satu Hummasti, Gail Jaffe-Bennek, Elizabeth Weber Johnson, Anne Johnston, Lisa S. Kahn, Wendy Kagan, Evelyn Kanter, Diana Niles King, Donna Kirdahy, Wendy Liberatore, Karen Little, Margaret Mittelbach, Jennifer Paull, Janet Pope, Jeanne Sager, Patti Singer, Sarah S. Sper, Tom Steele, Mark Sullivan

Maps: David Lindroth, *cartographer*; Bob Blake and Rebecca Baer, *map editors*

Design: Fabrizio La Rocca, *creative director*; Guido Caroti, *art director*; Moon Sun Kim, *cover designer*; Melanie Marin, *senior picture editor*

Production/Manufacturing: Colleen Ziemba

Cover Photo (Mohonk Preserve): Peter Guttman

First Edition

ISBN 1–4000–1378–X

SPECIAL SALES
This book is available for special discounts for bulk purchases for sales promotions or premiums. Special editions, including personalized covers, excerpts of existing books, and corporate imprints, can be created in large quantities for special needs. For more information, write to Special Markets/Premium Sales, 1745 Broadway, MD 6-2, New York, New York 10019, or e-mail specialmarkets@randomhouse.com.

AN IMPORTANT TIP & AN INVITATION
Although all prices, opening times, and other details in this book are based on information supplied to us at press time, changes occur all the time in the travel world, and Fodor's cannot accept responsibility for facts that become outdated or for inadvertent errors or omissions. So **always confirm information when it matters,** especially if you're making a detour to visit a specific place. Your experiences—positive and negative—matter to us. If we have missed or misstated something, **please write to us.** We follow up on all suggestions. Contact the New York State editor at editors@fodors.com or c/o Fodor's at 1745 Broadway, New York, New York 10019.

PRINTED IN THE UNITED STATES OF AMERICA

10 9 8 7 6 5 4 3 2 1

ON THE ROAD WITH FODOR'S

When you're on the road, concerns of life at home completely disappear, driven away by more immediate thoughts—about, say, what marvels will beguile the next day or where you'll have dinner. That's where Fodor's comes in. We make sure that you know all your options, so that you don't miss something that's around the next bend just because you didn't know it was there. Because the best memories of your trip might well have nothing to do with what you came to New York to see, we guide you to sights large and small all over the state. You might set out to see Niagara Falls, but back at home you find yourself unable to forget those extra-spicy Buffalo wings you had in a pub. With Fodor's at your side, serendipitous discoveries are never far away.

Our success in showing you every corner of New York State is a credit to our extraordinary writers, nearly all of whom live, work, and play in the Empire State. Although there's no substitute for travel advice from a good friend who knows your style, our contributors are the next best thing—the kind of people you would poll for travel advice if you knew them.

For their research, reporting, and writing for this guide, the editor gratefully acknowledges Gary Allen, Karen Bjornland, Doug Blackburn, Mary Bulkot, Collin Campbell, Mary Catt, Andrew Collins, Kathie Connelly, Tania Garcia de Rosier, Ruth Fantasia, Erica Freudenberger, Joanne Furio, Bob Goepfert, Gwendolen Groocock, Ann Hammerle, Breath A. V. Hand, Richard Haubert, Steve Hopkins, Jan Hughes, Gail Jaffe-Bennek, Elizabeth Weber Johnson, Anne Johnston, Wendy Kagan, Donna Kirdahy, Wendy Liberatore, Janet Pope, Jeanne Sager, and Patti Singer.

CONTENTS

ABOUT THIS BOOK

The best source for travel advice is a like-minded friend who's just been where you're headed. But with or without that friend, you'll be in great shape to find your way around New York State once you've learned to find your way around your Fodor's guide.

SELECTION

Our goal is to cover the best properties, sights, and activities in their category, as well as the most interesting communities to visit. We make a point of including local food lovers' hot spots as well as neighborhood options, and we avoid all that's touristy unless it's really worth your time. You can go on the assumption that everything in this book is recommended by our writers and editors. It goes without saying that no property pays to be included.

RATINGS

Orange stars ★ denote places that our editors and writers consider the very best in the area covered by the entire book. Most of these, the best of the best, are listed in the Fodor's Choice section in the front of the book. Black stars ★ highlight the sights and properties we deem Highly Recommended, the don't-miss sights within any region. In cities, sights pinpointed with numbered map bullets ❶ in the margins tend to be more important than those without bullets.

SPECIAL SPOTS

Pleasures & Pastimes and the chapter-title pages focus on experiences that reveal the spirit of the destination. Off the Beaten Path sights may be out of the way or quirky; all are worthwhile. When the munchies hit, look for Need a Break? suggestions.

TIME IT RIGHT

Check On the Calendar up front and the chapters' Timing sections for weather and crowd overviews and best times to visit.

SEE IT ALL

Use Fodor's exclusive Great Itineraries as a model for your trip. (For a good overview of the state, mix regional itineraries from several chapters.) Good Walks guide you to important sights in New York City and Albany; ▶ indicates the starting point of walks and itineraries in the text and on the map.

BUDGET WELL

Hotel and restaurant price categories from ¢ to $$$$ are defined in the opening pages of each chapter—expect to find a balanced selection for every budget. For attractions, we always give standard adult admission fees; reductions are usually available for children, students, and senior citizens. Want to pay with plastic? AE, D, DC, MC, V following restaurant and hotel listings indicate whether American Express, Discover, Diners Club, MasterCard, or Visa are accepted.

BASIC INFO

Smart Travel Tips lists travel essentials for the state; city- and region-specific basics end each chapter. To find the best way to get around, see the transportation section; see individual modes of travel ("Car Travel," "Train Travel") for details.

ON THE MAPS	Maps throughout the book show you what's where and help you find your way around. Black and orange numbered bullets ❶ ❶ in the text correlate to bullets on maps.
BACKGROUND	We give background information within the chapters in the course of explaining sights as well as in **CloseUp** boxes and in **Understanding New York** at the end of the book, which includes a **chronology** section.
FIND IT FAST	Within the book, chapters are arranged in a roughly counterclockwise direction, starting with New York City. Chapters are divided into small regions, within which towns are covered in geographical order; attractive routes and interesting places between towns are flagged as **En Route**. Heads at the top of each page help you find what you need.
DON'T FORGET	**Restaurants** are open for lunch and dinner daily unless we state otherwise; we mention dress only when there's a specific requirement and reservations only when they're essential or not accepted—it's always best to book ahead. **Hotels** have private baths, phone, TVs, and air-conditioning and operate on the European Plan (EP, meaning without meals) or, if indicated at the end of the service information after the review, CP (Continental Plan, with Continental breakfast), BP (Breakfast Plan, with full breakfast), MAP (Modified American Plan, with breakfast and dinner), or AI (all-inclusive, with breakfast, lunch, and dinner). We always list facilities but not whether you'll be charged extra to use them.
SYMBOLS	

Many Listings
- ★ Fodor's Choice
- ★ Highly recommended
- ⊠ Physical address
- ↔ Directions
- ⌂ Mailing address
- ☎ Telephone
- 🖷 Fax
- ⊕ On the Web
- ✉ E-mail
- 🎟 Admission fee
- ☉ Open/closed times
- ► Start of walk/itinerary
- Ⓜ Metro stations
- ☴ Credit cards

Outdoors
- 🏌 Golf
- ⚠ Camping

Hotels & Restaurants
- 🏨 Hotel
- 🛏 Number of rooms
- ⌂ Facilities
- ⏣ Meal plans
- ✕ Restaurant
- ⌂ Reservations
- 🏛 Dress code
- ↘ Smoking
- 🆋 BYOB
- ✕🏨 Hotel with restaurant that warrants a visit

Other
- ☾ Family-friendly
- 🛈 Contact information
- ⇨ See also
- ⊠ Branch address
- ☞ Take note

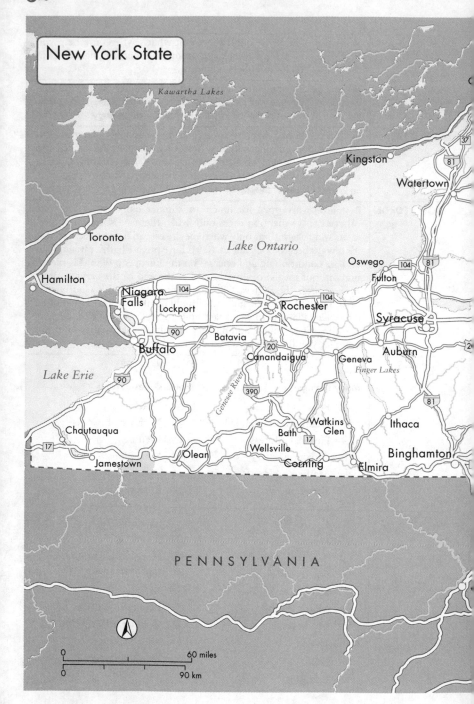

New York State

Kawartha Lakes

Kingston

Watertown

Toronto

Lake Ontario

Oswego

Hamilton

Fulton

Niagara Falls

104

Lockport

Rochester

104

Syracuse

90

Batavia

Auburn

Buffalo

Canandaigua

20

Geneva

Finger Lakes

Lake Erie

90

390

81

Watkins Glen

Ithaca

Chautauqua

Bath

17

Binghamton

Olean

Wellsville

Corning

Elmira

Jamestown

17

Genesee River

PENNSYLVANIA

0   60 miles

0   90 km

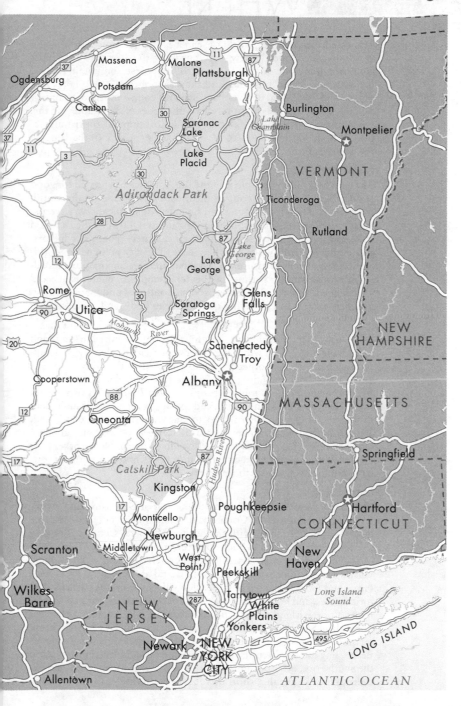

WHAT'S WHERE

The essence of the Empire State can be distilled down to a single word: diversity. Indeed, New York has more to see and do than most countries. It has miles of oceanfront, rolling forests, mountain ranges, dizzying peaks, and plunging cataracts. More than 4,000 lakes and ponds, and 70,000 mi of rivers and streams course through its almost 50,000 square mi. This section reflects the order of the chapters in this guide. New York City, by far the state's most popular tourist attraction, is first; western New York, on the opposite side of the state, is the final region.

1 New York City

More than 35 million people visit the Big Apple each year, and for good reason. New York City is one of the most exciting cities in the world. It's a national hub for banking and finance, communications, advertising, fashion, sports, and publishing. And it can rightly be called a world cultural capital: Artists, actors, musicians, writers, poets, conductors, and craftspeople all work and play here. The city is home to world-renowned museums of nature, film, and fine and contemporary art; Broadway showcases and experimental theaters; temples of haute cuisine and streets lined with ethnic eateries; stylish boutiques and mammoth department stores; and glittering dance palaces and standing-room-only jazz clubs.

Some insist that the real New York inhabits only Manhattan, an island 13 mi long and 2.3 mi wide, but others counter that the city is incomplete without the four other boroughs—Brooklyn, the Bronx, Queens, and Staten Island. Including Manhattan, the boroughs encompass 301 square mi and house 8 million people. Staten Island is its own island (to the southwest of Manhattan), and the Bronx is part of the mainland. Brooklyn and Queens swarm over the far western end of Long Island. With so much ground to cover, New York can feel overwhelming at times. One key to staving off this feeling is to do as native New Yorkers do: view the city as a collection of neighborhoods. Choose one area as your base and then venture forth into a few others.

2 Long Island

The island stretches about 120 mi to the east of New York City, parallel to the southern coast of Connecticut. A narrow spurt of land, its shape resembles that of a fish, with the head, or far west section, belonging to the New York City boroughs of Brooklyn and Queens. The tail, or east, end is split into two narrow fingers referred to as forks. Although known for its suburban sprawl, Long Island also has rural areas with farms and vineyards, charming seaside villages, glorious gardens, historic houses, and magnificent mansions of the omnipresent rich and famous. On the island's northern shore are the beaches and harbors of Long Island Sound, where Great Gatsby châteaux politely elbow for room on the Gold Coast. Spectacular sandy stretches, including those of Jones Beach, hug the southern flank of the island. The fabled Hamptons, on the South Fork, offer fashionable shopping streets, art galleries, and excellent restaurants, all a short drive away from the ocean.

③ The Hudson Valley

The region stretches along the scenic Hudson River from just north of New York City to Columbia County's northern border, narrowing as you travel north. On the west side of the river are the Palisades, Shawangunks, and Catskills; on the east are the Taconic Mountains. The beauty of the untamed valley—dramatic palisades, pine forests, cool mountain lakes and streams—inspired early American landscape painters and spurred the creation of the Hudson River school of art, which originated in the 19th century. It also prompted Vanderbilts, Rockefellers, Astors, and many other wealthy families to build spectacular riverfront mansions, some of which are now open to the public. Among these is Springwood, the birthplace and home of Franklin Delano Roosevelt. Nearby, occupying its own spot on the river, is the Culinary Institute of America, one of the top training grounds for up-and-coming restaurateurs—many of whom ultimately open up shop in the valley.

Throughout the region, historic sites chronicle the development of the state as well as of the country. West Point, for one, has been molding young men (and now young women) into army officers since 1802. River villages harbor intimate cafés, small museums, art galleries, antiques shops, and quirky boutiques. Deeper inland are sleepy hamlets scattered along country roads that bring you to apple orchards, dairy farms, wine trails, and farm markets. The numerous state parks serve as four-season playgrounds, and rock climbers come from around the world to conquer the Shawangunks (aka the Gunks). The Storm King Art Center and Dia:Beacon are highlights for art lovers, and the Woodbury Common outlet center lures hordes of shoppers. Seven Hudson River bridges allow travelers to sample the best of both shores.

④ The Catskills

This huge region to the west of the Hudson Valley encompasses parts of Ulster, Greene, Schoharie, Sullivan, Orange, and Delaware counties. At its heart are the Catskill Mountains, which rise between the Hudson River to the east and the upper Delaware and Susquehanna rivers to the south and west. They are one of the most visited, written-about, and painted mountain ranges in the country. The peaks climb as high as 4,200 feet, so it's no wonder that the Algonquins called them Onteora, or "land in the sky." These "fairy mountains," as writer Washington Irving once referred to them, contain dense forests, rock-walled gorges, and large lakes, and are veined with hiking and skiing trails.

The Catskills tradition of hospitality started during the 19th-century resort boom, when thousands of vacationers came to escape the city's swelter in the cool, dry atmosphere of the region. The first resort, the Catskill Mountain House, was built near Haines Falls, in the northern Catskills, in the 1820s. Later, Russian and Eastern European Jews, who weren't always welcome in other resort areas, started coming to the southern Catskills, and the area around Liberty and Monticello was nicknamed the Borscht Belt. Big resort hotels and abundant golf courses are the main draws for the young families and retirees who vacation in this area today. Throughout the region, one-traffic-light hamlets and small villages, including the arts colony of Woodstock, are the rule, and the great outdoors is the main attraction. World-class trout streams (namely the Beaver Kill, the Esopus, and the east and west branches of the Delaware River) flow through the region, which also encompasses wide valleys and open farmland. The high-peaks region of Greene and Ulster counties lures hikers and skiers.

⑤ The Capital Region

Near the juncture of the Hudson and Mohawk rivers lies Albany, the state capital and regional commercial center. Despite startling differences in architectural eras, Albany's stylistic juxtaposition achieves a curious harmony. The Empire State Plaza provides a spectacular introduction to the city's center. Against the modern backdrop of this government complex and its futuristic landmark Egg (formally the Empire State Performing Arts Center) stands the state capitol, an impressive example of château architecture that boasts the Romanesque Million Dollar Staircase. The sculptures and modern artworks that populate the plaza constitute a don't-miss attraction in their own right. Within 10 mi of Albany are the smaller cities of Troy and Schenectady.

To the north is Saratoga Springs, which at the turn of the 20th century was one of the nation's premier summer resorts. Whether visitors came to take the mineral waters or to wager on their favorite racehorse, Saratoga offered hedonistic seduction. Today the main street is lined with shops, hotels, galleries, and bistros, and Saratoga Springs remains a cultural and recreational draw. Visitors still come to soak in the soothing mineral springs, to see and hear world-class music and dance at the Saratoga Performing Arts Center, and from late July through August to watch the races at the nation's oldest Thoroughbred track. Nearby are several Revolutionary War sites, including that of the Battle of Saratoga, which halted the British invasion from Canada and turned the war in the rebels' favor.

⑥ Central New York

The region forms a triangle in the area bounded by Albany in the east, Syracuse in the west, the Adirondacks in the north, and the Catskill Mountains in the south. It's often referred to as Leatherstocking Country, so named for the leather breeches worn by the region's New England settlers. Dairy farms and white-spired churches reflect the area's Yankee heritage. The region's crown jewel is Cooperstown. Most people know it as the home of the National Baseball Hall of Fame, but its small-town charms appeal even to those who aren't fans of the national pastime. Classical-music lovers schedule trips in July and August, so as not to miss the highly regarded Glimmerglass Opera.

Along the region's northern edge is the historic Mohawk Valley, which winds through the Adirondack foothills, following the Mohawk River as it slices through rolling woodlands, farms, and pastures. The area was of great tactical importance during the American Revolution. The bloodiest battle of the war is said to have occurred at the Oriskany Battle-field, near Rome. Erie Canal Village marks the spot in Rome where, in 1817, the first shovelful of dirt was turned for the 363-mi waterway between Albany and Buffalo. Utica, the region's largest city, is at the west end of the Mohawk Valley and near the exact geographic center of the state. It's home to the Munson-Williams-Proctor Arts Institute, a museum that occupies an 1850 Italianate mansion and a 1960 Philip Johnson structure; the collection of Hudson River school paintings is a highlight here. Oneida and Amsterdam are the other cities in the region.

⑦ The Finger Lakes

Water and wineries are two of the defining features of this region, which stretches from the Pennsylvania border in the south to Lake Ontario in the north. The 11 long and skinny north–south lakes, collectively called the Finger Lakes, were created by retreating Ice Age glaciers that gouged deep holes in the earth a million years ago. Deep gorges and rushing falls contrast with wide fertile valleys and lend drama to the surrounding landscape. Watkins Glen State Park alone has 19 waterfalls, and the cascade in Taughannock Falls State Park is 30 feet higher than Niagara Falls. Ithaca, an urbane college town at the south end of Cayuga Lake, is surrounded by spectacular gorges. The glaciers also created excellent conditions for growing grapes, and the region today is home to 70-plus vineyards and wineries, most with tasting rooms.

The major cities are Syracuse and Rochester, in the region's more industrial and urban northern tier. In Rochester, the birthplace of the Kodak camera and film, Kodak founder George Eastman's mansion and lovely gardens are open for tours. Most of the rest of the region still shows its rural roots, with dairy farms, small villages, and stunning examples of 19th-century architecture dotting the landscape. Overlooking Cayuga Lake, Aurora has a main street lined with colonial, Federal, and Victorian architecture as well as examples of other building styles. Historic sites include Seneca Falls, where the first Women's Rights Convention was held in 1848. In Geneva, Frederick Douglas and Sojourner Truth participated in Emancipation celebrations in the 1800s. The Seneca Lake city is also known for the rich variety of its architecture, which includes Federal, Victorian Gothic, and Jeffersonian styles, among others. Corning, a few miles from the Pennsylvania border in the region's southern tier, is home to the must-see Corning Museum of Glass, one of the top attractions in the state.

⑧ The North Country

The region is bordered by the Mohawk River valley on the south, Lake Ontario and the St. Lawrence River valley on the west and north, and Lake Champlain on the east. It encompasses the Adirondacks and the Thousand Islands area. Much of the region is covered by Adirondack Park, a checkerboard of public and private lands that encompasses 6 million acres (an area larger than the state of New Jersey), 1,000 mi of rivers, 30,000 mi of brooks and streams, more than 3,000 lakes and ponds, and 1.3 million acres of forest. Nearly half the park has been designated "forever wild" by the state. The famed High Peaks area contains the 46 highest peaks in the Adirondacks, most of them surpassing 4,000 feet. On Mt. Marcy, the highest at 5,344 feet, Lake Tear of the Clouds is considered to be the source of the Hudson River. Just north is Lake Placid, site of the 1980 Winter Olympics and still a year-round sports hub. Nearby are Whiteface Mountain, the east's highest ski slope, and the pristine St. Regis Wilderness Canoe Area. The Champlain Valley, which skirts the region on the east, starts just north of the Lake George summer resort area and stretches to the border with Canada. Prime among its attractions are Fort Ticonderoga, built by the French in the 18th century, and Ausable Chasm, a 1½-mi-long geological spectacle.

The St. Lawrence Seaway forms a portion of the world's longest unfortified international border. The Thousand Islands area is a 50-mi section of the St. Lawrence River that begins at Lake Ontario's eastern end and curves northwest around the Adirondacks like a mother's protective arm. There are actually nearly 2,000 islands dotting the river, some quite small. Alexandria Bay is the vacation center and heart of this recreational area. Boat tours from here often stop at Boldt Castle, a Rhineland-style castle built on Heart Island at the turn of the 20th century. The waters surrounding the islands offer fine fishing.

⑨ Western New York

The westernmost section of the state is bordered by Lake Erie on the west and Lake Ontario on the north. The Niagara River, which connects the two lakes, and Niagara Falls—both shared by the United States and Canada—are in the northwest corner of the region. "Spectacular" is not too strong an adjective to describe Niagara Falls, which in summer gushes more than 750,000 gallons a second. For an adrenaline rush, don a slicker and take a *Maid of the Mist* tour to the very foot of the cataracts. A few miles south, on Lake Erie, is Buffalo. The second-largest city in New York, it boasts a lively waterfront area and theater district to go with its collection of architectural landmarks. To the south and east lie acres of rolling farmland, part of the Great Lakes Plain, which stretches north from the Appalachian Plateau. More than 10,000 acres of swamps, woodlands, marshes, meadows, and other wildlife habitat at the Iroquois National Wildlife Refuge attract migratory waterfowl and other birds, as well as resident wildlife. Letchworth State Park, at the edge of the Finger Lakes region, is often called the Grand Canyon of the East. The centerpiece of the 14,350-acre park is the 17-mi Genesee River gorge, which has three large waterfalls and sheer cliff walls that climb 600 feet.

Tucked away in the region's southwest corner is the Chautauqua-Allegheny area. When pioneers and settlers headed west from the terminus of the Erie Canal, they largely ignored this territory and left it relatively undeveloped and sparsely populated. It's an area of small towns, soft hills, vineyards, fish-filled lakes, and vast forests. A major draw is the Chautauqua Institution, a respected educational and cultural institution that in summer offers a packed program of lectures, art exhibits, outdoor concerts, theater, dance, and opera. It's in the lakeside Victorian village of Chautauqua (you see the name again and again in these parts), which was founded in 1874 as a school for Methodist teachers and allows no automobile traffic. To the east is the 65,000-acre Allegany State Park, New York's largest state park as well as one if its most primitive. The 50-mi drive from Silver Creek to Ripley, along the Lake Erie shore, is known as the Chautauqua Wine Trail. Along the route are wineries, roadside farm stands, and antiques shops.

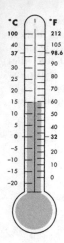

°C / °F
100 — 212
40 — 105
37 — 98.6
30 — 90
25 — 80
20 — 70
15 — 60
10 — 50
5 — 40
0 — 32
-5 — 20
-10 — 10
-15 — 0
-20

The best months for visiting depend on which area of the state you plan to visit and what you wish to do. While some museums and historic sites in the Catskills, Adirondacks, and Hudson Valley may close for winter, for instance, there are still enough places to visit, sights to see, and cold-weather sports to enjoy. In general, summer is the high season throughout much of the state. And while New York City can get very hot and humid in summer, particularly in July and August, that's also when the city is most crowded—not only with tourists but also with New Yorkers enjoying hosts of street fairs, outdoor concerts, and other activities. Winter is also a popular time to visit the Big Apple, especially during the December holiday season, when store windows are decked out with festive and imaginative holiday displays.

For the rest of the state, the weather can be pleasantly warm in summer. Ocean breezes help to cool Long Island's shores; New York's waterways attract people with boats, swimsuits, fishing poles, and sunscreen; and the Catskills, Adirondacks, and Shawangunks offer invigorating hikes and cool refuges. Fall months can be glorious throughout the state. Beginning in late September, the Adirondacks shimmer with spectacular fall foliage, and soon after most of the countryside in the rest of the state follows suit. Peak foliage times usually result in full hotels and B&Bs, so reserve early if you'll be traveling during this time. Vineyards celebrate harvests and new issues in fall, making this a great time to visit wineries in the Hudson Valley, along Lake Erie, on Long Island, and in the Finger Lakes region.

Climate

The weather varies widely throughout the state. It could be sunny in New York City and snowing in the Hudson Valley, for instance. Away from coastal areas, there's plenty of snow in New York, with a statewide seasonal average of 40 inches. More than half the state receives over 70 inches of snow per year. In summer, temperatures range from 70 to 85°F in the higher elevations of the Adirondacks and Catskills. The summer air can be much more humid in the lower Hudson Valley and the New York City area than the rest of the state. What follows are average daily maximum and minimum temperatures for four major cities in the state.
🛈 Forecasts **Weather Channel** ⊕ www.weather.com.

ALBANY

Jan.	30F	– 1C	May	58F	14C	Sept.	74F	23C
	17F	– 8C		35F	2C		54F	12C
Feb.	30F	– 1C	June	70F	21C	Oct.	73F	23C
	11F	– 12C		45F	7C		49F	9C
Mar.	33F	1C	July	79F	26C	Nov.	62F	17C
	14F	– 10C		55F	13C		39F	4C
Apr.	44F	7C	Aug.	84F	29C	Dec.	47F	8C
	25F	– 4C		60F	16C		34F	1C

BUFFALO

Month	High		Month	High		Month	High	
Jan.	37F	3C	May	66F	19C	Sept.	71F	21C
	26F	− 4C		47F	8C		53F	13C
Feb.	32F	0C	June	75F	24C	Oct.	73F	23C
	17F	− 8C		57F	14C		60F	16C
Mar.	42F	6C	July	80F	17C	Nov.	59F	15C
	26F	− 4C		62F	17C		43F	6C
Apr.	54F	12C	Aug.	78F	26C	Dec.	52F	11C
	36F	2C		60F	16C		36F	− 2C

NEW YORK CITY

Month	High		Month	High		Month	High	
Jan.	39F	4C	May	71F	22C	Sept.	75F	24C
	27F	− 3C		53F	12C		60F	16C
Feb.	48F	9C	June	79F	26C	Oct.	64F	18C
	35F	− 2C		63F	17C		50F	10C
Mar.	50F	10C	July	84F	29C	Nov.	35F	2C
	35F	− 2C		69F	21C		21F	− 6C
Apr.	61F	16C	Aug.	75F	24C	Dec.	34F	1C
	44F	7C		61F	16C		18F	− 8C

SYRACUSE

Month	High		Month	High		Month	High	
Jan.	33F	1C	May	77F	25C	Sept.	48F	9C
	15F	− 10C		54F	12C		33F	1C
Feb.	43F	6C	June	82F	28C	Oct.	35F	2C
	25F	− 4C		59F	15C		18F	− 8C
Mar.	56F	13C	July	79F	26C	Nov.	35F	2C
	36F	2C		58F	14C		23F	5C
Apr.	68F	20C	Aug.	72F	22C	Dec.	42F	6C
	46F	8C		51F	11C		27F	− 3C

ON THE CALENDAR

New York State brims with festivals, fairs, and seasonal happenings year-round. Many events are listed below; find details about these events, as well as information about other events, throughout this guide. For exact dates, which vary from year to year, consult ⊕ www.iloveny.com, the Web site of the New York State Division of Tourism.

ONGOING

Mid-June–early September	The celebrated **Hudson Valley Shakespeare Festival** (☎ 845/265–7858 ⊕ www.hvshakespeare.org) graces Garrison with contemporary interpretations of the Bard's work.
October–December	The Brooklyn Academy of Music's **Next Wave Festival** (☎ 718/636–4100 ⊕ www.bam.org) attracts artsy crowds with its program of local and international cutting-edge dance, opera, theater, and music.

WINTER

Late December–early January	The nine-day **New York National Boat Show** (☎ 212/984–7000 ⊕ www.nyboatshow.com), at the Jacob Javits Convention Center in Manhattan, shows off the latest in pleasure craft, yachts, and nautical equipment.
January	New York City's famous **ball drop in Times Square** (☎ 212/768–1560 ⊕ www.timessquarebid.org) is televised all over the world. Arrive early and plan to stay for a while.
	Outside of New York City and Boston, Albany's **First Night** (☎ 518/434–2032 ⊕ www.albanyevents.org), is one of the East Coast's largest New Year's Eve celebrations.
February	On weekends throughout the month, the **Lake George Winter Carnival.** (☎ 518/668–2233 ⊕ www.lakegeorgewintercarnival.com) offers cold-weather activities, a chili cook-off, and fireworks.
	Nearly 3,000 well-bred canines and their human overseers take over New York City's Madison Square Garden for the **Westminster Kennel Club Dog Show** (☎ 212/465–6741 or 800/455–3647 ⊕ www.westminsterkennelclub.org), which, after the Kentucky Derby, is the nation's second-longest-running sporting event.

SPRING

March	New York's first **St. Patrick's Day Parade** (☎ 212/484–1222) took place in 1766, making this boisterous mid-month tradition one of the city's oldest annual events. The parade heads up 5th Avenue, from 44th Street to 86th Street.
Late March–early April	The week before Easter, the **Macy's Flower Show** (☎ 212/494–4495) creates lush displays in its flagship Manhattan emporium and sets

its Broadway windows abloom. Exquisite flower arrangements are also on display in Rockefeller Center.

The Jacob Javits Center is host to the annual New York International Automobile Show (☎ 212/216–2000 ⊕ www.autoshowny.com), where hundreds of the latest and hottest cars, along with auto oddities, get drivers' motors running.

April	The three-ring Ringling Bros. and Barnum & Bailey Circus (☎ 212/465–6741 ⊕ www.ringling.com) comes to Manhattan annually, early in the month. Just before opening night, the Animal Walk takes the show's four-legged stars from the train yard in Queens through the Queens Midtown tunnel and west along 34th Street to Madison Square Garden; it happens around midnight but is well worth waiting up for.

Later in the month, the Cherry Blossom Festival (☎ 718/623–7200 ⊕ www.bbg.org) at the Brooklyn Botanic Garden celebrates the trees' peak flowering.

May	Held the week before and after Mother's Day, the Lilac Festival (☎ 585/256–4960 ⊕ www.lilacfestival.com) heralds the start of Rochester's festival season.

About 30,000 cyclists turn out for the annual Bike New York: The Great Five Boro Bike Tour (☎ 212/932–2453 ⊕ www.bikenewyork. org). The low-key, 42-mi tour begins in Battery Park and ends with a ride across the Verrazano-Narrows Bridge into Staten Island.

In early May, the Hudson River Maritime Museum in Kingston hosts a Shad Festival (☎ 845/338–0071 ⊕ www.ulster.net/~hrmm/ museum/festival.htm), celebrating the shad's seasonal swim up the river with shad and shad-roe dinners, music, crafts, and boat rides.

On the second or third Saturday of the month, booths of Manhattan's Ninth Avenue Food Festival (☎ 212/484–1222) line 20 midtown blocks of 9th Avenue and cook up every conceivable type of food.

Albany's Dutch heritage gets a nod mid-month at the three-day Tulip Festival (☎ 518/434–2032 ⊕ www.albanyevents.org).

The biannual Millbrook Antiques Show (☎ 845/677–5247 ⊕ www. showsfairsfestivals.com) is a three-day event held in late May or early June and again in mid-October.

The week before Memorial Day, ships from the armed forces of the United States and from other countries join up with Coast Guard ships during Manhattan's Fleet Week (☎ 212/245–0072 ⊕ www. intrepidmuseum.org) for a parade up the Hudson River.

The juried Woodstock/New Paltz Art and Crafts Fair (☎ 845/679–8087 or 845/246–3414 ⊕ www.quailhollow.com), held Memorial Day and Labor Day weekends, showcases artisans from around the country and includes better-than-usual fair fare, with many vegetarian and unusual dishes.

SUMMER

June	During the Hudson Valley Food and Wine Festival (☎ 845/758–5461 ⊕ www.hudsonvalley.org), held early in the month, local restaurants, New York State wineries, and regional farms come together for a weekend of tastings, demonstrations, and lectures.
	More than 35,000 motorcycle enthusiasts flock to the Lake George area for the six-day Americade Motorcycle Tour & Rally (☎ 518/798–7888 ⊕ www.tourexpo.com) in early June.
	Over 40 hot-air balloons participate in the three-day Balloon Fest (☎ 315/451–7275 or 315/435–5252 ⊕ onondagacountyparks.com/balloonfest), held the second weekend of the month in Jamesville.
	Later in the month, the JVC Jazz Festival New York (☎ 212/501–1390 ⊕ www.festivalproductions.net) brings giants of jazz and new faces alike to Carnegie Hall, Lincoln Center, Birdland, Bryant Park, and other venues around Manhattan.
	In late June, New York City's Lesbian & Gay Pride Week (☎ 212/807–7433 ⊕ www.nycpride.org) includes a film festival, concerts aplenty, and many other events. It culminates with the world's biggest annual gay-pride parade, which heads down 5th Avenue and then to Greenwich Village on the last Sunday of the month.
Late June–early July	Hunter and jumper competitions punctuate the Lake Placid Horse Shows (☎ 518/523–9625 ⊕ www.lakeplacidhorseshow.com).
Late June–August	On Monday nights, filmgoers head to Bryant Park, the New York Public Library's "backyard," for the Bryant Park Summer Film Festival (☎ 212/512–5700 ⊕ www.bryantpark.org). The lawn turns into a picnic ground as fans of classic films claim space hours before the show begins, at dusk.
	Shakespeare in the Park (☎ 212/539–8750 ⊕ www.joespub.com), sponsored by the Joseph Papp Public Theater and staged in Central Park's Delacorte Theater, tackles the Bard and other classics, often with star performers.
July	Lower Manhattan celebrates Independence Day with the Great 4th of July Festival (☎ 212/484–1222), which includes arts, crafts, ethnic food, and live entertainment. South Street Seaport also puts on a celebration.
	Macy's 4th of July Fireworks (☎ 212/494–4495) fill the night sky over Manhattan's East River. The best viewing points are FDR Drive from East 14th to 41st streets (access via 23rd, 34th, and 48th streets) and the Brooklyn Heights Promenade. The FDR Drive

is closed to traffic, but arrive early, as police sometimes restrict even pedestrian traffic.

On each of seven nights in early July, the Hill Cumorah Pageant (☎ 315/597–2757 or 315/597–6808 ⊕ www.hillcumorah.com) in Palmyra tells the story of the founding of the Mormon Church. The cast of more than 600 and the assorted high-tech visual and sound effects are what make the performances notable.

Monster trucks, racing pigs, and 4-H livestock competitions are highlights of the Cayuga County Fair (☎ 315/834–6606 or 800/499–9615 ⊕ www.cayugacountyfair.homestead.com), held for five days mid-month in Weedsport.

The two-day Corn Hill Arts Festival (☎ 585/262–3142 ⊕ www.cornhill.org), held the weekend after July 4, brings more than 200,000 people to one of Rochester's oldest neighborhoods.

Live-animal and gardening exhibits, crafts, and rides are the draw at the week-long Saratoga County State Fair (☎ 518/885–9701 ⊕ www.saratogacountyfair.org) in Ballston Spa.

World musicians join local artisans and farmers for the two-day Mountain Culture Festival (☎ 518/263–4908 Ext. 202 ⊕ www.catskillmtn.org) at the Hunter Mountain ski resort on the second weekend of the month.

The Stony Brook Film Festival (☎ 631/632–2787 ⊕ www.stonybrookfilmfestival.com), during the last two weeks of the month, presents features and shorts from filmmakers around the world.

A parade of restored wooden boats on Skaneateles Lake is the highlight of the three-day Antique and Classic Boat Show (☎ 315/685–0552 ⊕ www.skaneateles.com), held the last weekend of July.

Hear folk-scene luminaries belt their stuff or strap on your own dancing shoes at the four-day Falcon Ridge Folk Festival (☎ 860/364–0366 ⊕ www.falconridgefolk.com) in the Berkshire foothills late in the month.

Early July–August	Spend the day as an Elizabethan at the Sterling Renaissance Festival (☎ 315/947–5783 or 800/879–4446 ⊕ www.sterlingfestival.com), held near Lake Ontario over seven summer weekends starting early in the month.
	Scenic Amagansett is literally the backdrop for the Bard's tales at the annual Hamptons Shakespeare Festival (☎ 631/267–0105 ⊕ www.hamptons-shakespeare.org), typically scheduled during July and August.
August	Lincoln Center Out of Doors (☎ 212/875–5766 ⊕ www.lincolncenter.org) is a series of music, dance, and family-oriented events lasting almost the entire month.

National and international groups perform at the Cooperstown Chamber Music Festival (☎ 607/547–1450 ⊕ www.cooperstownmusicfest. com), held at the Farmers' Museum throughout the month.

Chamber music reigns during the month-long Skaneateles Festival (☎ 315/685–7418 ⊕ www.skanfest.org), which begins early in the month.

Preserves competitions and pig races are among the festivities at the week-long Ulster County Fair (☎ 845/255–1380 ⊕ www. ulstercountyfair.com), held early in the month.

Tractor pulls, a demolition derby, and beauty pageants enliven the week-long Herkimer County Fair (☎ 315/895–7464 ⊕ www. dreamscape.com/frankfpd/fair.htm) mid-month in Frankfort.

Caber tossing, Irish step dancing, and a march of bagpipers down Hunter Mountain are just some of what you can expect during the Celtic Festival (☎ 518/263–4223 or 800/486–8376 ⊕ www. huntermtn.com), held the second weekend of the month.

Over two consecutive weekends in Annandale-on-Hudson, Bard College's annual Bard Music Festival (☎ 845/758–7900 ⊕ www. bard.edu) focuses on a single composer with performances, discussions, and lectures.

Giant puppets dominate the Esopus Creek Festival of Mask and Puppet Theater (☎ 845/246–7873 ⊕ www.armofthesea.org), held in Saugerties during the last weekend of the month.

Butter-sculpting contests and lumberjack demonstrations are among the delights that draw major crowds to the Great New York State Fair (☎ 315/487–7711 ⊕ www.nysfair.org). Held in Syracuse, the fair traditionally closes its 12-day run on Labor Day.

August–September	From early August through late September, the New York Renaissance Faire (☎ 845/351–5174 ⊕ www.renfair.com) recreates 16th-century England in the town of Tuxedo.
	From late August through early September, the U.S. Open Tennis Tournament (☎ 866/673–6849 Ticketmaster ⊕ www.usopen.org) in Flushing Meadows–Corona Park, Queens, is one of the New York City's premier annual sporting events.

FALL

September	Garlands and lights bedeck Little Italy's Mulberry Street and environs for the Feast of San Gennaro (☎ 212/768–9320 ⊕ www. sangennaro.org), New York City's oldest, grandest, largest, and most crowded *festa,* held in honor of the patron saint of Naples.
	Each Labor Day weekend, the Columbia County Fair (☎ 518/758–1811 ⊕ www.columbiafair.com) in Chatham celebrates all things rural.

Pipe bands, highland dance performances, and traditional contests are the highlights of Altamont's **Capital District Scottish Games** (☎ 518/438–4297 or 518/785–0507 ⊕ www.scotgames.com), held on the Saturday and Sunday of Labor Day weekend.

Live music, artisans, and food enliven **JAS** (☎ 845/246–2321 ⊕ www.saugerties.ny.us), an acronym for Jazz and Art at Saugerties.

Statewide jazz groups converge at the Shepard Park bandstand for the **Lake George Jazz Weekend** (☎ 518/668–2616 ⊕ www.lakegeorgearts.org), usually on the weekend after Labor Day.

More than 100 crafts and food booths line the streets in the heart of Albany during the day-long **Larkfest** (☎ 518/434–3861 ⊕ www.larkstreet.org), held early in the month.

On a Saturday early in the month, the **Whiteface Mountain Scottish Highland Festival** (☎ 518/946–2223 ⊕ www.whiteface.com) includes a fair amount of piping and drumming as well as a Scottish heavy athletics competition.

Typically mid-month, self-described "traveling roadies" drive hot rods and muscle cars around Rhinebeck during the **Good Guys Classic Rod and Custom Car Show** (☎ 845/876–4001 ⊕ www.good-guys.com).

In the middle of the month, area restaurants, farm markets, breweries, and wineries offer a day-long **Taste of New Paltz** (☎ 845/255–0243 ⊕ newpaltzchamber.org).

More than 100 hot-air balloons participate in the four-day **Adirondack Hot Air Balloon Festival** (☎ 518/761–6366 ⊕ www.adirondackballoonfest.org), held around the third weekend of the month at the Floyd Bennett Memorial Airport in Queensbury.

Participate in grape-stomping contests or just enjoy the food and live music at the **Naples Grape Festival** (☎ 585/374–2240 ⊕ www.naplesvalleyny.com), held on the fourth full weekend of the month.

Upwards of 40,000 people make a pilgrimage to Saugerties at the end of the month to sample garlic ice cream and other savories at the **Hudson Valley Garlic Festival** (☎ 845/246–3090 ⊕ www.hvgf.org).

Late September–mid-October	Begun in 1963, the **New York Film Festival** (☎ 212/875–5600 ⊕ www.filmlinc.com) is New York City's most prestigious annual film event. Cinephiles pack various Lincoln Center venues—advance tickets to afternoon and evening screenings are essential to guarantee a seat.
October	Considered one of the world's top art fairs, Manhattan's **International Fine Art and Antique Dealers Show** (☎ 212/642–8572 ⊕ www.haughton.com) brings dealers from the United States and Europe, who show treasures dating from antiquity to the 20th century.

	Watching men imitate the courting rituals of the wood grouse is just part of the fun at the Hunter Mountain ski resort–based **Oktoberfest** (☎ 518/263–4223 or 800/486–8376 ⊕ www.huntermtn. com), during the first two weekends of the month.
	During the **Burning of Kingston** (☎ 845/331–7517 or 800/331–1518 ⊕ www.firstulster.org) mid-month, redcoats and colonial bluecoats occupy the city for three days following a reenactment of the 1777 British landing and battle at Kingston Point.
	The big annual event of the **Woodstock Film Festival** (☎ 845/679–4265 ⊕ www.woodstockfilmfestival.com) takes place around mid-month, with film screenings, concerts, and panels in and around Woodstock, Rhineback, and Hunter.
	On the third weekend of the month, the **FilmColumbia Festival** (☎ 518/392–1162 ⊕ www.filmcolumbia.com) brings together film buffs and industry members for screenings of pre-release films at Chatham's 1920 Crandell Theater.
	Thousands of revelers, many in bizarre-but-brilliant costumes or manipulating huge puppets, march up 6th Avenue from Spring to West 23rd streets in the rowdy **Greenwich Village Halloween Parade** (☎ 212/484–1222 ⊕ www.halloween-nyc.com).
November	The **New York City Marathon** (☎ 212/860–4455 ⊕ www.nycmarathon. org), the world's largest, begins on the Staten Island side of the Verrazano-Narrows Bridge and snakes through all five boroughs before finishing in front of Tavern on the Green in Central Park. New Yorkers turn out in droves to cheer on the runners.
	The **Macy's Thanksgiving Day Parade** (☎ 212/494–4495 ⊕ www. macysparade.com) is a New York City tradition. The huge balloons float down Central Park West from West 77th Street to Broadway and Herald Square. The parade begins at 9 AM; when it comes to getting a good spot, the earlier the better.
	Nearly 200 floats wind through downtown the day after Thanksgiving during the **Schenectady Gazette Christmas Parade** (☎ 518/372–5656 ⊕ www.schenectadychamber.org), the largest nighttime parade in the Northeast.
Late November–December	Scrooge strolls the streets of Skaneateles during **Dickens' Christmas** (☎ 315/685–0552 ⊕ www.skaneateles.com), held from Thanksgiving weekend through the Sunday before Christmas.

FODOR'S CHOICE

LODGING

$$$$	**Lake Placid Lodge, Lake Placid.** Get your fill of rustic chic at this lakefront retreat; or just stop by the restaurant, which prepares New American fare with flair and precision. Either way you'll have views of Lake Placid or the mountains.
$$$$	**The Lowell, New York City.** This old-money Upper East Side refuge was built as an upscale apartment hotel in the 1920s and still delivers genteel sophistication, including comforts of home like stocked bookshelves and umbrellas.
$$$$	**Mercer Hotel, New York City.** Owner Andre Balazs has a knack for channeling a neighborhood sensibility—it's SoHo loft all the way at this serene but achingly hip hotel, with its long entryways, high ceilings, and muted colors.
$$$$	**Mohonk Mountain House, New Paltz.** Spend the night—or even just the day—at this Victorian-style mountaintop hotel with acres of private gardens, woodlands, and a beautiful lake.
$$$$	**Old Drovers Inn, Dover Plains.** With its Victorian-style rooms and hearty Tap Room menu, this inn near Millbrook retains the feel of another era. One of the oldest inns in the country, it used be a cattle-herder haunt. Today it's part of the high-end Relais & Châteaux group.
$$$$	**Otesaga Resort Hotel, Cooperstown.** Grand architecture, fine-dining options, and activities such as golf, tennis, and fishing make this stately resort on the water a luxurious and relaxing getaway.
$$$$	**The Paramount, New York City.** Details like gilt-framed headboards and conical steel sinks speak volumes about the style and quality at this Midtown hotel, which caters to a somewhat bohemian, fashionable crowd.
$$$$	**Sagamore Resort, Bolton Landing.** You'll have plenty of opportunities to enjoy the elegant, country-chic decor at the Sagamore. The resort offers so many activities and dining options that you won't have to leave the property—a 72-acre island on Lake George.
$$$$	**W Times Square, New York City.** This super-sleek 57-floor monolith, the flagship of the white-hot W line, feels like it's out of the Jetsons, with a space-age, white-on-white lobby and futuristic room touches like glowing resin boxes.

$$$–$$$$	**Garden City Hotel, Garden City.** Go for real extravagance at this historic Long Island hotel, and indulge in a first-rate meal at the hotel's Polo Restaurant.
$$–$$$$	**Inn at Lake Joseph, Forestburgh.** Luxurious accommodations, exquisite natural surroundings, and quirky architectural details—like sleeping lofts and cupolas—make this lakeside inn a standout.
$–$$$$	**The Gershwin, New York City.** Andy Warhol is the muse at this hip hotel-cum-hostel-cum-palace of Pop Art in Manhattan's Murray Hill neighborhood.
$–$$$$	**Ram's Head Inn, Shelter Island.** Tucked away at the end of Ram Island is a little oasis consisting of this charming colonial-style inn, an exceptional restaurant, and a small private beach.
$–$$$$	**Turning Stone Resort & Casino, Oneida.** Spend the day playing golf, relax at the spa and fitness center, have dinner, and then hit the casino or take in a show at this resort.
$$$	**Beaverkill Valley Inn, Lew Beach.** This small lodge, tucked away in a corner of the Catskill Forest Preserve near Roscoe, has plenty of recreational facilities to keep both kids and adults busy. The Beaverkill runs right through the property, so you don't have to leave the grounds to fish its fabled waters.
$$–$$$	**Belhurst Castle, Geneva.** Plush furnishings, two-person showers, and fireplaces in the guestrooms make this 1889 stone castle a perfect romantic getaway.
$–$$$	**Inn at Green River, Hillsdale.** Cozy up to the fireplace or settle into a candlelit breakfast at this 1830 Federal home filled with carefully arranged furnishings and old-school charm.
$–$$	**Mansion on Delaware Ave., Buffalo.** Although the mansion was built in the 1860s, the decor is all about up-to-the-minute elegance. The amenities, including free car service to downtown, are what you'd expect to find in a much larger lodging.
$–$$	**Roycroft Inn, East Aurora.** Colorful pillows and throw rugs play off the original and reproduction Roycroft Arts and Crafts furnishings at this three-story inn.

BUDGET LODGING

¢–$$	**Hungry Trout Motor Inn & Restaurant, Wilmington.** This refined motor inn on the west branch of the Ausable River (bring your fishing gear) is known for its spacious, mountain-view rooms and a restaurant that specializes in trout. Whiteface Mountain Ski Center is nearby.
¢–$	**Larchmont Hotel, New York City.** You might miss the entrance to this homey residential-style town house, whose geranium boxes and lanterns blend right in with the street's Old New York feel.

¢–$ | **The Roxbury, Roxbury.** The rooms at this small motel have modern amenities and a dramatic flair, proving that cutting costs doesn't necessarily mean sacrificing style.

¢ | **Glen Iris Inn, Castile.** The country inn overlooks the Genesee River in Letchworth State Park. Interiors are decked out in Victorian style, but in such gorgeous natural surroundings you won't notice them much.

RESTAURANTS

$$$$ | **Daniel, New York City.** Internationally renowned chef Daniel Boulud has paired his extensive prix-fixe menu with genteel service and an impeccable wine list to create one of the most memorable dining experiences in Manhattan.

$$$$ | **Four Seasons, New York City.** One of America's most famous restaurants, the Four Seasons is the birthplace of the power lunch and the brainchild of architect Philip Johnson.

$$$$ | **Jean Georges, New York City.** Celebrity chef Jean-Georges Vongerichten's elegant Asian-accented French cooking is responsible for the legendary status of this prix-fixe restaurant.

$$$$ | **Le Bernardin, New York City.** The power-lunch set lines up for a seat in the plush, teak-paneled dining room at this classic French seafood restaurant.

$$$$ | **Peter Luger Steak House, New York City.** If you're after the best porterhouse steak in New York, then Peter Luger's—where the same highest-quality beef has been served since 1887—is worth the trip to Brooklyn.

$$$$ | **Xaviars at Piermont, Piermont.** Xaviars is a special-occasion kind of place, with extraordinary contemporary dishes and a smash-up (and quite reasonably priced) prix-fixe menu. The service is as impeccable as the food.

$$$–$$$$ | **Craft, New York City.** Crafting your ideal meal here is like picking and choosing from a gourmand's well-stocked kitchen—one overseen by the gifted Tom Colicchio, who is also chef at the renowned Gramercy Tavern.

$$$–$$$$ | **DePuy Canal House, High Falls.** Chef-owner John Novi, called "the father of new American cooking" in *Time* in 1984, is still turning out innovative seasonal fare in his cozy, antiques-filled 1797 stone tavern.

$$$–$$$$ | **Stone Creek Inn, Quogue.** Elegantly spare dining spaces are as fresh as the fish and produce used in the French-inspired menu. Expect a memorable experience.

$$–$$$$ | **Mirko's, Water Mill.** With Mediterranean, Continental, contemporary, and American dishes on the menu, there's something for everyone at this sophisticated foodie haven of freshness.

$–$$$$	**Nobu, New York City.** Reserve at least a month in advance to get into this Japanese restaurant—arguably New York's most famous. A wall of river-worn pebbles, a hand-painted beech floor, and sculptural birch trees set the stage for Nobu Matsuhisa's dramatic food.
$$$	**Babbo, New York City.** Mario Batali's ethereal homemade pastas (and the tender suckling pig) have given his flagship Greenwich Village restaurant quite the following, not to mention a waiting list.
$$–$$$	**Escoffier Restaurant, Hyde Park.** Classic French dishes with an international twist mark the repertoire of this elegant restaurant at the famed Culinary Institute of America.
$$–$$$	**The Frisky Oyster, Greenport.** Contemporary cuisine and a stylish atmosphere make vacationing city dwellers feel at home in this dynamic North Fork restaurant and bar.
$$–$$$	**Mina, Red Hook.** Diners are *encouraged* to linger at Mina, where fresh, seasonal ingredients punctuate a fierce commitment to simple, elegant food.
$$–$$$	**Wawbeek on Upper Saranac Lake, Tupper Lake.** A meal at the restaurant is in order whether or not you stay at this lodge, built in 1880 as a great camp. The seasonal North Country cuisine highlights local ingredients, and walls of windows frame views of Upper Saranac Lake.
$–$$$	**Quarter Moon Café, Delhi.** You might not expect to find innovative cuisine and cool decor in an intimate eatery in a small northern Catskills village, but here it is. The kitchen serves creative fusions of international flavors in eclectic surroundings.
$–$$	**La Parmigiana, Southampton.** With its warm atmosphere and generous plates of everyone's favorite Italian dishes, this casual spot is a hit.

BUDGET RESTAURANTS

$	**Calico, Rhinebeck.** This little storefront patisserie-restaurant brims with exquisite pastries and well-executed French-inspired cuisine.
¢	**Dallas Hot Weiners, Kingston.** Grab a spot at the counter of this narrow hot-dog haven and order one with everything—a dog with onions, mustard, and their famous sauce. Don't worry; the sauce doesn't bite.

MANSIONS & ESTATES

Kykuit, Tarrytown. Crowning a hill overlooking the Hudson River, this mansion housed four generations of Rockefellers—and still has a mean collection of art and antiques. The grounds and gardens, scattered with sculptures, are worth a trip on their own.

Olana State Historic Site, Hudson. Hudson River school painter Frederic Church applied his own special touches to this Moorish-style castle on a hill, which was designed for him by Calvert Vaux. You don't need an appointment to stroll the grounds, which offer magnificent Hudson River views.

Sonnenberg Mansion and Gardens, Canandaigua. The grounds of this 52-acre estate are a magnificent example of late-Victorian gardening and design. Take a tour of the 4,000 rose bushes, rock gardens, and other themed plantings before heading inside the stunning 1852 Queen Anne mansion.

Franklin D. Roosevelt National Historic Site, Hyde Park. Pay homage to the country's 32nd president with a tour of his Hudson River estate, which includes his birthplace and burial site, a museum, a library designed by FDR himself, and documents and memorabilia galore.

Staatsburg State Historic Site, Staatsburg. The grand 65-room mansion is known for its lavish interiors; the grounds offer some of the best views (and sledding) in the Hudson Valley.

Vanderbilt Mansion National Historic Site. Take your time walking through the Italian gardens and absorb the opulence and grandeur of this Hudson River mansion built for Cornelius Vanderbilt's grandson.

MUSEUMS

Adirondack Museum, Blue Mountain Lake. Nearly every aspect of Adirondack life is covered at this museum with 23 exhibit areas on 32 lakefront acres. Highlights include wood crafts and furnishings.

Corning Museum of Glass, Corning. Reflect on the history of glassmaking through a survey of the museum's enormous collection. After watching a glassblowing demo, make your own glass souvenir; walk-in workshops are offered daily.

Metropolitan Museum of Art, New York City. The largest art museum in the western hemisphere and one of the supreme cultural institutions in the world has a permanent collection of nearly 3 million works spanning the ages and the globe. For unbelievable Central Park views, don't miss seeing the rooftop terrace when it's open.

Munson-Williams-Proctor Arts Institute, Utica. The eclectic spaces of the museum yield diverse collections, including a rich sampling of Victorian-era furnishings and spectacular paintings by the Hudson River school's foremost artists.

Museum of Modern Art, New York City. Displaying more art in more space was the successful goal of MoMA's extensive renovation and redesign overseen by Japanese architect Yoshio Taniguchi. The museum reopened in Manhattan in November 2004 after temporarily residing in Queens.

National Baseball Hall of Fame and Museum, Cooperstown. Find out everything you've ever wanted to know about the national pastime's great legends at this museum.

Old Rhinebeck Aerodrome, Rhinebeck. Many of the vintage planes at this museum take to the air during weekend air shows. You may join them, wearing goggles and a Snoopy-style cap, on an open-cockpit-biplane ride.

Parrish Art Museum, Southampton. Important traveling exhibitions and a full program of educational activities complement the museum's extensive collection of American and Italian Renaissance art and get you out of the Hamptons sun for a few hours.

Solomon R. Guggenheim Museum, New York City. The Frank Lloyd Wright–designed structure is an icon of modernist architecture designed specifically to showcase and complement modern art.

Storm King Art Center, Mountainville. This outdoor museum has 500 acres of hills, fields, and meadows dotted with sculptural works by major international artists.

Strong Museum, Rochester. Kids love the interactive exhibits, antique-doll collection, and other attractions at the country's second-largest children's museum.

PARKS & NATURE

Jones Beach State Park, Wantagh. Its 6½ mi of white sand make this park one of Long Island's most popular beaches. The amphitheater presents big-name musicians throughout the summer.

Kaaterskill Falls, Haines Falls. You might recognize the 260-ft cascade from paintings, because Kaaterskill Falls was a popular subject for Hudson River artists. A hike of just under a mile brings you to the base of the two-tiered falls. **Lilac Festival, Rochester.** More than 500 varieties of lilacs burst into bloom for the two weeks surrounding Mother's Day; if mother nature doesn't cooperate, you can still wander the crisscrossing paths of Highland Park and enjoy garden tours, live music, and arts and crafts.

Letchworth State Park, Castile. The Genesee River courses through the park's 17-mi gorge, where the sheer cliff walls reach nearly 600 ft in some places. No wonder the park is often called the Grand Canyon of the East.

Minnewaska State Park Preserve, New Paltz. Bike the historic carriageways or hike past glorious streams and waterfalls at this jewel of a park in the Shawangunks. Or just take a walk around the lake and stop for a picnic.

Niagara Falls. Nothing compares with the rush of the three cascades that make up this natural wonder. Goat Island, part of Niagara

Falls State Park, offers spectacular vantage points for both the U.S. and Canadian falls.

Watkins Glen State Park, Watkins Glen. Glen Creek drops about 500 ft in a span of 2 mi at this stunning park, where you can count 19 waterfalls. A 1½-mi gorge trail runs parallel to the creek, and 300-ft cliffs border the water.

PERFORMING ARTS

Bardavon 1869 Opera House, Poughkeepsie. The artfully restored auditorium of this opera house, the oldest in the state, hosts performances of all kinds, including concerts by the resident Hudson Philharmonic.

Brooklyn Academy of Music, New York City. With a stellar record of cutting-edge performances in a variety of media, BAM also has the honor of being America's oldest performing-arts center.

Maverick Concert Series, Woodstock. Every summer, this chamber-music festival in a chapel renowned by audiophiles features a world-class roster of musicians.

Metropolitan Opera, New York City. The titan of American opera companies brings premier singers to its massive stage at Lincoln Center's Metropolitan Opera House; the music is executed with intensity and precision by an orchestra rivaling the world's finest.

Richard B. Fisher Center for the Performing Arts, Annandale-on-Hudson. The massive stainless-steel ribbons of Bard College's Frank Gehry–designed arts center reflect the sky and surroundings. Its main theater hosts world-class opera, dance, drama, and music performances throughout the year.

Saratoga Performing Arts Center, Saratoga Springs. Why stay in the city when the Philadelphia Orchestra, New York City Ballet, and various other big-name performers in jazz and pop come to roost every summer in this open-air venue?

QUINTESSENTIAL NEW YORK

Bethesda Fountain, New York City. Few New York views are more romantic than the one from the top of the magnificent stone stair case that leads to the ornate, three-tier Bethesda Fountain in Central Park.

Bronx Zoo, New York City. There are 843 animals and 265 acres to check out—plus the famous Congo Gorilla Forest exhibit—at this zoo, the largest urban zoo in the world.

Cathedral Church of St. John the Divine, New York City. Everything about this cathedral is on the scale of the giants; though technically unfinished, it's already the largest Gothic cathedral in the world, and it contains the biggest stained-glass window in the country.

Cutchogue Village Green and Old Burial Ground, Cutchogue. See 300 years of history by touring some of the region's oldest buildings, which are still fitted with period furnishings.

Ellis Island, New York City. Ellis Island received and processed the ancestors of more than 40% of Americans living today. Now it stands as a monument to the experiences of more than 12 million immigrants, with galleries full of artifacts, photographs, and taped oral histories.

Empire State Building, New York City. On a clear day you can see up to 80 mi from the 86th-floor observatory of this iconic art-deco skyscraper.

Grand Central Terminal, New York City. The ornate Grand Central is not only the world's largest railway station (76 acres), but also the nation's busiest (500,000 commuters and subway riders use it daily). While you're here, have a drink in the Campbell Apartment, a magnificent space that was a cushy private executive office in the '30s.

Governor Nelson A. Rockefeller Empire State Plaza, Albany. Among the important buildings on this ¼-mi concourse are the Performing Arts Center, the New York State Museum, the State Library, and its crowning feature, the 19th-century New York State Capitol, where a 45-minute tour guides you through the legislative chambers and the impressive Great Western Staircase. The plaza's sculptures and modern artworks constitute a don't-miss attraction in their own right.

Statue of Liberty, New York City. Millions of American immigrants first glimpsed their new land when they laid eyes on the 152-ft Statue of Liberty. This national monument still stands as a near-universal symbol of freedom and democracy.

Union Church of Pocantico Hills, Tarrytown. The English Gothic influences interest architects, but most other visitors are no doubt drawn to the stained-glass windows, which were designed by Marc Chagall and Henri Matisse.

United States Military Academy at West Point. It's one of the nation's most prestigious military academies, the oldest continually garrisoned post in the U.S. Army, and the site of the world's largest military museum.

SMART TRAVEL TIPS

Finding out about your destination before you leave home means you won't squander time organizing everyday minutiae once you've arrived. You'll be more streetwise when you hit the ground as well, better prepared to explore the aspects of New York State that drew you here in the first place. The organizations in this section can provide information to supplement this guide; contact them for up-to-the-minute details, and consult the A to Z sections that end each chapter for facts on the various topics as they relate to New York State's many regions. Happy landings!

AIR TRAVEL

New York is one of the easiest states in America to reach by plane, and international fares to New York City are among the least expensive in the United States (except for Asian and Australian flights, which are cheaper to California). Just about every major international airline with U.S. service flies to New York City, via either JFK or Newark airports. Nearly a dozen other airports in New York State have direct service throughout the United States and Canada on anywhere from 3 to 12 airlines.

BOOKING

When you book, look for nonstop flights and remember that "direct" flights stop at least once. Try to avoid connecting flights, which require a change of plane. Two airlines may operate a connecting flight jointly, so ask whether your airline operates every segment of the trip; you may find that the carrier you prefer flies you only part of the way. To find more booking tips and to check prices and make online flight reservations, log on to www.fodors.com.

CARRIERS

There's an abundance of large and small airlines with flights to and from New York City.

🛫 **International Carriers Air Canada** ☎ 888/247-2262 ⊕ www.aircanada.ca. **Alitalia Airlines** ☎ 800/223-5730 ⊕ www.alitalia.com. **Austrian Airlines** ☎ 800/843-0002 ⊕ www.aua.com. **British Airways** ☎ 800/247-9297, 0870/85-098-50 in U.K. ⊕ www.ba.com. **Qantas** ☎ 800/227-4500, 13-1313 in Australia ⊕ www.qantas.com. **Virgin Atlantic Airways** ☎ 800/862-8621, 01293/450-150 in U.K. ⊕ www.virgin-atlantic.com.

Major Domestic Airlines America West ☎ 800/235-9292 ⊕ www.americawest.com. **American** ☎ 800/433-7300 ⊕ www.americanairlines.com. **Continental** ☎ 800/525-0280 ⊕ www.continental.com. **Delta** ☎ 800/221-1212 ⊕ www.delta.com. **Northwest/KLM** ☎ 800/225-2525 ⊕ www.nwa.com. **United** ☎ 800/241-6522 ⊕ www.united.com. **US Airways** ☎ 800/428-4322 ⊕ www.usairways.com.

Smaller Domestic Airlines AirTran Airways ☎ 800/247-8726 ⊕ www.airtran.com. **Independence Air** ☎ 800/359-3594 ⊕ www.flyi.com. **jetBlue** ☎ 800/538-2583 ⊕ www.jetblue.com. **Midwest** ☎ 800/452-2022 ⊕ www.midwestairlines.com. **Pan Am Clipper Connection** ☎ 800/359-7262 ⊕ www.flypanam.com. **Southeast Airlines** ☎ 800/359-7325 ⊕ www.southeastairlines.com. **Southwest Airlines** ☎ 800/435-9792 ⊕ www.southwest.com. **TransMeridian Airlines** ☎ 866/435-9862 ⊕ www.iflytma.com.

CHECK-IN & BOARDING

Always **find out your carrier's check-in policy.** Plan to arrive at the airport about two hours before your scheduled departure time for domestic flights and 2½ to 3 hours before international flights. You may need to arrive earlier if you're flying from one of the busier airports or during peak air-traffic times. You can probably get away with arriving a bit later (1 to 1½ hours ahead of departure) for domestic flights from some of the smaller airports upstate; always check first with your airline. To avoid delays at airport-security checkpoints, try not to wear any metal. Jewelry, belt and other buckles, steel-toe shoes, barrettes, and underwire bras are among the items that can set off detectors.

Assuming that not everyone with a ticket will show up, airlines routinely overbook planes. When everyone does, airlines ask for volunteers to give up their seats. In return, these volunteers usually get a several hundred-dollar flight voucher, which can be used toward the purchase of another ticket, and are rebooked on the next flight out. If there are not enough volunteers, the airline must choose who will be denied boarding. The first to get bumped are passengers who checked in late and those flying on discounted tickets, so get to the gate and check in as early as possible, especially during peak periods.

Always **bring a government-issued photo I.D.** to the airport; even when it's not required, a passport is best.

CUTTING COSTS

The least expensive airfares to New York are priced for round-trip travel and must usually be purchased in advance. Airlines generally allow you to change your return date for a fee; most low-fare tickets, however, are nonrefundable. It's smart to call a number of airlines and check the Internet; when you are quoted a good price, book it on the spot—the same fare may not be available the next day, or even the next hour. Always check different routings and look into using alternate airports. Also, price off-peak flights, which may be significantly less expensive than others. Travel agents, especially low-fare specialists (⇨ Discounts & Deals), are helpful.

Consolidators are another good source. They buy tickets for scheduled flights at reduced rates from the airlines, then sell them at prices that beat the best fare available directly from the airlines. (Many also offer reduced car-rental and hotel rates.) Sometimes you can even get your money back if you need to return the ticket. Carefully read the fine print detailing penalties for changes and cancellations, purchase the ticket with a credit card, and confirm your consolidator reservation with the airline.

Consolidators AirlineConsolidator.com ☎ 888/468-5385 ⊕ www.airlineconsolidator.com; for international tickets. **Best Fares** ☎ 800/880-1234 ⊕ www.bestfares.com; $59.90 annual membership. **Cheap Tickets** ☎ 800/377-1000 or 800/652-4327 ⊕ www.cheaptickets.com. **Expedia** ☎ 800/397-3342 or 404/728-8787 ⊕ www.expedia.com. **Hotwire** ☎ 866/468-9473 or 920/330-9418 ⊕ www.hotwire.com. **Now Voyager Travel** ✉ 45 W. 21st St., Suite 5A, New York, NY 10010 ☎ 212/459-1616 🖷 212/243-2711 ⊕ www.nowvoyagertravel.com. **Onetravel.com** ⊕ www.onetravel.com, **Orbitz** ☎ 888/656-4546 ⊕ www.orbitz.com. **Priceline.com** ⊕ www.priceline.com. **Travelocity** ☎ 888/709-

5983, 877/282-2925 in Canada, 0870/111-7061 in U.K.
⊕ www.travelocity.com.

ENJOYING THE FLIGHT

State your seat preference when purchasing your ticket, and then repeat it when you confirm and when you check in. For more legroom, you can request one of the few emergency-aisle seats at check-in, if you're capable of moving obstacles comparable in weight to an airplane exit door (usually between 35 pounds and 60 pounds)—a Federal Aviation Administration requirement of passengers in these seats. Seats behind a bulkhead also offer more legroom, but they don't have under-seat storage. Don't sit in the row in front of the emergency aisle or in front of a bulkhead, where seats may not recline. SeatGuru.com has more information about specific seat configurations, which vary by aircraft.

Ask the airline whether a snack or meal is served on the flight. If you have dietary concerns, request special meals when booking. These can be vegetarian, low-cholesterol, or kosher, for example. It's a good idea to pack some healthful snacks and a small (plastic) bottle of water in your carry-on bag. On long flights, try to maintain a normal routine, to help fight jet lag. At night, get some sleep. By day, eat light meals, drink water (not alcohol), and **move around the cabin** to stretch your legs. For additional jet-lag tips consult *Fodor's FYI: Travel Fit & Healthy* (available at bookstores everywhere).

FLYING TIMES

Some sample flying times to New York City: from Chicago (2½ hours), London (7 hours), Los Angeles (6 hours), Sydney via Los Angeles (21 hours).

HOW TO COMPLAIN

If your baggage goes astray or your flight goes awry, complain right away. Most carriers require that you **file a claim immediately.** The Aviation Consumer Protection Division of the Department of Transportation publishes *Fly-Rights,* which discusses airlines and consumer issues and is available online. You can also find articles and information on mytravelrights.com, the Web site of the nonprofit Consumer Travel Rights Center.

🛂 Airline Complaints **Aviation Consumer Protection Division** ⊠ U.S. Department of Transportation, Office of Aviation Enforcement and Proceedings, C-75, Room 4107, 400 7th St. SW, Washington, DC 20590 🕾 202/366-2220 ⊕ airconsumer.ost.dot.gov. **Federal Aviation Administration Consumer Hotline** ⊠ For inquiries: FAA, 800 Independence Ave. SW, Washington, DC 20591 🕾 800/322-7873 ⊕ www.faa.gov.

RECONFIRMING

Check the status of your flight before you leave for the airport. You can do this on your carrier's Web site, by linking to a flight-status checker (many Web booking services offer these), or by calling your carrier or travel agent.

AIRPORTS

The major air gateways to New York City are LaGuardia Airport (LGA) and JFK International Airport (JFK) in the borough of Queens, and Newark Liberty International Airport (EWR) in New Jersey. Generally, more international flights go in and out of JFK, more domestic flights go in and out of LaGuardia, and Newark serves both domestic and international travelers. The following regional airports have direct service on several commercial carriers to many cities, mostly around the eastern United States and Canada: Albany International Airport (ALB), Buffalo Niagara International Airport (BUF), Greater Binghamton Airport (BGM), Greater Rochester International Airport (ROC), Long Island Islip Macarthur (ISP), Stewart International Airport in Newburgh (SWF), Syracuse Hancock International Airport (SYR), and Westchester County Airport in White Plains (HPN).

Although flights in and out of the main New York City airports are generally cheaper than those for smaller airports elsewhere in the state, there are some exceptions. Macarthur on Long Island and Buffalo are served by the discount airline Southwest, which spurs competition among the other airlines that serve these airports; Buffalo also has jetBlue service, which is often cheaper than other domestic airlines, via JFK. Other airports outside of New York City that have discount-airline service include Rochester (jetBlue), Stewart (Southeast Airlines and TransMeridian Airlines), and Syracuse (jetBlue and Trans-Meridian Airlines). With so many airports throughout the state, it's best to compare fares and flying times into a few airports. If you're not spending time in New York City, it's best to avoid its often chaotically busy facilities, where airport car-rental rates also tend to be astronomically high. If you're headed directly to the Adirondacks, it might make sense to fly into Montréal (Aéroports de Montréal; YMQ), which is about a two-hour drive from Lake Placid. Except for some rural areas upstate, nearly every major region in New York is within a 90-minute drive of two or more airports, so **shop around** and be sure to factor in differences in local car-rental rates and the number of connections required to reach different airports from your departure point.

⚐ Aéroports de Montréal ☎ 514/394-7200 ⊕ www.admtl.com. **Albany International Airport** ☎ 518/242-2200 ⊕ www.albanyairport.com. **Buffalo Niagara International Airport** ☎ 716/630-6000 ⊕ www.nfta.com/airport. **Greater Binghamton Airport** ☎ 607/763-4471 ⊕ www.binghamtonairport.com. **Greater Rochester International Airport** ☎ 585/464-6020 ⊕ www.rocairport.com. **JFK International Airport** ☎ 718/244-4444 ⊕ www.kennedyairport.com. **LaGuardia Airport** ☎ 718/533-3400 ⊕ www.laguardiaairport.com. **Long Island Islip Macarthur** ☎ 631/467-3210 ⊕ www.macarthurairport.com. **Newark Liberty International Airport** ☎ 888/397-4636 or 973/961-6000 ⊕ www.newarkairport.com. **Stewart International Airport** ☎ 845/564-2100 ⊕ www.stewartintlairport.com. **Syracuse Hancock International Airport** ☎ 315/454-4330 ⊕ www.syrairport.org. **Westchester County Airport** ☎ 914/995-4850 ⊕ www.westchestergov.com/airport.

BOAT & FERRY TRAVEL

Two car-and-passenger-ferry services connect Long Island with Connecticut. The Bridgeport & Port Jefferson Ferry runs between Port Jefferson, on the North Shore of Long Island, and the town of Bridgeport in southwestern Connecticut; the ride takes 1¼ hours. Cross Sound Ferry runs between Orient Point, at the northeastern tip of Long Island, and New London in southeastern Connecticut; this trip also takes 1¼ hours. In addition, Cross Sound Ferry offers high-speed passenger-ferry service (no vehicles) between Orient Point and New London; the ride takes 40 minutes. All ferries run year-round.

There's also extensive ferry service within New York City, including the famous and free Staten Island Ferry. The 25-minute ride between lower Manhattan and Staten Island affords spectacular views of the city skyline and the Statue of Liberty.

FARES & SCHEDULES

Ferry reservations are strongly recommended, particularly in summer, and in some cases they are required for automobiles. Fares are about $14 for pedestrians and $40 for autos on the Bridgeport & Port Jefferson Ferry, and $10 for pedestrians and $40 for autos on the Cross Sound Ferry. Both ferries run about a dozen times daily. Pedestrians pay $16 for the high-speed Cross Island Ferry. Ferries leave both Rochester and Toronto three times daily. There's no charge to ride the Staten Island Ferry, which runs 24 hours.

⚐ Bridgeport & Port Jefferson Ferry ☎ 888/443-3779 or 631/473-0286, 203/335-2040 ⊕ www.bpjferry.com. **CATS Fast Ferry** ☎ 877/825-3774 or 585/663-0790 ⊕ www.catsfastferry.com. **Cross Sound Ferry** ☎ 860/443-5281 or 631/323-2525 ⊕ www.longislandferry.com. **Staten Island Ferry** ☎ 718/815-2628 ⊕ www.siferry.com.

BUS TRAVEL

Several bus lines provide extensive regional service throughout New York State. Although they won't give you the same freedom as a car, buses can be a convenient and somewhat affordable means of getting around, as they travel many routes —particularly in upstate New York—that trains do not. Remember that buses sometimes make frequent stops, which may extend your journey but may also provide you the chance to see parts of the region you might not otherwise.

Reservations are required on some bus lines (such as Hampton Jitney, which runs from Manhattan and Boston to eastern

Long Island), and they're a good idea for just about any bus trip.

Within most large cities it's possible to use municipal bus service to get around town; service is especially convenient and pervasive within New York City. Still, relatively few nonlocals use city buses extensively, as bus schedules and routes take a bit of learning. *See* the A to Z sections within regional chapters for information on municipal buses.

CUTTING COSTS

Greyhound's North America Discovery Pass allows unlimited travel in the United States (and certain parts of Canada and Mexico) within any 7-, 10-, 15-, 21-, 30-, 45-, or 60-day period ($209–$569). You can also buy similar passes covering different areas, including the East Coast of North America, and non-U.S. residents can purchase similar international versions of these passes.

FARES & SCHEDULES

On some bus lines tickets can run 10% to 50% higher if you don't purchase them seven days in advance. The following are approximate one-way fares, times (which can vary greatly depending on the number of stops), and routes on major carriers: Boston or Washington, D.C., to New York City, 4–5 hours, $30; Atlantic City to New York City, 2½ hours, $23; Montréal to New York City, 7–9 hours, $70; Chicago to Buffalo, 10–13 hours, $60; Toronto to Buffalo, 2–3 hours, $17; Toronto to Kingston/Woodstock (mid–Hudson Valley), 10–13 hours, $89; Philadelphia to Ithaca (Finger Lakes), 7–9 hours, $60; New York City to Niagara Falls, 8–9½ hours, $80; Washington, D.C., to Cooperstown (Leatherstocking Country), 10 hours, $50; Cleveland to Albany, 9–11 hours, $50; New York City to eastern Long Island, 3–4 hours, $23; Boston to eastern Long Island, 6½ hours, $59.

Adirondack, Pine Hill, and New York Trailways has service from New York City to several communities in upstate New York and parts of Canada. Bonanza Bus Lines connects New York to New England. Greyhound Lines has extensive na-

tional service. Hampton Jitney connects New York City and Boston to eastern Long Island. Peter Pan Trailways, which sometimes operates in conjunction with Greyhound, serves New York City, Boston, Philadelphia, Baltimore, and Washington, D.C. For a little extra money ($69), you can pay for a cushier ride between Boston and New York City on LimoLiner buses, which are outfitted with leather recliner seats and satellite TV. Martz Trailways has limited service between New York City and Pennsylvania and New Jersey. Vermont Transit serves the Northeast. Shortline connects New York City to upstate New York and parts of New Jersey and Pennsylvania.

🚌 **Adirondack, Pine Hill, and New York Trailways** ☎ 800/225-6815 ⊕ www.trailways.com. **Bonanza Bus Lines** ☎ 401/751-8800 or 888/751-8800 ⊕ www.bonanzabus.com. **Greyhound Lines** ☎ 800/231-2222 ⊕ www.greyhound.com. **Hampton Jitney** ☎ 631/283-4600, 800/327-0732 in New England ⊕ www.hamptonjitney.com. **LimoLiner** ☎ 617/424-5469 or 888/546-5469 ⊕ www.limoliner.com. **Martz Trailways** ☎ 800/233-8604 ⊕ www.martztrailways.com. **New Jersey Transit** ☎ 973/762-5100 ⊕ www.njtransit.state.nj.us. **Peter Pan Trailways** ☎ 413/781-2900 or 800/343-9999 ⊕ www.peterpanbus.com. **Shortline** ☎ 800/631-8405 ⊕ www.shortlinebus.com. **Vermont Transit** ☎ 800/451-3292 or 802/864-6811 ⊕ www.vermonttransit.com.

BUSINESS HOURS

Shops and other businesses tend to keep later hours in New York City and its suburbs than in rural parts of the state.

BANKS & POST OFFICES

Banks are usually open weekdays 9–3 and sometimes Saturday morning. Post offices are generally open weekdays 8–5 and often on Saturday morning.

MUSEUMS & SIGHTS

Most major museums and attractions are open daily or six days a week (with Monday the most likely closed day). Hours are often shorter on Saturdays and especially Sundays. Some prominent museums, especially in New York City, stay open late one or two nights a week, usually Tuesday, Thursday, or Friday. New York's less poplous areas have quite a few smaller museums and sights—historical societies, small art galleries, specialized collections—that open only a few days a week, and sometimes only by appointment off-season.

SHOPS

Shops in urban and suburban areas, particularly in indoor and strip malls, typically open at 9 or 10 daily and stay open until anywhere from 6 to 10 on weekdays and Saturday, and until 5 or 6 on Sunday.

On major highways and in densely populated areas there are usually at least one or two supermarkets, drugstores, and gas stations open 24 hours, and in a few big cities and some college towns you'll find a smattering of all-night fast-food restaurants, diners, and coffeehouses. In New York City most bars and discos stay open until 4 AM; elsewhere in the state, closing time at bars is usually 2 AM.

CAMERAS & PHOTOGRAPHY

The *Kodak Guide to Shooting Great Travel Pictures* (available at bookstores everywhere) is loaded with tips.

7 **Photo Help Kodak Information Center** ☎ 800/242-2424 ⊕ www.kodak.com.

EQUIPMENT PRECAUTIONS

Don't pack film or equipment in checked luggage, where it is much more susceptible to damage. X-ray machines used to view checked luggage are extremely powerful and therefore are likely to ruin your film. Try to ask for hand inspection of film, which becomes clouded after repeated exposure to airport X-ray machines, and keep videotapes and computer disks away from metal detectors. Always keep film, tape, and computer disks out of the sun. Carry an extra supply of batteries, and be prepared to turn on your camera, camcorder, or laptop to prove to airport security personnel that the device is real.

CAR RENTAL

Choosing the right car-rental strategy depends significantly on whether you intend to spend any time in New York City, which has exorbitant rental rates and myriad driving obstacles, from expensive off street parking to heavy traffic. It's prudent to tackle New York City, with its excellent public transportation, without a vehicle and rent a car only to explore the rest of the state.

Rates at New York City airports, as well as at Long Island's Macarthur airport, begin at around $60 a day and $220 a week for an economy car with air-conditioning, automatic transmission, and unlimited mileage; in Manhattan itself, rates begin at around $60 a day but increase greatly for weekly rentals to about $320 a week and up. These rates do not include state tax on car rentals, which is 13.62%. The New York City Yellow Pages list countless local car-rental agencies, some renting secondhand vehicles, in addition to the national chains.

If you're traveling during a holiday period, make sure that a confirmed reservation guarantees you a car; if in doubt, call the local branch of the car-rental agency.

7 **Major Agencies Alamo** ☎ 800/327-9633 ⊕ www.alamo.com. **Avis** ☎ 800/331-1212, 800/879-2847 or 800/272-5871 in Canada, 0870/606-0100 in U.K., 02/9353-9000 in Australia, 09/526-2847 in New Zealand ⊕ www.avis.com. **Budget** ☎ 800/527-0700 ⊕ www.budget.com. **Dollar** ☎ 800/800-4000, 0800/085-4578 in U.K. ⊕ www.dollar.com. **Enterprise Rent-a-Car** ☎ 800/261-7331, 0870/350-3000 in U.K. ⊕ www.enterprise.com. **Hertz** ☎ 800/654-3131, 800/263-0600 in Canada, 0870/844-8844 in U.K., 02/9669-2444 in Australia, 09/256-8690 in New Zealand ⊕ www.hertz.com. **National Car Rental** ☎ 800/227-7368 ⊕ www.nationalcar.com. **Thrifty** ☎ 800/847-4389 or 918/669-2168 ⊕ www.thrifty.com.

CUTTING COSTS

For a good deal, book through a travel agent who will shop around. Also, price local car-rental companies—whose prices may be lower still, although their service and maintenance may not be as good as those of major rental agencies—and research rates on the Internet. Consolidators that specialize in air travel can offer good rates on cars as well (⇨ Air Travel). Remember to ask about required deposits, cancellation penalties, and drop-off charges if you're planning to pick up the car in one city and leave it in another.

You can save money and avoid New York City's traffic by taking a bus or train to a suburban station near car-rental agencies, such as Hoboken (in New Jersey), North White Plains, Poughkeepsie, or even Stamford, Connecticut, which borders New York's Westchester County. In North White Plains, for example, expect to pay from $33 per day and $160 per week. As you travel farther upstate, rates continue to decrease, meaning that if you're spending part of your time in the northern or western parts of the state, it may make sense to fly or take a train or bus to Albany, Rochester, Buffalo, or elsewhere upstate and rent a car once you arrive there. Rates at these destinations usually begin at around $25 per day and $135 per week.

INSURANCE

When driving a rented car you are generally responsible for any damage to or loss of the vehicle. You also may be liable for any property damage or personal injury that you may cause while driving. Before you rent, see what coverage you already have under the terms of your personal auto-insurance policy and credit cards.

For about $9 to $25 a day, rental companies sell protection, known as a collision- or loss-damage waiver (CDW or LDW), that eliminates your liability for damage to the car; it's always optional and should never be automatically added to your bill. Some states, including New York, have capped the price of the CDW and LDW. If you're renting a vehicle in New York State for more than 48 hours, you may choose to cancel the LDW coverage within 24 hours of signing the rental agreement. (To do so you must bring the car, which is subject to inspection, to one of the rental company's branches.)

REQUIREMENTS & RESTRICTIONS

In New York you must be 18 to rent a car. Although rental agencies based in New York are technically required to rent to qualified drivers under 25, hefty surcharges of as much as $115 a day effectively remove this option. Surcharges in New Jersey tend to be lower.

SURCHARGES

Before you pick up a car in one city and leave it in another, ask about drop-off charges or one-way service fees, which can be substantial. Also inquire about early-return policies; some rental agencies charge extra if you return the car before the time specified in your contract, whereas others give you a refund for the days not used. Most agencies note the tank's fuel level on your contract; to avoid a hefty refueling fee, return the car with the same tank level. If the tank was full, refill it just before you turn in the car, but be aware that gas stations near the rental outlet may overcharge. It's almost never a deal to buy a tank of gas with the car when you rent it; the understanding is that you'll return it empty, but some fuel usually remains. Surcharges may apply if you're under 25 or if you take the car outside the area approved by the rental agency. You'll pay extra for child seats (about $8 a day), which are compulsory for children under five, and usually for additional drivers (up to $25 a day, depending on the location).

CAR TRAVEL

New York has a bit of a Jekyll-and-Hyde complex when it comes to car travel. You need a car to explore the upper reaches of the state, where driving is generally painless, but a car can be more hindrance than help in New York City, and even on parts of Long Island. Manhattan is often a nightmare of gridlocked streets, aggressive drivers and bicyclists, and seemingly suicidal jaywalkers. Driving immediately outside Manhattan—in the outer boroughs, on Long Island, and just north of the city in Westchester County—can be just as frustrating owing to traffic-choked highways that seem forever hampered by construction projects, and to the complex and confusing network of interstates and parkways enveloping New York City.

Morning and evening rush-hour traffic ranges from ugly to catastrophic on the highways leading in and out of every decent-size city in New York. Also, most bridges and tunnels in and out of New York City charge significant tolls (as high as $6 each way for any of the six major

...dge and tunnel crossings between New ...ork City and New Jersey), as do those ...stretches of New York's interstate system that fall under the auspices of the New York Thruway (I–90 from the New York–Pennsylvania border east to the New York–Massachusetts border, and I–87 from Albany south to New York City). Toll booths in New York State all accept E-ZPass, an automated electronic toll pass used by many residents and frequent travelers; if you don't have the pass, be careful not to pull into one of the E-ZPass-only lanes when you approach a toll.

Despite the congested city areas, the state has quite a few scenic drives, even along certain spans of interstate (notably I–87 north of Albany to the Canadian border and parts of I–90 across the center of the state). The suburbs outside Manhattan are traversed by a series of narrow, twisting, and in many places beautiful parkways, mostly consisting of limited-access roads often bordered by verdant landscaping. (Note that although these parkways often make for pleasant drives, some of the twists and turns can be harrowing in snow or rain.) New York also has hundreds of miles of U.S. and state highways that pass through dense forests, open farmland, and pastoral historic hamlets. When time permits, it's worth venturing off the interstate system to behold some of the delightful scenery fringing the state's country roads.

GASOLINE
⊕ NewYorkGasPrices.com provides sample gas prices (within the past 84 hours) at a wide selection of stations throughout the state; you can also search specifically for stations with the lowest gas prices in a particular region. For typical gas prices, *see* Car Travel *in* For International Travelers.

PARKING
In most of New York State parking is not a serious problem—this is true even for larger cities, with the exception of New York City, which has arguably the most expensive and hard-to-find parking of any U.S. city. Free or even metered street parking is difficult to come by, and garages and parking lots in Manhattan charge as much as $25 for a few hours. If you find a spot on the street, be sure to **check parking signs carefully.** Rules differ from block to block, and they're nearly all confusing. The state's most touristy communities also suffer from limited or expensive visitor parking, including the Hamptons and some of the suburbs in Nassau, Westchester, and Rockland counties.

RULES OF THE ROAD
On city streets the speed limit is 30 mph unless otherwise posted; on rural roads, the speed limit is 55 mph unless otherwise posted. Interstate speeds range from 50 to 65 mph. Within New York City limits you may not turn right on a red light; you're permitted to do so elsewhere in the state unless signs indicate otherwise. Be alert for one-way streets and "no left turn" intersections.

State law requires that front-seat passengers wear seat belts at all times. Children under 16 must wear seat belts in both the front and back seats. Always strap children under age five into approved child-safety seats. It is illegal to use a handheld cell phone while driving in New York State. Police will immediately seize the car of any DWI (driving while intoxicated) offenders in New York.

CHILDREN IN NEW YORK
New York is an enjoyable part of the country for family road trips, and it's relatively affordable once you get outside of greater New York City—there are plenty of comparatively inexpensive kid-friendly hotels and family-style restaurants in the northern and western sections of the state, and these regions offer some of the top kid-oriented attractions. Favorite New York destinations for family vacations are the Long Island shoreline (including much of Fire Island and parts of the Hamptons), Lake George, the Catskills, the Finger Lakes, the Adirondacks, and Niagara Falls. Note that some of the quieter and more rural parts of the region—although exuding history—lack child-oriented attractions.

New York City is full of fun things for kids as well. Cultural institutions host programs introducing children to the arts; large stores put on fun promotional events; and many attractions, from skyscrapers to museums, engage the whole family. For listings of children's events, consult *New York* magazine and *Time Out New York,* both available at newsstands. The Friday *New York Times* "Weekend" section also includes children's activities. *Fodor's Around New York City with Kids* (available in bookstores everywhere) can also help you plan your days together. For general advice about traveling with children, consult *Fodor's FYI: Travel with Your Baby* (available in bookstores everywhere).

FLYING

If your children are two or older, ask about children's airfares. As a general rule, infants under two not occupying a seat fly at greatly reduced fares or even for free. But if you want to guarantee a seat for an infant, you have to pay full fare. Consider flying during off-peak days and times; most airlines will grant an infant a seat without a ticket if there are available seats.

Experts agree that it's a good idea to use safety seats aloft for children weighing less than 40 pounds. Airlines set their own policies: if you use a safety seat, U.S. carriers usually require that the child be ticketed, even if he or she is young enough to ride free, because the seats must be strapped into regular seats. And even if you pay the full adult fare for the seat, it may be worth it, especially on longer trips. Do **check your airline's policy about using safety seats during takeoff and landing.** Safety seats are not allowed everywhere in the plane, so get your seat assignments as early as possible.

When reserving, request children's meals or a freestanding bassinet (not available at all airlines) if you need them. But note that bulkhead seats, where you must sit to use the bassinet, may lack an overhead bin or storage space on the floor.

LODGING

Many of the state's fine, antiques-filled bed-and-breakfasts and inns really aren't suitable for kids; many flat-out refuse to accommodate children. Rooms in New York City, particularly in Manhattan, are small by national standards, so ask just how large the room is into which you're adding a cot or fold-out couch. Most hotels in New York allow children under a certain age to stay in their parents' room at no extra charge, but others charge for them as extra adults; be sure to find out the cutoff age for children's discounts.

SIGHTS & ATTRACTIONS

Places that are especially appealing to children are indicated by a rubber-duckie icon (🐤) in the margin.

CONSUMER PROTECTION

Whether you're shopping for gifts or purchasing travel services, **pay with a major credit card** whenever possible, so you can cancel payment or get reimbursed if there's a problem (and you can provide documentation). If you're doing business with a particular company for the first time, contact your local Better Business Bureau and the attorney general's offices in your state and (for U.S. businesses) the company's home state as well. Have any complaints been filed? Finally, if you're buying a package or tour, always consider travel insurance that includes default coverage (⇨ Insurance).

🔢 **BBBs Council of Better Business Bureaus** ✉ 4200 Wilson Blvd., Suite 800, Arlington, VA 22203 ☎ 703/276-0100 🖷 703/525-8277 ⊕ www. bbb.org.

CUSTOMS & DUTIES

IN AUSTRALIA

Australian residents who are 18 or older may bring home A$400 worth of souvenirs and gifts (including jewelry), 250 cigarettes or 250 grams of cigars or other tobacco products, and 1,125 ml of alcohol (including wine, beer, and spirits). Residents under 18 may bring back A$200 worth of goods. Members of the same family traveling together may pool their allowances. Prohibited items include meat products. Seeds, plants, and fruits need to be declared upon arrival.

🔢 **Australian Customs Service** 🏢 Regional Director, Box 8, Sydney, NSW 2001 ☎ 02/9213-2000 or 1300/363263, 02/8334-7444 or 1800/020-504 quarantine-inquiry line 🖷 02/9213-4043 ⊕ www. customs.gov.au.

IN CANADA

Canadian residents who have been out of Canada for at least seven days may bring in C$750 worth of goods duty-free. If you've been away fewer than seven days but more than 48 hours, the duty-free allowance drops to C$200. If your trip lasts 24 to 48 hours, the allowance is C$50. You may not pool allowances with family members. Goods claimed under the C$750 exemption may follow you by mail; those claimed under the lesser exemptions must accompany you. Alcohol and tobacco products may be included in the seven-day and 48-hour exemptions but not in the 24-hour exemption. If you meet the age requirements of the province or territory through which you reenter Canada, you may bring in, duty-free, 1.5 liters of wine or 1.14 liters (40 imperial ounces) of liquor or 24 12-ounce cans or bottles of beer or ale. Also, if you meet the local age requirement for tobacco products, you may bring in, duty-free, 200 cigarettes, 50 cigars or cigarillos, and 200 grams of tobacco. You may have to pay a minimum duty on tobacco products, regardless of whether or not you exceed your personal exemption. Check ahead of time with the Canada Customs and Revenue Agency or the Department of Agriculture for policies regarding meat products, seeds, plants, and fruits.

You may send an unlimited number of gifts (only one gift per recipient, however) worth up to C$60 each duty-free to Canada. Label the package UNSOLICITED GIFT—VALUE UNDER $60. Alcohol and tobacco are excluded.

Canada Border Services Agency ⊠ Customs Information Services, 191 Laurier Ave. W, 15th floor, Ottawa, Ontario K1A 0L5 ☎ 800/461-9999 in Canada, 204/983-3500, 506/636-5064 ⊕ www.cbsa.gc.ca.

IN NEW ZEALAND

All homeward-bound residents may bring back NZ$700 worth of souvenirs and gifts; passengers may not pool their allowances, and children can claim only the concession on goods intended for their own use. For those 17 or older, the duty-free allowance also includes 4.5 liters of wine or beer; one 1,125-ml bottle of spirits; and either 200 cigarettes, 250 grams of tobacco, 50 cigars, or a combination of the three up to 250 grams. Meat products, seeds, plants, and fruits must be declared upon arrival to the Agricultural Services Department.

New Zealand Customs ⊠ Head office: The Customhouse, 17-21 Whitmore St., Box 2218, Wellington ☎ 09/300-5399 or 0800/428-786 ⊕ www.customs.govt.nz.

IN THE U.K.

From countries outside the European Union, including the United States, you may bring home, duty-free, 200 cigarettes, 50 cigars, 100 cigarillos, or 250 grams of tobacco; 1 liter of spirits or 2 liters of fortified or sparkling wine or liqueurs; 2 liters of still table wine; 60 ml of perfume; 250 ml of toilet water; plus £145 worth of other goods, including gifts and souvenirs. Prohibited items include meat, dairy products, seeds, plants, and fruits.

HM Customs and Excise ⊠ Portcullis House, 21 Cowbridge Rd. E, Cardiff CF11 9SS ☎ 0845/010-9000 or 0208/929-0152 advice service, 0208/929-6731 or 0208/910-3602 complaints ⊕ www.hmce.gov.uk.

DISABILITIES & ACCESSIBILITY

New York has come a long way toward making life easier for people with disabilities. On most Manhattan street corners, curb cuts allow wheelchairs to roll along unimpeded. Statewide, many restaurants, shops, and movie theaters with step-up entrances have wheelchair ramps.

LODGING

Most hotels in New York comply with the Americans with Disabilities Act. The definition of accessibility, however, seems to differ from hotel to hotel. Some properties may be accessible by ADA standards for people with mobility problems but not for people with hearing or vision impairments, for example. When you call to make reservations, specify your needs and make sure the hotel can accommodate them. Newer and chain hotels are likely to be the most accessible.

If you have mobility problems, ask for the lowest floor on which accessible services are offered. If you have a hearing impairment, check whether the hotel has devices to alert you visually to the ring of the telephone, a knock at the door, and a fire/emergency alarm. Some hotels provide these devices without charge. Discuss your needs with hotel personnel if this equipment isn't available, so that a staff member can personally alert you in the event of an emergency.

If you're bringing a guide dog, get authorization from the hotel ahead of time and write down the name of the person with whom you spoke.

RESERVATIONS

When discussing accessibility with an operator or reservations agent, ask hard questions. Are there any stairs, inside *or* out? Are there grab bars next to the toilet *and* in the shower/tub? How wide is the doorway to the room? To the bathroom? For the most extensive facilities meeting the latest legal specifications, opt for newer accommodations. If you reserve through a toll-free number, consider also calling the hotel's local number to confirm the information from the central reservations office. Get confirmation in writing when you can.

SIGHTS & ATTRACTIONS

Most sights in New York, whether museums, parks, or theaters, can accommodate people who use wheelchairs. Some attractions have tours or programs for people with mobility, vision, or hearing impairments.

TRANSPORTATION

Drivers with disabilities may use windshield cards from their own state or Canadian province to park in designated handicap parking.

In Manhattan, other than at major subway exchanges, most stations are all but impossible to navigate for people with disabilities; people in wheelchairs should stick to public buses, most of which have wheelchair lifts at the rear door and "kneelers" at the front to facilitate getting on and off. Bus drivers will provide assistance. Reduced fares are available to all passengers with disabilities displaying a Medicare

card. Visitors to the city are also eligible for the same Access-a-Ride program benefits as New York City residents.

🚹 **Access-a-Ride** ☎ 877/337-2017, 646/252-5252, 646/252-5104 TTY ⊕ www.mta.nyc.ny.us.

🚹 Complaints **Aviation Consumer Protection Division** (⇨ Air Travel) for airline-related problems. **Departmental Office of Civil Rights** ✉ For general inquiries, U.S. Department of Transportation, S-30, 400 7th St. SW, Room 10215, Washington, DC 20590 ☎ 202/366-4648 🖷 202/366-9371 ⊕ www.dotcr. ost.dot.gov. **Disability Rights Section** ✉ NYAV, U.S. Department of Justice, Civil Rights Division, 950 Pennsylvania Ave. NW, Washington, DC 20530 ☎ 800/514-0301, 202/514-0301 ADA information line, 800/514-0383 or 202/514-0383 TTY ⊕ www. ada.gov. **U.S. Department of Transportation Hotline** ☎ 800/778-4838, 800/455-9880 TTY for disability-related air-travel problems.

TRAVEL AGENCIES

In the United States, the Americans with Disabilities Act requires that travel firms serve the needs of all travelers. Some agencies specialize in working with people with disabilities.

🚹 Travelers with Developmental Disabilities **New Directions** ✉ 5276 Hollister Ave., Suite 207, Santa Barbara, CA 93111 ☎ 888/967-2841 or 805/967-2841 🖷 805/964-7344 ⊕ www.newdirectionstravel.com. **Sprout** ✉ 893 Amsterdam Ave., New York, NY 10025 ☎ 888/222-9575 or 212/222-9575 🖷 212/222-9768 ⊕ www.gosprout.org.

🚹 Travelers with Mobility Problems **Access Adventures/B. Roberts Travel** ✉ 1876 East Ave., Rochester, NY 14610 ☎ 800/444-6540 ⊕ www. brobertstravel.com, run by a former physical-rehabilitation counselor. **Access Aloha Travel** ✉ 414 Kuwili St., Suite 101, Honolulu, HI 96817 ☎ 800/480-1143 🖷 808/545-7657 ⊕ www.accessalohatravel.com. **Accessible Vans of America** ✉ 9 Spielman Rd., Fairfield, NJ 07004 ☎ 877/282-8267, 888/282-8267, 973/808-9709 reservations 🖷 973/808-9713 ⊕ www.accessiblevans.com. **Flying Wheels Travel** ✉ 143 W. Bridge St., Box 382, Owatonna, MN 55060 ☎ 507/451-5005 🖷 507/451-1685 ⊕ www. flyingwheelstravel.com.

DISCOUNTS & DEALS

In most cities, and especially in Manhattan, numerous tourist-oriented publications available at hotels, stores, and attractions have coupons good for disounts of all kinds, from restaurants and shopping to sightseeing and sporting activities. Some major museums have evenings with free or pay-what-you-wish admission one day a week.

Be a smart shopper and compare all your options before making decisions. A plane ticket bought with a promotional coupon from travel clubs, coupon books, and direct-mail offers or purchased on the Internet may not be cheaper than the least expensive fare from a discount ticket agency. And always keep in mind that what you get is just as important as what you save.

DISCOUNT RESERVATIONS
To save money, look into discount reservations services with Web sites and toll-free numbers, which use their buying power to get a better price on hotels, airline tickets (⇨ Air Travel), even car rentals. When booking a room, always **call the hotel's local toll-free number** (if one is available) rather than the central reservations number—you'll often get a better price. Always ask about special packages or corporate rates.

🏨 **Hotel Rooms Accommodations Express** ☎ 800/444-7666 or 800/277-1064. **Central Reservation Service (CRS)** ☎ 800/555-7555 or 800/548-3311 ⊕ www.crshotels.com. **Hotels.com** ☎ 800/246-8357 ⊕ www.hotels.com. **Quikbook** ☎ 800/789-9887 ⊕ www.quikbook.com. **Steigenberger Reservation Service** ☎ 800/223-5652 ⊕ www.srsworldhotels.com. **Turbotrip.com** ☎ 800/473-7829 ⊕ w3.turbotrip.com.

PACKAGE DEALS
Don't confuse packages and guided tours. When you buy a package you travel on your own, just as though you had planned the trip yourself. Fly/drive packages, which combine airfare and car rental, are often a good deal. In cities ask the local visitor's bureau about hotel and local transportation packages that include tickets to major museum exhibits or other special events.

EATING & DRINKING
New York has developed an impressive reputation for creative, sometimes downright daring, cuisine—and not just in Man-

hattan, one of the world's great dining hubs. You can expect to find stellar restaurants, many of them helmed by culinary luminaries, throughout the Hamptons and much of Long Island, up and down the Hudson Valley, and in some of the more tourism-driven areas in northern and western New York, such as the Finger Lakes and parts of the Adirondacks. That said, restaurant food tends to become simpler, more traditional, and more conservative as you move away from the greater New York City area.

New York's so-called melting-pot status accounts for the wide variety of ethnic restaurants statewide; the state excels in particular at Italian, French, Japanese, Indian, and Thai cuisines. Proximity to the ocean accounts for the state's fine bounty of seafood restaurants, especially on Long Island. And in the interior regions, where both hunting and organic farming have strong followings, a slew of boutique dairy, meat, and vegetable suppliers have sprung up in the past couple of decades. Menus throughout the state often note which Hudson Valley dairy or Leatherstocking Country farm produced a particular goat cheese or heirloom tomato. Many New York restaurants also sell wine produced in the Long Island wine region and even the up-and-coming Finger Lakes wine region.

The restaurants we list are the cream of the crop in each price category. Properties indicated by ✕🏠 are lodging establishments whose restaurant warrants a special trip.

MEALTIMES
Unless otherwise noted, the restaurants listed in this guide are open daily for lunch and dinner.

RESERVATIONS & DRESS
Reservations are always a good idea; we mention them only when they're essential or not accepted. Book as far ahead as you can, and reconfirm as soon as you arrive. (Large parties should always call ahead to check the reservations policy.) We mention dress only when men are required to wear a jacket or a jacket and tie.

GAY & LESBIAN TRAVEL

Attitudes toward same-sex couples are very tolerant throughout the state, and certain areas rank among the most gay-friendly in the nation, including New York City, much of eastern Long Island (especially the Hamptons, and Cherry Grove and the Pines on Fire Island), and much of the Hudson Valley and Catskills regions. Several New York college towns—notably Ithaca and New Paltz—have strong gay and lesbian communities. Although upstate New York is considerably more conservative on gay issues, cities such as Albany, Rochester, Syracuse, and Buffalo all have neighborhoods with relatively high gay visibility, especially Albany's Lark Street section. The world's biggest gay-pride parade takes place along New York City's 5th Avenue the last Sunday in June.

For details about the gay and lesbian scene, consult *Fodor's Gay Guide to the USA* (available in bookstores everywhere), which covers Albany, Fire Island, the Hamptons, the Hudson Valley, and New York City.

Contact the Gay & Lesbian Switchboard of NY for gay-friendly lodging, nightlife, dining, and community resources. You can obtain advice and materials about New York City's lesbian and gay scene at the Lesbian, Gay, Bisexual & Transgender Community Center, which also hosts lectures, parties, and other events to which visitors are welcome.

🔢 Local Information **Gay & Lesbian Switchboard of NY** 📞 212/989-0999 🌐 www.glnh.org. **Lesbian, Gay, Bisexual & Transgender Community Center** ✉ 208 W. 13th St., between 7th and 8th Aves., Greenwich Village, New York, NY 10011 📞 212/620-7310 🌐 www.gaycenter.org.

🔢 Gay- & Lesbian-Friendly Travel Agencies **Different Roads Travel** ✉ 1017 N. LaCienega Blvd., Suite 308, West Hollywood, CA 90069 📞 310/289-6000 or 800/429-8747, Ext. 14 for both 🖶 310/855-0323 📧 lgernert@tzell.com. **Kennedy Travel** ✉ 130 W. 42nd St., Suite 401, New York, NY 10036 📞 800/237-7433 or 212/840-8659 🖶 212/730-2269 🌐 www.kennedytravel.com. **Now, Voyager** ✉ 4406 18th St., San Francisco, CA 94114 📞 800/255-6951 or 415/626-1169 🖶 415/626-8626 🌐 www.nowvoyager.com. **Skylink Travel and Tours/Flying Dutchmen Travel** ✉ 1455 N. Dutton Ave., Suite A, Santa Rosa,

CA 95401 📞 800/225-5759 or 707/546-9888 🖶 707/636-0951; serving lesbian travelers.

HEALTH

There are relatively few health issues specific to New York. Hospitals are as common and medical care as proficient as elsewhere in the United States.

In coastal regions, especially along the Atlantic seaboard, swimmers and boaters should **be respectful of the ocean's powerful surf.** Adhere to posted riptide warnings, and to be perfectly safe stick to areas that have lifeguards. Summers can be exceptionally hot and humid throughout much of New York, especially at lower altitudes and in the southern part of the state; wear light-color, loose-fitting clothing in summer, drink plenty of fluids (and bring along bottled water on hikes, boat trips, and bike rides), and consider staying indoors during the hottest times of the day.

PESTS & OTHER HAZARDS

Mosquitoes, seasonal black flies, and just about every other annoying insect known to North America proliferates in humid and often lush New York. Exercise common precautions and wear lotions or sprays that keep away such pests.

Lyme disease, which is spread by bites from tiny deer ticks, is not uncommon in New York, especially where you find significant deer populations (eastern Long Island, the Hudson Valley, and most rural parts of the state). Symptoms vary considerably; most victims show a red ring-shape rash around the deer-tick bite, somewhat resembling a little bull's-eye and appearing from one to several weeks after the incident. Flulike symptoms (fever, achy joints, swelling) often follow. One common problem is delayed diagnosis; the longer you go without treatment, the more severe the disease's effects.

When spending time in areas **where tick infestation is a problem,** wear long-sleeve clothing and slacks, tuck your pants legs into your boots and/or socks, apply insect repellent generously, and check yourself carefully for signs of ticks or bites. It's a good idea to don light-color clothing, as you'll have an easier time sighting ticks, which are dark. Remember that the more commonly found wood ticks do not carry the disease, and that deer ticks are extremely small—about the size of a pinhead.

HOLIDAYS

Major national holidays are New Year's Day (January 1); Martin Luther King Day (third Monday in January); Presidents' Day (third Monday in February); Memorial Day (last Monday in May); Independence Day (July 4); Labor Day (first Monday in September); Columbus Day (second Monday in October); Thanksgiving Day (fourth Thursday in November); Christmas Eve and Christmas Day (December 24 and 25); and New Year's Eve (December 31).

INSURANCE

The most useful travel-insurance plan is a comprehensive policy that includes coverage for trip cancellation and interruption, default, trip delay, and medical expenses (with a waiver for preexisting conditions).

Without insurance you'll lose all or most of your money if you cancel your trip, regardless of the reason. Default insurance covers you if your tour operator, airline, or cruise line goes out of business—the chances of which have been increasing. Trip-delay covers expenses that arise because of bad weather or mechanical delays. Study the fine print when comparing policies.

U.K. residents can buy a travel-insurance policy valid for most vacations taken during the year in which it's purchased (but check preexisting-condition coverage).

Always **buy travel policies directly from the insurance company**; if you buy them from a cruise line, airline, or tour operator that goes out of business you probably won't be covered for the agency or operator's default, a major risk. Before making any purchase, review your existing health and home-owner's policies to find what they cover away from home.

🖪 Travel Insurers In the U.S.: **Access America** ✉ 2805 N. Parham Rd., Richmond, VA 23294 ☎ 800/284-8300 🖷 800/346-9265 or 804/673-1491 ⊕ www.accessamerica.com. **Travel Guard International** ✉ 1145 Clark St., Stevens Point, WI 54481 ☎ 800/826-1300 or 715/345-1041 🖷 800/955-8785 ⊕ www.travelguard.com.

FOR INTERNATIONAL TRAVELERS

For information on customs restrictions, *see* Customs & Duties.

CAR RENTAL

When picking up a rental car, non-U.S. residents need a reservation voucher for any prepaid reservations that were made in the traveler's home country, a passport, a driver's license, and a travel policy that covers each driver.

CAR TRAVEL

Gas stations are common along major highways and in most communities throughout the state, the exception being New York City, where they can be hard to come by. Try to **fill up at stations outside of New York City,** where prices can be anywhere from 10¢ to 50¢ less expensive per gallon. At this writing, the average price of a gallon of regular unleaded gas was just under $2 throughout much of New York State; Manhattan and Long Island consistently register the highest prices, whereas western and upstate New York are typically a bit less expensive. Most stations stay open late (24 hours along large highways and in big cities), except in rural areas, where Sunday hours are limited and where you may drive long stretches without a refueling opportunity.

Highways are well paved. Interstate highways—limited-access, multilane highways whose numbers are prefixed by "I–"—are the fastest routes. Interstates with three-digit numbers encircle urban areas, which may have other limited-access expressways, freeways, and parkways as well. Tolls may be levied on limited-access highways. So-called U.S. highways and state highways are not necessarily limited-access but may have several lanes. Along larger highways, roadside stops with restrooms, fast-food restaurants, and sundries stores are well spaced. State police and tow trucks patrol major highways and lend assistance. If your car breaks down on an interstate, pull onto the shoulder and wait for help, or have your passengers wait while you walk to an emergency phone (available in most states). If you carry a cell phone, dial 911, noting your location on the small green roadside mileage markers.

Driving in the United States is on the right. Do obey speed limits posted along roads and highways. Watch for lower limits in small towns and on back roads. State law requires that front-seat passengers wear seat belts at all times. On weekdays between 6 and 10 AM and again between 4 and 7 PM expect heavy traffic. To encourage carpooling, some freeways have special lanes for so-called high-occupancy vehicles (HOV)—cars carrying more than one passenger.

Bookstores, gas stations, convenience stores, and rest stops sell maps (about $3) and multiregion road atlases (about $10).

CONSULATES

🇦🇺 **Australia Australian Consulate General** ✉ 150 E. 42nd St., 34th floor, between Lexington and 3rd Aves., Midtown East, New York, NY 10017 ☎ 212/351-6500 🖷 212/351-6501 ⊕ www.australianyc.org. 🇨🇦 **Canada Consulate General of Canada** ✉ 1251 Ave. of the Americas, between W. 49th and W. 50th Sts., Midtown West, New York, NY 10020-1175 ☎ 212/596-1628 🖷 212/596-1793 ⊕ www.canada-ny.org. 🇳🇿 **New Zealand New Zealand Consulate-General** ✉ 780 3rd Ave., 19th floor, Midtown East, New York, NY 10017-6702 ☎ 212/832-4038 🖷 212/832-7602. 🇬🇧 **United Kingdom British Consulate-General** ✉ 845 3rd Ave., between E. 51st and E. 52nd Sts., Midtown East, New York, NY 10022 ☎ 212/745-0200 🖷 212/745-3062 ⊕ www.britainusa.com/ny.

CURRENCY

The dollar is the basic unit of U.S. currency. It has 100 cents. Coins are the copper penny (1¢); the silvery nickel (5¢), dime (10¢), quarter (25¢), and half-dollar (50¢); and the golden $1 coin, replacing a now-rare silver dollar. Bills are denominated $1, $5, $10, $20, $50, and $100, all mostly green and identical in size; designs and background tints vary. In addition, you may come across a $2 bill, but the chances are slim. The exchange rate at this writing is US$1.77 per British pound, US$0.72 per Canadian dollar, US$0.69 per Australian dollar, and US$0.60 per New Zealand dollar.

ELECTRICITY

The U.S. standard is AC, 110 volts/60 cycles. Plugs have two flat pins set parallel to each other.

EMERGENCIES

For police, fire, or ambulance, **dial 911** (0 in rural areas).

INSURANCE

Britons and Australians need extra medical coverage when traveling overseas. 🇬🇧 In the U.K.: **Association of British Insurers** ✉ 51 Gresham St., London EC2V 7HQ ☎ 020/7600-3333 🖷 020/7696-8999 ⊕ www.abi.org.uk. In Australia: **Insurance Council of Australia** ✉ Insurance Enquiries and Complaints, Box 561, Collins St. W, Melbourne, VIC 8007 ☎ 1300/780808 or 03/9629-4109 🖷 03/9621-2060 ⊕ www.iecltd.com.au. In Canada: **RBC Insurance** ✉ 6880 Financial Dr., Mississauga, Ontario L5N 7Y5 ☎ 800/668-4342 or 905/816-2559 🖷 905/813-4704 ⊕ www.rbcinsurance.com. In New Zealand: **Insurance Council of New Zealand** ✉ Level 7, 111-115 Customhouse Quay, Box 474, Wellington ☎ 04/472-5230 🖷 04/473-3011 ⊕ www.icnz.org.nz.

MAIL & SHIPPING

You can buy stamps and aerograms and send letters and parcels in post offices. Stamp-dispensing machines can occasionally be found in airports, bus and train stations, office buildings, drugstores, and the like. You can also deposit mail in the stout, dark blue, steel bins at strategic locations everywhere and in the mail chutes of large buildings; pickup schedules are posted. You can deposit packages at public collection boxes as long as the parcels are affixed with proper postage and weigh less than one pound. Packages weighing one or more pounds must be taken to a post office or handed to a postal carrier.

For mail sent within the United States, you need a 37¢ stamp for first-class letters weighing up to 1 ounce (23¢ for each additional ounce) and 23¢ for postcards. You pay 80¢ for 1-ounce airmail letters and 70¢ for airmail postcards to most other countries; to Canada and Mexico, you need a 60¢ stamp for a 1-ounce letter and a 50¢ stamp for a postcard. An aerogram—a single sheet of lightweight blue paper that folds into its own envelope, stamped for overseas airmail—costs 70¢.

To receive mail on the road, have it sent c/o General Delivery at your destination's main post office (use the correct five-digit ZIP code). You must pick up mail in person within 30 days and show a driver's license or passport.

PASSPORTS & VISAS

When traveling internationally, carry your passport even if you don't need one (it's always the best form of I.D.) and **make two photocopies of the data page** (one for someone at home and another for you, carried separately from your passport). If you lose your passport, promptly call the nearest embassy or consulate and the local police.

Visitor visas aren't necessary for Canadian or European Union citizens, or for citizens of Australia who are staying fewer than 90 days.

Australian Citizens Passports Australia ☎ 131-232 ⊕ www.passports.gov.au. **United States Consulate General** ⊠ MLC Centre, Level 59, 19-29 Martin Pl., Sydney, NSW 2000 ☎ 02/9373-9200, 1902/941-641 fee-based visa-inquiry line ⊕ usembassy-australia.state.gov/sydney.

Canadian Citizens Passport Office ⊠ to mail in applications: 70 Cremazie St., Gatineau, Québec J8Y 3P2 ☎ 800/567-6868, 819/994-3500, 866/255-7655 TTY ⊕ www.ppt.gc.ca.

New Zealand Citizens New Zealand Passports Office ⊠ For applications and information, Level 3, Boulcott House, 47 Boulcott St., Wellington ☎ 0800/22-5050 or 04/474-8100 ⊕ www.passports.govt.nz. **Embassy of the United States** ⊠ 29 Fitzherbert Terr., Thorndon, Wellington ☎ 04/462-6000 ⊕ usembassy.org.nz. **U.S. Consulate General** ⊠ Citibank Bldg., 3rd floor, 23 Customs St. E, Auckland ☎ 09/303-2724 ⊕ usembassy.org.nz.

U.K. Citizens U.K. Passport Service ☎ 0870/521-0410 ⊕ www.passport.gov.uk. **American Consulate General** ⊠ Danesfort House, 223 Stranmillis Rd., Belfast, Northern Ireland BT9 5GR ☎ 028/9038-6100 🖷 028/9068-1301 ⊕ www.usembassy.org.uk. **American Embassy** ⊠ For visa and immigration information or to submit a visa application via mail (enclose an SASE), Consular Information

Unit, 24 Grosvenor Sq., London W1A 2LQ ☎ 090/5544-4546 or 090/6820-0290 for visa information (per-minute charges), 0207/499-9000 main switchboard ⊕ www.usembassy.org.uk.

TELEPHONES

All U.S. telephone numbers consist of a three-digit area code and a seven-digit local number. Within many local calling areas you dial only the seven-digit number. Within some area codes you must dial "1" first for calls outside the local area. To call between area-code regions, dial "1" then all 10 digits; the same goes for calls to numbers prefixed by "800," "888," "866," and "877"—all toll-free. For calls to numbers preceded by "900" you must pay—usually dearly.

For international calls, dial "011" followed by the country code and the local number. For help, dial "0" and ask for an overseas operator. The country code is 61 for Australia, 64 for New Zealand, 44 for the United Kingdom. Calling Canada is the same as calling within the United States. Most local phone books list country codes and U.S. area codes. The country code for the United States is 1.

For operator assistance, dial "0." To obtain someone's phone number, call directory assistance at 555–1212 or occasionally 411 (free at many public phones). To have the person you're calling foot the bill, phone collect; dial "0" instead of "1" before the 10-digit number.

At pay phones, instructions often are posted. Usually you insert coins in a slot (usually 25¢–50¢ for local calls) and wait for a steady tone before dialing. When you call long-distance, the operator tells you how much to insert; prepaid phone cards, widely available in various denominations, are easier. Call the number on the back, punch in the card's personal identification number when prompted, then dial your number.

LODGING

The lodgings we list are the cream of the crop in each price category. We always list the facilities that are available, but we don't specify whether they cost extra; when pricing accommodations, always ask what's included and what costs extra. Properties are assigned price categories based on the range between their least and most expensive standard double rooms at high season (excluding holidays). You'll be charged a hotel tax, which varies between towns and counties throughout the state from approximately 10% to 14%. Properties marked ✕ are lodging establishments whose restaurants warrant a special trip. Assume that hotels operate on the European Plan (EP, with no meals) unless we specify that they use either the Continental Plan (CP, with a Continental breakfast), Breakfast Plan (BP, with a full breakfast), or the Modified American Plan (MAP, with breakfast and dinner) or are AI (all-inclusive, including all meals and most activities).

New York City commands the highest hotel prices in the nation, and occupancy rates can be quite high, too. In seasonal destinations, such as the Hamptons and Fire Island, it can be tough to find weekend hotel rooms in summer, so it's wise to **book several weeks or months ahead in season**; you'll also pay the steepest rates in seashore destinations in summer. These same rules apply to popular fall-foliage destinations, especially the Catskills, Finger Lakes, and Hudson Valley. When visiting towns with a large college presence (Poughkeepsie, Ithaca, Hamilton), be aware that rooms can be extremely tough to come by on weekends throughout the school year. Also take into consideration major cultural and sporting events, which can push up prices and greatly reduce availability in certain places—everything from New Year's Eve in New York City to the Baseball Hall of Fame inductions in Cooperstown.

APARTMENT & HOUSE RENTALS

If you want a home base that's roomy enough for a family and comes with cooking facilities, consider a furnished rental. These can save you money, especially if you're traveling with a group. Home-exchange directories sometimes list rentals as well as exchanges. Some parts of New York are popular for short- and long-term vacation rentals, such as Long Island (especially the Hamptons and Fire Island), the Finger Lakes, and the Adirondacks. For information about rental listings in these locations, *see* the A to Z sections within the appropriate regional chapters.

f International Agents Hideaways International ✉ 767 Islington St., Portsmouth, NH 03801 ☎ 800/843-4433 or 603/430-4433 🖷 603/430-4444 ⊕ www.hideaways.com, annual membership $185. **Hometours International** ✉ 1108 Scottie La., Knoxville, TN 37919 ☎ 866/367-4668 or 865/690-8484 ⊕ thor.he.net/~hometour/.

BED & BREAKFASTS

Historic B&Bs and inns are plentiful throughout New York, including a handful in New York City. In many rural or less touristy areas B&Bs offer an affordable and homey alternative to chain properties, but in tourism-dependent destinations you can expect to pay about the same or more for a historic inn as for a full-service hotel. Although many B&Bs and inns are low-key and lack TVs and other amenities, the scene has changed somewhat in cities and upscale resort areas, where many such properties now cater to business and luxury leisure travelers with high-speed Internet, voice mail, whirlpool tubs, and VCRs. Many of the state's finest restaurants are also found in country inns. Quite a few inns and B&Bs serve substantial full breakfasts—the kind that may keep your appetite in check for the better part of the day.

American Country Collection is a reservation service for eastern upstate New York, from the Hudson Valley up through the eastern Adirondacks to the Canadian border. A Reasonable Alternative serves Long Island, and Bed and Breakfast Network of New York serves New York City.

f Reservation Services American Country Collection ☎ 800/810-4948 or 518/370-4948 ⊕ www.bandbreservations.com. **A Reasonable Alternative** ☎ 631/928-4034 ⊕ www.areasonablealternative.com. **Bed and Breakfast Network of New York** ☎ 800/900-8134 or 212/645-8134 ⊕ www.bedandbreakfastnetny.com.

CAMPING

Within New York's extensive state-park system, much of it concentrated in the

Adirondacks and the Catskills, campgrounds offering both primitive and developed sites abound. For state parks, you
can call or book online through Reserve
America to reserve a campsite at any of
the state's 66 camping parks as early as
nine months in advance and as late as two
days before you arrive. Most park campgrounds are open from Memorial Day
through Labor Day; some of them remain
open throughout the year, even in winter.
Some have cabin rentals, too. Based on
availability, state parks also accept walk-
ins without reservations, but it's best to
call ahead to avoid disappointment.

New York also has hundreds of private
commercial campgrounds for RV and tent
camping.

🏕 **Reserve America** ☎ 800/456-2267 ⊕ www.
reserveamerica.com. **Campground Owners of New
York** ⌂ Box 497, Dansville, NY 14437 ☎ 585/335-
2710 ⊕ www.nycampgrounds.com.

HOSTELS

No matter what your age, you can save on
lodging costs by staying at hostels. In some
4,500 locations in more than 70 countries
around the world, Hostelling International
(HI), the umbrella group for a number of
national youth-hostel associations, offers
single-sex, dorm-style beds and, at many
hostels, rooms for couples and family accommodations. HI has hostels in New
York City, Buffalo, Niagara Falls, Syracuse, and Cape Vincent (in the Thousand
Islands). Membership in any HI national
hostel association, open to travelers of all
ages, allows you to stay in HI-affiliated
hostels at member rates; one-year membership is about $28 for adults (C$35 for a
two-year minimum membership in
Canada, £14 in the U.K., A$52 in Aus-
tralia, and NZ$40 in New Zealand); hos-
tels charge about $10–$30 per night.
Members have priority if the hostel is full;
they're also eligible for discounts around
the world, even on rail and bus travel in
some countries.

🏕 **Organizations Hostelling International–USA**
⊠ 8401 Colesville Rd., Suite 600, Silver Spring, MD
20910 ☎ 301/495-1240 🖨 301/495-6697 ⊕ www.
hiusa.org. **Hostelling International–Canada**
⊠ 205 Catherine St., Suite 400, Ottawa, Ontario

K2P 1C3 ☎ 800/663-5777 or 613/237-7884 🖨 613/
237-7868 ⊕ www.hihostels.ca. **YHA England and
Wales** ⊠ Trevelyan House, Dimple Rd., Matlock,
Derbyshire DE4 3YH, U.K. ☎ 0870/870-8808, 0870/
770-8868, 0162/959-2600 🖨 0870/770-6127
⊕ www.yha.org.uk. **YHA Australia** ⊠ 422 Kent St.,
Sydney, NSW 2001 ☎ 02/9261-1111 🖨 02/9261-1969
⊕ www.yha.com.au. **YHA New Zealand** ⊠ Level 1,
Moorhouse City, 166 Moorhouse Ave., Box 436,
Christchurch ☎ 03/379-9970 or 0800/278-299
🖨 03/365-4476 ⊕ www.yha.org.nz.

MEDIA

NEWSPAPERS & MAGAZINES

The most prominent newspapers in New
York are based in New York City: the
*New York Times, Wall Street Journal,
New York Sun,* and the *New York Ob-
server,* all broadsheets, and the *Daily
News, Newsday,* and the *New York Post,*
which are tabloids. There are about 40
other daily newspapers throughout the
state, including major papers out of Al-
bany (the *Times Union*), Rochester (the
Rochester Democrat & Chronicle), and
Buffalo (the *Buffalo News*).

Free alternative news weeklies, distributed
in most big cities, can be a great source of
information on dining, arts, culture, and
sightseeing. In New York City, look for the
Village Voice and the *New York Press.*
Local magazines include the *New Yorker,
New York,* and *Time Out New York.* All
of these are widely available at newsstands
and bookstores around the state.

RADIO & TELEVISION

All of the major urban markets in New
York have their own radio and television
stations, New York City being the media
hub of the lower part of the state. New
York City has its own 24-hour cable TV
news station, New York 1 (Channel 1),
with local and international news an-
nouncements around-the-clock.

MONEY MATTERS

Prices for services and travel vary tremendously throughout the state. In Manhattan, New York City suburbs, eastern Long
Island, and even parts of the Hudson Valley, it's easy to get swept up in a debt-in-
ducing cyclone of $60-per-person dinners,
$100 theater tickets, $20 nightclub covers,

$10 cab rides, and $300 hotel rooms. Elsewhere in the state, prices for dining, hotels, and entertainment tend to be consistent with national averages. But one of the good things about New York, even in Manhattan, is that there's such a wide variety of options; you can spend in some areas and save in others. Within Manhattan and much of the metro area, a cup of coffee costs from 50¢ to $4, a pint of beer from $4 to $7, and a sandwich from $5 to $10; in upstate New York, especially rural areas, expect to pay 25% to 50% less for the same items.

Prices throughout this guide are given for adults. Substantially reduced fees are almost always available for children, students, and senior citizens. For information on taxes, *see* Taxes.

ATMS
Cash machines are abundant throughout New York and are found not only in banks but in many grocery stores, Laundromats, delis, and hotels. Note, however, that many bank ATMs charge users a fee of up to $2, and the commercial ATMs in retail establishments can charge even more.

CREDIT CARDS
Throughout this guide, the following abbreviations are used: AE, American Express; D, Discover; DC, Diners Club; MC, MasterCard; and V, Visa.

Reporting Lost Cards American Express ☎ 800/992-3404. **Diners Club** ☎ 800/234-6377. **Discover** ☎ 800/347-2683. **MasterCard** ☎ 800/622-7747. **Visa** ☎ 800/847-2911.

NATIONAL PARKS
Probably the most famous of New York's well-visited national parks, monuments, seashores, and forests are Fire Island National Seashore (on the south shore of Long Island) and the Statue of Liberty National Monument (off the southern tip of New York City, in New York Harbor). You'll also find several history- and culture-related national-park sites around the state.

Look into discount passes to save money on park entrance fees. For $50, the National Parks Pass admits you (and any passengers in your private vehicle) to all national parks, monuments, and recreation areas, as well as other sites run by the National Park Service, for a year. (In parks that charge per person, the pass admits you, your spouse and children, and your parents, when you arrive together.) Camping and parking are extra. The $15 Golden Eagle Pass, a hologram you affix to your National Parks Pass, functions as an upgrade, granting entry to all sites run by the NPS, the U.S. Fish and Wildlife Service, the U.S. Forest Service, and the Bureau of Land Management. The upgrade, which expires with the parks pass, is sold by most national-park, Fish-and-Wildlife, and BLM fee stations. A major percentage of the proceeds from pass sales funds National Parks projects.

Both the Golden Age Passport ($10), for U.S. citizens or permanent residents who are 62 and older, and the Golden Access Passport (free), for persons with disabilities, entitle holders (and any passengers in their private vehicles) to lifetime free entry to all national parks, plus 50% off fees for the use of many park facilities and services. (The discount doesn't always apply to companions.) To obtain them, you must show proof of age and of U.S. citizenship or permanent residency—such as a U.S. passport, driver's license, or birth certificate—and, if requesting Golden Access, proof of disability. The Golden Age and Golden Access passes are available only at NPS-run sites that charge an entrance fee. The National Parks Pass is also available by mail and phone and via the Internet.

National Park Foundation ✉ 11 Dupont Circle NW, 6th floor, Washington, DC 20036 ☎ 202/238-4200 ⊕ www.nationalparks.org. **National Park Service** ✉ National Park Service/Department of Interior, 1849 C St. NW, Washington, DC 20240 ☎ 202/208-6843 ⊕ www.nps.gov. **National Parks Conservation Association** ✉ 1300 19th St. NW, Suite 300, Washington, DC 20036 ☎ 202/223-6722 ⊕ www.npca.org.

Passes by Mail & Online National Park Foundation ⊕ www.nationalparks.org. **National Parks Pass** National Park Foundation ✍ Box 34108, Washington, DC 20043 ☎ 888/467-2757 ⊕ www.nationalparks.org; include a check or money order payable to the National Park Service, plus $3.95 for shipping and handling (allow 8 to 13 business days from date of receipt for pass delivery), or call for passes.

PACKING

In New York, especially in New York City and the surrounding suburbs, jackets and ties are required for men at a very few high-end restaurants; in general, New Yorkers tend to dress a bit more formally than their Midwest or West Coast counterparts for special events. Jeans and sneakers are acceptable for casual dining and sightseeing just about anywhere in the state. Be sure to **pack sneakers or other walking shoes** for pounding the pavement in urban areas, and hiking boots if you plan to hit the trails.

In spring and fall, pack at least one warm jacket and sweater, since moderate daytime temperatures can drop after nightfall. Bring shorts for summer, which can be quite humid. You need a warm coat, hat, scarf, and gloves in winter; boots for often slushy streets are also a good idea. Upstate New York has some of the coldest weather in the eastern United States, so pack particularly warm gear if you're spending time in the state's northern and western regions in winter.

Pack light—porters and luggage trolleys can be hard to find at New York airports. And bring a fistful of quarters for renting a trolley.

In your carry-on luggage, pack an extra pair of eyeglasses or contact lenses and enough of any medication you take to last a few days longer than the entire trip. You may also ask your doctor to write a spare prescription using the drug's generic name, as brand names may vary from country to country. In luggage to be checked, **never pack prescription drugs, valuables, or undeveloped film.** And don't forget to carry with you the addresses of offices that handle refunds of lost traveler's checks. Check *Fodor's How to Pack* (available at online retailers and bookstores everywhere) for more tips.

To avoid customs and security delays, carry medications in their original packaging. Don't pack any sharp objects in your carry-on luggage, including knives of any size or material, scissors, nail clippers, and corkscrews, or anything else that might arouse suspicion.

To avoid having your checked luggage chosen for hand inspection, don't cram bags full. The U.S. Transportation Security Administration suggests packing shoes on top and placing personal items you don't want touched in clear plastic bags.

CHECKING LUGGAGE

You're allowed to carry aboard one bag and one personal article, such as a purse or a laptop computer. Make sure what you carry on fits under your seat or in the overhead bin. Get to the gate early, so you can board as soon as possible, before the overhead bins fill up.

Baggage allowances vary by carrier, destination, and ticket class. On international flights, you're usually allowed to check two bags weighing up to 70 pounds (32 kilograms) each, although a few airlines allow checked bags of up to 88 pounds (40 kilograms) in first class. Some international carriers don't allow more than 66 pounds (30 kilograms) per bag in business class and 44 pounds (20 kilograms) in economy. If you're flying to or through the United Kingdom, your luggage cannot exceed 70 pounds (32 kilograms) per bag. On domestic flights, the limit is usually 50 to 70 pounds (23 to 32 kilograms) per bag. In general, carry-on bags shouldn't exceed 40 pounds (18 kilograms). Most airlines won't accept bags that weigh more than 100 pounds (45 kilograms) on domestic or international flights. Expect to pay a fee for baggage that exceeds weight limits. Check baggage restrictions with your carrier before you pack.

Airline liability for baggage is limited to $2,500 per person on flights within the United States. On international flights it amounts to $9.07 per pound or $20 per kilogram for checked baggage (roughly $640 per 70-pound bag), with a maximum of $634.90 per piece, and $400 per passenger for unchecked baggage. You can buy additional coverage at check-in for about $10 per $1,000 of coverage, but it often excludes a rather extensive list of items, shown on your airline ticket.

Before departure, itemize your bags' contents and their worth, and label the bags with your name, address, and phone number. (If you use your home address, cover it so potential thieves can't see it readily.) Include a label inside each bag and **pack a copy of your itinerary.** At check-in, make sure each bag is correctly tagged with the destination airport's three-letter code. Because some checked bags will be opened for hand inspection, the U.S. Transportation Security Administration recommends that you leave luggage unlocked or use the plastic locks offered at check-in. TSA screeners place an inspection notice inside searched bags, which are re-sealed with a special lock.

If your bag has been searched and contents are missing or damaged, file a claim with the TSA Consumer Response Center as soon as possible. If your bags arrive damaged or fail to arrive at all, file a written report with the airline before leaving the airport.

⑦ Complaints U.S. Transportation Security Administration Contact Center ☎ 866/289–9673 ⊕ www.tsa.gov.

SAFETY

Most of New York is comparable to the rest of the country with respect to safety and crime. And although outsiders have sometimes viewed New York City as being dangerous or crime-ridden, it is in fact one of the safest large cities in the country today. However, don't let yourself be lulled into a false sense of security. New York City and the state's other urban areas still have significantly higher rates of crime—both violent and nonviolent—than suburban and rural areas. Tourists can be relatively easy targets for pickpockets and thieves, especially in New York City. Your wisest approach in the state's urban and touristy areas is to avoid venturing out alone at night, to rely on cabs when getting around at night, and if you're driving, to lock your car and never leave important articles unattended. Keep jewelry out of sight on the street; better yet, **leave valuables at home.**

In the wake of the World Trade Center disaster, security has been greatly heightened in New York City and generally increased statewide. Expect thorough inspections of your apparel and personal belongings in airports, sports stadiums, museums, and government buildings.

In New York City it's best to ignore the panhandlers on the streets and subways, people who offer to hail you a cab (they often appear at Penn Station, the Port Authority, and Grand Central), and limousine and gypsy-cab drivers who (illegally) offer you a ride. Men should carry their wallets in their front pants pocket rather than in their back pockets. When in bars or restaurants, never hang your purse or bag on the back of a chair or put it underneath the table. Avoid deserted blocks in unfamiliar neighborhoods. A brisk, purposeful pace helps deter trouble wherever you go.

New York City's subway runs around the clock and is generally well trafficked until midnight (even later on Friday and Saturday nights); overall it is very safe. If you do take the subway at night, ride in the center car, with the conductor, and wait on the center of the platform or right in front of the station agent. Watch out for unsavory characters lurking around the inside or outside of stations, particularly at night. When waiting for a train, stand far away from the edge of the subway platform, especially when trains are entering or leaving the station. Once the train pulls into the station, **avoid empty subway cars.** While on the train, don't engage in verbal exchanges with aggressive riders, who may accuse others of anything from pushing to taking up too much space. If a fellow passenger makes you nervous while on the train, trust your instincts and change cars. When disembarking, stick with the crowd until you reach the street.

Travelers Aid International helps crime victims and stranded travelers and works closely with the police. Its office at JFK airport is staffed weekdays 10–6 and weekends 11–7.

⑦ Resources Travelers Aid International ☎ 718/656–4870 ⊕ www.travelersaid.org.

LOCAL SCAMS

Someone who appears to have had an accident at the exit door of a bus may flee with your wallet or purse if you attempt to give aid. The individual who approaches you with a complicated story probably hopes to get something from you. **Beware of people jostling you in crowds,** or someone tapping your shoulder from behind. Never play or place a bet on a sidewalk card game, shell game, or other guessing game—they're all rigged to get your cash, and they're illegal.

SENIOR-CITIZEN TRAVEL

To qualify for age-related discounts, mention your senior-citizen status up front when booking hotel reservations (not when checking out) and before you're seated in restaurants (not when paying the bill). Be sure to have identification on hand. When renting a car, ask about promotional car-rental discounts, which can be cheaper than senior-citizen rates.

The Metropolitan Transit Authority (MTA) offers lower fares for passengers 65 and over for New York City buses and subways. Show your Medicare card to the bus driver or station agent, and for the standard fare ($2) you will be issued a MetroCard and a return-trip ticket.

ⓘ Educational Programs Elderhostel ✉ 11 Ave. de Lafayette, Boston, MA 02111-1746 ☎ 877/426-8056, 978/323-4141 international callers, 877/426-2167 TTY 🖷 877/426-2166 ⊕ www.elderhostel.org.

SPORTS & OUTDOORS

Gorp.com is a terrific general resource for just about every kind of recreational activity; choose New York from the "Destinations" section and you'll be flooded with links to myriad topics, from wildlife refuges to ski trips to backpacking advice.

BICYCLING

New York's terrain is tremendously varied, and apart from Long Island it tends to be hilly. Long Island, however, especially Suffolk County, which is less congested than other parts of the island, affords cycling enthusiasts of all abilities miles of great riding. At the other end of the spectrum, traffic, theft, and a lack of suitable roads make New York City unappealing for biking. Depending on your fitness

level, upstate New York and the Hudson Valley can be terrific for cycling, especially if you're using a mountain bike.

The New York State Department of Transportation maintains three official long-distance bike routes through the state: Route 17, which runs across the southern tier of the state from the Hudson Valley to Lake Erie and in 2004 started being called Interstate 86 (aka the Quickway); Route 5, which runs across the middle tier of the state from Albany to Buffalo; and Route 9, which runs up the Hudson Valley from Westchester County to the Canadian border. Be prepared to bike alongside automobile traffic along these routes.

The New York Bicycling Coalition Web site has a resources page with links to biking organizations, maps, and itineraries. Several bike clubs throughout the state welcome visitors and can provide detailed advice on local routes and rental shops (which are plentiful in the state's most popular destinations); contact local tourist boards, many of which also distribute bike-trail maps, for more information.

ⓘ New York Bicycling Coalition ⬠ Box 8868, Albany, NY 12208 ☎ 518/436-0889 ⊕ www.nybc.net. **New York State Department of Transportation** ⊕ www.dot.state.ny.us.

BOATING

You can find marinas and yacht clubs throughout New York State, which has some 7,500 lakes and is fringed by the Atlantic Ocean, two of the five Great Lakes (Erie and Ontario), and Lake Champlain. There's also excellent boating along central New York's Finger Lakes, in the many pristine lakes of the Adirondacks, and along the lower Hudson River. Canoeing, kayaking, and rafting are popular in all these destinations, too, as well as in hundreds of smaller rivers, streams, and lakes statewide.

ⓘ New York State Department of Environmental Conservation, Bureau of Marine Resources ✉ 625 Broadway, Albany, NY 12233 ☎ 518/402-8920 ⊕ www.dec.state.ny.us.

FISHING

Much of interior New York is famous for its outstanding lake (lake trout, walleye, bass, perch) and river (coho and chinook salmon, brown and rainbow trout) fishing. Champlain, Ontario, Erie, George, Chautauqua, and the Finger Lakes all offer exceptional lake fishing. Top rivers for casting a line include the Delaware, upper Hudson, Mohawk, Salmon, St. Lawrence, Niagara, Beaver Kill, and Susquehanna. Off of Long Island, the state excels as a saltwater-fishing hub—top catches include Atlantic cod, mackerel, flounder, and bluefish.

Anglers 16 and older must obtain a license (often available at sporting-goods stores) for all freshwater fishing, except for the Hudson River below Troy Dam. For saltwater fishing you must observe the state's daily limits on the size and number of fish you're permitted to catch. Contact the New York State Department of Environmental Conservation for details on licenses, limits, and other fishing regulations.
🚩 **New York State Department of Environmental Conservation, Bureau of Fisheries** ✉ 625 Broadway, Albany, NY 12233 ☎ 631/444-0430 ⊕ www.dec.state.ny.us.

GOLF
New York abounds with golf courses, and some of the leading facilities around the state have hosted top pro-golf tournaments over the years, including the PGA's U.S. Open, which took place at Long Island's Shinnecock Hills Golf Club in 2004; the U.S. Open is scheduled to be held at Winged Foot Golf Club in Mamaroneck in 2006 and at Long Island's Bethpage State Park (in Farmingdale) in 2009. Many of the top courses, especially those on Long Island and in Westchester County, are private, but you can often arrange visits in advance if you're a member of a private club back home. Of *Golf Digest*'s top 50 U.S. golf courses, an impressive nine are in New York, but only one of these, Bethpage, is open to the public. Still, you can find some exceptional public courses all around the state.
🚩 **New York State Golf Association** 📬 Box 15333, Syracuse, NY 13215 ☎ 888/697-4223 or 315/471-6979 ⊕ www.nysga.org.

HIKING
Although New York is rife with great hiking regions, two areas stand head and shoulders above the rest: the Adirondacks, with some 42 peaks rising more than 4,000 feet and some of the most challenging hiking in the Northeast; and an 88½-mi swath of the Appalachian Trail cutting through New York's southern Hudson Valley. You'll also find hundreds of miles of trails in the Catskills and among New York's more than 160 state parks. Long Island, with its flat and sandy topography, presents less-challenging but pleasant rambles, many near the ocean or Long Island Sound.

The New York–New Jersey Trail Conference, a consortium of some 85 regional hiking clubs throughout both states, posts advice and resources on its Web site.
🚩 **Adirondack Mountain Club** ✉ 814 Goggins Rd., Lake George, NY 12845 ☎ 800/395-8080 or 518/668-4447 ⊕ www.adk.org. **Appalachian National Scenic Trail** ✉ NPS Park Office, Harpers Ferry Center, Harpers Ferry, WV 25425 ☎ 304/535-6331 or 304/535-6278 ⊕ www.nps.gov/appa. **New York–New Jersey Trail Conference** ✉ 156 Ramapo Valley Rd./U.S. 202, Mahwah, NJ 07430 ☎ 201/512-0348 ⊕ www.nynjtc.org.

SKIING
With one of the East Coast's premier ski facilities, Lake Placid, New York affords skiers plenty of action from early November through mid-April. There are more than 50 downhill ski areas in New York, plus about 120 properties or facilities geared toward cross-country skiing. The Adirondacks and Catskills have the best downhill mountains and cross-country terrain, but you can cross-country ski throughout much of the state. Refer to the state tourism Web site (⊕ www.iloveny.com) and regional chapters for more information.

STUDENTS IN NEW YORK
With several prominent private universities and colleges and 64 State University of New York (SUNY) campuses throughout the state, it's no wonder that New York offers countless discounts for students. Wherever you go, especially museums, sightseeing attractions, and performances,

identify yourself as a student up front and ask if a discount is available. **Be prepared to show your student I.D.** for discounts.

I.D.s & Services STA Travel ✉ 10 Downing St., New York, NY 10014 ☎ 800/777-0112 24-hr service center, 212/627-3111 🖷 212/627-3387 ⊕ www.sta.com. **Travel Cuts** ✉ 187 College St., Toronto, Ontario M5T 1P7, Canada ☎ 800/592-2887 in U.S., 416/979-2406 or 866/246-9762 in Canada 🖷 416/979-8167 ⊕ www.travelcuts.com.

TAXES

Municipalities throughout the state charge a variety of taxes on hotel rooms, car rentals, and parking in commercial lots or garages. These range typically from 10% to 14% for hotels and rental cars, and from 10% to 19% for parking.

SALES TAX

New York City's sales tax of 8.625% applies to almost everything you can buy retail, including restaurant meals. Nonprepared foods (from grocery stores) and prescription drugs are tax-exempt. Long Island's Nassau and Suffolk counties have the highest sales-tax rate in the state: 8.75%. Rates elsewhere in the state are 7.25%–8.5%.

TIME

New York operates on Eastern Standard Time. When it is noon in New York it is 9 AM in Los Angeles, 11 AM in Chicago, 5 PM in London, and 3 AM the following day in Sydney.

TIPPING

The customary tipping rate for taxi drivers is 15%–20%, with a minimum of $2; bellhops are usually given $2 per bag in luxury hotels, $1 per bag elsewhere. Hotel maids should be tipped $3 or $4 a night for rooms that cost up to $250 a night (before taxes), $5–$7 a night for rooms in the $250–$350 range, and $8–$10 a night when you stay in more-expensive lodgings. If the hotel charges a service fee, be sure to ask what it covers, as it may include this gratuity. A doorman who hails or helps you into a cab can be tipped $1–$2. You should also tip your hotel concierge for services rendered; the size of the tip depends on the difficulty of your request, as well as the quality of the concierge's work.

For an ordinary dinner reservation or tour arrangements, $3–$5 should do; if the concierge scores seats at a popular restaurant or show or performs unusual services (such as getting your laptop repaired or finding a good pet sitter), $10 or more is appropriate.

Waiters should be tipped 15%–20%, though at higher-end restaurants, a solid 20% is more the norm. Many restaurants add a gratuity to the bill for parties of six or more. Ask what the percentage is if the menu or bill doesn't state it. Tip $1 per drink you order at the bar; at an upscale establishment, those $15 martinis might warrant a $2 tip, however.

TOURS & PACKAGES

Because everything is prearranged on a prepackaged tour or independent vacation, you spend less time planning—and often get it all at a good price.

BOOKING WITH AN AGENT

Travel agents are excellent resources. But it's a good idea to collect brochures from several agencies, as some agents' suggestions may be influenced by relationships with tour and package firms that reward them for volume sales. If you have a special interest, find an agent with expertise in that area; the American Society of Travel Agents (ASTA; ⇨ Travel Agencies) has a database of specialists worldwide. You can log on to the group's Web site to find an ASTA travel agent in your neighborhood.

Make sure your travel agent knows the accommodations and other services of the place being recommended. Ask about the hotel's location, room size, beds, and whether it has a pool, room service, or programs for children, if you care about these. Has your agent been there in person or sent others whom you can contact?

Do some homework on your own, too: local tourism boards can provide information about lesser-known and small-niche operators, some of which may sell only direct.

BUYER BEWARE

Each year consumers are stranded or lose their money when tour operators—even large ones with excellent reputations—go out of business. So check out the operator. Ask several travel agents about its reputation, and try to **book with a company that has a consumer-protection program.** (Look for information in the company's brochure.) In the United States, members of the United States Tour Operators Association are required to set aside funds (up to $1 million) to help eligible customers cover payments and travel arrangements in the event that the company defaults. It's also a good idea to choose a company that participates in the American Society of Travel Agents' Tour Operator Program; ASTA will act as mediator in any disputes between you and your tour operator.

Remember that the more your package or tour includes, the better you can predict the ultimate cost of your vacation. Make sure you know exactly what is covered, and beware of hidden costs. Are taxes, tips, and transfers included? Entertainment and excursions? These can add up.

Tour-Operator Recommendations American Society of Travel Agents (⇨ Travel Agencies). **National Tour Association** (NTA) ✉ 546 E. Main St., Lexington, KY 40508 ☎ 800/682-8886 or 859/226-4444 📠 859/226-4404 🌐 www.ntaonline.com. **United States Tour Operators Association** (USTOA) ✉ 275 Madison Ave., Suite 2014, New York, NY 10016 ☎ 212/599-6599 📠 212/599-6744 🌐 www.ustoa.com.

TRAIN TRAVEL

Compared with most of the country, New York enjoys extensive rail service and utilizes it heavily, especially in and out of New York City. Amtrak routes traverse two key regions of New York: the Hudson Valley, running south–north from New York City through Albany and the Adirondacks to Montréal; and central New York, running east–west across the state from western Massachusetts through Albany, Syracuse, Rochester, and Buffalo before heading down into Erie, Pennsylvania, and on into Ohio. Both of these routes are extremely scenic, especially the Hudson River run. There are also several major Amtrak routes in the northeastern United States that cut through New York City, most of them connecting stations on the Washington–Boston corridor. New York City's Penn Station is the hub for all of the state's Amtrak service except for the central New York runs.

Nowhere else in the country can you find more comprehensive commuter-rail service than in greater New York City. From Manhattan, Metro-North Commuter Railroad trains take passengers from Grand Central Terminal to points north, both in New York State and Connecticut. For trains to Long Island and New Jersey, take the Long Island Railroad and New Jersey Transit, respectively; both operate from Penn Station. The PATH trains run between Manhattan and the New Jersey towns of Newark and Jersey City.

CUTTING COSTS

You can often save money by avoiding travel at peak periods (generally Friday and Sunday on Amtrak, and weekdays during rush hour on the commuter rails), when tickets are generally more expensive. Amtrak occasionally offers deals that allow a second or third accompanying passenger to travel for half price or free. Amtrak's North America rail pass allows unlimited travel within the United States and Canada during any 30-day period ($699 June–mid-October, $495 mid-October–May). Amtrak also sells several USA Rail passes, available to non-U.S. residents only, offering unlimited travel for 15 to 30 days.

FARES & SCHEDULES

Tickets can run 10% to 50% higher if you don't purchase them seven days in advance. The following are approximate one-way fares, times, and routes on Amtrak (times and fares vary depending on the train service and number of stops): Boston to New York City, 3½–4¼ hours, $65–$85; Washington, D.C., to New York City, 2¾–3¼ hours, $75–$125; Montréal to New York City, 10 hours, $65; Chicago to Buffalo, 12–14 hours, $50; Toronto to Buffalo, 3¼ hours, $26; Toronto to Rhinecliff (mid–Hudson Valley), 10½ hours, $71; Philadelphia to Syracuse, 8–10 hours, $70; New York City to Niagara Falls, 9 hours, $65; Cleveland to Albany, 8½ hours, $50.

One-way fares on the commuter lines are usually $5–$12, and the cost is highest during peak hours (morning and early-evening rush hours). Also, you pay a small surcharge if you purchase your tickets on the train rather than at the station.

⁊ Amtrak ☎ 800/872-7245 ⊕ www.amtrak.com. **Long Island Railroad** ☎ 718/217-5477 ⊕ www.mta.nyc.ny.us/lirr. **Metro-North Commuter Railroad** ☎ 212/532-4900 ⊕ www.mta.nyc.ny.us/mnr. **New Jersey Transit** ☎ 973/762-5100 ⊕ www.njtransit.com. **PATH** ☎ 800/234-7284 ⊕ www.pathrail.com.

TRANSPORTATION AROUND NEW YORK STATE

If you're primarily visiting New York City and regions relatively nearby, it makes sense to use public transportation to get to New York (planes, trains, and buses) and to get around the region (trains and buses). In New York City, cars are enough of a hassle and parking is enough of an expense that you're better off relying solely on public transportation. You may need to rent a car for extensive forays outside the city, but even then, it's prudent to take a train to an outlying suburb, where you can often expect to pay less for a rental car. If you're driving your own car mostly around New York City and southern New York and you want to visit Manhattan, it often makes sense to park in a garage outside the city (such as Brewster's Southeast Station, New York; Stamford, Connecticut; or Princeton, New Jersey) and take the train.

Many of the more popular destinations within striking distance of New York City can be managed fairly easily without a car, either because trains or buses pull right into town within walking distance of attractions, or because the communities have reliable local bus service or plenty of cabs. This is the case throughout much of Long Island (including the Hamptons but excluding the North Fork, where a car is necessary) and for such popular Hudson Valley destinations as Rhinebeck, Hudson, Cold Spring, and Woodstock. It's also true of Cooperstown, Ithaca, Niagara Falls, and most of the larger upstate cities, including Albany and Buffalo. In these areas, a car allows maximum flexibility and freedom but is not necessary.

In general, if you're relying on public ground transportation it's a good idea to **compare travel times and costs between bus and train routes** to and within New York; in some cases, it's faster and even cheaper to take the train.

For northern and western New York, you really need a car to visit attractions, explore different towns, and travel between your hotel and restaurants and shops. In rural areas, such as the Adirondacks, the Catskills, and the Finger Lakes, a car is necessary. With several regional airports throughout upstate New York, as well as train and bus service to most major cities, you can generally count on traveling to New York by plane, train, or bus and then renting a car once you arrive.

TRAVEL AGENCIES

A good travel agent puts your needs first. Look for an agency that has been in business at least five years, emphasizes customer service, and has someone on staff who specializes in your destination. In addition, **make sure the agency belongs to a professional trade organization.** The American Society of Travel Agents (ASTA)—the largest and most influential in the field with more than 20,000 members in some 140 countries—maintains and enforces a strict code of ethics and will step in to help mediate any agent-client disputes involving ASTA members if necessary. ASTA (whose motto is "Without a travel agent, you're on your own") also maintains a Web site that includes a directory of agents. (If a travel agency is also acting as your tour operator, *see* Buyer Beware *in* Tours & Packages.)

⁊ Local Agent Referrals American Society of Travel Agents (ASTA) ✉ 1101 King St., Suite 200, Alexandria, VA 22314 ☎ 800/965-2782 24-hr hotline, 703/739-2782 ☎ 703/684-8319 ⊕ www.astanet.com. **Association of British Travel Agents** ✉ 68-71 Newman St., London W1T 3AH ☎ 020/7637-2444 ☎ 020/7637-0713 ⊕ www.abta.com. **Association of Canadian Travel Agencies** ✉ 130 Albert St., Suite 1705, Ottawa, Ontario K1P 5G4 ☎ 613/

237-3657 613/237-7052 www.acta.ca. Australian Federation of Travel Agents ✉ Level 3, 309 Pitt St., Sydney, NSW 2000 02/9264-3299 or 1300/363-416 02/9264-1085 www.afta.com.au. Travel Agents' Association of New Zealand ✉ Level 5, Tourism and Travel House, 79 Boulcott St., Box 1888, Wellington 6001 04/499-0104 04/499-0786 www.taanz.org.nz.

VISITOR INFORMATION

Tourist Information New York State Division of Tourism 800/225-5697 or 518/474-4116 www.iloveny.com.

Government Advisories Australian Department of Foreign Affairs and Trade 300/139-281 travel advice, 02/6261-1299 Consular Travel Advice Faxback Service www.dfat.gov.au. Consular Affairs Bureau of Canada 800/267-6788 or 613/944-6788 www.voyage.gc.ca. U.K. Foreign and Commonwealth Office ✉ Travel Advice Unit, Consular Division, Old Admiralty Building, London SW1A 2PA 0870/606-0290 or 020/7008-1500 www.fco.gov.uk/travel. New Zealand Ministry of Foreign Affairs and Trade 04/439-8000 www.mft.govt.nz.

WEB SITES

Do check out the World Wide Web when planning your trip. You'll find everything from weather forecasts to virtual tours of famous cities. Be sure to visit Fodors.com (www.fodors.com), a complete travel-planning site. You can research prices and book plane tickets, hotel rooms, rental cars, vacation packages, and more. In addition, you can post your pressing questions in the Travel Talk section. Other planning tools include a currency converter and weather reports, and there are loads of links to travel resources.

Check out the New York State home page (www.state.ny.us) for information on state government, and for links to state agencies on doing business, working, learning, living, and traveling in the Empire State. Citysearch.com and Digitalcity.com both post reviews of and links to restaurants, cultural venues, and various services in major cities and destinations throughout the state.

NEW YORK CITY

1

RELISH THE QUIET
of early-morning Bryant Park ⇨*p.27*

PAY HOMAGE TO THE LADY
on a trip to Liberty Island ⇨*p.10*

GET LOST IN THE HALLS
of the Metropolitan Museum of Art ⇨*p.35*

SEE WHAT THE FUSS IS ABOUT
at the redesigned Museum of Modern Art ⇨*p.31*

TICKLE YOUR TASTEBUDS
with "love letters" at Babbo ⇨*p.59*

SIP A RETRO DRINK
in the 1930s Campbell Apartment ⇨*p.95*

JOIN THE RITZY CROWD
shopping Madison Avenue ⇨*p.97*

SEE A SHOW FOR A SONG
by buying tickets at TKTS ⇨*p.116*

MANHATTAN IS A WALKER'S CITY. Along its busy streets an endless variety of sights unfolds everywhere you go. Attractions, many of them world-famous, crowd close together on this narrow island, and because the city can only grow up, not out, the new simply piles on top of the old. Manhattan's character changes every few blocks, so quaint town houses stand shoulder to shoulder with sleek glass towers, gleaming gourmet supermarkets sit around the corner from dusty thrift shops, and chic bistros inhabit the storefronts of soot-smudged warehouses. Many visitors, beguiled into walking a little farther, then a little farther still, stumble upon their trip's most memorable moments.

Look up at the tops of skyscrapers, and you see a riot of mosaics, carvings, and ornaments. Step into the lobby of an architectural landmark and study its features; take a look around to see the real people who work, live, or worship there today. Peep down side streets, even in crowded midtown, and you may find fountains, greenery, and sudden bursts of flowers. Find a bench or ledge on which to perch and take time just to watch the crowd passing by. New York has so many faces that every visitor can discover a different one.

EXPLORING MANHATTAN

Updated by
Melisse
Gelula,
Melissa
Hantman,
Evelyn Kanter,
Margaret
Mittelbach,
and Mark
Sullivan

The map of Manhattan has a Jekyll-and-Hyde aspect. The rational Dr. Jekyll part prevails above 14th Street, where the streets form a regular grid pattern. Numbered streets run east and west (crosstown), and broad avenues, most of them also numbered, run north (uptown) and south (downtown). The chief exceptions are Broadway and the thoroughfares that hug the shores of the Hudson and East rivers. Broadway runs the entire length of Manhattan. At its southernmost end it follows the city's north–south grid; at East 10th Street it turns and runs on a diagonal to West 86th Street, then at a lesser angle until West 107th Street, where it merges with West End Avenue.

Fifth Avenue is the east–west dividing line for street addresses: on either side, addresses begin at 1 where a street intersects 5th Avenue and climb higher in each direction, in regular increments. Above 59th Street, where Central Park interrupts the grid, West Side addresses start numbering at Central Park West, an extension of 8th Avenue. Avenue addresses are much less regular, for the numbers begin wherever each avenue begins and increase at different increments. Even many New Yorkers cannot master the complexities of this system, so they give addresses in terms of intersections: 5th Avenue and 55th Street, for instance.

Below 14th Street, Manhattan streets reflect the disordered personality of Mr. Hyde. They may be aligned with the shoreline, or they may twist along the route of an ancient cow path. Below 14th Street you find West 4th Street intersecting West 11th Street, Greenwich Street running roughly parallel to Greenwich Avenue, and Leroy Street turning into St. Luke's Place for one block and then becoming Leroy again. There's an East Broadway and a West Broadway, both of which run north–south and neither of which is an extension of plain old Broadway. Logic won't help you below 14th Street; only a good street map and good directions will.

Enjoying everything New York City has to offer during a short trip is more than a challenge—it's an impossibility. Whether your bent is sightseeing or shopping, museums or music, New York does indeed have it all. In five days you can squeeze in only the best of the best.

If you have 3 days

For a small bite of the Big Apple, begin your first day at the Empire State Building, taking in a bird's-eye view of the city. Then head up to the Metropolitan Museum of Art. You could easily spend a whole day here, but you'll exhaust yourself if you do. Luckily, just behind the museum lies beautiful Central Park, where you can collapse onto a bench, rowboat, or meadow and watch the world go by. Exit the park's south end at 5th Avenue and work your way through the world-class shopping. At dusk, walk south on 7th Avenue toward the bright lights of Times Square.

1

On Day 2 set off in search of history via ferry to the Statue of Liberty and Ellis Island. An early start helps you beat the crowds, and after a thorough visit, complete with guided tours, you can expect to return six hours later. Back in Manhattan, walk through the Wall Street area, home of the colonial-era Fraunces Tavern and mid-19th-century Trinity Church. St. Paul's Chapel is Manhattan's oldest surviving church building and site of September 11 remembrances. Just north are the neo-Gothic Woolworth Building (don't miss the splendid gilded lobby) and City Hall. Board an N or R train to 8th Street, where you can begin a tour of Washington Square Park and Greenwich Village.

On your last day in town, do what many New Yorkers like to do on their days off—wander. Make your way to Chinatown for a dim sum breakfast or tapioca-filled soft drink. From here head north to SoHo and NoLita for galleries and chic boutiques and restaurants. If you haven't eaten by now, hit a café a few blocks north in the happening East Village, home to yet more shops and vintage stores. From Union Square, walk up Broadway to the fashionable Flatiron District with its inimitable Flatiron Building. Have dinner in one of the neighborhood's noted restaurants.

If you have 5 days

Early on Day 4, head west to the American Museum of Natural History. Take a gander at the dinosaurs and stop by John Lennon's last home, the Dakota apartment building on Central Park West at 72nd Street. Walk into lush, green Central Park to see its Shakespeare Garden, Belvedere Castle, Bethesda Fountain, and Wildlife Center (more familiarly known as the Central Park Zoo). After your dose of fresh air, treat yourself to dinner followed by a performance at Carnegie Hall or Lincoln Center for the Performing Arts.

Dedicate Day 5 to New York icons. Stroll up 5th Avenue past the leonine guardians of the New York Public Library and step inside to behold the gleaming Main Reading Room. Forty-second Street takes you east to the beaux-arts Grand Central Terminal, a hub of frenetic activity and architectural wonder. Move on to the Chrysler Building, an art deco stunner. Make your way west across 49th Street to the triumvirate of Saks Fifth Avenue, Rockefeller Center, and St. Patrick's Cathedral. Shopping, ice-skating at the Rockefeller rink, or visiting a nearby museum could fill the rest of your day.

You may also be confused by the way New Yorkers use *uptown, downtown,* and *midtown.* These terms designate both directions and location. Uptown means north of wherever you are at the moment; downtown means to the south. But Uptown, Downtown, and Midtown are also specific parts of the city. Unfortunately, there is no consensus about where these areas are: Downtown may mean anyplace from the tip of lower Manhattan through Chelsea. Midtown is generally considered to be between 34th and 59th streets. Be prepared for misunderstandings.

Wall Street & the Battery

Bustling seaborne commerce once glutted the harbor that built the "good city of old Manhatto," Herman Melville's moniker from the second chapter of *Moby-Dick.* It was here that the Dutch established the colony of Nieuw Amsterdam in 1625. The first capitol building of the United States was built on Wall Street in 1789, and George Washington was sworn in as president on its steps. The city did not really expand beyond these precincts until the middle of the 19th century. Wall Street, both an actual street and a shorthand name for the vast financial center that clusters around the New York and American stock exchanges, continues to dominate much of Lower Manhattan. It's fitting that this setting of feverish entrepreneurship and capitalism is within sight of enduring symbols of America: the Statue of Liberty and Ellis Island, port of entry for countless immigrants looking for a new life in a new land.

The famous skyline of Lower Manhattan was permanently altered after the terrorist attacks on the World Trade Center on September 11, 2001. Surrounding buildings were destroyed as well, and some businesses and residents moved elsewhere; but most stayed if they could, and many new faces have since moved to the area, helping to restore its busy storefronts and streets. Despite its changed profile and the difficulties businesses and residents have faced, Lower Manhattan is slowly rebuilding itself and will continue to do so in the years to come.

Numbers in the text correspond to numbers in the margin and on the Downtown map.

a good walk

At the tip of the island, the **Staten Island Ferry** ❶ ► affords a big-picture perspective on Wall Street and the Battery, and you can double the ride's scenic pleasures by taking it at sunset. Just north of the terminal, across the street from the Shrine of St. Elizabeth Ann Seton at Our Lady of the Rosary, the verdant **Battery Park** ❷ curves up the west side of the island. It's filled with sculptures and monuments, including the circular **Castle Clinton National Monument** ❸. The venerable fort is the place

Manhattan Neighborhoods

Randalls Island

Wards Island

HARLEM

W. 116th St.

Columbia University

MORNINGSIDE HEIGHTS

Morningside Park

E. 110th St.

E. 106th St.

Henry Hudson Pkwy.

Riverside Dr.

Broadway

Amsterdam Ave.

W. 96th St.

E. 96th St.

UPPER WEST SIDE

UPPER EAST SIDE

Riverside Park

W. 86th St.

Central Park West

E. 86th St.

Gracie Mansion

Central Park

Metropolitan Museum of Art

E. 79th St.

American Museum of Natural History

Columbus Ave.

West End Ave.

W. 72nd St.

Park Ave.

E. 72nd St.

Lexington Ave.

E. 65th St.

FDR Dr.

Roosevelt Island

QUEENS

Broadway

E. 59th St.

Lincoln Center

TimeWarner Center

Queensboro Bridge

W. 57th St.

E. 57th St.

11th Ave.

10th Ave.

9th Ave.

8th Ave.

Rockefeller Center

5th Ave.

E. 50th St.

Times Square

W. 42nd St.

Grand Central Terminal

1st Ave.

United Nations

Lincoln Tunnel

Port Authority Bus Terminal

MIDTOWN

E. 42nd St.

Madison Ave.

Queens-Midtown Tunnel

W. 34th St.

Javits Convention Center

Madison Square Garden

Empire State Building

East River

Broadway

3rd Ave.

2nd Ave.

MURRAY HILL

W. 23rd St.

Ave. of the Americas

7th Ave.

CHELSEA

Flatiron Building

E. 23rd St.

GRAMERCY

Union Sq.

W. 14th St.

E. 14th St.

GREENWICH VILLAGE

EAST VILLAGE

Washington Sq.

E. Houston St.

West Side Hwy.

W. Houston St.

NOLITA

LOWER EAST SIDE

Williamsburg Bridge

Hudson River

Canal St.

SOHO

LITTLE ITALY

Holland Tunnel

TRI-BECA

CHINA-TOWN

Manhattan Bridge

West St.

Broadway

Chambers St.

LOWER MANHATTAN

Brooklyn Bridge

NEW JERSEY

World Trade Center Site

South Street Seaport

BROOKLYN

Battery Park

Brooklyn-Battery Tunnel

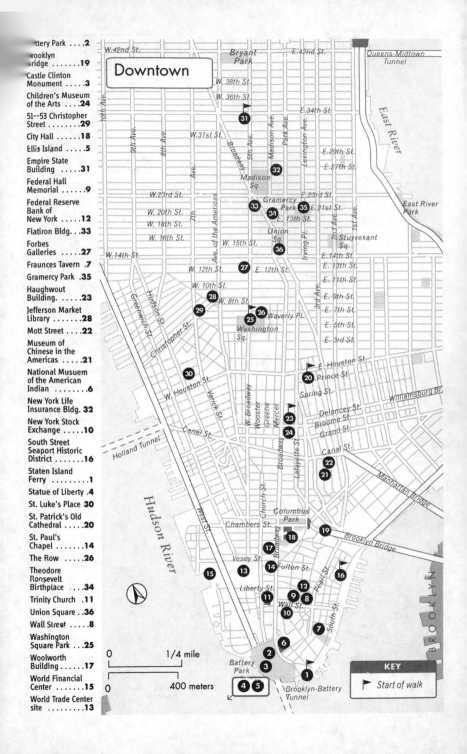

Downtown

W.42nd St.   Bryant Park   E.42nd St.   Queens-Midtown Tunnel

W. 38th St.

W. 36th St.

W.31st St.

E.34th St.

East River

E. 29th St.

E. 27th St.

Madison Sq.

New York Life Insurance Bldg. 32

Gramercy Park   E. 23rd St.
E. 21st St.

E. 10th St.

Union Sq.

E.14th St.

East River Park

Stuyvosant Sq.

E. 13th St.

E. 11th St.

E. 9th St.

E. 7th St.

E. 5th St.

E. 3rd St.

Waverly Pl.

Washington Sq.

E. Houston St.

Prince St.

Spring St.

Williamsburg Br.

Delancey St.
Broome St.
Grand St.

Canal St.

Manhattan Bridge

Holland Tunnel

Hudson River

Columbus Park

Chambers St.

Brooklyn Bridge

Vesey St.

Fulton St.

Liberty St.

Wall St.

South St.

Battery Park

Brooklyn-Battery Tunnel

BROOKLYN

0   1/4 mile

0   400 meters

KEY

► Start of walk

to buy tickets for ferries to the **Statue of Liberty** ➍ and **Ellis Island** ➎. From Castle Clinton, walk away from the water, following the path running alongside the rose-filled Hope Garden to *The Sphere,* by Fritz Koenig. The damaged bronze sculpture once stood at the center of the World Trade Center plaza. The path ends near Bowling Green, an oval greensward at the foot of Broadway that in 1733 became New York's first public park. On the south side of Bowling Green is the beaux-arts Alexander Hamilton U.S. Custom House, home of the **National Museum of the American Indian** ➏.

Follow Whitehall Street (the continuation of Broadway) down the east side of the museum. Turn left onto Bridge Street. As you approach Broad Street, the two-tone Georgian **Fraunces Tavern** ➐ appears on the right, on Pearl Street. Next head north on Pearl Street to Hanover Square, a quiet tree-lined plaza. Continue north on Pearl Street, then turn left on **Wall Street** ➑. For a jaw-dropping display of the money that built Manhattan, take a look at the massive arcade of 55 Wall Street, a former bank and now home of the Regent Wall Street Hotel. One block west on Wall Street, where Broad Street becomes Nassau Street, a statue of George Washington stands on the steps of **Federal Hall National Memorial** ➒. The temple-front **New York Stock Exchange** ➓ is the central shrine of Wall Street.

The focal point at the west end of Wall Street is the brownstone **Trinity Church** ⓫. From here, head north on Broadway two blocks and turn right on Liberty Street. North of the Chase plaza, Liberty Street converges with William Street and Maiden Lane under the massive, rusticated **Federal Reserve Bank of New York** ⓬. Walk west past Broadway on Maiden Lane (which will turn into Cortlandt Street) to Church Street. There the 16-acre **World Trade Center site** ⓭ once contained New York's tallest buildings, the twin towers. Displays along the west side of Church Street list the names of those who were lost on September 11, and tell the history of the towers. Walk north two blocks to Fulton Street to visit **St. Paul's Chapel** ⓮ (enter on Broadway). This is the oldest surviving church building in Manhattan. Across West Street, through Battery Park City, is the lovely Hudson River esplanade. At the north end of the esplanade is the **World Financial Center** ⓯, a four-tower complex designed by Cesar Pelli.

TIMING   The Manhattan portion of this tour takes most of a day—allow a lot more time to ferry out to the Statue of Liberty and Ellis Island. Visit on a weekday to capture the district's true vitality—but expect to be jostled on the crowded sidewalks if you stand still too long. If you visit on a weekend, in some areas you feel like a lone explorer in a canyon of buildings. The perimeter of the World Trade Center site is most crowded on the weekends. When visiting Liberty and Ellis islands, start early, preferably taking the first ferry to beat the crowds. The best place to end the day is on the Hudson River, watching the sunset.

What to See

➋ **Battery Park.** Jutting out as if it were Manhattan's green toe, Battery Park (so named because a battery of 28 cannons was placed along its shore in colonial days to fend off the British) is built on landfill. The park's main structure is Castle Clinton National Monument, the takeoff point for ferries to the Statue of Liberty and Ellis Island. The interior of the park is loaded with various monuments and statues. Climb the steps of the East Coast Memorial for a fine view of the main features of New York Harbor; from left to right: Governors Island, a former Coast Guard installation whose future is somewhat undecided; hilly Staten Island in the distance; the Statue of Liberty, on Liberty Island; Ellis Island, gateway to the New World for generations of immigrants; and the old railway terminal in Liberty State Park, on the mainland in Jersey City, New Jersey. The Verrazano-Narrows Bridge, between Brooklyn and Staten Island, is visible from here, just beyond Governors Island. ⊠ *Broadway and Battery Pl., Lower Manhattan* Ⓜ *Subway: 4, 5 to Bowling Green.*

Ⓒ ❸ **Castle Clinton National Monument.** The circular red-stone fortress, built in 1811, first stood on an island 200 feet from shore as a defense for New York Harbor. In 1824 it became Castle Garden, an entertainment and concert facility that reached its zenith in 1850 when more than 6,000 people attended the U.S. debut of the Swedish Nightingale, Jenny Lind. After landfill connected it to the city, Castle Clinton became, in succession, an immigrant processing center, an aquarium, and now a restored fort, museum, and ticket office for ferries to the **Statue of Liberty** and **Ellis Island.** Inside the old fort are dioramas of lower Manhattan in 1812, 1886, and 1941. If you're catching a ferry, be sure to leave adequate time for security checks, which include X-ray machines. Large packages and oversize bags and backpacks will not be permitted on board. ⊠ *Lower Manhattan* ☎ *212/344–7220 for Castle Clinton, 212/269–5755 for ferry information* ✆ *Castle Clinton free; ferry $10 round-trip* ☉ *Daily 8:30–5, ferry departures daily every 45 mins 9:30–3:30; more departures and extended hrs in summer* Ⓜ *Subway: 4, 5 to Bowling Green.*

Ⓒ ❺ **Ellis Island.** Between 1892 and 1924 approximately 12 million men,
Fodor'sChoice women, and children first set foot on U.S. soil at this 27½-acre island's
★ federal immigration facility. By the time Ellis Island closed in 1954 it had processed the ancestors of more than 40% of Americans living today. The island's main building, now a national monument, reopened in 1990 as the **Ellis Island Immigration Museum.** More than 30 galleries of artifacts, photographs, and taped oral histories chronicle the immigrant experience, from what someone's native village was like to where a particular national group took root in America and what industries employed them. Check at the visitors desk for free film tickets, ranger tour times, or special programs. At a computer terminal in the **American Family Immigration Center** you can search Ellis Island's records for your own ancestors (a $5 fee). ⊠ *Lower Manhattan* ☎ *212/363–3200 for Ellis Island, 212/883–1986 for Wall of Honor information* ⊕ *www. ellisisland.org* ✆ *Free* ☉ *Daily 9:30–5; extended hrs in summer.*

❾ **Federal Hall National Memorial.** The site of this memorial is rich with both the country's and the city's history. The City Hall here hosted the 1765 Stamp Act Congress and, beginning in 1789, served as the Federal Hall of the new nation. On its steps George Washington took his oath as the country's first president. After the capital moved from New York to Philadelphia in 1790, Federal Hall reverted to its role as New York's

City Hall, then was demolished in 1812 when the present City Hall was completed. The present Greek-revival building, built as a U.S. Customs House in 1842, was modeled on the Parthenon. Inside the hall is a museum with exhibits on New York and Wall Street. ⊠ *26 Wall St., at Nassau St., Lower Manhattan* ☏ *212/825–6888* 🎫 *Free* ☉ *Weekdays 9–5* Ⓜ *Subway: 4, 5 to Wall St.*

⑫ **Federal Reserve Bank of New York.** Built in 1924, this neo-Renaissance structure made of sandstone, limestone, and ironwork goes five levels underground. The gold ingots in the vaults here are worth roughly $140 billion—reputedly a third of the world's gold reserves. Tours of the bank include the gold vault, the trading desk, and "FedWorks," an interactive multimedia exhibit center where you can track trades that you "make." ⊠ *33 Liberty St., between William and Nassau Sts., Lower Manhattan* ☏ *212/720–6130* ⊕ *www.newyorkfed.org* 🎫 *Free* ☉ *1-hr tour by advance (at least 1 wk) reservation, weekdays 9:30–2:30* Ⓜ *Subway: A, C to Fulton St.; 2, 3, 4, 5 to Wall St.*

⑦ **Fraunces Tavern.** Red brick along one side, cream-color brick along another, the tavern's main building is a stately colonial house with a white-marble portico and coffered frieze, built in 1719 and converted to a tavern in 1762. It was the meeting place for the Sons of Liberty until the Revolutionary War, and in 1783 George Washington delivered a farewell address here to his officers celebrating the British evacuation of New York. Today a museum occupies the five-building complex. Fraunces Tavern contains two fully furnished period rooms and other displays of 18th- and 19th-century American history. ⊠ *54 Pearl St., at Broad St., Lower Manhattan* ☏ *212/425–1778* ⊕ *www.frauncestavernmuseum. org* 🎫 *$3* ☉ *Tues., Wed., and Fri. 10–5, Thurs. 10–7, Sat. 11–5* Ⓜ *Subway: R, W to Whitehall St.; 4, 5 to Bowling Green.*

⑥ **National Museum of the American Indian.** This museum, a branch of the Washington, D.C.–based Smithsonian Institution, is the first of its kind to be dedicated to Native American culture. The heritage of indigenous peoples of the Western Hemisphere is documented and explored through well-mounted exhibits, dance performances, lectures, readings, film, and crafts. Native Americans of all backgrounds participate in visiting programs and work at all levels of the staff. George Gustav Heye, a wealthy New Yorker, amassed most of the museum's collection—more than a million artifacts, including pottery, weaving, and basketry from the southwestern United States; carved jade from the Mexican Olmec and Maya cultures; and contemporary Native American paintings. The museum is in one of lower Manhattan's finest buildings, the beaux-arts **Alexander Hamilton U.S. Custom House** (1907). ⊠ *1 Bowling Green, between State and Whitehall Sts., Lower Manhattan* ☏ *212/514–3700* ⊕ *www.americanindian.si.edu* 🎫 *Free* ☉ *Mon.–Wed. and Fri.–Sun. 10–5, Thurs. 10–8* Ⓜ *Subway: R, W to Whitehall St.*

⑩ **New York Stock Exchange.** The largest securities exchange in the world, the NYSE nearly bursts from this relatively diminutive neoclassical 1903 building with an august Corinthian entrance—a fitting temple to the almighty dollar. Today's "Big Board" can handle trades of a trillion shares of stock per day. ⊠ *20 Broad St., between Wall St. and Exchange*

Pl., Lower Manhattan ☎ *212/656–5165* ⊕ *www.nyse.com* Ⓜ *Subway: 2, 3, 4, 5 to Wall St.*

⑭ **St. Paul's Chapel.** The oldest (1766) public building in continuous use in Manhattan, this Episcopal house of worship, built of rough Manhattan brownstone, was modeled on London's St. Martin-in-the-Fields. A prayer service here followed George Washington's inauguration as president; Washington's pew is in the north aisle. The gilded crown adorned with plumes above the pulpit is thought to be the city's only vestige of British rule. St. Paul's and its 18th-century cemetery abut the World Trade Center site. ⊠ *Broadway and Fulton St., Lower Manhattan* ☎ *212/602–0800* ⊕ *www.trinitywallstreet.org* Ⓜ *Subway: 2, 3, 4, 5 to Fulton St.*

🐾 ☞ ❶ **Staten Island Ferry.** The free 20- to 30-minute ride across New York Harbor provides great views of the Manhattan skyline, the Statue of Liberty, the Verrazano-Narrows Bridge, and the New Jersey coast. ⊠ *State and South Sts., Lower Manhattan* ☎ *718/390–5253* Ⓜ *Subway: 4, 5 to Bowling Green; 1, 9 to South Ferry.*

🐾 ❹ **Statue of Liberty.** Millions of American immigrants first glimpsed their
FodorsChoice new land when they laid eyes on the Statue of Liberty, a national monument and UNESCO World Heritage Site that still awes all those who
★ encounter it. *Liberty Enlightening the World*, as the statue is officially named, was sculpted by Frederic-Auguste Bartholdi and presented to the United States in 1886 as a gift from France. Since then she has become a near-universal symbol of freedom and democracy, standing a proud 152 feet high on top of an 89-foot pedestal on Liberty Island. Gustav Eiffel designed the statue's iron skeleton.

A limited number of tickets to tour the inside of the monument is available daily, and you have a choice of two tours. The promenade tour includes the lobby and museum area. The observatory tour includes the promenade tour as well as time on the pedestal observation platform. An elevator ascends 10 stories to the viewing area atop the pedestal, and 354 double-helix steps (the equivalent of a 22-story building) climb to the crown, which isn't accessible at this writing. ⊠ *Liberty Island, Lower Manhattan* ☎ *212/363–3200, 212/269–5755 for ferry information* ⊕ *www.nps.gov* ☞ *Free; ferry $10 round-trip* ⊙ *Daily 9–5; extended hrs in summer.*

⑪ **Trinity Church.** The present Trinity Church, the third on this site since an Anglican parish was established here in 1697, was designed in 1846 by Richard Upjohn. It ranked as the city's tallest building for most of the second half of the 19th century. The three huge bronze doors were designed by Richard Morris Hunt to recall Lorenzo Ghiberti's doors for the Baptistery in Florence, Italy. The church's Gothic Revival interior is light and elegant. On the church's north and south sides is a 2½-acre graveyard: Alexander Hamilton is buried beneath a white-stone pyramid. ⊠ *74 Trinity Pl., Broadway at the head of Wall St., Lower Manhattan* ☎ *212/602–0800* ⊕ *www.trinitywallstreet.org* ⊙ *Weekdays 8:30–6, weekends 8:30–4* Ⓜ *Subway: 4, 5 to Wall St.*

❽ **Wall Street.** Named after a wooden wall built across the island in 1653 to defend the Dutch colony against the Native Americans, ⅓-mi-long

Wall Street is arguably the most famous thoroughfare in the world—shorthand for the vast, powerful financial community that clusters around the New York and American stock exchanges. "The Street," as it's also widely known, began its financial career with stock traders conducting business along the sidewalks or at tables beneath a sheltering buttonwood tree. ⊠ *Lower Manhattan* Ⓜ *Subway: 4, 5 to Wall St.*

🅼 **World Financial Center.** The four towers of this complex, 34–51 stories high and topped with different geometric shapes, were designed by Cesar Pelli and continue to serve as company headquarters for the likes of American Express and Dow Jones. The sides of the buildings facing the World Trade Center towers were damaged during the September 11 attacks, but have been fully restored. The elegant glass-domed **Winter Garden** atrium houses shops, cafés, and restaurants as well as a display of architectural plans for the WTC site. ⊠ *West St. between Vesey and Liberty Sts., Lower Manhattan.*

🅼 **World Trade Center site.** On September 11, 2001, terrorist hijackers steered two commercial jets into the World Trade Center's 110-story towers, demolishing them and five outlying buildings and killing nearly 3,000 people. Dubbed Ground Zero, the fenced-in 16-acre work site that emerged from the rubble has come to symbolize the personal and historical impact of the attack. In an attempt to grasp the reality of the destruction, to pray, or simply to witness history, visitors come to glimpse the site, clustering at the two-story see-through fence surrounding it. Temporary panels listing the names of those who died in the attacks and recounting the history of the twin towers have been mounted along the fence on the west side of Church Street and the north side of Liberty Street. ⊠ *Lower Manhattan* Ⓜ *Subway: R, W to Cortlandt St.*

The Seaport & the Courts

New York's role as a great seaport is easiest to understand Downtown, with both the Hudson River and East River waterfronts within walking distance. Although the deeper Hudson River came into its own in the steamship era, the more sheltered waters of the East River saw most of the action in the 19th century, during the age of clipper ships. This era is preserved in the South Street Seaport restoration, centered on Fulton Street between Water Street and the East River. Only a few blocks away you can visit another seat of New York history: the City Hall neighborhood, which includes Manhattan's magisterial court and government buildings.

Numbers in the text correspond to numbers in the margin and on the Downtown map.

a good walk

Begin at the intersection of Water and Fulton streets. Extending to the river is the 11-block **South Street Seaport Historic District** 🔟 ►, which is grounded on 19th-century landfill. Return to Fulton Street and walk away from the river to Broadway, to St. Paul's Chapel. Two blocks north of Fulton Street, on Broadway, is one of the finest skyscrapers in the city, the Gothic **Woolworth Building** 🔟, for which Frank Woolworth paid $13 million—in cash. Wedged between Broadway and Park Row is triangular City Hall Park, originally the town common, which gives way to a slew of government offices. **City Hall ⑱**, built between 1803 and 1812, is unexpectedly modest. To the east of City Hall, just steps south of the Municipal Building, a ramp curves up into the pedestrian walkway over the **Brooklyn Bridge ⑲**. The views from the bridge of the river and four boroughs are wondrous.

What to See

★ ⑲ **Brooklyn Bridge.** "A drive-through cathedral" is how the critic James Wolcott describes one of New York's noblest and most recognized landmarks. Spanning the East River, the Brooklyn Bridge connects Manhattan island to the once-independent city of Brooklyn. Its twin Gothic-arch towers, supporting a span of 1,595½ feet, rise 272 feet from the river below; the bridge's overall length of 6,016 feet made it four times longer than the longest suspension bridge of its day. From roadway to water is about 133 feet, high enough to allow the tallest ships to pass. The roadway is supported by a web of steel cables, the main ones attached to block-long anchorages on either shore.

A walk across the bridge's promenade—a boardwalk elevated above the roadway and shared by pedestrians, in-line skaters, and bicyclists—takes about 40 minutes, from Manhattan's civic center to the heart of Brooklyn Heights. A word of caution to pedestrians: do obey the lane markings on the promenade—pedestrians on the north side, bicyclists on the south. Ⓜ *Subway: 4, 5, 6 to Brooklyn Bridge/City Hall.*

⑱ **City Hall.** Reflecting the classical refinement and civility of Enlightenment Europe, New York's decorous City Hall is a diminutive palace with a facade punctuated by arches and columns and a cupola crowned by a statue of Lady Justice. A sweeping marble double staircase leads from the domed rotunda to the second-floor public rooms. The small, Victorian-style **City Council Chamber** in the east wing has mahogany detailing and ornate gilding. The **Governor's Room** at the head of the stairs, used for ceremonial events, is filled with historic portraits and furniture, including a writing table that George Washington used in 1789 when New York was the U.S. capital. ⊠ *City Hall Park, Lower Manhattan* ☎ *212/788–6865 for tour information* 🎟 *Free* ☉ *Tours by advance (1–2 wks) reservation, weekdays 10, 11, and 2* Ⓜ *Subway: 4, 5, 6 to Brooklyn Bridge/City Hall.*

♟ ⌐ ⑯ **South Street Seaport Historic District.** Restored early-19th-century commercial buildings and cobblestone streets make up this historic-district and shopping-mall hybrid. Many of its streets' 18th-, 19th-, and early-20th-century architectural details recall the city's historic seafaring era.

At the intersection of Fulton and Water streets, the gateway to the Seaport, stands the **Titanic Memorial,** a small white lighthouse that commemorates the sinking of the RMS *Titanic* in 1912. Just to the left of Fulton, at 211 Water Street, is **Bowne & Co. Stationers,** a reconstructed working 19th-century print shop. On the south side of Fulton Street is the seaport's architectural centerpiece, **Schermerhorn Row,** a redbrick terrace of Georgian- and Federal-style warehouses and countinghouses built in 1811–12. Also here is the visitor center and gift shop of the **South**

Street Seaport Museum (☎ 212/748–8600 ⊙ Apr.–Sept., Fri.–Wed. 10–6, Thurs. 10–8; Oct.–Mar., Wed.–Mon. 10–5), which hosts walking tours, hands-on exhibits, and fantastic creative programs for children, all with a nautical theme. ⊠ *Visitor center, 211 Water St., South St. Seaport* ☎ *212/732–7678 for events and shopping information* ⊕ *www.southstseaport.org* ✉ *$5 to ships, galleries, walking tours, Maritime Crafts Center, films, and other seaport events* Ⓜ *Subway: A, C, 2, 3, 4, 5 to Fulton St./Broadway Nassau.*

⓱ Woolworth Building. Called the Cathedral of Commerce, this ornate white terra-cotta edifice was, at 792 feet, the world's tallest building when it opened in 1913. The lobby's extravagant Gothic-style details include sculptures set into the portals to the left and right; one represents an elderly F. W. Woolworth pinching his pennies, another depicts the architect, Cass Gilbert, cradling in his arms a model of his creation. Glittering mosaic tiles fill the dome and archways. ⊠ *233 Broadway, between Park Pl. and Barclay St., Lower Manhattan* Ⓜ *Subway: 2, 3 to Park Pl.; N, Q, R, W to City Hall.*

Little Italy & Chinatown

Mulberry Street is the heart of Little Italy; in fact, at this point it's virtually the entire body. In 1932 an estimated 98% of the inhabitants of this area were of Italian birth or heritage, but since then the expansion of Chinatown to the south has encroached on the Italian neighborhood to such an extent that merchants and community leaders of the Little Italy Restoration Association negotiated with Chinatown to let at least Mulberry remain an all-Italian street. Since the late 1990s, trendy shops and restaurants have sprouted in what were Little Italy's northern reaches, and the area is now known as NoLita (North of Little Italy).

With restaurants serving up steaming bowls of soup and shops overflowing with electronic gadgets, Chinatown attracts busloads of visitors, but it's more than a tourist attraction. Roughly a quarter of the city's 400,000 Chinese residents live in the neighborhood's tangle of streets. Many of these are immigrants from China, Taiwan, and Hong Kong; in fact, roughly half speak little or no English. Chinatown was once divided from Little Italy by Canal Street, the bustling artery that links the Holland Tunnel (to New Jersey) and the Manhattan Bridge (to Brooklyn). But the neighborhood now spills over its traditional borders into Little Italy to the north and the formerly Jewish Lower East Side to the east. Sidewalk markets burst with stacks of fresh seafood and strangely shaped fruits and vegetables and souvenir shops and restaurants occupy funky pagoda-style buildings.

Numbers in the text correspond to numbers in the margin and on the Downtown map.

a good walk

Start your tour at the corner of Mott and Prince streets, among the pricey, jewel-box-size boutiques and cafés that form chic NoLita. Mulberry, Mott, and Elizabeth streets between Houston and Kenmare streets are the core of this largely gentrified neighborhood that has wedged itself into the increasingly less visible mix of family-owned Italian, Latino, and Asian businesses. Windows artfully dressed with everything from wrist bags to baby clothes continue to debut, making the area a zestier sort of SoHo. Among these neighborhood debutantes sits the stately dowager **St. Patrick's Old Cathedral** ⑳ ▶, the oldest Roman Catholic church in New York City. Tour the church and walk west on Prince Street to Mulberry Street, Little Italy's main thoroughfare. Amble along Mulberry until you reach Chinatown's traffic-clogged Canal Street. Its sidewalks are lined with street vendors, and on weekends the crowds move at a snail's pace. A good place to get oriented is the **Museum of Chinese in the Americas** ㉑, in an 1893 schoolhouse at the corner of Bayard and Mulberry streets. Catercorner from the museum is Columbus Park. This gathering spot occupies the area once known as the Five Points, the tough 19th-century slum ruled by Irish gangs that provided the backdrop for Martin Scorsese's film *Gangs of New York*. One block east of Mulberry Street, **Mott Street** ㉒ is another of the neighborhood's main drags.

TIMING   Since Little Italy consists of little more than one street, a tour of the area shouldn't take more than one hour. Most attractions are food-related, so plan on visiting around lunchtime. A fun time to visit is during the San Gennaro festival, which runs for two weeks each September, starting the first Thursday after Labor Day. Come on a weekend to see Chinatown at its liveliest; locals crowd the streets from dawn till dusk, along with a slew of tourists. For a more relaxed experience, opt for a weekday. Allowing for a stop at the museum and a lunch break, a Chinatown tour will take about two additional hours.

What to See

★ ㉒ **Mott Street.** Broadway's Rogers and Hart immortalized this street in their 1925 hit "Manhattan," waxing poetic about the "sweet pushcarts gently gliding by." That's what Mott Street was like in the late 1880s when Chinese immigrants settled in tenements in a small area that included the lower portion of Mott Street as well as nearby Pell and Doyers streets. It soon became Chinatown's main thoroughfare. Today the busy street overflows with fish and vegetable markets, restaurants, bakeries, and souvenir shops.

㉑ **Museum of Chinese in the Americas.** On the second floor of an 1893 schoolhouse is the first U.S. museum devoted to preserving the history of Chinese immigration. The permanent exhibit—*Where Is Home? Chinese in the Americas*—explores the Chinese-American experience through displays of artwork, personal and domestic artifacts, and historical documentation. Slippers for binding feet, Chinese musical instruments, a reversible silk gown worn at a Cantonese opera performance, and antique business signs are some of the objects on display. ⊠ *70 Mulberry St., at Bayard St., Chinatown* ☎ *212/619–4785* ⊕ *www.moca-nyc.org* ✉ *$3 suggested admission* ☉ *Tues.–Sun. noon–5* Ⓜ *Subway: N, Q, R, W, 6 to Canal St.*

▶ ⑳ **St. Patrick's Old Cathedral.** The cornerstone of the original St. Pat's was laid in 1809, making it the city's oldest Roman Catholic church. It was completed in 1815 and completely restored after a fire in 1866. The first American cardinal, John McCloskey, received his red hat in this building. Pierre Toussaint, a former slave who later donated most of his earnings to the poor, was buried in the graveyard. He was reburied at St. Patrick's Cathedral on 5th Avenue in 1983. ⊠ *233 Mott St., between Houston and Prince Sts., NoLita* ☎ *212/226–8075* ◷ *Mon., Tues., Thurs. 8–1 and 3:30–6, Fri. 8–1 and 3:30–9, Sat. 8–1, Sun. 8–4* Ⓜ *Subway: F, V to Broadway–Lafayette St.; R, W to Prince St.*

SoHo & TriBeCa

Today the name of this downtown neighborhood is synonymous with a certain style—an amalgam of black-clad artists, hotshot investors, and media moguls darting between expansive loft apartments, chic boutiques, and packed-to-the-gills restaurants. It's all very urban, very cool, very now. Before the 1970s, though, SoHo (so named because it is the district *South of Houston* Street, roughly bounded by Lafayette, Canal Street, and 6th Avenue) was regularly referred to as "Hell's Hundred Acres" because of the many fires that raged through the untended warehouses crowding the area. It was saved by two factors: first, preservationists discovered the world's greatest concentration of cast-iron architecture and fought to prevent demolition; and second, artists discovered the large, cheap, well-lighted spaces that these cavernous structures provide.

All the rage between 1860 and 1890, cast-iron buildings were popular because they did not require massive walls to bear the weight of the upper stories. Since there was no need for load-bearing walls, these buildings had more interior space and larger windows. They were also versatile, with various architectural elements produced from standardized molds to mimic any style—Italianate, Victorian Gothic, Greek revival, to name but a few visible in SoHo. At first it was technically illegal for artists to live in their loft studios, but so many did that eventually the zoning laws were changed to permit residence.

By 1980 SoHo's trendy galleries, shops, and cafés, together with its marvelous cast-iron buildings and vintage Belgian-block pavements (the 19th-century successor to traditional cobblestones), had made SoHo such a desirable area that only the most successful artists could afford it. Seeking similar space, artists moved downtown to another half-abandoned industrial district, for which a new SoHo-like name was invented: TriBeCa (the *Tri*angle *Be*low *Ca*nal Street, although in effect it goes no farther south than Murray Street and no farther east than West Broadway). In SoHo, meanwhile, the arrival of large chain stores such as Pottery Barn and J. Crew has given some blocks the feeling of an outdoor shopping mall.

Numbers in the text correspond to numbers in the margin and on the Downtown map.

a good walk

Starting at Houston (pronounced *how*-ston) Street, walk south down Broadway, stopping to browse the stores and street vendors between Houston and Prince streets. At the Prada store at 575 Broadway, Dutch architect Rem Koolhaas has created a high-tech setting for the Italian house of fashion. Several art galleries share these blocks as well, most notably at 568 Broadway, which houses a handful of galleries. Just south of Prince

Street, 560 Broadway, on the east side of the street, is home to a dozen or so galleries.

Across Broadway is the charming Little Singer Building, a beaux-arts beauty that outshines all its neighbors. One block south of the Little Singer Building, between Spring and Broome streets, a cluster of lofts that were originally part of the 1897 New Era Building share an art nouveau copper mansard at No. 495. At the northeast corner of the intersection of Broadway and Broome Street is the **Haughwout Building** ㉓, a restored classic of the cast-iron genre. At the southeast corner the former Mechanics and Traders Bank at 486 Broadway is a Romanesque and Moorish Revival building with half-round brick arches.

If you have youngsters in tow, head east on Grand Street two blocks to the **Children's Museum of the Arts** ㉔, where the interactive exhibits provide a welcome respite from SoHo's mostly grown-up pursuits. Otherwise, walk west on Grand Street three short blocks to discover several of SoHo's better exhibition spaces clustered on the south end of Greene and Wooster streets near Grand and Canal streets.

From here you may continue north on Wooster Street for Prince Street shops or first head east one block to Greene Street, where cast-iron architecture is at its finest. The block between Canal and Grand streets represents the longest row of cast-iron buildings anywhere. Two standout buildings on Greene Street are the so-called Queen of Greene Street and the King of Greene Street. Greene Street between Prince and Spring streets is notable for the SoHo Building (Nos. 104–110). At Prince Street, walk one block west to Wooster Street. Like a few other SoHo streets, Wooster still has its original Belgian paving stones.

From Wooster Street, continue one block west on Prince Street to SoHo's main shopping drag, West Broadway. It's worth taking a detour west on Spring Street four blocks to see the New York City Fire Museum. Stay on West Broadway on the west side of the street and proceed south; between Grand and Canal streets stands the SoHo Grand Hotel. From here follow West Broadway south past Canal Street, the official boundary between SoHo and TriBeCa.

Continue south on West Broadway to Duane Street. Turn right on Duane to Hudson Street and walk one block north on Hudson Street. On the right-hand side you see the art-deco Western Union Building at No. 60, where 19 subtly shaded colors of brick are laid in undulating patterns. Turn off Hudson Street onto quiet Jay Street and pause at narrow Staple Street, whose green pedestrian walkway overhead links two warehouses. Continue west on Jay Street and turn left on Greenwich street. At Chambers Street, head west toward the Hudson River. At the end of the block, take the overpass across the West Side Highway, and walk past the Stuyvesant High School building to reach the Parks of Battery Park City.

TIMING To see SoHo and TriBeCa at their liveliest, visit on a Saturday, when the fashion-conscious crowd is joined by smartly dressed uptowners and suburbanites who come down for a little shopping and gallery hopping.

If you want to avoid crowds, take this walk during the week. Keep in mind that most galleries are closed Sunday and Monday. If you allow time for browsing in a few galleries and museums, as well as a stop for lunch, this tour can easily take up to an entire day.

What to See

© ㉔ **Children's Museum of the Arts.** In this bilevel space a few blocks from Broadway, children ages 1 to 10 can amuse and educate themselves with various activities, including diving into a pool of colorful balls; playacting in costume; music making with real instruments; and art making, from computer art to old-fashioned painting, sculpting, and collage. ✉ *182 Lafayette St., between Grand and Broome Sts., SoHo* ☎ *212/274-0986* ⊕ *www.cmany.org* ✉ *$6, Thurs. 4–6 pay as you wish* ⊙ *Wed., Fri.–Sun. noon–5, Thurs. noon–6* Ⓜ *Subway: 6 to Spring St.*

▶ ㉓ **Haughwout Building.** Nicknamed the Parthenon of Cast Iron, this five-story Venetian palazzo–style structure was built in 1857 to house Eder Haughwout's china and glassware business. Each window is framed by Corinthian columns and rounded arches. Inside, the building once contained the world's first commercial passenger elevator, a steam-powered device invented by Elisha Graves Otis. Otis went on to found an elevator empire and made high-rises practical possibilities. ✉ *488–492 Broadway, at Broome St., SoHo* Ⓜ *Subway: N, Q, R, W to Canal St.*

Greenwich Village

Greenwich Village, which New Yorkers invariably speak of simply as "the Village," enjoyed a raffish reputation for years. The area was originally a rural outpost of the city—a haven for New Yorkers during early-19th-century smallpox and yellow fever epidemics—and many of its blocks still look relatively pastoral, with brick town houses and low-rises, tiny green parks and hidden courtyards, and a crazy-quilt pattern of narrow, tree-lined streets (some of which follow long-ago cow paths). In the mid-19th century, however, as the city spread north of 14th Street, the Village became the province of immigrants, bohemians, and students. Its politics were radical and its attitudes tolerant, which is one reason it became such a large lesbian and gay community.

Several generations of writers and artists have lived and worked here: in the 19th century, Henry James, Edgar Allan Poe, Mark Twain, Walt Whitman, and Stephen Crane; at the turn of the 20th century, O. Henry, Edith Wharton, Theodore Dreiser, and Hart Crane; and during the 1920s and '30s, John Dos Passos, Norman Rockwell, Sinclair Lewis, John Reed, Eugene O'Neill, Edward Hopper, and Edna St. Vincent Millay. In the late 1940s and early 1950s the Abstract Expressionist painters Franz Kline, Jackson Pollock, Mark Rothko, and Willem de Kooning congregated here, as did the Beat writers Jack Kerouac, Allen Ginsberg, and Lawrence Ferlinghetti. The 1960s brought folk musicians and poets, notably Bob Dylan and Peter, Paul, and Mary.

Today, block for block, the Village is still one of the most vibrant parts of the city. Locals and visitors rub elbows at dozens of small restaurants, cafés spill out onto sidewalks, and an endless variety of small shops pleases everyone. Except for a few pockets of adult-entertainment shops and divey bars, the Village is as scrubbed as posher neighborhoods.

Numbers in the text correspond to numbers in the margin and on the Downtown map.

a good walk

Begin your tour of Greenwich Village at the foot of 5th Avenue at Washington Memorial Arch in **Washington Square Park** ㉕ ▶. Most buildings bordering the leafy square belong to New York University. On Washington Square North, between University Place and MacDougal Street, stretches **The Row** ㉖, two blocks of lovingly preserved Greek revival and Federal-style town houses.

From Washington Memorial Arch and the park, cross Washington Square North and continue up the west side of 5th Avenue; you pass the Church of the Ascension, a Gothic Revival brownstone building. At 12th Street you can stop in the **Forbes Galleries** ㉗. Backtrack to West 11th Street and turn right to see one of the best examples of a Village town-house block. Turn left on Avenue of the Americas (6th Avenue) and go south one block. On the west side of the street, the triangle formed by West 10th Street, 6th Avenue, and Greenwich Avenue originally held a market, a jail, and the magnificent towered courthouse that is now the **Jefferson Market Library** ㉘. West of 6th Avenue on 10th Street is the wrought-iron gateway to a tiny courtyard called Patchin Place; around the corner, on 6th Avenue just north of 10th Street is a similar cul-de-sac, Milligan Place.

Next, proceed to Christopher Street, which veers off from the south end of the library triangle. Christopher Street has long been the symbolic heart of New York's gay and lesbian community. Cross Waverly Place. At **51–53 Christopher Street** ㉙, the historic Stonewall riots marked the beginning of the gay rights movement. West of 7th Avenue South, the Village turns into a picture-book town of twisting tree-lined streets, quaint houses, and tiny restaurants. Starting from Sheridan Square West, follow Grove Street past the house at No. 59 where Thomas Paine died and the onetime home (No. 45) of poet Hart Crane. Turn right onto Bedford Street, and walk until you get to Barrow Street. Turn left onto Barrow and then right onto Hudson Street, so named because this was originally the bank of the Hudson River. Two blocks south of Barrow Street, turn left at **St. Luke's Place** ㉚ (this is Leroy Street west of Hudson Street), a one-block row of classic 1860s town houses. Across 7th Avenue South, St. Luke's Place becomes Leroy Street again, which terminates in an old Italian neighborhood at Bleecker Street.

TIMING Greenwich Village lends itself to a leisurely pace, so allow yourself most of a day to explore its backstreets and stop at shops and cafés.

What to See

㉙ **51–53 Christopher Street.** On June 27, 1969, a gay bar at this address named the Stonewall Inn was the site of a clash between gay men and women and the New York City police. As the bar's patrons were being forced into police wagons, sympathetic onlookers protested and started fighting back, throwing beer bottles and garbage cans. Protests, addressing the indiscriminate raids on gay bars, lasted for days. Every June the Stonewall Riots are commemorated around the world with gay pride parades and celebrations that honor the gay rights movement. ⊠ *51–53 Christopher St., between Waverly Pl. and 7th Ave. S, Greenwich Village* Ⓜ *Subway: 1, 9 to Christopher St./Sheridan Sq.*

Ⓒ ㉗ **Forbes Galleries.** The late publisher Malcolm Forbes's idiosyncratic personal collection fills the ground floor of the limestone Forbes Magazine Building. Rotating exhibits are displayed in the large painting gallery and one of two autograph galleries; permanent highlights include U.S. presidential papers, more than 500 intricate toy boats, 10,000 toy soldiers, and some of the oldest Monopoly game sets ever made. ⊠ *62 5th Ave., at 12th St., Greenwich Village* ☎ *212/206–5548* 🆓 *Free* 🕐 *Tues.–Sat. 10–4* Ⓜ *Subway: R, W to 8th St.; F, V to 14th St.*

㉘ **Jefferson Market Library.** After Frederick Clarke Withers and Calvert Vaux's magnificent, towered building was constructed in 1877, critics variously termed its hodgepodge of styles Venetian, Victorian, or Italian. Villagers, noting the alternating wide bands of red brick and narrow strips of granite, dubbed it the "lean bacon style." Inside are handsome interior doorways and a graceful circular stairway. If the gate is open, visit the flower garden behind the library. ⊠ *425 6th Ave., at 10th St., Greenwich Village* ☎ *212/243–4334* Ⓜ *Subway: A, C, E, F, V to W. 4th St./Washington Sq.*

㉖ **The Row.** Built from 1829 through 1839, this series of beautifully preserved Greek-revival town houses along Washington Square North, on the two blocks between University Place and MacDougal Street, once belonged to merchants and bankers, then writers and artists such as John Dos Passos and Edward Hopper. Now the buildings serve as NYU offices and faculty housing. The oldest building on the block, No. 20, was constructed in 1829 in the Federal style, and with Flemish bond brickwork—alternate bricks inserted with the smaller surface (headers) facing out—which before 1830 was considered the best way to build stable walls. ⊠ *1–13 and 19–26 Washington Sq. N, between University Pl. and MacDougal St., Greenwich Village.*

★ ㉚ **St. Luke's Place.** Shaded by graceful gingko trees, this street has 15 classic Italianate brownstone and brick town houses (1852–53). Novelist Theodore Dreiser wrote *An American Tragedy* at No. 16, and poet Marianne Moore resided at No. 14. Mayor Jimmy Walker (first elected in 1926) lived at No. 6. This block is often used as a film location, too: No. 12 was shown as the Huxtables' home on *The Cosby Show,* and No. 4 was the setting of the Audrey Hepburn movie *Wait Until Dark.* Before 1890 the playground on the south side of the street was a graveyard where, according to legend, the dauphin of France—the lost son of Louis XVI and Marie Antoinette—is buried. ⊠ *Between Hudson St. and 7th Ave. S, Greenwich Village* Ⓜ *Subway: 1, 9 to Houston St.*

★ Ⓒ ⚑ ㉕ **Washington Square Park.** Earnest-looking NYU students, Frisbee players, street musicians, skateboarders, jugglers, chess players, and bench warmers generate a maelstrom of playful activity in this physical and spiritual heart of the Village. This lively 9½-acre park started out as a cemetery, principally for yellow fever victims—an estimated 10,000–22,000 bodies lie below. In the early 1800s it was a parade ground and the site of public executions; bodies dangled from a conspicuous Hanging Elm that still stands at the northwest corner of the square. Made a public park in 1827, the square became the focus of a fashionable residential neighborhood and a center of outdoor activity. Tourists and locals alike are drawn toward the large central fountain. The triumphal **Washington Memorial Arch** stands at the square's north end, marking the start of glorious 5th Avenue. ⊠ *5th Ave. between Waverly Pl. and 4th St., Greenwich Village* Ⓜ *Subway: A, C, E, F, V to W. 4th St.*

Murray Hill, Flatiron District & Gramercy

As the city grew progressively northward throughout the 19th century, one neighborhood after another became fashionable for a time, only to fade from glory. But three neighborhoods east of 6th Avenue roughly between 14th and 40th streets have preserved much of their historic charm: Murray Hill, with its brownstone mansions and town houses; the Flatiron District, dotted with turn-of-the-20th-century skyscrapers; and Gramercy, which surrounds a leafy square that evokes those in London.

The Flatiron District, anchored by Madison Square in the north and Union Square to the south, is once again one of the city's hottest neighborhoods, brimming over with boutique hotels and trendy restaurants. The Flatiron District is also an important center of the city's new-media technology companies. Before the bubble burst on the dot-com frenzy, the area was often referred to in the press as "Silicon Alley." Here you find the Flatiron Building, the symbol of an older but ever-impressive technology.

Although its name is unknown to many people, Murray Hill is a charming residential neighborhood. Its main attraction, however, is one of the most recognizable structures in the world, the Empire State Building.

Numbers in the text correspond to numbers in the margin and on the Downtown map.

a good walk

Begin at the corner of 5th Avenue and 34th Street, where you can't miss the **Empire State Building** ③ ⌐, one of the world's most recognizable silhouettes. Walk a block west on 34th Street to 6th Avenue. The slender triangle before you is Herald Square, and across the street is the venerable Macy's department store.

At West 29th Street, head a block east back to 5th Avenue. East of here, toward Lexington Avenue in the high 20s, is a neighborhood dubbed Little India for its concentration of Indian restaurants, spice shops, and clothing emporiums. Four blocks farther south on 5th Avenue is Madison Square, a perfect spot for a brown-bag lunch. A walk through the shady square leads to Madison Avenue, where you can see the gold-topped **New York Life Insurance Building** ②, which occupies the entire block between East 26th and 27th streets. On the southern edge of the park is one of New York's most photographed buildings—the 1902 **Flatiron Building** ③. This tall triangular building tapers to the point made by the intersection of 23rd Street, Broadway, and 5th Avenue. It lends its name to the now trendy Flatiron District, which lies to the south between 6th Avenue and Park Avenue South.

Continue south on Broadway and turn left on East 20th Street to the **Theodore Roosevelt Birthplace National Historic Site** ③. East of Park Avenue South, the historically commercial Flatiron District quickly segues into the tony residential neighborhood of Gramercy. Its defining and exclusive feature is **Gramercy Park** ③, at the top of Irving Place between East 20th and 21st streets.

Return to Broadway, and head south along what was part of *the* most fashionable shopping area in the city during the Gilded Age. If you continue down Broadway, it leads to **Union Square** ③.

TIMING Half a day should suffice for this tour. Allow 1½ hours for the Empire State Building. Before traipsing up to the top, consider the weather and how it is likely to affect visibility. Sunsets from the observation deck are spectacular, so you may want to end your day there. Keep in mind that some office buildings included in the walk are open only during the week. The Union Square Greenmarket, a must-visit, is open all day every Monday, Wednesday, Friday, and Saturday.

What to See

Ⓒ ▶ ③ **Empire State Building.** It may no longer be the world's tallest building (it
FodorśChoice currently ranks seventh), but it's certainly one of the best-known
★ skyscrapers, its pencil-slim silhouette a symbol for New York City and, perhaps, the 20th century. The art-deco behemoth opened on May 1, 1931, after a mere 13 months of construction; the framework rose at a rate of 4½ stories per week, making the Empire State Building the fastest-rising skyscraper ever built. In 1951 a TV transmittal tower was added to the top, raising the total height to 1,472 feet. Ever since the 1976 American bicentennial celebration, the top 30 stories have been spotlighted at night with colors honoring dozens of different holidays and events.

Tickets are sold on the concourse level and on the building's Web site (a good way to avoid the considerable line). The 86th-floor observatory (1,050 feet high) is open to the air and circles the building; on clear days you can see up to 80 mi. Time your visit for early or late in the day (morning is the least crowded time), when the sun is low on the horizon and the shadows are deep across the city. ✉ *350 5th Ave., at E. 34th St., Murray Hill* ☎ *212/736–3100 or 877/692–8439* ⊕ *www. esbnyc.com* ✉ *$11* ⊘ *Daily 9 AM–midnight; last elevator up leaves at 11:15 PM* Ⓜ *Subway: B, D, F, N, Q, R, V, W to 34th St./Herald Sq.*

③ **Flatiron Building.** When completed in 1902, the Fuller Building, as it was originally known, caused a sensation. Architect Daniel Burnham made ingenious use of the triangular wedge of land and employed a revolutionary steel frame, which allowed for its 20-story, 286-foot height. Covered with a limestone and terra-cotta skin in the Italian Renaissance style, the ship's bowlike structure appears to sail intrepidly up 5th Avenue. ✉ *175 5th Ave., bordered by E. 22nd and E. 23rd Sts., 5th Ave., and Broadway, Flatiron District* Ⓜ *Subway: R, W to 23rd St.*

③⑤ **Gramercy Park.** In 1831 Samuel B. Ruggles, an intelligent young real estate developer, bought and drained a tract of what was largely swamp and created a charming park inspired by London's residential squares. Hoping that exclusivity would create demand, he limited access to the park to those who bought the surrounding lots. Sixty-six of the city's fashionable elite did just that, and were provided with golden keys to unlock the park's cast-iron gate. Although no longer golden, keys to the city's only private park are still given only to residents. Passersby can enjoy the carefully maintained landscaping through the 8-foot-high fence. ⊠ *Lexington Ave. between E. 20th and E. 21st Sts., Gramercy* Ⓜ *Subway: 6, R, W to 23rd St.*

③② **New York Life Insurance Building.** Cass Gilbert, better known for the Woolworth Building, capped this 1928 building with a gilded octagonal spire that is stunning when illuminated. The soaring lobby's coffered ceilings and ornate bronze doors are equally grand. P. T. Barnum's Hippodrome (1890–1925) formerly occupied this site, and after that Madison Square Garden, designed by architect and playboy Stanford White. White was shot in the Garden's roof garden by Harry K. Thaw, a partner in White's firm and the jealous husband of actress Evelyn Nesbit, with whom White was purportedly having an affair—an episode more or less accurately depicted in E. L. Doctorow's book *Ragtime.* ⊠ *51 Madison Ave., between E. 26th and E. 27th Sts., Flatiron District* Ⓜ *Subway: R, V to 28th St.*

③④ **Theodore Roosevelt Birthplace National Historic Site.** The 26th U.S. president—the only one from New York City—was born on this site in 1858. The original 1848 brownstone was demolished in 1916, but this Gothic Revival replica, built in 1923, is a near-perfect reconstruction of the house where Teddy lived until he was 15 years old. Administered by the National Park Service, the house has a fascinating collection of Teddyana in five Victorian period rooms. ⊠ *28 E. 20th St., between Broadway and Park Ave. S, Flatiron District* ☎ *212/260–1616* ⊕ *www. nps.gov/thrb* ⊠ *$3* ⊙ *Daily 9–5; guided tours 10–4* Ⓜ *Subway: 6, R, W to 23rd St.*

③⑥ **Union Square.** A park, outdoor market, meeting place, and site of rallies and demonstrations, this pocket of green space is the focus of a bustling residential and commercial neighborhood. The name "Union" originally signified that two main roads—Broadway and 4th Avenue—crossed here.

Union Square is at its best on Monday, Wednesday, Friday, and Saturday (8–6), when the largest of the city's 28 **greenmarkets** brings farmers and food purveyors from all over the Northeast. Crowds browse among the stands of fresh produce, flowers, plants, homemade baked goods, cheeses, cider, New York State wines, and fish and meat. ⊠ *E. 14th to E. 17th Sts. between Broadway and Park Ave. S, Flatiron District* Ⓜ *Subway: N, Q, R, W, 4, 5, 6 to Union Sq./14th St.*

42nd Street

Few streets in America claim as many landmarks as midtown Manhattan's central axis, from Times Square, Bryant Park, and the main branch of the New York Public Library on its western half to Grand Central Terminal and the United Nations on its eastern stretch. And few can claim as colorful a reputation. Before World War II it was known as the thoroughfare where Ziegfeld and other impresarios staged dazzling spectacles. In the decades that followed it took a nosedive, and the once-grand theaters around Times Square switched to screening second-run and X-rated movies. With that decline came prostitutes, drug dealers, and petty crime.

But 42nd Street began to turn around in the 1990s. The city, eager to clear space for corporate giants, passed legislation that sent the seedy movie theaters packing. Today there's a steady stream of headline-grabbing ground breakings; traffic-stopping celebrity appearances outside the Virgin Megastore and the MTV studios; and new shops, restaurants, and hotels, each more lavish than the last. In Times Square itself, however, the neon lights shine brighter than ever—a local ordinance requires that massive billboard-style ads be included in all new construction.

Numbers in the text correspond to numbers in the margin and on the Midtown map.

a good walk

Begin at the corner of West 42nd Street and 8th Avenue, where the monolithic Port Authority Bus Terminal dispenses commuters, tourists, and those in search of some excitement onto the street or into the subway running beneath it. The block of 42nd Street between 9th and 10th avenues is lined with a string of off-Broadway playhouses called Theatre Row. Literally the biggest attraction in this part of town is the **Intrepid Sea-Air-Space Museum** ③⑦ ▶, at West 46th Street and the Hudson River.

At the corner of 42nd and 7th Avenue, the dazzling billboards of **Times Square** ③⑧ will grab your attention. Head two blocks north to the southwest corner of 44th Street, where you'll probably run into a crowd of teenagers gawking at the second-floor studios of MTV. Directly across 7th Avenue are the studios of ABC, distinguished by two ribbons of light that flash up the latest headlines. Also on this corner is an enormous Toys R Us with a three-story-tall indoor Ferris wheel. Head through Times Square to Duffy Square, a triangle between West 46th and 47th streets, the home of the TKTS booth. You can score good seats to some of the hottest Broadway shows for half the going rate. On the east side of Broadway, the Times Square Visitors Center in the historic Embassy Theater is a helpful all-in-one resource.

At West 42nd Street between 5th and 6th avenues, steps rise into the shrubbery and trees of handsome **Bryant Park** ③⑨, a perfect place to stop for a picnic. The park stretches between West 42nd and West 40th streets and has been adopted by many Midtown workers. It's directly behind the magnificent beaux-arts **New York Public Library Humanities and Social Sciences Library** ④⓪, the central research branch of the city's library system. A well-kept public bathroom is between the park and library, next to West 42nd Street.

Continue east on 42nd Street to **Grand Central Terminal** ④①. Park Avenue wraps around Grand Central on an elevated roadway and continues to the north. The art-deco **Chrysler Building,** ④②, most New Yorkers' favorite

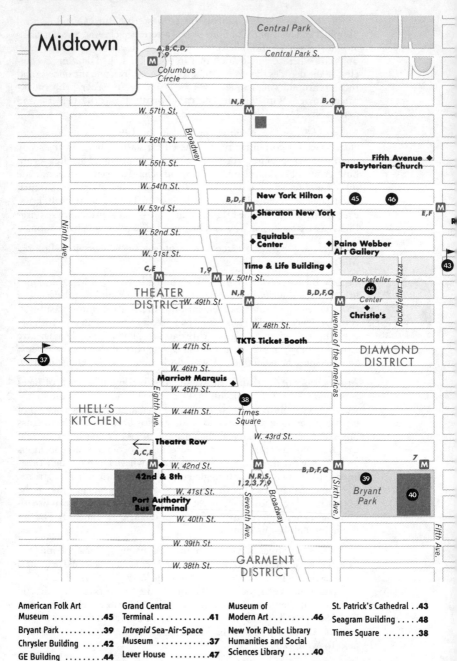

Midtown

Central Park

Central Park S.

A,B,C,D,
1,9

Columbus
Circle

W. 57th St.

N,R

B,Q

Fifth Avenue ◆
Presbyterian Church

Broadway

W. 56th St.

W. 55th St.

W. 54th St.

W. 53rd St.

B,D,E

New York Hilton ◆

45   46

E,F

Sheraton New York

W. 52nd St.

Equitable
Center

Paine Webber
Art Gallery

W. 51st St.

C,E   1,9

Time & Life Building ◆

43

Rockefeller Plaza

Ninth Ave.

W. 50th St.

Rockefeller

THEATER
DISTRICT

N,R

B,D,F,Q

44
Center

W. 49th St.

Christie's

W. 48th St.

Avenue of the Americas

DIAMOND
DISTRICT

W. 47th St.

TKTS Ticket Booth

W. 46th St.

← 37

Marriott Marquis ◆

Eighth Ave.

W. 45th St.

HELL'S
KITCHEN

W. 44th St.

38

Times
Square

W. 43rd St.

← Theatre Row

A,C,E

◆ W. 42nd St.

7

M

M

42nd & 8th

W. 41st St.

N,R,S,
1,2,3,7,9

B,D,F,Q
(Sixth Ave.)

39
Bryant
Park

40

Port Authority
Bus Terminal

W. 40th St.

Seventh Ave.

Broadway

W. 39th St.

Fifth Ave.

GARMENT
DISTRICT

W. 38th St.

E. 60th St.

E. 59th St.

4,5,6
M E. 58th St.

0 _____ 1/2 mile

0 _____ 800 meters

Four Seasons Hotel ◆

E. 57th St.

◆ **Dahesh Museum**

E. 56th St.

E. 55th St.

St. Peter's Church ◆ E. 54th St.

47

E,F
M

48

aquet & Tennis Club ◆

TURTLE BAY

E. 53rd St.

E. 52nd St.

6
M

E. 51st St.

E. 50th St.

Park Ave. ◆ **Waldorf-Astoria**

E. 49th St.

E. 48th St.

E. 47th St.

E. 46th St.

Madison Ave.

United Nations

E. 45th St.

E. 45th St.

E. 44th St.

E. 44th St.

Vanderbilt Ave.

Grand Central Terminal

Lexington Ave.

Third Ave.

Second Ave.

First Ave.

Beekman Pl.

Sutton Pl.

FDR Drive

East River

E. 43rd St.

41

42

M E. 42nd St.
4,5,6,7,S

Tudor City

Midtown Tunnel

Queens-Midtown Tunnel

E. 41st St.

Park Ave.

E. 40th St.

E. 39th St.

E. 38th St.

KEY

M *Subway stops*

▶ *Start of walk*

SUBWAY STORY

NEW YORK CITY HAS *always had a reputation for innovation and speed, so it's not surprising that the world's first elevated railcar ran on tracks between Prince and 14th streets. The steam-powered train known as an "el" made its fledgling journey in 1832, marking the advent of New York City public transit. By the end of the 19th century, underground railways had arrived in cities around the world— but not in New York, the largest commercial and industrial metropolis in the world. "Public" transportation still consisted primarily of horse-drawn streetcars. The city's proposed subway system spent the last three decades of the 19th century on hold, a victim of bureaucratic corruption and incompetence.*

The stranglehold finally broke in 1894 when New Yorkers voted overwhelmingly for public ownership of the subway. The decision gave the city ownership of the yet-to-be-built subway system's physical plant. On March 24, 1900, Mayor Robert A. Van Wyck, using a silver spade from Tiffany & Co., broke ground for the city's first subway. Over the next four years, 12,000 laborers—most of them immigrants—built the first tunnels, working 10-hour days for 20¢ an hour. More than 50 men died and thousands were maimed while building what became the Interborough Rapid Transit (IRT) line. The 9.1 mi of track began at City Hall, continued north to Grand Central, crossed town, and then ran up Broadway to West 145th Street.

The IRT finally opened on October 27, 1904. A nickel bought a ticket, and in the IRT's first year, passengers took more than a billion rides. Turnstiles appeared in 1928, and it would be another 20 years before the fare rose to a dime. In 1953 tokens replaced tickets and the fare rose to 15¢. By the late 1990s the fare reached $1.50 and the new MetroCard allowed unlimited-ride options. In 2003, the fare was increased to $2 and tokens were discontinued.

Those original 9.1 mi of track have grown to more than 700 today—more miles than any other subway system in the world. The newest of the 5,800 subway cars have digital displays and recorded messages that cheerfully advise, "Stand clear of the closing doors, please." (Nevertheless, some riders prefer the often amusing and grouchy exhortations of the live train operators.)

The 24 subway lines operate 24 hours a day, 365 days a year. Some platforms don't have any subway maps, or may display outdated versions, so carry a current map when navigating the system. (Be aware that some lines change their routes at night or on the weekend.) Although it's not foolproof, the subway system services more than 1.5 billion rides a year, proving that it's still one of this city's great bargains.

To learn more about the subway, visit the **New York Transit Museum** (✉ Boerum Pl. at Schermerhorn St., Brooklyn Heights ☎ 718/243-3060 ⊕ www.mta.nyc.ny. us Ⓜ Subway: 2, 4, 5 to Borough Hall; A, C, F to Jay St.; A, C, G to Hoyt St.). The museum, housed in a decommissioned subway station, includes an exhibition incorporating elements of a New York City intersection and displays more than 200 trolley models. It's open 10–4 Tuesday through Friday, noon–5 on weekends; admission is $5. The free **New York Transit Museum Gallery Annex & Store** (✉ Grand Central Terminal, main entrance, E. 42nd St. at Park Ave., Midtown East ☎ 212/ 878-0106 Ⓜ Subway: 4, 5, 6, 7, S to 42nd St./Grand Central), in Grand Central, has exhibitions and sells subway-related souvenirs. It's open weekdays 8–8 and weekends 10–6.

skyscraper, is farther east, at East 42nd Street and Lexington Avenue. Although the Chrysler Corporation itself moved out long ago, this graceful shaft culminating in a stainless-steel spire still captivates the eye and the imagination.

TIMING This long walk covers vastly different types of sights, from frenzied Times Square to bucolic Bryant Park, and from the ornate Grand Central Terminal to the sleek United Nations complex. If you start at the *Intrepid*, you could easily eat up half a day even before you reach 5th Avenue. The spectacle of Times Square is best appreciated at night.

What to See

39 Bryant Park. Midtown's only major green space has become one of the best-loved and most beautiful small parks in the city. America's first World's Fair, the Crystal Palace Exhibition, was held here in 1853–54. Today London plane trees and formal flower beds line the perimeter of its central lawn. At the east side of the park, near a squatting bronze statue of Gertrude Stein, are the open-air Bryant Park Café, which is open April 15 to October 15, and the stylish Bryant Park Grill, which has a rooftop garden. ⊠ *6th Ave. between W. 40th and W. 42nd Sts., Midtown West* ☎ *212/768–4242* ⊕ *www.bryantpark.org* ☉ *Oct.–Apr., daily 7–7; May–Sept., weekdays 7 AM–8 PM, weekends 7 AM–11 PM* Ⓜ *Subway: B, D, F, V to 42nd St.; 7 to 5th Ave.*

★ **42 Chrysler Building.** An art-deco masterpiece designed by William Van Alen and built between 1928 and 1930, the Chrysler Building is one of New York's most beloved skyscrapers. It's at its best at dusk, when the stainless-steel spire reflects the sunset, and at night, when its illuminated geometric design looks like the backdrop to a Hollywood musical. The Chrysler Corporation moved out in the mid-1950s, but the building retains its name and many automotive details: gargoyles shaped like car-hood ornaments sprout from the building's upper stories—wings from the 31st floor, eagle heads from the 61st. At 1,048 feet, the building only briefly held the world's-tallest title—for 40 days before the Empire State Building snatched it away. ⊠ *405 Lexington Ave., at E. 42nd St., Midtown East* Ⓜ *Subway: 4, 5, 6, 7, S to 42nd St./Grand Central.*

41 Grand Central Terminal. Grand Central is not only the world's largest railway station (76 acres) and the nation's busiest (500,000 commuters and subway riders use it daily), but also one of the world's greatest public spaces.

Fodor'sChoice ★

The south side of East 42nd Street is the best vantage point from which to admire Grand Central's dramatic beaux-arts facade. At the top are a graceful clock and a crowning sculpture, *Transportation*, which depicts Mercury flanked by Hercules and Minerva. The majestic **main concourse** is 200 feet long, 120 feet wide, and 120 feet—roughly 12 stories—high. Overhead, a celestial map of the zodiac constellations covers the robin's egg–blue ceiling.

The Grand Central Market on the east end of the main floor is a great place to buy fresh fruit, fish, dairy goods, and breads. Dozens of restaurants and shops, many in spaces long closed to the public, make the downstairs **dining concourse** a destination in its own right. *Main en-*

trance ⊠ *E. 42nd St. at Park Ave., Midtown East* ☎ *212/935–3960* ⊕ *www.grandcentralterminal.com* Ⓜ *Subway: 4, 5, 6, 7, S to 42nd St./Grand Central.*

☝ ▶ **㊲** **Intrepid Sea-Air-Space Museum.** Formerly the USS *Intrepid,* this 900-foot aircraft carrier is serving out its retirement as the centerpiece of Manhattan's only floating museum. An A-12 Blackbird spy plane, lunar landing modules, helicopters, seaplanes, and other aircraft are on deck. Docked alongside, and also part of the museum, are the *Growler,* a strategic-missile submarine; the *Edson,* a Vietnam-era destroyer; and several other battle-scarred naval veterans. For an extra thrill (and an extra $8), children can try the Navy Flight Simulator and "land" an aircraft on board. ⊠ *Hudson River, Pier 86, 12th Ave. and W. 46th St., Midtown West* ☎ *212/245–0072* ⊕ *www.intrepidmuseum.org* ᗌ *$14; free to active U.S. military personnel* ⊙ *May–Sept., weekdays 10–5, weekends 10–6; Oct.–Apr., Tues.–Sun. 10–5; last admission 1 hr before closing* Ⓜ *Subway: A, C, E to 42nd St.; M42 bus to pier.*

㊵ **New York Public Library Humanities and Social Sciences Library.** This 1911 masterpiece of beaux-arts design (Carrère and Hastings, architects) is one of the great research institutions in the world, with 6 million books, 12 million manuscripts, and 2.8 million pictures. The grand entrance is at 5th Avenue just south of 42nd Street, where a pair of **marble lions** guard a flagstone plaza. The library's bronze front doors open into the magnificent marble **Astor Hall,** flanked by a sweeping double staircase. Upstairs on the third floor, the magisterial **Rose Main Reading Room** has original chandeliers, oak tables, and gleaming bronze reading lamps. Exhibitions on photography, typography, literature, bookmaking, and maps are held regularly in the **Gottesman Exhibition Hall,** the Edna B. **Salomon Room,** the **Third Floor Galleries,** and the **Berg Exhibition Room.** ⊠ *5th Ave. between E. 40th and E. 42nd Sts., Midtown West* ☎ *212/ 930–0800, 212/869–8089 for exhibit information* ⊕ *www.nypl.org* ⊙ *Thurs.–Sat. 10–6, Tues. and Wed. 11–7:30; exhibitions until 6* Ⓜ *Subway: B, D, F, V to 42nd St.*

★ **㊳** **Times Square.** Whirling in a chaos of competing lights and advertisements, Times Square is New York's white-hot energy center. Hordes of people jostle for space on the sidewalks to walk and gawk. Like many New York City "squares," it's actually two triangles formed by the angle of Broadway slashing across 7th Avenue between West 42nd and 47th streets. Times Square (the name also applies to the general area, beyond the intersection of these streets) has been the city's main theater district since the turn of the 20th century: from West 44th to 51st streets, the cross streets west of Broadway are lined with some 30 major theaters.

On December 31, 1904, the *New York Times* celebrated the opening of its new headquarters, at Times Tower, with a fireworks show at midnight, thereby starting a New Year's Eve tradition. Now resheathed in marble and called **One Times Square Plaza** (⊠ W. 42nd St. between Broadway and 7th Ave., Midtown West), the building is topped with the world's most famous rooftop pole, down which an illuminated 200-pound ball is lowered each December 31.

Times Square's everyday high-wattage thunder includes two-story-high cups of coffee that actually steam; huge billboards of underwear models; mammoth, superfast digital displays of world news and stock quotes; and countless other technologically sophisticated allurements. The traffic island in front of the Armed Forces Recruiting Office provides the best angles on the whole of Times Square's helter-skelter welter. ⊠ *W. 42nd to W. 47th Sts. at Broadway and 7th Ave., Midtown West* Ⓜ *Subway: 1, 2, 3, 9, N, Q, R, W to 42nd St./Times Sq.*

Rockefeller Center & Midtown Skyscrapers

Athens has its Parthenon and Rome its Colosseum. New York's temples are its steel-and-glass skyscrapers. Many of them, including the Lever House and the Seagram Building, have been pivotal in the history of modern architecture, and the 19 limestone-and-aluminum buildings of Rockefeller Center constitute one of the world's most famous pieces of real estate.

Conceived by John D. Rockefeller during the Great Depression of the 1930s, the Rockefeller Center complex occupies nearly 22 acres of prime real estate between 5th and 7th avenues and West 47th and 52nd streets. Its central cluster of buildings consists of smooth shafts of warm-hue limestone streamlined with glistening aluminum. Plazas, concourses, and shops create a sense of community for the nearly quarter of a million people who use it daily.

Midtown now rivals the Wall Street area in its number of prestigious tenants. Rockefeller Center itself is a capital of the communications industry, containing the headquarters of a TV network, several major publishing companies, and the world's largest news-gathering organization, the Associated Press.

Numbers in the text correspond to numbers in the margin and on the Midtown map.

a good walk

This tour along six avenues and five streets is full of skyscrapers that can make the streets seem like canyon washes. An anchor of midtown Manhattan is Rockefeller Center (☎ 212/632–3975 for information, ⊕ www.rockefellercenter.com), one of the greatest achievements in 20th-century urban planning. Directly across the street, on 5th Avenue between East 50th and 51st streets, is **St. Patrick's Cathedral** ㊺ ☞. Head one block south on 5th Avenue and turn west to walk along the Channel Gardens, a promenade of rock pools and seasonal flower beds. At the far end is the sunken Lower Plaza and its famous gilt statue of *Prometheus*. The backdrop to this scene is the 70-story **GE Building** ㊸, originally known as the RCA Building, whose entrance is guarded by a striking statue of *Wisdom*. Peer around the corner of West 50th Street to see the pink-and-blue neon sign of the titanic Radio City Music Hall on 6th Avenue.

Head north on 6th Avenue and turn right on West 52nd Street. A shortcut through the outdoor public space close to the CBS Building or through a shopping arcade farther east, at 666 5th Avenue, takes you to West 53rd Street's museums: the **American Folk Art Museum** ㊺ and the

Museum of Modern Art ㊻. Walk eastward on East 55th Street to Park Avenue and head a bit south to see two prime examples of the functionalist International Style: **Lever House** ㊼ and the **Seagram Building** ㊽, the only New York building designed by Ludwig Mies van der Rohe.

TIMING   To see only the buildings, block out an hour. Allow more time depending on your interest in the museums en route. Keep in mind that some parts of Rockefeller Center are open only during the week.

What to See

㊺ **American Folk Art Museum.** The facade of this eight-story building consists of 63 hand-cast panels of alloyed bronze, revealing individual textures, sizes, and reflections of light. Inside, four gallery floors—dedicated to exhibitions and the collection of arts and decorative objects from the 18th century to the present day—are naturally lighted through a central skylight. Works include paintings, weather vanes, quilts, pottery, scrimshaw, and folk sculpture such as carousel animals and trade figures. ⊠ *45 W. 53rd St., between 5th and 6th Aves., Midtown West* ☎ *212/ 265–1040* ⊕ *www.folkartmuseum.org* ⊠ *$9; free Fri. 5:30 PM–7:30 PM* ⊙ *Wed. and Thurs. and weekends 10:30 AM–5:30 PM, Fri. 10:30–7:30* Ⓜ *Subway: E, V to 5th Ave./53rd St.*

㊹ **GE Building.** The tallest tower in Rockefeller Center is more than just the backdrop to the Channel Gardens, *Prometheus,* and the ice-skating rink—it's also the backdrop to the Rockefeller Center Christmas tree. The 70-story (850-foot-tall) building is the headquarters of the NBC television network. Inside the lobby is a monumental mural by José María Sert, *American Progress.* Sert's 1937 mural depicts the muses of poetry, dance, and music along with those of science, technology, and physical effort. Sert's mural replaced the work of Diego Rivera, which was ordered destroyed because it centered around the likeness of Joseph Stalin.

Some of the first TV programs emanated from 30 Rock, including the *Today* show, broadcast from ground-floor studios at the southwest corner of 49th Street and Rockefeller Plaza. The two-level, monitor-spiked NBC Experience Store, across West 49th Street from the *Today* studio, is the departure point for 70-minute tours of the **NBC Studios** and of Rockefeller Center itself. ⊠ *30 Rockefeller Plaza, between 5th and 6th Aves. at 48th St., Midtown West* ☎ *212/664–7174* ⊠ *Tour $17.75* ☞ *Children under 6 not permitted* ⊙ *Tours depart from NBC store at street level of GE Bldg. every 15 mins. Mon.–Sat. 8:30–5:30, Sun. 9:30–4:30* Ⓜ *Subway: B, D, F, V to 47th–50th Sts./Rockefeller Center.*

Poised above the GE Building's entrance doors on Rockefeller Plaza is a striking sculpture of Zeus by Lee Lawrie, the same artist who sculpted the big *Atlas* in front of the **International Building** on 5th Avenue. ⊠ *Bounded by Rockefeller Plaza, 6th Ave., and 49th and 50th Sts., Midtown West.*

㊼ **Lever House.** According to the *AIA Guide to New York City,* this 1952 skyscraper built for the Lever Brothers soap company is "where the glass curtain wall began." Gordon Bunshaft, of Skidmore, Owings & Merrill, designed a sheer, slim glass box that rests on the end of a one-story-thick shelf balanced on square chrome columns. The whole building seems to float above the street. ⊠ *390 Park Ave., between E. 53rd and E. 54th Sts., Midtown East* Ⓜ *Subway: 6 to 51st St./Lexington Ave.; E, V to Lexington–3rd Aves./53rd St.*

46 **Museum of Modern Art.** A major overhaul, led by Japanese architect Yoshio
Fodor'sChoice Taniguchi, has radically changed the look and feel of MoMA. After a
★ renovation that nearly doubled its square footage—and after a stint in Long Island City, in Queens—the museum reopened its 53rd Street site in November 2004. The museum moved to this block in 1939, into a six-story building designed by Edward Durell Stone and Philip Goodwin. The stylish former entrance, marked by the piano-shape canopy, now serves as an entrance to the restaurant and bookstore as well. A second entrance faces West 54th Street with two new buildings: the eight-story Education and Research Center and the Gallery Building, which house the main galleries. ⊠ *11 W. 53rd St., between 5th and 6th Aves., Midtown East* ☎ *212/708–9400* ⊕ *www.moma.org* ⊠ *$20* ☉ *Wed.–Mon. 10:30–5:30 (Fri. until 8)* Ⓜ *Subway: E, V to 5th Ave./53rd St.*

48 **Seagram Building.** Ludwig Mies van der Rohe (1886–1969), a leading interpreter of International Style architecture, built this simple, boxlike bronze-and-glass tower in 1958. The austere facade belies its wit: I-beams, used to hold buildings up, are here attached to the surface, representing the *idea* of support. The Seagram's innovative ground-level plaza, extending out to the sidewalk, has since become a common element in urban skyscraper design. ⊠ *375 Park Ave., between E. 52nd and E. 53rd Sts., Midtown East* ⊠ *Free* ☉ *Tours Tues. at 3* Ⓜ *Subway: 6 to 51st St./Lexington Ave.; E, V to Lexington–3rd Aves./53rd St.*

★ ⌐ **43** **St. Patrick's Cathedral.** The Gothic, double-spired, Roman Catholic cathedral of New York is one of the city's largest (seating approximately 2,400) and most striking churches. Dedicated to the patron saint of the Irish, the 1859 white marble-and-stone structure by architect James Renwick was consecrated in 1879. Additions over the years include the archbishop's house and rectory, the two 330-foot spires, and the intimate Lady Chapel. Among the statues in the alcoves around the nave is a modern depiction of the first American-born saint, Mother Elizabeth Ann Seton. ⊠ *5th Ave. between E. 50th and E. 51st Sts., Midtown East* ☎ *212/753–2261 rectory* ☉ *Daily 8* AM–*8:45* PM Ⓜ *Subway: E, V to 5th Ave./53rd St.*

Museum Mile

Once known as Millionaires' Row, the stretch of 5th Avenue between East 79th and 104th streets has been fittingly renamed Museum Mile, for it now contains New York's most distinguished cluster of cultural institutions. The connection is more than coincidental: many museums are housed in what used to be the great mansions of merchant princes and wealthy industrialists. A large number of these buildings were constructed of limestone and reflect the beaux-arts style so popular among the wealthy at the turn of the 20th century.

Numbers in the text correspond to numbers in the margin and on the Upper East Side & Museum Mile map.

This walk from East 70th to 105th Street covers around 2 mi. Walk on the west side of the avenue to be under the canopy of Central Park and have a good view of the mansions and apartments across the street. The **Frick Collection** ㊾ ☛ is housed at East 70th Street in an ornate, imposing beaux-arts mansion. To visit the **Asia Society and Museum** ㊿, an educational center dedicated to the art of South, Southeast, and East Asia, or the distinctive **Whitney Museum of American Art** ㊱, you have to venture off Fifth Avenue a bit. Head east two blocks to reach the Asia Society Museum at Park Avenue; from there, walk up five blocks and one block west to Madison Avenue for the Whitney. Heading one block west will put you back on Fifth Avenue.

Continuing along Fifth Avenue, you can't miss the **Metropolitan Museum of Art** ㊲, one of the world's largest art museums, making room for itself on Central Park's turf. One block north you encounter the **Neue Galerie New York** ㊳, a museum devoted to German and Austrian art in a 1914 Carrère and Hastings mansion.

At East 88th Street, Frank Lloyd Wright's striking **Solomon R. Guggenheim Museum** ㊴ is the architect's only major New York building. A block north stands the **National Academy of Design** ㊵, a prestigious museum and school of fine arts. At East 91st Street you find the former residence of industrialist Andrew Carnegie, now the **Cooper-Hewitt National Design Museum–Smithsonian Institution** ㊶.

As you continue north, look for the **Jewish Museum** ㊷ at East 92nd Street. Designed to look like a French Gothic château, it was originally built for financier Felix Warburg in 1908. The handsome, well-proportioned Georgian-style mansion on the corner of 5th Avenue and 94th Street was built in 1914 for another 5th Avenue magnate, Willard Straight, founder of *The New Republic* magazine. At East 103rd Street, the intimate **Museum of the City of New York** ㊸ has exhibits related to Big Apple history.

TIMING   It would be impossible to do justice to all these collections in one outing; the Metropolitan Museum alone contains too much to see in a week, much less a day. Consider selecting one or two museums or exhibits in which to linger and simply walk past the others, appreciating their exteriors. Save the rest for another day—or for your next trip.

Be sure to pick the right day for this tour: most museums are closed at least one day of the week, usually Monday, and a few have free admission during extended hours on specific days.

What to See

㊿ **Asia Society and Museum.** The eight-story red-granite building that houses this museum and educational center complements Park Avenue's older, more traditional architecture. Founded in 1956, the society hosts a regular program of lectures, films, and performances, in addition to exhibitions of art from the Asia-Pacific region. The Asian art collection of Mr. and Mrs. John D. Rockefeller III forms the museum's major hold-

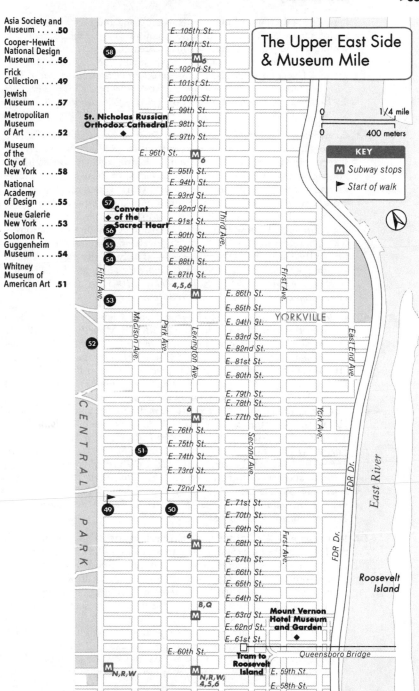

E. 105th St.
E. 104th St.
E. 102nd St.
E. 101st St.
E. 100th St.
E. 99th St.
St. Nicholas Russian E. 98th St.
Orthodox Cathedral E. 97th St.
E. 96th St.
E. 95th St.
E. 94th St.
E. 93rd St.
57 Convent E. 92nd St.
◆ **of the** E. 91st St.
56 Sacred Heart E. 90th St.
55 E. 89th St.
54 E. 88th St.
E. 87th St.
4,5,6
53 E. 86th St.
E. 85th St.
E. 04th St. YORKVILLE
E. 83rd St.
E. 82nd St.
E. 81st St.
E. 80th St.
E. 79th St.
E. 78th St.
6 E. 77th St.
E. 76th St.
51 E. 75th St.
E. 74th St.
E. 73rd St.
E. 72nd St.
49 E. 71st St.
50 E. 70th St.
E. 69th St.
6 E. 68th St.
E. 67th St.
E. 66th St.
E. 65th St.
E. 64th St.
B,Q
E. 63rd St. **Mount Vernon**
E. 62nd St. **Hotel Museum**
E. 61st St. **and Garden** ◆
E. 60th St. Queensboro Bridge
N,R,W **Tram to**
Roosevelt
N,R,W, **Island** E. 59th St
4,5,6 E. 58th St.

58
52

Fifth Ave.
Madison Ave.
Park Ave.
Lexington Ave.
Third Ave.
Second Ave.
First Ave.
York Ave.
East End Ave.
FDR Dr.

CENTRAL PARK
East River
Roosevelt Island

The Upper East Side & Museum Mile

0   1/4 mile
0   400 meters

KEY
M Subway stops
► Start of walk

ings. The collection includes South Asian stone and bronze sculptures; art from India, Nepal, Pakistan, and Afghanistan; bronze vessels, ceramics, sculpture, and paintings from China; Korean ceramics; and paintings, wooden sculptures, and ceramics from Japan. ☒ *725 Park Ave., at 70th St., Upper East Side* ☎ *212/288–6400 for general information, 212/ 517–2742 for the box office* ⊕ *www.asiasociety.org* ☜ *$7; free Fri. 6–9* ☉ *Tues.–Thurs. and weekends 11–6, Fri. 11–9* Ⓜ *Subway: 6 to 68th St./Hunter College.*

56 **Cooper-Hewitt National Design Museum–Smithsonian Institution.** The core of the museum's collection was assembled in 1897 by the two Hewitt sisters, granddaughters of inventor and industrialist Peter Cooper. Major holdings focus on aspects of contemporary and historical design, including drawings, prints, textiles, furniture, metalwork, ceramics, glass, wood-work, and wall coverings. The Smithsonian Institution took over the museum in 1967, and in 1976 the collection was moved into its current digs, formerly Andrew Carnegie's mansion. Changing exhibitions—which have covered such subjects as jewelry design and the construc-tion of the Disney theme parks—are invariably enlightening and often amusing. ☒ *2 E. 91st St., at 5th Ave., Upper East Side* ☎ *212/849–8400* ⊕ *www.si.edu/ndm* ☜ *$10* ☉ *Tues.–Thurs. 10–5, Fri. 10–9, Sat. 10–6, Sun. noon–6* Ⓜ *Subway: 4, 5, 6 to 86th St.*

★ ☞ **49** **Frick Collection.** Coke-and-steel baron Henry Clay Frick (1849–1919) amassed this superb art collection. Édouard Manet's *The Bullfight* (1864) hangs in the Garden Court. Two of the Frick's three Vermeers—*Officer and Laughing Girl* (circa 1658) and *Girl Interrupted at Her Music* (1660–61)—hang by the front staircase. Fra Filippo Lippi's *The An-nunciation* (circa 1440) hangs in the Octagon Room. Gainsborough and Reynolds portraits are in the dining room; canvases by Gainsborough, Constable, Turner, and Gilbert Stuart are in the library; and several Titians, Holbeins, a Giovanni Bellini, and an El Greco are in the "living hall." Three Rembrandts, including *The Polish Rider* (circa 1655) and *Self-Portrait* (1658), as well as a third Vermeer, *Mistress and Maid* (circa 1665–70), hang in the former; paintings by Whistler, Goya, Van Dyck, Lorrain, and David in the latter. ☒ *1 E. 70th St., at 5th Ave., Upper East Side* ☎ *212/288–0700* ⊕ *www.frick.org* ☜ *$12* ☞ *Children under 10 not admitted* ☉ *Tues.–Thurs. 10–6, Fri. 10–9, Sat. 10–6, Sun. 1–6* Ⓜ *Subway: 6 to 68th St./Hunter College.*

57 **Jewish Museum.** One of the largest collections of Judaica in the world, the Jewish Museum explores the development and meaning of Jewish identity and culture over the course of 4,000 years. Housed in a gray-stone Gothic-style 1908 mansion, the exhibitions draw on the mu-seum's collection of artwork and ceremonial objects, ranging from a 3rd-century Roman burial plaque to 20th-century sculpture by Elie Nadelman. The two-floor permanent exhibition, "Culture and Conti-nuity: The Jewish Journey," displays nearly 800 objects. ☒ *1109 5th Ave., at E. 92nd St., Upper East Side* ☎ *212/423–3200* ⊕ *www. jewishmuseum.org* ☜ *$10; Thurs. 5–8 pay what you wish* ☉ *Sun.–Wed. 11–5:45, Thurs. 11–8, Fri. 11–3* Ⓜ *Subway: 6 to 96th St.*

52 **Metropolitan Museum of Art.** The largest art museum in the Western Hemi-
Fodor$Choice sphere (spanning four blocks, it encompasses 2 million square feet), the
★ Met is one of the city's supreme cultural institutions. Its permanent collection of nearly 3 million works of art from all over the world includes
objects from the Paleolithic era to modern times—an assemblage whose
quality and range make this one of the world's greatest museums.

Past the admission booths, a wide marble staircase leads up to the **European paintings** galleries, whose 2,500 works include Botticelli's *The
Last Communion of St. Jerome* (circa 1490), Pieter Brueghel's *The Har-
vesters* (1565), Johannes Vermeer's *Young Woman with a Water Jug*
(circa 1660), Velázquez's *Juan de Pareja* (1648), and Rembrandt's *Aris-
totle with a Bust of Homer* (1653). The arcaded **European Sculpture
Court** includes Auguste Rodin's massive bronze *The Burghers of Calais*
(1884–95).

To the left of the Great Hall on the first floor are the **Greek Galleries.**
Grecian urns and mythological marble statuary are displayed beneath
a skylighted, barrel-vaulted stone ceiling. Although renovations are still
in progress, Roman galleries are slated to open behind the Greek galleries, with a court for Roman sculpture and space for the museum's
collection of rare Roman wall paintings excavated from the ash of Mt.
Vesuvius. The Met's awesome **Egyptian collection**, spanning some 4,000
years, is on the first floor, directly to the right of the Great Hall.

Also on the first floor are the **Medieval Galleries.** The Gothic sculptures,
Byzantine enamels, and full-size baroque choir screen built in 1763 are
impressive. To the north of the Medieval Galleries is the **Arms & Armor**
exhibit, which is full of chain mail, swords, shields, and fancy firearms.
On the lower level, the **Costume Institute** has changing exhibits of
clothing and fashion spanning seven centuries that focus on subjects ranging from undergarments to Gianni Versace. ⊠ *5th Ave. at 82nd St., Upper
East Side* ☎ *212/535-7710* ⊕ *www.metmuseum.org* ✑ *$12*
☉ *Tues.–Thurs. and Sun. 9:30–5:30, Fri. and Sat. 9:30–9* Ⓜ *Subway:
4, 5, 6 to 86th St.*

★ ☺ **58** **Museum of the City of New York.** Unique aspects of the city are drawn together in this massive Georgian mansion built in 1930. Period rooms,
dioramas, films, prints, paintings, sculpture, and clever displays of memorabilia cover the Dutch settlers of Nieuw Amsterdam to the present day.
An exhibit on Broadway illuminates the history of American theater with
costumes, set designs, and period photographs; the noteworthy toy
gallery has several meticulously detailed dollhouses. Maps, nautical artifacts, Currier & Ives lithographs, and furniture collections constitute
the rest of the museum's permanent displays. ⊠ *1220 5th Ave., at E. 103rd
St., Upper East Side* ☎ *212/534-1672* ⊕ *www.mcny.org* ✑ *$7 sug-
gested donation* ☉ *Wed.–Sun. 10–5* Ⓜ *Subway: 6 to 103rd St.*

55 **National Academy of Design.** Since its founding in 1825, the academy has
required each member elected to its Museum and School of Fine Arts
to donate a representative work of art. This criterion has produced a
strong collection of 19th- and 20th-century American art, as members
have included Mary Cassatt, Samuel F. B. Morse, Winslow Homer,

Frank Lloyd Wright, Jacob Lawrence, I. M. Pei, Robert Rauschenberg, Maya Lin, Frank Gehry, and Red Grooms. ✉ *1083 5th Ave., between E. 89th and E. 90th Sts., Upper East Side* ☎ *212/369–4880* 🌐 *www.nationalacademy.org* 🎟 *$8; pay what you wish Fri. 5–6* ⏲ *Wed. and Thurs. noon–5, Fri.–Sun. 11–6* Ⓜ *Subway: 4, 5, 6 to 86th St.*

(53) **Neue Galerie New York.** Organized by the late art dealer Serge Sabarsky and cosmetics heir Ronald S. Lauder, the Neue Galerie specializes in early-20th-century German and Austrian art and design as epitomized by Gustav Klimt, Vasily Kandinsky, Paul Klee, Egon Schiele, and Josef Hoffman and other designers from the Wiener Werkstätte. The two-floor gallery, along with a café serving Viennese pastries and a top-notch design shop, are in a 1914 mansion designed by Carrère and Hasting and originally the home of Mrs. Cornelius Vanderbilt III, the top society hostess of the Gilded Age. ✉ *1048 5th Ave., at E. 86th St., Upper East Side* ☎ *212/628–6200* 🌐 *www.neuegalerie.org* 🎟 *$10* ☞ *Children under 12 not admitted; under 16 must be accompanied by an adult* ⏲ *Mon. and weekends 11–6, Fri. 11–9* Ⓜ *Subway: 4, 5, 6 to 86th St.*

(54) Fodor'sChoice ★ **Solomon R. Guggenheim Museum.** Frank Lloyd Wright's landmark museum building is visited as much for its famous architecture as it is for its superlative art. Opened in 1959, shortly after Wright died, the Guggenheim is an icon of modernist architecture, designed specifically to showcase—and complement—modern art. Outside the curvaceous building, Wright's attention to detail is strikingly evident—in the portholelike windows on its south side, the circular pattern of the sidewalk, and the smoothness of the hand-plastered concrete. Inside, under a 92-foot-high glass dome, a ¼-mi-long ramp spirals down past changing exhibitions. The museum has strong holdings in Vasily Kandinsky, Paul Klee, Marc Chagall, Pablo Picasso, and Robert Mapplethorpe. In its Tower galleries, double-high ceilings accommodate extraordinarily large art pieces, and the Tower's fifth-floor sculpture terrace has a view overlooking Central Park. On permanent display, the museum's Thannhauser Collection comprises primarily works by French Impressionists and post-Impressionists, including Matisse, van Gogh, Toulouse-Lautrec, and Cézanne. ✉ *1071 5th Ave., between E. 88th and E. 89th Sts., Upper East Side* ☎ *212/423–3500* 🌐 *www.guggenheim.org* 🎟 *$15; Fri. 6–8 pay what you wish* ⏲ *Mon.–Wed. and weekends 10–5:45, Fri. 10–8* Ⓜ *Subway: 4, 5, 6 to 86th St.*

(51) **Whitney Museum of American Art.** This museum grew out of a gallery in the studio of the sculptor and collector Gertrude Vanderbilt Whitney, whose talent and taste were fortuitously accompanied by the wealth of two prominent families. She established an independent museum for her collection of 20th-century American art in 1930. The fifth floor's eight sleek galleries house "Hopper to Mid-Century," with works by Reginald Marsh, George Bellows, Robert Henri, Georgia O'Keeffe, and Marsden Hartley. Postwar and contemporary highlights from the permanent collection include paintings and sculpture by such artists as Jackson Pollack, Jim Dine, Jasper Johns, Mark Rothko, Frank Stella, Chuck Close, Cindy Sherman, and Roy Lichtenstein. ✉ *945 Madison Ave., at E. 75th St., Upper East Side* ☎ *212/570–3676* 🌐 *www.whitney.org*

$12; Fri. 6–9 pay what you wish ⊙ *Wed. and Thurs., and weekends 11–6, Fri. 1–9* Ⓜ *Subway: 6 to 77th St.*

Central Park

For many residents Central Park is the greatest—and most indispensable—part of New York City. Without the park's 843 acres of meandering paths, tranquil lakes, ponds, and open meadows, New Yorkers might be a lot less sane. Every day thousands of joggers, cyclists, in-line skaters, and walkers make their daily jaunts around the park's loop, the reservoir, and various other parts of the park. Come summertime the park serves as Manhattan's Riviera, with sun worshippers crowding every available patch of grass. Throughout the year pleasure seekers of all ages come to enjoy horseback riding, softball, ice-skating or roller-skating, rock climbing, croquet, tennis, and more—or simply to escape the rumble of traffic, walk through the woods, and feel, at least for a moment, far from the urban frenzy.

No matter how close to nature New Yorkers feel when reveling in it, Central Park was in fact the first artificially landscaped park in the United States. The design was conceived in 1857 by Frederick Law Olmsted and Calvert Vaux, the founders of the landscape architecture profession in the United States. The Greensward Plan, as it was called, combined pastoral, picturesque, and formal elements: open rolling meadows complement fanciful landscapes and grand, formal walkways. The southern portion of the park has many formal elements, whereas the north end is deliberately more wild.

Numbers in the text correspond to numbers in the margin and on the Central Park map.

a good walk

To explore the park on foot, begin at the southeast corner, at Grand Army Plaza, at 59th Street and 5th Avenue. The first path off the main road (East Drive) leads to **The Pond** ⑤⑨ ⌐, where Gapstow Bridge provides a great vantage point for the oft-photographed midtown skyscrapers. Heading north on the path, you come to Wollman Memorial Rink, whose popularity is second only to that of the rink at Rockefeller Center. Turn your back to the rink, and you see **The Dairy** ⑥⓪, which serves as the park's main visitor center.

As you leave the Dairy, to your right (west) is the Playmates Arch. Coming through the arch, you hear the jaunty music of the antique Friedsam Memorial Carousel, the second-oldest carousel on the East Coast. From the carousel, climb the slope to the left of the Playmates Arch and walk beside Center Drive, which veers to the right. Stop for a look at the Sheep Meadow, a 15-acre expanse. The grand, formal walkway farther up the drive is **The Mall** ⑥①, which is lined with statuary and magnificent American elms. The road ahead is the 72nd Street transverse. Pass beneath it through a lovely tile arcade—elaborately carved birds and fruit trees adorn the upper parts of both staircases—to get to **Bethesda Fountain** ⑥②, set on an elaborately patterned paved terrace on the edge of the lake.

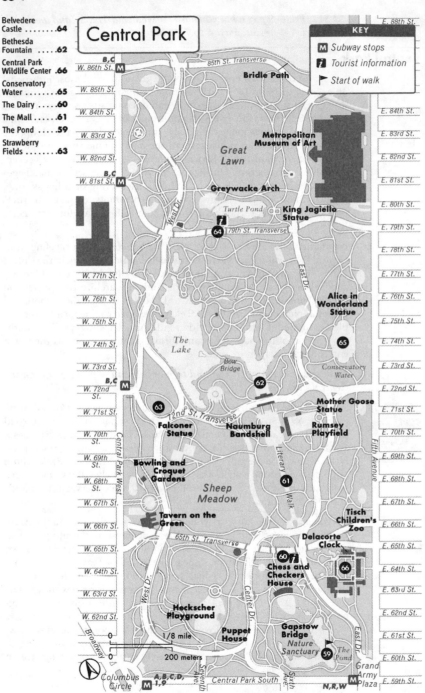

Central Park

KEY

M Subway stops

i Tourist information

▶ Start of walk

E. 88th St.

85th St. Transverse

B,C
W. 86th St. **M**

Bridle Path

W. 85th St.

E. 84th St.

W. 84th St.

Metropolitan Museum of Art

E. 83rd St.

W. 83rd St.

Great Lawn

E. 82nd St.

W. 82nd St.

B,C
W. 81st St. **M**

Greywacke Arch

E. 81st St.

E. 80th St.

Turtle Pond

King Jagiello Statue

i
64
79th St. Transverse

E. 79th St.

West Dr.

E. 78th St.

W. 77th St.

E. 77th St.

W. 76th St.

Alice in Wonderland Statue

E. 76th St.

W. 75th St.

E. 75th St.

W. 74th St.

The Lake

65

E. 74th St.

W. 73rd St.

Bow Bridge

Conservatory Water

E. 73rd St.

B,C
W. 72nd St. **M**

62

E. 72nd St.

W. 71st St.

63

72nd St. Transverse

Mother Goose Statue

E. 71st St.

W. 70th St.

Falconer Statue

Naumburg Bandshell

Rumsey Playfield

E. 70th St.

W. 69th St.

Central Park West

Bowling and Croquet Gardens

E. 69th St.

W. 68th St.

61

Literary Walk

Fifth Avenue

E. 68th St.

W. 67th St.

Sheep Meadow

E. 67th St.

Tavern on the Green

Tisch Children's Zoo

E. 66th St.

W. 66th St.

Delacorte Clock

E. 65th St.

W. 65th St.

65th St. Transverse

60 i

W. 64th St.

Chess and Checkers House

66

E. 64th St.

W. 63rd St.

West Dr.

Center Dr.

E. 63rd St.

W. 62nd St.

Heckscher Playground

E. 62nd St.

0

Broadway

1/8 mile

Puppet House

Gapstow Bridge

E. 61st St.

0

200 meters

Nature Sanctuary

59

The Pond

E. 60th St.

East Dr.

Columbus Circle

A,B,C,D,
M
1,9

Seventh Ave.

Central Park South

Sixth Ave.

N,R,W **M**

Grand Army Plaza

E. 59th St.

The path east from the terrace leads past Chinese massage purveyors and the Loeb Boathouse, where in season you can rent rowboats and bicycles. There are public restrooms on the southeast side of the café, as well as on the staircase leading to the Bethesda Fountain. The path to the west of the fountain's terrace leads to Bow Bridge, a splendid cast-iron bridge arching over a neck of the lake.

Take the path back to the 72nd Street transverse; on the rocky outcrop across the road is a statue of a falconer gracefully lofting his bird. Turn to the right, and you can see a more prosaic statue, the pompous bronze figure of Daniel Webster, and tramp up the winding walk into **Strawberry Fields** ⑥, a memorial to John Lennon.

If you need a break at this point, head out of the park at W. 72nd St. Otherwise, at the top of Strawberry Fields' hill turn right through a rustic wood arbor thickly hung with wisteria vines and follow the path downhill. A view of the lake will open on your right. Start up West Drive to 79th Street and head east to **Belvedere Castle** ⑥. Look out from the castle terrace over Turtle Pond; stretching out in front of you is the Great Lawn.

Walk out the south end of the terrace, turn left, and make your way downhill along the shaded path above Turtle Pond. At the east end of the pond curve left past the statue of King Jagiello of Poland, where groups gather on weekends for folk dancing.

Continue around the pond and head uphill to Cleopatra's Needle, an Egyptian obelisk just across East Drive from the Metropolitan Museum of Art. Return south from Cleopatra's Needle, following the path through Greywacke Arch under East Drive. Then angle right (south), around the back corner of the Metropolitan Museum, and take the first right.

After you pass the dog-walking stretch of Cedar Hill on the right, continue south to one of the park's most formal areas: the symmetrical stone basin of the **Conservatory Water** ⑥, which is often crowded with remote-control model sailboats. Climb the hill at the far end of the water, cross the 72nd Street transverse, and follow the path south. When you see a rustic wooden shelter atop an outcrop of rock, take the path on the right to see Balto, a bronze statue of the real-life sled dog. The path circles back to the Tisch Children's Zoo, then passes under the Denesmouth Arch to reach the **Central Park Wildlife Center** ⑥.

TIMING Allow three to four hours for this route so that you can enjoy its pastoral pleasures at a leisurely pace. The circular drive is closed to auto traffic weekdays 10 AM–3 PM (except for the southeast portion of the road, up to 72nd Street) and 7 PM–10 PM, and weekends and holidays. Nonautomotive traffic is often heavy and sometimes fast moving, so always be careful when you're crossing the road, and stay toward the inside when you're walking.

Central Park has one of the lowest crime rates in the city. Just use common sense and stay within sight of other park visitors. Take this walk only during the day, since the park is fairly empty after dark.

For a recorded schedule of park events, call 888/697–2757. For a schedule of walking tours in Central Park, call 212/360–2727. Or visit the park's Web site at www.centralparknyc.org. Directions, park maps, and event calendars can also be obtained from volunteers at two 5th Avenue information booths, at East 60th Street and East 72nd Street.

What to See

🐤 64 **Belvedere Castle.** Standing regally atop Vista Rock, Belvedere Castle was built in 1872 of the same gray Manhattan schist that thrusts out of the soil in dramatic outcrops throughout the park. From here you can also see the stage of the Delacorte Theater and observe the picnickers and softball players on the Great Lawn. The castle is a typically 19th-century mishmash of styles—Gothic with Romanesque, Chinese, Moorish, and Egyptian motifs. Inside, the Henry Luce Nature Observatory has nature exhibits, children's workshops, and educational programs. Free discovery kits containing binoculars, bird guides, maps, and sketching materials are available in exchange for two pieces of identification. ⊠ *Midpark at 79th St. Transverse, Central Park* ☎ *212/772–0210* ⌑ *Free* ☉ *Tues.–Sun. 10–5* Ⓜ *Subway: B, C to 81st St.*

62 **Bethesda Fountain.** Few New York views are more romantic than the one

Fodor'sChoice from the top of the magnificent stone staircase that leads down to the
★ ornate, three-tier Bethesda Fountain. You might recognize it from one of the many films that have been shot here. The fountain was dedicated in 1873 to commemorate the soldiers who died at sea during the Civil War. Named for the biblical pool in Jerusalem, which was supposedly given healing powers by an angel, it features the statue *The Angel of the Waters* rising from the center. The four figures around the fountain's base symbolize Temperance, Purity, Health, and Peace. Beyond the terrace stretches the lake, filled with swans and amateur rowboat captains. ⊠ *Midpark at 72nd St. Transverse, Central Park* Ⓜ *Subway: B, C to 72nd St.*

🐤 66 **Central Park Wildlife Center.** Even a leisurely visit to this small but delightful menagerie, which has more than 130 species, will take only about an hour. The biggest specimens here are the polar bears. Clustered around the central Sea Lion Pool are separate exhibits for each of the Earth's major environments. The Polar Circle has a huge penguin tank and polar-bear floe; the open-air Temperate Territory is highlighted by a pit of chattering monkeys; and the Rain Forest contains the flora and fauna of the tropics. The **Tisch Children's Zoo,** on the north side of the Denesmouth Arch, has interactive, hands-on exhibits where you can pet such domestic animals as pigs, sheep, goats, and cows. Above a redbrick arcade near the Zoo is the **Delacorte Clock,** a delightful glockenspiel. ⊠ *Entrance at 5th Ave. and E. 64th St., Central Park* ☎ *212/439–6500* ⊕ *www.centralparkzoo.org* ⌑ *$6* ⌲ *No children under 16 admitted without adult* ☉ *Apr.–Oct., weekdays 10–5, weekends 10–5:30; Nov.–Mar., daily 10–4:30* Ⓜ *Subway: 6 to 68th St./Hunter College; N, R, W to 5th Ave./59th St.; F to Lexington Ave./63rd St.*

🐤 65 **Conservatory Water.** The sophisticated model boats that sail this Renaissance Revival–style stone basin are raced each Saturday morning at

10, spring through fall. At the north end is one of the park's most beloved statues, José de Creeft's 1960 bronze sculpture of **Alice in Wonderland,** sitting on a giant mushroom with the Mad Hatter, March Hare, and leering Cheshire Cat in attendance. On the west side of the pond, a bronze statue of **Hans Christian Andersen,** the Ugly Duckling at his feet, is the site of storytelling hours on summer Saturdays at 11 AM. Model sailboats can be rented from a concession by the boat pond. ⊠ *East side of park, from E. 73rd to E. 75th Sts., Central Park* Ⓜ *Subway: 6 to 77th St.*

🕸 **The Dairy.** When it was built in the 19th century, the Dairy sat amid grazing cows and sold milk by the glass. Today the Dairy's painted, pointed eaves, steeple, and high-pitched slate roof harbor the **Central Park Visitor Center,** which has exhibits on the park's history, maps, a park reference library, and information about park events. ⊠ *Midpark south of 65th St. Transverse, Central Park* ☎ *212/794–6564* ⊘ *Apr.–Oct., Tues.–Sun. 10–5; Nov.–Mar., Tues.–Sun. 10–4.*

★ 🕸 **The Mall.** Around the turn of the 20th century, fashionable ladies and gentlemen used to gather to see and be seen on this broad, formal walkway. Today the Mall looks as grand as ever. The south end of its main path, the **Literary Walk,** is covered by the majestic canopy of the largest collection of American elms in North America and lined by statues of authors and artists such as Robert Burns, Shakespeare, and Sir Walter Scott. ⊠ *Midpark between 66th and 72nd Sts., Central Park* Ⓜ *Subway: 6 to 68th St./Hunter College.*

▶ 🕸 **The Pond.** Swans and ducks can sometimes be spotted on the calm waters of the Pond. For an unbeatable view of the city skyline, walk along the shore to **Gapstow Bridge.** From left to right you can see the brown peak-roof Sherry-Netherland Hotel; the black-and-white CBS Building; the rose-color Chippendale-style top of the Sony Building; the black-glass shaft of Trump Tower; and, in front, the green gables of the Plaza hotel. ⊠ *Central Park S and 5th Ave., Central Park* Ⓜ *Subway: N, R, W to 5th Ave.*

🕸 **Strawberry Fields.** This memorial to John Lennon, who penned the classic 1967 song "Strawberry Fields Forever," is sometimes called the "international garden of peace." Its curving paths, shrubs, trees, and flower beds donated by many countries create a deliberately informal landscape reminiscent of the English parks of Lennon's homeland. ⊠ *W. Park Dr. and W. 72nd St., Central Park* Ⓜ *Subway: B, C to 72nd St.*

Upper West Side & Morningside Heights

The Upper West Side—never as exclusive as the tony East Side—has always had an earthy appeal. Although real-estate prices have gone sky high (its restored brownstones and co-op apartments are among the city's most coveted residences), the Upper West Side is still a haven for families who give the area a pleasant, neighborhood feel. On weekends, stroller-pushing parents cram the sidewalks and shoppers jam the fantastic gourmet food stores and fashion emporiums that line Broadway.

In the evenings, the action moves inside as singles from the city and suburbs mingle in bars and restaurants along Columbus and Amsterdam
avenues. Altogether, the neighborhood's lively avenues, quiet tree-lined
side streets, two flanking parks—Central on its east, Riverside on its west—
and leading cultural complexes, such as the American Museum of Natural History and Lincoln Center, allow residents and visitors a great variety
of things to do in a relatively compact area.

Morningside Heights, on the high ridge north and west of Central Park,
grew up at the end of the 19th century, spearheaded by a triad of institutions: the relocated Columbia University, which developed the
mind; St. Luke's Hospital, which cared for the body; and the Cathedral of St. John the Divine, which tended the soul. Idealistically conceived as an American Acropolis, the cluster of academic and religious
institutions that developed here managed to keep these blocks stable
during years when neighborhoods on all sides were collapsing. This is
an *Uptown* student neighborhood—less hip than the Village, but
friendly, fun, and intellectual.

*Numbers in the text correspond to numbers in the margin and on the
Upper West Side map.*

a good
walk

The West Side story begins at 72nd Street and Central Park West at **The Dakota** ⑥ ➤, the châteaulike apartment building that presides over the block. Its neighbors to the north include several other famous apartment buildings. The Langham (135 Central Park W, at W. 73rd St.) is an Italian Renaissance–style high-rise that was designed by leading apartment architect Emery Roth in 1929–30. Roth also designed the twin-tower San Remo (145–146 Central Park W, at W. 74th St.), which was built in 1930; over the years it has been home to Rita Hayworth, Dustin Hoffman, Raquel Welch, Paul Simon, Tony Randall, and Diane Keaton. The Kenilworth (151 Central Park W, at W. 75th St.), built in 1908, with its immense pair of ornate front columns, was once the address of Basil Rathbone (Hollywood's quintessential Sherlock Holmes) and Michael Douglas. The row of massive buildings along Central Park West breaks between West 77th and 81st streets to make room for the **American Museum of Natural History** ⑥. Across 77th Street is the **New-York Historical Society** ⑥. The final residential beauty on Central Park West by Emery Roth is the cubic Beresford (211 Central Park W, at W. 81st St.), built in 1929, whose lighted towers romantically haunt the night sky.

If you feel like walking along the charming tree- and brownstone-lined park blocks that make up this neighborhood, West 71st Street or West 74th Street between Broadway and Central Park West are perfect for casual strolling; or follow Riverside Drive up to West 116th Street and Columbia University in Morningside Heights. The latter leads past **Riverside Park** ⑳, which many neighborhood residents use as their backyard. At West 112th Street, head east to Amsterdam Avenue to see the **Cathedral Church of St. John the Divine** ㉑.

TIMING This tour can easily take two or three hours at a relaxed clip. The exhibits at the New-York Historical Society shouldn't take more than one or two hours to view, but the mammoth and often crowded American Museum of Natural History can eat up most of a day. If you're here on a Sunday, check out the upscale flea market at the southwest corner of West 77th Street and Columbus Avenue.

What to See

 ★ ☺ ⑥ **American Museum of Natural History.** With 45 exhibition halls and more than 32 million artifacts and specimens, this is the world's largest and most important museum of natural history. Dinosaur mania begins in the massive, barrel-vaulted **Theodore Roosevelt Rotunda,** where a 50-foot-tall skeleton of a barosaurus rears on its hind legs, protecting its fossilized baby from an enormous marauding allosaurus. Three spectacular dinosaur halls on the fourth floor—the **Hall of Saurischian Dinosaurs,** the **Hall of Ornithischian Dinosaurs,** and the **Hall of Vertebrate Origins**—use real fossils and interactive computer stations to present interpretations of how dinosaurs and pterodactyls might have behaved. Other highlights include the 34-ton *Ahnighito*—the largest meteorite on display in the world—in the **Hall of Meteorites;** and the popular 94-foot blue whale model, which swims high above the **Hall of Ocean Life.** The spectacular **Hayden Planetarium** is in a 90-foot aluminum-clad sphere that appears to float inside an enormous glass cube, which in turn is home to the **Rose Center for Earth and Space.**

Films on the museum's 40-foot-high, 66-foot-wide **IMAX Theater** (☎ 212/769–5034 for show times) screen are usually about nature and cost $19, including museum admission. ✉ *Central Park W at W. 79th St., Upper West Side* ☎ *212/769–5200 for museum tickets and programs, 212/769–5100 for museum general information* ⊕ *www.amnh.org* ▧ *Museum $12 suggested donation; museum and planetarium show combination ticket $22. Prices may vary for special exhibitions* ⊙ *Daily 10–5:45; Rose Center for Earth and Space stays open on Fri. until 8:45 PM* Ⓜ *Subway: B, C to 81st St.*

⑦ Cathedral Church of St. John the Divine. Everything about the cathedral
Fodor'sChoice is colossal, from its cavernous 601-foot-long nave to its 162-foot-tall
★ dome crossing. Even though this divine behemoth is unfinished—the transepts and tower are the most noticeably uncompleted elements—it is already the largest Gothic cathedral in the world. To get the full effect of the building's size, approach it from Broadway on West 112th Street. On the wide steps climbing to the Amsterdam Avenue entrance, five portals arch over the entrance doors. The central **Portal of Paradise** depicts St. John witnessing the Transfiguration of Jesus, and 32 biblical characters, all intricately carved in stone. The doors have relief castings of scenes from the Old Testament on the left and the New Testament on the right. High above the doors, the **Great Rose Window,** made from more than 10,000 pieces of colored glass, is the largest stained-glass window in the United States.

Inside, along the cathedral's side aisles, some chapels are dedicated to contemporary issues such as sports, poetry, and AIDS. The **Saint Saviour Chapel** contains a three-panel bronze altar in white-gold leaf with religious scenes by artist Keith Haring. The more conventional **baptistry,** to the left of the altar, is an exquisite octagonal chapel with a 15-foot-high marble font and a polychrome sculpted frieze commemorating New York's Dutch heritage. Seventeenth-century Barberini tapestries hang throughout the cathedral.

A precinct of châteaulike Gothic-style buildings known as the **Cathedral Close** is behind the cathedral on the south side. In a corner by the Cathedral School is the **Biblical Garden,** with perennials, herbs, and an arbor. Around the bend from here is a rose garden. Back at Amsterdam Avenue, the **Peace Fountain** depicts the struggle of good and evil. ✉ *1047 Amsterdam Ave., at W. 112th St., Morningside Heights* ☎ *212/316–7540, 212/662–2133 box office, 212/932–7347 tours* ⊕ *www.stjohndivine. org* ▧ *Tours $5* ⊙ *Mon.–Sat. 7–6, Sun. 7–7; July and Aug. cathedral closes at 6 on Sun.; tours Tues.–Sat. at 11, Sun. at 1* Ⓜ *Subway: 1, 9 to 110th St./Cathedral Pkwy.*

▶ ⑥ The Dakota. The most famous of all the apartment buildings lining Central Park West, the Dakota set a high standard for the many that followed it. This buff-color château has picturesque gables and copper turrets and housed some of the West Side's first residents. The building's entrance is on West 72nd Street; the spacious, lovely courtyard is visible beyond the guard's station. At the Dakota's gate, in December 1980, a deranged fan shot John Lennon as he came home from a recording session. Other celebrity tenants have included Boris Karloff, Rudolf Nureyev, José Ferrer and Rosemary Clooney, Lauren Bacall, Rex Reed, Leonard Bernstein, Gilda Radner, and Connie Chung. ⊠ *1 W. 72nd St., at Central Park W, Upper West Side* Ⓜ *Subway: B, C to 72nd St.*

🟢 **New-York Historical Society.** Founded in 1804, the New-York Historical Society is the city's oldest museum and one of its finest research libraries, with a collection of 6 million pieces of art, literature, and memorabilia. Highlights of the collection include George Washington's inaugural chair, 500,000 photographs from the 1850s to the present, original watercolors for John James Audubon's *Birds of America,* the architectural files of McKim, Mead & White, and one of the most in-depth collections of pre-20th-century American paintings in the world, including seminal landscapes by Hudson River School artists Thomas Cole, Asher Durant, and Frederic Church. ⊠ *2 W. 77th St., at Central Park W, Upper West Side* ☎ *212/873–3400* ⊕ *www.nyhistory.org* 🖃 *Museum $8 suggested donation* ☉ *Museum Tues.–Sun. 10–6; library Tues.–Sat. 10–5; library closed Sat. Memorial Day–Labor Day* Ⓜ *Subway: B, C to 81st St.*

🌣 🟢 **Riverside Park.** Long and narrow, tree-lined Riverside Park—laid out by Central Park's designers Olmsted and Vaux between 1873 and 1888—runs along the Hudson River between West 72nd and West 159th streets. From the corner of West 72nd Street and Riverside Drive—where a statue of **Eleanor Roosevelt** stands at the park's entrance—head down the ramp (through an underpass beneath the West Side Highway) to the **79th Street Boat Basin,** a rare spot in Manhattan where you can walk right along the river's edge and watch a flotilla of houseboats bobbing in the water. Behind the boat basin, the **Rotunda** is home in summer to the Boat Basin Cafe, an open-air spot for a snack and river views. From the Rotunda, head up to the **Promenade,** a broad formal walkway extending a few blocks north from West 80th Street, with a stone parapet overlooking the river. ⊠ *W. 72nd to W. 159th Sts. between Riverside Dr. and the Hudson River, Upper West Side* Ⓜ *Subway: 1, 2, 3, 9 to 72nd St.*

Harlem

In an astonishing confluence of talent known as the Harlem Renaissance, black novelists, playwrights, musicians, and artists—many of them seeking to escape discrimination and persecution in other parts of the country—gathered here. Black performers starred in chic jazz clubs where, ironically enough, only whites could attend. Throughout the Roaring '20s, while whites flocked here for the infamous parties and nightlife, blacks settled in for the opportunity this self-sustaining community represented. But the Depression hit Harlem hard. By the late 1930s it was no longer a hot spot for the downtown set, and many African-American families began moving out to houses in the suburbs of Queens and New Jersey.

By the 1960s Harlem's population had dropped dramatically, and many of those who remained were disillusioned enough with social injustices to join in civil rights riots. A combination of deteriorating housing, crush-

ing poverty, and petty crime turned the neighborhood into a simmering ghetto. Today, however, Harlem is restoring itself. Deserted buildings and yards of rubble still scar certain streets, but shining amid them are old jewels such as the Apollo Theater, countless architecturally splendid churches, and cultural magnets such as the Studio Museum in Harlem. The economic turnaround has been billed as the second Harlem Renaissance. Former President Bill Clinton chose West 125th Street as the site of his official office, and many residents have warmly greeted his arrival as evidence that a new era has arrived.

Note that the city's north–south avenues acquire different names in Harlem, commemorating heroes of black history: 6th Avenue becomes Lenox Avenue or Malcolm X Boulevard, 7th Avenue is Adam Clayton Powell Jr. Boulevard, and 8th Avenue is Frederick Douglass Boulevard; West 125th Street, the major east–west street, is Martin Luther King Jr. Boulevard. Many people still use the streets' former names, but the street signs use the new ones.

Numbers in the text correspond to numbers in the margin and on the Harlem map.

a good walk

West 125th Street (also known as Martin Luther King Jr. Boulevard) is the main artery of Harlem's cultural and economic life. Walk west from 5th Avenue and you pass a number of African-theme stores. On Malcolm X Boulevard, between West 125th and 124th streets, you find the art-deco Lenox Lounge, which opened in the 1930s and hosts jazz and blues nights. Hungry tourists make the pilgrimage to Sylvia's Soul Food Restaurant, on Malcolm X Boulevard, between West 126th and 127th streets.

A community standout on West 125th Street between Malcolm X and Adam Clayton Powell Jr. boulevards is the **Studio Museum in Harlem** ⑫ ▶. Continuing west, you pass the striking Theresa Towers office building before arriving at one of the city's great cultural landmarks, the world-famous **Apollo Theater** ⑬. The glass-and-chrome Harlem USA shopping center a half block farther west is credited with being a big part of Harlem's recent upswing.

If you have time, backtrack east to Adam Clayton Powell Jr. Boulevard and continue north, passing numerous large churches. At West 138th Street is a neighborhood landmark, the Abyssinian Baptist Church, one of the first black institutions to settle in Harlem. Across Adam Clayton Powell Jr. Boulevard from the church is a handsome set of town houses known as Strivers' Row.

TIMING The walk takes about an hour, including a stop at the Studio Museum. Sunday is a good time to tour Harlem, especially if you'd like to attend one of the many churches to hear the rousing gospel music. If you do attend a service, remember that most people are there to worship and don't think of themselves or their churches as tourist attractions. Show up on time for services, and be respectful of ushers, who may ask you to sit in a special section. Don't take pictures or videos; dress in your Sunday best (not shorts and flip-flops); make a contribution when the collection comes around; and be prepared to stay for the full service, which may last as long as two hours.

What to See

⑬ **Apollo Theater.** When it opened in 1913, it was a burlesque hall for white audiences only, but after 1934 music greats such as Billie Holiday, Ella Fitzgerald, Duke Ellington, Count Basie, Nat "King" Cole, Lionel Hampton, and Aretha Franklin performed at the Apollo. Included in an hour long guided tour is a spirited, audience-participation-encouraged oral history of the theater, with many inside stories about past performers, as well as a chance to perform in a no-boos-allowed show. Tour goers also get to touch what's left of the Tree of Hope (a stump) as they walk across the stage. ⊠ *253 W. 125th St., between Adam Clayton Powell Jr. and Frederick Douglass Blvds., Harlem* ☎ *212/531–5301 for performances, 212/531–5337 for tours* ⊕ *www.apollotheater.com* 🎫 *Tours $11 weekdays, $13 weekends* ☉ *Tours Mon., Tues., Thurs., and Fri. 11, 1, 3, Wed. 11, weekends 11, 1* Ⓜ *Subway: A, B, C, D to 125th St.*

▶ ⑫ **Studio Museum in Harlem.** Focusing on African-American, Caribbean, and African art, this small museum houses a collection of paintings, sculp-

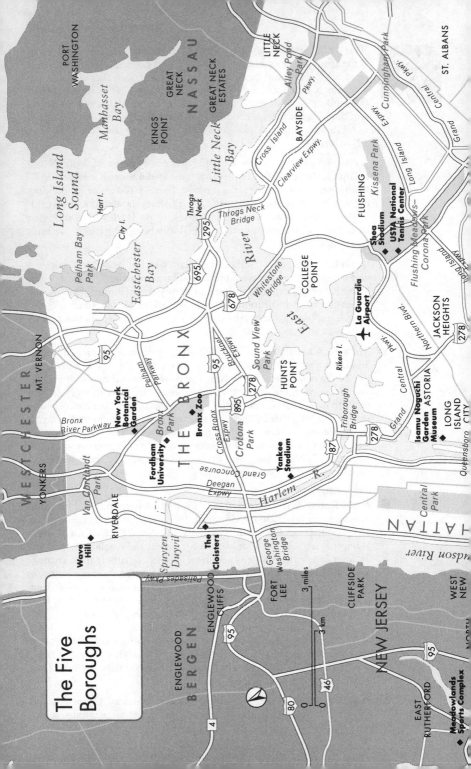

The Five Boroughs

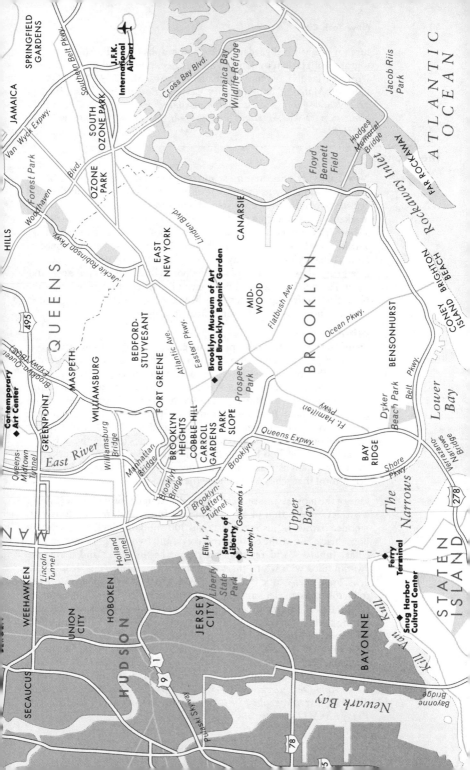

ture (in a light-filled garden), and photographs (including historic photographs of Harlem by James Van Der Zee, popular in the 1930s, and works by Jacob Lawrence and Romare Bearden). ✉ *144 W. 125th St., between Malcolm X and Adam Clayton Powell Jr. Blvds., Harlem* ☎ *212/864–4500* ⊕ *www.studiomuseuminharlem.org* ✐ *$7 suggested admission* ⊘ *Wed.–Fri. and Sun. noon–6, Sat. 10–6* Ⓜ *Subway: 2, 3 to 125th St.*

The Bronx

New York City's northernmost and only mainland borough (the others are all on islands) was the retreat of wealthy New Yorkers in the 19th century, when the area consisted of a picturesque patchwork of farms, market villages, and country estates. In the 1920s the Bronx experienced a short-lived golden age: the new elevated subway line attracted an upwardly mobile population, and the Grand Concourse was fashioned as New York City's Champs-Elysées. Although the Bronx has a reputation as a gritty, down-and-out place, the borough is full of vital areas like the Italian neighborhood of Belmont. It has its cultural gems, too—the New York Botanical Garden, the Bronx Zoo, and, of course, Yankee Stadium, home of the celebrated Bronx Bombers.

What to See

Ⓒ **Bronx Zoo.** When the zoo opened its gates in 1899, 843 animals were
Fodor'sChoice exhibited in small cages and enclosures. Today the 265-acre spread is
★ the world's largest urban zoo. The zoo's more than 4,500 animals, representing more than 600 species, mostly live in outdoor settings designed to re-create their habitats. You're often separated from them by no more than a moat. Planning your trip is important, as it's impossible to see everything here in one day. Try to visit the most popular exhibits, such as Congo Gorilla Forest, early to avoid lines later in the day. Take advantage of the **Zoo Shuttle** (✉ $2) that circles the entire park. You can get back on as many times as you wish. The **Skyfari** (✉ $2) is an aerial tram that whisks you above the trees.

One of the most fascinating exhibits is the **Congo Gorilla Forest** (✉ $3), a 6½-acre re-creation of an African rain forest with treetop lookouts, wooded pathways, lush greenery, and 300 animals—including red-river hogs, black-and-white colobus monkeys, and two troops of lowland gorillas. **Jungle World** re-creates a tropical rain forest and mangrove swamp filled with white-cheeked gibbons, tree kangaroos, black leopards, and other exotic critters. In **Wild Asia** (✉ $3), open from April to October, Asian elephants roam free on nearly 40 acres of open meadows and dark forests. Siberian tigers roam through **Tiger Mountain**, a setting that re-creates the Amur Valley, which borders China and Russia. From late May to September, 1,000 butterflies and moths of 35 species dazzle visitors in the **Butterfly Zone** (✉ $2). ✉ *Bronx River Pkwy. and Fordham Rd., Fordham* ☎ *718/367–1010* ⊕ *www.wcs.org* ✐ *$11; free Wed., donation suggested; extra charge for some exhibits; parking $7* ⊘ *Apr.–Oct., weekdays 10–5, weekends 10–5:30; Nov.–Mar., daily 10–4:30; last ticket sold 1 hr before closing* Ⓜ *Subway: 2, 5 to Pelham Pkwy.; BxM11 express bus to zoo entrance.*

New York Botanical Garden. Considered one of the leading botany centers of the world, this 250-acre garden built around the dramatic gorge of the Bronx River is one of the best reasons to make a trip to the Bronx. The grounds encompass the historic **Lorillard Snuff Mill,** built by two French Huguenot manufacturers in 1840 to power the grinding of tobacco for snuff. Outdoor plant collections include the **Peggy Rockefeller Rose Garden,** with 2,700 bushes of more than 250 varieties; the spectacular **Rock Garden,** which displays alpine flowers; and the **Everett Children's Adventure Garden,** 8 acres of plant and science exhibits for children, including a boulder maze, giant animal topiaries, and a plant discovery center. Inside the historic **Enid A. Haupt Conservatory** (✉ $5), a Victorian-era glass house with 17,000 individual panes, are year-round re-creations of misty tropical rain forests and arid African and North American deserts as well as changing exhibitions. ⊠ *200th St. and Kazimiroff Blvd., Bedford Park* ☎ *718/817–8700* ⊕ *www.nybg. org* ✉ *$3; free Sat. 10–noon and Wed.; parking $5* ⊙ *Apr.–Oct., Tues.–Sun. 10–6; Nov.–Mar., Tues.–Sun. 10–5* Ⓜ *Subway: B, D, 4 to Bedford Park Blvd.; Metro-North to Botanical Garden.*

Brooklyn

Hardly Manhattan's wimpy sidekick, Brooklyn is a metropolis in its own right, full of world-class museums, spacious parks, landmark buildings, excellent restaurants, and lively neighborhoods. In fact, it's the most populous of all the boroughs, with nearly 2.5 million residents; even if it were sheared from the rest of New York, it would still be among the 20 largest cities in the United States.

Some of Brooklyn's neighborhoods are as trendy as downtown Manhattan. Williamsburg is a catwalk of stylish young people who have built a lively nightlife scene. DUMBO, with its galleries and residential lofts, is often compared to SoHo. Fort Greene, with the Brooklyn Academy of Music as its anchor, is on the brink of becoming a performing arts enclave in full bloom. Brooklyn Heights, Cobble Hill, and Park Slope are favored more than ever by young families and professionals, who are drawn by the dignified brownstone- and tree-lined streets, handsome parks, cultural institutions, and the less frenetic pace of life.

What to See

★ **Brooklyn Museum of Art.** A world-class museum, the BMA was founded in 1823 as the Brooklyn Apprentices' Library Association and was a pioneer in the collection of non-Western art. With approximately 1.5 million pieces in its permanent collection, from Rodin sculptures to Andean textiles and Assyrian wall reliefs, it ranks as the second-largest art museum in New York—only the Met is larger. As you approach the massive, regal building designed by McKim, Mead & White (1893), look for the allegorical figures of Brooklyn and Manhattan, originally carved by Daniel Chester French for the Manhattan Bridge. The spectacular glass-fronted entranceway and the lobby were designed by Polshek Architects, the same firm that did the Rose Center for Earth and Space at the American Museum of Natural History.

Beyond the changing exhibitions, highlights include **Egyptian Art** (third floor), considered one of the best collections of its kind, and **African and Pre-Columbian Art** (first floor). In the gallery of **American Painting and Sculpture** (fifth floor), *Brooklyn Bridge* by Georgia O'Keeffe hangs alongside nearly 200 first-rate works by Winslow Homer, John Singer Sargent, Thomas Eakins, George Bellows, and Milton Avery. The **Period Rooms** (fourth floor) include the complete interior of the Jan Martense Schenck House, built in the Brooklyn Flatlands section in 1675, as well as a Moorish-style room from the since-demolished 54th Street mansion of John D. Rockefeller. **Asian Art** (second floor) includes galleries devoted to Chinese, Korean, Indian, and Islamic works. On the third floor is the **Beaux-Arts Court,** a gracious, skylighted space where changing exhibits and events are held. Outdoors, the **Frieda Schiff Warburg Memorial Sculpture Garden** showcases architectural fragments from demolished New York buildings, including Penn Station. On the first Saturday of each month, "First Saturdays" offers a free evening of special programs, including live music, dancing, film screenings, and readings. ⊠ *200 Eastern Pkwy., Prospect Heights* ☎ *718/638–5000* ⊕ *www. brooklynmuseum.org* ⊠ *$6 suggested donation* ⊙ *Wed.–Fri. 10–5, weekends 11–6; 1st Sat. every month 11–11; call for program schedule* Ⓜ *Subway: 2, 3 to Eastern Pkwy.*

Queens

Home of the LaGuardia and John F. Kennedy International airports and many people who commute to Manhattan, Queens is seen by most visitors only from the window of an airplane and cab. Its population of nearly 2,230,000 is the city's most diverse, with 36% of those living in its countless ethnic neighborhoods born on foreign soil. Its inhabitants represent almost all nationalities and speak scores of languages, from Hindi to Portuguese. Queens communities such as Astoria (Greek and Italian), Jackson Heights (Colombian, Mexican, and Indian), Sunnyside (Turkish and Romanian), Woodside (Irish), and Flushing (Korean and Chinese) are fascinating to explore, particularly if you're interested in experiencing some of the city's tastiest—and least expensive—cuisine.

What to See

Isamu Noguchi Garden Museum. The museum is dedicated to the work of Japanese-American sculptor Isamu Noguchi (1904–88). The building, a photo-engraving plant, was bought by Noguchi in 1975 as a place to display his work. The large, open-air garden and the 13 galleries that border it provide ample room to show more than 250 pieces done in stone, metal, clay, and other materials. ⊠ *32–37 Vernon Blvd., at 33rd Rd., Long Island City* ☎ *718/204–7088 or 718/721–1932* ⊕ *www. noguchi.org* ⊠ *$5 suggested donation* ⊙ *Wed.–Fri. 10–5, weekends 11–6* Ⓜ *Subway: N to Broadway, then walk west to Vernon Blvd.*

P.S. 1 Contemporary Art Center. A pioneer in the "alternative-space" movement, P.S. 1 rose from the ruins of an abandoned school in 1976 as a sort of community arts center for the future. P.S. 1, now a partner of the Museum of Modern Art, has an enormous exhibition space, and every available corner is used—four floors, rooftop spaces, staircases and landings, bathrooms, the boiler room and basement, and outdoor galleries. Exhibitions reflect the center's mission to present experimental and formally innovative contemporary art, from the progressive and interactive to the merely incomprehensible. ⊠ *22–25 Jackson Ave., at 46th Ave., Long Island City* ☎ *718/784–2084* ⊕ *www.ps1.org* 🗃 *$5 suggested donation* ⊗ *Thurs.–Mon. noon–6* Ⓜ *Subway: 7 to 45 Rd.–Courthouse Sq.; E, V (weekdays only) to 23rd St.–Ely Ave.; G to 21 St.–Van Alst.*

WHERE TO EAT

Updated By
Tom Steele

The city's lingering economic murkiness may have put a pinch on New Yorkers' wallets, but it's done little to slake their insatiable appetite for dining out. Besides satisfying a taste for the finer things in life, restaurants serve Gothamites in other crucial ways. They're a vital catalyst for exploring the city (the hunt through Brooklyn streets for a bite before a performance at BAM), a communication device ("Let me tell you about this great little Mexican place way uptown"), and a resource of cocktail-party one-upmanship ("What? You haven't been to Alain Ducasse yet?!"). Restaurants have consistently demonstrated a savvy sensitivity to the financial times, and a wide array of mid-priced restaurants somehow manages to serve high-end food. Quite a few have devised bargain prix-fixe three-course dinners. Many menus around town are market-driven and seasonal. Use the recommendations that follow as guidelines and you won't be disappointed.

Reservations

At the hottest restaurants reservations need to be made weeks in advance, no matter how well connected the concierge at your hotel is. Though it is by no means a guarantee, sometimes just showing up at a restaurant that has turned you away on the phone will get you a seat, if you are willing to wait for it. Last-minute cancellations and no-shows unexpectedly free up tables, and if you happen to be in the right place at the right time, one of those tables might be yours.

If you change your mind or your plans, cancel your reservation—it's only courteous, plus some of the busiest places have started to charge up to $25 a head for a no-show. Many restaurants will ask you to call the day before or the morning of your scheduled meal to reconfirm: remember to do so or you could lose out. If your original time isn't ideal, ask when you confirm if a better one has become available.

What It Costs

Entrée prices hover around the high $20s. Many restaurants charge $5–$10 for side dishes, but the $60-plus prix-fixe menu has given way to the standard à la carte. Beware of the $10 bottle of water poured eagerly for unsuspecting diners. If you are watching your budget, be sure to ask the price of daily specials recited by the waiter or captain.

If you eat early or late you may be able to take advantage of a prix-fixe deal not offered at peak hours, and get more attentive service in the bargain. Most upscale restaurants offer fantastic lunch deals with special menus at cut-rate prices designed to give a true taste of the place.

	$$$$	**$$$**	**$$**	**$**	**¢**
WHAT IT COSTS In New York City					
AT DINNER	over $30	$22–$30	$15–$21	$8–$14	under $8

Prices are per person for a main course at dinner.

Little Italy & Chinatown

CHINESE
¢–$$$

✗ **Joe's Shanghai.** Joe opened his first Shanghai restaurant in Queens, but buoyed by the accolades accorded his steamed soup dumplings—magically filled with a rich, fragrant broth and a pork or pork-and-crabmeat mixture—he saw fit to open in Manhattan's Chinatown, and then Midtown. There's always a wait, but the line moves fast. Menu highlights include turnip shortcakes and dried-bean-curd salad to start, and succulent braised pork shoulder, ropey homemade Shanghai noodles, and traditional lion's head—rich pork meatballs braised in brown sauce—to follow. ⊠ *9 Pell St., between the Bowery and Mott St., Chinatown* ☎ *212/233–8888* ▭ *No credit cards* Ⓜ *Subway: 6, N, R, Q, J, M, Z to Canal St.*

★ ¢–$$

✗ **Sweet 'n' Tart Café & Restaurant.** You are handed four different menus at this multilevel restaurant. One lists an extensive selection of dim sum prepared to order; another offers special dishes organized according to principles of Chinese medicine; a third lists more familiar-sounding dishes, such as hot-and-sour soup; and the final one lists curative "teas" (more like soups or fruit shakes, really). Don't miss the yam noodle soup with assorted dumplings, or the fried rice with taro and Chinese sausage served in a bamboo container. ⊠ *20 Mott St., between Chatham Sq. and Pell St., Chinatown* ☎ *212/964–0380* ▭ *AE* Ⓜ *Subway: 6, N, R, Q, W, J, M, Z to Canal St.*

PIZZA
★ $–$$

✗ **Lombardi's.** Brick walls, red-and-white check tablecloths, and the aroma of thin-crust pies emerging from the coal oven set the mood for some of the best pizza in Manhattan. Lombardi's has served pizza since 1905 (though not in the same location), and business has not died down a bit. The mozzarella is always fresh, resulting in an almost greaseless slice, and the toppings, such as homemade meatballs, pancetta, or imported anchovies, are also top quality. ⊠ *32 Spring St., between Mott and Mulberry Sts., Little Italy* ☎ *212/941–7994* ▭ *No credit cards* Ⓜ *Subway: 6 to Spring St.; F, V to Broadway–Lafayette St.*

TriBeCa

AMERICAN/
CASUAL
$–$$$

✗ **Bubby's.** Crowds clamoring for coffee and freshly squeezed juice line up for brunch at this TriBeCa mainstay. The dining room is homey and comfortable with attractive furnishings and plate-glass windows; in summer, neighbors sit at tables outside with their dogs. For breakfast you can order grits, homemade granola, or such entrées as sour cream pancakes with bananas and berries, and huevos rancheros with guacamole and grits. Eclectic comfort food and a quartet of Mexican dishes make up the lunch and dinner menus. ⊠ *120 Hudson St., at N. Moore St., TriBeCa* ☎ *212/ 219–0666* ▭ *AE, DC, MC, V* Ⓜ *Subway: 1, 9 to Franklin St.*

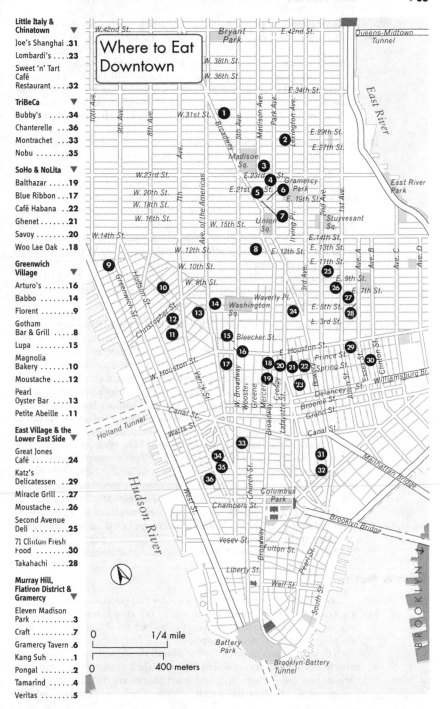

Little Italy & Chinatown ▼

Joe's Shanghai . **31**

Lombardi's **23**

Sweet 'n' Tart Café Restaurant **32**

TriBeCa ▼

Bubby's **34**

Chanterelle . . **36**

Montrachet . . **33**

Nobu **35**

SoHo & NoLita ▼

Balthazar **19**

Blue Ribbon . . . **17**

Café Habana . . **22**

Ghenet **21**

Savoy **20**

Woo Lae Oak . . **18**

Greenwich Village ▼

Arturo's **16**

Babbo **14**

Florent **9**

Gotham Bar & Grill **8**

Lupa **15**

Magnolia Bakery **10**

Moustache **12**

Pearl Oyster Bar **13**

Petite Abeille . . **11**

East Village & the Lower East Side ▼

Great Jones Café **24**

Katz's Delicatessen . . **29**

Miracle Grill . . . **27**

Moustache **26**

Second Avenue Deli **25**

71 Clinton Fresh Food **30**

Takahachi **28**

Murray Hill, Flatiron District & Gramercy ▼

Eleven Madison Park **3**

Craft **7**

Gramercy Tavern **.6**

Kang Suh **1**

Pongal **2**

Tamarind **4**

Veritas **5**

FRENCH   ✕ **Chanterelle.** Soft peach walls, luxuriously spaced tables, towering flo-
$$$$ ral arrangements, and stylish servers set the stage for what is certainly
the most understated of New York's fancy French restaurants. Unassuming service complements chef David Waltuck's simple creations.
The delicious signature grilled seafood sausage will always be available,
but the bulk of the prix-fixe menu is dictated by the season. ✉ *2 Harrison St., at Hudson St., TriBeCa* ☎ *212/966–6960* ⚐ *Reservations essential* ▤ *AE, DC, MC, V* ⊘ *Closed Sun. No lunch Mon.* Ⓜ *Subway:
1, 9 to Franklin St.*

$$$ ✕ **Montrachet.** Every chef Drew Nieporent selects for this, his first (and
one suspects dearest) restaurant, excels. Currently Chris Gesualdi of-
fers seasonal three- and five-course menus. If you're lucky, you may be
able to choose the sautéed frogs' legs with red-wine fricasée of escar-
gots and morel mushrooms to start, and follow it up with a truffle-crusted
salmon. Pastel walls, plush mauve banquettes, engaging works of art,
and the occasional line cook traversing the dining room to the incon-
venient walk-in refrigerator set an unpretentious tone. The distinguished
wine list emphasizes diminutive regional vineyards; Monday evenings
you may bring your own bottle with no corkage fee. ✉ *239 West
Broadway, between Walker and White Sts., TriBeCa* ☎ *212/219–2777*
⚐ *Reservations essential* ▤ *AE* ⊘ *Closed Sun. No lunch Mon.–Thurs.
and Sat.* Ⓜ *Subway: A, C to Chambers St.*

JAPANESE   ✕ **Nobu.** Unless you're Robert De Niro (he's a partner and eats here reg-
$–$$$$ ularly), you need to make reservations a month in advance at New York's
Fodor'sChoice   most famous Japanese restaurant. A curved wall of river-worn black peb-
★   bles, a hand-painted beech floor, bare wood tables, and sculptural birch
trees set the stage for Nobu Matsuhisa's dramatic food. The vast menu
can take you down two paths. One road is the way to classic Japanese
sushi and sashimi, among the best in town. Another leads you to con-
temporary dishes, such as the paper-thin hamachi spiced up with jalapeño
or sea bass topped with black truffle slivers. It's easiest to put yourself
in the hands of the chef by ordering the *omakase omikase*—specify how
much you want to spend (the minimum is $80 per person) and the kitchen
does the rest. Can't get reservations? Try your luck at Next Door Nobu,
where diners can enjoy a slightly less expensive menu on a first-come,
first-served basis. ✉ *105 Hudson St., at Franklin St., TriBeCa* ☎ *212/
219–0500, 212/219–8095 for same-day reservations* ⚐ *Reservations
essential* ▤ *AE, DC, MC, V* ⊘ *No lunch weekends* Ⓜ *Subway: 1, 9 to
Franklin St.* ◪ *Next Door Nobu* ✉ *105 Hudson St., at Franklin St.,
TriBeCa* ☎ *212/334–4445* Ⓜ *Subway: 1, 9 to Franklin St.*

Soho & NoLita

CONTEMPORARY   ✕ **Savoy.** Chef-owner Peter Hoffman serves an eclectic mix of dishes in-
$$$ spired by the Mediterranean in this cozy restaurant on a quiet cobble-
stone corner. A bronze wire-mesh ceiling, arched wood accents, and blazing
fireplace lend the downstairs space a rural feel, the perfect setting for
such down-to-earth dishes as braised lamb shank with lentils and crispy
artichokes, and salt-crust baked cod with shell bean stew. Upstairs, the
original tin ceiling, artwork, and open hearth are the backdrop for an
expensive nightly prix-fixe menu, which includes a special grilled dish

(cooked in the dining-room hearth). The wine list emphasizes small producers. ✉ *70 Prince St., at Crosby St., SoHo* ☎ *212/219–8570* ⌕ *Reservations essential* 🖃 *AE, MC, V* ⊘ *No lunch Sun.* Ⓜ *Subway: R, W to Prince St.; 6 to Spring St.; F, V to Broadway–Lafayette St.*

ECLECTIC ✕ **Blue Ribbon.** After more than a decade, Blue Ribbon remains *the* late-
★ **$–$$$** night food hangout. After the big boys—like Rocco, Bobby, and Mario—have closed their own kitchens, they join the genial hubbub on occasion for some midnight specialness, namely the bone marrow with oxtail marmalade and the renowned raw-bar platters. Flush trust funders, literary types, sassy singletons, austerely dressed designers—a good-looking gang fills this dark box of a room until 4 AM. The menu *appears* standard but it's not. Instead of the usual fried calamari, exceptionally tender squid is lightly sautéed in olive oil and garlic and served like a savory pudding in a Japanese rice bowl. ✉ *97 Sullivan St., between Prince and Spring Sts., SoHo* ☎ *212/274–0404* ⌕ *Reservations not accepted* 🖃 *AE, MC, V* ⊘ *No lunch* Ⓜ *Subway: 6, C, E, to Spring St.; R, W to Prince St.*

ETHIOPIAN ✕ **Ghenet.** A rotating exhibit of local, African-inspired art hangs on the
★ **$–$$** walls of this welcoming spot where the Ethiopian food is authentic and delicious. Order one of the combination platters to sample various dishes, mounded on a platter lined with spongy *injera* flat bread, which is your edible utensil. In addition to the tasty poultry and meat options is a good selection of vegetarian dishes such as rich collard greens with Ethiopian spices, fiery potatoes and cabbage, and carrots in an onion sauce. ✉ *284 Mulberry St., between E. Houston and Prince Sts., No-Lita* ☎ *212/343–1888* 🖃 *AE, MC, V* ⊘ *Closed Mon. No dinner Sun.* Ⓜ *Subway: 6 to Spring St.*

FRENCH ✕ **Balthazar.** You're no longer guaranteed to sit next to a celebrity at
$$–$$$$ Keith McNally's grand brasserie, but it's still difficult to get an 8 PM reservation. The raw bar may be the best in town, with an outstanding selection of impossibly fresh crustaceans and bivalves. Nightly specials are French dishes that are as classic as the painstakingly accurate reproduction of a Parisian eatery. Steak tartare, steak frites, duck shepherd's pie—it's all good. Breakfast is a civilized affair, with croissants and pains au chocolat coming from the restaurant's own bakery. ✉ *80 Spring St., between Broadway and Crosby St., SoHo* ☎ *212/965–1414* ⌕ *Reservations essential* 🖃 *AE, MC, V* Ⓜ *Subway: 6 to Spring St.; R, W to Prince St.*

KOREAN ✕ **Woo Lae Oak.** If you thought Korean food was a cheap bowl of
$$–$$$ bibimbop, think again: Woo Lae Oak uses traditional flavors to create an elevated cuisine. The food is spicy and flavorful: kimchi burns the lips and prepares the palate for such dishes as *kesalmari* (Dungeness crab wrapped in spinach crepes), and *o ree mari* (duck slices wrapped in miso blini sweetened with a date sauce). But fans of tabletop grilling can still get their *bul go gi.* Since this is SoHo, the tables are dark marble slabs, the lighting is low, and attractive servers are dressed head to toe in black. ✉ *148 Mercer St., between Prince and W. Houston Sts., SoHo* ☎ *212/925–8200* ⌕ *Reservations essential* 🖃 *AE, DC, MC, V* Ⓜ *Subway: R, W to Prince St.*

LATIN   ✗ **Café Habana.** The simple Cuban-Latin menu at this small neighbor-
¢–$ hood hangout reflects the friendly, casual atmosphere: Cubano sand-
wiches, rice and beans, and *camarones al ajillo* (shrimp in garlic sauce),
all at budget prices. Just try to get a seat, though: on any given night
the sidewalk outside the cheery space with blue booths and pale green
Formica tables is littered with belly-baring people waiting to get in. ⊠ *17
Prince St., at Elizabeth St., NoLita* ☎ *212/625–2001* ⊟ *AE, DC, MC,
V* ⊠ *229 Elizabeth St., between Houston and Prince Sts., NoLita*
☎ *212/625–2002* ⊟ *AE, DC, MC, V* Ⓜ *Subway: 6 to Spring St.*

Greenwich Village

BELGIAN   ✗ **Petite Abeille.** The eight small tables of the original closet-size Hud-
$–$$$ son Street storefront of this expanding chain of Belgian bistros re-
mains the most inviting outpost. The menu tempts with salads, frites,
sandwiches, omelets, poached salmon, and other light fare for early in
the day. Come evening, steak, stew, roasted duck breast, and mussels
satisfy. Two styles of waffles are always available; de Bruxelles (made
fresh to order and topped with ice cream, whipped cream, and fresh
fruit) and the true Belgian waffle, de Liège (imported from Belgium and
reheated until the subtle caramelized sugar coating crunches and melts
in your mouth). ⊠ *466 Hudson St., at Barrow St., Greenwich Village*
☎ *212/741–6479* ⊟ *AE, MC, V* Ⓜ *Subway: 1, 9 to Christopher
St.–Sheridan Sq.*

CAFÉS   ✗ **Magnolia Bakery.** Sky-high home-style cakes, fabulous cupcakes, pud-
★ ¢–$ dings, and pies keep this adorable bakery packed into the wee hours.
They will even serve you a glass of milk to wash it all down with.
⊠ *401 Bleecker St., at W. 11th St., Greenwich Village* ☎ *212/462–2572*
⊟ *AE, DC, MC, V* Ⓜ *Subway: A, C, E to 14th St.; L to 8th Ave.*

CONTEMPORARY   ✗ **Gotham Bar & Grill.** A culinary landmark, Gotham Bar & Grill is every
★ $$$$ bit as thrilling as it was when it opened in 1985. Celebrated chef Al-
fred Portale, who made the blueprint for architectural food, builds on
a foundation of simple, clean flavors. On weekends, a steady stream
of limos deposits people who come to gorge on transcendent dishes:
no rack of lamb is more tender, no scallop sweeter. Portale wrings max-
imum taste from the best the earth has to offer. A stellar 20,000-bot-
tle cellar provides the perfect accompaniments—at a price. A perfectly
splendid three-course $25 prix-fixe lunch is served from noon to 2:30
weekdays. ⊠ *12 E. 12th St., between 5th Ave. and University Pl.,
Greenwich Village* ☎ *212/620–4020* ⌂ *Reservations essential* ⊟ *AE,
DC, MC, V* ☉ *No lunch weekends* Ⓜ *Subway: L, N, Q, R, W, 4, 5,
6 to 14th St./Union Sq.*

FRENCH   ✗ **Florent.** This true pioneer of dining in the Meatpacking District stays
$–$$ open each night until 5 AM (Thursday through Sunday it stays open 24
hours). The brushed steel–and–Formica diner is always a blast; expect
loud music, drag queens, and members of every walk of city life. The
simple French menu features decent versions of everything you crave—
onion soup, mussels steamed in white wine, pâté—and in the early
morning hours you can also order from a full breakfast menu. ⊠ *69
Gansevoort St., between Greenwich and Washington Sts., Greenwich*

Village ☎ 212/989–5779 ▭ *No credit cards* Ⓜ *Subway: A, C, E to 14th St.; L to 8th Ave.*

ITALIAN
$$$
Fodor'sChoice
★

✕ **Babbo.** After your first bite of the kitchen's ethereal homemade pasta or the tender suckling pig, you won't wonder why it's so hard to get reservations at Mario Batali's flagship restaurant (make them before you arrive in New York). A five-course pasta tasting menu is the best way to get your fill of fresh noodles, such as the luscious lamb and fresh mint "love letters," or the rich beef-cheek ravioli. Adventuresome eaters will rejoice in the delicious lamb's-tongue salad or the custardy brain ravioli, but more timid diners gravitate toward such simple dishes as succulent whole fish baked in salt. Service is friendly and helpful. ✉ *110 Waverly Pl., between MacDougal St. and 6th Ave., Greenwich Village* ☎ *212/777–0303* ⌂ *Reservations essential* ▭ *AE, MC, V* ⊘ *No lunch* Ⓜ *Subway: A, B, C, D, E, F, V to W. 4th St.*

$–$$

✕ **Lupa.** Even the most hard-to-please Italian-food connoisseurs have a soft spot for Lupa, Mario Batali and Joseph Bastianich's "downscale" Roman trattoria. Rough-hewn wood, great Italian wines, and simple preparations of top-quality ingredients are what Lupa is about. People come repeatedly for dishes such as bucatini with sweet-sausage ragù, house-made salamis and hams, and fried baby artichokes. The front room of the restaurant is seated on a first-come, first-served basis; reservations are taken for the back. ✉ *170 Thompson St., between Bleecker and W. Houston Sts., Greenwich Village* ☎ *212/982–5089* ▭ *AE, DC, MC, V* ⊘ *Closed Sun.* Ⓜ *Subway: A, B, C, D, E, F, V to W. 4th St.*

MIDDLE EASTERN
$

✕ **Moustache.** There's always a crowd waiting outside for one of the copper-top tables at this appealing Middle Eastern restaurant. The focal point is the pita, steam-filled pillows of dough rolled before your eyes and baked in a searingly hot oven. They are the perfect vehicle for the tasty salads—lemony chickpea and spinach, and hearty lentil and bulghur among them. For entrées, try the leg of lamb or merguez sausage sandwiches. Although the service can be slow, it's always friendly. ✉ *90 Bedford St., between Barrow and Grove Sts., Greenwich Village* ☎ *212/229–2220* ⌂ *Reservations not accepted* ▭ *No credit cards* Ⓜ *Subway: 1, 9 to Christopher St.–Sheridan Sq.* ✉ *265 E. 10th St., between Ave. A and 1st Ave., East Village* ☎ *212/228–2022* ⌂ *Reservations not accepted* ▭ *No credit cards* Ⓜ *Subway: 6 to Astor Pl.*

PIZZA
$–$$$

✕ **Arturo's.** Few guidebooks list this brick-walled Village landmark, but the jam-packed room and the smell of well-done pies augur a good meal to come. The pizza is terrific, smoky from its roast in a coal-fired oven. Basic pastas as well as seafood, veal, and chicken concoctions with mozzarella and lots of tomato sauce come at giveaway prices. Let everyone else stand in line at John's Pizzeria on Bleecker Street. ✉ *106 W. Houston St., near Thompson St., Greenwich Village* ☎ *212/677–3820* ▭ *AE, MC, V* Ⓜ *Subway: 1, 9 to Houston St.; F, V to Broadway–Lafayette St.*

SEAFOOD
★ $$–$$$

✕ **Pearl Oyster Bar.** Chances are that you may have a bit of a wait for a table at this wildly popular spot. The draw is the fresh seafood: chilled oysters followed by bouillabaisse, a whole fish, or perhaps the famous lobster roll. Locals know to come by for a lazy lunch at the bar, when

you can down some bluepoints and beer in peace. ✉ *18 Cornelia St.,
between Bleecker and W. 4th Sts., Greenwich Village* ☎ *212/691–8211*
🖃 *MC, V* ☺ *Closed Sun. No lunch Sat.* Ⓜ *Subway: A, B, C, D, E, F,
V to W. 4th St.*

East Village & Lower East Side

CAJUN/CREOLE ✕ **Great Jones Cafe.** When you pass through the bright-orange door into
$–$$ this small, crowded Cajun joint you feel like you're in a honky-tonk. The
daily changing menu, posted on the brightly colored walls, always has
cornmeal-fried or blackened catfish, gumbo, jambalaya, po' boy sandwiches, popcorn shrimp, and rice. Brunch is also festive. ✉ *54 Great Jones
St., between the Bowery and Lafayette St., East Village* ☎ *212/674–9304*
🖃 *No credit cards* Ⓜ *Subway: R, W to 8th St.; 6 to Bleecker St.*

CONTEMPORARY ✕ **71 Clinton Fresh Food.** The name does little to indicate the sophisticated
★ $$–$$$ experience that awaits at this off-the-beaten-path fashionista favorite
(Calvin Klein and Michael Kors are spotted here). Food really is the focus—
Matt Reguin's short seasonal menu tempts with clean modern dishes with
clever twists. Winter might bring pan-roasted monkfish with a cranberry
bean *brandade,* or tender and rare rack of wild boar in a smoked mushroom consommé. The cramped dining room adds to the friendly, neighborhood charm of the place. Reservations can be hard to come by, so
call in advance. ✉ *71 Clinton St., between Stanton and Rivington Sts.,
Lower East Side* ☎ *212/614–6960* ⚑ *Reservations essential* 🖃 *AE,
MC, V* ☺ *No lunch* Ⓜ *Subway: F, V to 2nd Ave.*

DELICATESSENS ✕ **Second Avenue Deli.** A face-lift may have removed the wrinkles of time,
$$–$$$ but the kosher food is as good as ever at this East Village landmark.
The deli's bevy of Jewish classics includes chicken in the pot, matzo-
ball soup, chopped liver, Romanian tenderloin, and *cholent* (a Sabbath
dish of meat, beans, and grain). A better pastrami sandwich you can't
find (don't ask for it lean). A welcome bowl of pickles, sour green tomatoes, and coleslaw satisfies from the start, but at the finish forgo dessert—
it's nondairy to comply with the rules of kashruth. ✉ *156 2nd Ave., at
E. 10th St., East Village* ☎ *212/677–0606* 🖃 *AE, DC, MC, V* Ⓜ *Subway: 6 to Astor Pl.; F, V to 2nd Ave.*

¢–$$ ✕ **Katz's Delicatessen.** Everything and nothing has changed at Katz's since
it first opened in 1888, when the neighborhood was dominated by Jew-
ish immigrants. The rows of Formica tables, the long self-service counter,
and such signs as "send a salami to your boy in the army" are all com-
pletely authentic. What's different are the area's demographics, but the
locals still flock here for succulent hand-carved corned beef and pas-
trami sandwiches, soul-warming soups, juicy hot dogs, crisp half-sour
pickles, and a little old-school attitude thrown in for good measure. ✉ *205
E. Houston St., at Ludlow St., Lower East Side* ☎ *212/254–2246*
🖃 *AE, MC, V* Ⓜ *Subway: F, V to 2nd Ave.*

JAPANESE ✕ **Takahachi.** Of the pack of inexpensive East Village Japanese restau-
★ ¢–$$$ rants, Takahachi is one of the best. Well-done sushi standards attract a
loyal following, including the occasional celebrity. The food is not ex-
actly distinctive, but the freshness and the price make the restaurant stand
out. ✉ *85 Ave. A, between E. 5th and E. 6th Sts., East Village* ☎ *212/*

505–6524 ⚠ *Reservations not accepted* 🍽 *AE, MC, V* ⊘ *No lunch*
Ⓜ *Subway: 6 to Astor Pl.; F, V to 2nd Ave.*

SOUTHWESTERN ✕ **Miracle Grill.** In fair weather your long wait for an outdoor table is
$–$$$ rewarded by a seat in a large and pretty garden. The margaritas are fab-
ulous and the food reasonably priced and tasty—after all, this is where
Bobby Flay got his start. Appetizers such as cornmeal-crusted catfish
soft tacos are crowd pleasers. Entrée portions are huge, and vegetari-
ans appreciate the grilled or roasted vegetable dishes. One of the East
Village's best and most inexpensive brunches is in that garden on warm
Sundays. ✉ *112 1st Ave., between E. 6th and E. 7th Sts., East Village*
☎ *212/254–2353* ⚠ *Reservations not accepted* 🍽 *AE, MC, V* ⊘ *No
lunch weekdays* Ⓜ *Subway: 6 to Astor Pl.*

Murray Hill, Flatiron District & Gramercy

AMERICAN ✕ **Gramercy Tavern.** Danny Meyer's ever-popular restaurant is at the top
★ $$$$ of many New Yorkers' "favorite restaurant" list. In front, the first-come,
first-served tavern presents a somewhat lighter menu than the main din-
ing room, prepared in the wood-burning oven on view, plus a menu of
small dishes and desserts between lunch and dinner service. The more
formal dining room has a prix-fixe American table d'hôte menu care-
fully conceived by executive chef John Schaefer, overseen by founding
chef and co-owner Tom Colicchio. For $68 (plus an occasional sup-
plement), choose from seasonal dishes such as roasted cod in a sauce of
cèpes or a trio of beef sirloin, short ribs, and duck foie gras. ✉ *42 E.
20th St., between Broadway and Park Ave. S, Flatiron District* ☎ *212/
477–0777* ⚠ *Reservations essential* 🍽 *AE, DC, MC, V* Ⓜ *Subway: 6,
R, W to 23rd St.*

$$$–$$$$ ✕ **Craft.** Crafting your ideal meal here is like picking and choosing from
Fodor'sChoice a gourmand's well-stocked kitchen—one overseen by the gifted Tom Col-
★ icchio, who is also chef at Gramercy Tavern. The bounty of simple yet
intriguing starters and sides on the menu makes it easy to forget there
are main courses to pair them with as well. Seared scallops, braised veal,
seasonal vegetables—just about everything is exceptionally prepared with
little fuss. The serene dining room is an impressive modern American
Arts and Crafts experiment, with dark wood, custom tables, a curved
leather wall, and sculptural light arrangements of small radiant bulbs.
✉ *43 E. 19th St., between Broadway and Park Ave. S, Flatiron District*
☎ *212/780–0880* ⚠ *Reservations essential* 🍽 *AE, D, DC, MC, V*
⊘ *No lunch weekends* Ⓜ *Subway: R, W, 6 to 23rd St.*

CONTEMPORARY ✕ **Veritas.** What do you do when you own more wine than you can drink?
★ $$$$ Veritas's wine-collecting owners decided to open a restaurant. The wine
list originally included more than 1,300 producers, and although much
of the initial inventory has been drunk, the list remains exemplary. Chef
Scott Bryan's prix-fixe contemporary menu runs from such rich, earthy
dishes as braised short ribs with parsnip puree to seared diver scallops
with minted couscous and spicy Thai red curry nage. The dining room
is distinguished by clean, natural lines, with one wall made of Italian
tile and another displaying a collection of hand-blown vases. ✉ *43 E.
20th St., between Broadway and Park Ave. S, Flatiron District* ☎ *212/*

353–3700 ⚛ *Reservations essential* 🖃 *AE, DC, MC, V* ⊘ *No lunch* Ⓜ *Subway: R, W, 6 to 23rd St.*

★ **$$$–$$$$** ✕ **Eleven Madison Park.** Like Tabla, this Danny Meyer restaurant occupies the lobby of the landmark Metropolitan Life Building and has views of Madison Square Park. The design incorporates the original art-deco fixtures, but the place feels like a modern train station—in a good way. Chef Kerry Heffernan's seasonal menu always includes a delicious braised beef dish (the short ribs are superb), plus skate, squab, lobster, and rarities such as pig's feet, each prepared in his simple, elegant French manner. The bar is beautiful. ✉ *11 Madison Ave., at E. 24th St., Flatiron District* ☎ *212/889–0905* ⚛ *Reservations essential* 🖃 *AE, D, DC, MC, V* ⊘ *No lunch Sun.* Ⓜ *Subway: R, W, 6 to 23rd St.*

INDIAN ✕ **Tamarind.** Trading the usual brass, beads, and dark tones for a sleek
$–$$$$ contemporary skylighted dining room awash in soothing neutral colors and tantalizing fragrances, this modern Indian restaurant breaks from tradition. A multiregional menu contains not only such familiar dishes as tandoori chicken (prepared in a spotless glass-encased display kitchen) and a searing lamb vindaloo, but also such fusion-inspired options as rapturous venison chops in a spicy cranberry sauce and she-crab soup with saffron, ginger juice, and sweet spices. As a rule, the more intriguing a dish sounds, the better it is. ✉ *41–43 E. 22nd St., between Broadway and Park Ave. S, Flatiron District* ☎ *212/674–7400* ⚛ *Reservations essential* 🖃 *AE, DC, MC, V* Ⓜ *Subway: N, R, 6 to 23rd St.*

¢–$ ✕ **Pongal.** One of the city's best inexpensive Indian restaurants is also vegetarian-only and kosher. Its menu is a mix of southern Indian comfort foods (many that would be served at breakfast or on the streets of Bombay) and expertly prepared home-style dishes. Try the spicy, potato-filled samosas or chickpea-battered vegetable *pakoras* (unapologetically served with the traditional ketchup, in addition to tamarind and coconut dipping sauces). ✉ *110 Lexington Ave., between E. 27th and E. 28th Sts., Murray Hill* ☎ *212/696–9458* 🖃 *D, DC, MC, V* Ⓜ *Subway: 6 to 28th St.*

KOREAN ✕ **Kang Suh.** "Seoul" food at its best is served at this lively, second-floor
¢–$$ restaurant. Cook thin slices of ginger-marinated beef (*bul go gui*) or other meats over red-hot coals; top them with hot chilies, bean paste, and pickled cabbage; and wrap them all up with lettuce for a satisfying meal. Dinner starts with 10 or more delicious types of kimchi, spicy pickles, and other condiments that are almost a meal in themselves. A crisp oyster-and-scallion pancake, sautéed yam noodles, and other traditional dishes are all expertly prepared. The waitstaff speaks little English, but the menu has lots of pictures, so you can just point and smile. ✉ *32 W. 32nd St., between 5th and 6th Aves., Murray Hill* ☎ *212/947–8482* 🖃 *AE, MC, V* Ⓜ *Subway: B, D, F, N, Q, R, S, W to 34th St.*

Midtown West

AMERICAN ✕ **Beacon.** Chef Waldy Malouf has established himself as a past master
$$$–$$$$ of grilling in this multilevel restaurant where meat, fish, and even vegetables are seared and roasted to a succulent crisp juiciness in enormous wood-fired ovens. Just about everything on the seasonal menu sounds

delectable, but particularly delicious are lamb T-bone, Catskill mountain trout, and dry-aged sirloin with red wine and shallot confit. The crusty bread, baked on the premises, is especially delicious. Although the feel is Midtown business, the simple, almost rustic food delights people from all walks of life. ⊠ *25 W. 56th St., between 5th and 6th Aves., Midtown West* ☎ *212/332–0500* ▤ *AE, D, MC, V* ⊘ *No lunch Sat. and Sun.* Ⓜ *Subway: R, W to 5th Ave.*

$$$–$$$$ ✗ **"21" Club.** It's undeniably exciting to hobnob with celebrities and tycoons at this four-story brownstone landmark, a former speakeasy that opened on December 31, 1929. The Grill Room has roomy banquettes and a ceiling hung with toys, and the new Upstairs at "21" is an intimate 32-seat restaurant with a luscious $85 four-course prix-fixe menu. Thus chef Erik Blauberg can satisfy everyone, retaining signature dishes like the famous "21" burger and other New American food downstairs, while offering more eclectic fare upstairs, such as cinnamon lavender duck and pistachio mint poached turbot. Service is seamless throughout. ⊠ *21 W. 52nd St., between 5th and 6th Aves., Midtown West* ☎ *212/582–7200* ⚐ *Reservations essential* 🏛 *Jacket and tie* ▤ *AE, D, DC, MC, V* ⊘ *Closed Sun. No lunch Sat.* Ⓜ *Subway: B, D, F, V to 47–50th Sts./Rockefeller Center.*

BRAZILIAN ✗ **Churrascaria Plataforma.** This sprawling, boisterous shrine to meat,
★ $$$$ with its generous all-you-can-eat prix-fixe menu, is best experienced with a group of ravenous friends. Order a full pitcher of *caipirinhas* (a cocktail of sugarcane liquor and lime), and head for the vast salad bar that beckons with vegetables, meats, and cheeses, plus hot tureens of *feijoada* (the Brazilian national dish of beans, pork, greens, and manioc). But exercise restraint—the real show begins with the parade of lamb, beef, chicken, ham, sausage, and innards, brought to the table on skewers. ⊠ *316 W. 49th St., between 8th and 9th Aves., Midtown West* ☎ *212/245–0505* ⚐ *Reservations essential* ▤ *AE, DC, MC, V* Ⓜ *Subway: C, E to 50th St.*

CONTEMPORARY ✗ **Town.** It's difficult to decide which is more chic in this bilevel restau-
$$$$ rant: the design or the crowd. Ubiquitous architect David Rockwell has created a contemporary restaurant with an international feel, manipulating scale and using a variety of materials, including plastic and glass. Geoffrey Zakarian's cooking is every bit as sophisticated as the environment. The prix-fixe menu's descriptions are far simpler than the food that arrives. Escargot risotto, cod in porcini puree, and duck steak with buckwheat pilaf are intricate exercises in culinary craft. The "Balcony" lounge has a limited selection of light fare. ⊠ *15 W. 56th St., between 5th and 6th Aves., Midtown West* ☎ *212/582–4445* ⚐ *Reservations essential* ▤ *AE, D, DC, MC, V* Ⓜ *Subway: F to 57th St.*

FRENCH ✗ **Le Bernardin.** Owner Maguy LeCoze presides over the power scene
$$$$ in the plush, teak-paneled dining room at this trendsetting French
FodorsChoice seafood restaurant. Chef-partner Eric Ripert works magic with anything
★ that swims—preferring at times not to cook it at all. Deceptively simple dishes such as Spanish mackerel tartare with osetra caviar and steamed halibut on a pea puree are typical of his style. In Ripert's hands, a lowly croque monsieur becomes a four-star feast. There's no beating

64 <

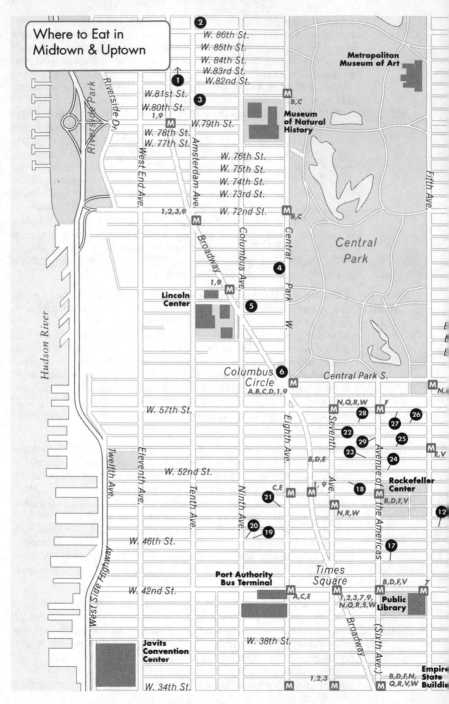

Where to Eat in
Midtown & Uptown

Le Bernardin for thrilling French cuisine, seafood or otherwise, coupled with some of the finest desserts in town. ⊠ *155 W. 51st St., between 6th and 7th Aves., Midtown West* ☎ *212/489–1515* ⌕ *Reservations essential* ⌂ *Jacket required* ▭ *AE, DC, MC, V* ☽ *Closed Sun. No lunch Sat.* Ⓜ *Subway: R, W to 49th St.; B, D, F, V to 47th–50th Sts.*

$$$–$$$$ ✕**db bistro moderne.** Daniel Boulud's "casual bistro" (it's neither, really) consists of two elegantly appointed rooms, one in front where the tables are not clothed, and one in back where they are. The menu is organized by the French names of seasonal ingredients—lobster (*homard*), beet (*betterave*), beef (*boeuf*), and mushroom (*champignon*), *par exemple*. Within each category, appetizers and main courses are listed. Much has been made of the $29 hamburger. But considering it is superbly stuffed with braised short ribs, foie gras, and black truffles, it's almost a deal. ⊠ *55 W. 44th St., between 5th and 6th Aves., Midtown West* ☎ *212/ 391–5353* ⌕ *Reservations essential* ▭ *AE, MC, V* ☽ *No lunch Sun.* Ⓜ *Subway: B, D, F, V to 42nd Sts.*

GREEK   ✕**Molyvos.** Fresh ingredients, bold flavors, fine olive oil, and fragrant
$$–$$$ herbs emerge from Jim Botsacos's marvelous kitchen at this upscale taverna. Meals start with a selection of salads, or *meze*. They include gigantes beans stewed with tomatoes, *taramasalata* (a creamy spread made with smoked carp roe), garlicky *skordalia* (potato puree), *saganaki* (fried *kefalotiri* cheese), and a real Greek salad with vegetables, olives, and feta—but no lettuce. Seasonal entrées include traditional Greek dishes, such as moussaka, lamb *yuvetsi* (marinated lamb shanks braised in a clay pot), and cabbage *dolmades* (cabbage stuffed with ground lamb in a lemon-dill sauce). ⊠ *871 7th Ave., between W. 55th and W. 56th Sts., Midtown West* ☎ *212/582–7500* ⌕ *Reservations essential* ▭ *AE, D, DC, MC, V* Ⓜ *Subway: F, N, R, Q, W to 57th St.*

ITALIAN   ✕**Osteria del Circo.** Opened by the sons of celebrity restaurateur Sirio
$$$–$$$$ Maccioni (of Le Cirque fame), this less formal place celebrates the Tuscan cooking of their mother, Egi. The contemporary menu offers a wide selection and includes some traditional Tuscan specialties, such as Egi's ricotta-and-spinach-filled ravioli, tossed in butter and sage and gratinéed with imported Parmesan. The pizza *pazza* (crazy pizza) has a delicate layer of mascarpone cheese and porcini mushroom sauce topped with thin slices of prosciutto di Parma. Don't miss the fanciful Circo desserts, especially the filled *bomboloncini* doughnuts. ⊠ *120 W. 55th St., between 6th and 7th Aves., Midtown West* ☎ *212/265–3636* ⌕ *Reservations essential* ▭ *AE, DC, MC, V* ☽ *No lunch Sun.* Ⓜ *Subway: F, N, R, Q, W to 57th St.*

$$$ ✕**Remi.** A Venetian sensibility pervades this stylish restaurant designed by Adam Tihany. A skylighted atrium, blue-and-white-striped banquettes, Venetian glass chandeliers, and a soaring room-length mural of the city of canals make this the perfect spot for a power lunch or a meal before a night on the town. Chef Francesco Antonucci's contemporary Venetian cuisine is highly favored among Italians living in New York. Fresh sardines make a lovely beginning, with their contrasting sweet-and-sour onion garnish, and you can't go wrong with the sumptuous pastas, expertly prepared rack of lamb, or any of the wonderful desserts. ⊠ *145 W. 53rd St., between 6th and 7th Aves., Midtown West* ☎ *212/*

581–4242 ⌕ *Reservations essential* ▤ *AE, DC, MC, V* ⊘ *No lunch weekends* Ⓜ *Subway: E, V to 5th Ave.–53rd St.*

$$–$$$ ✕ **Becco.** An ingenious concept makes Becco a prime Restaurant Row choice for time-constrained theatergoers. There are two pricing scenarios: one includes an all-you-can-eat selection of antipasti and three pastas served hot out of pans that waiters circulate around the dining room; the other adds a generous entrée. The selection changes daily but often includes gnocchi, fresh ravioli, and something in a cream sauce. The entrées include braised veal shank, rack of lamb, and fish. ✉ *355 W. 46th St., between 8th and 9th Aves., Midtown West* ☎ *212/397–7597* ⌕ *Reservations essential* ▤ *AE, DC, MC, V* Ⓜ *Subway: A, C, E to 42nd St.*

$ ✕ **Mangia–57th Street.** Office workers looking for out-of-the-ordinary takeout come here for sandwiches and salads that include fresh mozzarella, prosciutto, focaccia, grilled eggplant, and sun-dried tomatoes. In the sit-down restaurant upstairs, small pizzas and pastas are a regular feature, and special dishes might include grilled swordfish with puttanesca sauce or rib-eye steak with porcini mushrooms. It's one of the most reasonably priced lunches in midtown. ✉ *50 W. 57th St., between 5th and 6th Aves., Midtown West* ☎ *212/582–5882* ▤ *AE, D, DC, MC, V* ⊘ *Closed weekends. No dinner* Ⓜ *Subway: F to 57th St.*

RUSSIAN **$$$–$$$$** ✕ **Firebird.** Eight dining rooms full of objets d'art and period antiques lie within these two brownstones resembling a pre-Revolutionary St. Petersburg mansion. Staples of the regional cuisine include caviar, *zakuska* (assorted Russian hors d'oeuvres), porcini-crusted monkfish, or tea with cherry preserves. Great desserts (an assortment of Russian cookies steals the show) and an extraordinary vodka selection are giddy indulgences. ✉ *365 W. 46th St., between 8th and 9th Aves., Midtown West* ☎ *212/586–0244* ⌕ *Reservations essential* ▤ *AE, DC, MC, V* ⊘ *Closed Mon. No lunch Sun.* Ⓜ *Subway: A, C, E to 42nd St.*

Midtown East

AMERICAN **$$$$** ✕ **Four Seasons.** The landmark Seagram Building houses one of America's most famous restaurants, designed by architect Philip Johnson in a timeless moderne style. The stark Grill Room, birthplace of the power lunch, has inviting leather banquettes, a floating sculpture, and one of the best bars in New York. Illuminated trees and a gurgling Carrara marble pool distinguish the more romantic Pool Room. The eclectic menu changes seasonally. The pretheater prix-fixe dinner is relatively inexpensive; otherwise, the menu is pricey. You can't go wrong with Dover sole, steak tartare, or crispy duck, which has a final tableside preparation. ✉ *99 E. 52nd St., between Park and Lexington Aves., Midtown East* ☎ *212/754–9494* ⌕ *Reservations essential* ⛨ *Jacket required* ▤ *AE, DC, MC, V* ⊘ *Closed Sun. No lunch Sat.* Ⓜ *Subway: E, F, 6 to 51st St.–Lexington Ave.*

FRENCH **$$–$$$** ✕ **Brasserie.** This midtown ultramodern brasserie has an unmistakable Downtown vibe. The design by architects Diller & Scofidio uses molded pear wood, lime-green resin, pastry-bag sculptures, and digital flat-screen technology to create an otherworldly eating environment. As an added bonus, the contemporary brasserie fare—served from morning to late night—is excellent. The baguettes are superb and the daily specials speak French without an accent. Don't leave without sampling dessert. ⊠ *100 E. 53rd St., between Lexington and Park Aves., Midtown East* ☎ *212/751–4840* ⌂ *Reservations essential* ⊟ *AE, D, DC, MC, V* Ⓜ *Subway: 6 to 51st St.*

ITALIAN ✕ **Felidia.** Manhattanites frequent this *ristorante* as much for the win-
$–$$$$ ning enthusiasm of owner/cookbook author/Public Television chef Lidia Bastianich as for the food. The menu emphasizes authentic regional Italian cuisines, with a bow to dishes from Bastianich's homeland, Istria, on the Adriatic. Sit in an attractive front room with a wooden bar, a rustic room beyond, or in the elegant second-floor dining room. Order risotto, fresh homemade pasta, or roasted whole fish, and choose from a wine list representing Italy's finest vineyards. ⊠ *243 E. 58th St., between 2nd and 3rd Aves., Midtown East* ☎ *212/758–1479* ⌂ *Reservations essential* 🏛 *Jacket required* ⊟ *AE, DC, MC, V* ⊘ *Closed Sun. No lunch Sat.* Ⓜ *Subway: N, R, W, 4, 5, 6 to 59th St.–Lexington Ave.*

JAPANESE ✕ **Kuruma Zushi.** Only a small sign in Japanese indicates the location of
$$–$$$$ this extraordinary restaurant that serves only sushi and sashimi. Bypass the tables, sit at the sushi bar, and put yourself in the hands of Toshihiro Uezu, the owner and chef. Uezu imports hard-to-find fish directly from Japan, and on a typical night he will offer several different types of tuna, the prices of which vary according to the degree of fattiness and the size of the fish from which they are cut. The most quietly attentive service staff in the city completes the wildly expensive experience. ⊠ *7 E. 47th St., 2nd fl., between 5th and Madison Aves., Midtown East* ☎ *212/ 317–2802* ⌂ *Reservations essential* ⊟ *AE, MC, V* ⊘ *Closed Sun.* Ⓜ *Subway: 4, 5, 6, 7 to 42nd St.–Grand Central.*

MEXICAN ✕ **Pampano.** Richard Sandoval, who gave New Yorkers the great Maya
★ $$$ uptown, turned his culinary attention to Mexican seafood, and Pampano hit the ground running, immediately attracting a conspicuously international crowd. Bas-relief palm trees and fronds decorate the cathedral-high walls. Start with a tart, meaningful margarita, or choose from about 50 tequilas available by the snifter. An addictive smoked swordfish spread with tomatoes, onion, and cilantro is served with freshly fried tortilla chips. Continue with a sampling of three highly complex ceviches, then go Latin American with sautéed pompano with plantain, black rice, garlic, and chile guajillo sauce. Finish with a nice warm corn cake with coconut ice cream and hibiscus sauce. ⊠ *209 E. 49th St., at 3rd Ave., Midtown East* ☎ *212/751–4545* ⌂ *Reservations essential* ⊟ *AE, DC, MC, V* ⊘ *No lunch Sat. and Sun.* Ⓜ *Subway: 6 to 51st St.–Lexington Ave.*

PAN-ASIAN ✕ **Vong.** A tour of duty at Bangkok's Oriental Hotel inspired Jean-
$$–$$$$ Georges Vongerichten to create this radiant restaurant of potted palms and gold-leaf ceilings. Presentation is vital here: the food is showcased on dazzling dishes of varying sizes, colors, and shapes. The menu changes seasonally, but reliable standbys include chicken and coconut soup with *galangal* (a gingerlike root) and shiitake mushrooms, braised rabbit curry, and grilled beef and noodles in a ginger broth. A good strategy

for two or more: order set assortments of five appetizers ($21 per person) and five terrific desserts ($14). It's not authentic Thai—more like French-Thai fusion—but the food is intensely delicious. ✉ *200 E. 54th St., at 3rd Ave., Midtown East* ☎ *212/486–9592* ⌂ *Reservations essential* ▤ *AE, DC, MC, V* ⊘ *No lunch weekends* Ⓜ *Subway: 6 to 51st St./Lexington Ave.; E, V, to Lexington–3rd Aves./53rd St.*

SCANDINAVIAN   ✕ **Aquavit.** Cool as a dip in the Baltic Sea, this airy atrium that was once
★ **$$$$**   Nelson Rockefeller's town house is decorated with contemporary art and an inspiring waterfall. The nouveau Swedish fare of wunderkind chef Marcus Sammuelsson is dressed in chic contemporary garb. Forget herring, lingonberries, and pea soup (although they're better here than anywhere else): think molten foie gras ganache with truffle ice cream. Desserts are equally creative and scrumptious. An upstairs dining room is less formal and less expensive. New York's largest selection of aquavits (a strong Scandinavian liquor) partners with the well-chosen wine list. Sunday brunch is literally a smorgasbord. ✉ *65 E. 55th St., between Madison and Park Aves., Midtown East* ☎ *212/307–7311* ⌂ *Reservations essential* ▤ *AE, DC, MC, V* Ⓜ *Subway: E, V to 5th Ave.–53rd St.*

STEAK   ✕ **Sparks Steak House.** Magnums of wines that cost more than most peo-
$$$–$$$$ ple earn in a week festoon the large dining rooms of this classic New York steak house. Black-tie waiters at the door seem so sincerely pleased to see you it's startling to realize there are about 600 other people inside. Although seafood is given fair play on the menu, Sparks is about dry-aged steak. The lamb chops and veal chops are also noteworthy. Classic sides of hash browns, spinach (not creamed!), mushrooms, onions, and broccoli are all you need to complete the experience. ✉ *210 E. 46th St., between 2nd and 3rd Aves., Midtown East* ☎ *212/687–4855* ⌂ *Reservations essential* ▤ *AE, D, DC, MC, V* ⊘ *Closed Sun. No lunch Sat.* Ⓜ *Subway: S, 4, 5, 6, 7 to 42nd St.–Grand Central.*

Upper East Side

FRENCH   ✕ **Daniel.** In this grand space inside the historic Mayfair Hotel, celebrity
$$$$ chef Daniel Boulud has created one of the most memorable dining ex-
Fodor'sChoice   periences available in Manhattan today. The lengthy prix-fixe–only
★   menu is predominantly French, with such modern classics as roasted venison loin with a honey-juniper glaze and kabocha squash. Equally impressive are the professional service and primarily French wine list. Don't forget the decadent desserts and overflowing cheese trolley. For a more casual evening, you can reserve a table in the lounge area, where entrées range from $36 to $39. ✉ *60 E. 65th St., between Madison and Park Aves., Upper East Side* ☎ *212/288–0033* ⌂ *Reservations essential* 𝕸 *Jacket required* ▤ *AE, DC, MC, V* ⊘ *Closed Sun. No lunch* Ⓜ *Subway: 6 to 68th St.–Hunter College.*

★ **$$–$$$$**   ✕ **Café Boulud.** Both the food and service are top-notch at Daniel Boulud's conservative (but not overly stuffy) bistro in the Surrey Hotel. The kitchen is run by chef Andrew Carmellini, who has teamed up with Boulud to create a four-part menu. Under *La Tradition* you find such classic French dishes as braised and roasted rabbit with fennel; *Le Potager* has tempting vegetarian dishes like oven-roasted vegetable casserole; *La Saison* follows the rhythms of the season and really shines in early autumn; and *Le Voyage* is where the kitchen reinterprets the myriad cuisines of the world. ⊠ *20 E. 76th St., between 5th and Madison Aves., Upper East Side* ☎ *212/772–2600* ⚑ *Reservations essential* 🖃 *AE, DC, MC, V* ⊘ *No lunch weekends* Ⓜ *Subway: 6 to 77th St.*

MEXICAN
★ $$–$$$

✕ **Maya.** The upscale hacienda look of this popular restaurant is an appropriate setting for some of the best Mexican food in the city. Begin with a delicious fresh mango margarita, then order such flavorful dishes as a roasted poblano pepper stuffed with seafood and manchego cheese, or *mole poblano*—a grilled chicken breast covered with mole sauce and accompanied by cilantro rice and plantains, or lobster and shrimp marinated in adobo seasoning and paired with roasted corn puree and spicy watercress salad. Service can be a little rushed at times, especially on a busy weekend night. ⊠ *1191 1st Ave., between E. 64th and E. 65th Sts., Upper East Side* ☎ *212/585–1818* ⚑ *Reservations essential* 🖃 *AE, DC, MC, V* ⊘ *No lunch* Ⓜ *Subway: 6 to 68th St.–Hunter College.*

Upper West Side

AMERICAN
CASUAL
$$–$$$

✕ **Sarabeth's.** Lining up for brunch here is as much an Upper West Side tradition as taking a sunny Sunday afternoon stroll in nearby Riverside Park. Filled with bric-a-brac and imbued with a homespun charm, Sarabeth's is loved by locals for its eclectic menu featuring such dishes as old-fashioned chicken potpie and herb-crusted halibut. The baked goods like muffins, scones, and a cranberry-pear bread pudding are outstanding. The affordable wine list includes some unexpected bottles from small producers. ⊠ *423 Amsterdam Ave., between W. 80th and W. 81st Sts., Upper West Side* ☎ *212/496–6280* ⚑ *Reservations not accepted* 🖃 *AE, DC, MC, V* Ⓜ *Subway: 1, 9 to 79th St.*

¢–$$

✕ **Barney Greengrass.** The self-proclaimed "Sturgeon King," this Jewish deli dates back to 1908 and offers the basic formula of high-quality food, abrupt service, Formica tables, wooden chairs, and plenty of salt. Split a platter with smoked salmon, sturgeon, or whitefish and you get two bagels, cream cheese, potato salad, lemons, olives, tomato, and onion on the side. Omelets are also available, with such scrumptious fillings as salami and caramelized onions. Beware: the wait for a table can take an hour or more during weekend brunch time. ⊠ *541 Amsterdam Ave., between W. 86th and W. 87th Sts., Upper West Side* ☎ *212/724–4707* ⚑ *Reservations not accepted* 🖃 *No credit cards* ⊘ *Closed Mon.* Ⓜ *Subway: 1, 9 to 86th St.*

CONTEMPORARY
$$–$$$$

✕ **Ouest.** The menu at this contemporary American restaurant is the brainchild of celebrity chef Tom Valenti, who rewards patrons with signature dishes such as petit filet with braised short ribs, sweet-pea stew, and Parmesan pudding. There are also simple grilled meats, and lighter but such equally satisfying dishes as tuna "mignon" with white-bean puree, black olive-lemon compote, and red pepper coulis. Request one of the circular red-leather booths near the open kitchen to see Valenti and his crew at work. ⊠ *2315 Broadway, between W. 83rd and W. 84th Sts., Upper West Side* ☎ *212/580–8700* ⌦ *Reservations essential* ⊟ *AE, D, MC, V* ⊗ *No lunch* Ⓜ *Subway: 1, 9 to 86th St.*

CONTINENTAL   ✕ **Café des Artistes.** Howard Chandler Christy's murals of naked nymphs
$$$–$$$$ at play grace the walls of this thoroughly romantic restaurant, which first opened in 1917. Although the haute French food may no longer be among the best in New York, the menu still always has some stunners, such as pan-roasted squab with chanterelle mushrooms and garlic flan over a potato cake. Desserts like hot-fudge napoleon or perfect apple strudel are classic and appealing. The prix-fixe dinner is $45 (no substitutions allowed). ⊠ *1 W. 67th St., at Central Park W, Upper West Side* ☎ *212/877–3500* ⌦ *Reservations essential* ⊟ *AE, DC, MC, V* Ⓜ *Subway: 1, 9 to 66th St.–Lincoln Center.*

FRENCH   ✕ **Jean Georges.** Celebrity chef Jean-Georges Vongerichten's prix-fixe
$$$$ restaurant near Central Park is a true culinary destination. The main
Fodor'sChoice   dining room is dressed in neutral colors, with beige banquettes and min-
★   imal decoration. Vongerichten's Asian-accented French cooking shows a like-minded restraint, with some unusual combinations: sea scallops in caper-raisin emulsion with caramelized cauliflower is an outstanding example. Elegant desserts, exceedingly personalized service, and a well-selected wine list contribute to the overall experience. The **Nougatine** serves a more moderate à la carte menu in the front area, with a view of the open kitchen. ⊠ *1 Central Park W, at W. 59th St., Upper West Side* ☎ *212/299–3900* ⌦ *Reservations essential* ⬛ *Jacket required* ⊟ *AE, DC, MC, V* ⊗ *Closed Sun.* Ⓜ *Subway: A, B, C, D, 1, 9 to 59th St.–Columbus Circle.*

$$$–$$$$ ✕ **Picholine.** The elegant dining room in this mellow restaurant has soft colors, wood floors, and gorgeous dried flowers. Chef Terrance Brennan's French food with Mediterranean accents is considered by many to be among the very best in Manhattan. Top dishes include the "macaroni and cheese" risotto with wild mushrooms, prosciutto, and vacherin cheese, and saddle of venison with chestnut spaetzle, cabbage confit, and huckleberry sauce. The wine list is extensive and includes a good selection of wine by the glass. ⊠ *35 W. 64th St., between Broadway and Central Park W, Upper West Side* ☎ *212/724–8585* ⌦ *Reservations essential* ⊟ *AE, DC, MC, V* ⊗ *No lunch Sun. and Mon.* Ⓜ *Subway: 1, 9 to 66th St.–Lincoln Center.*

Brooklyn

CONTEMPORARY   ✕ **River Café.** When this gorgeous prix-fixe–only restaurant opened in
$$$$ 1977, no one imagined that such top New York chefs as Charlie Palmer
of Aureole would get their start here; however, owner Buzzy O'Keefe
has always been able to attract new talent (and customers) by promoting
the concept of seasonal-based American cuisine. Chef Brad Steelman's
menu remains true to this philosophy, with such tantalizing dishes
as Maine lobster poached with artichokes and basil. The flower-filled
main dining room has views of the Brooklyn Bridge and lower Manhattan.
⊠ *1 Water St., at Old Fulton St., Brooklyn Heights* ☎ *718/522–
5200* ⌫ *Reservations essential* 🏛 *Jacket required* 🖃 *AE, DC, MC, V*
Ⓜ *Subway: A, C to High St.–Brooklyn Bridge.*

STEAK   ✕ **Peter Luger Steak House.** Sure, steak houses in Manhattan have bet-
$$$$ ter lighting, more elegant dining, bigger wine lists, and comfortable chairs
FodorsChoice   instead of wooden benches, but if you're after the best porterhouse steak
★   in New York, then Peter Luger's is worth the trip to Brooklyn. Serving
the same highest-quality beef since 1887, it originally opened as a German
beer hall. You probably won't see a menu, but here's all you need
to know: shrimp cocktail, beefsteak tomato and onion salad, home
fries, creamed spinach, pecan pie, and of course steak—ordered according
to how many are in your party. Free parking is available. ⊠ *178 Broadway, at Driggs Ave., Williamsburg* ☎ *718/387–7400* ⌫ *Reservations
essential* 🖃 *No credit cards* Ⓜ *Subway: J, M, Z to Marcy Ave.*

WHERE TO STAY

Updated by
Elise Harris

New York life weaves in and out of the city's hotels. Whether a New
Yorker is invited to a wedding, a premiere, or dinner, there's a fair chance
it will take place in one of Manhattan's luxurious old standbys or in
one of the latest chic newcomers. New York hotels grant a loftier standard
of service and glamour to locals and visitors alike. Whatever your
preference, your hotel has a significant effect on the quality of your stay
in New York. Choose carefully. Some are visual dreamscapes, others offer
the kind of service that is effective without being overly attentive, but
many are simply adequate places to sleep. Increasingly, hotels have such
high-tech accessories as plasma TVs, wireless laptops, and DVD vending
machines. Wherever you stay, one design standard is universal:
you're pampered with 400-plus thread counts, goose-down duvets,
satin coverlets, and terry slippers.

Reservations

Hotel reservations are an absolute necessity when planning your trip to
New York. When booking inquire about any ongoing renovations lest
you get a room within earshot of noisy construction. In this ever-changing
city, travelers can find themselves temporarily, and most inconveniently,
without commonplace amenities such as room service or spa access
if their hotel is upgrading. Once you decide on a hotel, use a major credit
card to guarantee the reservation—another essential in a market where
"lost" reservations are not unheard of.

What It Costs

WHAT IT COSTS In New York City				
$$$$	$$$	$$	$	¢
over $250	$200–$250	$150–$199	$100–$149	under $100

Prices are for a standard double room, excluding 13.625% city and state taxes.

Lower Manhattan

★ $$$$ 🏨 **The Ritz-Carlton New York, Battery Park.** A stone's throw from the Financial District, this hotel has stunning views of the city's waterfront. The rooms are minimalist and monochromatic, with down pillows, feather beds, duvets wrapped in Frette linens, and luxurious marble baths. A fleet of service providers includes water sommelier, bath and technology butlers, and on-call aestheticians and masseurs. Come evening, locals flock to the Rise bar to drink martinis while admiring New York Harbor and the Statue of Liberty at sunset. ⊠ *2 West St., at Battery Pl., Battery Park 10004* ☎ *212/344–0800 or 800/241–3333* 🖷 *212/344–3801* ⊕ *www.ritzcarlton.com* ⇔ *254 rooms, 44 suites* ᐧ *Restaurant, in-room data ports, minibars, cable TV with video games, in-room DVD players, 2 bars, laundry service, Internet, meeting rooms, parking (fee), no-smoking rooms* ⊟ *AE, D, DC, MC, V.*

$$–$$$$ 🏨 **Holiday Inn Wall Street.** You know the future has arrived when a Holiday Inn provides T-1 Internet access in every room, express check-in lobby computers that dispense key cards, and both Web TV and Nintendo on 27-inch televisions. Half the rooms have desktop PCs, and on the "smart floor" wireless laptops and printers are at the ready. The comfortable rooms are surprisingly spacious—many have 14-foot ceilings. Thoughtful touches include ergonomically designed work spaces with L-shape desks, full-length mirrors that open to reveal ironing boards, and oversize showerheads that simulate falling rain. ⊠ *15 Gold St., at Platt St., Lower Manhattan 10038* ☎ *212/232–7700 or 800/465–4329* 🖷 *212/425–0330* ⊕ *www.holidayinnwsd.com* ⇔ *136 rooms, 1 suite* ᐧ *Restaurant, room service, in-room data ports, in-room safes, minibars, cable TV with movies and video games, gym, bar, dry cleaning, laundry service, Internet, business services, meeting rooms, parking (fee), some pets allowed (fee), no-smoking floors* ⊟ *AE, D, DC, MC, V* Ⓜ *Subway: A, E, J, M, 2, 3, 4, 5 to Fulton St./Broadway Nassau.*

SoHo

$$$$ 🏨 **Mercer Hotel.** Owner Andre Balazs, known for his Château Marmont in Hollywood, has a knack for channeling a neighborhood sensibility. Here it's SoHo loft all the way. In the hushed lobby the reception desk is unmarked. Guest rooms are generously sized with long entryways, high ceilings, and walk-in closets. Dark African woods and custom-designed furniture upholstered in muted solids lend serenity. The bathrooms steal the show with their decadent two-person marble tubs—some surrounded by mirrors—but beware: not all rooms come with a tub. ⊠ *147 Mercer St., at Prince St., SoHo 10012* ☎ *212/966–6060 or 888/918–*

Fodor's Choice
★

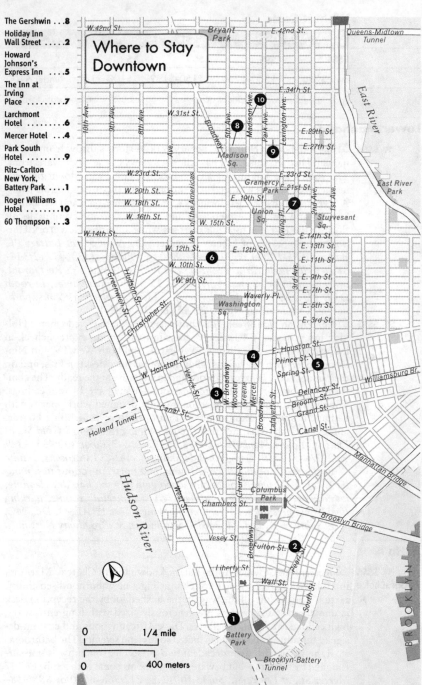

Where to Stay
Downtown

6060 🕾 212/965–3838 ⊕ *www.mercerhotel.com* ✂ *67 rooms, 8 suites* ♣ *Restaurant, room service, in-room data ports, in-room safes, mini-bars, cable TV, cable TV with movies and video games, in-room VCRs, 2 bars, concierge, business services, some pets allowed, no-smoking rooms* ▤ *AE, D, DC, MC, V* Ⓜ *Subway: R, W to Prince St.*

★ **$$$$** 🖼 **60 Thompson.** A superb and original design by Thomas O'Brien, along with a popular lounge and restaurant, instantly anchored this stunning hotel into the Downtown scene. The generous use of dark woods and full-wall leather headboards give the retro-classic rooms a welcoming warmth. The high-backed Thompson Chair has become a signature style statement. Amenities include CD stereos and Frette linens. Marble-swathed bathrooms are positively hedonistic. ✉ *60 Thompson St., between Broome and Spring Sts., SoHo 10012* 🕾 *212/431–0400* 🖷 *212/431–0200* ⊕ *www.60thompson.com* ✂ *90 rooms, 11 suites* ♣ *Restaurant, room service, in-room data ports, in-room fax, minibars, cable TV with movies, in-room DVD players, in-room VCRs, 2 bars, concierge, Internet, meeting rooms, parking (fee), no-smoking rooms* ▤ *AE, D, DC, MC, V* Ⓜ *Subway: C, E to Spring St.*

Greenwich Village & the East Village

★ **$–$$** 🖼 **Howard Johnson's Express Inn.** This hotel at the nexus of East Village and Lower East Side nightlife is perfect if you want to check out the Downtown scene. A corner location increases your chances of having a view when you eventually rise to meet the day, and next door is a century-old knish bakery. The tastefully done rooms each have enough space for a desk; a few have hot tubs or microwaves and mini-refrigerators. With amenities such as in-room hair dryers, irons, coffeemakers, and voice mail, plus free local calls, you're getting more than your money's worth in New York's hotel market. ✉ *135 E. Houston St., at Forsyth St., Lower East Side 10002* 🕾 *212/358–8844 or 800/446–4656* 🖷 *212/473–3500* ⊕ *www.hojo.com* ✂ *46 rooms* ♣ *In-room data ports, some microwaves, cable TV, laundry service, no-smoking floors* ▤ *AE, D, DC, MC, V* Ⓜ *Subway: F, V to 2nd Ave.*

¢–**$** 🖼 **Larchmont Hotel.** You might miss the entrance to this beaux-arts town
Fodor'sChoice house, whose geranium boxes and lanterns blend right in with the Old
★ New York feel of West 11th Street. If you don't mind shared bathrooms and no room service, the residential-style accommodations are all anyone could ask for, for the price. The small rooms have a tasteful safari theme; your own private sink and stocked bookshelf will make you feel right at home. You have access to a communal kitchen. ✉ *27 W. 11th St., between 5th and 6th Aves., Greenwich Village 10011* 🕾 *212/989–9333* 🖷 *212/989–9496* ⊕ *www.larchmonthotel.com* ✂ *60 rooms, none with bath* ♣ *Café, fans, business services, no-smoking rooms* ▤ *AE, D, DC, MC, V* Ⓜ *Subway: A, B, C, D, E, F, V to W. 4th St./Washington Sq.*

Gramercy & Murray Hill

★ **$$$$** 🖼 **The Inn at Irving Place.** The city's most charming small inn occupies two grand 1830s town houses just steps from Gramercy Park. Its cozy tea salon, antiques-filled living room, and original curving banister evoke a more genteel era. Rooms have ornamental fireplaces, four-poster beds with embroidered linens, wood shutters, and glossy cherrywood floors. The room named after Madame Olenska (the lovelorn Edith Wharton character) has a bay window with sitting nook. In the morning, steaming pots of tea and coffee are served in the tea salon, along with a free Continental breakfast including homemade pastries and breads. ⊠ *56 Irving Pl., between E. 17th and E. 18th Sts., Gramercy 10003* ☎ *212/533–4600 or 800/685–1447* 🖷 *212/533–4611* ⊕ *www.innatirving.com* ⤴ *5 rooms, 6 suites* ⚱ *Restaurant, room service, in-room data ports, minibars, refrigerators, cable TV, cable TV with movies, in-room VCRs, massage, bar, dry cleaning, laundry service, business services, parking (fee); no kids under 8* ▤ *AE, D, DC, MC, V* Ⓜ *Subway: 4, 5, 6, L, N, Q, R, W to 14th St./Union Sq.*

$$–$$$$ ⊡ **Park South Hotel.** In this beautifully transformed 1906 office building, rooms are smartly contemporary and even a bit regal, given the majestic, oversize wooden headboards. Some have views of the Chrysler Building. The New York flavor permeates from a mezzanine library focusing on local history to the ubiquitous black-and-white photos of city scenes from the 1880s through 1950s. The Black Duck bar and restaurant warms patrons with its wood-burning fireplace. Unlike at other boutique hotels where locals have made the lounges their watering holes, you won't have to contend with crowds here. ⊠ *122 E. 28th St., between Lexington and Park Aves., Murray Hill 10016* ☎ *212/448–0888 or 800/315–4642* 🖷 *212/448–0811* ⊕ *www.parksouthhotel.com* ⤴ *143 rooms* ⚱ *Restaurant, room service, in-room data ports, in-room fax, minibars, cable TV, in-room DVD players, gym, bar, dry cleaning, laundry service, concierge, business services* ▤ *AE, D, DC, MC, V* Ⓜ *Subway: 6 to 28th St.*

$–$$$$ ⊡ **The Gershwin.** Young foreign travelers flock to this budget hotel–cum-
Fodor'sChoice hostel housed in a converted 13-story Greek-revival building adjacent
★ to the Museum of Sex. A giant Plexiglas and metal sculpture of glowing pods by Stefan Lindfors creeps down the facade and winds its way into the lobby. With Andy Warhol as muse, there's Pop Art on every floor. Rooms are painted in bright colors. Dormitories have 2 to 10 beds and a remarkable $33 to $53 rate. In 2003 the hotel opened a new lounge and tapas bar. On any given night there's something going on—film series, stand-up comedy, performance art. ⊠ *7 E. 27th St., between 5th and Madison Aves., Murray Hill 10016* ☎ *212/545–8000* 🖷 *212/684–5546* ⊕ *www.gershwinhotel.com* ⤴ *120 rooms, 64 beds in dorm rooms, 12 suites* ⚱ *Restaurant, café, cable TV, bar, Internet, no-smoking floors; no TV in some rooms* ▤ *AE, MC, V* Ⓜ *Subway: 6, R, W to 28th St.*

★ **$$$** ⊡ **Roger Williams Hotel.** A masterpiece of industrial chic, the cavernous Rafael Viñoly–designed lobby—clad with sleek maple walls accented with fluted zinc pillars—was dubbed "a shrine to modernism" by *New York* magazine. What rooms lack in space they make up for in high-style, custom-made blond-birch furnishings—including sliding shoji screens behind the beds—and dramatic downlighting. Some baths have a cedarwood-floor shower stall. There's a complimentary breakfast and 24-hour cappuccino. ⊠ *131 Madison Ave., at E. 31st St., Murray Hill 10016* ☎ *212/448–7000 or 877/847–4444* 🖷 *212/448–7007* ⊕ *www.*

rogerwilliamshotel.com ↩ *185 rooms, 2 suites* ↻ *In-room data ports, cable TV, in-room VCRs, exercise equipment, gym, piano, concierge, Internet, business services, parking (fee), no-smoking rooms, no-smoking floors* ▤ *AE, D, MC, V* Ⓜ *Subway: 6 to 33rd St.*

Midtown West

$$$$ 🏨 **The Bryant Park.** Carved out of the bones of the former American Radiator Building that towers over the New York Public Library and Bryant Park, this brilliant blend of '20s Gothic Revival exterior and sleekly modern rooms delivers the pizzazz worthy of the city's moniker, Gotham. Though the stark red lobby disappoints, rooms are furnished at the apex of minimalist chic with sumptuous travertine bathrooms, hardwood floors, killer views, and wireless laptops that connect to the Internet via large TV monitors. Ilo, a rave-garnering restaurant, rises a few steps from the lobby bar popular with the after-work crowd. ⊠ *40 W. 40th St., between 5th and 6th Aves., Midtown West 10018* ☏ *212/869–0100 or 877/640–9300* 🖷 *212/869–4446* ⊕ *www.bryantparkhotel.com* ↩ *107 rooms, 22 suites* ↻ *Restaurant, room service, in-room data ports, in-room safes, minibars, cable TV with movies, gym, health club, massage, spa, steam room, 2 bars, dry cleaning, laundry service, concierge, Internet, business services, meeting rooms, parking (fee), some pets allowed (fee), no-smoking floors* ▤ *AE, DC, MC, V* Ⓜ *Subway: B, D, F, V to 42nd St.; 7 to 5th Ave.*

$$$$ 🏨 **Chambers.** Midtown is the new Downtown in David Rockwell's gorgeous showcase, where more than 500 works of art hang and each guestroom floor has a mural installation. Loftlike rooms with hand-troweled concrete walls are decorated warmly, and the bathroom floors of poured concrete shimmer with glass mosaic tiles. Enter through the magnificent carved teak doors and pass through the intimate yet grand lobby with soaring ceilings, double-sided fireplace, and Hugo Boss–uniformed staff. ⊠ *15 W. 56th St., off 5th Ave., Midtown West 10019* ☏ *212/974–5656 or 866/204–5656* 🖷 *212/974–5657* ⊕ *www.chambershotel.com* ↩ *72 rooms, 5 suites* ↻ *Restaurant, in-room data ports, in-room safes, minibars, cable TV with movies, in-room DVD players, bar, lounge, dry cleaning, laundry service, concierge, parking (fee), some pets allowed, no-smoking floors* ▤ *AE, D, DC, MC, V* Ⓜ *Subway: F, V to 57th St.*

$$$$ 🏨 **Marriott Marquis.** This brash behemoth in the heart of the theater district is a place New Yorkers love to hate. With its own little city of restaurants, a sushi bar, shops, meeting rooms, and ballrooms—there's even a Broadway theater—it virtually defines "over-the-top." As at other Marriotts, all of the nearly 2,000 rooms here look alike and are pleasant and functional. Some have more dramatic urban views than others. The View, the revolving restaurant and bar on the 49th floor, provides one of the most spectacular panoramas in New York, but it's open only in the evening. Make a reservation to get in. ⊠ *1535 Broadway, at W. 45th St., Midtown West 10036* ☏ *212/398–1900 or 800/843–4898* 🖷 *212/704–8930 or 212/704–8931* ⊕ *www.marriott.com* ↩ *1,889 rooms, 58 suites* ↻ *3 restaurants, café, coffee shop, room service, in-room data ports, in-room safes, minibars, cable TV, exercise equipment, health club, hair salon, hot tub, massage, 3 bars, theater, babysitting, dry cleaning, laun-*

Where to Stay in Midtown & Uptown

Metropolitan Museum of Art

Museum of Natural History

Central Park

Lincoln Center

Columbus Circle

Rockefeller Center

Grand Central Terminal

Port Authority Bus Terminal

Times Square

Public Library

Javits Convention Center

Empire State Building

Herald Square

Penn Station

Madison Square Garden

Hudson River

Riverside Park

Riverside Dr.

West End Ave.

Amsterdam Ave.

Broadway

Columbus Ave.

Central Park W.

Fifth Ave.

Madison Ave.

Park Ave.

Ninth Ave.

Eighth Ave.

Seventh Ave.

Avenue of the Americas

Sixth Ave.

Twelfth Ave.

Eleventh Ave.

West Side Highway

W. 86th St.
E. 86th
W. 79th St.
E. 79th
W. 72nd St.
Central Park S.
W. 57th St.
W. 52nd St.
W. 46th St.
W. 42nd St.
W. 38th St.
W. 34th St.
E. 32nd St.

KEY

Ⓜ Subway stops

dry service, concierge, Internet, business services, meeting rooms, parking (fee), some pets allowed, no-smoking rooms 🖃 AE, D, DC, MC, V Ⓜ Subway: 1, 2, 3, 7, 9, S, N, Q, R, W to 42nd St./Times Sq.

★ $$$$ 🔲 **The Michelangelo.** Italophiles will feel that they've been transported to the good life in the boot at this deluxe hotel whose long, wide lobby lounge is clad with multihue marble and Veronese-style oil paintings. Upstairs the decor of the relatively spacious rooms (averaging 475 square feet) varies. You can choose contemporary, neoclassical, art deco, or French country—all have marble foyers and marble bathrooms equipped with bidets and oversize 55-gallon tubs. The larger rooms have sitting areas and king beds. Complimentary cappuccino, pastries, and other Italian treats are served each morning in the baroque lobby lounge. 🖂 152 W. 51st St., at 7th Ave., Midtown West 10019 ☎ 212/765–1900 or 800/237–0990 📠 212/581–7618 🌐 www.michelangelohotel.com 🛏 123 rooms, 55 suites ♨ Restaurant, room service, in-room data ports, in-room fax, in-room safes, minibars, cable TV with movies, in-room DVD players, exercise equipment, gym, bar, babysitting, dry cleaning, laundry service, concierge, business services, meeting rooms, parking (fee), no-smoking floors 🖃 AE, D, DC, MC, V Ⓜ Subway: B, D, E to 7th Ave.; 1, 9 to 50th St.; B, D, F, V to 47th–50th Sts./Rockefeller Center.

$$$$ 🔲 **The Paramount.** The Paramount caters to a somewhat bohemian,
Fodor'sChoice fashionable, yet cost-conscious clientele. The tiny rooms have white fur-
★ nishings and walls, gilt-framed headboards, and conical steel bathroom sinks. In the lobby a sheer platinum wall and a glamorous sweep of staircase lead to the Mezzanine Restaurant, where you can enjoy cocktails or dinner while gazing down on the action below. The bar, once fiercely trendy, draws a somewhat diluted crowd now that other Whiskey Bars have opened in many of the W Hotels around town. Hotel drawbacks include limited room amenities and a sometimes harried staff. 🖂 235 W. 46th St., between Broadway and 8th Aves., Midtown West 10036 ☎ 212/764–5500 or 800/225–7474 📠 212/354–5237 🛏 590 rooms, 10 suites ♨ 2 restaurants, café, room service, in-room data ports, in-room safes, minibars, cable TV, in-room VCRs, gym, 2 bars, dry cleaning, laundry service, concierge, Internet, business services, meeting rooms, no-smoking floors 🖃 AE, D, DC, MC, V Ⓜ Subway: 1, 2, 3, 7, 9, S, N, Q, R, W to 42nd St./Times Sq.

$$$$ 🔲 **The Plaza.** Towering like a giant wedding cake opposite the fleet of horse-drawn carriages lining Central Park, this is New York's most beloved hotel. The fictional Eloise ran riot in it, Zelda Fitzgerald jumped into the fountain outside of it, countless films have featured it, and its comely Palm Court and handsome Oak Bar welcome all like a favorite aunt and uncle. The management carefully maintains its high-traffic public areas, which New Yorkers feel belong to them as much as the Statue of Liberty. Suites are magnificent, but even the smallest guest rooms have crystal chandeliers and 14-foot ceilings. 🖂 5th Ave. at W. 59th St., Midtown West 10019 ☎ 212/759–3000 or 800/759–3000 📠 212/546–5324 for reservations, 212/759–3167 for guests 🌐 www.fairmont.com 🛏 805 rooms, 60 suites ♨ 4 restaurants, room service, in-room data ports, in-room fax, in-room safes, minibars, refrigerators, cable TV, in-room VCRs, gym, health club, hair salon, massage, sauna, spa, steam room, 2 bars, children's programs (ages 6–18), babysitting, dry clean-

ing, laundry service, concierge, Internet, business services, meeting rooms, parking (fee), some pets allowed ▭ *AE, D, DC, MC, V* Ⓜ *Subway: N, R, W to 5th Ave.*

★ **$$$$** 🏨 **Ritz-Carlton New York, Central Park South.** Formerly the St. Moritz, this glamour palace sits on a strategic spot with some of the best views in the city. Its renovation yielded larger but fewer rooms, and the 1930s facade was kept intact. Adding to the value are technology butlers, butlers who draw your bath, on-call personal trainers, complimentary Bentley limousine service within Midtown, and a La Prairie salon. Rooms and suites are furnished in shades of celadon, taupe, and pale rose, with plush upholsteries, brocade drapes, and richly patterned carpets. ⊠ *50 Central Park S, at 6th Ave., Midtown West 10019* 🕾 *212/ 308–9100 or 800/241–3333* 🖷 *212/207–8831* ⊕ *www.ritzcarlton.com* 🛏 *237 rooms, 40 suites* ⚅ *Restaurant, in-room data ports, minibars, cable TV, in-room DVD players, bar, Internet, meeting rooms* ▭ *AE, D, DC, MC, V* Ⓜ *Subway: F, V to 57th St.*

$$$$ 🏨 **Royalton.** During the '90s, the lobby restaurant "44" started the craze of local media, music, and fashion folk meeting and greeting in hotel boîtes. Although many of the movers and shakers have moved on, the minimalist Philippe Starck space with its sumptuous sofas and inconspicuous Vodka Bar still gives off a cool vibe. Each guest room has a low-lying, custom-made bed, tasteful lighting, and fresh flowers. Some of the rooms have working fireplaces, and all have CD players. Slate bathrooms with stainless-steel and glass fixtures may also have round, two-person tubs. ⊠ *44 W. 44th St., between 5th and 6th Aves., Midtown West 10036* 🕾 *212/869–4400 or 800/635–9013* 🖷 *212/575– 0012* ⊕ *www.ianschragerhotels.com* 🛏 *168 rooms* ⚅ *Restaurant, room service, in-room data ports, in-room safes, minibars, refrigerators, cable TV, cable TV with movies, in-room VCRs, exercise equipment, gym, massage, bar, babysitting, dry cleaning, laundry service, concierge, business services, meeting rooms, parking (fee), some pets allowed, no-smoking rooms* ▭ *AE, DC, MC, V* Ⓜ *Subway: B, D, F, V to 42nd St.*

★ **$$$$** 🏨 **The Shoreham.** This is a miniature, low-attitude version of the ultra-cool Royalton—and it's comfortable to boot. Almost everything is metal or of metal color, from perforated steel headboards to steel sinks in the shiny, tiny bathrooms to the silver-gray carpets. Pleasant touches include CD players and cedar-lined closets. The Shoreham Restaurant & Bar serves an eclectic, light menu of sandwiches and salads. The legendary French restaurant La Caravelle is next door. ⊠ *33 W. 55th St., between 5th and 6th Aves., Midtown West 10019* 🕾 *212/247–6700 or 877/847– 4444* 🖷 *212/765–9741* ⊕ *www.shorehamhotel.com* 🛏 *174 rooms, 37 suites* ⚅ *Restaurant, room service, in-room safes, cable TV, in-room VCRs, bar, babysitting, dry cleaning, laundry service, concierge, Internet, business services, parking (fee), some pets allowed, no-smoking floors* ▭ *AE, D, DC, MC, V* Ⓜ *Subway: E, V to 5th Ave.*

$$$$
Fodor'sChoice
★
🏨 **W Times Square.** Times Square finally goes hip on a grand scale with the opening of this super-sleek 57-floor monolith, the flagship of the white-hot W line. After passing through an entrance of cascading, glass-enclosed water, you alight to the seventh-floor lobby where Kenneth Cole–clad "welcome ambassadors" await. The Jetsons experience continues in the space-age, white-on-white lobby and the futuristic rooms

with their glowing resin boxes and multiple shades of gray. The bilevel Blue Fin restaurant with its sushi bar and floor-to-ceiling windows caps the architectural wonderment. ⊠ *1567 Broadway, at W. 47th St., Midtown West 10036* ☎ *212/930–7400 or 877/946–8357* 🖷 *212/930–7500* ⊕ *www.whotels.com* 🖅 *466 rooms, 43 suites* ⚭ *Restaurant, café, room service, in-room data ports, in-room safes, minibars, cable TV with movies, in-room DVD players, exercise equipment, gym, massage, 4 bars, shop, dry cleaning, laundry service, concierge, Internet, business services, parking (fee), some pets allowed (fee), no-smoking rooms, no-smoking floors* ▱ *AE, D, DC, MC, V* Ⓜ *Subway: 1, 2, 3, 7, 9, S, N, Q, R, W to 42nd St./Times Sq.*

\$\$\$\$ 🖪 **Warwick.** Astonishingly, this palatial hotel was built by William Randolph Hearst in 1927 as a private hotel for his friends and family. The Midtown favorite is well placed for the Theater District. The marble-floor lobby buzzes with activity; the Randolph restaurant is on one side, and Murals on 54, a Continental restaurant, is on the other. Handsome Regency-style rooms have soft pastel color schemes, mahogany armoires, and marble bathrooms, and some have fax machines. The Cary Grant suite was the actor's New York residence for 12 years, and encapsulates a more refined moment in New York glamour. ⊠ *65 W. 54th St., at 6th Ave., Midtown West 10019* ☎ *212/247–2700 or 800/223–4099* 🖷 *212/713–1751* ⊕ *www.warwickhotels.com* 🖅 *358 rooms, 68 suites* ⚭ *2 restaurants, room service, in-room data ports, in-room safes, minibars, cable TV, cable TV with movies and video games, exercise equipment, gym, bar, dry cleaning, laundry service, concierge, Internet, business services, meeting rooms, parking (fee), no-smoking rooms* ▱ *AE, DC, MC, V* Ⓜ *Subway: E, V to 5th Ave.; N, Q, R, W to 57th St.*

★ **\$–\$\$\$\$** 🖪 **Broadway Inn.** In the heart of the Theater District, this Midwestern-friendly B&B welcomes with a charmingly comfy brick-walled reception room with hump-backed sofa, bentwood chairs, fresh flowers, and stocked book shelves that encourage lingering. Impeccably clean neodeco–style rooms with black-lacquer beds are basic but cheerful. An extra \$70 or \$80 gets you a suite with an additional fold-out sofa bed and a kitchenette hidden by closet doors. Single travelers can get their own room for as little as \$89, which very well might be one of the best deals in town. ⊠ *264 W. 46th St., between Broadway and 8th Ave., Midtown West 10036* ☎ *212/997–9200 or 800/826–6300* 🖷 *212/768–2807* ⊕ *www.broadwayinn.com* 🖅 *28 rooms, 12 suites* ⚭ *Some in-room data ports, some kitchenettes, some microwaves, refrigerators, cable TV, concierge, parking (fee), no-smoking rooms* ▱ *AE, D, DC, MC, V* Ⓜ *Subway: 1, 2, 3, 7, 9, N, Q, R, S, W to 42nd St./Times Sq.*

Midtown East

\$\$\$\$ 🖪 **Four Seasons.** Architect I. M. Pei designed this limestone-clad stepped
FodorsChoice spire amid the prime shops of 57th Street. Everything here comes in epic
★ proportions—from the rooms averaging 600 square feet (and *starting* at \$595) to the sky-high Grand Foyer, with French limestone pillars, marble, onyx, and acre upon acre of blond wood. The soundproof guest rooms have 10-foot ceilings, enormous English sycamore walk-in closets, and blond-marble bathrooms with tubs that fill in 60 seconds. If

you really want epic, a night in the one-bedroom penthouse suite may run to $19,000. ⊠ *57 E. 57th St., between Park and Madison Aves., Midtown East 10022* ☎ *212/758–5700 or 800/487–3769* 🖶 *212/758–5711* ⊕ *www.fourseasons.com* 🛏 *300 rooms, 68 suites* 🕭 *Restaurant, room service, in-room data ports, in-room fax, in-room safes, minibars, some microwaves, cable TV, cable TV with movies and video games, in-room DVD players, gym, health club, massage, sauna, spa, steam room, bar, lobby lounge, piano, babysitting, dry cleaning, laundry service, concierge, business services, meeting rooms, car rental, parking (fee), some pets allowed, no-smoking floors* ⊟ *AE, D, DC, MC, V* Ⓜ *Subway: 4, 5, 6, N, Q, R, W to 59th St./Lexington Ave.*

$$$$ 🏨 **Library Hotel.** This handsome landmark building (1900) gets its intellectual inspiration from the nearby New York Public Library. Each of its 10 floors is dedicated to one of the 10 categories of the Dewey Decimal System (such as technology or literature) with modern rooms stocked with art and books relevant to a subtopic (such as medicine or poetry). Neil Armstrong's preference is the astronomy room; a green thumb might choose Room 500.004, the botany room. The property delivers tremendous comfort, and you can unwind in front of the fire in the library or relax in the roof garden. ⊠ *299 Madison Ave., at E. 41st St., Midtown East 10017* ☎ *212/983–4500 or 877/793–7323* 🖶 *212/499–9099* ⊕ *www.libraryhotel.com* 🛏 *60 rooms* 🕭 *Restaurant, room service, in-room data ports, in-room safes, minibars, cable TV with movies, in-room VCRs, massage, bar, 3 lounges, babysitting, dry cleaning, laundry service, concierge, Internet, business services, meeting rooms, parking (fee), no-smoking floors* ⊟ *AE, DC, MC, V* Ⓜ *Subway: 4, 5, 6, 7, S to 42nd St./Grand Central.*

$$$$ 🏨 **New York Palace.** Connected mansions built in the 1880s by railroad baron Henry Villard make up this palatial hotel. The lobby, with its sweeping staircases and arched colonnades fit for royalty, is host to the stunning New American restaurant Istana. The tower provides a choice of glamorous deco-style guest rooms or traditional Empire-style rooms. For terrific views of St. Patrick's Cathedral head to the 7,000-square-foot health club, where TVs with videos and headphones await at every treadmill. ⊠ *455 Madison Ave., at E. 50th St., Midtown East 10022* ☎ *212/888–7000 or 800/697–2522* 🖶 *212/303–6000* ⊕ *www.newyorkpalace.com* 🛏 *808 rooms, 80 suites* 🕭 *2 restaurants, room service, in-room data ports, in-room fax, in-room safes, minibars, some refrigerators, cable TV with movies, health club, massage, spa, 2 bars, babysitting, dry cleaning, laundry service, concierge, business services, meeting rooms, some pets allowed, no-smoking rooms, no-smoking floors* ⊟ *AE, D, DC, MC, V* Ⓜ *Subway: 6 to 51st St./Lexington Ave.; E, V to Lexington–3rd Aves./53rd St.*

★ $$$$ 🏨 **The St. Regis.** A one-of-a-kind New York classic, this 5th Avenue beaux-arts landmark is a hive of activity in its unparalleled public spaces. The King Cole Bar is an institution in itself, with its famous Maxfield Parrish mural. Guest rooms, all serviced by accommodating butlers, are straight out of the American Movie Channel, with high ceilings, crystal chandeliers, silk wall coverings, Louis XVI antiques, and refined amenities like Tiffany silver services. Marble bathrooms with tubs, stall showers, and double sinks are outstanding. ⊠ *2 E. 55th St., at 5th Ave.,*

Midtown East 10022 ☎ *212/753–4500 or 800/325–3589* 🖷 *212/787–3447* ⊕ *www.stregis.com* ➥ *222 rooms, 93 suites* ♿ *Restaurant, room service, in-room data ports, in-room fax, in-room safes, minibars, cable TV, in-room VCRs, gym, health club, hair salon, massage, sauna, spa bar, shops, babysitting, dry cleaning, laundry service, concierge, business services, meeting rooms, parking (fee), no-smoking rooms, no-smoking floors* ▭ *AE, D, DC, MC, V* Ⓜ *Subway: 7 to 5th Ave.; B, D, F, V to 42nd St.*

$$$$ 🏨 **W New York.** This W brought nature to Midtown with calming earth tones and flowing curtains meant to conjure up the wind. Vast floor-to-ceiling windows pour sunlight into the airy lobby, where a fireplace and bar flank a sunken sitting area. Although tiny, the rooms display custom craftsmanship in natural materials, and soothe with feather beds and CD players. In the slate-floor baths, not a sliver of the all-too-familiar polished marble is to be found. Downstairs, a mezzanine dining area makes breakfast a quick buffet affair. The attached Whiskey Blue draws a young, hip, and moneyed crowd. ✉ *541 Lexington Ave., between E. 49th and E. 50th Sts., Midtown East 10022* ☎ *212/755–1200 or 877/946–8357* 🖷 *212/319–8344* ⊕ *www.whotels.com* ➥ *551 rooms, 62 suites* ♿ *Restaurant, snack bar, room service, in-room data ports, in-room fax, in-room safes, minibars, cable TV, health club, massage, spa, steam room, bar, lobby lounge, dry cleaning, laundry facilities, laundry service, concierge, business services, meeting rooms, no-smoking floors* ▭ *AE, D, DC, MC, V* Ⓜ *Subway: 6 to 51st St./Lexington Ave.; E, V to Lexington–3rd Aves./53rd St.*

★ **$$–$$$$** 🏨 **Roger Smith.** The elusive Roger Smith (see if *you* can find out who he is) lends his name to this colorful boutique hotel and adjacent gallery. Riotous murals cover the walls in Lily's, the café. The art-filled rooms are homey and comfortable, and some have stocked bookshelves and fireplaces. An eclectic mix of room service is provided by five local restaurants. You have access to the nearby New York Sports Club ($10 fee). Rates can drop by as much as $75 per night in winter and summer, so ask when booking. ✉ *501 Lexington Ave., between E. 47th and E. 48th Sts., Midtown East 10017* ☎ *212/755–1400 or 800/445–0277* 🖷 *212/758–4061* ⊕ *www.rogersmith.com* ➥ *102 rooms, 28 suites* ♿ *Restaurant, room service, in-room data ports, some kitchenettes, refrigerators, cable TV with movies and video games, massage, bar, babysitting, dry cleaning, laundry service, Internet, meeting rooms, parking (fee), some pets allowed, no-smoking floors* ▭ *AE, D, DC, MC, V* Ⓜ *Subway: 6 to 51st St./Lexington Ave.; E, V to Lexington–3rd Aves./53rd St.*

$–$$$ 🏨 **Pickwick Arms Hotel.** This no-frills but convenient East Side establishment is regularly booked solid by bargain hunters. Privations you endure to save a buck start and end with the Lilliputian size of some rooms, all of which have cheap-looking furnishings. However, some rooms look over the Manhattan skyline, and all are renovated on a regular basis. There's also a rooftop garden. ✉ *230 E. 51st St., between 2nd and 3rd Aves., Midtown East 10022* ☎ *212/355–0300 or 800/742–5945* 🖷 *212/755–5029* ⊕ *www.pickwickarms.com* ➥ *360 rooms, 175 with bath* ♿ *Café, in-room data ports, some refrigerators, cable TV, bar, airport shuttle, parking (fee)* ▭ *AE, DC, MC, V* Ⓜ *Subway: 6 to 51st St./Lexington Ave.; E, V to Lexington–3rd Aves./53rd St.*

Upper East Side

★ **$$$$**   **The Carlyle.** European tradition and Manhattan swank come together at New York's most lovable grand hotel. Everything about this Madison Avenue landmark suggests refinement, from the Mark Hampton–designed rooms with their fine antique furniture and artfully framed Audubons and botanicals to the first-rate service. Cabaret luminaries Barbara Cook and Bobby Short take turns holding court at the clubby Café Carlyle, but the canny Peter Mintun steals the show at Bemelmans Bar, named after the illustrator responsible for the bar's wall murals and the beloved children's book character Madeline. ⊠ *35 E. 76th St., between Madison and Park Aves., Upper East Side 10021* ☎ *212/744–1600* ⊕ *www.thecarlyle.com* ⤳ *145 rooms, 52 suites* ♻ *Restaurant, café, room service, in-room data ports, in-room fax, in-room safes, some in-room hot tubs, kitchenettes, minibars, microwaves, cable TV, in-room VCRs, gym, health club, massage, spa, bar, dry cleaning, laundry service, concierge, business services, meeting room, parking (fee), some pets allowed, no-smoking floors* ▤ *AE, DC, MC, V* Ⓜ *Subway: 6 to 77th St.*

$$$$ **The Lowell.** This old-money refuge was built as an upscale apartment
Fodor'sChoice hotel in the 1920s and still delivers genteel sophistication. Guest rooms,
★   most of which are suites, have all the civilized comforts of home, including stocked bookshelves, luxe bathrooms, and even umbrellas. Thirty-three of the suites have working fireplaces and 11 have private terraces, the better for spying on posh neighboring abodes. A gym suite has its own fitness center, and a garden suite has two beautifully planted terraces. ⊠ *28 E. 63rd St., between Madison and Park Aves., Upper East Side 10021* ☎ *212/838–1400 or 800/221–4444* ☎ *212/319–4230* ⊕ *www.lhw.com* ⤳ *23 rooms, 47 suites* ♻ *2 restaurants, room service, in-room data ports, in-room fax, in-room safes, kitchenettes, minibars, refrigerators, cable TV, in-room VCRs, exercise equipment, health club, massage, bar, babysitting, dry cleaning, laundry service, concierge, Internet, business services, parking (fee), some pets allowed* ▤ *AE, D, DC, MC, V* Ⓜ *Subway: 4, 5, 6, N, R, W to 59th St./Lexington Ave.; F to 63rd St./Lexington Ave.*

$$$$ **The Mark.** A member of the Mandarin Oriental hotel group, the Mark, whose motto is "No jacket, no tie, no attitude," is refreshingly unpretentious considering its luxurious atmosphere. An art-deco marble lobby leads into a clubby bar where even lone women travelers feel comfortable, and to the Mark's restaurant, where afternoon tea is served. Elegant bedrooms have English and Italian furnishings and prints, Frette linens, and deep soaking tubs in the sleek marble bathrooms. Special touches here include hidden pantries with small kitchenettes in many of the rooms, a free shuttle to Wall Street, and free cell phones. ⊠ *25 E. 77th St., at Madison Ave., Upper East Side 10021* ☎ *212/744–4300 or 800/843–6275* ☎ *212/472–5714* ⊕ *www.mandarinoriental.com* ⤳ *122 rooms, 54 suites* ♻ *Restaurant, room service, in-room data ports, in-room fax, in-room safes, some kitchenettes, minibars, cable TV, in-room VCRs, exercise equipment, health club, massage, sauna, steam room, bar, babysitting, dry cleaning, laundry service, concierge, Internet, business services, meeting rooms,* *parking (fee), some pets allowed, no-smoking floors* ☰ *AE, D, DC, MC, V* Ⓜ *Subway: 6 to 77th St.*

$$ 🏨 **The Franklin.** The Upper East Side's hippest, funkiest hotel has a pint-size lobby decorated with black granite, brushed steel, and cherrywood. Most rooms are also tiny (some measure 100 square feet), but what they lack in size they make up for in style: all have custom-built steel furniture, gauzy white canopies over the beds, cedar closets, and CD players. Added bonuses are the generous complimentary breakfast, fresh fruit in the evenings, and 24-hour cappuccino. ✉ *164 E. 87th St., between Lexington and 3rd Aves., Upper East Side 10128* ☎ *212/369–1000 or 877/847–4444* 🖷 *212/894–5220* ⊕ *www.franklinhotel.com* ⤏ *48 rooms* ⎙ *In-room data ports, in-room safes, cable TV, in-room VCRs, lounge, library, dry cleaning, laundry service, no-smoking floors* ☰ *AE, DC, MC, V* Ⓜ *Subway: 4, 5, 6 to 86th St.*

Upper West Side

$$$$ 🏨 **Trump International Hotel and Towers.** Rooms and suites in this expensive, showy hotel resemble mini-apartments: all have fully equipped kitchens with black-granite countertops, entertainment centers with stereos and CD players, and mini-telescopes, which you can use to gaze through the floor-to-ceiling windows. Creamy-beige marble bathrooms are equipped with Jacuzzis and Frette bathrobes, and slippers hang in the closets. Complimentary cellular phones and personalized stationery and business cards are also provided. The restaurant, Jean Georges, is one of the city's finest, and for a price a Jean Georges sous-chef will prepare a meal in your kitchenette. ✉ *1 Central Park W, between W. 59th and W. 60th Sts., Upper West Side 10023* ☎ *212/299–1000 or 888/448–7867* 🖷 *212/299–1023* ⊕ *www.trumpintl.com* ⤏ *37 rooms, 130 suites* ⎙ *Restaurant, café, room service, in-room data ports, in-room fax, in-room safes, in-room hot tubs, kitchenettes, minibars, microwaves, refrigerators, cable TV, in-room DVD/VCR players, in-room VCRs, indoor pool, gym, health club, massage, sauna, spa, steam room, bar, babysitting, dry cleaning, laundry service, concierge, Internet, business services, meeting rooms, parking (fee), no-smoking rooms, no-smoking floors* ☰ *AE, D, DC, MC, V* Ⓜ *Subway: 1, 9, A, B, C, D to 59th St./Columbus Circle.*

$$$–$$$$ 🏨 **Hotel Beacon.** The Upper West Side's best buy is three blocks from Central Park and Lincoln Center, and footsteps from Zabar's gourmet bazaar. All of the generously sized rooms and suites include marble bathrooms, kitchenettes with coffeemakers, pots and pans, stoves, and ironing facilities. Closets are huge, and some of the bathrooms have Hollywood dressing room–style mirrors. High floors have views of Central Park, the Hudson River, or the midtown skyline. ✉ *2130 Broadway, at W. 75th St., Upper West Side 10023* ☎ *212/787–1100 or 800/572–4969* 🖷 *212/787–8119* ⊕ *www.beaconhotel.com* ⤏ *120 rooms, 110 suites* ⎙ *Café, in-room safes, kitchens, kitchenettes, microwaves, refrigerators, cable TV, babysitting, laundry facilities, business services, meeting rooms, parking (fee), no-smoking rooms* ☰ *AE, D, DC, MC, V* Ⓜ *Subway: 1, 2, 3, 9 to 72nd St.*

NIGHTLIFE & THE ARTS

Updated by
John J.
Donohue and
Lynne Arany

There are enough committed club crawlers in Manhattan to support venues for almost every idiosyncratic taste. But keep in mind that when you go is just as important as where you go. These days, night prowlers are more loyal to floating parties, DJs, even party promoters, than they are to addresses. A spot is only hot when it's hopping, and you may find the same party or bar that raged last night completely empty tonight. The other thing to remember is to dress properly, something that is easily accomplished by wearing black and leaving your sneakers at home.

New York has somewhere between 200 and 250 legitimate theaters, and many more ad hoc venues—parks, churches, universities, museums, lofts, galleries, streets, rooftops, and even parking lots. The city also keeps up a revolving door of festivals and special events: summer jazz, one-act-play marathons, international film series, and musical celebrations from the classical to the avant-garde, to name just a few. It is this unrivaled wealth of culture and art that many New Yorkers cite as the reason why they're here.

The Arts

Performing Arts Centers

Fodor's Choice
★

Brooklyn Academy of Music. America's oldest performing arts center opened in 1859 and has a solid reputation for daring and innovative dance, music, opera, and theater productions. Acclaimed international companies are often on the bill. Its annual Next Wave Festival in the fall draws a global audience for its cutting-edge productions. ✉ *30 Lafayette Ave., at Ashland Pl. off Flatbush and Atlantic Aves., Fort Greene* ☎ *718/636–4100* ⊕ *www.bam.org.*

Carnegie Hall. Performances in this world-famous hall are given in the beautifully restored 2,804-seat Isaac Stern Auditorium and the far more intimate Weill Recital Hall, where many young talents make their New York debuts, as well as the new intimate and acoustically superb Judy and Arthur Zankel Hall on the lower level. ✉ *881 7th Ave., at W. 57th St., Midtown West* ☎ *212/247–7800* ⊕ *www.carnegiehall.org* Ⓜ *Subway: N, Q, R, W to 57th St.; B, D, E to 7th Ave.*

City Center. Major dance troupes such as Alvin Ailey and Paul Taylor perform here. You can also catch concert versions of classic American musicals. ✉ *131 W. 55th St., between 6th and 7th Aves., Midtown West* ☎ *212/581–1212* ⊕ *www.citycenter.org* Ⓜ *Subway: N, R, Q, W to 57th St./7th Ave.; F, V to 57th St./6th Ave.*

Lincoln Center. The 16-acre complex houses the Metropolitan Opera, New York Philharmonic, New York City Ballet, New York City Opera, Juilliard School, Lincoln Center Theater, New York Public Library for the Performing Arts, Film Society of Lincoln Center, Chamber Music Society of Lincoln Center, Jazz at Lincoln Center, School of American Ballet, the Vivian Beaumont Theater, the Mitzi E. Newhouse Theater, and the Walter Reade Theater. ✉ *W. 62nd to W. 66th Sts., Broadway to Amsterdam Ave., Upper West Side* ☎ *212/546–2656* ⊕ *www.lincolncenter. org* Ⓜ *Subway: 1, 9 to 66th St./Lincoln Center.*

P.S. 122. The former public school property has served as an incubator for talent like Eric Bogosian, Spalding Gray, Meredith Monk, and Blue Man Group. This scruffy, vibrant East Village venue presents productions in various media that come and go quickly, and they're never boring. ⊠ *150 1st Ave., at E. 9th St., East Village* ☎ *212/477–5288* ⊕ *www.ps122.org* Ⓜ *Subway: 6 to Astor Pl.; F, V to 2nd Ave.*

Ballet

American Ballet Theatre (ABT). The company is renowned for its brilliant renditions of the great 19th-century classics (*Swan Lake, Giselle, The Sleeping Beauty,* and *La Bayadère*), as well as its eclectic contemporary repertoire, including works by all the 20th-century masters such as Balanchine, Tudor, Robbins, and de Mille. The ballet has two New York seasons—eight weeks beginning in early May at its home in the Metropolitan Opera House in Lincoln Center (⇨ **Performing Arts Centers**) and two weeks beginning in late October at City Center (⇨ **Performing Arts Centers**). The two theaters handle ticket orders for the ballet. ☎ *212/477–3030* ⊕ *www.abt.org.*

★ **New York City Ballet.** The winter season, which runs from mid-November through February, includes the beloved annual holiday production of George Balanchine's *The Nutcracker.* The spring season lasts from late April through June. The company continues to stress the works themselves rather than individual performers. NYCB performs in Lincoln Center's **New York State Theater** (⇨ **Performing Arts Centers**) ☎ *212/870–5570* ⊕ *www.nycballet.com.*

Opera

Fodor'sChoice **Metropolitan Opera.** The titan of American opera companies brings the
★ world's leading singers to its massive stage at Lincoln Center's **Metropolitan Opera House** (⇨ **Performing Arts Centers**) ☎ *212/362–6000* ⊕ *www.metopera.org.* from October to mid-April. Under the direction of James Levine, the Met's artistic director and principal conductor, and principal guest conductor Valery Gergiev, the opera orchestra performs with an intensity and quality that rival the world's finest symphony orchestras.

New York City Opera. Although not as widely known as the Met, this opera company is just as vital to the city's operagoers. Under the leadership of artistic director Paul Kellogg, City Opera stages a diverse repertoire, including rarely seen baroque operas such as *Acis and Galatea* and *Rinaldo,* adventurous new works such as *Dead Man Walking,* and beloved classic operas such as *La Bohème* or *Carmen.* Placido Domingo and Beverly Sills began their careers at City Opera. City Opera performs from September through November and in March and April at Lincoln Center's **New York State Theater** (⇨ **Performing Arts Centers**). ☎ *212/870–5570* ⊕ *www.nycballet.com.*

Theater

BROADWAY The monthly **Broadway Theatre Guide,** published by the League of American Theatres and Producers, is available at the **Times Square Visitors Center** (⊠ 1560 Broadway, between W. 46th and W. 47th Sts., Midtown West); it may also be found at hotels around town. The **Broadway Line**

(☎ 888/276–2392 toll-free, 212/302–4111 in CT, NJ, and NY) provides show times, plot summaries, theater addresses, and ticket prices.

Playbill On-Line (⊕ www.playbill.com) is a good resource for both daily news and feature articles on Broadway and off-Broadway theater. **TheaterMania** (⊕ www.theatermania.com) is an excellent online theater source. For plot summaries, cast, and more on off-Broadway shows, go to **SmartTix** (⊕ www.smarttix.com).

The magazines and newspapers with a Downtown orientation, such as *Time Out New York* and the *Village Voice,* are an especially good source of information on what's going on off-off-Broadway and in performance art. Some off-Broadway venues sell tickets through the major agencies, but to obtain tickets to most off-off-Broadway and performance art events, contact the theater directly or **SmartTix** (☎ 212/868–4444).

BEYOND
BROADWAY   The best of New York theater is often found far away from 42nd Street. Off- and off-off-Broadway is where Eric Bogosian, Ann Magnuson, John Leguizamo, Danny Hoch, and Laurie Anderson often make their home. In terms of quality and popularity, productions at many of the best-known off-Broadway theaters rival those seen in the larger houses on Broadway. In fact, some of Broadway's biggest hits had their start off-Broadway.

★ **Manhattan Theatre Club.** These performers present their work in the magnificently restored 650-scat Biltmore Theatre, and, for smaller productions and their famous Writers in Performance series, they occupy two stages in City Center (⇨ **Performing Arts Centers**). ✉ *Biltmore Theatre, 261 W. 47th St., between Broadway and 8th Aves., Midtown West* ☎ *212/581–1212* ⊕ *www.mtc-nyc.org* Ⓜ *Subway: R, W to 49th St.*

New York Theater Workshop. Playwrights such as Paul Rudnick, Tony Kushner, and Claudia Shear produce new work here. Jonathan Larson's musical *Rent* debuted here in 1996 before moving within three months to Broadway's Nederlander Theater. ✉ *79 E. 4th St., between 2nd and 3rd Aves., East Village* ☎ *212/460–5475* ⊕ *www.nytw.org* Ⓜ *Subway: F, V to 2nd Ave.; 6 to Bleecker St.*

Playwrights Horizons. Promising new works are produced here, and the theater has the Pulitzers to prove it—for the plays *Driving Miss Daisy* and *The Heidi Chronicles* and the musical *Sunday in the Park with George.* ✉ *416 W. 42nd St., between 9th and 10th Aves., Midtown West* ☎ *212/ 564–1235* ⊕ *www.playwrightshorizons.org* Ⓜ *Subway: 1, 2, 3, 7, 9, N, Q, R, W to 42nd St./Times Sq.*

Nightlife

Dance Clubs

Arc. Video installations and a mammoth DJ booth that runs the width of the room enhance the vibe at this gallerylike TriBeCa space, which once housed the legendary dance hall Vinyl. Perhaps the no-alcohol policy here draws a more determined gang, but whatever the reason, the crowd is friendly, the vibe is good, and the dancing is among the city's hottest. Expect house music and a great time. ✉ *6 Hubert St., at Hudson St., TriBeCa* ☎ *212/226–9212* Ⓜ *Subway: 1, 9 to Canal St.*

Canal Room. This attractive and intimate club with its polished wood floor, simple white walls, potted palms, and stylish Barcelona chairs is a far cry from its former life as a somewhat worn live-music venue called Shine. The new room has a small stage, and musicians still occasionally perform, but they really just come here to enjoy themselves. Its owners' record-business connections, spectacular speaker system, and DJs who keep the crowds moving have drawn the likes of Backstreet Boy Nick Carter, Mariah Carey, and singer PM Dawn. ⊠ *285 West Broadway, at Canal St., TriBeCa* ☎ *212/941–8100* Ⓜ *Subway: 1, 9 to Canal St.*

FodorsChoice ★ **Club Shelter.** This warehouse-like space is the home to some of the best dancing in the city, which is no surprise, as it takes its name and its low-key attitude from a long-running after-hours party that was once found at the old TriBeCa club Vinyl. ⊠ *20 W. 39th St., between 5th and 6th Aves., Midtown West* ☎ *212/719–4479* Ⓜ *Subway: B, D, F, V to 42nd St.*

★ **Exit.** This extravagant multilevel club has everything from a massive dance floor to an outdoor patio. You'll find A-list DJs spinning for an enthusiastic crowd that can often include a hip-hop star or two. ⊠ *610 W. 56th St., between 11th and 12th Aves., Midtown West* ☎ *212/582–8282* Ⓜ *Subway: 1, 9, A, B, C, D to 59th St.*

Nell's. Nell Campbell (of *Rocky Horror* fame) opened this sophisticated club back in the '80s, and it's still going strong. The tone in the upstairs live-music jazz salon is Victorian; downstairs the DJ spins everything from R&B to reggae. ⊠ *246 W. 14th St., near 8th Ave., Greenwich Village* ☎ *212/675–1567* Ⓜ *Subway: A, C, E to 14th St.; L to 8th Ave.*

Rainbow Room. Heavenly views top the bill of fare at this romantic 65th-floor institution, where the revolving dance floor and 12-piece orchestra ensure high spirits, even on a cloudy night. ⊠ *30 Rockefeller Plaza, between 5th and 6th Aves., Midtown West* ☎ *212/632–5000* Ⓜ *Subway: B, D, F, V to 47th–50th Sts./Rockefeller Center.*

Show. With its blood-red walls, festive heart-shape balloons, and early evening burlesque show, this nightspot aims to bring back the days of the Moulin Rouge. It's popular with a young, energetic crowd, professional basketball players, and wayward pop stars (Britney Spears once did a striptease on stage). ⊠ *135 W. 41st St., between 6th Ave. and Broadway, Midtown West* ☎ *212/278–0988* Ⓜ *Subway: B, D, F, V to 42nd St.*

Sound Factory. A cavernous, super-high-energy dance mecca, this club is open only on Saturday nights, though the action continues through noon on Sunday. ⊠ *618 W. 46th St., between 11th and 12th Aves., Midtown West* ☎ *212/489–0001.*

Jazz Clubs

Arthur's Tavern. Unless there's a festival in town, you won't find any big names jamming here. But you will find live jazz nightly, without a cover charge, amid the dark-wood ambience of the Greenwich Village of old. The acts tend to be bluesier and funkier for the late shows. ⊠ *57 Grove St., between 7th Ave. S and Bleecker St., Greenwich Village* ☎ *212/675–6879* Ⓜ *Subway: 1, 9 to Christopher St.*

★ **Blue Note.** Considered by many to be the jazz capital of the world, the Blue Note could see on an average month Spyro Gyra, Ron Carter, and Jon Hendricks. Expect a steep music charge except on Monday, when record labels promote their artists' new releases for an average ticket price of less than $20. ⊠ *131 W. 3rd St., near 6th Ave., Greenwich Village* ☎ *212/475–8592* Ⓜ *Subway: A, C, E, F, V to W. 4th St.*

Iridium. This cozy club is a sure bet for big-name talent. It has good sight lines, and the sound system was designed with the help of Les Paul, the inventor of the solid-body electric guitar, who takes the stage on Monday night. ⊠ *1650 Broadway, at W. 51st St., Midtown West* ☎ *212/ 582–2121* Ⓜ *Subway: 1, 9 to 50th St.; R, W to 49th St.*

Jazz Standard. This sizable underground room is a reliable spot to hear the top names in the business. As a part of Danny Meyer's Southern-food restaurant Blue Smoke, it's one of the few spots where you can get dry-rubbed ribs to go with your bebop. ⊠ *116 E. 27th St., between Park and Lexington Aves., Murray Hill* ☎ *212/576–2232* Ⓜ *Subway: 6 to 28th St.*

Fodor's Choice **Village Vanguard.** This former Thelonious Monk haunt and prototypi-
★ cal old-world jazz club lives on in a cellar, where you might hear jams from the likes of Wynton Marsalis and James Carter, among others. ⊠*178 7th Ave. S, between W. 11th and Perry Sts., Greenwich Village* ☎ *212/ 255–4037* Ⓜ *Subway: A, C, E to 14th St.; L to 8th Ave.*

Rock Clubs

Arlene Grocery. This rock club on the Lower East Side is known for recruiting new bands with promising futures. Low cover charges (usually only on weekends), a welcoming atmosphere, and punk-rock/heavy-metal karaoke sessions on Monday night set it apart. ⊠ *95 Stanton St., between Ludlow and Orchard Sts., Lower East Side* ☎ *212/358–1633* Ⓜ *Subway: F, V to 2nd Ave.*

Bitter End. This old Village standby has served up its share of talent, Billy Joel, David Crosby, and Dr. John are among the stars who have played here. These days you're more likely to find unknown but talented musicians on their way up. Patrons, mostly seated in front of the stage, rotate with the bands billed each night—blues, country, rock, and jazz all make an appearance here. ⊠ *147 Bleecker St., between Thompson St. and LaGuardia Pl., Greenwich Village* ☎ *212/673–7030* Ⓜ *Subway: A, C, E, F, V to W. 4th St.*

Fodor's Choice **Bowery Ballroom.** This tastefully clean, balconied space is the city's pre-
★ mier midsize concert venue. You can sit at one of the few tables upstairs or stand and dance on the main floor. P. J. Harvey, Shelby Lynne, and Superchunk are the caliber of musicians who perform here. There's a comfortable bar in the basement. ⊠ *6 Delancey St., near the Bowery, Lower East Side* ☎ *212/533–2111* Ⓜ *Subway: F, J, M to Delancey St.*

CBGB & OMFUG. American punk rock and New Wave (the Ramones, Blondie, the Talking Heads) were born in this long, black tunnel of a club. Today expect Shirley Temple of Doom, Xanax 25, and other inventively named performers. **CB's 313 Gallery,** next door at 313 Bowery, attracts a quieter (and older) crowd with mostly acoustic music. ⊠*315 Bowery, at Bleecker St., East Village* ☎ *212/982–4052* Ⓜ *Subway: 6 to Bleecker St.; F, V to Broadway–Lafayette St.*

Irving Plaza. Looking for Joan Osborne, Weezer, or Wilco? You'll find them in this perfect-sized place for general-admission live music. There's a small balcony with a bar and a tiny lounge area. ⊠ *17 Irving Pl., at*

E. 15th St., Gramercy ☎ *212/777–6800* Ⓜ *Subway: 4, 5, 6, L, N, R to 14th St./Union Sq.*

Mercury Lounge. With one of the best sound systems in the city, this small club holds a quiet cachet with bands and industry insiders. One small problem: there's no coat check, and it can get hot in there. ✉ *217 E. Houston St., between Ludlow and Essex Sts., Lower East Side* ☎ *212/ 260–4700* Ⓜ *Subway: F, V to 2nd Ave.*

World Music Venues

Copacabana. The granddaddy of Manhattan dance clubs (it has been open almost continuously since 1940) moved into a massive new space in fall 2002. In typical Copa fashion, little restraint was shown, and the club now hosts music and dancing on three levels. From the disco on the lower level to the main ballroom where the top names in salsa and merengue perform, few other clubs can compare. ✉ *560 W. 34th St., between 10th and 11th Aves., Midtown West* ☎ *212/239–2672* Ⓜ *Subway: A, C, E to 34th St.*

Knitting Factory. This cross-genre venue regularly hosts performers from far and wide. The intimate Old Office space is a great place to catch a Cuban guitarist or an African folk singer. ✉ *74 Leonard St., between Broadway and Church St., TriBeCa* ☎ *212/219–3055* Ⓜ *Subway: 1, 9 to Franklin St.*

SOB's. The initials stand for Sounds of Brazil at *the* place for reggae, Trinidadian carnival, zydeco, African, samba, and especially Latin tunes and salsa rhythms. The decor is à la Tropicana; the favored drink, a caipirinha, a mixture of Brazilian sugarcane liquor and lime. Dinner is served as well. ✉ *204 Varick St., at W. Houston St., SoHo* ☎ *212/243–4940* Ⓜ *Subway: 1, 9 to Houston St.*

Comedy Clubs

Caroline's on Broadway. This high-gloss club presents established names as well as comedians on the edge of stardom. Janeane Garofalo, Bill Bellamy, Colin Quinn, and Gilbert Gottfried have appeared. ✉ *1626 Broadway, between W. 49th and W. 50th Sts., Midtown West* ☎ *212/ 757–4100* Ⓜ *Subway: 1, 9 to 50th St.*

Chicago City Limits. This troupe's been doing improvisational comedy for a long time, and it seldom fails to whip its audiences into a laughing frenzy. Chicago City Limits performs in a renovated movie theater and is very strong on audience participation. At this writing the troupe was leaving this location in search of a new venue. ✉ *1105 1st Ave., at E. 61st St., Upper East Side* ☎ *212/888–5233* Ⓜ *Subway: 4, 5, 6, N, R to 59th St.*

Upright Citizens Brigade Theatre. Sketch comedy, audience-initiated improv, and even classes are available at this venue. ✉ *161 W. 22nd St., between 6th and 7th Aves., Chelsea* ☎ *212/366–9176* Ⓜ *Subway: F, V to 23rd St.*

Cabaret & Performance Spaces

Fodor'sChoice
★

The Carlyle. Bobby Short plays the hotel's discreetly sophisticated Café Carlyle when he's in town, and Barbara Cook and Eartha Kitt also often purr by the piano. Stop by on a Monday night and take in Woody Allen, who swings on the clarinet with his New Orleans Jazz Band. Bemelmans

Bar, with murals by the author of the Madeline books, regularly stars pianist-singers Loston Harris and Peter Mintun. ⊠ *35 E. 76th St., between Madison and Park Aves., Upper East Side* ☎ *212/744–1600* Ⓜ *Subway: 6 to 77th St.*

★ **Joe's Pub.** Wood paneling, red-velvet walls, and comfy sofas make a lush setting for top-notch performers and the A-list celebrities who come to see them. There's not a bad seat in the house, but if you want to sit, arrive a half hour early and enjoy the finger foods. ⊠ *425 Lafayette St., between E. 4th St. and Astor Pl., East Village* ☎ *212/539–8770* Ⓜ *Subway: 6 to Astor Pl.*

Oak Room. One of the great classic cabarets, the Oak Room is formal (jacket and tie for men). You might find the hopelessly romantic singer Andrea Marcovicci, among other top-notch performers, crooning here. ⊠ *Algonquin Hotel, 59 W. 44th St., near 6th Ave., Midtown West* ☎ *212/840–6800* Ⓜ *Subway: B, D, F, V to 42nd St.*

Bars

SOHO & TRIBECA **Bar 89.** This bilevel lounge has the most entertaining bathrooms in town; the high-tech doors of unoccupied stalls are transparent, and (ideally) turn opaque as you lock the door. Like the neighborhood, the crowd at the perennially popular spot is hip and moneyed, but the help manages to be remarkably friendly. ⊠ *89 Mercer St., between Spring and Broome Sts., SoHo* ☎ *212/274–0989* Ⓜ *Subway: C, E to Spring St.*

Lush. One of TriBeCa's hottest lounges, this modern-looking space has a cool banquette running the length of its loftlike room, as well as a couple of round chambers where celebrities retire. ⊠ *110 Duane St., between Church St. and Broadway, TriBeCa* ☎ *212/766–1275* Ⓜ *Subway: A, C to Chambers St.*

★ **MercBar.** A chic European crowd and New Yorkers in the know come to this dark, nondescript bar for the wonderful martinis. Its street number is barely visible—look for the French doors, which stay open in summer. ⊠ *151 Mercer St., between Prince and W. Houston Sts., SoHo* ☎ *212/966–2727* Ⓜ *Subway: R, W to Prince St.*

Naked Lunch. Dazzlingly popular, this William Burroughs–inspired, earth-tone SoHo haunt is frequented by celebrities and other beautiful people. On weekends the crowd dances late into the night. ⊠ *17 Thompson St., at Grand St., SoHo* ☎ *212/343–0828* Ⓜ *Subway: C, E to Spring St.*

Raoul's. One of the first trendy spots in SoHo, this French restaurant has yet to lose its touch. Expect a chic bar scene filled with model-pretty men and women. ⊠ *180 Prince St., between Sullivan and Thompson Sts., SoHo* ☎ *212/966–3518* Ⓜ *Subway: C, E to Spring St.*

CHELSEA & **Automatic Slim's.** A cramped, sweaty, eternally popular joint where the
GREENWICH patrons often end up dancing on the bar to loud music, Slim's also
VILLAGE has amazingly good food. ⊠ *733 Washington St., at Bank St., Greenwich Village* ☎ *212/645–8660* Ⓜ *Subway: 1, 9 to Christopher St./Sheridan Square.*

★ **Chumley's.** There's no sign to help you find this place—they took it down during Chumley's speakeasy days—but when you reach the corner of Bedford and Barrow streets you're very close (just head a little north on Barrow, and use the doorway on the east side of the street). A fireplace warms the relaxed dining room, where the burgers are hearty and the clientele collegiate. ✉ *86 Bedford St., at Barrow St., Greenwich Village* ☎ *212/675–4449* Ⓜ *Subway: 1, 9 to Christopher St./Sheridan Square.*

Hogs & Heifers. This raucous place is all about the saucy barkeeps berating men over their megaphones and baiting women to get up on the bar and dance (and add their bras to the collection on the wall). Celebrities drop in to get their names in the gossip columns. ✉ *859 Washington St., at W. 13th St., Greenwich Village* ☎ *212/929–0655* Ⓜ *Subway: A, C, E to 14th St.; L to 8th Ave.*

White Horse Tavern. According to (dubious) New York legend, Dylan Thomas drank himself to death in 1953 at this historic tavern founded in 1889. From April through October there's sidewalk seating. ✉ *567 Hudson St., at W. 11th St., Greenwich Village* ☎ *212/989–3956* Ⓜ *Subway: 1, 9 to Christopher St./Sheridan Square.*

LOWER EAST SIDE & EAST VILLAGE THROUGH EAST 20S

Beauty Bar. Grab a seat in a barber chair or under a hair dryer at this former parlor. During happy hour, if the manicurist is around, you can get your nails done. There's no room to dance, but a DJ spins funky tunes on weekends. ✉ *231 E. 14th St., between 2nd and 3rd Aves., East Village* ☎ *212/539–1389* Ⓜ *Subway: 4, 5, 6, L, N, R to 14th St./Union Sq.*

★ **Fez.** Tucked away in the popular Time Café, this Moroccan-theme casbah hosts nightly events, including drag and comedy shows, readings, and jazz and pop music (make reservations in advance for big-name bands). ✉ *380 Lafayette St., between E. 4th and Great Jones Sts., East Village* ☎ *212/533–2680* Ⓜ *Subway: 6 to Astor Pl.*

Kush. A Moroccan-themed hideout in a neighborhood full of trendy lounges, Kush stands out. DJs spin a mix of world-inspired beats nightly. Belly dancers make appearances, and most remarkably, you can smoke legally here—Kush even has hookahs. ✉ *183 Orchard St., between Houston and Stanton Sts., Lower East Side* ☎ *212/677–7328* Ⓜ *Subway: F, V to 2nd Ave.*

★ **Ludlow Bar.** This bar is one of the main draws on the main drag of the Lower East Side. The nearly subterranean space (you descend four steps at the entrance) has a pool table and a tiny dance floor. The DJs spin everything from house music to R&B to Brazilian soul. ✉ *165 Ludlow St., between E. Houston and Stanton Sts., Lower East Side* ☎ *212/353–0536* Ⓜ *Subway: F, V to 2nd Ave.*

McSorley's Old Ale House. One of New York's oldest saloons (they claim to have opened in 1854) and immortalized by *New Yorker* writer Joseph Mitchell, this is a must-see for beer-loving first-timers to Gotham, even if only two kinds of brew are served: McSorley's light and McSorley's dark. Go on a weekday or go early. The line on Friday and Saturday often stretches down the block. ✉ *15 E. 7th St., between 2nd and 3rd Aves., East Village* ☎ *212/473–9148* Ⓜ *Subway: 6 to Astor Pl.*

Rehab. Every night from Wednesday to Saturday Time Café transforms itself (hot new furniture, hot new sound system, and hot new patrons) into an upscale lounge where some of the drinks are served in syringes. ✉ *380 Lafayette St., between E. 4th and Great Jones Sts., East Village* ☎ *212/475–7878* Ⓜ *Subway: 6 to Astor Pl.*

Remote. The tables here have science-fiction-movie video consoles on them, and you control the cameras that scan the room. For a technology that's designed to work over long distances, the effect, strangely enough, is to bring people closer together. Perhaps there are just more show-offs in New York City than elsewhere. It might be just a novelty, but it's a fun one. ✉ *327 Bowery, at 2nd St., East Village* ☎ *212/228–0228* Ⓜ *Subway: 6 to Bleecker St.*

Telephone Bar. Imported English telephone booths and a polite, handsome crowd mark this pub, which has great tap brews and killer mashed potatoes. ✉ *149 2nd Ave., between E. 9th and E. 10th Sts., East Village* ☎ *212/529–5000* Ⓜ *Subway: 6 to Astor Pl.*

Temple Bar. Romantic and upscale, this unmarked haunt is famous for its martinis and is a treat at any price. Look for the painted iguana skeleton on the facade, and walk past the slim bar to the back where in near-total darkness you can lounge on a plush banquette surrounded by velvet drapes. ✉ *332 Lafayette St., between Bleecker and E. Houston Sts., East Village* ☎ *212/925–4242* Ⓜ *Subway: 6 to Bleecker St.; F, V to Broadway–Lafayette St.*

MIDTOWN & THE THEATER DISTRICT

Algonquin Hotel Lounge. This venerable hotel bar plays up its heritage as the site of the fabled literary Algonquin Roundtable. The clubby, oak-paneled lobby and overstuffed easy chairs encourage lolling over cocktails and conversation. ✉ *59 W. 44th St., between 5th and 6th Aves., Midtown West* ☎ *212/840–6800* Ⓜ *Subway: B, D, F, Q to 42nd St.*

Fodor's Choice
★

Campbell Apartment. One of Manhattan's more beautiful rooms, this restored space inside Grand Central Terminal dates to the 1930s, when it was the private office of an executive named John W. Campbell. He knew how to live, and you can enjoy his good taste from an overstuffed chair. ✉ *15 Vanderbilt Ave., at E. 41st St., Midtown East* ☎ *212/953–0409* Ⓜ *Subway: 4, 5, 6, 7, S to 42nd St./Grand Central.*

Divine Bar. Zebra-stripe bar chairs downstairs and cozy velvet couches upstairs make this bar unusually chic for Midtown. There's a selection of tapas, wines, and beers, but no hard liquor is served. Wine samplers, known as flights, are organized by country and varietal. The wine list is updated each quarter and includes such hard-to-come-by bottles as those produced by Robert Mondavi's Opus One label. ✉ *244 E. 51st St., between 2nd and 3rd Aves., Midtown East* ☎ *212/319–9463* Ⓜ *Subway: 6 to 51st St.*

King Cole Bar. A famed Maxfield Parrish mural is a welcome sight at this classic, gorgeous midtown meeting place, which happens to be the birthplace of the Bloody Mary. ✉ *St. Regis Hotel, 2 E. 55th St., near 5th Ave., Midtown East* ☎ *212/753–4500* Ⓜ *Subway: E, V to 53rd St.*

Monkey Bar. Once a fabled spot where the likes of Tennessee Williams and hard-living actress Tallulah Bankhead gathered, this lounge was restored in the '90s. Despite the monkey decor, there's very little barbarism in the mannered banker types who shoot back scotch here. ✉ *60 E. 54th St., between Park and Madison Aves., Midtown East* ☎ *212/838–2600* Ⓜ *Subway: E, V to 53rd St.*

Oak Bar. Bedecked with plush leather chairs and oak walls, this old favorite continues to age well. The three Everett Shinn murals of early-20th-century city life were restored in 2001. Its great location draws sophisticates, shoppers, businesspeople, tourists in the know, and stars.

✉ *Plaza Hotel, 768 5th Ave., at W. 59th St., Midtown West* ☎ *212/ 759–3000* Ⓜ *Subway: N, R, W to 5th Ave.*

★ **Royalton.** Philippe Starck's modernistic hotel has two places to drink—the large lobby bar furnished with armchairs and chaise longues and, specifically for vodka and champagne, the banquette-lined Round Bar in a separate, circular room to your right as you enter. The entrance to the hotel is hidden (look for the curved silver railings). ✉ *44 W. 44th St., between 5th and 6th Aves., Midtown West* ☎ *212/869–4400* Ⓜ *Subway: B, D, F, V to 42nd St.*

Gay & Lesbian Bars

MEN **g lounge.** A huge circular bar and two airy, relaxed rooms lined with leather settees pack in the gays at this Chelsea favorite. ✉ *223 W. 19th St., between 7th and 8th Aves., Chelsea* ☎ *212/929–1085* Ⓜ *Subway: C, E to 23rd St.*

The Monster. A long-standing Village contender, the Monster has a piano bar upstairs and a disco downstairs that continue to draw a busy blend of ages, races, and sexes. ✉ *80 Grove St., between W. 4th St. and 7th Ave. S, Greenwich Village* ☎ *212/924–3558.*

WOMEN **Henrietta Hudson.** Two rooms, a pool table, and party nights attract young professionals, out-of-towners, and longtime regulars to this laid-back bar. ✉ *438 Hudson St., at Morton St., Greenwich Village* ☎ *212/924– 3347* Ⓜ *Subway: 1, 9 to Christopher St.*

Meow Mix. The East Village's only lesbian bar hosts live music, literary readings, cheap drinks, and the cutest girls in town. The crowd's young and outrageous, especially those that come for Gloss, on Thursday. ✉ *269 E. Houston St., at Suffolk St., East Village* ☎ *212/254–0688* Ⓜ *Subway: F, V to 2nd Ave.*

SHOPPING

Updated by Jennifer Paull

True to its nature, New York shops on a grand scale, from the glossy couture houses along Madison Avenue to the quirky spots downtown. No matter which threshold you cross, shopping is an event. The foremost American and international designers stake their flagship stores here; meanwhile, small neighborhood shops guarantee a reservoir of both the down-to-earth and the unexpected. One of Manhattan's biggest shopping lures is the bargain—a temptation fueled by Century 21, H&M, and other discount divas. Hawkers of not-so-real Rolex watches and Kate Spade bags are stationed at street corners, and Canal Street is lined with counterfeit Gucci logos and Burberry plaid. Malls are not the New York shopper's natural habitat, so save the chain stores for home and seek out the shops that are unique to New York, or at least unique to the world's shopping capitals.

Once an abandoned warehouse district, then lined with artists' studios and galleries, the cobbled streets of **SoHo** are now packed with high-rent boutiques, national chains, big fashion guns, and secondary-line designer outposts.

Fodor'sChoice ★ A cache of stylish shops selling clothing, handbags, shoes, and jewelry will start your sartorial engines running in **NoLita,** shorthand for "North of *Little Italy*." Stores in this crowded weekend-shopping destination downtown remain mostly one-of-a-kind.

The spirit of "Have I got a bargain for you!" still fills narrow Orchard Street, the center of the **Lower East Side**. It's crammed with tiny, no-non-sense clothing and lingerie stores and open stalls; some, however, are giving way to edgy boutiques. Note that many Orchard Street stores are closed on Saturday in observance of the Jewish Sabbath. In the **East Village**, to the north, East 7th and East 9th streets have diverse, offbeat specialty stops, kitsch, and some great vintage-clothing boutiques.

In the **Flatiron District**, stores on Fifth Avenue south of 23rd Street and on the streets fanning east and west are a mix of the hip and the hard-core. Broadway has a smattering of stores dear to New Yorkers' hearts. In the teens on 6th Avenue is a cluster of superstores, and several blocks west, between 10th and 11th avenues, a few intrepid retailers took root amid the flourishing **Chelsea** art galleries. Farther south, the **Meatpacking District** has become chic.

Glamazons Louis Vuitton, Yves Saint Laurent, and Christian Dior are surrounded by big-name art galleries and other swank flagships on **57th Street** near 5th Avenue. The block isn't limited to top-echelon shopping, however; a **NikeTown** sits cheek by jowl with the couture houses.

Fifth Avenue from Rockefeller Center to Central Park South still wavers between the money-is-no-object crowd, like Versace, Prada, and Gucci, and an influx of more accessible stores, such as Swedish retailer H&M. The perennial favorites will eat up a lot of shoe leather: Saks Fifth Avenue, Cartier jewelers, Salvatore Ferragamo, Takashimaya, Henri Bendel, Tiffany and Bulgari jewelers, and Bergdorf Goodman.

Fodor'sChoice ★ **Madison Avenue** from East 57th to about East 79th streets can satisfy almost any couture craving with Italian and French houses, boutiques, and full-fledged department store Barneys. A couple of marvelous book-stores, several outstanding antiques dealers, and numerous art galleries are here as well.

Department Stores

★ **Barneys New York.** Barneys continues to provide fashionistas with irre-sistible objects of desire at its Uptown flagship store. The extensive menswear selection has a handful of edgier designers, and the women's department showcases cachet designers of all stripes. ⊠ *660 Madison Ave., between E. 60th and E. 61st Sts., Upper East Side* ☎ *212/826–8900* Ⓜ *Subway: N, R, W, 4, 5, 6 to 59th St./Lexington Ave.*

★ **Bergdorf Goodman.** Good taste reigns in an elegant and understated set-ting, but remember that elegant doesn't necessarily mean sedate. Bergdorf's carries some brilliant couture and designer lines. Also notable are the basement Level of Beauty, the home department, and the menswear store across the street. ⊠ *754 5th Ave., between W. 57th and W. 58th Sts., Midtown West* ⊠ *Men's store* ⊠ *745 5th Ave., at 58th St., Midtown East* ☎ *212/753–7300* Ⓜ *Subway: N, R, W to 5th Ave./59th St.*

Bloomingdale's. The main floor is a stupefying maze of cosmetic counters, mirrors, and black walls. Get past this to find some good buys on dependable designers, bedding, and housewares. ✉ *1000 3rd Ave., main entrance at E. 59th St. and Lexington Ave., Midtown East* ☎ *212/ 705–2000* Ⓜ *Subway: N, R, W, 4, 5, 6 to 59th St./Lexington Ave.*

Century 21. For many New Yorkers this is the mother lode of discount shopping. Four large floors are crammed with everything from J. P. Tod's driving moccasins to Ralph Lauren bedding. Join the throngs of bargain hunters scouring the full floor of women's designer clothing, the men's merchandise, the collection of name-brand luggage, or the lingerie. ✉ *22 Cortlandt St., between Broadway and Church St., Lower Manhattan* ☎ *212/227–9092* Ⓜ *Subway: R, W to Cortlandt St.*

Lord & Taylor. Comfortably conservative and never overwhelming, Lord & Taylor is a stronghold of classic American designer clothes and casual wear. ✉ *424 5th Ave., between W. 38th and W. 39th Sts., Midtown West* ☎ *212/391–3344* Ⓜ *Subway: B, D, F, N, Q, R, V, W to 34th St./Herald Sq.*

Macy's. Macy's headquarters store claims to be the largest retail store in America; expect to lose your bearings at least once. Fashion-wise, there's a concentration on the mainstream rather than the luxe. ✉ *Herald Sq., 151 W. 34th St., between 6th and 7th Aves., Midtown West* ☎ *212/695– 4400* Ⓜ *Subway: B, D, F, N, Q, R, V, W to 34th St./Herald Sq.*

★ **Pearl River Mart.** The ground floor devotes plenty of space to clothing and some housewares. A waterfall guides you downstairs for a motley assortment of slippers, paper lanterns, Buddha figures, and more furnishings. ✉ *477 Broadway, between Broome and Grand Sts., SoHo* ☎ *212/431–4770* Ⓜ *Subway: N, R, Q, W to Canal St.*

Saks Fifth Avenue. A fashion-only department store, Saks sells an astonishing array of apparel. The choice of American and European designers is impressive without being esoteric, and the footwear collections are gratifyingly broad. ✉ *611 5th Ave., between E. 49th and E. 50th Sts., Midtown East* ☎ *212/753–4000* Ⓜ *Subway: E, V to 5th Ave./53rd St.*

Fodor'sChoice **Takashimaya New York.** This pristine branch of Japan's largest department
★ store carries stylish accessories and fine household items, all of which reflect a combination of Eastern and Western designs. In the Tea Box downstairs, you can have a *bento* box lunch in the serene, softly lighted tearoom or stock up on green tea. The florist-cum-front-window-display provides a refreshing mini botanical garden. ✉ *693 5th Ave., between E. 54th and E. 55th Sts., Midtown East* ☎ *212/350–0100* Ⓜ *Subway: E, V to 5th Ave./53rd St.*

Specialty Stores

Antiques

Chelsea Antiques Building. With a full 12 floors of antiques and collectibles here, the options include finds like antique books, vintage Georg Jensen silver, or lunch boxes. ✉ *108–110 W. 25th St., between 6th and 7th Aves., Chelsea* ☎ *212/929–0909* Ⓜ *Subway: F, V, 1, 9 to 23rd St.*

Florian Papp. The shine of gilt lures casual customers in, but this store has an unassailed reputation among knowledgeable collectors. ✉ *962*

Madison Ave., between E. 75th and E. 76th Sts., Upper East Side ☎ *212/288–6770* Ⓜ *Subway: 6 to 77th St.*

Israel Sack Inc. This is widely considered one of the best places in the country for 17th-, 18th-, and early-19th-century American furniture. ✉ *730 5th Ave., between W. 56th and W. 57th Sts., Midtown West* ☎ *212/ 399–6562* Ⓜ *Subway: F, N, R, Q, W to 57th St.*

Leigh Keno American Antiques. Twins Leigh and Leslie Keno have a good eye and an interesting inventory; gaze up at a tall case clock or down at the delicate legs of a tea table. It's best to make an appointment. ✉ *127 E. 69th St., between Park and Lexington Aves., Upper East Side* ☎ *212/ 734–2381* Ⓜ *Subway: 6 to 77th St.*

Leo Kaplan Ltd. The impeccable items here include Art Nouveau glass and pottery, porcelain from 18th-century England, antique and modern paperweights, and Russian artwork. ✉ *114 E. 57th St., between Park and Lexington Aves., Upper East Side* ☎ *212/249–6766* Ⓜ *Subway: N, R, W, 4, 5, 6 to 59th St./Lexington Ave.*

Manhattan Art & Antiques Center. Art Nouveau perfume bottles and samovars, samurai swords, pewter pitchers, and more fill 100-plus galleries. ✉ *1050 2nd Ave., between E. 55th and E. 56th Sts., Midtown East* ☎ *212/355–4400* Ⓜ *Subway: N, R, W, 4, 5, 6 to 59th St./Lexington Ave.*

Beauty

FACE Stockholm. Besides the pretty pastels and neutrals, FACE carries some brazenly colored nail polish, juicy red glosses, and little pots of jewel-tone glitter. ✉ *110 Prince St., at Greene St., SoHo* ☎ *212/966–9110* Ⓜ *Subway: R, W to Prince St.* ✉ *1263 Madison Ave., between E. 90th and E. 91st Sts., Upper East Side* ☎ *212/987–1411* Ⓜ *Subway: 6 to 96th St.* ✉ *226 Columbus Ave., between W. 70th and W. 71st Sts., Upper West Side* ☎ *212/769–1420* Ⓜ *Subway: 1, 2, 3, 9 to 72nd St.*

Jo Malone. Unisex scents like lime blossom and vetiver can be worn alone or, in the Malone style, layered. ✉ *949 Broadway, at 5th Ave., Flatiron District* ☎ *212/673–2220* Ⓜ *Subway: R, W to 23rd St.*

Fodor'sChoice

★ **Kiehl's Since 1851.** At this favored haunt of top models and stylists, white-smocked assistants can advise you on the relative merits of the incredibly effective and somewhat expensive skin lotions and hair potions, all packaged in disarmingly simple bottles. ✉ *105 3rd Ave., at E. 13th St., East Village* ☎ *212/677–3171* Ⓜ *Subway: 4, 5, 6, L, N, R, Q, W to 14th St./Union Square.*

M.A.C. Fashion hounds pile into these boutiques for the basics and the far-out. Salespeople can offer expert advice—many of them also work as professional makeup artists. ✉ *113 Spring St., between Mercer and Greene Sts., SoHo* ☎ *212/334–4641* Ⓜ *Subway: C, E to Spring St.* ✉ *14 Christopher St., between 6th and 7th Aves., Greenwich Village* ☎ *212/ 243–4150* Ⓜ *Subway: 1, 9 to Christopher St./Sheridan Sq.* ✉ *1 E. 22nd St., between 5th Ave. and Broadway, Flatiron District* ☎ *212/677– 6611* Ⓜ *Subway: F, V, R, W to 23rd St.*

Books, CDs & Records

BOOKS **Crawford Doyle Booksellers.** Peruse a thoughtful selection of fiction, non-
★ fiction, and biographies, plus some rare books here. ✉ *1082 Madison*

Ave., between E. 81st and E. 82nd Sts., Upper East Side ☎ 212/288–6300 Ⓜ Subway: 4, 5, 6 to 86th St.

Rizzoli. A marble entrance and oak paneling create a posh setting for books and magazines on art, architecture, dance, design, photography, and travel. ✉ 31 W. 57th St., between 5th and 6th Aves., Midtown West ☎ 212/759–2424 Ⓜ Subway: F, N, R, Q, W to 57th St.

★ **St. Mark's Bookshop.** Extending far beyond the New York Times best-seller list, this store's New Titles section might have a study of post-modernism next to the latest Nick Hornby. Cultural and critical theory books are right up front. ✉ 31 3rd Ave., at 9th St., East Village ☎ 212/260–7853 Ⓜ Subway: 6 to Astor Pl.

Shakespeare & Co. Booksellers. The stock here represents what's happening in just about every field of publishing today. ✉ 939 Lexington Ave., between E. 68th and E. 69th Sts., Upper East Side ☎ 212/570–0201 Ⓜ Subway: 6 to 68th St./Hunter College ✉ 137 E. 23rd St., at Lexington Ave., Gramercy ☎ 212/505–2021 Ⓜ Subway: 6 to 23rd St. ✉ 716 Broadway, at Washington Pl., Greenwich Village ☎ 212/529–1330 Ⓜ Subway: R, W to 8th St. ✉ 1 Whitehall St., at Beaver St., Lower Manhattan ☎ 212/742–7025 Ⓜ Subway: 4, 5 to Bowling Green.

The Strand. The Broadway branch proudly claims to have "8 miles of books"; craning your neck among the tall-as-trees stacks will likely net you something from the mix of new and old. ✉ 828 Broadway, at E. 12th St., East Village ☎ 212/473–1452 Ⓜ Subway: L, N, Q, R, W, 4, 5, 6 to 14th St./Union Sq. ✉ 95 Fulton St., between Gold and William Sts., Lower Manhattan ☎ 212/732–6070 Ⓜ Subway: A, C, J, M, Z, 1, 2, 4, 5 to Fulton St./Broadway–Nassau.

Three Lives & Co. Three Lives has one of the city's best book selections, highlighting the latest literary fiction and serious nonfiction, classics, quirky gift books, and gorgeously illustrated tomes. ✉ 154 W. 10th St., at Waverly Pl., Greenwich Village ☎ 212/741–2069 Ⓜ Subway: 1, 9 to Christopher St./Sheridan Sq.

CAMERAS & ELECTRONICS **Apple Store SoHo.** A former post office now displays the darlings of the e-mail set. Carve out some elbow room and try out the latest in Power-Books, iMacs, digital moviemaking, and more. ✉103 Prince St., at Greene St., SoHo ☎ 212/226–3126 Ⓜ Subway: R, W to Prince St.

B & H Photo Video and Pro Audio. Plunge into the excellent selection of imaging, audio, video, and lighting equipment. Low prices, good customer service, and a liberal returns policy make this a favorite with pros and amateurs alike. ✉ 420 9th Ave., between W. 33rd and W. 34th Sts., Midtown West ☎ 212/444–5000 Ⓜ Subway: A, C, E, 1, 2, 3 to 34th St./Penn Station.

CDS, TAPES & RECORDS **Bleecker Bob's Golden Oldies Record Shop.** The staff sells punk, new wave, and reggae, plus good old rock on vinyl until the wee hours. ✉ 118 W. 3rd St., at MacDougal St., Greenwich Village ☎ 212/475–9677 Ⓜ Subway: A, C, E, F, V to W. 4th St./Washington Sq.

Gryphon Record Shop. One of the city's best rare-record stores, it stocks some 90,000 out-of-print and rare LPs. ✉ 233 W. 72nd St., between Broadway and West End Ave., Upper West Side ☎ 212/874–1588 Ⓜ Subway: 1, 2, 3, 9 to 72nd St.

Kim's Video & Music. With its top-20 list a mix of electronica, jazz, lounge, and experimental, Kim's crystallizes the downtown music scene. ⊠ *6 St. Marks Pl., between 2nd and 3rd Aves., East Village* ☎ *212/598–9985* Ⓜ *Subway: 6 to Astor Pl.* ⊠ *144 Bleecker St., between Thompson St. and LaGuardia Pl., Greenwich Village* Ⓜ *Subway: A, C, E, F, V to W. 4th St./Washington Sq.* ☎ *212/260–1010* ⊠ *2906 Broadway, between W. 113th and W. 114th Sts., Morningside Heights* ☎ *212/864–5321* Ⓜ *Subway: 1, 9 to 116th St.*

★ **Other Music.** This spot carries hard-to-find albums on CD and vinyl, from Japanese remixes to French free jazz to American roots music. ⊠ *15 E. 4th St., between Lafayette St. and Broadway, East Village* ☎ *212/477–8150* Ⓜ *Subway: 6 to Astor Pl.*

Clothing

CHILDREN'S **Bu and the Duck.** Clothes for the young in an old setting set this infants'
CLOTHING and children's clothing shop apart from the rest. Owner Susan Lane designs the shop's complete line of clothing and accessories. ⊠ *106 Franklin St., at Church St., TriBeCa* ☎ *212/431–9226* Ⓜ *Subway: 1, 9 to Franklin St.*

Calypso Enfant et Bébé. Sailor-stripe tops, polka-dot PJs, lovely party dresses . . . you may find yourself dressing vicariously through your children. ⊠ *426 Broome St., between Lafayette and Crosby Sts., NoLita* ☎ *212/966–3234* Ⓜ *Subway: 6 to Spring St.*

Space Kiddets. The funky (Elvis-print rompers) mixes with the tried-and-true (patterned flannel PJs) at this casual, trendsetting store. ⊠ *46 E. 21st St., between Broadway and Park Ave., Flatiron District* ☎ *212/420–9878* Ⓜ *Subway: 6 to 23rd St.*

DISCOUNT **Loehmann's.** Label searchers can turn up $40 Polo/Ralph Lauren chinos
CLOTHING and Donna Karan and Yves Saint Laurent suits in the men's department here on a regular basis. ⊠ *101 7th Ave., at W. 16th St., Chelsea* ☎ *212/352–0856* Ⓜ *Subway: 1, 2, 3, 9 to 14th St.*

Syms. There are some excellent buys to be had on designer suits and separates. Men can flip through racks of Bill Blass and Cerruti, and women can uncover Calvin Klein and Versus Versace without even trying. ⊠ *400 Park Ave., at E. 54th St., Midtown East* ☎ *212/317–8200* Ⓜ *Subway: 6 to 51st St./Lexington Ave.; E, V to Lexington–3rd Aves./53rd St.* ⊠ *42 Trinity Pl., at Rector St., Lower Manhattan* ☎ *212/797–1199* Ⓜ *Subway: R, W to Rector St.*

MEN'S & **Brooks Brothers.** The clothes at this classic American haberdasher are,
WOMEN'S as ever, traditional, comfortable, and fairly priced. A modernizing trend
CLOTHING has resulted not only in slightly modified styles, but also in a foray into digital tailoring. ⊠ *666 5th Ave., at W. 53rd St., Midtown West* ☎ *212/261–9440* Ⓜ *Subway: E, V to 5th Ave./53rd St.* ⊠ *346 Madison Ave., at E. 44th St., Midtown East* ☎ *212/682–8800* Ⓜ *Subway: S, 4, 5, 6, 7 to 42nd St./Grand Central* ⊠ *1 Church St., at Liberty St., Lower Manhattan* ☎ *212/267–2400* Ⓜ *Subway: R, W to Cortlandt St.*

Burberry. The signature plaid is hardly square these days, as bikinis, leather pants, and messenger-style bags join the traditional gabardine trench coats. ⊠ *9 E. 57th St., between 5th and Madison Aves., Midtown West* ☎ *212/407–7100* Ⓜ *Subway: N, R, W to 5th Ave./59th St.* ⊠ *131 Spring St.,* *between Greene and Wooster Sts., SoHo* ☎ *212/925–9300* Ⓜ *Subway: R, W to Prince St.*

Club Monaco. This chain strikes the balance between manageable prices, neutral palettes, and mild designer knockoffs. ⊠ *121 Prince St., between Wooster and Greene Sts., SoHo* ☎ *212/533–8930* ⊠ *160 5th Ave., at W. 21st St., Flatiron District* ☎ *212/352–0936* Ⓜ *Subway: L, N, Q, R, W, 4, 5, 6 to 14th St./Union Sq.* ⊠ *8 W. 57th St., between 5th and 6th Aves., Midtown West* ☎ *212/459–9863* ⊠ *520 Broadway, between Broome and Spring Sts., SoHo* ☎ *212/941–1511* Ⓜ *Subway: F, V to Broadway–Lafayette St.*

DKNY. Not only does DKNY embrace the lifestyle store concept, but it's a lifestyle with a relatively short attention span. Cocktail-party ensembles, chunky-knit sweaters, and knockaround denim vie for notice; the "pure" line is reserved for all-natural fibers. ⊠ *655 Madison Ave., at E. 60th St., Upper East Side* ☎ *212/223–3569* Ⓜ *Subway: N, R, W, 4, 5, 6 to 59th St./Lexington Ave.* ⊠ *420 West Broadway, between Prince and Spring Sts., SoHo* ☎ *646/613–1100* Ⓜ *Subway: C, E to Spring St.*

Dolce & Gabbana. It's easy to feel like an Italian movie star amid these extravagant clothes. Pinstripes are a favorite. ⊠ *825 Madison Ave., between E. 68th and E. 69th Sts., Upper East Side* ☎ *212/249–4100* Ⓜ *Subway: 6 to 68th St./Hunter College.*

Donna Karan. Collections may vary from raw-edged to refined, but the luxurious materials remain a constant. Cashmere jersey, silk, and deerskin are drawn into carefully un-precious pieces. ⊠ *819 Madison Ave., between E. 68th and E. 69th Sts., Upper East Side* ☎ *212/861–1001* Ⓜ *Subway: 6 to 68th St./Hunter College.*

Gianni Versace. The five-story flagship store, in a restored turn-of-the-20th-century landmark building on 5th Avenue, hums with colored neon lights. Although the sometimes outrageous designs and colors of Versace clothes might not be to everyone's taste, they're never boring. ⊠ *647 5th St., near E. 51st St., Midtown East* ☎ *212/317–0224* Ⓜ *Subway: E, V to 5th Ave./53rd St.* ⊠ *815 Madison Ave., between E. 68th and E. 69th Sts., Upper East Side* ☎ *212/744–6868* Ⓜ *Subway: 6 to 68th St./Hunter College.*

Giorgio Armani. The space here has a museumlike quality, reinforced by the refined clothes. Suits for men and women have a telltale perfect drape. ⊠ *760 Madison Ave., between E. 65th and E. 66th Sts., Upper East Side* ☎ *212/988–9191* Ⓜ *Subway: 6 to 68th St./Hunter College.*

Gucci. The white-hot label shows no signs of cooling off. The most touted designs are often overtly sexy, but there's also subtler attire. ⊠ *685 5th Ave., between 54th and 55th Sts., Midtown East* ☎ *212/826–2600* Ⓜ *Subway: N, R, W to 5th Ave./59th St.* ⊠ *840 Madison Ave., between E. 69th and E. 70th Sts., Upper East Side* ☎ *212/717–2619* Ⓜ *Subway: 6 to 68th St./Hunter College.*

Helmut Lang. Lang's men's and women's clothes and accessories are tough distillations of his skinny-pants aesthetic. Black, mirror-ended walls slice up the space, which is punctuated by the digital ticker tape designed by artist Jenny Holzer. ⊠ *80 Greene St., between Spring and Broome Sts., SoHo* ☎ *212/334–3921* Ⓜ *Subway: 6 to Spring St.* ⊠ *80 Greene St., between Spring and Broome Sts., SoHo* ☎ *212/925–7214* Ⓜ *Subway: C, E to Spring St.*

Hermès. Sweep up and down the curving stairway in this contemporary flagship while on the prowl for the classic, distinctively patterned silk scarves and neckties, the coveted Kelly and Birkin handbags, or the beautifully simple separates. ⊠ *691 Madison Ave., at E. 62nd St., Upper East Side* ☎ *212/751–3181* Ⓜ *Subway: N, R, W, 4, 5, 6 to 59th St./Lexington Ave.*

H&M. Crowds swarm over the racks in search of up-to-the-minute trends at unbelievably low prices. Although you can get the latest in flared jeans or glittery tees, it's not all for teenyboppers; turtleneck sweaters, cords, and button-downs have their place, too. ⊠ *640 5th Ave., at W. 51st. St.* ☎ *212/489–0390* Ⓜ *Subway: B, D, F, V to 47th–50th St./Rockefeller Center* ⊠ *1328 Broadway, at W. 34th St., Midtown West* ☎ *646/473–1165* Ⓜ *Subway: A, C, E, 1, 2, 3, 9 to 34th St./Penn Station* ⊠ *558 Broadway, between Prince and Spring Sts., SoHo* ☎ *212/343–2722* Ⓜ *Subway: R, W to Prince St.* ⊠ *515 Broadway, between Spring and Broome Sts., SoHo* ☎ *212/965–8975* Ⓜ *Subway: R, W to Prince St.*

Jeffrey. The Meatpacking District really arrived when this Atlanta-based mini-Barneys opened its doors. You find an incredible array of shoes, both in terms of design and size, plus the ultimate in labels. ⊠ *449 W. 14th St., between 9th and 10th Aves., Chelsea* ☎ *212/206–1272* Ⓜ *Subway: A, C, E, L to 14th St./8th Ave.*

Marc Jacobs. Next door to a SoHo garage stands Jacobs's sleek boutique displaying piles of perfect (and pricey) cashmere, silk, and wool. The Bleecker Street spaces carry relatively casual clothes with a stronger sense of humor, such as stripes in sherbet colors. ⊠ *163 Mercer St., between W. Houston and Prince Sts., SoHo* ☎ *212/343–1490* Ⓜ *Subway: R, W to Prince St.* ⊠ *Accessories boutique* ⊠ *385 Bleecker St., at Perry St., Greenwich Village* ☎ *212/924 6126* Ⓜ *Subway: 1, 9 to Christopher St./Sheridan Sq.* ⊠ *403-405 Bleecker St., at W. 11th St., Greenwich Village* ☎ *212/924–0026* Ⓜ *Subway: 1, 9 to Christopher St./Sheridan Sq.*

Patricia Field. Field was the costume designer for *Sex and the City.* Fetishes are good-humoredly indulged, with teeny kilts, mesh tops, lamé, marabou, and vinyl thrown into the mix. ⊠ *382 West Broadway, between Spring and Broome Sts., SoHo* ☎ *212/966–4066* Ⓜ *Subway: C, E to Spring St.*

Polo/Ralph Lauren. One of New York's most distinctive shopping experiences, Lauren's flagship store is in the turn-of-the-20th-century Rhinelander mansion. Clothes range from summer-in-the-Hamptons madras to exquisite silk gowns and Purple Label men's suits. **Polo Sport** (⊠ 888 Madison Ave., at 72nd St., Upper East Side ☎ 212/434–8000 Ⓜ Subway: 6 to 68th St./Hunter College ⊠ 381 West Broadway, between Spring and Broome Sts., SoHo ☎ 212/625–1660 Ⓜ Subway: R, W to Prince St.) carries casual clothes and sports gear, from puffy anoraks to wick-away tanks. At **Double RL** (⊠ 271 Mulberry St., between Prince and E. Houston Sts., NoLita ☎ 212/343–0841 Ⓜ Subway: R, W to Prince St.) vintage flannel shirts, denim, motorcycle leathers, and accessories provide the models for new jeans, barn jackets, and the like. ⊠ *867 Madison Ave., at E. 72nd St., Upper East Side* ☎ *212/606–2100* Ⓜ *Subway: 6 to 68th St./Hunter College.*

Prada. Prada's gossamer silks, slick black suits, and luxe shoes and leather goods are among the all-time great Italian fashion coups. The SoHo location, an ultramodern space designed by Rem Koolhaas, incorporates so many technological innovations that it was written up in *Popular Science*. The dressing-room gadgets alone include liquid crystal displays, changeable lighting, and scanners that link you to the store's database. ✉ *724 5th Ave., between W. 56th and W. 57th Sts., Midtown West* ☎ *212/664-0010* Ⓜ *Subway: Q, W to 5th Ave./60th St.* ✉ *45 E. 57th St., between Madison and Park Aves., Midtown East* ☎ *212/308-2332* Ⓜ *Subway: E, V to 5th Ave./53rd St.* ✉ *841 Madison Ave., at E. 70th St., Upper East Side* ☎ *212/327-4200* Ⓜ *Subway: 6 to 68th St./Hunter College* ✉ *575 Broadway, at Prince St., SoHo* ☎ *212/ 334-8888* Ⓜ *Subway: R, W to Prince St.*

Valentino. The mix here is at once audacious and beautifully cut; the fur or feather trimmings, low necklines, and opulent fabrics are about as close as you can get to celluloid glamour. ✉ *747 Madison Ave., at E. 65th St., Upper East Side* ☎ *212/772-6969* Ⓜ *Subway: 6 to 68th St./Hunter College.*

Yves Saint Laurent Rive Gauche. Hedi Slimane's suits—meant for men but sometimes pilfered by women—follow boyishly slender, narrow lines. ✉ *855 Madison Ave., between E. 70th and E. 71st Sts., Upper East Side* ☎ *212/988-3821* Ⓜ *Subway: 6 to 68th St./Hunter College* ✉ *3 E. 57th St., between 5th and Madison Aves., Midtown East* ☎ *212/980-2970* Ⓜ *Subway: N, R, W to 5th Ave./59th St.*

MEN'S CLOTHING **Agnès b. Homme.** This French designer's love for the movies makes it easy to come out looking a little Godard around the edges. Turtleneck sweaters, lean black suits, and black leather porkpie hats demand the sangfroid of Belmondo. ✉ *79 Greene St., between Broome and Spring Sts., SoHo* ☎ *212/431-4339* Ⓜ *Subway: R, W to Prince St.*

Dunhill. Corporate brass come here for finely tailored clothing, both ready-made and custom-ordered, and smoking accessories. ✉ *711 5th Ave., between E. 56th and E. 55th Sts., Midtown East* ☎ *212/753-9292* Ⓜ *Subway: F to 57th St.*

John Varvatos. A degree of ease marks Varvatos' soft-shoulder suits, cotton crewneck shirts, and jeans in leather, velvet, or denim. ✉ *149 Mercer St., between W. Houston and Prince Sts., SoHo* ☎ *212/965-0700* Ⓜ *Subway: R, W to Prince St.*

Paul Smith. Dark mahogany Victorian cases complement the dandyish British styles they hold. Embroidered vests, brightly striped socks, scarves, and shirts, and tongue-in-cheek cuff links leaven the classic, dark, double-back-vent suits. Ashtrays, photography books, cordial glasses, and other such oddments beg for a toff bachelor pad. ✉ *108 5th Ave., at E. 16th St., Flatiron District* ☎ *212/627-9770* Ⓜ *Subway: F, V to 14th St.*

Sean. These snug shops carry low-key, well-priced, and comfortable apparel from France, including a respectable collection of suits and dress shirts. ✉ *132 Thompson St., between W. Houston and Prince Sts., SoHo* ☎ *212/598-5980* Ⓜ *Subway: R, W to Prince St.* ✉ *224 Columbus Ave., between W. 70th and W. 71st Sts., Upper West Side* ☎ *212/ 769-1489* Ⓜ *Subway: B, C to 72nd St.*

VINTAGE & **Resurrection.** With original Courrèges, Puccis, and foxy boots, this store
RESALE is a retro-chic gold mine. ✉ *217 Mott St., between Prince and Spring
CLOTHING Sts., NoLita* ☎ *212/625-1376* Ⓜ *Subway: 6 to Spring St.*

INA. Although you may spot something vintage, like a 1960s Yves Saint Laurent velvet bolero, most clothing at these small boutiques harks back only a few seasons, and in some cases, it's never been worn. The Mott Street location racks up menswear; the other two stores carry women's resale. ✉ *101 Thompson St., between Prince and Spring Sts., SoHo* ☎ *212/941–4757* Ⓜ *Subway: C, E to Spring St.* ✉ *21 Prince St., between Elizabeth and Mott Sts., NoLita* ☎ *212/334–9048* Ⓜ *Subway: R, W to Prince St.* ✉ *262 Mott St., between Prince and E. Houston Sts., NoLita* ☎ *212/334–2210* Ⓜ *Subway: R, W to Prince St.*

What Comes Around Goes Around. Thanks to the staff's sharp eyes, the denim and leather racks here are reliably choice. The tidy selection also provides hip-again items like rabbit-fur jackets and decorative belt buckles. ✉ *351 West Broadway, between Grand and Broome Sts., SoHo* ☎ *212/343–9303* Ⓜ *Subway: J, M, N, Q, R, W, Z, 6 to Canal St.*

WOMEN'S
CLOTHING

Agnès b. With this quintessentially French line you can look like a Parisienne schoolgirl—in snap-front tops, slender pants, sweet floral prints—or like her chic *maman* in tailored dark suits and leather jackets. ✉ *79 Greene St., between Prince and Spring Sts., SoHo* ☎ *212/925–4649* Ⓜ *Subway: R, W to Prince St.* ✉ *13 E. 16th St., between 5th Ave. and Union Sq. W, Flatiron District* ☎ *212/741–2585* Ⓜ *Subway: F, V to 14th St.* ✉ *1063 Madison Ave., between E. 80th and E. 81st Sts., Upper East Side* ☎ *212/570–9333* Ⓜ *Subway: 6 to 77th St.*

Anna Sui. The violet-and-black salon, hung with Beardsley prints and alterna-rock posters, is the perfect setting for Sui's bohemian, flapper- and rocker-influenced designs. ✉ *113 Greene St., between Prince and Spring Sts., SoHo* ☎ *212/941–8406* Ⓜ *Subway: R, W to Prince St.*

BCBG. If flirtation's your sport, find your sportswear here among the fluttering skirts, beaded camisoles, and leather pants. ✉ *120 Wooster St., between Prince and Spring Sts., SoHo* ☎ *212/625–2723* Ⓜ *Subway: R, W to Prince St.* ✉ *770 Madison Ave., at E. 66th St., Upper East Side* ☎ *212/717–4225* Ⓜ *Subway: 6 to 68th St./Hunter College.*

Calypso. Spring for something with a tropical vibe, like a sweeping, ruffled skirt in guava-color silk, an embroidered kurta-style top, or a fringed shawl. ✉ *424 Broome St., at Crosby St., SoHo* ☎ *212/274–0449* Ⓜ *Subway: 6 to Spring St.* ✉ *280 Mott St., between E. Houston and Prince Sts., NoLita* ☎ *212/965–0990* Ⓜ *Subway: 6 to Bleecker St.* ✉ *935 Madison Ave., at E. 74th St., Upper East Side* ☎ *212/535–4100* Ⓜ *Subway: 6 to 77th St.*

Catherine Malandrino. More monochromatic than in years past—with cream and black nudging out the lavender and red—these designs still get worked over with ruching, appliquéing, and crochet. ✉ *468 Broome St., at Greene St., SoHo* ☎ *212/925–6765* Ⓜ *Subway: 6 to Spring St.*

Chanel. The Midtown flagship has often been compared to a Chanel suit—slim, elegant, and timeless. Inside wait the famed suits themselves, along with other pillars of Chanel style: chic little black dresses and evening gowns, chain-handled bags, and yards of pearls. Downtown's branch concentrates on more contemporary forays, including ski gear, whereas Madison's boutique is dedicated to shoes, handbags, and other accessories. ✉ *139 Spring St., at Wooster St., SoHo* ☎ *212/334–0055* Ⓜ *Subway: C, E to Spring St.* ✉ *15 E. 57th St., between 5th and Madison*

Aves., Midtown East ☎ 212/355–5050 Ⓜ *Subway: N, R, W to 5th Ave./59th St.* ✉ *737 Madison Ave., at E. 64th St., Upper East Side* ☎212/ 535–5505 Ⓜ *Subway: 6 to 68th St./Hunter College.*

Chloé. Phoebe Philo stepped up to the plate as house designer after Stella McCartney's departure; her saucy trousers and puffed-sleeve blouses may induce you to roll out some Philo dough. ✉ *850 Madison Ave., at E. 70th St., Upper East Side* ☎ 212/717–8220 Ⓜ *Subway: 6 to 68th St./Hunter College.*

Christian Dior. The New York outpost of one of France's most venerable fashion houses makes its home in the dazzlingly modern LVMH tower. The designs bring elements of everything from raceways to skate punks to haute couture. ✉ *21 E. 57th St., at Madison Ave., Midtown East* ☎ 212/931–2950 Ⓜ *Subway: E, V to 5th Ave./53rd St.*

Destination. The model pigs guarding this store fit right in with the Meatpacking District. Inside are clothes and accessories that marry handmade and sophisticated styles. Polished Jacques Le Corre boots and bags could be paired with nubbly knit scarves or tops using vintage fabric. ✉ *32–36 Little West 12th St., between Greenwich and Washington Sts., Greenwich Village* ☎ 212/727–2031 Ⓜ *Subway: 1, 9 to Christopher St./Sheridan Square.*

Kirna Zabête. A heavy-hitting lineup of cachet designers—Balenciaga, Cacharel, Clements Ribeiro—is managed with an exceptionally cheerful flair. Step downstairs for Burberry dog coats, e.vil tees to announce your true colors ("Little Miss Drama"), and even giant gum balls. ✉ *96 Greene St., between Spring and Prince Sts., SoHo* ☎ 212/941–9656 Ⓜ *Subway: R, W to Prince St.*

Michael Kors. In his deft reworkings of American classics, Kors gives sportswear the luxury treatment, as with car coats using cashmere or fur. ✉ *974 Madison Ave., at E. 76th St., Upper East Side* ☎ 212/452– 4685 Ⓜ *Subway: 6 to 77th St.*

Miu Miu. Prada front woman Miuccia Prada established a secondary line to showcase her more experimental ideas. Look for Prada-esque styles in more daring colors and fabrics. ✉ *100 Prince St., between Mercer and Greene Sts., SoHo* ☎ 212/334–5156 Ⓜ *Subway: R, W to Prince St.* ✉ *831 Madison Ave., at E. 69th St., Upper East Side* ☎ 212/249– 9660 Ⓜ *Subway: 6 to 68th St./Hunter College.*

Nanette Lepore. The insouciant looks here put retro references—pom-pom trim, yoked tops, floral, tapestry, and paisley prints—to good use. ✉ *123 Broome St., between Lafayette and Crosby Sts., NoLita* ☎ 212/ 219–8265 Ⓜ *Subway: 6 to Spring St.*

Stella McCartney. You could put together an outfit of head-to-toe satin or chiffon, but it's more in keeping to mix it with shredded denim. As leather is verboten at this devout vegetarian's shop, shoes and accessories come in satin, canvas, and synthetics. ✉ *429 W. 14th St., at Washington St., Meatpacking District* ☎ 212/255–1556 Ⓜ *Subway: A, C, E to 14th St.*

Vera Wang. The made-to-order bridal and evening wear glows with satin, beading, and embroidery. Periodic pret-a-porter sales offer the dresses for a (relative) song. ✉ *991 Madison Ave., at E. 77th St., Upper East Side* ☎ 212/628–3400 Ⓜ *Subway: 6 to 77th St.*

Vivienne Tam. Tam is known for her playful, "China chic" take on familiar Asian images: embroidered flowers and Chinese dragons spill down soft net dresses, and Mao's image gazes impassively from PVC jackets or throw pillows. ⊠ *99 Greene St., between Prince and Spring Sts., SoHo* ☎ *212/966–2398* Ⓜ *Subway: R, W to Prince St.*

Home Furnishings

★ **ABC Carpet & Home.** ABC seems to cover most of the furnishings alphabet; over several floors it encompasses everything from rustic furniture to 19th-century repros, refinished Chinese chests and Vitra chairs, not to mention that loose category "country French." ⊠ *888 Broadway, at E. 19th St., Flatiron District* ☎ *212/473–3000* Ⓜ *Subway: L, N, Q, R, W, 4, 5, 6 to 14th St./Union Sq.*

Aero. Accessories such as ebonized wood trays and opalescent glass pieces are interspersed with quietly luxurious furniture. ⊠ *419 Broome St., SoHo* ☎ *212/966–1500* Ⓜ *Subway: 6 to Spring St.*

c.i.t.e. Housewares in this showroom wander from industrial (Pyrex containers) to amusing (bulbous fiberglass chairs) to kid-friendly (chairs that double as toy storage). ⊠ *100 Wooster St., between Prince and Spring Sts., SoHo* ☎ *212/431–7272* Ⓜ *Subway: R, W to Prince St.*

Design Within Reach. "An interesting plainness is the most difficult and precious thing to achieve" reads one of the quotes discreetly placed on the walls here. You can get a lot closer to Mies van der Rohe's ideal with these tasteful midcentury pieces and contemporary furnishings. ⊠ *408 W. 14th St., at 9th Ave., Meatpacking District* ☎ *212/242–9449* Ⓜ *Subway: A, C, E to 14th St.* ⊠ *142 Wooster St., between Prince and W. Houston Sts., SoHo* ☎ *212/475–0001* Ⓜ *Subway: F, V to Broadway–Lafayette.*

★ **De Vera.** The objets d'art and jewelry here all seem to have stories behind them. Many are antique and hint of colonial travels, whereas others exemplify modern forms of traditional workmanship. ⊠ *1 Crosby St., at Howard St., SoHo* ☎ *212/625–0838* Ⓜ *Subway: N, R, Q, W, 6 to Canal St.*

Fishs Eddy. The dishes, china, and glassware for resale here come from all walks of crockery life—corporate dining rooms, failed restaurants, etc. New wares often look retro and there are lots of oddball pieces such as finger bowls. ⊠ *2176 Broadway, at W. 77th St., Upper West Side* ☎ *212/873–8819* Ⓜ *Subway: 1, 9 to 79th St.* ⊠ *889 Broadway, at E. 19th St., Flatiron District* ☎ *212/420 9020* Ⓜ *Subway: L, N, Q, R, W, 4, 5, 6 to 14th St./Union Sq.*

Jonathan Adler. Adler gets midcentury modern and Scandinavian styles to lighten up with his striped, striated, or curvy handmade pottery as well as the hand-loomed wool pillow covers, rugs, and throws with blunt graphics. ⊠ *47 Greene St., between Broome and Grand Sts., SoHo* ☎ *212/941–8950* Ⓜ *Subway: N, R, Q, W, 6 to Canal St.*

Mood Indigo. For a retro rush, drift through Stork Club paraphernalia, Bakelite bangles, novelty salt-and-pepper sets, martini shakers, and Fiestaware. ⊠ *181 Prince St., between Sullivan and Thompson Sts., SoHo* ☎ *212/254–1176* Ⓜ *Subway: R, W to Prince St.*

★ **Moss.** International designers, many of them Italian or Scandinavian, put a fantastic spin on even the most utilitarian objects, which are carefully brought together by Murray Moss at his store-cum–design museum. ☒ *146 Greene St., between W. Houston and Prince Sts., SoHo* ☎ *212/ 226–2190* Ⓜ *Subway: R, W to Prince St.*

Mxyplyzyk. Hard to pronounce (*mixyplitsick*) and hard to resist, this is a trove of impulse buys—creative riffs on household standbys such as soap dispensers (here a stylized bird), first-aid kits (cross-shape), and doormats (polka-dotted). ☒ *125 Greenwich Ave., at W. 13th St., Greenwich Village* ☎ *212/989–4300* Ⓜ *Subway: A, C, E, L to 14th St./8th Ave.*

Room. The assortment at the first freestanding store from the Australian home-product line of the same name is random but complete—everything from doormats to credenzas to blocky poufs. ☒ *182 Duane St., between Hudson and Greenwich Sts., TriBeCa* ☎ *212/226–1045* Ⓜ *Subway: 1, 9 to Franklin St.*

Terence Conran Shop. The British style monger has made a victorious return to New York City. The small glass pavilion beneath the 59th Street Bridge caps a vast underground showroom of kitchen and garden implements, fabrics, furniture, and glassware. ☒ *407 E. 59th St., at 1st Ave., Midtown East* ☎ *212/755–9079* Ⓜ *Subway: N, R, W to 59th St./Lexington Ave.*

Troy. In this spare space the clean lines of Lucite, leather, cedar, and resin furniture and home accessories may well wreak havoc with your credit card. Less imposing are the limited-edition items, like puzzles, board games, and reissued Lennon and Ono "War Is Over" T-shirts. ☒ *138 Greene St., between Prince and W. Houston Sts., SoHo* ☎ *212/941–4777* Ⓜ *Subway: R, W to Prince St.*

William-Wayne & Co. Silver julep cups, Viennese playing cards, butler's trays: these whimsical decorative items are hard to resist. A low-key monkey theme puts smiling simians on dishes, candleholders, wall sconces, and tea towels. ☒ *40 University Pl., at E. 9th St., Greenwich Village* ☎ *212/533–4711* Ⓜ *Subway: 6 to Astor Pl.* ☒ *846 Lexington Ave., at E. 64th St., Upper East Side* ☎ *212/737–8934* Ⓜ *Subway: 6 to 68th St./Hunter College* ☒ *850 Lexington Ave., at E. 64th St., Upper East Side* ☎ *212/288–9243* Ⓜ *Subway: 6 to 68th St./Hunter College.*

Jewelry, Watches & Silver

Bulgari. This Italian company is certainly not shy about its name, which encircles gems, watch faces, even lighters. There are beautiful weighty rings and pieces mixing gold with stainless steel or porcelain, as well as the lighter Lucea line. ☒ *730 5th Ave., at W. 57th St., Midtown West* ☎ *212/315–9000* Ⓜ *Subway: N, R, W to 5th Ave.* ☒ *783 Madison Ave., between E. 66th and E. 67th Sts., Upper East Side* ☎ *212/717–2300* Ⓜ *Subway: 6 to 68th St./Hunter College.*

Cartier. Pierre Cartier allegedly won the 5th Avenue mansion location by trading two strands of perfectly matched natural pearls with Mrs. Morton Plant. The jewelry is still incredibly persuasive, from such established favorites as the interlocking rings to the more recent additions such as the handcufflike Menotte bracelets. ☒ *653 5th Ave., at E. 52nd St., Midtown East* ☎ *212/753–0111* Ⓜ *Subway: E, V to 5th Ave./53rd St.* ☒ *828 Madison Ave., at E. 69th St., Upper East Side* ☎ *212/472– 6400* Ⓜ *Subway: 6 to 68th St./Hunter Collge.*

David Yurman. The signature motifs here—cables, quatrefoil shapes—add up to a classic, go-anywhere look, and the use of semiprecious stones keeps prices within reason. ☒ *729 Madison Ave., at E. 64th St., Upper East Side* ☎ *212/752–4255* Ⓜ *Subway: 6 to 68th St./Hunter Collge.*

Fragments. This SoHo spot glitters with pieces by nimble new jewelry designers whose work is splashed across the pages of glossy fashion magazines. ☒ *116 Prince St., between Greene and Wooster Sts., SoHo* ☎ *212/334–9588* Ⓜ *Subway: R, W to Prince St.*

Fred Leighton. If you're in the market for vintage diamonds, this is the place, whether your taste is for tiaras, art-deco settings, or sparklers once worn by a Vanderbilt. ☒ *773 Madison Ave., at E. 66th St., Upper East Side* ☎ *212/288–1872* Ⓜ *Subway: 6 to 68th St./Hunter College.*

H. Stern. Sleek designs pose in an equally modern 5th Avenue setting; smooth cabochon-cut stones, most from South America, glow in pale wooden display cases. The designers make notable use of semiprecious stones such as citrine, tourmaline, and topaz. ☒ *645 5th Ave., between E. 51st and E. 52nd Sts., Midtown East* ☎ *212/688–0300* Ⓜ *Subway: E, V to 5th Ave./53rd St.* ☒ *301 Park Ave., between E. 49th and E. 50th Sts., in Waldorf-Astoria, Midtown East* ☎ *212/753–5595* Ⓜ *Subway: 6 to 51st St.*

Harry Winston. Oversize stones of impeccable quality sparkle in Harry Winston's inner sanctum—no wonder the jeweler was immortalized in the song "Diamonds Are a Girl's Best Friend." ☒ */18 5th Ave., at W. 56th St., Midtown West* ☎ *212/245–2000* Ⓜ *Subway: F to 57th St.*

Me + Ro. Eastern styling has gained these designers a cult following. The Indian-inspired, hand-finished gold bangles and earrings covered with tiny dangling rubies or sapphires may look bohemian, but the prices target the well-to-do. ☒ *241 Elizabeth St., between Prince and E. Houston Sts., NoLita* ☎ *917/237–9215* Ⓜ *Subway: R, W to Prince St.*

Mikimoto. The Japanese originator of the cultured pearl, Mikimoto presents a glowing display of perfectly formed, high-luster pearls. Besides the creamy strands from their own pearl farms, there are dazzlingly colored South Sea pearls and some freshwater varieties. ☒ *730 5th Ave., between W. 56th and W. 57th Sts., Midtown West* ☎ *212/457–4600* Ⓜ *Subway: F to 57th St.*

Stuart Moore. Many designs here are minimalist or understated, but stunning: the twinkle of a small diamond offset by gold or brushed platinum. Pieces tend to be modest in scale. ☒ *128 Prince St., at Wooster St., SoHo* ☎ *212/941–1023* Ⓜ *Subway: R, W to Prince St.*

Fodor's Choice
★ **Tiffany & Co.** The display windows can be elegant, funny, or just plain breathtaking. Alongside the $80,000 platinum-and-diamond bracelets, a lot here is affordable on a whim—and everything comes wrapped in that unmistakable Tiffany blue. ☒ *727 5th Ave., at E. 57th St., Midtown East* ☎ *212/755–8000* Ⓜ *Subway: N, R, W to 5th Ave./59th St.*

Tourneau. The three-level 57th Street TimeMachine is a high-tech merchandising extravaganza. A museum downstairs has timepiece exhibits, both temporary and permanent. The shops carry more than 70 brands, from status symbols such as Cartier and Rolex to more casual styles by Swatch or Swiss Army. ☒ *500 Madison Ave., between E. 52nd and E. 53rd Sts., Midtown East* ☎ *212/758–6098* Ⓜ *Subway: 6 to 51st St./Lexington Ave.; E, V to Lexington–3rd Aves./53rd St.* ☒ *12 E. 57th St.,*

between 5th and Madison Aves., Midtown East ☎ *212/758–7300*
✉ *200 W. 34th St., at 7th Ave., Midtown West* ☎ *212/563–6880*
Ⓜ *Subway: A, C, E, 1, 2, 3 to 34th St./Penn Station* ✉ *10 Columbus
Circle, at W. 59th St., Midtown West* ☎ *212/823–9425* Ⓜ *Subway: 1,
9, A, C, B, D to Columbus Circle.*

Van Cleef & Arpels. The jewelry here (lots of classically set diamonds and
floral motifs) is sheer perfection. ✉ *744 5th Ave., at W. 57th St., Midtown West* ☎ *212/644–9500* Ⓜ *Subway: E, F, N, R to 5th Ave.*

Shoes

MEN'S &
WOMEN'S SHOES

Arche. These molded natural latex soles make pounding the pavement
decidedly less painful, and besides the usual brown and black, the soft
leather or nubuck uppers come in colors like burgundy or forest green.
✉ *995 Madison Ave., at E. 77th St., Upper East Side* ☎ *212/439–
0700* Ⓜ *Subway: 6 to 77th St.* ✉ *123 Wooster St., between Prince and
Spring Sts., SoHo* ☎ *646/613–8700* Ⓜ *Subway: R, W to Prince St.* ✉ *128
W. 57th St., between 6th and 7th Aves., Midtown West* ☎ *212/262–
5488* Ⓜ *Subway: F to 57th St.*

Camper. Whether you choose a slide-on or laced-to-the-toe style of the
established Euro-fave walking shoe, all have comfortably round toes and
a springy feel. ✉ *125 Prince St., at Wooster St., SoHo* ☎ *212/358–1841*
Ⓜ *Subway: R, W to Prince St.*

Cole-Haan. With endless variations on the basic elements of its woven,
moccasin, and loafer styles in brown and black, Cole-Haan provides up-
to-date styles for a conservative crowd. ✉ *620 5th Ave., at Rockefeller
Center, Midtown West* ☎ *212/765–9747* Ⓜ *Subway: E, V to 5th
Ave./53rd St.* ✉ *667 Madison Ave., at E. 61st St., Upper East Side* ☎ *212/
421–8440* Ⓜ *Subway: N, R, W, 4, 5, 6 to 59th St./Lexington Ave.*
✉ *10 Columbus Circle, at W. 59th St., Midtown West* ☎ *212/823–9420*
Ⓜ *Subway: 1, 9, A, C, B, D to Columbus Circle.*

J. M. Weston. Specially treated calfskin for the soles and carefully handcrafted construction have made these a French favorite; they could also
double the price of your outfit. High heels, a more recent addition to
the selection, started gradually with stacked-heel pumps. ✉ *812 Madison Ave., at E. 68th St., Upper East Side* ☎ *212/535–2100* Ⓜ *Subway:
6 to 68th St./Hunter College.*

Otto Tootsi Plohound. Downtown New Yorkers swear by this large selection of supercool shoes. Many, including the store's own line, are Ital-
ian-made, and styles jump from vampy pumps to men's wing tips to Prada
Sport boots. ✉ *413 West Broadway, between Prince and Spring Sts., SoHo*
☎ *212/925–8931* Ⓜ *Subway: C, E to Spring St.* ✉ *273 Lafayette St.,
between Prince and E. Houston Sts., East Village* ☎ *212/431–7299*
Ⓜ *Subway: R, W to Prince St.* ✉ *137 5th Ave., between E. 20th and
21st Sts., Flatiron District* ☎ *212/460–8650* Ⓜ *Subway: F, V to 23rd St.*
✉ *38 E. 57th St., between Park and Madison Aves., Midtown East* ☎ *212/
231–3199* Ⓜ *Subway: N, R, W, 4, 5, 6 to 59th St./Lexington Ave.*

Salvatore Ferragamo. Elegance typifies these designs. The company re-
works some of their women's styles from previous decades, like the girl-
ish Audrey (as in Hepburn) flat, available in the original black or
seasonal takes like bone or leopard. ✉ *655 5th Ave., at E. 52nd St.* ☎ *212/
759–3822* Ⓜ *Subway: E, V to 53rd St.*

Sigerson Morrison. The details—just-right T-straps, small buckles, interesting two-tones—make the women's shoes irresistible. Prices hover around $300. ✉ *28 Prince St., between Mott and Elizabeth Sts., No-Lita* ☎ *212/219–3893* Ⓜ *Subway: F, V to Broadway–Lafayette St.*

MEN'S SHOES **Church's English Shoes.** The high quality of these shoes is indisputable; you could choose something highly polished for an embassy dinner or a loafer or a crepe-soled suede ankle boot for a weekend. ✉ *689 Madison Ave., at E. 62nd St., Upper East Side* ☎ *212/758–5200* Ⓜ *Subway: N, R, 4, 5, 6 to 59th St.*

John Lobb. These British shoes often use waxed leather, the better to contend with London levels of damp. Ankle boots with padded collars or zips join the traditional oxfords and derbys. ✉ *680 Madison Ave., between E. 62nd and E. 61st Sts., Upper East Side* ☎ *212/888–9797* Ⓜ *Subway: N, R, 4, 5, 6 to 59th St.*

WOMEN'S SHOES **Christian Louboutin.** Bright-red soles are the signature of Louboutin's delicately sexy couture slippers and stilettos. Look for brocade, mink trim, and tassels. ✉ *941 Madison Ave., between E. 74th and E. 75th Sts., Upper East Side* ☎ *212/396–1884* Ⓜ *Subway: 6 to 77th St.*

Hollywould. Colorful ballet flats with long grosgrain ties close ranks along the floorboards, and cinematic high heels patrol the shelves above. Padded soles make even the most soaring pumps surprisingly wearable. ✉ *198 Elizabeth St., between Prince and Spring Sts., NoLita* ☎ *212/343–8344* Ⓜ *Subway: 6 to Spring St.*

Jimmy Choo. Pointy toes, low vamps, narrow heels, ankle-wrapping straps—these British-made shoes are undeniably hot to trot, and sometimes more comfortable than they look. ✉ *716 Madison Ave., between E. 63rd and E. 64th Sts., Upper East Side* ☎ *212/759–7078* Ⓜ *Subway: 6 to 68th St./Hunter College* ✉ *645 5th Ave., at E. 51st St., Midtown East* ☎ *212/593–0800* Ⓜ *Subway: B, D, F, V to 47th–50th Sts./Rockefeller Center.*

Manolo Blahnik. These are, notoriously, some of the most expensive shoes money can buy. They're also devastatingly sexy, with pointed toes, low-cut vamps, and spindly heels. ✉ *31 W. 54th St., between 5th and 6th Aves., Midtown West* ☎ *212/582–3007* Ⓜ *Subway: E, V to 5th Ave./53rd St.*

Peter Fox. Combining old-fashioned lines, such as Louis heels, and such modern touches as thin platforms, these shoes defy categorization. ✉ *105 Thompson St., between Prince and Spring Sts., SoHo* ☎ *212/431–7426* Ⓜ *Subway: C, E to Spring St.*

Robert Clergerie. High-priced and highly polished, these shoes are not without their sense of fun. Pick up a pump and you may find a prowlike toe or a round pillar heel. ✉ *681 Madison Ave., between E. 61st and E. 62nd Sts., Upper East Side* ☎ *212/207–8600* Ⓜ *Subway: N, R, W, 4, 5, 6 to 59th St./Lexington Ave.*

Tod's. Diego Della Valle's coveted driving moccasins, casual loafers, and boots in colorful leather, suede, and ponyskin are right at home on Madison Avenue. ✉ *650 Madison Ave., near E. 60th St., Upper East Side* ☎ *212/644–5945* Ⓜ *Subway: N, R, W to 5th Ave./59th St.*

STATIONERY   **Kate's Paperie.** Heaven for avid correspondents and gift-givers, Kate's rus-
★   tles with fabulous wrapping papers, ribbons, blank books, writing implements of all kinds, and more. ✉ *561 Broadway, between Prince and
Spring Sts., SoHo* ☎ *212/941–9816* Ⓜ *Subway: R, W to Prince St.* ✉ *8
W. 13th St., between 5th and 6th Aves., Greenwich Village* ☎ *212/633–
0570* Ⓜ *Subway: F, V to 14th St.* ✉ *140 W. 57th St., between 6th and
7th Aves., Midtown West* ☎ *212/459–0700* Ⓜ *Subway: F to 57th St.*

TOYS & GAMES   **Enchanted Forest.** Stuffed animals peer out from almost every corner of
★   this fantastic shop. It's packed with all manner of curiosity-provoking
gadgets like pinhole-camera kits, puppets, and vintage tin toys. ✉ *85
Mercer St., between Spring and Broome Sts., SoHo* ☎ *212/925–6677*
Ⓜ *Subway: C, E to Spring St.*

Geppetto's Toy Box. Many toys here are handmade. They carry everything from extravagant costumed dolls to tried-and-true rubber duck-
ies. ✉ *10 Christopher St., at Greenwich Ave., Greenwich Village* ☎ *212/
620–7511* Ⓜ *Subway: 1, 9 to Christopher St./Sheridan Sq.*

Kidding Around. This unpretentious shop emphasizes old-fashioned
wooden toys, fun gadgets, craft and science kits, and a small selection
of infant clothes. ✉ *60 W. 15th St., between 5th and 6th Aves., Flatiron District* ☎ *212/645–6337* Ⓜ *Subway: L, N, Q, R, W, 4, 5, 6 to
14th St./Union Sq.*

NEW YORK CITY A TO Z

*To research prices, get advice from other travelers, and book travel ar-
rangements, visit www.fodors.com.*

ADDRESSES

In Manhattan, the grid layout makes getting around easy. Avenues run
north and south, with 5th Avenue dividing the east and west sides above
8th Street—the lower the address number on a street, the closer it is to
5th Avenue. The streets below 14th Street on the west and below 1st
Street on the east were settled before the grid system and follow no particular pattern.

To locate the cross street that corresponds to a numerical avenue address, or to find the avenue closest to a numerical street address, check
the Web site below.

🏢 **Manhattan Address Locator** ⊕ www.manhattanaddress.com.

AIR TRAVEL TO & FROM NEW YORK

For information, *see* Air Travel *in* Smart Travel Tips.

AIRPORTS & TRANSFERS

The major air gateways to New York City are LaGuardia Airport (LGA)
and JFK International Airport (JFK) in the borough of Queens, and
Newark Liberty International Airport (EWR) in New Jersey. (*See* Air
Travel *in* Smart Travel Tips A to Z for more information about LaGuardia,
JFK, and Newark airports, as well as for airline contact information.)
Cab fares are generally higher to and from Newark, and LaGuardia is
closer to Manhattan and easier to navigate than JFK. The Air Train link

between Newark Airport and Penn Station in Manhattan makes the journey in less than 30 minutes.

The Air-Ride Transportation Information Service provides detailed, up-to-the-minute recorded information on how to reach your destination from any of New York's airports. Outside the baggage-claim area at each of New York's major airports is a taxi stand where a uniformed dispatcher helps passengers find taxis. Note that if you arrive after midnight at any airport you may wait a long time for a taxi. Consider calling a car service, as there is no shuttle service at that time.

Car services can be a good option since the driver often meets you on the concourse or in the baggage-claim area and helps you with your luggage. New York City Taxi and Limousine Commission rules require that all car services be licensed and pick up riders only by prior arrangement; if possible, call 24 hours in advance for reservations. Drivers of nonlicensed vehicles ("gypsy cabs") often solicit fares outside the terminal in baggage-claim areas. Don't take them: even if you do have a safe ride you pay more than the going rate.

Shuttle services generally pick up passengers from a designated spot along the curb. New York Airport Service runs buses between JFK and LaGuardia airports, and buses from those airports to Grand Central Terminal, Port Authority Bus Terminal, Penn Station, and hotels between 27th and 63rd streets in Manhattan. The cost is between $10 and $15. Buses operate from 6 AM to 11:10 PM from the airport; between 5 AM and 10 PM going to the airport. A $5 bus leaves either airport on the hour from 8 AM to 8 PM for Long Island Railroad's Jamaica Station. The ride between both airports and the station is 30 minutes. SuperShuttle vans travel to and from Manhattan to JFK, LaGuardia, and Newark. These blue vans can stop at your home, office, or hotel. Courtesy phones are at the airports. For travel to the airport, the company requests 24-hour advance notice. Fares range from $13 to $22.

🛈 Transfer Information Air-Ride Transportation Information Service ☎ 800/247-7433 ⊕ www.panynj.gov/aviation.html.

🛈 Car Reservations Carmel Car Service ☎ 212/666-6666 or 800/922-7635 ⊕ www.carmelcarservice.com. **London Towncars** ☎ 212/988-9700 or 800/221-4009 ⊕ www.londontowncars.com. **Tel Aviv Car and Limousine Service** ☎ 212/777-7777 or 800/222-9888 ⊕ www.telavivlimo.com.

🛈 Shuttle Service New York Airport Service ☎ 718/875-8200 ⊕ www.nyairportservice.com. **SuperShuttle** ☎ 212/258-3826 ⊕ www.supershuttle.com.

FROM JFK
INTERNATIONAL
AIRPORT
Taxis charge a flat fee of $45 plus tolls (which may be as much as $6) to Manhattan only, and take 35–60 minutes. Prices are $16–$55 for trips to other locations in New York City. You should also tip the driver.

AirTrain JFK links to the A subway line's Howard Beach station, and to Long Island Railroad's Jamaica Station, which is adjacent to the Sutphin Boulevard/Archer Avenue E/J/Z subway station, with connections to Manhattan. The light-rail system runs 24 hours, leaving from the Howard Beach and LIRR stations every 4 to 8 minutes during peak times and every 12 minutes during low traffic times. From midtown Manhattan, the longest trip to JFK is via the A train, a trip of less than an hour that costs

$2 in subway fare in addition to $5 for the AirTrain. The quickest trip is with the Long Island Railroad (about 30 minutes), for a total cost of about $12. When traveling to the Howard Beach station, be sure to take the A train marked FAR ROCKAWAY or ROCKAWAY PARK, **not** LEFFERTS BOULEVARD. ⚃ JFK Transport Information AirTrain JFK ⊕ www.airtrainjfk.com. Long Island Railroad Jamaica Station ⊠ 146 Archer Ave., at Sutphin Blvd. ☎ 718/217-5477.

FROM LAGUARDIA AIRPORT

Taxis cost $15–$30 plus tip and tolls (which may be as high as $6) to most destinations in New York City, and take at least 20–40 minutes.

For $2 you can ride the M-60 public bus (there are no luggage facilities on this bus) to 116th Street and Broadway, across from Columbia University in Manhattan. From there you can transfer to the No. 1 subway to Midtown. Alternatively, you can take Bus Q-48 to the Main Street subway station in Flushing, where you can transfer to the No. 7 train. Allow at least 90 minutes for the entire trip to Midtown.

Triboro Coach Corp. runs its Q-33 line from the airport to the Jackson Heights subway stop in Queens, where you can transfer to the E or F train; it also stops at the Roosevelt Avenue–Jackson Heights station, where you can pick up the No. 7 subway line. The cost is $2. ⚃ LaGuardia Transport Information Triboro Coach Corp. ☎ 718/335-1000 ⊕ www. triborocoach.com.

FROM NEWARK AIRPORT

Taxis to Manhattan cost $40–$65 plus tolls ($5) and take 20–45 minutes. "Share and Save" group rates are available for up to four passengers between 8 AM and midnight—make arrangements with the airport's taxi dispatcher. If you're heading to the airport from Manhattan, there's an extra $10 surcharge.

AirTrain Newark is an elevated light-rail system that connects to New Jersey Transit and Amtrak trains at the Newark Liberty International Airport Station. Total travel time to Penn Station in Manhattan is approximately 20 minutes and costs $11.15 if you connect to a New Jersey train. AirTrain runs from 5 AM to 2 AM daily.

Before heading to Manhattan, the AirTrain makes a stop at Newark's Penn Station. The five-minute ride here costs $6.80. From Newark Penn Station you can catch PATH trains, which run to Manhattan 24 hours a day. PATH trains run every 10 minutes on weekdays, every 15 to 30 minutes on weeknights, and every 20 to 30 minutes on weekends. They travel along 6th Avenue in Manhattan, making stops at Christopher Street, West 9th Street, West 14th Street, West 23rd Street, and West 33rd Street. The fare is $1.50.

Olympia Trails buses leave for Grand Central Terminal and Penn Station in Manhattan about every 20 minutes until midnight. The trip takes roughly 45 minutes, and the fare is $12. Between the Port Authority or Grand Central Terminal and Newark, buses run every 20 to 30 minutes. The fare is $12. ⚃ Newark Transport Information AirTrain Newark ☎ 888/397-4636 ⊕ www. airtrainnewark.com. Olympia Trails ☎ 212/964-6233 or 877/894-9155 ⊕ www. olympiabus.com. PATH Trains ☎ 800/234-7284 ⊕ www.pathrail.com.

BOAT & FERRY TRAVEL

The Staten Island Ferry runs across New York Harbor between White-hall Street next to Battery Park in lower Manhattan and St. George terminal in Staten Island. The free 25-minute ride gives you views of the Financial District skyscrapers, the Statue of Liberty, and Ellis Island.

New York Water Taxi shuttles riders to the city's waterfront attractions between the West and East sides and Lower Manhattan, the South Street Seaport, and Brooklyn's waterfront parks. The 24-hour hop-on, hop-off ticket is $15 for adults.

NY Waterway is primarily a commuter service but also has sightseeing cruises. Its *Yankee Clipper* and *Mets Express* ferries take passengers from Manhattan and New Jersey to Yankee Stadium and Shea Stadium for $16 round-trip. NY Waterway also travels to Hoboken and Jersey City, New Jersey, from four Manhattan piers.

New York Water Taxi (NYWT) ☎ 212/742-1969 ⊕ www.newyorkwatertaxi.com. **NY Waterway** ☎ 800/533-3779 ⊕ www.nywaterway.com. **Staten Island Ferry** ☎ 718/815-2628.

BUS TRAVEL TO & FROM NEW YORK CITY

Most long-haul and commuter bus lines feed into the Port Authority Terminal, on 8th Avenue between West 40th and 42nd streets. For information, *see* Bus Travel *in* Smart Travel Tips.

BUS TRAVEL WITHIN NEW YORK CITY

Most city buses follow easy-to-understand routes along the Manhattan street grid. Routes go up or down the north–south avenues, or east and west on the major two-way crosstown streets: 96th, 86th, 79th, 72nd, 57th, 42nd, 34th, 23rd, and 14th. Most bus routes operate 24 hours. Certain bus routes provide "Limited-Stop Service" during weekday rush hours, stopping only at major cross streets and transfer points. A sign posted at the front of the bus indicates it has limited service. To find a bus stop, look for a light-blue sign (green for a limited bus) on a green pole; bus numbers and routes are listed, with the stop's name underneath.

Bus fare is $2. Pay when you board with exact change in coins or with a MetroCard. When using cash you can ask the driver for a free transfer coupon, good for one change to an intersecting bus route, but not the subway system. Legal transfer points are listed on the back of the slip. Transfers generally have time limits of two hours. MetroCards allow you one free transfer between buses or from bus to subway

Route maps and schedules are posted at many bus stops in Manhattan and at major stops throughout the other boroughs. The best places to obtain them are the MTA booth in the Times Square Visitors Center, or the information kiosks in Grand Central Terminal and Penn Station.

Metropolitan Transit Authority ☎ 718/330-1234 travel information center, 718/243-7777 status-information hotline ⊕ www.mta.nyc.ny.us.

CAR TRAVEL

Driving within Manhattan can be a nightmare. Narrow and one-way streets are common, particularly Downtown. The most congested streets of the city lie between 14th and 59th streets and 3rd and 8th avenues. Try to avoid the morning and evening rush hours as well as lunch hour.

Free parking is difficult to find in Midtown, and violators may be towed away literally within minutes. All over town, parking lots charge exorbitant rates—as much as $23 for two hours—so use your car sparingly in Manhattan. Instead, park it in a guarded parking garage for at least several hours, or, if you do find a spot on the street be sure to check parking signs carefully.

On city streets the speed limit is 30 miles per hour, unless otherwise posted. Turning right on red isn't allowed within city limits. Be alert for one-way streets and "no left turn" intersections.

DISCOUNTS & DEALS

Numerous tourist-oriented publications available at hotels, stores, and attractions have coupons good for discounts of all kinds. Cut-rate theater tickets are sold at TKTS booths in Times Square and South Street Seaport. Some major museums have evenings with free or pay-what-you-wish admission one day a week.

Consider purchasing a CityPass, a group of tickets to six top-notch attractions in New York—the Empire State Building (including the SkyRide), the Guggenheim Museum, the American Museum of Natural History, the Museum of Modern Art, Circle Line Cruises, and the *Intrepid* Sea-Air-Space Museum. The pass, which saves you half the cost of each individual ticket, is good for nine days from first use. It also allows you to beat long ticket lines at some attractions. You can buy a CityPass online or at any of the participants' ticket offices.

🔒 **CityPass** ☎ 208/787-4300 or 888/330-5008 ⊕ www.citypass.com.

EMERGENCIES

New Yorkers are sympathetic to out-of-towners in need of help. Dial 911 for police, fire, or ambulance services in an emergency (TTY is available for people with hearing impairments).

🔒 Hospitals **Bellevue** ⊠ 462 1st Ave., at E. 27th St., Gramercy ☎ 212/562-4141. **Beth Israel Medical Center** ⊠ 1st Ave. at E. 16th St., Gramercy ☎ 212/420-2000. **Lenox Hill Hospital** ⊠ 100 E. 77th St., between Lexington and Park Aves., Upper East Side ☎ 212/434-3030. **New York Presbyterian Hospital** ⊠ 525 E. 68th St., at York Ave., Upper East Side ☎ 212/746-5454. **NYU Hospital Downtown** ⊠ 170 William St., between Beekman and Spruce Sts., Lower Manhattan ☎ 212/312-5000. **NYU Health Center** ⊠ 550 1st Ave., at E. 32nd St., Murray Hill ☎ 212/263-5550. **St. Luke's-Roosevelt Hospital** ⊠ 10th Ave. at 59th St., Midtown West ☎ 212/523-6800. **St. Vincent's Hospital** ⊠ 7th Ave. and W. 12th St., Greenwich Village ☎ 212/604-8000.

🔒 Hotlines **Crime Victims** ☎ 212/577-7777. **LIFENET (counseling information and referrals)** ☎ 800/543-3638. **Mental Health** ☎ 212/219-5599. **Sex Crimes Report Line** ☎ 212/267-7273. **Terrorism** ☎ 888/692-7233.

🔒 24-Hour Pharmacies **CVS** ⊠ 342 E. 23rd St., between 1st and 2nd Aves., Gramercy ☎ 212/505-1555 ⊠ 630 Lexington Ave., at E. 53rd St., Midtown East ☎ 917/369-8688 ⊕ www.cvs.com. **Rite-Aid** ⊠ 303 W. 50th St., at 8th Ave., Midtown West ☎ 212/247-8736 ⊕ www.riteaid.com.

SUBWAY TRAVEL

The 714-mi subway system operates 24 hours a day and serves nearly all the places you are likely to visit. During the workweek it is often faster than either taxis or buses. The trains are clean, well lighted, and almost always air-conditioned. Still, many trains are crowded, the older ones are noisy, and homeless people and panhandlers are often on board.

Most subway entrances are at street corners and are marked by lamp-posts with an illuminated Metropolitan Transit Authority (MTA) logo or globe-shape green or red lights—green means open and red means closed. Each station entrance has a sign indicating the lines that run through the station. Some entrances are also marked "uptown only" or "downtown only." Subway lines are designated by numbers and letters, such as the 3 Line or the A Line. Some lines run "express" and skip stops, and others are "locals" and make all stops. One of the most frequent mistakes visitors make is taking the train in the wrong direction. Maps of the full subway system are posted in every train car and usually on the subway platform. You can usually pick up free maps at station booths.

For the most up-to-date information on subway lines, call the MTA's Travel Information Center or visit its Web site. Alternatively, ask a station agent.

FARES &
TRANSFERS
Subway fare is $2. Pay your subway fare at the turnstile, using a Metro-Card purchased at the station booth or from a vending machine. You can transfer between subway lines an unlimited number of times at any of the stations where lines intersect. You can also transfer to intersecting MTA bus routes for free if you use a MetroCard to pay your fare.
🚇 **Metropolitan Transit Authority** ☎ 718/330-1234 travel information center, 212/712-4500 lost-property office, 718/243-7777 status-information hotline ⊕ www.mta.nyc.ny.us.

TAXIS & CAR SERVICES

Yellow cabs are in abundance almost everywhere in Manhattan, cruising the streets looking for fares. They are usually easy to hail on the street or from a taxi rank in front of major hotels, though finding one at rush hour or in the rain can take some time. You can see if a taxi is available by checking its rooftop light: the center panel should be lighted and the side panels dark. Taxi fares cost $2.50 for the first ⅓ mi, 40¢ for each ⅓ mi thereafter, and 40¢ for every two minutes not in motion. A $1 surcharge is added to rides begun between 4 PM and 8 PM, and a 50¢ surcharge is added to rides begun between 8 PM and 6 AM. You must pay any bridge or tunnel tolls incurred during your trip. Taxi drivers expect a 15% to 20% tip.

Know where you want to go and how to get there before you hail a cab. Direct your cabdriver by the cross streets of your destination (for instance, "5th Avenue and 42nd Street"), rather than the numerical address, which means little to many drivers. A quick call to your destination will give you cross-street information.
🚖 Car Services **Carmel Car Service** ☎ 212/666-6666. **Highbridge Car Service** ☎ 212/927-4600. **Tel-Aviv** ☎ 212/777-7777.

SIGHTSEEING TOURS

BOAT TOURS   In good weather a Circle Line Cruise is one of the best ways to get oriented. Once you've finished the three-hour, 35-mi circumnavigation of Manhattan, you have a good idea of where things are and what you want to see next. Narrations are as interesting and individual as the guides who deliver them. The Circle Line operates daily, and the price is $26. Semi-Circle cruises, a more limited tour of three hours, also run daily; the price is $21.

NY Waterway runs two-hour harbor cruises for $24. Dates and times vary, but the cruises run year-round; the Twilight Cruise ($19) operates from May through early November.

Several cruises leave from South Street Seaport's Pier 16. The cargo schooner *Pioneer* makes two-hour voyages Tuesday through Sunday, from after Memorial Day through mid-September.

Seaport Liberty Cruises run daily, hour-long sightseeing tours of New York Harbor and lower Manhattan; the cost is $13. There are also two-hour cruises with live jazz and blues on Wednesday and Thursday nights, from June through August. For serious water fans, four- and six-hour Saturday trips are run from April through October aboard the wooden *W. O. Decker* tugboat, operated by the South Street Seaport Museum. Adult fare starts at $125.

Spirit City New York sets out on lunch ($30–$45) and dinner ($50–$85) cruises. The meal is accompanied by live music and dancing. Private parties can also be arranged.

World Yacht Cruises serves Sunday brunch ($42) on two-hour cruises, and dinner ($70–$80) on three-hour cruises. The Continental cuisine is restaurant quality, prepared by some of New York's leading chefs, and there's music and dancing on board. Dinner cruises run daily from April through December, and weekends only from January through March (weather permitting). Brunch cruises run only April through December. Reservations are necessary.

BUS TOURS   Gray Line New York runs a number of "hop-on, hop-off" double-decker bus tours in various languages, including a downtown Manhattan loop, upper Manhattan loop, Harlem gospel tour, and evening tours of the city. Packages include entrance fees to attractions and one-day MetroCards. The company also books sightseeing cruises, as well as day trips to Atlantic City, West Point, and other locations in the New York area.

New York Double-Decker Tours runs authentic London double-decker buses year-round, 9 AM–6 PM in summer, 9 AM–3 PM in winter, making stops every 15–30 minutes. Tickets, which are valid for boarding and reboarding all day for five days, cost $26 for a Downtown loop, $26 for an Uptown loop, and $40 for a combination ticket. For all tours, you can hop on and off as often as you like.

HELICOPTER TOURS   Liberty Helicopter Tours has six pilot-narrated tours from $56 per person on up to $849 for a tour of up to eight people. Some tours depart from Pier 6 in Lower Manhattan.

PRIVATE GUIDES   Arthur Marks creates customized tours on which he sings show tunes about the city. Private tours start at $350; you may wish to inquire about group tours, which Marks gives from May through November.

Walk of the Town tailors tours to your interests; special themes include "Cops, Crooks, and the Courts," "When Harlem Was Jewish," and "The Lullaby of Broadway." Tours are available by appointment only; most start at $300.

SPECIAL-   Central Park Walking Tours cover the park daily. Some of its 90-minute
INTEREST TOURS   tours are thematic, investigating such features as prominent trees and the park's unique bridges and arches. Bite of the Big Apple Central Park Bicycle Tour organizes two-hour bicycle trips through Central Park with stops along the way, including Strawberry Fields and Belvedere Castle. One tour is devoted to areas of the park used in movies.

Ellen Sax Tours & Events arranges architectural sightseeing, visits to museums, galleries, the Theater District, the Financial District, and other neighborhoods in Manhattan for groups of six or more.

Harlem Spirituals leads combination bus and walking tours and Sunday gospel trips to Harlem. Also in Harlem, you can trace the history of jazz backstage at the Apollo Theater.

The Lower East Side Tenement Museum runs a tour of the Lower East Side, retracing its history as an immigrant community; it's available weekends, April through December.

Opera buffs can tour scenery and costume shops and the stage area on Metropolitan Opera House Backstage Tours.

Quintessential New York has more than a dozen specialty tours for groups of six or more, each with a behind-the-scenes take. For example, during "The Artist Colony: SoHo" tour, guests visit an artist's studio and an antiques dealer's workshop. Another plus is the chauffeured car.

The South Street Seaport Museum has tours of historic ships and the waterfront, as well as predawn forays through the fish market.

WALKING TOURS: Howard Goldberg's Adventure on a Shoestring is an organization dat-
GUIDED   ing from 1963 that explores New York neighborhoods. The weekend tours run rain or shine, and cost $5 per person. Occasional tours cover the haunts of celebrities such as Katharine Hepburn and Jacqueline Onassis. Reservations are a must.

The wisecracking PhD candidates of Big Onion Walking Tours lead themed tours such as "New York in War & Peace" and "The Multi-Ethnic Eating Tour: From Naples to Bialystock to Beijing" in addition to neighborhood walks. The Downtown Alliance conducts free, history-rich tours of the Wall Street area on Thursday and Saturday at noon. Meet on the steps of the U.S. Customs House (the National Museum of the American Indian) at Bowling Green.

The Municipal Art Society conducts a series of walking tours on weekdays and both bus and walking tours on weekends. Tours emphasize the architecture and history of particular neighborhoods. New York City

Cultural Walking Tours have covered such sundry topics as buildings' gargoyles and the old Yiddish theaters of the East Village. Tours are run every Sunday from March to December; private tours can be scheduled throughout the week. Urban Explorations runs tours with an emphasis on architecture and landscape design. Chinatown is a specialty.

The Urban Park Rangers conducts free weekend walks and workshops in city parks. The knowledgeable Joyce Gold has been conducting tours since 1976. Regular historical walks include Harlem, Gramercy Park, and the Lower East Side. The contributions of immigrants and artists to various neighborhoods are often highlighted in other tours.

WALKING TOURS: The SoundWalk line of tour CDs, published by Oversampling, Inc., cov-
SELF-GUIDED   ers unusual sights in a nonstuffy manner. They get you off the main drags and on to the less traveled parts of such areas as the Bronx, Times Square, and Dumbo. The tours sell for around $20 and are available online and through various stores in the city, including Tower Records. For a narrated tour of Central Park, pick up an audio guide from the bike rental shop Pedal Pusher. It costs $10 for the day.

🚣 Boat Tours **Circle Line Cruise** ✉ Pier 83 at W. 42nd St., Midtown West ☎ 212/563-3200 ⊕ www.circleline.com. **NY Waterway** ✉ Pier 17 at South St. Seaport, Lower Manhattan ✉ Pier 78 at W. 38th St. and 12th Ave., Midtown West ☎ 800/533-3779 ⊕ www.nywaterway.com. *Pioneer* ✉ Pier 16 at South St. Seaport, Lower Manhattan ☎ 212/748-8786 ⊕ www.southstseaport.org. **Seaport Liberty Cruises** ✉ Pier 16 at South St. Seaport, Lower Manhattan ☎ 212/563-3200, 212/630-8888 blues cruise ⊕ www.circleline.com. *Spirit City New York* Cruise ✉ Pier 61 at W. 23rd St. and 12th Ave., Chelsea ☎ 212/742-7278 ⊕ www.spiritcruises.com. *W. O. Decker* Tugboat ✉ Pier 16 at South St. Seaport, Lower Manhattan ☎ 212/748-8786 ⊕ www.southstseaport.org. **World Yacht Cruises** ✉ Pier 81 at W. 41st St. and 12th Ave., Midtown West ☎ 212/630-8100 ⊕ www.worldyacht.com.

🚌 Bus Tours **Gray Line New York** ✉ Port Authority Bus Terminal, 625 8th Ave., at 42nd St., Midtown West ☎ 800/669-0051 ⊕ www.graylinenewyork.com. **New York Double-Decker Tours** ☎ 877/693-3253

🚁 Helicopter Tours **Liberty Helicopter Tours** ✉ Heliport, W. 30th St. at 12th Ave., Midtown West ☎ 212/967-6464 ⊕ www.libertyhelicopters.com.

🚶 Private Guides **Arthur Marks** ☎ 212/673-0477. **Walk of the Town** ☎ 212/222-5343.

🎭 Special-Interest Tours **Apollo Theater** ☎ 212/531-5305 ⊕ www.apollotheater.com. **Bite of the Big Apple** ☎ 212/541-8759 ⊕ www.centralparkbiketour.com. **Central Park Walking Tours** ☎ 212/721-0874 ⊕ www.centralparkwalkingtours.com. **Ellen Sax Tours** ☎ 212/832-0350. **Harlem Spirituals** ☎ 212/391-0900 or 800/660-2166 ⊕ www.harlemspirituals.com. **Lower East Side Tenement Museum** ☎ 212/431-0233 ⊕ www.tenement.org. **Metropolitan Opera House Backstage** ☎ 212/769-7020 ⊕ www.metguild.org/education. **Quintessential New York** ☎ 212/595-6510 ⊕ www.qny.com. **South Street Seaport Museum** ☎ 212/748-8590 ⊕ www.southstseaport.com.

🚶 Walking Tours: Guided **Adventure on a Shoestring** ☎ 212/265-2663. **Big Onion Walking Tours** ☎ 212/439-1090 ⊕ www.bigonion.com. **Downtown Alliance** ☎ 212/606-4064 ⊕ www.downtownny.com. **Joyce Gold** ☎ 212/242-5762 ⊕ www.nyctours.com. **Municipal Art Society** ☎ 212/935-3960, 212/439-1049 for recorded information ⊕ www.mas.org. **New York City Cultural Walking Tours** ☎ 212/979-2388 ⊕ www.nycwalk.com. **Urban Explorations** ☎ 718/721-5254. **Urban Park Rangers** ☎ 866/692-4295 ⊕ www.nycparks.org.

Walking Tours: Self-Guided **Pedal Pusher** ☒ 1306 2nd Ave., between E. 68th and E. 69th Sts., Upper East Side ☎ 212/288-5592. **SoundWalk** ☎ www.soundwalk.com.

VISITOR INFORMATION

The Grand Central Partnership has installed a number of unstaffed information kiosks near Grand Central Terminal, loaded with maps and helpful brochures on attractions throughout the city. There are also seasonal outdoor carts sprinkled throughout the area, staffed by friendly, knowledgeable, multilingual New Yorkers. The 34th Street Partnership runs a kiosk on the concourse level at Penn Station (33rd Street and 7th Avenue) and a cart at the Empire State Building (5th Avenue at 34th Street). New York City & Company has brochures, subway and bus maps, MetroCards, a calendar of events, listings of hotels and weekend hotel packages, and discount coupons for Broadway shows. In addition to its main center in Times Square, the bureau also runs kiosks at the south tip of City Hall Park and in Harlem at 163 West 125th Street, near Adam Clayton Powell Jr. Boulevard. The Downtown Alliance has information on the area encompassing City Hall south to Battery Park, and from the East River to West Street. For a free booklet listing New York City attractions and tour packages, contact the New York State Division of Tourism.

Brooklyn Information & Culture Inc. (BRIC) ☒ 647 Fulton St., 2nd fl., Brooklyn 11217 ☎ 718/855-7882 ⊕ www.brooklynX.org. **Downtown Alliance** ☒ 120 Broadway. Suite 3340, between Pine and Thames, Lower Manhattan 10271 ☎ 212/566-6700 ⊕ www. downtownny.com. **NYC & Company Convention & Visitors Bureau** ☒ 810 7th Ave., between W. 52nd and W. 53rd Sts., 3rd fl., Midtown West ☎ 212/484-1222 ⊕ www. nycvisit.com. **Times Square Visitors Center** ☒ 1560 Broadway, between 46th and 47th Sts., Midtown West ☎ 212/768-1560 ⊕ www.timessquarebid.org.

LONG ISLAND

2

STAKE OUT YOUR SPOT
on the sands of Jones Beach ⇨ *p.169*

GET A GLIMPSE OF GOLD
touring Old Westbury Gardens ⇨ *p.134*

SATISFY YOUR SHOPPING ITCH
in charming Southampton ⇨ *p.182*

STOP OFF FOR LUNCH
at the famed Lobster Roll ⇨ *p.201*

FOLLOW THE TRAIL
to the North Fork wineries ⇨ *p.150*

MAKE TIME TO SMELL THE ROSES
at Planting Fields Arboretum ⇨ *p.136*

TEE OFF
at the legendary Bethpage State Park ⇨ *p.171*

OGLE WATERFRONT MANSIONS
as you stroll along Cooper's Beach ⇨ *p.182*

Revised by Ann
Hammerle

AT 1,377 SQUARE MI, Long Island is the largest island on the East Coast, as well as the most varied. From west to east the island shifts from overcrowded roads and suburban sprawl to verdant farmland and fruit-laden vineyards punctuated by historic seaside villages. The island is notable for having one of the nation's finest stretches of white-sand beach, along its South Shore, as well as one of its most congested highways, the notorious Long Island Expressway. In addition to superb beaches, nature has given Long Island bountiful harbors and coves, rich soil, and a fascinating geology, whereas its inhabitants have given it a long and distinguished history, beautiful old homes, and, more recently, wonderful places to eat and stay.

Although two of New York City's boroughs, Brooklyn and Queens, occupy the island's western section, the *real* Long Island begins only when you leave the city behind and cross into Nassau County. East of Nassau is the more rural Suffolk County, with its North and South forks extending far into the Atlantic Ocean. The north–south distinction also applies to the North and South shores that run the length of the island. Noteworthy attractions of the North Shore, which stretches from Great Neck to Port Jefferson, include Teddy Roosevelt's summer home at Sagamore Hill, Walt Whitman's birthplace at Huntington Station, and Gold Coast mansions. North Fork highlights include quiet villages, bountiful farm stands, and the vineyards and tasting rooms of a burgeoning wine industry. Fronting Long Island Sound, the beaches on the North Shore are tame, particularly in comparison with the ocean waves of the South Shore beaches. The spectacular sandy stretches at Jones Beach, Fire Island, and Robert Moses State Park make the South Shore unforgettable. The cultured yet buzzing Hamptons, the fascinating old whaling village of Sag Harbor, and majestic Montauk Point are the essence of the South Fork.

Native Americans inhabited the area long before the Europeans arrived. In the early 1500s Verrazano reported seeing campfires on the shore as he sailed toward what is now New York. Settlers arrived in the 17th century, and the area was colonized quickly, in part because two nations were building settlements here simultaneously. While the Dutch were pushing eastward from their stronghold on New Amsterdam (today's Manhattan), the English were sailing down from newly settled Connecticut and Massachusetts to set up outposts at Hempstead, East Hampton, Southampton, Southold, and Brookhaven.

Agriculture, particularly potato farming, was the basis of Long Island's early economy, and later, in the 18th and early 19th centuries, whaling brought a brief period of wealth and prominence to Sag Harbor, Greenport, and Cold Spring Harbor. After the Civil War, when well-to-do Americans discovered the pleasures of saltwater bathing and cool sea breezes, the farming and fishing communities of the Hamptons were slowly transformed into fashionable summer resorts, and the North Shore became the playground of the Vanderbilts, Whitneys, and Roosevelts. It wasn't until after World War II, when highways were constructed and Americans began owning cars as a matter of course, that vast numbers of the middle class moved out to Long Island, converting farm fields into new suburbs and shopping centers.

Today, even amid the sprawl of new homes and commercial districts, old village centers remain intact. Historic sites and museums protect many of the oldest, finest, and most magnificent homes. New farms growing wine grapes, herbs, and nursery plants have been established on old potato farms. Beyond the hubbub of development and traffic, the beaches and the waters of the sound and ocean beckon swimmers, anglers, sailors, sunbathers, and beachcombers as they always have.

Exploring Long Island

From the Nassau–Queens border to its eastern terminus at Montauk Point, Long Island is 103 mi long and from 12 to 20 mi wide. There's plenty to see on the island, but you'll spot little but traffic from the Long Island Expressway (U.S. 495, known to most residents as the LIE), which runs through the middle of the island from Long Island City in Queens all the way east to Riverhead in Suffolk. Summer weekends can be particularly problematic, when people head straight for either the South Shore's Fire Island or the South Fork's Hamptons and points east to Montauk. If you're more interested in the museums, stately mansions, nature preserves, and other attractions of the North and South shores, take the more leisurely roads that follow the two coastlines. On the North Shore, your best bet is Route 25A; on the South Shore, follow Route 27 (Sunrise Highway). Many north–south roads connect the shores, so cutting back and forth is easy. If your schedule is tight, stick to the LIE or the Northern State or Southern State parkways to make the best time between points of interest.

By choosing the most direct route, it's possible to drive from Manhattan to Montauk Point in less than three hours—although rush-hour and weekend traffic can cause significant delays. Once you reach Riverhead on the LIE, Long Island separates into the North and South forks. Each fork is traversed by a two-lane highway (Route 25 on the North Fork, Route 27 on the South Fork), and the surroundings become increasingly rural the farther east you go. Be prepared for travel to slow considerably once you are on the forks, especially in the height of summer; there are, however, lots of interesting farm stands and shops along the way to take your mind off the slowdown. Shelter Island, between the two forks, is a destination in itself; the only way to get here is by a short ferry ride from either Sag Harbor, on the South Fork, or Greenport, on the North Fork.

About the Hotels & Restaurants

Every conceivable cuisine is served at restaurants, cafés, and diners across Long Island, but fresh seafood is the most notable regional specialty. It's not uncommon for chefs to prepare delectable dishes in the evening using seafood caught on the morning of the same day. A trend toward using organic foods and fresh local produce has increased the quality of restaurant meals here. If you enjoy good wine with your meal, try the Long Island chardonnays and merlots. The soil and climate on the North Fork have been compared to the finest wine-producing areas of France, and the wines reflect that quality. On the North and South forks, many restaurants change their schedules depending on the time of year, so it's always a good idea to call ahead in the off-season.

Long Island, 118 mi long, is strewn with interesting sights and diversions. Travel via your own vehicle is essential for exploring many of these places and activities; it also gives you the greatest amount of flexibility. That said, traffic can add hours to your travel times, regardless of where you go on the island. If you have only a few days for a visit, focus on one or two regions.

Numbers in the text correspond to numbers in the margin and on the Long Island map.

2

**If you have
1 day**

If you're starting from New York City, the North Shore's **Oyster Bay** ⑥, **Northport** ⑨, and **Port Jefferson** ⑪ make for easy day-trip destinations. If seeing a beach is your primary focus, head for the South Shore: **Long Beach** ⑲, **Jones Beach State Park** ⑳, or Robert Moses State Park, on the western end of **Fire Island** ㉔. Another option is to head straight for the wineries around **Riverhead** ⑫.

**If you have
3 days**

The Hamptons offer recreational opportunities galore, including hiking, horseback riding, surfing, tennis, and biking (depending on the season), but the beaches are the main attraction. Pick a base—whether it's ▦ **Westhampton Beach** ㉕, ▦ **Southampton** ㉗, ▦ **East Hampton** ㉛, or ▦ **Montauk** ㉜—from which to visit nearby villages. You can loll about on a beach, take a fishing trip, eat at top restaurants, shop at stylish boutiques, and see a few sights.

Alternatively, break up a stay on laid-back ▦ **Shelter Island** ⑰ with a visit to **Greenport** ⑮. Stop at a couple of North Fork wineries and antiques stores on your way to or from Shelter Island.

**If you have
5 days**

You can easily combine tastes of the North and South forks by staying in ▦ **Westhampton Beach** ㉕, ▦ **Sag Harbor** ㉚, **Greenport** ⑮, or ▦ **Shelter Island** ⑰. Let the weather dictate your schedule. Rainy and cold days are good for checking out the wineries, museums, and shops. On the hottest days, head for the beach either in the morning or in the late afternoon. On your way to or from eastern Long Island, stop to see Teddy Roosevelt's summer home, in **Oyster Bay** ⑥, or Old Westbury Gardens, in **Old Westbury** ④.

More than 340 lodging properties across Long Island—chain hotels, oceanfront condos, cottages, and bed-and-breakfasts—provide close to 15,000 rooms. Most resort-town lodgings are booked far in advance in summer, but occasional cancellations mean you can sometimes travel on a whim. In beach areas, many lodging properties offer their guests day-use beach passes, giving you access to sandy stretches reserved for residents. Some places on Fire Island and on the North and South forks institute three-night minimums during the peak season. Island real-estate agents have listings for seasonal and weekly rentals, and local chambers of commerce can point you in the right direction for a place to stay.

WHAT IT COSTS				
$$$$	$$$	$$	$	¢
RESTAURANTS over $30	$22–$30	$15–$21	$8–$14	under $8
HOTELS over $250	$200–$250	$150–$199	$100–$149	under $100

Restaurant prices are for a main course at dinner (or at the most expensive meal served). Hotel prices are for two people in a standard double room in high season, excluding tax.

Timing

Long Island beach connoisseurs know that early autumn is the best time to visit; the water stays warm into September and sometimes even early October, and the crowds thin considerably. Of course, if you love the action, you'll want to be here in summer, when everything's open and the weather is most predictable. Book rooms a couple of months in advance for summer travel. Spring usually bursts onto Long Island in late March; suddenly everything is newly green, the gardens awaken, the shorebirds build their nests, and even the ocean loses its winter gray and starts to sparkle. Winter is good for solitary, though cold and windy, beach walks, and it's the only time of year you can see seals and sea turtles.

THE NORTH SHORE

Revised by Donna Kirdahy

Jagged in its coastal outline and gentle in its topography, the North Shore is lapped by Long Island Sound, which F. Scott Fitzgerald called "the most domesticated body of saltwater in the Western Hemisphere." The Gold Coast, a string of wealthy suburbs, stretches along the shore for about 18 mi from Great Neck, 22 mi east of New York City, east to Huntington. As you drive east along Route 25A into Nassau County, you cut across the bases of two peninsulas that make up the towns of Great Neck and Port Washington, the West Egg and East Egg of Fitzgerald's *The Great Gatsby.*

Great Neck

❶ *22 mi east of New York City.*

The western gateway to the North Shore of Long Island, Great Neck sits on a peninsula jutting into Long Island Sound. Ever since Dutch settlers founded the city in 1681, people have been attracted by its tranquil setting and proximity to Manhattan. The mansions here inspired the wealthy estates F. Scott Fitzgerald wrote about in his classic novel *The Great Gatsby.* Today the city is a thriving residential, shopping, and business area. Great Neck Plaza, a small village within the greater community that is filled with upscale shops, is its hub.

Kings Point Park. The 175 acres at this park hold 5 mi of hiking trails, 26 picnic areas, four softball diamonds, a soccer field, and two all-weather basketball courts. There are also four clay tennis courts, but a permit is necessary for summer play. ✉ *Steamboat Rd.* ☎ *516/482-9257* 🎫 *Free* ☉ *Daily 8–sunset.*

Beaches Clean white-sand beaches are Long Island's main attraction for most visitors, whether their idea of beach fun is lounging on the warm sand, watching the sun drop slowly into the water, swimming or surfing in the rolling waves, or just strolling along the shore and breathing the fresh salt air. For serious waves, head to the magnificent South Shore, which includes Jones Beach, Robert Moses, and Fire Island. The seashore tends to get crowded on summer weekends, but as you move out east, the crowds thin—especially all the way out in Montauk. Most Hamptons beaches are open only to residents, but lodging properties usually have beach passes for their guests. The North Shore beaches, on Long Island Sound, draw smaller crowds, and although they lack the drama of the pounding surf and endless horizons, their calmer waters are ideal for young children.

Fishing Lined on one side by the Long Island Sound and on the other by the Atlantic Ocean, and nicked by numerous bays and harbors, Long Island provides countless chances for anglers to indulge their passion and fisherfolk to make their living. The waters here draw commercial-fishing vessels and sporting boats, pros and weekend warriors. In virtually every village that snuggles up against the water, you find docks, marinas, bait-and-tackle shops, and people willing to discuss the tides, weather, and best places to fish. Depending on the season and area, you can try your rod at striped bass, fluke, bluefish, flounder, skate, and even tuna and shark offshore. There's good surf casting at Montauk Point and Jones Beach. Charter boats glide in and out of harbors at Greenport, Shelter Island, and Montauk, filled with people seeking a prize for their wall or freezer.

Wineries The white-sand beaches of the North Fork encircle a broad, central agricultural belt that, it turns out, has near-perfect conditions for ripening European grape varieties like merlot and chardonnay. Now that the quality of Long Island wines rivals that of the world's top labels, the North Fork draws serious wine lovers and sightseeing fun seekers alike. Navigating the North Fork wine trail is really about deciding how often to stop, as all but three of the region's 30 wineries are on Route 25, which runs east–west through the fork, or on Route 48, running north of and parallel to Route 25. Each winery has its own personality; some encourage a quiet focus on the wine, whereas at others you jostle for a place at the lively bar. Some are in old barns that retain rural charm in wide-planked wood floors, heavy beams, and old farming equipment. Summer weekends—particularly when bad weather foils beach plans—attract droves of winery-hoppers. Fall brings harvest festivals and day-trippers buying fresh vegetables at farm stands and mixed cases of wines for the holidays. Off-season, the wineries are very quiet, and you're likely to be showered with extra attention.

Saddle Rock Grist Mill. This is one of the few tidal gristmills still in operation in the United States, and a miller is often on hand to distribute samples of ground corn and wheat. Although the mill has been restored to look as it did in the early 1800s, it's actually much older than this: the mill records date to 1702. ⊠ *Grist Mill La.* ☎ *516/572–0257* 🎫 *Free* ⊙ *Mid-May–mid-Oct., Sun. tours 1–5.*

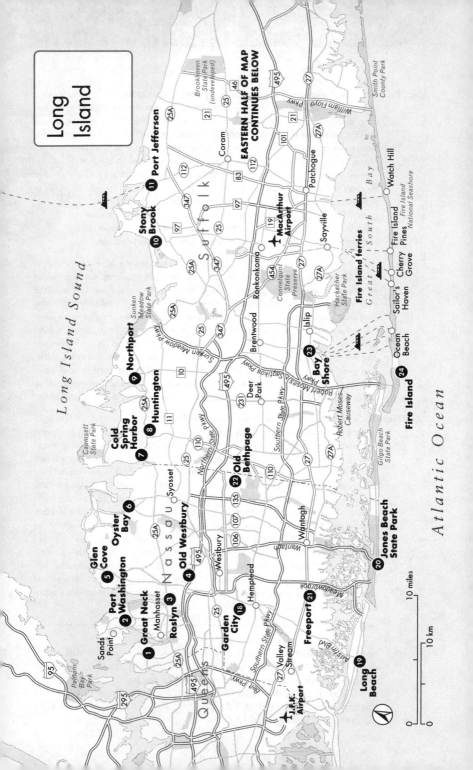

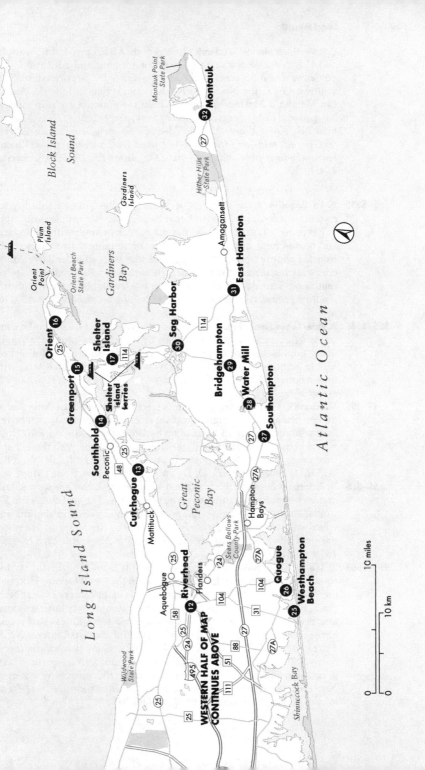

U.S. Merchant Marine Academy. Officers of the Merchant Marine Academy and U.S. Naval Reserve come here for training and education. The academy, set on 80 acres of the former Walter P. Chrysler estate, 3 mi southwest of Great Neck, has lovely grounds that include the **American Merchant Marine Museum.** Within the museum are ship models, navigational instruments, and other naval paraphernalia. ⊠ *300 Steamboat Rd., Kings Point* ☎ *516/773–5000* ⊕ *www.usmma.edu* 🖼 *Free* ☉ *Grounds mid-Jan.–June and Aug.–mid-Dec., weekdays 8–4:30; museum mid-Jan.–June and Aug.–mid-Dec., Tues.–Fri. 10–3:30, weekends 1–4:30.*

Where to Stay & Eat

$$$–$$$$ ✕ **La Coquille.** Lace curtains decorate the windows of this French restaurant a few miles east of Great Neck, and a harpist plays on Monday evenings. Try the duck à l'orange or rack of lamb with a mustard-and-bread-crumb crust, paired with one of the more than 150 selections from the wine list. Sunday through Thursday you can order a five-course chef's tasting dinner for $50, or $70 with wine. Reservations are essential on Saturday. A children's menu is available. ⊠ *1669 Northern Blvd., Manhasset* ☎ *516/365–8422* 🏛 *Jacket required* ⊟ *AE, DC, MC, V.*

$$$–$$$$ ✕ **Peter Luger Steak House.** With its vaulted ceiling, exposed wood beams, stained-glass window, and oak floors, this spacious restaurant, a branch of the famous Brooklyn steak house, resembles an English Tudor beer hall. In addition to first-rate steaks, you can order a grilled lobster with drawn butter. ⊠ *255 Northern Blvd.* ☎ *516/487–8800* ⚖ *Reservations essential* ⊟ *No credit cards.*

$$–$$$ ✕ **Bruzell's.** Contemporary cuisine is served in this art-deco dining room done in teal and black. Signature dishes include sumptuously rich calves' liver with red onions and Canadian bacon, Atlantic salmon with citrus beurre blanc, prime aged shell steak, and rack of lamb with thin, crispy, fried onions. A children's menu is available. ⊠ *451 Middle Neck Rd.* ☎ *516/482–6600* ⊟ *AE, D, DC, MC, V* ☉ *No lunch Sat.–Mon.*

$$–$$$ ✕ **Ristorante Bevanda.** Half a dozen kinds of fresh fish are served daily at this elegant restaurant with white tablecloths. The veal chops à la Bevanda, stuffed with cheese and prosciutto and sautéed in shallots and white wine, are a good choice for landlubbers. Reservations are essential on Friday and Saturday. ⊠ *570 Middle Neck Rd.* ☎ *516/482–1510* ⊟ *AE, DC, MC, V.*

$$$–$$$$ 🏨 **Inn at Great Neck.** Art deco–style motifs dominate the lobby and rooms of this four-story hotel, a member of the Small Luxury Hotels of the World group. The inn, opened in 1995, is in the center of Great Neck Plaza, surrounded by shops and restaurants. Rooms have large windows and desks, plush carpeting, and streamlined furnishings. Bathrooms have marble vanities; some have whirlpool tubs. ⊠ *30 Cuttermill Rd., 11021* ☎ *516/773–2000* 🖨 *516/773–2020* ⊕ *www.innatgreatneck. com* ⇆ *79 rooms, 6 suites* ⚮ *Restaurant, room service, in-room data ports, some in-room hot tubs, minibars, cable TV, in-room VCRs, gym, bar, concierge, Internet, business services, meeting rooms, some pets allowed, no-smoking rooms* ⊟ *AE, D, DC, MC, V.*

Shopping

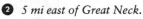

Immortalized as the "miracle mile" in Long Island–native Billy Joel's song "It's Still Rock and Roll to Me," **Americana Manhasset** (✉ 2060 Northern Blvd., Manhasset ☎ 516/627–2277 or 800/818–6767) is the ultimate shopping destination for the Gold Coast elite. Prada, Fendi, Giorgio Armani, Yves St. Laurent, Louis Vuitton, and Burberry are among the dozens of upscale shops for the rich, famous, and merely curious.

Port Washington

② *5 mi east of Great Neck.*

Antiques and collectibles stores, gift shops, and old buildings line this town's Main Street, and tall ships bob in the water beyond the town dock at Port Washington Harbor. This area was originally settled in 1674; early residents made their living farming oysters and raising cattle until the 20th century, when the sand and gravel industry took off. About 90% of New York City's skyscrapers were made with Port Washington sand.

Sands Point Preserve. Overlooking Long Island Sound, this 216-acre preserve, once part of a Gold Coast estate, occupies the tip of the Port Washington Peninsula. The grounds include natural and landscaped areas, with forests, meadows, freshwater ponds, and shore cliffs. Also here are three castlelike mansions. The 1904 Castlegould, the visitor center, houses changing exhibits on natural history. Falaise is a Normandy-style manor house built for Harry F. Guggenheim in 1923; the home is notable for its medieval and Renaissance style and artwork. The Tudor-style Hempstead House, used for various exhibits, overlooks the harbor. Tours through Falaise and nature walks are available. ✉ *95 Middle Neck Rd., Sands Point* ☎ *516/571–7900* ⊕ *www.sandspointpreserve.org* 🎫 *Preserve weekdays free, weekends $2; Falaise $6* ☉ *Preserve daily 9:30–4:30; Falaise May–Oct., Wed.–Sun. noon–3.*

Sands Willets House. The Sands family, early area settlers, built the kitchen, the oldest part of this house, in 1735. In 1845 Edmund Willets, an abolitionist and Quaker, bought the house and added on to it. His descendants lived here until 1967. Several rooms are furnished and open to the public. ✉ *336 Port Washington Blvd.* ☎ *516/365–9074* ⊕ *www.cowneck.org* 🎫 *Free* ☉ *Sun., by appointment.*

Where to Eat

$–$$$ ✕ **Finn MacCool's.** Part restaurant, part post-work social pub, Finn's has the feel of an Irish tavern, with lots of wood and a noise level that rises as the evening wears on. In addition to a large selection of domestic and imported beers, the pub serves hearty homemade stews and sandwiches. ✉ *205 Main St.* ☎ *516/944–3439* ▭ *AE, D, DC, MC, V.*

$–$$ ✕ **Louie's Oyster Bar and Grill.** This rustic, wood-paneled seafood restaurant with high ceilings, moldings, and brass railings at the wooden bar affords views of the harbor. Try the classic fish-and-chips or the salmon fillet with a soy-ginger glaze, asparagus, and black olives. ✉ *865 Main St.* ☎ *516/883–4242* ▭ *AE, D, DC, MC, V.*

Nightlife & the Arts

The 450-seat **Landmark on Main Street** (⊠ 232 Main St. ☎ 516/767–6444 ⊕ www.landmarkonmainstreet.org), which presents mostly musical performances, has hosted the likes of opera star Marilyn Horne and folk singers Judy Collins and John Sebastian.

Shopping

Among the many antiques shops in Port Washington is **Angels by the Sea** (⊠ 274 Main St. ☎ 516/767–0750), which sells artwork, vintage Italian silks, Victorian ephemera, chandeliers, and plenty of decorative angels. The shop occupies two stores separated by a garden filled with stone angels, bronze statuary, Victorian garden furniture, and fountains.

Roslyn

❸ *3 mi southeast of Port Washington.*

Roslyn, at the head of Hempstead Harbor, has an attractive downtown, popular restaurants, trendy boutiques, and charming residential areas. It's also the site of approximately 100 pre–Civil War buildings. However, its tree-lined Main Street and quiet family life have not escaped some of the ill effects of urbanization. Traffic and parking are problems here, as they are in most of Nassau County today.

Cedarmere. The prominent 19th-century poet, civic leader, and newspaper editor William Cullen Bryant lived in this house, built in 1787 by Quaker farmer William Kirk, from 1843 until his death in 1878. Bryant purchased the house as a rural retreat where he could work on his poetry and indulge his love of nature. He renovated and enlarged the original farmhouse, and planted exotic trees and flowers on the grounds, transforming the estate into a horticultural showplace. ⊠ *225 Bryant Ave., Roslyn Harbor* ☎ *516/571–8130* ⊆ *Free* ⊙ *May–Nov., Sat. 10–4:45, Sun. 1–4:45.*

Nassau County Museum of Art. A wedding gift in 1919 from industrialist Henry Clay Frick to his son and daughter-in-law, this Georgian brick mansion, designed by Ogden Codman Jr., in 1900, now houses an art museum. The permanent collection contains 600 works from 19th- and 20th-century European and American artists, including Edouard Vuillard, Roy Lichtenstein, Moses Soyer, George Segal, Auguste Rodin, Alex Katz, and Frederick Warren Freer. The museum sits amid 145 groomed acres with rose, azalea, and other gardens. Scattered across the grounds are 20 unique abstract and stylized sculptures, including *Jaguar* by Anna Vaughn Hyatt, *Moonlight Goddess* by Reuben Nakian, and *Caring* by Chaim Gross. The **Tee Ridder Miniatures Museum**, also on the grounds, holds a collection of 26 miniature rooms. ⊠ *1 Museum Dr., Roslyn Harbor* ☎ *516/484–9338* ⊕ *www.nassaumuseum.com/ ncma/* ⊆ *$6* ⊙ *Tues.–Sun. 11–5.*

Sea Cliff. This tiny village 4 mi north of Roslyn is filled with turn-of-the-20th-century homes, most lovingly restored to their original grandeur. Shops and restaurants in the village make it a pleasant destination for an afternoon visit. At the **Sea Cliff Village Museum,** displays of documents and photos trace the history of Sea Cliff. A scale model of a village Victorian house is also on exhibit. ⊠ *95 10th Ave., Sea Cliff* ☎ *516/671–0090* ⊕ *www.seacliff.org* ☎ *$1 suggested donation* ☉ *Weekends 2–5.*

Where to Stay & Eat

$$$$ ✕ **La Parma.** Ample portions draw crowds to this well-known southern Italian restaurant 4 mi south of Roslyn. It's noisy, but you can go into the kitchen and watch the food being prepared. Winners here include the chicken and the veal parmigiana. ⊠ *707 Willis Ave., Williston Park* ☎ *516/294–6610* ⚱ *Reservations not accepted* ⊟ *AE, DC, MC, V.*

$$–$$$$ ✕ **Bryant and Cooper Steak House.** The owners of this traditional steak house buy prime meat and age it themselves. Weekdays are much less crowded than weekends here. ⊠ *2 Middle Neck Rd.* ☎ *516/627–7270* ⊟ *AE, DC, MC, V* ☉ *No lunch weekends.*

$$–$$$$ ✕ **Jolly Fisherman and Steak House.** Waiters in tuxedos serve simple dishes such as broiled fish at this seafood restaurant with white-linen tablecloths, fireplaces, and paintings of old Roslyn. Children get their own menu. ⊠ *25 Main St.* ☎ *516/621–0055* ⊟ *AE, D, DC, MC, V* ☉ *Closed Mon.*

$$–$$$ ✕ **Classico.** Paintings by local artists hang on the walls, and the tables are spread with linen cloths at this Tuscan-style restaurant a mile northeast of Roslyn. Try the Dover sole with Mornay sauce, rabbit roasted with rosemary and potatoes, or the quail with polenta. ⊠ *1042 Northern Blvd., Roslyn Estates* ☎ *516/621–1870* ⊟ *AE, D, DC, MC, V* ☉ *No lunch Sat.–Tues.*

$$–$$$ ✕ **George Washington Manor.** George Washington is said to have eaten in this mansion that dates to 1740. The menu focuses on such traditional fare as prime rib, fillet of sole almondine or with champagne sauce, and salmon cooked to order. ⊠ *1305 Old Northern Blvd.* ☎ *516/621–1200* ⊟ *AE, D, DC, MC, V.*

$–$$$ ✕ **La Marmite.** Formality reigns at this glass-front restaurant with several dining areas. The menu mixes such staples as Caesar salad, shrimp cocktail, and rack of lamb with contemporary options like ostrich carpaccio and quail stuffed with wild rice and goose liver. La Marmite is 4 mi south of Roslyn. Reservations are essential for weekend dining. ⊠ *234 Hillside Ave., Williston Park* ☎ *516/746–1243* ⊟ *AE, DC, MC, V* ☉ *No lunch weekends.*

$$$–$$$$ ▨ **Roslyn Claremont.** Guest rooms at this posh three-story hotel are spacious and have marble bathrooms. Most suites have king-size four-posters beds with flouncy canopies and sitting areas with fireplaces. ⊠ *1221 Old Northern Blvd., 11576* ☎ *516/625–2700 or 800/626–9005* ⊟ *516/625–2731* ⊕ *www.roslynclaremonthotel.com* ⇗ *69 rooms, 7 suites* ⚱ *Restaurant, room service, in-room data ports, minibars, cable TV with movies and video games, gym, bar, laundry service, business services, no-smoking rooms* ⊟ *AE, D, DC, MC, V.*

Old Westbury

❹ *3 mi east of Roslyn.*

A wealthy residential community, Old Westbury, part of the larger town of Westbury, is one of the least-populated areas of Nassau County, thanks to zoning restrictions. Its roots date to 1657, when Captain John Seamann purchased 12,000 acres from the local Algonquin tribe. Later, in 1700, Quakers fleeing persecution settled in the area, naming their settlement Westbury after their hometown in England. Over time, estates replaced the farms of early settlers, and today horse trails wind across the area's soft hills.

★ **Old Westbury Gardens.** This is one of the few former Long Island estates still intact, and today the grounds and 1906 Gold Coast mansion built by financier-sportsman John S. Phipps are open to the public. The mansion showcases the home's original furniture and the family's art and belongings; the beautiful 160-acre property includes formal gardens, fountains, woodlands, and lakes. ⊠ *71 Old Westbury Rd.* ☎ *516/333–0048* ⊕ *www.oldwestburygardens.org* ⊠ *$10* ☉ *Apr.–mid-Dec., Wed.–Mon. 10–5.*

Where to Stay & Eat

$$$–$$$$ ✕ **Westbury Manor.** Six acres of lavish gardens with ponds, waterfalls, and gazebos surround this restaurant housed in a Victorian mansion. The dining room is equally lovely, with antique heirlooms, plush upholstery, and polished wood. The rack of lamb for two and the fish and pasta dishes are highlights here. A guitarist plays on Tuesday, and there's piano music Wednesday through Sunday. ⊠ *South side of Jericho Tpke., Westbury* ☎ *516/333–7117* ⊕ *www.scottobrothers.com* 🖃 *AE, DC, MC, V.*

$–$$ ✕ **Cafe Spasso.** At night, pink neon lights make this Italian restaurant ½ mi east of Old Westbury gleam. The rigatoni in vodka sauce, tortellini da Vinci (cheese tortellini with mushrooms and shrimp in pink cream sauce), calamari, and mussels marinara are local favorites. ⊠ *307 Old Country Rd., Carle Place* ☎ *516/333–1718* ⚖ *Reservations not accepted* 🖃 *AE, DC, MC, V.*

¢–$ 🏨 **Howard Johnson Express Inn.** Guest rooms here are fairly standard, with wall-to-wall carpets, coffeemakers, and hair dryers. French toast, waffles, and pancakes are part of the breakfast, included in the rate. The hotel is ¼ mi from Westbury Music Fair. ⊠ *120 Jericho Tpke., Westbury 11753* ☎ *516/333–9700 or 800/406–1411* 🖷 *516/333–9393* ⊕ *www.hojo.com* ➳ *80 rooms* ᕔ *In-room data ports, cable TV, pool, meeting room, no-smoking rooms* 🖃 *AE, D, DC, MC, V* ⦿ *BP.*

Nightlife & the Arts

The **Westbury Music Fair** (⊠ Brush Hollow Rd., ¼ mi north of LIE, near Exit 40W ☎ 516/334–0800 ⊕ www.musicfair.com), a theater-in-the-round, attracts top musical performers and pop artists of all genres. Children's shows are offered occasionally.

Glen Cove

⑤ *8 mi north of Old Westbury.*

Ever since Glen Cove was established in 1668, its waterfront, woodlands, and varied topography have been constant attractions. It takes only one look at a sunset on Hempstead Harbor to understand why. Once home to J. P. Morgan and F. W. Woolworth, Glen Cove was at the heart of the North Shore's Gold Coast. At one time, Gold Coast mansions occupied half of the town's land; the estates of Standard Oil's co-founder, Charles Pratt, and his sons alone covered more than 1,000 acres. Many of these mansions remain today in and around the more than 300 acres of nature preserves overlooking the harbor.

Garvies Point Museum and Preserve. Prehistoric Native American culture, the science of archaeology, and the area's geological past form the basis of this county-run museum's main exhibits. Woodland thickets, sediments, and meadows fill the preserve's 62 acres overlooking Hempstead Harbor. ⌂ *50 Barry Dr.* ☎ *516/571–8010* 💲 *$2* ☉ *Tues.–Sun. 10–4.*

Holocaust Memorial and Educational Center of Nassau County. Through its pictorial history of the Holocaust, special exhibits, seminars, and research library, this museum serves as a living memorial to the millions of victims who died at the hands of the Nazis. ⌂ *100 Crescent Beach Rd., at Welwyn Preserve* ☎ *516/571–8040* ⊕ *www.holocaust-nassau.org* 💲 *Free* ☉ *Weekdays 9:30–4:30, Sun. 11–4.*

Where to Eat

$$$$ ✕ **Veranda.** Plants and fresh flowers add to the cozy, warm spirit of this restaurant serving dishes from the northern region of Italy. Fresh fish is popular. For a local treat, try Long Island duck with raspberries and apples. A $25 prix-fixe menu is available Sunday through Thursday. ⌂ *75 Cedar Swamp Rd.* ☎ *516/759–0394* 🖃 *AE, D, DC, MC, V.*

$$$–$$$$ ✕ **Barney's.** A cozy roadhouse that was popular in the early 20th century houses this restaurant 20 minutes northeast of Glen Cove. The main dining room, downstairs, has a fireplace. There are also two smaller rooms with a bar in the center where you can try such dishes as crab cakes, Long Island roast duck, or seared ahi tuna. A children's menu is available. ⌂ *315 Buckram Rd., Locust Valley* ☎ *516/671–6300* 🖃 *AE, MC, V* ☉ *Closed Mon. No lunch.*

$$$–$$$$ ✕ **La Bussola.** Classic Italian dishes of chicken, veal, beef, and fish are served at candlelit tables in this romantic restaurant with French doors and lace curtains. A wooden bar leads into the main dining room. ⌂ *40 School St.* ☎ *516/671–2100* 🖃 *AE, D, DC, MC, V.*

$$$ ✕ **La Pace.** Green- and beige-fabric-covered walls, sconces, fresh roses on the tables, a chandelier, and fireplaces decorate this Tuscan-style restaurant. Try the fusilli served with *cimedirapa* (broccoli rabe) or scampi La Pace (sautéed shrimps stuffed with fontina cheese, rolled with bacon, and grilled with mustard sauce). ⌂ *51 Cedar Swamp Rd.* ☎ *516/671–2970* 🖃 *AE, DC, MC, V* ☉ *No lunch weekends.*

★ **$$–$$$** ✕ **Coles House Restaurant and Coppertop Pub.** One of Glen Cove's historic landmarks, built around 1810, houses eight dining rooms, many with working fireplaces. The American cuisine includes such dishes as pan-seared chicken breast with whipped sweet potatoes and sautéed spinach, and grilled Black Angus steak with a bourbon sauce. The Pub Room serves sandwiches and what has been called the best burger on Long Island. ⌂ *149 Glen St.* ☎ *516/676–4343* 🖃 *AE, D, DC, MC, V* ☉ *Closed Mon. No lunch.*

Nightlife

Friday and Saturday evenings local bands play classic rock, jazz, and blues at the **Downtown Cafe** (⌂ 4 School St. ☎ 516/759–2233 ⊕ www.

thedowntowncafe.com), and Tuesday is open-mike night. A small dance floor and a big-screen TV are here, and summer highlights include karaoke and an outdoor café. The well-stocked bar has imported beers on tap, and the menu lists pastas, steaks, wraps, and salads.

Oyster Bay

6 *6 mi east of Glen Cove.*

The history of this quaint town on an inlet off Long Island Sound can be traced to 1615, when a Dutch explorer, impressed by the area's bountiful shellfish, named it Oyster Bay. The hamlet's distance from Long Island's more urbanized areas has helped preserve a small-town feel.

The area's most famous resident was President Teddy Roosevelt, who built his home, Sagamore Hill, here in 1885. Not all of Oyster Bay's visitors had such positive pedigrees, however. It is reported that Oyster Bay was the last port of call for Captain Kidd before he was arrested in Boston and sent back to London to be hanged in 1701. A local cook, Mary Mallon, received lots of publicity in 1906 after being dubbed Typhoid Mary for allegedly infecting dozens of people with typhoid fever. Singer Billy Joel is the town's most recent claim to fame.

Humes Japanese Stroll Garden. Within this tranquil 4-acre garden are a teahouse, paths of gravel and stepping-stones, stone lanterns, and a waterfall, plus various mosses and Asian plants. Guided tours, which include a tea ceremony, are usually given once a day on alternate Saturdays; call for more information. ⊠ *Oyster Bay Rd. at Dogwood La., Mill Neck* ☎ *516/676–4486* ⊕ *dir.gardenweb.com/directory/hjsg* ⬚ *Garden $5, tours $10* ☉ *Late Apr.–mid-Oct., weekends 11:30–4:30.*

★ **Planting Fields Arboretum State Historic Park.** The home of insurance magnate William Robertson Coe from 1910 to 1955, Planting Fields is now a public arboretum with 160 acres of gardens and plant collections and 250 acres of lawns and woodlands. Two greenhouse complexes nurture native plants. **Coe Hall,** the estate's magnificent Tudor manor, is filled with period furnishings and antiques, including windows from the home of Henry VIII's second wife, Anne Boleyn. Guided tours of the house are available. ⊠ *Planting Fields Rd.* ☎ *516/922–9210 for manor, 516/922–8600 for arboretum* ⊕ *www.plantingfields.org* ⬚ *Parking $6, manor $5* ☉ *Daily 9–5.*

Raynham Hall Historical House Museum. Three generations of the Townsend family, renowned merchants and ship traders, lived in this colonial saltbox structure dating from the American Revolution. Sally Townsend was responsible for alerting her father to the fact that a certain Benedict Arnold was going to betray his country. Many of the original family furnishings are in the house, and there are rotating exhibits of Civil War memorabilia and holiday decorations. The house-museum reveals much about Oyster Bay from the time of the revolution through the town's affluent Victorian period. ⊠ *20 W. Main St.* ☎ *516/922–6808* ⊕ *www.raynhamhallmuseum.org* ⬚ *$3* ☉ *Labor Day–June, Tues.–Sun. 1–5; rest of yr, Tues.–Sun. noon–5.*

★ **Sagamore Hill National Historic Site.** Known for a time as the "summer White House," this 23-room Victorian was President Teddy Roosevelt's cherished family retreat from 1885 until his death in 1919. In addition to the original furnishings and some personal effects, the house contains animal heads and skins from Roosevelt's many hunting expeditions. The servants' quarters offer a behind-the-scenes look at life here. ⊠ *Cove Neck Rd.* ☎ *516/922–4788 or 516/922–4447* ⊕ *www.nps.gov/sahi* ☞ *$5* ⊘ *Grounds daily dawn–dusk. House Memorial Day–Labor Day, daily 10–4; rest of yr, Wed.–Sun. 10–4.*

Theodore Roosevelt Sanctuary and Audubon Center. Down the road from Sagamore Hill, Teddy Roosevelt's family home, is this 12-acre bird sanctuary—the perfect legacy of the environmentally active president. More than 125 species of birds live here. Roosevelt is buried in a cemetery on the grounds. ⊠ *134 Cove Rd.* ☎ *516/922–3200* ☞ *Free* ⊘ *Grounds daily 9–5; center Mon.–Thurs. 8–4:30, Fri. 8–2, weekends 1–4:30.*

Where to Stay & Eat

$$$–$$$$ ✕ **Mill River Inn.** A fireplace, white linens, fresh flowers, and candlelight are among the romantic touches at this quiet restaurant. Dishes are contemporary—sautéed Hudson Valley foie gras, grilled rack of lamb with poached pears and spinach, and pork chops stuffed with Swiss chard, roasted peppers, and pecorino cheese, for example. On weekends, dinner is a prix-fixe affair. ⊠ *160 Mill River Rd.* ☎ *516/922–7768* ⚑ *Reservations essential* 🖃 *AE, DC, MC, V* ⊘ *No lunch.*

$$–$$$$ ✕ **Steve's Pier I.** Maritime memorabilia such as an 8-foot replica of the USS *Rotterdam* and a stuffed 9-foot hammerhead shark decorate this restaurant on Long Island Sound. Lobster is seasoned and flame-roasted in a custom-made broiler that reaches more than 1,000°F. The result, fans say, is the tastiest, tenderest lobster around. Weather permitting, a deck is open for outdoor dining. In Bayville, the restaurant is 10 mi north of Oyster Bay. ⊠ *33 Bayville Ave., Bayville* ☎ *516/628–2153* 🖃 *AE, D, DC, MC, V.*

$–$$$ ✕ **Canterbury Ales Oyster Bar and Grill.** This bistro-grill serves everything from horseradish–honey mustard salmon and Japanese ahi tuna to Parmesan-and-herb-crusted chicken and wild game. To wash down your meal you have a choice of 99 beers from around the world. A children's menu is available. ⊠ *46 Audrey Ave.* ☎ *516/922–3614* ⊕ *www. canterburyalesrestaurant.com* 🖃 *AE, DC, MC, V.*

¢ ✕ **Oyster Bay Railz.** Open until 1 AM, this is the place to indulge late-night cravings. Chicken wings, mozzarella sticks, and burgers go great with a beer. You can play darts or pool, catch a game on TV, or enjoy live music on the weekend. ⊠ *115 Audrey Ave.* ☎ *516/624–6911* 🖃 *AE, MC, V.*

$ 🏨 **East Norwich Motor Inn.** The inn, a brick-and-stucco complex with Tudor-style touches, is a modern facility in a country setting about 1¼ mi south of Oyster Bay. You can choose from standard rooms, duplex suites, or the cottage, which has a full kitchen. The accommodations are spare but tidy. ⊠ *6321 Northern Blvd., East Norwich 11732* ☎ *516/ 922–1500 or 800/334–4798* 🖷 *516/922–1089* ⊕ *www.eastnorwichinn. com* ⇥ *72 rooms, 5 suites, 1 cottage* ⚒ *In-room data ports, some* *kitchens, some kitchenettes, cable TV with movies, pool, gym, sauna, laundry service, business services, meeting rooms, no-smoking rooms* ⊟ *AE, D, DC, MC, V* ⑩ *CP.*

Cold Spring Harbor

❼ *5 mi east of Oyster Bay.*

One of the North Shore's most enchanting towns, Cold Spring Harbor has always been valued for its location on the water. The Matinecock Indians are said to have called it Wawapex, meaning "place of good water." In 1653 three Englishmen from Oyster Bay bought the land around the harbor from the Matinecocks and named it Cold Spring after the area's freshwater springs. It became a U.S. Port of Entry in 1799 and during the mid-1800s was home to a fleet of nine whaling vessels and numerous cargo ships.

Time hasn't eroded any of the landscape surrounding this attractive village. As you drive east along Route 25A, the town's harbor suddenly comes into view from beyond the trees. After you take the turn that leads up the hill around Cold Spring Harbor, breathtaking trees draw the eye. At the crest of the hill, the shops and restaurants on Main Street (part of Route 25A) merit a stop. Note that parking is at a premium in the village's few and small lots.

Cold Spring Harbor Fish Hatchery and Aquarium. Eight outdoor tanks at this educational center hold the largest collection of native freshwater fish, turtles, and amphibians in New York State. It's 1½ mi from downtown Cold Spring Harbor. ⊠ *South side of Rte. 25A at Rte. 108* ☎ *631/692–6768* ⊕ *www.cshfha.org* 🎫 *$4* ☺ *Daily 10–5.*

Cold Spring Harbor State Park. Great horned owls and red-tailed hawks are among the many birds that make their home in this 40-acre park overlooking Cold Spring Harbor. The bird-watching is particularly good during the spring and fall migrations, and there are trails for hiking in warm weather and cross-country skiing in winter. ⊠ *Rte. 25A* ☎ *631/423–1770* 🎫 *Free* ☺ *Daily sunrise–sunset.*

Cold Spring Harbor Whaling Museum. One of the highlights of this museum's permanent exhibits exploring Long Island's whaling industry is a fully equipped 19th-century whaleboat. Whaling implements, paintings, scrimshaw, and ship models are also on display. ⊠ *Main St./Rte. 25A* ☎ *631/367–3418* ⊕ *www.cshwhalingmuseum.org* 🎫 *$4* ☺ *Memorial Day–Labor Day, daily 11–5; rest of yr, Tues.–Sun. 11–5.*

Where to Stay & Eat

$$–$$$$ ✕ **Inn on the Harbor.** The stately dining room in this Victorian house is a great place from which to view magnificent summer sunsets over Cold Spring Harbor. The food is Continental, with dishes such as rack of lamb with mustard sauce and filet mignon with peppercorn sauce; dessert runs to fruit tarts and cheesecake. The restaurant has dock space. ⊠ *105 Harbor Rd.* ☎ *631/367–3166* ⊟ *AE, DC, MC, V* ☺ *Closed Mon.*

$$-$$$ ✗ **Trattoria Grasso III.** Entrées are inspired by Tuscan, Sardinian, and Sicilian cooking, and the wine list is similarly inclusive. Try the *branzini* (Mediterranean sea bass), which is roasted whole and then filleted at your table. You can dine on the porch overlooking the village, or sit at a candlelit table inside, where you'll be surrounded by photographs of Europe and serenaded by live jazz bands on Wednesday through Saturday nights. ☒ *134 Main St.* ☎ *631/367–6060* ☐ *AE, D, DC, MC, V.*

$ ▣ **Swan View Manor.** The Victorian house, 1½ blocks from the center of town, overlooks the harbor. When the weather's warm you may eat breakfast on the front porch, which is cozy with flowers and wicker chairs. The guest rooms are frilly, with queen- and king-size beds and floral duvets fluffed to perfection. Complimentary tea is served every afternoon in the sitting room, which is warmed by a fireplace in winter. ☒ *45 Harbor Rd., 11724* ☎ *631/367–2070* 🖷 *631/367–2085* ⊕ *www.swanview. com* ⇗ *18 rooms, 1 suite* ⚐ *Dining room, cable TV, Internet; no kids under 10, no smoking* ☐ *AE, D, DC, MC, V* ⑩ *CP.*

Shopping
Heritage Candle and Home (☒ 29 Main St. ☎ 631/692–5788), in a circa-1850 wooden merchant's building, sells delightful candles of all types and scents, as well as sconces, electric lights, and brass accessories for every room of your home.

Huntington

❽ *2 mi east of Cold Spring Harbor.*

The township of greater Huntington embraces five navigable harbors, several beaches on the gentle waters of Long Island Sound, and 17 communities, including the attractive Huntington village (the township also includes Cold Spring Harbor and Northport). The township's original tracts of land were purchased from Native Americans in the mid-17th century, and its most famous resident, the poet Walt Whitman, was born here in 1819. Later, he founded a local newspaper, the *Long Islander,* which is still published today. The late 1800s and early 1900s saw the development of this region of the North Shore's Gold Coast, which attracted estate owners William K. Vanderbilt, Marshall Field III, and Walter B. Jennings, among others.

Today, Huntington village is the heart of the township; historic buildings and excellent restaurants and shops pepper the bustling downtown. Among the stores here are a large independent bookstore, charming gift shops, trendy boutiques, and antiques stores.

Caumsett State Historic Park. Set in magnificent Lloyd Neck, which juts into Long Island Sound, this park covers 1,500 acres and includes a sliver of beach and a bridle path for those who bring horses in by trailer. You can also hike, fish, bike, and cross-country ski here. The park was originally the estate of Marshall Field III; his mansion, which you can view from the outside, is now part of Queen's College. ☒ *W. Neck Rd., off Rte. 25A* ☎ *631/423–1770* ⊕ *nysparks.state.ny.us* ☒ *$6 (Memorial Day–Labor Day)* ☉ *Daily sunrise–sunset.*

Fleets Cove Beach. This Town of Huntington beach, which stretches for 1,600 feet on Northport Bay, includes a boardwalk and a playground. ⊠ *Off Fleets Cove Rd., Centerport* ☎ *631/261–7574, 631/351–3089 off-season* 🖼 *$15 (Memorial Day–Labor Day)* ⊗ *Daily 9–7:30.*

Gold Star Battalion Beach. The 400-foot beach, with a playground and beach house, faces Huntington Bay. ⊠ *Off West Shore Rd.* ☎ *631/261–7574, 631/351–3089 off-season* 🖼 *$15 (Memorial Day–Labor Day)* ⊗ *Daily 9–7:30.*

Heckscher Museum of Art. The museum, a wonderful example of beaux-arts architecture two blocks from downtown Huntington, houses more than 1,800 paintings, sculptures, and drawings. The permanent collection spans more than five centuries of European and American art, and the museum hosts impressive traveling exhibits. It's on the grounds of pleasant **Heckscher Park**, which has a playground, pond, tennis courts, and a band shell. ⊠ *2 Prime Ave.* ☎ *631/351–3250* ⊕ *www.heckscher. org* 🖼 *$5* ⊗ *Tues.–Fri. 10–7, weekends 1–5.*

Walt Whitman Birthplace State Historic Site & Interpretive Center. This was the boyhood home of Walt Whitman, considered by many to be America's greatest poet. A typical example of native Long Island craftsmanship of the time, the snug house, built by the poet's father circa 1819, has survived virtually intact since the Whitmans left it in 1823. Whitman portraits, letters, and manuscripts are on display. The home is off Route 110, across from Walt Whitman Mall. ⊠ *246 Old Walt Whitman Rd., Huntington Station* ☎ *631/427–5240* ⊕ *nysparks.state.ny.us* 🖼 *$3* ⊗ *Wed.–Fri. 1–4, weekends 11–4.*

Where to Stay & Eat

$$$$ ✕ **Panama Hatties.** Artful cuisine is served in this upscale yet relaxed art-deco dining room. Dinner is a prix-fixe three-course affair for $65; the prix-fixe lunch is more reasonable at $21. Specialties include rare seared tuna, foie gras, pistachio-crusted rack of lamb with roasted eggplant, and New Zealand venison with wild rice, cling peaches, and macadamia nuts. ⊠ *872 E. Jericho Tpke., Huntington Station* ☎ *631/351–1727* ⊟ *AE, D, DC, MC, V.*

$$–$$$$ ✕ **Abel Conklin's.** Dark mahogany woodwork shows off the original charm of this mid-19th-century building. Abel Conklin's is known for aged broiled steaks, sautéed liver, lobsters, and seafood. Reservations are essential on Friday and Saturday. There's open-air dining on a patio, and a children's menu is available. ⊠ *54 New St.* ☎ *631/385–1919* ⊟ *AE, MC, V* ⊗ *No lunch weekends.*

$$–$$$$ ✕ **Frederick's.** The upstairs room, where dinner is served at the bar, is the quaintest of the three dining rooms at this cozy restaurant in a little house. Try the rack of lamb roasted with rosemary, calves' liver with onions and bacon, or tuna with pecan-and-poblano-chili sauce. ⊠ *1117 Walt Whitman Rd., Melville* ☎ *631/673–8550* ⊟ *AE, DC, MC, V* ⊗ *Closed Sun. No lunch Sat.*

$–$$ 🏨 **Hilton.** Business travelers frequent this five-story hotel 10 minutes from Huntington. The airy, plant-filled atrium lounge is a pleasant place to sit and relax. ⊠ *598 Broad Hollow Rd., Melville 11747* ☎ *631/*

845–1000 🖷 *631/845–1223* ⊕ *www.hiltonlongisland.com* ⇔ *289 rooms, 16 suites* ⚐ *Restaurant, in-room data ports, some minibars, cable TV, tennis court, 2 pools, exercise equipment, hot tub, bar, business services* ☰ *AE, D, DC, MC, V* �🍽 *CP.*

$ 🏨 **Executive Inn at Woodbury.** This four-story chain hotel is close to restaurants, shops, and movie theaters. It's a few miles west of Huntington on Jericho Turnpike (Route 25). ✉ *8030 Jericho Tpke., Woodbury 11797* 🕿 *631/921–8500* 🖷 *631/921–1057* ⊕ *www. executiveinnatwoodbury.com* ⇔ *102 rooms, 5 suites* ⚐ *In-room data ports, some kitchenettes, some microwaves, cable TV, pool, business services* ☰ *AE, D, DC, MC, V* �🍽 *CP.*

$ 🏨 **Huntington Country Inn.** Walt Whitman's boyhood home and the Walt Whitman Mall are near this modest, modern hotel. Each room has a cordless phone, a CD player, and aromatherapy bath products. ✉ *270 W. Jericho Tpke., Huntington Station 11746* 🕿 *631/421–3900* 🖷 *631/ 421–5287* ⊕ *www.huntingtoncountryinn.com* ⇔ *62 rooms, 1 suite* ⚐ *Microwaves, refrigerators, cable TV, pool, exercise equipment* ☰ *AE, D, DC, MC, V* �🍽 *CP.*

Nightlife & the Arts

★ **Cinema Arts Centre** (✉ 423 Park Ave. 🕿 631/423–3456 or 631/423–7611 ⊕ www.cinemaartscentre.org) shows independent American and foreign films and hosts lectures by and about filmmakers and actors. A café on the premises serves organic vegetarian soups, salads, Greek spinach

★ pies, hot knishes, and baked goods. The nonprofit **Inter-media Art Center** (IMAC; ✉ 370 New York Ave. 🕿 631/549–2787 ⊕ www.imactheater. org) hosts well-known performers and bands who play jazz, blues, folk, country, and world music; the center occasionally stages dance and theater performances as well.

Sports & the Outdoors

The **Willow Tree Farm** (✉ W. Neck Rd., off Rte. 25A 🕿 613/427–6105) equestrian center offers horseback-riding lessons on the grounds of Caumsett State Historic Park.

Shopping

One of the largest independent bookstores in the country, **Book Revue** (✉ 313 New York Ave. 🕿 631/271–1442) is an important community fixture, thanks to a comfortable environment that lends itself to browsing new and used books, an excellent children's section, quirky murals, a café, and readings by renowned authors. One of Long Island's oldest malls, the **Walt Whitman Mall** (✉ Rte. 110 and Jericho Tpke., Huntington Station 🕿 631/271–1741) has grown increasingly upscale over the years. Among the 100 retailers are Bloomingdale's, Macy's, Saks Fifth Avenue, Banana Republic, Williams Sonoma, and J. Crew.

Northport

❾ *4 mi east of Huntington.*

The Matinecock Indians were the first inhabitants of what is now one of the North Shore's oldest and most charming villages. Originally known as Cow Harbor, Northport was incorporated in 1895. Victorian houses, some built by old sea captains, fill the scenic harbor area. The downtown shopping district is east of the harbor. Northport retains a rarity on Long Island, a true main street that runs through the heart of the village and still bears the original tracks of the trolley line, now defunct, built in 1902 to relieve town horses of the chore of meeting trains.

Asharoken Beach. One of five major beaches in the township of Huntington, Asharoken stretches for 535 feet along Long Island Sound. ⊠ *Asharoken Rd.* ☎ *631/261–7574, 631/351–3089 off-season* 🚗 *Parking $15 (Memorial Day–Labor Day)* ⊙ *Daily 9–7:30.*

Crab Meadow Beach. Basketball and volleyball courts, a playground, a restaurant, a snack bar, a boardwalk, outdoor showers, and an aid station are set along 1,000 feet of beachfront on Long Island Sound's Northport Bay. Lifeguards are on duty 10–6. ⊠ *447 Waterside Ave.* ☎ *631/261–7574* 🚗 *Parking $15 (Memorial Day–Labor Day)* ⊙ *Daily sunrise–sunset.*

Hobart Beach. The largest of the major beaches in the town of Huntington offers 1,725 feet of shore on Huntington Bay, plus a playground and three boat ramps. ⊠ *Eatons Neck, off Asharoken Ave.* ☎ *631/261–7574, 631/351–3089 off-season* 🚗 *$15 (Memorial Day–Labor Day)* ⊙ *Daily 9–7:30.*

Northport Historical Society and Museum. Built by Andrew Carnegie in 1914 as the village library, this structure now houses exhibits about the history, culture, and geography of Northport and its environs. Walking tours of Northport, educational programs, and lectures are offered. ⊠ *215 Main St.* ☎ *631/757–9859* ⊕ *www.northporthistorical.org* 🚗 *$2 suggested donation* ⊙ *Tues.–Sun. 1–4:30.*

★ **Suffolk County Vanderbilt Museum and Planetarium.** William K. Vanderbilt's 24-room Moroccan-style mansion, called Eagle's Nest, sits on 43 acres and houses collections that Vanderbilt acquired as he traveled throughout the world. Summer brings various theatrical performances to the mansion's courtyard. The adjacent planetarium is one of the best-equipped in the nation, with a 60-foot domed Sky Theater. Sky and laser shows are held regularly. ⊠ *180 Little Neck Rd., Centerport* ☎ *631/854–5555* ⊕ *www.vanderbiltmuseum.org* 🚗 *Grounds $5, mansion tour $8, planetarium show $7* ⊙ *May and June, and Sept. and Oct., Tues.–Fri. noon–5, weekends 11:30–5; July and Aug., Tues.–Sat. 10–5, Sun. noon–5; Nov.–Apr., Tues.–Fri. noon–4, Sat. noon–5, Sun. 11:30–5; call for planetarium schedule.*

Sunken Meadow State Park (Governor Alfred E. Smith State Park). A 3-mi beach edges this 1,200-acre park, which also has three 9-hole golf courses, a driving range, playgrounds, basketball courts, softball fields, a soccer field, and trails for biking, running, and cross-country skiing. Facilities include showers and an aid station. Take Sunken Meadow Parkway north and follow signs for the park. ⊠ *Off Sunken Meadow State Pkwy.* ☎ *631/269–4333* ⊕ *nysparks.state.ny.us* 🚗 *Parking $8 (Memorial Day–Labor Day)* ⊙ *Daily sunrise–sunset.*

Where to Stay & Eat

$$–$$$$ ✕ **Pumpernickels Restaurant.** This cozy German restaurant at the edge of Northport village is known for its sauerbraten and seafood. Candles and fresh flowers adorn the dining room, and there's often live music on the weekends. ✉ *640 Main St.* ☎ *631/757–7959* ☰ *AE, D, DC, MC, V* ☉ *No lunch Sun.*

$–$$ ✕ **Ship's Inn.** Sit in a candlelit booth and dig into mussels marinara, crab cakes, soft-shell crabs, or prime rib (on Wednesdays). Polished mahogany and brass nautical details highlight the ship theme. A children's menu is available. ✉ *78 Main St.* ☎ *631/261–3000* ☰ *AE, D, DC, MC, V.*

$ ▥ **Hampton Inn.** Three miles south of Northport, this five-story chain motel is convenient to North Shore businesses and shopping areas. It's also 2 mi from the nearest Long Island Rail Road stop and 10 mi from the ocean. ✉ *680 Commack Rd., Commack 11725* ☎ *631/462–5700 or 800/426–7866* ☒ *631/462–9735* ⊕ *www.hampton-inn.com* ⤴ *144 rooms* ⚬ *Refrigerators, in-room data ports, cable TV with movies, gym, laundry service, no-smoking rooms* ☰ *AE, D, DC, V* ⏺ *CP.*

Sports & the Outdoors

The challenging 18-hole **Crab Meadow Golf Course** (✉ Waterside Ave. ☎ 631/757–8800) is hilly and windy. Most holes have panoramic views of Long Island Sound and Connecticut's waterways. Greens fees are $40–$45 for nonresidents; carts are available for $14.

Shopping

Although **Four-Star Variety Stores** (✉ 35 Main St. ☎ 631/261–7223) is one of the few old five-and-tens left on Long Island, you'll be hard-pressed to find anything that costs only a nickel these days. Still, the creaking wood floors, aisles of candies, and various notions give you a sense of old-time Long Island. Organdy, tulle, and satin petal dresses that wouldn't be out of place in *The Nutcracker* ballet are among the items sold at **Main Street Kids Boutique** (✉ 139 Main St. ☎ 631/262–1949), where the forte is special-occasion clothes for young girls.

Stony Brook

🔟 *11 mi east of Northport.*

In Revolutionary times, Washington's spy ring operated in the Stony Brook area, and the village's gristmill was regularly visited by British soldiers for supplies. The village's shopping area, the Stony Brook Village Green, was the country's first planned business center, built in 1941 by philanthropist Ward Melville. Today 45 colonial-style shops and restaurants are clustered along brick-paved walkways with old-fashioned street lamps that surround a small park overlooking Stony Brook Harbor. The idyllic view from the Stony Brook Post Office at the top of the hill has been captured in countless photographs and paintings by tourists and locals alike.

☾ **Long Island Museum of American Art, History and Carriages.** Three small museums and several historic structures make up this complex. The **Margaret Melville Blackwell History Museum** depicts interior design from the late 1600s through the 1930s and includes an exhibit of miniature rooms, which are decorated for the holidays in December. The **Dorothy and Ward Melville Carriage Museum** displays 100 horse-drawn carriages, sleighs, and fire-fighting wagons. One interactive exhibit here, with a horse and carriage, a post office, and shops, is meant to show what life was like in Stony Brook at the turn of the 20th century. The **Art Museum** houses a permanent collection of works by Long Island artist William Sidney Mount, plus rotating exhibits. On the grounds are the beaux-arts fountain and horse trough that once stood at the corner of Madison Avenue and 23rd Street in New York City, the circa-1875 Samuel H. West Blacksmith Shop, and the Nassakeag One-Room Schoolhouse, which served the children of South Setauket until 1910. There's also a gift shop that sells inexpensive souvenirs for children, books, lace tablecloths, and glass suncatchers. ✉ *Main St. and Rte. 25A* ☎ *631/751–0066* ⊕ *www.longislandmuseum.org* 💲 *$7 (including all three museums)* 🕙 *Wed.–Sat. 10–5, Sun. noon–5.*

State University of New York at Stony Brook. The state university here is considered one of the top public-research universities in the country. The Stony Brook University Hospital and Medical Center is a major teaching facility. The university's **Staller Center for the Arts** hosts student productions as well as professional performers. ✉ *100 Nichols Rd.* ☎ *631/689–6000.*

Stony Brook Grist Mill. The mill dates from 1751 and is Long Island's most completely equipped working mill. A visit here might include milling demonstrations. ✉ *Harbor Rd.* ☎ *631/751–2244* ⊕ *www.wardmelvilleheritage.org* 💲 *$2* 🕙 *June–Aug., Wed.–Sun. noon–4:30; Apr. and May, and Sept.–Nov., weekends noon–4:30.*

Where to Stay & Eat

★ **$$$–$$$$** ✕ **Country House.** Built in 1710, this big white house on a hill at the entrance of Stony Brook village is listed with two historical societies, and includes many of the building's original 12-pane windows. The restaurant has a nice lounge and a beautiful large fireplace that was once used as an oven. Try one of the steaks, the Long Island duck with apple-walnut-and-sausage stuffing, or the lobster royale (diced lobster meat stuffed into the cleaned shell with shrimp and scallops and served with risotto). ✉ *Rte. 25A and Main St.* ☎ *631/751–3332* 🍴 *Reservations essential* 🍽 *AE, DC, MC, V.*

★ **$$–$$$$** ✕ **Paula Jean's Supper Club.** A culinary and soulful surprise in a yellow-and-purple colonial on East Setauket's main street, Paula Jean's dishes up spicy Cajun and creole food to go along with down-home blues. Chef-owner Peter Lutzen, who trained with Louisiana legend Paul Prudhomme, prepares authentic crawfish étouffée and Southern-fried catfish, plus unique creations such as blackened lamb chops. Delicious garlic mashed potatoes accompany many of the entrées. A surcharge, which varies with the performance, is added to your bill for the music. ✉ *130 Old Town Rd., East Setauket* ☎ *631/751–5483* 🍴 *Reservations essential* 🕙 *Closed Mon. and Tues. No lunch.*

$–$$$ ✕ **The Curry Club.** One of the few restaurants in the area serving both northern and southern Indian cuisine, the Curry Club specializes in southern *dosas*—huge, delicate crepes filled with a choice of mostly vegetarian stuffings, and served with coconut chutney and yellow dal. Another good choice are the *malai* kebabs—roasted tender chicken marinated in a sauce of mild spices and almonds. It's 2 mi east of Stony Brook. ⊠ *Rte. 25A and Nicolls Rd., East Setauket* ☎ *631/751–4845* ☐ *AE, DC, MC, V.*

$–$$ ✕⊡ **Three Village Inn.** You can stay in the main white clapboard house or in one of the small outlying private cottages overlooking Stony Brook Harbor. Built in 1751, the main house retains much of its original design and decor. Laura Ashley patterns decorate the rooms, some of which have fireplaces and brick patios. Staff members dress in colonial costume and are especially festive around the holidays. Specialties in the restaurant ($$–$$$) include New England seafood pie, roast prime rib, and basil-crusted salmon fillet. A children's menu is available. ⊠ *150 Main St.* ☎ *631/751–0555* 🖷 *631/751–0593* ⊕ *www.threevillageinn. com* ⟷ *26 rooms, 6 cottages* ⟨⟩ *Restaurant, picnic area, cable TV, bar, business services* ☐ *AE, DC, MC, V.*

Nightlife & the Arts

THE ARTS The university's **Staller Center for the Arts** (⊠ State University of New York at Stony Brook, 100 Nichols Rd. ☎ 631/632–7230 or 631/632–7235 ⊕ www.stallercenter.com) is Suffolk County's primary performing-arts venue. Popular singers and international dance companies and orchestras perform here, and the center also hosts student music and theater performances. July brings the Stony Brook Film Festival.

NIGHTLIFE The club **Saints and Sinners** (⊠ 558 Smithtown Bypass, Smithtown ☎ 631/979–9561), a small local favorite a few miles west of Stony Brook, hosts bands from Long Island and New York City. The crowd is young, and the music ranges from grunge and emo to techno and industrial. The cover charge is usually less than $5.

Shopping

There are plenty of quaint shops at the **Stony Brook Village Green,** near Stony Brook Harbor, plus several pleasant eateries, including an old-fashioned luncheonette and a tea shop. On the National Register of Historic Places, the 1857 **St. James General Store** (⊠ 516 Moriches Rd., ½ mi north of Rte. 25A, St. James ☎ 631/862–8333) is the oldest continually operating general store in the country. Adults and children alike love the huge candy selection displayed in old-fashioned glass cases. A twisty narrow staircase leads to a second floor filled with books, toys, and holiday goods. It's 3 mi east of Stony Brook.

Port Jefferson

⑪ *5 mi east of Stony Brook.*

Because of its port and deep harbor, Port Jefferson has long served as a gateway to Long Island. The Setauket Indians, the first to live here, began selling the land to settlers in the mid-1600s. By the time of the Revolutionary War the village was home to many patriots, and during the War of 1812 the harbor was attacked. In 1836 the local residents named the village after Thomas Jefferson. Construction of a large dock began several years later. The area had once been named "Drowned Meadow" because it was so marshy, and during the building of the dock, landfill was added to what is now Main Street.

Shipbuilding was Port Jefferson's major industry until the size and weight of ships required larger shipyards in the late 1800s. Since then, the village has become a Long Island tourist destination. A passenger ferry that crosses Long Island Sound to Bridgeport, Connecticut, docks here. Across from the busy harbor you find a slew of restaurants, souvenir shops, antiques stores, and art galleries. Waterfront estates, charming Victorians, and old sea-captains' homes crowd its downtown. Along its cliffs lies some of the most cherished real estate on Long Island, including such posh neighborhoods as Belle Terre.

Mather House Museum. If you're interested in learning about shipbuilding, head to this site, which includes the mid-19th-century home of shipbuilder John Mather, a marine barn and sail loft, and a tool shed with early shipbuilding tools. A country store, butcher and barbershop, crafts house with pre–Civil War furnishings, and perennial and herb gardens are also on the grounds. ⊠ *115 Prospect St.* ☎ *631/473–2665* ⊕ *www. portjeffhistorical.org* ⊠ *$3 suggested donation* ۞ *July–mid-Sept., Tues. and Wed. and weekends 1–4.*

Where to Stay & Eat

$$–$$$$ ✕ **Dockside.** Etched-glass windows overlook the harbor at this spacious family-style restaurant known for its seafood. The dining room has a nautical theme; a saltwater fish tank sits by the bar. There's open-air dining on a deck, and a pianist plays Friday through Sunday. A children's menu is available. ⊠ *111 W. Broadway* ☎ *631/473–5656* ⊟ *AE, D, DC, MC, V.*

$$–$$$ ✕ **Village Way.** The ship's stern just outside this restaurant 100 feet from the harbor is a Port Jefferson landmark. Inside, you find a child-friendly, casual restaurant serving seafood, beef, and pasta dishes. Good choices include stuffed shrimp, steak, shrimp scampi, and crabmeat-stuffed salmon. A patio opens for seasonal open-air dining. Thursday through Saturday there's live music. A children's menu is available. ⊠ *106 Main St.* ☎ *631/928–3395* ⊟ *AE, D, DC, MC, V.*

★ ¢–$ ✕ **Salsa Salsa.** This spot is popular for Mexican takeout for the working crowd. With only a handful of stools and counters lining the perimeter and a busy galley kitchen, Salsa Salsa is tiny, so it's best to time your arrival to beat the lunch and dinner crushes. All the expected fare is done well, but it's truly the salsa that is memorable. ⊠ *142 Main St.* ☎ *631/ 473–9700* ⊟ *MC, V.*

★ ¢ ✕ **Tiger Lily Cafe.** There's a definite West Coast vibe to this café. Head to the counter to order chicken salad, a wrap, carrot-ginger soup, or one of the satisfying home-cooked vegetarian selections, then settle into a big comfortable chair or couch in the rear (adults only here). Occasionally there's live music on weekend afternoons. The place is open only until 5 PM. ⊠ *156 E. Main St.* ☎ *631/476–7080* ⊟ *No credit cards* ۞ *No dinner.*

$$ ✕▥ **Danfords Inn on the Sound.** This inn near a marina on the harbor has spacious rooms with antiques and views of Long Island Sound. The inn's restaurant, American Bistro ($$–$$$$), also has great views of the water. It serves seafood and meat dishes and offers a $36 prix-fixe pre-theater dinner in conjunction with nearby Theatre Three. ⊠ *25 E. Broadway, 11777* ☎ *631/928–5200 or 800/332–6367* 🖷 *631/928–9092* ⊕ *www.danfords.com* ⬧ *85 rooms, 7 suites* ⚙ *Restaurant, room service, some kitchenettes, cable TV, exercise equipment, library, business services* ▤ *AE, D, DC, MC, V.*

$ 🖭 **Miss Scarlet's Bed and Breakfast.** French provincial and English country antiques fill this small cottage-style B&B. ⊠ *305 California Ave., 11777* ☎ *631/928–5064* 🖷 *631/928–3067* ⊕ *www.miss-scarletts.com* ⬧ *3 rooms* ⚙ *In-room data ports, some refrigerators, cable TV, some in-room VCRs; no kids under 12, no smoking* ▤ *AE, MC, V* 〫 *BP.*

The Arts

The 400-seat **Theatre Three** (⊠ 412 Main St. ☎ 631/928–9100 ⊕ www. theatrethree.org) stages productions ranging from classics like *A Christmas Carol* to offbeat comedies.

THE NORTH FORK & SHELTER ISLAND

By Heather Buchanan, Lisa S. Kahn

Updated by Gwendolen Groocock

The North Fork was formed many eons ago by a glacier that crept down from the north, leaving behind a moraine of sandy soil. Stretching from Riverhead in the west to Orient Point at its easternmost tip, this sedate sister of the South Fork forms the upper finger of what looks like a sideways peace sign. Not long after you take the last exit of the LIE the roads become distinctly rural. As you head east, tidy wood-frame farmhouses and fancier Victorians are followed by acres of green, once chiefly potato farms, that now hold row after row of meticulously tended grape vines.

The New England–style hamlets of the western North Fork, particularly Jamesport, Cutchogue, and Southold, are peppered with unpretentious restaurants and interesting shops that seem transported from another era. Clean, uncrowded beaches lie to the south on Great Peconic Bay and to the north on Long Island Sound.

Farther east is the fishing village of Greenport. From here you can take a short ferry ride to Shelter Island, a small, quiet island that lies between Long Island's North and South forks.

Riverhead

❷ *22 mi east of Port Jefferson.*

The town of Riverhead was established in 1792 at the junction of the North and South forks, with the Peconic River and Great Peconic Bay bordering the town on the south and Long Island Sound on the north. Riverhead, like most other places on the North Fork, began as a farming village. Although agriculture remains a key factor in its economy, the town's main industries today are shopping and tourism. The sprawling Tanger Outlet Stores annually draws thousands of bargain hunters and tour groups, and several major shopping centers have sprung up along Route 58.

★ ☺ **Atlantis Marine World.** Indoor exhibits, such as a natural rockscape pool and a sand-shark lagoon, offer a compelling glimpse of regional marine life. Kids love watching the frisky resident sea lions that put on outdoor shows in summer. The aquarium even has a submarine-simulator ride. ⊠ *431 E. Main St.* ☎ *631/208–9200* ⊕ *www.atlantismarineworld. com* ⊠ *$13.50* ☉ *Daily 10–5.*

Indian Island County Park. Winding trails take you through 275 acres of indigenous pine-scrub forest, wetlands, and creeks to a small beach on Flanders Bay. Under the trees by the entrance are 150 campsites, full re-strooms and showers, picnic tables, and barbecue grills, and nearby there's a large field for ball games. ⊠ *Rte. 105 between Rtes. 24 and 25* ☎ *631/ 854–4949* ⊕ *www.co.suffolk.ny.us* ⊠ *Parking $5* ☉ *Apr.–Oct., daily 8–dusk; Nov.–Mar., Thurs.–Sun. daily 8–dusk.*

Jamesport Vineyards. A wood-shingled, circa-1850 barn holds a mod-ern winery and tasting room; the feel is casual and friendly, with knowledgeable pourers willing to give extra attention. The crisp sauvi-gnon blanc is a highly accomplished expression of a grape that's gain-ing ground in this region. ⊠ *Main Rd., Jamesport* ☎ *631/722–5256* ⊕ *www.jamesport-vineyards.com* ⊠ *Tasting $4* ☉ *Daily 10–6, tours by appointment.*

Martha Clara Vineyards. Once a roadside farm stand, Martha Clara now has a large, barn-style summer tasting room and patio as well as a more intimate winter tasting room. Original old barns serve as art galleries and event spaces; pet goats, live music, and antique-carriage tours pulled by resident Clydesdales add to the down-on-the-farm feel. ⊠ *6025 Sound Ave., Jamesport* ☎ *631/298–0075* ⊕ *www.marthaclaravineyards. com* ⊠ *Tasting $3, tour $4* ☉ *Weekdays and Sun. 11–5:30, Sat. 11–6.*

Palmer Vineyards. A small, old-fashioned tasting room leads out to a wooden deck and lawn—a top spot for watching the sun set over acres of vines and farm fields. Palmer wines regularly impress top critics, es-pecially its "41/72" merlot cuvée. ⊠ *Sound Ave. off Osborne Ave., Aque-bogue* ☎ *631/722–9463* ⊕ *www.palmervineyards.com* ⊠ *Tasting fees vary, tour free* ☉ *Daily 11–6.*

Paumanok Vineyards. The Massoud family tends the vines, makes the wine, and greets visitors in a tasting room that has a great view of the whole winemaking operation; ask and you might be shown the exten-sive catwalk system. Paumanok wines, traditionally crafted, consis-tently receive top marks. ⊠ *1074 Main Rd., Aquebogue* ☎ *631/722–8800* ⊕ *www.paumanok.com* ⊠ *Tasting fees vary, tour free* ☉ *Tast-ings daily 11–5, tours by appointment.*

Peconic River Herb Farm. The working farm on 13 riverfront acres west of Riverhead grows more than 700 varieties of plants, including herbs, heirloom vegetables, beautiful shrubs, and roses. Wander through the trail gardens or visit (in season) the farm's market. Garden-related workshops and other events are offered off-season. ⊠ *2749 River Rd., Calverton* ☎ *631/369–0058* ⊕ *www.prherbfarm.com* ⊠ *Free* ☉ *Apr.–June, daily 9–5; July–Oct., daily 9–4.*

Riverhead Raceway. From April through September this stock-car track with a figure-eight course hosts NASCAR events, spectator drag racing, and demolition derbies. In season, early-evening races are scheduled for each Saturday and one Sunday a month; gates open at 3. ⊠ *Rte. 58 ½ mi east of the LIE* ☎ *631/842–7223* ⊕ *www.riverheadraceway. com* ⊠ *$18–$30.*

South Jamesport Beach. On Peconic Bay, this 3,000-foot-long beach has shallow-water areas for children. Lifeguards are on duty weekends from mid-May through June and daily in July to early September. ⊠ *Off Peconic Bay Blvd., Jamesport* ☎ *631/727–5744* ⊠ *Parking $25 (Memorial Day–Labor Day).*

🖑 **Splish Splash.** At this 96-acre water park you may ride an inner tube down the 1,300-foot-long Lazy River, passing waterfalls, geysers, and wave pools. Other attractions include Monsoon Lagoon, Mammoth River Ride, and Kiddie Cove. The park has three pools, a beach area, and two restaurants. ⊠ *2549 Splish Splash Dr.* ☎ *631/727–3600* ⊕ *www.splishsplashlongisland.com* ⊠ *$24* ⊙ *Memorial Day–Labor Day, daily 10–6.*

off the beaten path

THE BIG DUCK – Duck farming was a major industry on Long Island when this 20-foot-tall duck-shape building was erected in 1931. The duck farmer who built it sold Long Island's famously delicious ducks here, but today it serves as a tourism center and gift shop carrying T-shirts, mugs, and other souvenirs bearing the aquatic birds. Long Island's most recognized landmark, the Big Duck is on the National Register of Historic Places. It's a few miles east of Riverhead on Route 24. ⊠ *At entrance to Sears Bellows County Park, Rte. 24, Flanders* ☎ *631/852–8292* ⊕ *www.co.suffolk.ny.us/exec/parks* ⊠ *Free* ⊙ *Memorial Day–Labor Day, daily 10–5.*

Where to Stay & Eat

$–$$ ✕ **Digger O'Dells.** In addition to such pub standards as shepherd's pie, fish-and-chips, and corned beef and cabbage, the menu here includes prime rib, steaks, and pasta and chicken dishes. The pub-restaurant hosts live music on Friday and Saturday. A children's menu is available. ⊠ *58 W. Main St.* ☎ *631/369–3200* ⊟ *AE, D, DC, MC, V.*

★ $–$$ ✕ **Jamesport Country Kitchen.** The food outshines the decor at this eatery, which looks like a simple, wood-shingled country store. The menu is contemporary, and dishes feature local ingredients such as fresh seafood and Long Island duck. The wine list also has a local focus. It's in Jamesport, about 7 mi northeast of Riverhead. ⊠ *Main Rd., Jamesport* ☎ *631/722–3537* ⊟ *AE, DC, MC, V.*

$–$$ ✕ **Meetinghouse Creek Inn.** The seafood at this waterside restaurant 4 mi east of Riverhead is a big draw, but the kitchen also turns out good steaks and pasta dishes. A patio offers open-air dining, and a pianist plays here Friday and Saturday. A children's menu is available. ⊠ *177 Meeting House Creek Rd., Aquebogue* ☎ *631/722–4220* ⊟ *AE, D, MC, V* ⊙ *Closed Tues. from Labor Day to late May.*

$–$$ ✕ **Modern Snack Bar.** At this unpretentious family-owned café beloved by locals and out-of-towners alike, you can savor sauerbraten with

CloseUp

THE NORTH FORK WINE TRAIL

WHEN LOUISA AND ALEX HARGRAVE PLANTED *their first grape vines at their eponymous vineyard in 1973, they also planted the seeds of a new North Fork industry. Little more than a quarter-century later, the area's burgeoning wine industry is attracting ever-more attention. (The Hargraves sold the winery in 1999 and the place was renamed Castello di Borghese Vineyard.)*

Chardonnay and merlot together account for more than 60% of the varietals grown on Long Island; cabernet franc, cabernet sauvignon, sauvignon blanc, chenin blanc, malbec, pinot blanc, pinot gris, pinot noir, Riesling, and viognier are among the others planted here. Land devoted to vineyards on the East End exceeds 3,000 acres.

From Aquebogue to Greenport, 20-plus wineries and vineyards—the majority on or close to routes 25 or 48—are open to the public for tastings and, at some, tours; most host special events as well. To follow the North Fork Wine Trail, take the last LIE exit (73) and follow it to Route 25 (via Route 58), where green WINE TRAIL *road signs guide you to the wineries. Before making a special trip or taking a detour to visit a winery or vineyard, call to confirm hours. At the Tasting Room (2885 Peconic La., Peconic, 631/765–6404), open Wednesday through Monday 11–6, you may try (and buy) wines from small North Fork producers not open to the public.*

potato dumplings, delectable lobster salad, and home-baked strawberry-rhubarb and lemon-meringue pies. ⊠ *628 Main Rd., Aquebogue* ☎ *631/722–3655* ⌕ *Reservations not accepted* ⊟ *AE, D, MC, V* ☉ *Closed Mon. and Dec.–Mar.*

$$–$$$$ 🏨 **Best Western East End.** This chain property, next to the Tanger outlet center (just off the LIE) and 1 mi from Splish Splash and the Riverhead Raceway, earns high marks for comfort and convenience. ⊠ *1830 Rte. 25, 11901* ☎ *631/369–2200* 🖷 *631/369–1202* ⊕ *www.bestwestern. com* ⇔ *100 rooms* ⚲ *Restaurant, room service, in-room data ports, cable TV with movies, pool, gym, laundry facilities, business services, meeting rooms, car rental, some pets allowed, no-smoking rooms* ⊟ *AE, D, DC, MC, V* � *CP.*

$$–$$$$ 🏨 **Red Barn Bed & Breakfast.** At this lovingly restored 1877 farmhouse you can relax in a hammock, sip lemonade on the porch, and stargaze through the owner's telescope. Rooms are tidy and uncluttered. Breakfast features free-range local eggs, homemade scones, and desserts such as strawberry-rhubarb cobbler. ⊠ *733 Herricks La., Jamesport 11947* 🏨 *631/722–3695* ⊕ *www.redbarnbandb.com* ⇔ *3 rooms* ⚲ *Dining room, croquet, horseshoes, some pets allowed; no room TVs, no smoking* ⊟ *MC, V* ⎪⎪ *BP.*

$$–$$$ ▦ **Motel on the Bay.** All rooms at this motel overlook Peconic Bay and its sandy beach. Some units have full kitchens. The two- and three-room suites, furnished in a contemporary style, are especially roomy. ⊠ *Front St., South Jamesport 11970* ☎ *631/722–3458* 🖷 *631/722–5166* ⊕ *www.northforkmotels.com* 🛏 *7 studios, 10 suites* ♿ *Some kitchens, some kitchenettes, refrigerators, cable TV, beach, no-smoking rooms* ▤ *AE, D, MC, V.*

¢–$$ ▦ **Budget Host Inn.** This motel-style budget option is on 6 acres 6 mi from the Splish Splash water park. The grounds include play and picnic areas. Rooms are carpeted and colorful. ⊠ *30 E. Moriches Rd., 11901* ☎ *631/727–6200* 🖷 *631/727–6466* ⊕ *www.budgethost.com* 🛏 *68 rooms* ♿ *Restaurant, coffee shop, picnic area, some kitchenettes, cable TV, pool, lounge, playground, business services, meeting rooms, no-smoking rooms* ▤ *AE, D, DC, MC, V.*

Sports & the Outdoors

CANOEING & KAYAKING Renting a canoe or kayak at **Peconic Paddler** (⊠ 89 Peconic Ave. ☎ 631/369–9500 ⊕ www.peconicpaddler.com) is the best way to see the ecologically diverse Peconic River, which flows for 15 mi before emptying into Flanders Bay.

GOLF **Long Island National Golf Course** (⊠ 1793 Northville Tpke. ☎ 631/727–4653 ⊕ www.islandsendgolf.com), designed by Robert Trent Jones Jr., is an 18-hole, 6,838-yard course surrounded by farmland. Greens fees are $80–$125, depending on the season.

Fodor'sChoice ★

Shopping

Coach, Nike, DKNY, and Pottery Barn are among the more than 170 brand-name factory stores at the popular **Tanger Outlet Stores** (⊠ 1770 W. Main St., at Rte. 25 ☎ 631/369–2732 or 800/407–4894).

Cutchogue

⑬ *12 mi east of Riverhead.*

White steepled churches and a small collection of old-fashioned shops line Cutchogue's Main Street. Here you can stroll to an ice-cream parlor, browse a handful of art and crafts boutiques, and eat blueberry pie at the landmark Cutchogue Diner. In summer, people flock to the antiques fairs, tag sales, and concerts on the village green.

Bedell Cellars. Merlot is the benchmark of the region, and Bedell's reputation as the area's premier maker of this wine attracts serious wine lovers. The tasting room, in a New England farm-style building, has a modern-art collection and a stainless-steel bar. ⊠ *36225 Main Rd.* ☎ *631/734–7537* ⊕ *www.bedellcellars.com* 🍷 *Tasting $5, tour free* ☉ *Tastings daily 11–5, tours weekends at 3 and by appointment.*

Bidwell Vineyards. This low-key, family-run winery has a large tasting room with an industrial feel. You can get good values on house blends. ⊠ *18910 Rte. 48, near Depot La.* ☎ *631/734–5200* 🍷 *Tasting $1, tour free* ☉ *Tastings daily 11–6, tours by appointment.*

Castello di Borghese Vineyard & Winery. Long Island's founding vineyard has been transformed into a lively venue for festivals, opera, and art exhibits in a former barn off to the side of the tasting room. The Novella wine, a fruity pinot noir bottled young in the classic Italian style, is an annual sellout. ⊠ *Rte. 48 at Alvah's La.* ☎ *631/734–5111* ⊕ *www. castellodiborghese.com* ⊠ *Tasting $3, tour free* ⊙ *Jan.–Mar., Thurs.–Mon. 11–5; Apr.–Dec., weekdays 11–5, weekends 11–6.*

Fodor'sChoice **Cutchogue Village Green and Old Burial Ground.** Five old buildings, main-
★ tained by the Cutchogue–New Suffolk Historical Council, inhabit the village green. The 1649 Old House is one of the oldest frame houses in the country. Also here are the 1840 Old School House and the 1890 Red Barn, both filled with period furnishings. To see the interiors, you must take the tour, which lasts one hour. ⊠ *Main Rd. at Case La.* ☎ *631/734–7122* ⊠ *Free* ⊙ *Late June–Labor Day, Sun. and Mon. 1–4.*

Fort Corchaug/Downs Farm Preserve. You may walk along peaceful wood-land trails lined with native flora and fauna at this National Historic Landmark and important archaeological site. The fort dates to at least the early 1600s and is largely intact. At the visitor center, a volunteer can explain exhibits about the native Corchaug Indians, who built the fort, and the early colonial settlers. ⊠ *Main Rd.* ☎ *631/734–5630* ⊕ *southoldtown.northfork.net* ⊠ *Free* ⊙ *Daily dawn–dusk.*

Galluccio Family Wineries. A busy tasting room has cozy couches in front of a large fireplace and a wide deck leading to lawns that invite a stroll among the vines. An annual pig roast kicks off the new releases, like the Cru George Allaire series. ⊠ *24385 Main Rd.* ☎ *631/734–7089* ⊕ *www. galluciofamilywineries.com* ⊠ *Tasting fees vary, tour $25* ⊙ *Tastings week-days 11–5, weekends 11–6; tours May–Sept., by appointment.*

Laurel Lake Vineyards. The winery, built in 1998, has an antique bar sal-vaged from an old hotel. Laurel Lake grows its own chardonnay and obtains red grapes from other North Fork growers. ⊠ *3165 Main Rd., Laurel* ☎ *631/298–1420* ⊠ *Tasting and tour free* ⊙ *Tastings daily 11–6, tours by appointment.*

Lenz Winery. This iconoclastic winery enjoys pitting its wines against top international pours in blind tastings, and critics are often generous with their praise. An enclosed courtyard flanked by old vines leads into an old barn, now a large tasting room. ⊠ *Main Rd. west of Peconic La., Peconic* ☎ *631/734–6010* ⊕ *www.lenzwine.com* ⊠ *Tasting fees vary, tour free* ⊙ *Tastings daily 10–6, tours by appointment.*

Lieb Family Cellars. Premium Wine Group is a custom crush facility, a unique place where dozens of labels are produced for private clients with small vineyards. Lieb wines are poured in a no-frills room at the front; try the pinot blanc, a unique wine for this region. ⊠ *35 Cox Neck Rd., Mattituck* ☎ *631/734–1100* ⊕ *www.liebcellars.com* ⊠ *Tasting $3, tour free* ⊙ *Daily 11–6.*

Macari Vineyards & Winery. The family-owned winery is committed to organic and sustainable vineyard practices, and wines like its Bergen Road red enjoy consistent critical acclaim. The tasting room is big and mod-ern; vineyards nestle below the Long Island Sound bluffs. ⊠ *150 Bergen Ave., south side of Sound Ave., Mattituck* ☎ *631/298–0100* ⊕ *www.*

macariwines.com ✉ *Tasting fees vary, tour $10* ☉ *Tastings daily 11–5, tours by appointment.*

Osprey's Dominion Vineyards. Osprey's top wines, like the rich cabernet sauvignon, are becoming serious players, whereas a sweet wine made from strawberries is a great picnic pour. During a late-afternoon summer tasting on the patio, you might see the owners, avid flyers, buzz in for a 4 PM "visit" on an antique plane. ✉ *44075 Main Rd., Peconic* ☎ *631/765–6188* ⊕ *www.ospreysdominion.com* ✉ *Tasting fees vary, tour free* ☉ *Daily 11–5.*

Peconic Bay Winery. Although Peconic Bay's small blue-and-white tasting barn and patio are across from a shopping center, the surrounding vines buffer them from the bustle. A special tour of the winery, "Wednesday with the Winemaker," includes barrel tastings. ✉ *31320 Main Rd.* ☎ *631/734–7361* ⊕ *www.peconicbaywinery.com* ✉ *Tasting free–$1, tour free* ☉ *Tastings Sun.–Thurs. 11–6, Fri. and Sat. 11–5; tours May–mid-Oct., weekends at 2.*

Pellegrini Vineyards. With a tower over the tasting room, a professional kitchen, and an interior courtyard, this winery is an architectural standout. Weddings are held here almost every weekend in warm-weather months. ✉ *23005 Main Rd.* ☎ *631/734–4111* ⊕ *www. pellegrinivineyards.com* ✉ *Tasting fees vary, tour free* ☉ *Daily 11–5.*

Pindar Vineyards. At the region's largest producer, it can be three-deep at the bar, with a fun crowd enjoying ample free tastes of approachable wines. Tours are a real education for beginners and experienced hands alike; on November weekends, a special tour shows how sparkling wine is made. ✉ *Main Rd. between Bridge La. and Peconic La., Peconic* ☎ *631/ 734–6200* ⊕ *www.pindar.net* ✉ *Tasting free–$2, tour free* ☉ *Daily 11–6.*

Pugliese Vineyards. The Pugliese family makes down-to-earth wines that are local favorites. Its sparklers really shine: the Blanc de Blanc Brut regularly ranks in national competitions, and the off-dry sparkling merlot is an unusual treat. ✉ *Main Rd. between Cox La. and Bridge La.* ☎ *631/734–4057* ✉ *Tasting free* ☉ *Daily 10–5.*

Raphael. The winery is a boutique producer of high-end merlot, but the lavish Spanish mission–style winery, built with wrought iron and stone, is worth a visit on its own. ✉ *39390 Main Rd., Peconic* ☎ *631/765– 1100* ⊕ *www.raphaelwine.com* ✉ *Tasting $8, tour $10* ☉ *Daily noon–5.*

Waters Crest Winery. Shoehorned into an industrial center, Waters Crest is a venture by home winemakers who decided to go pro. The owners seem to truly enjoy chatting with the intrepid tasters who seek them out. ✉ *22355 Rte. 48, Unit 6* ☎ *631/734–5065* ⊕ *www.waterscrest.com* ✉ *Tasting $1.50* ☉ *Fri.–Sun. noon–5.*

Where to Stay

$$$–$$$$ 🏨 **Santorini Hotel.** Location is everything at this motel-style complex, which sits amid 17 acres with a 500-foot-long beach on Long Island Sound. Rooms are spare and simple. ✉ *3800 Duck Pond Rd., 11935* ☎ *631/ 734–6370* ⊕ *www.santorinibeach.com* ⇌ *45 rooms* ♿ *Restaurant,*

cable TV, pool, wading pool, beach, basketball, some pets allowed, no-smoking rooms; no phones in some rooms ⊟ *AE, D, MC, V* ⦿ *CP.*

Nightlife & the Arts

Legend's (⊠ 725 1st St., New Suffolk ☎ 631/734–5123) is a casual yet classy sports bar and restaurant in tiny, nautical New Suffolk village, a few miles south of Cutchogue. Wednesday evenings in summer you may want to bring a chair or blanket to the nearby beach to watch the Robins Island sailing race at 6 PM; afterward you can join the sailors and spectators at the bar.

Sports & the Outdoors

Matt-A-Mar Marina (⊠ 2255 Wickham Ave., Mattituck ☎ 631/298–4739 ⊕ www.mattamar.com), 3 mi west of Cutchogue, rents craft and offers guided canoe and kayak tours.

Shopping

The local artists and craftspeople of the **Old Town Arts and Crafts Guild** (⊠ 28265 Rte. 25 ☎ 631/734–6382), first established in the late 1940s, sell their artwork in this converted old house. It's open daily in July, August, November, and December; it's open weekends only in June, September, and October. In summer you can buy fresh fruit at **Wickham's Fruit Farm stand** (⊠ Rte. 25 ☎ 631/734–6441); the Wickham family has been growing apples, peaches, and vegetables on Long Island for more than 300 years.

---

en route At **Punkinville,** a mini-zoo in Peconic, between Cutchogue and Southold, kids can feed and pet farm and other animals and take

 pony rides. ⊠ 26085 Rte. 48, Peconic ☎ 631/734–5530 ⊡ $5
⊙ May–Nov., Thurs.–Sun. 10–5.

Southold

14 *6 mi east of Cutchogue.*

With its wineries and beautiful farmland, the village of Southold is at the heart of the North Fork. Like its neighboring villages and hamlets, it exudes New England charm. Southold was settled in 1640, at the same time as the South Fork's Southampton, making them the oldest towns in New York State. Southold Township originally stretched from Orient Point all the way west to Wading River, but the new western boundary was drawn in Laurel when Riverhead Township was created. Southold Township today comprises several villages, including Cutchogue, Greenport, and the eponymous Southold, where you'll find the town hall.

Back in 1757, a young surveyor from Virginia, George Washington, recommended that a lighthouse be built off Cliff Lot to assist sailors who had to face the perilous glacier boulders just below the surface of Long Island Sound's Deadman's Cove. This lighthouse still stands atop a 110-foot bluff.

Corey Creek Vineyards. A short, winding road leads you to this airy, chalet-like tasting house with a spacious deck and one of the best vineyard views in the area. The wines are made under the Corey Creek label at Bedell Cellars. ⊠ *45470 Main Rd.* ☎ *631/765–4168* ⊕ *www.coreycreek.com* ⊠ *Tasting $5* ☉ *Tastings weekdays 11–5, weekends 11–6.*

Custer Institute. Taking advantage of some of the darkest night skies on Long Island, this observatory is a prime viewing spot for astronomy buffs and star-deprived urbanites. Atop the barnlike structure is a motorized dome with a telescope you can use to track the heavenly view. ⊠ *Main Bayview Rd.* ☎ *631/765–2626* ⊕ *www.custerobservatory.org* ⊠ *Free* ☉ *Sat. after dusk–midnight.*

Historic Museums of Southold. The complex encompasses a dozen buildings, including the **Ann Currie-Bell Home,** which has antique dolls and toys, costume collections, and period rooms; the **Thomas Moore House,** a mid-18th-century carriage house and blacksmith shop; the circa-1821 **Old Bay View School,** which now looks as it did in 1914; and a buttery and icehouse. ⊠ *Main Rd. and Maple La.* ☎ *631/765–5500* ⊕ *www.southoldhistoricalsociety.org* ⊠ *Free* ☉ *July and Aug., Wed. and weekends 1–4.*

Horton Point Lighthouse and Nautical Museum. The 58-foot-tall lighthouse, operated by the Southold Historical Society, was built in 1847. Together with the adjoining lighthouse keeper's home, it resembles a church. The museum, in the keeper's residence, displays sea captains' journals, sea chests, paintings, and maps. The 8-acre park surrounding the lighthouse includes public barbecue grills. ⊠ *Lighthouse Rd.* ☎ *631/ 765–5500 or 631/765–3262* ⊕ *www.longislandlighthouses.com* ⊠ *$2 suggested donation* ☉ *Memorial Day–Columbus Day, weekends 11:30–4.*

Old Field. Christian and Rosamund Baiz's family homestead is the only place on Long Island where rows of vines run right up to sparkling Peconic Bay. The wines are made by one of the area's top winemakers. Tastings are in an old barn or picnic-style by the beach. ⊠ *59600 Main Rd.* ☎ *631/ 765–2465* ⊕ *www.theoldfield.com* ⊠ *Tasting $2–$3, tour free* ☉ *Fri.–Sun. 11:30–5.*

Southold Indian Museum. At this museum focused on natural history and archaeology, permanent exhibits record the cultural evolution of Native Americans. A large collection of Algonquin pottery is among the highlights, and most of the artifacts and handiworks here are relics of local tribes. ⊠ *1080 Bayview Rd.* ☎ *631/765–5577* ⊕ *www. southoldindianmuseum.org* ⊠ *$1 suggested donation* ☉ *July and Aug., weekends 1:30–4:30; Sept.–June, Sun. 1:30–4:30.*

Where to Eat

$$–$$$ ✕**Coeur des Vignes.** The name of this family-run restaurant in Long Island's wine country translates as "heart of the vines." Lace curtains, candlelight, and fine china are part of the romantic setting. The fine fare served here is French: seared duck breast and confit, braised sweetbreads, grilled filet mignon with béarnaise sauce. An extensive wine list accompanies the menu. ⊠ *57225 Main Rd.* ☎ *631/765–2656* ☉ *Closed Mon. in Nov.–Apr., Tues. all yr. No lunch Sun.–Fri.* ▭ *AE, D, DC, MC, V.*

★ **$$–$$$**   ✕ **Seafood Barge.** The airy, nautically themed restaurant—one of the best on the North Fork—offers sweeping views of Peconic Bay and refined seafood and other contemporary dishes, including sushi. Local ingredients are emphasized. Try the pan-seared local fish or the grilled salmon over lobster succotash with sweet-potato sticks. ⊠ *Port of Egypt Marina, 62980 Main Rd.* ☎ *631/765–3010* ▭ *AE, DC, MC, V.*

Sports & the Outdoors

CANOEING &   **Eagle's Neck Paddling Company** (⊠ 49295 Main Rd. ☎ 631/323–2660
KAYAKING   ⊕ www.eaglesneck.com) offers guided kayak tours and rents boats. **Sound View Scuba** (⊠ 46770 Rte. 48 ☎ 631/765–9515 ⊕ www. soundviewscuba.com) runs kayak tours in the area.

Shopping

Jan Davis Antiques (⊠ 45395 Main Rd. ☎ 631/765–2379) sells and restores antique dolls along with some vintage toys and other small items.

Greenport

⑮ *6 mi east of Southold.*

A fleet of commercial fishing boats still operates out of this down-to-earth, working-class village, but shops and restaurants have grown increasingly upscale due to an influx of summer visitors and second-home owners. Since the late 1600s, Greenport's saga—which includes a brisk rum-running business during Prohibition—has depended on the sea. In summer the deep waters of Long Island Sound still summon home tall ships reminiscent of the whaling boats that once docked in the safe waters of Greenport Harbor. Waterfront Mitchell Park is the perfect place to watch yachts and sailboats, or to catch an outdoor performance in the landscaped amphitheater.

★ **East End Seaport and Maritime Museum.** A former Long Island Rail Road passenger terminal contains exhibits about lighthouses, ships, East End shipbuilding, and yacht racing. ⊠ *3rd St. at ferry dock* ☎ *631/477–2100* ⊕ *www.eastendseaport.org* ☜ *$2* ☉ *Late May, weekends 11–5; June–Sept., Wed.–Mon. 11–5.*

☾ **Mitchell Park Carousel.** The 1920s carousel, housed in a round, gleaming glass structure that allows year-round enjoyment, is the highlight of Greenport's renovated waterfront. ⊠ *Front St., near the post office* ☎ *No phone* ☜ *$1* ☉ *June–Labor Day, daily 10–10; rest of yr, weekends (call for hrs).*

Railroad Museum of Long Island. The museum, in an 1892 Greenport freight station, exhibits a Reading Railroad track car, a 1907 snow-plow, and a 1925 Long Island Rail Road caboose. ⊠ *440 4th St.* ☎ *631/727–7920* ⊕ *www.rmli.org* ☜ *$3* ☉ *Memorial Day–Columbus Day, weekends 11–4.*

Stirling Historical Society. Maritime exhibits emphasize whaling and oyster industries; whaling tools and oil lamps are on display, along with a collection of artifacts, furniture, and tools from the 1800s. ⊠ *Main and Adams Sts.* ☎ *631/477–1719* ☜ *Free* ☉ *July–Sept., weekends 1–4.*

Ternhaven Cellars. You can make wine anywhere, as this former gas station in the village of Greenport proves. Billed as "the last winery before France," Ternhaven offers wines in a tiny, art-filled room. ⊠ *331 Front St.* ☎ *631/477–8737* ⊕ *www.ternhaven.com* 🖃 *Tasting fees vary* ⏱ *Apr.–Dec., Thurs.–Mon. 11–6.*

Where to Stay & Eat

$$–$$$ ✕ **Chowder Pot Pub.** The views of Peconic Bay at this casual seafood spot are best at sunset. You may eat outside when the weather's nice. The place hosts live music on weekends. ⊠ *104 3rd St.* ☎ *631/477–1345* 🖃 *AE, MC, V* ⏱ *Closed Jan.–Mar.; Mon.–Wed. in Apr.–June and Labor Day–Dec.*

$$–$$$ ✕ **The Frisky Oyster.** This sophisticated, modern restaurant is a little piece
Fodor'sChoice of Manhattan in Greenport. North Fork sophisticates come for the
★ small, lively bar and contemporary fare, such as seared foie gras atop roasted pineapple and mâche, and penne with pancetta, littleneck clams, leeks, and tomatoes. ⊠ *27 Front St.* ☎ *631/477–4265* 🖃 *AE, D, DC, MC, V* ⏱ *No lunch.*

$$ ✕ **Claudio's Clam Bar/Claudio's Restaurant/Crabby Jerry's.** These three restaurants share a 2½-acre waterfront property. The Clam Bar, right on the dock, serves salads, hot dogs, fried clams, mussels, and soft-shell crab. Claudio's is known for seafood, porterhouse steaks, and lobsters; the bar dates from the late 1800s. Crabby Jerry's offers self-service with picnic tables on the Main Street Dock. ⊠ *111 Main St.* ☎ *631/477–0627* 🖃 *MC, V* ⏱ *Closed Dec.–mid-Apr.*

$$$$ 🏨 **Shady Lady Inn.** The Victorian-style inn, decorated to the hilt with furnishings and objets d'art from the owner's collections, offers an over-the-top, frilly rendezvous. Rooms have 14-foot ceilings, fireplaces, marble bathrooms, featherbeds, and massive antique headboards and armoires. Both the formal Scarlet Room and more casual Pine Lounge serve sophisticated Continental cuisine. ⊠ *305 North Rd., 11944* ☎ *631/477–4500* ⊕ *www.shadyladyinn.com* 🖃 *6 rooms, 2 suites* ♺ *Restaurant, cable TV, lounge, Internet; no kids under 18, no smoking* 🖃 *AE, D, DC, MC, V* ⏱ *CP.*

$$$–$$$$ 🏨 **The Greenporter Hotel & Spa.** A 1950s motel a block from the waterfront has been converted into this sleek, minimalist lodging with a cool green interior scheme. Rooms have light-wood platform beds, graphic rugs, and metal accents. Until the spa is completed (at this writing expected by 2005), you may schedule in-room treatments, from shiatsu and reflexology to body polishes. ⊠ *326 Front St., 11944* ☎ *631/477–0066* 🖨 *631/477–2317* ⊕ *www.thegreenporter.com* 🖃 *15 rooms* ♺ *Restaurant, in-room data ports, cable TV, pool, hot tub, massage, bar, some pets allowed (fee), no-smoking rooms* 🖃 *AE, MC, V.*

★ **$$$–$$$$** 🏨 **The Harborfront Inn.** Most rooms at this three-story, gray-and-white inn have balconies, some with harbor views; all rooms have high-speed Internet access, flat-screen TVs, and CD players. Interiors are contemporary and bright, with cherrywood furniture, leather armchairs, and light-color carpeting. Down comforters and Frette linens outfit the beds. For a really big splurge, you might consider the Terrace Suite; at 800 square feet, it's double the size of the regular rooms, *and* it has a 1,000-square-foot deck. The property, which opened in 2004, is within walking distance of restaurants and shops. ⌧ *209 Front St., 11944* ☎ *631/477–0707* 🖷 *631/477–8603* ⊕ *www.theharborfrontinn.com* 🛏 *32 rooms, 4 suites* ♺ *Refrigerators, in-room safes, cable TV, pool, gym, Internet, meeting rooms; no smoking* ⊟ *AE, D, MC, V* |◎| *CP.*

$$–$$$ 🏠 **The Victorian Lady.** The delightful in-town B&B has a sizable front porch where you can sit while savoring a confection from the fudge factory across the street. The rooms, each named after a flower, are furnished with antiques and Victorian-period pieces. The Lilac Room is the most flowery of the three. A resident dog shares common rooms with guests. ⌧ *151 Bay Ave., 11944* ☎ *631/477–1837* ⊕ *www.victorianladybnb.com* 🛏 *3 rooms* ♺ *Dining room, fans, cable TV, library; no smoking* ⊟ *MC, V* |◎| *BP.*

$–$$$ 🏠 **Watson's by the Bay.** Built in 1873, this three-story Victorian home sits on a quiet cul-de-sac two blocks from the village, overlooking the Peconic Bay and Shelter Island. Rooms have period antiques and bay views. The wraparound porch is a great place to relax while sipping some local wine. ⌧ *104 Bay Ave., 11944* ☎ *631/477–0426* 🖷 *631/477–8441* ⊕ *www.greenport.com/watsons* 🛏 *3 rooms* ♺ *Dining room, fans, cable TV, pool; no kids, no smoking* ⊟ *No credit cards* ☾ *Closed early Sept.–Memorial Day* |◎| *CP.*

$$ 🏠 **Sound View Inn.** Each room in this complex of modern motel-style buildings has a deck overlooking the 1,400-foot-long private beach. Interiors are bright, with contemporary wood furniture in light tones and pale wood paneling. ⌧ *57185 North Rd., 11944* ☎ *631/477–1910* 🖷 *631/477–9436* ⊕ *www.soundviewinn.com* 🛏 *49 rooms, 31 suites* ♺ *Restaurant, some in-room data ports, some kitchenettes, refrigerators, cable TV, 4 tennis courts, pool, sauna, beach, bar, no-smoking rooms* ⊟ *AE, D, DC, MC, V.*

Nightlife

Late at night, the funky, eclectic **Bay & Main Restaurant** (⌧ 300 Main St. ☎ 631/477–1442) turns into a busy bar that specializes in martinis. In warm weather the older crowd gravitates to the outdoor patio, where there's live acoustic music. Saturday nights draw twentysomethings who dance to the local rock, jazz, and funk bands. **The Whiskey Wind** (⌧ 30–32 Front St. ☎ 631/477–8764), a bar that's popular with fisherfolk and laborers, is the real Greenport. A fixture from the old days, it's still frequented mainly by local residents and their dogs, and has dartboards, a pool table, and a jukebox.

Sports & the Outdoors

FISHING Seasonal freshwater licenses in the township of Southold cost $14 for New York State residents, $35 for nonresidents; they're available at the town hall (in the village of Southold) and local sporting-goods stores. Temporary shellfish permits cost $10.

Island Star Lines (⌧ Railroad Dock, 3rd St. ☎ 631/696–0936 ⊕ islandstarfishing.com) can provide rods and bait for free, if you need them, for trips on its 65-foot open fishing boat, *Island Star.* You can go out from May through November and bring the kids. A day ticket costs $45. The 90-foot, 150-passenger ***Peconic Star II*** (⌧ Railroad Dock, 3rd St. ☎ 631/289–6899 ⊕ www.peconicstar.com) regularly offers fishing trips from May through December. Full-day rates are $49 per person and include bait and a rod and reel.

GOLF The semiprivate **Island's End Golf & Country Club** (⊠ Rte. 25 ☎ 631/477–0777 ⊕ www.islandsendgolf.com) has a well-maintained 18-hole, 6,639-yard course with great views. One hole overlooks Long Island Sound. High-season (June through October) greens fees are $37–$48.

Shopping

An old-time emporium with wide-plank floors, **Arcade Department Store** (⊠ 14 Front St. ☎ 631/477–1440) carries a little bit of everything, including boots, buttons, and North Fork necessities like lobster crackers. The owners of the antiques shop **Beall & Bell** (⊠ 18 South St. ☎ 631/477–8239) source serious treasures from the area, where many of the grand houses are passed down through the generations and have odds and ends in their attics going back centuries. Originally a wharfside ship's chandlery dating from 1880, **S. T. Preston's & Sons** (⊠ 102 Main St. ☎ 631/477–1990) is now a marine supply and clothing store, with a gift shop selling scrimshaw, sailing books, and all things nautical for the boat and home.

Orient

⑯ *6 mi east of Greenport.*

Orient, a seaside village, sits on sheltered Orient Harbor, a few miles west of the North Fork's easternmost tip. Beyond the village—jutting into the rough waters of Plum Gut, where Long Island Sound meets the Atlantic Ocean—is Orient Point, a wild, rocky spit that can be reached on foot after Route 25 ends. Corchaug Indians inhabited the area originally; in 1661 six English families settled here and called the land Oysterponds, a reference to the rich supply of shellfish. Orient village is still very much a rural hamlet, with well-tended old homes surrounded by farmland and wetlands.

Orient Beach State Park. The park occupies a tendril of land that extends southward from Orient Point and stretches west, surrounded by Gardiner's Bay on its south side and Orient Harbor and Long Beach Bay on its north side. The beach nestles beside a waterfront forest. In addition to swimming (from late June to early September), you may fish, picnic, hike, and bike here. ⊠ *South of Rte. 25* ☎ *631/323–2440* ⊕ *nysparks.state.ny.us* 🅿 *Parking $7 (Memorial Day–Labor Day)* 🕙 *Daily sunrise–sunset.*

Oysterponds Historical Society. Several old buildings in this complex, including the 19th-century Village House and the 18th-century Orange Webb House, depict the maritime and rural past of Orient and nearby East Marion. Antique furniture, art, and scrimshaw fill the buildings. ⊠ *Village La.* ☎ *631/323–2480* 🅾 *$3* 🕙 *June–Sept., Thurs. and weekends 2–5.*

Where to Stay & Eat

$$–$$$ ✕ **Orient by the Sea.** The casual marina restaurant overlooks Gardiner's Bay. Dishes include a broiled-seafood combo of lobster tail, stuffed flounder, shrimps, and scallops, as well as steaks, chicken, and pasta.

Outdoor dining is on the deck. A children's menu is available. ✉ *Main Rd.* ☎ *631/323–2424* ▭ *D, DC, MC, V* ⊙ *Closed Nov.–Apr.*

★ ¢–$$ ✕ **Hellenic Snack Bar.** Heavenly homemade lemonade—well known on the North Fork—and authentic Greek appetizers and main courses are the draws at this East Marion restaurant. The outdoor patio is covered and has a huge rotisserie for roasting lamb. ✉ *5145 Main Rd., East Marion* ☎ *631/477–0138* ▭ *AE, D, DC, MC, V.*

$$$$ ▦ **Quintessentials Bed & Breakfast.** Fresh flowers, Caribbean colors, chocolates, and maximum pampering await in this gingerbread Victorian set amid feng shui gardens. The spa offers such extras as massage, reflexology, facials, and body wraps. Sylvia's homemade corned-beef hash and fried plantains are a breakfast specialty. ✉ *8985 Main Rd., East Marion 11939* ☎ *631/477–9400 or 877/259–0939* ⊕ *www.quintessentialsinc.com* ➪ *6 rooms* ↻ *Dining room, fans, in-room data ports, some in-room hot tubs, cable TV, in-room VCRs, spa, library, Internet; no smoking* ▭ *AE, MC, V* ⊠ *BP.*

$$–$$$ ▦ **Blue Dolphin Resort.** This neat and welcoming resort makes it easy to vacation with the whole family, including the dog. There's even a dog run on the premises. Rooms are simple and bright. ✉ *7850 Main Rd., East Marion 11939* ☎ *631/477–0907* ⊕ *www.bluedolphinmotel.net* ➪ *29 studios* ↻ *Café, picnic area, kitchenettes, refrigerators, cable TV, pool, lounge, video game room, playground, laundry facilities, some pets allowed (fee), no-smoking rooms* ▭ *AE, MC, V.*

Shelter Island

🄱 *3 mi south of Greenport, via ferry.*

Shelter Island lies between Long Island's North and South forks. Reachable only by boat (there's regular ferry service), the 11½-square-mi island offers at least a partial escape from the summer traffic and crowd snarls of the Hamptons. Quiet country lanes wind across the island's rolling land, nearly a third of which has been set aside as a nature preserve that's a bird-watcher's delight.

Taking advantage of its hilltop elevation, Shelter Island Heights is the island's center of activity. Its Queen Anne, Victorian, and colonial-revival houses, stores, and inns show off embellished porches, scalloped shingles, and carved friezes. This relaxed place becomes even mellower in the off-season, when many restaurants and other businesses reduce their hours or close for extended periods. If you're planning an off-season visit, call ahead to see what's open.

Crescent Beach. The bay beach, a long sandy strip across the street from the trendy Sunset Beach restaurant, faces northeast and is especially popular at sunset. It has picnic tables and restrooms. Island lodging properties have parking permits for guests; otherwise, contact the town clerk to get one. ✉ *Shore Rd. off W. Neck Rd.* ☎ *631/749–1166* 🖾 *Weekly parking $25 (mid-June–Labor Day).*

Havens House. Listed on the National Register of Historic Places, the home of First Colonial Congress member William Havens was built in 1743. The Shelter Island Historical Society maintains a museum here—

seven rooms with period furnishings and a toy collection. ⊠ *16 S. Ferry Rd.* ☎ *631/749–0025* ⊕ *www.shelterislandhistsoc.org* ✉ *$2 suggested donation* ☉ *Mid-May–mid-Sept., Fri.–Sun. 1–5.*

★ **Mashomack Nature Preserve.** Marked hiking trails of 1½ to 11 mi lace the preserve's 2,000-plus acres of beech and oak forest, meadows, tidal wetlands, beach, and freshwater ponds. A large population of ospreys nests here, along with many other bird species. The preserve is also home to harbor seals, turtles, and foxes. At the visitor center, ask for directions to the nearby gazebo, which has a water view. The Nature Conservancy, which owns the preserve, also runs tours and educational programs here. ⊠ *79 S. Ferry Rd.* ☎ *631/749–1001* ⊕ *www.nature. org* ✉ *$2.50 suggested donation* ☉ *July and Aug., daily 9–5; Sept. and Apr.–June, Wed.–Mon. 9–5; Oct.–Mar., Wed.–Mon. 9–4.*

Wades Beach. The shallow, sandy beach, on the island's south side, has picnic tables, restrooms, and a lifeguard. Locals comb the beach's salt-marsh area for clams and crab. Island lodging properties have parking permits for guests, or contact the town clerk for one. ⊠ *Heron La., off Shorewood Rd.* ☎ *631/749–1166* ✉ *Weekly parking $25 (mid-June–Labor Day).*

Where to Stay & Eat

$$–$$$ ✕ **Vine Street Cafe.** Husband-and-wife team Terry and Lisa Harwood create casual but sophisticated dishes, and their staff provides exceptional service. Daily specials such as bouillabaisse and crispy duck confit augment the limited menu, which lists staples such as steak *frites* (with fries) and miso-glazed salmon. The simple interior employs beige walls, exposed beams, and a wooden bar. In warm weather you may dine alfresco under tiki lights. Save room for dessert. ⊠ *41 S. Ferry Rd.* ☎ *631/ 749–3210* ♿ *Reservations essential* ▤ *AE, MC, V* ☉ *Closed Tues. and Wed.*

$–$$$ ✕ **Planet Bliss.** You can't miss this brightly painted, funky restaurant in a converted Victorian. The menu of healthful but delicious fare includes everything from rice-and-bean dishes to fruit smoothies and fine wine. Weekend brunch on the porch and patio is busy. ⊠ *23 N. Ferry Rd.* ☎ *631/749–0053* ▤ *AE, MC, V* ☉ *Closed Mon.–Thurs. Oct.–May.*

$–$$ ✕ **The Dory.** At this relaxed spot, seafood dishes are served on a scenic deck along Chase Creek. Daily specials round out a regular menu that includes fish-and-chips and chowder. In the off-season locals gather in the pub and dining room for a beer and a game of pool. ⊠ *Bridge St., Shelter Island Heights* ☎ *631/749–8871* ▤ *AE* ☉ *Closed Feb.*

¢–$ ✕ **Pat & Steve's Family Restaurant.** Head here for good old-fashioned home cooking for breakfast or lunch in a kid-friendly environment. Pancakes, omelets, and sandwiches come in ample portions. ⊠ *63 N. Ferry Rd.* ☎ *631/749–1998* ♿ *Reservations not accepted* ▤ *MC, V* ☉ *No dinner. Closed Wed.*

¢–$ ✕ **Tom's Coffee Shoppe.** An old-fashioned soda shop with stools at the counter and a few plastic tables outside, Tom's serves breakfast and lunch items such as grilled-cheese sandwiches and lobster rolls. ⊠ *S. Ferry Rd. next to fire station* ☎ *631/749–2655* ♿ *Reservations not accepted* ▤ *No credit cards* ☉ *No dinner.*

$$$$ ✕▦ **Sunset Beach.** An international crowd has flocked to this trendy hotel ever since celebrity hotelier Andre Balazs (of Los Angeles's Chateau Marmont and SoHo's Mercer) opened it in the late 1990s. Each retro-style guest room has a sundeck that looks out over the parking lot to the water. The beachfront restaurant ($$–$$$$; reservations essential) provides the best sunset- and people-watching around. You can stick your toes in the sand during cocktail hour or dine on the open-air deck under Japanese lanterns. French bistro dishes, such as *moules frites* (mussels and fries) and fried calamari, are the things to get here, but choose an American finale and go for the chocolate sundae. Service can be slow in season, but you can stay all night, enjoying the world music that plays until the wee hours. ⊠ *35 Shore Rd., 11965* ☎ *631/749–2001* ⊕ *www. sunsetbeachli.com* ➳ *20 rooms* ⚭ *Restaurant, picnic area, some kitchenettes, cable TV, beach, bar, business services, some pets allowed (fee), no-smoking rooms* ⊟ *AE, D, MC, V* ⊘ *Closed Oct.–Apr.* ⦿❘ *CP.*

$$–$$$$ ✕▦ **Olde Country Inn.** Privacy and romance are yours at this Victorian inn on a country lane. Rooms are named after their color schemes ("Rose Room," "Emerald Room"), which are subdued, and include antique furnishings. You can relax in the library, which has a fireplace, or sip a drink on the wraparound porch. The intimate French restaurant ($$–$$$) serves dinner in cozy rooms or outside on the porch in summer. The menu includes simple country French favorites such as steamed mussels in cream sauce and rack of lamb with ratatouille. ⊠ *11 Stearns Point Rd., Shelter Island Heights 11965* ☎ *631/749–1633* ⊕ *www. oldecountryinn.com* ➳ *9 rooms, 4 suites, 1 cottage* ⚭ *Restaurant, fans, some in-room hot tubs, bar, library; no room phones, no room TVs, no kids under 14, no smoking* ⊟ *AE, MC, V* ⦿❘ *BP.*

$–$$$$ ✕▦ **Ram's Head Inn.** At this 1929 colonial-style inn, Adirondack
Fodor'sChoice chairs are scattered across lawns sloping down to Coecles Harbor. The
★ secluded spot at the end of Ram Island has a small beach for swimming (bring insect repellant) or sailing. Rooms, furnished in a simple country style, are bright; they often book up months ahead of time. The restaurant ($$$–$$$$; reservations essential) is known for its outstanding seasonal fare. Sauces, such as the aged-sherry syrup that accompanies quail, set the restaurant apart, as does the attentive and knowledgeable service. Jazz musicians play during Sunday brunch, served late May to late October. ⊠ *Ram Island Dr., 11965* ☎ *631/ 749–0811* 🖷 *631/749–0059* ⊕ *www.shelterislandinns.com* ➳ *13 rooms, 9 with bath; 4 suites* ⚭ *Restaurant, tennis court, gym, sauna, beach, boating, bar, playground; no room TVs, no smoking* ⊟ *AE, MC, V* ⊘ *Closed Nov.–Mar.* ⦿❘ *CP.*

$–$$$ ✕▦ **Chequit Inn.** The 1872 Victorian inn sits in the center of activity in the Heights. The main building, which houses the restaurant and bar, has a tree-shaded patio and a sitting room. Guest rooms, furnished sparingly with country antiques and reproductions, are bright and comfortable. In summer two adjunct buildings, the Cedar House and Summer Cottage, also accommodate overnighters; front rooms and those near the doors may get some street and foot-traffic noise. As a guest here, you may use the facilities at the Ram's Head, a sister property. The inn's formal restaurant ($$–$$$$) feels like a country club; the menu ranges from curried chicken breast to mustard-coated rack of lamb. In warm weather, crowds swarm the tree-covered patio, where lighter fare is served. The pub hosts live music on some weekends. ⊠ *23 Grand Ave., Shelter Island Heights 11965* ☎ *631/749–0018* 🖶 *631/749–0183* ⊕ *www. shelterislandinns.com* ↩ *35 rooms* ⚘ *Restaurant, dining room, room service, fans, billiards, bar; no TV in some rooms, no smoking* ▤ *AE, MC, V* ⦿ *CP.*

$$$–$$$$ 🏨 **Dering Harbor Inn.** With spectacular views of Dering Harbor, this co-op complex offers motel studios, which are by the road, as well as one- and two-bedroom units. The two-bedroom waterfront suites have a fireplace and private deck. The marina dock is a few steps away. ⊠ *13 Winthrop Rd., Shelter Island Heights 11965* ☎ *631/749–0900* ⊕ *www. deringharborinn.com* ↩ *4 rooms, 21 suites* ⚘ *Restaurant, picnic area, some kitchenettes, some microwaves, some refrigerators, cable TV, some in-room VCRs, 2 tennis courts, saltwater pool, marina, volleyball, bar, laundry facilities, no-smoking rooms* ▤ *AE, D, MC, V* ⦿ *Closed Mid-Oct.–mid-May.*

$$$ 🏨 **Belle Crest Inn & Aimee's Cottage.** Built in the 1920s, the cozy inn decorated with period antiques and personal artifacts remains family-owned and -operated. Oriental rugs, a piano, and family photos grace the front parlor. Bedrooms have floral wallpaper, canopy beds, and lace curtains. The cottage out back has a kitchenette and its own patio. Breakfast is served on the front or back porch, both of which are filled with an eclectic mix of wicker furniture. The town dock and historic district are a short walk away. ⊠ *163 N. Ferry Rd., Shelter Island Heights 11965* ☎ *631/749–2041* ↩ *7 rooms, 2 with shared bath; 1 cottage* ⚘ *Dining room, some kitchenettes, cable TV, piano, Internet, some pets allowed, no-smoking rooms; no room phones* ▤ *MC, V* ⦿ *Closed mid-Oct.–early May* ⦿ *BP.*

$$$ 🏨 **Pridwin.** The rambling, old-timey, family-friendly resort is on Crescent Beach. In summer, meals may be served on the deck, and there's outdoor dancing at night. Rooms, some with water views, are simple but comfortable; some of the cottages have fireplaces. ⊠ *Shore Rd., 11964* ☎ *631/749–0476 or 800/273–2497* 🖶 *631/749–2071* ⊕ *www. pridwin.com* ↩ *40 rooms, 8 cottages* ⚘ *Restaurant, some kitchens, some microwaves, some refrigerators, cable TV, 3 tennis courts, pool, beach, dock, boating, fishing, bicycles, billiards, Ping-Pong, shuffleboard, bar, laundry facilities, no-smoking rooms* ▤ *AE, D, MC, V* ⦿ *Closed Nov.–Apr.* ⦿ *BP.*

Sports & the Outdoors

FISHING Fluke, flounder, striped bass, and skate are some of what you might catch in these parts. Guides and full- and half-day captained charters are available; a half day for two anglers costs about $325. **Jack's Marine & True Value Hardware** (⊠ Bridge St. at Rte. 114 ☎ 631/749–0114) offers transient mooring and a marine-supply store. **Light Tackle Challenge** (⊠ 91 W. Neck Rd. ☎ 631/749–1906 ⊕ reel-time.com/guides/captjimhull) conducts full- and half-day sportfishing trips for striped bass and bluefish.

GOLF The **Shelter Island Country Club** (⊠ 26 Sunnyside Ave., Shelter Island Heights ☎ 631/749–0416) has a well-maintained 2,510-yard, 9-hole public golf course with small greens on slightly rolling grass. It's open from April to late October. Greens fees are $15–$18.

KAYAKING The waters around Shelter Island are perfect for kayaking. If you set out on a kayak you have the option of exploring on your own or taking a guided tour. The Mashomack Nature Preserve, rich with bird life and other animals, is a favorite kayaking destination. A solo kayak from **Shelter Island Kayak Tours** (✉ Rte. 114 at Duval Rd. ☎ 631/749–1990 ⊕ www.kayaksi.com) rents for about $26 for two hours; tours are $45.

MINIATURE GOLF The 18-hole, lighted minigolf course at **Whale's Tale** (✉ 3 Ram Island Rd. ☎ 631/749–1839 ⊕ www.onisland.com/whalestale) has an ice-cream stand and outdoor terrace for taking a break after the game. The cost is $6.50 per person, and it's open daily Memorial Day through Labor Day and on weekends April through late May and early September through mid-October.

THE SOUTH SHORE & FIRE ISLAND

Revised by Janet Pope

The Atlantic Ocean sends its rollers onto the white-sand beaches that fringe the South Shore. Several of these beach areas, including Jones Beach and Fire Island, are actually long, narrow barrier islands that wind and tide have thrown up as a kind of sandy protection for Long Island's southern coast. The South Shore stretches from Nassau County to Suffolk County and encompasses diverse communities, from residential suburbia to hard-partying summer-resort areas.

Garden City

⑱ *19 mi east of New York City.*

In 1869, the "Merchant Prince of Broadway," Alexander T. Stewart, put his considerable talents, creativity, and wealth into the creation of a model city, reportedly a century ahead of its time. *Harpers Weekly* said of the venture, "it will be the most beautiful suburb in the vicinity of New York. Godspeed the undertaking!" To service this model city, he also developed the original department-store concept.

By the mid-20th century, the retail stores of Mr. Lord, Mr. Taylor, and Mr. Bloomingdale—all modeled after Stewart's department store—opened along Garden City's Franklin Avenue, which came to be known as the 5th Avenue of Long Island. Lord & Taylor is still here, but Sears has replaced Bloomingdale's, which moved to the Roosevelt Field mall. Today, thanks to an influx of more than two dozen banks, insurance companies, and brokerages, however, Franklin Avenue's nickname has changed to the "Wall Street of Long Island." On 7th Street you find specialty and food emporiums and fine restaurants.

Village highlights include the imposing Cathedral of the Incarnation and the posh Garden City Hotel. Mitchel Center, which includes the Cradle of Aviation Museum, the Long Island Children's Museum, and the Long Island Museum of Science & Technology (under expansion at this writing), occupies what was Mitchel Field, the home of Long Island aviation.

Cathedral of the Incarnation. The 1876 Gothic-style cathedral, the bishop's house, and the St. Mary's and St. Paul's school buildings were all part of an elaborate memorial for Garden City's founder, A. T. Stewart, commissioned by his wife, Cornelia. The bells, purchased at the Philadelphia Centennial exposition in 1876, are replicas of the Liberty Bell; there are 13 of them, one for each of the original colonies. The church is noted for its hand-carved mahogany woodwork and rare marble. The Casavant organ, the largest pipe organ on Long Island, has 103 ranks of pipes. ✉ *50 Cathedral Ave.* ☎ *516/746–2955* ⊕ *www.dioceselongisland.org* ▣ *Free* ☉ *Tues.–Fri. 10–4, Sat. 8–noon, Sun. 11:30–2 (excluding service times).*

☺ **Cradle of Aviation Museum.** The museum, housed in two 1932 hangars, is a tribute to Long Island's reputation as the "cradle of aviation." Displays here include a 1929 Brunner Winkle Bird, a biplane; a 1938 Grumman G-21 Goose, originally intended for civilian use; a Republic P-47 Thunderbolt, and a Grumman F6F Hellcat, both World War II fighter planes; a supersonic F-14 Tomcat, a strike fighter in service today; and one of only three existing original Apollo lunar modules, as well as dozens of other planes. Special exhibits have focused on space-theme toys and the Wright brothers. The museum encompasses the **Leroy R. & Rose W. Grumman IMAX Dome Theater** and a restaurant, the Red Planet Café. ✉ *Mitchel Center, 1 Davis Ave., off Charles Lindbergh Blvd.* ☎ *516/572–4111* ⊕ *www.cradleofaviation.org* ▣ *Museum $7, IMAX $8.50* ☉ *Tues. 9:30–2, Wed.–Sun. 9:30–5.*

Hofstra University. The 240-acre Hofstra campus includes the **Hofstra Arboretum** (☎ 516/463–6623), which basically is spread throughout the entire campus. It counts more than 8,000 trees of 425 varieties, 50 outdoor sculptures, a 2-acre bird sanctuary, and a 40-foot stone labyrinth for meditation. The **Hofstra Museum** (☎ 516/463–5672 ▣ Free) has three main spaces in which it shows paintings, drawings, photographs, sculptures, decorative arts, African and Asian artifacts, and other objects from its permanent collection: the Emily Lowe Gallery (open June–late July, Mon.–Thurs. 10–4; rest of year, Tues.–Fri. 10–5 and weekends 1–5), in Emily Lowe Hall, and the Rochelle and Irwin A. Lowenfeld Conference and Exhibition Hall and the David Filderman Gallery, both in the main library (open June–Aug., Mon.–Thurs. 9–8, Fri. 9–4, and weekends 1–5; rest of yr, Mon.–Thurs. 8 AM–midnight, Fri. 8 AM–9 PM, Sat. 9–9, Sun. 10 AM–11 PM). Temporary exhibits have covered a range of subjects from Web design to Long Island history. ✉ *1000 Fulton Ave., Hempstead* ☎ *516/463–6600* ⊕ *www.hofstra.edu.*

☺ **Long Island Children's Museum.** Housed in an old airplane hangar, this is a learning laboratory with hands-on exhibits. Children ages 2 to 12 can inspect a steam engine, climb into big bubbles, ride a wild wheelchair, play musical instruments, or pretend they're TV-news anchors. ✉ *Mitchel Center, 11 Davis Ave., off Charles Lindbergh Blvd.* ☎ *516/224–5800* ⊕ *www.licm.org* ▣ *$8* ☉ *Sept.–June, Wed.–Sun. 10–5; July and Aug., Tues.–Sun. 10–5.*

Where to Stay & Eat

$$–$$$ ✕ **Akbar.** Tables at this northern Indian restaurant are set with candles and draped with tablecloths. The buffet (lunch and dinner) is one draw; popular dishes include tandoori chicken and charcoal-grilled prawns. ⊠ *1 Ring Rd. W* ☎ *516/357–8300* ⊟ *AE, D, DC, MC, V.*

$$–$$$ ✕ **Orchid.** You have more than 26 house specialties to choose from at this restaurant dressed in red and gold. The spicy and sweet orange beef and the Grand Marnier shrimp are favorites. Paintings of birds and a dramatic mirrored ceiling adorn the space. ⊠ *730 Franklin Ave.* ☎ *516/ 742–1116* ⊟ *AE, MC, V.*

$$–$$$ ✕ **Victor Koenig's.** The food at this German restaurant is well worth the trip to Floral Park, 2 mi west of Garden City. Beer steins and curios lend a traditional European spirit to the space. The menu includes sauerbraten, pot roast with gingersnap gravy, Wiener schnitzel, beef roulade with spaetzle, and Long Island duckling. Long Islanders come here to get their German-food fix, so reservations are essential on weekends. ⊠ *86 S. Tyson Ave., Floral Park* ☎ *516/354–2300* ⊟ *AE, MC, V.*

$$ ✕ **Seventh Street Cafe.** Ceiling fans whir above white linen–cloaked tables and terra-cotta floors at this Italian restaurant, which specializes in brick-oven pizza and homemade pastas, like shrimp-and-porcini tortellini and farfalle with salmon and Gorgonzola. You may also eat on an outdoor patio. ⊠ *126 Seventh St.* ☎ *516/747–7575* ⊟ *AE, DC, MC, V.*

$$$$ ▦ **Long Island Marriott Hotel & Conference Center.** The 11-story chain property, where interiors show nautical flair, is geared to the business market. Each guest room has a desk, an ergonomic chair, and high-speed Internet access. ⊠ *101 James Doolittle Blvd., Uniondale, 11553* ☎ *516/ 794–3800* ⊟ *516/794–5936* ⊕ *www.marriotthotels.com* ⤸ *609 rooms, 9 suites* ⚭ *Restaurant, café, room service, in-room data ports, cable TV, indoor pool, gym, hair salon, hot tub, sauna, sports bar, dry cleaning, laundry service, business services, meeting rooms; no-smoking rooms* ⊟ *AE, D, DC, MC, V.*

$$$–$$$$ ✕▦ **Garden City Hotel.** Outstanding service and stylish interiors are two **Fodor's**Choice high points at this luxury hotel, in operation since 1874. The complex ★ has several buildings; the youngest was completed in the 1980s. Charles Lindbergh, who slept here the night before his transatlantic flight, is one of the many illustrious guests who have lodged here. The Polo Restaurant ($$$$), a popular special-occasion venue, serves refined American fare with contemporary touches—rack of lamb with ricotta gnocchi and stewed artichokes, for example, or arctic char with a pistachio crust and citrusy crab sauce. ⊠ *45 7th St.,* ☎ *516/747–3000, 800/547–0400 outside NY* ⊟ *516/747–1414* ⊕ *www.gardencityhotel.com* ⤸ *280 rooms, 20 suites* ⚭ *Restaurant, room service, in-room data ports, in-room safes, minibars, cable TV with movies, some kitchenettes, indoor pool, health club, hair salon, massage, bar, Internet, business services, meeting rooms, airport shuttle; no-smoking rooms* ⊟ *AE, D, DC, MC, V.*

$$ ▦ **Wingate Inn.** Bright, clean, and modern, this high-rise hotel is a mid-price alternative. Standard rooms are at least 300 square feet, with a separate work area and desk. Warm tones, neutral colors, and light wood furnishings all help make the rooms cheery. During the week the technologically up-to-date inn draws mostly business travelers; families join the mix on weekends. A common area is equipped with both Internet access and printers. ⊠ *821 Stewart Ave., 11530* 📞 *516/705–9000* 📠 *516/705–9100* ⊕ *www.wingateinn.com* 🛏 *118 rooms, 12 suites* ♨ *In-room data ports, some microwaves, some refrigerators, cable TV with movies and video games, exercise equipment, hot tub, dry cleaning, laundry service, concierge, Internet, business services, meeting rooms; no-smoking rooms* 🖃 *AE, D, DC, MC, V* 🍽 *CP*.

Sports & the Outdoors

GOLF The popular **Eisenhower Park** (⊠ Hempstead Tpke., East Meadow 📞 516/572–0327 information, 516/542–4653 tee times ⊕ www.co. nassau.ny.us/parks.html) has three regulation 18-hole courses, a 300-yard driving range, and a restaurant, all open to nonresidents. The **Red Course,** originally designed by Devereux Emmet, is the longest of the three (6,756 yards) and is considered the most challenging. The **Blue Course** and the **White Course** were designed by Robert Trent Jones. Red Course greens fees are $52–$60 for nonresidents; greens fees for the other two are $50–$60. (Fees are lower in winter.) All are open daily year-round, weather permitting.

ICE HOCKEY Home games of the **New York Islanders** (⊠ 1535 Old Country Rd., Plainview 📞 516/501–6700, 800/882–4753 Ext. 1 tickets ⊕ www. newyorkislanders.com), a National Hockey League team, are played at **Nassau Veterans Memorial Coliseum.**

Nightlife & the Arts

The **Nassau Veterans Memorial Coliseum** (⊠ 1255 Hempstead Tpke., Uniondale 📞 516/794–9300 ⊕ www.nassaucoliseum.com) showcases various forms of entertainment, including rock concerts and family shows. The **Tilles Center for the Performing Arts** (⊠ CW Post Campus, Long Island University, 720 Northern Blvd., Old Brookville 📞 516/299–2752 ⊕ www.tillescenter.org), a 2,242-seat concert hall, host all kinds of entertainment. The Big Apple Circus, Wynton Marsalis, Art Garfunkel, and the Alvin Ailey American Dance Theater have performed here.

Shopping

Nordstrom, Macy's, Bloomingdale's, and JCPenney anchor the two-level ★ **Roosevelt Field** mall (⊠ Old Country Rd. and Meadowbrook Pkwy. 📞 516/742–8000), a blend of high-end and midrange retailers. The more than 245 specialty stores include Apple, Banana Republic, Bang & Olufsen, Betsey Johnson, Brooks Brothers, Coach, the Disney Store, H&M, J. Jill, Modell's, Movado, Papyrus, Perlina, Pottery Barn, Swarovski Crystal, Timberland, Urban Outfitters, and Zara, as well as a food court, several restaurants, and a Loews Cinema.

Long Beach

⑲ *11 mi south of Garden City.*

A series of large barrier islands, which protect the mainland from ocean surges, sits off the south shore of Long Island. The city of Long Beach occupies the westernmost of these islands, in Nassau County. Thanks to the ocean breezes, the weather is moderate—on average 10 degrees warmer in winter and 10 degrees cooler in summer than the rest of the county.

The city, aptly named for its 5-mi-long stretch of pristine beach, was established as a warm-weather resort community in the 1870s. Teeming with restaurants, nightlife, and shops, it's still a popular vacation spot. The 2-mi-long boardwalk is a hub of activity, especially in summer, when the permanent population of 35,000 swells to 50,000. The Long Island Rail Road makes it easy to get here from New York City. The water's edge is only a ⅓-mi walk from the last stop on the railroad's Long Beach line.

Boardwalk. The 2-mi boardwalk, overlooking a beautiful stretch of Atlantic Ocean beach, is the heart of the community. It was constructed in the early 1900s with the help of elephants from Coney Island's Dreamland Park. The pachyderms pulled materials for the boardwalk's pilings along what is known today as Sunrise Highway. You can hear live music throughout summer; on weekends, vendors and entertainers attract lively crowds. ⊠ *Between New York Ave. and Neptune Blvd.* ☏ *516/431–3890* ⊠ *Free.*

Ocean Beach Park. Sun worshippers throng this beach park, which stretches for 5 mi on the barrier island's south side, to play volleyball, surf, swim, and sunbathe—all under the watchful eyes of lifeguards (on duty weekends late May to mid-June, daily mid-June to early September). The park's indoor pool is open to the public all year. ⊠ *Magnolia St. between Nevada Ave. and Maple Blvd.* ☏ *516/431–1810, 516/431–1021, 516/431–5533* ⊠ *Beach $6 (late May–early Sept.), pool $5* ☉ *Pool daily 9–6.*

Where to Eat

$$$$ ✕ **Kitchen off Pine Street.** Works by local artists are on display at this restaurant, where the eclectic furnishings change with the seasons. The fare is diverse as well: roasted rack of lamb with ancho-spiked mashed potatoes and bean salsa, grilled yellow-fin tuna, bananas Foster. Patio dining is a summertime option. Reservations are essential on Saturday. ⊠ *670 Long Beach Rd.* ☏ *516/431–0033* ⊟ *AE, DC, MC, V* ☉ *Closed Sun.–Tues. No lunch.*

$$$–$$$$ ✕ **Jimmy Hays Steak House.** Great steaks are the draw at this fun and lively restaurant. Favorite main dishes include Black Angus rib eye, paired with sautéed spinach and a potato pancake, and Lobster Jimmy (pan-sautéed lobster with lemon, butter, and garlic). For dessert, consider chocolate mousse, peach melba, or crème brûlée. The restaurant is about a five-minute drive from Long Beach. ⊠ *4310 Austin Blvd., Island Park* ☏ *516/432–5155* ⊟ *AE, D, DC, MC, V* ☉ *No lunch.*

$$–$$$ ✕ **Duke Falcon's Global Grill.** Memorabilia from around the world adorn this casual but intimate eatery. The menu is all over the globe, too, covering a range of cuisines from new American to South American. Argentine gaucho steak, grilled rib eye served with garlic-mashed potatoes and roasted peppers, is a popular choice. Sidewalk café–style dining is available in summer. ⊠ *36 W. Park Ave.* ☏ *516/897–7000* ⊟ *AE, D, DC, MC, V.*

$$–$$$ ✕ **Josie's.** This dimly lighted spot has the feel of a 1920s speakeasy. Highback black-velvet booths separate candlelit tables, so you can talk qui-

etly and have some privacy during your meal, and jazz plays in the background. Even the Victorian-style bathroom is adorable. Fresh fish dishes are a house specialty. Also consider the crabmeat-stuffed baked clams, the caramelized onion soup, and the cavatelli with sausage. ⊠ *232 W. Park Ave.* ☎ *516/897–3600* ⊟ *AE, MC, V* ⊘ *No lunch.*

$–$$$ ✕ **Baja California Grill.** Bright colors and tropical motifs set the stage at this upbeat restaurant and lively bar where 10 kinds of margaritas are served. The owner, a huge music fan, selects the sounds played here from his collection of 3,000 CDs. Coconut popcorn shrimp is a popular dish. Or choose from a variety of chicken wings, including Iguana (very hot with green chili sauce), buffalo-style, and Chinese-spiced. The Tuesday night special is $1 tacos; Wednesday night it's "wings at the bar" for 10¢ each. A patio has tables for warm-weather dining. ⊠ *1032 W. Beech St.* ☎ *516/889–5992* ⊟ *MC, V* ⊘ *No lunch.*

Nightlife & the Arts

During warm-weather months free concerts are held on the boardwalk on many afternoons and evenings. Bar-strewn Beech Street is the setting for a lively "bar crawl"; each place has a distinct flair and flavor. **The Inn** (⊠ 943 West Beech St. ☎ 516/432–9220) is the only live-music venue in the area that's open four nights a week (Thursday through Sunday). A mixed-age crowd enjoys the music as well as brunch, lunch, dinner, and late-night noshes. With a large bar and 10 TV screens that are usually tuned to a game, **Minnesota's Grill & Bar** (⊠ 959 West Beech St. ☎ 516/432–4080) attracts sports fans. Dancing is also a favorite here. **The Saloon** (⊠ 1016 West Beech St. ☎ 516/431–9185), the local neighborhood classic, has large windows opening to the sidewalk; there's always a crowd (mostly twentysomethings) spilling out onto the backyard deck.

Jones Beach State Park

20 *11 mi east of Long Beach.*

Fodor'sChoice ★ Its 6½ mi of white sand make Jones Beach State Park one of the best known and popular of Long Island's beaches. The 2,500-acre park is loaded with facilities, including two pools, bathhouses, piers, a bait station, two surf-casting areas (by permit), picnic areas, and four basketball courts. A 1½ mi-long boardwalk has deck games and hosts special events. Lifeguards are on duty from late May to mid-September. The restaurant (open daily in season) is being remodeled; at this writing, completion is scheduled for mid-2005.

The **Tommy Hilfiger at Jones Beach Theater** (☎ 516/221–1000 ⊕ www. tommyhilfigerjonesbeach.com), a 14,000-seat amphitheater in Jones Beach State Park, presents such big-name musicians as Alanis Morissette, David Bowie, and Tom Petty, as well as other performers. The concert season usually runs June through August. The park can be reached from the Wantagh and Meadowbrook parkways (head south). ⊠ *Ocean Pkwy., Wantagh* ☎ *516/785–1600* ⊕ *nysparks.state.ny.us* ⊟ *Parking $8 (June–Aug.).*

Freeport

㉑ *9 mi north of Jones Beach State Park.*

This busy harbor community along the fast-moving Sunrise Highway has residential districts to the north and south that hint at an earlier glory. The original Native American inhabitants reportedly were attracted to the area's beauty and wealth of seashells. Later such notables as bandleader Guy Lombardo and actor Broderick Crawford called Freeport home. Freeport's Nautical Mile, along Woodcleft Canal, attracts throngs to its busy wharfs, where a plethora of waterside restaurants and open-air fish markets serve fresh seafood. Antiques shops, thrift stores, and nautically flavored retailers line the main streets.

Cow Meadow Park and Preserve. This recreational facility and 150-acre wetland preserve has a hiking trail that runs through a bayberry thicket, ball fields, a playground, a picnic area, and a 1-mi jogging course. The saltwater marsh here is home to more than 15 species of mammals and 150 species of nesting, migrating, and wintering birds. There's also a small bird-watching tower. ⊠ *End of S. Main St.* ☎ *516/571–8685* ⊕ *www.co.nassau.ny.us* ⊑ *Free* ⊙ *Daily 8–6.*

Long Island Marine Education Center. Often called the "Seaport at Freeport," the center is an annex of the South Street Seaport Museum in Manhattan. Interactive exhibits focus on marine life and trades, taking a historical approach. On the Nautical Mile, the center aims to promote conservation and a clean marine environment. ⊠ *202 Woodcleft Ave.* ☎ *516/771–0399* ⊕ *www.southstseaport.org/places/li.marine.html* ⊑ *$2* ⊙ *Tues.–Fri. 11–4, weekends 1–5.*

Nautical Mile. Restaurants, shops, and open-air fish markets line the Nautical Mile, which runs parallel to Woodcleft Canal (one of several canals in Freeport). Also here are commercial-fishing and charter boats. Brick walkways and old-fashioned light fixtures add to the charm. The **Shoppes at the Crow's Nest Cove** encompass six distinctive shops. ⊠ *Woodcleft Ave. south of Front St.*

Where to Stay & Eat

$$–$$$$ ✕ **Otto's Sea Grill.** Established in 1929, this casual eatery is run by third-generation owners. You may watch boats going by as you dig into flounder stuffed with shrimp and crab, or scrod casino—broiled scrod topped with diced peppers, garlic, onions, and bacon. In warm weather, you can sit on the deck and, on weekends, listen to live music. ⊠ *271 Woodcleft Ave.* ☎ *516/378–9480* ⊟ *AE, MC, V.*

$$–$$$$ ✕ **Schooner.** The view of Woodcleft Canal underscores the nautical theme of this seafood restaurant, in business since 1969. The menu offers steaks and chicken dishes, in addition to shellfish, such as giant lobster tails, and other seafood preparations. ⊠ *435 Woodcleft Ave.* ☎ *516/378–7575* ⊟ *AE, DC, MC, V.*

¢–$ ▥ **Freeport Motor Inn.** You can dock your boat at the marina of this comfortable waterfront inn where exterior corridors connect the rooms. ⊠ *445 S. Main St., 11520* ☎ *516/623–9100* ⎙ *516/546–5739* ⇥ *60 rooms*

ᐳ *Cable TV, refrigerators, in-room data ports, marina, no-smoking rooms* ☰ *AE, DC, MC, V.*

Sports & the Outdoors

Charter fishing boats leave daily at 8 AM and 1 PM for fluke fishing. **Captain Lou** (⊠ 28 Woodcleft Ave. ☎ 516/623–5823) rents both 85- and 75-foot fishing boats for $28 (half day) and $38 (full day). **Super Spray** (⊠ 540 Guy Lombardo Ave. ☎ 516/223–2507), a 90-footer, goes out at 8 AM, 1 PM, and 6 PM daily. Reservations aren't needed; just come down a half hour before departure. Rates are $26; fishing-pole rentals are $2.

Old Bethpage

㉒ *14 mi northeast of Freeport.*

The area is home to the Old Bethpage Restoration Village, a re-creation of a pre–Civil War farm community on 200 acres. Bethpage State Park, in nearby Farmingdale, thrills golfers with its five municipal courses; the Black Course, host of the 2002 U.S. Open, is considered one of the top courses in the United States.

Bethpage State Park. The 1,500-acre park is renowned for its golf complex, one of the best public golf facilities in the country. It also encompasses bridle, hiking, biking, and cross-country-skiing trails; tennis courts; and picnic areas. A polo field hosts weekly matches from mid-June to mid-October. ⊠ *Off Powell Ave. east of Rte. 135, Farmingdale* ☎ *516/249–0701* ⊕ *nysparks.state.ny.us* ⊠ *Free* ☉ *Daily dawn–dusk.*

ᗡ **Old Bethpage Village Restoration.** A re-created pre–Civil War farm village, this living-history museum sits on 200 pastoral acres with soft hills and lovely meadows. The buildings were moved to this spot from other parts of Long Island; the 45 structures, all original, include two general stores, nine homes, a schoolhouse, a tavern, a church, and a working farm with animals. The guides, dressed in period costume, love sharing their knowledge. ⊠ *1303 Round Swamp Rd., 1 mi south of LIE Exit 48* ☎ *516/572–8401* ⊕ *www.oldbethpage.org* ⊠ *$7* ☉ *Late Feb.–late May and mid-Oct.–late Oct., Wed.–Fri. 10–4, weekends 10–5; late May–mid-Oct., Wed.–Sun. 10–5; late Oct.–Dec., Wed.–Sun. 10–4.*

Where to Stay & Eat

$$–$$$ ✕ **56th Fighter Group.** The World War II–theme restaurant sits on a local airport runway with real planes and jeeps out back. Big-band music is piped throughout the place, enhancing the 1940s mood. You can watch planes take off and land while you dig into steaks, chops, or seafood. Signature items include beer-cheese soup, prime rib with cheddar mashed potatoes, and pot roast with chive dumplings. ⊠ *Rte. 110, Republic Airport Gate 1, E. Farmingdale* ☎ *631/694–8280* ᐱ *Reservations essential* ☰ *AE, D, DC, MC, V.*

$–$$$ ✕ **Melanie's, a Bistro.** A Victorian aura pervades this turn-of-the-20th-century brick building with stained-glass windows. Dining areas are bright and cheerful, with soft floral wallpaper and white-clothed tables. The menu includes Italian and French dishes. The starters and pastas offer several choices for vegetarians, such as a napoleon of grilled portobello, tomato, and mozzarella. Simple preparations include pan-seared salmon with spinach and a citrusy butter sauce. ⊠ *169 Main St., Farmingdale* ☎ *516/293–0004* ⊟ *AE, MC, V* ⊘ *Closed Tues.*

$$ ✕**Ozumo Japanese Restaurant.** At $21, the dinner box—soup; salad; steamed dumplings; fruit; California roll; and chicken, beef, salmon, or shrimp teriyaki, or another main dish—is a deal. The sushi cuts are high quality and the prices are moderate. ⊠ *164 Hicksville Rd., Bethpage* ☎ *516/731–8989* ⊟ *AE, MC, V* ⊘ *Closed Tues. No lunch weekends.*

$$$ 🏨**Residence Inn.** Abundant on-site amenities and services put this all-suites property a step above the typical chain hotel. Business travelers make up the bulk of the clientele here. Rooms are average in size and include a desk and data ports. Bethpage State Park is less than a mile away, and the ocean is about 10 mi to the south. ⊠ *9 Gerhard Rd., Plainview 11803* ☎ *516/433–6200 or 800/331–3131* ᕉ *516/433–2569* ⊕ *www.residenceinn.com* ⇄ *170 suites* ⚭ *Restaurant, room service, in-room data ports, some kitchenettes, cable TV with movies, in-room VCRs, 2 pools (1 indoor), gym, hot tub, sauna, bar, babysitting, laundry facilities, laundry service, concierge, Internet, business services, some pets allowed (fee)* ⊟ *AE, MC, V* ⦿| *CP.*

Sports & the Outdoors

GOLF **Bethpage State Park** (⊠ 99 Quaker Meetinghouse Rd., Farmingdale
Fodor'sChoice ☎ 516/249–0700 ⊕ nysparks.state.ny.us) has five 18-hole regulation
★ golf courses, most designed by A. W. Tillinghast. The renowned par-71 **Black Course,** site of the U.S. Open in 2002 and 2009, is tough to play and tough to get on, especially on weekends. With small greens, soft slopes, and a good selection of holes, the par-71 **Green Course** is much less difficult. At the par-72 **Blue Course,** the level of difficulty drops after the challenging front 9 holes. The par-70 **Red Course** is formidable overall, but its opening hole is considered particularly tough. Although it has some steep slopes, the par-71 **Yellow Course** is probably the easiest course in the complex. Black Course greens fees are $62–$78 (nonresidents); at the other four courses, greens fees are $24–$29 (regardless of whether you're a resident) and carts are available. All are open daily year-round, weather permitting, except for the Black Course, which is closed Monday.

Bay Shore

㉓ *15 mi southeast of Old Bethpage.*

About 40 mi east of New York City, Bay Shore is close to Robert Moses and Jones Beach state parks; Fire Island is a short ferry ride away across Great South Bay. Houses ring the active waterfront, which attracts locals as well as out-of-towners to its boat launches, abundant dock space, and excellent restaurants. The Bay Shore Marina, host to big boat shows and fishing tournaments, is one of the largest publicly owned marinas on the East Coast.

Bayard Cutting Arboretum State Park. The original plans for this arboretum, which had its beginnings in 1887, were drawn up by Frederick Law Olmstead's landscape-architecture firm. Some of the oaks and other trees on the property pre-date that period. The 125-acre park, along the

Connetquot River 8 mi east of Bay Shore, also has one of the largest collections of conifers—fir, yew, pine, hemlock, and spruce, to name a few—on Long Island. Hiking trails run along the shoreline, which draws bird-watchers. The shingle-style mansion, built in 1886, overlooks a great lawn that sweeps down to the water. The first floor of the house, which includes a café, is open to the public. ⊠ *Montauk Hwy. east of the Heckscher State Pkwy (extension of Southern State Pkwy), East Islip* ☎ *631/581–1002* ⊕ *www.bcarboretum.com* 🖾 *Parking $6 (Apr.–early Sept., Tues.–Sun. 10–5; early Sept.–Oct., weekends 10–5)* ☉ *Tues.–Sun. 10–dusk.*

Gibson-Mack-Holt House. One of Bay Shore's oldest houses, this typical 1850s tradesman's house is still authentically furnished. On the property are a Victorian herb garden, a two-seater outhouse, and a chicken coop. The research library, in the basement, has maps, antique postcards, old newspapers, and books about the Bay Shore/Brightwaters area. Temporary exhibits display memorabilia and artifacts relating to topics ranging from the world wars to crafts and sports. ⊠ *22 Maple La.* ☎ *631/665–7003* 🖾 *Free* ☉ *Tues. and Sat. 2–4; closed Jan. and Feb.*

Sagtikos Manor. The original sections of this house were built between 1692 and 1697. The manor served as a military headquarters for the British Army during the Revolutionary War. George Washington also slept here, but not until after the war, in 1790. Today the 150-acre estate holds a substantial collection of antiques and historical exhibits depicting its early days. ⊠ *Montauk Hwy. between Gardiner Dr. and Manor La., West Bay Shore* ☎ *631/321–8829* ⊕ *www.sagtikosmanor.com* 🖾 *$5* ☉ *Tours July and Aug., Wed., Thurs., and Sun. 1–4; June, Sun. 1–4.*

Where to Eat

$$–$$$ ✕ **Molly Malone's.** The restaurant, on the pier for the Fire Island Ferry, serves Irish standards, including corned beef and cabbage, but also is known for its fresh seafood. Tiffany-style lamps illuminate the bar and dining areas of this casual place. A deck is open for warm-weather dining. Tuesday through Sunday, there's live Irish music. ⊠ *124 Maple Ave.* ☎ *631/969–2232* 🖃 *AE, MC, V.*

$–$$$ ✕ **Fat Fish Bar and Bistro.** Steamers, mussels, and fresh fish are the mainstays at this casual, nautical-theme restaurant with an open-air view of the water. Steak and chicken are also available, and you may eat outside on the deck under a tent canopy. Service is family style. ⊠ *28 Cottage Ave.* ☎ *631/666–2899* 🖃 *AE, D, DC, MC, V.*

$–$$ ✕ **Siam Lotus Thai.** For many faithful locals, this is the best spot for Thai food on Long Island. Try the fried red snapper with chilies or the pad thai. Small and casual, the place fills up quickly on weekends. ⊠ *1664 Union Blvd.* ☎ *631/968–8196* 🖃 *AE, D, MC, V* ☉ *Closed Mon.*

Fire Island

㉔ *8 mi south of Bay Shore.*

With the Atlantic Ocean to its south and the Great South Bay to its north, Fire Island is basically a long stretch of pristine beach. Most of the 32-mi-long barrier island belongs to the **Fire Island National Seashore.** Deer roam freely here, finding shelter in the thickets, and migrating ducks and geese seek sanctuary in the marshes; wildlife is abundant along the seashore. Vehicles aren't allowed on most of the island, which is accessible by ferry, private boat, and water taxi, although you can drive to Robert Moses State Park and Smith Point County Park, on opposite ends of the island.

One of the outer playgrounds of Long Island's majestic coastline, Fire Island is home to a string of small communities, each with its own personality. In most, boardwalks lead to a vast expanse of beach. Slightly funky Cherry Grove and the male-dominated Pines are the two gay-and-lesbian communities. Ocean Beach, the largest residential area, has restaurants, stores, and bars and attracts day-trippers and families as well as summer-house sharers. In Ocean Bay Park, weekending twentysomethings whoop it up late into the night. Kismet, Saltaire, Fair Harbor, Seaview, and Robbins Rest, mostly inhabited by private-home owners, are more exclusive. Kismet is also known for its restaurants.

In summer the population swells to the tens of thousands. The island doesn't have many lodging places, so most of these fair-weather visitors rent houses. You can see them and Fire Island homeowners coming off the ferries, pulling behind them little red wagons filled with their belongings. Enterprising youngsters meet the boats with their own wagons, in hopes of making a few dollars by helping you to your destination. After Columbus Day, the island pretty much shuts down until Memorial Day, and only a few hundred souls live here in winter.

Fire Island Lighthouse. The 168-foot-tall lighthouse—Long Island's tallest—marks the western tip of Fire Island. The black-and-white-striped beauty, built in 1858, replaced the original, 1826 lighthouse, which, at 74 feet tall, was deemed too short to be effective. Tours of the tower are offered; call for tour times and reservations. On clear days Manhattan skyscrapers are visible from the top of the lighthouse, a climb up 192 winding steps. To get to the lighthouse, park in Field 5 of **Robert Moses State Park** (park on the lot's east side) and then walk ¾ mi following the marked trail. ⊠ *Off southern end of Robert Moses Causeway* ☎ *631/661–4876* ⊕ *www.fireislandlighthouse.com* ☜ *$5* ☉ *Apr.–June, daily 9:30–5, July–Labor Day, daily 9:30–5:30, rest of yr, weekends noon–4.*

Robert Moses State Park. A 5-mi stretch of ocean beach is the highlight of this 1,000-acre park. Facilities include four bathhouses, a fishing pier, a picnic area, and miniature golf; a boat basin with pump-out and bait stations is nearby. The park, one of only two parts of Fire Island accessible by car, is open year-round (fields 2 and 5 only). Special summer events include fishing contests. To get here, take the Sagtikos Parkway south to Robert Moses Causeway and follow the latter to the end. ⊠ *Off southern end of Robert Moses Causeway* ☎ *631/669–0470* ⊕ *nysparks.state.ny.us* ☜ *Parking $7 (early Apr.–late Nov.)* ☉ *Daily dawn–dusk.*

Sunken Forest. Protected by big dunes and stunted by the wind and the salt air, the Sunken Forest actually does look like it's sunken. Some of the trees here, which include sassafras and pine, are thought to be more than 200 years old. A 1½-mi boardwalk winds through flora, marsh, and swamp, offering viewing spots and benches at various points. Twisted trees form a canopy overhead. The area is protected, so you must stick to the marked trails. (Doing so also decreases your chances of encountering poison ivy and ticks.) Guided tours are an option in summer; call for tour times. The Sunken Forest is part of **Sailors Haven** (☎ 631/597–6183 visitor center ⊕ www.nps.gov/fiis), which is near the middle of Fire Island and has a beach with lifeguards, on duty from late June through Labor Day; picnic areas; a snack bar; a marina; changing rooms; and a visitor center. Sailors Haven doesn't have lodgings, however, so you can't overnight here. ⊠ *Free* ⊙ *Mid-May–mid-Oct.*

Smith Point County Park. The 2,295-acre park at the southern end of William Floyd Parkway includes a visitor center, hiking trails, barbecue facilities, and a long stretch of ocean beach (lifeguards are on duty from late June through Labor Day). A campground is adjacent to the park. ⊠ *Off southern end of William Floyd Parkway* ☎ *631/852–1313* ⊕ *www.co.suffolk.ny.us* ⊠ *Parking $10 (mid–May–mid-Sept.)* ⊙ *Daily 7 AM–10 PM.*

Watch Hill. This area in the eastern section of the national seashore, across the bay from Patchogue, has a marina with a pump-out station, wilderness camping, a visitor center, nature trails, and changing rooms. Lifeguards patrol the beach from late June through Labor Day. ☎ *631/597–6455 visitor center* ⊕ *www.nps.gov/fiis* ⊠ *Free* ⊙ *Visitor center mid-May–late Sept., daily 9–5.*

Where to Stay & Eat

$$$ ✕ **The Hideaway.** The views at this casual waterside eatery are spectacular, whether you eat on the deck or inside. The food is American with contemporary touches; seafood is emphasized. Pan-seared day-boat scallops, for example, are flavored with preserved lemons and carrot-ginger juice and served with couscous. The menu also includes duck, veal chops, and filet mignon. The earlier you come, the less rambunctious the crowd. ⊠ *Houser's Hotel, Bay Walk, Ocean Beach* ☎ *631/583–8900* ⊟ *AE, MC, V* ⊙ *Closed Oct.–mid-May.*

$$$ ✕ **Top of the Bay.** You can eat outside at this harborside eatery, one of the more upscale places on Fire Island. Winners include stone-crab cakes and rack of lamb. ⊠ *1 Dock Walk, Cherry Grove* ☎ *631/597–6699* ⊟ *AE, MC, V* ⊙ *Closed Sept.–May and Tues.*

$$$$ ▣ **The Seasons Bed & Breakfast.** The small white house with a porch is a couple of blocks away from the ocean and half a block from the bay. You're sent off to the water with beach chairs, umbrellas, and towels. Rooms have hardwood floors and either a full or queen bed or two twins. Rates include "afternoon tea," really a small meal—pizzas, sandwiches, salads, or quiches, with options for vegetarians. On weekends, the tea takes the form of a big barbecue. Breakfast is served buffet style in the great room. The owners also run the Bay House, which has one-, two-, or three-bedroom apartments. ⊠ *468 Dehnhoff Walk, Ocean Beach 11770* ☎ *631/583–8295* 🖷 *631/583–9482* ⊕ *www.fivacations.com* 🛏 *9 rooms with shared baths, 1 cottage* ♦ *Cable TV, bicycles; no room phones, no kids, no smoking* ⊟ *AE, MC, V* ⊙❙ *BP.*

$–$$$$ 🏨 **Fire Island Hotel & Resort.** The hotel has water views and is a short walk (100 yards) to the beach. The pool, an uncommon find on Fire Island, is a plus. Rooms have either one double bed, two doubles, or a twin and a double. The suites sleep six. Bathrooms have been updated. There's a three-night minimum on weekends, which includes a $50 voucher for the hotel restaurant. Rates are significantly less expensive on weekdays. The hotel also has a few cabins, studios, and apartments, but these are usually booked up by its time-share members. ⊠ *25 Cayuga Walk, Ocean Bay Park 11770* 🕾 *631/583–8000* 🖷 *631/583–9404* 🛏 *30 rooms, 4 suites* ⚐ *Restaurant, fans, pool, bar; no a/c in some rooms, no room phones* ⊟ *AE, D, MC, V* ☉ *Closed early Oct.–mid-May.*

$–$$$ 🏨 **Clegg's Hotel.** In the center of hopping Ocean Beach, this friendly hotel is across from the ferry dock and a five-minute walk from the beach. The place, which feels a bit like a boardinghouse, offers simple accommodations. Studios have water or garden views and private bathrooms; regular rooms face the garden and share bathrooms. ⊠ *478 Bayberry Walk, Ocean Beach 11770* 🕾 *631/583–5399* 🖷 *631/583–9375* 🛏 *13 rooms with shared baths, 6 studios* ⚐ *Some kitchenettes, bicycles; no room TVs* ⊟ *AE, MC, V* ☉ *Closed Oct.–Apr.* ⊠ *BP.*

Nightlife & the Arts

Flynn's (⊠ Cayuga St., Ocean Bay Park 🕾 631/583–5000), a Fire Island institution at the ferry terminal, overflows with not-long-out-of-college singles. If you want to skip the scene, come for lunch. At **Tequila Jack's Grill & Cantina** (⊠ 85 Compass Walk, Robbins Rest 🕾 631/583–2628), a Fire Island favorite, locals and visitors come to relax and take in the great bay and sunset views. The place is huge, with 400 seats, and serves lunch and dinner. Umbrellas shade outdoor tables.

Sayville

11 mi east of Bay Shore.

At various times in its history, Sayville has been a major exporter of pine to New York City as well as the oyster capital of the United States. Thanks to its large Victorian homes and its proximity to Fire Island, it became a resort town. Today residents occupy these beautiful homes year-round and the area blends small-town simplicity with suburbia. Ferries leave Sayville for Fire Island, a 30-minute trip across the Great South Bay.

Long Island Maritime Museum. A 19th-century oystering vessel as well as a small collection of local craft are on display at this museum 1½ mi west of Sayville village. Changing exhibits focus on boating and maritime history. Actual boatbuilding can be observed most days. Guided tours are available by appointment. ⊠ *86 West Ave., West Sayville* 🕾 *631/854–4974* ⊕ *www.limaritime.org* 💰 *$4 suggested donation* ☉ *Mon.–Sat. 10–4.*

off the beaten path

WILLIAM FLOYD ESTATE – The 613-acre site includes the ancestral home of William Floyd, a signer of the Declaration of Independence, as well as several outbuildings and a cemetery. Over a 250-year period, eight generations of his family occupied the estate, a satellite property of the Fire Island National Seashore that's 18 mi east of

Sayville. The house began as a two-story wood-frame structure in 1724. Over the years it saw several renovations; in 1857 the house took on a Greek-revival style during a major expansion. It was expanded to its current 25 rooms in the 1920s. Tours of the property are available. ⊠ *245 Park Dr., off William Floyd Pkwy., Mastic Beach* ☎ *631/399–2030* ⊕ *www.nps.gov/fiis* ⊠ *Free* ⊙ *Memorial Day–Labor Day, Fri.–Sun. 11–4:30.*

Where to Stay & Eat

$$$–$$$$ ✕ **Collins & Main.** Muted hues of yellow and cream and soft lighting provide an amber glow at this sophisticated and popular place. Specials are themed some nights: Wednesday is pasta night and Thursday is lobster night. Contemporary dishes make up most of the menu. Mahimahi comes in a white wine–sweet chili sauce; tuna is pan seared and served with wasabi and sesame risotto. ⊠ *100 Old S. Main St.* ☎ *631/563–0805* ⊟ *AE, DC, MC, V* ⊙ *Closed Sun. and Mon. No lunch Sat.*

$$$–$$$$ ✕ **Riverview.** A wall of windows overlooks the Great South Bay at this restaurant known for its seasonal, seafood-focused menu. Starters include crab cakes and lobster ravioli; entrées include flounder meunière and seared, teriyaki-marinated yellowfin tuna as well as grilled filet mignon and baby rack of lamb. The place is popular for Sunday brunch, too. In warm weather, patio dining is available. The restaurant is 3½ mi west of Sayville. To eat here on a weekend, make a reservation. ⊠ *3 Consuelo Pl., Oakdale* ☎ *631/589–2694* ⊟ *AE, D, DC, MC, V* ⊙ *No lunch Sat.*

$$–$$$$ ✕ **Le Soir.** A Tudor-style building 1¾ mi east of Sayville houses this classy but casual restaurant with white-linen-draped tables. The fare is French— steamed lobster in whiskey sauce, baked salmon in champagne vinaigrette—and has many loyal fans. In winter, the menu includes game dishes. ⊠ *825 Montauk Hwy., Bayport* ☎ *631/472–9090* ⊟ *AE, MC, V* ⊙ *Closed Mon. No lunch.*

$–$$$ ✕ **Cafe Joelle on Main Street.** Ceiling fans, wood floors, and a series of small, pendant lights add homey touches to this intimate storefront café. Chef-owner Steve Sands, a Culinary Institute of America graduate, is in the kitchen. The menu lists dinner salads and burgers as well as more-substantial dishes, such as rack of lamb encrusted with walnuts and fettuccine studded with chicken, shrimp, andouille, and scallops. Sunday brunch is a hit with the locals. ⊠ *25 Main St./Railroad Ave.* ☎ *631/589–4600* ⊟ *AE, DC, MC, V.*

$$–$$$ ▣ **Holiday Inn MacArthur Airport.** The two-story hotel, 1 mi away from MacArthur Airport, is particularly busy with business travelers during the week. Each room has Wi-Fi Internet access, a desk, and two telephones. Suites have bathrooms with whirlpool tubs. ⊠ *3845 Veterans Memorial Hwy., Ronkonkoma 11779* ☎ *631/585–9500 or 800/422–9150* ⊟ *631/585–9550* ⊕ *www.ichotelsgroup.com* ⇌ *289 rooms, 9 suites* ⇕ *Restaurant, room service, in-room data ports, some in-room hot tubs, minibars, cable TV with movies, pool, exercise equipment, bar, babysitting, dry cleaning, laundry facilities, laundry service, business services, airport shuttle, car rental, no-smoking rooms* ⊟ *AE, D, DC, MC, V.*

$–$$ 🖥 **Radisson MacArthur.** The chain property is 7 mi north of Sayville and about 15 minutes from MacArthur Airport. Rooms are spacious, fresh, and cheery, with large TVs and desks and either two double beds or one king bed. A glass-enclosed atrium houses the pool and hot tub. ✉ *1730 N. Ocean Ave., Holtsville 11742* 🕾 *631/758–2900* 🖷 *631/758–2612* ⊕ *www.radisson.com* 📞 *188 rooms, 2 suites* ♦ *Restaurant, snack bar, in-room data ports, cable TV with movies and video games, indoor pool, gym, hot tub, bar, dry cleaning, laundry service, business services, meeting rooms, airport shuttle, no-smoking rooms* ▤ *AE, D, DC, MC, V* ¶◎¶ *CP.*

THE SOUTH FORK & THE HAMPTONS

Updated by
Ann Hammerle

The sand-and-pine-covered finger of land that is Long Island's South Fork starts about 75 mi east of Manhattan and stretches another 50 mi east into the Atlantic Ocean. It is home to several communities dating from the 1600s, as well as a group of celebrated villages known as the Hamptons. At the eastern tip of the South Fork is Montauk, a low-key, family-friendly fishing community; just beyond the village is Montauk Point, the very end of the island. The beaches—making up one of the finest stretches of white sand in the United States—are the main draw here. Rolling farmland and vineyards are juxtaposed with historic villages, sophisticated restaurants and shops, and spectacular mansions and farms.

One could say the Hamptons mystique began in the late 1800s, when residents of Westhampton Beach and other villages out east began renting rooms to travelers who reached the area first by horse-drawn stage and later on the newly constructed Long Island Rail Road. It wasn't long before the Hamptons had become a resort area of renown, to which affluent city dwellers would escape for cool sea breezes, relaxed country living, and a hefty dose of high society. Today the villages are a curious mix of year-round communities and full-blown summer resorts, drawing vacationers, summer-home owners, and twentysomething "summer share" renters by the carload between Memorial Day and Labor Day. June is still relatively quiet, however, and in May and September you can enjoy pleasant weather while avoiding the peak-season prices and crowds.

Westhampton Beach

❷❺ *78 mi east of New York City, 27 mi east of Sayville.*

So many seasonal visitors have fallen in love with Westhampton that it has become one of the fastest-growing year-round communities on eastern Long Island. Excellent restaurants, chic shops, a regionally famous performing-arts center, and magnificent ocean beaches are the major draws. Along scenic Dune Road, which you can follow east to the nearby village of Hampton Bays, extravagant mansions are interspersed with simple beach houses and condominium complexes.

Cupsogue Beach County Park. This 296-acre barrier-beach park on Moriches Inlet has lifeguards from late May to early September, a 1-mi stretch of white-sand beach, a snack bar, restrooms and showers, and a first-aid station. Outer-beach camping and saltwater fishing are permitted away from swimming areas. ⊠ *West end of Dune Rd.* ☎ *631/852–8111 park, 631/288–7670 snack bar* ⊕ *www.co.suffolk.ny.us* ⊠ *$10 (May–Sept.)* ⊗ *Daily 8:30–4:30.*

Lashley Beach. A secret spot for locals and surfers, this is a pristine white-sand beach with parking, showers, restrooms, and lifeguards (on duty weekends 10–5 from mid-May to mid-June and daily 10–5 from mid-June through Labor Day). ⊠ *Dune Rd.* ☎ *631/288–6306* ⊠ *Seasonal nonresident permit $225.*

Rogers Beach. Parking is by village permit only at this white-sand beach. In addition to a lifeguard (on duty weekends 10–5 from mid-May to mid-June and daily 10–5 from mid-June through Labor Day), there's a pavilion with showers and restrooms. ⊠ *Beach La.* ☎ *631/288–6306* ⊠ *Seasonal nonresident permit $225.*

Westhampton Beach Historical Society and Tuthill House Museum. Exhibits in this early-19th-century house depict life in the area from the 1700s through 1850. Photographs of early Westhampton Beach are on display, as are several spinning wheels and a turn-of-the-20th-century peanut-roasting machine used at the local general store. ⊠ *115 Mill Rd.* ☎ *631/288–1139* ⊕ *www.whbvillage.com* ⊠ *Free* ⊗ *Mid-June–Labor Day, weekends 2–5.*

Where to Stay & Eat

$$$–$$$$ ✕ **Starr Boggs.** The dining room of this sophisticated see-and-be-seen restaurant has artwork, white linens, large windows, and simple wooden chairs. The new American fare is just as attractive. The menu changes daily, and each dish, while on the expensive side, is unforgettable. There's open-air dining on the patio, which has a waterfall. ⊠ *6 Parlato Dr.* ☎ *631/288–3500* ⚑ *Reservations essential* ⊗ *Closed mid-Oct.–mid-May. No lunch* ⊟ *AE, MC, V.*

$$$–$$$$ ✕ **Tierra Mar.** Stunning ocean views are surpassed only by the quality of food that emerges from the kitchen of chef Todd Jacobs. Try the lobster bisque with plum tomatoes, local organic mesclun salad, tempura-battered crab cakes, or the delectable roast breast of free-range Long Island duck. If you really want to eat here, make a reservation. ⊠ *231 Dune Rd.* ☎ *631/288–2700* ⊟ *AE, DC, MC, V.*

$$–$$$ ✕ **Rene's Casa Basso.** Sculptures dot the front and side lawns of this upscale, traditional restaurant. To enter, you walk under the swords of two concrete 12-foot-tall fencing musketeers, after which you come upon a miniature castle complete with mythological figures. The fare, a mix of northern and southern Italian, includes well-prepared pasta, seafood, veal, and steak dishes. Try the delectable osso buco, veal Milanese, or fresh seafood-laden bouillabaisse. ⊠ *59 Montauk Hwy.* ☎ *631/288–1841* ⊟ *AE, MC, V* ⊗ *Closed Mon. No lunch.*

$–$$$ ✕ **Belle's Cafe.** Caribbean, Cajun, and creole specialties such as blackened catfish and jambalaya are among the soul-satisfying dishes on the ever-changing menu at this small, homey café. In the old officer's club at the airport and overlooking the landing strip, Belle's is favored by locals, visitors, and pilots. Hot bands play music ranging from blues to funk weekend nights and during Sunday brunch, and there's a courtyard for alfresco dining. ⊠ *Francis Gabreski Airport, County Rd. 31* ☎ *631/288–3927* ⊟ *AE, MC, V* ⊘ *No dinner Mon.–Wed.*

$$$–$$$$ 🏨 **Harborside Hotel.** The bright, clean, airy rooms at this hotel on the beach have their own terraces, and most have an ocean view. Interiors are mostly outfitted in cool blues or greens, with contemporary furnishings. Studios and suites have kitchenettes and comfy leather couches. ⊠ *538 Dune Rd., 11978* ☎ *631/288–4450* 🖷 *631/288–2083* ⊕ *www.harborsidehotel.com* ⇨ *4 rooms, 20 studios, 2 suites* ⚷ *Some kitchenettes, cable TV, pool, no-smoking rooms* ⊟ *AE, MC, V* ⊘ *Closed mid-Nov.–Apr.*

$$–$$$$ 🏨 **1880 House.** The rooms in this antiques-filled B&B built in 1880 have private baths, and the common area has a fireplace. Two rooms have an adjoining sitting room, and the third is a suite in an old carriage house. The ocean is a five-minute walk away. ⊠ *2 Seafield La.* Ⓓ *Box 648, 11978* ☎ *631/288–1559 or 800/346–3290* 🖷 *631/288–0721* ⊕ *www.1880seafieldhouse.com* ⇨ *3 rooms* ⚷ *Microwaves, refrigerators, tennis court, pool, Internet; no room phones* ⊟ *AE, MC, V* ⧆ *BP.*

$–$$$ 🏨 **The Inn on Main.** Clean, bright rooms with floral quilts and wooden dressers and mirrors ensure a comfortable stay at this cheerful Victorian inn built in 1890. The beach is ¾ mi away, and a short stroll takes you to Main Street's trendy shops and fine restaurants. ⊠ *191 Main St., 11978* ☎ *631/288–8900* ⊕ *www.theinnonmain.com* ⇨ *9 rooms* ⚷ *Cable TV, Internet; no room phones* ⊟ *AE, MC, V* ⧆ *CP.*

Nightlife & the Arts

Well-known artists perform in professional theater, music, and dance events at the **Westhampton Beach Performing Arts Center** (⊠ 76 Main St. ☎ 631/288–2350 for information, 631/288–1500 for box office ⊕ www.whbpac.org). The center also screens classic and contemporary films.

Shopping

Main Street is dotted with small shops selling antiques, gifts, clothing, and area specialties. **Baby Shock/Shock Kids** (⊠ 99 Main St. ☎ 631/288–2522) carries all manner of stylish clothing and accessories for babies and kids. **Koala** (⊠ 130 Main St. ☎ 631/288–0444) sells unique clothing for sophisticated, fun-loving women. At the **Little Red Wagon** (⊠ 128 Main St. ☎ 631/288–9633) you can browse through a delightful selection of fine designer clothing, shoes, accessories, and furniture for kids and moms-to-be. Unique pottery pieces and gifts are for sale at **O'Suzanna** (⊠ 108 Main St. ☎ 631/288–2202).

Quogue

🟆 *3 mi east of Westhampton Beach.*

Settled in the mid-17th century, Quoque, part of the greater Westhampton area, is one of the oldest communities on Long Island. Today, thanks to the stately Victorians nestled along its tree-lined streets and the contemporary mansions along the ocean on Dune Road, Quoque is one of the most desirable residential areas in the Hamptons. Just east is East Quogue, which was settled in 1686 and was originally known as Fourth Neck. Its acres of farmland and pine forest, beautiful bay, and ocean beaches are enlivened by Main Street shopping and the seasonal influx of visitors.

Quogue Wildlife Refuge. The 300-acre wildlife preserve, managed by the State Department of Environmental Conservation, has self-guided trails and a wildlife-rehabilitation center, plus a Nature Center with exhibits and a library. Classes about field ecology and wildlife photography are available, and the refuge also has children's programs. ⊠ *3 Old Country Rd.* ☎ *631/653–4771* ⊕ *www.quoguerefuge.com* ⊠ *Free* ☉ *Daily dawn–dusk.*

Tiana Beach. In addition to 1,000 feet of white sand on the ocean, this beach has lifeguards, showers, restrooms, picnic tables, a food stand, and volleyball. A town of Southampton parking permit is required here. ⊠ *Dune Rd., East Quogue/Hampton Bays* ☎ *631/283–6000* ⊠ *Parking $10 (Memorial Day–Labor Day).*

Where to Stay & Eat

$$$-$$$$ ✕ **Stone Creek Inn.** At this bright and airy restaurant, the talented chef-
Fodor's Choice owner relies on the freshest local produce and seafood—as well as on
★ his considerable talent—to provide a memorable dining experience. Oven-roasted halibut, rack of lamb with Mediterranean spice, and braised Montauk lobster with baby vegetables are among the dishes on the French-leaning menu. Homemade desserts—such as ricotta mousse and lemon tart—may make you swoon. The dining spaces are elegantly spare, with polished hardwood floors, countless windows, and white-clothed tables. ⊠ *405 Montauk Hwy., East Quogue* ☎ *631/653–6770* ▤ *AE, D, DC, MC, V* ☉ *No lunch.*

$$-$$$$ ✕ **Dockers.** People stop in at this casual, lively waterfront restaurant on their way home from the beach just across the road. Try the calamari appetizer, Black Angus aged steak, clambake platter, or lobster. The large deck overlooking the bay has good views of the sunset. There's live music Friday through Sunday, and early-bird dinner specials are available. ⊠ *94 Dune Rd., East Quogue* ☎ *631/653–0653* ⌿ *Reservations not accepted* ▤ *AE, D, DC, MC, V* ☉ *Closed mid-Sept.–mid-May.*

$-$$$ ✕ **New Moon Cafe.** This rustic, noisy restaurant has bright colors and lots of windows. Try the mesquite-smoked barbecued brisket served with Texas pinto beans and corn-on-the-cob. A children's menu is available. Occasionally there's live music, with a guitar, keyboards, and a singer. ⊠ *524 Montauk Hwy., East Quogue* ☎ *631/653–4042* ▤ *AE, D, MC, V.*

$$$-$$$$ ✕▥ **Inn at Quogue.** This tranquil complex in the center of Quogue village consists of a house from the 18th century, another from the 19th century right across the road, and private cottages. Ralph Lauren designers supervised the interior scheme here, and each comfortable, antiques-filled room is different. The beach is just minutes away. The inn's restaurant ($$-$$$$; reservations essential) has a hint of the antebellum South about it. The chef is known for such innovative dishes as apple-and-Gorgonzola salad, seared ahi tuna, and tangy lemon-lobster risotto. ⊠ *47–52 Quogue St., 11959* ☎ *631/653–6560* ▤ *631/723–4517* ⊕ *www.innatquogue.com* ⇌ *67 rooms, 2 cottages* ⌂ *Restaurant, din-*

ing room, some kitchens, some microwaves, cable TV, pool, spa, bicycles, volleyball, bar, some pets allowed (fee) ⊟ *AE, D, MC, V.*

Sports & the Outdoors

At **Quogue Wildlife Refuge** (⊠ 3 Old Country Rd. ☎ 631/653–4771 ⊕ www.quoguerefuge.com) you can bird-watch, hike along a self-guided trail, or visit a complex where injured animals are rehabilitated. It's open daily dawn to dusk; admission is free.

Shopping

In addition to greenhouses with tropical plants, the **Old Quogue Farm and Florist** (⊠ Montauk Hwy. and Depot Rd. ☎ 631/653–4145) has a shop full of flowers, Trapp candles, paintings by a local artist, birdhouses, and hand-painted china. **Once Upon a Time** (⊠ Montauk Hwy., East Quogue ☎ 631/653–8197) is a well-stocked consignment boutique that sells women's clothing. **New Leaf Antiques** (⊠ 140 Jessup Ave. ☎ 631/653–6010) sells an eclectic mix of furniture, paintings, mirrors, and china. **Respectable Collectibles** (⊠ Montauk Hwy., East Quogue ☎ 631/653–4372) carries 19th- and 20th-century English, Continental, and country antiques.

Southampton

㉗ *15 mi east of Quogue.*

Southampton is not only steeped in rich history but also in contemporary affluence. Pristine area beaches framed by sparkling Atlantic waters are a draw, but so are upscale shops, fine restaurants, polo matches and other horsey events, and antiques shows.

The village was settled in the 17th century by Puritans who had set sail from Lynn, Massachusetts, and landed at what is today known as Conscience Point. Southampton, which was formally incorporated in 1894, was named after the third earl of Southampton, Henry Wriothesly, who was sympathetic to the early British settlers and widely respected.

Southampton has several districts and buildings included on the National Register of Historic Places. The village is part of the much larger town of Southampton, which spans from parts of Eastport to the west all the way east to Sagaponack, with its potato farms and seaside estates. A drive through the "estate section" of Southampton takes you past graceful mansions surrounded by 20-foot privet hedges. Gin Lane, in particular, is worth a peek.

★ **Cooper's Beach.** For a fee, you can stretch out on the sand of this Southampton Village beach, studying the sea in one direction and historic mansions—including Calvin Klein's massive manse (the one with the turrets)—in the other. Facilities include lifeguards (9–5 daily from Memorial Day through Labor Day), restrooms, outdoor showers, and a snack bar. ⊠ *268 Meadow La.* ☎ *631/283–0247* ⊕ *www. southamptonvillage.org* ⌚ *Memorial Day–Labor Day $25 weekdays, $30 weekends.*

Long Island University, Southampton College. In summer the campus hums with such musical events as Pianofest in the Hamptons and the All for the Sea fund-raising concert, which draws the likes of Jimmy Buffett and Paul Simon here in July. Throughout the season several organizations sponsor plays, art shows, readings, workshops, and other activities for adults and children. ⊠ *239 Montauk Hwy.* ☎ *631/283–4000* ⊕ *www.southampton.liu.edu.*

Old Halsey House. This 1648 saltbox was built by town founder Thomas Halsey. The English general William Erskine had his headquarters here during the American Revolution. Today it's a museum that includes furniture from the 17th and 18th centuries and a 16th-century "breeches" Bible that has an interesting take on what Adam and Eve actually wore after the Fall. ⊠ *189 S. Main St.* ☎ *631/283–2494* ⊠ *$3* ☉ *Mid-Apr.–mid-Sept., Tues.–Sun. 11–5.*

Fodor'sChoice ★ **Parrish Art Museum.** Samuel Longstreth Parrish built this museum in 1898 as a repository for his Italian Renaissance art. Through the years the museum has also developed a strong collection of American paintings, including works by renowned Long Island artists. Traveling exhibits have ranged from pieces by sculptor August Saint-Gaudens to photographs of the civil rights movement by Herbert Randall. The gardens are filled with reproductions of sculpture from the museum's permanent collection. There's a full calendar of lectures, workshops, concerts, and children's programs. Juried art exhibitions hang on the walls during the year. ⊠ *25 Jobs La.* ☎ *631/283–2118* ⊕ *thehamptons.com* ⊠ *$5 suggested donation* ☉ *Mon.–Sat. 11–5, Sun. 1–5.*

Ponquogue Beach. This beach, a 15-minute drive west of Southampton Village and at the end of Ponquogue Bridge, has lifeguards, changing and shower facilities, and a snack bar. ⊠ *Dune Rd., Hampton Bays* ☎ *631/728–8585* ⊕ *www.town.southampton.ny.us* ⊠ *$15 (late June–mid-Sept.).*

Southampton Historical Museum. The museum encompasses seven historic structures, including an 1843 whaling captain's home, a country store, an old-fashioned apothecary, a pre–Revolutionary War barn, and a blacksmith shop. Montauk and Shinnecock Indian artifacts are also on display. ⊠ *17 Meeting House La.* ☎ *631/283–2494* ⊕ *www.town.southampton.ny.us* ⊠ *$3* ☉ *Mid-June–Sept., Tues.–Sat. 11–5, Sun. 1–5.*

Where to Stay & Eat

$$$–$$$$ ✕ **Lobster Inn.** This crowded, family-friendly seafood restaurant was once a marina and boat shop. It's still nautical and rustic—the perfect place to dine on Manhattan clam chowder, lobster, and mussels. There's also a salad bar. ⊠ *162 Inlet Rd.* ☎ *631/283–1525* ⚲ *Reservations not accepted* ⊟ *AE, D, DC, MC, V* ☉ *Closed Dec.–mid-Feb.*

★ $$$–$$$$ ✕ **Red Bar Brasserie.** Candle sconces line the wonderful wraparound windows at this popular American restaurant. Fried calamari, grilled salmon with local corn, filet mignon, and grilled tuna with steamed baby bok choy are all good choices. Part of the space, which has bentwood chairs and white-clothed tables, is devoted to the bar. The social scene is lively here on summer nights. ⊠ *210 Hampton Rd.* ☎ *631/283–0704* ⊟ *AE, MC, V* ☉ *Closed Tues. No lunch.*

$$–$$$$ ✕ **Basilico.** The upscale patrons who favor this restaurant in Southampton Village come for the brick-oven pizzas and the Tuscan-tinged entrées. The pasta is homemade, and the portions are large. In the evening the interior's wood trim and terra-cotta tiles seem to glow in the candlelight. Weekend lunches are leisurely events. ⊠ *10 Windmill La.,* ☎ *631/283–7987* ▭ *AE, D, DC, MC, V.*

$$–$$$$ ✕ **Belle's East.** This fancy outpost of Belle's Cafe in Westhampton Beach serves such New Orleans–style dishes as barbecued shrimp alongside more standard American fare. If possible, opt for a table on the patio, which is open in the spring and fall as well as in the summer thanks to the use of heaters. Inside, the lounge has live music—often Latin or reggae—six nights a week and a late-night menu of barbecue fare on weekends. There's also a buffet brunch on Sunday. ⊠ *256 Elm St.* ☎ *631/204–0300* ▭ *AE, MC, V* ۞ *Closed Tues.*

$$–$$$$ ✕ **George Martin.** The new American takes on steak and seafood, the regional specialties, the stellar desserts, and the generous portions earn this restaurant high marks. Try the herb-roasted free-range chicken or the signature steak, a dry-aged, prime New York sirloin. There's also a $20 prix-fixe menu daily. ⊠ *56 Nugent St./Main St.* ☎ *631/204–8700* ▭ *AE, MC, V* ۞ *No lunch.*

$$–$$$$ ✕ **Q, a Thai Bistro.** Inventive Thai cuisine and nightly Asian-fusion spe-
Fodor'sChoice   cials are the draws at this Noyac spot. A stylish cocktail lounge and a
★   patio encourage you to linger here. ⊠ *129 Noyac Rd., North Sea* ☎ *631/204–0007* ⌖ *Reservations essential* ▭ *AE, MC, V* ۞ *Closed Tues. and Dec.–Mar. No lunch.*

$$$ ✕ **Le Chef.** A warm, welcoming, busy little bistro, Le Chef serves mainly French food. Standouts include rack of lamb and lobster with a tomato-cognac cream sauce. All meals are prix fixe. ⊠ *75 Jobs La.* ☎ *631/283–8581* ▭ *AE, MC, V.*

$$–$$$ ✕ **John Duck Jr.** This restaurant in a converted farmhouse on a terraced hill has been a family business for more than a century. It has five dining rooms, one of which is a glassed-in porch. Local produce is key, as are seafood and steak dishes. The roast Long Island duckling is a good bet. Sunday brunch is available, as is a children's menu. ⊠ *15 Prospect St.* ☎ *631/283–0311* ▭ *AE, D, DC, MC, V* ۞ *Closed Mon.*

$–$$$ ✕ **Barrister's.** Simple but good American fare is the rule here, as are friendly service and a general conviviality. Try for a table at the front for an entertaining view of Main Street. There are daily specials as well as a steady menu of burgers, seafood entrées, and pasta dishes; salads rise above the usual. The bar draws locals for after-work drinks. ⊠ *36 Main St.* ☎ *631/283–6206* ⌖ *Reservations not accepted* ▭ *AE, D, DC, MC, V.*

$–$$$ ✕ **Driver's Seat.** The dining room, whose huge stone fireplace is often ablaze in winter, hums with diners eager to order one of the daily seafood specials or such stick-to-your-ribs dishes as pot roast, meat loaf and mashed potatoes, burgers, and homemade soups. The bar business is brisk, too. ⊠ *62 Jobs La.* ☎ *631/283–6606* ▭ *AE, MC, V.*

$–$$ ✕ **Golden Pear.** Make your way to the counter of this small, often-crowded café and then sit at a table and watch Southampton's scene from the large windows while you wait to be served. For breakfast, try scrambled eggs on a croissant with a side of fruit. Good lunch choices include chili, vegetable lasagna, and the interesting combo sandwiches. The coffee is delicious at any time of day. ⊠ *97–99 Main St.* ☎ *631/283–8900* ⊟ *AE, MC, V* ⊙ *No dinner.*

$–$$ ✕ **La Parmigiana.** Everyone seems to love this family-style place for its **Fodor'sChoice** "red-sauce" Italian menu, its huge portions, and its reasonable prices. ★ Spaghetti *celestino* (with tomato-cream sauce) and prosciutto with tomato and basil are favorites. Be prepared for a wait on summer weekends. ⊠ *44–48 Hampton Rd.* ☎ *631/283–8030* ⊟ *AE, MC, V* ⊙ *Closed Mon.*

¢ ✕ **Sip 'n Soda.** Open for breakfast, lunch, and dinner, this retro luncheonette serves the usual casual fare: burgers, sandwiches, omelets, salads, and ice cream. ⊠ *40 Hampton Rd.* ☎ *631/283–9752* ⌂ *Reservations not accepted* ⊟ *No credit cards.*

$$$$ ▥ **Southampton Village Latch Inn.** A collective of local artists owns and runs this hotel. The interior design reflects their tastes: Burmese puppets, New Guinea masks, African artifacts, and Tibetan rugs are among the furnishings. Some rooms and duplexes have balconies and decks. The inn is on 5 acres in Southampton Village and just over a mile from the beach. ⊠ *101 Hill St., 11968* ☎ *631/283–2160 or 800/545–2824* 🖷 *631/283–3236* ⊕ *www.villagelatch.com* ⊸ *43 rooms, 18 suites, 6 duplexes* ⌂ *Dining room, some refrigerators, cable TV with movies, tennis court, pool, bicycles, business services, some pets allowed (fee); no smoking* ⊟ *AE, D, DC, MC, V* ⊨⊙⊨ *CP.*

$$$–$$$$ ▥ **The Bentley.** Each large suite overlooks Peconic Bay and has a patio or a deck. Richly hued paint effects, accent pieces, and contemporary Italian furniture either complement or tastefully contrast with the overall palette of beiges and creams. Breakfast bars face kitchenettes equipped with microwaves, coffeemakers, and java from Starbucks. In the bathroom, it's all about Aveda products. The 4½-acre property has a kidney-shape pool with a large sundeck. ⊠ *161 Hill Station Rd., 11968* ☎ *631/283–0908* 🖷 *631/283–6102* ⊕ *www.hrhresorts.com* ⊸ *39 suites* ⌂ *Picnic area, in-room data ports, kitchenettes, minibars, microwaves, cable TV, in-room VCRs, tennis court, pool, laundry facilities, business services, some pets allowed (fee); no smoking* ⊟ *AE, D, DC, MC, V* ⊙ *Closed Labor Day–Memorial Day* ⊨⊙⊨ *CP.*

$$–$$$$ ▥ **Arlington Shores.** You might see a gorgeous Hamptons sunset from the common balcony at this condominium resort on Shinnecock Bay, 10 mi west of Southampton. Standard condos have a queen-size bed, kitchen, and oak floors. Stay for a week, a month, a season, or even a year. A shuttle to the train or bus stops is provided. ⊠ *40 Penny La., Hampton Bays 11946* ☎ *631/723–6000* 🖷 *631/723–4517* ⊕ *www.arlingtonshores.com* ⊸ *28 condos* ⌂ *Picnic area, kitchens, cable TV, tennis court, pool, volleyball* ⊟ *AE, MC, V* ⊨⊙⊨ *CP.*

$$–$$$$ ▥ **The Atlantic.** On the outside it looks like any other raised ranch circa 1975. Inside, however, rooms are up-to-date with sleek, contemporary maple furniture, stainless-steel headboards, lamps, and other details. Plump white duvets, soft sheets, and Aveda bath goodies are among the comforts. The grounds are well manicured, and the pool seems to stretch on for an eternity. ⊠ *1655 Rte. 39, 11968* ☎ *631/283–6100* 🖷 *631/*

283–6102 ⊕ *www.hrhresorts.com* ⟶ *62 rooms, 5 suites* ﾐ *In-room data ports, some in-room hot tubs, some kitchenettes, minibars, cable TV, in-room VCRs, tennis court, pool, gym, business services, some pets allowed (fee); no smoking* ⊟ *AE, MC, V* ⦿ *CP.*

$$–$$$$ ▦ **Evergreen on Pine.** Tall, carefully groomed hedges front a house with a pretty porch and flower-filled window boxes on each sill. The five guest rooms are singular: one room has an ornamental fireplace and a brass bed; another has a French-lace canopy bed. There's also a suite with a sitting area and Laura Ashley bedding. The beach is less than a mile away. ✉ *89 Pine St., 11968* ☎ *631/283–0564 or 877/824–6600* ⊕ *www. evergreenonpine.com* ⟶ *4 rooms, 1 suite* ﾐ *Dining room, in-room data ports, cable TV, Internet; no kids under 12, no smoking* ⊟ *AE, DC, MC, V* ⦿ *CP.*

$$–$$$$ ▦ **Mainstay Inn.** Every bedroom in this shingle-covered colonial has antique cast-iron beds and country pine furniture. Each also seems to be filled with yard upon yard of fabric: generous floral table covers and drapes, white duvets, and quilted spreads. Whether the gardens were inspired by the guest-room fabrics or the fabrics were chosen to mirror the gardens is hard to know. Southampton's main street is a 15-minute walk away, and the public beach is a mile away. ✉ *579 Hill St., 11968* ☎ *631/283–4375* 🖶 *631/614–6300* ⊕ *www.themainstay.com* ⟶ *8 rooms, 5 with bath; 1 suite* ﾐ *Dining room, some fans, cable TV, pool, business services; no a/c in some rooms, no TV in some rooms, no smoking* ⊟ *AE, DC, MC, V* ⦿ *CP.*

$$–$$$$ ▦ **1708 House.** It's truly a colonial, from the wide clapboards outside to the wood beams within. Antiques, Asian rugs, and rich fabrics fill this B&B in the heart of Southampton Village. Public areas include an informal card room, a more formal dining room, and an even more formal parlor. Guest quarters in the house and in the two-bedroom cottages have four-poster beds. Some rooms are elegantly rustic; others are simply elegant. All are true to the age and style of the house. ✉ *126 Main St., 11968* ☎ *631/287–1708* 🖶 *631/287–3593* ⊕ *www.1708house.com* ⟶ *6 rooms, 3 suites, 3 cottages* ﾐ *Dining room, some kitchens, cable TV; no kids under 12, no smoking* ⊟ *AE, MC, V* ⦿ *BP.*

$$–$$$$ ▦ **Southampton Inn.** The interior of this modern inn is dressed in refined contemporary-country furniture and fittings. Beds have down comforters and lots of pillows. Adirondack chairs are scattered throughout the expansive, formally landscaped grounds, and there's a patio courtyard and a pool. There's plenty of on-site parking, and a shuttle runs to the beach. Great shopping, dining, and sightseeing are steps away. ✉ *91 Hill St., 11968* ☎ *631/283–6500 or 800/832–6500* 🖶 *631/283–6559* ⊕ *www.southamptoninn.com* ⟶ *90 rooms* ﾐ *Restaurant, in-room data ports, refrigerators, cable TV, tennis court, pool, badminton, billiards, croquet, shuffleboard, volleyball, bar, library, video game room, business services, meeting rooms, some pets allowed (fee), no-smoking rooms* ⊟ *AE, D, DC, MC, V* ⦿ *CP weekends.*

$–$$$$ ▦ **Enclave Inn.** Not all motels have to be about '50s kitsch. Rooms in this one have chunky, country-style furniture and accessories that work well with highly polished wood floors, floral drapes, crisp white window sheers, and lacy white bed linens. The hotel and its tree-filled grounds are just minutes from the Hampton Jitney bus stop and a few miles from area beaches. ✉ *450 Rte. 39, 11968* ☎ *631/537–2900* 🖷 *631/537–5436* ⊕ *www.enclaveinn.com* ⇄ *11 rooms* ♪ *Fans, refrigerators, cable TV, pool, Internet, business services, meeting room; no smoking* ⊟ *AE, MC, V* ⦶ *CP May–Oct.*

$–$$$ ☒ **The Capri.** Outside clapboards, shingles, and creatively used bits of canvas all recall classic seaside properties. Inside, the fluffy white duvets and pillows do, too. But all the other interior details seem to be about mid-20th-century modern, from the custom headboards to the bold, linear paint effects. All rooms face the pool in the central courtyard. The hotel is 3 mi from the beach and ½ mi from Southampton Village. ✉ *281 Rte. 39A, 11968* ☎ *631/283–4220* 🖷 *631/283–6102* ⊕ *www.hrhresorts.com* ⇄ *27 rooms, 4 suites* ♪ *Restaurant, in-room data ports, minibars, some refrigerators, cable TV, pool, business services, some pets allowed (fee); no smoking* ⊟ *AE, D, MC, V* ⊙ *Closed Labor Day–Memorial Day* ⦶ *CP.*

CAMPING △ **Shinnecock East County Park.** This beach park has 100 RV campsites
¢ (no tents are allowed) on either the Atlantic or on the inlet to Shinnecock Bay. If you're not a resident of Suffolk County, call to check rules about staying here. ✉ *Dune Rd., 11968* ☎ *631/852–8899 or 631/852–8290* ⊕ *www.co.suffolk.ny.us* ⇄ *100 sites* ♪ *Dump station, drinking water, public telephone, swimming (ocean)* ⊛ *Reservations not accepted* ⊟ *MC, V.*

Nightlife

At **Jet East** (✉ 1181 N. Sea Rd. ☎ 631/283–0808), a super-trendy club, regulars regularly shell out hundreds of dollars to reserve weekend tables and buy bottles of champagne. Expect a wait at the velvet rope if you're not plugged in. The place is usually open Thursday through Sunday from Memorial Day through Labor Day; there's a $15 cover on Friday and a $20 cover Saturday.

Sports & the Outdoors

MINIATURE GOLF The 18-hole miniature-golf course at **Lynch's Links** (✉ 375 David Whites La. ☎ 631/283–0049) is open daily from Memorial Day to Labor Day and then on weekends until Columbus Day. The cost per person is $8.

WINDSURFING The area's many protected waterways, including Cold Spring Pond and Peconic Bay, are popular with windsurfers and kiteboarders. You can rent gear or bring your own. If you rent, experts will assess your ability, steer you to an appropriate spot, and haul the equipment there and back. Instruction is also available; the cost for two hours on the water runs about $40 with rentals, $85 for a full day.

Windsurfing Hampton, Inc. (✉ 1688 North Hwy./Rte. 27 ☎ 631/283–9463 ⊕ www.w-surf.com), a premier, full-service, sailboarding shop, has windsurfing and kiteboarding equipment, kayak and Sunfish rentals, lessons with certified instructors, demo clinics, and swap meets.

Shopping

Ann Madonia Antiques (⊠ 36 Jobs La. ☎ 631/283–1878) is packed with 18th- and 19th-century American and European furnishings and decorative items, many of which came from Hamptons-area estates. You might find a French daybed with carved classical urns, a Venetian headboard, or a Second Empire bed with mother-of-pearl accents. The shop is closed October through late May, except by appointment. The independent ★ **BookHampton** (⊠ 91 Main St. ☎ 631/283–0270) combines an autonomous spirit with chain-store selection and pricing (hardcovers are always 20% off). There's plenty of contemporary fiction and nonfiction, as well as classical literature, cookbooks, children's books, and titles on the Hamptons. The scent of homemade fudge wafts into the street in front of the cheery **Fudge Co.** (⊠ 67 Main St. ☎ 631/283–8108), which is closed Christmas through Easter. Storefront displays of colorful, scrumptious confections—including many novelty items—delight kids as well as grown-ups.

To say that **Hildreth's** (⊠ 51 Main St. ☎ 631/283–2300) is a Hamptons institution is an understatement. This home-furnishings store has been in business—on this spot and owned by the same family—since 1842. It's fun to shop for 21st-century carpets, lamps, furniture, linens, and table settings amid 19th-century architectural details. There are other outlets in the Hamptons, but this is the original. The posh **Mecox Gardens** (⊠ 257 Rte. 39A ☎ 631/287–5015), which sells furnishings for indoor and outdoor spaces, is all about steeply pitched gables, cascading ivy, and tasteful topiary. Look for antique, reproduction, and contemporary furniture; unusual garden ornaments; and intriguing accessories. A whitewashed interior with flea-market furnishings forms the perfect backdrop for the casual but upscale men's and women's resort wear and accessories at the **Ralph Lauren Polo Country Store** (⊠ 41 Jobs La. ☎ 631/287–6953); it's closed Tuesdays and Wednesdays October through late March. Family-owned **Rose Jewelers** (⊠ 57 Main St. ☎ 631/283–5757) sells gems, crystal, estate jewelry, and watches by Rolex, TAG Heuer, and Baume & Mercier.

Southampton's former town hall makes an intimate outpost for the venerable **Saks Fifth Avenue** (⊠ 1 Hampton Rd. ☎ 631/283–3500) department store. It's all about designer stuff here: resort wear by Donna Karan and Calvin Klein, bags by Burberry and Prada, cosmetics and skin-care products by Chanel and Kiehl's. **Stevenson's Toys and Games** (⊠ 68 Jobs La. ☎ 631/283–2111), an old-fashioned toy shop, stocks Madame Alexander dolls, Playmobil toys, stuffed animals, art-and-crafts supplies, and puzzles for the diminutive set. **Tate's Bake Shop** (⊠ 43 N. Sea Rd. ☎ 631/283–9830) is famous for its sinfully yummy chocolate-chip cookies but also sells freshly baked pies, scones, muffins, and specialty cakes.

Water Mill

 1 mi east of Southampton.

This small village, settled in the mid-17th century, is the nation's only community with a functional, working water mill and windmill. The original settlers used the mills as power sources to grind grain, saw wood, and make paper and clothing materials. Today there are several restaurants in this tiny village, and the block-long Main Street has the South Fork's only old-time penny-candy store, in existence for more than 50 years.

Duck Walk Vineyards. A Normandy-style château sits on 56 acres of vineyards. There are daily tours (free, at noon, 2, and 4) and tastings. Special events include live music on the patio overlooking the vineyards weekends in summer and fall, as well as complimentary hot mulled wine on December weekends. ⊠ *231 Montauk Hwy.* ☎ *631/726–7555* ⊕ *www.duckwalk.com* ⊠ *Free* ⊙ *Daily 11–6.*

Water Mill Museum. Originally built in 1644, the oldest operating water mill on Long Island is still fully operational today. You can work the lathe and learn the arts of quilting and weaving here. Uncle Fred's workshop, also on-site, has handmade toys. ⊠ *41 Old Mill Rd.* ☎ *631/ 726–4625* ⊕ *www.watermillmuseum.org* ⊠ *$3 suggested donation* ⊙ *June–Sept., Thurs.–Mon. 11–5, Sun. 1–5.*

Where to Stay & Eat

$$–$$$$
Fodor's Choice
★

✕ **Mirko's.** The warm atmosphere and the talented chef-owner's use of only the freshest local ingredients have consistently won this gem of a restaurant rave reviews from respected foodies. The menu is a blend of Mediterranean, Continental, contemporary, and American dishes. Try the pan-roasted striped bass, the herb-crusted rack of lamb, or the grilled veal chop with corn-tomato salsa. You can dine inside by the fireplace or out on the terrace. ⊠ *Water Mill Sq., 670 Montauk Hwy.* ☎ *631/726–4444* ⊘ *Reservations essential* ⊟ *AE, DC, MC, V* ⊙ *Closed Jan.–mid-Sept. No lunch.*

$$–$$$

🏠 **Inn at Box Farm.** A colonial farmhouse dating from the late 1600s, this shingled structure has been expanded over the years and derives its form and style from early English and Dutch traditional houses. Rooms are bright and furnished with antiques, the beds are covered with thick comforters, and the innkeepers pamper you with afternoon cocktails and the like. Beaches are within ½ mi of the inn, which provides passes. ⊠ *78 Mecox Rd.* ☎ *212/371–7191* ⊕ *www.boxfarm.com* ⊠ *7 rooms* ⊘ *Internet, bicycles* ⊟ *AE, D, DC, MC, V* ⊙I *BP.*

Shopping

The **Animal Rescue Fund Thrift Shop** (⊠ Main St. ☎ 631/726–6613) sells china, lamps, paintings, furniture, and clothing at bargain prices. The items are mostly secondhand, but castoffs in the Hamptons can be pretty fabulous. At the old-time, wooden-floored **Penny Candy Store** (⊠ Main St. ☎ No phone) kids (and adults) can decide what sweets to put in their little brown paper sacks. This shop has been here for more than 50 years, and the storekeepers are very patient and friendly. The **Water Mill Shops** (⊠ 760 Montauk Hwy. ☎ No phone) complex includes a candy-and-gift shop called Double Rainbow and fine-foods store Citarella.

Bridgehampton

㉙ *7 mi east of Water Mill.*

The beautiful beaches are just part of the attraction at this quiet, classy Hamptons community. Elegant Bridgehampton has antiques shops, art galleries, and restaurants in which you can sip wine made from locally grown grapes. This is also horse country, and in summer Bridgehampton hosts the prestigious annual Hampton Classic Horse Show and the Mercedes-Benz Polo Challenge. South of the village of Bridgehampton, running along the ocean, is the area called Sagaponack, a traditional agricultural community dating from 1656 and known for having some of the richest soil on Long island. Even though more grand homes are being built on this precious farmland every year, you can still buy outstanding local berries, vegetables, and flowers at the farm stands here.

Madoo Conservancy. A stroll around this whimsical, plant- and sculpture-studded 2-acre preserve designed by artist Robert Dash reveals why *HomeStyle* magazine once described it as one of the 10 most beautiful gardens in America. Photographs are permitted, but not dogs, strollers, or children under six. ⊠ *618 Sagg Main St., off Rte. 27, Sagaponack* ☎ *631/537–8200* ⊕ *www.madoo.org* ☜ *$10* ☉ *May–Sept., Wed. and Sat. 1–5.*

Poxabogue County Park. Woods, fields, marshland, and numerous plants and animals appeal to hikers and nature lovers who venture through this 26-acre preserve. Members of the local trail-preservation society lead guided hikes here, and there's an easy ½-mi nature walk. ⊠ *Old Farm Rd. north of Rte. 27* ☎ *631/854–4949* ☜ *Free* ☉ *Daily dawn–dusk.*

Sagg Main Beach. This Town of Southampton beach stretches along the ocean for 1,500 feet. Lifeguards are on duty (weekends 10–5 from late May to late June and daily 10–5 from late June to early September), and facilities include showers, restrooms, a food stand, picnic tables, and volleyball. Beachgoers must have a parking permit. ⊠ *Sagg Main St., Sagaponack* ☎ *631/283–6011* ☜ *Parking $10 (late May–early Sept.).*

Where to Stay & Eat

$$$$ ✕ **Bobby Van's.** The French doors and large ceiling fans give this restaurant a distinctly *Casablanca* feel. Originally a popular gathering place for local artists and writers, today it is known as much for people-watching near its open doors as for its food. Try the great steaks for which it is famous or the fresh local seafood dishes and daily specials. The bar scene is lively. Reservations are essential on Friday and Saturday. ⊠ *2636 Main St.* ☎ *631/537–0590* ⊟ *AE, D, DC, MC, V.*

$$–$$$$ ✕ **Almond.** This cozy spot, with a pressed-tin ceiling and loads of wood, is known for its brasserie-style food. The flounder served on a bed of spinach in a tureen is sublime, as is the striped bass Provençal. The menu also includes chicken, lamb, and veal dishes; casual fare, like sandwiches and burgers; and a raw bar. French names dominate the wine list. Surprisingly fair prices and friendly service add to Almond's appeal. ⊠ *1970 Montauk Hwy.* ☎ *631/537–8885* ⊟ *AE, MC, V.*

¢–$$ ✕ **World Pie.** A friendly staff and mouthwatering Italian food make this down-to-earth eatery a popular choice. Artichoke hearts, goat cheese, and basil are among the toppings used on the more than 20 varieties of pizza baked in the wood-burning oven. The fresh salads—such as the chopped romaine with tomatoes, red onions, and blue cheese—are delectable, as are such daily specials as seared lamb chops with polenta. ⊠ *2402 Main St.* ☎ *631/537–7999* ⊟ *AE, MC, V.*

★ ¢–$ ✕ **Bridgehampton Candy Kitchen.** This is a classic luncheonette and soda fountain where locals rub elbows with celebrities—and no one makes a big deal of it. The waitstaff is efficient and friendly, and the food is simple and good. Try a burger with fries, an omelet, or one of the Greek specialties, followed by the delicious homemade ice cream. ⊠ *Main and School Sts.* ☎ *631/537–9885* ⊟ *No credit cards.*

$$$$ 🏨 **Bridgehampton Inn.** On Main Street and within walking distance of the village center is this stately 1795 clapboard inn, operated by the same family that owns the Loaves & Fishes food shop in Sagaponack. Beautiful antique dressers and mirrors decorate the rooms, many of which have four-poster beds. The sumptuous English breakfast, served in the dining room or on the veranda, is one of the biggest treats here. ⊠ *2266 Main St., 11932* ☎ *631/537–3660* ⊕ *www.bridgehamptoninn.com* ⇨ *5 rooms, 1 suite* ⚒ *Dining room, cable TV; no smoking* ⊟ *AE, MC, V* ⟲ *BP.*

$–$$$$ 🏨 **Enclave Inn.** The modern, high-tech rooms at this small inn that resembles a motel are clean, comfortable, and well equipped, with hair dryers and irons. Some of the rooms have high-speed Internet access. The inn, within walking distance of the village, has well-designed landscaping and a secluded pool. Passes to nearby beaches are available. ⊠ *2668 Montauk Hwy., 11932* ☎ *631/537–2900* 🖷 *631/537–5436* ⊕ *www.enclaveinn.com* ⇨ *10 rooms* ⚒ *Some in-room data ports, refrigerators, cable TV, pool, business services* ⊟ *AE, MC, V* ⟲ *CP May–Oct. 15.*

Sports & the Outdoors

Late in August, the Hampton Classic show grounds in Bridgehampton, about 10 minutes east of Southampton, host the **Hampton Classic Horse Show** (⊠ Snake Hollow Rd, ☎ 631/537–3177 ⊕ www.hamptonclassic. com), one of North America's most prestigious equestrian shows. Participants from around the globe compete in several events that challenge their hunter and jumper skills. Huge cash prizes are put up by Calvin Klein, David Yurman jewelers, and other deep-pocketed entities.

Shopping

Numerous antiques, clothing, and specialty shops line Main Street. Just west of town is **Bridgehampton Commons** (⊠ 2044 Montauk Hwy. ☎ 631/ 537–2174), a shopping complex that attracts people from the surrounding communities. Among the chain stores here are the Gap, Yankee Candle, Banana Republic, T. J. Maxx, Athlete's Foot, Hallmark, and Williams-Sonoma. Specialty stores include Hampton Photo Arts, Razzano's Italian Specialties, and Wild Bird Crossing, for bird lovers.

Sag Harbor

③⓪ *5 mi northeast of Bridgehampton.*

On the South Fork's north coast, Sag Harbor has a strong maritime flavor that largely stems from its history as a whaling port. The first white settlers arrived in the late 1600s, learned a thing or two about whaling from the resident Native Americans, and started sending out whaleboats in the mid-1700s. By the time the industry hit its peak in the mid-1800s, Sag Harbor had become one of the world's busiest ports.

Sag Harbor's centuries-old Main Street, lined with boutiques, galleries, and restaurants, leads to the wharf where tall ships from around the world would arrive. Today impressive sailboats and powerboats line the marina and bay. Thanks to careful preservation, much of Sag Harbor's 18th- and 19th-century architecture remains intact, including Greek-revival houses once owned by whaling captains. Also abundant are early-colonists' homes as well as Victorian houses built for wealthy industrialists.

Custom House. Henry Packer Dering, the port's first U.S. custom master, lived in this beautifully appointed 1789 Federal home that doubled as customhouse and now serves as a museum. Historical documents and period furnishings are on display. ⊠ *Garden and Main Sts.* ☎ *631/725–0250* ⊕ *www.splia.org* ⊠ *$3* ☉ *July and Aug., daily 10–5; Sept.–June, weekends 10–5.*

First Presbyterian/Old Whaler's Church. Majestic by day and mysterious by night, the 1844 Egyptian-revival church has a simple but grand design. Its original steeple soared 180 feet but was destroyed by a hurricane in the 1930s. The church cemetery contains many empty graves for sailors who perished at sea. ⊠ *44 Union St.* ☎ *631/725–0894* ⊠ *Free* ☉ *Tours by appointment.*

Foster Memorial Beach. The slightly rocky bay beach, also known as Long Beach, runs along Noyac Bay a couple of miles west of Sag Harbor and is a great spot from which to watch sunsets. In season, the beach has a snack truck, lifeguard, and restrooms. You need a nonresident daily permit, sold at the beach, for parking. ⊠ *Long Beach Rd.* ☎ *631/728–8585* ⊠ *Parking $15 (Memorial Day–Labor Day).*

Havens Beach. A walk or bike ride from the village center, this long sandy stretch of bay beach has calm waters for swimming, a swing set and playing field, and public restrooms. It's necessary to obtain a parking permit at the Sag Harbor municipal hall, at 55 Main Street. ⊠ *Off Bay St. near Hempstead St.* ☎ *631/725–0222* ⊠ *Parking $10 (Memorial Day–Labor Day).*

Morton National Wildlife Refuge. The 187-acre refuge, on a small peninsula that juts into Little Peconic and Noyac bays a few miles west of Sag Harbor, encompasses beaches and woody bluffs inhabited by terns, osprey, and wading birds as well as deer. Hiking trails vein the area. ⊠ *Noyac Rd., Noyac* ☎ *631/286–0485* ⊠ *Parking $4* ☉ *Daily ½ hr before sunrise–½ hr after sunset.*

Sag Harbor Fire Department Museum. Sag Harbor, which saw four severe blazes in the 1800s, established the first volunteer fire department in New York State. The museum, housed in an 1833 building that served as fire-company quarters as well as town hall, displays an 1890 hand-pulled hose cart, a 1920s fire chief's vehicle, model fire trucks, and other old firefighting equipment. ⊠ *Sage and Church Sts.* ☎ *631/725–0779* ⊠ *$1* ☉ *July 4–Labor Day, daily 11–4.*

Sag Harbor Whaling Museum. Noted 19th-century architect Minard Lafever designed this striking 1845 Greek-revival mansion for shipowner Benjamin Huntting and his family. Museum displays include scrimshaw pieces, a boat collection, period furnishings, and model ships. ⊠ *200 Main St.* ☎ *631/725–0770* ⊕ *www.sagharborwhalingmuseum.org* ⊑ *$3* ⊙ *Mid-May–Sept., Mon.-Sat. 10–5, Sun. 1–5; Oct.–Dec., weekends noon–4.*

Where to Stay & Eat

$$–$$$ ✕ **B. Smith's.** The world's finest yachts sit at your feet when you're on the deck of B. Smith's, on Long Wharf. The restaurant attracts crowds on sunny days and steamy nights. Seafood preparations and a raw-bar menu are mixed with a dose of Southern cooking. Be prepared for slower service when things get busy here. ⊠ *1 Bay St.* ☎ *631/725–5858* ⊟ *AE, D, MC, V* ⊙ *Closed mid-Oct.–Memorial Day.*

$$–$$$ ✕ **Il Capuccino.** Chianti bottles hang from the ceiling over tables draped in red-and-white-check cloths. Consistently good cooking and service make the three rooms of this Italian family eatery a year-round favorite. The garlic bread and the ravioli, made in-house, are the must-haves. ⊠ *30 Madison St.* ☎ *631/725–2747* ⊲ *Reservations not accepted* ⊟ *AE, DC, MC, V* ⊙ *No lunch.*

$–$$$ ✕ **Estia's Little Kitchen.** A mile outside Sag Harbor center, this roadside restaurant serves good breakfasts and lunch, as well as fresh, creative American dishes for lunch and dinner. ⊠ *1615 Bridgehampton–Sag Harbor Tpke.* ☎ *631/725–1045* ⊲ *Reservations not accepted* ⊟ *MC, V* ⊙ *Closed Mon. and Tues.*

$–$$$ ✕ **La Superica.** From the fresh lime juice in the margaritas to the fresh tuna in the tacos, the Mexican offerings here are well prepared and tasty. Traditional burritos and quesadillas are large, with many options for vegetarians. Next to the wharf, this casual eatery attracts sailors. At the large bar in back you can watch the sun set while sipping a tequila sunrise. ⊠ *Main St. and Long Island Ave.* ☎ *631/725–3388* ⊲ *Reservations not accepted* ⊟ *AE, MC, V* ⊙ *No lunch.*

$–$$$ ✕ **New Paradise Café.** You may browse the bookstore in front before walking to the restaurant in back for a cappuccino or a meal. A copper bar with tall café tables leads to a main dining room with original artwork on the walls. A covered patio is used in summer. The diverse dinner menu ranges from couscous to Tuscan-style pot roast. Sunday brunch is available all year. ⊠ *126 Main St.* ☎ *631/725–6080* ⊟ *AE, MC, V.*

$–$$$ ✕ **Sen.** An attractive, black-clad staff serves sushi and other Japanese dishes to the hip crowd that frequents this place. Sashimi and rolls of all varieties are available; vegetable, noodle, and fresh-fish dishes help fill out the menu, which includes an extensive sake list. You may encounter a wait, but the beeper system lets you be mobile. ⊠ *23 Main St.* ☎ *631/725–1774* ⊲ *Reservations not accepted* ⊟ *AE, MC, V* ⊙ *Closed Tues. No lunch Sun.–Thurs.*

$–$$ ✕ **Conca D'oro.** Large portions, down-home cooking, and reasonable prices make this a good choice for families. A casual pizza parlor in front serves slices to go, whereas the Italian restaurant in back can seat the whole gang for platters of antipasto, spaghetti and meatballs, and carafes of Chianti. ⊠ *Main St. near Washington St.* ☎ *631/725–3167* ⊲ *Reservations not accepted* ⊟ *AE, MC, V.*

$–$$ ✕ **Dockside Bar & Grill.** On the first warm day of the season, locals flock to the umbrella-shaded patio tables of this casual spot next to the American Legion Hall. Have a bowl of steamers and watch the boats head into the marina. Traditional seafood favorites such as seared scallops and fried oysters share the menu with paella and chicken potpie. Inside are two simple dining rooms and a small bar. ☒ *26 Bay St.* ☎ *631/725–7100* ⚓ *Reservations not accepted* ▭ *AE, MC, V.*

★ **$$$$**   ✕▥ **The American Hotel.** Victorian elegance defines this hotel dating from 1846. The three-story brick facade and white-pillared porch look out on Main Street. Guest rooms have turn-of-the-20th-century antiques and spacious bathrooms with fine Italian towels and bathrobes. The restaurant ($$$–$$$$) and bar inhabit four intimate antiques-filled rooms, including a front room with a piano and a bar room with a fireplace. The fare is largely French but encompasses other cuisines, so you might find sushi and sashimi, or grilled local seafood mixed with cilantro-spiked Asian noodles on the menu. The wine list runs 85 pages. The bar and lounge attract a sophisticated crowd. ☒ *Main St., 11963* ☎ *631/725–3535* ☒ *631/725–3573* ⊕ *www.theamericanhotel.com* ⌁ *8 rooms* ⚘ *Restaurant, in-room hot tubs, minibars, lounge, piano bar, no-smoking rooms; no room TVs* ▭ *AE, D, DC, MC, V* ⦿| *CP.*

$$$$ ▥ **Baron's Cove Inn.** Well suited for families, the casual and comfortable rooms here vary in size from a standard room, which can accommodate three, to a loft, which sleeps six. The rooms in back look out over the parking lot and tennis court; those in front have views of the pool and bay. Baron's Cove, which is the largest hotel in the area, is a short walk from the village center and across the street from a marina. ☒ *31 W. Water St., 11963* ☎ *631/725–2100* ☒ *631/725–2144* ⊕ *www. baronscove.com* ⌁ *66 rooms* ⚘ *Microwaves, refrigerators, cable TV, tennis court, pool, business services, meeting room, no-smoking rooms* ▭ *AE, MC, V.*

$$$$ ▥ **Sag Harbor Inn.** The two-story hotel is across from the marina and within walking distance of Main Street. Each room is simple but spacious, with a sitting area and modern pine furniture. French doors open onto patios and balconies, which look over the water in front rooms and the pool in back rooms. The breakfast room and promenade deck have harbor views. ☒ *W. Water St., 11963* ☎ *631/725–2949* ☒ *631/725–5009* ⊕ *www.sagharborinn.com* ⌁ *42 rooms* ⚘ *Dining room, cable TV, pool, meeting rooms, no-smoking rooms* ▭ *AE, MC, V* ⦿| *CP.*

Nightlife & the Arts

NIGHTLIFE   Locals and out-of-towners gather to drink to the strains of lounge music at **Cigar Bar** (☒ 2 Main St. ☎ 631/725–2575 ⊕ www. hamptonscigarbar.com), a late-night hot spot and intimate space. During the day, before things get hopping, the place serves as an Internet café. For true local flavor head for the **Corner Bar** (☒ 1 Main St. ☎ 631/725–9760). Open when everything else has closed for the night, it's ideal for a late-night snack—the burger is one of the best in town. Bands play some weekends.

THE ARTS   The regional **Bay Street Theater** (☒ Bay St. at Long Wharf ☎ 631/725–9500 ⊕ www.baystreet.org) presents new plays on their way to Broadway as well as time-honored classics. Bay Street also mounts holiday shows, comedy and musical performances, and children's programs.

Sports & the Outdoors

BOATING &
KAYAKING
Everything from kayaks to luxury yachts ply the protected bays that lead out to Long Island Sound. At the **Sag Harbor Sailing School** (⊠ Hidden Cove Marina, Noyac Rd. ☎ 631/725–5100), a sailboat rental runs from $225 for a half day to $275 for a full day, excluding the captain's fee. Two-day introductory sailing courses are offered on weekends; tuition is about $450. More-advanced courses also are available.

GOLF
The dense woods of Barcelona Neck surround the **Sag Harbor State Golf Course** (⊠ Golf Club Rd., off Rte. 114 ☎ 631/725–2503 ⊕ nysparks. state.ny.us), a 9-hole, 2,660-yard public course. Greens fees are $12–$18, and tees are on a first-come, first-served basis. The course is open all year, weather permitting, and has a clubhouse.

Shopping

Vintage and new rugs, pillows, lamp shades, and nautical prints are part of the mix at **Beach Bungalow** (⊠ 26 Main St. ☎ 631/725–4292), a stylish home-furnishings store. You can browse for favorite volumes at **Black Cat Books** (⊠ 78 Main St. ☎ 631/725–8654), a discriminating used-book store. The gleaming wood shelves at **BookHampton** (⊠ 20 Main St. ☎ 631/725–8425) are filled with contemporary and classic fiction and nonfiction, with a large section of books of local interest. **Canio's Books** (⊠ 290 Main St. ☎ 631/725–4926) carries new and used poetry, literary-fiction, art, nature, and history books as well as cookbooks. Readings and other events are regularly scheduled.

Only the finest fabrics with the highest thread counts grace the shelves of **Carriage House** (⊠ 42 Main St. ☎ 631/725–8004). A great place for a hostess gift or a treat for yourself, the boutique stocks bed and table linens, hand towels, soaps, candles, and even a smattering of fine lingerie. At **Christy's Art and Design** (⊠ 3 Madison St. ☎ 631/725–7000), housed in a Victorian, you may buy antiques as small as a vintage vase or as large as enormous fireplaces and columns. Modern tableware is also for sale here, and everything is from Europe. Indonesian crafts, penny candy, candles, and a large selection of casual women's clothes and shoes populate the eclectic but chic **Flashbacks** (⊠ 69B Main St. ☎ 631/725–9683). A working glassblowing studio, **Megna Hot Glass Studio** (⊠ 11 Bridge St. ☎ 631/725–1131) sells handmade doorknobs, lighting, sculptures, and art glass. You can watch the work in process here.

The two floors at **Paradise Books** (⊠ 126 Main St. ☎ 631/725–1114) are filled with classics, best sellers, and children's books. In back is the New Paradise Café. **Punch** (⊠ 80 Main St. ☎ 631/725–2741), a source for preppy clothes for kids, sells everything from hand-knit sweaters and brightly colored galoshes to baby bikinis. The mix of international artwork, music, and books at the **Romany Kramoris Gallery** (⊠ 41 Main St. ☎ 631/725–2499) makes for good browsing. Goods include Brazilian CDs and Indonesian jewelry. **Simpatico** (⊠ 82 Main St. ☎ 631/725–2210) is a brightly painted shoe boutique that carries name-brand sandals, dress shoes, boots, and sneakers for men and women. You can match your pairs with the purses and wallets on display.

East Hampton

31 *7 mi east of Bridgehampton, 5 mi southeast of Sag Harbor.*

Graced with ancient elm trees, majestic gray-shingled homes, and historic windmills, the village of East Hampton has evolved into a busy, expensive, and sophisticated combination of thriving summer resort and year-round community of hardworking locals and transplanted urbanites. A group of Puritan farmers and fisherfolk from Connecticut and Massachusetts settled the village in 1648, and agriculture remained its main source of livelihood until the 1800s, when the area began to develop into a fashionable resort. Cooled by Atlantic Ocean breezes, East Hampton is noted today for its lovely beaches and fine food and shopping. Its considerable wealth and the sustained effort by local government and residents to maintain East Hampton's precious heritage have combined to preserve much of the village architecture and landscape as it was during the 18th century.

East Hampton Historical Society. The society operates several local historic sites and museums, all near stately Main Street. The society's headquarters are in the circa-1740 **Osborn-Jackson House,** a period museum. The 1784 **Clinton Academy** (tours scheduled upon request) was the town's first preparatory academy for young men and women. Dating from approximately 1731, **Town House** is the only remaining town government building from colonial times. It's also the oldest surviving one-room schoolhouse on Long Island. The circa-1680 **Mulford Farm,** complete with a farmhouse and barn, hosts several wonderful programs each year, including a Colonial Kids Club, A Day in 1776, and various colonial reenactments. Each year, the farm plants Rachel's Garden with heirloom flowers and vegetables. The **Marine Museum** has three floors of exhibits devoted to East Hampton maritime history, including the eerie Shipwreck Hall. Call the society or visit the Web site for a complete list of activities at all the sites. ⊠ *101 Main St.* ☎ *631/324–6850* ⊕ *www.easthamptonhistory.org* ✉ *Marine Museum $4, other buildings free* ☉ *Osborn-Jackson House (society headquarters), daily 9–5; opening days and hours vary for other sites.*

Guild Hall Museum. Changing exhibitions at this fine-arts museum and cultural center focus on regional artists. The **John Drew Theater** presents several stage productions a year and also hosts concerts, film festivals, lectures, and readings. ⊠ *158 Main St.* ☎ *631/324–0806 or 631/324–4050* ⊕ *www.guildhall.org* ☉ *June–Labor Day, Mon.–Sat. 11–5, Sun. noon–5; rest of yr, Thurs.–Sat. 11–5, Sun. noon–5.*

"Home Sweet Home" House. This circa-1680 saltbox house was once the home of the 19th-century poet, playwright, and actor John Howard Payne, who wrote the words to "Home Sweet Home." Guided tours lead you through the collections of English ceramics, American furniture, and textiles. The museum is in a historic district, within walking distance of 19th-century windmills, including the Old Hook Mill. ⊠ *14 James La.*

☎ *631/324–0713* ✉ *$4* ☉ *May–Sept., Mon.–Sat. 10–4, Sun. 2–4; Apr., and Oct. and Nov., Fri. and Sat. 10–4, Sun. 2–4.*

★ **Long House Reserve.** The gallery, arboretum, sculpture gardens, and special programs at this 16-acre preserve all underscore the mission of Long House—to show that experiencing art and nature together is essential to living a whole and creative life. You can explore the grounds on your own or call ahead to sign up for a tour of the ever-changing gardens. The reserve also hosts evening musical performances. ⊠ *133 Hands Creek Rd., off Stephen Hands Path* ☎ *631/329–3568* ⊕ *www.longhouse.org* ✉ *$10* ☉ *Late Apr.–mid-Sept., Wed. and Sat. 2–5.*

Old Hook Mill. Built in 1806 by Nathaniel Dominy, the mill, which once ground corn and wheat, is still operational. It's a popular spot for photographs, and you can walk around inside and pick up informative brochures here. ⊠ *N. Main St.* ☎ *631/324–4150* ✉ *$2.50* ☉ *June–Aug., Mon.–Sat. 10–4, Sun. 2–4.*

Pollock-Krasner House. The house where Abstract Expressionist Jackson Pollock painted his masterpieces is now a museum and study center. You can see the paint-splattered floor of his studio, plus exhibits on Pollock and his wife and fellow artist, Lee Krasner. Call for a schedule of art exhibits, lectures, workshops, and guided tours. ⊠ *830 Fireplace Rd.* ☎ *631/324–4929* ⊕ *www.pkhouse.org* ✉ *$5* ☉ *Guided tours May–Oct. by appointment.*

Where to Stay & Eat

$$$–$$$$ ✕ **Nick and Toni's.** The dining room at this upscale, trendy restaurant has a wood-burning brick oven in which Mediterranean and northern Italian house specialties are cooked daily. Local artist Eric Fischl designed the oven's mosaic mural. Wood-roasted chicken and fish are popular, and on Sunday you can order oven-roasted pizza. There's open-air dining on the porch. ⊠ *136 N. Main St.* ☎ *631/324–3550* ♨ *Reservations essential* ▭ *AE, MC, V* ☉ *No lunch Sun.*

$$$–$$$$ ✕ **The Palm.** The Palm's old-fashioned decor fits perfectly with the building, parts of which were constructed in 1699. Usually crowded, the restaurant is well known for its aged prime beef, veal, lobster (3–6 pounds), and other kinds of seafood, as well as high prices. Side dishes are served family style. ⊠ *Hunting Inn, 94 Main St.* ☎ *631/324–0411* ♨ *Reservations essential* ▭ *AE, D, DC, MC, V* ☉ *No lunch.*

$$–$$$$ ✕ **East Hampton Point.** You can watch the sun go down over Three Mile Harbor through a wall of windows at this resort restaurant known for its fresh, creative, contemporary menu. The emphasis is on seafood, like 3-pound lobsters with roasted potatoes and corn salad or pan-seared halibut served with black olives, tomatoes, fennel, and baby artichokes. Outside tables have umbrellas for shade. ⊠ *295 Three Mile Harbor Rd.* ☎ *631/329–2800* ♨ *Reservations essential* ▭ *AE, MC, V.*

$$–$$$ ✕ **The Farmhouse.** The dining room is done up like a country farmhouse, with an antique bar and fireplaces. An extensive wine list accompanies the menu of dry-aged rib-eye steak with garlic mashed potatoes, Farmhouse chicken (a whole baby chicken on a bed of mashed potatoes), salmon with creamy risotto, and other dishes. Large parties are no problem here, and there's open-air dining on the enclosed patio or the

open courtyard. A children's menu and early-bird dinners are available. ⊠ *341 Montauk Hwy.* ☎ *631/324–8585* ▤ *AE, MC, V* ☯ *No lunch.*

$–$$$ ✕ **The Blue Parrot.** The killer margaritas complement the intensely flavored Tex-Mex food at this busy, colorful spot. Shell steak comes with jalapeño mashed potatoes; Southwestern paella is a spicy version of the popular shellfish-and-rice dish. It's on an alley off Main Street. ⊠ *33A Main St.* ☎ *631/324–3609* ▤ *AE, MC, V.*

$–$$$ ✕ **Nichols.** This cozy, wooden-antiques-filled restaurant serves good, old-fashioned, home-style food. Try the meat loaf and mashed potatoes, roast-turkey dinner, or fresh local seafood. ⊠ *100 Montauk Hwy.* ☎ *631/ 324–3939* ▤ *AE, MC, V.*

$–$$$ ✕ **Turtle Crossing.** Paintings of rodeo riders and dented old signs decorate the rustic interior of this Southwestern restaurant. The hardwood-smoked barbecue platters are laden with mouthwatering chicken, ribs, and sides. ⊠ *221 Pantigo Rd.* ☎ *631/324–7166* ⌨ *Reservations not accepted* ▤ *AE, MC, V* ☯ *Closed Dec.–Apr.*

$$$$ ✕▦ **Hedges' Inn.** With their chintz wall coverings, fluffy quilts, and wall-to-wall carpeting, the individually decorated rooms at this clapboard inn overlooking Town Pond surround you with comfort and charm. Less than ¼ mi from the beach, the inn is also within walking distance of shops, a movie theater, and restaurants. The complimentary Continental breakfast includes muffins, bagels, fruit, and Starbucks coffee. The James Lane Cafe ($$–$$$; no lunch) has family-style service and is known for its aged prime beef, lobsters, and crab cakes. Open-air dining is on a tented and screened garden terrace. A children's menu is available. ⊠ *74 James La., 11937* ☎ *631/324–7100* ⟰ *631/324–5816* ⤳ *11 rooms* ⌂ *Restaurant, business services; no room phones, no room TVs* ▤ *AE, DC, MC, V* ⍾ *CP.*

★ **$$$$** ✕▦ **Maidstone Arms Inn.** This Greek-revival inn in the center of town has been in operation since the 1870s. The front porch has wicker rocking chairs, and the garden in back is filled with rhododendrons. Antiques furnish the comfortable, individually decorated rooms. At the restaurant, the chef prepares sumptuous daily specials using fresh local seafood and produce. Breads and desserts are baked fresh daily. The Boat Bar and Bistro has a lighter menu and cocktails. There's an open-air garden, plus live music on weekends. ⊠ *207 Main St., 11937* ☎ *631/324– 5006* ⊕ *www.maidstonearms.com* ⤳ *12 rooms, 4 suites, 3 cottages* ⌂ *Restaurant, room service, some refrigerators, some in-room VCRs, bar* ▤ *AE, MC, V* ⍾ *CP.*

$$–$$$$ ✕▦ **1770 House.** Rooms at this 18th-century inn have canopy beds, fine bedding, and an eclectic collection of early-American and English antiques. Outside are a flower-bordered patio and a yard. The restaurant ($$$$) consistently earns rave reviews for its innovative and fresh approach to preparing food. Risotto includes Montauk lobster, basil, and asparagus; more fanciful is the roast loin of pork, which comes with mustard custard, brussels-sprout leaves, candied-apple preserves, and rosemary jus. ⊠ *143 Main St., 11937* ☎ *631/324–1770* ⟰ *631/324– 3504* ⊕ *www.1770house.com* ⤳ *8 rooms* ▤ *AE, MC, V* ⌂ *Restaurant, business services; no kids under 12* ⍾ *BP.*

$$$$ ▦ **Hunting Inn.** Old elms and maples surround this charming white clapboard inn, home of The Palm restaurant, in the center of town. Each room is individually furnished with reproductions of 18th-century antiques. The gardens are delightful. ⊠ *94 Main St., 11937* ☎ *631/324–0410* 🖷 *631/324–8751* ⊕ *www.thepalm.com* ↩ *19 rooms* ⚹ *Restaurant, business services* ☰ *AE, D, DC, MC, V* ⦿ *CP.*

$$$$ 🏠 **Mill House Inn.** Built in the 1790s as a classic Cape Cod cottage, this B&B has been turned into anything but typical. Each room has a fireplace and private bathroom, but from there they diverge stylistically, with influences ranging from Asian to nautical to floral. Beds, either queen or king, have feather mattresses and high-count cotton sheets that would be hard to leave if it weren't for the savory smell of the professionally cooked brunch wafting up the stairs. ⊠ *31 N. Main St., 11937* ☎ *631/324–9766* 🖷 *631/324–9793* ⊕ *www.millhouseinn.com* ↩ *8 rooms* ⚹ *Some in-room hot tubs, cable TV, in-room VCRs* ☰ *AE, DC, MC, V* ⦿ *BP.*

$$–$$$$ 🏠 **Bassett House–a Country Inn.** Within walking distance of shops and restaurants is this Victorian inn built in 1830 as a farmhouse. Trees and gardens surround the house, and eclectic antiques fill the rooms. Beds range from twin to queen-size. Two rooms have fireplaces. ⊠ *128 Montauk Hwy., 11937* ☎ *631/324–6127* 🖷 *631/324–5944* ⊕ *www.bassetthouseinn.com* ↩ *12 rooms* ⚹ *Dining room, Internet, business services, some pets allowed (fee); no TV in some rooms* ☰ *AE, D, MC, V* ⦿ *BP.*

Nightlife & the Arts

Musical and theatrical performances by local groups and celebrities alike fill the schedule at the 387-seat **John Drew Theater** (⊠ 158 Main St. ☎ 631/324–4050 ⊕ www.guildhall.org) at Guild Hall. The theater also hosts lectures and film festivals. If you make it past the velvet ropes, you can dance the night away at **NV Resort** (⊠ 44 Three Mile Harbor Rd. ☎ 631/329–6000), an opulent celebrity-studded club.

Sports & the Outdoors

For beach clothing and accessories, as well as biking, surfing, and skating gear and rentals, check out **Khanh's Sports** (⊠ 60 Park Pl. ☎ 631/324–2703).

BOWLING   You can have a good old-fashioned game of bowling at **East Hampton Bowl** (⊠ 71 Montauk Hwy. ☎ 631/324–1950). They'll even put bumpers in the gutters if you need them.

KAYAKING &   You can explore the beauty of Accabonac Harbor in a stable, easy-to-
SURFING   paddle kayak available for rent by the hour from **Kayak at Springs General Store** (⊠ 29 Old Stone Hwy., off Springs Fireplace Rd. ☎ 631/329–5065). **Main Beach Surf and Sport** (⊠ Montauk Hwy. 1 mi west of East Hampton, Wainscott ☎ 631/537–2716 ⊕ www.mainbeach.com), a premier surf, skate, and snowboard shop with great clothing and equipment, rents two- and four-person kayaks for excursions on Georgica Pond and other local bodies of water.

Shopping

East Hampton's Main Street and the perpendicular Newtown Lane are lined with upscale shops that are great for browsing. **BookHampton** (⊠ 20 Main St. ☎ 631/324–4939) is a fully stocked bookstore with a friendly and knowledgable staff, the latest releases, and a relaxing reading area upstairs. **East Coast Cowboy** (✉ 47 Newtown La. ☎ 631/329–7676) sells well-designed western-style clothing, boots, and belts. **London Jewelers** (✉ 2 Main St. ☎ 631/329–3939) has stunning and expensive jewelry and watches. The **Polo Country Store** (✉ 31–33 Main St. ☎ 631/324–1222) sells Ralph Lauren's classic clothes and accessories. **Steph's Stuff** (✉ 38 Newtown La. ☎ 631/329–2943) has a mind-boggling and absolutely delightful assortment of toys and other whimsical goodies for kids.

Amagansett

3 mi east of East Hampton.

Amagansett takes its name from a Native American word meaning "place of good water." From the very beginning, the town's tranquil setting was perfectly suited to fishing and offshore whaling. Downtown Main Street has retained many of its original buildings as private residences, shops, B&Bs, and good restaurants. There's also a small outlet center on the village green.

Atlantic Avenue Beach. The beach is convenient to the center of Amagansett, and there are food concessions right on the sand, making it possible to stay all day. Lifeguards are on duty daily 10–5 from Memorial Day through Labor Day. An East Hampton parking permit is required on weekends and holidays, but during the week you can pay to park without a permit. ✉ *South end of Atlantic Ave. off Bluff Rd.* ☎ *631/ 324–2417* 🅿 *Parking $10 (weekdays; parking permit required weekends and holidays).*

Miss Amelia's Cottage and Roy Lester Carriage Museum. Built in 1725 and full of beautifully preserved colonial antiques—including a collection of rare Dominy furniture—the museum contains artifacts and exhibits illustrating Amagansett life from the colonial period through the 20th century. On summer weekends, pony rides are given on the museum lawn from 10 to 2, and twice during the season there are huge antiques sales full of local treasures. In a barn to the rear of the property is the Roy Lester Carriage Museum, which displays locally made horse-drawn carriages. ✉ *Main St.* ☎ *631/267–3020* 🅿 *Museum $2, pony rides $5* ⏱ *Late May–early Sept., Fri.–Sun. 10–4.*

Where to Stay & Eat

$–$$$ ✕ **Estia.** The talented chef uses only the finest organic ingredients to create sumptuous, mouthwatering meals. The pasta dishes and entrées change according to what ingredients are available, but you can't go wrong with potato-crusted flounder, barbecued salmon, and pulled-pork tacos. ✉ *177 Main St.* ☎ *631/267–6320* 🍴 *MC, V* ⏱ *No dinner Mon.–Wed. mid-Sept.–early May.*

$–$$$ ✕ **Napeague Stretch.** You might feel as if you are standing on the deck of a fabulous yacht inside this sleek restaurant with gleaming wooden floors and teak and white-canvas accents. The three-sided bar serves infused cocktails such as fresh strawberry margaritas and pineapple-rum punch. Everything about this restaurant is fresh, from the baby-spinach

salad and the sesame-crusted tuna to the exquisite lobster salad, bouillabaisse, and steaks. Attentive service and an outdoor terrace with stunning northeast views round out your experience. ⊠ *2095 Montauk
Hwy.* ☎ *631/267–6980* ⊟ *AE, MC, V* ☉ *Closed Nov.–Mar.*

★ **$–$$** ✕**Lobster Roll.** Set along the no-man's-land between Amagansett and Mon-
tauk, this local institution (affectionately known as "Lunch") is the prover-
bial shanty by the sea. Its booths and outdoor picnic tables are filled
with people coming and going from the beach. They come for the fresh
lobster rolls, fish-and-chips, puffers (blowfish), and mouthwatering
grilled tuna and swordfish. ⊠ *1980 Montauk Hwy.* ☎ *631/267–3740*
⊟ *MC, V* ☉ *Closed Nov.–Apr.*

$$$–$$$$ 🏨 **Sea Crest on the Ocean.** Many of the one- and two-bedroom units at
this family-friendly resort have direct beach access. Accommodations,
furnished in neutral tones, are bright and airy and have dinette sets. The
two-bedroom units are especially large. Barbecue pits allow you to grill
near the dunes. ⊠ *2166 Montauk Hwy., 11930* ☎ *631/267–3159*
🖷 *631/267–6840* ⊕ *www.duneresorts.com* ➥ *60 suites, 6 studios*
 ⟐ *Picnic area, some kitchens, some kitchenettes, cable TV, 2 tennis courts,
pool, beach, basketball, shuffleboard, laundry facilities, business services,
no-smoking rooms* ⊟ *D, MC, V.*

$$–$$$$ 🏨 **White Sands Resort Hotel.** The beach is steps away from this peaceful
seaside hotel nestled between open ocean and gorgeous flower gardens.
Uncluttered, simple rooms have private decks and lounge chairs; all have
views of the ocean. ⊠ *28 Shore Rd., 11930* ☎ *631/267–3350* 🖷 *631/
267–2728* ⊕ *www.whitesands-resort.com* ➥ *20 rooms* ⟐ *Fans, some
kitchens, refrigerators, cable TV, beach; no smoking* ⊟ *MC, V* ☉ *Closed
mid-Oct.–mid-Apr.*

$–$$$ 🏨 **Mill Garth Country Inn.** This two-story antiques-filled B&B is a mile
from the beach and within walking distance of Amagansett restaurants
and shops. Suites in the main house have living rooms and kitchenettes,
and additional lodging is available in charming separate cottages. There's
a lovely terrace, and guests receive complimentary beach-parking passes.
⊠ *23 Windmill La., 11930* ☎ *631/267–3757* ➥ *2 rooms, 4 suites, 5
cottages* ⟐ *Picnic area, some kitchenettes; no phones in some rooms,
no TV in some rooms, no smoking* ⊟ *MC, V.*

Nightlife & the Arts

You can hear live rock, jazz, and blues music, including many well-known
acts, nearly every summer night and most off-season weekend nights
★ at the **Stephen Talkhouse** (⊠ 161 Main St. ☎ 631/267–3117 ⊕ www.
stephentalkhouse.com). With two bars, a small stage, and a dance
floor, it's usually a laid-back scene, but the place can get packed on the
weekends. Cover charges start at around $20. Doors open one hour
before showtime.

Shopping

Beneath the 200-year-old elm and chestnut trees at **Amagansett Square**
(⊠ 154 Main St. ☎ 631/267–6200) are clothing, shoe, flower, and gift
shops. **Lume** (⊠ 167 Main St. ☎ 631/267–7551) sells one-of-a-kind
jewelry, candles, home accents, and gift items. **Outdoors of Amagansett**
(⊠ 171 Main St. ☎ 631/267–3620) has just the sort of country cloth-
ing and footwear you might need for your visit to the Hamptons.

Montauk

 12 mi east of Amagansett.

Twelve long miles of windswept road, aptly named the Napeague Stretch, separate Montauk from the Hamptons, and as you roll into the small seaside village it becomes immediately apparent that here is a place apart in other respects as well. Surrounded by water on three sides, Montauk is known for its distinct natural beauty. The spectacular undeveloped beaches and parks attract surfers and hikers, and the waters are superb for fishing.

Continue east past the village center and you arrive at land's end, where the Montauk Lighthouse, commissioned by President George Washington in 1792 and the oldest operating lighthouse in the state, perches on a rocky bluff overlooking the wild surf and craggy coastline of Montauk Point State Park.

More than 50 hotels, inns, and guesthouses, along with top-notch restaurants and shops, are concentrated in two distinct sections of Montauk—the village center, including Old Montauk Highway, and the harbor area, which is home to the local fishing fleet as well as dozens of party, charter, and whale-watching boats.

Fort Pond Bay Park. Sitting at the western end of Fort Pond Bay, near Rocky Point, this park is perfect for picnics and beachcombing, but not suitable for swimming. You can comb the shore for shells or walk to the end of the sturdy pier and do some fishing. There are shorefront trails that tie into the Hither Woods trail system, a parking lot (follow Navy Road to the end), and portable bathrooms. A resident permit is required for parking. ⊠ *End of Navy Rd., off 2nd House Rd.* ☢ *Free* ☉ *Daily dawn–dusk.*

Gin Beach. On Block Island Sound, this beach east of the jetty has calm water and sparkling clean sand—perfect for families with little ones. You can watch the boats go in and out of the harbor all day. There are public restrooms, a snack trailer, and outdoor showers. Lifeguards are on duty Memorial Day to early September (weekends only from May to late June and after Labor Day). A resident permit is required for parking. ⊠ *End of East Lake Dr., off Montauk Hwy.* ☎ *631/324-2417* ☢ *Free (resident pass required for parking).*

Hither Hills State Park. This 1,755-acre park, with rolling moors and forests of pitch pine and scrub oak, encompasses a campground, picnic areas, a playground, general store, miles of ocean beach, and hiking and bicycling trails. An unusual natural phenomenon in the park is known as the Walking Dunes, so named because strong northwest winds cause the 80-foot dunes to travel 3 or more feet per year. The ¾-mi loop through cranberry bogs, beaches, and pine forests submerged in sand is not too far for little feet to travel, and most people find the natural lore of the area fascinating. Pick up the descriptive brochure, which includes trail maps, at the park office or the chamber of commerce before you set out. ⊠ *Old Montauk Hwy.* ☎ *631/668-2554, 800/456-2267 camping reservations* ⊕ *nysparks.state.ny.us* ☢ *Parking $8 (late May–early Sept.)* ☉ *Daily dawn–dusk.*

Kirk Park Beach. This sandy, clean, protected ocean beach has a picnic area across the street; public restrooms are in the parking lot. Lifeguards are on duty Memorial Day weekend through late September (weekends only from late May to June 20 and Labor Day to the end of the season). ✉ *Montauk Hwy. near IGA supermarket* ☎ *631/324–2417* 🚗 *Parking $10 (Memorial Day weekend–late Sept.)* ☉ *Daily dawn–dusk.*

Montauk Downs State Park. An 18-hole Robert Trent Jones–designed championship-length golf course is the main draw at this park. The park also has six well-maintained Har-Tru tennis courts ($16 per hour on weekends), a locker room, showers, a pro shop, a snack bar, a restaurant, a children's pool, and a large, sparkling recreational pool surrounded by comfortable lounge chairs. ✉ *50 S. Fairview Ave.* ☎ *631/668–3781* ⊕ *nysparks.state.ny.us* 🚗 *Park free, pool $3.50* ☉ *Daily dawn–dusk.*

Montauk Point State Park. About 6 mi east of the village, the 724 acres of rocky shoreline, grassy dunes, and bayberry-covered moors surrounding Montauk's lighthouse have been so well protected that you might feel as if you're standing at an undiscovered frontier of pounding surf and pristine land. Frequently, a wild riptide (this is not a swimming beach) sets up perfect conditions for exciting surf casting. This is one of the best spots in Montauk to try your luck at catching the "big one." A fishing permit isn't necessary. Other activities include hiking (trail maps are available at the information booth), bird-watching, and beachcombing. Every weekend from early December to late April, weather permitting, naturalists lead two- to three-hour **Guided Seal Walks** (☎ 631/668–5000) in Montauk Point State Park. Hikers are guided to the haul-out sites along the north beach to observe seals and winter birds, and to learn about marine geology. Tours are $5, call for tour times.

The **Montauk Lighthouse** (☎ 631/668–2544 ⊕ www.montauklighthouse. com), the oldest lighthouse still in operation in the state and a well-known Long Island landmark, is perched solidly on a bluff in Montauk Point State Park. President George Washington signed an order to build the lighthouse in 1792. Climb the 137 iron steps to the top for spectacular views of the Atlantic Ocean and, to the northeast, Block Island, or take a moment to ponder the touching memorial to local fishermen lost at sea. The museum, in the former lightkeeper's quarters, displays a wealth of photos and artifacts. ✉ *East end of Rte. 27* ☎ *631/668–3781* ⊕ *nysparks.state.ny.us* 🚗 *Parking $6* ☉ *Park daily dawn–dusk. Lighthouse Mar.–late May and mid-Oct.–Nov., weekends 10:30–4:30; late May–early Sept., daily 10:30–6; early Sept.–mid-Oct., weekdays 10:30–4:30, weekends 10:30–5.*

Montauk Trolley. This old-fashioned trolley traverses the sights of Montauk—the village, the lighthouse, the harbor, and several parks—on 90-minute tours from Memorial Day weekend through Columbus Day. The friendly tour director answers questions and gives interesting observations. Same-day-ticket holders are allowed all-day boarding privileges (15 stops), which makes this a great way to get around. Pick up a map and schedule at the chamber of commerce or at any of several businesses in town. Tours begin at the chamber of commerce. ✉ *Main St. across* *from village green* ☎ *631/668–6868* ⊕ *www.montaukchamber.com* ☞ *$15.*

⏱ **Puff and Putt Family Fun Center.** On a narrow strip of land between Montauk Highway and sparkling Fort Pond, this complex encompasses a miniature-golf course, video game room, and boat-rental center. Boats for hire include Sunfish, pedal boats, canoes, rowboats, and kayaks. The waters of Fort Pond are usually quite calm, and sightings of local waterfowl are common. ⊠ *Montauk Hwy. across from IGA supermarket* ☎ *631/668–4473* ☜ *Miniature golf $5, boat rentals $13–$22* ⊙ *July and Aug., daily; Sept.–June, weekends. Hrs vary; call for details.*

Second House Museum. The second house built in Montauk, this 1700s farmhouse holds a collection of early photos and artifacts that depict the era when it was surrounded by pastures, sheep, and cattle. Now enveloped by gorgeous lawns, rose gardens, and hydrangeas, it is the site of daily tours and two well-attended summer crafts fairs. ⊠ *Montauk Hwy. at 2nd House Rd.* ☎ *631/668–5340* ☜ *$2* ⊙ *Memorial Day–Columbus Day, Thurs.–Tues. 10–4.*

Shadmoor State Park. With 99 acres of steep bluffs, sand beach, rare plants, and hiking trails, this gem of a park is a quiet place to walk, think, and take in the view. Parking is at the entrance, just east of Montauk center on Montauk Highway (look for the sign). ⊠ *Montauk Hwy. east of Montauk center* ☎ *631/324–2417* ☜ *Free* ⊙ *Daily dawn–dusk.*

Theodore Roosevelt County Park. Miles of hiking and horseback-riding trails vein this 1,126-acre park, which also includes an exhibit about the Spanish-American War. At the close of the war in Cuba, Teddy Roosevelt and his band of Roughriders and 28,000 soldiers came to this site for a long season of rest and recovery after their ordeal. The museum is a memorial to their courage and tenacity. The gift shop sells related books and souvenirs. In July and August, the annual Hamptons Shakespeare Festival takes place in the park. Activities at the park include fishing, outer-beach camping (self-contained trailers only), picnicking, and bird-watching. ⊠ *Off Montauk Hwy. 3 mi east of Montauk village* ☎ *631/852–7878* ☜ *Free* ⊙ *Park daily dawn–dusk, museum daily 10–5.*

Where to Stay & Eat

Most lodgings and eateries here are family-friendly, and you can leave your heels and neckties at home.

★ **$$$–$$$$** ✕ **Harvest on Fort Pond.** The glass-enclosed dining room of this seafood restaurant affords stunning views of sunsets on Fort Pond. There's family-style service—entrées are huge and serve at least two. Try the calamari salad and the sizzling whole red snapper. You can dine outside in the herb garden in summer. ⊠ *11 S. Emory St.* ☎ *631/668–5574* ⌂ *Reservations essential* ⊟ *AE, MC, V.*

$$–$$$$ ✕ **East by Northeast.** Earth tones and Asian accents decorate this sophisticated and soothing restaurant. Entrées are served family-style. Try the crisp duck tacos or the seared sesame tuna as you settle back into comfortable chairs or banquettes and watch the sun set over Fort Pond. The service is attentive, the bar cosmopolitan. ⊠ *51 Edgemere St.* ☎ *631/668–2872* ⌂ *Reservations essential* ⊟ *AE, MC, V.*

$$–$$$ ✕ **Dave's Grill.** Unpretentious yet stylish, Dave's is at the Montauk fishing docks next to Salivar's. Indoor seating is in a small, candlelit room or around a cozy adjoining bar; outdoor seating is on a deck next to the harbor. Come for succulent steaks and contemporary dishes prepared with fresh local seafood. This is a popular spot with locals, and there's always a wait for a table. ⊠ *468 W. Lake Dr.* ☎ *631/668–9190* ⚑ *Reservations not accepted* ▭ *MC, V* ⊘ *Closed Nov.–Apr. No lunch.*

★ $$–$$$ ✕ **Shagwong Tavern.** The specials at this local hangout next to Herb's Market change daily, but are straightforward, well-prepared dishes such as cedar-planked salmon, beer-battered fish-and-chips, and chicken saltimbocca. The bar scene makes the wait for a table on weekends bearable. ⊠ *774 Main St.* ☎ *631/668–3050* ⚑ *Reservations not accepted* ▭ *AE, D, DC, MC, V.*

$–$$$ ✕ **Inlet Cafe at Gosman's Dock.** The view from the waterside tables and sushi bar is so mesmerizing that you may forget to bite into the sushi or succulent local lobster on your plate. There are four Gosman's eating establishments on the dock; this one serves fresh seafood right off the boat. ⊠ *Gosman's Dock, Montauk Harbor* ☎ *631/668–2549* ⚑ *Reservations not accepted* ▭ *AE, MC, V* ⊘ *Closed mid-Oct.–mid-May.*

$–$$ ✕ **The Dock.** Seafaring-related antiques festoon the rustic wood walls and ceiling of Montauk's favorite dockside restaurant. Great nachos, burgers, fish sandwiches, specials, and a cozy, local bar scene are hallmarks here. ⊠ *Montauk Harbor near the town dock* ☎ *631/668–9778* ⚑ *Reservations not accepted* ▭ *No credit cards* ⊘ *Closed Dec.–Mar.*

$–$$ ✕ **Salivar's.** This dockside eatery serves classic diner food with a lot of local flavor. You can have breakfast with local fisherfolk at 4 AM, grab a bite of lunch while you watch the boats sail in and out of the harbor, or stop by in the evening for an ice-cold beer under the watchful eye of the biggest great white shark ever caught (4,500 pounds). ⊠ *470 W. Lake Dr.* ☎ *631/668–2555* ⚑ *Reservations not accepted* ▭ *No credit cards* ⊘ *No dinner Nov.–Apr.*

¢–$$ ✕ **Gianni's.** The best brick-oven pizza and focaccia sandwiches in Montauk are served here. Try one of the special salads; Margherita pizza, with basil and garlic; "grandma" pizza, a square, thin-crust pizza with fresh mozzarella, plum-tomato sauce, and basil; or Sicilian pizza, with caramelized onions and sausage. There's no seating here, only takeout and delivery. ⊠ *54 S. Erie Ave.* ☎ *631/668–8888* ▭ *No credit cards.*

¢–$ ✕ **John's Pancake House.** Omelets and delicious pancakes are served all day at this bustling Main Street restaurant, along with hearty homemade soups and chowders, thick burgers and shakes, spicy chicken-salad wraps, and fried ice cream. Come at off-hours especially on weekends, because there's always a line. Breakfast begins at 6:15. ⊠ *Main St.* ☎ *631/668–2383* ⚑ *Reservations not accepted* ▭ *No credit cards* ⊘ *No dinner.*

¢–$ ✕ **Joni's.** This casual spot serves good coffee, salads, rejuvenating fresh-squeezed juices and smoothies, daily breakfast and lunch specials, and exotic wraps such as the Zen Rabbit, with mixed greens, avocado, goat cheese, tomato, onion, and calamata olives on a spinach tortilla. Eat at the outdoor picnic tables or bring your meal to the beach or hotel. ⊠ *9 S. Edison St.* ☎ *631/668–3663* ⚑ *Reservations not accepted* ▭ *MC, V.*

$$$$ ▣ **Beachcomber Resort.** The four two-story buildings that make up this airy, modern resort overlook the ocean and are right across from the beach. Studio and apartment-style suites are clean and comfortable, with contemporary furnishings. Complimentary beach stickers are provided. ⊠ 727 *Old Montauk Hwy., 11954* ☎ *631/668–2894* 🖷 *631/668–3154* ⊕ *www.beachcomber-montauk.com* 🛏 *88 suites* ♨ *Kitchenettes, cable TV, in-room VCRs, tennis court, pool, sauna, beach, laundry facilities, business services, no-smoking rooms* ⊘ *Closed Nov.–Mar.* ▤ *AE, D, DC, MC, V.*

$$$$ ▣ **Gurney's Inn Resort and Spa.** Long popular for its fabulous location on a bluff overlooking 1,000 feet of private ocean beach, Gurney's has become even more famous in recent years for its European-style spa. The large, luxurious rooms and suites all have ocean views. ⊠ *290 Old Montauk Hwy., 11954* ☎ *631/668–2345* 🖷 *631/668–3576* ⊕ *www.gurneys-inn.com* 🛏 *100 rooms, 4 suites, 5 cottages* ♨ *2 restaurants, room service, refrigerators, cable TV, pool, health club, hair salon, hot tub, sauna, spa, steam room, beach, bar, business services, no-smoking rooms* ▤ *AE, D, DC, MC, V* ❙❙❙ *MAP.*

$$$–$$$$ ▣ **Hartman's Briney Breezes Motel.** This two-story motel is steps from the dunes and the beach, just across the two-lane Old Montauk Highway. The bright, clean, one- and two-room suites have full kitchens and ocean views. You can walk the seaside path to town and restaurants. Beach passes are provided. ⊠ *693 Old Montauk Hwy., 11954* ☎ *631/668–2290* 🖷 *631/668–2987* ⊕ *www.brineybreezes.com* 🛏 *18 studios, 64 suites* ♨ *Kitchens, microwaves, refrigerators, cable TV, pool, no-smoking rooms* ▤ *MC, V* ⊘ *Closed mid-Nov.–early Mar.*

★ **$$$–$$$$** ▣ **Montauk Manor.** The sprawling, family-friendly "American castle" has views of the bay and myriad amenities. The Tudor-style Manor, built in 1927 as a luxury resort, today is a condominium, so each unit is decorated differently. Most units are bright and have contemporary furnishings; some have loft bedrooms with skylights, patios, or balconies. Jitneys take you to the beaches, and beach passes are available. The restaurant, Breakwater Café, offers New American fare accented with Japanese dishes and flavors. ⊠ *236 Edgemere St., 11954* ☎ *631/668–4400* 🖷 *631/668–3535* ⊕ *www.montaukmanor.com* 🛏 *18 studios, 81 suites* ♨ *Restaurant, picnic area, cable TV, putting green, 3 tennis courts, 2 pools (1 indoor), gym, hot tub, sauna, basketball, boccie, shuffleboard, squash, meeting rooms, no-smoking rooms* ▤ *AE, D, DC, MC, V.*

$$$–$$$$ ▣ **Surf Club.** A cluster of low, gray-shingled buildings with one- and two-bedroom duplex apartments sits on 8½ beachfront acres within walking distance of the village. Each unit has a large, private terrace. The apartments are spacious and fully carpeted and have contemporary furnishings. ⊠ *Surfside Ave. and S. Essex St.* ✑ *Box 1174, 11954* ☎ *631/668–3800* ⊕ *www.duneresorts.com* 🛏 *92 apartments* ♨ *Kitchenettes, cable TV, some in-room VCRs, tennis court, pool, sauna, beach, no-smoking rooms* ▤ *MC, V* ⊘ *Closed mid-Nov.–mid-Apr.*

$$–$$$$ ▣ **Burcliffe by the Sea.** Peace and quiet are the hallmarks of this beautifully landscaped property only 1 mi from town and right across from the beach. The small inn has studio efficiencies with alcove bedrooms and one- and two-bedroom cottages; some units have ocean views and three have fireplaces. Beach permits are provided. ⊠ *397 Old Montauk*

Hwy., 11954 ☎ *631/668–2880* ⊕ *www.montauklife.com* ➭ *4 efficiencies, 3 cottages* ⚘ *Picnic area, kitchenettes, cable TV, beach, some pets allowed, no-smoking rooms* ⊟ *MC, V.*

$$–$$$$ 🏨 **Montauk Yacht Club, Resort and Marina.** The plush resort on Star Island, in Montauk Harbor, has its own mini-replica of the Montauk Lighthouse as well as a 232-slip marina. Rooms, contemporary and bright, have floor-to-ceiling windows and private terraces. The waterfront villas contain 23 oversize rooms. ✉ *32 Star Island Rd., 11954* ☎ *631/ 668–3100, 800/832–4200 in NY* 🖷 *631/668–6181* ⊕ *www. montaukyachtclub.com* ➭ *107 rooms* ⚘ *2 restaurants, room service, in-room data ports, cable TV, 3 tennis courts, 3 pools (1 indoor), health club, spa, boating, marina, 2 bars, business services, no-smoking rooms* ⊟ *AE, DC, MC, V* ⊗ *Closed mid-Dec.–early Mar.*

$$–$$$$ 🏨 **Panoramic View.** Tucked into a treed hillside that rises directly from the beach, this hotel complex has landscaped lawns and flower gardens. In the wood-paneled, carpeted guest rooms, picture windows frame the ocean views. The beach houses have wood floors, a fireplace, a porch and patio, and two bathrooms. ✉ *272 Old Montauk Hwy., 11954* ☎ *631/668–3000* 🖷 *631/668–7870* ⊕ *www.panoramicview.com* ➭ *101 rooms, 14 suites, 3 beach houses* ⚘ *In-room data ports, kitchenettes, refrigerators, cable TV, pool, gym, beach, laundry facilities, business services, no-smoking rooms; no kids under 10* ⊟ *No credit cards* ⊗ *Closed mid-Nov.–mid-Apr.*

$$$ 🏨 **Wavecrest Resort.** This modern complex was built on a rise so that each room would have an ocean view from its private terrace. Rooms are carpeted and have wood furniture. The resort is popular with couples and families because of its beach access and proximity to Hither Hills State Park. ✉ *Old Montauk Hwy., Box 952, 11954* ☎ *631/ 668–2141* 🖷 *631/668–2337* ⊕ *www.wavecrestonocean.com* ➭ *65 rooms* ⚘ *Picnic area, kitchenettes, cable TV, in-room VCRs, indoor pool, beach, no-smoking rooms* ⊟ *AE, D, MC, V* ⊗ *Closed mid-Nov.–mid-Apr.*

$$–$$$ 🏨 **Ocean Resort Inn.** Hanging baskets of flowers and picnic tables on the deck invite you to relax and enjoy the surroundings at this in-town two-story inn, a half block from the ocean. Some rooms have whirlpool baths and more than one bathroom; all are well maintained and clean. Complimentary beach permits are available. ✉ *95 S. Embassy St., 11954* ☎ *631/668–2300* 🖷 *631/668–4075* ⊕ *www.oceanresortinn.com* ➭ *17 rooms* ⚘ *Picnic area, some in-room hot tubs, microwaves, refrigerators, cable TV, no-smoking rooms* ⊟ *AE, MC, V* ⊗ *Closed Nov.–early Mar.*

$–$$ 🏨 **Sunrise Guest House.** Small and romantic, this country home by the sea has an old-fashioned porch with rockers overlooking the ocean. Tables are garnished with wildflowers, and there's an outdoor hot tub. The common living-dining area has a fireplace. Rooms have hardwood floors and are done in soft vintage-floral prints. ✉ *681 Old Montauk Hwy., 11954* ☎ *631/668–7286* ⊕ *www.sunrisebnb.com* ➭ *4 rooms* ⚘ *Dining room, cable TV, outdoor hot tub; no kids under 12, no smoking* ⊟ *MC, V* ⦿ *CP.*

¢–$$ 🏨 **Culloden House Motel.** The modern accommodations at this motel, a three-minute walk from famous Gosman's Dock and the Harbor area, are sparkling clean and reasonably priced. Barbecues are on-site, and beach passes are available. ✉ *540 W. Lake Dr., 11954* ☎ *631/668–9293* ☏ *631/668–3228* ⊕ *www.montauklife.com* ⇥ *29 rooms* ♦ *Some kitchenettes, refrigerators, cable TV, no-smoking rooms* ▤ *AE, MC, V* ⊘ *Closed late Oct.–mid-May.*

CAMPING ⚠ **Hither Hills State Park.** The campsites in this popular park are just off
¢ a gorgeous, protected beach. They book up quickly, sometimes nearly a year in advance. The campground has a softball field and daily planned activities for the kids. The park has basketball, volleyball, tetherball, sportfishing, and hiking and biking trails. ✉ *Old Montauk Hwy., 11937* ☎ *631/668–2554 or 800/456–2267* ⊕ *www.reserveamerica.com* ⇥ *165 sites* ♦ *Flush toilets, dump station, guest laundry, showers, picnic tables, public telephone, general store, play area* ⚓ *Reservations essential* ▤ *MC, V* ⊘ *Closed mid-Nov.–mid-Apr.*

Sports & the Outdoors

FISHING Excellent surf casting (at Montauk Point or along the ocean beaches) and inshore or offshore trips on party and charter boats make Montauk one of the premier fishing destinations on the East Coast. A trip to the chamber of commerce on Main Street or to the Harbor area (off West Lake Drive) yields the information you need to choose from the many fishing options.

For summer trips, make reservations in advance.

Breakaway (✉ Montauk Harbor ☎ 631/668–2914), a 42-foot Downeaster, can take up to six people inshore fishing for striped bass and fluke, or offshore for tuna and shark. Half-day fishing for up to 40 people takes place on **Lazy Bones** (✉ Montauk Harbor ☎ 631/668–5671), a popular party boat. You might catch flounder, fluke, striped bass, or bluefish, depending on the season. Choose from deep-sea fishing or a half-day inshore haul for bass and bluefish on the **Oh Brother** (✉ Montauk Harbor ☎ 631/668–2707), which welcomes families. **Viking Fleet** (✉ Montauk Harbor ☎ 631/668–5700 ⊕ www.vikingfleet.com) offers half- or full-day offshore or night-fishing trips aboard its party boats.

Freddie's Bait and Tackle (✉ S. Edgemere St. south of The Plaza ☎ 631/668–5520 ⊕ www.freddiesofmontauk.com) sells lures, hooks and tackle, and fresh and frozen bait. You can also have your rod or reel repaired here. **Johnny's Tackle Shop** (✉ Montauk Hwy. ☎ 631/668–2940) is the place to go for custom-designed rods, excellent surf-casting advice, and a complete selection of fishing tackle. **Montauk Sportfishing** (☎ 631/668–2019 or 800/280–5565 Captain Gene Kelly ⊕ www.montauksportfishing.com) lists tide tables, fishing reports, marinas, charter boats, tackle shops, and other information. **Star Island Yacht Club** (✉ Star Island Rd. ☎ 631/668–5052 ⊕ www.starislandyc.com) includes a marina, yacht club, restaurant, and the East End's largest nautical store, which is filled with bait and tackle, clothing, footwear, and supplies. Star Island hosts Montauk's famous shark tournaments in summer.

GOLF The 18-hole, par-72, Robert Trent Jones–designed golf course at **Mon-**
★ **tauk Downs State Park** (✉ 50 S. Fairview Ave. ☎ 631/668–5000, 631/668–1234 reservations) is one of the top public courses in the nation.

Club and cart rentals, instruction, a driving range, a putting green, and a restaurant are available. Greens fees are $30–$36 for New York residents and $60–$72 for nonresidents. Call at least a week in advance in summer to reserve tee times. The Downs is off West Lake Drive, near the harbor.

HIKING Miles of hiking trails meander through peaceful, beautiful **Hither Hills State Park** (⊠ Old Montauk Hwy. ☎ 631/668–2554 ⊕ nysparks.state.ny.us). On the western edge of the park you can wander the Walking Dunes trail, a ¾-mi loop through some of the most interesting local ecology around. At the eastern edge, the trails connect to Fort Pond Bay Park. Pick up a map at the campground office before you go. **Montauk Point State Park** (⊠ Montauk Point, at end of Rte. 27 ☎ 631/668–3781 ⊕ nysparks.state. ny.us), a 724-acre preserve with miles of trails, surrounds Montauk Lighthouse. The northern paths lead you through the woods or along the rocky beach to the seal haul-out sites; the southern paths lead through the moors and along the bluffs for spectacular ocean views.

HORSEBACK RIDING Established in 1658, **Deep Hollow Ranch** (⊠ Montauk Hwy. across from Theodore Roosevelt County Park ☎ 631/668–2744 ⊕ www. deephollowranch.com) claims to be the oldest working cattle ranch in the country. The sunset beach rides are unforgettable, as are the trail rides through Theodore Roosevelt County Park, across the road. Pony rides keep little ones occupied. English and Western riding lessons, outdoor barbecue dinners and bonfires, wagon tours, and historical reenactments are among the special things to do and see here.

SURFING ★ If you want to surf in Montauk, head for **Ditch Plains** (⊠ Ditch Plains Rd.). It's an insider's spot, but the locals welcome newcomers who have a modicum of surfing etiquette. You can grab a wrap sandwich or an iced coffee at Lily's Ditch Witch wagon. You need a town parking permit or temporary beach sticker to park here. Take Montauk Highway east through town, make a right on Ditch Plains Road, and follow it to the beach.

The **Air and Speed Board Shop** (⊠ 7 The Plaza ☎ 631/668–0356) offers group and private surfing lessons. The shop also sells surfing, snowboarding, and skateboarding equipment, plus the latest in clothing and accessories. **Plaza Sports** (⊠ 716 Main St. ☎ 631/668–9300) sells surfing equipment as well as biking paraphernalia, outdoor toys, and beach and sportswear.

Shopping

Downtown Montauk has an eclectic mix of shops that sell books, clothing, jewelry, antiques, home furnishings, and gifts. At a similar but more limited grouping of shops in the harbor area, you can find Irish knits, pricier clothing shops, and a great toy store.

At Home en Provence (⊠ 625 Tuthill Rd., Fort Pond Bay ☎ 631/668–4808) carries European-style home accessories, quilts, clothing, jewelry, and linens. The small, charming, and friendly **Book Shoppe** (⊠ The Plaza South ☎ 631/668–4599) has a good selection of books in all categories, including new releases. The harborside **Captain Kid Toys** (⊠ Gosman's Dock, Montauk Harbor ☎ 631/668–4482) brims with fabulous toys, colorful trinkets, and artistic and educational kits. **Seagrass Cove** (✉ Edgemere St. ☎ 631/668–8886) sells handmade one-of-a-kind jewelry, along with antique furniture and other unusual items. Walk into **Strawberry Fields Flowers and Gifts** (✉ Main St. ☎ 631/668–6279) and your senses are filled with the fragrance of flowers and spice and a riot of color. Flowers, baskets, plants, unusual gifts, candles, and wrought-iron wall hangings are just the beginning. The talented owner of **Willow** (✉ 41 The Plaza ☎ 631/668–0772) designs and sews beautifully crafted quilts, as well as outfits for American Girl dolls. The assortment of unusual gifts includes garden ornaments, linens, stationery, and candles.

LONG ISLAND A TO Z

To research prices, get advice from other travelers, and book travel arrangements, visit www.fodors.com.

AIR TRAVEL

Long Island is served by LaGuardia Airport and John F. Kennedy International Airport, both in the New York City borough of Queens, as well as by the smaller but more centrally located Long Island MacArthur Airport. American Eagle, Atlantic Southeast, Comair, Continental, Delta, Southwest Airlines, and US Airways fly into MacArthur. *See* Air Travel *in* Smart Travel Tips A to Z for more information about LaGuardia and JFK airports, as well as for airline contact information.

🛪 Airports **Long Island MacArthur Airport (ISP)** ✉ 100 Arrivals Ave., Ronkonkoma ☎ 631/467–3210 ⊕ www.macarthurairport.com.

BOAT & FERRY TRAVEL

FIRE ISLAND   Three passenger ferries service Fire Island. The Sayville Ferry Service shuttles from Sayville to Cherry Grove, the Pines, and Sailor's Haven. Fire Island Ferries links Bay Shore, on the mainland, with eight Fire Island communities, including Fair Harbor, Kismet, Ocean Bay Park, Ocean Beach, Saltaire, and Seaview. Davis Park Ferry runs from Patchogue to Watch Hill. The services offer long-term parking (from $7 a weekday to $38 a weekend) on the mainland side. Round trips are $10–$12.50, depending on your destination.

SHELTER ISLAND   The North Ferry and the South Ferry service Shelter Island from Long Island's north and south forks. The North Ferry, which leaves from Greenport, is the best way to get to the Chequit Inn and other places in Shelter Island Heights from the North Fork. The fare is $8 one way for a car and driver, and a same-day round-trip is $9.75. The South Ferry leaves from Sag Harbor; the fare (cash only) is $7 one way for a car and driver, and a same-day round-trip is $8. On both ferries, pedestrians and additional car passengers pay $1 each way. North and south ferry lines are prone to backups on summer weekends, in both directions.

🛥 Fire Island **Davis Park Ferry** ☎ 631/475–1665 ⊕ www.davisparkferry.com. **Fire Island Ferries** ☎ 631/665–3600 ⊕ www.fireislandferries.com. **Sayville Ferry Service** ☎ 631/589–0810 ⊕ www.sayvilleferry.com.

🛥 Shelter Island **North Ferry** ☎ 631/749–0139 ⊕ www.northferry.com. **South Ferry** ☎ 631/749–1200 ⊕ www.southferry.com.

BUS TRAVEL

Long Island Bus, part of the Metropolitan Transportation Authority, travels throughout Nassau County and western Suffolk County, stopping at nearly 50 Long Island Rail Road stations. From late May through August, the LIRR offers special train-bus packages to Jones Beach State Park. The plush Hampton Jitney and Hampton Luxury Liner link Manhattan with the South Fork towns and offer connections to MacArthur Airport. Fares are $24–$37 one way. Reservations are required for all trips.

Sunrise Coach Lines serves the North Fork, offering direct daily service from Manhattan and Queens to Riverhead, Mattituck, Cutchogue, Southold, and Greenport, for $16 one way during peak travel times. Seats must be reserved.

🚍 **Hampton Jitney** ☎ 631/283-4600 or ⊕ www.hamptonjitney.com. **Hampton Luxury Liner** ☎ 631/537-5800 ⊕ www.hamptonluxuryliner.com. **Long Island Bus** ☎ 516/228-4000 weekdays 7-5 ⊕ www.mta.nyc.ny.us. **Sunrise Coach Lines** ☎ 631/477-1200 or 800/527-7709 ⊕ www.sunrisecoach.com.

CAR RENTAL

The Avis, Budget, Dollar, Enterprise, Hertz, and National companies rent cars at John F. Kennedy International and LaGuardia airports. Avis, A-Car Auto Rental, Enterprise, and PAM Rent a Car are represented at Long Island MacArthur Airport. *See* Car Rental *in* Smart Travel Tips A to Z for national agencies' contact information.

🚗 **A-Car Auto Rental** ☎ 631/363-5300 or 877/296-2277 ⊕ www.acarautorental.com. **PAM Rent a Car** ☎ 631/979-6100 ⊕ www.pamrent.com.

CAR TRAVEL

The Queens Midtown Tunnel (leading to the Long Island Expressway), Queensboro Bridge (Northern Boulevard, Route 25A), and the Triborough Bridge (I–278) connect Long Island with Manhattan. The Throgs Neck Bridge (I–295) and the Bronx Whitestone Bridge (I–678) provide access from the Bronx and New England. From points south, take the Verrazano Narrows Bridge (I–278). Traffic in and around the metropolitan area is always heavy; the 7–9:30 morning rush and the 4–6:30 evening peak are the most harrowing times. The heavily traveled Long Island Expressway (aka the LIE or I–495), and the Northern State and Southern State parkways are the most-utilized east–west thoroughfares, whereas the Meadowbrook and Wantaugh state parkways are major north–south connectors. Although mass transit makes Long Island very accessible, a car is necessary to explore the island's nooks and crannies. On Fire Island, only Robert Moses State Park, on the west end, and Smith Point County Park, on the opposite end, are accessible by car. Long-term parking is available near the Fire Island ferry services.

EMERGENCIES

In an emergency, dial 911.

🏥 **North Shore Long Island Jewish Medical Center** ✉ 270-05 76th Ave., New Hyde Park ☎ 516/470-7000. **North Shore University Hospital at Glen Cove** ✉ 101 St. Andrews La., Glen Cove ☎ 516/674-7300. **Stony Brook University Hospital** ✉ Nicolls Rd. at East Loop Rd., Stony Brook ☎ 631/689-8333.

🔢 North Fork & Shelter Island **Central Suffolk Hospital** ✉ 1300 Roanoke Ave., Riverhead ☎ 631/548-6000.
🔢 South Shore & Fire Island **Good Samaritan Hospital** ✉ 655 Deer Park Ave., Babylon ☎ 631/376-3850. **Long Beach Medical Center** ✉ 455 East Bay Dr., Long Beach ☎ 516/897-1000.
🔢 South Fork & the Hamptons **Southampton Hospital** ✉ 240 Meeting House La., Southampton ☎ 631/726-8200.

LODGING

The Long Island Convention and Visitors Bureau lists B&Bs, hotels, motels, inns, and resorts on its Web site and offers a free Long Island lodging guide. The Web site of the North Fork Bed & Breakfast Association includes pictures of various North Fork properties. Cherveny Real Estate, Fire Island Homes, Fire Island Living, and Kitty King Real Estate list rentals on Fire Island. Several real-estate companies post available North and South Fork rentals on Hamptons Real Estate Online; Hampton Retreats also handles weekly and longer-term rentals. The Sunday real-estate section of the *New York Times* is another good source for listings (also posted online).

🔢 **Cherveny Real Estate** ☎ 631/583-8718 ⊕ www.chervenyrealestate.com. **Fire Island Homes** ☎ 631/583-6661 ⊕ www.fihomes.net. **Fire Island Living** ☎ 631/583-5600 ⊕ www.fireislandliving.com. **Hampton Retreats** ✉ 425 Rte. 39A, Suite 202, Southampton ☎ 631/259-8000 or 866/307-0999 ⊕ www.hamptonretreats.com. **Kitty King Real Estate** ☎ 631/583-8927 ⊕ www.kittykingrealestate.com. **Long Island Convention and Visitors Bureau** ☎ 631/951-3440 or 800/441-4601 ⊕ www.licvb.com. **Hamptons Real Estate Online** ⊕ www.hreo.com. *New York Times* ⊕ www.nytimes.com. **North Fork Bed & Breakfast Association** ⊕ www.northfork.com/nfbba.

SPORTS & THE OUTDOORS

Ticks are an issue on Long Island; wear insect repellant, cover exposed skin, and check for ticks after spending time outdoors.

BIKING Long Island has a relatively flat terrain that makes it good for biking. On its Web site, the Long Island Convention and Visitors Bureau outlines more than two dozen suggested routes all over the island. The Web site of the Paumonok Bicycling Advocacy, an umbrella group of Long Island's major bike clubs, lists cycling events; it also gives nearly 20 suggested routes. You can take your bike on the Long Island Rail Road if you have a permit ($5); applications are available on the LIRR Web site.

GOLF Long the home of great private courses, Long Island today is also known for its excellent public courses. Bethpage State Park has five municipal courses, including the Black Course, which hosted the U.S. Open in 2002 and is considered one of the top places to play golf in the United States. Montauk Downs State Park and Long Island National are fantastic options. Getting onto a course can be tough, especially from Memorial Day through Labor Day, the peak season. The Long Island Convention and Visitors Bureau has an extensive list of courses on the island.

HIKING A beautifully preserved and extensive system of trails veins Long Island, leading through peaceful woodlands and fields and past windswept dunes. Most trails are open to the public and free of charge; trail maps are available at local chambers of commerce and visitor centers as well as at parks and trailheads. The Nassau-Suffolk and the Long Island Greenbelt trails are north–south paths. The Paumanok Path starts in Rocky Point, on the North Shore about 9 mi east of Port Jefferson, and stretches south and then east to Montauk Point; several preserves and parks are strung along it. The Long Island Convention and Visitors Bureau details many other routes on its Web site.

SURFING   The Long Island chapter of the Surfrider Foundation has information about current conditions and surf forecasts on its Web site. Surf Long Island has links to other sources of information about surfing on the island.
🚹 Biking **Long Island Convention and Visitors Bureau** ☎ 631/951–3440 or 800/441–4601 ⊕ www.licvb.com. **Paumonok Bicycling Advocacy** ⊕ www.bicyclelongisland.com.
🚹 Golf **Long Island Convention and Visitors Bureau** ☎ 631/951–3440 or 800/441–4601 ⊕ www.licvb.com.
🚹 Hiking **Long Island Convention and Visitors Bureau** ☎ 631/951–3440 or 800/441–4601 ⊕ www.licvb.com. **Paumanok Path** ☎ 631/563–4354 ⊕ www.paumanokpath.org.
🚹 Surfing **Surf Long Island** ⊕ www.surfli.com. **Surfrider Foundation, Long Island Chapter** ⊕ www.surfriderli.org.

TOURS
BOAT TOURS   Atlantis Explorer Environmental Boat Tours organizes two-hour boat tours ($17) down the Peconic River, during which naturalists explain the geological history of the Peconic Estuary system and discuss local flora and fauna. There's also a shoreline walking tour. The tours, run by the Cornell Cooperative Extension Marine Program, are offered twice daily April through September.

From April through October, you may take a 2½-hour tour from Greenport around Long Island Sound aboard the *Mary E.*, a 1906 schooner, for $20–$25.

Nautical Cruise Lines offers dinner cruises (starting at $65 per person) year-round on the 100-foot *Nautical Princess,* a trilevel yacht, and the 85-foot *Nautical Belle,* an old-style paddle wheeler. Specialty cruises include magic shows, brunches, and seal watching.
🚹 Boat Tours **Atlantis Explorer Environmental Boat Tours** ✉ 431 E. Main St., Riverhead ☎ 631/208–9200 ⊕ www.atlantismarineworld.com. *Mary E.* ✉ Preston's Dock, Main St., Greenport ☎ 631/477–8966 ⊕ themarye.netfirms.com. **Nautical Cruise Lines** ✉ 395 Woodcleft Ave., Freeport ☎ 516/623–5712 ⊕ www.nauticalcruiselines.com.

TRAIN TRAVEL
The Long Island Rail Road has 124 stations (including those in Brooklyn, Queens, and Manhattan) and frequent service. Bicycles are allowed with a permit ($5; applications are available on the LIRR Web site). On weekdays trains are congested during the 7–9:30 morning rush and the 4–6:30 evening peak. In summer the LIRR offers Hamptons Reserve service (aka "the Cannonball"), express trains with reserved seats, air-conditioning, and bar and snack service.
🚹 **Long Island Rail Road** ☎ 516/822–5477 or 631/231–5477 ⊕ www.lirr.org

TRANSPORTATION AROUND LONG ISLAND

Unless you plan to stay in one town or resort for the duration of your visit, a car is necessary for exploring and getting from place to place on Long Island. If you're coming from more than 200 mi away, consider flying into one of the airports and renting a car. Although train and bus service is regular, you may have to wait around for connections, depending on your destination. Taxi and car services can get you from place to place, but this is an expensive way to go if you're using them as your only mode of transportation.

Most of Fire Island isn't accessible by car, so plan on taking a ferry. If you drive to the ferry, park your car in one of the lots by the boat terminals. Alternatively, consider taking the Long Island Rail Road to a South Shore village with ferry service (Sayville or Patchogue, for example). Shelter Island also is reached by ferry service, but you can bring your car aboard. Shelter Island ferries leave from Sag Harbor and Greenport; in Greenport, the terminal is a short walk from the LIRR station.

VISITOR INFORMATION

Long Island's Page of Pages, a Web site, lists links to other Long Island–related sites. The Friday edition of *Newsday*, Long Island's daily paper, includes listings for movies, theaters, museums, children's activities, musical performances, and other diversions.

🛈 General **Long Island Convention and Visitors Bureau** ⊠ 350 Vanderbilt Motor Pkwy., Suite 103, Hauppauge 11788 ☎ 631/951-3440 or 800/441-4601 ⊕ www.licvb.com. **Long Island's Page of Pages** ⊕ www.fordyce.org. *Newsday* ⊕ www.newsday.com.

🛈 The North Shore **Glen Cove Chamber of Commerce** ⊡ Box 721, Glen Cove 11542 ☎ 516/676-6666 ⊕ www.glencovechamber.org. **Long Island Gold Coast** ⊕ www.ligoldcoast.com. **Northport Chamber of Commerce** ⊠ 24 Larkfield Rd., East Northport 11731 ☎ 631/261-3573 ⊕ www.northportny.info. **Port Jefferson Chamber of Commerce** ⊠ 118 W. Broadway, Port Jefferson 11777 ☎ 631/473-1414 ⊕ www.portjeffchamber. com. **Port Washington Chamber of Commerce** ⊡ Box 121, Port Washington 11050 ☎ 516/883-6566. **Visitor Information Centers** ⊠ Southern State Pkwy. between Exits 13 and 14, Valley Stream ⊠ LIE between Exits 52 and 53, Dix Hills-Deer Park.

🛈 North Fork & Shelter Island **Greenport-Southold Chamber of Commerce** ⊡ Box 1415, Southold 11971 ☎ 631/765-3161 ⊕ www.greenportsouthold.org. **Long Island Wine Council** ☎ 631/369-5887 ⊕ www.liwines.com. **North Fork Promotion Council** ⊡ Box 1865, Southold 11971 ☎ 631/298-5757 ⊕ www.northfork.org ⊠ Tourist Information Booth, Main Rd. near Chapel La., Greenport. **Riverhead Chamber of Commerce** ⊠ 524 E. Main St., Riverhead 11901 ☎ 631/727-7600 ⊕ www.riverheadchamber.com. **Riverhead Tourist Information Booth** ⊠ Tanger Outlet Stores, 1770 W. Main St., at Rte. 25, Riverhead ☎ 631/727-0048. **Shelter Island Chamber of Commerce** ⊠ 47 W. Neck Rd., Shelter Island 11964 ☎ 631/749-0399 ⊕ www.shelter-island.org. **Shelter Island Town Hall** ⊠ 38 N. Ferry Rd., Shelter Island ☎ 631/749 0015 ⊕ www.shelterislandtown.us.

🛈 South Shore & Fire Island **Fire Island Chamber of Commerce** ⊕ www.fireislandcc. org. **Fire Island Online** ⊕ www.fireisland.com. **Fire Island Tourist Bureau** ⊠ 49 N. Main St., Sayville 11782 ☎ 631/563-8448. **Garden City Chamber of Commerce** ⊠ 230 7th St., Garden City 11530 ☎ 516/746-7724. **Greater Sayville Chamber of Commerce** ⊠ Montauk Hwy. and Lincoln Ave., Sayville 11782 ☎ 631/567-5257 ⊕ www.sayville.com.

🛈 South Fork & the Hamptons **East Hampton Chamber of Commerce** ⊠ 79A Main St., East Hampton 11937 ☎ 631/324-0362 ⊕ www.easthamptonchamber.com. **Greater**

Westhampton Chamber of Commerce ⌖ Box 1228, Westhampton Beach 11978 ☎ 631/288-3337 ⊕ www.whbcc.org. **Montauk Chamber of Commerce** ✉ Main St., Montauk 11954 ☎ 631/668-2428 ⊕ www.montaukchamber.com. **Sag Harbor Chamber of Commerce** ⌖ Box 2810, Sag Harbor 11963 ☎ 631/725-0011 ⊕ www.sagharborchamber.com. **Sag Harbor Town Hall** ✉ Main St., Sag Harbor ☎ 631/725-0222 ⊕ www.sagharborvillage.com. **Southampton Chamber of Commerce** ✉ 72 Main St., Southampton 11968 ☎ 631/283-0402 ⊕ www.southamptonchamber.com.

THE HUDSON VALLEY

3

By Wendy
Kagan

IN 1609 EXPLORER HENRY HUDSON SAILED HIS SHIP, the *Half Moon*, up the great river that would later bear his name. He was seeking a short-cut from Europe to spice-rich Asia, but instead found heady treasures of a different sort—plunging rock cliffs, lush green highlands, jagged black ridges, and massive granite domes. More than 200 years later, the untamed beauty of the Hudson River valley fueled the imaginations of America's early landscape painters. Today the valley's forces of nature retain every bit of their impact and majesty, and the region remains, as Hudson put it, "as pleasant a land as one can tread upon."

In the 19th century New York City folk believed the valley held thera-peutic powers. Even today you could say they're still coming north for the so-called mountain cure, headed for places such as Bear Mountain in the Hudson Highlands, glacier-scarred Minnewaska outside New Paltz, or any of the dozen-plus other state parks in the Hudson corridor. Craggy peaks, pine-scented forests, cool mountain waterways, and the sapphire ribbon of the river itself serve as superb venues for hiking, climb-ing, biking, kayaking, fishing, and other outdoor diversions.

A vibrant tableau of American history unfolds along the Hudson's shores, culminating in the Gothic facades of the United States Military Academy at West Point, where you can walk in the footsteps of Civil War heroes and U.S. presidents. Grand, antiques-filled mansions, the legacies of prominent New York families of yore, command breath-steal-ing Hudson River views. Many—including the Boscobel Restoration in Garrison; Kykuit, the Rockefeller estate near Tarrytown; and Montgomery Place, the Livingston mansion in Annandale-on-Hudson—open their doors and gardens for seasonal touring.

The true spirit of the valley lives in the little river towns, scattered gems where clusters of cafés, boutiques, and galleries arrange themselves along storybook main streets. You find a treasure chest of antiques shops in Nyack, Cold Spring, and newly revitalized Hudson, where more than 60 vendors jostle for ascendancy over a span of five blocks. Beacon, home to the expansive Dia:Beacon museum, lays claim to an edgy contem-porary-arts scene, and the festival town of Saugerties hosts yearly cele-brations of jazz and garlic. Deeper inland, particularly in the sleepy hamlets nestled near Millbrook and New Paltz, country roads wend their way to apple orchards, wine trails, horse paddocks, and farm stands.

Modern-day explorers can follow in Hudson's wake, finding a passage to adventure and inspiration in a valley some have compared to Germany's stunning Rhine. It's easy to skip upriver from New York City for a day trip to the region, but scores of country inns and bed-and-breakfasts hold all the enticements for a longer, more leisurely Hudson Valley sojourn.

Exploring the Hudson Valley

The region stretches from just north of New York City all the way to Columbia County's northern border, narrowing the farther north you go. Beacon and Newburgh demarcate the northern edge of the lower Hudson Valley, which includes parts of Rockland, Orange, Westches-ter, and Putnam counties. The Mid-Hudson Valley runs to the northern boundaries of Ulster and Dutchess counties, where it's bound by the Catskill Mountains on the west and the Berkshires on the east. Columbia County makes up the bulk of the Upper Hudson Valley.

Six bridges connect the west and east banks of the river in the region: the Tappan Zee Bridge, the Bear Mountain Bridge, the Newburgh-Beacon Bridge, the Mid-Hudson Bridge, the Kingston-Rhinecliff Bridge, and the Rip Van Winkle Bridge. Interstate 84 runs east–west across the northern section of the lower valley, crossing the Newburgh-Beacon Bridge. I–87, the New York Thruway, runs northward through the Bronx and lower Westchester, on the east side of the Hudson River, before crossing west at the Tappan Zee Bridge and heading north toward Albany.

The Palisades Interstate Parkway is the other major north–south road on the west side, sometimes referred to as the "left bank"; Route 17 (to be called I–86, aka the Quickway) cuts northwest across the lower valley and into the southern Catskills. U.S. 9W travels the west bank from Nyack to Catskill, through Newburgh and Kingston.

On the east side of the river, the Saw Mill River Parkway runs north of Yonkers, hooking up with I–684 in the northeast corner of Westchester County. The Taconic State Parkway, which starts north of White Plains, winds its way northward the length of the Hudson Valley. U.S. 9 mostly hugs the east bank of the Hudson River, passing through many picturesque towns, including Tarrytown, Hyde Park, and Rhinebeck.

About the Hotels & Restaurants

The area is home to a slew of talented chefs, many of whom attended the Culinary Institute of America in Poughkeepsie and decided to stay close by after graduation. Excellent cuisine is available throughout the region, and at the culinary institute itself. Rhinebeck and Nyack brim with high-quality restaurants. Such quality often means high prices, but you can also find appealing inexpensive eateries and high-end delis. With few exceptions (which are noted in individual restaurant listings), dress is informal. Where reservations are indicated as essential, you may need to reserve a week or more ahead. In summer and fall you may need to book several months ahead.

The majority of places to stay in the Hudson Valley are inns, bed-and-breakfasts, hotels, and motels, and they range from quaint to fairly luxurious. The area does also include a smattering of full-service resorts. A few places have pools, but these are the exception rather than the rule. On weekends, two-night minimum stays are commonly required, especially at smaller inns and B&Bs. Many B&Bs book up long in advance of summer and fall, and they're often not suitable for children.

WHAT IT COSTS					
	$$$$	$$$	$$	$	¢
RESTAURANTS	over $30	$22–$30	$15–$21	$8–$14	under $8
HOTELS	over $250	$200–$250	$150–$199	$100–$149	under $100

Restaurant prices are for a main course at dinner (or at the most expensive meal served). Hotel prices are for two people in a standard double room in high season.

With your own transportation, you can easily see many of the places outlined below on day trips from New York City. That said, you can get a better feel for the valley by taking to the open road over three days. Along the way you'll stop at a historic site, have a leisurely lunch, and watch the countryside glide past your windshield. You could spend a month exploring the Hudson Valley—the historic sites and mansions alone could easily consume a few weeks—but three days will give a good overview. A six-day stay allows you to spend more time exploring additional villages and combines tours of the area's many stately homes with outdoor time.

If you're driving, it's not difficult to combine explorations of the western Hudson Valley with excursions into the Catskills region. Woodstock, for instance, is just a few miles from Kingston and Saugerties. ⇨ For information about the Catskills, *see* Chapter 4.

Numbers in the text correspond to numbers in the margin and on the Lower Hudson Valley and Mid- & Upper Hudson Valley maps.

If you have 1 day

The Lower Hudson Valley is a great day-trip destination from New York City. You could spend the morning hiking in **Harriman & Bear Mountain State Parks** ❸, eat a picnic lunch, and then head for some pre-dinner shopping in either the Woodbury Common Premium Outlets or in **Nyack** ❷, or center a trip on a visit to **West Point** ❻ or **Storm King** ❻. On the east side of the Hudson River, you can head for **Tarrytown** ❿, touring Kykuit or one of the other magnificent homes in the area and then treating yourself to dinner at Blue Hill at Stone Barns (reserve a month ahead) or another local spot. **Katonah** ❾ is a good option with or without kids. **Beacon** ⓭ is a blend of cool art, old buildings, funky shops, and laid-back restaurants. **Cold Spring** ⓬ is your best bet if you're traveling by train; if the shops and eateries don't interest you, take a hike—in Hudson Highlands State Park, that is.

If you have 3 days

With just three days, it's best to concentrate on one or two areas and to avoid repeatedly crisscrossing the Hudson River. Make **Hyde Park** ⓴ your first stop and tour Franklin D. Roosevelt's home and/or the Vanderbilt Mansion. If you're here on a Friday or Saturday, have dinner at one of the Culinary Institute of America restaurants before continuing on to 🚆 **New Paltz** ⓮, the 🚆 **High Falls** ⓯ area, 🚆 **Kingston** ⓱, 🚆 **Millbrook** ㉑, or 🚆 **Rhinebeck** ㉓, where you'll spend the next two nights. (If it's not Friday or Saturday, eat in whichever town you end up overnighting in.)

If you're staying on the west side of the Hudson River, spend Day 2 exploring the sights and other diversions in your base village. From Kingston you can take a cruise on the Hudson River (May through October) and float past several historic mansions. On Day 3, head for the great outdoors—the Minnewaska State Park Preserve or the Mohonk Preserve, specifically—and go walking, hiking, biking, rock climbing, or cross-country skiing.

If you're staying in Rhinebeck, visit **Staatsburg** ㉒, **Annandale-on-Hudson & Tivoli** ㉔, or **Hudson** ㉓ on Day 2. The stately beaux-arts mansion at the Staatsburg State Historic Site; Bard's Frank Gehry–designed performing-arts center; the stunning gardens and classical revival–style mansion of Montgomery Place; and Frederic Church's Moorish-style home, Olana, are all highlights. If you're staying in Millbrook, check out a winery and one of the gardens. On Day 3, spend time strolling and shopping in either village.

If you have
6 days

Follow Day 1 of the three-day itinerary above and choose a base on either the west or east side of the Hudson. On the second and third days, follow the suggestions given in the above itinerary for this area. At the end of Day 3, head to a new base on the opposite side of the river. On the fourth and fifth days, follow the suggestions given in the three-day itinerary. On Day 6, drive to one of the day-trip destinations mentioned in the one-day itinerary.

Timing

Summer and fall are the peak seasons in the valley; this is when most of the biggest festivals take place. Winter can be cold and dreary, but many of the villages look quite magical with a fresh layer of snow. If winter road conditions worry you, consider traveling by train.

THE LOWER HUDSON VALLEY

Revised by
Elizabeth
Weber
Johnson,
Wendy
Kagan, Joanne
Furio

The lower Hudson Valley splits its allegiance between urban New York City and rural upstate, and a little of both can be found here. Many lower-valley residents work in New York City, and some areas are overwhelmed with such trappings of suburbia as strip malls and multiplexes. But the lower valley still has a sense of place, and its rich history has become part of everyday life. Many American Indian names, such as Nyack, Taconic, and Ramapo, remain in use today. Historical markers locate the numerous Revolutionary War battles that were fought along the Hudson. And although modern-day housing developments are prevalent, old family farms and the downtowns with clusters of Victorian and Dutch colonial buildings aren't very far away.

Piermont

❶ *24 mi north of New York City.*

Piermont doesn't hide its gritty, blue-collar history. A century-old flywheel, which supplied power to factories in the village until 1983, is displayed as sculpture in the village's park. Art is what helped establish Piermont as a destination for visitors; many galleries surround Flywheel Park, which has a clear view of the Hudson River and the Tappan Zee Bridge. Nowadays shops and restaurants have filled the void that industry left, and the downtown thrives with day-trippers as well as residents doing errands or enjoying a night out with friends.

Tallman Mountain State Park. The 689-acre park along the Hudson River has 3 mi of hiking trails, a pool, picnic areas, a ball field, a track, tennis courts, and a basketball court. ⊠ *Rte. 9 W, Sparkill* ☎ *845/359–*

0544 ⊕ *nysparks.state.ny.us* ⌦ *June–Labor Day parking $5, pool $2*
☉ *Daily dawn–dusk.*

Where to Eat

$$$$
Fodor'sChoice
★
✗ **Xaviars at Piermont.** Impeccable service, elegant decor, and extraordinary food by chef and owner Peter X. Kelly make this 40-seat restaurant a not-to-be-missed special-occasion place. Dinner is a relative bargain: $60 gets you a four-course, prix-fixe meal with an *amuse-bouche* (bite-size appetizer) and petits fours. The menu, which changes seasonally, might include roasted breast of squab served with Hudson Valley foie gras, lobster with vanilla beurre blanc and parsnip puree, and a tasting of raw fish. The wine cellar stores more than 600 bottles. Lunch, served Friday and Sunday, is $38 prix fixe. ⊠ *506 Piermont Ave.* ☎ *845/359–7007* ⚑ *Reservations essential* 🏛 *Jacket required* 🖃 *No credit cards* ☉ *Closed Mon. and Tues. No lunch Wed., Thurs., and Sat.*

$$–$$$
✗ **Freelance Café & Wine Bar.** On weekends a line forms outside for this casual, less expensive sister to Xaviars at Piermont, with which it shares an address. Bistro-style dishes include osso buco with barley risotto, steak *frites,* (with fries) and pan-roasted chicken with spaetzle and morels. The coconut shrimp are outstanding. ⊠ *506 Piermont Ave.* ☎ *845/365–3250* ⚑ *Reservations not accepted* 🖃 *No credit cards* ☉ *Closed Mon.*

★ **$$–$$$**
✗ **Relish.** Although the decor is nothing fancy (the floor is painted plywood), the food and the earnest, efficient service make this restaurant worth a visit. Creative fusion cuisine—Niman Ranch lamb ribs with Peruvian spices, for instance—and classic dishes such as New York strip steak au poivre draw crowds on weekends. Sparkill is off the Palisades Parkway about 4 mi south of Piermont. ⊠ *4 Depot Sq., Sparkill* 🖃 *845/398–2747* 🖃 *AE, MC, V* ☉ *Closed Tues. No dinner Mon.–Thurs.*

$–$$
✗ **Pasta Amore.** Families, foursomes, and large groups come to this northern Italian restaurant for its signature dish, chicken Amore (with white wine and roasted peppers), as well as for its pastas, especially the penne with vodka sauce. Try to snag a table near the windows overlooking Flywheel Park (and, farther away, the Tappan Zee Bridge). ⊠ *200 Ash St.* ☎ *845/365–1911* 🖃 *AE, DC, MC, V* ☉ *Closed Mon.*

$–$$
✗ **Sidewalk Cafe.** The best people-watching in Piermont is from this casual restaurant's sidewalk tables, but outdoor dining is also available on the back patio. Southwestern dishes are the specialty; pastas and sandwiches are also part of the repertoire. ⊠ *482 Piermont Ave.* ☎ *845/359–4439* 🖃 *AE, D, DC, MC, V.*

Nightlife & the Arts

Long a bastion of live music, the **Turning Point** (⊠ 468 Piermont Ave. ☎ 845/359–1089 ⊕ www.turningpointcafe.com) specializes in jazz, blues, and folk, and attracts big names on occasion. Seating is general admission; tickets are usually $10–$30, depending on the act.

Sports & the Outdoors

BIRD-WATCHING Bird-watchers search the skies for migratory birds such as great blue heron and American avocet at the 500-acre **Piermont Marsh,** part of Hudson River National Estuarine Research Reserve, itself part of **Tallman Mountain State Park** (⊠ Rte. 9 W, Sparkill ☎ 845/359–0544 ⊕ nysparks.

state.ny.us ✉ June–Labor Day, parking $5). The park is open daily from dawn to dusk.

Shopping

Abigail Rose & Lily Too (✉ 516 Piermont Ave. ☎ 845/359–4649), a boutique for women and girls, carries trendy designers such as Dosa and Michael Stars. The gift shop **Boondocks** (✉ 490 Piermont Ave. ☎ 845/365–2221) focuses on earth- and eco-friendly merchandise. Along with fresh flowers, **Ned Kelly & Company** (✉ 485 Piermont Ave. ☎ 845/359–4480) offers unusual home and garden furnishings.

Nyack

② *3 mi north of Piermont.*

Although only a 35-minute car ride from Manhattan, the Hudson River village of Nyack retains a small-town charm. Elegant mansions and Victorian stunners mix with modest homes as well as delightful shops and fine restaurants. For a scenic drive with glimpses of the river, take Main Street to North Broadway and turn left to follow it north to Hook Mountain.

The arts have long played an important role in Nyack, the birthplace of realist painter Edward Hopper. Today Hopper's house is a community cultural center and exhibit space. Nyack was also the longtime home of stage actress Helen Hayes, for whom a thriving local theater is named.

Hopper House Art Center. The childhood home of artist Edward Hopper now serves as a community center and exhibition space. The famed painter owned the Federal-style house, which was built in 1858 by his grandfather, until his death in 1967. A group of Nyack citizens saved the structure from ruin in 1971. Jazz concerts are held in the backyard on Thursday evenings in July. ✉ *82 N. Broadway* ☎ *845/358–0774* ⊕ *www.edwardhopperhouseartcenter.org* ✉ *$1 suggested donation* ◷ *Thurs.–Sun. 1–5.*

Nyack Beach State Park. The 61-acre park, known as **Hook Mountain** to locals, includes a main trail that stretches alongside the Hudson River and attracts bicyclists, dog walkers, and runners. Bird-watchers look for hawks, and area residents come with their lawn chairs and Sunday papers. Bring lunch and enjoy it at a waterfront picnic table. Parking is free weekdays in May, September (after Labor Day), and October. ✉ *North end of N. Broadway* ☎ *845/268–3020* ⊕ *nysparks.state.ny. us* ✉ *Parking $6 (May–Columbus Day)* ◷ *Daily dawn–dusk.*

Oak Hill Cemetery. The graves of many of Nyack's artists and writers, including Edward Hopper, Carson McCullers, and Helen Hayes, are in this cemetery. Occasional walking tours of Oak Hill Cemetery are led by **Friends of the Nyacks** (☎ 845/359–4973); call for dates and times. ✉ *140 N. Highland Ave./Rte. 9W, near Charles St.*

Where to Stay & Eat

$$–$$$$ ✗ **Hudson House of Nyack.** Save room for banana cream pie or one of the other amazing desserts at this American restaurant in the former village hall. (The wine is stored behind bars in the old jail.) Entrée favorites

3

Hiking

One of the most popular—and satisfying—ways to experience the natural beauty of the Hudson Valley and its mountain ranges is to take a walk, whether it be a casual stroll along a flat riverside trail or a challenging climb up a craggy path. Often you won't walk far before being rewarded with stunning scenery. The proximity of some of these hiking venues to New York City may surprise you; Bear Mountain and Harriman state parks, for example, are just 50 mi north of the city. Wherever you go in the region, you're likely to find places to hike. Highlights include Anthony's Nose, Hudson Highlands State Park, Minnewaska State Park Preserve, Mohonk Preserve, Mills-Norrie State Park, and Stissing Mountain. The grounds of many of the Hudson River mansions open to the public are also great places to stretch your legs.

Shopping

More than 12 million visitors head for the sprawling Woodbury Common outlet center each year, making it one of the top tourist destinations in the state. You could easily spend the day browsing the 200-plus stores at this outdoor complex. If you want to get away from the retail chains and get out of the malls, head for the small shopping hubs that dot the region: Nyack, Katonah, High Falls, Kingston, Rhinebeck, Millbrook, Hudson. Nyack's laid-back commercial district has used-book stores, antiques and thrift shops, and home-furnishings boutiques. In Rhinebeck and Millbrook the retail scene is more refined, with high-end antiques and other goods. Katonah and uptown Kingston have a smattering of attractive gift shops. Stylish shops—most selling furniture and home goods—keep opening up in tiny High Falls, where you can easily spend a couple of hours browsing. Although still gritty around the edges, Hudson offers an urbane shopping experience. Posh antiques stores; cool and kitschy shops selling clothing, lotions and potions, accessories, and home props; and art galleries line the city's main arteries.

---

include tricolor pasta with smoked chicken, Gorgonzola, and pine nuts, as well as duck breast with pecan-jalapeño cornmeal stuffing and raspberry sauce. ⊠ *134 Main St.* ☎ *845/353–1355* ▤ *MC, V* ⊗ *Closed Mon.*

$$–$$$$ ✕ **Hunter's Steakhouse.** Inspired by an Adirondack lodge but named for the chef-owner's son, this steakhouse turns out excellent (and expensive) aged beef. Also consider the sinful stuffed burger with steak fries; you choose a filling of either shrimp and cheese or bacon, onions, and shiitake. ⊠ *162 Main St.* ☎ *845/358–0055* ▤ *AE, MC, V* ⊗ *Closed Mon. No lunch weekends.*

$$–$$$ ✕ **Heather's Open Cucina.** Locals pack this bustling, modern Italian restaurant, where they dine on squid-ink pasta with lobster, gnocchi with wild-boar ragout, and sautéed chicken cutlets with asparagus gratiné. Reservations are essential on weekends. ⊠ *12 N. Broadway* ☎ *845/358–8686* ▤ *AE, MC, V* ⊗ *Closed Mon.*

$$–$$$ ✕ **LuShane's.** The long copper bar displays the raw-bar selection on one end. Order the house martini, made with Lillet, and browse the menu, which is bistro with Asian touches. Daring diners might choose one of

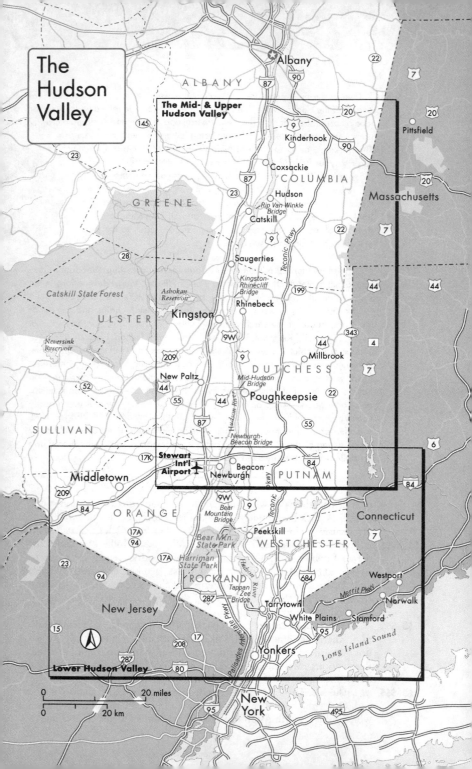

the game dishes, but also excellent are the bouillabaisse and the seared tuna steak with perfect fries. ⊠ *8 N. Broadway* ☏ *845/358–5556* ⊕ *www.lushanes.com* ⊟ *AE, MC, V* ☉ *Closed Mon.*

$$–$$$ ✕ **Restaurant X.** Fireplaces warm this rustic restaurant overlooking picturesque ponds and gardens. Try tartare of Japanese hamachi, grilled swordfish in a bouillabaisse broth, or classic beef Wellington. The restaurant is in Congers, 4 mi north of Nyack. ⊠ *117 N. Rte. 303, Congers* ☏ *845/268–6555* ⊟ *AE, MC, V* ☉ *Closed Mon. No lunch Sat.*

$–$$$ ✕ **Lanterna Tuscan Bistro.** The pastas and the Parmesan-basket salad are your best bets at this casual bistro with a good wine list. The frittatas are an excellent option for Sunday brunch. ⊠ *3 S. Broadway* ☏ *845/ 353–8361* ⊟ *AE, DC, MC, V.*

$–$$$ ✕ **Wasabi.** The stylish surroundings are a match for the hip, Asian-fusion cuisine served at this spot. Winners include salmon with lemon and olive oil and black cod with miso. Reservations are essential on weekends. ⊠ *110 Main St.* ☏ *845/358–7977* ⊟ *AE, DC, D, MC, V.*

$–$$ ✕ **King and I.** The decor at this busy Thai restaurant is rather basic, but the menu is varied and includes excellent dishes. Crispy duck and steamed dumplings are standouts; weekend specials often are, too. ⊠ *93 Main St.* ☏ *845/353–4208* ⊟ *AE, MC, V* ☉ *Closed Tues.*

$–$$ ✕ **River Club.** Take in sweeping views of the river, marina, and Tappan Zee Bridge from this restaurant. Popular dishes include salmon Wellington and chicken Arezzio (chicken breast sautéed with pine nuts and spinach). A covered waterside deck is used for warm-weather dining. ⊠ *11 Burd St.* ☏ *845/358–0220* ⊟ *AE, D, DC, MC, V* ☉ *Closed Mon.*

$ $$ ✕ **Thai House.** Chicken and basil, red-curry dishes, and seafood steamed in banana leaf are standouts at this Thai place in an old silver diner. ⊠ *12 Park St.* ☏ *845/358–9100* ⊟ *MC, V* ☉ *No lunch Mon.–Thurs.*

¢–$ ✕ **Runcible Spoon Bakery.** Day-tripping bicyclists and locals favor this popular bakery, where you can nibble on scones, muffins, and pastries that satisfy any sweet tooth. A cup of well-made coffee washes it all down. ⊠ *37–9 N. Broadway* ☏ *845/358–9398* ⊟ *AE, D, MC, V* ☉ *No dinner.*

¢–$ ▭ **Best Western.** Near the New York State Thruway and the Hudson River, this chain motel has a three-story conference room–lobby area enclosed in smoked glass. Avoid rooms in the back, however, as they're noisy. The family-style restaurant is open until 1 AM. ⊠ *26 Rte. 59, 10960* ☏ *845/358–8100* 🖷 *845/358–3644* ⊕ *www.bestwestern.com* ⟿ *80 rooms* ⌂ *Restaurant, cable TV, bar* ⊟ *AE, D, DC, MC, V.*

¢–$ ▭ **Super 8.** This pleasant Tudor-style motel offers reasonable rates and is convenient to major highways. All single rooms have king-size beds and recliners. ⊠ *47 Rte. 59, 10960* ☏ *845/353–3880 or 800/800– 8000* 🖷 *845/353–0271* ⟿ *43 rooms* ⌂ *In-room data ports, cable TV, business services* ⊟ *AE, D, DC, MC, V.*

Nightlife & the Arts

NIGHTLIFE Don't let the velvet rope outside **Luna Lounge** (⊠ *4 S. Broadway* ☏ *845/ 358–1954*) fool you. Everyone's welcome at this comfortable, gay-friendly club that serves top-notch cocktails and has great music. The outdoor patio is a bonus for smokers. If you want to meet the locals,

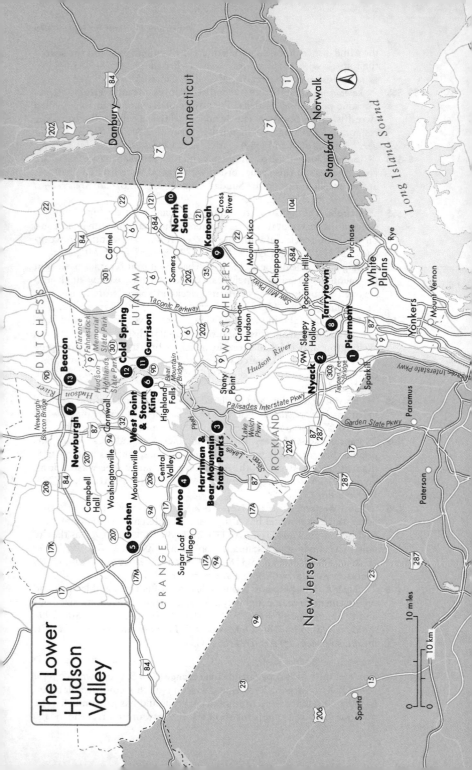

The Lower Hudson Valley

Connecticut

Danbury

Norwalk

Stamford

Long Island Sound

Rye

White Plains

Yonkers

Mount Vernon

Purchase

DUTCHESS

PUTNAM

WESTCHESTER

ROCKLAND

ORANGE

Carmel

Somers

Mount Kisco

Chappaqua

Pocantico Hills

Croton-on-Hudson

Sleepy Hollow

Hudson River

Stony Point

Cross River

Taconic Parkway

Saw Mill Pkwy.

Taconic Parkway

Tappan Zee Bridge

Palisades Interstate Pkwy

Palisades Interstate Parkway

Garden State Pkwy

New Jersey

Paramus

Paterson

Sparta

Newburgh-Beacon Bridge

Hudson River

Campbell Hall

Washingtonville

Mountainville

Central Valley

Sugar Loaf Village

Cornwall

Highland Falls

Fahnestock Memorial State Park

Clarence Fahnestock State Park

Hudson Highlands State Park

Bear Mountain Bridge

Lake Welch Pkwy

Lakes Sebago

- **10** North Salem
- Katonah **9**
- **8** Tarrytown
- **1** Piermont
- **2** Nyack
- **13** Beacon
- **7** Newburgh
- **12** Cold Spring
- Garrison **11**
- **6** West Point & Storm King
- **3** Harriman & Bear Mountain State Parks
- **4** Monroe
- **5** Goshen

10 miles

10 km

sidle up to the bar at **O'Donoghue's Tavern** (✉ 66 Main St. ☎ 845/358–0180), get a beer pulled from the tap, and listen to their stories. The menu stretches beyond standard pub fare and draws families (mostly for lunch and early dinner) and couples. **Olde Village Inne** (✉ 97 Main St. ☎ 845/358–1160), an Irish pub, caters to all crowds—into the wee hours. Where else can you get a burger, shepherd's pie, or enchiladas at 3 AM?

THE ARTS Named for the late actress and Nyack native Helen Hayes, the **Helen Hayes Theatre Company** (✉ 117 Main St. ☎ 845/358–6333 box office ⊕ www.hhtco.org) hosts dramatic, dance, comedy, and musical performances. You might see Sally Struthers or Jackie Mason on stage.

Shopping

If you plan to shop in Nyack, don't visit on Monday, because most places won't be open. For trendy designer clothing for women, check out **Adrienne's** (✉ 6 S. Broadway ☎ 845/353–1377). **Christopher's** (✉ 71 S. Broadway ☎ 845/358–9574) brims with antique furniture and reproductions, as well as housewares and decorative items. Pet the sleeping dog on your way out. The **Franklin Antique Center** (✉ 142 Main St. ☎ 845/353–0071) houses many antiques dealers under one roof. The goods—art-deco furnishings, old cameras and typewriters, Victrolas, jadeite—are just as varied. In addition to African, Mexican, and South American furnishings and housewares, **Hacienda** (✉ 70 S. Franklin St. ☎ 845/348–0300) also has beautiful textiles. Local art, midcentury furnishings, and colorful home accessories make up the mix at the small **Re: fresh Home** (✉ 95½ Main St. ☎ 845/353–3165).

Lord & Taylor, Filene's, and JCPenney anchor the mammoth **Palisades Center** (✉ Rtes. 59 and 303, West Nyack ☎ 845/348–1000), which has more than 170 stores, including Pottery Barn, J. Crew, and Restoration Hardware. The four-level mall, 3 mi west of Nyack, also has a skating rink, a Ferris wheel, a carousel, an IMAX theater, a Loews multiplex, and many chain restaurants, including Legal Sea Foods.

Harriman & Bear Mountain State Parks

❸ *23 mi north of Nyack.*

Bear Mountain, which some say resembles the profile of a reclining bear, presides over the four-season Bear Mountain State Park. A beautiful weekend can attract swarms of picnickers, but the commotion rarely extends beyond the lawns and into the wooded trails, which the park shares with adjacent Harriman State Park—a rambling wilderness of mountain peaks, dense forests, and beach-fringed lakes that straddles the Orange-Rockland county line. A 21-mi stretch of the Appalachian Trail, including its first completed section, snakes through both parks, traversing nine peaks before crossing the Hudson River via the Bear Mountain Bridge.

Bear Mountain State Park. The mass of pinkish-gray granite known as Bear Mountain looms over this enormously popular 5,067-acre park, which hugs the Hudson River at the northern end of the Palisades Interstate Parkway. The park's varied terrain affords hiking, road biking, and cross-country skiing; boat rentals and fishing are available on Hessian Lake, and small craft can moor at a dock on the river. Of the three picnic areas, the prettiest edges the lake. Open to the public are the Bear Mountain Inn and its restaurant, a swimming pool, an ice rink (rentals $3 plus $2 deposit), a merry-go-round, a playground, and playing fields. The **Trailside Museums & Wildlife Center** (⊙ Daily 10–4:30) consists of a nature trail with outdoor exhibits and animal enclosures, as well as four museum buildings with exhibits interpreting such themes as colonial and American Indian history, geology, and wildlife.

Fort Montgomery State Historic Site was the scene of a 1777 Revolutionary War battle for the Hudson River. The foundation of the fort is still visible on the 14½-acre site, which is on a cliff with stunning Hudson River views. To get to the site from New York City, take the Palisades Parkway north to Route 9W north and proceed just over ½ mi. The parking area is on the right.

To enter the park, take the Palisades Parkway to Exit 19 and follow signs. Parking fills up quickly on nice weekends, so plan accordingly. The parking fee is charged daily from Memorial Day through Labor Day and on weekends only the rest of the year. ⊠ *Rte. 9W, Bear Mountain* ☎ *845/ 786–2701* ⊕ *nysparks.state.ny.us* ⊠ *Parking $6, museum and wildlife center $1, pool $2* ⊙ *Daily 8 AM–dusk.*

Harriman State Park. Miles of hiking trails and biking roadways link this park with contiguous Bear Mountain State Park, with which it is considered one unit of the Palisades Interstate Park system. Nearly 10 times as large as its neighbor, the park encompasses more than 46,000 acres in the Ramapo Mountains of the Hudson Highlands. Mostly vast, pristine wilderness in which are scattered 31 lakes, ponds, and reservoirs, the park has several recreational areas, including three beaches (at lakes Welch, Sebago, and Tiorati); two camping facilities; fishing areas; and cross-country skiing, hiking, and bridle trails. In a wooded valley the **Anthony Wayne Recreation Area** (Exit 17 off the Palisades Parkway) has picnic areas with fireplaces, playing fields, and access to hiking and skiing trails. The Silver Mine area (Exit 18 off the parkway) has lakeside picnic grounds and biking roads, as well as boat-launch sites and fishing. A visitor center, in the parkway median between exits 16 and 17, sells trail maps and books. ⊠ *Palisades Parkway Exits 15–18* ☎ *845/786–2701* ⊕ *nysparks.state.ny.us* ⊠ *Parking $6 (beach parking $7)* ⊙ *Daily 8 AM–dusk.*

Stony Point Battlefield State Historic Site. This is the only Revolutionary War battleground in Rockland County. A museum with exhibits and a slide show describes the battle, and reenactments in period costume are common. It is also the home of the oldest lighthouse on the Hudson River. For magnificent river views, climb to the top of the lighthouse, which was restored in 1995. ⊠ *Park Rd., off Rte. 9W* ☎ *845/786–2521* ⊕ *nysparks.state.ny.us* ⊠ *Museum $2, weekend parking $5* ⊙ *Mid-Apr.–Oct., Wed.–Sat. and Mon. 10–4:30, Sun. 11–4:30.*

Where to Stay & Eat

$–$$$ ✕**Gasho of Japan.** Housed in a 400-year-old samurai farmhouse— shipped to America from Japan and reconstructed on-site in Central Valley—this hibachi chophouse claims to deliver both "steak and theater." Skillful chefs slice, dice, flip, and grill your dinner before your eyes, while kimono-clad servers fetch appetizers and umbrella-topped specialty drinks. Proximity to Woodbury Common Premium Outlets makes this a convenient post-shopping spot. ⊠ *365 Rte. 32, Central Valley* ☎ *845/ 928–2277* ⊟ *AE, D, DC, MC, V.*

$–$$ ✕**Cub Room Restaurant.** Seasonal outdoor dining on a covered porch gives you a bird's-eye view of the boaters on Hessian Lake at this casual eatery within Bear Mountain State Park. The varied menu covers all the bases, from burgers and pastas to barbecued ribs and Parmesan-encrusted salmon. Some dishes err on the greasy side, but the service is cheerful and attentive, and weekends bring a steady stream of families, inn guests, and hungry hikers. ⊠ *Bear Mountain Inn, Rte. 9W off Palisades Parkway Exit 19, Bear Mountain* ☎ *845/786–2731* ⊟ *AE, D, MC, V* ☻ *Closed Mon. and Tues. Jan.–Mar.*

¢–$$ 🏨 **Sebago Cabin Camp.** Rustic cabins, built in the 1930s, offer a step up from tent camping on the grounds by Lake Sebago in Harriman State Park. Ranging from two to four bedrooms (each with two military cots), the cabins have heat, electricity, refrigerators, and hot plates, but no running water. Bathrooms are communal. Also available are two furnished cottages with private bathrooms and full kitchens. The site has swimming, tennis courts, rowboat rentals, and a recreation hall with kids' activities. Rangers are on duty all night and make Saturday bonfires. From late June through Labor Day, rentals are by the week only (cabins $190–$310, cottages $580–$640). To get here take Exit 16, Lake Welch Drive, off the Palisades Parkway. ⊠ *Seven Lakes Dr., off Lake Welch Drive, Harriman State Park 10911* ☎ *845/351–2360 information, 800/456–2267 reservations* ⊕ *nysparks.state.ny.us* ⊃ *36 cabins with shared baths, 2 cottages* ⚘ *Picnic area, some kitchens, refrigerators, 2 tennis courts, lake, boating, fishing, basketball, hiking, playground, laundry facilities; no a/c, no room phones, no room TVs, no smoking* ⊟ *MC, V* ☻ *Closed mid-Oct.–mid-Apr.* ❑ *EP.*

¢ 🏨 **Bear Mountain Inn.** A convenient setting and inexpensive room rates are the draw at this family-friendly place within Bear Mountain State Park. Constructed in 1915 of native stone and timber found on the site, the Main Inn has 12 rooms, a restaurant and bar, and a vast, rustic lobby with a fireplace, a cathedral ceiling, and exposed chestnut-log posts and beams. About a mile away, on the other side of Hessian Lake, are two additional buildings called the Stone Lodges. These have large windows (some with lake views) but get traffic noise from nearby highways. Overlook Lodge, in a quiet wooded area, has 24 spacious, serviceable rooms and a lobby with Hudson River vistas. With the inn undergoing a major renovation that is expected to last through 2005, you may want to request a room in one of the stone lodges. ⊠ *Rte. 9W, Bear Mountain 10911* ☎ *845/786–2731* 🖶 *845/786–2543* ⊕ *www.bearmountaininn.com* ⊃ *60 rooms* ⚘ *Restaurant, some cable TV, pool, lake, boating, fishing, hiking, cross-country skiing, bar, playground, meeting rooms, no-smoking rooms* ⊟ *AE, D, MC, V* ❑ *CP.*

CAMPING ⛺ **Beaver Pond Campgrounds.** Adjacent to Lake Welch in Harriman State Park, the campground occupies an open area dotted with trees.

Man-made Lake Welch has the largest beach—½ mi long—in the park and is popular for swimming, fishing, boating, and picnicking. Some 14-by-14-foot platforms for freestanding tents are available. Access is from Route 106, Exit 14 off the Palisades Parkway. ⚐ *Flush toilets, dump station, running water, showers, fire pits, grills, picnic tables, public telephone, swimming (lake)* ⊠ *800 County Rte. 106, Stony Point 10980* ☎ *845/947–2792 information, 800/456–2267 reservations* ⊕ *nysparks. state.ny.us* ⇥ *73 regular tent sites, 55 platform tent sites, 12 RV sites without hookups* ⊠ *$13 ($14 platforms)* ⚐ *Reservations essential* ⊟ *MC, V* ⊘ *Closed mid-Oct.–mid-Apr.*

Sports & the Outdoors

BIKING   Some 55 mi of roadways snake through the linked **Bear Mountain and Harriman state parks** (⊠ Palisades Parkway Exits 15–19 ☎ 845/786–2701 ⊕ nysparks.state.ny.us), giving you numerous options for biking expeditions. Expect a vigorous ride through hilly areas; you'll be rewarded with fine lake and river views. Popular routes include Seven Lakes Drive east from the Palisades Parkway and Perkins Memorial Drive to the Hudson River; Tiorati Brook Road off Tiorati Circle; and Arden Valley Road. Many park roads are closed to truck traffic and have 40 mph speed limits.

CROSS-COUNTRY SKIING   The 1777E Trail begins near the ice rink and merry-go-round at **Bear Mountain State Park** (⊠ Rte. 9W off Palisades Parkway Exit 19 ☎ 845/786–2701 ⊕ nysparks.state.ny.us), cutting an approximately 5-mi loop through the park's Doodletown area. Marked but not groomed, the trail follows an old wood road; mostly flat and fairly wide open, it's suitable for beginner to intermediate skiers. To get there, go to the south end of parking lot No. 2, pass through the stone tunnel, and look for a white trail marker with red lettering. Equipment rentals aren't available.

Many miles of marked, ungroomed trails crisscross the vast **Harriman State Park** (⊠ Palisades Parkway Exits 17 and 18 ☎ 845/786–2701 ⊕ nysparks.state.ny.us), so bring a map and keep your bearings. Better yet, bring a compass. At Lake Sebago (Exit 18 off the Palisades Parkway), you can pick up a trail near the "fishermen's parking lot." Crossing Seven Lakes Drive, this trail follows peaceful, traffic-free Wood Town Road to Pine Meadow Lake and Lake Wanoksink. The terrain here can vary and is suitable for all levels. Alternately, pick up one of many trails starting near the Anthony Wayne Recreation Area (Exit 17 off the parkway). Beachy Bottom Road is one of several woods roads fit for intermediate-level skiing. The park doesn't offer gear rentals.

HIKING   Along all the hiking trails of this region is evidence of old iron mines, active here from colonial times through the Civil War. In Bear Mountain and Harriman state parks, abandoned shafts, pits, and dumps from these mines are a fascinating aspect of many hikes. Take care to stick to the trails and resist the temptation to explore the old mines, which can be unstable and dangerous.

The first completed section of the Appalachian Trail (AT) opened in **Bear Mountain State Park** (⊠ Rte. 9W off Palisades Parkway Exit 19 ☎ 845/786–2701 ⊕ nysparks.state.ny.us) in 1923; today this section is only a small piece of the 2,160-mi trail that stretches from Georgia to Maine. The moderately vigorous, two-hour trek up Bear Mountain is popular with day-hikers. Begin just past the southern side of the Bear Mountain Inn, following the white AT blazes, which first lead you along a paved road. The trail then splits off to the right, ascending amid open woods. At the peak you may climb to the top of Perkins Memorial Tower for panoramic views of four states (New York, New Jersey, Connecticut, and Pennsylvania) and even glimpse the New York City skyline.

Scores of trails weave through the enormous **Harriman State Park** (⊠ Palisades Parkway Exits 15–18 ☎ 845/786–2701 ⊕ nysparks.state.ny.us), giving you countless choices for easy, moderate, or vigorous hikes. Stop at the visitor center, in the median between exits 16 and 17 of the Palisades Parkway, and pick up a trail map before you go. Popular routes include the Pine Meadow Trail, a 2½-mi loop that begins at the Reeves Meadow Visitors Center, and the Harriman-Iron Mine Trail, a moderately vigorous 3-mi hike from the Lake Skannatati parking area. The latter trail passes the site of the Pine Swamp iron mine, which dates from the 1830s.

Shopping

Fodor'sChoice More than 220 designer outlets fill the **Woodbury Common Premium Out-
★ lets** (⊠ 498 Red Apple Ct., off Rte. 32, Exit 16 off I–87, Central Valley ☎ 845/928–4000 or 845/928–6840), a sprawling shopping complex about a 20-minute drive north of Bear Mountain. Many of the top fashion retailers are here, including Giorgio Armani, Gucci, J. Crew, and Donna Karan. Beyond clothing, the goods range from shoes and leather goods to housewares and jewelry, with outlets for Nike, Kenneth Cole, and Williams-Sonoma. Deals can be found, but don't expect everything to be a bargain. One of the most popular destinations in the state, the center draws about 10 million visitors a year. The parking lots fill quickly and traffic can be a tangle on weekends (and certain holidays).

Monroe

❹ *15 mi west of Harriman State Park.*

Although it's largely residential, Monroe blends industrial grit and old-fashioned living: it's the birthplace of Velveeta as well as home to Museum Village, a living-history museum. The town offers dining just off Exit 130 of Route 17 (at this writing morphing into I–86, the Quickway), which makes it a relatively convenient place to eat near Harriman State Park and Sterling Forest, site of a well-known Renaissance festival.

Museum Village. The daily life of colonial America is depicted at this re-created village. Twenty-five buildings, including a century-old general story, house crafts workshops and old-time equipment and furnishings. Interpreters dressed in period costumes perform daily activities such as publishing the weekly newspaper, hammering horseshoes in the blacksmith's shop, and making pots at the pottery workshop. ⊠ 1010 Rte. 17M ☎ 845/782–8248 ⊕ www.museumvillage.com ⌦ $8 ⊙ June and Sept.–Nov., weekdays 10–2, weekends 11–4; July and Aug., Wed.–Sun. 11–4.

off the
beaten
path

BROTHERHOOD WINERY – The oldest continually operating winery in the United States, Brotherhood includes some European-style stone buildings that date from 1839. Tours and tastings are available. The winery is about 8 mi north of Monroe. ⊠ *100 Brotherhood Plaza Dr., off Rte. 208 N, Washingtonville* ☎ *845/496–9101* ⊕ *www. wines.com/brotherhood* 🍷 *Tour and tasting $5* ⊙ *Store daily 11–6. Tours May–Dec., daily 11–4; Jan.–Apr., weekends 11–4.*

SUGAR LOAF VILLAGE – The hamlet of Sugar Loaf, about 3 mi southwest of Monroe, encompasses more than 50 shops and artists' studios. Painters, sculptors, and other craftspeople ply their trade and sell their wares here, some in buildings dating from the mid-1800s. Most of the shops are open Wednesday through Sunday. ⊠ *King's Hwy., off Rte. 94 south of Rte. 17/I–86* ☎ *845/469–9181* ⊕ *www. sugarloafartsvillage.com.*

Where to Eat

$$ ✕ **Rainbow.** Northern Italian dishes, including seafood dinners and fresh pastas served in hearty portions, are the highlights at this comfortable, softly lighted family restaurant. ⊠ *16 Rte. 17M* ☎ *845/783–2670* ⊟ *D, MC, V.*

¢–$$ ✕ **Goodfellows.** The casual spot, a local favorite, bustles with diners who come for the traditional Italian dishes. Chicken Romeo, for one, combines chicken with Italian sausage, broccoli, artichoke hearts, and roasted peppers in white-wine sauce. ⊠ *590 Rte. 208* ☎ *845/783–1133 or 845/246–9371* ⊟ *AE, D, MC, V.*

$ ✕ **Cafe Fiesta.** The come-as-you-are family-friendly eatery in Highland Mills serves authentic Mexican fare, including vegetarian and low-fat renditions. ⊠ *530 Rte. 32, Highland Mills* ☎ *845/928–2151* ⊟ *AE, D, MC, V.*

Goshen

❺ *12 mi west of Monroe.*

With a huge park, old trees, nice restaurants, and two side-by-side hardware stores, Goshen is the kind of walkable, slow-paced village ideal for an afternoon visit. And though it remembers its past with places like the Historic Track and the Trotting Horse Museum, it is not a place that time forgot. You find a smattering of restaurants and interesting shops, as well as beautiful churches and statues to admire.

Goshen Historic Track. The oldest harness track in the United States is also a National Historic Landmark. You can watch daily training or take a self-guided walking tour of the premises, but these days races are run only in July. ⊠ *44 Park Pl.* ☎ *845/294–5333* 🎫 *Free* ⊙ *Daily; call for times.*

Trotting Horse Museum. Overlooking the track is this museum and hall of fame dedicated to harness racing. Exhibits include a three-dimensional racing simulator, prints, and paintings. Original track stables house some of the displays. ⊠ *240 Main St.* ☎ *845/294–6330* 🎫 *$7.50* ⊙ *Daily 10–6.*

Where to Stay & Eat

\$\$–\$\$\$ ✕ **Bull's Head Inn.** The kitchen of this restaurant in a restored 1786 building turns out contemporary American fare: grilled swordfish with cilantro-lime sauce, grilled chicken and pancetta over rigatoni with sherry cream sauce, baby rack of lamb with mashed sweet potatoes. A gazebo, an herb garden, and a fountain make outdoor dining appealing. Fireplaces warm the place in winter. The restaurant is about 6 mi north of Goshen. ⊠ *120 Sarah Wells Trail, Campbell Hall* ☎ *845/496–6758* ⊟ *AE, DC, MC, V* ⊗ *Closed Mon. No lunch.*

\$\$–\$\$\$ ✕ **Catherine's.** Long popular, this restaurant serves as both local watering hole and midrange dining room. The menu lists American classics like steaks and Caesar salad, seafood dishes, and some pastas. ⊠ *153 W. Main St.* ☎ *845/294–8707* ⊟ *AE, MC, V* ⊗ *Closed Sun. and Mon.*

\$\$–\$\$\$ ✕ **Ile de France Restaurant.** Classic French cuisine, such as frogs' legs and pâté, is served in a space with 15th-century tapestries on the walls and roses and candles on the tables. Desserts are all baked on the premises; try crème brûlée or lemon tart. Lunch is less formal and less expensive. ⊠ *6 N. Church St.* ☎ *845/294–5759* ⊟ *No credit cards* ⊗ *Closed Sun. and Mon.*

\$\$–\$\$\$\$ 🏠 **Anthony Dobbins Stagecoach Inn.** Built in 1747 as a farmhouse, this quiet Georgian B&B sits peacefully on 3 wooded acres near the foothills of the Catskills. Rooms are English and colonial in style, filled with family antiques and liberal doses of floral fabrics; some rooms have a fireplace. The suite is really a semidetached house with three small bedrooms, a kitchen, a living room, two bathrooms, and a back porch. ⊠ *268 Main St., 10924* ☎ *845/294–5526* ⊕ *www.dobbinsinn.com* ⛌ *7 rooms, 2 with shared bath; 1 suite* ⚬ *Dining room, cable TV, library; no smoking* ⊟ *AE, D, MC, V* ⟡ *CP weekdays, BP weekends.*

West Point & Storm King

❻ *West Point is 5 mi north of Bear Mountain State Park.*

Though very different in purpose—one site is dedicated to military education and the other to celebrating art and nature—West Point and Storm King are among the most interesting of the lower Hudson Valley's attractions. Storm King, in Mountainville, is closed in winter, but that is high season for traveling shows at the theater at West Point's Eisenhower Hall.

🕒 **Storm King Art Center.** More than 100 sculptures by major international artists—including David Smith, Alexander Calder, and Isamu Noguchi—are spread out on 500 acres of hills, fields, meadows, and woodlands. The relationship between art and nature is a focus for the center. For the best overview of the grounds and collection, ride the shuttle (wheelchair-accessible), which runs every half hour. Free "Highlights of the Collection" walk-in tours are offered daily at 2 and summer evenings at 5:30. Designated picnic areas have tree-shaded tables. Whether or not you picnic, consider wearing bug repellent. Kids love to run around the grounds and the sculptures; you just need to make sure they don't touch the installations. ⊠ *Old Pleasant Hill Rd., Mountainville* ☎ *845/*

FodorsChoice
★

534–3115 ⊕ www.stormking.org ✉ $9 ⊙ Apr.–late Oct., Wed.–Sun. 11–5:30 (late May–Labor Day Sat. until 8 PM); late Oct.–mid-Nov., Wed.–Sun. 11–5.

Fodor'sChoice
★ **United States Military Academy at West Point.** Occupying the western shore of one of the most scenic bends in the Hudson River, the academy consists of some 16,000 acres of training grounds, playing fields, and buildings constructed of native granite in the Military Gothic style. The oldest continually garrisoned post in the U.S. Army, the citadel was founded in 1778 and opened as a military academy in 1802. Distinguished graduates include Robert E. Lee, Ulysses S. Grant, and Douglas MacArthur. The world's oldest and largest military museum, the **West Point Museum** in Olmstead Hall, showcases a vast collection of uniforms, weapons, flags, American military art, and other memorabilia. **Fort Putnam,** built in 1778 and a key component of West Point's defense during the Revolutionary War, was restored in the 1970s. Campus visits are by bus tour only (bring photo ID), but you do get a chance to step off the bus, look at a few memorials and cannons up close, and perhaps glimpse cadets in action. Civilians are also allowed on campus for sporting and cultural events, including football games, theater presentations, parades, and concerts. You can visit the museum and visitor center without taking the tour. Tours aren't given during graduation week (usually late May) and on Saturdays of home football games. ✉ *Rte. 9 W 5 mi north of Bear Mountain State Park, Highland Falls* ☎ *845/938–2638* ⊕ *www.usma.edu* ✉ *Tour $7, museum and visitor center free* ⊙ *Visitor center daily 9–4:45, museum daily 10:30–4:15.*

Where to Stay & Eat

$–$$$ ╳ **Prima Pizza.** The pizzeria is well known for its Internet pizzas—it'll ship a pie anywhere overnight and promise it's never frozen. But it also serves out-of-the-ordinary pizzas like lemon chicken and stuffed steak, as well as pastas and subs. ✉ *252 Main St., Cornwall* ☎ *845/534–7003* ⌂ *Reservations not accepted* ▭ *AE, D, MC, V* ⊙ *Closed Mon.*

$$$–$$$$ ╳▥ **Thayer Hotel.** Elegant accommodations and ethereal Hudson River views ennoble this imposing brick-and-granite hotel on the grounds of the United States Military Academy at West Point. (You pass through two security checkpoints on your way to the hotel, which has long housed military officers and their guests.) Sleek marble floors, iron chandeliers, and portraits of military leaders bedeck the main lobby; dark, regal furnishings and prints of river scenes adorn guest rooms. Request an odd-numbered room for river vistas or an even-numbered room for commander's-eye views of the academy. The restaurant lures crowds to its Sunday champagne brunch buffet ($26 prix fixe); pastries, salads, pastas, quiches, and even omelet, waffle, and beef-carving stations amount to a veritable food orgy. In summer, angle for a table on the outdoor terrace, where you can savor the panoramic Hudson River views. Dinner specialties ($$–$$$) include rack of lamb, stuffed shrimp, and the house pasta dish, fettuccine with artichokes, black olives, and tomatoes. Restaurant reservations are essential. ✉ *674 Thayer Rd., West Point 10996* ☎ *845/446–4731 or 800/247–5047* ▤ *845/446–0338* ⊕ *www. thethayerhotel.com* ➷ *117 rooms, 8 suites* ⌂ *Restaurant, room service,*

in-room data ports, cable TV with video games, hair salon, lounge, comedy club, business services, meeting rooms, no-smoking rooms ▤ *AE, D, DC, MC, V* ▢ *EP.*

¢ ✕▣ **The Inn at Painter's.** Funky artwork fills the guest rooms and public spaces of this inn above a popular eatery. A slightly disheveled East Village flavor prevails here. Simple furnishings reminiscent of the 1970s are a backdrop for the eclectic paintings, multimedia works, and bright murals. Motel prices make these bohemian digs one of the area's best deals. Down-home cooking with creative twists keeps the locals coming to the restaurant ($–$$) downstairs. Beyond burgers and steaks, the extensive menu mixes in Southern favorites (such as buttermilk fried chicken) and other inspired choices (like the "Dragon Bowl" of Chinese noodles and silky peanut sauce). Berry-red ceilings, steel I-beams, and quirky paintings adorn the spacious dining room. Art and revelry spill over into the bar/gallery on weekends. The service can be uneven and the volume high, but the casual crowd and families don't seem to mind. ✉ *266 Hudson St., Cornwall-on-Hudson 12520* ☎ *845/534–2109* 📠 *845/534–8428* ⊕ *www.painters-restaurant.com* 🛏 *6 rooms, 1 suite* ♻ *Restaurant, room service, bar, laundry service; no room phones, no smoking* ▤ *AE, D, DC, MC, V* ▢ *EP.*

$$–$$$$ ▣ **Cromwell Manor Inn.** After you arrive at this stately Greek revival mansion and pass through the grand columns of the portico, any hint of formality dissolves as the innkeepers greet you with a plate of fresh-baked cookies. Combining manor-house elegance with bed-and-breakfast-style warmth, this 1820 architectural treasure is surrounded by lawns, gardens, and a patio with sunset views. Many rooms have four-poster beds with sheer panels or crocheted canopies; cavernous marble bathrooms are a feature of the suites, which are plush. Windows provide pastoral vistas without another house in sight—except the 1764 Chimney's Cottage, which contains four bedrooms filled with period antiques. ✉ *174 Angola Rd., Cornwall 12518* ☎ *845/534–7136* 📠 *845/534–0354* ⊕ *www.cromwellmanor.com* 🛏 *10 rooms, 3 suites* ♻ *Dining room, Internet; no room phones, no room TVs, no kids under 7, no smoking* ▤ *AE, MC, V* ▢ *BP.*

$$–$$$ ▣ **Storm King Lodge.** A vast, light-filled great room with exposed beams, comfy couches, and a massive hearth welcomes you to this white-clapboard country B&B. Rolling lawns and a peaceful feng shui garden surround the early-1800s carriage house, which was converted to a guesthouse in the 1920s. The covered back porch—often a setting for breakfast or an evening drink by candlelight—looks out over the Storm King Art Center's sculpture-strewn meadows across the thruway. Upstairs guest rooms have higher ceilings and are bright; the Lavender Room has a fireplace, rocker, and wide-board floors. ✉ *100 Pleasant Hill Rd., Mountainville 10953* ☎ *845/534–9421* 📠 *845/534–9416* ⊕ *www.stormkinglodge.com* 🛏 *4 rooms* ♻ *Kitchenette, piano; no room phones, no room TVs, no smoking* ▤ *AE, MC, V* ▢ *BP.*

Sports & the Outdoors

HIKING Peaceful hiking trails traverse the 3,750-acre **Black Rock Forest Preserve and Consortium** (✉ Rte. 9W, Cornwall ☎ 845/534–4517 ⊕ www.blackrockforest.org), just north of Storm King in Cornwall. In the 1800s loggers cut down the old-growth forest here to make way for farms. By the next century a restoration project was under way to bring the forest back, and the preserve remains an important educational and research site. Black Rock, the forest's highest peak, can be accessed from a number of trails. The Stillman Trail climbs through mountain laurel to the summit, which affords views of Storm King, the Schunnemunk Mountains, and the Shawangunks.

At the heart of the 1,900-acre **Storm King State Park** (⊠ Off Rte. 9W between Cornwall and West Point ☎ 845/786–2701 ⊕ nysparks.state.ny. us) is Storm King Mountain, which is veined with hiking trails, many with spectacular views. The park is undeveloped, so there are no bathrooms and parking is limited. Hikers must heed posted warnings and restrictions and stick to marked trails here, because unexploded artillery shells from the neighboring military academy might be found off trails in area B of the park, in the south. (In 1999 severe forest fires set off the unexploded ordnance, or UXO, which apparently would land in the park whenever a particular target range at the military academy was overshot, and resulted in a three-year closure of the park.)

Newburgh

❼ *15 mi north of West Point.*

Toward the close of the Revolutionary War, George Washington kept his headquarters and residence here. Although the riverside city has lost much of its original architecture to urban renewal, Newburgh retains the largest historic district in the state, with elaborate Italianate mansions and fanciful Queen Anne Victorians lining Montgomery, Grand, and Liberty streets. Although the city's interior is rough, the waterfront area has rebounded, thanks partly to the bevy of restaurants, bars, and shops that opened at Newburgh Landing in 2000. A parade of tour boats departs from here, and piers, pathways, and alfresco tables make it a prime spot from which to enjoy valley views.

Newburgh Landing. Newburgh's revitalized waterfront is a lively spot where you may stroll, catch a tour boat, and sample the creations of the riverfront restaurants. The cluster of businesses here, which also includes bars and a day spa, definitely benefits from the breezy marina setting and panoramic Hudson Highlands views. Torches has an expansive bar and floor-to-ceiling windows; it also lays claim to one of the biggest aquariums in the country—a 5,700-gallon tank filled with exotic fish. ⊠ *Front and 4th Sts.*

Washington's Headquarters State Historic Site. From April 1782 to August 1783, General George Washington made his military headquarters and home in this Dutch fieldstone house, where he attended to the final years of Revolutionary War activity. Guided tours show how Washington, his wife, Martha, and his aides-de-camp lived and worked here as the war drew to a close. Filled with period furniture and reproductions, the house opened to the public in 1850, becoming the first official historic site in the United States. A monument to peace, the Tower of Victory, was erected here in the late 1880s. Adjacent to the house is a small museum containing artifacts collected since the mid-1880s. Lectures, live music, military and crafts demonstrations, and family programs honor Washington's birthday during a three-day extravaganza over Presidents' Day weekend. ⊠ *84 Liberty St.* ☎ *845/562–1195* ⊕ *nysparks.state.ny. us* ⊠ *$3* ⊘ *Mid-Apr.–Oct., Mon. and Wed.–Sat., 10–5; Sun. 11–5.*

Where to Stay & Eat

$$–$$$ ✕ **Il Cena'colo.** The flavors of Tuscany take center stage at this highly regarded eatery tucked into an unlikely corner of commercial Newburgh. You'll want to toss the menu aside in favor of the exhaustive list of daily specials, many of which appear with regularity. Fresh buffalo mozzarella, porcini mushrooms, and sun-dried tomatoes pop up in many dishes; the osso buco is a signature dish, and the pasta with shaved black truffles has acquired nearly a cult following. For dessert, don't miss the chocolate soufflé cake. The cordial waitstaff, outfitted in ties and crisp white aprons, presides over the softly lighted dining room, which has a pressed-copper ceiling and blond-wood beams. ⊠ *228 S. Plank Rd.* ☎ *845/564–4494* ⚑ *Reservations essential* ▤ *AE, D, DC, MC, V* ⊘ *Closed Tues. No lunch.*

¢–$ ✕ **Cafe Pitti.** Riverfront tables under a mandarin-orange canopy make for a relaxed meal at this small café, perfect for lunch, dessert, or a light bite in warm weather. When the air is nippy, head inside to the slightly cramped but warm space. The chairs are rickety and the service can be slow, but all is forgiven upon the arrival of the authentic Italian fare. Try a warm panini with brie, arugula, and truffle oil, or a thin-crusted, prosciutto-topped pizzetta from the wood-burning oven. Tiramisu and cappuccino cake pair well with a selection of dessert wines and ports. ⊠ *40 Front St.* ☎ *845/565–1444* ▤ *AE, MC, V.*

$–$$$ ▦ **Stockbridge Ramsdell House on Hudson.** Every bedroom in this rambling 1870 Queen Anne Victorian commands sweeping views of the Hudson River, with some windows framing scenes of Bannerman's Island and the Beacon-Newburgh Bridge. Among the spacious rooms, Beau Rivage has a high canopy bed and private enclosed porch, and Ferry Crossing has an outdoor deck with top-of-the-world vistas. The multicourse breakfast fuels a day's worth of sightseeing. Wander the block to see the 19th-century mansions, but if you stray too far west you'll come to rough-around-the-edges inner Newburgh. ⊠ *158 Montgomery St., 12550* ☎ *845/562–9310* ⊕ *www.stockbridgeramsdell.com* ➲ *5 rooms* ⚱ *Dining room, cable TV, in-room VCRs; no room phones, no smoking* ▤ *AE, D, MC, V* ⎛⎝ *BP.*

Yonkers

Just north of the Bronx border.

Settled by the Dutch in the 17th century, Yonkers takes its name from a word meaning "Djonk Herr's land." The Bronx border is to the south and Manhattan is a short drive away. The farming villages of colonial times grew into an industrial stronghold during the 19th century and home to burgeoning immigrant populations who worked in its factories. Now a modern city of shopping malls and corporate parks, Yonkers is home to almost 200,000 people. The city was made famous by author Thornton Wilder as the home of Dolly Levi, the main character in his play *The Matchmaker,* which became the hit musical *Hello, Dolly!*

Today downtown Yonkers is in the midst of an urban renaissance. Many grand 19th-century structures, including a beaux-arts train station and a Victorian pier, are being rehabilitated; artists are moving into lofts; and new restaurants and businesses are being fueled by an influx of private and municipal funding. North and east of the downtown are smaller, quainter neighbors.

Hudson River Museum. In an 1877 Victorian Gothic mansion, the museum displays changing exhibits of 19th- and 20th-century American art and has the county's only planetarium. Its specializes in combining art, history, and science in its shows. ⊠ *511 Warburton Ave.* ☎ *914/963–4550* ⊕ *www.hrm.org* ➰ *$3* ⊙ *Wed.–Sun. noon–5.*

Philipse Manor Hall State Historic Site. Frederick Philipse I, a wealthy Dutch merchant, began building this house in the 1680s. After the Revolutionary War his great-grandson Frederick Philipse III, a loyalist to the British Crown, had to leave behind the house and a 52,000-acre estate stretching from the Bronx to Croton. The home, the oldest in Westchester County, includes some of the finest surviving examples of American rococo architecture and decor. ⊠ *29 Warburton Ave.* ☎ *914/965–4027* ⊕ *nysparks.state.ny.us* ➰ *Free* ⊙ *Wed. and Thurs. 11–2, Sun. 2–5, or by appointment.*

St. Paul's Church National Historic Site. The parish that built St. Paul's church was established in 1665. The present fieldstone-and-brick Georgian church begun in 1763 was used by British and Hessian soldiers as a military hospital during the Revolutionary War. The historic cemetery, one of the oldest in New York, contains footstones dating back to 1704, a mass grave for Hessian soldiers, and the graves of former slaves. The church is in Mount Vernon, about 2 mi east of Yonkers. ⊠ *897 S. Columbus Ave., Mount Vernon* ☎ *914/667–4116* ⊕ *www.nps.gov/sapa* ➰ *Free* ⊙ *Weekdays 9–5.*

> **off the beaten path**

PLAYLAND PARK – One of the oldest amusement parks of its type in the country, this National Register site on Long Island Sound is known for its art-deco architecture and the fact that it retains some of its original rides (its carousel was built in 1915). You can swim, boat, fish, and picnic on the grounds, or skate indoors in winter at the Ice Casino. The park is 10 mi east of Yonkers. ⊠ *Playland Pkwy., off I–95 Exit 19, Rye* ☎ *914/813–7000* ⊕ *www.ryeplayland.org* ➰ *Parking $5, rides $2.50–$5* ⊙ *Call for hrs.*

Where to Eat

$$–$$$ ✕ **Zuppa.** Exposed brick walls contribute to the SoHo feel of this pioneering Italian restaurant in the city's up-and-coming downtown. The food is lighter and more experimental than standard red-sauce fare. All pastas are made in-house, and include parsnip gnocchi served with braised oxtail, and ricotta cavatelli served with red-wine-soaked bacon. Lamb *due volte* (two ways) comes with mint-spiked wheat berry, a grain that's slow-cooked like risotto. ⊠ *59 Main St.* ☎ *914/376–6500* 🖃 *AE, V, MC.*

Sports & the Outdoors

Yonkers Raceway (⊠ 810 Central Ave. ☎ 914/968–4200 ⊕ www. yonkersraceway.com 🎟 Clubhouse $2.25, parking $2), a harness-racing track, opened in 1899 as the Empire City Trotting Club. The current facility dates from 1958 and was renovated in the mid-1980s. You can see live races daily (except Sunday). Post time is 7:40 PM.

Tarrytown

❽ *10 mi north of Yonkers.*

On the east bank of the Hudson River, Tarrytown has a bustling downtown with a rich artistic history. In the mid-1600s this Westchester County village was settled by the Dutch, who called it Tarwe, which means "wheat." Filled with boutiques, antiques shops, art galleries, restaurants, bed-and-breakfasts, and beautiful parks, Tarrytown is a popular tourist destination whose most famous son was Washington Irving, considered the first American writer to make a living solely from his work. His classic works include *Rip Van Winkle* and *The Legend of Sleepy Hollow.* (Sleepy Hollow is the neighboring village to the north.) Irving's house, Sunnyside, is a popular attraction.

FodorśChoice **Kykuit.** On a hill surrounded by gardens, stone terraces, and fountains
★ sits the stunning classical-revival mansion that was home to four generations of Rockefellers, one of America's most famous families. From its regal position, Kykuit (pronounced "kie-cut"), which means "lookout" in Dutch, has breathtaking views of the Hudson River. Antiques, ceramics, and famous artworks fill the house, which was finished in 1913; sculptures by Alexander Calder, Constantin Brancusi, Louise Nevelson, and Pablo Picasso adorn the grounds, which encompass 87 acres. You must take a tour to see the estate, which is accessible only by shuttle bus from Philipsburg Manor (381 N. Broadway, Sleepy Hollow). Four tours are offered, from an introductory house-and-garden tour to the Estate Life Tour, which includes the ⇨ **Stone Barns Center for Food and Agriculture.** ⊠ *200 Lake Rd., Pocantico Hills* ☎ *914/631–9491* ⊕ *www. hudsonvalley.org* 🎟 *$22–$35* ☉ *Late Apr.–early Nov., Wed.–Mon. by appointment only.*

☺ **Lyndhurst.** Noted architect Alexander Davis Jackson designed this magnificent marble mansion overlooking the Hudson River. Built in 1838, Lyndhurst is widely considered the premier Gothic revival home in the United States. You may tour the mansion's elaborate interior and stroll the 67 landscaped acres. The estate also includes a turn-of-the-20th-century bowling alley and an original child's playhouse, open for children to play in today. ⊠ *635 S. Broadway* ☎ *914/631–4481* ⊕ *www. lyndhurst.org* 🎟 *$10* ☉ *Mid-Apr.–Oct., Tues.–Sun. 10–5; Nov.–mid-Apr., weekends 10–4.*

Old Dutch Church of Sleepy Hollow. Built in 1685, this is the oldest church in New York State. It figures prominently in *The Legend of Sleepy Hollow,* by Washington Irving. Made of stone and hand-hewn lumber, the church is in a style typical of the northern Netherlands. Surrounding the Old Dutch Church is the famous **Sleepy Hollow Cemetery** (✉ 540 N. Broadway ☎ 914/631–0081 ⊕ www.sleepyhollowcemetery.org), which is mentioned in *The Legend of Sleepy Hollow* and was the source of some of Irving's characters' names. The cemetery is open daily 8:30–4:30. Free tours of the church and cemetery are given Sunday at 2 from Memorial Day through October. *✉ 430 N. Broadway, Sleepy Hollow ☎ 914/631–1123 ⊕ www.sleepyhollowchamber.com ☜ Free ☉ Memorial Day–early Sept., weekends 2–4 and Mon., Wed., and Thurs. 1–4; early Sept.–Oct., weekends 2–4; rest of yr by appointment.*

Philipsburg Manor. On the bank of the Pocantico River sits this 18th-century farm and provisioning plant owned by Frederick Philipse III, whose Dutch family owned most of the land in the region. Guides in period costume conduct tours of the Dutch stone house filled with 17th- and 18th-century antiques. The museum focuses, however, on the lives and stories of the 23 enslaved Africans who lived here and on slavery in the colonial north. Check out the water-powered gristmill, 18th-century barn, slave garden, and reconstructed tenant house. *✉ 381 N. Broadway, Sleepy Hollow ☎ 914/631–8200 Historic Hudson Valley ⊕ www.hudsonvalley. org ☜ $9 ☉ Mar., weekends 10–4; Apr.–Oct., Wed.–Mon. 10–5; Nov.–Dec., Wed.–Mon. 10–4.*

★ **Stone Barns Center for Food and Agriculture.** Founded by David Rockefeller in honor of his late wife, Peggy, Stone Barns is a groundbreaking nonprofit educational center that aims to promote sustainable, community-based agriculture. The 80-acre working farm encompasses Norman-style barn buildings, a restaurant and café, a greenhouse, and livestock, including sheep and swine. Garden tours, greenhouse workshops, and introductions to local environmentalists, winemakers, and organic farmers are among the programs. Self-guided tours are free; guided tours are $9. The dinner-only restaurant, **Blue Hill at Stone Barns,** is an outpost of Manhattan's famed Blue Hill. The Blue Hill Café serves light fare and sandwiches until 4:30. *✉ 630 Bedford Rd., Pocantico Hills ☎ 914/366–6200 ⊕ www.stonebarnscenter.org ☜ Free; fees for programs ☉ Wed.–Sun. 10–5.*

Sunnyside. A guide in period costume escorts you through the1830s home of Washington Irving, whose writings include *The Legend of Sleepy Hollow* and *Rip Van Winkle*. The eclectic building, one of the nation's earliest examples of romantic architecture, includes stepped gables that recall Dutch architecture and a curved roof modeled after that of a Spanish monastery. Sunnyside was often called America's Home, because it appeared in many landscape illustrations of the period. Irving's book-lined study is a highlight. *✉ 89 W. Sunnyside La. ☎ 914/631–8200 Historic Hudson Valley ⊕ www.hudsonvalley.org ☜ $9 ☉ Mar., weekends 10–4; Apr.–Oct., Wed.–Mon. 10–5; Nov. and Dec., Wed.–Mon. 10–4.*

Tarrytown Lighthouse. Great views of the Hudson River and the Tappan Zee Bridge can be seen from this 65-foot-tall all-metal beacon built in 1883. Guided tours show how the keeper once lived. *✉ Kingsland Point Park, Palmer Ave. (off Pierson St. west of Rte. 9), Sleepy Hollow ☎ 914/366–5109 ⊕ www.sleepyhollowchamber.com ☜ $5 ☉ By appointment.*

Fodor'sChoice **Union Church of Pocantico Hills.** The nondenominational stone church built
★ in 1922 on land donated by John D. Rockefeller is loosely based on early
English Gothic buildings but deliberately devoid of sectarian detailing.
The real stars of the site, however, are the stained-glass windows by Marc
Chagall and Henri Matisse, also gifts of the Rockefeller family. ⊠ *555
Bedford Rd./Rte. 448, Pocantico Hills* ☎ *914/631–8200 Historic Hud-
son Valley* ⊕ *www.hudsonvalley.org* ⊠ *$4* ☉ *Apr.–Dec., Wed.–Mon.,
11–5, Sat. 10–5, Sun. 2–5.*

Van Cortlandt Manor. At this living-history museum, costumed guides are
strategically placed throughout the estate, which includes an 18th-cen-
tury stone manor house and an 18th-century tavern. The house includes some of its original Georgian and Federal furnishings. Spinning,
weaving, and other demonstrations are held in a tenant house adjacent
to the tavern. ⊠ *S. Riverside Ave., off Rte. 9, Croton-on-Hudson*
☎ *914/631–8200 Historic Hudson Valley* ⊕ *www.hudsonvally.org*
⊠ *$9* ☉ *Apr.–Oct., Wed.–Mon., 10–5; Nov. and Dec., weekends 10–4.*

off the
beaten
path
DONALD M. KENDALL SCULPTURE GARDENS AT PEPSICO – The
world headquarters of the global soft-drinks giant, about 10 mi east
of Tarrytown, is home to a 145-acre sculpture garden with 20th-
century works by the likes of Henry Moore, Alexander Calder, and
Isamu Noguchi. This is not a public park (so no dogs or Frisbees); the
corporation welcomes visitors "as guests." A self-guided tour
brochure, restrooms, and a small picnic area are available.
⊠ *Anderson Hill Rd., Purchase* ☎ *914/253–2001* ⊠ *Free* ☉ *Daily
9–5 (until dusk in winter).*

Where to Stay & Eat

★ $$$$ ✕ **Blue Hill at Stone Barns.** This outpost of Dan Barber's famed Blue
Hill restaurant (in Manhattan) occupies an old barn on the grounds of
the Stone Barns Center for Food and Agriculture. The menu features
the center's own produce and meats as well as the bounty of many other
local farms. That said, neither the food nor the decor is rustic. The space
is beautiful in its restraint, which puts the focus on the high picture windows and the barn rafters. Banquettes, dressed in brown and set off
against white tablecloths and cream walls, are elegant. Dinner is prix
fixe, two to four courses. With such an intense focus on seasonal fare,
the menu changes frequently; you might find pea-green gazpacho, roast
pork with braised bacon, or lobster-filled cannelloni. Desserts, including a molten chocolate-and-caramel cake and passion-fruit soufflé, are
extra but worth it. ⊠ *630 Bedford Rd., Pocantico Hills* ☎ *914/366–
9600* ⊟ *AE, D, MC, V* ⚛ *Reservations essential* ☉ *Closed Mon. and
Tues. No lunch.*

$$$$ ✕ **Equus.** A grand experience awaits at this lavishly appointed restaurant at the Castle at Tarrytown, a century-old mansion on an 11-acre
estate. Choose from three dining rooms, all of them formal—the Oak
Room, with ornately carved built-ins from France; the Tapestry Room,
and the Garden Room, which has breathtaking Hudson River views—
and an outdoor terrace. French influences make their way into the fare,
which ranges from hazlenut-crusted Hudson Valley foie gras to pan-seared

veal sweetbreads. A $35 prix-fixe lunch and $66 four-course dinner is also served. The restaurant hosts regular wine tastings, afternoon tea, and, on Wednesday evenings, jazz. A children's menu is available. ⊠ *400 Benedict Ave.* ☎ *914/631–1980* ▤ *AE, D, MC, V* ⌖ *Reservations essential* ⌂ *Jacket required.*

$–$$$$ ✕ **Santa Fe.** Locals flock to this casual restaurant for its fresh specialties and colorful Southwestern atmosphere. Pasta de Mesilla is semolina–and–green chili linguine with cilantro pesto; *cochinita pibil* consists of boneless pork marinated in orange juice and achiote and slow-cooked in banana leaves. The menu lists more than 30 premium tequilas. ⊠ *5 Main St./Rte. 9* ☎ *914/332–4452* ▤ *AE, D, DC, MC, V.*

$$–$$$ ✕ **Horsefeathers.** A main-drag institution, the restaurant serves traditional pub fare, which includes its famous burgers and more than 80 microbrews from around the globe. The seemingly endless menu also features lighter fare and 13 kinds of omelets, all served continuously so you can have lunch at dinnertime or dinner at lunchtime. Weekend brunch is served 11–4, however. Dine indoors in a dark, pub-like environment or outdoors on the sidewalk when weather permits. ⊠ *94 S. Broadway* ☎ *914/631–6606* ▤ *AE, D, MC, V.*

$$ ✕ **Caravela.** Although small and informal, this Portuguese and Brazilian restaurant is highly regarded. Paella brims with shrimp, clams, mussels, chicken, and sausage; fresh cod mixes with shrimp, scallops, and clams in fennel-and-saffron broth. Reservations are essential on Saturday. Outdoor dining is at sidewalk tables. ⊠ *53 N. Broadway* ☎ *914/ 631–1863* ▤ *AE, D, DC, MC, V.*

$–$$ ✕ **Lefteris Gyro.** At a busy downtown corner, this family-friendly fixture is known for using fresh ingredients and taking a light approach to traditional Greek fare. Favorites are the enormous Greek salad, which can be shared, and platters of souvlaki, *bifteki* (Greek-style hamburger), and gyros, served with pita, tomato, and yogurt sauce. ⊠ *1 Main St.* ☎ *914/524–9687* ▤ *AE, D, DC, V, MC.*

$$$$ ⌖ **Castle on the Hudson.** The magnificent mansion, completed in 1910, sits amid 11 hilltop acres overlooking the Hudson River. With two impressive towers and a stone exterior, the mansion was modeled after Lismore Castle in County Waterford, Ireland. Rooms occupy the original house and a stucco wing, where a spa is planned (to open in early 2005). Rooms are elegant, decorated with antiques, silk curtains, and four-poster beds. The food at the Equus restaurant is as refined as the surroundings. ⊠ *400 Benedict Ave., 10591* ☎ *914/631–1980* 🖷 *914/ 631–4612* ⊕ *www.castleattarrytown.com* ⇝ *26 rooms, 5 suites* ⌖ *Restaurant, room service, in-room data ports, in-room fax, in-room safes, minibars, in-room VCRs, tennis court, indoor pool, gym, outdoor hot tub, massage, boccie, croquet, bar, dry cleaning, laundry facilities, Internet, business services, convention center, meeting rooms; no smoking* ▤ *AE, D, DC, MC, V* ¶O¶ *CP.*

$–$$$ ⌖ **Westchester Marriott.** A beautiful atrium houses an indoor pool and a full-service health club; some rooms overlook the pool courtyard. A favorite of business travelers, the hotel is convenient to Tarrytown's corporate parks and the nearby city of White Plains. A Ruth's Chris Steak House and a Pizza Hut are on the premises. ⊠ *670 White Plains Rd.*

☎ *914/631–2200* 🖷 *914/631–7819* ⊕ *www.westchestermarriott.com* 🛏 *439 rooms, 5 suites ⚓ 2 restaurants, room service, in-room data ports, cable TV with movies, indoor pool, gym, hair salon, hot tub, sauna, 3 bars, dry cleaning, laundry facilities, laundry service, concierge, concierge floor, Internet, business services, meeting rooms, car rental, no-smoking floors* ▤ *AE, D, DC, MC, V.*

$$ 🏨 **Dolce Tarrytown House.** Two 19th-century mansions—one Georgian, the other a stone Gothic revival that's a National Trust site—dominate this conference-oriented property, once home to tobacco heiress Mary Duke Biddle. The grounds, high above the Hudson River, are loaded with recreational diversions and include massive specimen trees and antique garden statues. Most of the mansion rooms serve as restaurants and other public meeting places; modern wings provide the bulk of the guest rooms, each with a desk and high-speed Internet access. ⊠ *49 E. Sunnyside La., 10591* ☎ *914/591–8200 or 800/553–8118* 🖷 *914/591–3131* ⊕ *www.tarrytownhouse.dolce.com* 🛏 *212 rooms, 4 suites ⚓ Restaurant, in-room data ports, cable TV with movies, 3 tennis courts, 2 pools, gym, hot tub, massage, steam room, basketball, billiards, boccie, bowling, horseshoes, racquetball, volleyball, bar, dry cleaning, laundry service, Internet, business services, convention center, no-smoking rooms* ▤ *AE, D, DC, MC, V* ❏ *BP.*

¢–$$ 🏨 **Tarrytown Courtyard.** Set back from a busy commercial strip, the low-lying, circa 1988 hotel has a ranchlike feel and residential neighbors. Contemporary in style, the lobby has a swirl-patterned rug and the rooms have homey details, such as black-and-white photos resting on a shelf. Business travelers dominate on weekdays. ⊠ *475 White Plains Rd., 10591* ☎ *914/631–1122* 🖷 *914/631–1357* ⊕ *www.marriott.com* 🛏 *120 rooms, 19 suites ⚓ Restaurant, in-room data ports, microwaves, refrigerators, cable TV with movies, indoor pool, gym, hot tub, bar, dry cleaning, laundry facilities, Internet, business services, meeting rooms; no smoking* ▤ *AE, D, DC, MC, V.*

¢–$$ 🏨 **Tarrytown Hilton.** Near the intersection of two major highways, I–87 and I–287, the hotel attracts business travelers during the week and Manhattan families on summer weekends. Rooms have reproductions of American Empire furniture with glass handles and sleigh beds. The sunny restaurant overlooks a courtyard, one of two where you can relax outdoors on wrought-iron lawn furniture. ⊠ *455 S. Broadway, 10591* ☎ *914/631–5700* 🖷 *914/631–0075* ⊕ *www.hilton.com* 🛏 *244 rooms, 7 suites ⚓ Restaurant, room service, in-room data ports, minibars, cable TV, tennis court, indoor-outdoor pool, hot tub, gym, sports bar, dry cleaning, laundry service, business services, some pets allowed, no-smoking rooms* ▤ *AE, D, DC, MC, V.*

Nightlife & the Arts

The 1885 **Tarrytown Music Hall** (⊠ 13 Main St. ☎ 914/631–3390), a National Historic Landmark and the oldest live theater in Westchester County, serves as a cultural-arts center best known for its jazz concerts. The interior combines Victorian workmanship and design with art-deco playfulness. Performers have included Wynton Marsalis, the Preservation Hall Jazz Band, and Tony Bennett. Theater, opera, and art films fill out the offerings.

Sports & the Outdoors

Hiking trails, fishing ponds, carriage paths, woodlands, and lush meadows make up the more than 1,000 acres of the **Rockefeller State Park Preserve** (⊠ Rte. 117 near Rte. 9, Mount Pleasant ☎ 914/631–1470 ⊕ nysparks.state.ny.us), 4 mi northeast of Tarrytown. The wetlands portion is home to a number of migratory bird species, such as the scarlet tanager and Baltimore oriole, which breed here. Panoramic views of the Hudson River can be seen from the former site of Rockwood Hall, William Rockefeller's estate. What's left of it is a dramatic Frederick Law Olmstead landscape that includes a century-old alley of copper beeches. The park is open daily from 8:30 AM to sunset; parking is $6.

Shopping

Tarrytown is a walking village that prides itself on having only two national-chain stores. Most of its shops occupy old buildings, and the two main drags—Main Street and Broadway—have an old-fashioned feel. **Belkind-Bigi** (⊠ 21 Main St. ☎ 914/524–9626) is one of the few shops specializing in midcentury modern furniture and accessories. Choose from designer pieces—Mies van der Rohe's Barcelona chairs, George Nelson's platform bench—or those with idiosyncratic pedigrees that hold their own among such heavyweights. Antiques dealers love the low prices and large and diverse selection at **Hank's Alley** (⊠ 15 N. Washington St. ☎ 914/524–9895), set back from the street in what was once a trolley shop. You can find 1920s mahogany dining sets and '60s Danish modern pieces as well as vintage jewelry, beaded bags, and clothing. **Razzmatazz** (⊠ 35 N. Broadway ☎ 914/631–4646), an all-around gift shop, has a small yet interesting selection of women's and children's clothing, glassware and ceramics, bath products, and books and prints on local history and sites.

Katonah

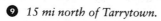 *15 mi north of Tarrytown.*

Named after an American Indian chief who sold the town its land, Katonah was a 19th-century farming center that shipped produce and milk to New York City via railroad. When New York City planned to flood parts of the old village to make way for reservoirs, some enterprising residents decided to move their homes to a newly combined commercial and residential district, Katonah's current downtown. In all, some 55 buildings were relocated in 15 years, including some gingerbread Victorian homes that make up the core of this charming village.

Katonah's downtown encompasses a shopping district populated with upscale galleries, boutiques, and restaurants, as well as a few family-owned stores that have managed to retain the feel of yesteryear. The village is also a cultural hub for northern Westchester, with the Katonah Museum of Art, Caramoor Center for Music and the Arts, and John Jay Homestead luring visitors from the tri-state region.

John Jay Homestead State Historic Site. The estate of John Jay (1745–1849), the first chief justice of the United States Supreme Court, has many American classical furnishings from the period and traces Jay's life and career. The house, built in 1801, was, until the early 1950s, home to five generations of Jay's family. You can stroll the property, which includes formal gardens. ⊠ *400 Jay St./Rte. 22* ☎ *914/232–5651* ⊕ *nysparks. state.ny.us* ⬚ *$7* ⊙ *Apr.–Nov., Tues.–Sat. 10–4, Sun. 11–4; Dec.–Mar., call for hrs.*

Katonah Museum of Art. The museum's changing exhibitions span a wide range of cultures, mediums, historical periods, and social issues. It's not uncommon to see a show about banjos or puzzles followed by a more traditional art exhibit—a review of Latin-American works or a retrospective of Richard Diebenkorn's prints, for example. In addition to lectures, symposia, and tours of private collections, the museum offers workshops for children and families. Guided tours start at 2:30 Tuesday through Sunday. ⊠ *Rte. 22 at Jay St.* ☎ *914/232–9555* ⊕ *www. katonahmuseum.org* ⬚ *$3 (free 10–noon)* ⊙ *Tues.–Sat. 10–5, Sun. noon–5.*

♻ **Muscoot Farm.** The county park, first a gentleman's farm, was named after a Lenape word meaning "by the swamp," because of its location near what is now part of the New York City watershed. A lively seasonal roster of special events is offered, including hay rides and demonstrations of blacksmithing, maple sugaring, and sheep shearing. Farm animals—sheep, chickens, pigs, goats, cows, horses—are permanent residents. ⊠ *Rte. 100 south of Rte. 35* ☎ *914/864–7282* ⊕ *www. westchestergov.com* ⬚ *Free* ⊙ *Daily 10–4.*

Ward Pound Ridge Reservation. The 4,700-acre reserve, 5 mi east of Katonah, is the largest park in Westchester County. More than 35 mi of deep woodland trails and cross-country-skiing, hiking, horse, mountain-biking, and nature trails crisscross the park, which encompasses picnic areas, ponds, rivers, and marshes. You can camp here, too, in Adirondack-style lean-tos or tent sites. Adjacent to a wildflower garden is the **Trailside Nature Museum,** a resource center that houses a collection of American Indian artifacts. ⊠ *Rtes. 35 and 121, Cross River* ☎ *914/864–7317* ⊕ *www.westchestergov.com* ⬚ *Parking $8 (May–Sept.), museum free* ⊙ *Park daily 8–dusk, museum Wed.–Sun. 9–4.*

Where to Eat

$$–$$$ ✕ **Blue Dolphin.** What looks like a kitschy old diner on the outside might as well be a trattoria in Capri on the inside: photos of the island adorn the walls and the food is authentic Italian. That's why locals wait in long lines to get in. Its pastas—veal-stuffed ravioli, baked pasta with eggplant and loads of cheese—are renowned. Vegetables such as wilted broccoli rabe are also a specialty. ⊠ *175 Katonah Ave.* ☎ *914/232–4791* ⚎ *Reservations not accepted* ⊟ *AE, MC, V.*

$$–$$$ ✕ **Cafe Antico.** Subdued lighting and fresh flowers at each table set a romantic mood at this Italian restaurant. Try the spaghetti with imported baby octopus or the pasta *bianco e nero*, black and white spaghetti with calamari and shrimp in a mildly spicy lobster consommé. The Venetian winged lions at the bar add a nice touch. ⊠ *251 Lexington Ave., Mount Kisco* ☎ *845/242–7490* ⊟ *AE, D, DC, MC, V.*

$–$$ ✕ **Willy Nick's.** Across the street from the Katonah train station, this is the place to get a cup of joe and a freshly baked scone to go. Or stay for a lunch or dinner of classic American comfort food (such as burgers and meat loaf) and updated variations on that theme (lobster macaroni and cheese). On weekends, families pack the place for brunch. ✉ *17 Katonah Ave.* ☎ *914/232–8030* ▭ *AE, MC, V* ⊙ *No dinner Mon. and Tues.*

$ ✕🏨 **Crabtree's Kittle House.** Gardens surround this elegant colonial-style inn, 8 mi south of Katonah, that dates to 1790. Rooms with quilts and four-poster beds combine historic character with country charm. The restaurant ($$–$$$$) is known for creative dishes such as a starter of grilled Hudson Valley foie gras with toasted brioche, candied orange, and Bordeaux syrup. Portobello mushrooms, served as a main course, are roasted and given the Wellington treatment—encased in puff pastry and served with wild mushroom sauce. ✉ *11 Kittle Rd., Chappaqua 10514* ☎ *914/666–8044* 🌐 *www.kittlehouse.com* *12 rooms* *Restaurant, in-room data ports, some refrigerators, cable TV, in-room VCRs, bar, piano, some pets allowed; no smoking* ▭ *AE, D, DC, MC, V* 🍽 *CP.*

$$ 🏨 **Holiday Inn.** This branch of the national chain has a quiet lobby with knotty pine paneling and a roaring fire, but on Friday and Saturday evenings the place rocks with the sounds of a DJ in the bar, which has a mirrored ceiling and a disco ball. Some of the guest rooms have small sofas; executive rooms have large work areas. ✉ *1 Holiday Inn Dr., Mount Kisco 10549* ☎ *914/241–2600* 🖷 *914/241–4742* 🌐 *www.hudsonvalleymanor.com* *122 rooms* *Restaurant, room service, in-room data ports, cable TV with movies, pool, bar, video game room, dry cleaning, laundry facilities, laundry service, Internet, business services, some pets allowed (fee), no-smoking rooms* ▭ *AE, D, DC, MC, V.*

Nightlife & the Arts

Some of the world's finest classical and jazz performers can be heard at the **Caramoor Center for Music and the Arts** (✉ 149 Girdle Ridge Rd. ☎ 914/232–5035 🌐 www.caramoor.org) during its summer concert season, June through August. Music is also offered year-round in the house museum, which contains an extraordinary collection of Renaissance and Asian art. Ninety acres of lovely gardens are another highlight.

Shopping

Katonah has a wonderful array of independently owned shops. At **Boo Girls** (✉ 155 Katonah Ave. ☎ 914/232–8082), which targets "tweens," the leopard rug and cow-patterned dressing-room curtains compete for attention with lacy tops and lip gloss. **Charles Department Store** (✉ 113 Katonah Ave. ☎ 914/232–5200) has been selling clothing, housewares, and hardware since 1939. The salesperson-to-customer ratio is high, so expect some old-fashioned service. At **Sticky Fingers** (✉ 155 Katonah Ave. ☎ 914/232–8078), a children's boutique, girls flip for the sequined shoes.

North Salem

⑩ *9 mi northeast of Katonah.*

The town of North Salem encompasses idyllic rural landscapes: gentle hills, streams, ponds, horse farms, narrow winding roads, and lovely old houses. The area served as a camp for General de Rochambeau and his French troops after their Yorktown victory, which ended the Revolutionary War. Shortly thereafter, North Salem bustled with factories and mills, churning out everything from dairy and lumber products to tools and clothes. The area was also known for its contribution to the early circus. Several townsfolk invested in early circus shows, and others established the first touring circus syndicate. Their travels introduced new circus animals, including the hippopotamus, to American audiences.

Hammond Museum and Japanese Stroll Gardens. The center shows changing exhibitions related to Eastern and Western cultures. The 3½-acre Japanese stroll garden is beautiful in all seasons. There is also a café with outdoor dining on a tree-lined terrace. ⊠ *28 Deveau Rd.* ☎ *845/669–5033* ⊕ *www.hammondmuseum.org* ⌑ *$5* ☉ *Wed.–Sat. noon–4.*

Museum of the Early American Circus and the Somers Historical Society. The museum (about 8 mi west of North Salem) exhibits artifacts related to the American traveling circus, which came into being in Somers. Hachaliah Bailey (later of Barnum & Bailey), a dairy farmer, purchased an African elephant in 1807 and soon thereafter featured it in a traveling menagerie. A vest coat worn by P. T. Barnum's protégé during an 1844 audience with Queen Victoria is among the items on display. ⊠ *Rtes. 100 and 202, Somers* ☎ *914/277–4977* ⊕ *www.somersmuseum.org* ⌑ *Free* ☉ *Thurs. 2–4, 2nd and 4th Sun. of each month 1–4.*

North Salem Vineyard. Westchester's only vineyard and winery has 18 acres of grapes planted in 1965. You can sample the vineyard's bounty at wine tastings in a rustic, beamed barn, or picnic on the grounds with a basket lunch for two ($15). The winery offers an array of wines, from sparkling varieties to red table wine. ⊠ *441 Hardscrabble Rd.* ☎ *914/669–5518* ⊕ *www.northsalemwine.com* ⌑ *Free* ☉ *Weekends 1–5.*

Where to Eat

$$–$$$$ ✕ **Purdys Homestead.** The updated 18th-century farmhouse is sophisticated and welcoming, with hand-hewn beams and stone fireplaces. The menu includes mainstays such as roasted oysters with leeks and vermouth, and crispy Long Island duck, as well as seasonal dishes like hearty wild-mushroom potpie with rosemary crust. Chocolate bread pudding with chocolate sauce and chocolate diamonds (shards of white chocolate) and espresso sauce is a chocoholic's dream. ⊠ *100 Titicus Rd.* ☎ *914/277–2301* ☐ *AE, MC, V* ☉ *Closed Mon. No lunch.*

$$$ ✕ **Auberge Maxime.** Elegance reigns at this French restaurant where candlelight warms the interior and white tablecloths offset floral draperies. Specialties include roast duck with berry medley and braised lamb shank. In warm weather you may opt to dine on the terrace for a view of the manicured grounds and tree-covered hills beyond. Sunday brunch is available. ⊠ *721 Titicus Rd.* ☎ *914/669–5450* ☐ *AE, DC, MC, V* ☉ *Closed Tues. and Wed. No lunch.*

Garrison

❶ *35 mi northwest of North Salem, 35 mi north of Tarrytown.*

Sleepy Garrison takes full advantage of its riverside setting with a rambling waterfront park. Pleasure boats dock at the marina, and a gazebo and willow tree–shaded benches are front-row seats to the mighty Hudson River; across the shore, on the west bank, loom the buildings of the United States Military Academy at West Point. At Garrison's Landing, as the waterfront area is known, a small clutch of art galleries, offices, and homes surrounds the old train station, now a community theater called the Philipstown Depot.

Beyond the Landing, restored homes and artful landscapes bespeak the region's rich aesthetic history. Boscobel showcases architecture and decorative arts from the early-19th-century Federalist period, whereas Manitoga—the home, studio, and woodlands of industrial designer Russel Wright—fast-forwards into the mid-20th century. In summer the celebrated Hudson Valley Shakespeare Festival comes to town, gracing Boscobel with contemporary interpretations of the hallowed plays in a tent-theater. The Appalachian Trail passes through the region, crossing the Hudson River at Bear Mountain and meandering through Garrison's many acres of protected land.

Boscobel Restoration. High-style period furniture and collections of crystal, silver, and porcelain fill this restored 1808 mansion, now a museum of Federal-period decorative arts. Built by States Morris Dyckman, a descendant of one of New Amsterdam's early Dutch families, the house originally stood in Montrose, some 15 mi south. It's open by tour only, but the grounds are reason enough to visit: the 30 sweeping acres give way to Hudson River views and encompass multiple gardens, an orangery, and a 1-mi woodland trail. ⊠ *1601 Rte. 9D* ☎ *845/265–3638* ⊕ *www. boscobel.org* ☞ *Tour $10* ⊙ *House Apr.–Nov., Wed.–Mon. 10–4:15 (last tour); Dec., Wed.–Mon. 10–3:15 (last tour). Grounds Apr.–Nov., Wed.–Mon. 9:30–dusk.*

Constitution Marsh Audubon Center and Sanctuary. An extensive boardwalk leads you deep into the reeds and rushes of this lush, wildlife-filled tidal marshland. In winter the boardwalk is a prime lookout spot for bald eagles. Tromp through the 200-acre sanctuary's bluffs and woodlands, or visit the Educational Center, where a 500-gallon aquarium offers an up-close look at fish, crabs, and other resident wildlife. ⊠ *Indian Brook Rd. off Rte. 9D south* ☎ *845/265–2601* ⊕ *ny.audubon.org/ cmac.htm* ☞ *Free* ⊙ *Trails daily 9–6, center Tues.–Sun. 9–5.*

Garrison Art Center. Exhibits by local artists working in various mediums are shown at this gallery and educational center housed in three 19th-century buildings by the waterfront. ⊠ *23 Garrison's Landing* ☎ *845/ 424–3960* ⊕ *www.garrisonartcenter.org* ☞ *Free* ⊙ *Daily noon–5.*

★ **Manitoga–The Russel Wright Design Center.** Nature and art blend seamlessly throughout the home, studio, and 75-acre grounds of mid-20th-century industrial designer Russel Wright. Boulders protrude through the ground floor of **Dragon Rock,** Wright's experimental home, which is built on a rock ledge and spans 11 levels; fist-size stones serve as door handles. Four miles of paths weave through a landscape that appears natural but is actually a studied design of native trees, rocks, mosses, and wildflowers. Daily 90-minute tours take in the buildings and woodlands (wear comfortable walking shoes), or you can take a self-guided tour of the grounds. ⊠ *Rte. 9D 2½ mi north of Bear Mountain Bridge* ☎ *845/424–3812* ⊕ *www.russelwrightcenter.org* ☒ *Guided house-and-grounds tour $15, grounds $5 suggested donation* ⊙ *Grounds Apr.–Oct., daily dawn–dusk. Tours by appointment only.*

Where to Eat

$$–$$$ ✕ **Valley Restaurant.** The seasonal menu of regional American fare features meats, produce, and cheeses from artisinal area farms as well as from the restaurant's own kitchen garden. Ravioli are filled with Hudson Valley foie gras and scallops and served with wild chervil–and–wine sauce; jumbo crab cakes are dressed with grainy mustard sauce and tea leaves; and organic pork gets an Asian barbecue glaze. There is also a raw bar. At Sunday brunch ($28 prix fixe) the buffet table is laden with omelets, crepes, smoked fish, and scones. Large windows frame swoon-inducing valley views. Lunch and dinner may be served on a river-view terrace, weather permitting. ⊠ *The Garrison, 2015 Rte. 9* ☎ *845/424–3604* ▤ *AE, D, DC, MC, V* ⊙ *Closed Mon.–Wed.*

Sports & the Outdoors

GOLF   Top-of-the-world vistas of the Hudson Highlands enhance 18 holes of championship golf at the **Garrison Golf & Country Club** (⊠ 2015 U.S. 9 ☎ 845/424–3604 ⊕ www.garrisongolfclub.com). The river and valley views from the driving range are positively jaw-dropping. Greens fees range from $65 weekdays to $85 on weekends. Pick up refreshments at the snack bar next to the pro shop or from the circulating beverage cart.

KAYAKING   For a leisurely afternoon excursion, slip into the river from the boat launch at **Garrison's Landing,** near the Garrison train stop. Across the Hudson River loom the buildings of the United States Military Academy at West Point. Paddle upriver, past Constitution Island and Constitution Marsh, and land at Cold Spring. For quicker access to the marsh, enter the water in Cold Spring, where kayak rentals ($30 to $70 a day) are available. Removed from the river's currents, **Constitution Marsh** is one of the most peaceful places on the Hudson to dip your paddle. Wide canals let you steer amid the marsh plants and wildlife—but take care not to lose your sense of direction in this maze of waterways. Keep in mind that because the Hudson is actually an estuary, tides affect the marsh. Avoid getting yourself grounded in the mud by leaving plenty of time to get back to the shore by low tide.

Cold Spring

⑫ *5 mi north of Garrison.*

The well-preserved 19th-century village edges one of the most dramatic bends of the Hudson River, and its true showpiece may well be the breath-stealing river-valley views. The village has a handful of sights, but the chief pleasures of Cold Spring are its mix of shops and its proximity to green spaces and hiking trails. Main Street, a few steps from the Metro-North train stop, is the commercial heart.

You might not guess that this small, laid-back Putnam County village once bustled with an industry pivotal to the fate of the entire nation. When the West Point Foundry opened here in 1817, Cold Spring laid claim to the most innovative and productive ironworks in the United States. The facility turned out Civil War munitions as well as iron cast for the nation's first commissioned locomotive and steamboat. In 1884 the ironworkers' furnaces ceased blazing, and the foundry site succumbed to neglect and the hand of nature. Only one office building still stands in Foundry Cove; a small cache of artifacts and objects tells the foundry's story at the local museum.

Chapel of Our Lady. Greek revival architecture finds expression in this 1833 chapel atop a bluff facing the Hudson River. Passing sailors have long taken pleasure in the landmark, originally built to support the spiritual lives of West Point Foundry workers. Initially a Catholic church, the nondenominational chapel now hosts ecumenical services, weddings, and other events. The chapel has no set open hours, but the facade is worth a look, and the columned porch is a great place for river gazing. ⊠ *45 Market St.* ☎ *845/265–5537.*

Foundry Cove. The ruins of a 19th-century iron foundry stand (barely) here amid a tangle of vines, a babbling brook, and 85 acres of preserved marshland and woodland. The original commercial hub of Cold Spring village, the West Point Foundry once buzzed with activity, as ironworkers manufactured Civil War cannons, cannon balls, and guns, as well as cast-iron facades for SoHo warehouses and even the nation's first domestically made locomotive. To get here from Main Street, turn south onto Kemble Avenue and take it to the end, proceed through the gate, turn left, and follow the path to the site. You can also follow the marked woodland trail to a waterfall at the site's edge. ⊠ *Off Kemble Ave., south of Main St.* ☎ *No phone.*

Heritage Way Guided Walking Tours. The Putnam County Historical Society leads a 60- to 90-minute walking tour of Cold Spring village that takes you past the village's oldest intact homes along Market and Main streets as well as the spot where General George Washington drank from the spring for which the village is named. Reservations aren't required. Tours meet at 72 Main Street. ☎ *845/265–4010* ⊕ *www.pchs-fsm.org* ☒ *$5 suggested donation* ⊙ *Mid-May–mid-Nov., Sun. at 2.*

Putnam County Historical Society and Foundry School Museum. Local historical memorabilia and changing exhibits fill this former 19th-century schoolhouse, once attended by children of West Point Foundry workers. A permanent installation and video chronicle the history of the foundry. Paintings, drawings, photographs, and other objects and artifacts round out the museum's collection. ⊠ *63 Chestnut St.* ☎ *845/265–4010* ⊕ *www.pchs-fsm.org* ☒ *$5 suggested donation* ⊙ *Mar.–Dec., Tues.–Thurs. 10–4 and weekends 2–5.*

Riverfront Bandstand and Dock. The majesty of the Hudson Highlands surrounds this 100-by-100-foot dock, where you can stroll, fish, lounge, or simply behold the views of Bear Mountain, Crow's Nest, and Storm King. Free concerts bring musicians to the bandstand on Sunday evenings in July and August. ⊠ *Lower Main St. at the Hudson River* ☎ *No phone.*

★ **Stonecrop Gardens.** Sixty-three acres showcase the landscape design of Francis Cabot, founder of the Garden Conservancy. Display gardens span

12 of the acres, in settings ranging from rock cliffs and woodlands to placid pools and verdant lawns. Don't overlook the picture-perfect conservatory, where the winter garden includes trees and flowers native to South Africa, New Zealand, and Australia. ⊠ *81 Stonecrop La., off Rte. 301 between U.S. 9 and the Taconic State Parkway* ☎ *845/265–2000* ⊕ *www.stonecrop.org* ▦ *$3* ⊙ *By appointment only.*

off the beaten path

CHUANG YEN MONASTERY – The largest indoor statue of the Buddha in the Western Hemisphere resides here, standing 37 feet tall and surrounded by 10,000 Buddha figurines on a lotus terrace in Great Buddha Hall. The extensive grounds invite walking, with pathways leading to Seven Jewels Lake. The largest monastery in the eastern United States, Chuang Yen holds Sunday-morning English-language programs in Tai-Hsu Hall. Its vegetarian lunch ($5), at noon on weekends, may be the best deal in town. The monastery is in Carmel, east of Cold Spring. ⊠ *2020 Rte. 301, Carmel* ☎ *845/225–1819* ⊕ *www.baus.org/baus* ▦ *Free* ⊙ *Daily 9–5.*

Where to Stay & Eat

$$$–$$$$ ✕ **Hudson House River Inn.** Watch sailboats drift by from the veranda tables at this riverfront restaurant, or dine by the window in the country-style River Room. A crust of red and blue tortillas gives crab cakes a new twist. Notable entrées include salmon filled with sun-dried-tomato pesto and arugula, and filet mignon wrapped in a crusty sleeve of pancetta. Sunday brunch is $23 prix fixe. ⊠ *2 Main St.* ☎ *845/265–9355* ▤ *AE, DC, MC, V* ⊙ *Closed Tues. No lunch Wed.*

$–$$$ ✕ **Brasserie Le Bouchon.** It's France-on-the-Hudson at this village hot spot with crimson walls, lipstick-hued banquettes, and Edith Piaf on the stereo. Although purists might claim the fare is more bistro than brasserie, the extensive menu and wine lists give you many choices. Expertly executed classics range from *croque monsieur* (egg batter–dipped ham-and-cheese sandwich) to steak au poivre with cognac-and-cream dressing. The rum-infused crème brûlée and cloud-light profiteroles have gained a following. ⊠ *76 Main St.* ☎ *845/265–7676* ▤ *AE, MC, V* ⊙ *Closed Tues.*

$–$$$ ✕ **Cathryn's Dolcigno Tuscan Grill.** Swaths of sheer fabric and vibrant murals romance the interior of this rustic trattoria—a paean to northern Italian food and fresh herbs. Transplanted New Yorkers sip reds and whites from an extensive wine list. Sage-browned butter laces silky calves' liver, and an espresso demi-glace enlivens grilled hanger steak. Vegetarians choose from pasta dishes such as whole-wheat fusilli primavera. Sunday brunch, from noon to 3, is $20 prix fixe. ⊠ *91 Main St.* ☎ *845/265–5582* ▤ *AE, D, MC, V.*

$–$$ ✕ **Café Maya.** Authentic Mexican fare and congenial service make up for the strip-mall setting of this tiny eatery. Homemade *mulato* sauce, a blend of four kinds of peppers, flavors the steak-filled house burrito; *mojo de ajo* (Mexican garlic sauce) envelops a dish of sautéed shrimp. The guacamole is served in the *molcajete* (stone bowl or mortar and pestle) in which it's made to order. ⊠ *Perks Plaza, 3182 U.S. 9* ☎ *845/265–4636* ⚇ *Reservations not accepted* ▤ *AE, D, MC, V* ▯ *BYOB* ⊙ *Closed Tues.*

¢–$$ ✕ **East Side Kitchen.** At this relaxed Main Street eatery, a stamping ground for local families, you can tuck into a chili-cheese dog with curly fries or a plate of barbecued ribs, or sample signature fare like tortilla-wrapped chicken with jack cheese, spicy remoulade, and sweet-potato fries. Kids cozy up to the ice-cream counter, which turns out milk shakes and floats. Retro-hip 1950s decor, comfy banquettes, and oldies music set a feel-good tone. ⊠ *124 Main St.* ☎ *845/265–7223* ▭ *AE, MC, V* ◯ *Closed Mon.*

$$ ✕▦ **Riverview.** A popular village restaurant ($–$$) offers a couple of spacious and airy upstairs lodgings. Windows in the north-facing room—including one over the whirlpool tub for two—look out onto the Hudson River and Storm King. Extra-large bathrooms, shabby-chic armchairs, and other homey furnishings are inviting. Downstairs, transcendent views accompany "modern Continental" fare. Handblown sconces lend a golden glow to the dining room come evening. Wood-oven pizzas are praiseworthy, as are grilled rib-eye steak, fusilli Bolognese, and fish specials. Reservations are essential for the highly coveted terrace tables and on Wednesday nights, when special prices lure a spirited crowd. ⊠ *45 Fair St., 10516* ☎ *845/265–4778* 🖷 *845/265–5596* ➳ *1 room, 1 suite* ⌂ *Restaurant, 1 in-room hot tub, cable TV; no phone in 1 room, no smoking* ▭ *No credit cards* ¶⦿ EP.

$–$$ ✕▦ **Plumbush Inn.** The 19th-century Victorian inn a short hop from the village center was once the home of a U.S.-born marquess. The rooms, commodious and serviceable, overlook the gardens. Vaulted ceilings and velvet furnishings bedeck the largest room, which is billed as a suite. An armchair-filled common parlor has a TV and a pay phone. The landscaped grounds often host weddings on weekends. The restaurant ($$$$; reservations essential on weekends) has several dining rooms: two rooms, one dark with oak paneling and one abloom with rose wallpaper, have fireplaces, whereas the veranda and garden room look out at landscaped grounds. Chef Ans Benderer serves Continental fare with Swiss accents and makes the terrines and pâtés on-site. Consider such starters as Swiss mushroom crepe or polenta torte, then move on to pecan-breasted chicken, pork medallions, or fresh trout. ⊠ *1656 Rte. 9D, 10516* ☎ *845/265–3904* 🖷 *845/265–3997* ➳ *2 rooms, 1 suite* ⌂ *Restaurant, bar; no room phones, no room TVs, no smoking* ▭ *AE, DC, MC, V* ¶⦿ CP ◯ *Closed Mon.–Wed.*

$$–$$$ ▦ **Pig Hill Inn.** An 1825 brick inn in the heart of the village re-creates a 19th-century country house. Guest rooms and lounges teem with antiques, from Chippendale to chinoiserie—and if you fall in love with that four-poster bed or mahogany armoire, you can buy it (price tags hang from nearly every furnishing). Most rooms have a wood-burning stove or a fireplace; one has a whirlpool tub. Breakfasts, served in the light-filled Victorian conservatory or on the garden patio, are ample. Sweet aromas also waft from the kitchen in early afternoon, when the innkeeper often bakes cookies or pound cakes to serve with tea. ⊠ *73 Main St., 10516* ☎ *845/265–9247* 🖷 *845/265–4614* ⊕ *www.pighillinn.com* ➳ *9 rooms, 4 with shared bath* ⌂ *Dining room, tea shop, some in-room hot tubs, lounge; no room phones, no room TVs, no smoking* ▭ *AE, MC, V* ¶⦿ BP.

$$ 🏨 **Hudson House Inn.** A stunning riverfront setting and a wraparound porch distinguish this simple three-story clapboard inn built in 1832 to house steamboat passengers. Farmhouse antiques and French-country furnishings adorn the rooms, two of which have toile de Jouy wallpaper and bedspreads. Be sure to request a room with a private terrace looking out onto the Hudson River or quiet Main Street. Hiking trails, river sports, and antiques shops are a short walk away. ⊠ *2 Main St., 10516* ☎ *845/265–9355* 🖷 *845/265–4532* ⊕ *www.hudsonhouseinn. com* ⇆*11 rooms, 1 suite* ⚘ *Restaurant, cable TV, bar; no smoking* ⊟*AE, DC, MC, V* ⦿*BP weekends, CP weekdays.*

Sports & the Outdoors

CROSS-COUNTRY
SKIING

Nearly 10 mi of groomed trails vein the meadows, woodlands, and snowed-over lake of **Fahnestock Winter Park** (⊠ 12 Dennytown Rd. ☎ 845/225–3998 ⊕ nysparks.state.ny.us), part of Clarence Fahnestock Memorial State Park. Old pasture lanes weave through hemlock and hardwood groves, passing old stone walls and granite outcroppings. Come with your own gear or rent skis, boots, and poles on-site ($15 a day). Trail passes are $6. The park, open daily 9–4:30, also rents skate skis and snowshoes, as well as inner tubes for use on the groomed sledding hill. Call ahead to check weather conditions, and for information about lessons and ski clinics. You can warm up with hot food and drinks in the park's lodge.

HIKING

A vigorous climb of about an hour leads you through an oak and hickory forest to the top of **Anthony's Nose** (⊠ Rte. 9D immediately north of Bear Mountain Bridge), a 900-foot mountain, for spectacular views of the Hudson Highlands and Bear Mountain across the Hudson River. The first ½ mi of the hike is part of the Appalachian Trail (at the trailhead you see traffic pullouts and an Appalachian Trail sign); at the fork in the trail halfway up, turn right onto the Hudson River Trail to reach the peak.

Hike past hemlock gorges and an old iron mine in **Clarence Fahnestock Memorial State Park** (⊠ Rte. 30 ½ mi west of the Taconic State Pkwy. [Cold Spring exit] ☎ 845/225–7207 ⊕ nysparks.state.ny.us), which encompasses some 11,000 acres of protected land. More than 70 mi of trails, including a segment of the Appalachian Trail, wend through the wilderness here. **Canopus Lake** has picnic spots and a beach for swimming. Another lake and four ponds dot the landscape, with excellent bass, perch, pickerel, and trout fishing. The park office has trail maps. Admission is free, but parking for the beach area is $7 per car. The park is open daily from sunrise to sunset; the beach area is open 9–7 (swimming 10–6) on weekends from Memorial Day through late June and then daily through Labor Day.

Hudson Highlands State Park (⊠ Rte. 9D ½ mi north of Main St. ☎ 845/225–7207 ⊕ nysparks.state.ny.us), an easy walk from the Metro-North train station at Cold Spring, encompasses 5,800 acres of undeveloped land just north of town along the Hudson River. The trail to Bull Hill is the closest to the village. A moderately easy climb of about an hour through a forest offers successively grander views of Cold Spring and the river, culminating in a wide vista of the Hudson River Valley at the summit. Stop for a picnic at the rocky ledge overlooking the village halfway up and watch the trains trace the shore and, in summer, sailboats, freighters, and other riverboats ply the waterway. A more challenging hike is the aptly named Breakneck Ridge, whose trail climbs a cliff face over Route 9D halfway between Cold Spring and Beacon. The especially ambitious climb the cliff face itself; if you prefer a more leisurely but still fairly strenuous climb, stick to the trail. Metro-North trains stop at the Breakneck Ridge trailhead on weekends. The park is free and open daily from sunrise to sunset.

Two trails—one to a sandy beach, another to a small peak with panoramic views—traverse **Little Stony Point State Park** (⊠ Rte. 9D ½ mi north of Main St. ☎ 845/265–7815 Little Stony Point Citizens Association ⊕ www.hvgateway.com/stonypt.htm), a short walk from the center of Cold Spring. Although swimming isn't officially permitted at the beach, hikers often dip their toes in the river on hot days. The park is free and open daily from sunrise to sunset.

KAYAKING The relatively calm river waters close to the local shoreline make kayaking here a serene yet invigorating experience whether you're a novice or an experienced kayaker. To access **Constitution Marsh** from Cold Spring, set out from the boat launch directly across the road from the train-station parking lot. Once you're in the water, paddle downriver a short distance to the railroad bridge, and pass under it to enter the marsh. Because the Hudson is an estuary, tides affect the marsh; leave yourself plenty of time to get back to the shore by low tide so that you don't get grounded in the mud.

Hudson Valley Outfitters (⊠ 63 Main St. ☎ 845/265–0221 ⊕ www. hudsonvalleyoutfitters.com) runs tours for beginning to advanced kayakers that include some instruction. Half-day tours (four hours) are $50; full-day tours are $100. Rentals alone are $45–$60 a day. At **Outdoor Sports** (⊠ 141 Main St. ☎ 845/265–2048), kayak rentals start at $25 for two to four hours; three-hour tours are $30–$40, depending on the day. The outfitter also offers sailing lessons and charters of a 32-foot sloop.

Shopping

Back-to-back antiques and specialty shops line Cold Spring's Main Street. Browse amid hanging lanterns, funky glassware, wall tiles, and garden torches at **Archipelago** (⊠ 119 Main St. ☎ 845/265–3992), an out-of-the-ordinary home-furnishings and gift shop. More than 25 dealers in antiques, vintage clothes, jewelry, art, and collectibles hawk their wares in **Bijou Galleries, Ltd.** (⊠ 50 Main St. ☎ 845/265–4337), a jam-packed emporium. The largest antiques center in the county, the 5,000-square-foot **Downtown Gallery** (⊠ 40 Main St. ☎ 845/265–2334) teems with furniture from Victorian through modern periods, vintage textiles and clothes, and collectible toys. You may try on a Zulu necklace, a jade pendant, or a string of Tahitian pearls at **Momminia** (⊠ 113 Main St. ☎ 845/265–2260), an avant-garde jewelry boutique.

Beacon

13 *8 mi north of Cold Spring.*

For a touch of urban grit, arty cool, and coffeehouse grunge, head to this small river city in Dutchess County's southwestern corner. Dia:Beacon, an expansive contemporary-art museum in a former Nabisco printing plant, has put Beacon on the map. While Dia prepared its 2003 debut, artists and bargain seekers infiltrated the area, snatching up real estate that sold for a song; the renovated colonials and Victorians are already fetching a prettier penny. Gentrification has progressed along the eastern end of Beacon's Main Street and continues its march toward the river, bringing funky clothing boutiques, java shops, galleries, and enough antiques dealers to give neighboring Cold Spring a run for its money.

★ **Dia:Beacon.** Works by some of the biggest names in modern art from the 1960s to today fill this former Nabisco printing plant on the bank of the Hudson River. The Dia Art Foundation's collection of mid-20th-century art finds a home here, along with works commissioned expressly for the museum. Highlights include Andy Warhol's *Shadows,* which includes several canvases, and works by minimalist icons Robert Ryman and Agnes Martin. Expansive spaces and luxuriant light make the nearly 300,000-square-foot building—on 34 acres with artistic landscaping—an experience in itself. If you don't know much about modern art, take the tour to gain some context. ✉ *3 Beekman St.* ☎ *845/440–0100* ⊕ *www.diabeacon.org* 💵 *$10* ☉ *Mid-May–mid-Oct., Thurs.–Mon. 11–6; mid-Oct.–mid-May, Fri.–Mon. 11–4.*

Madam Brett Homestead. The oldest surviving home in Dutchess County, this white-clapboard dwelling housed seven generations of the Brett family from 1709 to 1954. During the Revolutionary War the homestead was used to store military supplies, and George Washington and the Marquis de Lafayette attended a Christmas party here. Original furnishings include 18th- and 19th-century pieces; hand-hewn beams, handcrafted shingles, and wide-board floors are among the architectural details. ✉ *50 Van Nydeck Ave.* ☎ *845/831–6533 or 845/896–6897* 💵 *$4* ☉ *Sept.–Dec., 1st Sun. each month 1–4, or by appointment.*

Where to Eat

$–$$ ✕ **The Piggy Bank.** Beacon's restaurant scene has yet to catch up with its vibrant arts arena, but this neighborhood mainstay dishes out slow-cooked Southern barbecue favorites. It's not Memphis, but the sweet-potato fries, hickory-smoked ribs, and barbecued pulled pork over tossed greens have won over the stomachs of some locals. The restaurant occupies a circa-1880 bank building where the vault now serves as wine cellar. The dining room, with glowing copper sconces and pink-brick walls, is open and airy but visually warm. ✉ *448 Main St.* ☎ *845/ 838–0028* 🍴 *AE, MC, V.*

Nightlife & the Arts

You can get a good early-morning cup of joe (or tea) and a muffin or other baked treat at **Chthonic Clash Coffeehouse** (✉ 418 Main St. ☎ 845/ 831–0359 ⊕ www.chthonicclash.com), a brick-walled neighborhood hangout, and then return in the evening to hear live music. Open-mike nights are held on the second and fourth Wednesday each month. Admission to events starts at $3. The coffeehouse stays open until midnight Friday and Saturday.

Shopping
The selection at the eclectic **Beacon Hill Antiques** (✉ 474 Main St. ☎ 845/831–4577) includes period furniture, accessories, decorative items, and folk art. The assortment of antiques, collectibles, jewelry, glassware, and furnishings at **Past Tense Antiques** (✉ 457 Main St. ☎ 845/838–4255) ranges from the primitive to the classic. At **Relic** (✉ 484 Main St. ☎ 845/440–0248) the mix includes vintage home accessories from Pyrex bowls to collectibles by Russel Wright and Eva Zeisel, as well as a smattering of furniture, old books, and clothing. If art deco is your quarry, you're in luck at **20th Century Fox Antiques** (✉ 466 Main St. ☎ 845/831–6059), a showroom of lamps, furnishings, and decorative arts. It's open only on weekends.

THE MID-HUDSON VALLEY

Revised by
Gary Allen,
Erica
Freudenberger,
Jan Hughes,
Gail Jaffe-
Bennek, Diana
Niles King

As you head north of the Newburgh-Beacon Bridge, the number of rural pockets increases and the suburban areas become sparser. You don't find as many New York City commuters here as in the lower valley, but some residents, especially those on the "right bank" of the Hudson River, do make the trip daily. On weekends, however, an ever-growing number of New Yorkers—writers, professionals, artists—make their way up north, many to their own vacation homes. These weekenders come to enjoy the proximity to water and mountains, the simple pleasures of yard sales and farm stands, and the seemingly endless opportunities for sporty endeavors. They share their appreciation of the area's history and its cultural offerings with the locals, many of whom were once New Yorkers themselves.

New Paltz

 18 mi north of Newburgh.

A vibrant cultural scene, a magnificent natural setting, and abundant outdoor activities are among the draws of this small college town, home to a State University of New York (SUNY) campus. The school lures serious students of the arts, many of whom end up living in the area after graduation. These artists, craftspeople, writers, and musicians have helped make this an energetic place with diverse shopping, dining, and arts offerings.

Founded in 1677 by Huguenots who received a patent from the colonial governor, New Paltz is one of the oldest communities in the United States. The settlers originally wanted to build on the flats, on the west side of the Wallkill River, but rethought that plan after the American Indians warned them about the river's spring floods. Building on the higher, eastern bank was an excellent decision: buildings dating from the early 1700s still stand throughout town. Several serve as bed-and-breakfasts today, so you can experience them personally.

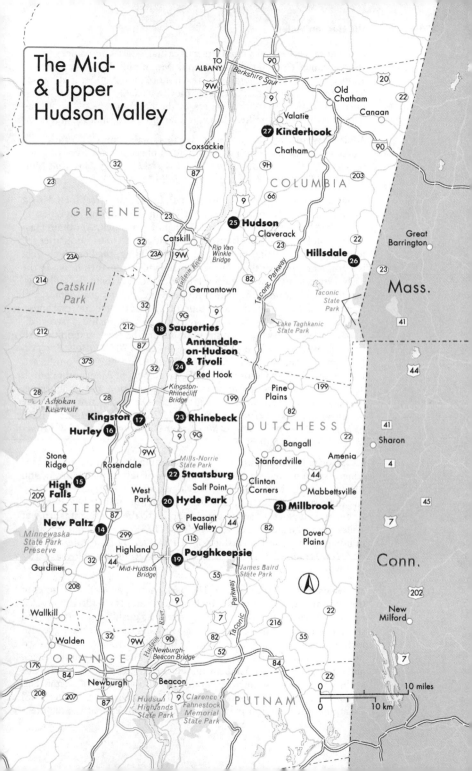

The Mid-
& Upper
Hudson Valley

TO ALBANY

Berkshire Spur

90

9W

9

Old Chatham

20

22

Coxsackie

Valatie

27 **Kinderhook**

Canaan

Chatham

90

32

87

9H

66

9

203

COLUMBIA

23

GREENE

23

Catskill

Rip Van Winkle Bridge

25 **Hudson**

Claverack

Great Barrington

23

23A

32

23A

9W

23

82

Hillsdale

22

26

Mass.

214

Catskill Park

Germantown

Taconic State Park

Lake Taghkanic State Park

23

41

212

32

9G

9

Hudson River

Taconic Parkway

212

18 **Saugerties**

375

Annandale-on-Hudson & Tivoli

44

28

87

32

24

Red Hook

Kingston-Rhinecliff Bridge

Pine Plains

199

41

Ashokan Reservoir

28

199

82

DUTCHESS

22

41

Kingston

17

23 **Rhinebeck**

Bangall

Sharon

Hurley

16

9

9G

Stanfordville

Amenia

4

Stone Ridge

Rosendale

9W

Mills-Norrie State Park

44

Mabbettsville

45

High Falls

15

22 **Staatsburg**

Salt Point

Clinton Corners

7

209

West Park

20 **Hyde Park**

82

ULSTER

New Paltz

14

299

Pleasant Valley

44

Dover Plains

Conn.

Minnewaska State Park Preserve

Highland

9G

115

21 **Millbrook**

82

Gardiner

32

44

Mid-Hudson Bridge

19 **Poughkeepsie**

James Baird State Park

208

Mohonk

55

202

Wallkill

9

7

Taconic Parkway

216

New Milford

Walden

32

9W

9D

82

55

22

17K

84

Newburgh-Beacon Bridge

52

7

ORANGE

84

22

208

207

87

Newburgh

Beacon

9

Hudson Highlands State Park

Clarence Fahnestock Memorial State Park

PUTNAM

0   10 miles

0   10 km

In the distance, beyond a main street of casual eateries and quirky shops, rise the craggy cliffs of the Shawangunk Mountains. With steep faces of white quartzite conglomerate that reach more than 2,000 feet above sea level at some points, the Gunks, as they're casually known, are a premier destination for rock climbers in the northeast. Sky Top Tower, which sits atop a prominent ledge, is a landmark for miles around.

Adair Vineyards. Tastings are offered in this small winery's centuries-old Dutch barn. The mountain views provide a pleasant backdrop for a picnic. ⊠ *52 Allhusen Rd.* ☎ *845/255–1377* 🖅 *Free* ☼ *May, and Nov. and Dec., Fri.–Sun. 11–5; June–Oct., daily 11–6.*

Huguenot Street. A National Historic Landmark, the street includes six stone houses that date from before 1720 and are among the oldest in the United States. Indeed, parts of the **Jean Hasbrouck, Abraham Hasbrouck, and Bevier-Elting houses** were built in the 1680s, soon after the founding of New Paltz, in 1677. Another building, the **French church,** is a reconstruction of the 1717 structure, which was torn down in the early 19th century. The Huguenot Historical Society owns the buildings, many of which contain original furnishings and architectural details, and runs tours of them. The 55-minute tour includes an orientation, one house, and the church; the longer tour, nearly two hours, includes two additional houses. Tours begin on the hour during the week and on the half hour on weekends. The tour office is in the **1705 DuBois Fort,** on Huguenot Street between Broadhead Avenue and North Front Street. During the one-day **Colonial Street Festival,** held in August, the church and the stone houses are all open; weaving, quilting, butter churning, musket firing, sheep shearing, and African-American storytelling are demonstrated. ⊠ *64 Huguenot St.* ☎ *845/255–1889 or 845/255–1660* ⊕ *www.hhs-newpaltz.net* 🖅 *Short tour $7, long tour $10* ☼ *Tours May–Oct., Tues.–Sun. 9–4.*

Locust Lawn. Josiah Hasbrouck—a lieutenant in the Revolution and U.S. congressman during the presidential terms of Jefferson, Madison, and Monroe—built the 1814 Federal-style mansion, which has an impressive three-story central hall. Exhibits include 18th- and 19th-century furniture and an ox cart used to carry supplies to the Continental army at Valley Forge. Nearby is **Terwilliger House** (1738), a Huguenot-era stone building with period furnishings. ⊠ *400 Rte. 32, Gardiner* ☎ *845/ 255–1660 Huguenot Historical Society* ⊕ *www.hhs-newpaltz.net* 🖅 *$7* ☼ *By appointment.*

Fodor'sChoice **Minnewaska State Park Preserve.** The park encompasses 12,000 acres in
★ the Shawangunk Mountains. Much of the terrain is wooded and rocky, but you also come across trickling streams, gushing waterfalls, and spectacular valley views. Lake Minnewaska is its jewel; the park also includes Awosting Lake. A network of historic carriageways, now used by hikers, mountain bikers, horseback riders, and cross-country skiers, and other trails veins the land. Swimming is restricted to designated areas; scuba divers must be certified. Boating is allowed with a permit. Nature programs include walks and talks. The entrance to the **Peter's Kill Escarpment,** where you may rock climb, is 1 mi east of the main en-

trance. ⊠ *U.S. 44/Rte. 55 5 mi from Rte. 299* ☎ *845/255–0752* ⊕ *nys-parks.state.ny.us* ☜ *Parking $6* ⊙ *Daily 9–dusk.*

Mohonk Mountain House. Even if you don't stay at this grand Victorian resort, you can spend the day here. The 2,200-acre property includes Lake Mohonk, 85 mi of hiking trails, a 9-hole golf course, extensive gardens, and a restaurant, and is adjacent to Mohonk Preserve. If you come for breakfast, lunch, or dinner, admission to the grounds and the house (off-limits to day visitors who don't eat here) is included. Meal reservations are required, even for breakfast and lunch. ⊠ *1000 Mountain Rest Rd.* ☎ *845/255–1000* ⊕ *www.mohonk.com* ☜ *Weekends $12, weekdays $10* ⊙ *Daily dawn–1 hr before sunset.*

Mohonk Preserve. The 6,400-acre preserve has more than 60 mi of hiking trails and carriageways and four trailheads: **Visitor Center,** on U.S. 44/Route 55; **West Trapps,** about 1⅓ mi east of the visitor center; **Coxing,** 1 mi off Clove Road (about ¼ mi east of West Trapps); and **Spring Farm,** on Mountain Rest Road near the entrance to the Mohonk Mountain House. The mountain views are spectacular. A visit to the preserve, which accommodates picnickers, walkers, hikers, bikers, rock climbers, and horseback riders, gives you access to the adjacent Mohonk Mountain House grounds (with some restrictions) and the Minnewaska State Park Preserve. ⊠ *Mohonk Preserve Visitor Center, 3197 U.S. 44/Rte. 55, ½ mi west of Rte. 299, Gardiner* ☎ *845/255–0919* ⊕ *www. mohonkpreserve.org* ☜ *Weekdays $6, weekends $8* ⊙ *Daily sunrise–sunset. Visitor center Tues.–Sun. 9–5.*

Rivendell Winery. Tastings of Rivendell wines are offered alongside more than 50 other New York State wines. You may also picnic on the grounds and pick up local foods at the deli counter here. ⊠ *714 Albany Post Rd.* ☎ *845/255–2494* ⊕ *www.rivendellwine.com* ☜ *Free* ⊙ *Daily 10–6.*

State University of New York at New Paltz. The college, which long has attracted arts students, presents the community with a host of cultural offerings on its 216-acre campus. At the **Samuel Dorsky Museum of Art** (☎ 845/257–3844), 19th- and 20th-century photographs and American and European paintings, along with a core collection of works on paper, are focal points. ⊠ *75 S. Manheim Blvd./Rte. 32S* ☎ *845/257–2121, 845/257–3880 box office* ⊕ *www.newpaltz.edu.*

Trapeze Club at Stone Mountain Farm. From May through September, the center offers several two-hour trapeze classes each week on a 350-acre farm. All levels, from beginner to expert, are welcome; flyers may be as young as four. Classes are limited to 10 students; call to reserve a spot. ⊠ *475 River Rd. Extension* ☎ *845/658–8540* ⊕ *www.trapeze-club.org* ⊙ *May–Sept.; call for class schedule.*

off the beaten path

SLABSIDES AND JOHN BURROUGHS SANCTUARY – Naturalist and area resident John Burroughs built Slabsides, a rustic cabin, as a retreat and study in 1895. The cabin, which has built-in twig furniture, holds an open house only twice a year, but you may stroll the 170-acre nature sanctuary year-round, from dawn to dusk. West

Park is 7 mi east of New Paltz, and the cabin itself is about a ⅓-mi uphill walk from the parking area. ⊠ *Burroughs Dr. off Floyd Ackert Rd., West Park* ☎ *845/679–5169 or 845/384–6320* ⊕ *research. amnh.org/burroughs/* ☜ *$2 suggested donation* ☉ *May, 3rd Sat. 12:30–4:30; Oct., 1st Sat. 12:30–4:30; or by appointment.*

FESTIVALS &
FAIRS **Taste of New Paltz.** Nosh and nibble at this one-day event during which area restaurants, farm markets, breweries, and wineries sell tasting portions. Activities include music acts and children's games, as well as pony and other rides. ⊠ *Ulster County Fairgrounds, Libertyville Rd.* ☎ *845/255–0243* ⊕ *newpaltzchamber.org.*

Ulster County Fair. Livestock, local crafts, baking and preserves competitions, pig races, and amusement rides constitute a genuine old-fashioned county fair. Held in early August, it runs Tuesday through Sunday. ⊠ *Ulster County Fairgrounds, Libertyville Rd.* ☎ *845/255–1380* ⊕ *www.ulstercountyfair.com.*

Woodstock/New Paltz Art and Crafts Fair. The juried fair, held Memorial Day and Labor Day weekends, showcases potters, photographers, jewelry designers, and other artisans from across the nation. The food is better than usual fair fare, with many vegetarian and unusual dishes. ⊠ *Ulster County Fairgrounds, Libertyville Rd.* ☎ *845/679–8087 or 845/ 246–3414* ⊕ *www.quailhollow.com.*

Where to Stay & Eat

$$-$$$ ✕ **Ristorante Locust Tree.** A historic building houses this formal Italian restaurant, where dishes such as roast of "pasture-raised" veal with creamy polenta and truffle sauce or seared Hudson Valley foie gras with figs, prosciutto, and port sauce display the kitchen's love for organic, local ingredients and regional Italian cuisines (the chef hails from northern Italy). The menu changes daily, and tasting menus, $48–$70 depending on the number of courses, are available. Part of the restaurant inhabits a stone Dutch colonial with fireplaces, beamed ceilings, and hand-carved woodwork that dates from 1759. (The addition was built in the late 1920s.) ⊠ *215 Huguenot St.* ☎ *845/255–7888* ⚓ *Reservations essential* ⚲ *Jacket required* ⊟ *DC, MC, V* ☉ *Closed Mon. and Tues. No lunch.*

$$-$$$ ✕ **The Would.** The white-tablecloth restaurant was once a resort catering to Italian families from New York City; boccie is still played here on summer evenings. The food is no throwback, however; organic produce and poultry blend with ingredients and techniques from around the world. Pineapple-soy glazes pan-seared Hudson Valley duck breast, and papaya-wasabi sauce and shrimp cakes accompany sautéed scallops. In winter a fireplace warms the dining room. ⊠ *120 North Rd., west of U.S. 9W, Highland* ☎ *845/691–9883* ⚓ *Reservations essential* ⊟ *AE, MC, V* ☉ *Closed Mon. and Tues.*

$-$$$ ✕ **Hokkaido Japanese Restaurant.** Sample sushi and other tidbits beneath handcrafted Japanese lanterns at this informal spot. Spider rolls, hot crisp-fried soft-shell crabs in cool nori-wrapped sushi rice, are a delight. ⊠ *18 Church St.* ☎ *845/256–0621* ⊟ *AE, D, MC, V* ☉ *No lunch weekends.*

$–$$$ ✕ **La Stazione.** Dim lighting and dark mahogany trim lend romance to this Italian restaurant in a converted railroad station. For starters consider "La Stazione," a small pizza topped with artichokes, black olives, ham, and onions, or a bowl of escarole and creamy cannellini beans; garlic-laced tomato-sauced clams are a savory main course. Crowds flock to the $7.95 prix-fixe dinner, offered Monday and Tuesday. ☒ *5 Main St.* ☎ *845/256–9447* ▤ *AE, D, MC, V.*

$–$$ ✕ **Loft Restaurant.** An airy loft, sloping skylights, and a simple but elegant American menu define this eatery. Featured entrées include lobster ravioli in creamy tomato sauce and duck roasted with a black currant–and–brandy glaze. ☒ *46 Main St.* ☎ *845/255–1426* ▤ *AE, D, MC, V* ⊘ *Closed Mon. and Tues.*

$–$$ ✕ **Mountain Brauhaus Restaurant.** Time (fortunately) has not changed this family-style restaurant. The wood paneling and Alpine decor complement the menu, which includes sauerbraten, schnitzels, wursts, and *Kassler Rippchen* (smoked pork chops). The selection of German beers, in bottles and on tap, is excellent. ☒ *U.S. 44/Rte. 55 and Rte. 299, Gardiner* ☎ *845/255–9766* ▤ *AE, D, MC, V* ⊘ *Closed Mon. and Tues.*

¢–$$ ✕ **The Gilded Otter.** A gleaming copper brewery, live music, tasty pub grub and more substantial food, and views of the Gunks—what could be better after a day of rock climbing or hiking? Just don't expect much quiet on weekends. Two brews to try: New Paltz Crimson Lager and Stone House Irish Stout. Among the more unusual dishes here is pizza topped with caramelized pear, bacon, onions, Gorgonzola, fontina, mozzarella, and mesclun. ☒ *3 Main St.* ☎ *845/256–1700* ▤ *D, DC, MC, V.*

$$$$
Fodor'sChoice
★
✕▦ **Mohonk Mountain House.** The rambling Victorian-era hotel—a jumble of towers, chimneys, porches, and turrets—sits at the edge of a mountaintop lake. The resort's 2,200 acres encompass private woodland and elaborate gardens and overflow with options for recreation, including 85 mi of hiking trails. Antiques fill the guest rooms, which are luxurious and spacious. Choice accommodations in the towers have original Victorian woodwork, working fireplaces, and balconies. Breakfast and lunch are buffet-style; dinner is a formal affair for which men (and boys 12 and older) must wear jackets. The three dining rooms are elegant backdrops for dishes like pan-seared tournedos of filet mignon, made modern with blue-crab succotash and lemon-peppercorn butter, and smoked breast of duck, which comes with field greens, New Zealand figs, and maple-cognac vinaigrette. Dinner is prix fixe ($47–$50, including tax and tip); reservations are essential. If you're not overnighting here, come early to enjoy the grounds before dinner. ☒ *1000 Mountain Rest Rd., 12561* ☎ *845/255–1000 or 800/772–6646, 845/256–2056 restaurant* ▤ *845/256–2180* ⊕ *www.mohonk.com* ⇆ *269 rooms, 6 suites, 4 cottages* ⌂ *3 restaurants, room service, in-room data ports, 9-hole golf course, putting green, 6 tennis courts, gym, spa, boating, fishing, croquet, hiking, horseback riding, lawn bowling, shuffleboard, cross-country skiing, ice-skating, library, children's programs (ages 2–12), laundry facilities, Internet; no a/c, no room TVs* ▤ *AE, DC, MC, V* ⊘ *Cottages closed mid-Oct.–mid-May* ⎮◯⎮ *FAP; EP in cottages.*

☾ $$$–$$$$ ▦ **Rocking Horse Ranch.** Seven miles southeast of New Paltz, this all-inclusive dude ranch is loaded with activities, including a petting zoo and waterslide. Accommodations include rooms in the main lodge, where the lobby is hung with wagon wheels, and motel-style buildings. ✉ *Rte. 44/55 at Pancake Hollow Rd., Highland 12528* ☎ *845/691–2927, 800/647–2624 reservations* 🖷 *845/691–6434* ⊕ *www.rhranch. com* 🖙 *119 rooms* ⊟ *AE, D, DC, MC, V* ⚒ *2 dining rooms, coffee shop, snack bar, some refrigerators, cable TV, miniature golf, 2 tennis courts, 3 pools (1 indoors), lake, exercise equipment, hot tub, sauna, boating, waterskiing, fishing, archery, basketball, boccie, hiking, horseback riding, horseshoes, Ping-Pong, shuffleboard, softball, volleyball, downhill skiing, ice-skating, sleigh rides, bar, dance club, video game room, shop, babysitting, children's programs (ages 4–12), playground, laundry service; no smoking* ⊙ *Closed some weekdays in March* ⊯ *FAP.*

$$–$$$ 🏨 **Lefevre House Bed & Breakfast.** Contemporary European paintings, many of them for sale, fill this 1870 pink-and-white gingerbread Victorian. The name of each room—Red Hot, Am I Blue, Purple Rain, and Green with Envy—corresponds to its color scheme. Although bold, the palettes tend toward rich jewel tones rather than headache-inducing primary colors. Beds, some king-size four-posters, have Frette sheets and Versace comforters and shams. Breakfast is served in the formal dining room or on the wraparound porch, which has a perfectly framed view of Sky Top Tower. The house has wireless Internet access and is within walking distance of the university. ✉ *14 Southside Ave., 12561* ☎ *845/255–4747 or 845/430–5689* 🖷 *845/255–0808* ⊕ *www.lefevrehouse.com* 🖙 *3 rooms, 1 suite* ⚒ *Dining room, some in-room hot tubs, some kitchenettes, cable TV, in-room DVD players, outdoor hot tub, Internet; no room phones, no smoking* ⊟ *AE, D, DC, MC, V* ⊯ *BP.*

★ **$$–$$$** 🏨 **Minnewaska Lodge.** Cathedral ceilings, Arts and Crafts styling, and towering windows with views of white cliffs or deep forests contribute to the delight of this lodge. Works by local artists and photographers add interest. Some guest rooms have balconies. A Culinary Institute–trained chef prepares breakfast. ✉ *3116 U.S. 44/Rte. 55, Gardiner 12525* ☎ *845/255–1110* 🖷 *845/256–0629* ⊕ *www.minnewaskalodge.com* 🖙 *26 rooms, 1 suite* ⚒ *Dining room, in-room data ports, gym; no smoking* ⊟ *AE, MC, V* ⊯ *CP weekdays, BP weekends.*

$–$$ 🏨 **Super 8 Motel.** Not even ½ mi from the thruway entrance and on the edge of the village, this two-story chain property offers reasonable rates and no surprises. ✉ *7 Terwilliger La., at Main St., 12561* ☎ *845/255–8865 or 800/800–8000* 🖷 *845/255–1629* ⊕ *www.super8.com* 🖙 *67 rooms, 2 suites* ⚒ *Restaurant, in-room data ports, some microwaves, some refrigerators, cable TV; no-smoking rooms* ⊟ *AE, D, DC, MC, V* ⊯ *CP.*

¢–$$ 🏨 **Days Inn.** The single-story motel is 2 mi east of SUNY New Paltz and convenient to shopping and restaurants. The thruway entrance is less than ½ mi away. ✉ *601 Main St./Rte. 299, 12561* ☎ *845/883–7373* ⊕ *www.daysinn.com* 🖙 *20 rooms* ⚒ *In-room data ports, cable TV, no-smoking rooms* ⊟ *AE, D, DC, MC, V* ⊯ *CP.*

$ 🏨 **Mountain Meadows Bed & Breakfast.** Linger over breakfast by the pool, which faces the Shawangunk cliffs, or in the country kitchen. Later you may throw some horseshoes or shoot some pool. Frills and florals adorn furnishings in the guest rooms. ✉ *542 Albany Post Rd., 12561* ☎ *845/255–6144 or 845/527–8359* ⊕ *www.mountainmeadowsbnb.com* 🖙 *4 rooms* ⚒ *Pool, outdoor hot tub, badminton, billiards, croquet, horse-*

shoes, Ping-Pong, recreation room, laundry facilities; no room phones, no room TVs, no smoking ⊟ *No credit cards* ⦶ *BP.*

Nightlife & the Arts

NIGHTLIFE Thursday it's '80s Night, and Friday it's Latin salsa at **Cabaloosa's/The Odyssey** (⊠ 58 Main St. ☎ 854/255–3400), a gritty downstairs club on a little alley off Main. It's big with the college crowd. A lively sports-bar ambience, a good beer menu, tasty food, and generous portions make **McGillcuddy's Restaurant & Tap House** (⊠ 84 Main St. ☎ 845/256–9289) a popular spot. Choose from 14 kinds of chicken wings. The "Inferno" wings are hotter than hot. ("Get the fire extinguisher," says the description in the menu—and it's not kidding.) **Oasis Cafe** (⊠ 58 Main St. ☎ 845/255–2400), upstairs from Cabaloosa's, is a slightly more polished venue for live music.

THE ARTS The **New Paltz Summer Repertory Theatre** (⊠ 75 S. Manheim Blvd./Rte. 32S ☎ 845/257–3880 box office ⊕ www.newpaltz.edu) mounts comedies, dramas, and musicals in Parker Theatre at the State University of New York. Public concerts are part of **PianoSummer at New Paltz Festival/Institute** (⊠ 75 S. Manheim Blvd./Rte. 32S ☎ 845/257–3880 box office ⊕ www.newpaltz.edu), at SUNY New Paltz; Vladimir Feltsman is the program's artistic director.

Sports & the Outdoors

Eastern Mountain Sports (⊠ 4124 U.S. 44/Rte. 55, Gardiner ☎ 845/255–3280 or 800/310–4504 ⊕ www.emsclimb.com), originally a catalog store, has been a favorite among campers, climbers, and hikers for decades. It carries everything a climber might need—to rent or buy—and offers classes in rock and ice climbing. Opened in 1970 by Dick Williams, one of the pioneers of climbing in the Shawangunk Mountains, **Rock & Snow** (⊠ 44 Main St. ☎ 845/255–1311 ⊕ www.rocksnow.com) sells everything you need for rock and ice climbing, camping, hiking, and cross-country skiing. It also carries maps, and can hook you up with lessons and licensed guides. You can rent some of the equipment.

BIRD-WATCHING The open meadows and broken woods of the **Shawangunk Grasslands National Wildlife Refuge** (⊠ Hoagerburgh Rd., 1½ mi north of Bruyn Tpke., Wallkill ☎ 973/702–7266 ⊕ shawangunk.fws.gov) shelter kildeers, broad-winged and red-tailed hawks, several types of flycatchers, a few warblers, woodpeckers, eastern kingbirds, and bluebirds. In spring, listen for the evening mating rituals of American woodcocks. In fall, watch for the occasional peregrine falcon–a few breeding pairs nest in the nearby cliffs.

CROSS-COUNTRY
SKIING **Minnewaska State Park Preserve** (⊠ U.S. 44/Rte. 55, 5 mi west of Rte. 299 ☎ 845/256–0579, 845/256–0752 trail conditions ⊕ nysparks.state.ny.us) has 27 mi of carriage trails—8 of them ungroomed—available for cross-country skiing. Winter scenery here includes frosted cliffs and frozen lakes and waterfalls. The 2,200-acre property of the **Mohonk Mountain House** (⊠ 1000 Mountain Rest Rd. ☎ 845/255–1000 ⊕ www.mohonk.com), a Victorian resort, includes 38 mi of cross-country-skiing trails; equipment is available only to resort guests. Approximately 25 mi of groomed trails lace **Mohonk Preserve** (⊠ Mohonk Preserve

Visitor Center, 3197 U.S. 44/Rte. 55, ½ mi west of Rte. 299 ☎ 845/255–0919 ⊕ www.mohonkpreserve.org) and lead to spectacular views.

HIKING Some area trails are rather challenging, but less demanding options, including those for casual walkers, are plentiful. Crystalline streams and mountaintop lakes highlight 27 mi of carriage trails and 30 mi of footpaths at **Minnewaska State Park Preserve** (⊠ U.S. 44/Rte. 55, 5 mi west of Rte. 299 ☎ 845/256–0579 ⊕ nysparks.state.ny.us). At the **Mohonk Preserve** (⊠ Mohonk Preserve Visitor Center, 3197 U.S. 44/Rte. 55, ½ mi west of Rte. 299 ☎ 845/255–0919 ⊕ www.mohonkpreserve.org), hikers can use more than 100 mi of carriageways and paths and are allowed access to the trails of the Minnewaska State Park Preserve and the Mohonk Mountain House Resort. A popular route at the latter starts from the lake and leads through a maze of giant boulders and up the Lemon Squeeze (not for claustrophobic or tall people); the rewards are cool winds and spectacular cliff-top views.

MOUNTAIN BIKING The area has an extensive network of well-maintained trails peppered with jaw-dropping views. The 27 mi of carriage trails open to bikers at **Minnewaska State Park Preserve** (⊠ U.S. 44/Rte. 55, 5 mi west of Rte. 299 ☎ 845/256–0579 ⊕ nysparks.state.ny.us) are hilly, sometimes quite steep, and have a gravel or rocky surface. The carriageways may take you through woods and meadows, around lakes and beaches, and to ledges with panoramic views. On weekends, the earlier in the day you go, the better. The 25 mi of carriage roads at the **Mohonk Preserve** (⊠ Mohonk Preserve Visitor Center, 3197 U.S. 44/Rte. 55, ½ mi west of Rte. 299 ☎ 845/255–0919 ⊕ www.mohonkpreserve.org) connect to those of the Mohonk Mountain House resort and the Minnewaska State Park Preserve. The carriage trails, mostly covered in shale, are hilly and sometimes steep but are interspersed with level stretches. Weekends are crowded.

The friendly folks at **Bicycle Depot** (⊠ 15 Main St. ☎ 845/255–3859 ⊕ www.bicycledepot.com) can sell or rent you a bike, but they can also make any kind of repair, and they know *everything* about biking in the area. The **Bistro Mountain Store** (⊠ 3124 U.S. 44/Rte. 55, at Rte. 299, Gardiner ☎ 845/255–2999), at the foot of the cliffs, is a little deli and ice-cream parlor that also rents bikes. It's a good place to start and end a day trip through the Gunks.

ROCK CLIMBING The long ridge of the Shawangunk Mountains offers plenty of cliffs for climbers of all abilities. Because the Gunks are a major draw for climbing enthusiasts, routes can be extremely crowded on weekends, especially on some of the more accessible cliffs, such as the Trapps and Near Trapps areas. If you want climbing instruction, use a guide accredited by the American Mountain Guide Association. Check with the preserves and local outfitters for guide recommendations.

At **Minnewaska State Park Preserve** (⊠ U.S. 44/Rte. 55, 4 mi west of Rte. 299 ☎ 845/256–0752 ⊕ nysparks.state.ny.us), rock climbing is restricted to the lower Peter's Kill Escarpment, a west-facing escarpment, ½ mi long, with a talus area offering excellent bouldering. In order to climb here you first must obtain a climbing permit, on the day you plan to use it, from the office next to the Peter's Kill parking area. The park limits the number of permits it hands out. More than 1,000 technical rock-climbing routes attract 40,000-plus climbing visits to the **Mohonk Preserve** (⊠ Mohonk Preserve Visitor Center, 3197 U.S. 44/Rte. 55, ½ mi west of Rte. 299 ☎ 845/255–0919 ⊕ www.mohonkpreserve.org) each year. A small camping area is available (for climbers only) near Trapps Bridge.

Shopping
Shopping in New Paltz is eclectic, largely aimed at students, creative individuals (of all ages), and outdoors enthusiasts. Nearly all the shops are on or near Main Street and within easy walking distance of one another. Farm stands are outside the village center, so you need a car to get to them.

★ Regional books and remainders are among the strengths of **Ariel Booksellers** (⊠ 3 Plattekill Ave. ☎ 845/255–8041). Readings include well-known—and, often, local—authors, such as Gail Godwin and Valerie Martin. Although it specializes in crafts and jewelry, **Handmade and More** (⊠ 6 N. Front St. ☎ 845/255–6277 ⊠ Water Street Market, 10 Main St. ☎ 845/255–1458) also carries toys, clothing, and a selection of quirky cards at its two locations. More than 20 varieties of apples, from Macoun and Red Delicious to Empire and Ida Red, as well as other produce, are sold at **Jenkins-Lueken Orchards** (⊠ Yankee Folly Rd. at Rte. 299 ☎ 845/255–0999 ☉ Closed Apr.–mid-Aug.). You can pick pumpkins, and the apple cider, made on the premises, is fresh and good. The **Wallkill View Farm Market** (⊠ 15 Rte. 299 ☎ 845/255–8050 ☉ Closed Dec. 23–wk before Easter) sells local produce, cheeses, baked goods, jams and preserves, maple syrup, garden supplies, fresh-pressed apple cider, and pumpkins you can pick yourself. **Water Street Market** (⊠ 10 Main St. ☎ 845/255–1458), an unassuming pedestrian mall, includes antiques stores, crafts and art galleries, cafés, clothing boutiques, and custom-furniture and other specialty shops.

High Falls

⓯ *9 mi northwest of New Paltz.*

The tiny hamlet of High Falls is a weekender's delight. Cool shops, old buildings, excellent restaurants, and cozy places to stay nestle beside the ancient locks of the Delaware and Hudson Canal. From 1828 to 1898 the canal connected Pennsylvania's coal mines to the Hudson River. "Canawlers" also shipped bluestone for New York City's sidewalks and Rosendale cement for the Brooklyn Bridge. You can see some of the locks right in town; a brochure (available at the D&H Canal Museum) outlines a walking tour. In fall, pick your own apples or taste freshly pressed cider at one of the local orchards.

D&H Canal Museum. At this museum in a former church a collection of maps, photographs, documents, boat models, and artifacts traces the history of the canal, an important 19th-century waterway. ⊠ *Rte. 6A/ Mohonk Rd. off Rte. 213* ☎ *845/687–9311* ⊕ *www.canalmuseum.org* 🖾 *$3* ☉ *May–Oct., Mon. and Thurs.–Sat. 11–5, Sun. 1–5.*

> **off the beaten path**

A. J. SNYDER ESTATE – The estate includes the Widow Jane Mine, cement kilns, and parts of the D&H Canal. A museum concentrates on the local cement industry and showcases antique sleighs and carriages. ⊠ *Rte. 213 ½ mi west of Rte. 32, Rosendale* ☎ *845/658–9900* ☞ *$2* ⊙ *May–Oct., weekends 1–4; or by appointment.*

Where to Stay & Eat

$$$–$$$$ ✕ **DePuy Canal House.** The food at this 1797 stone tavern, a National
FodorsChoice Historic Landmark, is eclectic and elaborate. Chef-owner John Novi
★ opened the place in 1969, and in 1984 was referred to as "the father of new American cooking" in a *Time* magazine article. After all these years he still manages to be creative. The menu is seasonal and often incorporates Hudson Valley ingredients. You might find chicken-and-fish consommé with salmon-mousse wonton or sautéed lobster with steamed spinach, caramelized-shallot beurre blanc, and mango salsa. The restaurant has five antiques-jammed dining rooms; you can also dine at a balcony table overlooking the kitchen. ⊠ *Rte. 213* ☎ *845/687–7700* ⌕ *Reservations essential* ⊟ *AE, MC, V* ⊙ *Closed Mon.–Wed. and late Jan.–mid-Feb. No lunch.*

$–$$ ✕ **Chefs on Fire.** In the former wine cellar of the DePuy Canal House, this is a casual and tasty offshoot of the elegant main restaurant. Flavors are more Italian than they are upstairs, and dishes include frittatas, panini, pastas, and pizza (including one with a topping of arugula, cannellini beans, and bacon). Breads and pastries, baked here, are also available at the New York Store, next door. Sunday brunch is served 11:30–2. ⊠ *Rte. 213* ☎ *845/687–7778* ⊟ *AE, MC, V* ⊙ *Closed Mon. and Tues.*

¢–$ ✕ **The Egg's Nest.** Playfully cluttered and wildly painted, the Egg's Nest is fun, whether for a casual meal or a couple of drinks. "Praeseux" are house favorites—crisp, pizzalike dishes with various toppings baked on flour tortillas. The Thanksgiving sandwich layers turkey breast with provolone cheese and apple-walnut stuffing on whole-wheat bread dipped in egg batter. Pasta dishes, wraps, soups, and chili also are offered. ⊠ *Rte. 213 at Bruceville Rd.* ☎ *845/687–7255* ⊟ *No credit cards.*

★ $$ ✕▦ **The Inn at Stone Ridge.** The 18th-century Dutch stone mansion sits on 40 landscaped acres in the village of Stone Ridge, about 3 mi west of High Falls. Period antiques, including an old billiard table, furnish the parlors, library, and guest rooms. Room 10 has a balcony with private access. The suites are especially spacious. Suite 3, for example, has two bedrooms, a dining table for four, and a sitting area with a TV. The inn frequently hosts weddings, often in a massive tent in back. The first floor has an intimate bar area and a restaurant ($$–$$$; closed Monday and Tuesday), where you can dine on updated American dishes—mulled butternut-squash soup, smoked duck–and–spinach salad with pancetta vinaigrette, pork tenderloin with smoked bacon and horseradish on apple-potato pancake. Furnishings in the main dining room have a refined country appeal; the Jefferson Room and Tavern are more casual. ⊠ *U.S. 209, Stone Ridge, 12484* ☎ *845/687–0736* ☐ *845/687–0112* ⊕ *www.innatstoneridge.com* ☞ *3 rooms, 2 suites* ⌕ *Restaurant, some in-room data ports, some in-room hot tubs, lake, billiards, bar, library, some pets allowed; no TV in some rooms, no smoking* ⊟ *AE, D, DC, MC, V* ⏀ *BP.*

$$ ☒ **The 1712 House at Hardenbergh Pond.** You pass a duck- and goose-filled pond before you reach the unmarked driveway of this lodge a little more than ½ mi off U.S. 209. The house, built in the mid-1990s, blends wood from the property with Catskill bluestone. Guest rooms have handcrafted quilt-covered beds (including four-posters and canopies), small tables with a couple of chairs, VCRs, and lace-fringed windows. Breakfast is served by the dining-room fireplace, in the kitchen, on the deck, or in your room. ⊠ *93 Mill Dam Rd., Stone Ridge, 12484* ☎ *845/687–7167* ⊕ *www.1712house.com* ↪ *5 rooms, 1 suite ⚭ Dining room, in-room data ports, some in-room hot tubs, cable TV, in-room VCRs, pond; no kids, no smoking* ⊟ *AE, D, MC, V* ⫶⫶⫶ *BP.*

$–$$ ☒ **Captain Schoonmakers B&B.** Guest rooms, each with a private balcony and a canopy or brass bed, are in an 1810 carriage house at this B&B. Breakfast, including eggs from the owners' hens, is served amid antiques in front of the fireplace in the 1760 stone main house. The library leads to the solarium and, just beyond, 10 acres of gardens, woods, waterfalls, and a trout stream. ⊠ *913 Rte. 213, at Mossy Brook Rd., 12440* ☎ *845/687–7946* ⊕ *www.captainschoonmakers.com* ↪ *4 rooms ⚭ Fishing, library; no room phones, no room TVs, no kids under 10, no smoking* ⊟ *No credit cards* ⫶⫶⫶ *BP.*

$–$$ ☒ **Hardenbergh House.** Antiques fill this six-gabled Victorian B&B with high ceilings and floral wall coverings. The Grand Room is lush with patterned and textured fabrics; a salmon-and-sage palette is the focal point in the Asia Room. Both rooms have a cast-iron bathtub. The house is in Rosendale, about 3 mi east of High Falls; it sits on 3 acres with huge trees and a small pond. Your host, a baker trained at the Culinary Institute, prepares breakfast. ⊠ *118 Maple Hill Dr., Rosendale, 12472* ☎ *845/658–9147* 🖷 *845/658–3845* ⊕ *www.hardenberghhouse.com* ↪ *2 rooms ⚭ Dining room, cable TV, pond; no room phones, no kids under 13, no smoking* ⊟ *MC, V* ⫶⫶⫶ *CP.*

$–$$ ☒ **The Sheeley House.** Built in the 1830s, this quiet brick Italianate B&B has two dining rooms, a sitting room, a porch, and a grand piano. In the spacious Rose Room, which can accommodate up to four people, white bedding offsets floral garlands. The Gold Room is also airy and uncluttered. ⊠ *6 Fairview Ave., 12440* ☎ *845/687–4360* 🖷 *845/687–4360* ⊕ *www.thesheeleyhouse.com* ↪ *4 rooms, 2 with shared bath; 1 cottage* ⊟ *No credit cards ⚭ Dining room, piano; no room phones, no kids under 13, no smoking* ⫶⫶⫶ *CP weekdays, BP weekends.*

$ ☒ **The Locktender Cottage.** The small, historic house sits beside a lock of the old Delaware and Hudson Canal in the center of High Falls. Across the street is the highly regarded DePuy Canal House restaurant, which is where you check in, and quirky antiques and gift shops are a few doors away. In the rooms, pale walls dilute flowery bedspreads and curtains. The Chef's Quarters suite, under the eaves, has a kitchenette, dining area, and laundry facilities. Two additional suites are across the street in a building next to the Canal House. One has a full kitchen and a screened-in porch. ⊠ *Rte. 213, 12440* ☎ *845/687–7700* 🖷 *845/687–7073* ⊕ *www.depuycanalhouse.net* ↪ *2 rooms, 3 suites ⚭ Some in-room hot tubs, some kitchens, some kitchenettes, some cable TV, some pets allowed (fee); no smoking* ⊟ *AE, MC, V* ⫶⫶⫶ *CP.*

¢ ☒ **Baker's B&B.** On frosty days you can cuddle up by one of the wood-stoves or by the fireplace in this antiques-filled 1780 stone farmhouse in the Rondout Valley. Breakfast, served in front of a fireplace or out on the deck, includes homemade jams and jellies and home-smoked salmon or trout. ☒ *24 Old King's Hwy., Stone Ridge, 12484* ☎ *845/687–9795 or 888/623–5513* 🖷 *845/687–4153* ⊕ *www.bakersbandb.com* ◞*5 rooms, 1 suite* ⚭ *Dining room; no room phones, no room TVs, no kids under 12, no smoking* ⊟ *MC, V* ⦿| *BP.*

Nightlife & the Arts

★ An early-1900s firehouse was converted into the **Rosendale Theatre** (☒ 401 Main St., Rosendale ☎ 845/658–8989 ☜ $5) in 1949—and few changes have been made to the movie theater since. Instead of a concession counter, two ancient vending machines discharge candy. Movies ($5) run the gamut from action blockbusters to small foreign films, and include first-runs.

Sports & the Outdoors

MOUNTAIN BIKING Although it sells, rents, and repairs bicycles, **Table Rock Tours & Bicycles** (☒ 292 Main St., Rosendale ☎ 845/658–7832 ⊕ www.tablerocktours.com) specializes in arranging custom tours, including nature rides, antiques-hunting tours, and D&H Canal–focused trips.

Shopping

Antiques fill the warren of rooms at the **Barking Dog** (☒ 7 2nd St., off Rte. 213 ☎ 845/687–4834), in business since 1984. You won't find the ubiquitous here, and nearly everything dates from before the 1920s. The shop specializes in country pieces, such as pine tables and cupboards, and folk art, and also offers old prints and paintings. For about three weeks in May and sometimes in November, the store showcases its stock of vintage linens, textiles, and clothing (call for details). Birds—wild birds, in particular—are the theme at the **Bird Watcher's Country Store** (☒ Rte. 213 about ¼ mi west of High Falls center ☎ 800/947–2347). In addition to bird feeders, seed, houses, and baths, the store has chimes, field guides, window ornaments, and weathervanes. The inventory at **Cathouse Antiques** (☒ 136 Bruceville Rd., ½ mi off Rte. 213 ☎ 845/687–0457) favors the 1940s, but pieces from the 1930s and '50s are here, too. Kitchen items and housewares in bright hues mingle with collectibles, glass and pottery pieces, and some furniture. The **Green Cottage** (☒ 1204 Rte. 213 ☎ 845/687–4810) is part florist and part gift boutique. It creates interesting bouquets and carries small gift items such as handcrafted and estate jewelry (one of the owners has a jewelry studio), ceramic vases, prettily packaged soaps, sculptural candles, children's books, and a few toys. The mix changes seasonally; garden gear is featured in summer. A bright, lovingly restored space is home to **High Falls Mercantile** (☒ 113 Main St. ☎ 845/687–4200), which carries new and antique furniture, 1920s European paintings, scented lotions and candles, and by-the-yard printed fabrics. A bevy of white platters comes in assorted shapes. Sunny, colorful clothes and accessories fill **Le Petit Boutique** (☒ 8 2nd St., off Rte. 213 ☎ 845/687–4600), a truly petite space. The men's and women's clothes are made by one of the owners; the kids kimono tops and tiny T-shirts are from the Lucky Wang line. Cool canvas bags round out the mix. At **Linger** (✉ 8 2nd St., off Rte. 213 ☎ 845/687–7907), you may indeed want to stay awhile to browse through the diverse collection of home furnishings and decorative items (most new, some antique), bath-and-body lotions and potions, garden accessories, and affordable jewelry. **Spruce** (✉ 105½ Main St. ☎ 845/687–4481), tucked behind the Canal House restaurant, juxtaposes furniture and objects from the 1940s to the '70s—Lucite lamps, mod couches, Eva Zeisel pottery—against rustic, wood-lined walls.

The **JMW Auction Gallery** (✉ Fann's Shopping Center, 1157 Rte. 32, Rosendale ☎ 845/658–8586 or 845/339–4133 ⊕ www.jmwauction.com) holds auctions at least every few months, and more frequently in summer. They're usually on Saturday, and may include antique furniture, arts and crafts pieces, old coins, wrought-iron outdoor dining sets, wicker chairs, and decorative items. The assortment is hit or miss, but half the fun is looking for that one treasure. Call, or check the Web site, for an auction schedule.

en route

Set back from U.S. 209 between the center of Stone Ridge and Hurley is the **Bevier House Museum** (✉ 2682 U.S. 209, Stone Ridge ☎ 845/338–5614 ⚏ $4), which dates from 1690 and is the headquarters of the **Ulster County Historical Society.** The house is open 1–5 Thursday through Sunday from June through September. Among the house-tour highlights are the scullery, which contains early building and food-prep tools (some from the 17th century), and an extensive collection of Civil War artifacts, including guns, photos, drums, and uniform pieces. The research library (open by appointment) contains 17th-century books and maps, diaries, and genealogical materials. A small gift shop has books about local history and architecture.

Hurley

⑯ *7 mi northeast of High Falls.*

Hurley, a National Historic Landmark, was founded by the Dutch in 1661. The area is surrounded by cornfields, which occupy the floodplain of the Esopus Creek, sitting on deep soils that accumulated during the last ice age. Hurley was burned by American Indians in 1663, during the Second Esopus War. It was rebuilt and today includes one of the largest clusters of stone houses in the United States. The 24 **Hurley Stone Houses,** as they're known collectively, date from the late 17th to early 19th century, and many are still home to descendants of the original families. On the second Saturday in July about a third of the homes are opened to the public. During Hurley's one-month stint as the state capital following the burning of Kingston by the British, the 1723 Van Deusen House (or Senate House) served as meeting space for the Colonists.

Col. Jonathan Elmendorf House. The house, built between 1783 and 1790, contains the **Hurley Heritage Society Museum.** It includes a good collection of Revolutionary War materials, and has changing exhibits about local history. Walking- and driving-tour brochures are available in its front lobby. ⊠ *52 Main St.* ☏ *845/338–1661* ⊕ *pws.prserv.net/ hurleyheritagesociety* ⊑ *Free* ⊙ *May–Nov., Sat. 10–4, Sun. 1–4.*

Hurley Patentee Manor. The original portion of this cottage was built for Cornelius Cole in 1696. The structure was then expanded in 1745 into a Georgian manor. Rooms are furnished with period antiques and colonial reproductions. Part of the Hurley Patent, a 1708 land grant from King George I, the house reflects the English style of its day. ⊠ *464 Old Rte. 209* ☏ *845/331–5414* ⊑ *$2* ⊙ *Mid-July–Labor Day, Wed.–Sat. 11–4, Sun. 1–5.*

Hurley Reformed Church. This church was built in 1853 to replace the 1801 stone church a few doors up the street. Look for the original family nameplates at the end of the pews. The parsonage is next door in the 1790 **Crispell House.** ⊠ *17 Main St.* ☏ *No phone.*

Hurley Stone House Day. During this one-day event many of Hurley's 24 stone houses are opened to the public, including the Crispell House (next to the Hurley Reformed Church), the Dr. Richard TenEyck House, the DuMond House, the Van Deusen House, and the Col. Jonathan Elmendorf House. Fourteen of the original stone houses are on Main Street (aka Route 29); a few more are across Esopus Creek, to the west. As a child, abolitionist Sojourner Truth was a slave in the Hardenberg House, on Schoolhouse Road, just south of Main. Additional houses sometimes open as well. Tours start at the Dutch Reformed Church. Costumed guides are part of the fun. ☏ *845/331–4121* ⊕ *pws.prserv.net/hurleyheritagesociety* ⊑ *$12* ⊙ *July, 2nd Sat., 10–4.*

Where to Eat

¢–$$ ✕ **Hurley Mountain Inn.** Once called "the Hurley Hilton," this early-19th-century restaurant-bar was featured in the 1980s film *Tootsie*. It's been remodeled since then, but it's still a casual place where country music, juicy burgers, spicy chicken wings, and large portions are the rule. ⊠ *Old Rte. 209* ☏ *845/331–1780* ⊟ *D, MC, V.*

Kingston

🟊 *2 mi northeast of Hurley.*

In 1609 Henry Hudson's ship landed at Kingston Point. Within five years a fur-trading post was established at the mouth of Rondout (from the Dutch word for a small fort) Creek. In 1658 a permanent village—Wiltwyck—was built. When the British took over in 1669, that tiny village was renamed Kingston.

It became the state's first capital in 1777. As such, Kingston became a target for the British, who set fire to every building but one (alleged to belong to a Tory sympathizer) in October of that year. Many stone houses were rebuilt, however; uptown Kingston's historic Stockade District has examples from the 17th and 18th centuries. The intersection of Crown and John streets is the only one in the United States with 18th-century stone houses occupying all four corners. The architecture throughout the city is rich and varied, and it includes representatives of Federal; Greek, Gothic, and Romanesque revival; Italianate; English Renaissance, colonial, Georgian; Second Empire; English Tudor; Dutch-colonial; and Victorian styles. The design of City Hall, which has a distinctive tower and was completed in 1875, was based on that of the Palazzo Vecchio in Florence.

Kingston thrived as a commercial port in the 19th century, especially between 1828 and 1898, when the D&H Canal was in operation and coal was shipped here from Pennsylvania for distribution elsewhere. Much of this commerce-related action occurred in the Rondout District, just west of where the Rondout Creek joins with the Hudson River. This waterfront area, which has seen extensive gentrification since the 1980s, has a lively arts and restaurant scene. River cruises embark from the pier at the foot of Broadway.

Fred J. Johnston Museum. Antiques dealer Fred J. Johnston rescued this 1812 Federal mansion from the wrecking ball in the 1930s; the Friends of Historic Kingston inherited the house in 1993 through Johnston's will. His collection of 18th- and 19th-century Hudson Valley furniture and decorative arts is on display. Adjacent is the Friends of Historic Kingston Museum. ⊠ *63 Main St., Stockade District* ☎ *845/339–0720* ⊕ *www. cr.nps.gov/nr/travel/kingston/k9.htm* ☜ *$3* ⊙ *May–Oct., weekends 1–4.*

Heritage Area Visitor Center. The Stockade and Rondout districts each have a visitor center. The one uptown, which is open seasonally and is staffed by volunteers, occupies an 1837 Federal House across the street from the Senate House. The center in the waterfront area is open all year and has full-time staff. Both centers have permanent exhibits. ⊠ *20 Broadway Rondout District* ☎ *845/331–7517 or 800/331–1518* ⊕ *www.ci. kingston.ny.us* ☜ *Free* ⊙ *May–Oct., weekdays 9–5, weekends 11–5; Nov.–Apr., weekdays 9–5* ⊠ *308 Clinton Ave., Stockade District* ☎ *800/ 331–1518* ⊕ *www.ci.kingston.ny.us* ☜ *Free* ⊙ *May–Oct., daily 11–5.*

Hudson River Maritime Museum. Models, artifacts, and photographs illustrate the region's maritime history. Changing exhibits show tugboats and antique fishing and sailing craft. You may board the *Half Moon,* a replica of Henry Hudson's ship, when it's in dock. Tours to the **Rondout Lighthouse** (also known as the Kingston Lighthouse) leave from the museum's dock. In mid-July the museum hosts the one-day **Steam Launch Meet Festival,** with displays of working steam engines and a launch parade. Other events include a boat show (in late July or early August) and the ⇨ **Shad Festival** in May. ⊠ *50 Rondout Landing, Rondout District* ☎ *845/338–0071* ⊕ *www.ulster.net/~hrmm/* ☜ *Museum $5, lighthouse $5* ⊙ *May–Oct., daily 11–5.*

Keegan Ales. This working microbrewery offers free tours and tastings. (Stout fans should try Mother's Milk.) It also holds quarterly rock concerts, either in the brewery itself or in the parking lot, and functions as a gallery and performance space. ⊠ *20 St. James St., Midtown* ☎ *845/ 331–2739* ⊕ *www.keeganales.com* ☜ *Tours and tastings free* ⊙ *Thurs. and Fri. 3–7, Sat. noon–7.*

Old Dutch Church Heritage Museum. The church was established in 1659, and a small wooden building was erected in 1661. It was burned down in 1663, during the Second Esopus War. Today's church (the fourth at

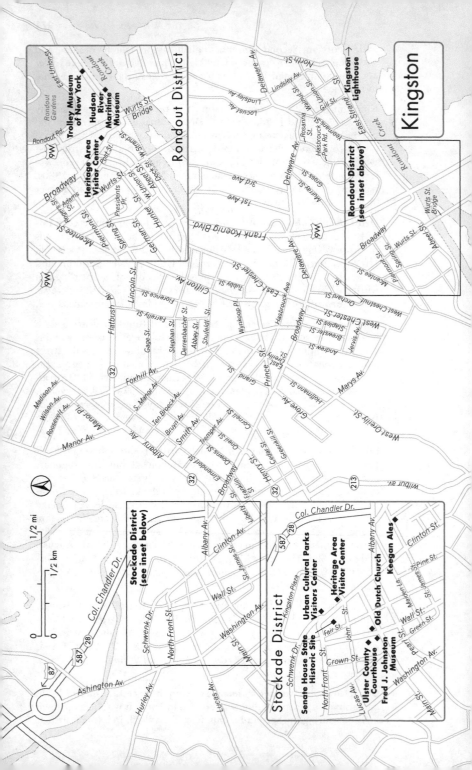

Kingston

Rondout District

- Trolley Museum of New York
- Hudson River Maritime Museum
- Heritage Area Visitor Center

Rondout Gardens
East Union St.
Rondout Creek
Wurts St. Bridge
Rondout Rd.
9W
Broadway
Rogers St.
Adams St.
McEntee St.
Piermont St.
Spring St.
Hunter St.
Presidents Pl.
Post St.
W. Union St.
Abeel St.
Dock St.
W. Strand St.
Wurts St.
German St.

Rondout District (see inset above)

Delaware Av.
Lindsley Av.
North St.
Gill St.
W. Union St.
Hasbrouck Av.
Rosanna St.
Park Rd.
Locust Av.
Kingston Lighthouse →
East Strand
Rondout Creek
Delaware Av.
Gross St.
Murray St.
3rd Ave
1st Ave
Frank Koenig Blvd.
9W
Broadway
Wurts St.
Wurts St. Bridge
Abeel St.
Spring St.
Piermont St.
McEntee St.
West Chestnut St.
West Chestnut St.

Lincoln St.
Florence St.
Farrelly St.
Clifton Av.
Tubby St.
East Chester St.
West Chester St.
Hasbrouck Av.
Orchard St.
Broadway
Delaware Av.
Flatbush
Gage St.
Stephan St.
Derrenbacher St.
Abbey St.
Shufeldt St.
Wynkoop Pl.
Prince St.
Grand St.
East O'Reilly St.
Brewster St.
Staples St.
Andrew St.
Jervis Av.
Marys Av.
32
Foxhill Av.
S. Manor Av.
Ten Broeck Av.
Bruyn Av.
Smith Av.
Cornell St.
Grove Av.
Hoffmann St.
West O'Reilly St.
Madison Av.
Wilson Av.
Roosevelt Pl.
Manor Av.
Manor Av.
Albany Av.
Elmendorf St.
Downs St.
O'Neil St.
Hasbrook Av.
Tremper Av.
Henry St.
Greenkill Av.
Broadway
Franklin St.
32
32
213
Wilbur av.

Stockade District (see inset below)

Col. Chandler Dr.
587
28
87
Col. Chandler Dr.
Ashington Av.
Hurley Av.
Lucas Av.
Albany Av.
Clinton Av.
James St.
Wall St.
Washington Av.
Schwenk Dr.
North Front St.

N

1/2 mi
1/2 km
0

Stockade District

- Urban Cultural Parks Visitors Center
- Heritage Area Visitor Center
- Senate House State Historic Site
- Ulster County Courthouse
- Old Dutch Church
- Fred J. Johnston Museum
- Keegan Ales

Col. Chandler Dr.
587
28
Kingston Plaza
Schwenk Dr.
North Front St.
Fair St.
John St.
Crown St.
Lucas Av.
Maiden Ln.
Albany Av.
Pearl St.
Wall St.
Green St.
Clinton St.
Pine St.
St. James St.
Washington Av.
Main St.

the site) went up in 1852 and features an 1891 window made by the Tiffany Studios. George Clinton (first governor of New York and vice president under Thomas Jefferson) and a number of Revolutionary War soldiers are buried in the graveyard. ⊠ *272 Wall St., Stockade District* ☎ *845/338–6759* 💲 *Free* ⊙ *Weekdays 10–4, tours by appointment.*

Senate House State Historic Site. The first State Senate met in this 17th-century Dutch house. In the modern museum across the garden, you can view works by John Vanderlyn (1775–1852), among other notable American painters, and an exhibit about the American Revolution. ⊠ *312 Fair St., Stockade District* ☎ *845/338–2786* ⊕ *nysparks.state. ny.us* 💲 *$4* ⊙ *Mid-Apr.–Oct., Wed.–Sat. 10–5, Sun. 1–5; Nov.–mid-Apr., by appointment.*

Trolley Museum of New York. The museum stands on the site of the eastern terminal of the Ulster & Delaware (U&D) Railroad, which ran from Kingston through the Catskills and was affectionately known as the Up & Down Railroad. Trolley cars dating from 1907 are on display; trolley tours of historic Kingston (included in the admission fee) leave from the museum. ⊠ *89 E. Strand, Rondout District* ☎ *845/331–3399* ⊕ *www.tmny.org* 💲 *$4* ⊙ *May–Oct., weekends noon–5.*

Ulster County Courthouse. New York's first constitution was drafted on this site in 1777, in an earlier building. Then its first chief justice, John Jay, was sworn in on the front steps of that courthouse. He then swore in its first governor, George Clinton. Shortly thereafter, in the same year, the British burned down Kingston; the current courthouse was built in 1818. Sojourner Truth was freed in 1827, and she immediately—and successfully—sued, in this courthouse, to have her son freed from slavery in Alabama. ⊠ *285 Wall St., Stockade District* ⊕ *www.cr.nps.gov/ nr/travel/kingston.*

FESTIVALS & FAIRS **Burning of Kingston.** Following the 1st Ulster County Militia's annual reenactment of the 1777 British landing and battle at Kingston Point (in mid-October), redcoats and colonial bluecoats occupy the city for three days. Spectators can watch the landing and invasion. Much of the activity takes place in the Stockade District. ☎ *845/331–7517 or 800/331–1518* ⊕ *www.firstulster.org.*

Shad Festival. In early May the Hudson River Maritime Museum celebrates the shad's seasonal swim up the Hudson River with shad and shadroe dinners, storytelling, crafts, jazz and blues, and boat rides. The Gourmet Society of the Culinary Institute of America prepares the food, and samplings from the menus of several waterfront restaurants are also available. ⊠ *50 Rondout Landing, Rondout District* ☎ *845/338–0071* ⊕ *www.ulster.net/~hrmm/museum/festival.htm.*

Where to Stay & Eat

$$–$$$$ ✕ **23 Broadway.** Friendly Culinary Institute graduates run this beautifully renovated 19th-century storefront restaurant, where a bar stretches along one wall and all the woodwork gleams. The menu changes frequently and is fairly eclectic, ranging from tapas style dishes to French bistro classics. Roasted beet salad and lobster cavatelli in cognac-cream

sauce are two good options. ⊠ *23 Broadway, Rondout District* ☎ *845/ 339–2322* ⊟ *AE, D, DC, MC, V* ⊗ *Closed Mon. and Tues.*

$$–$$$ ✕ **Hoffman House Tavern.** You can dine by a fireplace in this late-17th-century stone house, a National Historic Landmark. Try the aged steak or the special seafood of the day. On Saturday night, prime rib is served with Yorkshire pudding. The homemade pastas are also a treat. The dessert menu includes a different cheesecake for each day of the week. In summer, ask to sit on the patio. ⊠ *94 N. Front St., Stockade District* ☎ *845/ 338–2626* ⊟ *AE, D, DC, MC, V* ⊗ *Closed Sun.*

$$–$$$ ✕ **Le Canard Enchaîné.** This relaxed bistro offers a slice of France in uptown Kingston. Try modern versions of traditional dishes, like duck pâté served on a bed of red onions (a starter) or grilled New Zealand rack of lamb in a merlot–balsamic vinegar reduction. The prix-fixe menus offer good value. You can hear live jazz at the piano bar on Saturday night. ⊠ *276 Fair St., Stockade District* ☎ *845/339–2003* ⊟ *AE, D, MC, V.*

$$–$$$ ✕ **Ship to Shore.** The storefront restaurant, owned by a Culinary Institute alum, has great food: salmon fillet with citrus-basil lacquer, crab-meat ravioli in champagne-tomato beurre blanc, and the 12-ounce filet mignon in a black pepper–Chianti reduction are among the popular choices. The space—warm and inviting, with exposed-brick walls and dark-wood trim—includes a bar area. The service, friendly and professional, does the food justice. ⊠ *15 W. Strand, Rondout District* ☎ *845/ 334–8887* ⊟ *AE, D, MC, V.*

★ $–$$$ ✕ **El Coqui.** Puerto Rican food and music, both spicy and plentiful, are good reasons to visit this relaxed spot. The menu includes several different paellas, in portions for one or two, as well as cod fritters, mashed plaintains, and arroz con pollo. For such a small place, El Coqui can really pack in a crowd on Friday nights, when live salsa, merengue, and other Latin sounds are the draw. ⊠ *21 Broadway, Rondout District* ☎ *845/340–1106* ⊟ *AE, D, DC, MC, V* ⊗ *Closed Mon. in Sept.–Apr.*

$–$$$ ✕ **Hickory BBQ and Smokehouse.** Savory, slow-cooked smoked meats are the draw at this casual eatery with wooden booths and a bar. The traditional Southern-style sides—collard greens, macaroni and cheese, corn bread, and flaky biscuits—are another reason to come. ⊠ *743 Rte. 28 (3 mi west of traffic circle)* ☎ *845/338–2424* ⊟ *AE, D, MC, V.*

$$ ✕ **Cafe Nouba.** This corner restaurant specializes in the flavors of southeast Asia: Thailand, Indonesia, and Vietnam. Thai paella (with mussels, crab, calamari, chicken and shrimp), pan-roasted salmon with red curry, and Asian crab cakes (with cilantro, onions, shallots, garlic, and Thai fish sauce) are all worth a try. The eclectic, colorful decor takes its cues from Asia as well, and the crowd it attracts is fairly diverse. The apple martini is a signature drink. ⊠ *284 Fair St., Stockade District* ☎ *845/ 340–4770* ⊟ *AE, MC, V* ⊗ *Closed Mon. No lunch.*

$–$$ ✕ **El Dazante.** You get authentic Oaxacan food at this small and unpretentious place. Instead of ordering the usual Americanized dishes, go for the soft tacos, tamales (especially the ones filled with mole poblano and wrapped in plantain leaves), or the fried squid in chipotle sauce. El Dazante carries the best selection of Mexican beers and tequilas around. ⊠ *720 Broadway, Midtown* ☎ *845/331–7070* ⊟ *AE, D, DC, MC, V.*

¢–$ ✕**Bread Alone.** Although artisanal baked goods are the main attraction at this European-style bakery-café, its gourmet coffees and light lunches are also well worth a stop. The storefront space, with big windows and wooden tables, has an old-fashioned feel. ⊠ *34 N. Front St., Stockade District* ☎ *845/339–1295* ⟝ *Reservations not accepted* ▭ *MC, V.*

¢–$ ✕**Joyous Café.** This small, cheery refuge in midtown Kingston is perfect for breakfast or lunch, Sunday brunch, or just dessert. Everything here is fresh and homemade. The lunch menu includes salads, cold and hot sandwiches, burgers, and soup, as well as omelets, waffles, and other brunch items. The fries, served in a cone, come with your choice of sauce: roasted garlic, horseradish, chipotle, or Asian barbecue. On weekdays the place closes at 5:30. ⊠ *308 Broadway, Midtown* ☎ *845/334–9441* ▭ *AE, D, MC, V* ☉ *Closed Sat. No dinner.*

¢ ✕**Dallas Hot Weiners.** Hot dogs are the specialty at this narrow spot
Fodor'sChoice with a counter and a handful of tables. "One with everything" means
★ a steamed dog on a steamed bun topped with slightly spicy chili sauce, a dab of mustard, and a sprinkling of chopped onions. The sauce livens up fries, too; temper it with ketchup if it's too spicy for you. ⊠ *51 N. Front St., Stockade District* ☎ *845/338–6094* ⟝ *Reservations not accepted* ▭ *No credit cards* ☉ *Closed Sun.* ⊠ *490 Broadway, Midtown* ☎ *845/331–6311* ⟝ *Reservations not accepted* ▭ *No credit cards* ☉ *Closed Sun.*

¢ ✕**Jane's Homemade Ice Cream.** This is the place to find out how ice cream was meant to taste. The ice-cream flavors are deep and intense, and the variety is amazing: pumpkin, cinnamon, chocolate raspberry, and hazelnut fudge are only a few of the temptations. Light lunches are also available here; the salads and sandwiches are ethnically inspired eclectic delights. Do save room for dessert, though. ⊠ *305 Wall St., Stockade District* ☎ *845/338–8315* ⟝ *Reservations not accepted* ▭ *No credit cards* ☉ *Closed Sun. No dinner.*

$ ⊞**Ramada Inn.** The two-story chain property is about ¼ mi off Exit 19 of I–87 and is convenient to uptown Kingston, as well as to Rhinebeck and Woodstock. Rooms are fairly spacious, with the usual cookie-cutter decor. ⊠ *114 Rte. 28, 12401* ☎ *845/339–3900* ⊟ *845/338–8464* ⊕ *www.ramada.com* ⇆ *147 rooms, 3 suites* ⟝ *Restaurant, room service, in-room data ports, cable TV, indoor pool, gym, bar, babysitting, laundry service, business services, meeting rooms, no-smoking rooms* ▭ *AE, D, DC, MC, V* ⏶l *EP.*

$ ⊞**Rondout B&B.** The circa-1906 colonial-revival house, a 15-minute walk from the Rondout waterfront, sits on two hilltop acres surrounded by flower gardens, picnic tables, and a hammock. You can take in the the grounds from two furnished porches. Inside are antiques, eclectic portraits, sculptures, ceramics, two pianos, and two woodstoves, but the house is so airy and spacious that it doesn't look cluttered or precious. Two of the guest rooms share a bathroom and a sitting area, which has a TV. (The living room has another TV.) There are two resident dogs, so the owners welcome canine guests, too. ⊠ *88 W. Chester St., 12401* ☎ *845/331–8144* ⊟ *845/331–9049* ⊕ *www.rondoutbandb.com* ⇆ *4 rooms, 2 with shared bath* ⟝ *Dining room, piano, some pets allowed; no room phones, no room TVs, no smoking* ▭ *AE, MC, V* ⏶l *BP.*

¢–$ 🏨 **Holiday Inn.** The two-story chain hotel is ¼ mi off the Kingston exit of I–87 and close to uptown's commercial district. Many of the rooms are adjoining and there's an indoor courtyard with a pool, making this a good choice for families. Some rooms include large desks. ✉ *503 Washington Ave., 12401* ☎ *845/338–0400 or 800/465–4329* ⊕ *www.ichotelsgroup.com* ⊷ *212 rooms, 5 suites* ⚲ *Restaurant, room service, in-room data ports, cable TV, indoor pool, wading pool, gym, hot tub, sauna, billiards, Ping-Pong, bar, recreation room, laundry facilities, Internet, business services, some pets allowed (fee), no-smoking rooms* ▤ *AE, D, DC, MC, V* �’⨀❘ *EP.*

Nightlife & the Arts

NIGHTLIFE   DJs spin dance tunes at the club **Rive Gauche** (✉ 276 Fair St., Stockade District ☎ 845/339–2003), which comes to life after 10 PM Friday and Saturday. On Sunday, the gay set turns out for "tea dances," which start at 4 PM. The **West Strand Grill** (✉ 50 Abeel St., Rondout District ☎ 845/340–4272), in a refurbished 1892 temple high above the Rondout, hosts live music acts (mostly rock and grunge) in its downstairs space. The bar is the focal point of the main level, which includes a couple of pool tables.

THE ARTS   Kingston has a vibrant arts scene, with more galleries and art events than can be listed here. The Arts Society of Kingston (ASK; ☎ 845/338–0331 ⊕ www.askforarts.org) and the Ulster County Arts Council (☎ 845/339–9935 ⊕ www.ulstercountyartscouncil.org) are good sources of information about the latest happenings. Many galleries participate in **First Night,** keeping their doors open 5–7 on the first Saturday of each month.

Backstage Studio Productions (✉ 323 Wall St., Stockade District ☎ 845/338–8700) hosts live music, performance art, dance, open-mike nights, and stand-up poets. It also serves as a gallery space and has a cash bar. The **Coffey Gallery** (✉ 330 Wall St., Stockade District ☎ 845/334–9752) shows paintings, drawings, prints, sculpture, and one-of-a-kind furniture. Local artists are the focus. The avant-garde **Gallery at Deep Listening Space** (✉ 75 Broadway, Rondout District ☎ 845/338–5984 or 800/560–6955 ⊕ www.deeplistening.org/dls/), a gallery and performance space, was started by accordionist–performance artist–composer Pauline Oliveros and is run by her foundation. Events and exhibits here tend to be more cutting-edge and experimental. The **Ulster Performing Arts Center** (UPAC; ✉ 601 Broadway, Midtown ☎ 845/339–6088 ⊕ www.upac.org) resides in a beautifully restored 1927 art-deco movie palace. It's home to the 1,500-seat Broadway Theater and hosts local groups, such as the Hudson Valley Philharmonic, as well as well-known performers like Little Feat, Joan Rivers, and Randy Travis.

Shopping

The used and rare books at **Alternative Books** (✉ 35 N. Front St., Stockade District ☎ 845/331–5439), including a large collection of poetry and signed first editions, reflect the artistic nature of the Mid-Hudson Valley. **Blue-Byrd's** (✉ 21 W. Strand, Rondout District ☎ 845/339–3174) is a cool spot for the blues—the music, the look, the memorabilia—and for beautiful hats for guys and gals. It carries books, boxed sets, and posters of blues and jazz biggies. **Bop to Tottom** (✉ 299 Wall

St., Stockade District ☎ 845/338–8100), a whimsical mélange of gift items for children of all ages, sells fun jewelry, throw pillows, scented soaps and candles, spinning tops and jack-in-the-boxes, rice-paper lamp shades, and more. **NEXT Boutique** (⊠ 17 W. Strand, Rondout District ☎ 845/331–4537) carries quirky handcrafted and costume jewelry and flirtatious frocks that capture the delicate allure of vintage apparel with none of the mustiness of the real thing. Three Dots and other casual lines are also available here. If you love to pamper your pet, don't miss **Pawprints & Whiskers** (⊠ 292 Wall St., Stockade District ☎ 845/339–5735). Fido and Fifi will adore the souvenirs you bring home from this pet boutique. Multiple dealers of delightful antiques and other old stuff, much of it reflecting the neighborhood's nautical past, occupy **Skillypot Antiques** (⊠ 41 Broadway, Rondout District ☎ 845/338–6779). **The Well-Seasoned Nest** (⊠ 303 Wall St., Stockade District ☎ 845/338–4629), a sunny space in a converted bank, carries lovely pieces for the home and garden, including vine wreaths, fine table linens, ceramic and metal planters, and assorted candles.

Saugerties

⑱ *15 mi north of Kingston.*

Ever since Governor Andros negotiated a deal with the Esopus tribe in 1677, Saugerties, strategically located between the Catskill Mountains and the Hudson River, has lured entrepreneurs, visionaries, and working folk. It was for centuries a no-nonsense mix of agrarian and early industry, where farmers harvested ice from the Hudson in winter, quarried bluestone and brick from surrounding hills, milled lumber, and made paper. With one of the few deepwater ports along the river, Saugerties was once a thriving riverfront town, loading its wares onto southern-bound steamboats and building racing sloops.

Today, after decades of slumber, Saugerties is thriving for completely different reasons. Mint-condition Victorian houses line its streets, and the occasional stone house evokes memories of early Palatine settlers. Civic pride blooms in flower baskets in the downtown shopping area, especially along Main and Partition streets, where antiques shops, independent bookstores, and tantalizing restaurants draw weekend crowds.

Kiersted House. The stone house, parts of which date from the 1720s, serves as the home of the Saugerties Historical Society and a museum. Inside you can see original architectural details, including wide-plank floors and fireplace mantels. The front lawn is the site of summertime concerts, periodic colonial reenactments, and other special events. ⊠ *119 Main St.* ☎ *845/246-9529* ☺ *Free* ☺ *Memorial Day–Columbus Day, weekends 2–7, Fri. and Mon. by appointment.*

Opus 40. The late Harvey Fite put 37 years into the making of this 6-acre outdoor sculpture, created in the rock bed of an abandoned bluestone quarry. The architectural creation is an assemblage of curving bluestone walkways, swirling terraces, and finely fitted ramps around pools, trees, and fountains. The **Quarryman's Museum** contains 19th-century tools. The place sometimes closes for special events, so call ahead.

✉ *50 Fite Rd.* ☎ *845/246–3400* ⊕ *www.opus40.org* ✉ *$6* ⊗ *Memorial Day–Columbus Day, Fri.–Sun. noon–5.*

> **off the beaten path**

BRONCK MUSEUM – A group of 17th- and 18th-century buildings and 19th-century barns makes up this museum, which also serves as headquarters of the Greene County Historical Society. The oldest building here—indeed, in all of Greene County—is a stone Dutch-colonial house that was built in 1663. Additions to the one-room structure included a 1685 stone wing and a 1738 brick house. The rooms contain a hodgepodge of Federal, Victorian, and Empire furnishings and paintings by period notables. The wide expanse of lawn includes several barns, among them a 13-sided Dutch structure from the 1830s. The museum is 33 mi north of Saugerties. ✉ *U.S. 9W 3¾ mi south of I–87 Exit 21B, Coxsackie* ☎ *518/731–6490* ⊕ *www.gchistory.org* ✉ *$4* ⊗ *Late May–Oct. 15, Wed.–Fri. noon–4, Sat. 10–4, Sun. 1–4.*

THOMAS COLE NATIONAL HISTORIC SITE – You may feel the urge to pick up a paintbrush as you take in the Catskill Mountain views from the front porch of this yellow-brick Federal house. Well, at least you can understand what inspired Thomas Cole (1801–48), the painter credited with starting the Hudson River school of art. Cole came to know the 1815 house, called **Cedar Grove,** when he set up a studio in an outbuilding he rented on the property; he settled down here after marrying a niece of the owner. James Fenimore Cooper and Asher B. Durand are among the 19th-century luminaries who visited Cedar Grove, 13 mi north of Saugerties. Frederic Church, who later built his magnificent home, Olana, on the other side of the Hudson, spent two years here studying with Cole. Entry to the house, which includes exhibits of 19th-century artworks, is via guided tour. ✉ *218 Spring St., near Rip Van Winkle Bridge, Catskill* ☎ *518/943–7465* ⊕ *www.thomascole.org* ✉ *House $5, grounds free* ⊗ *House early May–late Oct., Fri. and Sat. 10–4, Sun. 1–5; grounds daily dawn–dusk.*

FESTIVALS & FAIRS **Esopus Creek Festival of Mask and Puppet Theater.** The last weekend in August you can watch giant puppets and imaginative spectacles unfold before the Esopus Creek in Tina Chorvas Waterfront Park. You'll be dazzled once the sun goes down and local puppeteers transform the park into an otherworldly extravaganza. ✉ *E. Bridge St.* ☎ *845/246–7873* ⊕ *www.armofthesea.org.*

Hudson Valley Garlic Festival. Upward of 40,000 people make a pilgrimage to Saugerties the last weekend of September for a celebration of the "stinking rose": garlic. Although you find much of the usual fair fare here—crafts booths, fried-dough stands, live musical performances—one vast section of the festival is devoted to farmers, arts and crafts people, and food vendors all providing tributes to garlic. You may learn about growing your own, or savor garlic soup and ice cream. ✉ *Cantine Field, between Washington Ave. and Market St.* ☎ *845/246–3090* ⊕ *www.hvgf.org.*

JAS. The village of Saugerties closes off its streets to car traffic for one day on the first weekend in September for JAS, Jazz and Art at Saugerties. Three stages of live music get people dancing to Latin and other jazz sounds; restaurants serve food outdoors; and local artists, including photographers and sculptors, line the streets with booths showing their works. ⊠ *Main and Partition Sts.* ☎ *845/246–2321* ⊕ *www. saugerties.ny.us.*

Where to Stay & Eat

$$–$$$ ✕ **Café Tamayo.** Sweep back the claret-colored velvet curtains at the entrance and you're transported to a turn-of-the-20th-century French bistro. Gourmands have enthused over the New American fare—smoked salmon–potato pancake and grilled loin of lamb, for example—since the place opened in 1987. Chef-owner James Tamayo, a Culinary Institute graduate, prides himself on using fresh local produce and is known for his duck confit. Upstairs are two guest rooms and a suite ($80–$120). All have antiques, queen brass beds, and private baths—one with a decadent 6-foot-long soaking tub. ⊠ *89 Partition St.* ☎ *845/246–9371* ⊟ *DC, MC, V* ☉ *Closed Mon. and Tues. No lunch.*

$–$$$ ✕ **New World Home Cooking Co.** Colorful accents and artwork adorn this lively restaurant. A large bar and a sapphire–and–stainless steel open kitchen are focal points. The eclectic menu includes a sampler with creole-mustard shrimp, Spanish manchego cheese, Sicilian olive-salad crostini, smoked Maine mussels, roasted chorizo, and pickled vegetables. Also here: chicken Punjabi, Thai barbecued fish, and Cajun peppered shrimp. The pan-blackened string beans will have you humming zydeco. Everything is prepared without "zappers," aka deep-fat fryers, or MSG, and a kids' menu is available. Live music gets the joint jumping Friday nights. ⊠ *1411 Rte. 212* ☎ *845/246–0900* ⊟ *AE, D, DC, MC, V* ☉ *No lunch Tues. and Wed.*

$–$$ ✕ **Chowhound Cafe.** Terra-cotta, brick, and lime-colored walls provide a backdrop to Candida Ellis's funky eatery, where jazz musicians jam during Sunday brunch. The menu's all over the map, with Italian, Latin, Asian, and American dishes, including salads, sandwiches, and inventive appetizers like coconut-fried shrimp. Spicy citrus coleslaw is the perfect foil for Cajun catfish tacos. ⊠ *112 Partition St.* ☎ *845/246–5158* ⊟ *AE, D, DC, MC, V* ☉ *Closed Mon. and Tues.*

¢–$$ ✕ **Main Street Bar & Grille.** Sweet potato–corn chowder and succulent pork tips that melt away on your tongue have kept generations of locals at the bar and in the booths of this casual eatery. Fish-and-chips, a beer batter–coated piece of scrod, puts other versions of this pub classic to shame. Heartier appetites relish linguine with clam sauce, the rack of ribs, and Asian stir-fry. ⊠ *244 Main St.* ☎ *845/246–6222* ⊟ *AE, D, DC, MC, V.*

$$ ⌂ **Saugerties Lighthouse Bed and Breakfast.** A ½-mi hike from a small parking lot near a Coast Guard station brings you to this romantic hideout, a restored lighthouse overlooking the Hudson River. Downstairs is a Victorian-style parlor. Accommodations are simple and rustic—you make up your own bed at night, and the shared bathroom has a composting toilet—but the two bedrooms are bright and have expansive views. Be sure to climb to the lantern house, which looks across the river at

the Clermont estate. Outdoor decks make for idyllic picnics; at low tide stairs lead to a beach. ✉ *Off Mynderse St., off U.S. 9W, 12477* ☎ *845/ 247–0656* ⊕ *www.saugertieslighthouse.com* ⇱ *2 rooms with shared bath* ⚿ *Beach, some pets allowed (fee); no a/c, no room phones, no room TVs* ☐ *AE, D, MC, V* ⊘ *Closed Mon. and Tues.* ⦿ *BP.*

$-$$ ▣ **The Villa at Saugerties.** Occupying a 1929 Mediterranean-style house on 4 gloriously landscaped and wooded acres, this B&B forgoes froufrou for a contemporary sensibility. The Flat, the largest and most modern of the rooms, has a birch platform bed and naked knotty-plank floors. Furniture is kept to a minimum in the Grange, the smallest of the rooms, which has burnt-red walls. All beds are dressed in 310-thread-count Egyptian-cotton sheets. Common areas include a stone fireplace, floor-to-ceiling paintings, and a breakfast nook with a picture window. The B&B is 6 mi from the center of Saugerties. ✉ *159 Fawn Rd., 12477* ☎☎ *845/ 246–0682* ⊕ *www.thevillaatsaugerties.com* ⇱ *4 rooms* ⚿ *Cable TV, pool; no room phones, no smoking, no kids* ☐ *MC, V* ⦿ *BP.*

¢   ▣ **Comfort Inn.** The two-story chain motel is in a residential area just off Exit 20 of the New York State Thruway and about 2 mi from village shops. Interior corridors connect the rooms, some of which have king beds and recliners. ✉ *2790 Rte. 32, 12477* ☎ *845/246–1565* 🖶 *845/246–1631* ⊕ *www.comfortinn.com* ⇱ *65 rooms* ⚿ *In-room data ports, some in-room hot tubs, some microwaves, some refrigerators, cable TV, business services, some pets allowed (fee), no-smoking rooms* ☐ *AE, D, DC, MC, V* ⦿ *CP.*

Shopping

★   Chocoholics beware: you could find yourself in serious trouble at **Krause's Candy** (✉ 41 S. Partition St. ☎ 845/246–8377), a second-generation-run confectionery. Candy-cane-striped columns beckon you inside, where the aroma of Karl Krause's closely guarded recipes envelop you. Grab a basket to hold your wares; this chocolate is so fresh it's likely to melt in your hands.

Sports & the Outdoors

HORSEBACK   From early May to early September you can join the horsey set in cele-
RIDING   brating all things equine during the seven-week-long hunter-and-jumper competitions at **HITS-on-the-Hudson** (✉ 454 Washington Ave. ☎ 845/ 246–8833 ⊕ www.hitsshows.com). The Catskill Mountains serve as backdrop for the international contests, which draw top talent—human and horse—with substantial winners' purses. It's open Wednesday through Sunday; admission is free weekdays and $5 on weekends. The horse-show facility also hosts antiques and equine-art shows and food-related events.

Poughkeepsie

⑲   *25 mi north of Beacon.*

Founded in 1687, this small Hudson River city has a population of about 30,000. After the British burned down Kingston in 1777, Poughkeepsie served as the state capital for several years. New York's first governor, George Clinton, lived in the city for more than two decades, and it was here that New York State ratified the Constitution in 1788. Today Poughkeepsie is the seat of Dutchess County and home to prestigious Vassar College. The downtown has seen better days, but you can see some signs of rejuvenation.

Absolute Auction Center. You never know what or who you'll find at an auction here: the what varies from fabulous to flea market, whereas the who ranges from well-known New York City dealers to local farmers. Auctions are held most Saturdays. ⊠ *45 South Ave., Pleasant Valley* ☎ *845/635–3169* ⊕ *www.absoluteauctionrealty.com.*

James Baird State Park. The Robert Trent Jones–designed championship golf course is a major draw at this park. Its 590 acres also include hiking and cross-country-skiing trails; basketball, volleyball, and tennis courts; picnic areas; a playground; and a softball field. A full-service restaurant overlooks the golf course. The park is off the Taconic Parkway 1 mi north of Poughkeepsie. ⊠ *122D Freedom Rd., Pleasant Valley* ☎ *845/452–1489* ⊕ *nysparks.state.ny.us* ☜ *Free* ⊙ *Daily dawn–dusk.*

Locust Grove. After Samuel F. B. Morse, the inventor of the telegraph, bought this circa-1830 house, he remodeled it into a Tuscan-style villa. It still contains the possessions and keepsakes of the family that lived here after him. The Morse Gallery, inside the visitor center, has exhibits of telegraph equipment and paintings by Morse. The grounds include hiking trails. ⊠ *370 South Rd./U.S. 9* ☎ *845/454–4500* ⊕ *www.morsehistoricsite.org* ☜ *House $7, grounds free* ⊙ *House May–Nov., daily 10–3; grounds daily 8 AM–dusk.*

Springside. You can walk the carriage roads and trails that vein this woodsy, 20-acre landscape. It is the only surviving example of a landscape design by A. J. Downing, the 19th-century tastemaker. Downing had designed the landscape in 1850 for the country estate of Matthew Vassar, the founder of Vassar College. A trail guide is available in the kiosk at the site. ⊠ *181 Academy St.* ☎ *845/454–2060* ☜ *Free* ⊙ *Daily dawn–dusk.*

Vassar College. Begun as a women's college in 1865, Vassar has since gone co-ed. Today about 2,400 students attend this well-respected liberal-arts school. Vassar was the first college in the United States to have an art gallery; that gallery grew into the **Frances Lehman Loeb Art Center** (⊕ www.fllac.vassar.edu ⊙ Tues.–Sat., 10–5; Sun. 1–5), housed in a 1993 Cesar Pelli building. The center's collections amount to more than 15,000 works, from Egyptian and Asian relics to 19th- and 20th-century paintings. At the free **A. Scott Warthin Geological Museum** (⊕ www.geologyandgeography.vassar.edu/museum.html ⊙ Weekdays 9–4), on the ground floor of Ely Hall, you can see fossil, mineral, and rock specimens. The 1,000-acre campus, with its lakes, gardens, and 200-plus tree varieties, is a lovely place for a walk. Other Vassar highlights include the Tiffany windows in the chapel. ⊠ *124 Raymond Ave.* ☎ *845/437–7000* ⊕ *www.vassar.edu.*

Where to Stay & Eat

$$$–$$$$ ✕ **Le Pavillon.** Classical music and European paintings add to the air of refinement at this French restaurant in a 200-year-old farmhouse surrounded by well-tended grounds. The kitchen makes use of local in-

gredients and turns out French standards: escargots in Pernod-garlic sauce (a starter), coq au vin with leeks and mashed potatoes, and steak au poivre, among others. When the weather's warm, you may also eat on an open-air patio. ⊠ *230 Salt Point Tpke.* ☎ *845/473–2525* ⊟ *AE, D, DC, MC, V* ☽ *Closed Sun. and 2 wks in July. No lunch.*

★ **$$–$$$**   ✕ **Busy Bee Café.** Outside the yellow building there's a sign with a bumblebee. Inside, white tablecloths are an elegant contrast against such homey touches as straw beehives and the occasional bee sculpture. Once you taste the contemporary American fare, you'll know what the buzz is about—and why this place is a local favorite. The menu, which changes frequently, might include crab cakes or filet-mignon satay as starters and grilled fish, lamb, or creative pasta dishes as entrées. Save room for desserts such as berry-topped warm flourless chocolate cake. ⊠ *138 South Ave.* ☎ *845/452–6800* ⊟ *AE, D, DC, MC, V* ☽ *Closed Sun. No lunch Sat.*

$–$$ ✕ **Beech Tree Grill.** You can unwind at this popular bistro-style eatery with brick walls and a bar along one wall. The menu includes Italian and Asian-inspired dishes, such as shrimp *fra diavolo* and sesame-dressed soba-noodle salad, as well as continental comfort classics like beef Stroganoff. A few options are vegetarian, and there's a long list of beers. It's in the commercial district adjacent to the Vassar College campus. ⊠ *1–3 Collegeview Ave.* ☎ *845/471–7279* ⊟ *AE, D, DC, MC, V* ☽ *No lunch Mon.*

$–$$ ✕ **96 Main.** The handsome pub is within walking distance of the train station. Look for the sign with the derby hat that hangs over the door—a leftover from the previous establishment. The bar interior has dark woods, booths, and fans. French doors lead into a more formal dining room. The fare, prepared by Culinary Institute grads, blends rustic Italian and spicy Asian flavors. Brick oven–baked pizza is a specialty, and the desserts are musts. ⊠ *96 Main St.* ☎ *845/454–5200* ⊟ *AE, D, DC, MC, V* ☽ *Closed Mon.*

$–$$ ✕ **Spanky's.** Zesty Cajun and Creole classics, including seafood jambalaya and chicken gumbo, are the main attraction here, but the menu also offers more pedestrian fare like tuna steaks and barbecued ribs, if you prefer something with a little less kick. The restaurant, in a historic building with embossed-tin ceilings, exposed-brick walls, and lots of potted greenery, has a full bar and two separate dining areas. ⊠ *85 Main St.* ☎ *845/485–2294* ⊟ *AE, D, DC, MC, V* ☽ *No lunch weekends.*

¢–$ ✕ **Saigon Café.** This tiny Vietnamese restaurant serves delicious noodle dishes and soups in a friendly atmosphere with prices that don't break the bank. Choices include tender marinated steak bits, beef *pho* (soup) with vermicelli, crispy spring rolls, lime-marinated chicken, and a few vegetarian options. Vietnamese beef and chicken sandwiches, dressed with lettuce, tomato, and pickled carrot, are also available. Vassar College is around the corner. ⊠ *6A LaGrange Ave.* ☎ *845/473–1392* ⊟ *AE, D, DC, MC, V* ☽ *No lunch Sun.*

$$–$$$ ▥ **Inn at the Falls.** The shingle-style inn, overlooking Wappingers Creek and its falls, has a rather European feel to it. Room furnishings and styles vary, from contemporary to country and Asian-inspired to English-manor; some rooms have canopy or four-poster beds. Windows are draped in yards of fabric, framing water views in some rooms. ⊠ *50 Red Oaks Mill Rd.,*

12603 ☎ 845/462–5770 📠 845/462–5943 ⊕ www.innatthefalls.com ➷ 24 rooms, 12 suites ⚅ In-room data ports, some in-room hot tubs, refrigerators, cable TV, exercise equipment, billiards, Ping-Pong, business services, no-smoking rooms ▭ AE, D, DC, MC, V ¶⊙¶ CP.

$–$$ ▦ **Courtyard by Marriott.** Rooms at this three-story chain hotel geared for the business traveler are fairly spacious and have sitting areas, large work desks, two phone lines, and high-speed Internet access. Vassar College is 6 mi away. ⊠ 2641 South Rd./U.S. 9, 12601 ☎ 845/485–6336 📠 845/485–6514 ⊕ www.courtyard.com ➷ 149 rooms, 12 suites ⚅ Restaurant, some in-room data ports, some refrigerators, cable TV with movies, indoor pool, gym, hot tub, bar, laundry facilities, laundry service, business services, meeting rooms, no-smoking rooms ▭ AE, D, DC, MC, V.

$ ▦ **Poughkeepsie Grand Hotel.** The Bardavon Opera House and the train station are within walking distance of this downtown hotel. Rooms have either one king or two double beds, three telephones (one in the bathroom), and high-speed Internet access; some have sofas. Executive rooms include office supplies, a fax machine/copier/printer, and large desks. ⊠ 40 Civic Center Plaza, 12601 ☎ 845/485–5300 📠 845/485–4720 ⊕ www.pokgrand.com ➷ 175 rooms, 9 suites ⚅ Restaurant, room service, in-room data ports, some in-room hot tubs, some refrigerators, cable TV with movies and video games, exercise equipment, bar, business services, meeting rooms, no-smoking rooms ▭ AE, D, DC, MC, V ¶⊙¶ BP.

¢–$ ▦ **Best Inn.** This friendly, budget-conscious chain property has two stories with exterior corridors. Vassar College is three blocks away. ⊠ 536 Haight Ave., 12603 ☎ 845/454–1010 📠 845/454–0127 ⊕ www.bestinn.com ➷ 41 rooms ⚅ In-room data ports, cable TV with movies, indoor pool, gym, business services, no-smoking rooms ▭ AE, D, DC, MC, V ¶⊙¶ CP.

Nightlife & the Arts

Fodor'sChoice The **Bardavon 1869 Opera House** (⊠ 35 Market St. ☎ 845/473–5288 ★ ⊕ www.bardavon.org), home of the Hudson Valley Philharmonic, is the oldest opera house in the state. The beautifully restored auditorium has an active program of theater, music, dance, and drama. Performances are scheduled for most weekends October through June. **The Chance** (⊠ 6 Crannell St. ☎ 845/471–1966 ⊕ www.thechancetheatre.com) is the premier live-music venue in the region. Bookings span all musical styles and include up-and-coming local bands as well as popular, internationally known performers. Housed in two Victorian buildings originally commissioned by the Vassar family, the **Cunneen-Hackett Cultural Center** (⊠ 9 & 12 Vassar St. ☎ 845/471–1221) houses nonprofit organizations, a dance studio, a workshop, an auditorium, and an art gallery. The center presents exhibits; dance, music, and drama performance; and lectures throughout the year. It's open weekdays 9–5. In the heart of downtown Poughkeepsie, the **Mid-Hudson Civic Center** (⊠ 14 Civic Center Plaza ☎ 845/454–5800 ⊕ www.midhudsonciviccenter.com) encompasses the 3,000-seat Mair Hall, the largest venue in the area for shows and concerts. It also includes the McCann Ice Arena, an NHL-size rink open to the public for recreational skating.

Sports & the Outdoors

GOLF Robert Trent Jones designed the 18-hole championship **James Baird State Park Golf Course** (✉ 122D Freedom Rd., off Taconic Pkwy 1 mi north of Poughkeepsie, Pleasant Valley ☎ 845/473–6200 pro shop, 845/452–6959 reservations ⊕ nysparks.state.ny.us), which, with greens fees of $19–$23, is a good value. The par-5, 560-yard 13th hole is considered the signature hole. The course is open from early April to mid-November. Club and cart rentals, lessons, and a driving range are available, and there's a full-service restaurant.

Hyde Park

❷⓿ *6 mi north of Poughkeepsie.*

Hyde Park dates from 1702, when an estate on this land was named for Edward Hyde, Lord Cornbury, then the provincial governor of New York. Most famous for being the boyhood home of Franklin Delano Roosevelt, it's also home to an impressive summer mansion built by one of the Vanderbilts, as well as to the East Coast campus of the renowned Culinary Institute of America (aka the CIA). Much of Dutchess County is blessed with outstanding restaurants, in part because so many CIA graduates decide to stay in the area after they've completed their training. The institute itself has five restaurants.

Culinary Institute of America (CIA). The East Coast branch of the country's most respected cooking school is on the grounds of a former Jesuit seminary overlooking the Hudson River. Tours are available Monday and Thursday when school's in session. Five student-staffed restaurants are open to the public. The Craig Claiborne Bookstore stocks more than 1,300 cookbooks in addition to culinary equipment and specialty foods. One- and two-day workshops and lectures are offered on weekends. ✉ *1946 Campus Dr.* ☎ *845/452–9600* ⊕ *www.ciachef.edu* ▤ *Tour $5* ☉ *Tours Mon. 10 and 4, Thurs. 4; call for details.*

Eleanor Roosevelt National Historic Site. An unpretentious cottage, **Val-Kill** was first a retreat and later the full-time residence for Eleanor Roosevelt. A biographical film, *First Lady of the World,* is shown at the site. The property encompasses 180 acres of trails and gardens. It's also the location of Val-Kill Industries, Eleanor's attempt to prevent farm workers from relocating to the city for employment; reproductions of early American furniture, pewter, and weavings were produced here. ✉ *Rte. 9G* ☎ *845/229–9115* ⊕ *www.nps.gov/elro* ▤ *Tour $8* ☉ *May.–Oct., daily 9–5; Nov.–Apr., Thurs.–Mon. 9–5.*

Fodor'sChoice **Franklin D. Roosevelt National Historic Site.** The birthplace and home of
★ the country's 32nd president, **Springwood** is just as it was when the Roosevelts lived here. It contains family furnishings and keepsakes, and Franklin and Eleanor are buried in the wonderful rose garden. At the **Franklin D. Roosevelt Library and Museum** (⊕ www.fdrlibrary.marist. edu.fdr), photographs, letters, speeches, and memorabilia document FDR's life; a multimedia exhibit examines World War II. The first of the presidential libraries, the building was designed by Roosevelt himself. A large floor mosaic based on a 1949 WPA artist's rendition of the

estate's grounds graces the entryway of the **Wallace Center,** the gateway to the tours, which include the home, library, and museum. ✉ *U.S. 9* ☎ *845/229–9115* ⊕ *www.nps.gov/hofr* ✎ *Tour $14, grounds free* ⊙ *Daily 9–5.*

☺ **Hyde Park Railroad Station.** Franklin D. Roosevelt used this 1914 train station, which today houses an extensive collection of railroad paraphernalia and has running displays of model trains all manned by knowledgeable enthusiasts. The station is at Riverside Park, which has picnic tables and sweeping Hudson River views. ✉ *34 River Rd.* ☎ *845/229–2338* ⊕ *www. hydeparkstation.com* ✎ *Free* ⊙ *June 15–Sept. 15, weekends 11–5.*

Fodor'sChoice **Vanderbilt Mansion National Historic Site.** The grand and imposing 1898
★ McKim, Mead, and White mansion, built for Cornelius Vanderbilt's grandson Fredrick, makes a striking contrast with its Roosevelt neighbor, Springwood. A fine example of life in the Gilded Age, the house is lavishly furnished and full of paintings. It conveys the wealth and privilege of one of the state's most prominent families. The grounds offer excellent views of the Hudson River and encompass lovely Italian gardens. ✉ *U.S. 9* ☎ *845/229–9115* ⊕ *www.nps.gov/vama* ✎ *Tour $8, grounds free* ⊙ *Daily 9–5.*

Where to Stay & Eat

$$–$$$$ ✕ **American Bounty.** Regional American fare is the specialty at this student-staffed restaurant at the Culinary Institute, and local and seasonal ingredients are emphasized. For instance, a salad with baked sheep-milk cheese and candied walnuts gets a dressing with Hudson Valley apple cider. The restaurant is in venerable Roth Hall, once a Jesuit seminary. ✉ *Culinary Institute of America, 1946 Campus Dr.* ☎ *845/471–6608* ✍ *Reservations essential* ⊟ *AE, D, MC, V* ⊙ *Closed Sun. and Mon., 3 wks in July, 2 wks in late Dec.*

$$–$$$ ✕ **Escoffier Restaurant.** The elegant Culinary Institute restaurant presents
Fodor'sChoice modern interpretations of classic French dishes such as lobster salad,
★ smoked salmon, and sautéed beef tenderloin. Other specialties include duck-liver terrine with mango chutney, seared sea scallops, and snails with basil cream sauce. ✉ *Culinary Institute of America, 1946 Campus Dr.* ☎ *845/471–6608* ✍ *Reservations essential* ⊟ *AE, D, MC, V* ⊙ *Closed Sun. and Mon., 3 wks in July, 2 wks in late Dec.*

$$–$$$ ✕ **St. Andrew's Café.** Contemporary fare takes on Asian influences at this casual restaurant at the CIA—chicken-and-shrimp soup, warm spinach salad with wood-fired quail, and grilled tuna with soba noodles, for example. The wood-fired pizza of the day is popular. ✉ *Culinary Institute of America, 1946 Campus Dr.* ☎ *845/471–6608* ✍ *Reservations essential* ⊟ *AE, D, MC, V* ⊙ *Closed weekends, 3 wks in July, 2 wks in late Dec.*

$–$$ ✕ **Hyde Park Brewing Company.** American pub fare and some of the best beer in the Hudson Valley are served in this relaxed restaurant-brewery. The menu includes sandwiches and pizzas as well as toothier fare like steaks and pastas. The breads, desserts, and ice creams are made on the premises. Live music three nights a week makes this a popular nightspot, too. ✉ *4076 Albany Post Rd./U.S. 9* ☎ *845/229–8277* ⊟ *AE, D, DC, MC, V.*

$-$$ ✕ **Ristorante Caterina de' Medici.** The Culinary Institute's terraced Colavita Center for Italian Food and Wine is the setting for this complex of Italian dining areas, each with its own character. The ornately decorated main dining room has Venetian light fixtures and is the most formal; the Al Forno room has an open kitchen with a colorfully painted wood-fired oven. Antipasti choices are plentiful, followed by first and second courses. Panna cotta is a good dessert pick. ⊠ *Culinary Institute of America, 1946 Campus Dr.* ☎ *845/471–6608* ♨ *Reservations essential* ▤ *AE, D, MC, V* ⊘ *Closed weekends, 3 wks in July, 2 wks in late Dec.*

¢ ✕ **Apple Pie Bakery Café.** The CIA's most casual dining option showcases luscious desserts and breads made daily. The light lunch menu lists soups, sandwiches, pizza, and salads. The atmosphere is relaxed, and prices are reasonable. The line can get quite long around noon on weekdays (the place isn't open on weekends) but moves fairly quickly. ⊠ *Culinary Institute of America, 1946 Campus Dr.* ☎ *845/905–4500* ♨ *Reservations not accepted* ▤ *AE, D, MC, V* ⊘ *Closed weekends.*

$ ▥ **Journey Inn.** Each room at this B&B, across the road from the entrance to the Vanderbilt Mansion, is tastefully decorated with treasures the owners have collected during their world travels. The Kyoto Room, with light-wood furniture and soft colors, is serene. The English-country suite has rich floral wallpaper, an Oriental carpet, softly ruffled window treatments, and a cozy nook with a daybed. The Roosevelt Room, dressed in subdued country-print fabrics, has two twin beds. The common living room is slightly formal but bright and comfortable. ⊠ *1 Sherwood Pl./U.S. 9, 12538* ☎ *845/229–8972* ⊕ *www.journeyinn.com* ☜ *4 rooms, 2 suites* ♨ *Dining room; no room phones, no room TVs, no kids under 9, &no smoking* ▤ *No credit cards* ⦿I *BP.*

¢ ▥ **Roosevelt Inn of Hyde Park.** The family-owned motel, painted presidential white, has two stories and exterior corridors. Rooms have a queen or king bed, one or two doubles, or a pair of twin beds. The smaller rooms have knotty-pine paneling, whereas the others are more contemporary in style. The property is in the heart of Hyde Park, within walking distance of antiques shops, restaurants, and museums. ⊠ *4360 Albany Post Rd./U.S. 9, 12538* ☎ *845/229–2443* ⊕ *www.rooseveltinnofhydepark.com* ☒ *845/229–0026* ☜ *24 rooms, 1 suite* ♨ *Coffee shop, some refrigerators, cable TV, no-smoking rooms* ▤ *AE, MC, V* ⊘ *Closed Jan. and Feb.* ⦿I *CP.*

Millbrook

㉑ *17 mi east of Hyde Park.*

For many, this Dutchess County village midway between the Hudson River and Connecticut is just the right blend of town and country. Historic downtown streets lined with shops and restaurants sit amid rolling farms, country estates, and dense woodlands all laced with hiking and equestrian trails. The area, settled in the 1700s, is largely agricultural. Locals take pride in preserving this environment and go to great lengths to protect working farms, open green space, and rural practices. Where you don't see cows you're likely to see horses; meadows of them are around almost every bend outside the village, and a horsey theme threads through the village, too.

Millbrook has long attracted the rich and famous, many of whom have eschewed the Hamptons to build luxurious weekend and summer homes here. Exploring the winding back roads you can see the long, private drives that lead to their sprawling retreats. The region is also known for its wineries, with vineyards stretched along soft hills, and magnificent gardens, such as Innisfree, where views of natural features are framed for you.

Cascade Mountain Winery. A Hudson Valley wine pioneer, the now well-established winery produces a collection of reds and whites. A well-regarded chalet-style restaurant is on-site. ⊠ *835 Cascade Mountain Rd., Amenia* ☎ *845/373–9021* ⊕ *www.cascademt.com* ⊡ *Tour free, tasting $5* ⊙ *Daily 10–5.*

Clinton Vineyards and Winery. Seyval blanc is the specialty of this family-run operation housed in an 1800s converted barn. The owner, when he's around and about, conducts tours himself, displaying wit, style, and a passion for wines and winemaking. ⊠ *212 Schultzville Rd., Clinton Corners* ☎ *845/266–5372* ⊕ *www.clintonvineyards.com* ⊡ *Tour free, tasting $5* ⊙ *Fri.–Sun. 11–5, or by appointment.*

★ **Innisfree Garden.** A unique contribution to garden design in America, Innisfree is based on Chinese-garden design and draws inspiration from ages-old Chinese paintings. The term *cup garden* is used to describe the concept; it refers to the way spaces frame, or "cup," features, such as striking rock formations or small pools. Cliffs, low hills, waterfalls, streams, and picnic spots surround the 40-acre lake at the center of the garden. A path takes you through Innisfree. ⊠ *362 Tyrrel Rd.* ☎ *845/677 8000* ⊕ *www.innisfreegarden.com* ⊡ *$3–$4* ⊙ *May–late Oct., Wed.–Fri. 10–4, weekends 11–5.*

Institute of Ecosystem Studies. The research center is part of the 2,000-acre **Mary Flagler Cary Arboretum**, which contains one of the largest perennial gardens in the Northeast, more than 1,000 species of plants, a fern glen, and miles of walking trails. Highlights include rose, butterfly, water, and hummingbird gardens. Other plant collections address such gardening issues as water conservation and deer resistance. The center also offers one-day courses about everything from Hudson Valley landscapes to rock-garden basics. ⊠ *181 Sharon Tpke.* ☎ *845/677–5359* ⊕ *www.ecostudies.org* ⊡ *Free* ⊙ *Oct.–Mar., Mon.–Sat. 9–4, Sun. 1–4; Apr.–Sept., Mon.–Sat. 9–6, Sun. 1–6.*

Millbrook Winery. At this 130-acre winery and vineyard you may savor a chardonnay or cabernet franc against a backdrop of spectacular views. Summer-weekend programs combine lunch with film screenings and musical performances. A wine bar in the winery's upstairs loft is open on weekends and offers a selection of the vineyard's reds and whites. ⊠ *26 Wing Rd.* ☎ *845/677–8383 or 800/662–9463* ⊕ *www.millbrookwine. com* ⊡ *Tour free, tasting $4* ⊙ *Memorial Day–Labor Day, daily 11–6; rest of yr, daily noon–5.*

Trevor Teaching Zoo. Wallabies, chinchillas, emus, otters, parrots, snakes, and lemurs are among the more than 100 exotic and indigenous small mammals and birds that reside at this zoo on the grounds of the Millbrook School. Students, along with full-time and consulting staff, run the zoo and care for the animals as part of their curriculum at the college-preparatory school; their enthusiasm for their charges is infectious. ⊠ *Millbrook School, Millbrook School Rd., off U.S. 44 about 5 mi east of Millbrook center* ☎ *845/677–3704* ⊕ *www.millbrook.org* ⊡ *$4* ⊙ *Daily 8–5.*

Wing's Castle. The artist owners of this out-of-the-ordinary attraction constructed the multitowered stone castle using salvaged materials from old buildings. It's amusing to try to spot the exotic bits and pieces woven into the structure. The views take in the Catskills and the Millbrook Winery vineyard. ⊠ *717 Bangall Rd., off Rte. 57* ☎ *845/677–9085* ⊡ *$7* ⊙ *June–Aug., Wed.–Sun. noon–4:30; Sept.–late Dec., weekends noon–4:30.*

Wethersfield. The late owner, philanthropist Chauncey Stillman, envisioned his property as a grand Edwardian estate and fully realized his dream. The Georgian-style brick mansion surveys formal gardens (complete with resident peacocks), fountains, a sculpture garden, and a dramatic view of the Catskills. The house has an important collection of paintings assembled by the owner. The stable block houses the carriage museum and a collection of coaching memorabilia. ⊠ *214 Pugsley Hill Rd., Amenia* ☎ *845/373–8037* ⊡ *Free* ⊙ *Gardens June–Sept., Wed., Fri., and Sat. noon–5; house and stables June–Sept. by appointment.*

Where to Stay & Eat

$$–$$$ ✗ **Allyn's Restaurant and Café.** An 1834 church has successfully morphed into a Millbrook dining fixture. Locals treat Allyn's like a club and do much of their entertaining here; don't be surprised if you encounter most of the Millbrook Hunt having breakfast. The owner-chef is devoted to freshness and obtains all ingredients locally. The menu is huge and includes pan-roasted chicken, grilled duck breast, and seafood dishes. The wine list gives you more than 300 choices. Follow the lead of the locals: request a table on the lawn in warm weather and a table in the bar by the fireplace in winter. ⊠ *42–58 U.S. 44* ☎ *845/677–5888* ⊟ *AE, D, DC, MC, V* ⊙ *Closed Tues.*

$$–$$$ ✗ **Quail Hollow Restaurant.** It's easy to drive right by this old farmhouse on the edge of an exit off the Taconic Parkway. Once inside with the antiques and art, you feel as if you're in a private house rather than a restaurant. The food is simple, unpretentious, well prepared, and nicely presented. Roast chicken is tender and moist, for example, and crab cakes come with an outstanding Dijon mustard sauce. The mixed-green salad that accompanies entrées is tossed with ginger dressing. The list of wines by the glass is long and includes some good values. ⊠ *360 Hibernia Rd., Salt Point* ☎ *845/266–8622* ⊟ *AE, MC, V* ⊙ *Closed Mon. and Tues. No lunch.*

$$–$$$ ✗ **TinHorn.** In warm weather you may watch the always-interesting doings in town while you have lunch or dinner on the restaurant's umbrella-sheltered front patio. The chef is a fanatic about using local organic produce, and you can taste the difference. The Black Angus rib-eye steak, 21-day dry aged and from a local farm, is absolutely sublime in taste and texture. On many Mondays, three-course dinners are de-

signed around an international theme—Spanish one week, perhaps French the next. The wine list is interesting and offers a good local selection. ⊠ *1129 Franklin Ave.* ☎ *845/677–5600* ▤ *AE, MC, V* ⊗ *Closed Tues. and Wed.*

$–$$$ ✕ **Café Les Baux.** The jolly sunburst graphic on the café sign and the banks of colorful flowers on the front steps are *très* French country. Warm terra-cotta–tone walls and vine-motif sconces continue the theme inside. The food is authentic French bistro fare, well prepared and presented. What a delight to find a really good croque monsieur and *moules* (mussels) or steak frites. Tarte tatin, baked by the chef and served with a scoop of crème fraîche, is not to be missed. ⊠ *152 Church St.* ☎ *845/677–8166* ▤ *AE, MC, V* ⊗ *Closed Tues.*

$–$$$ ✕ **Millbrook Café.** With a hunter-green awning over the entrance, walls covered with framed hunting prints, and wood paneling that recalls a stable, this restaurant plays up the horse-country theme. The food is billed as "authentic 19th-century cooking in a wood-fired oven." Everything is cooked in this oven; the open-plan kitchen invites you to watch. The house specialty, baked, stuffed Spanish onion, is a concoction of cheddar cheese and fresh vegetables that's worth trying. Entrées are served on sizzling cast-iron platters straight from the oven. ⊠ *3288 Franklin Ave.* ☎ *845/677–6956* ▤ *AE, D, DC, MC, V* ⊗ *Closed Mon. No dinner Sun.*

$–$$ ✕ **Copperfield's.** A large oval bar dominates the front room and provides plenty of space for a drink before dinner. The adjacent dining room has a casual feel with a combination of wooden booths and cloth-draped tables. The menu is long and varied, ranging from Mexican and pasta dishes to burgers and sushi. Brunch is served Sunday; the bartender makes a great Bloody Mary to go along. The restaurant is 3.8 miles west of Millbrook. ⊠ *U.S. 44, Salt Point* ☎ *845/677–8188* ▤ *AE, MC, V.*

$–$$ ✕ **Marcello's.** With floral wallpaper, soft lighting, and paintings of Italian scenes, the main dining room of this Italian restaurant is fairly formal; the roomy bar area, down several steps, is *the* spot for an after-dinner Amaretto. Outside is a patio for more casual dining. The signature chicken Marcello is topped with escarole, mozzarella, and bacon in white-wine sauce. *Zuppe di pesce* (fish soup), served for two, combines lobster, crab, clams, calamari, and shrimp in a thick, rich seafood stew; the portion is more than ample. Pasta dishes taste authentically Italian. ⊠ *18 Alden Pl.* ☎ *845/677–3080* ▤ *AE, D, DC, MC, V* ⊗ *Closed Mon. No lunch.*

¢–$$ ✕ **Millbrook Diner.** Since 1929 a diner has sat on this spot. The current edition, a stainless-steel boxcar version, dates from 1952. It's a great hangout for locals, who love how quickly that early-morning cup of coffee is served. Order hamburgers, french fries, BLTs, and other diner basics here. ⊠ *3266 Franklin Ave.* ☎ *845/677–5319* ▤ *MC, V.*

¢–$$ ✕ **Stage Stop.** Decorative horsey items—horseshoes, bits of old tack, antique carriage parts, horse-show posters—adorn every available wall. One corner houses James Cagney memorabilia; the photos of the actor on his nearby farm as well as stills from his old films are fascinating. The main dining room has a huge salad bar with more than 60 items; abundant and reasonably priced, it can serve as dinner. The menu also has pasta, burgers, steaks, pork chops, chicken, and lobster tails. ⊠ 7

Stage Stop Way, Bangall ☎ 845/868–7343 ▭ *AE, MC, V* ⊗ *No lunch Mon.–Sat.*

¢–$ ✕ **Mabbettsville Market.** This café–deli–specialty foods market, about 2 mi east of Millbrook, is about the only place around where you can get excellent cappuccino. Eat at a table inside, or outside under the awning, or get goodies to go. The market serves hot breakfast and offers an array of salad and sandwich options for lunch as well as a case of prepared foods. ⊠ *3809 U.S. 44, Mabbettsville* ☎ 845/677–5284 ▭ *AE, MC, V* ⊗ *Closed Mon. No dinner.*

$$$$ ✕▣ **Old Drovers Inn.** Cattle herders (aka drovers) bringing their stock
Fodor'sChoice to New York in the 18th century made a stopover at this inn, on 12 acres
★ 15 mi southeast of Millbrook. Today the Relais & Châteaux property is one of the oldest continuously operating inns in the United States. Rooms are Victorian in style; three have fireplaces. Weekend rates include full breakfast and dinner; weekday rates are considerably lower and include only Continental breakfast. In the low-ceilinged Tap Room ($$$–$$$$; closed Wednesday), old favorites such as rack of lamb and turkey hash blend with more contemporary dishes such as sesame-crusted tuna and marsala-braised Muscovy duck. The tavern menu includes hearty cheddar-cheese soup, offered here for more than 60 years and still a favorite. The wine list is extensive, and the drinks are legendary for their largesse. ⊠ *196 E. Duncan Rd., Dover Plains 12522* ☎ *845/832–9311* ⊟ *845/ 832–6356* ⊕ *www.olddroversinn.com* ⇋ *4 suites* ⊗ *Closed first 3 wks in Jan.* ⟁ *Restaurant, dining room, room service, fans, bicycles, mountain bikes, library, some pets allowed (fee); no room phones, no room TVs, no kids under 12, no smoking* ▭ *DC, MC, V* ⦿ *CP weekdays, MAP weekends.*

$$$$ ▣ **Bullis Hall.** The street-side facade of this once-derelict old building gives no hint about the surprises inside. The entrance through a garden at the back puts you in the front parlor. The owner's vision is of a small, European boutique hotel. Thick Turkish carpets are underfoot, and exquisite flowers adorn a mantel. Ice magically appears at cocktail time, and the self-serve bar is well stocked. If you wish to dine in, the in-house chef is happy to prepare a splendid meal. All of these to-the-manner-born touches come at a price and with certain expectations: tracksuit-and-sneakers travelers might not find this Relais & Châteaux property to be their cup of tea. ⊠ *Hunns Lake Rd., Bangall 12506* ☎ *845/868– 1665* ⊟ *845/868–1441* ⊕ *www.bullishall.com* ⇋ *2 rooms, 3 suites* ⟁ *Restaurant, dining room, some in-room hot tubs, cable TV, croquet, wine bar, library, laundry service, concierge, Internet; no kids, no smoking* ▭ *AE, MC, V* ⦿ *CP.*

$$$$ ▣ **Lakehouse Inn on Golden Pond.** Woods surround the lake at the center of the inn's 22 backcountry acres. Guest quarters are tucked into three buildings and have either water or woodland views. Each room has a whirlpool or soaking tub for two, a fireplace, and a deck; many beds have canopies and country quilts, and interior schemes swing from refined country to Victorian. ⊠ *419 Shelley Hill Rd., Stanfordville 12581* ☎ *845/266–8093* ⊟ *845/266–4051* ⊕ *www.lakehouseinn.com* ⇋ *6 rooms, 1 suite* ⟁ *Fans, some in-room hot tubs, some minibars, some refrigerators, cable TV, some in-room VCRs, lake, boating, fishing; no kids under 16, no smoking* ▭ *MC, V* ⦿ *BP.*

$$$$ ⌸ **Troutbeck.** Surrounded by elaborate landscaping and gardens, this resort on the bank of the Webatuck River encompasses 442 acres. The hotel, about 10 mi east of Millbrook, is exquisitely furnished with antiques. The library includes 12,000 books and videotapes. Rooms, some with fireplaces, have rich wood paneling and canopy beds. ⌂ *Leedsville Rd., Amenia 12501* ☎ *845/373–9681* 🖷 *845/373–7080* ⊕ *www. troutbeck.com* ⥰ *42 rooms, 6 suites* ⚼ *Restaurant, cable TV, in-room VCRs, 2 tennis courts, 2 pools (1 indoor), gym, sauna, spa, billiards, Ping-Pong, bar, library, business services, meeting rooms; no kids under 12, no smoking* ⊟ *AE, MC, V* ⦿ *CP.*

$$$ ⌸ **Millbrook Country House.** The house, built in 1810, was remodeled in 1838 when classical detailing was all the rage (witness the majestic columns in the front hall). If the interior recalls 17th-century Italy, it's probably because most of the furniture came from the current owner's palazzo near Modena. Elegant marquetry tables grace the parlors (where you may come across the owners' three cats), and lush silk draperies dress many windows. Extensive gardens—perennial, herb, cutting, border—surround the house, which also has a sculpture garden displaying works by local artists. Afternoon tea and full breakfast are included; in warm-weather months, they're served on the lawn under the shade of an enormous maple tree. ⌂ *506 Sharon Tpke./Rte. 44A, 12545* ☎🖷 *845/677–9570* ⊕ *www.millbrookcountryhouse.com* ⥰ *4 rooms* ⚼ *Dining room, bicycles, croquet; no kids under 10, no smoking* ⊟ *AE, MC* ⦿ *BP.*

$–$$ ⌸ **The Porter House Bed & Breakfast.** The original chestnut woodwork and wainscoting from this 1920 stone house are intact and restored. Their warm patina works well with the Victorian furniture that fills the sunny parlor. Bedrooms blend rustic pieces with more refined furnishings; printed fabrics are limited to accents. The B&B is a block from the heart of Millbrook. ⌂ *17 Washington Ave., 12545* ☎ *845/677–3057* ⊕ *www. porterhousebandb.com* ⥰ *2 rooms, 3 suites* ⚼ *Dining room, fans; no room phones, no room TVs, no kids under 12, no smoking* ⦿ *CP.*

$ ⌸ **Cottonwood Motel.** The design and decor of this roadside motel are standard issue: parking lot, vending machines in one corner, lobby in the other. What makes things interesting are the sights and sounds behind the motel. Each room has a little patio that looks out over acres of nature preserve. Local wildlife—deer, wild turkeys, pheasants—roam right up to your doorstep. Towering cottonwoods frame your view across the stream to soft hills beyond. ⌂ *2639 U.S. 44, 12545* ☎ *845/677–3283* 🖷 *845/677–3577* ⊕ *www.cottonwoodmotel.com* ⥰ *17 rooms, 1 suite, 1 cottage* ⚼ *Some in-room hot tubs, some refrigerators, cable TV, some pets allowed, no-smoking rooms* ⊟ *AE, MC, V.*

¢–$ ⌸ **Antrim House.** The 2 acres on which this Victorian-style contemporary sits are secluded enough to appeal to wildlife, and on most mornings various critters (deer, wild turkeys) can be seen around the grounds. Inside, family heirlooms coexist with 1920s wicker. The largest room has a queen-size bed and a deck overlooking the lawn. In winter the glow of the constantly stoked fireplaces in the library and living/dining room creates a cozy respite from the cold. The highlight of a stay may well be the full Irish-style cooked breakfast; being of Irish descent, the owner knows how to do it up right. ⌂ *33 Deer Pond Rd., 12545* ☎ *845/677–*

6265 ⇔ 3 rooms ⚭ Dining room, fans; no a/c, no room phones, no room TVs, no smoking ⊟ No credit cards ⟁ BP.

Nightlife & the Arts

On Saturday, and sometimes Friday, **Mary's Pub and Music Room** (⊠ 1364 Franklin Ave. ☎ 845/677–2282) hosts live music—rock, jazz, blues, folk, and classical acts. The music starts around 8:30 PM.

Sports & the Outdoors

HIKING The **Stissing Mountain Fire Tower** crowns the summit (elevation 1,403 feet) of **Stissing Mountain** (⊠ Off Lake Rd., about 1½ mi off Rte. 82, Pine Plains ☎ 518/398–5247, 518/398–5673 Friends of Stissing Landmarks), an isolated Precambrian mound; clear-day views from the 90-foot-tall structure stretch from Albany to Bear Mountain and across the Catskills. You also may see eagles, hawks, and other birds in flight from the tower, which is reached via hiking trails accessed at the mountain base. The mountain is undeveloped, with no facilities. Trails, steep in parts, are treed all the way up and have intermittent markers. Parking is limited to a small dirt lot across the road from a trailhead. Trail maps are available from local businesses and Dutchess County Tourism.

HORSEBACK Millbrook is heaven for the horsey set. All manner of horse-related ac-
RIDING tivity—polo, eventing, hunter pace (which has its roots in foxhunting)—takes place here. Bring your own horse to participate, or schedule a riding session. Eventing is an international (and Olympic) equestrian sport during which horse and rider compete over two to three days in dressage, cross-country, and show jumping. In the cross-country phase, competitors face a course of obstacles. The **Millbrook Horse Trials** (⊠ Bangall-Amenia Rd. opposite Coole Park Farm, Millbrook ☎ 845/677–3002 ⊕ www.millbrookhorsetrials.com) are an example of the highest level of the sport. They're held here over a Friday–Sunday period in mid-August; a training-beginner event is held the following weekend. Spectators are welcome; admission is free.

Cedar Crest Farm Equestrian Center (⊠ 2054 Rte. 83, Pine Plains ☎ 518/398–1034 ⊕ www.equestcenter.com/cedarcrest.htm), a 70-acre boarding and instruction facility, offers lessons in dressage, cross-country riding and jumping, and stadium jumping Tuesday through Sunday 8–4. Adult sessions start at $45 (group lesson) and climb to $75 (private lesson with senior staff member); most run 45 minutes. (Few horses here are suitable for small children.) The center requires you to wear a riding helmet with harness; shoes or boots (sneakers aren't allowed) must have a ¼- or ½-inch heel. At **Western Riding Stables** (⊠ 228 Sawchuck Rd., Millerton ☎ 518/789–4848 ⊕ www.westernridingstables.com) a western riding experience can include trail and moonlight rides and horseback pack trips. A 4-mi, 1- to 1½-hour introductory trail ride starts at $50; 9-mi moonlight rides are $100 and include dinner cooked over an open fire. Lessons are held on the trail or in an arena; pony rides are available as well.

Shopping

Antiquing is the highlight of Millbrook shopping. More than 100 dealers are represented along Franklin Avenue, the small main street, where trees shade old two-story buildings housing enticing stores. The biannual **Millbrook Antiques Show** (✉ Dutchess Day School, 415 Rte. 343 ☎ 845/677–5247 ⊕ www.showsfairsfestivals.com) is a three-day event held in late May or early June and again in mid-October.

Hedges and trees shield **British Sporting Arms** (✉ 3684 U.S. 44 ☎ 845/677–5756), which is set back from the road and easy to overlook. It's worth seeking out for its country-squire inventory: hand-carved walking sticks, flasks, bird sculptures, and all manner of shooting-related items, including antique and modern long guns. Upstairs are leather outerwear and European tweed pieces, including one local favorite—a tweedy bonnet with a large, flat bow in back. The owner of **Merritt Bookstore** (✉ 57 Front St. ☎ 845/677–5857) promises he can access any book in print, and he means it. The store also sells offbeat greeting cards. For the best prices in town, check out the **Millbrook Antique Center** (✉ 3283 Franklin Ave. ☎ 845/677–3921), an emporium with two floors of antiques and collectibles. A special Tiffany cabinet displays vintage Tiffany silver, objets d'art, and porcelain, all good values. With 38 dealers, the **Millbrook Antique Mall** (✉ 3301 Franklin Ave. ☎ 845/677–9311) is the largest fine-antiques center for miles around. Almost every antiques category is represented: country furniture, botanical prints, porcelain, brass fireplace tools. The dealer collections create a series of nicely edited and presented boutique spaces.

Because the **Red School House** (✉ 3300 Franklin Ave. ☎ 845/677–9786) is the only single-dealer location in Millbrook, the collections here are more edited and focused than at other shops in town. Specialties include 18th- and 19th-century furnishings, decorative arts, and European and American oil paintings. A two-story barn in Mabbettsville, east of Millbrook via U.S. 44, has additional collections that you can view by appointment. The dealers represented at the **Village Antique Center** (✉ 3278 Franklin Ave. ☎ 845/677–5160) are carefully chosen by the owner, and each collection is thoughtfully presented. The individual items are distinctive, with both personality and good provenance. Art-directed spiral-shape potted trees flank the double doors of the beautifully restored 1850s church that houses **Yellow Church Antiques** (✉ U.S. 44 ☎ 845/677–6779). The fine (usually very expensive) antiques include English, American, and Continental furniture, and paintings and carpets from the 17th, 18th, and 19th centuries. The pieces are displayed in cohesive groupings that can inspire multiple acquisitions. The shop is open Friday through Sunday.

Staatsburg

㉒ *21 mi northwest of Millbrook.*

On U.S. 9 midway between Rhinebeck and Hyde Park is Staatsburg, surrounded by soft hills overlooking the Hudson River. The main attraction here is the Staatsburg State Historic Site, of which the old Mills Mansion is the centerpiece. You may hike or stroll the estate grounds, which offer stunning Hudson River views.

Mills-Norrie State Park. Formed from Margaret Lewis Norrie State Park and Ogden Mills and Ruth Livingston Mills Memorial State Park, the park encompasses 1,000 scenic acres along the Hudson River, about 5 mi south of Rhinebeck. The grounds include 6 mi of hiking, biking, and horseback-riding trails; a marina; nature center; public golf course; and the **Staatsburg State Historic Site.** Eagles can sometimes be spotted from the nature center. ⊠ *Old Post Rd., off U.S. 9* ☎ *845/889–4646* ⊕ *nysparks.state.ny.us* ☜ *Free.*

FodorśChoice
★
Staatsburg State Historic Site. The well-known architectural firm of McKim, Mead, and White was responsible for the beaux-arts style of this grand 65-room mansion fronted with mammoth columns. Formerly known as Mills Mansion, the Hudson River estate was a family home of financier Ogden Mills and his wife, Ruth Livingston Mills, in the late 1800s to early 1900s. You may see the mansion's lavish interior by guided tour only. The estate, one of the most beautiful properties in the Hudson Valley, has hiking and cross-country-skiing trails, a huge hill for sledding in winter, and spectacular river views; state park land surrounds it. ⊠ *Old Post Rd., off U.S. 9* ☎ *845/889–8851* ⊕ *nysparks.state.ny.us* ☜ *House tour $5, grounds free* ☉ *Early Apr.–early Sept., Wed.–Sat. 10–5, Sun. noon–5; early Sept.–late Oct., Wed.–Sun. noon–5.*

Where to Stay & Eat

$-$$
✕ **Portofino Ristorante.** This out-of-the-way, good-value Italian restaurant, in a defunct inn on the historic postal route that once connected New York City and Albany, has a loyal following among locals and weekenders. The menu lists 25 pasta and main dishes; nightly specials add options. Baked artichokes with oregano, garlic, lemon, and butter are a good way to start your meal. A popular pasta dish combines seared sea scallops with sweet red-pepper cream sauce and basil. ⊠ *57 Old Post Rd.* ⚑ *Reservations not accepted* ▤ *AE, D, DC, MC, V* ☉ *Closed Mon. No lunch.*

$$–$$$$
▥ **Belvedere Mansion.** The commanding neoclassical-style house sits on a hill with distant Hudson River and mountain views across a sometimes-busy road. Trimmed with marble, crystal, silk, and damask, the main-house rooms are the most elegant lodgings on the property, which includes several other buildings. Most rooms in what's called the Hunt Lodge, in the woods behind the main house, are suites with fireplaces and private terraces. The more modest Carriage House building—a motel-like strip—has small rooms, some with fireplaces, and king beds. Four teeny rooms ($) are available as well. ⊠ *10 Old Rte. 9, 12580* ☎ *845/889–8000* ⊟ *845/889–8811* ⊕ *www.belvederemansion.com* ⇖ *30 rooms, 5 suites* ⚑ *Restaurant, picnic area, some fans, tennis court, pool, pond, volleyball, bar, no-smoking rooms; no room phones, no room TVs* ▤ *AE, DC, MC, V* ◉ *BP.*

CAMPING
⚠ **Mills-Norrie State Park.** The park totals 1,000 scenic acres along the Hudson River and encompasses two adjoining state parks as well as the Staatsburg State Historic Site (home of the old Mills Mansion). The grounds include 6 mi of hiking trails as well as a marina, nature center, and 18-hole public golf course. Cabins have two bedrooms and electricity (no heat). ⚑ *Flush toilets, dump station, drinking water, showers, grills, picnic tables, some electricity* ⊠ *Old Post Rd., off U.S. 9, 12580*

☎ *800/456–2267 reservations* ⊕ *nysparks.state.ny.us* ⟋ *32 tent sites, 16 RV sites without hookups, 10 cabins* ⊟ *$13–$62* ⟋ *Reservations essential* ⊟ *D, MC, V* ⊙ *Closed late Oct.–mid-May.*

Sports & the Outdoors

HIKING You can take an easy walk or an invigorating hike through the 6 mi of wooded trails at **Mills-Norrie State Park** (⊠ Old Post Rd., off U.S. 9 ☎ 845/889–4646 ⊕ nysparks.state.ny.us). The environmental center frequently offers guided walks. Numerous trails weave through the grounds of the magnificent **Staatsburg State Historic Site** (⊠ Old Post Rd., off U.S. 9 ☎ 845/889–8851), formerly called the Mills Mansion. A particularly scenic trail runs along the Hudson River as far as Mills-Norrie State Park and offers views of the Esopus Lighthouse as well as the Catskill Mountains. Be prepared to step over some tree roots; otherwise the hike, no more than a mile long, is easy, and the round-trip can be completed in a little over an hour. In winter, trails accommodate cross-country skiers.

Rhinebeck

㉓ *5 mi north of Staatsburg.*

At heart, Rhinebeck is a historic village with a dose of city sophistication. The influence of earlier times is present in the Victorian, Greek revival, colonial, and other architectural treasures scattered throughout the village. Some two dozen, including the early Dutch-style post office, are listed on the National Register of Historic Places. Meanwhile, up-to-the-minute shops, restaurants, and theaters keep bringing new life to the old churches, early educational institutions, and other repurposed buildings they occupy.

In summer and during the fall foliage season, peak times to visit, the village swells with sidewalk and car traffic, and reservations—for restaurants and lodgings—are in high demand.

ⓒ **Old Rhinebeck Aerodrome.** All the vintage aircraft at this museum still
Fodor'sChoice fly; indeed, many are used during air shows, held on weekends from mid-
★ June to mid-October (weather permitting). The collection includes a reproduction of Charles Lindbergh's *Spirit of St. Lewis* and fighter planes from World War I. For a thrill you can don a Snoopy-style cap and goggles and soar over the area in an open-cockpit biplane. Ride booths open at 10 on weekends of air shows, and the rides (less than 15 minutes long; $40 per person) book up quickly. Air shows start at 2. ⊠ *44 Stone Church Rd.* ☎ *845/752–3200* ⊕ *www.oldrhinebeck.org* ⊟ *Air-show weekends $12, otherwise $6* ⊙ *Mid-May–Oct., daily 10–5.*

Wilderstein. The grand, Queen Anne–style Victorian home with a dramatic five-story circular tower was owned by the Suckley family for more than 140 years. The last family member to occupy the estate was Margaret "Daisy" Suckley, a distant cousin of Franklin Delano Roosevelt; she assisted the president with his papers and was considered a close companion of his. The house, with main-floor interiors and stained-glass windows designed by J. B. Tiffany, is being restored in phases. Noted landscape architect Calvert Vaux designed the grounds, which have Hudson River views. ⊠ *330 Morton Rd.* ☎ *845/876–4818* ⊕ *www.*

wilderstein.org ✉ *$5* ✆ *May–Oct., Thurs.–Sun. noon–4; Dec., weekends 1–4 (Victorian holiday house tours).*

FESTIVALS & FAIRS **Good Guys Classic Rod and Custom Car Show.** For a weekend every September, "traveling roadies," as they call themselves, can be seen driving their brightly decorated hot rods, muscle cars, and custom classics around Rhinebeck. It's quite a sight when 2,000 pre-1964 cars converge on the fairgrounds for this swap meet, exhibition, and sale. Food and old-time music are part of the fun. ✉ *Dutchess County Fairgrounds, U.S. 9* ☎ *845/876–4001* ⊕ *www.good-guys.com.*

Where to Stay & Eat

$$–$$$ ✗ **Le Petit Bistro.** You might walk by this small French restaurant in the center of Rhinebeck and not give it a second glance, but Le Petit Bistro has quite a following. On weekends the crowd tends to be spirited. Chef Joseph Dalu is particular about ingredients, and uses local and organic when available; daily specials reflect his concept of "cooking with the season." The house pâté appetizer and English Dover sole are favorites on the regular menu. The dining room is warm, with worn pine floors and pale paneled walls. You may also order dinner at the bar. ✉ *8 E. Market St.* ☎ *845/876–7400* ▤ *AE, D, DC, MC, V* ✆ *No lunch Tues. and Wed.*

$–$$$ ✗ **Gigi Trattoria.** A lively, sophisticated clientele crowds the bar, patio, and dining rooms of this popular Italian restaurant, once the showroom of a Chevrolet dealership. The food, billed as "Hudson Valley Mediterranean," includes artfully crafted salads, house-made pasta dishes, and hearty entrées. Baby greens provide a bed for roasted butternut squash, beets, and asparagus dressed with walnuts and crumbled goat cheese. Toppings for the Skizzas (flatbread pizzas) range from a sausage–broccoli rabe–mozzarella combo to a version with goat cheese, mozzarella, arugula, pears, and figs. The restaurant tends to be noisy, especially on weekends. Expect a wait, too. ✉ *6422 Montgomery St.* ☎ *845/876–1007* ⌕ *Reservations not accepted* ▤ *AE, D, MC, V* ✆ *Closed Mon.*

★ $–$$$ ✗ **Osaka.** You can count on a cheerful greeting when you venture into this immaculate sushi bar and restaurant. The fish is super-fresh, the presentation artistic, and the sake assortment excellent. In addition to sushi, the menu covers teriyaki, tempura, and udon-noodle dishes. The place isn't large and it tends to fill up on weekends, but it is worth the wait. Nearby Tivoli is home to an Osaka branch. ✉ *22 Garden St.* ☎ *845/876–7338* ⌕ *Reservations not accepted* ▤ *AE, D, MC, V* ✆ *Closed Tues.*

★ $–$$$ ✗ **Terrapin.** An 1842 church contains two dining options within its soaring space: a bistro-bar, where reservations aren't taken, and a more-formal dining area. The bistro menu ($–$$) lists small plates, soups, stews, and a make-your-own sandwich board, as well as traditional entrées. Expect a lively crowd at the bar, especially on weekends. With white-cloth-draped tables, the main dining area ($$–$$$) is quieter. The food veers from creative to comforting. A popular starter is baby-arugula salad with goat-cheese wontons. Three sauces—roasted-shallot hollandaise, mole verde, and ancho chile—accompany the salmon dish. Warm chocolate cake with a molten center is a winner. ✉ *6426 Montgomery St.* ☎ *845/876–3330* ⌕ *Reservations essential for main dining room* ▤ *AE, D, DC, MC, V* ✆ *Closed Mon.*

$–$$$ ✕ **Traphagen.** The venerable Beekman Arms, the oldest operating inn in the country, is home to this multiroom restaurant. With its warm and woody setting, the low-ceilinged Tap Room recalls the days when the inn was a true travelers' stop back in the 1700s. The greenhouse room, a bright, 20th-century addition that's filled with plants and flowers, is a favorite for lunch and brunch. (The hearty Sunday brunch buffet is $22.) The food is solid American, fairly straightforward. For example, grilled Atlantic salmon, a specialty, comes with mashed potatoes and horseradish sauce. ⊠ *6387 Mill St.* ☎ *845/876–1766* ▭ *AE, D, DC, MC, V.*

$$ ✕ **Calico.** There's more to this little storefront patisserie-restaurant
Fodor'sChoice than meets the eye. Exquisite specialty cakes, tarts, and baked goods
★ fill the pastry case. The lunch, dinner, and Sunday brunch fare is mostly American and includes a vegetarian option or two, such as napoleon of polenta layered with goat cheese, vegetables, and pesto. Bouillabaisse, brimming with shellfish in lobster broth, is a good deal. ⊠ *6384 Mill St.* ☎ *845/876–2749* ▭ *AE, MC, V* ⊘ *Closed Mon. and Tues. No dinner Sun.*

¢–$ ✕ **Bread Alone.** The European-style bakery receives daily deliveries of fresh bread from its main facility in nearby Boiceville. The loaves, shaped by hand and baked in wood-fired ovens, come in such varieties as hearty whole-grain "health bread" and baguettes. Sensitive to gluten? Consider the spelt bread. The café, with six tables and a window bar, is a comfortable place for a light lunch. The cappuccino here is excellent. ⊠ *45 E. Market St.* ☎ *845/876–3108.*

¢–$ ✕ **Garden Street Cafe.** The tiny café–juice bar occupies one end of the Rhinebeck Health Foods store. The kitchen uses the freshest local and organic ingredients, turning them into flavorful wraps, salads, sandwiches, and soups, such as the hearty Avocado Supreme (avocado and melted Havarti on multigrain bread) and Chili Works (vegetarian black-bean chili over brown rice). Daily specials are posted on a white board decorated with funky art by a staff member. To create a custom smoothie or juice drink, simply choose your ingredients. Takeout is popular. ⊠ *24 Garden St.* ☎ *845/876–2005* ▭ *AE, MC, V* ⊘ *Closed Sun. No dinner.*

★ **$$$$** ▦ **Olde Rhinebeck Inn.** On a quiet tree-lined street 3 mi from Rhinebeck center, Jonna Paolella caringly tends to her guests. She can tell you the fascinating history of this house, built by Palatine German settlers, and about George, the resident ghost who reportedly appears with some regularity in the Spirited Dove room. Much of the original detail in this circa-1745 inn has been beautifully preserved. The country décor mixes rustic pieces with some finer furnishings. ⊠ *340 Wurtemburg Rd., 12572* ☎ *845/871–1745* ▭ *845/876–8809* ⊕ *www.rhinebeckinn.com* ⇨ *2 rooms, 1 suite* ⊘ *Dining room, some in-room hot tubs, refrigerators, cable TV, pond, fishing, no-smoking rooms; no room phones* ▭ *AE, MC, V* ▯◯▮ *BP.*

$$ ▦ **Gables Bed and Breakfast.** Wicker, lace, pastels, and gables everywhere (17 in all) contribute to the sweetness of this light and airy pre–Civil War cottage surrounded with a white picket fence. Enjoy a quiet moment on one of the porches or a long soak in an original cast-iron tub. Terry robes and a goodies drawer stocked with commonly forgotten items and little treats make this B&B special. The suite, roomy enough for three and awash in rose-patterned wallpaper and fabric, is popular for "girlfriend getaways." ✉ *6358 Mill St., 12572* ☎ *845/876-7577* ⊕ *www.gablesbnb.com* ⇔ *2 rooms, 1 suite* ⌕ *Dining room; no room phones, no TV in some rooms, no kids under 12, no smoking* ⊟ *D, DC, MC, V* ◯◯ *BP.*

$–$$ ⊡ **Whistlewood Farm Bed & Breakfast.** You can't help but leave the city behind as you drive up the fence-lined road to this farm where Thoroughbred horses graze. The main house is homey and rustic, with more-refined, contemporary-country guest rooms. You may sit on one of many decks and enjoy the display of wildflowers. In winter, the fieldstone fireplace is put to use. For more privacy, stay in the Carriage House, a converted barn with two suites. Breakfast—pancakes or egg dishes— is hearty, and home-baked pie and cake are readily available. After fueling up, explore one of the trails on the grounds. ✉ *52 Pells Rd., off Rte. 308, 12572* ☎ *845/876-6838* ⊟ *845/876-5513* ⊕ *www.whistlewood.com* ⇔ *3 rooms, 3 suites* ⌕ *Dining room, fans, some in-room hot tubs, some in-room VCRs, cross-country skiing, some pets allowed (fee), no-smoking rooms; no room phones, no TV in some rooms* ⊟ *AE* ◯◯ *BP.*

¢–$$ ⊡ **Beekman Arms and Delamater Inn.** America's oldest operating inn, the Beekman Arms is a welcoming presence in the center of town. Beyond the massive doors of this pre-Revolutionary lodging are wide-plank floors, beamed ceilings, and a stone hearth. The original 1766 building has smallish though cheery and comfortable colonial-style rooms with modern baths. Contemporary motel-style rooms are available in a separate building behind the Beekman Arms. One block north on U.S. 9 is "the Beek's" sister, the Delamater Inn. It contains the Delamater House, an American Gothic masterpiece designed by Alexander Jackson Davis, and a hidden courtyard with six guesthouses, perfect for family reunions or travel with friends. Many of the Delamater rooms have fireplaces. ✉ *6387 Mill St., 12572* ☎☎ *845/876-7077* ⊕ *www.beekmanarms.com* ⇔ *61 rooms, 6 suites* ⌕ *Restaurant, some in-room data ports, some kitchenettes, some refrigerators, cable TV, bar, business services, meeting room, some pets allowed, no-smoking rooms; no a/c in some rooms* ⊟ *AE, D, DC, MC, V* ◯◯ *EP Beekman Arms, CP Delamater Inn.*

$ ⊡ **Sleeping Beauty B&B.** The late-19th-century Folk Victorian on a quiet side street has a twin design, with two adjacent sections that mirror each other. Innkeepers Christine and Doug Mosley occupy one half and guests stay in the other. Rooms have period toile, floral, and striped wallpapers and fabrics. One has a separate entrance and its own enclosed porch. Details such as fish-scale shingles, tiny stained-glass windows, pocket doors, dentil molding, and antique wall-hung sinks make it all the more interesting. ✉ *28–30 Chestnut St., 12572* ☎ *845/876-8986* ⊕ *www.sleepingbeautybandb.com* ⇔ *4 rooms* ⌕ *Dining room, fans; no room phones, no room TVs, no kids under 10, no smoking* ⊟ *MC, V* ◯◯ *BP.*

Nightlife & the Arts

A large red barn about 3½ mi east of the village center houses the busy **Center for Performing Arts at Rhinebeck** (✉ 661 Rte. 308/E. Market St.

☎ 845/876–3080 ⊕ www.centerforperformingarts.org). Open year-round, the center hosts local, national, and international theater groups, dance troupes, and musicians. The ongoing series of Saturday-morning (11 AM) children's shows is popular. A cultural hub for everything about

★ film, the small **Upstate Films Theater** (✉ 6415 Montgomery St./U.S. 9 ☎ 845/876–2515 or 866/345–6688 ⊕ www.upstatefilms.org) shows documentaries, independent films, classics, and animation. Shows ($6.50) often sell out, so it's best to purchase tickets in advance. Talks and discussion groups are often held here. The theater is also a screening venue for the acclaimed Woodstock Film Festival, held in September.

Shopping

More than 350 artists show their crafts at **Crafts at Rhinebeck** (✉ Dutchess County Fairgrounds, U.S. 9 ☎ 845/876–4001 ⊕ www.dutchessfair. com), a prestigious and popular juried event held in mid-June and again in October. An impressive array of handcrafted items including jewelry, blown glass, pottery, musical instruments, and wearable art is for sale. Most booths are manned by artists eager to discuss their work. One of the best-known and -loved antiques fairs in the country, the **Rhinebeck Antiques Fair** (✉ Dutchess County Fairgrounds, U.S. 9 ☎ 845/876–4001, 845/876–1989 in May ⊕ www.rhinebeckantiquesfair.com) showcases more than 200 dealers in four large exhibition halls. The fair, held three times a year (in May, July, and October), interests both casual and serious collectors. Roomlike settings set the stage for an eclectic selection of antiques from different periods. Delivery service is available.

More than 30 antiques dealers sell their wares at the **Beekman Arms Antique Market** (✉ 6387 Mill St. ☎ 845/876–3477), which occupies a large red barn behind the Beekman Arms. The antiques mix is eclectic, with Americana, Victorian, country, and primitive pieces represented. The furniture has been spruced up and doesn't need work. Clinics, with appraisals and workshops, are occasionally held here. One-of-a-kind creations by local and international artisans are artfully displayed at the exquisite **Hummingbird Jewelers** (✉ 20 W. Market St. ☎ 845/876–4585 ⊗ Closed Tues.; call for winter hrs). An exceptional collection of designer wedding bands and engagement rings is showcased. **Oblong Books and Music** (✉ Montgomery Row, 6420 Montgomery St. ☎ 845/876–0500 or 800/625–6640), a well-stocked, all-purpose bookstore one block north of the Beekman Arms, offers a good selection of novels, books about area places and local history, and works by local writers. It also sells CDs. The children's room in the back occasionally hosts kids' events. Author signings are on Friday at 7; on many Sunday afternoons the store hosts music events. "Life is chaotic, you might as well look good" is the motto of Diana Brind, owner and creative force behind the **SugarPlum Boutique** (✉ 71 E. Market St. ☎ 845/876–6729), an accessories shop. (ChaosCosmetics is the name of her line of beauty products.) Her eye for the delicate is evident in the array of barrettes, scarves, hats, and personally designed silver jewelry here. Ever-changing, exotically decorated display windows set the stage for the side-by-side **Winter Sun/Summer Moon** (✉ 10 E. Market St. ☎ 845/876–2223 Winter Sun, 845/876–3555 Summer Moon). Luscious fabrics, bright colors, and rich textures give the shops the feel of a sophisticated bazaar. Comfortable, easy-to-wear, and elegant clothes, jewelry, and accessories are the signature of Winter Sun. Eileen Fisher, Flax, and Dansko are among the designers carried. Walk through to Summer Moon for natural personal-care products, yoga mats, and candles.

Red Hook

5 mi north of Rhinebeck.

Red Hook hasn't adopted the trendy edge of some of its nearby neighbors, so there's nothing slick or pretentious about this small village. Nevertheless, it has a surprisingly large number of restaurants for its size. Antiques and collectibles hunters enjoy the shops here.

Where to Stay & Eat

$$-$$$ ✕ **Mina.** The couple that owns this New American dinner spot is pas-
Fodor'sChoice sionate about food. The DiBenedettos make an art of searching for and
★ using only fresh, wholesome ingredients. The menu changes weekly, depending on what ingredients are available. Both the food and the restaurant display a simple elegance, and you're encouraged to linger and savor the dining experience. Grilled hanger steak with creamed spinach is a house favorite. Whole trout may be roasted and served with French lentils and warm bacon vinaigrette. Desserts, including the ice cream, are homemade. The wine list is carefully chosen and fairly priced. ⊠ *29 W. Market St./U.S. 9* ☎ *845/758–5992* 🖃 *AE, D, MC, V* ⊗ *Closed Mon.–Thurs. No lunch.*

¢-$$ ✕ **Max's Memphis BBQ.** A hickory smoke oven was imported from Louisiana to give authentic flavor to the Southern-style cooking found here. Slow cooking takes on a new meaning when meats are smoked for 4–15 hours. Hearty dishes of pulled pork, ribs, chicken, and crab cakes are served with sides of cheese grits and collard greens. Small-batch bourbons and fresh-juice margaritas are bar favorites. Chocolate–peanut butter pie is worth the calorie splurge. Every few weeks, local musicians perform here. ⊠ *136 S. Broadway* ☎ *845/758–6297* 🖃 *AE, D, MC, V* ⊗ *Closed Mon. and 2 wks in Jan. No lunch.*

$ ✕ **Luna 61.** Candles and Ella Fitzgerald tunes set the stage at this slightly artsy, slightly funky vegetarian eatery. Organic ingredients are used in most of the dishes, which are served in hearty portions. Even dedicated meat eaters leave full and satisfied. The challah French toast is an AM winner; pad thai is a good lunch or dinner choice. Desserts include banana cream pie. Beer and wine, all organic, are available, too. ⊠ *61 E. Market St.* ☎ *845/758–0061* 🖃 *AE, MC, V* ⊗ *Closed Mon. and Tues. No lunch Wed.*

¢ ✕ **White Rabbit.** The 1960s and '70s are mixed up in this coffeehouse café with murals of the Mad Hatter and Alice on the walls and painted clouds on the ceiling. People usually come and stay a while, working on laptops, playing chess, or just chatting. The menu includes coffee, baked goods, soups, salads, and sandwiches with funny names like Phunky Chicken (chicken salad) and Smoken' Sista (mozzarella, hummus, and veggies on a rosemary focaccia). The sesame-ginger salad dressing is delicious. Place your order at the counter. ⊠ *40 W. Market St.* ☎ *845/758–6500* 🖃 *MC, V.*

$–$$ ✕⊡ **Red Hook Inn.** Rooms in this 1840s inn with a wide front porch are mostly spacious and uncluttered; floral fabrics, some vintage, dress a couple of them. Breakfast is served in the restaurant, or on the porch if you're staying here. Three dining options are available at "the inn," as it's known locally. The main dining rooms have white tablecloths and lace curtains. The tavern, which has a fireplace, mahogany bar, and a few tables, offers a small menu. Dinner is also served on the front porch. The menu changes with the season. Local produce is used when available and the wine is exclusively from New York State. The cream of mushroom soup is outstanding. If you have room for dessert, try chocolate souffle cake. ⊠ *7460 S. Broadway, 12571* ☎ *845/758–8445* 📠 *845/758–3143* ⊕ *www.theredhookinn.com* 🛏 *5 rooms, 1 suite* ⚒ *Restaurant, some in-room hot tubs, some cable TV, some in-room VCRs, bar; no room phones, no TV in some rooms, no smoking* ⊟ *AE, DC, MC, V* ⦿ *CP.*

¢–$ ⊡ **Grand Dutchess Bed & Breakfast.** Pass through the center of Red Hook and you can't help but notice this stately blue Victorian mansion. The owners are antiques collectors, so the house has the feel of a museum, especially in the common rooms. All but one of the bedrooms are corner rooms. The proprietors also own the more relaxed Red Hook Inn. ⊠ *7571 Old Post Rd., 12571* ☎ *845/758–5818* 📠 *845/758–3143* ⊕ *www.granddutchess.com* 🛏 *5 rooms, 2 with shared bath; 1 suite* ⚒ *Dining room, some in-room hot tubs; no room phones, no room TVs, no kids under 6, no smoking* ⊟ *AE, DC, MC, V* ⦿ *BP.*

Annandale-on-Hudson & Tivoli

㉔ *3 mi west of Red Hook.*

Annandale-on-Hudson is home to the beautiful Bard College campus and its famous Fisher Center for the Performing Arts. If you travel north to the campus via River Road, which is shaded by trees and lined with old stone walls and orchards, you'll pass Poets' Walk and Montgomery Place. Tivoli, on Route 9G 2 mi north of Bard, is known for its restaurants and artistic community. It comes alive at night and is a popular spot for Bard students and professors.

Bard College. A winding tree-lined road leads to this small college of liberal arts and sciences. The beautiful 540-acre campus encompasses two Hudson River estates, parklike grounds and gardens, and wooded areas. The free **Center for Curatorial Studies** (☎ 845/758–7598 ☽ Wed.–Sun. 1–5), on the south end of the Bard campus, is known for cutting-edge exhibits of contemporary art. Museum exhibitions take place in summer and fall; student shows are exhibited in spring. Artists Chuck Close, Joseph Kosuth, and Nam June Paik have participated in the cultural-studies center's public lectures and conferences, which focus on contemporary-art issues, including public policy. Noted architect Frank Gehry designed Bard's extraordinary **Richard B. Fisher Center for the Performing Arts** (☎ 845/758–7900 🎫 tours $5). Brushed stainless-steel panels, draped like massive ribbons over the roof and sides of the 108,000-square-foot performing-arts center, reflect the light and colors of the sky as well as the hilly surroundings. Tours of the Fisher Center,

Fodor'sChoice
★

on the north end of the campus, are given daily at 11, 1, and 2 most of the year. ✉ *Annandale Rd., west of Rte. 9G, Annandale-on-Hudson* ☎ *845/758–6822* ⊕ *www.bard.edu.*

★ **Montgomery Place.** This 23-room mansion, once the Livingston family estate, sits on 434 acres along the Hudson River north of Rhinebeck. Janet Livingston Montgomery, the widow of American Revolution hero General Richard Montgomery, commissioned the original house in the early 1800s. Built in the Federal style, the mansion was remodeled in the mid-19th century by noted American architect Andrew Jackson Davis, who applied a classical revival style. The well-maintained house is open for tours, but the grounds alone are worth seeing; they encompass orchards, flower gardens, and ancient trees, and offer plenty of picnic-perfect spots as well as views of the Hudson River and the Catskill Mountains. During the **Hudson Valley Food and Wine Festival,** held in early June, New York State vineyards, local restaurants, and regional farms come together for a weekend of tastings, demonstrations, and lectures. Other special events include twilight walks, candlelight tours, and gardening workshops. ✉ *River Rd. off Rte. 9G, Annandale-on-Hudson* ☎ *845/758–5461* ⊕ *www.hudsonvalley.org* ✉ *House and grounds $7, grounds $4* ☉ *Apr.–Oct., Wed.–Mon. 10–5; Nov., weekends 10–5; first half of Dec., weekends noon–5.*

Poets' Walk. Spectacular views of the Hudson River and the Catskill Mountains are your reward for trekking through the fields and wooded trails (2¼ mi) at this 120-acre park. Rustic cedar benches, footbridges, and gazebos add to the park's charm and offer places to picnic and rest. The well-maintained paths are gravel in some places and dirt in others. ✉ *Rte. 103, ½ mi north of Kingston–Rhinecliff Bridge, Annandale-on-Hudson* ☎ *845/473–4440 Ext. 270* ⊕ *www.scenichudson.org* ✉ *Free* ☉ *Daily 9–dusk.*

off the beaten path

CLERMONT STATE HISTORIC SITE – Robert R. Livingston Jr. (1746–1813), who helped draft the Declaration of Independence, was just one of the illustrious Livingstons who made their home on this estate between Tivoli and Hudson. The stately white house reflects the changes made by several generations: it was burned by the British during the Revolutionary War and rebuilt in the late 1700s on the original foundations. The rooms are furnished with family heirlooms and include splendid examples of decorative objects and of cabinetmaking. Views of the Catskill Mountains across the Hudson River are stunning. Admission to the grounds is free (on weekends April through October, parking is $5). ✉ *Rte. 6W off Rte. 9G, Germantown* ☎ *518/537–4240* ⊕ *nysparks.state.ny.us* ✉ *$5* ☉ *House Apr.–Oct., Tues.–Sun. 11–5; Nov.–Mar., weekends 11–4. Grounds daily, 8:30–sunset.*

Where to Eat

★ **$-$$$** ✗ **Osaka.** This immaculate sushi bar and restaurant is popular with the college crowd as well as with the locals. A branch of the Rhinebeck restaurant, it offers the same high-quality sushi, teriyaki, tempura, and noodle dishes. There's also an extensive assortment of sake. The meal always ends with a perfectly chilled orange. ⊠ *74 Broadway, Tivoli* ☎ *845/757–5055* ᴬ *Reservations not accepted* ▤ *AE, D, MC, V* ⊘ *Closed Tues.*

$–$$$ ✕ **Santa Fe.** Every year or two, owner David Weiss travels to Mexico in search of new culinary inspiration—and then he changes the menu. Luckily some of the most popular dishes are mainstays, such as the grilled-pork taco and the goat cheese–and–spinach enchilada. The frozen margaritas are made from scratch. ⊠ *52 Broadway, Tivoli* ☎ *845/757–4100* ▤ *AE, D, MC, V* ⊘ *Closed Mon. No lunch.*

¢ ✕ **Milagros.** "A place with an identity crisis" is how owner Pamela Morin describes this 1892 church with a twist. It's a café, deli, bar, folk-art showcase, gallery, and convenience store under the same roof. Somehow it works. Locals, city folk, artists, and Bard College students come to shoot the breeze, drink coffee, and munch on wraps and salads. The quinoa wrap and BLT with chipotle mayonnaise are two favorites. Tables are large, great for spreading out papers. A patio beckons on nice days. ⊠ *73 Broadway, Tivoli* ☎ *845/757–5300* ▤ *MC, V* ⊘ *No dinner.*

Nightlife & the Arts

NIGHTLIFE At the lively **Black Swan Pub** (⊠ 66 Broadway, Tivoli ☎ 845/757–3777), an Irish pub, you can often overhear the bartenders having intense political discussions or see them playing chess with patrons. Musicians, some local and some from "the city," perform almost nightly, and on any given evening you might hear bluegrass, folk, ethnic, or rock music. Among the 10-plus beers on tap (bottled beer isn't served here) is Smithwicks, an Irish brew not found elsewhere locally. The pub's most enchanting aspect is the back patio with its twinkling white lights, lilac bushes, and organic peach trees from which you're invited to pluck a sample.

THE ARTS A cultural hub in the area, **Bard College** (⊠ Annandale Rd., west of Rte. 9G, Annandale-on-Hudson ☎ 845/758–7900 ⊕ www.bard.edu) hosts several outstanding performing-arts festivals. The mix of events during **Bard SummerScape**, which runs from mid-July to mid-August, might blend orchestral and choral concerts, operas, dance performances, puppetry and other theater presentations, films, and panel discussions. Performances, which may include world or American premieres, are staged throughout the campus; the Richard B. Fisher Center for the Performing Arts is the main venue.

The Fisher Center's main Sosnoff Theater also hosts world-class opera, dance, drama, and music performances throughout the year. The most notable performance series, the annual **Bard Music Festival** is devoted to a single composer deemed worthy of a new look and is held over two consecutive weekends in August. The approach is multidisciplinary and includes lectures, demonstrations, art exhibits, and panel discussions, in addition to musical performances. The music is a heady blend of virtuoso performances and symphonic, chamber, and solo works; examples of works by contemporaries are used to put the composer in the larger context of his or her cultural milieu.

Members of the **Tivoli Artists' Co-op** (⊠ 60 Broadway, Tivoli ☎ 845/757–2667 ⊕ www.tivoliartistsco-op.com) host festive openings every month or so. The art is diverse; themes may range from the garden to the erotic. The annual holiday show is popular for its multimedia works, which are priced in a wide range. The space is sometimes used for musical events, too.

Sports & the Outdoors

HIKING A 1,720-acre nature reserve stretching for 2 mi along the east bank of the Hudson River, **Tivoli Bays** (⊠ Rte. 9G and Kidd La., about 10 mi north of Kingston–Rhinecliff Bridge, Tivoli ☎ 845/758–7010 reserve office ⊕ nerrs.noaa.gov/hudsonriver) has several short trails that wind through and around a freshwater tidal wetland. The bays, part of the Hudson River National Estuarine Research Reserve, are used for long-term field research and education, as well as for hunting in season. Tide charts are available at the research reserve's main office, at Bard College Field Station on Tivoli South Bay, as well as at the visitor center in Watts de Peyster Fireman's Hall (86 Broadway) in Tivoli.

KAYAKING A popular put-in site for canoes and kayaks lies at the end of Route 78, off Route 9G, in Tivoli. Cross the railroad tracks to the small parking area. From here you can paddle across the river to the Saugerties Lighthouse or head south to explore Tivoli Bays. To reach the bays, travel along the river bank for about 1 mi and then pass under the railroad trestle. Follow the channels and you might see snapping turtles, beavers, blue herons, and an assortment of other wildlife and flora. Note that hunters use this area during duck season (usually in early October and most of November and December). Another entry point for the Tivoli Bays is from Kidd Lane, also off Route 9G. At this launch site you must carry your boat down—and, later, up—a steep hill.

THE UPPER HUDSON VALLEY

By Erica
Freudenberger,
Steve Hopkins

The fertile upper Hudson Valley, made verdant by winding rivers and copious lakes, is bordered on the east by the Berkshire Mountains. (The area west of the Hudson River is covered in Chapter 4.) The rural landscape is graced with homes and grand manors reflecting its history; drive on U.S. 9 or Route 23 and you pass Dutch-colonial, Georgian, and Federal architecture.

Henry Hudson first stepped ashore in the area in the early 17th century. Dutch settlers, and later the English, drove the native Mohican, Lenni-Lenape, and other tribes from the area, setting up farms, mills, and taverns. A few received vast parcels of land, and many places still bear their names, Van Rensselaer and Livingston among them. With the Industrial Revolution came the train and steamboat, and visitors flocked to the region, taking the waters at natural springs in Lebanon and environs. Artists toting paintbrushes and palettes came and stayed, founding the Hudson River school.

Dairy farms and orchards still cover much of the arable land, although they are slowly finding new life as seasonal getaways. Catering to the area's growing popularity as a weekend destination is a growing number of restaurants, lodgings, and high-end stores. In the throes of resurgence, the city of Hudson lures urbanites to Warren Street, where art galleries and antiques shops jostle for space.

Lake Taghkanic State Park

🕒 *10 mi northeast of Tivoli.*

Lake Taghkanic is the centerpiece of this 1,569-acre park, which has two sandy beaches, picnic areas, boat rentals, playgrounds, restrooms, and trails for hiking. You may camp here from early May through October, choosing between tent or trailer sites or rustic cabins (with bathrooms and hot and cold water). Kids enjoy climbing the water tower. Cross-country skiing, snowmobiling, ice-skating, and ice-fishing are options in winter. ✉ *1528 Rte. 82, Ancram* ☎ *518/851–3631* ⊕ *nysparks.state.ny.us* 🎫 *Parking $7 (late May–Labor Day)* ⊙ *Daily sunrise–sunset.*

Hudson

㉕ *15 mi north of Tivoli.*

Rising from decades of decay and decrepitude, Hudson has, over the past few years, finally arrived as a bona fide weekend destination for a growing cadre of hip New Yorkers. The beautifully restored architecture, the hundred-odd antiques emporiums, and the nascent reputation of the city as an upstate offshoot of Manhattan's SoHo neighborhood are what draw the hordes of aesthetes who descend on Hudson from Wednesday through Sunday each week.

Warren Street, the main drag, is lined with the lion's share of the city's antiques shops, scores of quirky boutiques and art galleries, and a rising number of increasingly trendy restaurants. At its foot is Promenade Hill Park, which offers views of the river, the Catskill Mountains, and the Hudson-Athens Lighthouse.

Settled in 1783 as a whaling port, Hudson was built—from scratch— on a planned grid by a group of Quaker seafarers, artisans, and businessmen from Nantucket and New Bedford. These hardy folks felt their hometowns were sitting ducks for British warships in the uncertain days following the Revolution and wanted a safe, inland, deepwater haven. Not so long ago, into the mid-20th century, the city became famous for another industry: vice. Its red-light district, on what today is Columbia Street, was notorious. These days the old brothels have been restored by weekenders.

American Museum of Firefighting. The museum, a country mile from the Warren Street hub, contains 43 examples of hand-pulled engines and hose carts, including a Newsham engine built in London, imported to Manhattan in 1731, and in active service for more than 150 years. A pair of horse-drawn trucks, five steam-powered vehicles, and 15 internal-combustion engines round out the hardware, which along with other artifacts purports to tell the history of firefighting. ✉ *125 Harry Howard Ave.* ☎ *518/828–7695* 🎫 *Free* ⊙ *Daily 9–4:30.*

Fodor'sChoice ★ **Olana State Historic Site.** In the 1870s, Hudson River school artist Frederic Church built this 37-room Moorish-style castle atop a hill with panoramic valley and river vistas. Architect Calvert Vaux came up with the design of the house, to which the artist applied his own eclectic touches. The interior is an extravaganza of tile and stone, carved screens, Persian rugs, and paintings, including some by Church. The house, about 4 mi south of Hudson, is open only for guided tours, which run about 45 minutes; reservations are strongly suggested. The grounds, open daily, offer great Hudson River views. ⊠ *Rte. 9G* ☎ *518/828–0135* ⊕ *www.olana.org* 🖳 *Tours $3, grounds free* ⊙ *House early Apr.–May and Oct., Wed.–Sun. 10–5; June–Sept., Wed.–Sun. 10–6; Nov., Wed.–Sun. 10–4; Dec., call for hrs. Grounds daily 8–sunset.*

Robert Jenkins House and Museum. This Federal home, built in 1811, now houses a museum containing various articles of Hudsoniana, including historic documents, maps and books relating to whaling, military artifacts, and other archaic goodies. Tours are generally by appointment only. ⊠ *113 Warren St.* ☎ *518/828–9764* 🖳 *$3* ⊙ *July and Aug., Sun. and Mon. 1–3 or by appt.*

Where to Stay & Eat

$$–$$$ ✕ **Bølgen & Moi.** Chefs Trond Moi and Lars Erik Vesterdal of Norway have put together an unusual menu of international flavors cooked in the classic French manner but with Scandinavian flair. The house specialty is a Norwegian fish–and–shellfish pot. The interior's uncluttered lines are meant to draw attention to the fine art: photographs by Norwegian Knut Bry in the bar and paintings by Frank Faulkner in the dining room. ⊠ *136 Warren St.* ☎ *518/671–6380* ▭ *AE, D, DC, MC, V* ⊙ *Closed Tues. No lunch Mon.–Thurs.*

$$–$$$ ✕ **Charleston.** Tin ceilings, sculptural metal lighting, and a calming beige backdrop provide this storefront restaurant with Hudsonian SoHo chic. Painstakingly described dishes fight for attention on the menu, including an appetizer of Saranac Ale–steeped Prince Edward Island mussels with jalapeño, leeks, and cilantro and an entrée of grilled pork medallions with mustard-bourbon sauce and roasted-red-pepper soft polenta. A decent wine list complements the gastronomic offerings. ⊠ *517 Warren St.* ☎ *518/828–4990* ▭ *AE, D, DC, MC, V* ⊙ *Closed Wed.*

$–$$$ ✕ **Ca' Mea.** The restaurant, clean and classic, serves northern Italian fare. A mahogany ceiling and cherrywood floor in the bar–dining room give way to a lighter, more-elegant birch-maple motif in the main dining room. Outdoor dining is also available. Veal scaloppine with mozzarella and eggplant in a light red sauce is a crowd pleaser. Watch for the grilled-octopus special. ⊠ *333 Warren St.* ☎ *518/822–0005* ▭ *MC, V* ⊙ *Closed Tues. and Wed. in winter.*

$–$$$ ✕ **Paramount Grill.** Fitting in comfortably with the muted, contemporary feel of the majority of Hudson's restaurants, the Paramount exhibits a simple, uncluttered design with wood floors, fine table linens, and original artwork. The food is also designed not to offend. Popular dishes include roasted rack of lamb with Moroccan spices and apricot-mango chutney. Vegetarian entrées are also available. ⊠ *321 Warren St.* ☎ *518/828–3657* ▭ *AE, MC, V* ⊙ *Closed Tues. and Wed.*

$–$$$ ✕ **Park Place Bistro.** Along with its mate, the Rip Van Winkle Tap Room across the lobby, this quiet restaurant in the St. Charles Hotel is said to be the oldest venue for vittles and grog in Hudson. Candles glow atop ivory tablecloths, casting warm light on the tin ceiling. A Culinary Institute–trained chef turns out the goods. Spice-rubbed New Zealand rack of lamb heads the list in price and stick-to-your-ribs satisfaction. ⊠ *16–18 Park Pl.* ☎ *518/822–9900* ⊟ *AE, D, DC, MC, V.*

$-$$ ✕ **Mexican Radio.** Come off Warren Street into this slice of contemporary Mexico—an outpost of Manhattan's Mexican Radio. High ceilings means there's plenty of room for thematic art on the orange-hued walls, which are dominated by wrought-iron crucifixes and augmented by Mexican art and still more crucifixes fashioned out of found objects. The cuisine is hearty, high-end Mexican; Cajun burritos filled with chorizo and shrimp and topped with jalapeño salsa, and steak and shrimp fajitas stand out. ⊠ *537 Warren St.* ☎ *518/828–7770* ⊟ *AE, D, DC, MC, V.*

¢–$$ ✕ **Red Dot Bar & Grill.** A trendy spot in the heart of the gallery district, this sleek 90-seat bar-restaurant with seasonal garden seating offers a varied menu, from hamburgers and quesadillas to soft-shell crabs (in season). The dining room has a large picture window overlooking the garden. The bar is open until 2 AM. ⊠ *321 Warren St.* ☎ *518/828–3657* ⊟ *MC, V* ☺ *Closed Mon. and Tues.*

¢–$$ ✕ **Wunderbar & Bistro.** The bar-restaurant is a casual place to mix and mingle without putting too much of a dent in your wallet. The menu includes hearty Hungarian dishes, such as braised beef with potato dumplings, as well as chicken and sirloin burgers and pasta combos. A piano player entertains from 7 to 10 on Saturday. ⊠ *744 Warren St.* ☎ *518/828–0555* ⊟ *AE, D, DC, MC, V* ☺ *Closed Sun.*

¢–$ ✕ **Muddy Cup Coffee House.** Unusually large and comfortable, this coffeehouse teems with overstuffed furniture upon which you may lounge, read, and telecommute. More than 21 flavors of coffee compete with 10 types of tea and a full menu of cappuccinos, lattes, coffee shakes, smoothies, and desserts. The owner is a crack studio musician with a long list of friends in the biz, so expect some musical surprises. ⊠ *742 Warren St.* ☎ *518/828–2210* ⌕ *Reservations not accepted* ⊟ *No credit cards.*

$–$$$ 🏨 **Hudson Guest House.** Occupying the floors above Alain Pioton Antiques in the heart of the antiques district, this chic haven of two four-room suites is populated by an appropriately eclectic blend of antiques and contemporary furnishings. You can easily imagine some of the rooms in *Elle Decor*. A credit card holds your reservation, but payment is by check. ⊠ *536 Warren St., 12534* ☎ *518/822–9148* ⊕ *www.hudsonguesthouse.com* ⇄ *2 suites* ⌂ *Kitchens; no kids under 12, no smoking* ⊟ *AE, MC, V (for deposit only).*

$–$$$ 🏨 **Inn at Blue Stores.** On U.S. 9 about 10 mi south of Hudson, this country B&B in the hamlet of Blue Stores is a 1908 Arts and Crafts gem on a 100-acre gentleman's farm. The stucco building has a clay-tile roof, lots of stained glass and dark oak woodwork, period furnishings, and extra-wide porches. The interior scheme is largely Victorian, with floral wallpaper, lace, and ruffles. ⊠ *2323 U.S. 9, Blue Stores 12534* ☎ *518/537–4277* ⊕ *www.innatbluestores.com* ⇄ *5 rooms, 2 with shared bath* ⌂ *Dining room, fans, some cable TV, pool; no room phones, no kids under 10, no smoking* ⊟ *No credit cards* ⦿ *BP.*

$–$$$ 🏨 **Union Street Guest House.** In an unassuming 1830 Greek revival, this small hideaway offers two suites with private bathrooms. The rooms are spacious, high-ceilinged, and furnished with a mix of antique and mid-20th-century furniture and art. One suite has two bedrooms with queen beds; the other has one bedroom with a queen and a twin. Feather pillows and quilts abound, and wireless Internet access is available. This is not a B&B and offers no food. ⊠ *349 Union St. 12534* ☎ *518/828–0958* ⊕ *www.unionstreetguesthouse.com* ➪ *2 suites* ⧉ *Refrigerators, cable TV; no smoking* ⊟ *MC, V.*

$–$$ ⊞ **Hudson City B&B.** The fanciful circa-1865 home has a broad veranda and tower and is chock-full of period antiques. A crackling fireplace beckons in the first-floor parlor; in warmer seasons you can relax on the porch or in the garden. Bedrooms are decked out in pinks and florals; some beds are draped with swags. ⊠ *326 Allen St., 12534* ☎ *518/822–8044* ⧉ *518/828–9139* ⊕ *www.hudsoncitybnb.com* ➪ *6 rooms* ⧉ *Some refrigerators, in-room VCRs, Internet, some pets allowed; no smoking* ⊟ *AE, D, DC, MC, V* ⦾ *BP.*

¢–$ ⊞ **St. Charles Hotel.** Rooms at this three-story brick Victorian hotel in downtown Hudson are bright, dressed in mostly muted tones with splashes of green, burgundy, and mauve, and have wi-fi (wireless) Internet access. Pick from king, queen, or twin beds. ⊠ *16–18 Park Pl., 12534* ☎ *518/822–9900* ⧉ *518/822–0835* ⊕ *www.stcharleshotel.com* ➪ *34 rooms, 6 suites* ⧉ *Restaurant, cable TV, bar, business services, meeting room, some pets allowed* ⊟ *AE, D, DC, MC, V* ⦾ *CP.*

Nightlife & the Arts

NIGHTLIFE   The misleadingly named **Hudson River Theater** (⊠ 521 Warren St. ☎ 518/822–8189 ⊕ www.hudsonrivertheater.com), a Hudson institution, offers a dizzying array of campy, gut-wrenchingly humorous entertainment, much of it involving men dressed in homage to various larger-than-life female stereotypes. Co-owner Dini Lamott, former vocalist for the band Human Sexual Response, frequently takes to the stage as the improbably voluptuous Musty Chiffon, whose repertoire is heavy with psychedelic '60s tunes like "Itchycoo Park" and "Incense and Peppermints." Shows are at 9 PM Friday and Saturday; disco dancing to DJ sounds starts at 10. Drag shows, movie nights, concerts, and puppet shows round out the fun. A full bar is on the premises.

THE ARTS   The **Carrie Haddad Gallery** (⊠ 622 Warren St. ☎ 518/822–9744) was the first art gallery to open in Hudson, in 1991, and shows a mix of established and newly discovered artists in a large two-floor complex. Paintings, photography, sculpture, and other works are $500 to $5,000. The annual **Hudson ArtsWalk,** sponsored by the Columbia County Council on the Arts (⊠ 209 Warren St. ☎ 518/671–6213 ⊕ www.artscolumbia. org), takes place in October. The event, a showcase for local visual artists, attracts thousands of visitors who come to ogle a wide array of exhibits and demonstrations as well as to see concerts, dance performances, lectures, and poetry readings. Most of the action is on Warren Street. A cultural anchor in the city center, the **Hudson Opera House** (⊠ 327 Warren St. ☎ 518/822–9003 ⊕ www.hudsonoperahouse.org) offers a steady program of low-cost culture, including jazz, folk, blues, and classical concerts; theater and dance presentations; readings and lectures; and exhibitions by emerging artists. It also serves as a community arts center. Despite its moniker, the 19th-century building was the old city hall. A performance space with a combined artistic-activist mission, **Time & Space Limited** (TSL; ⊠ 434 Columbia St. ☎ 518/822–8448 ⊕ www.

timeandspace.org), founded by unconventional dramatist-activists Linda Mussman and Claudia Bruce, is a stone-cold-serious proposition. All TSL offerings, be they theatrical productions, art and photography exhibitions, films, readings, or youth programs, are produced with an eye toward burning local, national, and international issues.

Shopping

Face Stockholm (✉ 401 Warren St. ☎ 518/822–9474), a makeup and spa services retailer, shares its store with Hedstrom & Judd, a purveyor of Swedish antiques and new furniture. Man, woman, and child can while away the hours getting massaged, waxed, pampered, styled, blow-dried, and generally made over using an array of Face products. **Historical Materialism** (✉ 601 Warren St. ☎ 518/671–6151), a large, airy corner store, offers antiques from all periods, with an emphasis on lighting and clean design. The company also manufactures a line of lamps. **Joovay** (✉ 623 Warren St. ☎ 518/822–1526) stocks fine European lingerie—teddies, slips, silk chemises, and assorted unmentionables—as well as kimono robes and vintage silk Haori jackets. **Keystone** (✉ 620 Columbia St. ☎ 518/822–1019) is a warehouse loaded with architectural salvage—immense bronze urns, fountains, cornices, and plenty of imposing statuary. If it's all too overwhelming, visit Keystone's more-conventional antiques outlet, at 734 Warren Street. **Lili and Loo** (✉ 259 Warren St. ☎ 518/822–9492) is where you go when you're bored with Pier One. The mix includes postmodern-, Asian-, and African-inspired pottery, furniture, and sundries; sculptures, bowls, and teapots; and lots of finely crafted bamboo. **Ornamentum** (✉ 506½ Warren St. ☎ 518/671–6770) is a jewelry store and art gallery combined. All the fanciful jewelry for sale is by fine artists whose work appears in museums around the world. **Rural Residence** (✉ 316 Warren St. ☎ 518/822–1061) carries an assortment of housewares, candles, coffee-table art books, Italian and Belgian linens, and other refined trifles. **Theron Ware** (✉ 548 Warren St. ☎ 518/822–9744) is the archetype of Hudson antiques shops: a single storefront populated with rare and pricey treasures. It specializes in European and American antiques and artworks from the 17th through the 19th century and tends toward the ornate. **Toad** (✉ 725 Warren St. ☎ No phone) operates under the subtitle "Summer of 1969 Revisited," which is no joke. The narrow storefront has since 1973 been loaded to the rafters with clothing from India—blouses, skirts, dresses—and tie-dyed clothing, the teetering piles of which conceal shelves stocked with incense and hemp candles, oils, and other 1960s accoutrements. Says proprietor Michael Martin: "We're sort of stuck in a time warp." The **Velvet Egg** (✉ 528 Warren St. ☎ 518/822–9556) is a small general store with a natural bent. Bath and baby items, books, and accessories vie for precious shelf space with jewelry and doodads for your garden and your pet.

Claverack

4 mi east of Hudson.

The Dutch Van Rensselaer family laid claim to the lands of Claverack in the 17th century, driving the native Mahicans from the land and establishing farms. The 18th century brought the Revolutionary War; with it came the English, who set up mills and brickyards in the area. Claverack College (now Washington Seminary) educated some of the best and the brightest of its day: Martin Van Buren, Herman Melville, Stephen Crane, and Margaret Sanger can be counted among alumni. Today, to drive through the town poised between the Hudson and the Berkshires is to be surrounded by the past; you can peek at Victorian and colonial homes, and many sites have been designated historic by both the state and national historic registries.

The brick First Columbia County Courthouse (549 Route 23B), built in 1788 and now in private hands, was where archrivals Alexander Hamilton and Aaron Burr practiced law. Martin Van Buren was also admitted to the bar here.

Reformed Dutch Church. The soaring windows of this brick 1767 church, perched atop a grassy knoll with views of the Catskills, inspire thoughts of the divine. Below sits a cemetery where you can find members of the Van Ness, Van Rensselaer, Livingston, and Van Wyck families, among others. The church is open only for Sunday worship, at 9:30 AM. ⊠ *Rte. 9H* ☎ *518/851–3811.*

Where to Stay

$ 🏨 **1805 House B&B.** If you're looking to get away from it all, this place fits the bill. The eyebrow colonial sits on 20 acres of pastoral land overlooking a pond and provides ample privacy and relaxation. You can spend the day in a king-size mahogany bed gazing out the window, or use the canoe to explore the pond and glimpse the resident snapping turtle. The bathroom has a whirlpool tub. ⊠ *775 Snydertown Rd., 12513* ☎ *518/ 851–3467* 🖨 *518/851–3465* ⊕ *www.1805house.com* 🛏 *1 room* ⚄ *In-room hot tub, some pets allowed; no room phone, no room TV, no smoking* ⊟ *AE, DC, MC, V* �101 *BP.*

Hillsdale

㉖   *11 mi east of Claverack.*

Five miles from the Massachusetts border, the hamlet of Hillsdale serves as a jumping-off point for the surrounding cultural attractions of Tanglewood, Great Barrington, and Jacob's Pillow. The Falcon Ridge Folk Festival, which draws tens of thousands to the area each July, is held here. Outdoors enthusiasts can fly-fish, hike, and bike the Harlem Rail Trail or nearby Taconic State Park, golf at three public courses, and ski at the Catamount Ski area.

Taconic State Park–Copake Falls Area. You can hike and bike trails shaded by oak and hickory trees, swim in an old iron-ore mine, cross-country ski, or snowshoe on 5,000 sylvan acres. Visit the site of the old Copake Iron Works along the bank of the Bash Bish Brook and venture just over the border to Massachusetts to enjoy the Bash Bish Falls, where a brook cascades in a series of waterfalls. ⊠ *253 Rte. 344, east of Rte. 22, Copake Falls* ☎ *518/329–3993* ⊕ *nysparks.state.ny.us* 🅿 *Parking $7 (Memorial Day–Labor Day)* ⊙ *Daily 8–dusk.*

Where to Stay & Eat

¢–$$ ✕ **Four Brothers Restaurant.** The pizza at this casual Greek eatery, part of a local chain owned by the Stefanopoulos brothers, is just as good as the gyros and baklava. Anything Greek is good here; regulars come from miles around for the salad with hunks of feta and gleaming olives. ⊠ *Rte. 23 east of Rte. 22* ☎ *518/325–7300* ▤ *MC, V.*

$–$$ ✕▥ **Swiss Hutte.** You can walk to the Catamount Ski lift from this chalet-style inn tucked away on 12 acres off Route 23. Double beds, wall-to-wall carpeting, and tiled bathrooms make up the unassuming rooms, each of which has its own balcony overlooking a pond and gardens. The draws here are the location and the food prepared by chef-owner Gert Alper, who insists on making everything from scratch. Spend the day working up your appetite, and then satiate it with honey-glazed duckling with plum-cherry compote and caramelized pineapple, double-thick pork chops, or schnitzel in front of one of the dining-room fireplaces. ⊠ *18 Nickelson Rd., 12529* ☎ *518/325–3333 or 413/528–6200* ▤ *413/528–6201* ⊕ *www.swisshutte.com* ▱ *13 rooms, 1 suite* ⚘ *Restaurant, in-room data ports, refrigerators, cable TV, pool, bar, babysitting, concierge, business services, meeting rooms, some pets allowed (fee); no smoking* ▤ *MC, V.*

¢–$ ✕▥ **Aubergine.** The decor in this Dutch colonial transports you to the Victorian age; most rooms have riotous floral wallpaper and lush wall-to-wall carpeting in rose and green hues. The Lavender Room, actually painted rich ocher, has a dramatic window under the eaves of the inn. The French Room has a queen-size brass bed. Artesian tiles accentuate the bathrooms and cut-glass lamps perch atop night tables. The restaurant ($$$; reservations essential) serves seasonal country cooking, such as crab boudin with leeks and smoked pork chops alongside escargot fritters and steamed mussels. The dining rooms run the gamut from Victorian folly to staid paneled and brick rooms; some have fireplaces. You can have a nightcap at the copper-topped bar. ⊠ *Rtes. 22 and 23, 12529* ☎ *518/325–3412* ▤ *518/325–7089* ⊕ *www.aubergine.com* ▱ *4 rooms, 2 with shared bath* ⚘ *Restaurant, bar, some pets allowed; no room phones, no room TVs, no smoking* ▤ *AE, D, MC, V* ✆ *Closed Mon. and Tues., 3 wks in Mar.*

$–$$$ ▥ **Inn at Green River.** Muted tones—celadon, rose, dusky blue, dove gray—
Fodor's Choice prevail throughout this 1830 Federal home perched on nearly an acre
  ★ in the foothills of the Berkshires. There's a fireplace in the front parlor, where antique tables hold bowls of miniature pinecones and old vases of dried hydrangea. Many of the rooms have toile curtains and bedspreads; a couple have four-poster beds and two have whirlpool tubs. In the spacious Martin Van Buren room, said to be haunted, a tall window overlooks an old graveyard. Arrange the time of your breakfast with your hostess, who staggers seatings in the candlelit dining room and is known for her lemon-ricotta hotcakes and other scrumptious morsels. ⊠ *9 Nobletown Rd., 12529* ☎ *518/325–7248* ⊕ *www.iagr.com* ▱ *7 rooms* ⚘ *Dining room, some in-room hot tubs; no room phones, no room TVs, no kids, no smoking* ▤ *AE, DC, MC, V* ▯ *BP.*

$$ ▥ **The Honored Guest.** You pass lilac bushes and well-tended gardens on the way to the front porch of this 1910 Prairie house. Inside the friendly B&B, Stickley furniture, original Frank Lloyd Wright lamps, and other mint-condition Mission pieces fill the common rooms. The guest rooms are awash in pastel colors. The Cottage Room has eight pieces of mid-1800s cottage pine furniture, and a claw-foot tub in the bathroom. A white wrought-iron queen bed takes center stage in the Rose Room. Turn-down service includes bedtime truffles. The dining room is where the magic happens; the hearty breakfasts might include lemon-soufflé pancakes, sausage, fruit parfaits, and freshly baked muffins. Don't miss afternoon tea, served outside or in front of the fireplace. ⊠ *20 Hunt Rd., 12529* 🕾🕾 *518/325–9100* ⊕ *www.honoredguest.com* ⊅ *4 rooms* ♢ *Dining room, fans, babysitting; no a/c in some rooms, no room phones, no room TVs, no smoking* ⊟ *AE, MC, V (for deposit only)* ⦿l *BP.*

$–$$ 🏨 **Linden Valley Lodge.** You can step off the slopes of Catamount and take a short stroll to your room, or in warm weather play a set of tennis and then swim in the pool or spring-fed pond at this 1970s-era lodge with soaring ceilings and extensive decks. Each room has a separate entrance and mountain views; four have private terraces. A rose garden scents the air, and perennials bloom across 5 acres. ⊠ *38 Nickelson Rd., off Rte. 23, 12529* 🕾 *518/325–7100* 🖷 *518/325–4107* ⊅ *7 rooms* ♢ *Cable TV, 2 tennis courts, pool, pond* ⊟ *AE, MC, V.*

$–$$ 🏨 **Silvanus Lodge.** Step inside this retro '50s motel, low slung on 5 acres at the foot of the Berkshires, and you're transported to a funky world where swirls of primary colors dance across carpets and whimsy rules. The amiable and honest owner, Steele, makes the ultimate concierge, arranging everything so you don't have to worry. Architectural drawings and witty contemporary art grace the walls of the rooms, which are immaculate; many rooms have CD players. If you're traveling with family, your best bet is the efficiency, which includes a kitchen. ⊠ *9350 Rte. 22, 12529* 🕾 *518/325–3000* ⊕ *www.silvanuslodge.com* ⊅ *9 rooms, 1 efficiency* ♢ *Some kitchens, cable TV, some in-room VCRs, pool, concierge, business services, some pets allowed; no smoking* ⊟ *AE, DC, MC, V.*

CAMPING 🏕 **Taconic State Park–Copake Falls Area.** You can get back to nature with a basic tent site or splurge on a cabin with electric heat, sofas, and a breakfast bar. Cook outdoors around your own campfire ring or grill, and dine at the comfort of individual picnic tables. Cabins have three bedrooms, electricity, and kitchens, and can be booked throughout the year. ♢ *Flush toilets, dump station, running water, showers, fire pits, grills, picnic tables, play area, swimming (pond)* ⊠ *253 Rte. 344, Copake Falls 12517* 🕾 *518/329–3993 information, 800/456–2267 reservations* ⊕ *nysparks.state.ny.us* ⊅ *43 regular tent sites, 20 platform tent sites, 34 RV sites, 14 cabins, 2 cottages* ▭ *$13 tents and RVs, $14 tent platforms, $78–$93 cabins and cottages* ⊟ *MC, V* ⊙ *Closed early Dec.–early May (cottages open all yr).*

Nightlife & the Arts

The **Falcon Ridge Folk Festival** (⊠ Long Hill Farm, Rte. 23 🕾 860/364–0366 ⊕ www.falconridgefolk.com) brings the foothills of the Berkshires to life with the sound of music for four days in late July. You can hear folk-scene luminaries belt their stuff from three stages or strap on your dancing shoes and pound out rhythm on 8,000 square feet of dance floor.

Sports & the Outdoors

SKIING   The **Catamount Ski Area** (✉ Rte. 23 ☎ 518/325–3200 or 413/528–1262 ⊕ www.catamountski.com) encompasses 110 acres straddling the border of New York and Massachusetts in the Berkshire Mountains. An unpretentious lodge sits at the base of Catamount, where the double-diamond Catapult descends 1,000 feet; full snowmaking facilities ensure active slopes all winter. You can leave the kids at the children's playroom or enroll them in one of numerous programs and grab a lift to the top, where you have 28 trails to choose from. A separate area accommodates snowboarders and has nighttime lighting. Ski and snowboard rentals and instruction are available; full-day lift tickets are $45. The lodge sits at the end of Nickelson Road, off Route 23.

Kinderhook

 **27** *11 mi northwest of Hillsdale.*

Henry Hudson disembarked from his ship, *Half Moon,* and stepped onto the fertile land we now know as Kinderhook in 1609. Shortly afterward, Dutch and Swedish settlers pushed the Lenni Lenape out, expanded their fur trade, tilled fields, established mills, made wagons, and, by the 18th century, set up taverns. Kinderhook's location at a heavily traveled crossroads made it a popular resting spot for travelers, including Benedict Arnold after he was wounded in battle.

One of Kinderhook's most notable residents was Martin Van Buren, eighth president of the United States. You can retrace the steps of early American history by walking or driving through the village, which brims with well-preserved Federal and Dutch-colonial architecture. From here it's a short hop to Chatham, where you can spend a day bouncing around the hip shopping district and checking out art galleries. Near Old Chatham, working farms yield to opulent estates with fenced-in paddocks and stables.

Columbia County Museum. The building that houses the museum and the offices of the Columbia County Historical Society was a Masonic temple and dates from 1916. You can trace your roots with the help of staff and extensive genealogical archives, peruse period postcards, and see fine examples of period furniture. ✉ *5 Albany Ave.* ☎ *518/758–9265* ⊕*www.cchsny.org* ✉ *Free* ⊙ *Memorial Day–Labor Day, weekdays 10–4, Sat. 1–4; rest of yr, Mon., Wed., and Fri. 10–4 (call for Sat. hrs).*

James Vanderpoel House. The 1818 Federal house in downtown Kinderhook displays historic exhibits about life in Columbia County. The rooms have plasterwork ceilings and graceful mantelpieces; the foyer, with its curved staircase, is especially graceful. Pieces by New York cabinetmakers are displayed throughout. ✉ *16 Broad St./U.S. 9* ☎ *518/ 758–9265* ✉ *$3* ⊙ *Memorial Day–Labor Day, Wed.–Sun. 10–4.*

Luykas Van Alen House. The 1737 restored Dutch farmhouse is especially noted for its collection of Hudson Valley paintings. The grounds include the **Ichabod Crane Schoolhouse,** a one-room schoolhouse that was actually used until the 1940s. It takes its name from the character in *The*

Legend of Sleepy Hollow, by Washington Irving. Irving, who tutored at Lindenwald, purportedly modeled the character after a schoolmaster who taught in the area. At this writing, the main house is closed for renovations, due for completion by 2005. ⊠ *Rte. 9H* ☎ *518/758–9265* ⊡ *$3* ☉ *Memorial Day–Labor Day, Thurs.–Sat. 11–5, Sun. 1–5.*

Martin Van Buren National Historic Site. Born in Kinderhook, Martin Van Buren (1782–1862)—the eighth president of the United States—decided to retire to this estate, which he purchased during his presidency and called **Lindenwald.** Built in the Federal style in 1797, the house took on Gothic and Italianate features following a revamp in the mid-1800s. The graceful building, which can be visited only as part of a guided tour, appears much the way it did when Van Buren lived here and includes many furnishings attributed to the period of his residency. It's also known for its large collection of historic wallpaper samples. ⊠ *1013 Old Post Rd., off Rte. 9H* ☎ *518/758–9689* ⊕ *www.nps.gov/maval* ⊡ *House $2, grounds free* ☉ *House late May–Oct. daily 9–4:30, Nov.–early Dec. weekends 9–4:30.*

Shaker Museum and Library. You can learn about the daily life of the Shakers from one of the largest collections focusing on their culture. The extensive array of clothing and household textiles on exhibit is a highlight. The series of red barns also displays furniture, tools, machinery, and decorative objects from all of the major Shaker communities. ⊠ *88 Shaker Museum Rd., off Rte. 13, Old Chatham* ☎ *518/794–9100* ⊕ *www. smandl.org* ⊡ *$8* ☉ *Late May–Oct., Wed.–Mon. 10–5.*

FESTIVALS & FAIRS
Columbia County Fair. Each Labor Day weekend, the fair celebrates all things rural. You can grab some cotton candy; watch antique-tractor pulls, horse shows, a fireman's parade, and livestock shows; and get tips at horticultural exhibits. The bright lights of the carnival rides draw people from neighboring counties for this time-honored event. ⊠ *32 Church St., Chatham* ☎ *518/758–1811* ⊕ *www.columbiafair.com.*

Where to Stay & Eat

$$–$$$$ ✕ **The Pillars Restaurant.** The first thing you see as you step into this carriage-house restaurant is a glass case showcasing Chef Paul Bock's exquisite dessert confections: mousse-filled blown-sugar apples and sculpted-chocolate pianos. Dining rooms cloaked in paisley or chintz wallpaper provide the backdrop for fine fare like smoked salmon with potato pancake; shrimp fritters with tangy honey-horseradish sauce; beer crepe with shiitake, spinach, and Gruyère; and flambéed roast duck in Grand Marnier sauce. The stone-walled bar has a fireplace and is a good place for a before- or after-dinner drink. ⊠ *Rte. 20, New Lebanon* ☎ *518/794–8007* ⊟ *AE, D, MC, V* ☉ *Closed Mon. and Tues. No lunch.*

$–$$$ ✕ **The Red Barn.** Glass bottles filled with jewel-toned syrups sit in front of a large mirror overlooking the dining room, paying homage to the original 1957 establishment famous for its homemade ice cream. You can still get homemade ice cream, pies, cakes, and other treats, but Chef Bert Goldfinger excels at comfort food like you wish your mother made: meat loaf, roasted chicken, homemade fries, mussels, and crispy roast duck with potato pancakes. You'll catch a whiff of a French influence, owing to the chef's training at New York City's Le Cirque. ☒ *47 Old Post Rd./Rte. 9H, Ghent* ☎ *518/828–6677* ▤ *AE, DC, MC, V* ☉ *Closed Feb. and Mon.–Wed. No lunch Thurs.*

$–$$ ✕ **Blue Plate.** The paper covering the white linen tablecloths and the crayons displayed in water glasses reflect the relaxed nature of this eatery. From shrimp étouffée to hamburgers, everything here is just right. The kitchen makes the most of organic, local produce and gets its cheese and lamb from the Old Chatham Sheepherding Company, well known among gourmands. Vegetarian entrées change nightly, drawing aficionados from miles around. ☒ *1 Kinderhook St., Chatham* ☎ *518/ 392–7711* ▤ *DC, MC, V* ☉ *Closed Jan. and Mon. No lunch.*

¢–$$ ✕ **Triple Nickel.** At this unusual combination of coffeehouse and miniature golf course, you can grab a latte or lunch and improve your swing in one stop. The place, in the heart of New Lebanon, is the brainchild of golf professional Kay McMahon. The fare is mostly casual: sandwiches, wraps, homemade soups. Special dinners are offered by reservation. (Call for details.) ☒ *555 Rte. 20/22, New Lebanon* ☎ *518/794– 7270* ▤ *MC, V.*

¢–$ ✕ **Our Daily Bread.** Baskets of fresh baguettes and focaccia scent the air, greeting you as you step inside. Glass counters hold lush chocolate temptations and bags of apricot rugalach. You can pick up goodies for a picnic, or sit down and dig into kasha varnishkas (a dish of buckwheat and pasta) with seared bok choi or grilled rainbow trout. The place is open until 5:30. ☒ *54 Main St., Chatham* ☎ *518/392–9852* ☉ *Closed Mon. and Tues. No dinner.* ▤ *No credit cards.*

¢ ✕ **The Summit.** Customers return to this popular spot several times a day to nosh on burritos, top off an espresso, or indulge in gourmet ice cream. A friendly crowd hangs out around the café tables, and while browsing the baked goods you can get lots of advice on where to go, what to do, or—more important—what to eat. Sidewalk tables make the most of the sunny side of the street. The place closes at 5:30 PM weekdays and at 4 PM Sunday. ☒ *20 Main St., Chatham* ☎ *518/392–3291* ☉ *No dinner.* ▤ *No credit cards.*

$–$$ ▦ **Churchill House B&B.** You can fish for trout in Wyomanock Creek, or loll on a wooden swing a few steps away from the wraparound porch of this rambling Greek-revival house. The rooms overlook perennial gardens and have luxurious featherbeds; two of the rooms have a queen and a twin bed. ☒ *228 Churchill Rd., New Lebanon 12125* ☎ *518/ 766–5852* ⊕ *www.churchillhousebb.com* ➳ *3 rooms* ♨ *Cable TV, basketball, boccie, croquet, business services; no phones in some rooms, no kids under 6, no smoking* ▤ *AE, DC, MC, V* ⦿ *BP.*

$–$$ ▦ **Inn at Silver Maple Farm.** Exposed timbers, wide-plank floors, antique trunks, and custom-made cupboards evoke a Shaker spirit at this 1830 dairy farm. On the way up to the Loft Room—which recalls a romantic, shabby-chic beach cottage—you pass a shimmering hallway mural of flower sprigs, silver maples, and a rogue bunny. Ralph Lauren sheets complement the elegantly simple rooms. You could lose hours pondering the Berkshires from the expansive back deck. ☒ *1871 Rte. 295, East Chatham 12060* ☎ *518/781–3600* ▤ *518/781–3883* ⊕ *www.*

silvermaplefarm.com ✍ *9 rooms, 2 suites* ☖ *Dining room, some refrigerators, cable TV with movies, croquet, business services; no smoking inside* ☰ *AE, DC, MC, V* ⭙❙ *BP.*

$-$$ ▢ **Van Schaack House.** Symmetrical topiaries flank the steps to this 1785 Georgian manor with leaded-glass windows. A major renovation in 1865 resulted in the Victorian demeanor you see today; amid all the original artwork, period architectural details, and antiques, you could easily mistake your surroundings for a museum. In the dramatic crimson hall, stairs rise to the four guest rooms, all stocked with plush bathrobes, 360-thread-count Egyptian cotton sheets, boxes of chocolates, bottled water, and fruit baskets. The smallest and simplest of the accommodations is Judge Benson's Room. In the morning, a Culinary Institute graduate prepares a sumptuous breakfast of fresh muffins and juices and other treats to tempt your palate. ⊠ *20 Broad St., 12106* ☎ *518/758–6118* 🖷 *518/ 758–2850* ⊕ *www.vanschaackhouse.com* ✍ *4 rooms* ☖ *Dining room, in-room VCRs, cable TV, croquet; no room phones, no kids, no smoking* ☰ *AE, MC, V* ⭙❙ *BP.*

¢-$$ ▢ **Spencertown Country House B&B.** Soft strains of bluegrass and the scent of cinnamon cookies greet you as you enter the foyer of this former saltbox dairy barn. The owners pride themselves on overseeing every detail, from the collection of folk-art portraits in the living room to the sumptuous homemade fruitbreads at breakfast. Colorful accents punch up many of the rooms. In Gunda's Room, painted a soothing periwinkle blue, windows on three sides overlook gardens. The Taconic suite opens onto a large, enclosed porch where you can sit and listen to the soft gurgling of a nearby brook. The breakfast is a highlight. ⊠ *1909 U.S. 9, Spencertown 12165* ☎ *518/392–5292 or 888/727–9980* 🖷 *518/ 392–7453* ⊕ *www.spencertowncntryhouse.com* ✍ *8 rooms, 2 suites* ☖ *Dining room, in-room data ports, cable TV, croquet, business services; no smoking* ☰ *AE, DC, MC, V* ⭙❙ *BP.*

¢ ▢ **Blue Spruce Inn & Suites.** You can sip your cider from Golden Harvest Farms, directly across the street, at one of several strategically placed picnic benches scattered on the front lawn. The motel-style accommodations here have dated decor but show signs of inspiration—some eschew the typical mundane art for handsome black-and-white photographs reminiscent of Ansel Adams. Rooms have one queen bed, two doubles, or two twins; suites have eat-in kitchens and living rooms with sleeper sofas. ⊠ *3093 U.S. 9, Valatie 12184* ☎ *518/758–9711 or 888/261– 9823* 🖷 *518/758–1638* ⊕ *www.bluespruceinnsuites.com* ✍ *22 rooms, 6 suites* ☖ *Coffee shop, in-room data ports, some fans, some kitchens, cable TV with movies, pool, badminton, croquet, business services, some pets allowed, no-smoking rooms* ☰ *AE, DC, MC, V.*

Nightlife & the Arts

Make a detour to explore cutting-edge contemporary sculpture at **Art Omi** (⊠ 59 Letter S Rd., off Rte. 22, 2 mi west of Rte. 66, Ghent ☎ 518/ 392–7656 ⊕ www.artomi.org), an international center for artists where giant heads spring fully formed from the ground in **Fields Sculpture Park;** about 80 artworks are scattered around 90 acres of the park. You can bring a picnic and spend a full afternoon roaming the park; bicycles are provided. The sculpture park is free and open daily from dawn to dusk.

On the third weekend of October, the **FilmColumbia Festival** (☎ 518/392–1162 ⊕ www.filmcolumbia.com) brings together film buffs and industry members for screenings of pre-release films at Chatham's 1920 Crandell Theater; many of the films shown here have gone on to win Academy Awards. The area has a high concentration of famous second-home owners, so expect to see stars promenading down Main Street during the festival.

Sports & the Outdoors

If you have the need for speed, check out the **Lebanon Valley Speedway** (⊠ 1746 U.S. 20, West Lebanon ☎ 518/794–9606 ⊕ www.lebanonvalley.com). The quintessential country dirt track has enthusiasts camping out all weekend. The gates open at 5 PM.

HUDSON VALLEY A TO Z

To research prices, get advice from other travelers, and book travel arrangements, visit www.fodors.com.

AIR TRAVEL

The Hudson Valley is served by Stewart International Airport and Westchester County Airport. Albany International Airport, at the north end of the Hudson Valley, is a good option for visits to Ulster, Columbia, and Dutchess counties. CommutAir, a Continental Airlines affiliate, connects Albany airport to the Finger Lakes region, Long Island, and western New York; the carrier also flies to Westchester County Airport, in the lower Hudson Valley, and links the Westchester airport to the Finger Lakes region. US Airways Express links Albany to New York City, Long Island, and western New York. Flights into Stewart, which is near Newburgh, come from outside New York State. The New York City–area airport closest to the Hudson Valley is LaGuardia. *See* Air Travel *in* Smart Travel Tips A to Z for more information about Albany, LaGuardia, Stewart, and Westchester airports and for major airlines' contact information.

🛈 **Carriers CommutAir** ☎ 800/525–0280 ⊕ www.commutair.com. **US Airways Express** ☎ 800/428–4322 ⊕ www.usairways.com.

BOAT & FERRY TRAVEL

A high-speed commuter ferry travels between Haverstraw, in Rockland County, and the Metro-North Railroad station in Ossining, in Westchester County, where you may board a train bound for New York City. The combined travel time to Grand Central Station is 70 minutes; the ferry ride alone takes about 17 minutes. NY Waterway operates the ferry. It also offers day-trip packages from New York City to Kykuit, Lyndhurst, Sunnyside, and Philipsburg Manor.

🛈 **Metro-North Railroad** ☎ 212/532–4900 or 800/638–7646 ⊕ mta.info/mnr/html/connectingservice.htm. **NY Waterway** ☎ 800/533–3779 ⊕ www.nywaterway.com.

BUS TRAVEL

Shortline buses link the Hudson Valley with New York City, Long Island, the Catskills, the Finger Lakes region, and western New York. Stops include Bear Mountain, Cornwall, Fort Montgomery, Goshen, Harriman, Highland Falls, Hyde Park, Monroe, Newburgh, Rhinebeck,

Staatsburg, West Point, White Plains, and the Woodbury Common outlets. It also serves the Culinary Institute of America, the Franklin D. Roosevelt National Historic Site, Marist College, Vassar College, and the Vanderbilt Mansion. Shortline also offers day-trip and overnight packages to Bear Mountain State Park, the Brotherhood Winery, Hyde Park, Locust Grove, Montgomery Place, the Storm King Art Center, West Point, and the Woodbury Common outlets.

Adirondack Trailways links Hudson Valley cities and villages (primarily to the west of the river) with New York City as well as with most regions in the rest of the state, including the northern Catskills, the Adirondacks, the Capital-Saratoga Region, central and western New York, the Finger Lakes, and Long Island. Buses stop in High Falls, Kingston, Nanuet, Newburgh, New Paltz, Rosendale, Saugerties, and White Plains.
🚍 **Adirondack Trailways** ☎ 800/858-8555 ⊕ www.trailways.com. **Shortline Coach USA** ☎ 800/631-8405 ⊕ www.shortlinebus.com.

CAR RENTAL

Avis, Hertz, and Enterprise all serve the Albany, Stewart, and Westchester airports. Avis also rents cars in Poughkeepsie and White Plains. Hertz rents in Poughkeepsie. Enterprise has locations in Beacon, Goshen, Kingston, Hudson, Monroe, Newburgh, North Tarrytown, Nyack, Poughkeepsie, and White Plains. *See* Car Rental *in* Smart Travel Tips A to Z for national agencies' contact information.

CAR TRAVEL

Although public transportation makes the Hudson Valley very accessible, a car is the best way to explore the region and its scenic backroads and byways. The Taconic State Parkway, a main route on the east side of the river, is particularly scenic, with good views of the Catskills to the west, but it's also narrow, with nearly nonexistent shoulders, and has patches of rough paving and poor drainage; fog and rain can make this curvy road dangerous. Deer are plentiful throughout the Hudson Valley; you may even come across them on I-8. Be on the lookout especially in the evening and at night. In more-rural areas, cattle and other livestock sometimes find their way into the road, and you may find yourself stuck behind a tractor or other slow-moving farm vehicle. (Don't tailgate; you never know when a hay bale will come tumbling off a wagon.)

Weekday traffic is busier during the morning and late-afternoon work rushes. On Friday evening, the major thoroughfares jam up with weekenders heading north from New York City; the southbound lanes can back up on Sunday evening, when these weekenders return home.

EMERGENCIES

In an emergency, dial 911.
🚑 **Lower Hudson Valley Nyack Hospital** ✉ 160 N. Midland Ave., Nyack ☎ 845/348-2000 ⊕ www.nyackhospital.org. **St. Luke's Cornwall Hospital** ✉ 70 Dubois St., Newburgh ☎ 845/561-4400 ⊕ stlukescornwallhospital.org. **White Plains Hospital Center** ✉ Davis Ave. at E. Post Rd., White Plains ☎ 914/681-0600 ⊕ www.wphospital.org.
🚑 **Mid-Hudson Valley Kingston Hospital** ✉ 396 Broadway, Kingston ☎ 845/331-3131 ⊕ www.kingstonhospital.org. **Northern Dutchess Hospital** ✉ 6511 Springbrook Ave.,

Rhinebeck ☎ 845/876-3001 ⊕ www.ndhosp.com. **Vassar Brothers Medical Center** ✉ 45 Reade Pl., Poughkeepsie ☎ 845/471-8500 ⊕ www.vassarbrothers.org.
🚩 **Upper Hudson Valley Columbia Memorial Hospital** ✉ 71 Prospect Ave., Hudson ☎ 518/828-7601 ⊕ www.columbiamemorial.com.

SPORTS & THE OUTDOORS

See Sports & the Outdoors *in* Smart Travel Tips A to Z for additional information.

BIKING   With a variety of terrain and countless scenic backroads, the Hudson Valley is a popular biking destination. U.S. 9W draws throngs of bikers who make their way north from the George Washington Bridge to Nyack. But you can find great bike routes wherever you go in the valley. On its Web site, Dutchess County Tourism outlines six suggested routes. Portions of the 46-mi Harlem Valley Rail Trail, which hugs the eastern border of Columbia County and travels south into Dutchess County, have been completed and are open to riders. The Mid-Hudson Bicycle Club organizes rides throughout the region, with a focus on Ulster and Dutchess counties. Members of the Westchester Cycle Club lead rides in Westchester and Putnam counties.

Mountain biking is also popular, especially in Minnewaska State Park Preserve, Mohonk Preserve, and Mills-Norrie State Park.

ROCK CLIMBING   The Shawangunk Mountains are one of the top destinations in the world for rock climbing. The cliffs, near New Paltz, are appropriate for climbers of all levels. If you want instruction, find a guide who is accredited by the American Mountain Guide Association. (The association's Web site lists accredited instructors.)

🚩 **Biking Dutchess County Tourism** ✉ 3 Neptune Rd., Suite M-17, Poughkeepsie 12601 ☎ 845/463-4000 or 800/445-3131 ⊕ www.dutchesstourism.com. **Harlem Valley Rail Trail Association** ⌂ Box 356, Millerton 1254 ☎ 518/789-9591 ⊕ www.hvrt. org. **Mid-Hudson Bicycle Club** ⌂ Box 1727, Poughkeepsie 12601 ☎ No phone ⊕ www. midhudsonbicycle.org. **Westchester Cycle Club** ☎ No phone ⊕ www. westchestercycleclub.org.

🚩 **Rock Climbing American Mountain Guide Association** ⌂ Box 1739, Boulder CO 80302 ☎ 303/271-0984 ⊕ www.amga.com.

TOURS

BOAT TOURS   The main season for Hudson River boat tours is May through October. Departing from West Point's South Dock, Hudson Highlands Cruises' World War I–era ferryboat *Commander* takes you north past Constitution Island and Storm King Mountain to Pollepel Island for a view of the ruins of Bannerman's Castle before returning to West Point 90 minutes later.

Hudson River Adventures' *Pride of the Hudson,* a modern yacht, departs from Newburgh Landing for two-hour sightseeing cruises that take you past the ruins of Bannerman's Castle on Pollepel Island and pass Cold Spring and Storm King Mountain before turning back at West Point. A special cruise to Pollepel Island operates twice a month and includes commentary about the castle, but the cruise doesn't land at the island.

The River Rose is a 150-passenger double-decker New Orleans paddle-wheel boat—with a fully stocked snack and wine bar—that first saw service in the 1980s on the Mississippi River. Cruises leave from Newburgh; most last two hours. Cruises to West Point's Constitution Island include a tour of the island; the entire trip takes 3½ hours.

Hudson Valley Cruises offers two-hour cruises aboard the *Rip Van Winkle*. The boat leaves from Kingston's Rondout Landing, passing near the Rondout Lighthouse, and then travels south on the Hudson River to the northern edge of Hyde Park before turning around. You see several Hudson Valley mansions on the way, including the Wilderstein, Vanderbilt, and Staatsburg estates (all on the east bank). The boat has a shaded deck and a snack-and-beverage bar.

Kingston-based North River Cruises offers custom Hudson River cruises on its 40-foot motorboat, *Minsis,* which it charters out to small groups (six or fewer). Rates are about $225 an hour; call for pricing details.
🚢 Boat Tours **Hudson Highlands Cruises** ⊠ South Dock, West Point ☎ 845/534-7245 ⊕ www.commanderboat.com. **Hudson River Adventures** ⊠ Newburgh Landing, Front and 4th Sts., Newburgh ☎ 845/220-2120 ⊕ www.prideofthehudson.com. **Hudson River Cruises** ⊠ Rondout Landing, foot of Broadway, Kingston ☎ 845/340-4700 or 800/843-7472 ⊕ www.hudsonrivercruises.com. **North River Cruises** ⊠ West Strand Park, foot of Broadway, Kingston ☎ 845/679-8205 ⊕ www.northrivercruises.com. **River Rose Cruises** ⊠ Newburgh Landing, Front and 4th Sts., Newburgh ☎ 845/562-1067 ⊕ www.riverrosecruises.com.

TRAIN TRAVEL

Metro-North's Hudson Line trains travel between New York City's Grand Central Station and Poughkeepsie, with stops in Yonkers, Tarrytown, Garrison, Cold Spring, and Beacon. Stops on the Harlem Line include White Plains, North White Plains, Mount Kisco, and Katonah. Bicycles are allowed only with a permit, which you can purchase for $5 (annual fee) in Grand Central.

Amtrak connects the Hudson Valley with New York City, the Finger Lakes region, and western New York; it stops in Yonkers, Poughkeepsie, Rhinecliff, Hudson, and Albany. To assure a spot, reserve a ticket in advance. Bikes are allowed only as checked baggage, but Amtrak lines that service the Hudson Valley don't usually have baggage cars.

The trains follow the Hudson River along the same route traveled by Cary Grant and Eva Marie Saint in the 1959 Alfred Hitchcock film *North by Northwest.* For many, the river views alone are worth the ticket price. (Be sure to sit on the left side going north and on the right side when you head south, toward New York City.)
🚆 **Amtrak** ☎ 800/872-7245 ⊕ www.amtrak.com. **Metro-North Railroad** ☎ 212/532-4900 or 800/638-7646 ⊕ mta.info/mnr.

TRANSPORTATION AROUND THE HUDSON VALLEY

The best way to explore the Hudson Valley and take in its sights and scenic backroads is by car. Public transportation within the region is limited. If you have to travel by train, consider visiting Cold Spring or Hudson; if you're coming by bus, Kingston, New Paltz, Rhinebeck are your best bets.

VISITOR INFORMATION

🚩 **General Hudson River Valley Travel & Tourism** ⬧ Box 284, Salt Point 12578 ☎ 800/232-4782 ⊕ www.travelhudsonvalley.org.

🚩 **Lower Hudson Valley Cold Spring/Garrison Area Chamber of Commerce** ⬧ Box 36, Cold Spring 10516 ☎ 845/265-3200 ⊕ www.hvgateway.com/chamber.htm. **Greater Cornwall Chamber of Commerce** ✉ 284 Main St., Cornwall 12518 ☎ 845/534-7826 ⊕ www.cornwallnychamberofcommerce.org. **Katonah Chamber of Commerce** ✉ 20 Woodsbridge Rd., Katonah 10536 ☎ 914/232-2668 ⊕ www.katonahchamber.org. **Newburgh Visitors Center** ✉ Rte. 9W between South and 3rd Sts., Newburgh 12550 ☎ 845/565-5559. **Orange County Chamber of Commerce** ✉ 30 Matthews St., Suite 111, Goshen 10924 ☎ 845/291-2136 or 800/762-8687 ⊕ www.orangetourism.org. **Palisades Parkway Tourist Information Center** ✉ Palisades Parkway between exits 16 and 17 ☎ 845/786-5003 ⊕ www.pipc.org. **Putnam County Visitors Bureau** ✉ 110 Old Rte. 6, Bldg. 3, Carmel 10512 ☎ 800/470-4854 ⊕ www.visitputnam.org. **Rockland County Tourism** ✉ 18 New Hempstead Rd., New City 10956 ☎ 845/708-7300 ⊕ www.rockland.org. **Sleepy Hollow Chamber of Commerce** ✉ 54 Main St., Tarrytown 10591 ☎ 914/631-1705 ⊕ www.sleepyhollowchamber.com. **Westchester County Office of Tourism** ✉ 222 Mamaroneck Ave., Suite 100, White Plains 10605 ☎ 914/995-8500 or 800/833-9282 ⊕ www.westchestertourism.com. **Yonkers Chamber of Commerce** ✉ 20 S. Broadway, Suite 1207, Yonkers 10701 ☎ 914/963-0332 ⊕ www.yonkerschamber.com.

🚩 **Mid-Hudson Valley Dutchess County Tourism** ✉ 3 Neptune Rd., Suite M-17, Poughkeepsie 12601 ☎ 845/463-4000 or 800/445-3131 ⊕ www.dutchesstourism.com. **Kingston Heritage Area Visitor Center** ✉ 20 Broadway, Kingston ☎ 845/331-7517 or 800/331-1510 ⊕ www.ci.kingston.ny.us ✉ 308 Clinton Ave., Kingston ☎ 800/331-1518 ⊕ www.ci.kingston.ny.us. **Kingston Uptown Business Association** ☎ 845/339-5822 ⊕ www.oldtownkingston.org. **New Paltz Chamber of Commerce** ✉ 124 Main St., New Paltz 12561 ☎ 845/255-0243 ⊕ www.newpaltzchamber.org. **Rhinebeck Chamber of Commerce** ✉ 6372 Mill St., Rhinebeck 12572 ☎ 845/876-4778 ⊕ www.rhinebeckchamber.com. **Ulster County Tourism** ✉ 10 Westbrook La., Kingston 12401 ☎ 800/342-5826 ⊕ www.ulstertourism.info.

🚩 **Upper Hudson Valley Columbia County Chamber of Commerce** ✉ 507 Warren St., Hudson 12534 ☎ 518/828-4417 ⊕ www.columbiachamber-ny.com. **Columbia County Tourism** ✉ 401 State St., Hudson 12534 ☎ 518/828-3375 or 800/724-1846 ⊕ www.columbiacountyny.org.

THE CATSKILLS

4

By Erica
Freudenberg

THE ALGONQUINS CALLED THIS AREA ONTEORA, or "land in the sky." Later, writer Washington Irving would refer to the Catskills as "these fairy mountains," and they are one of the most visited, written-about, and painted ranges in the country. Rising between the Hudson River to the east and the upper Delaware and Susquehanna rivers to the south and west, the Catskills provided an early outlet for those who had the time and money to leave the hustle and bustle of New York City for some peace and quiet. The first resort, the Catskill Mountain House, was built in the 1820s near Haines Falls. World-class trout streams flow through the region, which spawned the sport of fly-fishing.

Ask for a description of the Catskills, and a fair proportion of vacationers who've been here speak of the lakes and large resorts of Sullivan County. Skiers and hikers point to the high-peaks region of Greene and Ulster counties. Anglers measure the Catskills in miles of pristine trout streams—the Beaver Kill, the Esopus, the east and west branches of the Delaware River. If you're Irish you've likely heard of East Durham; Jewish vacationers congregate in the Monticello-Liberty area. There is a sizable Ukrainian population in the Lexington area (near Windham), and German, French, and Italian enclaves are scattered around the Catskills as well.

The Catskills represent something different to everyone who comes here. It's a huge region that encompasses parts of Ulster, Greene, Schoharie, Sullivan, Orange, and Delaware counties. This crooked arm of the ancient Appalachians contains dense forests on mountains that climb as high as 4,200 feet; twisting rivers bordered by open farmland; rock-walled gorges where bald eagles winter; and lush, wide valleys. Small towns and one-store crossroad hamlets abound, so forget big cities.

New York City is just two or three hours away though, which means the Catskills are an attractive getaway destination for urban weekenders and an increasingly popular site for second homes. Areas where until recently cows outnumbered humans are now targets for developers. The changing face of the Catskills has generated dollars and spawned new attractions, cultural events, and recreational opportunities. It also has caused concern among environmentalists, planners, and longtime residents fearful that newcomers are spoiling the very natural splendor that drew them here in the first place.

Much of the terrain, however, is protected land within the Catskill Forest Preserve, which the state intends to keep "forever wild." The nearly 700,000-acre preserve has more than 200 mi of marked hiking trails and several campgrounds that offer closer encounters with the special nature of the Catskills. Here, somewhat off the beaten path, among mossy boulders, delicate alpine flowers, and fragrant groves of evergreens, you can experience the beauty that has lured poets, writers, artists, and nature lovers to the region for nearly two centuries. John Burroughs reflected on his beloved Catskills and wrote: "To find the universal elements enough; to find the air and the water exhilarating; to be refreshed by a morning walk or an evening saunter; to be thrilled by the stars at night; to be elated over a bird's nest or a wildflower in spring—these are some of the rewards of the simple life." Although much has changed in the intervening years and some of the magnificence has been irrevocably altered, travelers who pack a sense of wonder may yet reap the rewards of the region themselves.

Exploring the Catskills

Most travelers first glimpse the Catskills from the New York State Thruway, which links New York City and Albany. About 10 mi west of the thruway the mountains rise abruptly from the valley floor in an uneven blue wall some 20 mi long. In the northern Catskills, the Hudson River towns of Kingston and Catskill (thruway exits 19 and 21) are jumping-off points for Routes 23, 23A, and 28, which climb the mountainous wall and snake through Greene and upper Ulster counties. The principal access routes through Delaware County, which lies to the west of the mountains separating the Hudson and Delaware river watersheds, are Routes 23, 28, and 30. Sullivan County and the Upper Delaware River region can most easily be accessed via Route 17 (at this writing morphing into I–86), which runs from the thruway westward through the Catskills.

Numbers in the text correspond to numbers in the margin and on The Catskills map.

About the Hotels & Restaurants

Winter is usually considered high season for most lodging places near the Belleayre, Windham, and Hunter ski centers. In the northern Catskills it's not unusual for places to charge high-season rates in summer and winter. That said, prices tend to be much lower during the week, regardless of the season.

Although Catskill cuisine used to be a misnomer, regional restaurants are changing their reputations, largely thanks to the not-so-far-away Culinary Institute of America. Many CIA students decide to settle in the area after graduation and open restaurants showcasing their skills. Combined with a movement to use fresh, local produce and farm products, the result is a plethora of superb dining choices. Most of the best restaurants are in areas that draw New York City money; Windham, Woodstock, and the Hunter area all cater to an upscale clientele, although smaller, more remote towns and villages yield pleasant surprises. Dining in the region remains a casual experience, and few people dress for dinner.

WHAT IT COSTS				
$$$$	$$$	$$	$	¢
RESTAURANTS over $30	$22–$30	$15–$21	$8–$14	under $8
HOTELS over $250	$200–$250	$150–$199	$100–$149	under $100

Restaurant prices are for a main course at dinner (or at the most expensive meal served). Hotel prices are for two people in a standard double room in high season, excluding tax.

Timing

Each season in the Catskill Mountains has its own majesty. Spring brings the reemergence of dormant fauna, mating and foraging for food

You can get a good feel for the Catskills, which aren't as filled with attractions as most other regions of the state, in just a couple of days. If you're driving it's not difficult to combine explorations of the Catskills with excursions into the Hudson Valley. Woodstock, for instance, is just a few miles from Kingston and Saugerties. ⇨ For information about the Hudson Valley, *see* Chapter 3.

Numbers in the text correspond to numbers in the margin and on The Catskills map.

4

If you have 2 days Focus on either the northern or southern Catskills. ▥ **Woodstock** ❶, which has a smattering of shops and restaurants, makes a good base in the northern Catskills. From here you can easily go hiking, canoeing, kayaking, tubing, or fishing, or go to see Kaaterskill Falls. The ski resorts are accessible from here as well: the ▥ **Hunter Mountain ski area** ❺, for example, is 19 mi to the north and the ▥ **Belleayre Mountain ski area** ❹ is about 30 mi to the west. The **Catskill Game Farm** ❻, about 25 mi north, is also doable from here. Or make quick jaunts into small villages in the area: ▥ **Mount Tremper** ❷ (which also makes a good base) and **Phoenicia** ❸ or, closer to Belleayre, Fleischmanns, Margaretville, and Arkville. Be sure to devote a few hours to exploring Woodstock.

In the southern Catskills the area around ▥ **Monticello** ⓬ has a few good lodging choices, including a magnificent inn in Forestburgh and a golf-focused resort in Kiamesha Lake. If you head west, you can see the site of the famed 1969 Woodstock music festival on the outskirts of Bethel. The area is known for golf and fishing, so you may want to spend time on either or both of these activities. The fishing town of **Roscoe** ⓫ is about 26 mi north of Monticello; if you're an avid angler, you'll want to base yourself here and focus on the fish. The Catskill Fly Fishing Center and Museum is in nearby Livingston Manor.

If you have 5 days During the warm-weather months, follow the two-day itinerary for the southern Catskills and then head to the northern Catskills on the morning of Day 3. Drive north on Route 17/I–86 to Route 30 and take that east into the ▥ **Belleayre Mountain ski area** ❹. Explore Fleischmanns, Margaretville, or Arkville in the afternoon, or go hiking or mountain biking. Spend Day 4 exploring **Woodstock** ❶ (driving through **Mount Tremper** ❷ and **Phoenicia** ❸ on the way back to your base) and leave Day 5 for Kaaterskill Falls. During ski season, spend only one day in the southern Catskills and devote much of the rest of the time to the ▥ **Hunter Mountain ski area** ❺, the ▥ **Belleayre Mountain ski area** ❹, or the ▥ **Windham ski area** ❼. In between time on the slopes, check out the surrounding villages. You may also want to spend a day in **Woodstock** ❶.

as buds strain to bursting on the branches. In summer the mountains fill with travelers roaming dense forests, splashing in cool rivers and watering holes, and attending myriad festivals. Leaves turn to golden amber, rich red, brilliant orange, and the occasional pink in autumn. In winter, bare, silvery branches stretch to the sky, laden with mounds of snow and icicles. The only time to avoid a visit is mud season, usually mid-March to mid-May, when the melting snow and rainfall turn the region into a gooey mess, and many businesses close.

THE NORTHERN CATSKILLS REGION
IN ULSTER, GREENE & DELAWARE COUNTIES

The lure of the northern Catskills seems obvious even at first glance: its verdant forests, undulating mountains, swiftly moving streams and rivers, meandering creeks, waterfalls, and abundance of wildlife are spectacular. But there is also a deep sense of mystery and spiritual vibrancy that has drawn visitors through the centuries and has come to characterize the region at least as much as its physical beauty. The looming, mist-shrouded Catskill Mountains were formed 2 million years ago after valley glaciers sliced through gray sandstone, giving them a bluish tint from a distance. Henry Hudson felt their pull in 1609, and was followed by Dutch and English colonists, who populated and farmed the fertile land in the small, upland valleys between the stony round-topped peaks over 3,500 feet in elevation. In the mid-19th century a group of artists led by Thomas Cole and Frederick Church, the rock stars of their day, followed old Indian trails into the deep clefts between the mountains and emerged with a series of cathedral-like, supernatural paintings that spoke to the popular imagination, drawing thousands of New York City urbanites to the mountains every summer in search of classic vistas and spawning an entire rugged tourism industry. More artists, writers and early environmentalists flocked to the area, followed in the 1900s by ethnic and religious groups looking to flee the heat and oppression of the city. Syrians, Armenians, Viennese, Ukrainians, Germans, Italians, Russians, Irish, and others came to the Catskills, giving it an indelible stamp that pervades the region today. The early environmentalists made their mark as well. Since 1904, 700,000 acres have been incorporated into the Catskill Park and Forest Preserve, with approximately 250,000 acres designated "forever wild."

As the old resorts faded with the advent of easy interstate highway travel, the region retrenched and accommodated itself to the long haul. Hunting and fishing are still significant draws, but the farms have slowly disappeared, supplanted along the major state highways by ski areas and other outdoor sports–oriented businesses catering to today's more active tourist. Today, hikers, climbers, kayakers and canoeists, bicyclists, and tubers join Bruderhof community members, Buddhists, and Orthodox and Hasidic Jews on the streets of mountain villages in summer; in winter most of these groups are gone, displaced by an influx of skiers from the New York metropolitan area, as well as a considerable number of snowmobilers and hardy ice climbers. Intrepid souls continue to flock to the northern Catskills, where dreamers, visionaries, artists, writers, poets, and musicians can still find a corner to call their own, and a community with which to share their talents.

4

Catskill Park
Designated a state treasure in 1904, Catskill Park spans Ulster, Green, Delaware, and Sullivan counties. It encompasses 700,000 acres of public and private land, and some of the wildest country south of Maine, with bears, coyotes, rattlesnakes, and other creatures. About 60 percent of the land is privately owned; the nearly 300,000 acres of state land within the park is called the Catskill Forest Preserve. The park has 200 mi of marked trails, campgrounds, ponds, lakes, and mountains; 98 peaks rising above 3,000 feet make for inspired hiking. At 4,190 feet, Slide Mountain is the highest of the Catskill peaks.

Fishing
Fly-fishing, one of the nation's greatest sports, is said to have gotten its start in the Catskills—more specifically, at Roscoe's Junction Pool, where the Willowemoc River runs into the Beaverkill. Serious anglers make it a point, at least once in their life, to fish the fabled waters around Roscoe, which is often called Trout Town, U.S.A. The state stocks brown trout to supplement the wild trout you can catch here. The Delaware River, another option, is much less heavily fished. Esopus Creek, which runs along part of Route 28 in and around Phoenicia, is one of the most productive wild-trout streams in the Northeast. Although the number of fish—mostly wild rainbow and brown trout, but also brook trout—in the Esopus is impressive, most fish are less than 12 inches in length.

Golf
When most people think of golfing in the Catskills, they think of the dozen-plus courses in Sullivan County. Indeed, several of the courses in the southern Catskills are highly rated and offer good value. Standouts include the Grossinger Country Club's Big G and Little G courses and the Concord Resort & Golf Club's Monster course; the course at the Villa Roma resort is another good option. For the best golf in the southern Catskills, however, detour to the Nevele Grand Resort & Country's Club's 27 holes, designed by Robert Trent Jones and Tom Fazio. The resort is in Ellenville, at the eastern edge of the Catskills. The northern Catskills aren't as well supplied with courses, but you can still find places to play, including the Windham Country Club course, which earns high marks. Regardless of where you play, the mountainous scenery provides a beautiful backdrop. Much of the terrain is rather curvy, with big elevation changes, but you'll also find gentler 9-hole courses.

Skiing
With several ski resorts and hundreds of trails, the Catskill Mountains draw loads of skiers. The northern Catskills, home to the region's main ski resorts—Hunter, Belleayre, and Windham, as well as the smaller and quieter Plattekill—see most of the action. Many skiers come for the weekend from the metro New York area, satisfied with vertical drops of 1,100 to 1,600 feet. The drive's not bad either: about 2½ to 3 hours from New York City. Buses also serve the ski areas. Facilities offer lessons and trails for all levels of experience. Snowboarding and snowtubing in terrain parks are popular too, in part thanks to the superlative snowmaking abilities of the area resorts. Winters here are usually long and cold, allowing for the season to stretch to six months.

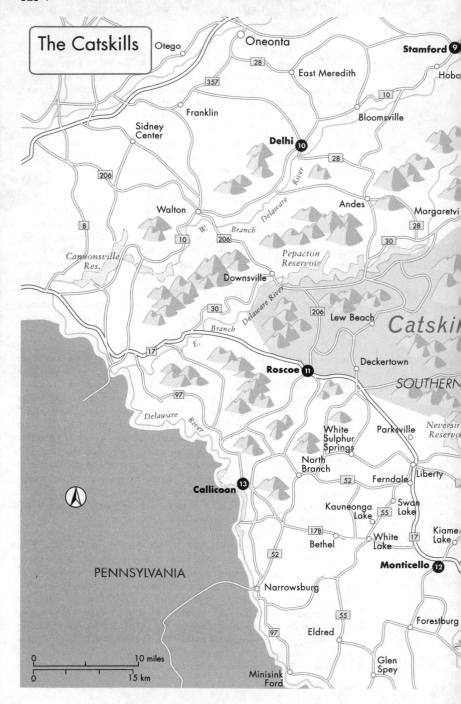

The Catskills

Otego
Oneonta
Stamford **9**
28
East Meredith
Hobo
357
10
Franklin
Bloomsville
Sidney
Center
Delhi 10
28
206
Andes
Margaretvi
Walton
W.
Branch
28
Delaware River
10
206
30
Pepacton Reservoir
8
Cannonsville
Res.
Downsville
30
Delaware River
206
Lew Beach
Catski
Branch
17
E.
Roscoe 11
Deckertown
SOUTHERN
97
White
Sulphur
Springs
Parksville
Neversi
Reservo
Delaware River
North
Branch
Callicoon 13
52
Ferndale
Liberty
Kauneonga
Lake
55
Swan
Lake
Kiame
Lake
17B
White
Lake
17
Bethel
Monticello 12
52
PENNSYLVANIA
Narrowsburg
55
Forestburg
97
Eldred
Glen
Spey
0   10 miles
0   15 km
Minisink
Ford

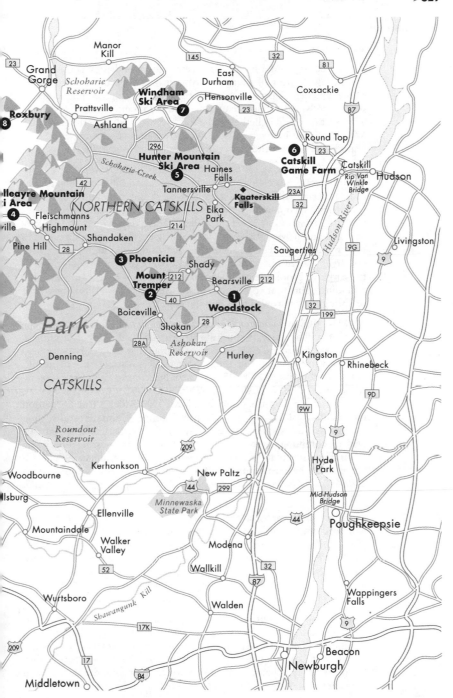

Manor
Kill

23 Grand
Gorge

*Schoharie
Reservoir*

145

East
Durham

32

81

Coxsackie

87

**Windham
Ski Area** 7

Hensonville

Prattsville

23

8 **Roxbury**

Ashland

Round Top

296

Schoharie Creek

**Hunter Mountain
Ski Area** 5

Haines
Falls

6 **Catskill
Game Farm**

23

Catskill
*Rip Van
Winkle
Bridge* Hudson

42

Tannersville

NORTHERN CATSKILLS

Elka
Park

**Kaaterskill
Falls** ♦

23A

32

4 **lleayre Mountain
i Area**

Fleischmanns

Highmount

214

Hudson River

Saugerties

9G

Livingston

•ille

28

Shandaken

9

Pine Hill

3 **Phoenicia**

Shady

**Mount
Tremper** 2 212

Bearsville

212

Boiceville

40

1
Woodstock

32

Park

Shokan

28

199

28A

*Ashokan
Reservoir*

Hurley

Kingston

Denning

Rhinebeck

CATSKILLS

9D

*Roundout
Reservoir*

9W

9

209

Hyde
Park

•Woodbourne

Kerhonkson

New Paltz

Mid-Hudson
Bridge

•lsburg

44

299

*Minnewaska
State Park*

44

Poughkeepsie

Ellenville

Mountaindale

Walker
Valley

Modena

52

Wallkill

32

87

Wurtsboro

Shawangunk Kill

Walden

Wappingers
Falls

17K

9

209

17

84

Beacon

Middletown

Newburgh

Woodstock

❶ *105 mi north of New York City.*

An arts colony and a haven for eccentricity, Woodstock is the almost mythical wellspring of alternative American culture and home to many of the now deified promulgators of the seemingly endless phenomenon of the 1960s. In having its name usurped for a seminal music festival in 1969 (actually held in Bethel, in the southwestern region of the Catskills), Woodstock has inadvertently been called upon to define an entire generation—or at least the amber-tinted soul of its lost youth.

Woodstock's main street hugs the small town green, where angst-ridden teenagers, musicians, political protesters, and the occasional pet parade convene. Although eclectic shops, art galleries, and a pervasive eccentricity help maintain the town's status as a countercultural magnet, the current scene is rather mellow. These days you're more likely to spot Land Rovers than VW buses in town, where aging hippies and baby boomers, families, and celebrities share sidewalks with out-of-towners. To enjoy Woodstock's charm, don't overlook the details—the gently gurgling brooks, the odd homegrown bench here and there, the twinkling lights that come on at dusk—and consider visiting in winter or spring, when crowds thin out and traffic eases.

Byrdcliffe. Ralph Radcliffe Whitehead, a wealthy Englishman under the sway of William Morris and John Ruskin, decided to create a utopian arts colony. His friend and conspirator Bolton Brown, an artist, suggested Woodstock; after a visit in 1902, Whitehead agreed. Here is the result: 300 acres dotted with 35 buildings, the only intact Arts and Crafts colony remaining on U.S. soil. Although Whitehead was considered dictatorial, his early efforts laid the groundwork for Woodstock's transformation into a colony of the arts. John Dewey, Thomas Mann, naturalist John Burroughs, and Isadora Duncan all fell under Byrdcliffe's spell. Artists, writers, composers, and dance and theater companies still call it home when they participate in its residency programs. Pamphlets in the mailbox outside the barn outline a self-guided walking tour. ⊠ *Upper Byrdcliffe Rd., off Glasco Tpke.* ☎ *845/679–2079* ⊕ *www.woodstockguild. org* ⌨ *Free.*

Center for Photography at Woodstock. If you come here, you're entering hallowed ground: what was once the Espresso Café, where Bob Dylan, Janis Joplin, and others entertained countercultural dreamers, remains indelibly imprinted on the town. Now a gallery space for photography, the center aims to provoke serious consideration of the medium, offering a dynamic series of exhibits, lectures, and workshops. ⊠ *59 Tinker St.* ☎ *845/679–9957* ⊕ *www.cpw.org* ⌨ *Free* ☉ *Wed.–Sun. noon–5.*

Karma Triyana Dharmachakra. A giant golden Buddha resides in the colorful shrine room of this Tibetan Buddhist monastery, where you can meditate or wander the grounds. Tours are given weekends at 1:30; stroll around to discover a fishpond, guesthouse, and solitary-retreat cabins. Because this is a religious center, you aren't allowed in the shrine room wearing shoes, hats, or revealing garments. Introductory instruction in *shinay* (mind-calming) meditation is also available. Call for the schedule or to make an appointment. The monastery is about 3 mi north of the village center. ⊠ *335 Meads Mountain Rd.* ☎ *845/679–5906 Ext. 10* ⊕ *www.kagyu.org* 🎟 *Free* ⊙ *Daily 6–6.*

Woodstock Artists Association Gallery. With three spaces able to run concurrent exhibitions, this gallery exercises its commitment to showing—and collecting—area artists' works in all mediums. One space has monthly group exhibits; another features solo shows of contemporary artists; and the Phoebe and Belmont Towbin Wing is devoted to art from the permanent collection. ⊠ *28 Tinker St.* ☎ *845/679–2940* 🎟 *Free* ⊙ *Thurs.–Mon. noon–5.*

Woodstock Artists Cemetery. Dead artists of all kinds reside here: poets, musicians, writers, painters, sculptors, dancers, and bons vivants. Many of the stones, in keeping with the wishes of their buried subjects, tell artfully rendered stories that reverberate in the bones of the living who pause overhead. Look for the grassy knoll behind the Evergreen Cemetery to commune with the spirits of Woodstock. ⊠ *On hill behind parking lot of Colony Cafe, which is at 22 Rock City Rd.* ☎ *No phone* 🎟 *Free.*

Woodstock Guild. A nonprofit arts organization with more than 600 members, the guild has been serving artists in the mid-Hudson Valley since 1939. Steward of the Byrdcliffe Arts Colony, the guild also oversees the **Fleur de Lis Gallery,** which showcases the works of 90-plus artisans, and hosts performing, visual, and literary artists at its **Kleinert/James Arts Center.** ⊠ *34 Tinker St.* ☎ *845/679–2079* ⊕ *www.woodstockguild.org* 🎟 *Free* ⊙ *Call for open days and hrs.*

off the beaten path

ELENA ZANG GALLERY – Meander through the terraced sculpture garden, past the babbling brook, several inspired birdhouses, and other delightful art objects to the studio of Elena Zang and Alan Hoffman, creators of minimalist functional pottery. Down the hill is the gallery space, where blond-wood floors and an infusion of light set off the contemporary art on the walls. Mary Frank, Judy Pfaff, and Joan Snyder are some of the contemporary luminaries exhibiting here. ⊠ *3671 Rte. 212, Shady* ☎ *845/679–5432* ⊕ *www.elenazang. com* 🎟 *Free* ⊙ *Daily 11–5.*

Where to Stay & Eat

$$–$$$ ✕ **Blue Mountain Bistro.** A barn with rough-hewn beams and siding from a corncrib makes for a cozy yet elegant atmosphere. The zinc tapas bar includes duck liver pâté, Moroccan carrot salad, and other goodies. Local wisdom holds that you can't get a bad meal here. Try mushroom *panzerotti* (pizzalike tart), jumbo sea scallops with wild-mushroom risotto, or *moules* Marseillaise, and see if you don't agree. Herb gardens border the outdoor patio. ⊠ *1633 Glasco Tpke.* ☎ *845/679–8519* ⚭ *Reservations essential* ▤ *AE, D, DC, MC, V* ⊙ *Closed Sun. and Mon.*

$$–$$$ ✕ **Joshua's.** At one of the oldest eateries on Woodstock's main street, the unassuming interior gives no hint of the wonders coming out of the

kitchen. The inventive Middle Eastern menu has zucchini flat cakes and tangy Cosmic Curry Chicken, which is served over brown-rice pilaf. Joshua's smorgasbord brings together hummus, baba ghanouj, tabbouleh, dolmas, and salad. ⊠ *51 Tinker St.* ☎ *845/679–5533* ▭ *AE, MC, V* ☺ *Closed Wed. in Jan.–Mar.*

$–$$$ ✕ **Bear Cafe.** Rock stars and actors find their way to this streamside restaurant 3 mi west of Woodstock, where a horseshoe bar adjoins two dining areas, one outdoors. Sit on the west side of the restaurant for an unfettered view of the Saw Kill stream. The patio is about as close to the water as you can get without falling in. The kitchen prepares American fare, such as its signature filet mignon dressed with port-garlic sauce and Stilton. The wine list includes 200 bottles from almost every continent, and ranges from $25 to $1,500. ⊠ *295A Tinker St., Bearsville* ☎ *845/679–5555* ▭ *MC, V* ☺ *Closed Tues. No lunch.*

¢–$$ ✕ **The Little Bear.** The wall of windows overlooking the Saw Kill inspires thoughts of feng shui as you ponder the extensive menu. Try chicken (or tofu) with honey walnuts or the vegetable–shark fin soup for two. Hunan shredded pork with black-bean sauce is one way to indulge carnivorous tendencies. The chef keeps it healthful by refusing to yield to the seduction of MSG, and the alert staff keeps things moving. ⊠ *295B Tinker St., Bearsville* ☎ *845/679–8899* ▭ *AE, MC, V.*

¢–$ ✕ **Taco Juan's.** The laid-back storefront eatery began as a humble stand behind the infamous Espresso Café. You can help yourself to utensils and sort your dirty dishes when you're finished. A rogues' gallery of Woodstock characters lines one wall. Nothing beats the enormous wet-tofu burrito; a scoop of Jane's homemade ice cream is the perfect chaser. Park benches outside provide front-row seats for watching bongo players on the village green. ⊠ *31 Tinker St.* ☎ *845/679–9673* ⚑ *Reservations not accepted* ▭ *No credit cards.*

$$$ ▦ **Woodstock Country Inn.** Hidden in a meadow of wildflowers several hundred yards from the quiet main road 2 mi west of Woodstock center, this bed-and-breakfast offers peaceful seclusion. The house includes paintings by Woodstock artist Jo Cantine, whose home this originally was, as well as hand-painted furnishings. Guest rooms keep frills to a minimum, instead offering simple luxuries such as 300-thread-count sateen sheets, mountain views, a porch or deck, and a private entrance. Breakfast is lavish and consists of organic fare. ⊠ *Cooper Lake Rd., 12498* ☎ *845/679–9380* ⊕ *www.woodstockcountryinn.com* ⚐ *3 rooms, 1 suite* ᗙ *Some cable TV, some kitchenettes, pool; no room phones, no TV in some rooms, no kids under 12, no smoking* ▭ *MC, V* ▮◯▮ *BP.*

$$–$$$ ▦ **Enchanted Manor.** The B&B eschews the farm aesthetic for the suburban. Seemingly endless decks lead to a heated pool, hot tub, and pond—all framed by 8 acres of forest. To enter the 1965 white-columned brick house you first must take off your shoes. A fireplace warms the large living room, where plush upholstery invites you to unwind. Cozy bedrooms and friendly hosts lend a comfortable vibe. The suite has its own living room and fireplace. ⊠ *23 Rowe Rd., 12401* ☎ *845/679–9012* ▤ *845/679–9871* ⊕ *www.enchantedmanorinn.com* ⚐ *2 rooms, 1 suite, 1 cabin (no bath in cabin)* ᗙ *Dining room, some in-room hot tubs, cable TV, in-room VCRs, pool, exercise equipment, outdoor hot tub,* *massage, laundry facilities; no room phones, no kids, no smoking* ▭ *AE, MC, V* 🍽 *BP.*

$$–$$$ **The Wild Rose Inn.** Beyond a white picket fence and a pleasant amble from central Woodstock is this rose-focused 1898 Victorian. Most rooms are draped in damask and organza swags and bedding. A dramatic, antique walnut-burl bed takes center stage in the Honeysuckle Rose Suite, which has a private entrance. The Sweetheart Room is the smallest of the accommodations, but the others are large. Complimentary brandy, truffles, and fruit add to the sweetness. The Continental breakfast is substantial. ✉ *66 Rock City Rd., 12498* ☎🖷 *845/679–8783* 🌐 *www.thewildroseinn.com* *2 rooms, 3 suites* *Dining room, in-room hot tubs, cable TV; no room phones, no smoking* ▭ *MC, V* 🍽 *CP.*

¢–$$ **Woodstock Inn on the Millstream.** Tall pines stand sentinel at this motel-style lodging, creating a private haven a short walk from the center of Woodstock. After splashing in the swimming hole you can relax on the landscaped lawn. In the rooms, more like B&B lodgings than motel units, hanging flower planters adorn front porches and quilts cover beds. The Continental breakfast spread is more bountiful than you might expect. ✉ *48 Tannery Brook Rd., 12498* ☎ *845/679–8211 or 800/420–4707* 🖷 *845/679–4550* 🌐 *www.woodstock-inn-ny.com* *11 rooms, 5 studios* *Some kitchenettes, cable TV with movies, Internet; no room phones* ▭ *AE, MC, V* 🍽 *BP.*

$ **Twin Gables.** The Victorian B&B in the center of Woodstock has served lodgers since the 1940s. Patterned wallpaper provides a backdrop for period furnishings and local artists' works. Several bedrooms share hall bathrooms. Shops, restaurants, and live-music venues are within strolling distance. ✉ *73 Tinker St., 12498* ☎ *845/679–9479* 🖷 *845/679–5638* 🌐 *www.twingableswoodstockny.com* *9 rooms, 6 with shared bath* *No room phones, no room TVs, no smoking* ▭ *AE, D, MC, V* 🍽 *CP.*

Nightlife & the Arts

NIGHTLIFE Local and national performers play at the **Colony Cafe** (✉ 22 Rock City Rd. ☎ 845/679–5342 🌐 www.colonycafe.com); after the first time, they always come back. A fireplace at one end and a stage at the other anchor the large space. Doors open at 7 nightly except Wednesday, when the place is closed; admission varies. Choose from beer, wine, espresso, and desserts. WDST, Woodstock's independent radio station, books top-notch acts that demonstrably enjoy performing at the open-to-the-elements **Woodstock Playhouse** (✉ Rtes. 212 and 375 ☎ 845/679–4101 🌐 www.woodstockplayhouse.org). You can expect to interact with the performers—if you're not pulled onto the stage, the performers may work their way through the crowd to you. Seating is stadium style, but you'll be hard-pressed to remain in your seat.

THE ARTS Hervey White broke with Ralph Whitehead to form his egalitarian enclave for the arts, Maverick, in the woods outside Woodstock. In order to subsidize his dream, White staged a music and dramatic festival in 1915, thus beginning the **Maverick Concert Series** (✉ 1 mi from junction of Rte. 375 and Maverick Rd. ☎ 845/679–8217 🌐 www.maverickconcerts.org), the country's oldest continuously running summer chamber-music series. Every summer since has seen a confluence of world-class musi-

Fodor's Choice ★

cians drawn by superlative acoustics in a chapel renowned by audiophiles. An open-admission policy reflects its beginnings as a collaborative colony of artists; the faithful gather early to secure good seats. The season runs from late June to early September.

Cinephiles flock to Woodstock for five autumnal days in September, when Hollywood converges with the fiercely independent for the well-regarded **Woodstock Film Festival** (☎ 845/679–4265 ⊕ www. woodstockfilmfestival.com). Celebrity-led seminars, film screenings, and raucous parties—most in Woodstock—find you pressing the flesh until morning. Poet laureates and Pulitzer Prize winners inspire the aspiring, read to the faithful, and hold workshops praising the muse during the **Woodstock Poetry Festival** (⌂ Box 450, 12498 ☎ No phone ⊕ www.woodstockpoetryfestival.com), held the last weekend in August. Venues include the Colony Cafe, the Maverick Concert Hall, and the Center for Photography at Woodstock.

Sports & the Outdoors

HIKING   Looming over Woodstock, **Overlook Mountain** (⌂ Off Meads Mountain Rd. ☎ 845/256–3000 ⊕ www.catskillcenter.org) has inspired generations of landscape artists as well as several rock musicians. The 3,140-foot peak offers one of the best views in the Catskills, on clear days taking in five neighboring states. On the way up the 2½-mi dirt road, an almost constant ascent, you see the ruins of the Overlook Mountain House, a once-grand hotel; an old fire tower is at the top. To get here from the Woodstock village green, turn onto Rock City Road. Proceed to the four-way stop, after which the road becomes Meads Mountain Road. Continue for another 2½ mi. The Overlook trailhead, and parking for it, are on the right, across the road from Karma Triyana Dharmachakra.

Stretching over 47,500 acres, the **Slide Mountain Wilderness** is the largest and most popular wilderness area in the Catskills. The area includes **Slide Mountain** (⌂ Off Rte. 47 10 mi south of Big Indian ☎ 607/652–7365, 607/652–5076, 607/652–5063 ⊕ www.dec.state.ny.us/website/outdoors), which at 4,190 feet is the range's highest peak, and encompasses several forest preserves. Its 35 mi of hiking trails take you over lofty peaks with spectacular views. The most straightforward way up Slide Mountain is via the Woodland Valley–Denning and Burroughs Range trails, accessed from the Slide Mountain trailhead parking area on Route 47, west of Woodstock. You trek 2.7 mi and climb 1,780 feet to the summit, where a plaque commemorates naturalist and poet John Burroughs.

Shopping

At **Golden Notebook** (⌂ 29 Tinker St. ☎ 845/679–8000), a venerable Woodstock institution open since 1978, the friendly staff helps you navigate the eclectic mix of local lore, children's books, fiction, and other titles. Wander through the labyrinth and you come across the Golden Bough, an adjacent gift shop. At **Loominus** (⌂ 3257 Rte. 212, Bearsville ☎ 845/679–6500), scarves, shawls, jackets, vests, hats, and pillows fashioned from piles of lush chenille fill the front of the store. Behind the counter women work sewing machines, trying to keep pace with orders from Barneys and Bergdorf. Incense tickles your nose as you enter **Mirabai** (⊠ 23 Mill Hill Rd. ☎ 845/679–2100), a decidedly spiritual bookstore. Crystals give way to books, tapes, and myriad other objects to help the flow of your chi. Two former Condé Nast graphic designers revamped Woodstock's old post office into the **Woodstock Wool Company** (⊠ 105 Tinker St. ☎ 845/679–0400), a 3,000-square-foot tribute to wool. A boisterous young crowd attends monthly karaoke-knitting sessions at this sleek contemporary space—this is not your grandmother's knitting store.

Mount Tremper

② *10 mi west of Woodstock.*

A Woodstock neighbor and home to the acclaimed Zen Mountain Monastery, Mount Tremper has attracted its share of artists and weekenders seeking a less-expensive address. The village sits along Esopus Creek, which lures anglers and is a popular spot for tubing. There's no precious shopping district here, just a few good restaurants worth checking out.

Emporium at Emerson Place. A darkened 60-foot silo, once used to store grain and animal feed, houses an enormous **kaleidoscope.** From the silo, wander through the cobblestone courtyard of this retail complex, where upscale boutiques sell clothing, furniture and antiques. ⊠ *146 Mount Pleasant Rd.* ☎ *845/688–5800* ⊕ *www.emersonplace.com* ☞ *Kaleidoscope $7* ☉ *Mid-Sept.–May, Wed.–Mon. 10–5; June–mid-Sept., daily 10–6.*

Zen Mountain Monastery. The monastery resides in a four-story bluestone–and–white oak church on 230 acres bordered by the Beaverkill and Esopus rivers. The building, constructed by Norwegian craftsmen at the turn of the 20th century, includes a 150-person meditation hall, a dining hall, and resident and guest quarters. The only way to visit is to partake in introductory Zen instruction, offered Wednesday evening and as weekend retreats, or in the Sunday session of services, *zazen* (or sitting) meditation, and lunch. ⊠ *South Plank Rd., off Rte. 212* ☎ *845/ 688–2228* ⊕ *www.mro.org* ☞ *Wed. free; Sun. $5 donation* ☉ *Wed. 7:30 PM–9 PM, Sun. 8:45 AM–noon.*

Where to Stay & Eat

$$–$$$ ✕ **La Duchesse Ann.** As you pull into the gravel driveway and climb the steps of this 1850s Victorian, visions of Grandma's house dance in your head. Crushed velvet and floral paper cover the walls, and period antiques grace dark rooms. Diners come from miles around to savor such French dishes as *cotriade bretonne* (fish stew), rack of lamb, and Black Angus steak with peppercorn-cognac cream sauce in formal surroundings with a glowing fireplace. ⊠ *1564 Wittenberg Rd.* ☎ *845/688–5260* ☐ *AE, D, MC, V* ☉ *Closed Wed.*

$$ ✕ **Catskill Rose.** Architectural glass blocks flank a magenta door, hinting at the funky art-deco motif inside. Herb gardens line the restaurant's perimeter, with brightly painted window boxes above. If you want to eat alfresco, head for the periwinkle tables and chairs on the brick courtyard. The menu, which changes with the seasons and is mostly New American, might include smoked duck with tamarind-raspberry sauce

or poached salmon flavored with lemon and basil. ✉ *5355 Rte. 212* ☎ *845/688–7100* 🖃 *D, DC, MC, V* ⊘ *Closed Mon.–Wed. No lunch.*

★ **$$$$**   ✕🏠 **The Emerson Inn & Spa.** You're cosseted from the minute you pull up to this 1870s Victorian building. Before you know it, your car is parked, your luggage is delivered to your room, and you're accepting a flute of champagne. Persian, Victorian, West Indies colonial, African, and Asian decorative schemes are manifested in tailored leopard-print curtains, Asian and African artifacts, fringed lampshades, and embroidered pillows. Bedrooms have cordless phones and Frette linens. One suite has a sauna; the duplex has two bathrooms and an indoor hammock. Fine china and crystal dress tables in the restaurant ($$–$$$$), where Continental fare meets contemporary flair. Roast rack of lamb, for instance, is paired with Parmesan soufflé. At the serene spa, which is open to the public, you may indulge in everything from algae wraps to shiatsu. ✉ *146 Mount Pleasant Rd., 12457* ☎ *845/688–7900 or 800/525–4800* 🖷 *845/688–2789* ∰ *www.theemerson.com* ⇨ *20 rooms, 4 suites* ⚴ *Restaurant, in-room data ports, some in-room hot tubs, exercise equipment, spa, mountain bikes, concierge, meeting rooms; no TV in some rooms, no kids under 13, no smoking* 🖃 *AE, D, DC, MC, V* †⊙† *BP.*

$$$–$$$$ 🏠 **Kate's Lazy Meadow Motel.** The exterior of this single-story 1950s motel reveals little of what's inside the meticulously appointed suites, owned by Kate Pierson of the B-52s and kept clean by Lady Estrogen, the drag-queen maid. The funky decor includes vintage pieces—Eames furniture, Russel Wright kitchenware—as well as custom wallpaper and handcrafted bathroom tiles and shower curtains. Most of the suites have a mint '50s kitchen and a sitting area with a gas fireplace; some suites have sleeping lofts and private decks. Lush gardens designed by Dean Riddle (a nationally known garden writer and green thumb) surround the red motel. A bonfire pit overlooks Esopus Creek, where you can fish for trout or—thanks to the motel's wireless Internet access—read e-mail on your laptop. ✉ *5191 Rte. 28, 12457* ☎ *845/688–7200* 🖷 *845/688–2447* ∰ *www.lazymeadow.com* ⇨ *7 suites* ⚴ *BBQs, in-room data ports, minibars, microwaves, refrigerators, some kitchens, cable TV, in-room VCRs, hot tub, fishing, Internet; no kids under 14, no smoking* 🖃 *AE, D, DC, MC, V.*

$$–$$$ 🏠 **Lodge at Emerson Place.** Antler chandeliers and a folksy mural greet you in the lobby; a welcome basket of fruit and wine awaits in your room. Plaid blanket–draped Adirondack twig beds and log walls are part of the country-cabin look. Some rooms have fireplaces and views of Esopus Creek. Access to the spa facilities at the Emerson Inn, the lodge's nearby sister property, is $15. ✉ *5368 Rte. 28, 12457* ☎ *845/688–2828* ∰ *www.catskillcorners.com* ⇨ *12 rooms, 15 suites* ⚴ *Restaurant, in-room data ports, in-room safes, some in-room hot tubs, refrigerators, cable TV, babysitting, some pets allowed (fee); no smoking* 🖃 *AE, D, MC, V* †⊙† *CP.*

★ **$$–$$$**   🏠 **Onteora the Mountain House.** Spectacular Catskills vistas leave you breathless at this B&B, the former summer home of mayonnaise magnate Richard Hellman. A massive stone fireplace presides over the great room, a truly great space with a soaring ceiling. Oriental rugs, scattered across wide-plank honey-colored floors, cushion your every step, and Asian antiques and American pieces enjoy an elegant coexistence. A couple of rooms have fireplaces, and one has a window seat with dazzling valley views. You may play billiards in the cavernous game room, or sweat it out in the sauna. Weekends in May through August usually book up a year in advance. ⊠ *96 Piney Point Rd., Boiceville 12412* 🏠🏠 *845/ 657–6233* ⊕ *www.onteora.com* ⤴ *4 rooms, 1 suite* ⚭ *Some in-room hot tubs, sauna, billiards, hiking; no a/c, no room phones, no room TVs, no kids under 12, no smoking* ⊟ *D, MC, V* ⧇ *BP.*

CAMPING ⚠ **Kenneth L. Wilson Campground.** At this campground, part of the Catskill Forest Preserve camping system, tall pine trees surround sites, which are near a lake with a sand beach. The lake includes chain pickerel, yellow perch, bullheads, white sucker, shiners, and sunfish. Fishing licenses are available at the campground, as are rowboat, canoe, paddleboat, and kayak rentals. The grounds, originally several farms, lie in the valley of Little Beaver Kill, a tributary of Esopus Creek. Each site has a picnic table and grill. Self-contained RVs are welcome. ⚭ *Flush toilets, dump station, showers, grills, picnic tables, public telephone, swimming (lake)* ⊠ *859 Wittenberg Rd., 12457* ☎ *845/679–7020, 800/456–2267 reservations* 🏠*845/679–6533* ⊕*www.dec.state.ny.us* ⤴*76 tent sites* 🗲*$17* ⚓*Reservations essential* ⊟ *MC, V* ☉ *Closed Columbus Day–Apr.*

Sports & the Outdoors

CANOEING & The owner of **Cold Brook Canoes** (⊠ 4181 Rte. 28, Boiceville ☎ 845/
KAYAKING 657–2189), Ernie Gardner began selling canoes out of his garage in 1970. Since then his selection has expanded, and the garage now overflows with canoes, kayaks, flotation devices, wet bags, and anything else you need to spend a day on the water. Ernie, who's always friendly, can also point you to the best paddling spots.

FISHING An especially productive area of Esopus Creek is just south of Boiceville (3 mi south of Mount Tremper), near the Ashokan Reservoir, where you may catch smallmouth bass and walleye in addition to wild rainbow trout, brown trout, and brook trout. Through **Ed's Fly Fishing & Guide Services** (⊠ 69 Ridge Rd., Shokan ☎ 845/657–6393), you can learn to fly-fish for trout in Esopus Creek or the Delaware or Neversink rivers for $150 a day. Because Ed doesn't take out more than three people at a time, personal attention is pretty much guaranteed. Book several weeks in advance, especially in spring and fall, and be sure to secure a New York State fishing permit.

Shopping

Soapbox-derby entries mingle with sculpture at **Fabulous Furniture** (⊠ Rte. 28, Boiceville ☎ 845/657–6317). Around back, owner Steve Heller does unimaginable things to rotting or dead wood and old Cadillacs and other cars. Inside are the amazing results: custom-made tables with tree-trunk bases, lamps, menorahs, and mirrors.

Phoenicia

❸ *8 mi north of Mount Tremper.*

Since the 1990s, when hipsters discovered this tiny hamlet—formerly boondocks—Phoenicia has been undergoing a transformation. The number of creative individuals who have found the natural world narcotic and have settled here, establishing funky boutiques and fine restaurants, is growing. Many out-of-towners come to Phoenicia to go tubing down Esopus Creek, and the Hunter and Belleayre ski resorts are an easy trip through the High Peaks area from here.

Upstate Art. A blue-sequined sign lures you inside this gallery. Upstairs, six brightly lighted rooms exhibit contemporary regional artists. Nita Friedman has been running the gallery since the late 1990s, and has created a place where lively openings draw local artists out of their homes in the surrounding wooded hills. ⊠ *60 Main St.* ☎ *845/688–9881* 🖅 *Free* ۞ *Call for hrs or to make an appointment.*

Where to Stay & Eat

¢–$ ✕ **Sweet Sue's.** French doors open into a bright, airy space filled with white wooden booths, marble-top café tables, and a stainless-steel counter where trays of fresh muffins cool. Folksy renditions of the house specialties decorate one wall; a blackboard announcing specials resides on another. Robert DeNiro haunts this place, as do other area glitterati. You'll see why when you tuck into the Blue Monkey, a stack of blueberry-banana buttermilk pancakes. Pumpkin-crusted tofu over polenta and sautéed kale topped with roasted red-pepper sauce are served alongside hot meat-loaf sandwiches and other comfort food. Efficient, friendly service caters to your needs. Take a note from the locals, who come armed with newspapers and books and stay a while. Reservations are essential on weekends. ⊠ *33 Main St.* ☎ *845/688–7852* ▭ *No credit cards* ۞ *Closed Tues. and Wed.*

CAMPING   ⚠ **Woodland Valley State Park Campground.** The woodsy sites here, with trails leading to Wittenberg and Cornell mountains, are favorites with hikers. Some sites are next to Woodland Valley Stream, which teems with fish. Fishing licenses are available. Self-contained RVs are welcome. ⚭ *Flush toilets, dump station, showers, picnic tables, public telephone* ⊠ *1319 Woodland Valley Rd., 12464* ☎ *845/688–7647* ⤶ *72 tent sites* 🖅 *$15* ⚭ *Reservations essential* ▭ *MC, V* ۞ *Closed mid-Oct.–mid-May.*

Nightlife & the Arts

The **Shandaken Theatrical Society** (⊠ Church St. ☎ 845/688–2279) produces a show each season: a spring musical, a summer melodrama, a fall comedy or drama, and a winter holiday event. Past performances include *Cabaret, Harvey,* and *The Sound of Music.*

Sports & the Outdoors

HIKING   Two trails lead you to the summit of **Tremper Mountain** (☎ 607/652–7365, 607/652–5076, 607/652–5063 ⊕ www.catskillcenter.org), where an early-20th-century fire tower stands. The red-blazed Phoenicia Trail, the much shorter but steeper of the two, begins off Route 40 about 1 mi southeast of Phoenicia and climbs the western side of the mountain for 2¾ mi to the summit (at 2,740 feet). The 4.2-mi Willow Trail starts just west of the post office in the village of Willow, on Route 212 about 5 mi southeast of Phoenicia.

TUBING   **F-S Tube and Raft Rentals** (⊠ 4 Church St. ☎ 845/688–7633 ⊕ www.catskillpark.com/fs.html), a tubing outfitter, offers a 4-mi run down Esopus Creek. A lower 3-mi course encounters milder rapids and is more appropriate for families. Children must be at least nine years old to go tubing. The season runs from Memorial Day to the third week in September; $10 covers tube rental and transport.

The red barn that stands guard as you enter Phoenicia houses the **Town Tinker** (⊠ 10 Bridge St. ☎ 845/688–5553 ⊕ www.towntinker.com), which has everything you need to spend a day riding the rapids or drifting on the currents of the Esopus. From mid-May through September you can rent tubes for beginner and advanced routes on Esopus Creek between Shandaken and Mount Pleasant. Don't feel like hiking back? Get out at a designated spot for a ride to Phoenicia on the Catskill Mountain Railroad. Tube and transport are $15. Children must be older than 12, and only strong swimmers should consider this.

Shopping

Garden gnomes occupy the front window of **Morne Imports** (⊠ 52 Main St. ☎ 845/688–7738), and camping and hunting gear hangs precariously above their heads. The general store sells everything you need to tackle nature, from fishing rods and hand-tied flies to hunting knives. Home goods are artfully displayed at **The Tender Land** (⊠ 45 Main St. ☎ 845/688–2001), a sophisticated country housewares shop. After browsing here, head down the street to Tender Land Home, a complementary contemporary store filled with small—aka easily transportable—delights. Chic pottery and luscious pillows, window treatments, and rugs make you want to move in.

Belleayre Mountain Ski Area

❹ *Highmount is 12 mi northwest of Phoenicia.*

Some of the villages and hamlets close to Belleayre have been experiencing a resurgence, spurred by an influx of city folk escaping the rat race. In Margaretville, 9 mi east of Belleayre, boutiques and upscale restaurants are beginning to stake a claim. A couple of miles before Margaretville is Arkville; blink and you might miss this tiny place, home to the Erpf Cultural Center. With half a dozen restaurants and places to stay, Pine Hill, a stone's throw from the Highmount-based ski resort, bustles by comparison. In Fleischmanns, 3 mi east of Belleayre, locals sit on their porches and Orthodox Jewish families stroll down the sleepy Main Street. Shandaken, at the junction of Routes 42 and 28, sits beside Esopus Creek.

Catskill Center for Conservation and Development. The center helps villages and hamlets in the region get grants for beautification and other economic stimulation programs. Its gallery in the **Erpf Cultural Center** hosts rotating exhibits of regional artists' works, with a focus on nature-inspired pieces. You can take part in a busy schedule of twice-monthly public events, including hikes, canoe trips, bird-watching, and lectures. ⊠ *43355 Rte. 28, Arkville* ☎ *845/586–2611* ⊕ *www.catskillcenter. org* ☑ *Free* ☉ *Weekdays 9–5, Sat. 10–2.*

Where to Stay & Eat

$$–$$$ ✕ **Loretta Charles' Natural Wood Grill.** Most dishes involve seafood at this New American restaurant overlooking Esopus Creek. The dining

room is rustic, with picture windows with water views and a wood-burning fireplace. The blackboard menu, which changes weekly, might include Thai-style grilled shrimp with chilies and garlic served with basmati rice. The food is all grilled over hickory and cherrywood, and entrées come with at least four vegetables. A piano player entertains at an upright in the dining room Friday and Saturday nights. ✉ *7159 Rte. 28, Shandaken* ☎ *845/688–2550* ▭ *AE, D, MC, V* ☺ *Closed Mon.–Wed. No lunch.*

$$ ✕ **Café on Main.** The menu changes every two weeks at this small café with chocolate-colored walls and matching toile-and-gingham tablecloths, but you always find fish and vegetarian entrées (and sometimes frogs' legs). The food is mostly Continental; the chef uses fresh local produce and is known for his osso bucco and calves liver. The walls serve as gallery space for local artists. ✉ *The Commons, Main St., Margaretville* ☎ *845/586–2343* ⚑ *Reservations essential* ▭ *AE, MC, V* ☺ *Closed Tues. No lunch.*

$–$$ ✕ **Pine Hill Arms Hotel.** The 1882 country inn has two dining rooms—the Catskill Mountain Room, with rustic barn-wood siding, and the Greenhouse Room—and a bar. Among the draws: charcoal-broiled steaks, blackened red snapper, a wide range of desserts, and the hearty country-style breakfast. The aprés ski crowd packs the place on winter weekends, when live bands play. ✉ *Main St., Pine Hill* ☎ *845/254–4012 or 800/932–2446* ▭ *AE, D, MC, V* ☺ *Closed Mon. and Tues. No lunch weekdays or Sun.*

$–$$ ✕ **Pine Hill Indian Restaurant.** Framed Indian textiles and embroidered curtains set the stage for tasty tandoori chicken, chicken korma, *biriani* (a layered dish of spicy meat and rice), and other Indian specialties. On weekend nights you can sample a chunk of the menu during an all-you-can-eat buffet; $12.95 lets you choose from a dozen entrées (many vegetarian) and includes dessert and coffee. You can bring your own beer or wine to accompany the meal or choose a refreshing *lassi* (a cold yogurt drink). ✉ *143 Main St., Pine Hill* ☎ *845/254–6666* ▭ *AE, D, MC, V* ☺ *Closed Tues. and Wed.*

¢–$ ✕ **El Rey Mexican Restaurant.** Traditional Mexican celebration banners in bright red, green, yellow, and pink hang from the ceiling of this convivial spot, where locals flock for good, inexpensive food. The menu leans toward Tex-Mex fare: fajitas, enchiladas, burritos, and tostadas. The salsa, infused with cilantro, is available to go, and diners inevitably grab a quart to take home. ✉ *297 Main St., Pine Hill* ☎ *845/254–6027* ▭ *MC, V* ☺ *Closed Tues.*

¢   ✕ **The Cheese Barrel.** Locals come to this upscale deli-grocery for breakfast and lunch or to pick up specialty ingredients. You can eat a sandwich or sip an organic-coffee drink at one of the café tables in the simple dining area. While waiting, study shelves of vinegars, olives, old-fashioned candy, and Italian lemonade. ✉ *Main St., Margaretville* ☎ *845/586–4666* ▭ *MC, V* ☺ *No dinner.*

¢–$ ▦ **Birch Creek Inn.** The antiques-filled 1896 inn is nestled on 23 acres in the woods and bounded by streams, stone bridges, and slate walks. The vintage billiards room has a pool table, piano, and board games; the library has a fireplace. Most guest rooms are spacious and furnished in a romantic country style, with floral fabrics and lace touches on canopy or sleigh beds and windows. The separate cottage suite has a queen bed, a gas fireplace, and a kitchenette. ⊠ *Rte. 28, Pine Hill 12465* ☎ *845/254–5222* ⊕ *www.abirchcreekinn.com* ➬ *8 rooms, 1 suite* ♨ *Dining room, fans, some kitchenettes, some refrigerators, cable TV, pool, exercise equipment, hot tub, fishing, billiards, hiking, library, piano, babysitting, Internet; no a/c, no room phones, no smoking* ▭ *AE, D, MC, V* ⦿ *BP.*

¢–$ 🏨 **Highlands Inn.** Fragrant lavender blooms near the entrance to this 1904 late Victorian. Original inlaid parquet floors and chestnut trim run through the 3,000 square feet of common space, which includes a sunroom, a library with an upright piano, two dining rooms, and a lounge with a 73-inch TV, a gas fireplace, leather couches, and a pool table. Guest rooms are outfitted in florals, toiles, or country quilts. Some have twin beds; all have private sinks. Third-floor rooms are nestled under the eaves. ⊠ *923 Main St., Fleischmanns 12430* ☎ *845/254–5650* ⊟ *845/254–6571* ⊕ *www.thehighlandsinn.com* ➬ *7 rooms, 3 with bath* ♨ *Dining room, fans, billiards, boccie, croquet, library, piano, Internet, business services; no a/c, no room phones, no room TVs, no smoking* ▭ *MC, V* ⦿ *BP.*

¢–$ 🏨 **Margaretville Mountain Inn.** The 1886 Queen Anne Victorian occupies 6 acres atop Margaretville Mountain, on the site of what was the region's first cauliflower farm. Bluestone steps lead to the 80-foot porch, where you can sit on wicker love seats and chairs while taking in sweeping views of the Catskill Mountains. Lace curtains veil the windows, and vintage photographs line the stairs leading to rooms with antiques. One room has a dramatic canopied brass bed. Breakfast is served on Royal Dalton china in a formal dining room. A hot tub occupies the old milk house. ⊠ *1478 Margaretville Mountain Rd., Margaretville 12455* ☎ *845/586–3933* ⊟ *845/586–1699* ⊕ *www.margaretvilleinn.com* ➬ *6 rooms* ♨ *Dining room, fans, some cable TV, hot tub, fishing, badminton, boccie, croquet, ski storage, babysitting, playground, some pets allowed (fee); no a/c, no room phones, no TV in some rooms, no smoking* ▭ *AE, MC, V* ⦿ *BP.*

¢–$ 🏨 **River Run Bed & Breakfast Inn.** Garden gnomes greet you on the front porch of this Queen Anne Victorian. The smell of freshly baked muffins permeates the 1887 house, which has antiques, original stained glass, and a pictorial history of the innkeeper's family. The suite, decorated with '50s furnishings and retro floral prints, has two bedrooms, two bathrooms, a private entrance, and a kitchen. You can fly fish for brown trout at the edge of the 1-acre yard, where the Bushkill Stream flows by old stone retaining walls, or wander through a stone labyrinth. A full vegetarian breakfast is served. ⊠ *882 Main St., Fleischmanns 12430* ☎ *845/254–4884* ⊕ *www.catskill.net/riverrun* ➬ *8 rooms, 4 with bath; 1 suite* ♨ *Dining room, picnic area, fans, refrigerator in common area, some kitchens, some cable TV, some in-room VCRs, fishing, library, babysitting, Internet, some pets allowed (fee); no a/c, no room phones, no TV in some rooms, no smoking* ▭ *MC, V* ⦿ *BP.*

Nightlife & the Arts

Lyle Lovett, the Neville Brothers, Herbie Hancock, and the Alvin Ailey American Dance Theater are among the performers who have appeared at the annual **Belleayre Music Festival** (⊠ Belleayre Mountain Ski Center, off Rte. 28, Highmount ☎ 845/254–5600 or 800/942–6904 ⊕ www.belleayre.com), held Saturday nights in July and August. Friday nights in August bring the Jazz Club, when the audience dances up a storm under the stars.

Sports & the Outdoors

SKI AREA The **Belleayre Mountain Ski Center** (⊠ Belleayre Mountain Rd., off Rte. 28, Highmount ☎ 845/254–5600 or 800/942–6904 ⊕ www.belleayre.com), in the Catskill Forest Preserve, has one section for expert skiers and another for intermediates and novices. Of the 38 trails that vein the peak's 171 acres of skiable terrain, 22% are for beginners and 58% are for intermediate skiers; the vertical drop is 1,404 feet. The resort, owned by the New York State Department of Environmental Conservation, has 96% snowmaking capability, eight lifts, and more than 5 mi of cross-country trails. Families appreciate the laid-back atmosphere, whereas serious skiers seek out the great snow, grooming, and single- and double-black-diamond trails. Skiing and snowboarding instruction and rentals are available. Full-day peak-season lift tickets are $42. A shuttle transports skiiers to and from nearby villages. From late April through October, the upper, lower, and cross-country areas offer biking tracks for beginners to experts; lifts aren't equipped for bikes, so you have to ride in both directions. From Memorial Day through Labor Day you may also swim, boat, and fish at Pine Hill Lake ($6 per car), where pedal boats, rowboats, and kayaks are for rent. A lift ($8 per person) takes you to the summit, from which you can hike or ride the lift back down. Belleayre hosts crafts, music, and other festivals, too.

Shopping

The Commons, a rustic version of a mini-mall, is home to **Frog's Leap** (⊠ The Commons, Main St., Margaretville ☎ 845/586–4466), which sells handcrafted, environmentally friendly, fair trade–oriented goods. Browse through piles of felt pillows, slippers, and wall hangings from Kyrgyzstan; gaze into mirrors from Israel; or choose from jewelry, home wares, candles, or natural oils. Owner Roger Mabery ships anywhere. Vintage housewares sit alongside Nigella Lawson's kitchen line at **Home Goods of Margaretville** (⊠ The Commons, Main St., Margaretville ☎ 845/586–4177), an emporium with everything for anyone who cooks or entertains. Le Creuset cast-iron pots, neat dish towels, and cookbooks fill the large, bright store. The nearly 7,000 square-foot **Margaretville Antique Center** (⊠ 801 Main St., Margaretville ☎ 845/586–2424), formerly a 1922 theater, holds a broad cross section of antiques and collectibles.

You never know what might be for sale at **Roberts' Auction Service** (⊠ 820 Main St., Fleischmanns ☎ 845/254–4490 ⊕ www.roberts-auction.com). The whole town—and antiques dealers from near and far—turns out for Saturday night auctions, held at 7, and the bidding can turn fierce. You can stop by Saturday afternoon to check out what will hit the auction block that night.

Hunter Mountain Ski Area

⑤ *Hunter is 12 mi northeast of Phoenicia.*

Nestled in the shadow of Hunter Mountain, the second-highest mountain in the Catskills, the village of Hunter is all about the slopes. On winter weekends thousands of skiers flock to the area, the oldest of the Catskill ski resorts. Although it was once dominated by twentysomething rowdies from the New York metropolitan area and still provides, along with nearby Tannersville (5 mi east), a raucous nightlife scene, Hunter is becoming more family oriented. In other seasons, fairs and special events, including a well-known Oktoberfest, are held here. The village's permanent arts scene, mostly the work of the not-for-profit Catskill Mountain Foundation (CMF), includes a gallery, movie theater, bookstore, and performing-arts center.

Hunter Mountain Skyride. A lift takes you over 1 mi to the 3,200-foot summit of Hunter Mountain, where you can look out at the Catskill, Berkshire, and Green mountain ranges. The autumn foliage is a knockout. ⊠ *Rte. 23A, Hunter* ☎ *518/263–4223 or 800/486–8376* ⊕ *www.huntermtn.com* ⊠ *$6* ☉ *Early July–Aug., Wed. noon–4 and weekends 10–5; Sept.–early Oct., weekends 10–5.*

Mountain Top Arboretum. The 11 acres of this preserve and garden are part of a 21-acre experiment that was begun in the late 1970s to see which temperate trees could grow at 2,500 feet above sea level. Wooded paths weave past lush ferns, oaks, beech, rhododendron, and mountain laurel. A circular path leads to a large, open meadow filled with finches, warblers, orioles, thrushes, sapsuckers, bluebirds, turkeys, and hummingbirds. In spring you may see ducks and geese at the pond, where great blue herons have moved in. ⊠ *Rte. 23C and Maude Adams Rd., Tannersville* ☎ *518/589–3903* ⊕ *www.mtarbor.org* ⊠ *Free* ☉ *April–Nov., daily dawn–dusk.*

FESTIVALS & FAIRS

Celtic Festival. Caber tossing, Irish step dancing, and a march of bagpipers down Hunter Mountain are just some of what you can expect during this celebration of all things Celtic, held the second weekend in August. ⊠ *Rte. 23A, Hunter* ☎ *518/263–4223 or 800/486–8376* ⊕ *www.huntermtn.com.*

Mountain Culture Festival. World musicians join local artisans and farmers for a two-day celebration of mountain life on the second weekend in July. Displays of handmade quilts, woodworking, and farm animals bring people from miles around to the streets of Hunter. Athletes compete at the Masters of the Mountains bike race. ⊠ *Rte. 23 A, Hunter* ☎ *518/263–4908 Ext. 202* ⊕ *www.catskillmtn.org.*

Oktoberfest. The Hunter Mountain ski resort stands in for the Alps during the first two weekends of October, when the harvest is celebrated with German and Austrian music, food, and dance. Watch men imitate courting rituals of the wood grouse during traditional dances; after a couple of beers, you may be tempted to try it yourself. Kids get free pumpkins. ⊠ *Rte. 23A, Hunter* ☎ *518/263–4223 or 800/486–8376* ⊕ *www.huntermtn.com.*

to Stay & Eat

...want to stay right on the slopes, consider booking a condo rental ...ugh the Hunter Mountain resort (☎ 518/263–4223, 800/486–8376, ...6/486–8376). Its modern condo cluster, called Liftside, is at the base of Hunter Mountain.

$ ✕ **Chateau Belleview.** The French restaurant, about a five-minute drive east of Hunter, has a Tudor facade, two dining rooms with fireplaces, walls of windows with mountain views, an outdoor deck, and a vast lawn where kids can run and play while their parents sup. Roast duck is the signature dish here; steak *au deux poivres* (with black and green peppercorns) in brandy cream sauce is also popular. ⊠ *Rte. 23A, Tannersville* ☎ *518/589–5525* ▭ *AE, D, MC, V* ☉ *Closed Tues. No lunch.*

$$–$$$ ✕ **Mountain Brook.** A space with high wood ceilings and a fireplace, this eatery serves an upscale version of comfort food: meat loaf with creamy chive mashed potatoes, grilled filet of tuna in ginger-soy marinade, Black Angus steak with black-truffle butter, and endive-and-radicchio salad with local goat cheese. A wall of windows overlooks Hunter Mountain and Schoharie Creek. ⊠ *Main St./Rte. 23A, Hunter* ☎ *518/263–5351* ▭ *MC, V* ☉ *Closed Tues. and Wed. No lunch.*

$–$$ ✕ **Last Chance Cheese and Antiques Café.** Antiques hang from the rafters, crowd into corners, and fill every nook and cranny of this restaurant and gourmet shop, in business since 1971. You can hang out on the front porch, choose from a selection of 320 beers, and dig into a hearty "knishwich" of potato knish, coleslaw, melted cheddar, pastrami, and turkey. A quick browse through the emporium yields artisanal cheeses, imported *soppressata* (a type of Italian salami), and baskets of old-fashioned candy. ⊠ *602 Main St./Rte. 23A, Tannersville* ☎ *518/589–6424* ▭ *AE, D, MC, V* ☉ *Closed Mon.–Thurs. in early Sept.–early Dec.*

¢–$$ ✕ **Yacht Club Restaurant.** Floor-to-ceiling windows overlook a small creek, a forest, the slopes of Hunter Mountain, and wraparound decks at this restaurant-nightclub. You can choose your own crustacean from the lobster tank, order a steak, or share a pizza. Night owls who crowd in for weekend laser-light shows, DJs, live bands, and dancing after a day of skiing order off the late-night menu of standard bar fare. ⊠ *6001 Main St./Rte. 23A, Hunter* ☎ *518/589–0039* ▭ *MC, V* ☉ *No lunch.*

¢–$ ✕ **Maggie's Krooked Café.** At this laid-back eatery with homemade muffins piled on the counter you can have breakfast all day—well, at least until closing time, at 4 or 5 PM. Mountain bikers and skiers fill the place in the morning to partake of challah French toast, steak and eggs, and freshly squeezed juices. Later in the day, sandwiches and salads are an option. Thumbtacks hold artwork on the white wood-plank walls, and aqua benches hold boisterous families. ⊠ *3066 Main St./Rte. 23A, Tannersville* ☎ *518/589–6101* ▭ *No credit cards* ☉ *No dinner.*

★ $$$$ ✕🏠 **Scribner Hollow Lodge.** As you step inside this complex with laid bricks underfoot, skylights, carved wooden balconies, and planters filled with greenery, you're transported to a European village square. Guest rooms are outfitted with mountain-lodge flair; most have exposed beams, river-stone fireplaces, Spanish tiles, handcrafted woodwork, and balconies with mountain views. The deluxe duplex suites have fireplaces. The indoor pool–hot tub area resembles a cavern and has seven waterfalls. Transportation to Hunter Mountain is available. At the Prospect restaurant ($$–$$$; no lunch), local organic produce, fresh herbs, and wild game figure prominently on the menu. Try the locally smoked (and local) rainbow trout, pheasant, elk, or venison. The wine list, with more than 250 selections, has garnered consistent praise from *Wine Spectator* magazine. ⊠ *Main St./Rte. 23A, Hunter 12442* ☎ *518/263–4211 or 800/395–4683* 🖷 *518/263–5266* ⊕ *www.scribnerhollow.com* 🛏 *21 rooms, 17 suites* ☐ *Restaurant, room service, in-room data ports, some in-room hot tubs, some refrigerators, cable TV with movies, some in-room VCRs, tennis court, 1 indoor and 2 outdoor pools, hot tub, massage, sauna, tobagganing, bar, video game room, babysitting, laundry service, concierge, Internet, business services, meeting rooms, no-smoking rooms* ▭ *AE, D, MC, V* ⊚ *MAP winter, BP rest of yr.*

¢–$ ✕▥ **The Redcoat's Country Inn & Restaurant.** The 1860 four-story home sits on 15 acres surrounded by mountains and adjacent to Schoharie Creek, where you can swim or fish for trout. A porch with hanging baskets of petunias and wooden rocking chairs wraps around two sides of the inn. With a fireplace in the bar and a book-lined dining room, the decor conjures an English country inn. Guest rooms are country-simple, with quilted and floral touches. The restaurant ($$–$$$) serves American country cuisine, with entrées such as pan-seared scallops wrapped in bacon and filet mignon in Portobello-and-port ragout. ⊠ *50 Dale La., Elka Park 12427* ☎ *518/589–9858* 🖷 *518/589–0309* ⊕ *www.redcoatsonline. com* 🛏 *14 rooms, 7 with shared bath* ☐ *Restaurant, fans, hiking, cross-country skiing, bar; no a/c, no room phones, no room TVs, no kids, no smoking* ▭ *AE, D, MC, V* ⊚ *BP.*

$$–$$$ ▥ **Hunter Inn.** The modern, chalet-style hotel is ¾ mi from the Hunter ski resort. Some rooms have mountainside patios or balconies with views of the surrounding forest and Hunter Mountain. Suites have a cathedral ceiling, a loft sleeping area, and a whirlpool tub, and are adorned with botanical prints on the walls. Odd-numbered rooms face the parking lot and road, which can be busy; even-numbered rooms face the mountains. ⊠ *7433 Main St./Rte. 23A, Hunter 12442* ☎ *518/263–3777* 🖷 *518/263–3981* ⊕ *www.hunterinn.com* 🛏 *27 rooms, 14 suites* ☐ *Dining room, in-room data ports, some in-room hot tubs, some refrigerators, cable TV with movies, gym, hot tub, Ping-Pong, bar, recreation room, laundry facilities, Internet, business services, meeting rooms, some pets allowed (fee), no-smoking rooms; no a/c in some rooms* ▭ *AE, D, MC, V* ⊚ *CP* ⊙ *Closed weekdays late May–late Nov.*

★ $–$$ ▥ **Washington Irving Inn.** Built in 1890 as a summer home for members of New York's high society, the inn retains many of its original architectural details, including lustrous dark-wood paneling, stained-glass windows, built-in bookcases, and carved fireplace mantels. Guest rooms contain antiques but aren't crowded with them; some have four-poster beds, and three have private balconies. Owner Stefania Jozic oversees every detail, from the fresh flowers in the rooms to the scrumptious afternoon tea served in the dining room, where lace doilies from her native Serbia cover tables. ⊠ *6629 Rte. 23A, Hunter 12442* ☎ *518/589–5560* 🖷 *518/589–5775* ⊕ *www.washingtonirving.com* 🛏 *13 rooms, 2 suites* ☐ *Dining room, some in-room hot tubs, cable TV, in-room VCRs,*

pool, ski storage, bar, Internet; no smoking ▭ *AE, MC, V* ¶◎ *BP* ⊙ *Closed late Apr.–early May.*

★ ¢–$$ 🏨 **Fairlawn Inn.** You can see the mountains from your room at this Queen Anne Victorian ½ mi from the Hunter resort and 2 mi from North-South Lake. Modern-day amenities join original oil paintings, stained-glass windows, antiques, paneling, parquet floors, and wood carvings to create a seamless whole. The pristine rooms have wrought-iron, four-poster, carved-wood, or brass queen beds; some bathrooms have claw-foot tubs and antique dressing tables. Victorian touches are used throughout. Owner Chuck Tomajko sets out bottled water, carbonated drinks, snack baskets, and cookie jars. ⊠ *7872 Main St./Rte. 23A, Hunter 12442* 🕾 *518/263–5025* ⊕ *www.fairlawninn.com* ⤳ *9 rooms* ⚘ *Dining room, in-room data ports, cable TV, boccie; no kids under 10, no smoking* ▭ *AE, MC, V* ¶◎ *BP.*

$ 🏨 **Eggery Inn.** Part of a working farm in 1898, this Dutch-colonial farmhouse took on a new life in the 1930s when it became a boardinghouse for Viennese guests. Many of the antiques that fill the inn are for sale. Guest rooms are simple, with brass or wooden beds covered in crocheted, matelassé, or quilted bedspreads. You may sit at the bar facing Hunter Mountain or in a glider on the wraparound front porch, or wander the 12½ acres. ⊠ *288 Platte Clove Rd./Rte. 16, Tannersville 12485* 🕾 *518/ 589–5363* 🖷 *518/589–5774* ⊕ *www.eggeryinn.com* ⤳ *15 rooms* ⚘ *Dining room, in-room data ports, cable TV, ski storage, bar, library, Internet; no smoking* ▭ *AE, MC, V* ¶◎ *BP* ⊙ *Closed Apr.*

CAMPING   ⚠ **Devil's Tombstone Campground.** The campground, one of the oldest in the state, attracts hikers, who access the popular Devil's Path trail at the north end of the campground parking lot. The terrain here, about 3 mi south of the Hunter Mountain ski resort, is mountainous and rocky. Within the campground sits the Devil's Tombstone, a large boulder typical of the area's natural rock formations, which came down the mountain many centuries ago either in a landslide or via glacier. Sites are wooded, with limited facilities (no electricity, hookups, or showers). Self-contained RVs are welcome. ⚘ *Flush toilets, running water, grills, picnic tables, public telephone, play area* ⊠ *Rte. 214, 12442* 🕾 *845/688–7160, 800/ 456–2267 reservations* ⊕ *www.dec.state.ny.us* ⤳ *24 tent sites* ▧ *$11* ⚘ *Reservations essential* ▭ *MC, V* ⊙ *Closed early Sept.–late May.*

Nightlife & the Arts

NIGHTLIFE   The bar at the **Hunter Village Inn** (⊠ 7746 Main St./Rte. 23A, Hunter 🕾 518/263–4788 ⊕ www.thehuntervillageinn.com), which has been around since 1965, has the biggest party scene on Hunter Mountain, and draws an après-ski crowd in its twenties to thirties. On weekends, live bands and DJs get everyone jumping, and the pool table doesn't get a rest.

THE ARTS   Part of Hunter Village Square, the **Catskill Mountain Foundation Gallery** (⊠ 7950 Main St./Rte. 23A, Hunter 🕾 518/263–4291) is a bright, well-lighted space showcasing high-quality crafts and fine arts by artists with ties to the region. Exhibits change every six to eight weeks and run the gamut from contemporary to outsider to native arts. The **Catskill Mountain Foundation Movie Theatre** (⊠ 7971 Main St./Rte. 23A, Hunter

☎ 518/263–4702 ⊕ www.catskillmtn.org) shows first-runs, indie films, and foreign movies on its two screens and has a small café in a restored single-story building. As part of the Mountain Culture Festival, the Best of Mountain Film screens movies dealing with environmental issues, mountain sports, and other topics related to mountain life. Housed in a red barn behind Hunter Village Square, the **Catskill Mountain Foundation Performing Arts Center** (✉ 7967 Main St./Rte. 23A, Hunter ☎ 518/263–4908 or 518/263–5157 ⊕ www.catskillmtn.org) hosts an active program of music, dance, theater, and family events. Verdigris copper onion domes perch atop cedar-shingled structures at the Ukrainian cultural complex surrounding **St. John the Baptist Ukrainian Catholic Church,** built in the 1960s by Ukrainian expatriates who settled in the surrounding mountains. Every Saturday night from July 4 through Labor Day weekend you can hear classical music at the **Grazhda Music and Art Center of Greene County** (✉ 78 Ukraine Rd./Rte. 23A, Jewett ☎ 518/263–4335 ⊕ www.grazhdamusicandart.org ☞ $15). During the first two weeks in August, Ukrainian arts-and-crafts workshops are offered.

Sports & the Outdoors

The year-round **Bear Creek Landing Family Sport Complex** (✉ Rte. 214 south of Rte. 23A, Hunter ☎ 518/263–3839 ⊕ www.bearcreeklanding. com) has 18 holes of miniature golf, a driving range, go-karts, a trout pond, an arcade room, ice-skating, snowmobiling, and a restaurant that specializes in barbecue. On some weekends you get live music with your smoked meat.

FISHING The **Hunter Mountain Fly Fishing School** (✉ Rte. 23A, Hunter ☎ 518/263–4223, 518/263–4666, 800/486–8376 ⊕ www.huntermtn.com) offers fly-fishing instruction, guide services, and equipment rentals from April through November. Once enrolled, you can expect to spend the day on Schoharie or Esopus creek, casting for rainbow, brown, or brook trout or bass. You must have a valid New York State fishing license.

HIKING **Devil's Path** (✉ O&ff Rte. 214, Hunter ☎ 607/652–7365, 607/652–5076, 607/652–5063 ⊕ www.dec.state.ny.us/website/outdoors), in the Westkill Mountain Wilderness area of the Catskills, winds through the Stony Clove mountain pass and around natural rock formations. Follow the red trail markers for the scenic 7-mi hike to the summit of Westkill Mountain (3,880 feet). The trailhead is at the north end of the parking lot at the Devil's Tombstone Campground, at Diamond Notch Lake. To get here from Hunter proper, take Route 23A east to Route 214 and head south for 4 mi.

SKI AREAS The sprawling **Hunter Mountain** resort (✉ Rte. 23A, Hunter ☎ 518/263–4223 or 800/486–8376 ⊕ www.huntermtn.com) has 53 trails on 240 acres, where you may ski, snowboard, snow tube, and snowshoe. In the Catskill Forest Preserve, Hunter has full snowmaking capability, a definite boon when natural conditions are less than optimal. The 3,200-foot peak offers a 1,600-foot vertical drop; 11 lifts move you up the slope. Fifteen of the trails are set aside for beginners, eight are designed for double-black-diamond skiers, and about 16 are for intermediates. Full-day lift tickets are $52. Rentals and instruction are available. From May to early October, mountain bikers take over. The single-track trails run through dense forest and cross streams. A lift transports bikers to the summit. Fly-fishing instruction and guidance also are available. Throughout summer and fall, music and ethnic festivals are held here.

At the **Mountain Trails Cross Country Ski Center** (✉ Rt. 23A between Hunter and Tannersville ☎ 518/589–5361 ⊕ www.mtntrails.com), you can cross-country ski 21 mi of groomed, wooded trails at the beginner, intermediate, or expert level, secure in the knowledge that the National Ski Patrol is on the beat. The lodge has a snack bar and rents snowshoes, cross-country skis, and sleds.

Shopping
The **Catskill Mountain Foundation Bookstore** (✉ Hunter Village Square, 7950 Main St./Rte. 23A, Hunter ☎ 518/263–4448) has the largest selection of regional books in the northern Catskills. It also has an extensive general-interest collection and gift items. You can pick up regional organic produce year-round at the **Catskill Mountain Foundation Farm Market** (✉ 7950 Main St./Rte. 23A, Hunter ☎ 518/263–4908 Ext. 204), where Francine Sherer, former owner of the Soho Charcuterie and Restaurant, presides. The staggering array of prepared foods, artisanal cheeses, and smokehouse products makes for good picnic fare.

Haines Falls

6 mi east of Hunter.

Haines Falls was once filled with tanneries and mills as well as mountain houses where wealthy urbanites came to play. For much of the 19th century the famous Catskill Mountain House, which stood near North-South Lake and the stunning Kaaterskill Falls, provided a respite to denizens of the increasingly industrialized cities to the south. Things have slowed down quite a bit in this hamlet, but the natural world is still the main attraction. Haines Falls also benefits from the overflow of visitors to nearby Hunter Mountain, which draws thousands of skiers each winter.

Catskill Mountain House site. A stone's throw from North-South Lake and Kaaterskill Falls, the mountain house was built in the early 1820s as an intimate retreat that appealed mostly to outdoorsy folks and artists. As the area's popularity increased, the resort expanded, topping out at just over 300 rooms. The area and its grand hotels fell out of favor in the early 20th century, as the automobile opened up more and more destination options for travelers. In the 1960s, following years of disrepair and neglect, the mountain house was burned down by the state. Still, many people make the hike to the site, about 2,300 above sea level. The site is a short hike from the North-South Lake Public Campground, which welcomes day-trippers. ✉ *Rte. 18 2 mi north of Rte. 23A* ☎ *518/589–5058 North-South Lake Public Campground* ⊕ *www.dec.state.ny.us* ▦ *Mid-May–late Oct., $6.*

Fodor'sChoice
★
Kaaterskill Falls. As you watch the waters cascade 260 feet down the gray rock of this two-tiered waterfall, you can see why the spot was so popular with Thomas Cole and other Hudson River school painters. To ac-

cess the trail that leads to the bottom of the falls, park in the public lot on Route 23A 3 mi west of Palenville. To get to the trailhead, walk about ¼ mi down (east) along the narrow shoulder of Route 23A, a very busy road with hairpin turns; you may find yourself hugging rocks as cars pass you. Signs point the way to the path, which leads you past the delicate Bastion Falls. Although largely level, the trail does have a few steep sections. Altogether the hike is less than 1 mi long and shouldn't take a full hour. You may be tempted to climb to the top of the falls, but this is really risky and can't be recommended: missteps on the slippery rocks here have resulted in many accidents and some fatalities. ☒ *Off Rte. 23A 3 mi west of Palenville* ☎ *No phone.*

Where to Stay

¢   🏨 **Silver Springs Ranch.** The centerpiece of this 33-acre family-friendly ranch is a turn-of-the-20th-century tavern. Above the old tavern are six modest rooms, five with shared baths but in-room sinks; an adjacent single-story building holds five motel-style rooms. A piano player provides the entertainment Sunday afternoon; open-mike nights or, in winter, DJs may be scheduled on other days. In summer, kids can sign up for horsemanship camp. ☒ *103 Rte. 25, 12436* ☎ *518/589–5559 or 800/258–2624* ⊕ *www.thesilverspringsranch.com* ⇨ *11 rooms, 5 with shared bath* ♿ *Restaurant, BBQs, some fans, some microwaves, some refrigerators, cable TV, some in-room VCRs, exercise equipment, massage, sauna, badminton, boccie, horseback riding, horseshoes, volleyball, ski storage, bar, piano, Internet, some pets allowed (fee), no-smoking rooms; no a/c in some rooms* ▤ *AE, MC, V* ▷ *CP.*

CAMPING   ⚸ **North-South Lake Campground.** In the Catskill Forest Preserve, the facility has a recreational program (July 4 through Labor Day) that keeps the kids engaged in the natural world. North-South Lake has sand beaches, and you can swim in the brisk water from late May through Labor Day, when lifeguards are on duty. If the water's too cold—the lakes are 2,000 feet above sea level—rent a boat and go fishing (with a license) for bass, perch, or catfish, or hit the surrounding trails on a mountain bike or on foot. From here it's a short hike to the site of the old Catskill Mountain House. The campground is 3 mi northeast of Haines Falls. Reservations are essential for summer weekends. Day-trippers pay $6 entry. ♿ *Flush toilets, dump station, showers, grills, picnic tables, public telephone, swimming (lake)* ☒ *Rte. 18 2 mi north of Rte. 23A, 12436* ☎ *518/589–5058 or 800/456–2267* ⊕ *www.dec.state.ny.us* ⇨ *219 tent and trailer sites* ▦ *$19.75* ▤ *MC, V* ☼ *Closed late Oct.–mid-May.*

Sports & the Outdoors

HIKING   The **Escarpment Trail,** part of the 340-mi Long Path from Albany to New York City, offers 23 mi of rigorous Catskills hiking and beautiful valley views. The trail follows the 1,600-foot-tall cliff known as the Great Wall of Manitou, leading you through rugged terrain and forests, over fallen trees, across creeks, and along rock outcroppings with stunning views of North-South Lake. If you want to hike just part of this rough trail, access it at the North-South Lake Public Campground (☒ Rte. 18 2 mi north of Rte. 23A ☎ 518/589–5058 ⊕ www.dec.state.ny.us);

the day-use fee is $6 from mid-May to late October and free the rest of the year.

Catskill Game Farm

🐾 **6** *14 mi northeast of Haines Falls.*

In 1933 German immigrant Roland Lindemann cleared the way for the zoo. His descendants continue to own and operate this popular attraction, where you can see tame and exotic animals, including rare wild Przewalski horses and reptiles; visit the animal nursery and bird garden; and pet llamas and sheep. There's also miniature golf, a large playground, a splash pad, daily wild-animal shows, and amusement rides. ✉ *400 Game Farm Rd., off Rte. 32, Catskill* ☎ *518/678–9595* ⊕ *www.catskillgamefarm.com* ✂ *$16.95* ⊙ *May–Oct., daily 9–5.*

> **off the beaten path**

MAHAYANA BUDDHIST TEMPLE – An oversize incense holder decorated with dragons sits before the main hall of the temple, where golden Buddhas have held court since 1971. The 130-acre Buddhist retreat houses several other Chinese architectural delights, including the seven-tiered Jade Pagoda. South Cairo is about 7 mi northwest of Catskill. ✉ *Ira Vail Rd., South Cairo* ☎ *518/622–3619* ✂ *Free* ⊙ *Daily 8–6.*

🐾 **ZOOM FLUME WATERPARK** – The Catskills' largest water park has a dozen squeaky-clean waterslides, tube rides, mat rides, and a lagoon activity pool with a giant waterfall, oversize raindrops. and other interactive features. The Black Vortex is a three-person enclosed tube ride; the Anaconda is an enclosed body slide; and Thrill Hill is a tube ride for little children. The park is about 2 mi north of the center of East Durham off Route 145. ✉ *91 Shady Glen Rd., East Durham* ☎ *518/239–4559 or 800/888–3586* ⊕ *www.zoomflume.com* ✂ *$19.95* ⊙ *Father's Day–Labor Day, weekdays 10–6, weekends 10–7.*

Where to Stay & Eat

★ ¢ ✕ **Hartmans Kaffeehaus.** Desserts are serious business at this simple café-bakery where a "periodic table" of sweets hangs on the wall. The Fürst Pückler torte—layers of marzipan, butter cream, sponge cake, and apricot jam—could spur a sugar shock. Strudels are delicious, too. The breakfast and lunch fare is good as well. A side of warm German potato salad accompanies midday plates, such as the bratwurst platter or chicken salad studded with bits of apple, bell pepper, and celery. Pick from the selection of German beers for something to wash it all down. ✉ *1507 Hearts Content Rd., Round Top* ☎ *518/622–3820* 🖃 *MC, V* ⊙ *Closed Mon. and Tues. and Christmas–Easter.*

$$$$ 🏨 **Blackhead Mountain Lodge and Country Club.** The German-American Maassmann family, which owns this golf-focused lodge, has presided over this section of the Blackhead Mountains since 1967. Some of the motel-style rooms open onto balconies overlooking playgrounds, tennis courts, and the mountains. The restaurant specializes in German food; bratwurst, pepper steak, potato pancakes, sauerbraten, and Rouladen

(German roulade), all with side orders of spaetzle, are served in a large, bright dining room with beer steins displayed on mantels. ☒ *Crow's Nest Rd., Round Top 12473* ☎ *518/622–3157 or 888/382–7474* ☐ *518/622–2331* ⊕ *www.blackheadmountaingolf.com* ☞ *24 rooms* ♢ *Restaurant, cable TV, driving range, 18-hole golf course, putting green, tennis courts, pro shop, pool, billiards, boccie, horseshoes, shuffleboard, 2 bars, babysitting, playground, business services; no room phones, no smoking* ▭ *AE, MC, V* ⦿ *BP or MAP.*

$$ ⊞ **Winter Clove Inn.** A weeping willow and a grove of birch trees stand on the front lawn of this early-19th-century colonial with an expansive front porch. Inside you find loads of hardwood and a vast collection of antiques and reproductions. The rooms, simple and tidy, all overlook the landscaped grounds. The lounge has a TV, stone fireplace, piano, and several wing chairs and sofas to relax in. Rates include all three meals. Children's programs are offered in summer. ☒ *2965 Winter Clove Rd., off Rte. 32, Round Top* ☎ *518/622–3267* ⊕ *www.winterclove.com* ☞ *50 rooms* ♢ *Restaurant, dining room, 9-hole golf course, tennis court, 2 pools, (1 indoor), fishing, badminton, bowling, horseshoes, Ping-Pong, shuffleboard, soccer, softball, volleyball, cross-country skiing, sleigh rides, piano, recreation room, video game room, children's programs (ages 3–16), playground, meeting rooms; no room phones, no smoking* ▭ *MC, V* ⦿ *AI.*

Sports & the Outdoors

Narrow tree-lined fairways, water hazards, undulating greens, and dramatic elevation changes make the par-72 **Blackhead Mountain Golf Course** (☒ Crow's Nest Rd. Round Top ☎ 518/622–3157 or 888/382–7474 ⊕ www.blackheadmountaingolf.com) challenging for golfers. The $40 greens fee includes a cart rental. A 19th-century barn with murals of dancing gnomes and Rip Van Winkle serves as clubhouse; a bar with a stone fireplace awaits inside, where you can order lunch.

Windham Ski Area

❼ *Windham is 17 mi west of Catskill Game Farm.*

Once a private club attracting politicians and business leaders, the Windham resort retains a somewhat exclusive air. Professionals from the New York metropolitan area and their broods flock to the slopes, which have a family-friendly reputation. Greater Windham is a favorite destination for hikers and hunters, and lodging options range from intimate inns and converted Victorian homes to a sprawling resort and modern hotels.

Where to Stay & Eat

$$–$$$ ✕ **Vesuvio Restaurant.** At this regional Italian restaurant, statues stand watch over bubbling fountains in the lush gardens that surround the outdoor seating area. Inside, a large bar dominates a corner of the front dining room; an arched white trellis separates the rear dining rooms. Seafood figures prominently on the menu, which is extensive. Dishes include crabmeat-stuffed artichoke hearts in Frangelico sauce and seafood Vesuvio, a combination of lobster, clams, mussels, calamari, scallops, and shrimp over pasta. ⊠ *40 Goshen Rd., Hensonville* ☎ *518/734–3663* ▭ *AE, DC, MC, V* ☉ *Closed Apr. No lunch.*

$$–$$$ ✕ **Madison's Restaurant.** Operating as Thetford's since the mid-1960s, this restaurant changed hands in 2004. The menu still lists steak-house specials and includes fish dishes like sautéed red snapper or salmon; rack of lamb with rosemary sauce; and roast duck. The dining room is casual, with white walls and dark-wood beams. On Saturday night, DJs and bands get people moving on the dance floor. ⊠ *5126 Rte. 23, Windham* ☎ *518/734–3322* ▭ *AE, MC, V* ☉ *No lunch.*

$–$$$ ✕ **Chalet Fondue Restaurant.** The decor at this German-Swiss restaurant in the heart of Windham combines a slice of Germany—owner Ute Seigies imported the two ceramic stoves, oversize wine casks, and all the ironwork and woodwork from her native country—with fireplaces, candlelight, and lush ficus and palm trees. The chef, who hails from Hungary, turns out authentic *Jaegerschnitzel,* Wiener schnitzel, and sauerbraten. Fondue offerings include cheese, Chinoise (veal and filet mignon cooked in broth), and chocolate. The wine-and-beer list is extensive, and the desserts are rich. ⊠ *Rte. 296, Windham* ☎ *518/734–4650* ▭ *AE, DC, MC, V* ☉ *Closed Tues. No lunch.*

¢–$$$ ✕ **Windhaven Pub & Restaurant.** A sly sense of humor imfuses this laid-back eatery, where dissembled toilets await cigarette butts on the front porch and the ultrafriendly staff makes you feel like a native. You can sit in a barbershop chair by a fireplace on the front porch, hang out at the rectangular bar, or take a table surrounded by an assortment of antiques and kitschy objects and tuck into chicken with apricot-cilantro salsa, raspberry duck, a sandwich, a burger, or a steak. The main menu is served until 10 PM, after which you can still satisfy your appetite with items from the pub menu. Reservations are essential in winter. ⊠ *Rte. 296 near Rte. 23, Hensonville* ☎ *518/734–4428* ▭ *AE, DC, MC, V.*

$$ ✕▣ **Christman's Windham House.** The centerpiece of this 260-acre golf resort is a white Greek-revival inn that's been taking in travelers since its opening in 1805. The rooms, although updated, retain the flavor of the past, with antiques, Victorian-inspired wallpaper, and wide-plank floors; some have fireplaces. Several attractive motel-style buildings surround the inn. If you tire of golf, you can fish in Batavia Kill or wander the grounds. Meals are served in the main building, where the excellent **Messina's La Griglia** ($$–$$$; no lunch) has three comfortable dining rooms with a mostly white-on-white decor. The fare is northern Italian. You can savor mussels, capellini with shrimp and scallops in white wine sauce, or roast duck in fig-and-honey sauce while eyeing the golf course's 9th hole through the large windows. ⊠ *5742 Rte. 23, Windham 12496* ☎ *518/734–4230 or 888/294–4053, 518/734–4499 restaurant* ⊕ *www.windhamhouse.com* ↩ *50 rooms* ♨ *Restaurant, some in-room hot tubs, some refrigerators, cable TV, some in-room VCRs, driving range, 18- and 9-hole golf courses, putting green, tennis court, pro shop, pool, billiards, croquet, horseshoes, paddle tennis, Ping-Pong, shuffleboard, 2 bars, recreation room, babysitting, playground, laundry facilities, business services, meeting rooms, no-smoking rooms* ▭ *AE, MC, V* ⋈ *MAP late Apr.–mid-Oct., CP late Dec.–late Mar.* ☉ *Closed mid-Oct.–Christmas and late Mar.–Apr.*

$$-$$$ 📷 **Winwood Mountain Inn.** The family-oriented property sits on 12 acres in the mountains and offers a variety of accommodations. The condos, which account for the bulk of the units, are roomy and have either private patios or balconies. Suites have one or two bedrooms. All the accommodations are outfitted in a comfortable American decor with cherrywood furniture. ⊠ *Rte. 23, Windham 12496* ☎ *518/734–3000 or 800/754–9463* 🖷 *518/734–5900* ⊕ *www.winwoodinn.com* ⏎ *5 rooms, 15 suites, 30 condos* ♻ *Restaurant, in-room data ports, some kitchenettes, some microwaves, some refrigerators, cable TV, putting green, tennis court, pool, gym, basketball, billiards, boccie, Ping-Pong, shuffleboard, ski storage, bar, cinema, video game room, playground, laundry facilities, Internet, business services, no-smoking rooms, some pets allowed (fee)* ▤ *AE, D, MC, V.*

★ ¢–$$ 📷 **Albergo Allegria.** Antiques are scattered throughout this handsome 1892 Queen Anne Victorian with stained-glass windows and other original features. You can warm up by the fireplace in the parlor, which is slightly formal but inviting, or help yourself to a snack in the kitchen. The house has 12 guest rooms and four suites, all with down comforters and plush carpeting; the decor is country-chic, and flounces are kept to a minimum. The master suite, with its king-size bed and featherbed, double whirlpool tub, and gas fireplace, is billed as honeymoon central. Behind the inn is a carriage house (formerly horse stable) with a courtyard and outdoor lounge. Its five suites have cathedral ceilings, skylights, double whirlpool tubs, gas fireplaces, and garden views. The inn also has two sister properties—the **Mountain Streams Cottage,** with two suites and one room, and the **Farmhouse,** with three apartments—in Windham. ⊠ *43 Rte. 296, Windham 12496* ☎ *518/734–5560 or 800/625– 2374* 🖷 *518/734–5570* ⊕ *www.albergousa.com* ⏎ *12 rooms, 9 suites* ♻ *Dining room, some fans, in-room data ports, some in-room hot tubs, some refrigerators, cable TV, in-room VCRs, hot tub, shuffleboard, ski storage, library, babysitting, laundry service, Internet, business services, meeting rooms; no smoking* ▤ *MC, V* ⦿ *BP.*

¢–$$ 📷 **Hotel Vienna.** The rooms at this tidy hotel have exposed ceiling beams, solid cherrywood furniture, lace curtains, cheery bed and window coverings, and sliding doors to a private, tiled balcony. You may eat breakfast in front of a wood-burning stove and, in the afternoon, unwind with homemade cookies and hot chocolate. The glass-enclosed pool opens onto a sundeck and provides 360-degree views of the countryside. ⊠ *107 Rte. 296, Windham 12496* ☎ *518/734–5300* 🖷 *518/ 734–4749* ⊕ *www.thehotelvienna.com* ⏎ *29 rooms* ♻ *In-room data ports, some in-room hot tubs, cable TV, some in-room VCRs, indoor pool, exercise equipment, hot tub, ski storage, recreation room, babysitting, Internet, business services, meeting rooms; no smoking* ▤ *D, MC, V* ⦿ *CP.*

Nightlife & the Arts

Two former Metropolitan Opera performers started the **Windham Chamber Music Festival** (⊠ Main and Church Sts., Windham ☎ 518/734–3868, 518/734–6378 tickets ⊕ www.windhammusic.com) in 1997. The festival makes the most of the soaring acoustics at the **Windham Performing Arts Center,** which occupies an 1826 Greek-revival church.

Saturday-evening concerts are scheduled throughout the year, but many take place in summer; tickets are $18. At **Windham Fine Arts** (⊠ 5380 Main St. Windham ☎ 518/734–6850 ⊕ www.windhamfinearts.com), a gallery in an 1855 Federal-style house, track lighting bounces off richly hued wooden floors and illuminates the work of regional and national artists. You may see contemporary, representational, and traditional works in all mediums here. The gallery is open Thursday through Monday (Friday through Monday from Labor Day to Memorial Day).

Sports & the Outdoors

GOLF   The par-71, 18-hole course at the **Windham Country Club** (⊠ 36 South St., Windham ☎ 518/734–9910 ⊕ www.windhamcountryclub.com), with a Catskills backdrop, is well groomed and has been a regional favorite since 1927. The 6,005-yard course, open daily from April through November, fills up on weekends. Greens fees of $55 cover your cart rental.

SKI AREA   Professionals and families come to ski the 1,600-foot verticals, two terrain parks, and tube park, or to test out the half pipe at **Ski Windham** (⊠ C. D. Lane Rd., Windham ☎ 518/734–4300 or 800/354–9463 ⊕ www.windhammountain.com). Of the 39 downhill trails, 10 are set aside for beginners. Eight trails are for black-diamond skiers; six are double-black-diamond trails. You can arrange for valet and caddy service to greet your vehicle, take your skis, and meet you at the lift. The facility also offers perks like First Tracks Tickets, which for $15 extra allow you to carve out a slice of the mountain for an hour before the lifts open to the public. At the slope-side business center, wireless Internet access keeps you connected, and the Children's Learning Center keeps kids busy while their parents are on the slopes. Night skiing and tubing are available until 10 PM. During the rest of the year Windham hosts special events; in fall, lift rides offer treetop views of the Catskills foliage. A shuttle bus operates from the town area.

Prattsville

10 mi west of Windham.

Thick hemlock forests, abundant wildlife, and cool mountain water lured Mohawks and Dutch, English, and German settlers to the area. In the early 1800s, Zadock Pratt, a tanner in nearby Jewett, saw an opportunity and seized it, utilizing the tannin from the trees to establish a tannery that yielded $500,000 in profits by 1825. To celebrate his success, Pratt built 100 Federal-style buildings in the area forming Prattsville—80 of which still stand. Not content to rest on his laurels, he went on to become a banker, and, eventually, a U.S. congressman. These days, second-home owners, out-of-towners, and locals enjoy a slow-paced life here. Main Street is lined with Arts and Crafts bungalows, Victorian houses, and Gothic-revival and Greek-revival buildings.

Pratt's Rocks. A steep, serpentine climb leads to gray sandstone carvings referencing Zadock Pratt's life. According to local lore, Pratt commissioned sculptor Andrew W. Pearse to create the carvings in exchange for room and board. Images of Pratt's son George, a colonel who was killed in the Civil War, and Pratt's favorite horse emerge from the mountainside as you hike. ⊠ *Main St./Rte. 23 1 mi east of Prattsville center* ☎ *518/299–3125* ☜ *Free.*

Zadock Pratt Museum. Antiques and memorabilia depicting life in the 1850s fill the former Greek-revival summer home of Prattsville's namesake. A tireless entrepreneur, Zadock Pratt, who outlived five wives, made his initial money in tanning but went on to develop a variety of industries, including several mills, factories, a general store, and a printing plant. The museum includes a cultural and educational center with changing exhibits related to the history of the Catskills. ⊠ *Main St./Rte. 23* ☎ *518/299–3395* ⊕ *www.prattmuseum.com* ☜ *Free* ☉ *Memorial Day–Columbus Day, Thurs.–Sun. 1–4:30.*

Where to Eat

¢–$$$ ✕ **Hitching Post.** Low lighting and lots of bare wood give this family-friendly restaurant about 5 mi northwest of Prattsville something of the aura of a roadhouse. The building dates from the turn of the 20th century and has a storied history; during Prohibition one enterprising owner set the attic on fire when his still blew up. The menu is loaded with well-prepared American favorites such as burgers and fries, steak-and-potato dinners, shareable appetizer baskets, and scrumptious home-made desserts—save room for co-owner Jennifer's apple crisp. Simple, reasonably priced rooms upstairs and a sizable cottage out back are available to rent. You might have company if you choose to stay here; guests have reported benign ghostly visitors. ⊠ *37690 Rte. 23, Grand Gorge* ☎ *607/588–7078* ▤ *MC, V.*

Roxbury

❽ *12 mi west of Prattsville.*

The headwaters of the Delaware River flow through bucolic Roxbury, meandering past tree-lined streets and the stone walls of the 11-acre Kirkside Park. The area was mainly known for its dairy farms, the number of which dwindled significantly in the second half of the 20th century. After naturalist John Burroughs (1837–1921) wrote lovingly about his home here and the surrounding mountains, the area captured the interest of city dwellers.

In the 19th-century Roxbury was shaped by financier Jay Gould and his family, whose fortune was made in railroads and the Western Union Telegraph Co. Ensuing Gould generations used their money philanthropically, building churches and community centers that still stand today.

Jay Gould Memorial Reformed Church. When two of Roxbury's churches were destroyed—one in a windstorm, the other by fire—Jay Gould offered to foot the bill to rebuild. The result was this church, built in 1893 at the edge of Kirkside Park under the direction of Henry Hardenburgh, architect of New York City's Dakota apartment building. Constructed of St. Lawrence limestone, the church has had only minor restoration work over the years. It has two stained-glass windows by Tiffany and two others by the Maitland Armstrong Co. ⊠ *53738 Main St.* ☎ *607/326–7101* ☜ *Free* ☉ *Early June–Labor Day, Sun. 10–11; rest of yr., Sun. 10:30–11:30.*

John Burroughs Memorial State Historic Site. Acres of fields, a small stone gravesite, and mountain views on the outskirts of Roxbury are the perfect memorial to John Burroughs, an early environmentalist whose books changed the way many Americans looked at the natural world. En route to the memorial you pass Woodchuck Lodge, a rustic summer home with quarter moons carved into closed shutters that Burroughs built in 1908 for his retirement years. You can stand on the front porch where Burroughs slept, and take in the vistas that inspired him. ⊠ *Burroughs Memorial Rd., west of Rte. 30* ☎ *607/326–7908* ⊕ *nysparks. state.ny.us* ☜ *Free* ☾ *Daily dawn–dusk.*

Where to Stay & Eat

¢   ✕ **Taste Bud's Country Store and Restaurant.** Don't be scared away by the worn linoleum and mismatched paint at this funky little breakfast and lunch spot. You can take in local color; everyone from the mailman to celebrities with weekend homes in the area comes for Sunday brunch, savoring the sausage gravy and spiced apples. A large collection of historic photographs hangs on the wall, including one taken of the premises a decade ago by *National Geographic.* ⊠ *53535 Main St.* ☎ *607/326–3663* ☐ *MC, V* ☾ *No dinner.*

¢–$ ☒ **The Roxbury.** From the moment you spot the chartreuse doors, you
Fodor'sChoice   know this is no ordinary motel. The owners' background in theater be-
★   comes evident when you step inside. A glass of wine or champagne is available at check-in, after which you're ushered to your stylish, modern room, where a pillow-top bed, high-speed Internet access, and Egyptian-cotton towels await. Some rooms have bright accent furnishings that pop against dove-gray and taupe walls; others employ chrome galore. In the mod-happy suite, you can channel Austin Powers. The top floor of the main house—as cool as the other spaces but more subdued—accommodates small groups; it has two bedrooms, a bathroom, and living area. Owner Gregory Henderson makes an obliging and energetic concierge. ⊠ *2258 Rte. 41, 12474* ☎ *607/326–7200* ☐ *607/326–3311* ⊕ *www.theroxburymotel.com* ➳ *10 rooms, 2 suites* ⚐ *In-room data ports, some kitchenettes, cable TV, in-room DVD players, fishing, croquet, shuffleboard, babysitting, laundry facilities, Internet, business services, meeting rooms* ☐ *AE, D, DC, MC, V* ☾ *Closed 1st wk in Apr. and 2nd wk in Nov.*

Nightlife & the Arts

At the **Enderlin Gallery** (⊠ Main St. ☎ 607/326–3200 ⊕ www. enderlingallery.com), open weekends and by appointment, a former hardware store with wooden floors and a tin ceiling serves as backdrop for regional artists' works. Under the direction of Zoe Randall, the gallery also hosts acoustic-music and literary events. The **Roxbury Arts Group** transformed a 1911 classical-revival building that had housed the village YMCA into the **Walt Meade Gallery and Hilt Kelly Hall** (⊠ 5025 Vega Mountain Rd. ☎ 607/326–7908 ⊕ www.roxburyartsgroup.org), which hosts year-round dance and theater performances, concerts, and children's programs. On Sunday of Columbus Day weekend, hundreds of North American fiddlers converge for a series of concerts, jam sessions, and dance. The Todd Mountain Theatre Project premieres new plays by New York playwrights for three weeks each August, and the gallery showcases works by local artists.

Sports & the Outdoors

GOLF The par-36, 3,127-yard golf course called **Shephard Hills** (⊠ Golf Course Rd. ☎ 607/326–7121 ⊕ www.shephardhills.com) was built in 1918 as part of the estate of Helen Gould Shephard. The 1911 stone clubhouse, which originally served as a summer guesthouse, recalls the turn of the 20th century; you can grab a quick bite in the casual dining room. Greens fees, including cart rental, are $32. It's open April through October.

MOUNTAIN BIKING From late April to early November, mountain bikers take over **Ski Plattekill** (⊠ 1 Plattekill Mountain Rd., east of Rte. 30, ☎ 607/326–3500 or 800/633–3275 ⊕ www.plattekill.com). With 70 trails covering 60-plus mi, a vertical drop of 1,100 feet, and two lifts, the park is considered one of the top mountain-biking venues in North America. Races for all ages and skills levels take place monthly, during which hundreds of aficionados pitch tents in the lower parking lot. An all-day trail-and-lift pass is $25. Instruction and rentals are available.

SKI AREA The family-oriented **Ski Plattekill** (⊠ 1 Plattekill Mountain Rd., east of Rte. 30, ☎ 607/326–3500 or 800/633–3275 ⊕ www.plattekill.com) sits on 75 acres with 40 mi of cross-country trails, 20 mi of downhill trails, a 1,100-foot vertical drop, and a snow-tubing area. It averages 165 inches of snowfall a year, and has 85% snowmaking capability. Of its 35 trails, 20% are for novices and 40% are for intermediates; 20% are deemed difficult and another 20% are for experts only. Expert skiers and snowboarders soar down the longest continuous vertical in the Catskills, while those in the learning stages can cruise for a couple of miles. Full-day passes are $37. The family-run lodge includes a cafeteria, ski shop, nursery, bar and lounge, and rental shop.

Stamford

⑨ *14 mi northwest of Roxbury, 13 mi northwest of Prattsville.*

Long before trappers and farmers settled in Stamford in 1790, American Indians spent time traveling the trail between the Schoharie Valley and the Catskills. With the advent of the Delaware & Ulster Railroad in 1872 came tourists, and the farms ceded way to boardinghouses, hotels, and inns, earning the village the moniker Queen of the Catskills. The village's heavy reliance on tourism suffered a blow after World War II, when the automobile became the preferred method of travel. Although many of the old boardinghouses still line the main streets, most have seen better days. Today this sleepy village of 3,000 has big plans that include extensive renovation at the park atop Mount Utsayantha, which it hopes will help it become a prime tourist destination once again.

☼ **Blenheim–Gilboa Power Project Visitors Center.** Housed in a 1905 barn, the visitor center sits above the Blenheim-Gilboa pumped-storage project, which generates power by recycling water between two reservoirs. Hands-on exhibits explain the science of energy production; an enclosed porch overlooking the lower reservoir has exhibits of local fauna. Picnic tables are scattered between the historic outbuildings. Hiking trails lead to Mine Kill State Park. ⊠ *Rte. 30, North Blenheim* ☎ *518/827–6121 or 800/724–0309* ⊕ *www.nypa.gov* 🎫 *Free* ⊙ *Daily 10–5.*

Greenbriar Farm. A single-story board-and-batten farm building constructed with logs from the property contains a sap house and cider mill. You can buy tangy apple cider, cider doughnuts, homemade pies, and maple syrup. If you bring your own apples, the Powell-Wagner family will happily custom press them for you. You can tour the premises by calling ahead. ⊠ *146 Berg Rd., South Gilboa* ☎ *607/652–7898* 🎫 *Free* ⊙ *Early Sept.–Thanksgiving, weekends 11–5.*

Lansing Manor. John Lansing, who served in the New York State Assembly (1780–88) and as mayor of Albany (1786–90), built this Federal-style manor in 1819 for his daughter Frances and son-in-law Honorable Jacob Sutherland so that they could collect rent from his tenant farmers. After the Sutherlands sold the manor, it passed to the Rosseter, Spring, and Mattice families before the New York Power Authority bought it in 1972. The manor, a window onto the 19th century, is filled with period antiques, some of which belonged to the resident families. In the ladies' reception area you can see where a young member of the Rosseter clan and his friend scratched their names into the window with a diamond. Tours take place each half hour. ⊠ *Rte. 30, North Blenheim* ☎ *518/827–6384* ⊕ *www.nypa.gov* 🎫 *Free* ⊙ *May–Oct., Wed.–Mon. 10–5.*

Mine Kill State Park. You may picnic, hike, swim, or walk the nature trails at this park 18 mi northeast of Stamford. The facilities include an Olympic-size pool as well as pools for divers and waders ($2 daily; open Memorial Day–Labor Day); basketball and volleyball courts; and soccer and softball fields. Because the park is adjacent to the Blenheim-Gilboa power project, you can fish from the shores of the reservoir, which is stocked with bass, trout, and walleye. A hike to Mine Kill Falls Overlook yields a glimpse of a series of small waterfalls. In winter, cross-country skiers, snowshoers, and snowmobilers hit the trails. The park doesn't have trash cans, so you must pack up and take out whatever you bring in. ⊠ *Rte. 30, North Blenheim* ☎ *518/827–6111* ⊕ *nysparks.state.ny. us* 🎫 *May–Oct., parking $6* ⊙ *Daily 7:30–dusk.*

Mount Utsayantha. You arrive at the top after a bone-rattling drive up a steep gravel road. Ever since a carriage road and observation tower were created in 1882, intrepid souls have ventured to the 3,365-foot summit to take in the sweeping vistas of Delaware and Schoharie counties and the Berkshire, Green, Adirondack, and Catskill mountains. A 1926 wooden observation tower is under renovation at this writing, as are the steel fire tower and hiking trails. According to local lore, the mountain takes its name from an American Indian princess who drowned herself in a lake after her father killed her white lover and their child; the princess is supposedly buried on the mountain. ⊠ *Tower Mountain Rd.* ☎ *607/652–6671* ⊕ *www.utsayantha.com* 🎫 *Free.*

Where to Eat

¢ ✕ **Greenbriar Farm Sweets, Treats and Eats.** The outgoing Powell-Wagner family runs this ice-cream parlor and casual eatery in addition to its sap house and cider mill (in nearby South Gilboa). You can reap the benefits of both with a visit here. Jars of homemade pickles, salsa, and fruit jams jostle for space with freshly baked pies and sweet breads. The Friday-night fish fry—when fresh pollack, flounder, and haddock are beer-battered and deep-fried—is becoming a local tradition. ⊠ *75 Main St.* ☎ *607/652–9164* ⊟ *No credit cards* ⊗ *Closed Dec.–Apr.*

¢ ✗**T. P's Café Restaurant**. At the counter of this luncheonette, locals fill the stools by the griddle at breakfast and lunch. The bright, cheerful dining room, with pale yellow walls and a tin ceiling, has five tables overlooking Veterans Memorial Park. The amiable staff lets you sit as long as you like. ⊠ *7 Railroad Ave.* ☎ *607/652–4752* ⊟ *No credit cards* ⊗ *Closed Mon.*

Nightlife & the Arts

The **Frank W. Cyr Center** (⊠ 159 W. Main St. ☎ 607/652–1200) inhabits the former Rexmere Hotel, which was built in 1898 by local hotel magnate Dr. Stephen E. Churchill. Surrounding the center is the 100-acre Churchill Park, which Churchill created complete with man-made lakes, tree clusters, meadows, and idyllic summer homes. Local arts organizations utilize the center. The **Friends of Music** present classical-music concerts using a Steinway grand piano flanked by Corinthian columns, and the **Mount Utsayantha Arts League** hangs regional artists' works in the gallery space. (Otsego-Northern Catskills BOCES and various administrative offices occupy other parts of the building.) On the back porch are rocking chairs from which you can survey the park's lakes and groves. Timothy Touhey runs **The Gallery** (⊠ 128 Main St. ☎ 607/652–4030 ⊕ www.touhey.com) in an old tin-ceilinged department store, where he showcases his sculptures and vibrant paintings. The congenial Touhey may let you peek into his studio, or he might play a tune for you on the upright piano. A second space, at the back of the building, displays regional artists' works.

Sports & the Outdoors

GOLF   Since 1897, the bucolic **Stamford Golf Club** (⊠ Taylor Mountain Rd. ☎ 607/652–7398 ⊕ www.stamfordgolfclub.com) has been delighting golfers with sweeping views of the Catskills and Mount Utsayantha. You can relax over lunch on a veranda and then head back to the greens. Greens fees at this 18-hole, 6,285-yard course are $50, which covers two golfers and a cart. Facilities include a driving range, practice trap, putting green, and pro shop.

Delhi

🔟 *19 mi southwest of Stamford.*

Pastures and soft hills surround this village of barely 3,000 residents. The government seat of Delaware County, Delhi has some notable Federal architecture, mostly along Main Street. The brick 1878 county clerk's building anchors the western edge of the village square, with its Victorian gazebo and Civil War monument. Farming is still the main industry here. Each Wednesday from Memorial Day through October, area farmers bring their wares to market on the square. The State University of New York at Delhi is the other industry in town. The courses offered here reflect the region's cultural shift; the school was once known for its agricultural program, but today's students are more interested in the culinary arts and golf-management programs.

Delaware County Historical Association Museum. The centerpiece of this museum property is the 1797 Federal-style farm of Gideon Frisbee, an original settler of Delhi. The complex includes six other historic buildings as well as an extensive genealogical library. One exhibit gallery holds a permanent collection of 19th-century farm implements; the other rotates displays of local historical interest. Special events re-create the daily life of the period. A nature trail leads to a covered bridge; when in bloom, more than 80 lilac bushes perfume the grounds. ☒ *46549 Rte. 10, 2½ mi north of Delhi center* ☎ *607/746–3849* ⊕ *www.dcha-ny.org* ☞ *$4* ☉ *Historic buildings Memorial Day–mid-Oct., Tues.–Sun. 11–3:30.*

> **off the beaten path**

HANFORD MILLS MUSEUM – An 1846 red barn overlooking a millpond was purchased in 1860 by David Josiah Hanford, who developed it into a working sawmill and gristmill. By 1898 the mill was supplying East Meredith with electricity, and it remained in operation until 1967, when it became a museum. The still-functional mill, powered by a waterwheel, is open for daily tours. The grounds include nature trails, a gallery space, and a picnic area. You can try your hand at ice harvesting during the annual Winter Ice Harvest, when period tools are used to cut ice from the frozen pond. The ice is then loaded onto a bobsled and stored until July 4, when it's used to make ice cream. ☒ *Rtes. 10 and 12, East Meredith* ☎ *607/278–5744 or 800/295–4992* ⊕ *www.hanfordmills.org* ☞ *$6* ☉ *May–Oct., daily 10–5.*

Where to Stay & Eat

$–$$$
Fodor'sChoice
★

✕ **Quarter Moon Café.** At this decidedly upscale spot at the edge of the village, cobalt-blue vases sit on blond-wood tables in sharp contrast with the deep-russet walls and tin-ceilinged bar area. Large photographs of Cuban scenes are hung between book racks, where a handpicked collection of art books await your browsing—that is, if you can pull yourself away from the seared tofu with pumpkin-seed mole, curry-crusted calamari, or truffle-and-soy risotto. Wednesday is sushi night. Reservations are essential on weekends and for sushi night. ☒ *53 Main St.* ☎ *607/746–8886* ☐ *AE, MC, V* ☉ *Closed Tues. and early Jan.–mid-Feb.*

$–$$
✕ **Olde Caledonia Restaurant.** Window boxes heavy with petunias lure you inside the dining room, which, with a white-trellis room divider and lace curtains, evokes a tearoom. Simple table settings and white linen tablecloths are the backdrop for veal Marsala and Cajun shrimp. Lunch includes burgers and wrap sandwiches. ☒ *106 Main St.* ☎ *607/746–9590* ☐ *AE, D, DC, MC, V* ☉ *Closed Sun.*

¢–$$
✕ **Angelos Family Restaurant.** This casual eatery has the feel of a pizzeria. The menu includes plenty of Greek specialties, along with pasta dishes, sandwiches, and pastries. Regulars return for the skirt steak, moussaka, and spinach-pie dinners. ☒ *82 Main St.* ☎ *607/746–7171* ☐ *D, DC, MC, V* ☉ *Closed Mon.*

¢
▦ **Buena Vista Motel.** A simple picket fence borders the grounds of this single-story motel. The rooms are motel-style with either two queen or

twin beds. A large cottage has a full kitchen, a sleeping alcove, a living room, and two bedrooms. ⊠ *18718 Rte. 28, 13753* ☎ *607/746–2135* 🖷 *607/746–6008* ⊕ *www.buenavistamotel.com* ⊃ *33 rooms, 1 cottage* ♿ *Some kitchenettes, some microwaves, some refrigerators, cable TV, some pets allowed (fee); no smoking* ⊟ *AE, D, DC, MC, V* ⦿ *CP.*

Sports & the Outdoors

GOLF The east branch of the Delaware River cuts through the par-72, 6,472-yard **Delhi College Golf Course** (⊠ 85 Scotch Mountain Rd. ☎ 607/746–4653). On weekends, $45 covers your greens fees and cart rental. A full pro shop, restaurant, and bar are on the premises.

Shopping

At **Good Cheap Food** (⊠ 53 Main St. ☎ 607/746–6562), a combination health-food shop and children's store, you can pick up everything you need for a lavish picnic as well as an outfit for your tyke. The front window holds wooden cases filled with fresh, organic local produce; handcrafted earrings are for sale behind the counter. Built in 1820 by Colonel Robert Parker, **Parker House** (⊠ 74 Main St. ☎ 607/746–3141 or 888/263–5573) now serves as an upscale gift emporium. The mix includes Wedgwood pieces, handwoven scarves, Vera Bradley handbags, and children's items.

THE SOUTHERN CATSKILLS

SULLIVAN COUNTY

By Jeanne
Sager

Although 15 championship golf courses are strewn throughout the region, Sullivan County also is the winter home of the bald eagle. There's a racino (a racetrack with gaming) with top-of-the-line video-game terminals at one portal, in Monticello, and an old-time single-screen theater at the other, in Callicoon. Fast-food restaurants and a few "box stores" (large retail-chain stores) are evidence of the county's development, but motorists still watch for deer and slow-moving tractors.

Roscoe

⓫ *120 mi northwest of New York City.*

Known as Trout Town, U.S.A., Roscoe is the site of the protected Beaverkill and Willowemoc creeks, some of the most famous angling waters in the Northeast. Fly-fishing enthusiasts make pilgrimages to this Sullivan County community on the western edge of the Catskills to fish for rainbow, brook, and brown trout. Like the early bird after the worm, the early fisherman who awakens first on April Fool's Day is awarded the chance to cast the first line in the fabled waters of Junction Pool, where American dry-fly fishing is said to have gotten its start. You would think that the people of this village breathe as if they have gills—it's all fishing, all the time.

Catskill Fly Fishing Center and Museum. The nonprofit center, 4 mi east of Roscoe, is devoted to the preservation of the sport of fly-fishing and of the delicate ecological environment that makes the sport possible. The center maintains a vast collection of fishing accoutrements, antique flies, and fishing-related artwork. It also conducts outreach and educational programs throughout the year, with twice-yearly cane rod–making classes and an October celebration of the latest legends to be named to the Fly Fishing Hall of Fame. ⊠ *1031 Old Rte. 17, Livingston Manor* ☎ *845/439–4810* ⊕ *www.cffcm.org* 🎫 *$3* ⊙ *Apr.–Oct., daily 10–4; Nov.–Mar., Tues.–Fri. 10–1, Sat. 10–4.*

New York State Catskill Fish Hatchery. A half-million brown trout are raised here each year to help stock the state's rivers and lakes. Spawning occurs in September, but you can stop in any time of year for a guided tour of the facility. Experts from the state environmental conservation department are always on hand to answer questions and explain the life cycle of the fish. ⊠ *402 Fish Hatchery Rd., Livingston Manor* ☎ *845/ 439–4328* 🎫 *Free* ⊙ *Weekdays 8:30–4, weekends 8:30–noon.*

Roscoe O&W Railway Museum. On those rainy days when fishing isn't an option, Roscoe's Wilmer Simpson can keep the entire family occupied with his stories of the old days when the trains still ran through the village. At this museum with a bright red caboose in the yard and original watchman's shanties, you can see firsthand the ins and outs of railroad life before the trains stopped running in 1957. ⊠ *7 Railroad Ave.* ☎ *607/498–4346 or 607/498–5289* ⊕ *www.nyow.org* 🎫 *Free* ⊙ *Memorial Day–Columbus Day, weekends 11–3.*

Where to Stay & Eat

$–$$$ ✕ **Roscoe Diner.** The quintessential upstate diner has been owned by the same family since 1969. The menu has a bit of everything: omelets for breakfast, soups and sandwiches for lunch, and hearty steaks, seafood, and chicken dishes for dinner. The restaurant holds a fond place in the hearts of regular Route 17 travelers who have stopped in for a slice of pie or a belly-bustin' breakfast, and they'll find that not much has changed since their last visit. ⊠ *Old Rte. 17* ☎ *607/498–4405* ▭ *AE, D, DC, MC, V.*

$–$$$ ✕ **Raimondo's Ristorante & Pizzeria.** The best pizza in town is at Raimondo's, on the main drag. The building has aged, and the decor isn't much, but the tables are clean and the service fast-paced. ⊠ *Stewart Ave.* ☎ *607/498–4702* ▭ *AE, MC, V.*

$$$ 🏨 **Beaverkill Valley Inn.** Tucked away in the southwest corner of the
Fodor's Choice   Catskill Forest Preserve, this family-friendly lodge has the amenities of
★   a small resort. The 1895 inn, which sits on a great lawn, houses guest rooms outfitted with brass and iron beds and muted country prints and quilts. A fireplace warms the game room, which is of the board, rather than video, variety. The grounds include a large barn building that contains a gym, a playroom, an indoor pool, a basketball court, and an all-you-can-eat ice-cream parlor (you serve yourself); access to these facilities costs an additional $100 per room or family. A stretch of the famous Beaverkill runs right through the property, which also has an herb garden and a pond. ⊠ *Off Beaverkill Rd., Lew Beach 12753* ☎ *845/439– 4844* 🖷 *845/439–3884* ⊕ *www.beaverkillvalleyinn.com* ⤶ *20 rooms, 15 with bath* ⚭ *Dining room, ice-cream parlor, 2 tennis courts, indoor pool, fishing, basketball, billiards, croquet, hiking, cross-country ski-*

ing, ice-skating, meeting rooms; no room phones, no room TVs, no smoking ⊟ *AE, MC, V* ⦿ *BP.*

¢–$ 🏨 **Baxter House Bed & Breakfast.** If you don't want to spend a minute out of the water while on your fishing vacation, the Baxter House is where you want to park your canoe. Breakfast comes with the latest information about water temperatures, and a guide downstairs tells you how the fish are running. Equipment rentals and fly-fishing lessons make this a fisherman's dream. ⊠ *2012 Old Rte. 17, 12776* ☎ *607/498–5811 or 800/905–5095* ⊕ *www.baxterhouse.net* 🛏 *6 rooms, 4 with bath* ⚲ *Dining room, kitchen, Cable TV, fishing; no room phones, no smoking* ⊟ *AE, DC, MC, V* ⦿ *CP.*

¢–$ 🏨 **Reynolds House & Motel.** A 1902 Victorian house with a wraparound porch holds six of the rooms at this B&B and motel. The B&B has a proud history of sharing Roscoe with visitors, which have included John D. Rockefeller, for whom the largest, most attractive room is named. Two of the rooms in the house have queen-size beds; the Rockefeller Room has a king bed and the others have doubles. Motel rooms, each with a couple of double beds, are spacious and bright. Common areas include a reading room and a lounge. Shops and eateries are within walking distance. ⊠ *Old Rte. 17, 12776* ☎ *607/498–4422* 🖷 *607/498–5808* ⊕ *www.reynoldshouseinn.com* 🛏 *18 rooms* ⚲ *Dining room, some kitchenettes, cable TV; no kids under 10 in main house, no smoking* ⊟ *MC, V* ⦿ *BP main-house rooms, EP motel rooms.*

¢ 🏨 **Roscoe Motel.** Popular with families on a budget, this small motel just off Route 17 has simple rooms within spitting distance of some of the world's best fishing holes. Some rooms have views of the Beaverkill River, and you can easily walk from the motel to local eateries and shops. ⊠ *Old Rte. 17, 12776* ☎ *607/498–5220* ⊕ *www.roscoemotel.com* 🛏 *18 rooms* ⚲ *Picnic area, some refrigerators, cable TV, pool, fishing, some pets allowed (fee)* ⊟ *AE, MC, V* ⦿ *CP.*

CAMPING ⛺ **Beaverkill Campground.** The campground, part of the Catskill Forest Preserve camping system, is adjacent to the famed Beaverkill creek, where you can fish for brown and brook trout. There's also an 1865 covered bridge on the property. Berrybrook Road is off Beaverkill Road, which you reach via Route 206 west of Route 17/I–86. ⚲ *Flush toilets, dump station, drinking water, showers, grills, picnic tables, public telephone* 🛏 *108 tent and trailer sites* ⊠ *792 Berrybrook Rd., off Beaverkill Rd., 12776* ☎ *845/439–4281, 800/456–2267 reservations* ⊕ *www.dec.state.ny.us* 🗊 *$15* ⊟ *MC, V* ☉ *Closed Labor Day–mid-May.*

Sports & the Outdoors

FISHING The pioneers of trout fishing took to Sullivan County's waterways in the 1800s and, with a flick of the wrist and knot on a fly, a tradition was born. Roscoe's **Junction Pool,** where the Beaverkill and Willowemoc creeks meet, is hallowed ground for anglers who wade into these waters—the supposed birthplace of dry-fly fishing. From the April 1 opening of trout season, folks are after the approximately 2.27 million catchable-size trout the state stocks each year.

At **Beaverkill Angler** (⊠ Stewart Ave. ☎ 607/498–5194 ⊕ www.beaverkillangler.com), the official Orvis dealer in Trout Town, U.S.A., you have the option to "test before buying" with a rental, and the fisherman-cashier can fill you in on the water temperature and fishing prospects before you climb into your waders. **Catskill Flies** (⊠ Stewart Ave. ☎ 607/498–6146 ⊕ www.catskillflies.com) has everything a fly-fisherman could ask for, from Columbia sportswear and hiking boots to waders and casting lessons. And you can arrange for a licensed guide to accompany you for a day of fishing. Serious anglers should make this their first stop for the latest stream and river conditions. Owner Dennis ties the dry flies himself—he can almost guarantee you'll catch the big one with his flies. A member of fly-fishing royalty, Joan Wulff breaks down the secret of the perfect cast into simple mechanics. **Wulff School of Fly Fishing** (⊠ 7 Main St., Livingston Manor ☎ 845/439–4060 or 800/ 328–3638 ⊕ www.royalwulff.com), the school she runs on the banks of the fabled Beaverkill, gives you a chance to crack the mysteries with the master.

FodorśChoice ★

Shopping
At the down-home **Annie's Place** (⊠ 51 Stewart Ave. ☎ 607/498–4139), named for the owner's placid poodle, you can browse for a memento from Trout Town, U.S.A., or a candle to light your way home.

Liberty

15 mi southeast of Roscoe.

In the pine-clad foothills at the southern edge of the Catskill Mountains, and roughly in the center of Sullivan County, this quiet community is one of the gateways to the so-called Borscht Belt resort area. The village itself doesn't have much to offer visitors; it's the surrounding area, with its hilly forests and renowned fly-fishing streams, that's the main attraction.

Where to Stay & Eat
$$-$$$ ✕ **Piccolo Paese.** Intimate surroundings with white tablecloths set against a burgundy backdrop and waiters clad in tuxedos make this a romantic spot. But it's not just couples who come to dine on the fine northern Italian fare. Handmade pastas are a specialty, and Caesar salad for two is made up tableside. Linguine is tossed with tuna, capers, olives, and wine sauce; penne in spicy tomato-cream sauce gets a splash of vodka; and shrimp are sautéed with mushrooms and proscuitto in champagne and cream. The menu also includes chicken, steak, and veal preparations. The list of wines is extensive. ⊠ 5 Rte. 52 E ☎ 845/292–7210 ⊟ AE, D, MC, V ☺ No lunch weekends.

$-$$$ ✕ **Manny's Steakhouse and Seafood.** If you're craving a hunk of prime meat or a slab of baby-back ribs, you won't go wrong at this classic steak house. Try the house specialty if you dare—a 50-ounce porterhouse steak for two. The seafood part of the menu includes daily fresh-fish dishes—grilled salmon, halibut, and swordfish—and stuffed lobster tails. The unassuming facade hides a spacious interior of warm woods. ⊠ 79 Sullivan Ave. ☎ 845/295–3170 ⊟ AE, D, MC, V.

$$$-$$$$ ☷ **Swan Lake Golf & Country Club.** Asian furnishings, paintings, and accents are scattered throughout this large, refurbished resort hotel, which overlooks Swan Lake and brings to mind the 1980s. Rooms lack the

THE BORSCHT BELT

LIBERTY AND MONTICELLO are jumping-off points for the legendary Catskills resorts. The cool, dry atmosphere of the region and its proximity to New York City attracted early sufferers of tuberculosis and other lung ailments. Later, Russian and Eastern European Jews flocked here to escape the heat and disease of New York City's immigrant ghettos.

Over time, this network of vacation spots came to be known as the Borscht Belt, and served as boot camp for innumerable entertainers who later gained national prominence. The Catskills churned out comedians Milton Berle, Freddie Roman, and Danny Kaye, to name a few. Old-time resorts like the Concord and Grossinger's are still standing, some as hotels and others as popular golf destinations. The influence of the resorts era has faded from the landscape, but the Yiddish sayings uttered by the local high-school kids are remnants of a period of Catskills history that affected a county and a country.

same flourish; most are furnished like those in a small motel, with two beds, two chairs, and a small table. The range of activities is the strong suit, and the 18-hole golf course is a big draw. The indoor sports center includes tennis, racquetball, and basketball courts. Bus groups predominate here. ⊠ *Hope Rd., Swan Lake 12783* ☎ *845/292–8000 or 877/800–0705* 🖶 *845/292–4194* ⊕ *www.swanlakeresorthotelcc.com* ↬ *216 rooms, 12 suites* ⚭ *Restaurant, dining room, cable TV, 18-hole golf course, 4 tennis courts, pro shop, 2 pools (1 indoor), gym, sauna, basketball, billiards, boccie, horseshoes, racquetball, shuffleboard, volleyball, ice-skating, bar, video game room, meeting rooms; no-smoking rooms* ▭ *MC, V.*

¢–$ 🏚 **Old House on a Hill.** If you're looking to get away from it all and want to avoid the cookie-cutter chains and mega-resorts that dot the region, consider this modest and friendly B&B. The three-story farmhouse, built in 1860, is on a hillside overlooking a meadow. Rooms are country simple and have iron beds, quilts, and pine and maple furnishings. ⊠ *295 Lt. Brender Hwy., Ferndale 12734* 🖶🖶 *845/292–3554* ⊕ *www. oldhouseonahill.com* ↬ *4 rooms* ⚭ *Dining room, fans; no room phones, no room TVs, no kids under 10, no smoking* ▭ *MC, V* ❘◎❘ *BP.*

Sports & the Outdoors

GOLF **Grossinger Country Club** (⊠ 26 Rte. 52 E ☎ 845/292–9000 or 888/448–
★ 9686 ⊕ www.grossingergolf.net) has two highly rated courses: the 18-hole, par-71 Big G course and the 9-hole, par-36 Little G course. Both were originally designed by A. W. Tillinghast. Greens fees are $20 for Little G and $45–$85 (including cart rental) for its 7,004-yard sibling. With big greens set amid beautiful scenery, the par-72, 6,820-yard course at the **Swan Lake Country Club** (⊠ Hope Rd., Swan Lake ☎ 845/292–0323 or 888/254–5818 ⊕ www.swanlakeresorthotel.com) is like a day in the park. Greens fees are $40–$55; cart rental is $15.

Shopping

A warren of 13 rooms on four floors, **Ferndale Marketplace Antiques** (✉ 52 Ferndale Rd., off Exit 101 of Rte. 17/I–86 ☎ 845/295–8701) brims with glassware, paintings, furniture, and vintage costume jewelry. Built in 1894, the building served as a post office and general store and is listed on the National Register of Historic Places. Exploring its nooks and crannies is as much fun as studying the objects for sale. **Memories** (✉ Rte. 17/ I–86, Parksville ☎ 845/292–4270 or 800/222–8463) has the pieces of your fondest memories. The acre-size antiques emporium has rooms devoted to carousels, lamps, the Victorian age, and collectibles.

Monticello

⑫ *11 mi south of Liberty.*

Sullivan County's largest population center, the village of Monticello is also the county's government seat. It's considered a gateway to the Catskills resort region and offers large-town conveniences. Attempts by American Indian tribes to open casinos in the area have kept Monticello in the news.

Monticello Raceway. Opened in 1958, the track has year-round harness racing, a daily-double race, and trifectas and perfectas with wagering. Inside is a Vegas-style racino with video lottery terminals. The all-you-can-eat buffet is first rate. ✉ *Rte. 17B 1 mi west of Rte. 17/I–86* ☎ *845/ 794–4100 or 800/777–4263* ⊕ *www.monticelloraceway.com* 🎫 *$1.50* ⊙ *Daily 10 AM–2 AM.*

Holiday Mountain Ski and Fun Park. Batting cages, miniature golf, a mechanical bull, paintball, a rock-climbing wall, go-karts, bumper cars, and an arcade are enough to keep the whole family engaged for a day of fun in the sun. The ski slopes are in business come December; the winter wonderland stays open until the snow is gone. ✉ *99 Holiday Mountain Rd., off Exit 107 of Rte. 17/I–86* ☎ *845/796–3161* ⊕ *www. holidaymtn.com* 🎫 *$1.50–$8, depending on activity* ⊙ *June–Aug., daily 10–10; Sept.–May, weekdays noon–9, Sat. 9–9, Sun. 9–5.*

> **off the beaten path**
>
> **WOODSTOCK MUSIC FESTIVAL MONUMENT** – On a former farm on the outskirts of Bethel, about 8 mi west of Monticello, this small stone monument marks the site of the legendary 1969 music festival. The site, which was purchased by Cablevision Industries mogul Gerry Allen in the mid-1990s, hosts Saturday farmers' markets (from July though late August) and themed Sunday festivals and crafts events (from Labor Day through Columbus Day weekends). Elaborate plans for the site include the Bethel Woods Center for the Performing Arts, under construction at this writing. It will include a 4,800-seat pavilion, scheduled to open in July 2006. ✉ *Hurd Rd., off Rte. 17B, Bethel* ☎ *845/295–2440* ⊕ *bethelwoods.us* 🎫 *Free.*

Where to Stay & Eat

$$–$$$ ✕ **Hana.** The Japanese eatery offers several tranquil dining rooms with an indoor water garden and bar. Sushi, sashimi, and tempura are the standouts. A popular spot with vegetarians, Hana is also a good choice for when you want something just a little different. ⊠ *166 Bridgeville Rd.* ☎ *845/794–3700* ⊟ *AE, MC, V.*

$$–$$$$
Fodor'sChoice
★
Inn at Lake Joseph. The inn, adjacent to a 250-acre lake and surrounded by forest, includes an 1860s manor house that's listed on the National Register of Historic Places, a carriage house, and a cottage. Most guest rooms are large and have working fireplaces and whirlpool tubs; several have decks. Manor-house rooms have Victorian wallpaper, Oriental rugs, four-poster beds, and antiques. Carriage-house rooms, outfitted in Adirondack-lodge style, have private entrances and beamed cathedral ceilings; one has a cupola skylight and another has a sleeping loft. Accommodations in the Adirondack-style cottage have cathedral ceilings and full kitchens. Breakfast is served on the manor's veranda (screened or glassed in, depending on the weather), and the complimentary snack bar is open all day. You have plenty of recreational choices, both on the 20-acre property and nearby, and inn owners Ivan and Ru Weinger provide most of the gear you'll need. ⊠ *400 St. Joseph Rd., Forestburgh 12777* ☎ *845/791–9506* ⊟ *845/794–1948* ⊕ *www. lakejoseph.com* ⤴ *11 rooms, 4 suites* ♿ *Dining room, snack bar, some fans, in-room data ports, some in-room hot tubs, some kitchens, some microwaves, some refrigerators, golf privileges, 2 tennis courts, pool, lake, massage, boating, fishing, mountain bikes, badminton, billiards, hiking, volleyball, cross-country skiing, massage, library, meeting rooms, some pets allowed (fee); no kids under 12 (July and Aug., and weekends Sept.–June), no smoking* ⊟ *AE, MC, V* ❑ *BP.*

$$
Best Western Monticello. Popular with race fans, this chain hotel is across from the Monticello Raceway and gives you plenty of bang for your buck. Rooms are nondescript (think white walls, cheap art prints, and basic furnishings), but the spacious, wood-paneled lobby is inviting, as are the heated indoor pool, sauna, and hot tub. Several restaurants are within walking distance or a few minutes' drive away. ⊠ *16 Raceway Rd., 12701* ☎ *845/796–4000* ⊟ *845/796–4000* ⊕ *www. bestwesternnewyork.com* ⤴ *62 rooms* ♿ *Some microwaves, some refrigerators, cable TV with movies, indoor pool, exercise equipment, hot tub, sauna, video game room, laundry service, Internet, meeting rooms, no-smoking rooms* ⊟ *AE, D, DC, MC, V* ❑ *CP.*

$
Concord Resort & Golf Club. Golf is the draw at this resort. Guests have access to the resort's Monster championship golf course and the highly rated Monster Golf Academy. Serious golfers like the convenience of the basic, no-frills rooms in the golf clubhouse. At this writing, big plans are in place for a huge resort on the 1,600-acre property to lure folks who do more than golf. ⊠ *219 Concord Rd., Kiamesha Lake 12751* ☎ *845/794–4000 or 888/448–9686* ⊟ *845/794–6944* ⊕ *www.concordresort.com* ⤴ *42 rooms* ♿ *Restaurant, minibars, refrigerators, cable TV, 18-hole golf course, pro shop, meeting rooms; no smoking* ⊟ *AE, D, DC, MC, V* ❑ *CP.*

Nightlife & the Arts

★
A mixture of professional and nonprofessional actors brings the words of famous playwrights to life at the **Forestburgh Playhouse** (⊠ 39 Forestburgh Rd., Forestburgh ☎ 845/794–1194 ⊕ www.fbplayhouse.com). The playhouse, one of a handful of small summer theaters left in the

country, has kick-started the careers of a number of Broadway stars. Shows change frequently from June through September, ranging from popular musicals to children's events.

Sports & the Outdoors

GOLF   Although both courses at the **Concord Resort & Golf Club** (⊠ 95 Chalet
★   Rd., Kiamesha Lake ☎ 845/794–4000 or 888/448–9686 ⊕ www. concordresort.com) earn high marks, the Monster course outshines its sibling, the International course. The 7,650-yard, par-72 Monster, opened in 1963, has greens fees of $45–$95; the 6,619-yard, par-71 International is $45–$55.

Callicoon

⓭ *22 mi west of Monticello.*

The hamlet is the restaurant capital of the Delaware River valley. You can walk from fine dining spots serving buffalo and other exotic fare to Italian eateries dishing out pasta dripping with pesto and vodka sauces, meander past antiques shops, and then head down to the banks of the Delaware. The yearly **tractor parade** (held the second Sunday in June, rain or shine) epitomizes the flavor of Callicoon: funny and fun-loving, with a reverence for its agricultural history. Pennsylvania is just on the other side of the Delaware.

Where to Stay & Eat

$$–$$$$ ✕ The **1906 Restaurant.** Ostrich, buffalo, and venison are served alongside traditional New York strip steak, pastas, and seafood dishes at this brick-storefront restaurant. At various times the building has housed a bank, a dry-goods store, a luncheonette, and a clothing store; the restaurant takes its name from the date of the building's construction, which appears prominently on the facade. ⊠ *41 Lower Main St.* ☎ *845/887– 1906* ▤ *AE, MC, V.*

★ ¢–$$ ✕ **Matthew's on Main.** The place combines the comfort and fun of a small-town tavern with a broad, ever-changing menu. Service on the deck gives you an eagle's-eye view of the hamlet. If you're in the mood for meat, you can't go wrong with the Big Mama Burger, a patty laden with ham, caramelized onions, and cheese on a toasted bun, and a basket of chef Matthew Lanes's hand-sliced potato chips. If you want a lighter meal, try a cheesy quesadilla and a cup of chunky gazpacho. ⊠ *19 Lower Main St.* ☎ *845/887–5636* ▤ *MC, V* ☉ *Closed Wed. in Sept.–May.*

$$–$$$$ ▥ **Villa Roma Resort Hotel.** Families have been coming to this bustling Catskills resort for generations. The casual, friendly atmosphere and wide range of activities also attract bus-tour groups and corporate gatherings. The extensive pool facilities, which include a waterslide and a bar, are a major draw, as is the indoor sports complex. Rooms, mostly dressed in pastels or neutrals, all have wall-to-wall carpeting and basic furnishings; some have balconies. Dining options are numerous. ⊠ *356 Villa Roma Rd., 12723* ☎ *845/887–4880 or 800/533–6767* ▤ *845/887– 4824* ⊕ *www.villaroma.com* ⇔ *182 rooms, 18 suites* ♧ *Restaurant, café, dining room, BBQ, snack bar, in-room data ports, some in-room hot tubs, some refrigerators, cable TV, 18-hole golf course, 2 tennis courts, pro shop, 5 pools (1 indoor), 2 wading pools, health club, massage, bil-*

liards, boccie, bowling, Ping-Pong, racquetball, shuffleboard, skiing, bar, lounge, nightclub, recreation room, video game room, babysitting, children's programs (ages 3–19), meeting rooms; no-smoking rooms ☰ *AE, D, DC, MC, V* ⚅ *BP.*

Nightlife & the Arts

★ Independent and foreign films are on the schedule at the **Callicoon Theater** (✉ 30 Upper Main St. ☎ 845/887–4460 ⊕ www.callicoontheater. com), one of the few single-screen theaters still operating in the country. The 1948 theater has changed with the times while retaining its old-time feel. At $5.50, tickets take you back in time, too.

Sports & the Outdoors

GOLF The outstanding course at the **Villa Roma Country Club** (✉ 356 Villa Roma Rd. ☎845/887–5097 or 800/727–8455), designed by David Postlethwaite, is 6,499 yards long and has a 71 par. The rather hilly setting is lovely, especially in fall. Greens fees are $50–$65, which includes cart rental.

Narrowsburg

13 mi south of Callicoon.

Taking its cues from the Delaware River, Narrowsburg lets life flow by at a slow pace. On the main drag, antiques shops and art galleries stand side by side with hardware stores and insurance agencies.

Eagle Institute. The nonprofit institute runs guided habitat tours from January through March, when nearly 200 bald eagles return to the area to breed. Barryville is a 20-minute drive southeast of Narrowsburg, but you can talk with trained volunteers and watch the birds at popular viewing sites throughout the region. The institute also hosts slide presentations and children's programs. ✉ *Rte. 97, Barryville* ☎ *845/557–6162* ⊕ *www.eagleinstitute.org.*

Ⓒ **Fort Delaware Museum of Colonial History.** The living-history site includes a replica of the 1755 stockaded fort-settlement that was the first of its kind in the Delaware River valley. Blockhouses, cabins, and gardens, along with exhibits, films, and demonstrations, give you a glimpse of the life of an 18th-century settler. ✉ *Rte. 97* ☎ *845/252–6660* 🎟 *$4* ☉ *Memorial Day–Labor Day, weekends 10–5:30.*

Where to Eat

$–$$$ ✗ **Dave's Big Eddy Diner.** This tiny casual eatery packs them in for breakfast and lunch, when diners fill up on overstuffed omelets, fresh berry pancakes, thick burgers, and veggie stir-fries. Dinner, served Friday and Saturday only, is more refined, with specialties like grilled stuffed flounder, rack of lamb, and steak au poivre. ✉ *40 Main St.* ☎ *845/ 252–3817* ☰ *AE, D, MC, V* ☉ *Closed Mon. and Tues. No dinner Sun., Wed., and Thurs.*

$–$$$ 🍴 **Eldred Preserve.** At the restaurant on this 3,000-acre preserve kids can slip into the kitchen to watch the chef clean and prepare the trout they caught in one of the ponds and lakes. You have 12 trout dishes to choose from, including trout champignon (pan-fried in butter and served with sautéed mushrooms and wine sauce). The bourbon-smoked salmon appetizer, which comes with toast points and red-pepper jelly, is another specialty. The menu also includes chicken, steak, veal, lamb, and duck. You may spot deer sipping from a stream outside the window as you sample cheesecake for dessert. The place also has rustic cabin-style buildings with motel rooms (¢) for overnighting in the forest. ☒ *1040 Rte. 55, Eldred* ☎ *845/557–8316 or 800/557–3474* 🖃 *AE, D, DC, MC, V.*

Nightlife & the Arts

The **Delaware Valley Arts Alliance** (☒ 37 Main St. ☎ 845/252–7576 ⊕ www.artsalliancesite.org) is a haven for the artists who flock to the hills and dales of Sullivan County to perfect their craft. Monthly receptions in its two gallery spaces bring visitors face to face with the artists who created the pots and paintings for sale.

Sports & the Outdoors

CANOEING &
RAFTING

Lander's Delaware River Trips (☒ 5666 Rte. 97 ☎ 800/252–3925 ⊕ www.landersrivertrips.com) operates guided canoeing and rafting trips—easy floats as well as white-water thrills—from April through December. Ten riverfront sites along the Delaware River help make family-owned and -operated Lander's king of the water. Overnight camping packages are available at sites along the Delaware River.

FISHING

Encompassing 3,000 acres of mostly untouched forest, the **Eldred Preserve** (☒ 1040 Rte. 55, Eldred ☎ 845/557–8316 or 800/557–3474 ⊕ www.eldredpreserve.com) has several ponds and lakes for bass, trout, and catfish fishing. Unless you fish in the catch-and-release trout pond ($12.50), you must keep and pay for the trout you catch ($2.50 to fish, $4.25 per pound of caught fish). At the preserve's popular restaurant, the kitchen will cook your trout for you. Bass fishing is catch-and-release only; two-person bass-boat rentals are $75 for a full day, and reservations are necessary. Catch-and-release catfish fishing is $15. Other activities here include sporting clays and deer and turkey hunting. The place also offers motel rooms (¢) in rustic buildings.

THE CATSKILLS A TO Z

To research prices, get advice from other travelers, and book travel arrangements, visit www.fodors.com.

AIR TRAVEL

The closest airports to the Catskills are Greater Binghamton Airport, Stewart International Airport, and Albany International Airport. The Albany airport puts you within an hour's drive of the northern Catskills. Continental Airlines affiliate CommutAir connects Albany airport to the Finger Lakes region, Long Island, and western New York; the carrier also flies to Westchester County Airport, in the lower Hudson Valley. US Airways Express links Albany to New York City, Long Island, and western New York.

Flights into Binghamton and Stewart come from outside New York State. *See* Air Travel *in* Smart Travel Tips A to Z for more information about

Binghamton, Albany, and Stewart airports and for major airlines' contact information.

Carriers CommutAir ☎ 800/525-0280 ⊕ www.commutair.com. **US Airways Express** ☎ 800/428-4322 ⊕ www.usairways.com.

BUS TRAVEL

Shortline buses link the Catskills with New York City, Long Island, the Hudson Valley, the Finger Lakes region, and central and western New York. Stops include Bethel, Liberty, Monticello, Roscoe, and Swan Lake; depending on your destination, you may have to wait at the Monticello terminal for your connecting bus.

Adirondack Trailways travels between the northern Catskills and New York City, the Hudson Valley, the Capital-Saratoga Region, and central New York; connecting service gets you to and from the other regions of the state. Buses stop in Arkville, Delhi, Fleischmanns, Haines Falls, Highmount, Hunter, Mount Tremper, Phoenicia, Prattsville, Shandaken, Tannersville, Windham, and Woodstock. During ski season, the Hunter-, Windham-, and Belleayre-bound buses are packed with twentysomethings from New York City heading for the slopes. Special packages include lift tickets.

Lines Adirondack Trailways ☎ 800/858-8555 ⊕ www.trailways.com. **Shortline Coach USA** ☎ 800/631-8405 ⊕ www.shortlinebus.com.

CAR RENTAL

Avis, Hertz, and Enterprise all serve Albany International Airport. Hertz also has a location at the Albany-Rensselaer Amtrak station. Monticello has an Enterprise representative that will pick you up at the bus station (about a five-minute drive away); the location is closed Saturday and Sunday, but after-hours drop-off is available. In Liberty, M&M Auto Group is a car dealer that also has rentals; it's about ½ mi from the bus station and is closed Sunday. Liberty also has a Hertz outlet, which is 1 mi from the bus station. *See* Car Rental *in* Smart Travel Tips A to Z for national agencies' contact information.

M&M Auto Group ✉ 127 Mill St., Liberty ☎ 845/292-8600 or 800/452-2217 ⊕ www.sweetestdeal.com.

CAR TRAVEL

Although you can get to the Catskills by bus, traveling by car is the best way to experience the region. It also allows you to easily detour into the adjacent Hudson Valley. You can enter the northeast Catskills via Exits 19 and 21 off the New York State Thruway (I-87). Route 17/I-86 (aka the Quickway) provides access to the southern and western Catskills. Weekenders heading north take to these highways on Friday evenings, when you can expect congestion and slower travel. The same is true heading south on Sunday, especially in the late afternoon and early evening.

The scenery is breathtaking on many of the region's roads. These include Route 23A, which, heading northwest toward Hunter, climbs steeply, passing Kaaterskill Falls; Route 10, which snakes its way across Delaware County past working farms and 19th-century homesteads; and Route 97, which runs parallel to the Delaware River.

Deer are plentiful throughout the region, so be on the lookout, especially at night. Also, cellular service in the region is spotty, so this is not a trip for the jalopy. You may want to skip a winter trip if you don't have four-wheel drive to help you negotiate the hilly (and often snowy and icy) terrain. In summer, slow-moving farm vehicles and animals along the roadside may impede travel; bikers and pedestrians on the road can also be hazards.

EMERGENCIES

In an emergency, dial 911.

The list below includes hospitals in the adjacent Hudson Valley region. **🖪 Northern Catskills Columbia Memorial Hospital** ✉ 71 Prospect Ave., Hudson ☎ 518/828-7601 ⊕ www.columbiamemorial.com. **Delaware Valley Hospital** ✉ 1 Titus Pl., Walton ☎ 607/865-4101 ⊕ www.uhs.net/aboutus/hospitals. **Kingston Hospital** ✉ 396 Broadway, Kingston ☎ 845/331-3131 ⊕ www.kingstonhospital.org. **Margaretville Memorial Hospital** ✉ Rte. 28, Margaretville ☎ 845/586-2631 ⊕ www.margaretville.com/hospital. **O'Connor Hospital** ✉ 460 Andes Rd., Delhi ☎ 607/746-0300 ⊕ www.oconnor-hospital.org. **Phoenicia Health Center/Benedictine Clinic** ✉ 9 Ave Maria Dr., Phoenicia ☎ 845/688-7513.
🖪 Southern Catskills Catskill Regional Medical Center ✉ Seelig Division, 68 Harris-Bushville Rd., Harris ☎ 845/794-3300 ⊕ www.catskillregional.org ✉ Grover Hermann Division, 8081 Rte. 97, Callicoon ☎ 845/887-5530 ⊕ www.catskillregional.org. **Crystal Run Healthcare** ✉ 61 Emerald Pl., Rock Hill ☎ 845/794-6999 ⊕ www.crystalrunhealthcare.com.

LODGING

All the county tourism bureaus and most local chambers of commerce list B&Bs, hotels, motels, inns, and resorts on their Web sites. The Web sites of the Sullivan County Bed & Breakfast Association and the Ulster County B&B Alliance include pictures of their member lodgings and links to individual properties' Web sites.

For weekly, monthly, and seasonal rentals, check listings in the Sunday real-estate section or on the Web site of the *New York Times*. The Sullivan County Board of Realtors can point you to real-estate agents who handle rentals in the southern Catskills.
🖪 New York Times ⊕ www.nytimes.com. **Sullivan County Bed & Breakfast Association** ✉ Box 69, Jeffersonville 12748 ☎ 845/482-5099 or 888/786-5287 ⊕ www.sullivanbandbs.com. **Sullivan County Board of Realtors** ✉ 19 St. John St., Monticello ☎ 845/794-2735. **Ulster County B&B Alliance** ✉ 110 Fairview Ave., Kingston ☎ 845/532-5466 ⊕ www.hudsonvalleybandbs.com.

SPORTS & THE OUTDOORS

Ticks are prevalent in the Catskills; wear bug repellant, cover skin with light-colored clothing, and check for ticks after outdoor excursions and activities.

BIKING   The Catskills offer a mix of endurance-testing hills and flat straightaways. Throughout the region you can find marked bike trails, wide country roads, and no-vehicles-allowed rail trails. Bike-rental places and tourism offices can provide information about specific routes. In its online biking guide, the Sullivan County Visitor's Association outlines 14 suggested rides. The Delaware County Chamber of Commerce has information about the 19-mi Catskill Scenic Trail, an old railway path, and lists five bike routes on its Web site.

For challenging mountain biking, head for the ski resorts—Belleayre, Plattekill, Hunter—in the off-season, when they turn their trails over to two-wheeled enthusiasts. The Ski Plattekill resort is actually one of the top mountain-biking spots in North America. You can also stay at a bike-focused lodging property. The Mountain Bike Inn, in Haines Falls, runs tours for beginning and experienced mountain and road bicyclists; the inn has seven rooms and a five-bedroom cottage.

CANOEING & The Class II–III Esopus Creek, which parallels Route 28 in and around
KAYAKING   Phoenicia, is a popular spot for canoeing and kayaking. Regulated by the state's Department of Environmental Conservation, releases from the nearby Schoharie Reservoir help maintain optimal conditions for recreational use of the creek waters—and create some awesome rapids. Contact the DEC for water-release schedules and additional information. If you're looking for a something tamer, try the Delaware River; public-access spots are scattered between Long Eddy and Port Jervis.

FISHING   For fishing regulations, license fees, seasons, and other specific information, contact the regional headquarters of the New York State Department of Environmental Conservation before heading off to the water.

HIKING   The Catksill 3500 Club, an organization of intrepid souls dedicated to hiking all 35 Catskills peaks with summits of 3,500 feet or more, outlines high-peaks hikes in its quarterly *Catskill Canister* ($10 annual subscription). The Catskill Center for Conservation and Development, in Arkville, occasionally runs guided hikes in the northern Catskills. Alternatively, you can join the Rip Van Winkle Hikers on one of their beginner, intermediate, or advanced group hikes; nearly every weekend the hikers congregate in Saugerties (a few miles east of the northern Catskills), at the parking lot on the corner of Market and Main streets, and then carpool to their destination. In the southern Catskills, the Catskill Hiking Shack (in Wurtsboro, about a 20-minute drive southeast of Monticello) carries hiking and camping gear and will point you to the area's best hiking spots.

Hiking in the Catskills can be amazing, but the rocky terrain and abundance of wildlife, including raccoons, skunks, porcupines, and bears, mean that extra care should be taken whenever you head away from populated areas. The state's Department of Environmental Conservation includes safety information on its Web site.

🚲 **Biking Delaware County Chamber of Commerce** ✉ 114 Main St., Delhi 13753 ☎ 607/746–2281 ⊕ www.delawarecounty.org. **Mountain Bike Inn** ✉ Rte. 23A, Haines Falls ☎ 518/589–9079 ⊕ www.mountainbikeinn.com. **Sullivan County Visitor's Association** ✉ 100 North St., Monticello 12701 ☎ 800/882–2287 ⊕ www.scva.net.
🚲 **Canoeing & Kayaking New York State Department of Environmental Conservation** ☎ 845/256–3161 Esopus water-release information ⊕ www.dec.state.ny.us.
🚲 **Fishing New York State Department of Environmental Conservation** ☎ 866/933–2257 fishing licenses, 845/256–3000 general information ⊕ www.dec.state.ny.us.
🚲 **Hiking Catskill Center for Conservation and Development** ✉ 43355 Rte. 28, Arkville ☎ 845/586–2611 ⊕ www.catskillcenter.org. **Catskill Hiking Shack** ✉ 169 Sul-

livan St., Wurtsboro 🕾 845/888-4453 ⊕ www.catskillhikes.com. **Catskill 3500 Club** ⊕ members.aol.com/howiedash/catskill_3500_club.htm. **New York State Department of Environmental Conservation** 🕾 845/256-3000 ⊕ www.dec.state.ny.us. **Rip Van Winkle Hikers** 🕾 845/246-8616 ⊕ www.newyorkheritage.com/rvw.

TOURS

TRAIN TOURS The Catskill Mountain Railroad runs train tours through the northern Catskills and also shuttles tubers back to their cars after they've floated down the Esopus. On weekends and holidays from late May through October, trains depart three times daily for the 14-mi tour ($12), which passes through Phoenicia and Boiceville.

From late May through October, the Delaware & Ulster Rail Road train travels along the Catskill Scenic Trail and the East Branch of the Delaware River, providing farm, field, and mountain views. It leaves Arkville for Roxbury (1 hour and 45 minutes round-trip), home of railroad magnate Jay Gould, who created the original railway in this area. On weekends you can opt for the shorter ride to Halcottsville, which takes about an hour there and back. Special excursions include a train ride to Highmount, where you transfer to a shuttle bound for the lift ride at Belleayre Mountain (a 3½-hour outing), and a ride pulled by Thomas the Tank Engine. From mid-September through October, leaf peepers pack the trains to take in the splendid Catskills foliage. Tickets are $7–$15.

🚺 **Catskill Mountain Railroad** ✉ Route 28, Mount Pleasant 🕾 845/688-7400 ⊕ www. catskillmtrailroad.com. **Delaware & Ulster Rail Road** ✉ 43510 Rte. 28, Arkville 🕾 845/586-3877 or 800/225-4132 ⊕ www.durr.org.

TRAIN TRAVEL

No trains service the Catskills. Amtrak stops in the Hudson Valley and in the Capital-Saratoga Region. The Rhinecliff, Hudson, and Albany stations all put you near the northeastern Catskills. From here you'll have to rent a car, however.

🚺 **Amtrak** 🕾 800/872-7245 ⊕ www.amtrak.com.

TRANSPORTATION AROUND THE CATSKILLS

The best way to get around and explore the Catskills is by car. Although you can get here by bus, public transportation within the region is limited and therefore impractical. In winter, snow and ice make for tough going, especially in the northern Catskills.

VISITOR INFORMATION

🚺 General **Catskill Association for Tourism Services** ⌂ Box 449, Catskill 12414 🕾 No phone ⊕ www.catskillvacation.net.

🚺 Northern Catskills Region **Delaware County Chamber of Commerce** ✉ 114 Main St., Delhi 13753 🕾 607/746-2281 ⊕ www.delawarecounty.org. **Greene County Tourism** ✉ 700 Rte. 23B, at Exit 21 off I-87, Catskill 12414 🕾 518/943-3223 or 800/355-2287 ⊕ www. greene-ny.com. **Ulster County Tourism** ✉ 10 Westbrook La., Kingston 12401 🕾 800/342-5826 ⊕ www.ulstertourism.info. **Woodstock Chamber of Commerce & Arts** ✉ 21 Tinker St., Woodstock 12498 🕾 845/679-8025 ⊕ woodstockchamber.com.

🚺 Southern Catskills Region **Callicoon Business Association** ⌂ Box 303, Callicoon 12723 🕾 845/887-4405 ⊕ www.visitcallicoon.com. **Liberty Chamber of Commerce** ⌂ Box

147, Liberty 12754 ☎ 845/292-1878 ⊕ www.libertyshops.com. **Livingston Manor Chamber of Commerce** ⫐ Box 122, Livingston Manor 12758 ☎ 845/439-4859 ⊕ www. livingstonmanor.org. **Narrowsburg Chamber of Commerce** ☎ 845/252-7434 or 888/ 252-7234 ⊕ www.narrowsburg.org. **Roscoe Chamber of Commerce** ⫐ Box 443, Roscoe 12776 ☎ 607/498-6055 ⊕ www.roscoeny.com. **Sullivan County Visitor's Association** ⊠ 100 North St., Monticello 12701 ☎ 800/882-2287 ⊕ www.scva.net.

THE CAPITAL REGION

ALBANY, SARATOGA SPRINGS, SCHENECTADY, TROY

5

SOAK AWAY YOUR WORRIES
at the Roosevelt Baths & Spa ⇨*p.393*

EXAMINE ARCHITECTURAL DETAILS
inside the New York State Capitol ⇨*p.386*

STAY AMID 2,200 PARK ACRES
at the Gideon Putnam Resort ⇨*p.398*

HEAR BIG-NAME MUSICIANS
at the Saratoga Performing Arts Center ⇨*p.400*

RISE AND SHINE WITH BREAKFAST
at the Saratoga Race Course ⇨*p.401*

HIKE THE INDIAN LADDER TRAIL
in John Boyd Thacher State Park ⇨*p.408*

By Tania
Garcia de
Rosier

EXPLORING THE CAPITAL REGION is like walking through a lesson in U.S. history. It was in this geographically diverse swath of land that the Iroquois Indians traded furs. In the 1600s the region was the destination of Dutch settlers who sailed here to stake out what eventually would become some of the oldest cities in the country. And this is also where the British forces were defeated in a defining moment of the American Revolution. In 1797, Albany was chosen as the state capital.

Rich in timber and iron ore from the nearby Adirondack Mountains, the region later would become a leader in the Industrial Revolution as the rise of factories and steel mills altered its agricultural landscape. Prosperity continued into the 19th century, when the landmark 363-mi Erie Canal across upstate New York was built, linking the Atlantic Ocean with the Great Lakes and opening up new trade and transportation routes. Evidence of the ensuing commerce and wealth can be seen today in the region's abundance of 19th- and early-20th-century architecture, from Saratoga Springs' historic avenues lined with majestic Victorian homes to Albany's châteaulike capitol.

With New York City to its south and Boston to its east, the Albany area has been at the center of much of the scientific and technological growth that defined the 20th century. This is where inventors such as Thomas Edison established what would later become General Electric, the source of pioneering contributions in power generation and distribution as well as in radio and television technology. Thanks to its roster of world-class universities and high-tech businesses, the region—a hub within New York's Tech Valley, which stretches from Orange County to the northern state border—remains a science-and-technology leader.

Yet the capital region is more than the government center and business magnet it professes to be. The region, encompassing a northern section of the Hudson River and bordered by the Adirondack and Catskill mountains, is rich in natural beauty. Opportunities for hiking, biking, golf, fishing, cross-country skiing, snowshoeing, and other outdoor pursuits abound. More passive activities include rooting for your favorite racehorse, soaking in a mineral bath, and watching a minor-league baseball game.

Perhaps even more appealing is the array of cultural diversions. Festivals celebrate opera, chamber music, and jazz; concert series cover everything from pop and rock to country and classical; the New York City Ballet and the Philadelphia Orchestra offer summertime performances; and small stages present blues, jazz, and folk sounds. You might stroll through the region's many art galleries, museums, and historic homes. The sculptures and modern artworks that populate Albany's Empire State Plaza constitute a don't-miss attraction in their own right.

Exploring the Capital Region

The capital region consists of Albany and three smaller cities: Troy, Schenectady, and Saratoga Springs. All are accessible via Interstate 87, which runs north–south the length of the state, and I–90, which runs east to west. Across the Hudson River and a few miles northeast of Albany is

Troy. Schenectady, which hugs the Mohawk River, is a few miles north-west of the capital. Traveling north on I–87 gets you to Saratoga Springs.

About the Hotels & Restaurants

Thanks to a culturally rich history, the capital region has restaurants that serve excellent Italian fare and other cuisines. Just about every neighborhood has a family-owned Italian restaurant that's been there for generations; these small establishments are worth considering for their authentic and delicious dishes. The region also has a number of good Asian, Indian, Caribbean, and Mexican eateries.

The area has many chain and independent full-service hotels; bed-and-breakfasts operate in the region's many historic neighborhoods and on the city outskirts. In Saratoga Springs, high-season prices jump considerably—even as much as 50%—during the racing season, which runs from late July to early September.

WHAT IT COSTS					
	$$$$	$$$	$$	$	¢
RESTAURANTS	over $30	$22–$30	$15–$21	$8–$14	under $8
HOTELS	over $250	$200–$250	$150–$199	$100–$149	under $100

Restaurant prices are for a main course at dinner (or at the most expensive meal served). Hotel prices are for two people in a standard double room in high season, excluding tax.

Timing

After a long, snowy Northeast winter there's nothing quite like the spring here. The remaining patches of snow are quickly overtaken by early spring flowers, namely the tulip, which is the focus of a weekend-long celebration every Mother's Day. Summer temperatures are mostly moderate, with the exception of a few 90°F days. With the warm weather comes the festival season, when many regional parks stage outdoor concerts and plays. The festivals last through the fall harvest season, when the weather cools and the trees burst with colorful foliage. August is a high point in Saratoga Springs, when the horse-racing season—with its attendant cultural and social activities—is in full swing.

ALBANY

Revised by
Bob Goepfert,
Ruth Fantasia

Since 1797 Albany has served as the capital of the state. You could say that the city, thanks to its role in state politics and to its location—about 150 mi north of New York City and roughly the same distance from Montréal—is in the thick of things. The state is the largest employer in the city (population 100,000), which helps to keep the economy fairly stable.

The heart of the state government is Empire State Plaza, where more than 35,000 people work. The city's most prominent architectural features are the towers that dominate the plaza's marble expanses. The imposing state capitol, on the north end of the plaza, looks across the mall to the classical modern New York State Museum. Other fine architec-

Numbers in the text correspond to numbers in the margin and on The Capital Region and Albany maps.

If you have 2 days

Touring ▣ **Albany** ❶–❿ is a good strategy if you have only two days to spend in the region. Exploring the New York State Capitol, the Empire State Plaza and its attractions and artworks, the Albany Heritage Area Visitors Center, and the Lark Street area consumes most of Day 1. On Day 2 either head south of the plaza and visit Historic Cherry Hill and the Schuyler Mansion State Historic Site or head north of the plaza and see the Ten Broeck Mansion and then, if the weather's nice, the Corning Preserve.

Alternatively, you could head out of town on Day 2 and tour **Saratoga Springs** ⓫. If you have tickets to a performance at the Saratoga Performing Arts Center, you can spend the good part of the day browsing through the shops. Have an early dinner before heading to your show.

If you have 3 days

Follow the two-day itinerary above, spending both days in ▣ **Albany** ❶–❿. On Day 2, in the late afternoon, drive north to ▣ **Saratoga Springs** ⓫. In the evening, go for a concert at the Saratoga Performing Arts Center or at the much smaller Spa Little Theatre; if you're really keen on seeing a certain performance, be sure to buy tickets in advance. Spend the next morning strolling through downtown and Congress Park. If you're visiting during racing season, head straight for the Saratoga Race Course for an early breakfast and then relax until the first race. If you're feeling energetic, consider visiting the Saratoga National Historical Park/Battlefield in the afternoon.

If you have 4 days

Spend two days in ▣ **Albany** ❶–❿, following the suggestions in the two-day itinerary above. On Day 3, explore the Historic Stockade District in **Schenectady** ⓬, tour the RiverSpark Visitor Center in **Troy** ⓭, or go hiking in **John Boyd Thacher State Park** ⓮. In the evening, head north to ▣ **Saratoga Springs** ⓫ (follow the suggestions in the three-day itinerary).

tural specimens are easily found, like the Romanesque City Hall. In addition to the many public buildings here are historic residences, good restaurants, and interesting shops. To the west is Washington Park, which was designed by Frederick Law Olmsted and Calvert Vaux and is the site of many annual festivals and events. To the east of the plaza is the Corning Preserve, a lively waterfront park.

Henry Hudson first visited the Albany area in 1609, while exploring the Hudson River. He claimed the river valley for the Dutch, and in 1624 Dutch settlers developed Fort Orange, the second-oldest permanent European settlement within the country's 13 original colonies. The area, a hub for the beaver-fur trade, was also known as Beverwyck. Under British control, the name was changed to Albany, for the Duke of York and Albany. The area was a strategic location during the American Revolution, and its importance was cemented after the state capital was moved here. The arrival of the Erie Canal in 1826 turned the city into a key transportation and commercial hub.

As the city grew more prosperous in the late 1800s, wealthy residents built homes in Mansion Hill, today a historic district south of the plaza. Although the district's historic structures suffered neglect for decades, recent years have seen a spate of renovation, fueled in part by federal grants. Adding prestige to the neighborhood is the governor's residence on Eagle Street.

Exploring Albany

Albany is a compact city that is easily negotiated on foot or by car. The downtown business area revolves around the state government and, thus, Empire State Plaza. During the plaza's construction, many older buildings were destroyed; the Center Square historic district, to the west of the plaza, was developed in order to preserve the remaining brick houses built between 1850 and 1900. The area is bounded by State, Jay, Swan, and Lark streets. Because of its nightlife, boutiques, and colorful characters, the stretch of Lark Street between Madison Avenue and State Street is often compared to New York City's Greenwich Village.

South of the plaza you find Mansion Hill and the Pastures, an area used for grazing in the city's earliest days; the largest concentration of Federal and Greek-revival buildings in the city is found in these two neighborhoods. Pearl Street, a few blocks southeast of the plaza, has small stores, restaurants, and clubs—all sandwiched between the Pepsi Arena to the north and the Palace Theater to the south. The Arbor Hill area, on the city's north side, is where the industrial barons built lavish brownstone homes.

A loop of highways creates Albany's boundaries and makes traveling around the city quick and easy. Route 5, known as Central Avenue, cuts through the city from I–787 to I–87 (aka the Northway), but traffic lights and shopping draws can slow travel on this road. Because the majority of the city's residents work for the state government, office hours are staggered to alleviate severe traffic congestion. Downtown has ample parking in public lots, garages, and metered spaces. North Pearl Street has several multilevel lots, and a number of smaller lots can be found along Broadway and Madison Avenue.

Start at the **Governor Nelson A. Rockefeller Empire State Plaza ❶** ▶, the sprawling complex at the city's center. At the south end of the plaza is the **New York State Museum ❷**. As you walk toward the museum you pass several examples of modernist and contemporary sculpture that complement the plaza's dramatic layout. At the corner of Madison Avenue and Eagle Street is the **Cathedral of the Immaculate Conception ❸**. From the museum, the **New York State Executive Mansion ❹** is a short walk south along Eagle Street. The mansion is open to the public only on Thursday, so you might want to skip this part of the walk on other days.

After a visit to the New York State Museum, exit to another striking view of the plaza, this time with the capitol in the distance. Go down one level

5

Summertime Shows

Summer is the season for music and entertainment, from weekend-long jazz festivals to dance performances. Many events—such as the Live at Five concert series at the Corning Preserve, in Albany—are free, whereas others charge moderate fees with no extra charge for children. Both the New York City Ballet and the Philadelphia Orchestra hold summer residencies at the Saratoga Performing Arts Center, a cultural gem that hosts pop, rock, and jazz concerts as well. Opera and chamber-music festivals are held at the Spa Little Theatre, part of Saratoga Spa State Park. Parks in Schenectady and nearby Scotia also host outdoor concerts.

to the enclosed concourse, which has shops, a restaurant, and the largest collection of public art in the country. Included in the collection are works by Alexander Calder, Robert Motherwell, Jackson Pollock, Mark Rothko, George Segal, Claes Oldenburg, and other 20th-century masters. Take the elevator to the 42nd-floor observation deck of the **Corning Tower** ❺, where you have a panoramic view of the city.

Return to the concourse and exit at the north end of the plaza, near the **New York State Capitol** ❻, one of the finest examples of 19th-century public architecture in the United States. From the front of the capitol you have a dramatic view of the plaza and its reflecting pools. To your left is the Egg (formally the Empire State Performing Arts Center), a modernist structure housing two theaters; to your right are four government buildings.

Right behind the capitol, on the north side of Washington Street, the multicolumned New York State Education Building hides the grand Episcopal Cathedral of All Saints, which you can see by walking a block west to Swan Street. Farther west on Washington is the **Albany Institute of History and Art** ❼. Continue west to the corner of Lark Street to see the interesting but vacant 1889 New York State Armory Building. Turn right onto Lark Street (the western edge of the Central Square historic district) for boutique shops, brownstone rows, and ethnic restaurants. Return to Washington Street and backtrack east; at the end of the street is **City Hall** ❽.

Facing City Hall, turn left onto Eagle Street, right onto Columbia Street, and finally left onto North Pearl Street. Pass the many shops and the Capitol Repertory Theatre before crossing the street to Clinton Square. This is the fourth site for the First Church of Albany, a building listed on the National Register of Historic Places; it includes the original church's pulpit from 1656—the nation's oldest. Across Clinton Avenue is the Palace Theatre, a restored 1931 vaudeville theater and a national historic site. Follow Clinton east (right) to the **Albany Heritage Area Visitors Center** ❾ and the Henry Hudson Planetarium. Next door to the visitor center is the 1736 Quackenbush House, now occupied by a restaurant.

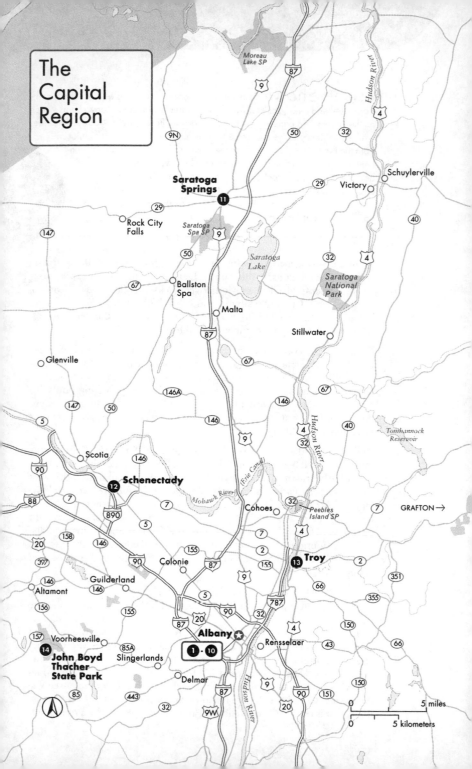

The Capital Region

Moreau Lake SP

87

9

Hudson River

4

50

32

9N

Schuylerville

29

Victory

40

Saratoga Springs 11

Rock City Falls

29

Saratoga Spa SP 9

147

Saratoga Lake

32

4

50

Saratoga National Park

67

Ballston Spa

Malta

87

Stillwater

Glenville

67

67

146A

146

40

Tomhannock Reservoir

147

50

146

9

4

32

Hudson River

5

Scotia

146

Schenectady 12

Mohawk River (Erie Canal)

32

Cohoes

Peebles Island SP

7

GRAFTON →

90

88

7

890

7

Cohoes

32

4

Troy 13

2

5

158

146

90

155

7

2

351

20

397

Colonie

87

155

66

355

146

Guilderland

9

787

Altamont

146

5

32

4

150

156

155

43

66

Albany ☆

157

Voorheesville

85A

John Boyd Thacher State Park 14

Slingerlands

Delmar

Rensselaer

150

85

443

32

87

Hudson River

9W

20

90

151

0   5 miles

0   5 kilometers

1 – 10

Walk south along Broadway and pass Albany's old train station, Union Station, which has been converted to private use.

Continue south to Pine Street. From here either turn right and head back toward Empire State Plaza, ending the walk, or turn left to Maiden Lane and cross over busy I–787 to the **Corning Preserve** ⓾, via the Hudson River Way Pedestrian Bridge. The preserve is a good place to walk or sit alongside the Hudson River. When you're ready, return over the pedestrian bridge and make a left. Continue south on Broadway past the Post Office and Federal Building (1879–83) to State Street. Here you see a massive curved building that once served as the headquarters for the Delaware & Hudson Railroad and is now the state-university administrative complex. A walk up the hill on State Street returns you to city hall and the capitol.

TIMING The walk takes three to four hours, but if you explore everything on the route, it can take a full day. To break the walk into two excursions, follow the first half of the walk to Lark Street. Pick up the walk at City Hall for the second half. Some shops and restaurants might be closed on weekends and state holidays.

What to See

Albany Aqua Ducks. From April through October, you can tour the city in a land-and-water vehicle. The 75-minute tour starts on dry ground, cruising the streets of Albany to historic sites. The U.S. Coast Guard–certified vessel then plunges into the Hudson River to give you another perspective of the city skyline. Tours start at the Albany Heritage Area Visitors Center and depart in the morning and early afternoon. Times vary; call for a schedule. ☎ 518/462–3825 or 888/258–3582 ⊕ www. albanyaquaducks.com ✍ $20.

Albany Center Galleries. Regional artists' works, which may include photographs, prints, drawings, paintings, and mixed-media pieces, are shown at these downtown galleries on the second floor of the public library. ✉ Albany Public Library, 161 Washington Ave. ☎ 518/462–4775 ⊕ www.albanycentergalleries.org ✍ Free ☉ Tues.–Sat. noon–5, or by appointment.

❾ **Albany Heritage Area Visitors Center.** The center's museum gallery is a good place for an orientation. Displays trace the city's history and define its neighborhoods; some include cultural artifacts. The center, downtown, has basic visitor information and often serves as a starting point for guided tours. Within the visitor center is the **Henry Hudson Planetarium** (✍ $2), which presents various shows and lectures. The star-sighting program, an interactive show, is held the second Saturday of each month at 1 PM. Call for schedules for special events and animal, holiday, and other themed shows. ✉ 25 Quackenbush Sq. ☎ 518/434–0405 ⊕ www.albany.org ✍ Free ☉ Weekdays 9–4, weekends 10–4.

❼ **Albany Institute of History and Art.** The 1791 museum, the state's oldest, has annual rotating exhibits and an impressive permanent collection that includes Hudson River school paintings and an Egyptian mummy exhibit. Silver, furniture, and contemporary-art collections cover regional history dating from the 1500s. The building, which combines a mod-

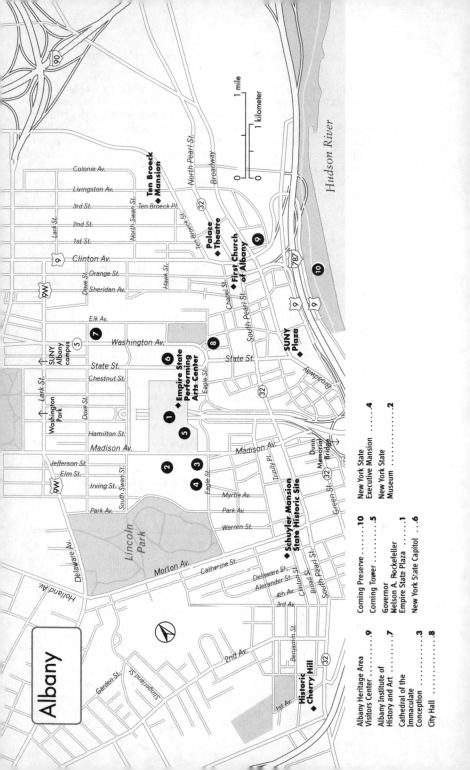

Albany

Hudson River

1 mile
1 kilometer

Ten Broeck Mansion
Colonie Av.
Livingston Av.
3rd St.
2nd St.
1st St.
Clinton Av.
Orange St.
Sheridan Av.
Lark St.
North Swan St.
Hawk St.
North Pearl St.
Broadway
Ten Broeck Pl.
Ten Broeck St.

Palace Theatre
Chapel St.
First Church of Albany

⑨

⑩

SUNY Plaza

Elk Av.
⑦
Washington Av.
⑥
State St.
Chestnut St.
SUNY Albany campus
Dove St.
Lark St.
South Pearl St.
State St.
⑧

Empire State Performing Arts Center
①
⑤

Washington Park
Hamilton St.
Madison Av.
②
③
④
Eagle St.
Madison Av.
Trinity Pl.
Dunn Memorial Bridge
Green St.
Broadway

Jefferson St.
Elm St.
Irving St.
South Swan St.
Park Av.

Myrtle Av.
Park Av.
Warren St.

Schuyler Mansion State Historic Site
Delaware St.
Alexander St.
4th Av.
3rd Av.
Clinton St.
Broad St.
South Pearl St.

Holland Av.
Delaware Av.
Lincoln Park
Morton Av.
Catherine St.

Historic Cherry Hill
Benjamin St.

Garden St.
Schuyler St.
1st Av.
2nd Av.

ern expansion with the original 18th-century space, is interesting architecturally. ⊠ *125 Washington Ave.* ☎ *518/463–4478* ⊕ *www.
albanyinstitute.org* ≦ *$7* ⊗ *Wed.–Sat. 10–5, Sun. noon–5.*

❸ **Cathedral of the Immaculate Conception.** The country's oldest neo-Gothic
cathedral, finished in 1852, has an imposing redbrick exterior with tall
twin spires. Inside you find a high vaulted ceiling, stained-glass windows,
and statues. A multimillion-dollar restoration was completed in 2004.
⊠ *Madison Ave. and Eagle St.* ☎ *518/463–4447* ⊕ *www.cathedralic.
com* ⊗ *Tours by appointment.*

❽ **City Hall.** American architect Henry Hobson Richardson, who also developed the state's capitol, designed this 1881 Romanesque revival–style
structure. A 49-bell carillon, one of about 200 in the country, was
added in 1927. ⊠ *25 Eagle St., Downtown* ☎ *518/434–5075* ⊕ *www.
albanyny.org.*

❿ **Corning Preserve.** The Hudson River Way Pedestrian Bridge leads to this
expansive green space along the Hudson River. A 5.3-mi trail, which
can be used for biking and hiking, snakes through the preserve. At the
north end are a public boat launch and a restaurant on a barge. June
through August, the 800-seat amphitheater hosts Live at Five, a free Thurs-
day-night concert series that attracts thousands of fans of jazz, bluegrass,
blues, and Celtic music. ⊠ *Off Maiden La., near Broadway* ☎ *No
phone* ≦ *Free.*

❺ **Corning Tower.** An elevator whisks you up 589 feet to the 42nd-floor observation deck of this building, the tallest structure in the state outside
New York City. The views on a clear day include the Berkshire, Catskill,
and Adirondack mountains. To get to the deck, you first must present
a photo ID at the plaza-level security desk. ⊠ *Empire State Plaza, off
Madison Ave. near Eagle St.* ☎ *518/474–2418* ⊕ *www.ogs.state.ny.us/
curatorial/* ≦ *Free* ⊗ *Daily 10–2:30.*

Five Rivers Environmental Center. Outdoor education programs, ¼- to 2-
mi hiking and skiing trails, a wildlife garden, and an exhibit center with
animals are at this 400-acre preserve 10 mi southwest of downtown.
You can picnic on the grounds. ⊠ *56 Game Farm Rd., Delmar* ☎ *518/
475–0291* ⊕ *www.dec.state.ny.us* ≦ *Free* ⊗ *Grounds daily dawn–dusk,
visitor center Mon.–Sat. 9–4:30 and Sun. 1–4:30.*

❶ **Governor Nelson A. Rockefeller Empire State Plaza.** The ¼-mi-long, 98-acre
FodorśChoice concourse includes modern art and sculpture, the New York State Mu-
★ seum, the State Library, the elliptical performing-arts center, and the New
York State Vietnam Memorial. At the center of the plaza is a rectangular reflecting pool. The capitol crowns the plaza's north end. On
weekdays you can take a free guided tour, which examines the plaza's
history, architecture, monuments, and artworks. Tours last about an hour
and start at the concourse-level visitor center. ⊠ *Bordered by Madison
Ave. and State, Eagle, and Swan Sts.* ☎ *518/474–2418* ⊕ *www.ogs.state.
ny.us* ≦ *Free* ⊗ *Tours weekdays 11 and 1.*

Historic Cherry Hill. The 1787 Georgian house was the home of Philip
Van Rensselaer, one of the region's original Dutch settlers. Guided tours

focus on Catherine Putnam, Rensselaer's niece, who lived in the house during the Civil War and World Wars I and II. The collection of family memorabilia encompasses more than 20,000 objects, including furniture, artworks, kitchen items, and pottery pieces; 3,000 photographs; and extensive documents and records. To visit the house you must take the tour, which lasts about an hour and starts on the hour. ☒ 523½ S. Pearl St. ☎ 518/434–4791 ⊕ www.historiccherryhill.org ☒ $4 ☉ July–Sept., Tues.–Sat. 10–3, Sun. 1–3; Apr.–June, Oct., and Nov., Tues.–Fri. noon–3, Sat. 10–3, Sun. 1–3.

❻ New York State Capitol. It took more than 30 years to complete this grand

Fodor'sChoice building (1867–99), which incorporates elaborate carvings, interesting

★ architectural elements, and eclectic styles. The 45-minute guided tour highlights the ornate Great Western Staircase (aka the Million Dollar Staircase)—which took 13 years and 600 stone carvers to complete— and, right over it, a 3,000-square-foot skylight that had been covered from World War II until 2002. Amid the carved faces adorning the staircase pillars are several famous visages. You can visit the legislative chambers and, when open, the governor's ceremonial offices. Tours begin at the visitor center on the concourse level of Empire State Plaza. ☒ Washington Ave. and State St., Downtown ☎ 518/474–2418 ⊕ www. ogs.state.ny.us ☒ Free ☉ Tours weekdays 10, noon, 2, and 3; weekends 11, 1, and 3.

❹ New York State Executive Mansion. Wraparound porches, a balconied gable, and turrets provide evidence of the 1856 building's progression of architectural phases, from Italianate to Second Empire and finally Queen Anne. The mansion has served as the official residence of New York's governors since 1875. To see the interior, you must take one of the guided tours, which last about an hour; because visiting times are so limited, reserve at least two weeks in advance. ☒ 138 Eagle St. ☎ 518/473–7521 ⊕ www.ogs.state.ny.us ☒ Free ☉ Tours Sept.–June, Thurs. noon, 1, and 2.

★ ❷ New York State Museum. The museum explores the state's history, geography, nature, and art; exhibits include a re-created Iroquois village, a display about New York birds, and a working 1916 carousel (with horses from the 1890s). A display about the September 11 terrorist attacks documents, through photographs and artifacts, rescue efforts at the World Trade Center. In February the museum hosts the regional flower show, "New York in Bloom." ☒ Empire State Plaza, Cultural Education Center, Madison Ave. ☎ 518/474–5877 ⊕ www.nysm.nysed.gov ☒ $2 suggested donation ☉ Daily 9:30–5.

Schuyler Mansion State Historic Site. Philip Schuyler, a Revolutionary War general, was the original owner of this 1763 Georgian mansion. George Washington and Benjamin Franklin were among the notable figures who visited the house. Tours of the national historic landmark (the only way to see the interior) feature original family furnishings, artifacts, and paintings. ☒ 32 Catherine St. ☎ 518/434–0834 ⊕ nysparks.state.ny.us ☒ $4 ☉ Mid-Apr.–Oct., Wed.–Sat. 10–5, Sun. 1–5; Nov.–mid-Apr., by appointment.

State University of New York at Albany. About 16,000 students are enrolled at this state university (aka SUNY), established in 1844. The quaint, traditional downtown campus, built in 1909, was modeled after that of the University of Virginia. The 1971 **uptown campus** is dominated by stark, massive arches. A large reflecting pool lies at the center of a quadrangle formed by four high-rise dorms and classrooms. The free **University Art Museum** (⊠ 1400 Washington Ave. ☎ 518/442–4035), open 11–4 Tuesday through Saturday, has three galleries with frequently rotating contemporary-art exhibits. The museum's permanent collection includes works by Richard Diebenkorn, Donald Judd, Ellsworth Kelly, and Robert Rauschenberg. ⊠ *Downtown campus, 135 Western Ave.* ☎ *518/442–5200* ⊠ *Uptown campus, 1400 Washington Ave.* ☎ *518/ 442–3300* ⊕ *www.albany.edu.*

Ten Broeck Mansion. Family portraits and period furnishings fill this 1798 Greek-revival home built for General Abraham Ten Broeck, a former Albany mayor. The tour takes you through the house and well-kept gardens. ⊠ *9 Ten Broeck Pl.* ☎ *518/436–9826* ⊡ *$4* ☉ *Tours May–Dec., Thurs. and Fri. 10–5, weekends 1–4.*

USS *Slater.* The Destroyer Escort warship is the last of 565 destroyer ships used by military personnel through World War II and the Cold War. Tours show the ship's restored armaments, crew and officers' quarters, radio room, and pilot house. ⊠ *Quay and Broadway* ☎ *518/431–1943* ⊕ *www.ussslater.org* ⊡ *$6* ☉ *Apr.–Nov., Wed.–Sun. 10–4.*

off the beaten path

SHAKER HERITAGE SOCIETY AND MEETING HOUSE – Through exhibits and tours, the preservation group details the history of the Shaker movement. The site was home to the first Shaker settlement in the United States; it started in 1776 with about a dozen members and grew to about 350 members at its peak, in the mid-1900s. The 1848 meetinghouse, a clapboard structure with a tin roof, was the third meetinghouse built here. Although it houses a museum and the preservation group's offices, the building looks much as it did originally. The property, which you can tour on your own, also encompasses several other buildings, a nature preserve, and a cemetery. Guided tours ($3; Saturday 11:30 and 1:30) are available June through October. ⊠ *875 Watervliet Shaker Rd., Colonie* ☎ *51/ 456–7890* ⊕ *www.crisny.org/not-for-profit/shakerwv/* ⊡ *Free* ☉ *Feb.–Oct., Tues.–Sat. 9:30–4; Nov. and Dec., Mon.–Sat. 10–4.*

FESTIVALS & FAIRS — **Capital District Scottish Games.** Pipe bands, highland dance performances, and traditional contests are the highlights of this annual Celtic arts festival held on the Saturday and Sunday of Labor Day weekend. ⊠ *Altamont Fair Grounds, Rte. 146, Altamont* ☎ *518/438–4297 or 518/785–0507* ⊕ *www.scotgames.com.*

First Night. Outside of New York City and Boston, this public New Year's Eve celebration is one of the East Coast's largest. A $10 button gives you access to more than 30 public and private spaces—all within a five-block area—that have been turned into one big alcohol-free, family-friendly entertainment zone. The general festivities start at 7 PM, but children's events start as early as 2 PM. Midnight fireworks conclude the shindig. ☎ 518/434–2032 ⊕ *www.albanyevents.org.*

Larkfest. During the daylong street festival, held in early September, more than 100 crafts and food booths line the streets. A separate area for kids has games and rides. Local bands perform, in addition to area dancers and magicians. ⊠ *Lark St. between Madison and Washington Aves.* ☎ 518/434–3861 ⊕ *www.larkstreet.org.*

Tulip Festival. Thousands of tulips are at their peak during this three-day weekend festival in mid-May celebrating Albany's Dutch heritage. Traditions include scrubbing the streets and crowning a Tulip Queen. On Saturday and Sunday, Washington Park has music, concerts, and food vendors. ⊠ *Washington Park, between State St., Madison Ave., Lake Ave., and Willett St.* ☎ 518/434–2032 ⊕ *www.albanyevents.org.*

Where to Stay & Eat

$$–$$$$ ✕ **Jack's Oyster House.** For great seafood, this Albany establishment with tiled floors, white tablecloths, dark wood, and polite service is the place to go. Two menus are offered at dinner: one has dishes from 1913, the year Jack's opened, and the other lists more contemporary preparations. Oysters, steak, and prime rib are regular features. Signature dishes from the 1913 menu include calves' liver sautéed with bacon, and Jack's Seafood Grille, which contains scallops, shrimp, and salmon. Pasta dishes, chicken fingers, and hamburgers are popular. The restaurant is down the hill from the state capitol and next door to the Pepsi Arena. ⊠ *42 State St., Downtown* ☎ 518/465–8854 ⊟ *AE, D, DC, MC, V.*

$$–$$$$ ✕ **McGuire's.** Whether you're looking for drinks or an interesting meal, this always-crowded spot is the place to see and be seen in Albany. The innovative chef has put together a menu that ranges from vegetarian pasta dishes to Kobe beef steaks. Mixed in are exotics such as kangaroo and venison, the latter served with Mexican chocolate and cinnamon sauce. Appetizers include ostrich pot stickers and peaches broiled with Gorgonzola. ⊠ *353 State St.* ☎ 518/463–2100 ⊟ *AE, D, MC, V* ☺ *No lunch.*

$$–$$$ ✕ **Yono's.** This intimate restaurant in the Armory Center draws mostly businesspeople, who come to savor curry and coconut-milk dishes in an elegant, colonial-style setting. The pale-periwinkle walls, fireplace, unfussy antique chandelier, white tablecloths, and lovely wood trim create a formal but comfortable space. The menu, a blend of Indonesian and Continental fare, includes winners such as pistachio-crusted chicken breast in Madeira sauce and rack of lamb. For dessert consider raspberry-walnut torte with cream-cheese frosting. The wine list, covering more than 700 bottles, has been lauded by *Wine Spectator.* ⊠ *64 Colvin Ave.* ☎ 518/436–7747 ⋔ *Jacket required* ⊟ *AE, D, DC, MC, V* ☺ *Closed Sun.–Tues. No lunch.*

$–$$$ ✕ **Café Capriccio.** A favorite of the Albany political establishment, this intimate, wood-paneled eatery serves northern Italian and Mediterranean food in small booths with beautiful lighting. The breads and pastas are made on-site, and you can't miss with the risotto of the day. ⊠ *49 Grand St.* ☎ 518/465–0439 ⊟ *AE, D, MC, V* ☺ *No lunch.*

$-$$$ ✕ **Lombardo's.** Young professionals, legislators, couples, and out-of-towners flock here to eat northern and southern Italian fare in a dining room where casual clothes mix easily with jackets and ties. Lombardo's is known for veal, pasta, and seafood dishes, and has some of the best waiters in the region. The Pepsi Arena is a block away; the Governor's Mansion and the State Library are up the street. ✉ *119–121 Madison Ave.* ☎ *518/462–9180* ▭ *MC, V* ⊘ *Closed Sun. No lunch Sat.*

$-$$ ✕ **Mangia Cafe.** Fresh bread, hearty pasta portions, and wood oven–baked pizzas are trademarks at this eatery, part of a small chain. The lunch crowd of professionals and shoppers gives way to families in the evening. The chicken tortellini with sun-dried tomatoes and mushrooms garners many requests for the recipe. ✉ *Stuyvesant Plaza, Western Ave. at I–87, Guilderland* ☎ *518/482–8000* ▭ *AE, D, MC, V* ✉ *1652 New Scotland Rd., Slingerlands* ☎ *518/439–5555* ▭ *AE, D, MC, V.*

¢   ✕ **Miss Albany Diner.** The Albany landmark is one of the few pre–World War II diners in nearly original condition in the United States. The menu has a selection of stick-to-your ribs favorites, such as fried eggs, pancakes, and ⅓-pound hamburgers. Daily blue-plate specials might include turkey and pot roast. The owners pay homage to Rhode Island— where diners originated—with quahog (clam) chowder and chocolate and coffee egg cremes. ✉ *893 Broadway* ☎ *518/465–9148* ▭ *No credit cards* ⊘ *No dinner.*

$-$$ ✕▢ **Mansion Hill Inn and Restaurant.** The inn, in the heart of downtown, was built in 1861 and has a central courtyard. Guest rooms are large and uncluttered, with reproduction antiques and tasteful watercolor prints. The real draw, however, is the dozen-table storefront restaurant ($$–$$$), which serves imaginative New American cuisine. Entrées include grilled duck breast, which is served with the sauce of the day, and sesame-crusted salmon fillet with sweet soy sauce; the menu also lists vegetarian and pasta dishes. In nice weather you may eat outside in the landscaped courtyard. The restaurant is closed Sunday and does not serve lunch. ✉ *115 Philip St., 12202* ☎ *518/465–2038 or 888/299–0455* ⊟ *518/434–2313* ⊕ *www.mansionhill.com* ⇦ *8 rooms* ⚲ *Restaurant, room service, some refrigerators, in-room data ports, in-room safes, cable TV, lounge, babysitting, dry cleaning, laundry facilities, laundry service, business services, meeting rooms, free parking, some pets allowed; no smoking* ▭ *AE, D, DC, MC, V* ⑩ *BP.*

$$-$$$ ▢ **Desmond Hotel & Conference Center.** Brick courtyards, hand-painted wooden signs, Early American furniture, and staff in 18th-century attire give this large hotel the air of a colonial village with modern conveniences. Some rooms have king-size canopy beds; all have large bathrooms with phones. The complex includes a casual all-day eatery (many patrons favor the cheese blintzes for breakfast); a fine dinner-only restaurant; and a lounge with cushy upholstery seats. The hotel is less than a mile from Albany International Airport. ✉ *660 Albany Shaker Rd., Colonie 12211* ☎ *518/869–8100 or 800/448–3500* ⊟ *518/869–7659* ⊕ *www.desmondhotels.com* ⇦ *323 rooms, 18 suites* ⚲ *2 restaurants, room service, in-room data ports, some microwaves, some refrigerators, cable TV, 2 pools, gym, hot tub, billiards, pub, business services, meeting rooms, airport shuttle, free parking; no smoking* ▭ *AE, D, DC, MC, V.*

★ **$–$$$**   🏨 **The State House.** Inside the **Morgan State House,** a late-19th-century town house on Washington Park, rich cherrywood wainscoting and trim complement high ceilings, hand-glazed walls, and fireplaces. Although the house is in the center of town, the views are of either the park or the inn's well-tended flower beds. The building has four floors and no elevator. Each room is different—yours might have a fireplace, a claw-foot tub, exposed brick walls, a skylight, or a reading area—but the over-all look is refined, and all rooms have down comforters, featherbeds, and terry robes. Regular rooms have queen or king beds, and the sec-ond-floor suite has two queens. Studios are available three doors away at the **Washington Park State House,** a sibling property with an eleva-tor. Breakfast is served in the town house. ⊠ *393 State St., 12210* ☎ *518/427–6063 or 888/427–6063* 🖷 *518/463–1316* ⊕ *www.statehouse. com* ➯ *4 rooms, 1 suite, 9 studios* ♿ *In-room data ports, some kitchens, some kitchenettes, cable TV, massage, laundry service, business ser-vices, meeting rooms, parking (fee); no kids, no smoking* ▤ *AE, D, DC, MC, V* ⏺*◎ BP.*

¢–$$ 🏨 **Crowne Plaza.** Two blocks from the state capitol, the 15-story hotel primarily serves businessmen and politicians, which means you'll get the best rates on weekends and in summer, when the legislature isn't in ses-sion. Rooms have wireless Internet access, dual-line phones, work desks, and CD players. The lobby-level bar serves 40 types of martinis. The hotel is a few blocks from the Pepsi Arena, the State Museum, histori-cal sights, and a half-dozen restaurants and nightspots. ⊠ *State and Lodge Sts., 12207* ☎ *518/462–6611* 🖷 *518/462–2901* ⊕ *www.crowneplaza. com* ➯ *384 rooms, 15 suites* ♿ *Restaurant, room service, in-room data ports, some refrigerators, cable TV with movies, indoor pool, hot tub, gym, bar, dry cleaning, laundry service, concierge, Internet, busi-ness services, convention center, meeting rooms, airport shuttle, car rental, parking (fee), no-smoking rooms* ▤ *AE, D, DC, MC, V.*

$ 🏨 **Days Inn of Albany.** The location of this three-story chain-motel property a few miles from the Albany airport gives you quick access to I–87 and I–90. Interior corridors and elevators connect the rooms, which are simple but offer voice mail and free local calls. Guests get day-use privileges at a nearby health club. ⊠ *16 Wolf Rd., 12205* ☎ *518/ 459–3600* 🖷 *518/459–3677* ⊕ *www.daysinn.com* ➯ *141 rooms, 8 suites* ♿ *In-room data ports, some kitchenettes, some microwaves, in-room safes, cable TV with movies, pool, dry cleaning, Internet, busi-ness services, free parking, no-smoking floors* ▤ *AE, D, DC, MC, V* ⏺*◎ CP.*

¢–$ 🏨 **State Street Mansion.** The intimate, neoclassical town home is near the state capitol, museums and other attractions, and restaurants. Rooms have either one king bed, one or two queens, or one or two doubles; some have working fireplaces. Guest-room furnishings are fairly sim-ple; breakfast is served in a more formal, parlorlike space with a fire-place and a European feel. ⊠ *281 State St., 12210* ☎ *518/462–6780* 🖷 *518/462–5889* ⊕ *www.statestreetmansion.com* ➯ *5 rooms* ♿ *Some in-room data ports, some refrigerators, cable TV, business services, meeting room, free parking, some pets allowed; no room phones, no smoking* ▤ *AE, MC, V* ⏺*◎ CP.*

Nightlife & the Arts

Nightlife

The Roaring Twenties theme at **Big House Brewing** (⊠ 90 N. Pearl St. ☎ 518/445–2739 ⊕ www.bighouseonline.com) makes this former warehouse a three-story party palace. The microbrewery has a good number of beers on tap. The first floor has a game room. Live entertainment on weekends makes conversation difficult, but upstairs levels are more sedate. In good weather you can dine outside. The high-energy, casual **Jillian's** (⊠ 59 N. Pearl St. ☎ 518/432–1997 ⊕ www.jillians.com) is a three-story club inside a downtown entertainment complex. You can watch sports on large televisions, play interactive video games, or shoot pool at one of the 12 tables. Take a turn on the dance floor in the Groove Shack, the restaurant's nightclub; or grab a burger, sandwich, or slice of pizza. Choose from four different levels of decks if you want to eat outside. At **Nick's Sneaky Pete's** (⊠ 711 Central Ave. ☎ 518/489–0000 ⊕ www.nickssneakypetes.com), the largest dance club in Albany, DJs start spinning at 10 PM Wednesday through Saturday.

The Arts

The **Capitol Repertory Theatre** (⊠ 111 N. Pearl St. ☎ 518/445–4531 ⊕ www.capitalrep.org) is an intimate space for musicals, comedies, and dramas. Though balanced on a platform that reaches six stories underground, the futuristic **Empire State Performing Arts Center** (⊠ Empire State Plaza, near Eagle St. ☎ 518/473–1845 ⊕ www.theegg.org), known as the Egg, appears to float above the plaza like a UFO. Shows here include acts by touring pop and folk musicians, comedy routines, modern-dance performances, and old-movie screenings. The 982-seat Hart Theater and the 445-seat Swyer Theater have good sightlines. The spectacular 2,800-seat **Palace Theatre** (⊠ 19 Clinton Ave. ☎ 518/465–3335 ⊕ palacealbany.com), a restored movie-and-vaudeville house, hosts pop concerts and touring Broadway shows. It's the home of the **Albany Symphony Orchestra**. National music acts, the circus, and wrestling all make stops at the 16,000-seat **Pepsi Arena** (⊠ 51 S. Pearl St. ☎ 518/ 487–2000 ⊕ www.pepsiarena.com).

Sports & the Outdoors

The **Pepsi Arena** (⊠ 51 S. Pearl St. ☎ 518/487–2000 ⊕ www.pepsiarena. com) is home to the River Rats hockey team, an affiliate of the New Jersey Devils, and the Albany Conquest arena-football team. Siena College's basketball team plays its Division I basketball home games here as well. The arena also hosts professional basketball games.

NORTH OF THE CAPITAL

Revised by
Marianne
Comfort

Since the late 1980s, the spa-resort city of Saratoga Springs has served as a somewhat distant suburb for the tri-city area of Albany, Schenectady, and Troy, and many of its residents make the 25-mi commute south to go to work. Beyond Saratoga Springs are several American Revolution sites. The Revolution's Battle of Saratoga, actually fought in nearby

Stillwater, halted the British invasion from Canada and turned the war in the rebels' favor, thus securing the area a place in U.S. history books.

Saratoga Springs

⑪ *25 mi north of Albany.*

Mineral-water springs first brought American Indians and, later, American settlers to this area just south of the Adirondack foothills. Gideon Putnam opened the first inn and commercial bathhouse here in 1791, to cater to early health seekers eager to drink from and bathe in the supposedly restorative waters. By the 1870s, Victorian society had turned Saratoga Springs into one of the country's principal vacation resorts, and the city became known as the "Queen of Spas."

In 1909, after the commercial exploitation of the mineral springs diminished their flow and even dried up some wells, New York State developed the Spa State Reservation (now called Saratoga Spa State Park) to protect against excessive pumping. Today you may sample the naturally carbonated waters of more than a dozen active springs, which were created by complex geological conditions centuries ago. A "tasting tour" brochure (available from the Saratoga Visitor Center) guides you to the springs in the Congress Park and High Rock Park areas, which are downtown, and in Saratoga Spa State Park, at the south end of the city. The springs differ, offering water rich in iron or sulfur or with minute quantities of radon gas. Geysers, or spouters, spray water out of a couple of springs.

By the 1890s the city had become a horse-racing hot spot, with the Travers Stakes a highlight of the racing season. These days, Thoroughbred racing has surpassed the springs as a draw, and the Travers, first run in 1864, remains a high point. The other major draw is the Saratoga Performing Arts Center. For a few summer weeks it's the residence of the Philadelphia Orchestra and the New York City Ballet; the open-air venue also hosts big-name jazz, rock, and pop concerts.

Ⓒ **Children's Museum of Saratoga.** At this museum with hands-on exhibits geared for kids three to nine years old, youngsters may slide down a fire pole to a pretend fire truck or imagine they're slinging hash in a model diner. ⊠ 69 *Caroline St.* ☎ 518/584–5540 ⊕ *www.childrensmuseumatsaratoga.org* 🎫 *$5* ⊙ *July–Labor Day, Mon.–Sat. 9:30–4:30; rest of yr, Tues.–Sat. 9:30–4:30, Sun. noon–4:30.*

Congress Park. Italian gardens, ponds, fountains, and statuary punctuate wide lawns at this park in the heart of the city. Fifty cents buys you a ride on a **carousel** with 28 horses that were carved and painted about a century ago. Crowds gather outside the Italianate Canfield Casino, a former gambling hall within the park, to watch the tuxedo set enter one of the August balls. The 1870s building also houses the **Historical Society Museum of Saratoga Springs** (☎ 518/584–6920 🎫 $4), where exhibits of Victorian furnishings, paintings, original gambling paraphernalia, and historic documents bring the city's history alive. From Memorial Day weekend through Labor Day, the museum is open Monday through

Saturday 10–4 and Sunday 1–4; the rest of the year it's closed Monday and Tuesday. ⊠ *Broadway between Circular and Spring Sts.* 🕾 *Free.*

Crystal Spa. The spa taps into water from the **Rosemary Spring,** on property it shares with the Grand Union Motel. The original motel owner built a gazebo and then drilled water underneath (in 1964) to honor his wife, who had just delivered their 12th child. The family-run, cash-only business offers everything from an aromatherapy sauna for $18 to a package of several treatments for $160. ⊠ *120 S. Broadway* 🕾 *518/584–2556* ⊕ *www.thecrystalspa.com* ⊙ *Sept.–June, Fri.–Tues. 8:30–4:30; July, Thurs.–Tues. 8:30–4:30; Aug., daily 8:30–5:30.*

Lincoln Mineral Baths. The bathhouse, in a grand building at the entrance to Saratoga Spa State Park, offers a slew of treatments, from massages to body wraps and facials. A mineral bath is $18, a half-hour massage $40. ⊠ *65 S. Broadway* 🕾 *518/584–2011 or 518/583–2880* ⊕ *www. gideonputnam.com* ⊙ *July and Aug., daily 9–4; June and Sept., Wed.–Mon. 9–4; Oct.–May, Wed.–Sun. 9–4.*

National Museum of Dance. Five galleries house photographs, videos, costumes, and archives that explore the history and development of dance as an art form. The Hall of Fame honors top dancers, choreographers, and costumers. You may even watch dancers rehearsing in the performing-arts studios. ⊠ *99 S. Broadway* 🕾 *518/584–2225* ⊕ *www. dancemuseum.org* 🖾 *$6.50* ⊙ *Late May–late Oct., Tues.–Sun. 10–5; late Oct.–late May, weekends 10–5.*

National Museum of Racing and Hall of Fame. Exhibits, including memorabilia from famed horse Seabiscuit, relate the story of Thoroughbred racing in the United States. In the Hall of Fame, video clips of races bring to life the horses and jockeys enshrined here. For an additional fee you may take a tour of the training track. ⊠ *191 Union Ave.* 🕾 *518/584– 0400* ⊕ *www.racingmuseum.org* 🖾 *$7* ⊙ *Mon.–Sat. 10–4:30, Sun. noon–4:30 (during the race meet, daily 9–5).*

Roosevelt Baths & Spa. After a seven-year closure and a major renovation, the 1930 Georgian-revival building reopened in 2004 with 42 treatment rooms and a 13,000-square-foot fitness center. A mineral bath is $18. Other treatments include reflexology, shiatsu, aromatherapy, body polishes, mud wraps, and assorted facials. ⊠ *Gideon Putnam Resort & Spa, 24 Gideon Putnam Rd.* 🕾 *518/584–3000 or 800/732– 1560* ⊕ *www.gideonputnam.com* ⊙ *Daily 7–7.*

Saratoga Automobile Museum. America's love affair with the car is celebrated in this museum in a former bottling plant in Saratoga Spa State Park. Included are three galleries and an orientation theater. Changing exhibits display classic and racing cars. ⊠ *110 Ave. of the Pines* 🕾 *518/ 587–1935* ⊕ *www.saratogaautomobilemuseum.org* 🖾 *$7* ⊙ *May–early Nov., daily 10–5; early Nov.–Apr., Tues.–Sun. 10–5.*

Saratoga County Arts Council. Changing exhibits in this 2,000-square-foot art gallery and theater-performance space showcase works by local as well as nationally known artists. At the theater here the **Saratoga Film Forum** shows mostly art-house movies (tickets $6) Thursday and Friday nights in fall, winter, and spring. ⊠ *320 Broadway* ☎ *518/584–4132* ⊕ *www.saratoga-arts.org* ▨ *Free* ☉ *Mon.–Wed. and Fri. 9–5, Thurs. 9–8, Sat. 11–5.*

Saratoga Harness Racing Museum and Hall of Fame. The museum, on the grounds of Saratoga Raceway, displays antique horseshoes, high-wheeled sulkies (the two-wheeled vehicles used for harness racing), and horse-related artwork. ⊠ *352 Jefferson St.* ☎ *518/587–4210* ⊕ *www. saratogaraceway.com* ▨ *Free* ☉ *July and Aug., Tues.–Sat. 10–4; Sept.–June, Thurs.–Sat. 10–4.*

Saratoga National Historical Park/Battlefield. The Battle of Saratoga, fought 12 mi southeast of Saratoga Springs at this site in 1777, is recognized as the turning point in the American Revolution. The visitor center at the Route 32 entrance provides historic information and an orientation to the park, which encompasses the battlefield and two sites in the nearby villages of Schuylerville and Victory. Ten stops along a 9½-mi tour road through the battlefield explain the battle and its significance. Reenactments and other living-history programs are scheduled throughout the summer. The road is popular with bicyclists in warm-weather months and, when closed to traffic in winter, with cross-country skiers. The **John Neilson House,** the only structure standing on the battlefield that was here in the time of the Battle of Saratoga, might have served as headquarters for Benedict Arnold. It's open sporadically; if you spot a park ranger nearby, ask to have a look inside.

The 155-foot **Saratoga Monument** (⊠ 53 Burgoyne St., Victory) commemorates the British surrender on October 17, 1777. The obelisk was built between 1877 and 1883, and has three niches commemorating generals Philip Schuyler, Horatio Gates, and Colonel Daniel Morgan. The fourth niche, where a statue of Benedict Arnold would have gone, has been left empty deliberately and cannot be entered. The monument is open from late May to Labor Day, Wednesday through Friday 9:30–4:30. The **General Philip Schuyler House** (⊠ 1072 U.S. 4, Schuylerville) was the general's country home before its destruction by the British in 1777. Schuyler and his soldiers rebuilt it in 29 days. The house includes some original furnishings. It's open from late May through Labor Day, Wednesday through Friday 9:30–4:30; tours are given every half hour. ⊠ *Visitor center, 648 Rte. 32, Stillwater* ☎ *518/664–9821 Ext. 224* ⊕ *www.nps.gov/sara* ▨ *Visitor center free, tour road $5 per car* ☉ *Visitor center daily 9–5; tour road Apr.–mid-Nov., daily dawn–dusk.*

Saratoga Spa State Park. Developed for the study and therapeutic use of the mineral springs here, this 2,200-acre park is now listed on the National Historic Register. It is home to the Gideon Putnam Resort & Spa, the Saratoga Performing Arts Center, the Lincoln and Roosevelt baths, the Spa Little Theatre, and eight active springs. Recreational facilities include walking trails, 36 holes of golf, two pools, clay and asphalt tennis courts, picnic facilities, an ice-skating rink, and 12 mi of cross-country skiing trails. ⊠ *S. Broadway and Rte. 50* ☎ *518/584–2535* ⊕ *nysparks.state.ny.us* ▨ *Parking $6 (May–Sept.)* ☉ *Memorial Day–Columbus Day daily 8 AM–dusk; limited access in winter.*

Skidmore College. This four-year coeducational college, founded in 1903, sponsors year-round cultural events and entertainment, and is the summer home of the New York State Writer's Institute. The **Frances Young Tang Teaching Museum and Art Gallery** (☎ 518/580–8080 ⊕ tang. skidmore.edu ⊠ $5 suggested donation) contains galleries large enough for oversize works and innovative installations, a 150-seat presentation room, and multimedia classrooms for lectures and film screenings. The rooftop is the setting for summer concerts. The museum is open Tuesday through Friday 10–5 and weekends noon–5. ⊠ *815 N. Broadway* ☎ *518/580–5000* ⊕ *www.skidmore.edu.*

Yaddo. Artists, writers, and musicians from all over the United States come to this highly regarded artists' colony to work. The estate was built in 1899 by philanthropist Spencer Trask as a gift to his wife, Katrina. Although you can't visit the house, you can tour the grounds, which include a formal rose garden with fountains and an informal rock garden. From mid-June through the racing season, tours are offered at 11 on weekends. ⊠ *Union Ave.* ☎ *518/584–07446* ⊕ *www.yaddo.org* ⊠ *Grounds free, tours $3* ☉ *Daily dawn–dusk.*

> off the beaten path

NATIONAL BOTTLE MUSEUM – The state-chartered museum's extensive collection of bottles dates from the 1700s. On-site is a glassworks that sometimes hosts a sale of contemporary art-glass pieces. The museum is 7 mi south of Saratoga Springs. ⊠ *76 Milton Ave., Ballston Spa* ☎ *518/885–7589* ⊕ *family.knick.net/ nbm* ⊠ *$2 suggested donation* ☉ *June–Sept., daily 10–4; Oct.–May, weekdays 10–4.*

FAIRS & FESTIVALS **Saratoga County State Fair.** The weeklong traditional county fair, held in July at the fairgrounds 8 mi south of Saratoga Springs and run by the Saratoga County Agricultural Society, includes live-animal and gardening exhibits, crafts and antiques vendors, and carnival rides. ⊠ *Saratoga County Fairgrounds, Prospect St. and Fairground Ave., Ballston Spa* ☎ *518/885–9701* ⊕ *www.saratogacountyfair.org.*

Where to Stay & Eat

$$$–$$$$ ✕ **Chez Sophie Bistro.** The second generation of owners has updated the classic French food served at this gleaming 1950s diner with an emphasis on ingredients from area farmers. But this is no casual eatery: inside are two refined dining rooms with cloth-covered tables and an abundance of artwork. The food is just as refined. Duck breast is glazed in green peppercorn–flecked apricot sauce; cassoulet is studded with bits of goose, pancetta, and lamb; and black sea bass is wrapped in parchment and steamed with herbs. A $25 three-course "pink plate special" dinner is available Tuesday through Thursday off-season. The restaurant is 4½ mi south of Saratoga Springs. ⊠ *2853 U.S. 9, Malta* ☎ *518/583–3538* ⊟ *AE, DC, MC, V* ☉ *Closed Mon. No lunch.*

$$$–$$$$ ✕ **Sargo's Restaurant and Lounge.** With high ceilings, draped tables, and mahogany-stained paneling and trim, this restaurant in the Saratoga National Golf Club's Victorian-style clubhouse exudes quiet elegance. The food lives up to the decor. The menu might include roast chicken with artichoke hearts and cremini mushrooms in spring, or Long Island duck

prepared three ways in fall. Chefs create pasta dishes table-side on Wednesday nights; on Sunday, live jazz accompanies an international brunch buffet. A lounge with a granite-and-wood bar and an outdoor terrace are more-casual dining options. ⊠ *458 Union Ave.* ☎ *518/583–4653* ⊟ *AE, MC, V* ☉ *No lunch Nov.–Mar.*

$$–$$$$ ✕ **43 Phila Bistro.** Old caricatures of patrons and Campari posters vie for space at this Saratoga hot spot known for innovative fare. Offerings might include pan-seared duck breast with lingonberry sauce or crab cakes with spicy coleslaw. The menu also lists prime steaks and ribs. ⊠ *43 Phila St.* ☎*518/584–2720* ⊟*AE, D, MC, V* ☉ *Closed Sun. in Sept.–May.*

$$–$$$$ ✕ **Saratoga Stakes.** A life-size replica of the racehorse Man-O-War greets you as you enter this enormous steak house, which wagers that a steak dinner here will top the best you've ever had. In the dining room, rich patterned fabrics break up expanses of dark, polished wood. The menu includes various Black Angus cuts and other meats, as well as chicken and seafood dishes; the kitchen prepares vegetarian (and vegan) meals upon request. ⊠ *86 Congress St.* ☎*518/587–5637* ⊟ *AE, MC, V.*

$$–$$$ ✕ **Eartha's Restaurant.** Vintage liquor ads adorn the walls of this funky small bistro in an old building painted purple. A hip crowd comes for the pastas and mesquite-grilled seafood. ⊠ *60 Court St.* ☎ *518/583–0602* ⌂ *Reservations essential* ⊟ *AE, D, DC, MC, V.*

$$–$$$ ✕ **Sperry's.** The 1930s art-deco design at this restaurant on a narrow side street includes a black-and-white tile floor and equestrian art; outside is a garden with herbs. Try the specialty, soft-shell crab (in season), or Maryland crab cakes, swordfish, or steaks. Reservations are not accepted in August. ⊠ *30½ Caroline St.* ☎ *518/584–9618* ⊟ *AE, D, DC, MC, V.*

$$–$$$ ✕ **Springwater Bistro.** The chef, who relies largely on locally sourced ingredients, changes the menu daily to reflect what's available from area farms. Carmelized-onion ravioli and spinach may accompany roast pork, for example. The bar area of this restaurant, which occupies a restored Victorian across from the track, serves tapas, and the kitchen prepares picnic baskets in summer. A tasting menu is available if your entire table orders it ($52 per person). Works by local artists adorn the converted Victorian residence. ⊠ *139 Union Ave.* ☎ *518/584–6440* ⊟*AE, D, DC, MC, V* ☉ *Closed Tues. Sept.–June. No lunch Sept.–June.*

$$–$$$ ✕ **The Wine Bar.** A sealed cigar room makes this one of the few restaurants in New York where you can still smoke. The lamb chops and the ahi tuna are two of the more popular items on the mostly American menu; small plates, with smaller prices, also are available. More than 50 wines are offered by the glass, but the bar pours other libations, too. ⊠ *417 Broadway* ☎ *518/584–8777* ⊟ *AE, D, DC, MC, V* ☉ *No lunch.*

$–$$ ✕ **Hattie's.** Since 1938 this casual restaurant has been serving such Southern favorites as fried chicken, ribs, pork chops, and jambalaya. Meals include homemade biscuits and corn bread and a choice of sides, including macaroni and cheese and sweet potatoes. In nice weather you may eat on the courtyard patio. Inside, tables—in checkered cloths—crowd together; overhead fans and a banging screen door keep the air circulating. The place does not take reservations in July and August; you just show up and wait. ⊠ *45 Phila St.* ☎ *518/584–4790* ⊟ *AE, MC, V* ☉ *Closed Mon. and Tues. in Sept.–June. No lunch.*

$–$$ ✕ **Olde Bryan Inn.** Built in the late 1700s, this three-level tavern-restaurant retains colonial-style fireplaces and exposed beams. The staff has also collected ghost stories of a woman sighted in period dress. The menu is broad, offering sandwiches as well as fresh seafood, chops, and pastas served with the popular homemade biscuits. ✉ *123 Maple Ave.* ☎ *518/ 587–2990* ⚑ *No reservations* ☰ *AE, D, DC, MC, V.*

$–$$ ✕ **Sushi Thai Garden Restaurant.** A hostess dressed in a kimono is likely to greet you at this bright and airy restaurant furnished in light wood. A sushi bar serves a large selection of sushi and sashimi combinations; entrées include Japanese teriyaki, tempura, and *kutsu* dishes as well as Thai curries and noodles. ✉ *44–46 Phila St.* ☎ *518/580–0900* ☰ *AE, D, MC, V.*

$–$$ ✕ **The Wheat Fields.** You can see fettuccine, lasagna, and other pastas squeezing out of the pasta machine in the front window of this main-street restaurant. Traditional Italian dishes share menu space with more creative fare. Smoked salmon, caviar, and scallions adorn angel-hair pasta in Alfredo sauce; the same sauce dresses breaded breast of chicken filled with asparagus mousse and served with tomato-tinted pasta. The menu includes selections for vegetarians and meat eaters. ✉ *440 Broadway* ☎ *518/587–0588* ☰ *AE, D, MC, V* ☺ *No lunch weekdays.*

¢–$$ ✕ **PJ's Saratoga Style Bar-B-Q.** You can smell the smoke pit for miles before you pass this '50s-style drive-in. Seating at this seasonal local favorite just south of Spa State Park on U.S. 9 is either under a roof shared with the kitchen and order counter or at outdoor picnic tables; a small section has table service. Chicken, ribs, and beef brisket are the specialties, but you can come just to have ice cream, listen to the DJ spinning oldies, and gaze at the classic cars that congregate in the lot on Saturday night. ✉ *1 Kaydeross Ave. W at S. Broadway* ☎ *518/583–2445* ☰ *No credit cards at counter; AE, MC, V for table service* ☺ *Closed mid-Sept.–Easter.*

¢–$ ✕ **Ravenous.** Savory and dessert crepes are the focus at this small eatery furnished with plain wooden tables and chairs. Side orders of Belgian-style *frites* (fries) come in paper cones sized for an individual or a table of diners, and may include several kinds of dipping sauce. ✉ *21 Phila St.* ☎ *518/581–0560* ⚑ *No reservations* ☰ *MC, V* ☺ *Closed Mon. Closed Tues. mid-Oct.–early Apr. No dinner Sun.*

★ ¢   ✕ **Esperanto.** The menu of this tiny basement eatery offers a smattering of inexpensive dishes from Thailand, Mexico, England, the Middle East, and Italy. There's counter service only and just a few tables. ✉ *6½ Caroline St.* ☎ *518/587–4236* ☰ *AE, D, DC, MC, V.*

$$$$ ⌂ **Prime Hotel & Conference Center–Saratoga Springs.** This five-story hotel offers a 24-hour business center and self-serve computerized check-in (and check-out) both curbside and at a lobby kiosk. Guest rooms are furnished in traditional American style and have work areas with wood desks. Stay here and you may stumble on one of the many weekend events held in the adjoining City Center. ✉ *534 Broadway, 12866* ☎ *518/584–4000* 🖷 *518/584–7430* ⊕ *www.primehotelsandresorts.com* ⇥ *235 rooms, 5 suites* ⚐ *Restaurant, room service, in-room data ports, some in-room hot tubs, some kitchenettes, some microwaves, some refrigerators, cable TV with movies, indoor pool, gym, sauna, pub, con-*

cierge, business services, car rental, no-smoking rooms ☰ AE, D, DC, MC, V ⦿ CP.

$$$–$$$$ 🏨 **Batcheller Mansion Inn.** The ornate architectural details of this High Victorian Gothic stunner include dormer windows crowned with clamshell arches and a mansard roof of alternating bands of red and gray slate. The common spaces include porches, a living room, and a dining room that seats 20. Two long plush-velvet couches invite lingering in the library. Some of the smaller rooms are tucked under the slope of the roof; on the other end of the size spectrum, the Diamond Jim Brady suite has a regulation-size pool table, a jetted tub for two, and a king bed. Congress Park is across the street. ⊠ *20 Circular St., 12866* ☎ *518/584–7012 or 800/616–7012* 🖷 *518/581–7746* ⊕ *www. batchellermansioninn.com* ⧠ *4 rooms, 5 suites* ♿ *Dining room, some in-room hot tubs, in-room data ports, refrigerators, cable TV, piano, library; no kids under 14, no smoking* ☰ *AE, MC, V* ⦿ *BP (racing season and weekends), CP.*

$$–$$$$ 🏨 **Adelphi Hotel.** The impressive lobby of one of the city's original late-19th-century hotels has slightly worn divans, elaborately stenciled walls and ceilings, and trompe-l'oeil details. The grand staircase leads to three floors of guest rooms and common spaces, including a second-story piazza overlooking Broadway. Bedroom styles—from Victorian and French country to Adirondacks and Arts and Crafts—are diverse. The bar, which spills off the lobby and into a courtyard, is a favorite evening gathering spot for drinks and desserts. ⊠ *365 Broadway, 12866* ☎ *518/587–4688* 🖷 *518/587–0851* ⊕ *www.adelphihotel.com* ⧠ *21 rooms, 18 suites* ♿ *Café, cable TV, pool, lounge, meeting rooms* ☰ *MC, V* ⊙ *Closed Nov.–Apr.* ⦿ *CP.*

$$–$$$$ 🏨 **Westchester House.** Antique and reproduction furnishings fill lace-curtained rooms in this 1885 Victorian painted lady. The property, with gardens, is on a leafy residential street within walking distance of downtown and the race track. A formal dining room is the setting for the full cold breakfast, which includes baked goods and meat and cheese platters. The parlor houses a library and baby grand piano. ⊠ *102 Lincoln Ave., 12866* ☎ *518/587–7613* ⊕ *www.westchesterhousebandb.com* ⧠ *7 rooms* ♿ *Dining room, some fans, in-room data ports, library, piano; no a/c in some rooms, no smoking* ⊙ *Closed Jan. and Feb.* ☰ *AE, D, DC, MC, V* ⦿ *BP.*

$$–$$$ 🏨 **Saratoga Arms.** The Smith family greets you at this 1870 Second Empire brick hotel in the heart of downtown. Rooms may have white country-cottage or Victorian furnishings; some have fireplaces or claw-foot tubs. Printed fabrics outfit beds and windows, and every room has a CD player. Shower stalls contain a tile with a quote about local history, characters, or landmarks painted on it. The wraparound porch is roomy and has antique wicker chairs. ⊠ *495–497 Broadway, 12866* ☎ *518/584–1775* 🖷 *518/584–4064* ⊕ *www.saratoga-lodging.com* ⧠ *16 rooms* ♿ *Dining room, in-room data ports, some in-room hot tubs, cable TV, concierge, business services, meeting rooms; no kids under 12, no smoking* ☰ *AE, D, DC, MC, V* ⦿ *BP.*

$$ 🏨 **Gideon Putnam Resort & Spa.** A product of the public works projects of the 1930s, this Georgian revival–style brick hotel sits amid the 2,200 acres of Saratoga Spa State Park. Tall windows look out onto front and

back gardens, and the interior scheme sticks to a gracious, traditional style. The Sunday brunch buffet of hot and cold entrées is a favorite among locals and visitors alike. ⊠ *24 Gideon Putnam Rd., 12866* ☎ *518/584–3000 or 800/732–1560* 🖷 *518/584–1354* ⊕ *www.gideonputnam.com* ⟿ *99 rooms, 22 suites* ⚘ *Restaurant, café, in-room data ports, cable TV, 4 tennis courts, pool, gym, spa, bicycles, ice-skating, bar, lounge, babysitting, dry cleaning, laundry service, concierge, Internet, business services, meeting rooms, no-smoking rooms* ▭ *AE, D, DC, MC, V.*

$$ 🏨 **Union Gables Bed and Breakfast.** A sweeping front porch graces this turreted and gabled Queen Anne Victorian inn, one in a row of equally impressive homes. Benches built into the wood paneling flank the foyer sitting area, and the dining room, dressed in purple, is a Victorian fantasy. A piano figures prominently in the living room. None of the guest rooms are cramped, and those on the second floor are particularly large. Pastels are coupled with busy florals in some rooms, and in others deep greens and blues set off paisleys or plaids. Hardwood floors gleam throughout. ⊠ *55 Union Ave., 12866* ☎ *518/584–1558 or 800/398–1558* 🖷 *518/583–0649* ⊕ *www.uniongables.com* ⟿ *11 rooms, 1 suite* ⚘ *Dining room, refrigerators, cable TV, tennis court, gym, outdoor hot tub, bicycles, piano, pets; no smoking* ▭ *AE, D, DC, MC, V* ⦿ *CP.*

$–$$ 🏨 **Inn at Saratoga.** At this 1848 inn, Victorian-inspired rooms with dark-wood furniture and tailored swags include such modern conveniences as high-speed Internet access. The four suites, in the Brunelle Cottage in the back, have heated floors. Your room key grants access to the fitness facilities at the YMCA. ⊠ *231 Broadway, 12866* ☎ *518/583–1890 or 800/274–3573* 🖷 *518/583–2543* ⊕ *www.theinnatsaratoga.com* ⟿ *38 rooms, 6 suites* ⚘ *Restaurant, in-room data ports, cable TV, lounge, Internet, meeting rooms; no smoking* ▭ *AE, D, DC, MC, V* ⦿ *BP.*

$–$$ 🏨 **The Mansion Inn.** Paper-bag inventor George West had this 23-room villa built in 1866 across from one of his mills, 7 mi west of Saratoga Springs. Today it serves as a luxurious B&B where special services may include being picked up at the train station by the inn's Bentley or having cocktails delivered to your room on a silver tray. Intricate moldings, mirrors, and mantels grace rooms with 14-foot ceilings and Victorian furnishings. Some rooms have four-poster beds; all have down comforters. In warm weather you may opt to have breakfast on the long porch overlooking the mansion's gardens and ponds. ⊠ *801 Rte. 29, Rock City Falls 12863* ☎ *518/885–1607 or 888/996–9977* 🖷 *518/884–0364* ⊕ *www.themansionsaratoga.com* ⟿ *7 rooms, 2 suites* ⚘ *Dining room, in-room data ports, some in-room hot tubs, cable TV, library, piano, Internet, some pets allowed (fee); no kids under 14, no smoking* ▭ *AE, D, MC, V* ⦿ *BP.*

¢–$ 🏨 **Saratoga Motel.** Small rooms with knotty-pine paneling bring to mind rustic cabins at this small motel, which sits on more than 4 acres that encompass trees and ponds. The motel is about 3 mi west of the Saratoga tracks and 2 mi west of the heart of the city. Next door (434 Church St.) and under the same ownership is a four-room B&B in an 1860s farmhouse. ⊠ *440 Church St., 12866* ☎ *518/584–0920* 🖷 *518/584–7177* ⊕ *www.saratogamotel.com* ⟿ *9 rooms, 2 efficiencies* ⚘ *Cable TV, some kitchenettes, refrigerators, some pets allowed* ▭ *AE, D, MC, V.*

Nightlife & the Arts

Recognized as the country's oldest folk-music venue, **Caffè Lena** (✉ 47 Phila St. ☎ 518/583–0022 🌐 www.caffelena.com ⏲ Wed.–Sun.; call for schedule) opened in 1960 and hosted Bob Dylan and Arlo Guthrie early in their careers. The tradition continues at this upstairs coffeehouse, thanks to staff members as well as volunteers who together work the shows, a mix of well-known musicians and newcomers. Admission starts at $1 for open-mike nights, and similar programs and can top $25 for big-name acts. Some of the hottest jazz musicians stop at the **Freihofer's Jazz Festival** (✉ Saratoga Performing Arts Center, 108 Ave. of the Pines, between U.S. 9 and Rte. 50, ☎ 518/587–3330 🌐 www.spac.org) in June for two days of music to kick off summer. Free pre-opera talks provide some background on the operas performed at the **Lake George Opera Festival** (✉ Spa Little Theatre, 19 Roosevelt Dr., off Ave. of the Pines ☎ 518/587–3330 🌐 www.lakegeorgeopera.org), which runs for two weeks at the start of the summer. Live jazz comes to the 40-seat **9 Maple Ave.** (✉ 9 Maple Ave. ☎ 518/583–2582 🌐 www.9mapleavenue.com) every Friday and Saturday evening. The centerpiece of the hand-built mahogany bar is a porcelain tap head thrown by potter Regis Brodie. The club claims to offer the largest selection of single-malt scotches in New York State. The **Saratoga Chamber Music Festival** (✉ Spa Little Theatre, 19 Roosevelt Dr., off Ave. of the Pines, Saratoga Springs ☎ 518/587–3330 🌐 www.spac.org), a celebration of music written for ensemble groups, is offered for several days through the Saratoga Performing Arts Center but presented at the more intimate Spa Little Theatre, next door. The **Saratoga Performing Arts Center** (SPAC ✉ Saratoga Spa State Park, 108 Ave. of the Pines, between U.S. 9 and Rte. 50 ☎ 518/587–3330 🌐 www.spac.org) is the summer home of the New York City Ballet and the Philadelphia Orchestra. The open-air venue, with both assigned amphitheater seats and lawn seating, also hosts the Freihofer's Jazz Festival and concerts by big-name pop acts. The box office is open from early May through September, 10–6 Monday through Saturday.

Fodor's Choice ★

Sports & the Outdoors

You may fish, rent boats from one of several marinas, learn to water-ski, or just watch weekend sailboat races at the 8½-mi-long, 1½-mi-wide **Saratoga Lake. Brown's Beach** (✉ 712 Rte. 9P ☎ 518/587–8280 🌐 www.brownsbeach.com), the only public beach on Saratoga Lake, is open June through Labor Day ($4). It's about 7 mi east of downtown Saratoga Springs.

GOLF

At the **Saratoga National Golf Club** (✉ 458 Union Ave. ☎ 518/583–4653 🌐 golfsaratoga.com), the 2½-story Victorian-style clubhouse and mile-long access road edged with ponds and stone walls gives the impression of an exclusive private club. But the 18-hole course, built on 400 acres of hills and wetlands in the style of the 1920s and '30s, is open to anyone willing to pay greens fees that top $100 in-season. **Saratoga Spa Golf** (✉ Saratoga Spa State Park, 60 Roosevelt Dr. ☎ 518/584–2008, 518/584–3137 Ext. 7 🌐 www.saratogaspagolf.com), a public 18-hole course in Saratoga Spa State Park, has a championship layout. Weekend greens fees of $25 make it a good value.

HORSE RACING Top jockeys compete for six weeks (starting in late July) each year at the **Saratoga Race Course** (✉ 262 Union Ave. ☎ 518/584–6200 ⊕ www.nyra.com), the nation's oldest Thoroughbred track. Breakfast at the track has become a tradition, with a buffet meal served 7–9:30, while the horses go through their morning workouts. You also can bring your own breakfast and sit in the stands for the free show. Afterward, get a behind-the-scenes look at the track with a free tram tour of the backstretch. The gates open at 11 AM on weekdays (except Tuesday) and 10:30 on weekends. Most first races of the day have a 1 PM post time. The first Saturday of August features the Whitney Handicap, one of Thoroughbred racing's most prestigious handicaps. The action at the **Saratoga Raceway** (✉ Nelson Ave. ☎ 518/584–2110 ⊕ www.saratogaraceway.com) is in the form of harness racing, and it's free and offered year-round. The air-conditioned clubhouse has a restaurant, but food concessions are options, too.

Starting in July, the **Saratoga Polo Club** (✉ Denton and Bloomfield Rds., Saratoga Springs ☎ 518/584–8108 ⊕ www.saratogapolo.com) hosts a weeks-long world-class polo competition, with renowned picnics and tailgate parties, at Whitney and Skidmore fields, off Route 9N.

Shopping

Chain stores have been encroaching on the small clothing boutiques and gift shops that make wandering down Broadway and its side streets so interesting, but the majority of storefronts are still unique to the city.

Designers Studio (✉ 492 Broadway ☎ 518/584–1977), a gallery, carries pottery, jewelry, kitchenwares, leather handbags, decorative pieces, and other items from top artisans. Out-of-print books, first editions, and antique prints are the specialties at **Lyrical Ballad Bookstore** (✉ 7–9 Phila St. ☎ 518/584–8779). The three covered pavilions at the **Saratoga Farmer's Market** (✉ High Rock Park, High Rock Ave., off Lake Ave., ☎ No phone) are a social gathering spot on Wednesday 3–6 and Saturday 9–1, from early May to mid-December. The variety of produce, poultry, and meats from area farms, baked goods, and jams (from local berries) is good. Although **Soave Faire** (✉ 449 Broadway ☎ 518/587–8448) specializes in framing and art and office supplies, it's also the place to buy any type of hat you might want to wear to the track or a picnic on the polo grounds.

WEST & EAST OF THE CAPITAL

Revised by Bob Goepfert, Karen Bjornland

Within 10 mi of Albany are the smaller cities of Troy and Schenectady. Although each has its own distinct character and attractions, the cities are tightly knit by common threads of industry and immigration that spin back to the 1600s. Troy, home of Rensselaer Polytechnic Institute, and Schenectady, with a General Electric Co. site, have been vital centers of science and technology for more than a century. A visit today could include marveling at a 1930s refrigerator in the Schenectady Museum or strolling down Troy's antique lamp–lined River Street. Parks, farms, and forest trails are never far away.

Schenectady

🔟 *8 mi northwest of Albany.*

Founded by Dutch traders in 1661, Schenectady is one of the oldest cities in the country. Both General Electric Co. and the now-defunct American Locomotive Co. had their headquarters here in the early 1900s, and Schenectady was dubbed "the city that lights and hauls the world." At night, a giant GE emblem still glows over downtown from atop a factory. Today, with a population of nearly 62,000, the city is an interesting blend of arts, architecture, and culture. Proctor's Theatre, an old vaudeville theater, hosted the upstate premiere of Schenectady native John Sayles's 2004 movie, *Silver City*. In the city's quiet, tree-lined Stockade District—a historic district away from the downtown area—18th- and 19th-century homes and churches nestle along the Mohawk River. European immigrants, especially Italians and Poles, have left an indelible imprint on the city's churches, restaurants, and markets; festivals celebrating Italian, Greek, Polish, and Jewish food and culture, held from June through September, attract thousands. The Christmas Parade—the largest nightime parade in the Northeast—winds through downtown the day after Thanksgiving, cheered by excited children and parents bundled in overcoats. In the 21st century, Guyanese newcomers have discovered Schenectady, and Indo-Caribbean grocery stores are not uncommon.

Empire State Aerosciences Museum. Cruise through aviation history via dioramas, models, photos, and interactive displays at the **Schenectady County Airport,** near the spot where Charles Lindbergh landed in 1928. Take a ride in the simulated-flight reality vehicle, or get an up-close look at dozens of restored aircraft, which are parked all around the 27-acre site and include an F-14A Tomcat. In September, a museum-sponsored air show roars over the city. ✉ *250 Rudy Chase Dr., off Rte. 50, Glenville* ☎ *518/377–1959* ⊕ *www.esam.org* ⊠ *$5* ⊗ *Wed. and Sun. noon–4, Thurs.–Sat. 10–4.*

Historic Stockade District. Examples of Federal, Dutch, Gothic, Victorian, and Greek-revival architecture are found among the homes and churches here, which date from 1690 to 1930. The Stockade is one of the oldest continuously occupied neighborhoods in the nation. (George Washington slept here.) In warm weather you see people running and relaxing in tiny Riverside Park, along the Mohawk River. Residents open their homes to the public for guided tours during **Walkabout Weekend,** held in September. At the **Stockade Villagers Art Show,** also in September, painters set up easels and tents to display their works. To tour the neighborhood on your own, pick up a self-guided walking tour brochure at the ⇨ Schenectady Museum & Suits-Bueche Planetarium, the ⇨ Schenectady Country Historical Society & Museum, or the Chamber of Schenectady County (306 State St.). ✉ *Between Erie Blvd. and Union St. along Mohawk River* ☎ *518/374–0263 or 518/372–5656* ⊕ *www. historicstockade.com.*

Schenectady County Historical Society & Museum. A stenciled floor and a huge 1930s dollhouse are among the highlights of this museum, which fills the 1896 Georgian-style **Dora Jackson House** with its 18th-century furniture, paintings, costumes, toys, and household and military items. The **Grems-Doolittle Library** has Revolutionary War records, newspapers from the 1800s, and the papers of Charles Steinmetz, an inventor who developed alternate-current motors. ⊠ *32 Washington Ave.* ☎ *518/ 374–0263* ⊕ *www.schist.org* 🖂 *Museum $3, library $5* ☉ *Tues.–Fri. 1–5, Sat. 10–4.*

☺ **Schenectady Museum & Suits-Bueche Planetarium.** Early televisions and kitchen appliances are part of a vast General Electric archive that traces the city's scientific and cultural history. Interactive children's displays explore science and technology. ⊠ *15 Nott Terrace Heights* ☎ *518/382– 7890* ⊕ *www.schenectadymuseum.org* 🖂 *Museum $5, museum and planetarium $6.50* ☉ *Tues.–Fri. 10–4:30, weekends noon–5.*

Union College. The 100-acre campus of this liberal-arts college founded in 1795 was the first in America to be designed by an architect. The grounds include **Jackson's Garden,** an oasis of perennials and herbs near a bubbling brook. At the campus center is the 1875 **Nott Memorial** (☉ *Daily 10–6*), a 16-sided structure with a colorful slate mosaic dome. The unusual building, a National Historic Landmark, is illuminated in the evening. The **Mandeville Gallery** (☎ *518/388–6004*), on the Nott Memorial's second floor, shows history-, science-, and art-related exhibits. ⊠ *807 Union St.* ☎ *518/388–6000* ⊕ *www.union.edu* 🖂 *Free.*

FESTIVALS & **Schenectady Gazette Christmas Parade.** The 150 to 200 floats of the
FAIRS largest nighttime parade in the Northeast wind through downtown the day after Thanksgiving, cheered by excited children and parents bundled in overcoats. The festivities start at 6 PM. ☎ *518/372–5656 Schenectady Chamber of Commerce* ⊕ *www.schenectadychamber.org.*

Where to Stay & Eat

$–$$$ ✕ **Cornell's.** Locals love this place and have savored its Italian specialties since 1943. Start with the clams in wine, butter, oil, and garlic, or a hot antipasto. For a main course, consider the braciola, a longtime favorite; the tender rolls of beef are filled with sausage and baked in meat sauce. The restaurant is part of Schenectady's emerging Little Italy community on North Jay Street. ⊠ *39 N. Jay St.* ☎ *518/370–3825* ▤ *AE, MC, V* ☉ *Closed Mon.*

¢–$ ✕ **Peter Pause.** Shirt-and-tie wearers mix with jeans-and–work boots types at this tiny, cash-only Italian diner across the street from Union College. The best seats are at the counter, where you can watch the soup simmer and smell the tomato sauce. Melt-in-your-mouth eggplant parmigiana sandwiches are the specialty. The purple veggie is pounded thin and layered before it's sauced and tucked between thick slabs of homemade Italian bread. Daily pasta dishes might include spaghetti, ravioli, or linguini with red or white clam sauce. On a cold day, warm up with a bowl of *stracciatelli* (a soup made with eggs, semolina, and cheese). ⊠ *535 Nott St.* ☎ *518/382–9278* ▤ *No credit cards* ☉ *Closed weekends.*

¢ ✕ **Cafe 1795.** Nab a sidewalk table and dip into a bowl of creamy lobster bisque at this café and deli. The alfresco seats have views of the colorful, shuttered Stockade District houses. House-baked *ciabatta* (flat Italian bread) is served throughout the day. Hefty sandwiches, like the egg-salad

Mohawk, are dressed with field greens and named for famous people and places. If you're in a hurry, get good stuff to go, such as red-skin-potato salad and citrus-thyme chicken salad. You can eat indoors here, too. ⊠ *35 N. Ferry St.* ☎ *518/372–4141* ▭ *AE, D, MC, V.*

$–$$$ ✕🔲 **Glen Sanders Mansion.** A former fur trapper's trading post–turned–Dutch mansion provides a swish backdrop for a room and a meal on the Mohawk River. Standard rooms have two queen beds; junior suites have a king-size sleigh bed, a desk, and a seating area. Gas fireplaces, patios, two-person whirlpool tubs, and three shower heads up the luxury quotient in the full suites. The decor throughout is a harmonious blend of patterned fabrics and wallpapers in elegant palettes. Candlelit tables set with fine china and table linens fill the pre-colonial dining room, which has two decorative fireplaces, hand-hewn beams, and thick, wooden Dutch doors. The Mediterranean-accented cuisine includes gnocchi with roasted shrimp and spinach; chili-lacquered sea bass with olives, feta, and pine nuts; and a daily risotto. Filet mignon, lamb chops, and wild-mushroom osso buco round out the menu. A cavelike, stone-walled pub downstairs offers lighter, less-expensive dishes. ⊠ *1 Glen Ave., off Rte. 5/Mohawk Ave., Scotia 12302* ☎ *518/ 374–7262* ⊕ *www.glensandersmansion.com* ⇆ *10 rooms, 10 suites* ᗜ *Restaurant, some in-room hot tubs, some refrigerators, some in-room safes, cable TV, some in-room VCRs, pub, no smoking* ▭ *AE, DC, D, MC, V* ¡◎¡ *CP.*

¢–$ ✕🔲 **The Stockade Inn.** Before its latest incarnation, this three-story, 1816 brick Federal building in the heart of the Stockade served as a bank and an exclusive men's club. The Victorian-style rooms, all on the top floor, have plush carpeting and reproduction antique poster beds; six have gas fireplaces. Guests may use the facilities at the local YMCA. The first two floors hold a swanky restaurant ($–$$$), which has upholstered armchairs, high ceilings, and chandeliers; a billiards room; and meeting rooms. Martinis are mixed behind a copper-topped antique bar in the carpeted lobby. The food is contemporary, with such creative appetizers as crab-mascarpone cheesecake and a house salad studded with olives and Gorgonzola. Seafood Newburg, in sherry-cream bisque, and roasted pork shanks with caramelized onions are among the dozen-plus entrées. ⊠*1 N. Church St., 12305* ☎*518/346–3400* ⇆*7 rooms, 2 suites* ᗜ *Restaurant, cable TV, billiards, bar, Internet, meeting rooms; no smoking* ▭ *AE, D, MC, V* ¡◎¡ *CP.*

$–$$ 🔲 **The Parker Inn.** When this hotel opened in 2003, it dramatically transformed the Parker Building, a narrow, eight-story structure that was the city's tallest building when it was erected in 1906. An antique, cage-style elevator takes you to contemporary rooms with dark-wood furniture and floral-fabric accents. Maroon velvet curtains and vintage movie posters in the lounge downstairs are a nod to the inn's neighbor, Proctor's Theatre; before and after shows, a chic crowd gathers for drinks, dinner, and snacks. ⊠ *434 State St., 12305* ☎ *518/688–1001* 🖷 *518/688– 1002* ⊕ *parkerinn.com* ⇆ *23 rooms, 6 suites* ᗜ *In-room data ports, cable TV, lounge, dry cleaning, laundry facilities, Internet, business services, meeting rooms; no smoking* ▭ *AE, D, MC, V* ¡◎¡ *CP.*

$ 🔲 **Holiday Inn.** A fountain babbles in the spacious lobby of this four-story chain hotel. Standard rooms have sliding doors, and some look down onto the indoor pool. Suites have wet bars and sofa beds. The hotel is downtown and within walking distance of Union College and Proctor's Theatre. ⊠ *100 Nott Terr., 12308* ☎ *518/393–4141* 🖷 *518/393–4174* ⊕ *www.holiday-inn.com* ⮌ *181 rooms, 3 suites* ⌂ *Restaurant, room service, some minibars, cable TV, indoor pool, exercise equipment, hot tub, bar, recreation room, Internet, business services, airport shuttle, some pets allowed; no-smoking rooms* ▤ *AE, D, DC, MC, V.*

¢–$ 🎬 **Days Inn.** Choose a room with a king-size bed or two doubles at this three-story, no-frills chain motel. Suites have whirlpool tubs. The downtown location is close to the Schenectady Museum and within walking distance of Union College and Proctor's Theatre. ⊠ *167 Nott Terr., 12308* ☎ *518/370–3297* 🖷 *518/370–5948* ⊕ *www.daysinn.com* ⮌ *64 rooms, 4 suites* ⌂ *Some in-room hot tubs, cable TV, dry cleaning, laundry facilities, Internet, business services, meeting room, some pets allowed (fee), no-smoking rooms* ▤ *AE, D, DC, MC, V* ⦿ *CP.*

Nightlife & the Arts

NIGHTLIFE One of the best clubs for jazz and blues in the capital region is **The Van Dyck** (⊠ 237 Union St., off Erie Blvd. ☎ 518/381–1111 ⊕ www.thevandyck.com), at the entrance to the Stockade District. Sip a martini at the first-floor antique bar before heading upstairs to the intimate, attic-like performance space. Tickets usually cost $15–$30.

THE ARTS Local, national, and internationally known musicians perform as part of the **Central Park Concert Series** (⊠ Ashmore Ave. and Iroquois Way ☎ 518/292–0368 ⊕ www.swconcerts.org). The outdoor concerts start
★ at 3, 4, or 7 PM on Sundays in July and August. **Proctor's Theatre** (⊠ 432 State St. ☎ 518/346–6204 ⊕ www.proctors.org), a 1926 vaudeville theater with chandeliers, balconies, and 2,700 seats, is one of the crown jewels of the capital region. Year-round schedules include Broadway shows performed by national touring companies; concerts; dance performances; and second-run movies. A window in Proctor's Arcade displays movie costume pieces, such as Vivien Leigh's petticoat from *Gone With the Wind* and the Wicked Witch's pointy black boots from *Wizard of Oz.*

Freedom Park (⊠ Schonowee Ave. near Rte. 5, Scotia ☎ No phone ⊕ www.freedomparkscotia.org) comes alive from June through August with free outdoor concerts of jazz, blues, rock, and polka. Shows start at 7 PM on Wednesday.

Shopping

A dozen or so shops line a pedestrians-only section of Jay Street. On Thursdays in summer you can browse to the sounds of the free lunchtime concerts that take place in front of City Hall. In addition to the shops listed below, pop into the Open Door Bookstore, Earthly Delights health-food store, Two Spruce Pottery gallery, and Bibliomania, a store of rare and used books.

Civitello's (⊠ 42 N. Jay St. ☎ 518/381–6165), a bakery and small café with booths and tables, has been selling cannoli, spumoni, and Italian cookies since 1911. In summer, you can cool off with fruity house-made Italian ices. The **New York Folklore Society** (⊠ 133 Jay St. ☎ 518/346–7008) sells one-of-a-kind items made by New York folk artists: carved birds and walking sticks, quilts, hand-knitted children's sweaters, American Indian jewelry, baskets, and Ukrainian *pysanky* (decorated eggs). A line forms every afternoon at **Perreca's Bakery** (✉ 33 N. Jay St. ☎ 518/ 372–1875), in business since 1914 and the cornerstone of the city's Little Italy project. It's a Schenectady tradition to wait for a loaf of Perreca's bread, still warm from the oven. Round or rectangular, large or small, the crusty bread is the city's best-known food item. Actor Jack Nicholson developed a craving for Perreca's when he was in Albany filming the 1987 movie *Ironweed* and has friends pick up a loaf when they're in the area.

Troy

13 *4 mi north of Albany.*

At the juncture of the Hudson River and the Erie Canal and just a few miles north of Albany, Troy was an important commercial city in the early 1800s. Although the development of the railroads curtailed its commercial dominance, Troy became one of the largest industrial cities on the East Coast. Uncle Sam—actually Sam Wilson, a meatpacker who acquired the moniker during the War of 1812—hailed from Troy and is buried in the Oakwood Cemetery. In the 20th century the city became known as the home of Cluett-Peabody, maker of Arrow shirts. Today Troy (population 52,000) has a host of cultural venues as well as several excellent restaurants. It's also rich in architecture, with Federal-style farmhouses, 19th-century Georgian-style buildings and brownstones, and 20th-century bungalow-style homes. It's also home to Rensselaer Polytechnic Institute and Russell Sage College.

Arts Center of the Capital Region. Two gallery spaces display contemporary and folk pieces by local and regional artists. One and two-day classes (mostly around $100) are offered in art, photography, writing, and crafts. ✉ *265 River St.* ☎ *518/273–0552* ⊕ *www.artscenteronline.org* ▣ *Free* ☉ *Mon.–Thurs. 9–7, Fri. and Sat. 9–5, Sun. noon–4.*

Grafton Lakes State Park. The Durham Reservoir, 20 mi of trails, and a series of ponds make this park a favorite place for such warm-weather activities as picnicking, swimming, fishing, hiking, and biking. In winter, cross-country skiers, snowshoers, and snowmobilers hit the trails, and ice-skaters take to the frozen water. The park is off Route 2 east of Troy. ✉ *61 N. Long Pond Rd., Grafton* ☎ *518/270–1155* ⊕ *nysparks. state.ny.us* ▣ *Free* ☉ *Daily dawn–dusk.*

Junior Museum. Kids can learn about Mohican life or bees and pollination through the interactive exhibits here, which cover science, history, and art. ✉ *105 8th St.* ☎ *518/235–2120* ⊕ *www.juniormuseum.org* ▣ *$5* ☉ *Fri. and Sat. 10–5.*

Rensselaer County Historical Society. The 19th-century **Carr Building** contains the historical society's offices as well as a research library that, through old photos, maps, diaries, and letters, documents Troy's development from the 1800s through the following century. Next door is the **Hart-Cluett House**, an 1827 Federal town house with a white marble exterior and period furnishings; tours are available by reservation.

⊠ *57 2nd St.* ☎ *518/272–7232* ⊕ *www.rchsonline.org* ☜ *$4* ⊗ *Museum Tues.–Sat. 10–4, library Tues.–Sat. noon–5.*

Troy RiverSpark Visitor Center. The staff offers an orientation to the area, including tips on local events. Exhibits cover the city's river history. ⊠ *251 River St.* ☎ *518/270–8667* ⊕ *www.troyvisitorcenter.org* ☜ *Free* ⊗ *May–Sept., Tues.–Fri. 10–6 and weekends 10–5; Oct.–Apr., Tues.–Sat. 11–5.*

Where to Stay & Eat

$$–$$$ ✕ **Lo Porto's.** Veal Scorsese, one of the more popular entrées at this casual, multilevel northern Italian restaurant, is named for Martin Scorsese, who dined here regularly while directing *The Age of Innocence* in town. The dish pairs wafer-thin pieces of veal with mushrooms, artichoke hearts, prosciutto, and capers, all covered with cooked tomatoes. Fresh seafood and pasta dishes are also good choices. ⊠ *85 4th St.* ☎ *518/273–8546* ▤ *AE, D, DC, MC, V* ⊗ *Closed Sun. and Mon. No lunch Sat.*

★ **$$–$$$** ✕ **River Street Café.** On your way upstairs to the dining room, you pass the chef working in an exposed kitchen. The comfortable brick-and-mahogany room overlooks the Troy marina on the Hudson River. The eclectic menu changes frequently to reflect the seasonal ingredients available and incorporates Asian, American, Mediterranean, and other flavors. ⊠ *429 River St.* ☎ *518/273–2740* ▤ *MC, V* ⊗ *Closed Sun. and Mon. No lunch.*

$–$$$ ✕ **Daisy Bakers.** Plank floors, small wood tables, old organ pipes, and a high ceiling flanked by rich wood walls are reminders of this dining room's former religious uses: at various times, the 1892 brownstone has been a fundamentalist church, a Christian Science reading room, and a YWCA. The menu, which changes frequently and doesn't stick to one cuisine, might include pancetta-wrapped veal rib chop with smashed red potatoes and a drizzle of basil oil; grilled swordfish with cucumber strips, tomato salad, and cilantro vinaigrette; or roasted free-range chicken with sautéed mushrooms and onions in cherry-wine sauce. After 10 PM, a young crowd fills the long bar, and local bands play until the wee hours. ⊠ *33 2nd St.* ☎ *518/266–9200* ▤ *AE, D, MC, V* ⊗ *Closed Sun.*

$ ✕ **Brown's Brewing Company.** The brewpub occupies a circa-1850 riverside warehouse. In warm weather, locals linger on the outdoor deck overlooking the Hudson; inside, exposed brick walls set off local memorabilia, antiques, and old photos. A slew of beers is concocted on-site, including the smooth oatmeal stout, which won a gold medal at the World Beer Cup. The classic but limited pub menu has half-pound burgers, salads, wraps, beer-battered chicken wings, and shepherd's pie. Weekend reservations aren't accepted. ⊠ *417–419 River St.* ☎ *518/273–2337* ▤ *AE, MC, V.*

¢–$ ▥ **Best Western Rensselaer Inn.** At this four-story hotel in downtown Troy, rooms are bright and uncluttered, with big windows and either two double beds or one king and a pullout couch. Although it's part of a chain, the property is independently owned. ⊠ *1800 6th Ave., 12180* ☎ *518/274–3210* 🖷 *518/274–3294* ⊕ *www.bestwestern.com* ⇥ *152 rooms* ₺ *Restaurant, in-room data ports, cable TV with movies, pool, gym,* *bar, video game room, meeting rooms, airport shuttle, some pets allowed (fee), no-smoking rooms* ⊟ *AE, D, DC, MC, V* ⦾ *CP.*

¢–$ ⊞ **Franklin Square Plaza Inn and Suites.** The modern, cheerful brick inn a block from the Hudson River is a good alternative to chain hotels. Standard rooms tend to be a bit run-of-the-mill and have either two double beds or a king. Suites, double the size of the standard rooms, have king-size beds, an adjoining sitting room, a refrigerator, and a whirlpool tub. Five restaurants are within a block of the property. ⊠ *1 4th St., 12180* ☎ *518/274–8800 or 866/708–2233* 🖷 *518/274–0427* ⊕ *www.franklinsquareinn.com* ⮐ *58 rooms, 4 suites* ♿ *In-room data ports, some in-room hot tubs, some refrigerators, cable TV with movies, business services, no-smoking rooms* ⊟ *AE, D, DC, MC, V* ⦾ *CP.*

Nightlife & the Arts

The **New York State Theatre Institute** (NYSTI ⊠ 37 1st St. ☎ 518/273–2337 ⊕ www.nysti.org), a family-oriented professional theater company, presents plays and musicals from September to May. The Schact Fine Arts Center at Russell Sage College houses the company. Tickets are usually $20. Local and touring bands play the popular **Revolution Hall** (⊠ 425 River St. ☎ 518/273–2337 ⊕ revolutionhall.com). The converted 18th-century warehouse hosts jazz, blues, and folk acts, and past shows have included Gaelic music and Tim Reynolds (of Dave Matthews Band fame). Brown's Brewing Company is a few doors away. The beaux-arts **Troy Music Hall** (⊠ State and 2nd Sts. ☎ 518/273–0038 ⊕ www. troymusichall.org), considered one of the few acoustically perfect concert halls in the world, attracts top international and U.S. musicians. A full lineup of classical, pop, and jazz concerts is held throughout the year, and the Albany Symphony plays a seven-concert season here from October through May.

Sports & the Outdoors

BASEBALL The **Tri-City ValleyCats** (⊠ Joseph Bruno Stadium, Hudson Valley Community College, South Rd. ☎ 518/629–2287 ⊕ www.tcvalleycats.com), a minor-league baseball team affiliated with the Houston Astros, plays at the Joseph Bruno Stadium from June through Labor Day. The stadium, built in 2003, has 4,500 seats.

John Boyd Thacher State Park

★ ⑭ *15 mi southwest of Albany.*

The park sits along the **Helderberg Escarpment,** one of the most fossil-rich formations in the world and the most dramatic natural feature of the regional landscape. From the escarpment ledge you can take in panoramic views of the Hudson-Mohawk Valley, with the Adirondack foothills and the western mountain ranges of Massachusetts and Vermont off in the distance. The park is the ending point for the Long Path, a 349-mi hiking trail that starts in Fort Lee, New Jersey, and crosses public and private land. Within the park you can hike the **Indian Ladder Trail,** which runs along the Helderberg cliff. The trail, open from May to mid-November, is furnished with interpretive signs, and guided hikes are available. Another 12 mi of trails are open all year. In warm weather the trails are used for hiking, biking, and nature walks; cross-country skiing (on groomed and ungroomed trails) and snowshoeing are available in winter. Facilities include an Olympic-size pool ($2 in season) and picnicking sites. ✉ *Rte. 157 off Rte. 85, Voorheesville* ☎ *518/872–1237* ⊕ *nysparks.state.ny.us* 🚗 *Parking $6 (late May–Labor Day)* ⊙ *Daily 8* AM*–dusk.*

CAPITAL REGION A TO Z

By Wendy Liberatore

To research prices, get advice from other travelers, and book travel arrangements, visit www.fodors.com.

AIR TRAVEL

The capital region is served by Albany International Airport (ALB). US Airways flies nonstop to Albany from New York City's LaGuardia Airport and Buffalo Niagara International Airport. Continental flies nonstop from Buffalo Niagara International Airport, Greater Rochester International Airport, and Syracuse Hancock International Airport. Travelers should try to avoid the airport rush from 5 to 7 AM weekdays. *See* Air Travel *in* Smart Travel Tips A to Z for more information about Albany, Buffalo, LaGuardia, Rochester, and Syracuse airports and for major airlines' contact information.

BUS TRAVEL

Greyhound and Adirondack Trailways provide almost hourly service from New York City's Port Authority Terminal to Albany, Schenectady, and Saratoga Springs; tickets for the two bus lines are interchangeable. Adirondack Trailways and Greyhound also connect the capital region with the Hudson Valley and northern, central, and western New York. Within the region, the Capital District Transportation Authority provides service in and around Albany, Schenectady, Troy, and Saratoga Springs. Service is more extensive around Albany, Troy, and Schenectady, but it's still infrequent on weekends.

🚍 **Adirondack Trailways** ☎ 800/858-8555 ⊕ www.trailways.com. **Capital District Transportation Authority** ☎ 518/482-8822 ⊕ www.cdta.org. **Greyhound** ☎ 800/231-2222 ⊕ www.greyhound.com.

CAR RENTAL

Avis, Budget, Enterprise, and Hertz rent cars at Albany International Airport. *See* Car Rental *in* Smart Travel Tips A to Z for these national agencies' contact information. Thrifty and Payless are off-site; a shuttle bus runs passengers to and from the airport.

🚗 **Payless** ✉ 955 Albany Shaker Rd., Latham ☎ 518/783-5353 or 800/729-5377 ⊕ www.paylessalbany.com. **Thrifty** ✉ 941 Albany Shaker Rd., Latham ☎ 518/782-7612 ⊕ www.thrifty.com.

CAR TRAVEL

The best way to explore the capital region is by car. Interstates 90 and 87 intersect in Albany. Traffic on both I–87 and Route 9 moves freely, except for the weekday rush hour in Albany from 4 to 6 PM.

On-street parking is allowed everywhere, though parking in downtown Albany during the week can be difficult. In summer, parking in Saratoga, which has only a few small, free public lots, can be frustrating. Most hotels in the region have their own parking lots; not all are free, however.

EMERGENCIES
In an emergency, dial 911.

🚩 Hospitals **Albany Medical Center** ⊠ 43 New Scotland Ave., Albany ☎ 518/262-3131 ⊕ www.amc.edu. **Ellis Hospital** ⊠ 1101 Nott St., Schenectady ☎ 518/243-4121 ⊕ www.ellishospital.org. **Samaritan Hospital** ⊠ 2215 Burdett Ave., Troy ☎ 518/271-3424 ⊕ www.northeasthealth.com. **Saratoga Hospital** ⊠ 211 Church St., Saratoga Springs ☎ 518/587-3222 ⊕ www.saratogahospital.org.

SPORTS & THE OUTDOORS
See Sports & the Outdoors *in* Smart Travel Tips A to Z for additional information.

BIKING   The scenic Mohawk-Hudson Bikeway has about 60 mi of paved trails for bikers and walkers. It winds around the Erie Canal and the Hudson River, from Schenectady to Albany and Troy, and is mostly flat with a few hills. You can access the bikeway from Route 5S in Rotterdam and Route 158 in Niskayuna. The New York State Canals Web site has additional information.

GOLF   The area has a few top-rated courses, the best being Saratoga National Golf Course. Public courses, such as Saratoga Spa Golf ($25 greens fee), are a good budget option. The Saratoga Visitor Center has more information about area golf courses, which it lists on its Web site.

🚩 Biking **New York State Canals** ⊕ www.canals.state.ny.us/exvac/.

🚩 Golf **Saratoga Visitor Center** ⊠ 297 Broadway, Saratoga Springs 12866 ☎ 518/587-3241 ⊕ www.saratoga.org.

TOURS
BOAT TOURS   From April through October, Dutch Apple Cruises runs daily Hudson River tours aboard the *Dutch Apple II*. Twice a month the boat travels through the locks in Troy and the Erie Canal Park in Waterford. Departure is from the docks in Albany.

🚩 **Dutch Apple Cruises** ⊠ 141 Broadway, Albany ☎ 518/463-0220 ⊕ dutchapplecruises.com.

TRAIN TRAVEL
Amtrak links the capital region with New York City, the Finger Lakes, central and western New York, the Hudson Valley, and the Adirondacks. Reservations are strongly recommended for weekday trains to Albany-Rensselaer and weekend trains to Saratoga Springs, which often sell out.

🚩 **Amtrak** ☎ 800/872-7245 ⊕ www.amtrak.com

TRANSPORTATION AROUND THE CAPITAL REGION
Getting to the capital region by train or bus is pretty easy, but a car is the best way to get around within the area. Summer in Saratoga Springs is an exception. Most Saratoga sites are within walking or cycling distance of downtown, and the city has a trolley that runs along Broadway from Skidmore College to the Saratoga Performing Arts Center. Rides are 50¢.

VISITOR INFORMATION

🚹 **Albany Convention and Visitors Bureau** ✉ 25 Quackenbush Sq., Albany 12207 ☎ 518/434–1217 or 800/258–3582 ⊕ www.albany.org. **Rensselaer County Chamber of Commerce** ✉ 31 Second St., Troy 12180 ☎ 518/274–7020 ⊕ www.renscochamber.com. **Saratoga Visitor Center** ✉ 297 Broadway, Saratoga Springs 12866 ☎ 518/587–3241 ⊕ www.saratoga.org. **Schenectady Chamber of Commerce** ✉ 306 State St., Schenectady 12305 ☎ 518/372–5656 or 800/962–8007 ⊕ www.schenectadychamber.org.

CENTRAL NEW YORK
LEATHERSTOCKING COUNTRY

By Richard
Haubert

PART OF NEW YORK'S AGRICULTURAL and dairy heartland, the region known as Leatherstocking Country epitomizes the pastoral lifestyle. As you move deep into the region, distances between towns grow and signs of industry dwindle. Rivers, streams, and brooks glisten between vivid green hillsides; forests of hardwood and pine and fields of corn and alfalfa form a shimmering patchwork.

Extending westward from the outskirts of Albany toward the Finger Lakes and Syracuse, the region encompasses 7,000 square mi. It is roughly defined by the Susquehanna River on the south and the Mohawk River on the north; these historic waterways, with their romantic Indian names, are traced by interstates 88 and 90.

The region's curious nickname is a reference to the leather leggings the early Yankees wore. Cooperstown, first made famous by James Fenimore Cooper's *Leatherstocking Tales,* a two-volume collection of novels, is the highlight of central New York. On the shores of Otsego Lake—Cooper's beloved Glimmerglass—Cooperstown provides the backdrop for a number of museums and attractions. Fans of the great American pastime make pilgrimages to the National Baseball Hall of Fame. Other notable sites are the Farmers' Museum, the Fenimore Art Museum, and, north of the lake, a one-of-a-kind Petrified Creatures Museum. This is also the home of the Glimmerglass Opera, which presents classics in English each summer. Nearby attractions such as Howe Caverns and the Old Stone Fort Museum Complex in Schoharie are easy detours from here.

Along the region's northern edge is the historic Mohawk Valley, winding through the Adirondack foothills. The area was of great tactical importance during the Revolutionary War, when the British attempted to capture the Mohawk waterway and thereby separate New England from the southern colonies. Rome's Fort Stanwix was attacked in August 1777 as part of the British force's three-pronged invasion. The Battle of Oriskany, one of the war's bloodiest conflicts, followed, laying the groundwork for the rebels' victory at the Battle of Saratoga—a turning point in the revolution. Today the Fort Stanwix National Monument and the Oriskany Battlefield State Historic Site are among the Revolutionary War–related sites you can visit in the region.

The region is also rich in American Indian history. The territory inhabited by the Six Nations of the Iroquois Confederacy—the Oneida, Mohawk, Onondaga, Cayuga, Seneca, and Tuscarora tribes—originally stretched from the Hudson River west to the Genesee River and north to the St. Lawrence River, and central New York was its heart. The Oneida Nation, the only Iroquois tribe to side with the colonists in the Revolutionary War, owns and operates the Turning Stone Resort & Casino. The Shako:wi Cultural Center, on the Oneida reservation, a few miles south of the city of Oneida, is one place to learn more about this tribe. Between Amsterdam and Canajoharie is Kanatsiohareke, a traditional Mohawk community with a bed-and-breakfast and a noteworthy crafts shop. Other American Indian sites are scattered throughout the region.

In the early and mid-1800s, the Erie Canal brought prosperity and settlers to this fertile heartland. With the canal's opening in 1825, the Mohawk Valley was transformed into a center of industrial development, and many of its cities and towns floated and then foundered a bit with its fortunes. Utica, the region's largest city, became a focus for that growth and drew waves of immigrants. Remnants of this industrialization include the many factories and plants that now sit idle or underused.

Exploring Central New York

The triangular Leatherstocking region, which includes Montgomery, Schoharie, Otsego, southern Herkimer, Chenango, Broome, Madison, and Oneida counties, is sandwiched between Albany to the east, Syracuse to the west, the Adirondacks to the north, and the Catskill Mountains to the south. The Mohawk, Susquehanna, Chenango, and other, less-important rivers cut through the region, as do several highways. U.S. 20, the longest continuous highway in the country, originated in these parts as the Great Western Turnpike. It runs west–east through the heart of the region. Fewer than 15 mi to the north, I–90 parallels U.S. 20. Defining the region's southern edge is I–88. The north–south I–81 skirts the region on the west, connecting Syracuse (part of the Finger Lakes region) and Binghamton; Route 12 links Binghamton and Utica. Several other north–south routes link I–90 and I–88, including (in east-to-west order) Routes 10, 28, and 8.

About the Hotels & Restaurants

From price to cuisine, eating out in the Leatherstocking region largely exemplifies middle-American dining. The region's best-known entrée is purely American and can be found on many restaurant menus on Friday: the fish fry, a breaded piece of haddock served with french fries and coleslaw. That said, new immigrant groups in the region continue to diversify the cuisines available here. And, although casual dining is the rule rather than the exception, the region does have several fine-dining places that hold up against the best restaurants in the state. Cooperstown, for one, has a cluster of excellent restaurants, and Utica is known for its Italian eateries.

With few exceptions, accommodations in the region fall within the inexpensive to moderate range. The cities usually have higher-end business-oriented properties (which tend to offer more amenities) as well as midrange and budget chain properties; independent motels are found throughout the region. Bed-and-breakfast and small inn properties are usually outside the big cities. Cooperstown is filled with this kind of lodging, but you should book six weeks in advance if you plan to visit in summer or early fall. Ask about minimum stays when booking; many B&Bs and inns require two-night stays on weekends, especially in July and August.

6

Many of the sights mentioned close in winter, so check the hours of the attractions you're interested in before planning an itinerary for the October-through-March period.

Numbers in the text correspond to numbers in the margin and on Central New York map.

If you have
3 days

Cooperstown ❶ ▶ deserves two full days, which will give you the chance to see the main sights and to walk about a bit. Classical music fans shouldn't miss the Glimmerglass Opera (July and August). Spend both nights in Cooperstown (many lodgings have a two-night minimum in season). On Day 3, head either north or east. If you're traveling with children, stop at the Petrified Creatures Museum in Richfield Springs on your way north before continuing on to **Herkimer ❻** to dig for "diamonds" (really quartz crystals) or to take an Erie Canal cruise. Without kids, head straight to Herkimer for the cruise. Boats leave from the Gems Along the Mohawk retail complex, which has a restaurant. If you choose to head east instead, you can do some underground exploring in **Howes Cave ❸**. A third option is to head northeast to **Sharon Springs ❷** for lunch.

If you have
4 days

Spend two days in **Cooperstown ❶** ▶ and then head north on Day 3 to **Herkimer ❻**, as described in the itinerary above. In the late afternoon, drive west to **Utica ❼** to see the Munson-Williams-Proctor Arts Institute and the magnificently restored Hotel Utica. The city also has a few sights to interest the kids. Check out the Italian bakeries or an Italian restaurant while you're here. On Day 4 take a trip into the Adirondack wilderness on the Adirondack Scenic Railroad, which leaves from stately Union Station. Check the excursion train's schedule so that you time Day 4 correctly, and book ahead for the popular holiday-themed rides.

If you have
6 days

Follow the four-day itinerary above. On Day 5, continue west to **Oneida ❾**, where the lodging options include the Turning Stone Resort. You can spend much of Day 5 relaxing at the resort, which has a spa, three championship golf courses, and several restaurants as well as a casino. If you're interested in the American Revolution, travel to see the related sights in and around **Rome ❽** before heading to Turning Stone for dinner and a show or to try your luck in the casino.

WHAT IT COSTS					
	$$$$	**$$$**	**$$**	**$**	**¢**
RESTAURANTS	over $30	$22–$30	$15–$21	$8–$14	under $8
HOTELS	over $250	$200–$250	$150–$199	$100–$149	under $100

Restaurant prices are for a main course at dinner (or at the most expensive meal served). Hotel prices are for two people in a standard double room in high season.

Timing

Although the Leatherstocking region draws visitors throughout the year, the most popular time to visit is summer, when antiques hunters are out in full force, seeking treasures in the hundreds of shops scattered throughout Schoharie, Madison, and Broome counties, and baseball enthusiasts converge on Cooperstown, the home of America's favorite pastime. With its apple harvests and spectacular displays of colorful foliage, fall is also a good time to visit. In winter the region sees 100-plus inches of snow. From mid-March to early May the combination of melting snow and spring showers creates what's known as mud season.

COOPERSTOWN & OTSEGO COUNTY

By Doug Blackburn, Breath A. V. Hand, Karen Little

Cooperstown is the jewel of Otsego County as well as of the Leatherstocking Region. The village sits beside Otsego Lake in the middle of the county, which is wedged between U.S. 20 on the north and I–88 on the south. The area is riddled with creeks, streams, and small lakes.

Cooperstown

❶ *215 mi northwest of New York City, 72 mi west of Albany.*

The village was founded in 1786 by William Cooper on the southern shore of Otsego Lake, also known as Lake Glimmerglass. William was the father of novelist James Fenimore Cooper (1789–1851), who set some of his epics in this region. By the late 19th century, word about the village and its beautiful lake spread, as New York's wealthy began building vacation homes upstate. The community is full of civic structures and residences from this period—many of them stately, most of them well preserved. Indeed, many of Cooperstown's accommodations are run by highly dedicated innkeepers in refurbished historic mansions, and are a big draw for visitors. All told, a third of a million people visit the village annually.

When thinking of Cooperstown, you can't help but think of the national pastime. Home to the National Baseball Hall of Fame and Museum as well as a beautiful baseball diamond, the village draws fans of the game who feel they need to make the pilgrimage at least once in their lives. Both sights, as well as several shops and restaurants, are along a four-block stretch of Main Street, roughly between Chestnut and Fair streets.

Brewery Ommegang. The affinity with *all* things Belgian, not just the beer, is palpable at this brewery, an elegant, white wooden structure with an unusual round wing that has slitlike windows and would probably be called Romanesque if it were built of stone. Brews include Hennepin Farmhouse Ale, Ommegang Abbey Ale, and Rare Vos Ale. Tours and tastings are possible throughout the year. In warmer months the staff makes waffles according to a traditional recipe. The brewery also hosts several seasonal events. ✉ *656 Rte. 33* ☎ *800/544–1809* 💲 *Tours $4* ☉ *Memorial Day–Labor Day, daily 11–6; rest of yr, daily noon–5.*

Farmers' Museum. The 10 acres on which this museum is set have been dedicated to farming in one way or another since the days of James Fen-

The Erie Canal

Central New York was the birthplace of the Erie Canal, which was key to the development of the state and, indeed, the country. The first portion of the cross-state canal was dug in Rome in the early 1800s, and the project drew thousands of laborers to central New York, many of them immigrants. The waterway opened in 1825 and, compared with road travel, was a much more affordable way to transport goods and resources. It fueled industrial development along its 363 mi, increased trade, and prompted a major westward migration. The boom in water traffic made New York City the busiest port in the country, and the canal was expanded.

6

You can experience the canal in different ways throughout the region. The place where the digging of the canal started is part of the Erie Canal Village, a re-created 19th-century settlement. The Schoharie Crossing State Historic Site, 5 mi west of Amsterdam, has structures dating from all stages of the canal's development. In addition, you may take a cruise or boat on the canal, bike or walk alongside it, and dine at a canalside restaurant.

Sports Halls of Fame

You could plan an entire itinerary through central New York that focuses on sports-related halls of fame. The region is home to four such attractions: the National Soccer Hall of Fame in Oneonta, the National Distance Running Hall of Fame in Utica, the International Boxing Hall of Fame in Canastota (southwest of Oneida), and the National Baseball Hall of Fame and Museum in Cooperstown The shrine to America's favorite pastime is the most popular of the bunch, and it's the one most likely to appeal to nonsports fans. The distance-running hall times its annual induction ceremonies for the night before Utica's Boilermaker, the largest 15K race in the country.

---

imore Cooper. Stone structures that were once part of an actual farm now contain permanent and changing exhibits on agriculture, homemaking, and other aspects of farm life. Docents in period costumes mill about a village created with buildings that date from the 18th and 19th centuries and were moved here from several upstate communities. You can also inspect the livestock in the barns, wander through vegetable patches and herb gardens, and play with such historic toys as stilts and hoops and sticks. The museum celebrates a harvest weekend every year around mid-September. ☒ *Lake Rd. off Rte. 80* ☎ *607/547–1500 or 888/547– 1450* ⊕ *www.farmersmuseum.org* ☒ *$9* ☽ *May–Oct., daily 10–5.*

Fenimore Art Museum. Native, folk, fine, and decorative American art is displayed in a brick neoclassical mansion that dates from the 1930s. Paintings of landscapes and everyday scenes enlighten you on what this country was like in the 19th century. Sculptor John H. I. Browere's (1792–1834) bronze busts were made from life masks, so they truly depict such luminaries as Thomas Jefferson and Dolley and James Madison. Furniture, portraits, other artifacts shed light on James Fenimore Cooper and

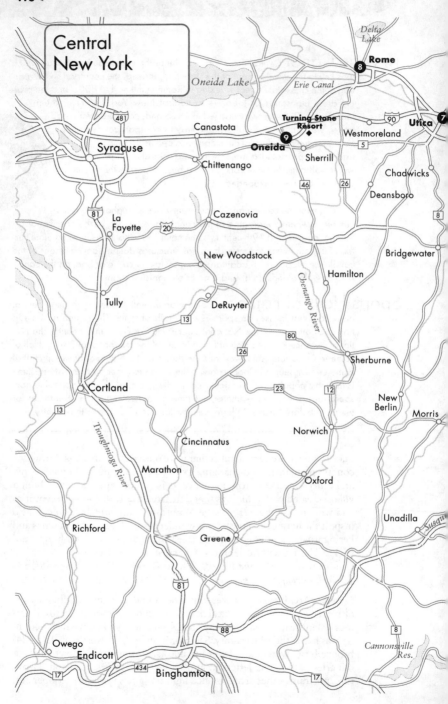

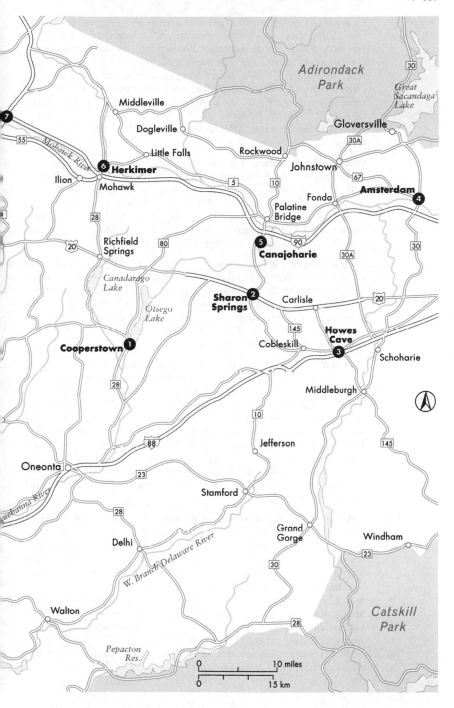

his family. Traveling exhibits are eclectic: one that explored the history of high-heel shoes was held concurrently with another that had paintings of America's Western frontier. Photography and modern works by contemporary artists have been showcased, and so have Norman Rockwell illustrations. There's also an ever-changing roster of lectures, specialty tours, and book signings. The café serves tasty salads, soups, and other light fare, and has a view across gardens and lawns to Otsego Lake. ✉ *Lake Rd. off Rte. 80* ☎ *607/547–1400 or 888/547–1450* ⊕ *www. fenimoreartmuseum.org* ✑ *$9* ☉ *June–Sept., daily 10–5; Apr., May, and Oct.–Dec., Tues.–Sun. 10–4.*

Glimmerglass State Park. Enjoy average summer temperatures of 72°F in the deep woods of this state park on Otsego Lake 8 mi north of the village of Cooperstown. In warm months you can swim, hike, and fish. There's a concession stand as well as 80 campsites. In winter you can snowshoe, snow-tube, cross-country ski, and ice fish. ✉ *1527 County Hwy.* ☎ *607/547–8662 park, 800/456–2267 reservations* ⊕ *nysparks. state.ny.us* ✑ *$6 per vehicle* ☉ *Daily 8 AM–dusk.*

Heroes of Baseball Wax Museum. It's great to read about and trade cards of your favorite players, but this museum puts you face-to-face with them. Thirty-odd baseball legends are immortalized here. When your interest in all that wax starts to wane, you can slug it out in the virtual-reality batting cage, buy a team pennant or jersey in the gift shop, or grab lunch in the café. ✉ *99 Main St.* ☎ *607/547–1273* ⊕ *www.baseballwaxmuseum. com* ✑ *$7.95* ☉ *May–Oct., daily 9 AM–10 PM.*

Hyde Hall. Its legacy is as remarkable as its architecture: from the time it was built in 1819 until it was sold to New York State in 1964, Hyde Hall remained in the same family. Money from estates here, in Europe, and in the Caribbean enabled George Clarke (1768–1835), a prominent figure in colonial New York, to finance what is, according to many historians, the largest residence built in this country before the Civil War. Ongoing restoration projects—and the chance to question artisans about their work—add texture to a tour of the 50-room mansion. The property adjoins Glimmerglass State Park on the north end of Otsego Lake. ✉ *Mill Rd.* ☎ *607/547–5098* ⊕ *www.hydehall.org* ✑ *$7* ☉ *Mid-Apr.–Oct., Tues.–Thurs. 10–4.*

Fodor'sChoice
★ **National Baseball Hall of Fame and Museum.** The ball that Babe Ruth hit for his 500th home run and Shoeless Joe Jackson's shoes are among the memorabilia that help to make this shrine to America's favorite pastime so beloved. Plaques bearing the pictures and biographies of major-league notables line the walls in the actual hall of fame. The museum also has multimedia displays, exhibits geared to children, and a research library with photos, documents, and videos. New hall members are inducted during a ceremony held on the grounds of Clark's Sport Center. The event, which may be scheduled for any weekend between June and August, is free. ✉ *25 Main St.* ☎ *607/547–7200 or 888/425–5633* ⊕ *www.baseballhalloffame.org* ✑ *$9.50* ☉ *Labor Day–Memorial Day, daily 9–9; rest of yr, daily 9–5.*

off the beaten path

NATIONAL SOCCER HALL OF FAME – This interactive, hands-on (and feet-on) museum displays soccer-related memorabilia, equipment, trophies, and photographs. In the Kicks Zone section, you can show off your kicking, heading, and dribbling skills and test your knowledge of the sport. The collection includes the world's oldest soccer ball. ✉ *18 Stadium Circle, Oneonta* ☎ *607/432-3351* ⊕ *www.soccerhall.org* 🏷 *$9* ☉ *Memorial Day–Labor Day, daily 9–7; rest of yr, daily 10–5.*

Where to Stay & Eat

$$–$$$ ✕ **Hoffman Lane Bistro.** The sunny alley bistro is 1½ blocks from the Baseball Hall of Fame. You can eat lunch or dinner on the patio or in the brightly painted dining rooms. The dinner menu includes good salads and pasta dishes as well as such classics as meat loaf with pan gravy. ✉ *2 Hoffman La.* ☎ *607/547-7055* ▤ *AE, MC, V.*

$$–$$$ ✕ **James Fenimore Cooper Room.** Part of the Tunnicliff Inn, this sparkling restaurant is quite cozy. Hallways to the guest areas are closed off, so that diners (no more than 30) can enjoy a peaceful and intimate dinner. The food and service are impeccable. Dishes range from regional American fare to Continental classics and contemporary preparations. One hearty choice: a grilled 12-ounce strip steak atop sautéed portobello and shiitake mushrooms and a pool of mustard cream sauce. Downstairs is the Pit, a historic pub where many a baseball player and fan has raised a glass. The bartender is full of good stories about serving the baseball greats. ✉ *34–36 Pioneer St.* ☎ *607/547-9611* ▤ *AE, D, MC, V* ☉ *No lunch.*

$–$$ ✕ **T. J.'s Place.** The large, family-style restaurant is filled with baseball memorabilia. The menu includes everything from omelets to burgers to Italian dishes. A bar, plasma-screen TV, and gift shop provide additional distractions. ✉ *124 Main St.* ☎ *607/547-4040* ▤ *AE, MC, V* ☉ *No dinner.*

$$$$ ✕▥ **Otesaga Resort Hotel.** There's something almost collegiate about

Fodor's Choice the stately Otesaga—maybe it's all the brick, or perhaps it's the cupola ★ or the neoclassical entryway. The same studied grace runs throughout the interior. But it would be hard to hit the books here, thanks to such distractions as the Leatherstocking Golf Course and fishing or canoeing on Otsego Lake. The water view from the circular back porch alone is enough to take you far from the everyday world. In the luxurious **Main Dining Room** ($$$$), elegant jabots frame massive windows. Dinner is prix fixe (four courses) and formal, with jackets required for men. The ever-changing menu lists contemporary dishes such as an appetizer of corn tortellini with Madeira sauce as well as classics like beef medallions in cognac-mushroom cream sauce. The kitchen prides itself on the high quality of its ingredients, including fish that comes fresh from Boston, and breads are baked on the premises. The much more relaxed **Hawkeye Bar & Grill** ($–$$$) spills out onto a lakeside patio. The dinner menu includes linguine topped with exceptionally fresh lobster, clams, shrimp, and scallops, as well as such casual fare as burgers and Caesar salad. Although the resort closes in winter, the grill is open throughout the year (closed Sunday and Monday and no lunch Saturday from late November to mid-April). ✉ *60 Lake St., 13326* ☎ *607/*

547–9931 or 800/348–6222 ⊕ *www.otesaga.com* ↝ *136 rooms* ♨ *Restaurant, dining room, in-room data ports, in-room safes, cable TV, 18-hole golf course, 2 tennis courts, pool, lake, gym, boating, fishing, lobby lounge, lounge, concert hall, business services, meeting rooms* ☱ *AE, D, DC, MC, V* ⊘ *Closed mid-Nov.–mid-Apr.* ¶⊙¶ *MAP.*

$–$$$$ ⌂ **Diastole Bed and Breakfast.** The breathtaking views from the huge porch of this hilltop B&B 3 mi from the village center are of woods and Otsego Lake's western shore. Shaker pieces are used throughout the house. The largest guest room, outfitted with Early American as well as Shaker furnishings, is impeccable. The property encompasses miles of private hiking trails, and you can arrange for horseback riding with a nearby outfitter. ☒ *276 Van Yahres Rd., 13326* ☎ *607/547–2665* ⊕ *www.cooperstownchamber.org/diastole* ↝ *5 rooms* ♨ *Dining room, some in-room hot tubs, hiking; no kids under 6, no smoking* ☱ *No credit cards* ¶⊙¶ *BP.*

$–$$$$ ⌂ **White House Inn.** The 1835 Greek revival sits on a half acre near the village's main sights. Behind the inn are the carriage house, pool, and shaded, landscaped yard. Public areas have Oriental rugs and rich palettes. Guest rooms feel more casual, thanks to pastel color schemes, country quilts, and touches of floral. Rooms can be combined to accommodate groups of up to six. ☒ *46 Chestnut St., 13326* ☎ *607/547–5054* ⊞ *607/547–1100* ⊕ *www.thewhitehouseinn.com* ↝ *6 rooms, 1 carriage house* ♨ *Dining room, cable TV, pool; no smoking* ☱ *AE, D, MC, V* ¶⊙¶ *BP.*

$–$$$ ⌂ **Stables Inn.** The Stables is in the heart of town, right near the Baseball Hall of Fame and above a store catercorner to T. J.'s Place, a popular baseball-themed restaurant that's affiliated with the inn. (The full breakfast is served at T. J.'s.) Guest quarters are all suites with queen and twin beds as well as such amenities as microwaves and coffeemakers. ☒ *124 Main St., 13326* ☎ *607/547–4040* ⊕ *www.tjs-place.com* ↝ *5 suites* ♨ *Restaurant, cable TV, microwaves, refrigerators; no smoking* ☱ *AE, MC, V* ¶⊙¶ *BP.*

$$ ⌂ **Angelholm Bed and Breakfast.** This impeccable 1805 Federal home is just off Main Street and adjacent to Doubleday Field. Innkeeper Dan Lloyd loves kids and baseball, as evidenced by his ever-full cookie jar and his baseball-card collection. Rooms have elegant wallpapers or traditional colonial paint schemes, baths (some with claw-foot tubs), lace curtains, and large beds. ☒ *14 Elm St., 13326* ☎ *607/547–2483* ⊕ *www.angelholmbb.com* ↝ *5 rooms* ♨ *Dining room, library, piano; no smoking* ☱ *AE, D, MC, V* ¶⊙¶ *BP.*

$$ ⌂ **Cooper Inn.** With white moldings, delicate plaster- and woodwork, and a flying staircase, the interior of this 1812 brick inn is as Federal as its exterior. A stay here gets you access to all the facilities at the nearby Otesaga Resort—including discounted greens fees—as well as to those at a sports center down the road. ☒ *15 Chestnut St., 13326* ☎ *607/547–2567 or 800/348–6222* ⊕ *www.cooperinn.com* ↝ *15 rooms* ♨ *Dining room, in-room data ports, cable TV; no smoking* ☱ *AE, MC, V* ¶⊙¶ *CP.*

$$ ⌂ **Inn at Cooperstown.** Rocking chairs are set all along the front porch, which runs the width of this glorious Second Empire building (circa 1874) near Main Street. Guest rooms are uncluttered, making them seem even roomier than they already are. Crisp clean walls, king- and queen-size beds, and wall-to-wall carpeting lend modernity. Pastel quilts in traditional patterns and period reproductions are nods to this inn's history and its place on the National Register of Historic Places. ⊠ *16 Chestnut St., 13326* ☎ *607/547–5767* ⊕ *www.innatcooperstown.com* ⤳ *17 rooms, 1 suite* ♧ *Dining room, some refrigerators, Internet; no room phones, no room TVs, no smoking* ▤ *AE, MC, V* ▥ *CP.*

$$ 🏨 **Landmark Inn.** An expansive front lawn rolls from Chestnut Street to the sheltered entry of this truly grand 1856 Italianate mansion. Common areas are large and sunny. Shiny wood floors and attractive furnishings are found throughout. Beds and chairs are so plump you can't resist flopping onto them as soon as you enter your room. Many rooms have special showers or tubs; one has an 11-head shower. Full breakfasts are served in a formal dining room. ⊠*64 Chestnut St., 13326* ☎*607/ 547–7225* ⊕ *www.landmarkinnbnb.com* ⤳ *9 rooms* ♧ *Dining room, some in-room hot tubs, refrigerators, cable TV, in-room VCRs, Internet; no smoking* ▤ *AE, D, MC, V* ▥ *BP.*

$$ 🏨 **Tunnicliff Inn.** This 1802 Federal-style hotel is one of Cooperstown's oldest brick structures. It was first used as a general store before being transformed, in 1848, into a hotel. A restaurant with an old-fashioned tap room adjoins the hotel, which is near the Baseball Hall of Fame and other village sights. ⊠ *34 Pioneer St., 13326* ☎ *607/547–961* ⊕ *www. cooperstownchamber.org/~tunnicliff* ⤳ *17 rooms* ♧ *Restaurant, dining room, cable TV, Internet; no smoking* ▤ *AE, D, MC, V.*

$–$$ 🏨 **Barnwell Inn.** The owners of this 1850 mansion are opera lovers, and the inn tends to book up with other opera buffs during the local company's July–August season. The house, on a tree-lined, flower-filled yard created from three city lots, includes rooms painted in salmon pink, malachite green, burgundy, and pale yellow. Each guest room is unique, and a coach-house apartment—a good value—has a bedroom, a living area, and a kitchenette. Breakfast includes fresh berry pies and fruit crisps as well as such standard fare as quiche. Note that a dog also resides here. ⊠*48 Susquehanna Ave., 13326* ☎ *607/547–1850* ⊕ *www.barnwellinn. com* ⤳*2 rooms, 2 suites, 1 apartment* ♧ *Dining room, fans, some kitchenettes, cable TV, piano; no kids under 2* ▤ *MC, V* ▥ *BP.*

$–$$ 🏨 **Bay Side Inn & Marina.** Otsego Lake is the focal point at this well-run motel, which has its own beach with docks, paddleboats, canoes, and gazebos—there's even a waterside swing set. The central building has large guest rooms, a sweeping porch, a lounge, and a room with pinball machines. There are also 11 freestanding cottages, the largest of which can accommodate 10 people. ⊠ *7090 Rte. 80, 13326* ☎ *607/ 547–5856* ⊕ *www.cooperstown.net/bayside* ⤳ *29 rooms, 11 cottages* ♧ *Picnic area, refrigerators, cable TV, beach, boating, recreation room, playground; no smoking* ▤ *AE, D, MC, V* ☉ *Closed Nov.–Apr.*

$–$$ 🏨 **Green Apple Inn.** This 1854 colonial-revival mansion near Otsego Lake has Victorian-style guest rooms, some with claw-foot bathtubs. Porches and an atrium facing a beautiful yard are great places to read in warmer months; on colder days you can curl up by a fireplace in one of the public areas. It's an easy walk to the museums just outside the village or to Main Street. ⊠ *81 Lake St., 13326* ☎ *607/547–1080*

⊕ *www.greenappleinn.com* ⌕ *4 rooms* ⚒ *Dining room, cable TV, Internet; no kids under 8, no smoking* ▤ *MC, V* ⍾ *BP.*

$–$$ ▦ **Lake Front Motel.** Rooms are large and tidy at this professionally run dockside motel. Rooms have lake or park views. Don't feel bad if you can't snag one with a water view; just head to the restaurant's patio, where you can eat while watching boats drift by. With so much lake activity, you tend to forget that the Baseball Hall of Fame is just over a pitch away. ☒ *10 Fair St., 13326* ☎ *607/547–9511* ⊕ *www. lakefrontmotelandrestaurant.com* ⌕ *44 rooms* ⚒ *Restaurant, cable TV, lake, dock, fishing; no smoking* ▤ *AE, MC, V.*

$ ▦ **Bryn Brooke Manor.** Atop a hill off Lake Street, this old mansion has lake and mountain vistas and provides a country-manor-house experience. The resident dog and cats pay you visits in the spacious public rooms, which have wood details, paneling, and floors. In the dining room the windows open so wide that you feel like you're on a porch. Guest rooms are done in dusty pastels, whites, and florals. Quilts cover queen-sized beds, and baths have plush robes and hair dryers. Some rooms can be joined with others. The innkeeper, a baseball expert, can help you plan walks and other activities. Note that to reach the B&B, you need to walk up a steep hill. ☒ *6 Westridge Rd., 13326* ☎ *607/544–1885* ⊕ *www.brynbrookemanor.com* ⌕ *4 rooms* ⚒ *Dining room, in-room data ports, in-room VCRs, pool; no smoking* ▤ *MC, V* ⍾ *BP.*

¢ ▦ **Cooperstown Motel.** The owners of this bargain motel—representing three generations of one family—are very knowledgeable about the area and, like so many folks in Cooperstown, about baseball. The motel, ½ mi from the Baseball Hall of Fame, is one of the few area lodgings with rooms for smokers. ☒ *101 Chestnut St., 13326* ☎ *607/547–2301* ⊕ *www.cooperstownmotel.com* ⌕ *40 rooms* ⚒ *Cable TV, no-smoking rooms* ▤ *No credit cards.*

CAMPING ⚠ **Glimmerglass State Park.** On Otsego Lake's northeast edge, this park has a shoreline as well as deep woods, an inland pond, picnic tables, trailer and tent campsites, and clean facilities. There's a limit to one hard-wheeled camping option (trailer or boat) per site. Leashed pets are allowed, but you must have proof of rabies vaccination. ⚒ *Flush toilets, dump station, showers, fire pits, food service, grills, picnic tables, public telephone, play area, swimming (lake)* ⌕ *80 tent and trailer sites* ☒ *1527 Hwy. 31, 13326* ☎ *607/547–8662, 800/456–2267 reservations* ⊕ *nysparks.state.ny.us* ☒ *$13* ▤ *MC, V.*

Nightlife & the Arts

National and international groups perform at the **Cooperstown Chamber Music Festival** (☒ Lake Rd., off Rte. 80 ☎ 607/547–1450 ⊕ www.cooperstownmusicfest.com), held at the Farmers' Museum throughout August. Area opera devotees staged a performance of *La Bohème* at the local high school in 1975. Twelve summers later the company they went on to form was successful enough to merit its own space.
★ In 1987 the **Glimmerglass Opera** (☒ 7300 Rte. 80 ☎ 607/547–5704 ⊕ www.glimmerglass.org) held its first production in the 900-seat **Alice Bush Opera Theater.** The company presents four operas during its July–August season. Picnics on the grounds are a good way to spend

time before a performance. Tickets are $28–$92 weekdays and $56–$100 weekends

Sports & the Outdoors

BASEBALL One glance at the brick entrance of **Doubleday Field** (✉ Main St. ☎ 607/547-7200 or 888/425-5633 ⊕ www.baseballhalloffame.org), just south of the Baseball Hall of Fame, will have you whistling "Take Me Out to the Ballgame" for the rest of the day. Local leagues play at this diamond, which opened around 1939 and can seat about 9,000 people in its bleachers. It's also used for the Baseball Hall of Fame Game held each summer, exhibition games, and other area events.

BOATING & From May through October, **C. P.'s Charter Service** (☎ 315/858-3922 FISHING ⊕ www.cooperstownfishing.com) offers 90-minute boat tours of Otsego Lake for as many as 20 people. Vessels can pick you up from many places along the shore, and trips include free soft drinks. Rates vary. C. P.'s also conducts excursions to fish for bass, carp, perch, salmon, trout, and other game fish. Prices are $160 for four-hour trips for two people and $250 for full-day trips; if you have more than two people in your group, add another $30 per person onto the fee.

GOLF The par-72, 6,416-yard **Leatherstocking Golf Course** (✉ 60 Lake St. ☎ 607/547-9931 or 800/348-6222 ⊕ www.otesaga.com), designed by Devereux Emmet in 1909 and part of the Otesaga Resort, has a championship green that runs along Otsego Lake's southwestern shore. There's an on-site pro shop as well as a practice facility down the road. Greens fees are $70–$80. You can arrange individual lessons or take part in two- or four-day weekday or weekend training sessions (fees include hotel accommodations) through the Leatherstocking Golf School.

Richfield Springs

16 mi northwest of Cooperstown.

Richfield Springs is known for its Great White Sulfur Springs, called Big Medicine Waters by the American Indians who visited the springs for ceremonies. The village here was established after colonists became aware of the waters' healing properties and as Indian raids subsided. In 1820 Dr. Horace Manley widely publicized the effectiveness of the springs in the treatment of many ailments; it was during this time that the "strongest sulfur waters on the American continent" drew visitors from far and wide. The remains of this golden spa era can be seen in **Spring Park**, on Main Street, where the spring still runs. Canandarago Lake is nearby. Forested hills, moist gullies, and long valley vistas surround the village.

Holy Trinity Russian Orthodox Monastery. The monastery, on 300 acres of farmland, is perhaps one of the most important seminaries in North America. The largest Orthodox monastery in America, this extensive complex, founded in the 1920s, includes a cathedral, a seminary, publishing and printing facilities, a vegetable garden, an apiary, and a large cemetery. Call ahead to arrange a tour. ✉ *Robinson Rd. at Rte. 167, Jordanville* ☎ *315/858-0940* ⊕ *omna.nettinker.com/htm.htm* 💲 *Free* ☉ *Weekdays 9–4.*

🐾 **Petrified Creatures Museum of Natural History.** You can stroll among life-size dinosaur statues and pan for fossils at this hands-on museum. Much of the region was covered by the Devonian Sea more than 300 million years ago, and this site is particularly rich in fossils. More than 40 types of invertebrates have been identified here. You get to keep whatever you dig up. ⊠ *Rte. 20 1½ mi west of Rte. 80* ☎ *315/858–2868* ⊕ *www.cooperstownchamber.org/~pcm/* 🔊 *$8* ⊙ *Mid-May–mid-Sept., daily 9–5.*

SCHOHARIE COUNTY

By Doug Blackburn, Breath A. V. Hand

This picturesque region is the bridge between the Capital Region and Cooperstown. It also serves as a buffer between the Catskills and the Adirondacks. Soft hills and rich farmland dominate Schoharie County. The lone college town here is Cobleskill, home to a state-university campus. State and town roads throughout display numerous Revolutionary War battle markers.

Sharon Springs

❷ *21 mi east of Richfield Springs.*

Sharon Springs is at the intersection of U.S. 20 and Route 10. A Victorian spa village with five sulfur springs, it was a forerunner to Saratoga Springs, which became the destination of choice for New York's society set. From the 1920s through the early '50s, Sharon Springs became a popular summer retreat for wealthy Jewish families. Since 1990 this tiny community has attracted new residents who have been fixing up 19th-century buildings and opening B&Bs and other tourism-minded businesses.

Where to Stay & Eat

$ ✕ **Gino's Restaurant.** The front half is a pizzeria; in back is a casual Italian eatery that can seat 50 people. The specialty is chicken a la Gino, sautéed chicken breast in pink cream sauce. The place doesn't have a liquor license, but you can bring your own wine or beer. ⊠ *166 Main St.* ☎ *518/284–2931* ⊙ *Closed Mon. and Jan.*

★ $–$$ ✕▦ **The American Hotel.** The handsome Greek-revival hotel, built in the mid-1800s, graces Main Street with its full-facade, two-tier porch. Although magnificently restored, the hotel forgoes the fancy for the comfortable. Rooms have either a queen bed or two twins; the mostly neutral decor is punched up by cheery wall colors or patterned curtains and upholstered headboards. In the restaurant ($$–$$$; closed Monday and Tuesday from September through June), a coffered ceiling, hardwood floors, painted wood chairs, and cloth-draped tables create a warm atmosphere. The contemporary American and Continental fare—roast duck in apricot-ginger glaze, trout stuffed with crab meat, New Zealand rack of lamb with mellow garlic sauce—is good, not gimmicky. The terrace has umbrella-shaded tables for warm-weather dining. ⊠ *192 Main St., 13459* ☎ *518/284–2105* 🖨 *518/284–2105* ⊕ *www.americanhotelny.com* 🔊 *9 rooms* ♿ *Restaurant, in-room data ports, pub; no room TVs, no smoking* ▤ *AE, D, MC, V* ¶⊙∣ *BP.*

$ 🏨 **Clausen Farms Bed & Breakfast.** The property, purchased as a summer getaway by the owner of the New York City–based Clausen Brewery, has been in the Clausen family since 1890. From April through October the 80-acre llama farm offers seven rooms in an 1892 turreted Victorian called the Casino. From the large porch, you have Mohawk Valley views. Inside, the place recalls a hunting lodge, with wood paneling, a massive brick fireplace, and dark-wood furniture. The restored antique bowling alley is old-fashioned fun; there's only one lane and you set the pins. Across the lawn is the main building, a late-1700s farmhouse with four guest rooms, available all year. Breakfast is all-you-can-eat. ⊠ *106 Clausen Ridge Dr., 13459* ☎ *518/284–2527* ⊟ *518/284–2929* ⊕ *www.reu.com/clausen* ❤ *11 rooms* ⚴ *Dining room, some fans, pool, bowling, hiking; no a/c, no room phones, no TV in some rooms, no smoking* ⊟ *AE, D, MC, V* ❢⊙❢ *BP* ☺ *Casino closed.*

$–$$ 🏨 **Edgefield B&B.** Patterned fabrics, cushy upholstery, leaded-glass doors, and tailored window treatments contribute to the B&B's English country-manor charm. This refinement carries into the guest rooms, which have a queen bed or a pair of twins. Afternoon tea is served in the parlor or on the veranda. The owner has a cat, but the property doesn't welcome other pets. ⊠ *153 Washington St., 13459* ☎ *518/284–3339* ⊕ *www.sharonsprings.com/edgefield.htm* ❤ *5 rooms* ⚴ *Dining room; no room phones, no room TVs, no smoking* ⊟ *No credit cards.* ❢⊙❢ *BP.* ☺ *Closed mid-Nov.–mid-May.*

$ 🏨 **New Yorker Guest House & Wellness Spa.** The sprawling structure, built around 1875 as a hotel, has a separate wing with six massage rooms where you can have facials, body wraps, Reiki, reflexology, and other treatments. Guest rooms, outfitted with country furnishings and quilts, are simple. The two two-bedroom suites are a good option for families. The long covered porch, lined with chairs, encourages lingering. ⊠ *110 Center St., 13459* ☎ *518/284–2126* ⊕ *www.nyguesthouse.com* ❤ *4 rooms, 2 suites* ⊟ *No credit cards* ⚴ *Dining room, fans, massage, piano; no room phones, no room TVs, no smoking* ☺ *Closed Nov.–Apr.* ❢⊙❢ *BP.*

Howes Cave

❸ *16 mi southeast of Sharon Springs.*

Caverns Creek Grist Mill. At this restored 1816 mill you can take a self-guided tour and watch the 12-foot-round waterwheel power the 1,400-pound millstone. ⊠ *Caverns Rd. north of Rte. 7* ☎ *518/296–8448* ⊕ *www.cavernscreekgristmill.com* 🎫 *$4* ☺ *June–early Sept., daily 11–6; early Sept.–Oct. and May, weekends 11–6.*

Howe Caverns. An elevator takes you down 156 feet to reach these caverns. The 80-minute guided tours lead you along paved walkways and include a ¼-mi boat ride on an underground lake. The temperature down under hovers just above 50°F all year, so dress appropriately. On Friday and Saturday evenings visitors (13 and older) can opt for a lantern-lighted tour; call ahead for a reservation. The grounds include a restaurant and a motel. ⊠ *255 Discovery Dr., off Exit 22 off I–88* ☎ *518/296–8900* ⊕ *www.howecaverns.com* 🎫 *$16–$25* ☺ *July–Labor Day, daily 8–8; rest of yr., daily 9–6.*

Iroquois Indian Museum. Displays of ancient and modern artworks, archaeological relics, and ever-changing cultural exhibits and events celebrate one of the mightiest American Indian confederacies of the Northeast. The museum, which sits on 45 park acres in a building designed to recall a longhouse, includes an area devoted to exhibits for children. ⊠ *Caverns Rd. north of Rte. 7* ☎ *518/296–8949* ⊕ *www.iroquoismuseum. org* ⊠ *$7* ☉ *July and Aug., Mon.–Sat. 10–5, Sun. noon–5; Apr.–June and Sept.–Dec., Tues.–Sat. 10–5, Sun. noon–5.*

Old Stone Fort Museum Complex. The site contains several 18th- and 19th-century buildings, including the 1772 church that served as a fort during its early years. A log stockade was erected in 1777, and the building came under attack by the British three years later. During the Civil War it was used as an armory. Converted to a museum in 1889, the interior serves as a museum within a museum, with hundreds of artifacts exhibited in cases that have changed little in the past century. Revolutionary War reenactments are held on Columbus Day, and Heritage Days are celebrated in August. ⊠ *145 Fort Rd., off Rte. 30, Schoharie* ☎ *518/295–7192* ⊕ *www.schohariehistory.net* ⊠ *$5* ☉ *May and June, and Sept. and Oct., Tues.–Sat. 10–5, Sun. noon–5; July and Aug., Mon.–Sat. 10–5, Sun. noon–5.*

Secret Caverns. The cave was discovered in 1928 on a farm just outside Cobleskill. An hour-long guided tour takes you 85 feet down, via winding stairs, and features fossils, stalagmites and stalactites, natural domes, and a 100-foot-high waterfall. The cavern temperature is usually 50°F, so dress accordingly. ⊠ *Secret Caverns Rd., off Rte. 7* ☎ *518/296–8558* ⊕ *www.secretcaverns.com* ⊠ *$12.50* ☉ *May and Sept., daily 10–5; Apr. and Oct., daily 10–4; June–Aug., daily 9–7; or by appointment.*

Where to Stay & Eat

$–$$ ✕ **Bull's Head Inn.** In the center of Schoharie County's lone college town, the inn—in operation since 1802—is considered the grande dame of steak houses in these parts. The space is rustic and intimate, with picks, whips, yolks, and long rifles mounted on the walls. Below the restaurant is the Timothy Murphy Brew Pub, which briefly made its own beer. ⊠ *2 Park Pl., Cobleskill* ☎ *518/234–3591* ⊟ *AE, MC, V* ☉ *Closed Mon. No lunch Sat.*

$–$$ ✕ **Dairy Deli.** The Thai owners present American, Continental, and Thai fare, a true novelty in rural upstate New York. The menu ranges from nachos to pad thai, all at eyebrow-raising low prices. ⊠ *141 E. Main St., Cobleskill* ☎ *518/234–7720* ⊟ *AE, MC, V.*

¢–$$ ▦ **Gables Bed and Breakfast Inn.** Two Victorian homes form this peaceful B&B option among other turn-of-the-20th-century homes 1 mi from I–88. Most rooms have queen-size beds, and all are decorated in a period style of florals, lace, and wicker. Wireless Internet access is a bonus. ⊠ *436 W. Main St., Cobleskill 12043* ☎ *518/234–4467* ⊕ *www.nyinn. com* ⇨ *4 rooms, 1 suite, 1 studio* ☖ *Dining room, some kitchens, some cable TV, some in-room VCRs, Internet; no room phones, no TV in some rooms, no smoking* ⊟ *MC, V* ⊠ *CP.*

¢–$$ ▦ **Howe Caverns Motel.** Rooms at this single-level motel, on the grounds of Howe Caverns, have mountain and valley views. Choose between a queen, a king, or two double beds; family suites have four doubles. Interiors are basic, but some rooms have whirlpool tubs. The restaurant is open from July through Labor Day. ✉ *255 Discovery Dr., 12092* ☎ *518/296–8950* 🖷 *518/296–8950* ⊕ *www.howecaverns.com* 🛏 *21 rooms* ⚬ *Restaurant, in-room data ports, some in-room hot tubs, some microwaves, some refrigerators, cable TV, pool, no-smoking rooms* ☰ *AE, D, MC, V* ▯ *CP.*

$ ▦ **Best Western Inn of Cobleskill.** The low-slung, two-story chain motel is about a 10-minute drive from Howe Caverns. Rooms have either a king-size bed or two doubles; some have desks, pull-out sofas, and dual phones. The decor is uninspired, but the facilities are extensive for this type of property. ✉ *121 Burgin Dr., Cobleskill 12043* ☎ *518/234–4321 or 800/528–1238* 🖷 *518/234–3869* ⊕ *www.bestwestern.com* 🛏 *76 rooms* ⚬ *Restaurant, in-room data ports, some microwaves, some refrigerators, cable TV with movies, indoor pool, wading pool, gym, bowling, recreation room, dry cleaning, business services, meeting rooms, some pets allowed (fee), no-smoking rooms* ☰ *AE, D, DC, MC, V.*

THE MOHAWK VALLEY

By Doug Blackburn, Karen Bjornland, Breath A. V. Hand

The Mohawk Valley, the ancestral home of the Mohawk Indians, is so peaceful and scenic that it catches you by surprise. This is big-sky country Northeast style: miles of rolling woodlands, farms, and pastures sliced through by the Mohawk River, a shimmering ribbon with mostly undeveloped banks. In the valley's small cities and tiny villages hidden treasures await, from Herkimer "diamonds" to Winslow Homer masterpieces.

Amsterdam

❹ *27 mi northeast of Howes Cave.*

In its heyday, this Erie Canal town bustled with mills and factories churning out manufactured goods, from carpets and curtains to carriage springs. Amsterdam was once the nation's biggest producer of brooms, crafting 7 million a year from corn grown in the Mohawk Valley. Today visitors stop in the former Rug City (population 21,000) on their way to many historic sites, both American Indian and colonial. Izzy Demsky, better known as Kirk Douglas, grew up poor in Amsterdam and wrote about it in his autobiography, *The Ragman's Son.* The city has one of the oldest upstate Hispanic communities and is the home of musicians Alex Torres and the Latin Kings.

Noteworthy Indian Museum. A detailed model of an Iroquois longhouse is on exhibit, along with 4,000 items from a 60,000-piece collection of American Indian artifacts—pottery, beaded clothing, tools, baskets—once owned by museum founder and paper manufacturer Thomas Constantino. ✉ *100 Church St.* ☎ *518/843–4761* ⊕ *www.greatturtle. net* 🎟 *Free* ☉ *July and Aug., Tues.–Fri. 11–5, Sat. 11–4; Sept.–June, by appointment.*

Schoharie Crossing State Historic Site. Five miles west of Amsterdam is the only site with structures dating from all three stages of the Erie Canal's evolution, including the Schoharie Aqueduct. The earliest parts date from

1817. Exhibits in the visitor center show how the canal developed and include dress-up and coloring activities for children. The site has a small-boat launch and hiking, cross-country skiing, and bike trails. ⊠ *129 Schoharie St., Fort Hunter* ☎ *518/829–7516* ⊕ *nysparks.state. ny.us* ☑ *Free* ☉ *Grounds daily dawn–dusk; visitor center May–Oct., Wed.–Mon. 10–5 and Sun. 1–5.*

Shrine of Our Lady of Martyrs. North America's first canonized saints, three Catholic priests killed by Mohawk Indians in the 1640s, are remembered at this shrine 6 mi west of Amsterdam. This was also the birthplace of Blessed Kateri Tekakwitha in 1656. The immense circular church, opened in 1931, has 72 doors and offers daily mass. Walking paths lace the 600-acre grounds and offer views of the Mohawk Valley. There's a gift shop, cafeteria, and picnic grove. ⊠ *144 Shrine Rd., Auriesville* ☎ *518/853–3033* ⊕ *www.martyrshrine.org* ☑ *Free* ☉ *May–Oct., daily 10–4.*

Walter Elwood Museum. Exhibits in a 1902 schoolhouse in downtown Amsterdam trace the natural history and industries of the Mohawk Valley through the early 20th century. ⊠ *300 Guy Park Ave.* ☎ *518/843–5151* ⊕ *www.walterelwoodmuseum.com* ☑ *Free* ☉ *Weekdays 10–3.*

Where to Stay & Eat

$–$$$$ ✕ **Raindancer Steak Parlour.** Everyone knows this big, busy restaurant 3 mi north of Amsterdam—including Hillary Clinton, who lunched here during her 1999 campaign for a U.S. Senate seat. Dining is casual, in cozy booths or at tables in wood-paneled nooks. Specialties include beef-and-seafood combo plates, such as salmon and filet mignon or Alaskan king crab and prime rib. Help yourself at the soup-and-salad bar. ⊠ *4582 Rte. 30* ☎ *518/842–2606* ☰ *AE, D, DC, MC, V.*

¢   ✕ **Happi Daze Charcoal Pit.** In the 1950s it was a teen hangout, with carhops zipping trays of burgers, fries, and colas to Chevys and Fords lined up in the parking lot. The Pit, 4 mi north of Amsterdam, is still a cool place, with tunes by Elvis and the Beatles playing from loudspeakers and babes in hot pants and go-go boots pictured on the big neon sign. Try the famous foot-long hot dogs or chill out with ice cream that's made on-site. You can eat in your car or relax at pine-shaded picnic tables. ⊠ *4479 Rte. 30* ☎ *518/843–8265* ⊛ *No reservations* ☰ *No credit cards* ☉ *Closed Oct.–Mar.*

¢   🏨 **Best Western Amsterdam.** The five-story chain hotel, in the city's business district, is 1 mi north of the thruway. Rooms have large windows and simple furnishings. The indoor pool is open only from Memorial Day through Labor Day. ⊠ *10 Market St.* ☎ *518/843–5760* 🖷 *518/842–0940* ⊕ *www.bestwestern.com* ↶ *125 rooms* ♧ *Restaurant, in-room data ports, cable TV, indoor pool, bar, recreation room, laundry facilities, business services, some pets allowed, no-smoking rooms* ☰ *AE, D, DC, MC, V.*

¢   🏨 **Mohawk Indian Bed & Breakfast.** This family-oriented B&B, about 10 mi west of Amsterdam, is part of Kanatsiohareke, a traditional Mohawk community established in 1993 on 400 acres once occupied by Mohawk villages. Spacious, comfortable rooms are named for deer, wolf, turtle, and bear and outfitted with American Indian fine-art paintings, baskets, and pottery. In nice weather you can hike in the forest or walk along the Mohawk River. Snowshoeing, sledding, and horse-drawn sleighs are options in winter. ⊠ *4934 Rte. 5, Fonda 12068* ☎ *518/673–5092* 🖷 *518/673–5575* ⊕ *www.mohawkcommunity.com* 🖙 *4 rooms* ♿ *Exercise equipment, hiking, sleigh rides, no-smoking rooms; no a/c, no room phones, no room TVs* ▭ *MC, V* ⏀ *CP.*

Shopping

Baskets, moccasins, beaded hair ornaments, and carved bone pendants, all handmade by American Indians, are available for purchase at the **Mohawk Indian Craft Shop** (⊠4934 Rte. 5, Fonda ☎518/673–2534) at Kanatsiohareke, a traditional Mohawk community and education center about 10 mi west of Amsterdam. The selection of books for adults and children is large; you'll also find American Indian–style cotton shirts and dresses adorned with flowing ribbons.

Canajoharie

❺ *22 mi west of Amsterdam.*

Canajoharie is on Route 5S, on the south bank of the Mohawk River. Founded in 1730, the village is now home to a large Beech-Nut food-processing plant. The wealth of its industrial past is evident in the Canajoharie Library and Art Gallery, which has a collection of fine art donated by the late Beech-Nut factory owner, Bartlett Arkell.

★ **Canajoharie Library and Art Gallery.** The collection of paintings, largely by American artists, includes works by such well-known painters as Winslow Homer, Gilbert Stuart, Edward Hopper, John Singer Sargent, Mary Cassatt, Childe Hassam, Charles Burchfield, and Thomas Eakins. Twenty-one Homer paintings are lent out regularly to museums around the world. ⊠ *2 Erie Blvd.* ☎ *518/673–2314* ⊕ *www.clag.org* 🖭 *Free* ⏱ *Mon.–Thurs., 10–7:30, Fri. 10–4:30, Sat. 10–1:30.*

Fort Klock. The 1750 limestone house and trading post, built to protect settlers from the American Indians during the French and Indian Wars, has managed to avoid much alteration over the years. Spread around its 30 acres are a blacksmith shop, a one-room schoolhouse, and some farm buildings. ⊠ *Rte. 5, St. Johnsville* ☎ *518/568–7779* ⊕ *www.fortklock.com* 🖭 *$1* ⏱ *Late May–mid-Oct., Tues.–Sun. 9–5.*

Fort Plain Museum. A Greek-revival house on the west side of Fort Plain is home to this museum, where you can see Revolutionary War artifacts and American Indian collections. The home was built in 1848 on what had been the site of a Revolutionary War fortification in the late 1700s. ⊠ *389 Canal St., Fort Plain* ☎ *518/993–2527* 🖭 *Free* ⏱ *Call for hrs.*

Where to Stay & Eat

¢ ✕ **Village Restaurant.** Locals craving a Spanish omelet, baked ziti, and other comfort food head for this downtown diner just off I–90. Everything is made from scratch, and seasonal decorations brighten the decor. ⊠ *59 Church St.* ☎ *518/673–2596* ▭ *No credit cards.*

¢–$ 🛏 **Window Box Guest House.** The B&B occupies two circa-1870 buildings, a Greek-revival house and a Federal-style building, which sit on a quiet street and have garden views. The Federal-style building includes a living area, where breakfast is served, and a small guest kitchen. Decorated in warm colors and with refined country furnishings, rooms are cozy and attractive. Beds are either doubles or queens. Wireless Internet access is available. ⊠ *23–29 Front St., 13317* 🏠 *518/673–3131* ⊕ *www.windowboxguesthouse.com* 🕤 *4 rooms* 🔥 *Cable TV, in-room VCRs, Internet; no smoking* 🚭 *AE, D, DC, MC, V* 🍽 *BP.*

Herkimer

❻ *29 mi west of Canajoharie.*

The village, on the north bank of the Mohawk River, takes its name from a Revolutionary War general whose home, now a state historic site, was several miles east, near Little Falls. The first road through Herkimer was built in 1794; the Erie Canal came in 1825, followed by the railroad in 1833 and the thruway in 1954. The arrival of these harbingers of historic, economic, and cultural transformation is analogous to the history of Herkimer. After settlement, this village transitioned from an agricultural base to producing bicycles, shoes, furniture, matches, coat hangers, carriages, and lumber. Later, as the 20th century approached, the local economy became more reliant on the service industry, and jobs shifted to the healthcare and education fields. Boosting tourism are Herkimer's "diamonds," which you may discover at one of the local mines. History buffs appreciate the pre–Civil War architecture and preservation efforts of the village.

☾ **Ace of Diamonds.** Bring your own sledgehammers and pry bars or rent them from the gift shop, stake a "claim," and begin your search for quarry. No matter where you prospect, you're not likely to be disappointed. Many open pits are an easy walk to the right or left of the visitor center, where you can see beads, stones, an extensive book section, and other rock-related items. You might venture up the steep hillside in hope of finding a pocket containing hundreds of "diamonds"—really quartz crystals with diamondlike facets. The views of the wooded valley and the Mohawk River are a find in themselves. ⊠ *Rte. 28, Middleville* 🕿 *315/891–3855* 🎫 *$7* 🕙 *Apr.–Oct., daily 9–5.*

Erie Canal Cruises. Canal-history tours aboard the *Lil' Diamond*, a 36-passenger motorboat, take you from the docks at the Gems Along the Mohawk retail complex through Lock 18 and back. The tour takes about two hours, and the season runs from May to early October. ⊠ *800 Mohawk St.* 🕿 *315/717–0077* ⊕ *www.eriecanalcruises.com* 🎫 *$18.*

☾ **Herkimer Diamond Mines.** Try your luck at prospecting: hammer open the right rocks and you'll find double-terminated quartz crystals, aka Herkimer diamonds. Two open pits are easy to reach. The first is adjacent to the gift shop. Upstairs you can watch an explanatory video or stroll through multiple scientific displays, including exhibits about dinosaurs and fluorescent minerals. A short walk up the dirt road, past the waterfall, is the second pit. The mines are just south of Middleville. ⊠ *Rte. 28 between Rtes. 5 and 29* 🕿 *315/891–7355 or 800/562–0897* ⊕ *www.herkimerdiamond.com* 🎫 *$8* 🕙 *Apr.–Nov., daily 9–5.*

Herkimer Home State Historic Site. You can stroll the gardens, attend a multimedia show, and tour the restored Georgian-style mansion that was home to Revolutionary War General Nicholas Herkimer. Costumed historical interpreters inform you about the history, crafts, and lifestyle of the 18th century. Picnicking is encouraged. ☒ *Rte. 5S ½ mi off Thruway Exit 29A, Little Falls* ☎ *315/823–0398* ⊕ *nysparks.state.ny. us* ☒ *$4* ⊙ *May–Oct., Tues.–Sat. 10–5, Sun. 11–5.*

Suiter Mansion. The 1884 Victorian mansion is one of four buildings, all within short walking distances of one another, that make up the Historic Four Corners. Upstairs at the 1834 **Herkimer County Jail** (☒ $2) is a large dollhouse assemblage. The **Reformed Church** (1835) and the **Herkimer County Court House** (1873), as well as the jail, may be visited by appointment. Adjacent to the Suiter Mansion, which you can tour, is the Eckler House, a simple Italianate house occupied by the Herkimer County Historical Society. Its holdings include gravestone files, photographs, maps, and a manuscript collection. ☒ *Herkimer County Historical Society, 400 N. Main St.* ☎ *315/866–6413* ⊕ *www.rootsweb. com/~nyhchs/* ☒ *Free* ⊙ *Sept.–June, weekdays 10–4; July and Aug., weekdays 10–4, Sat. 10–3.*

FESTIVALS &
FAIRS **Herkimer County Fair.** At the weeklong fair, held in mid-August, you can take in many daily shows, including the Wild West Follies and Amateur Radio Club demos. Games, rides, farming and livestock displays, tractor pulls, an ice-cream eating contest, and other diversions keep the kids busy. A demolition derby, beauty pageants, and fireworks round out the event. ☒ *Herkimer County Fairgrounds, Cemetery Rd. and Rte. 5S, Frankfort* ☎ *315/895–7464* ⊕ *www.dreamscape.com/frankfpd/fair.htm*

Where to Stay & Eat

★ **$$–$$$** ✕ **Beardslee Castle.** Thanks to the meticulous owners, you'd never know that this 1860 castle, now a fine American restaurant, had survived fires and years of abandonment. The place is said to be inhabited by ghosts, and that's not hard to imagine. Stone archways separate the five cozy dining rooms, where white cloths cover the tables. The food doesn't detract from the haunting ambience. Starters might include smoked-salmon "cheesecake" with Parmesan and caviar sauce or fried alligator cakes with cumin remoulade. Many entrées come grilled, such as pork loin with compote or honey-glazed duck with fig relish. Meat-free dishes like terrine of grilled vegetables also appear on the menu. The restaurant is 6 mi east of the center of Little Falls. ☒ *Rte. 5, Little Falls* ☎ *315/823–3000 or 800/487–5861* ☐ *AE, D, MC, V* ⊙ *Closed Sun.–Wed. No lunch.*

★ **$$–$$$** ✕ **Canal Side Inn.** At this warm, French restaurant about 100 yards from the Erie Canal, specialties include sesame-crusted tuna, roasted duck with seasonal fruit sauce, and rack of lamb with herbes de Provence. Upstairs, a gracious suite and a studio are available for overnighters; breakfast and an evening aperitif are included. ☒ *Historic Canal Place, 395 St. Ann St., Little Falls* ☎ *315/823–1170* ⊕ *www.canalside.com* ☐ *D, DC, MC, V* ⊙ *Closed Sun. and Mon. No lunch.*

¢ ☐ **Putnam Manor House Bed & Breakfast.** The ivy-covered Italianate home, built in 1902, has rooms with private balconies, Victorian antiques, Oriental rugs, European wall coverings, oak floors, and mahogany accents. Beds are either king- or queen-size. Strewn throughout the public rooms is a doll collection that includes antiques and reproductions. The formal sitting room has a fireplace, and the classic Italian-style garden has statuary pieces. ⊠ *112 W. German St.* ☎ *315/866–6738* 🖷 *315/866–3102* ⊕ *www.putnammanor.com* 🖘 *4 rooms, 1 suite* ♦ *Dining room, in-room data ports, some in-room hot tubs, cable TV, badminton; no smoking* ⊟ *AE, MC, V* ⫿⃝❘ *CP.*

Shopping
Gems Along the Mohawk (⊠ 800 Mohawk St. ☎ 866/717–4367), next to the Erie Canal, has more than 50 local and regional vendors. The complex includes a waterfront restaurant.

ONEIDA & MADISON COUNTIES
UTICA, ROME, ONEIDA

By Karen Bjornland, Richard Haubert

The area, a frontier in the 1750s, has played a pivotal role in the development of the state as well as of the country. It became a gateway to the West, especially after the Erie Canal opened in 1825, in what is called the Mohawk Valley. South of the valley are soft hills, lush forests, and farmed fields. North of the canal are the Adirondack foothills, and to the west are the glistening waters of Oneida Lake. The area is home to such notable industries as Revere Copper Products, Oneida Ltd., and Harden Furniture. The Oneida Indian Nation, which runs the Turning Stone Resort & Casino as well as several other businesses, is a major employer here.

Utica

❼ *13 mi west of Herkimer.*

Utica, near the exact geographic center of New York State, has been a magnet for immigrants since Erie Canal days. Thousands of Irish workers came here to dig the big ditch in the early 1800s; after the city was incorporated in 1832 there was a wave of German immigrants. Poles and Italians, attracted by the railroad, construction, brickyard, and mill jobs, poured into Utica in the late 1800s.

Although its industrial presence is no longer what it once was, the city continues to attract—and retain—immigrants. Some of the many Italian bakeries and restaurants for which Utica is known have been in business in the same neighborhoods for three generations. The inflow of immigrants since the 1990s has been mostly from Asia, Africa, Russia, and other parts of Eastern Europe. Indeed, 10% of the population of 60,000 is from Bosnia, and the daily newspaper even prints a weekly column in Serbo-Croatian.

☾ **Children's Museum of History, Natural History, Science and Technology.** A redbrick building in the historic Main Street district houses four floors of hands-on exhibits for all ages. There's a Dinorama, with dinosaur models and fossils, and a Weather Room, with Doppler radar. Kiddies can walk into a replica Iroquois longhouse, don firefighting gear, and pretend to fly a 17-foot-long airplane. Outside you can explore the inside of an old Adirondack locomotive, dining car, and caboose parked alongside the building. Next door to the museum, Amtrak trains roar into Union Station. ⊠ *311 Main St.* ☎ *315/724–6128* ⊕ *www. museum4kids.net* ✉ *Museum $6, train free* ⊙ *Museum Mon., Tues., and Thurs.–Sat. 9:45–3:45; train weekends 12:30–2:30.*

Fodor'sChoice **Munson-Williams-Proctor Arts Institute.** The institute is made up of a mu-
★ seum, an art school, and a performing-arts center. Its **Museum of Art** occupies two distinctly different buildings. The 1850 Italianate mansion, called Fountain Elms, has rooms of Victorian-era furnishings. The main gallery spaces are in the 1960 Philip Johnson structure, a rather austere building clad in polished granite. The holdings include 18th-, 19th-, and 20th-century American paintings, sculptures, and photographs; 19th- and 20th-century European paintings; Asian prints; and pre-Columbian artifacts. A highlight here is the collection of Hudson River school paintings, which include the four-part "Voyage of Life" series by Thomas Cole as well as works by Asher B. Durand and Frederic Church. ⊠ *310 Genesee St.* ☎ *315/797–0000* ⊕ *www.mwpi.edu* ✉ *Free* ⊙ *Tues.–Sat. 10–5, Sun. 1–5.*

Saranac Brewery Tour Center. Learn how the **F. X. Matt Brewing Co.** creates its Saranac-brand traditional lager, pale ale, pilsner, Adirondac amber, and old-fashioned root beer. The same family has operated the seven-story brick brewhouse for more than a century. Inhaling the yeasty aroma of fermenting hops and malt, you see every step of the process, from the giant copper cooking kettles to the rapid-fire bottling process. Tours are an hour long and end with a beer or root-beer sampling. ⊠ *830 Varick St., off Court St.* ☎ *315/732–0022 or 800/765–6288* ⊕ *www.saranac.com* ✉ *$3* ⊙ *June–Aug., Mon.–Sat. 1–4 and Sun. 1–3; Sept.–May, Fri.–Sat. 1–3.*

Union Station. The massive limestone-and-granite building has 47-foot-high vaulted ceilings, marble pillars, a terrazzo floor, original steam-heated wooden benches, and a vintage barbershop that still gives haircuts. Train tours operated by Adirondack Scenic Railroad leave from the 1914 Italian Renaissance–style station for day trips into the Adirondack wilderness. ⊠ *321 Main St.* ☎ *No phone.*

ⓒ **Utica Zoo.** Siberian tigers, Alaskan grizzly bears, and California sea lions are some of the 200 animals that reside in this city park with views of the Mohawk Valley. A petting zoo and live animal shows are options in summer. Ghosts and goblins inhabit the zoo in October during its annual "Spooktacular." ⊠ *99 Steele Hill Rd.* ☎ *315/738–0472* ⊕ *www. uticazoo.org* ✉ *Apr.–Oct. $4.50, Nov.–Mar. free* ⊙ *Daily 10–5.*

Where to Stay & Eat

$–$$$ ✕ **Ventura's Restaurant** Utica's Italian-Americans have gathered here for family celebrations since 1943. The semiformal dining room, with pink upholstered chairs, white linens, and tabletop candles, hums with conversation. Appetizers include escargots with mushrooms and, that regional favorite, "greens" (escarole sautéed with red cherry peppers, onions, and cheese). The lengthy list of entrées includes *zuppa di pesce* (fish-and-mussel soup), steak pizzaiola (beef with mushrooms, peppers, marinara, and mozzarella), and house-made melt-in-your mouth pastas like cannelloni, cavatelli, linguine, and fettuccine. On the walls hang signed photographs by Joe DiMaggio and Rocky Marciano. ⊠ *787 Lansing St.* ☎ *315/732–8381* ▭ *AE, D, DC, MC, V* ⊗ *Closed Mon.*

$–$$ ✕ **Dominique's Chesterfield Restaurant.** This family restaurant, a brick storefront with a full-service bar, serves traditional Italian dishes as well as local specialties such as chicken "riggies" (rigatoni and bite-size chunks of chicken breast tossed with hot and sweet peppers, cheese, onions, and marinara sauce). The dining room has Tiffany-style lamps and a tin ceiling. ⊠ *1713 Bleecker St.* ☎ *315/732–9356* ▭ *AE, MC, V.*

$–$$ ✕ **Kitty's on the Canal.** The city's best spot for outdoor dining, Kitty's overlooks the Erie Canal, with a dock for tugboats and pleasure craft. Enjoy dinner or snacks at one of the umbrella-shaded tables on the patio. When the weather isn't agreeable, head indoors to the spacious two-level dining rooms, which have floor-to-ceiling windows. The fare is largely American and includes steak, pork chops, and pasta and seafood dishes. Sandwiches and soups also are available. ⊠ *16 Harbor Lock Rd., off Rte. 790* ☎ *315/266–0629* ▭ *AE, D, MC* ⊗ *Closed Sun.*

$–$$ ✕ **The Phoenician.** Traditional Lebanese cuisine is the specialty of this small restaurant just outside Utica. Stuffed grape leaves, tabbouleh, and hummus with pita bread are among the appetizers. Kebabs of marinated and grilled lamb, pork, beef, and chicken are the most popular entrée. Also on the menu are *kafta* (skewered meatballs of finely ground beef and lamb), *kibbi* (raw, ground spiced lamb), stuffed cabbage, and several vegetarian dishes. A small patio offers outdoor dining. ⊠ *623 French Rd., New Hartford* ☎ *315/733–2709* ▭ *AE, D, MC, V.*

★ $–$$ ✕▣ **Hotel Utica.** Judy Garland once sang from the mezzanine to fans in the lobby, and Mae West, Rita Hayworth, and Jimmy Durante all spent the night at this 14-story Renaissance revival–style hotel in the downtown business district. The two-story lobby of the grand 1912 building has a coffered ceiling, faux marble pillars, large crystal chandeliers, a piano, and lovebirds that serenade you from their antique cage. Guest rooms, spacious and attractive, have swagged window treatments and traditional furnishings; many have Mohawk Valley views. There's no gym, but you have access to an off-site fitness facility. Floor-to-ceiling arched windows, potted palms, delicate chandeliers, and massive pillars grace the elegant 1912 Restaurant ($$–$$$). The food is contemporary, with Asian influences showing up here and there. Peppery shrimp and scallops are pan-seared and served with pasta and vanilla vodka butter sauce; salmon fillet in teriyaki-chili glaze comes with crab remoulade; and tangy barbecue sauce spices up braised pork shank. Lighter fare is served in the Lamplighter lounge. ⊠ *102 Lafayette St., 13502* ☎ *315/724–7829 or 877/906–1912* 🖷 *315/733–7663* ⊕ *www. hotelutica.com* ⤲ *98 rooms, 14 suites* ◔ *Restaurant, room service, in-room data ports, some in-room hot tubs, some refrigerators, cable TV with movies, some in-room VCRs, lobby lounge, laundry service, business services, meeting rooms, free parking, no-smoking rooms* ▭ *AE, D, DC, MC, V.*

$–$$　☒ **Radisson Hotel–Utica Centre.** The upscale chain hotel is in downtown, close to the Munson-Williams-Proctor Arts Institute and the Stanley Performing Arts Center. Free wireless Internet access is available throughout the Radisson. Guest rooms have either one king or two double beds and contemporary wood furniture. The skylit Garden Grille is popular with locals. ☒ *200 Genesee St., 13502* ☎ *315/797–8010 or 800/333–3333* 🖷 *315/797–1490* ⊕ *www.radisson.com* ⟿ *158 rooms, 4 suites* ♿ *Restaurant, refrigerators, cable TV with movies and video games, indoor pool, health club, hair salon, hot tub, sauna, lounge, Internet, business services, meeting rooms, parking (fee), no-smoking rooms* ⊟ *AE, D, DC, MC, V.*

¢–$　☒ **Rosemont Inn Bed & Breakfast.** A cupola crowns this handsome three-story brick Italianate villa built in 1866. The B&B has two large porches, a parlor with a marble fireplace, and bathrooms with claw-foot tubs. One guest room is on the first floor; the others are on the second floor. Most rooms have a queen bed, and all have rose-print bed coverings and down comforters. The Wine and Roses room, where walls are the color of claret, has a queen and a double bed. ☒ *1423 Genesee St., 13501* ☎ *315/792–8852 or 800/883–0901* ⊕ *www.borg.com/~rosemont* ⟿ *7 rooms* ♿ *Dining room, library, free parking; no room phones, no room TVs, no smoking* ⊟ *MC, V* ⦿ *BP.*

Nightlife & the Arts

The performing-arts division of the **Munson-Williams-Proctor Arts Institute** (☒ 310 Genesee St. ☎ 315/797–0000 ⊕ www.mwpi.org) offers jazz, classical, and contemporary concerts; children's programs; movies; and festivals. Some institute-sponsored performances are held at the Stanley Performing Arts Center.

At the 2,945-seat **Stanley Performing Arts Center** (☒ 259 Genesee St. ☎ 315/724–4000 ⊕ www.cnyarts.com) you can see touring Broadway shows and enjoy performances by the **Mohawk Valley Ballet** and the **Utica Symphony Orchestra.** The Mexican-baroque center was built as a movie house in 1928. It has an ornate marquee and terra-cotta and mosaic tile accents on its exterior; inside, walls are adorned with gold-leaf lions and angels, and the ceiling is scattered with stars.

Sports & the Outdoors

Attracting more than 10,000 runners, including Olympians and world-class athletes, the **Boilermaker** (☎ 315/724–7221 or 800/426–3132 ⊕ www.boilermaker.com) is the largest 15K race in the country. It's held annually on the second Sunday in July. The **National Distance Running Hall of Fame** (☒ 114 Genesee St. ☎ 315/724–4525 ⊕ www. distancerunning.com) holds its annual induction ceremony the night before the Boilermaker.

Shopping

A food lover's delight awaits at Bleecker and Albany streets 1 mi from downtown. Here, in the remnants of an old Italian neighborhood, Uticans wait patiently in line for freshly made pastries, bread, and tomato pie (pizzalike squares that are eaten at room temperature). **Caffe Caruso** (☒ 707 Bleecker St. ☎ 315/735–9712) has glass cases packed with fresh cookies, a giant copper espresso machine, and white wrought-iron chairs and glass-topped tables. Crisp-and-creamy cannoli are $1 each, and chocolate *pasticciotti* (small custard-filled pies) are 80¢ at the **Florentine Pastry Shop** (⊠ 667 Bleecker St. ☎ 315/724–8032), open since 1918. Enjoy your treat with a cup of coffee in an adjoining storefront room decorated with maps and photos of Italy. In business since 1908, **Rintrona's Bakery** (⊠ 744 Bleecker St. ☎ 315/732–2337) sells bread, meatballs, fried dough, pizza shells, and tomato pie.

Rome

❽ *15 mi northwest of Utica.*

The Mohawk River courses through Rome, about 10 mi north of I–90, and the route linking the Atlantic Ocean with the Great Lakes cuts through the area. The Oneida were the first to live in this area, and in the 1600s British and French fur traders came to barter for black-beaver pelts. In the 1750s the British built Fort Stanwix, which the Americans took over just before the Revolutionary War. And it was here, in 1817, that the first portion of the Erie Canal was dug. Today about 35,000 people live in Rome, where the former Griffiss Air Force Base has been converted into a high-tech community. The city is home to a number of historic sites that attract tens of thousands of visitors each year.

Delta Lake State Park. On a peninsula that juts into the Delta Reservoir, the park has a sandy beach with a swimming area, a snack bar, restrooms, and changing facilities. The fishing includes trout, walleye, bass, and perch; in winter there's ice fishing. Trails are used for hiking, biking, nature walks, snowmobiling, and cross-country skiing. Campsites (early May through Columbus Day) are on a bluff overlooking the water. Picnic tables, grills, and pavilions are scattered throughout the park. ⊠ *8797 Rte. 46* ☎ *315/337–4670, 800/456–2267 campground reservations* ⊕ *nysparks.state.ny.us* ⊠ *Parking $7 (early May–Columbus Day)* ⊙ *Daily dawn–dusk.*

Erie Canal Village. Digging of the Erie Canal started in 1817 on this site, now home to a re-created 19th-century canal settlement. You can visit a tavern, a blacksmith shop, a one-room schoolhouse, and settlers' houses from different eras of the 1800s. The complex also includes a cheese museum (in a former cheese factory), a carriage museum with horse-drawn vehicles, and a canal museum with displays about the construction of, and life along, the canal. A mule-drawn packet boat gives rides on the canal, or you can take a ride on a steam train. ⊠ *5789 New London Rd.* ☎ *315/337–3999 or 888/374–3226* ⊕ *www.eriecanalvillage. net* ⊠ *Village and museums $4, train or packet boat $5* ⊙ *Late May–Labor Day, Wed.–Sat. 10–5, Sun. noon–5; rest of Sept., Sat. 10–5, Sun. noon–5.*

Fort Stanwix National Monument. In 1758, during the French and Indian Wars, the British built a fort here to protect the strategic Oneida Carrying Place—a 1-mi-long area between the Mohawk River and Oneida Lake where boats had to be carried. It was part of the route from the Atlantic Ocean to the Great Lakes. A path here allows you to walk part of the Oneida Carrying Place. The British eventually abandoned the fort, which the American rebels took over at the start of the Revolutionary War. The fort came under attack by British forces, Tories, and their Indian allies for three weeks in August 1777, but the rebels were able to fend off the siege. The structure you see today is a reconstruction of that fort, which suffered a major fire and destructive floods after the Revolution. The ranger-staffed visitor center is inside Gregg Barracks. The 16-acre site also includes the Marinus Willett Center (at this writing under construction and expected to open in mid-2005), which is to house visitor orientation exhibits and artifacts. Living-history programs, encampments, military drills, and concerts are some of the summer events. ⊠ *112 E. Park St.* ☎ *315/336–2090* ⊕ *www.nps.gov/fost* ⊠ *Free* ⊙ *Apr.–Dec., daily 9–5.*

Oriskany Battlefield State Historic Site. The August 6, 1777, battle fought here is said to have been one of the bloodiest conflicts of the American Revolution, and is viewed as key to later rebel victories. It involved Brigadier General Nicholas Herkimer and the 800 men and 60 Oneida warriors he had assembled to march to the aid of the rebels at Fort Stanwix, which British forces had attacked. As Herkimer's group marched toward the fort, it was ambushed in a ravine by British forces, Tories, and their Seneca and Mohawk allies. The losses, heavy on both sides, caused the British side to retreat. The site includes interpretive signs and an 85-foot-tall monument. In summer, historic encampments take place here. ⊠ *7801 Rte. 69, Oriskany* ☎ *315/768–7224* ⊕ *nysparks.state. ny.us* ⊠ *Free* ⊙ *Mid-May–mid-Oct., Wed.–Sat. 9–5, Sun. 1–5.*

Where to Stay & Eat

$-$$$ ✕ **Michelina's.** The restaurant is part of the Beeches, an estate with a 1920s manor and an adjacent inn. The place serves top-quality Continental fare that's full of flavor and attractively presented. Rack of pork, rarely encountered on restaurant menus in these parts, is marinated and slow roasted so that the meat melts in your mouth. Salmon streaks are broiled and dressed with the restaurant's tasty dill sauce. The dining room, with a large fireplace and hand-painted ceiling panels, exudes 1920s style. The chandelier, crafted in 1920 by Raulli Ironworks of Rome, is original. ⊠ *7900 Turin Rd./Rte. 26* ☎ *315/336–1700* ▤ *AE, D, DC, MC, V* ⊙ *Closed Mon.*

¢-$$ ✕ **Savoy.** At this Italian restaurant you can come for an intimate meal or just to sip cocktails at the bar and listen to live piano music (Friday or Saturday evening). The menu offers homemade pastas and fresh seafood as well as such traditional preparations as sautéed chicken and artichoke hearts in white wine and butter or flavorful, red wine–marinated steak. The walls are covered with photographs of politicians, musicians, and other famous people that illustrate the long history of the restaurant, which opened in 1908 and is run by the family that runs the Beeches complex. The bar, separate from the dining room, has intimate seating. ⊠ *255 E. Dominick St.* ☎ *315/339–3166* ▤ *AE, D, DC, MC, V* ⊙ *No lunch weekends.*

¢-$$ ▦ **Beeches Paul Revere Lodge.** The family running this inn, part of the 52-acre Beeches estate, has been in the hotel business since 1908. Rooms, dressed in French-country style with floral patterns, have a king bed or one or two queen-size beds; bathrooms have marble trim. The suite has a sitting area and a whirlpool tub. ✉ *7900 Turin Rd., 13340* ☏ *315/336–1776 or 800/765–7251* 🖷 *315/339–2636* ⊕ *www.thebeeches.com* 🛏 *65 rooms, 1 suite* ⚒ *Restaurant, dining room, in-room data ports, 1 in-room hot tub, refrigerators, cable TV, pool, laundry service, business services, meeting rooms, some pets allowed (fee), no-smoking rooms* ☰ *AE, D, DC, MC, V.*

¢–$$ 🏨 **Quality Inn.** Rooms at this chain property have either two double beds or one king bed; some have balconies and sofa beds. Several rooms face Route 49, but most face away from the road. Half the rooms have interior entrances, whereas those overlooking the courtyard with the outdoor pool have exterior entrances. The connecting Denny's restaurant is open around the clock. ✉ *200 S. James St., 13440* ☏ *315/336–4300* 🖷 *315/336–4492* ⊕ *www.choicehotels.com* 🛏 *103 rooms* ⚒ *Restaurant, microwaves, refrigerators, cable TV, pool, gym, laundry facilities, business services, no-smoking rooms* ☰ *AE, D, DC, MC, V.*

Oneida

❾ *16 mi southwest of Rome.*

This small city off Route 5 and the thruway was settled in 1834. It's home to the Mansion House estate, where the former Oneida Community, a utopian religious sect, lived in the mid-19th century. The group produced assorted goods, including silverware, and in the 1880s, abandoning its communal way of life, it morphed into Oneida Community Ltd. This joint-stock company eventually became Oneida Ltd. In Verona, 4 mi northeast, is the Turning Stone Resort & Casino; it's run by the Oneida Nation and offers round-the-clock gambling, three hotels, and several restaurants. A few miles north, on the eastern end of Oneida Lake, Sylvan Beach offers warm-weather amusements.

Cottage Lawn. The 1849 Gothic-revival cottage, headquarters of the Madison County Historical Society, was designed by noted architect Alexander Jackson Davis. The group runs tours of the cottage, which contains period furnishings. Glassware from Canastota Glass and portraits of City of Oneida founder Sands Higinbotham and prominent abolitionist Garrett Smith are among the displays here. The building, which once belonged to Higinbotham's son Niles, includes a research library. Out back is the Hops Barn, where exhibits explain that the region was once the center of hop production for England. The annual summer Hops Festival celebrates this heritage. ✉ *435 Main St.* ☏ *315/363–4136 or 315/361–9735* ⊕ *www.dreamscape.com/mchs1900* 💲 *$2* ⊗ *Weekdays 9–4.*

International Boxing Hall of Fame. In 1982, residents of Canastota and boxing enthusiasts wanted to honor two hometown boxers, late 1950s welterweight and middleweight champion Carmen Basilio and his nephew Billy Backus, the 1970 winner of the world welterweight title. Their efforts resulted in the 1989 opening of boxing's first hall of fame and museum, where you may see memorabilia from such notable boxers as Muhammad Ali, Joe Louis, and Billy Graham. The hall of fame is 6 mi southwest of Oneida. ✉ *1 Hall of Fame Dr., Canastota* ☏ *315/697–7095* ⊕ *www.ibhof.com* 💲 *$7* ⊗ *Weekdays 9–5, weekends 10–4.*

Mansion House. The three-story brick house and its 34 acres were the home of the 19th-century utopian Oneida Community, founded in 1848 by John Humphrey Noyes. The sect believed that the second coming of Christ had already occurred and that a new Eden could be achieved on earth. Followers considered themselves sinless and believed in the sharing of property and spouses. The group, which supported itself by making silk thread, animal traps, canned foods, and silverware, eventually led to the formation of tableware manufacturer Oneida Ltd. The mansion, a 93,000-square-foot National Historic Landmark, was constructed in stages between 1861 and 1914 and contains 35 apartments (some occupied by descendants of the original community members), a large hall, a dining room, and a museum. Guided tours are the only way to see the interior. You can also overnight here. ⊠ *170 Kenwood Ave.* ☎ *315/363–0745* ⊕ *www.oneidacommunity.org* ⊠ *$5* ۞ *Mar.–Dec., Wed.–Sat. 10 and 2, Sun. 2; Jan. and Feb., Sat. 10 and 2, Sun. 2.*

Sylvan Beach Amusement Park. The amusement park, on the eastern shore of Oneida Lake, is loaded with old-fashioned fun. One of the highlights is Laffland, what's known as a dark ride—an indoor ride, like a haunted house, through which you're moved in a cart or other vehicle. Amusement-park fans come from across the country to experience the ride, which was built in the 1950s by the New Jersey–based Pretzel amusement-ride company and is one of the few Pretzel dark rides in existence today. Other attractions include an old-time carousel, bumper cars and boats, the Galaxi roller coaster, food vendors, and arcades. ⊠ *112 Bridge St., Sylvan Beach* ☎ *315/762–5212* ⊕ *www. sylvanbeach.org* ⊠ *Entry free* ۞ *Apr.–June, weekends; June–early Sept., daily. Call for hrs.*

Shako:wi Cultural Center. The center, in a log building on the grounds of the Oneida Indian Nation, has exhibits highlighting baskets, beadwork, dolls, and wampum. You may also learn about the role of the Oneida Nation during the American Revolution, when it sided with the rebels rather than with the British. ⊠ *Oneida Indian Nation, Rte. 46, off I–90 Exit 33, Verona* ☎ *315/829–8801* ⊕ *www.oneida-nation.net/shakowi/* ⊠ *Free* ۞ *Daily 9–5.*

Turning Stone Resort & Casino. The Oneida Indian Nation has transformed what began as a bingo hall in a trailer into a sprawling modern resort with hotels, restaurants, a convention center, and a 5,000-seat entertainment center. The casino has more than 100 table games, including baccarat, blackjack, craps, and roulette; a poker room; and 2,400-plus slot machines. Several areas are designated smoke-free zones. The spa and fitness facility has saunas, steam rooms, and an indoor pool. Available treatments include massages (hot-stone, couples, foot, full-body, etc.), facials, manicures and pedicures, exfoliation, body wraps, and waxing. A day pass for the fitness facility is $15; booking a massage is another way to gain all-day access to the facility. The resort presents concerts, comedy shows, and other entertainment, and the three championship golf courses are a major draw. ⊠ *5218 Patrick Rd., Verona* ☎ *315/361–7711 or 800/771–7711* ⊕ *www.turning-stone.com.*

Where to Stay & Eat

$–$$ ✕🏨 **Turning Stone Resort & Casino.** You have three lodging options at this huge resort: the all-suites **Lodge at Turning Stone** ($$$$), the 19-story **Tower at Turning Stone**, and the modern **Hotel at Turning Stone**. Rooms in the hotel have contemporary furnishings and dramatically lighted marble bathrooms; some suites have whirlpool tubs and patios. In the tower, which opened in fall 2004, bedspreads with geometric designs complement the up-to-date room decor. The tower's third floor is devoted to a health club and a 65-foot-long indoor lap pool; a rooftop terrace crowns the building. The more intimate and luxurious lodge has chic suites with balconies, streamlined furniture, Egyptian-cotton linens, plush bathrobes, separate tubs and showers, and high-speed Internet access. The resort's food offerings include a steak house, an Italian eatery, an Asian restaurant, a buffet bar, and a bakery. The elegant Dining Room at the Lodge serves seasonal Continental and contemporary fare, with some dishes prepared at your table to your specifications. ✉ *5218 Patrick Rd., Verona, 13478* ☎ *800/771–7711* ⊕ *www.turning-stone.com* ➯ *255 rooms, 30 suites in hotel; 98 suites in lodge; 266 rooms, 21 suites in tower* ♿ *6 restaurants, 2 cafés, patisserie, room service, in-room data ports, some in-room safes, some in-room hot tubs, some minibars, some refrigerators, cable TV with movies and video games, driving range, 3 18-hole and 2 9-hole golf courses, putting green, pro shop, indoor pool, health club, hair salon, spa, casino, concert hall, showroom, laundry service, concierge, business services, convention center, no-smoking rooms* ▤ *AE, D, DC, MC, V.*

¢–$$ ✕🏨 **Charlotte's Creekside Inn.** The colonial-style house, on three wooded acres along the Sconondoa Creek, was built in 1813 by State Assemblyman Sydney Breese, uncle of inventor Samuel Morse. The property includes a multilevel deck and manicured gardens. Guest rooms, painted in bright greens and other cheery colors, embrace the flair of the Caribbean. The coral-colored Jamaican Suite has a king-size bed and a sitting area; in the huge bathroom, potted plants and leafy-print wallpaper surround the large whirlpool tub. The Aruba Suite has a skylight and an in-room jet tub; the bathroom is adjacent but only semiprivate (it doesn't have doors), which is also the case in the Bahamian Room. The other two rooms have private bathrooms. The first floor houses the restaurant ($–$$$; closed Sunday), which has four intimate dining rooms. The food is mostly Italian—veal chop with mushrooms, hot peppers, and Chianti sauce; chicken, mushrooms, and broccoli over pasta with Alfredo sauce; cheese ravioli in vodka-cream sauce—but you also find fresh seafood dishes, such as grilled salmon with hollandaise sauce. ✉ *3960 Sconondoa Rd., Oneida 13421* ☎ *315/363–3377* ☒ *315/361–8868* ⊕ *www.charlottescreekside.com* ➯ *3 rooms, 2 suites* ♿ *Restaurant, fans, some in-room hot tubs, cable TV, bar, no smoking* ▤ *AE, D, DC, MC, V* ⊚❙ *CP.*

¢–$$ 🏨 **Governor's House Bed & Breakfast.** The pristine four-story brick Victorian, built in 1848, was intended to be the state capitol. The town, however, lost out by one vote to Albany, and the building was used as a rooming house and private residence thereafter. The B&B has spacious guest rooms furnished with period antiques and adorned with frills and ruffles. On weekends, complimentary wine and cheese are served in one of the two parlors. ⊠ *50 Seneca Ave., Oneida Castle, 13421* ☎ *315/ 363–5643 or 800/437–8177* ⊕ *www.bbhost.com/govhouse* ↩ *5 rooms* ⚘ *Dining room, cable TV, in-room VCRs, library, piano, laundry facilities, Internet, business services; no kids under 12, no smoking* ☰ *AE, D, MC, V* ⊗ *Closed Jan.–Mar.* ⏲ *BP weekends, CP weekdays.*

$ 🏨 **Oneida Community Mansion House.** This mammoth three-story brick home once belonged to the Oneida Community, a utopian religious group founded in 1848. Today it houses private rental apartments, a museum, and eight large guest rooms. Two rooms have twin beds; the others have one double. Most rooms include comfortable upholstered chairs, and the decor throughout is tasteful and restrained. You may stroll through the more than 33 acres of lawns and gardens that surround the mansion. ⊠ *170 Kenwood Ave., 13421* ☎ *315/363–0745* 🖷 *315/361– 4580* ⊕ *www.oneidacommunity.org* ↩ *8 rooms* ⚘ *Some refrigerators, cable TV, golf privileges, library, no-smoking rooms* ☰ *MC, V* ⏲ *CP.*

¢–$ 🏨 **Inn at Turning Stone.** The former Super 8 is affiliated with the Turning Stone Resort & Casino, 1 mi away. Staying here gives you access to the resort's facilities; a free shuttle brings you to and from the casino. Guest rooms here, less expensive than those on the resort property, are spacious and have wall-to-wall carpeting, either a king or two double beds, and simple wood furniture. ⊠ *5558 W. Main St., Verona 13478* ☎ *315/363–0096* 🖷 *315/363–2797* ⊕ *www.turning-stone.com* ↩ *62 rooms* ⚘ *In-room data ports, some microwaves, some refrigerators, cable TV, no-smoking rooms* ☰ *AE, D, MC, V* ⏲ *CP.*

¢ 🏨 **Super 8.** Rooms at this chain property, 3 mi from the Turning Stone Resort & Casino, are spacious, with either double beds or one king-size bed; some also have recliners. Interior corridors and stairs connect the two stories. Wireless Internet access is available, and the lobby has a computer for guest use. ⊠ *215 Genesee St., 13421* ☎ *315/363–5168* 🖷 *315/363–4628* ⊕ *www.super8.com* ↩ *39 rooms, 1 suite* ⚘ *In-room data ports, microwaves, refrigerators, cable TV, Internet, no-smoking rooms* ☰ *AE, D, DC, MC, V* ⏲ *CP.*

Sports & the Outdoors

Fodor'sChoice ★ The **Turning Stone Resort & Casino** (⊠ 5218 Patrick Rd., Verona ☎ 877/ 748–4653 ⊕ www.turning-stone.com) has three championship golf courses. *Golf Digest* chose the Rick Smith course at the **Shenendoah Golf Club** as one of the best-conditioned courses in the United States. The 7,129-yard course was designed with nature in mind, with efforts made to preserve delicate wetlands. Robert Trent Jones Jr. designed the challenging 7,105-yard course at the **Kaluhyat Golf Club,** a mix of open links-style stretches and tight tree-lined fairways. The course takes advantage of the rolling landscape, so you have to place shots to remain in play; attempt the shortcut and the tall native grasses surely will make you pay with a penalty stroke.

The newest of the resort's golf offerings is the 7,314-yard Tom Fazio course at the off-property **Atunyote Golf Club,** designed for the long-ball hitter. But this course, too, has a variety of challenges in its stretches of open space and gentle slopes. The course includes several lakes, the largest of which runs along three fairways. Greens fees run $90–$175 for resort guests and $125–$200 for nonguests. The resort also has two 9-hole courses.

Nightlife & the Arts

The **Turning Stone Resort & Casino** (✉ 5218 Patrick Rd. Verona ☎ 315/ 361–7469 or 877/833–7469 ⊕ www.turning-stone.com) presents nationally known entertainers and musicians such as Bill Cosby, Tim McGraw, Paul Anka, Jethro Tull, Olivia Newton-John, and the Irish Tenors. It has two venues: the 800-seat **Showroom at Turning Stone** and the 5,000-seat **Event Center.**

CENTRAL NEW YORK A TO Z

By Breath A. V. Hand

To research prices, get advice from other travelers, and book travel arrangements, visit www.fodors.com.

AIR TRAVEL

Central New York is serviced by Albany International Airport, which is just east of the region as defined in this chapter, and Syracuse Hancock International Airport, just west of the region.

CommutAir, a Continental Airlines affiliate, connects the Albany airport to the Finger Lakes region, Long Island, and western New York; the carrier also flies to Westchester County Airport, in the lower Hudson Valley. US Airways links Albany to New York City (LaGuardia Airport), Long Island, and western New York. If you use the Albany airport, avoid the weekday rush period, 5 to 7 AM.

Continental affiliates fly between Syracuse Hancock and New York City (Newark Liberty International Airport), western New York, and Long Island (via Albany). Low-cost carrier Independence Air links Syracuse with New York City (JFK International Airport as well as the Newark airport), and the Hudson Valley. JetBlue flies from Syracuse to JFK, whereas US Airways flies into LaGuardia.

Flights into Binghamton Regional Airport, in the southern part of the region, come from outside New York State. *See* Air Travel *in* Smart Travel Tips A to Z for more information about Binghamton, Albany, and Syracuse airports and for major airlines' contact information.

BUS TRAVEL

Greyhound and Adirondack Trailways link the region with New York City and much of the rest of the state. Tickets for the two bus lines are interchangeable. Buses stop in Amsterdam, Binghamton, Cooperstown, Herkimer, Oneonta, Richfield Springs, and Utica. Limited service is available to the Turning Stone Resort & Casino, near Oneida.

Vermont Transit Lines connects the region (Binghamton, Cobleskill, and Oneonta) with the capital region and the Finger Lakes. Shortline buses, which stop in Binghamton and Utica, link central New York with New York City, the Catskills, the Finger Lakes, and western New York. Within the region, Otsego Express offers weekday service between Cooperstown, Oneonta, and Richfield Springs.

⚽Adirondack Trailways ☎800/858-8555 ⊕www.trailways.com. **Greyhound** ☎800/
231-2222 ⊕www.greyhound.com. **Otsego Express** ☎315/822-6444 or 800/388-9853.
Shortline Coach USA ☎800/631-8405 ⊕www.shortlinebus.com. **Vermont Transit Lines**
☎800/451-3292 ⊕www.vermonttransit.com.

CAR RENTAL

Avis, Budget, Enterprise, and Hertz rent cars at Albany International
Airport. Thrifty and Payless are off-site; a shuttle bus takes renters to
and from the airport. Syracuse Hancock International Airport has
branches of Avis, Budget, Enterprise, Hertz, and National Car Rental.
Avis also rents cars in Rome and Binghamton. Enterprise has locations
in Amsterdam, Oneida, Oneonta, and Rome. Hertz rents in Binghamton, Oneonta, and Utica. National has a branch in Binghamton. Sensible Car Rental is 3 mi from the train station and bus terminal in Utica.
See Car Rental *in* Smart Travel Tips A to Z for national agencies' contact information.
⚽Local Agencies Sensible Car Rental of Utica ✉1430 Lincoln Ave., Utica ☎315/
735-3552.

CAR TRAVEL

Many scenic, well-maintained roads crisscross and border the region.
The interstates—I–90 (the New York State Thruway), I–81, and 1–88—
are the fastest way to get around central New York. The thruway parallels the Mohawk River, which flows west to east across the region.
Route 5, which also parallels the Mohawk River, is an alternative.
Route 20 is a more southerly east–west option. Off the interstates,
watch for wildlife and livestock, which sometimes wander into or near
the road; be especially alert in the early evening and at night. Farm vehicles and the occasional Amish buggy can slow traffic on the smaller
roads; given room, these vehicles will usually pull to the side so that you
can pass.

EMERGENCIES

In an emergency, dial 911.
⚽Hospitals Albany Medical Center ✉43 New Scotland Ave., Albany ☎518/262-
3131 ⊕www.amc.edu. **Binghamton General Hospital** ✉10-42 Mitchell Ave., Binghamton ☎607/762-2231 ⊕www.uhs.net. **Little Falls Hospital** ✉9 Gibson St, Dolgeville ☎315/823-5311 ⊕www.lfhny.org. **Mary Imogene Bassett Hospital** ✉1 Atwell
Rd., Cooperstown ☎607/547-3284 ⊕www.bassett.org. **University Hospital** ✉750
E. Adams St., Syracuse ☎877/464-5540 ⊕www.upstate.edu/uh/services.

SPORTS & THE OUTDOORS

See Sports & the Outdoors *in* Smart Travel Tips A to Z for additional
information.

BIKING   Bike routes covering a broad range of terrain lace the region. Canal trails
are especially popular here. The Mohawk-Hudson Bikeway, encompassing
about 60 mi of paved trails for bikers and walkers in central New York
and the capital region, follows the Erie Canal and Mohawk River between Waterford, northeast of Albany, and St. Johnsville, north of
Canajoharie. The Mohawk-Hudson Bikeway is a major segment of
what's known as the Canalway Trail System. The 36-mi Old Erie Canal

State Park Trail, another major segment of the trail system, runs from Rome to just east of Syracuse. You can obtain a free map of the Canalway Trail System from the New York State Canal System, which offers additional information about biking on its Web site.

The Mohawk Valley Bicycling Club runs training and other rides in the region; information is available on the group's Web site.

BOATING The Erie Canal is one of the many natural and man-made waterways in the region on which you may boat. You may order a copy of *The Cruising Guide to the New York State Canal System* ($19.95 plus tax, shipping, and handling) from the New York State Canal Corporation, which runs the New York State Canal System. The canal system's Web site includes limited boating information.

⚡ Biking Mohawk Valley Bicycling Club ⊕ www.mvbc.us. **New York State Canal System** ⌂ Box 189, Albany 12201 ☎ 800/422-6254 ⊕ www.canals.state.ny.us.
⚡ Boating New York State Canal System ⌂ Box 189, Albany 12201 ☎ 518/471-5016 boating information, 800/422-1825 to order canal-cruising guide ⊕ www.canals.state.ny.us.

TOURS

BOAT TOURS Boat tours, usually available from May through October, range from short excursions to multiday canal tours. The New York State Canal System has more information about canal tours and charters.

TRAIN TOURS From Memorial Day weekend through Columbus Day, the Adirondack Scenic Railroad's 1950s-era locomotive chugs and whistles from Utica's historic Union Station on day trips into the Adirondack Wilderness. Special events—such as Halloween- and Christmas-themed rides and murder-mystery and wine-tasting trips—are scheduled throughout the year. (Book as early as possible for the Christmas rides, which often sell out.) Most rides are $12–$32.

From late May to mid-October, the Leatherstocking Railway Historical Society offers rides from Milford (in the upper Susquehanna River valley) to Cooperstown on the Cooperstown & Charlotte Valley Railroad. The society owns and runs the railroad, which was built in 1869. The 16-mi round-trip is $8 and takes about two hours. Reservations are required for special events, which include murder-mystery trains, blues-and-drinks rides, and assorted holiday-themed rides.

⚡ Boat Tours New York State Canal System ⌂ Box 189, Albany 12201 ☎ 518/436-2700 or 800/422-6254 ⊕ www.canals.state.ny.us.
⚡ Train Tours Adirondack Scenic Railroad ✉ Main St., Utica ☎ 315/724-0700 or 877/508-6728 ⊕ www.adirondackrr.com. **Leatherstocking Railway Historical Society** ✉ Rte. 7, Cooperstown Junction ☎ 607/432-2429 main office, 607/286-7805 Milford depot ⊕ www.lrhs.com.

TRAIN TRAVEL

Amtrak connects Amsterdam, Rome, and Utica in central New York with Albany, the Finger Lakes, and western New York. From Albany you can go on to New York City, the Hudson Valley, and the Adirondacks. The Amsterdam station is open only 10–6:30, and it has no ticket office or machine, checked-baggage service, or taxi stand.

⚡ Amtrak ☎ 800/872-7245 ⊕ www.amtrak.com

TRANSPORTATION AROUND CENTRAL NEW YORK

Traveling to the region by bus gives you more destination choices than train travel. Depending on your starting point, however, air travel may be your best bet, especially if you don't want to spend a full day in transit. If you plan to travel within the region and explore more than one or two villages or cities, a car is recommended.

VISITOR INFORMATION

Broome County Convention & Visitors Bureau Metro Center ⊠ 49 Court St., Binghamton 13902 ☎ 607/772-8860 or 800/836-6740 ⊕ www.binghamtoncvb.com. **Cooperstown Chamber of Commerce** ⊠ 31 Chestnut St., Cooperstown 13326 ☎ 607/547-9983 or 877/867-4737 ⊕ www.cooperstownchamber.org. **Herkimer County Chamber of Commerce** ⊠ 28 W. Main St., Mohawk 13407 ☎ 315/866-7820 or 877/984-4636 ⊕ www.herkimercountychamber.com. **Madison County Tourism** ⚓ Box 1029, Morrisville 13408 ☎ 315/684-7320 or 800/684-7320 ⊕ www.madisontourism.com. **Mohawk Valley Chamber of Commerce** ⊠ 520 Seneca St., 3rd fl., Utica 13502 ☎ 315/724-3151 ⊕ www.mvchamber.org. **Montgomery County Chamber of Commerce** ⚓ Box 309, Amsterdam 12010 ☎ 518/842-8200 or 800/743-7337 ⊕ www.montgomerycountyny.com. **Oneida County Convention & Visitors Bureau** ⚓ Box 551, Utica 13503 ☎ 315/724-7221 or 800/426-3132 ⊕ www.oneidacountycvb.com. **Otsego County Tourism Program** ⊠ 242 Main St., Oneonta 13820 ☎ 607/643-0059 or 800/843-3394 ⊕ www.co.otsego.ny.us. **Rome Area Chamber of Commerce** ⊠ 139 W. Dominick St., Rome 13440 ☎ 315/337-1700 ⊕ www.romechamber.com. **Schoharie County Chamber of Commerce** ⊠ 315 Main St., Schoharie 12157 ☎ 518/295-7032 or 800/418-4748 ⊕ www.schohariechamber.com. **Sharon Springs Chamber of Commerce** ⚓ Box 182, Sharon Springs 13459 ☎ 518/284-2034 ⊕ www.sharonspringschamber.com.

THE FINGER LAKES

7

Updated by
Mary Bulkot

THE 11 PARALLEL FINGER LAKES STRETCH like narrow north–south slashes across western central New York. Their names evoke the tribes of the Iroquois Confederacy that dominated the area for more than two centuries. From east to west, the lakes are Otisco, Skaneateles, Owasco, Cayuga, Seneca, Keuka, Canandaigua, Honeoye, Canadice, Hemlock, and Conesus.

Iroquois legend has it that the Finger Lakes were formed when the Great Spirit placed his hand in blessing on this favored land, leaving behind an imprint. Geologists offer another explanation: the lakes were created by retreating Ice Age glaciers about a million years ago. The intense grinding pressure of the retreating ice masses gouged deep holes in the earth, creating the long, narrow lakes that lie side by side, the region's deep gorges and their rushing falls, and the wide fertile valleys that extend south for miles.

The dramatic landscape encompasses more than 1,000 waterfalls. The highest, Taughannock, is, at 215 feet, higher than Niagara Falls. It's in one of more than two dozen state parks and nature preserves in the region. Farther south, the rock walls and 19 waterfalls of Watkins Glen are reminiscent of a nascent Grand Canyon.

Veterans of the American Revolution settled in the region after receiving tracts of land in lieu of pay for their war service. In the 19th and early 20th centuries the Finger Lakes became the land of dreamers and doers—dreamers who founded a religion, began the women's rights movement, ran the Underground Railroad, invented the camera, and created great schools and universities.

As the home of statesmen, inventors, industrialists, and writers, the region has played a significant role in American social, economic, and political history. Mark Twain wrote many of his classics, including *The Adventures of Huckleberry Finn,* at his summer home in Elmira. Glenn H. Curtiss put Hammondsport on the aviation map after his *June Bug* flew just under a mile—the longest distance of a preannounced flight—in 1908. Harris Hill is considered the birthplace of soaring, and its National Soaring Museum has the country's largest display of sailplanes.

Seneca Falls is the birthplace of the women's rights movement, and the Women's Rights National Historical Park is on the site of the first Women's Rights Convention, held in 1848. Palmyra, on the banks of the Erie Canal, was the early home of Joseph Smith, whose vision led to the founding in 1830 of the Church of Jesus Christ of Latter-day Saints, or Mormons. This event is commemorated annually in late July with the Hill Cumorah Pageant, the oldest and largest religious pageant in the United States.

Auburn was the home of Secretary of State William Seward, who served in the Lincoln administration, and Harriet Tubman, who led more than 300 slaves to freedom via the Underground Railroad, which ran through the region. Seward and Tubman are buried at Fort Hill Cemetery, a Victorian graveyard.

Rochester is the birthplace of the Kodak camera and film and of the Xerox copy machine. You may tour Kodak founder George Eastman's mansion and lovely gardens, now home to a museum of photography and film. Eastman also founded a world-famous music school and theater that bear his name, home to the Rochester Philharmonic Orchestra.

Corning, in the southern part of the Finger Lakes, is famous for the Corning Glass Works and its Steuben Glass division. Steuben masterpieces have been presented as gifts to foreign heads of state and are in museums around the world. The Corning Museum of Glass gives you the opportunity to experience the world of glass hands-on. Ithaca, the home of Cornell University and Ithaca College, is a collegiate oasis with a cosmopolitan flair at the southern end of Cayuga Lake. Restaurants, cafés, and theaters line the downtown Commons. Surrounding the city are deep gorges that provide spectacular backdrops for hiking and swimming.

Much of the Finger Lakes region still shows its rural roots. Dairy farms, small villages, and stunning examples of 19th-century architecture dot the landscape. Viniculture is another of the region's many offerings. The retreating glaciers that created the Finger Lakes also created ideal growing conditions for grapes by depositing a shallow layer of topsoil on sloping shale beds above the lakes. The deep lakes are a perfect microclimate, protecting the vineyards from the cold winters and hot summers by moderating temperatures along their shores. Today the region has more than 70 vineyards and wineries. For the full Finger Lakes experience, be sure to visit pick-your-own orchards, farmer's markets, and wine-tasting rooms.

Exploring the Finger Lakes

The major cities in the region are Syracuse, in the northeast corner, and Rochester, in the region's northwest corner. Interstate 90 (the New York State Thruway) links the two cities. The region's east border is I–81, which crosses I–90 in Syracuse; I–390, the western border, runs north–south through Rochester.

The Finger Lakes are strung across the heart of the region, south of I–90. Parallel to I–90, U.S. 20/Route 5 travels through Skaneateles, Auburn, Seneca Falls, Geneva, and Canandaigua. The historic Erie Canal, part of the state park system, meanders its way west to east roughly parallel to I–90. To the north lie the high bluffs and sandy beaches of Lake Ontario; the Chemung and Susquehanna rivers border the region on the south.

The Seaway Trail along Lake Ontario makes for spectacular driving or biking. Other scenic routes wind along and around the lakes, passing through villages and farmland. Many wineries are located along these roads, which include Cayuga Lake's routes 89 and 90, and Route 14, on the western shore of Seneca Lake.

In this chapter we break down the region into smaller areas organized roughly from east to west and centered on the lakes, with Syracuse and Rochester serving as bookends. Another way to explore the region is to treat it as two halves, north and south; make your way across one half and then circle back across the other half.

The itineraries below have you switching lodgings almost nightly. If you prefer not to do this—or if the lodging places you've chosen require two-night minimum stays—you may have to condense the itineraries a bit by skipping a village or park here and there. Many attractions, restaurants, and lodgings close up for the winter, so check open information before planning an itinerary for the cold-weather months.

Numbers in the text correspond to numbers in the margin and on The Finger Lakes map.

7

If you have 3 days

Spend Day 1 in ▦ **Ithaca** ❻ ⊢, a good gateway into the region. On the morning of Day 2 take a quick trip to Taughannock Falls State Park in ▦ **Trumansburg** ❼, where the falls are higher than Niagara Falls. From here you have a couple of options.

You may reverse direction and head back east around Cayuga Lake to charming ▦ **Aurora** ❺, where you spend your second night. On Day 3, continue northward along the lake to Montezuma National Wildlife Refuge, which you can tour in your car. Or skip the refuge and instead head for **Seneca Falls** ❽, site of the Women's Rights National Historical Park.

Alternatively, travel from Ithaca to ▦ **Watkins Glen** ❿ on Day 2. Walk the awesome gorge trail at Watkins Glen State Park (note that the gorge trail is closed in winter) and check out a winery or two. On the morning of Day 3, swing down to **Corning** ⓬ to see the Corning Museum of Glass, which is a must if you're in the area.

If you have 5 days

Pick one of the three-day itineraries above and expand on it. If on Day 3 you end up in Seneca Falls, then continue west late that afternoon to ▦ **Geneva** ❾. Set aside time on Day 4 to tour the Rose Hill Mansion, which has lovely Seneca Lake views. In the afternoon you might continue westward to ▦ **Canandaigua** ⓰, where you have your choice of several lovely B&Bs. Save the morning of Day 5 for a tour of the Sonnenberg Mansion and Gardens.

If you wind up in Corning on Day 3, then head northwest in the afternoon to ▦ **Hammondsport** ⓭. Spend the last two days of your trip visiting local wineries and taking a lake cruise.

If you're coming from the north, you may want to stay closer to I–90. Start in tiny ▦ **Skaneateles** ❷. If you're here in August, consider taking in a chamber-music concert at the Skaneateles Festival. On Day 2, drive west to **Seneca Falls** ❽ and spend a few hours exploring the women's rights–related sights. In the afternoon, make the short trip to ▦ **Geneva** ❾. On Day 3, visit Rose Hill Mansion before driving on to ▦ **Canandaigua** ⓰. You can spend the last two days relaxing here, or you can head for the city sights in ▦ **Rochester** ⓱–㉗: the Strong Museum and the George Eastman House and International Museum of Photography and Film. In summer, save time for Ontario Beach Park, north of the city.

About the Hotels & Restaurants

Lodging options in the cities range from full-service hotels to budget chain properties, and include individually owned inns and bed-and-breakfasts. Outside the cities you're more likely to find accommodation in converted farmhouses and mansions and refurbished inns, where two-night minimum stays are often required on weekends, especially in summer and early fall. Many properties offer lake views and retain a sense of the past with impressive collections of antiques. Lakeside rentals, from simple cottages to luxury homes, are good options for families and for stays of a week or longer. Nature lovers can rent a cabin, throw up a tent, or park their RV in one of the many state and private campgrounds. The region is a popular weekend and summer getaway for New Yorkers from all corners of the state, so book ahead—particularly in summer and early fall.

The larger cities offer a full range of dining options, from trendy restaurants to ethnic eateries. Ithaca and Rochester, in particular, are havens for vegetarian and ethnic fare. Several inns and B&Bs, mostly outside the urban areas, are known for their fine restaurants and are worth checking out even if you're spending the night elsewhere. Regional wines often show up on menus. (The region's Rieslings, which have garnered high praise, are perfect summer and early-fall sips.) Otherwise, American restaurants, diners, family-style spots, and pizza parlors are the norm; steaks, chops, and prime rib are standards, as are Italian-American dishes.

WHAT IT COSTS					
	$$$$	**$$$**	**$$**	**$**	**¢**
RESTAURANTS	over $30	$22–$30	$15–$21	$8–$14	under $8
HOTELS	over $250	$200–$250	$150–$199	$100–$149	under $100

Restaurant prices are for a main course at dinner (or at the most expensive meal served). Hotel prices are for two people in a standard double room in high season, excluding tax.

Timing

Lined with beaches, parks, campgrounds, and marinas, the Finger Lakes are most enjoyable in the warm-weather months. The season is at its peak in July and August, and festivals and fairs celebrating regional theater, music, crafts, and other diversions are most plentiful in summer. Some attractions, especially the smaller ones, are open only in summer and early fall; the same is true of many campgrounds and other lodgings. Many places, including restaurants and inns, shut down in winter.

Although summer warmth can linger into September, Labor Day marks the end of the lake season. In early October, when the leaves start to change color, hiking and biking are good ways to take in the gorgeous foliage. Cold-weather sports enthusiasts might prefer winter, which tends to come early and leave late. Spring, when it finally does arrive, can be rainy, but there's a payoff: runoff from winter snows makes for dramatic waterfalls, and the returning wildlife and wildflowers are a welcome sight.

Fishing

Because of their unique physical attributes, each of the Finger Lakes is known for different species. Large- and smallmouth bass are found in all the lakes. Brown, lake, and rainbow trout inhabit most, except Conesus and Honeoye. Yellow perch, landlocked salmon, northern pike, pickerel, bullhead, and walleye are common, too. Cayuga Lake, the longest of the lakes, has the greatest fishing diversity. Seneca Lake is especially known for its rainbow and lake trout. Tiger muskie are found in Conesus and Otisco lakes.

The region is also veined with many rivers and streams teeming with trout, bass, pike, bullhead, and walleye. The major tributaries of Canandaigua, Cayuga, Keuka, Owasco, and Seneca lakes often offer up large specimens; most of these waters offer miles of public access. For game fishing, head north to Lake Ontario. Sodus Bay has some of the best fishing year-round, including ice fishing in winter.

Vines & Wines

The region has three American Viticultural Areas, a federal designation. The Finger Lakes AVA encompasses the four largest lakes; Cayuga and Seneca lakes, which are considered microclimates, have their own AVA designations. Because of their size and depth, the lakes heat up and cool down more slowly than the surrounding land, and the air circulating around them moderates shore temperatures and thus extends the growing season.

Pinot noir, chardonnay, Riesling, cabernet franc, merlot, and cabernet sauvignon are among the fine wines being produced in the region. These are created from European grapes, known as *vitis vinifera*. But before the second half of the 20th century only native American grapes, or *vitis labrusca*, which produced sweeter, heavier wines, were grown here. The belief was that the European varietals wouldn't survive the climate. Dr. Konstantin Frank, a Ukrainian immigrant who settled in the area in the 1950s, challenged that belief and started growing vinifera vines, proving that the conditions weren't an issue.

Today the region is home to more than 80 wineries, including Dr. Frank's Vinifera Wine Cellars. Many wineries sprang up as a result of the Farm Winery Act of 1976, which eased regulations for small wineries. And although native grapes (Concord, Catawba, Niagara, Delaware) are still grown here, winemakers have been experimenting with new varieties, often with the help of Cornell University's School of Agriculture.

The best way to enjoy the wineries is to sample several of them in a leisurely day trip. You may follow one of the four wine trails, named for the four largest lakes, or explore off the trails. Nearly all the wineries have tasting rooms and gift shops, and many have restaurants, cafés, or picnic grounds with panoramic lake views.

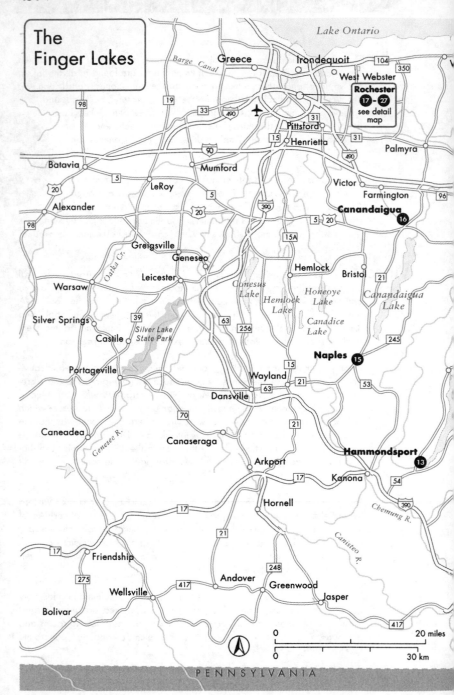

The Finger Lakes

Lake Ontario

Barge Canal

Greece

Irondequoit

104
350

West Webster

Rochester
17 – 27
see detail map

19

98

33

490

Pittsford

31

15

Henrietta

31

490

Palmyra

90

Batavia

5

Mumford

Victor

Farmington

96

20

LeRoy

5

Canandaigua

16

Alexander

20

390

5 20

98

Greigsville

15A

Geneseo

Hemlock

Bristol

21

Leicester

Warsaw

Oatka Cr.

Conesus Lake

Hemlock Lake

Honeoye Lake

Canandaigua Lake

Silver Springs

39

Silver Lake State Park

Castile

63

256

Canadice Lake

245

Portageville

15

Naples

15

Wayland

63

21

53

Dansville

Caneadea

70

21

Canaseraga

Genesee R.

Hammondsport

13

Arkport

Kanona

54

17

390

Hornell

Chemung R.

17

21

Canisteo R.

17

Friendship

275

Andover

248

Greenwood

Jasper

Wellsville

417

Bolivar

417

0   20 miles

0   30 km

PENNSYLVANIA

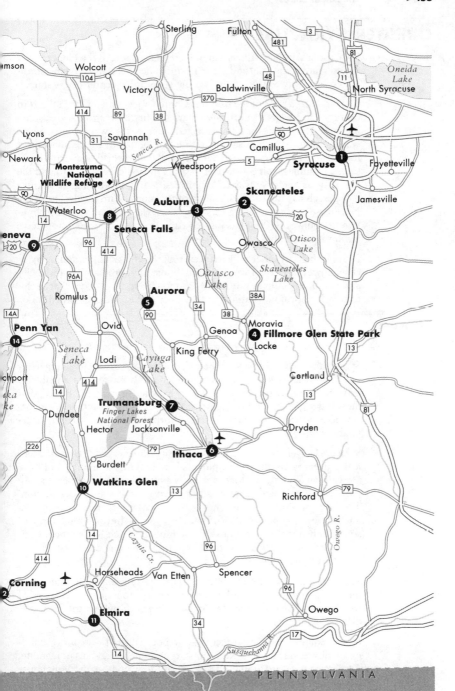

GREATER SYRACUSE

By Mary Catt   Syracuse sits at the southern tip of Lake Onondaga, in the Finger Lakes region's more industrial and urban northern tier. It's considered the north-eastern gateway to the region and the geographic center of the state.

The Onondaga tribe of the Iroquois Confederacy settled here in the 16th century. Europeans, mainly missionaries at first, came to the area start-ing in the 1600s. The fur trade attracted others to the swampy area, which was found to be rich in salt. The Erie Canal, one of the nation's most important waterways, floated Syracuse salt to the world on narrow boats pulled by mules. Salt production peaked during the Civil War, and the Salt City, as Syracuse was called, diversified by producing steel, auto-mobiles, china, and candles, among other goods. With the decline of the Northeast's manufacturing economy since the 1970s, Syracuse (popu-lation around 140,000) has lost jobs and people—some of whom have left for nearby suburbs.

Don't let belts of suburbia keep you from the villages surrounding Syra-cuse, however. Drive 15 minutes in almost any direction from the city and you'll find communities with country flavor, pre–Civil War archi-tecture, historical sites dating from the early 1800s, and uncrowded parks.

Syracuse

❶ *255 mi northwest of New York City, 135 mi west of Albany.*

Syracusans are fond of saying their city offers the best of city living with-out the traffic hassles. Thanks to quick-flow bypasses, it's possible to drive from one corner of Syracuse to another in minutes. But a good map and a game plan are essential; this is a loosely knit city, with at-tractions scattered throughout neighborhood nooks casual travelers might overlook.

Syracuse University and the State University of New York's Upstate Med-ical University are the top employers here in terms of numbers of jobs. Downtown Syracuse lost its footing as a retail leader by the 1980s, but parts of it have been reinvented as a cultural and nightlife destination. The Everson Museum, which has outdoor sculptures and a large piazza, anchors one corner of downtown; Armory, Clinton, and Hanover squares anchor other sections of downtown, which hosts ethnic festi-vals, outdoor winter ice-skating, and an hours-long St. Patrick's Day parade, among other events.

There are plans to convert and expand the existing Carousel Center mall into a mammoth retail and entertainment complex along the lines of Minnesota's Mall of America. At this writing, however, the project is delayed indefinitely.

Armory Square. The former factory-warehouse district of redbrick build-ings is now a vibrant area with shops, restaurants, and loads of nightlife. The district is named after the 1874 armory, now home to the Museum of Science and Technology, near its southern perimeter. ⊠ *On sections of Jef-ferson, Harrison, W. Fayette, and Clinton Sts.* ⊕ *www.armorysquare.com.*

Erie Canal Museum and Syracuse Heritage Area Visitor Center. Orient your-self to Syracuse and the region by watching the introductory film in the museum theater. Then make your way to a replica canal boat in the circa-1850 museum building, where real canal boats were weighed when the Erie was a major player in U.S. commerce. A re-created general store, an 1800s canal office, and a postal area are interspersed with exhibits about Syracuse musician Libba Cotten and others who shaped the re-gion. ⊠ *318 Erie Blvd. E* ☎ *315/471–0593* ⊕ *www.eriecanal.com* ⊠ *Free* ☉ *Tues.–Sat. 10–5, Sun. 10–3.*

Everson Museum of Art. Architect I. M. Pei designed the Everson, where you can see at least two familiar paintings: *Portrait of George Washington* by Gilbert Johnson and *The Peaceable Kingdom* by Edward Hicks. Jack-son Pollock and Andrew Wyeth works are part of the collection of more than 8,000 objects, which include ceramics, art videos, Arts and Crafts artifacts, photographs, and ancient art. Kids have their own gallery; there is also a café here. ⊠ *401 Harrison St.* ☎ *315/474–6064* ⊕ *www. everson.org* ⊠ *$5* ☉ *Tues.–Fri. and Sun. noon–5, Sat. 10–5.*

☺ **International Mask and Puppet Museum.** A multicultural approach helps children enjoy the fine arts through masks and puppets ranging from English marionettes to Indonesian shadow puppets. The museum also has a hands-on art studio and presents puppeteer performances. The gift shop is open 11–1 on weekdays. ⊠ *518 Prospect Ave.* ☎ *315/ 476–0466* ⊕ *www.openhandtheater.org* ⊠ *Free* ☉ *Sat. 10–3, and by appointment.*

☺ **Museum of Science and Technology.** Stand in a bubble, see your voice, walk in a kaleidoscope, take a ride in a motion simulator that feels like a wooden roller coaster, climb a wall: the MOST, as it's called, is a hands-on sci-ence museum built to entertain and educate. It occupies a former ar-mory and includes an IMAX theater, which is open until 8 on Saturday. ⊠ *500 S. Franklin St.* ☎ *315/425–9068* ⊕ *www.most.org* ⊠ *$4, IMAX $8* ☉ *Wed.–Sun. 11–5.*

☺ **Rosamond Gifford Zoo at Burnet Park.** Ramps at tree-top level allow you to traipse above fields of reindeer and other hoof-stock species. Asian elephants have been bred here for decades, so you have a good chance of seeing elephants of several age groups. A reptile house is among the indoor exhibits, and at this writing a penguin exhibit is slated to open in 2005. Red pandas and white Siberian tigers reside here, too, along with hundreds of other animals. ⊠ *1 Conservation Pl.* ☎ *315/435–8511* ⊕ *www.syracusezoo.org* ⊠ *$5* ☉ *Daily 10–4:30.*

Syracuse University. The school, founded in 1870 as a private coeduca-tional institution, enrolls more than 18,000 students in its undergrad-uate and graduate programs. Two centuries of building styles can be seen on the compact campus, which is crossed by city streets and includes a traditional collegiate quadrangle. A number of lectures and music per-formances are open to the public, as is the **Lowe Art Gallery** (☎ *315/ 443–3127* ☉ Tues. and Thurs.–Sun. noon–5, Wed. noon–8), in the Shaffer Art Building. Call ahead to make sure the gallery is open before heading over. Football, basketball, and lacrosse are played in the 50,000-

seat **Carrier Dome.** ✉ *University Ave. at University Pl.* ☎ *315/443–1870* ⊕ *www.syr.edu* 🗺 *Free.*

off the beaten path

BEAVER LAKE NATURE CENTER – Ten miles of trails are used year-round to visit the habitats of hundreds of species of plants and animals. A 200-acre lake is the centerpiece of the 596-acre preserve, 17 mi north of Syracuse. Activities include guided walks, snowshoeing, and canoeing. ✉ *8477 E. Mud Lake Rd., Baldwinsville* ☎ *315/638–2519* 🗺 *Parking $2* ☉ *Daily 7:30–dusk.*

FESTIVALS & FAIRS **Balloon Fest.** More than 40 hot-air balloons participate in this annual three-day event held the second weekend in June. Live bands, balloon rides, and food and crafts vendors are part of the fun. ✉ *Jamesville Beach Park, Apulia Rd. north of Rte. 20 E, Jamesville* ☎ *315/451–7275 or 315/435–5252* ⊕ *onondagacountyparks.com/balloonfest/.*

New York State Fair. Nearly a million people visited the 2004 fair, making it one of the most popular events in upstate New York. The 375-acre fairground hosts world-class musical entertainment, carnival rides and games, international equestrian competitions, 4-H animal shows, butter-sculpting contests, and assorted vendors. Free daily entertainments include concerts, circus acts, and lumberjack demonstrations. Dishes from around the world and an array of New York State wines are served, but sausage sandwiches and fried dough dominate the fare. The fair traditionally closes its 12-day run on Labor Day. ✉ *581 State Fair Blvd.* ☎ *315/487–7711* ⊕ *www.nysfair.org.*

Where to Stay & Eat

$$–$$$ ✕ **Pascale Wine Bar & Restaurant.** Much of the contemporary food here, including the signature mixed grills, is prepared on the wood-burning grill. The game-grill combo might include antelope, quail, sausage, duck, or venison, and come with black-currant or huckleberry sauce. The menu, tuned to the weather, changes three times a year. Breads and desserts come from Pascale Bakehouse, a nearby sister operation. A 12-page wine list includes hundreds of wines from France, California, Australia, and South America; 20 wines are available by the glass. Local artists created most of the stained-glass panels, paintings, and sculptures you see here. ✉ *204 W. Fayette St.* ☎ *315/471–3040* ▭ *AE, DC, MC, V* ☉ *No lunch.*

$–$$$ ✕ **Arad Evans Inn.** The 1843 Federal-style home offers several hundred wines, formal dining rooms, and a more casual bistro area. The food is largely Continental. Escargots arrive shelled, in a crock brimming with garlic butter, toasted pine nuts, tomato, and melted Gorgonzola. Many diners choose a tower of chocolate mousse to follow entrées of lamb, sea bass, filet mignon, or veal. The restaurant is in Fayetteville, 8 mi east of Syracuse. ✉ *7206 Genesee St., Fayetteville* ☎ *315/637–2020* ▭ *AE, MC, V* ☉ *No lunch.*

$–$$$ ✕ **Clam Bar.** More clams are sold here than anywhere else in the region, according to the Clam Bar, which also serves lobster, haddock, steaks, seafood, and chicken, plus daily specials. Clams come raw, steamed, in marinara sauce, and with garlic, butter, and wine. A full bar rounds out this comfortable, family-owned North Syracuse spot, which opened in

1959 in an old farmhouse. ⊠ *3914 Brewerton Rd./Rte. 11, North Syracuse* ☎ *315/458–1662* ☐ *AE, D, MC, V.*

$–$$$ ✕ **Dinosaur Bar-B-Que.** What started as a darling of the biker crowd has evolved into a regional hot spot for pork sandwiches, barbecued ribs, and, on most nights, live blues. On Friday and Saturday, table waits can run as long as 90 minutes; the former diner's full-service bar, with 16 beers on tap, helps pass the time. In July and August, you can eat at one of the sidewalk picnic tables. ⊠ *246 W. Willow St.* ☎ *315/476–4937* ⟐ *Reservations not accepted* ☐ *AE, D, DC, MC, V.*

$–$$$ ✕ **Pastabilities.** A funky, urban feel infuses this downtown Syracuse spot—a former union hall—which attracts a business crowd by day and a singles and dating crowd at night. Lunch is cafeteria style, and dinner is full service. There's always fresh pasta with sauces like the ever-popular spicy hot tomato oil. The restaurant bakes its own bread daily. You can eat in the dining room, which is decorated with mosaic-trimmed mirrors, or outside at a sidewalk table or in the back courtyard. ⊠ *311 S. Franklin St.* ☎ *315/474–1153* ☐ *AE, D, DC, MC, V* ☺ *No lunch on weekends.*

$$ ✕ **Phoebe's.** Choose bistro-style dining in the foliage-filled atrium or enjoy a more casual atmosphere in the front dining room, where large windows overlook a neighborhood anchored by Syracuse Stage. Both parts of the restaurant serve the same menu, led by Mediterranean and Tuscan-influenced fare. Try French onion soup and crème brûlée. ⊠ *900 E. Genesee St.* ☎ *315/475–5154* ☐ *AE, MC, V.*

$–$$ ✕ **Coleman's.** Crawl through the little front door built for the "wee people who come directly from Ireland" and you'll understand why this restaurant is the center of Tipperary Hill, Syracuse's Irish neighborhood. (Don't worry: there's also a regular-size front door.) Green beer flows freely every March 17 on the hill and in Coleman's, where corned beef and cabbage and open-faced reuben sandwiches are menu leaders year-round. Live Irish music plays Thursday through Sunday. Patio dining is a summer option. ⊠ *100 S. Lowell Ave.* ☎ *315/476–1933* ☐ *AE, D, DC, MC, V.*

$–$$$ 🏨 **Genesee Grande Hotel.** The hotel is a mile from downtown and five blocks from Syracuse University. Completely overhauled in 2004, rooms have elegant, streamlined furnishings; hypoallergenic bedding; granite bathrooms; and wireless Internet access. Blackout drapes are available. Suites come in several configurations. The restaurant offers fine contemporary fare with many seafood and Italian-inspired selections; the bistro area offers more casual fare. The 50-seat theater is used for both business and entertainment purposes. The hotel lounge has a grand piano. ⊠ *1060 E. Genesee St., 13210* ☎ *315/476–4212 or 800/365–4663* 🖷 *315/471–4663* ⊕ *www.geneseegrande.com* 🗗 *160 rooms, 49 suites* ♨ *2 restaurants, room service, in-room data ports, in-room fax, in-room safes, some in-room hot tubs, some kitchens, cable TV, health club, bar, lounge, piano, theater, babysitting, dry cleaning, laundry facilities, laundry service, Internet, business services, convention center, airport shuttle, free parking, some pets allowed, no-smoking floors* ☐ *AE, D, DC, MC, V.*

$–$$ 🏨 **Bed & Breakfast Wellington.** This 1914 Tudor-style home is a product of the Arts and Crafts movement and regionally acclaimed architect Ward Wellington Ward. The house, in a residential neighborhood, has hardwood floors, two Mercer-tile fireplaces, Oriental rugs, and antiques. One guest room has two queen-size beds, and the Lakeview Room has a screened-in porch. A multicourse breakfast is served on weekends. ✉ *707 Danforth St., 13208* ☎ *315/474–3641 or 800/724–5006* 🖷 *315/474–2557* ⊕ *www.bbwellington.com* ⟿ *4 rooms, 2 with shared bath; 1 suite ⌂ Dining room, snack bar, in-room data ports, 1 kitchen, cable TV with movies, in-room VCRs, library, Internet, business services, meeting rooms, free parking; no a/c in some rooms, no smoking ☱ AE, D, DC, MC, V* ⦁I *CP weekdays, BP weekends.*

$–$$ 🖷 **Dickenson House on James.** The inn, a 1920s English Tudor-style house, is in the city's prestigious Sedgewick neighborhood, 1½ mi east of downtown. The decor varies from room to room; one has a cottage-style pine sleigh bed, whereas another may have a cherry French-country bed or an iron-and-brass bed. Guests have use of a shared kitchen stocked with on-the-house beverages and snacks. ✉ *1504 James St., 13203* ☎ *315/423–4777 or 888/423–4777* 🖷 *315/425–1965* ⊕ *www.dickensonhouse.com* ⟿ *4 rooms, 1 suite ⌂ Dining room, in-room data ports, cable TV, dry cleaning, laundry service, concierge, business services, meeting room; no kids under 5, no smoking ☱ AE, D, MC, V* ⦁I *BP.*

$–$$ 🖷 **Holiday Inn Fairgrounds.** This two-story chain hotel is 9 mi west of downtown Syracuse and near I–90, Route 690, and the New York State Fairgrounds. Rooms have one or two beds and inoffensive dark-wood furniture. ✉ *100 Farrell Rd.* ☎ *315/457–8700 or 866/919–8700* 🖷 *315/457–2379* ⊕ *www.holiday-inn.com* ⟿ *150 rooms, 1 suite ⌂ Restaurant, room service, in-room data ports, some in-room hot tubs, some refrigerators, cable TV with movies and video games, pool, gym, bar, dry cleaning, laundry facilities, Internet, business services, free parking, some pets allowed (fee), no-smoking rooms ☱ AE, D, DC, MC, V*

¢–$$ 🖷 **Sheraton Syracuse University Hotel & Conference Center.** The nine-floor hotel is adjacent to the main campus of Syracuse University, in a high-energy neighborhood of casual eateries and quirky shops. In the rooms, rich jewel tones (think purple or deep red) punch up the updated-traditional furnishings. Accommodations on the club floor include such extras as triple-sheeted beds, robes, and complimentary evening appetizers. The business center is open around the clock. ✉ *801 University Ave., 13210* ☎ *315/475–3000 or 800/395–2105* 🖷 *315/475–3311* ⊕ *www.sheratonsyracuse.com* ⟿ *217 rooms, 19 suites ⌂ Restaurant, in-room data ports, some in-room hot tubs, some refrigerators, cable TV with movies and video games, some in-room VCRs, indoor pool, health club, sauna, steam room, lobby lounge, sports bar, babysitting, dry cleaning, laundry facilities, laundry service, concierge floor, business services, meeting rooms, airport shuttle, parking (fee), some pets allowed, no-smoking floors ☱ AE, D, DC, MC, V.*

¢–$$ 🖷 **Wyndham Syracuse.** The seven-story Wyndham, in an East Syracuse business district, is geared for the business traveler. Rooms are contemporary, with large desks and adjustable work chairs, cordless and speaker phones, bathrobes, and pillow-top mattresses. Wireless Internet access is available in the public spaces. ✉ *6301 Rte. 298, East Syracuse 13057* ☎ *315/432–0200* 🖷 *315/433–1210* ⊕ *www.wyndham.com* ⟿ *248 rooms, 2 suites ⌂ Restaurant, room service, in-room data* ports, some refrigerators, cable TV with movies and video games, indoor-outdoor pool, health club, hot tub, sauna, bar, dry cleaning, laundry facilities, business services, meeting rooms, airport shuttle, free parking, no-smoking floors ⊟ AE, D, DC, MC, V.

¢–$ ⊞ **Radisson at the Marx Hotel & Conference Center.** Staying at this upscale high-rise hotel puts you within a mile of most downtown sights and Syracuse University. Interiors show contemporary flair. Neutral palettes color the rooms, which have streamlined furnishings, including desks and ergonomic work chairs, and speaker phones. Redfield's is a two-level restaurant. Light fare is served in the Library Lounge, which offers live entertainment Wednesday through Saturday. ⊠ 701 E. Genesee St., 13210 ☎ 315/479–7000 or 877/843–6279 ⬛ 315/472–2700 ⊕ www.marxsyracuse.com ⊄ 280 rooms, 4 suites ⬧ Restaurant, room service, in-room data ports, in-room safes, cable TV with movies, gym, 2 bars, lobby lounge, library, piano, dry cleaning, laundry service, Internet, business services, meeting rooms, airport shuttle, free parking, some pets allowed (fee), no-smoking floors ⊟ AE, D, DC, MC, V.

¢ ⊞ **Cambridge Inn.** A pet deer named Daisy, two pheasants, and a peacock entertain you at this family-owned inn 8 mi west of Syracuse. Rooms are more B&B than motel in style. Some rooms have rocker-recliners and a small desk. Guests have use of the outdoor grill. The inn is on a roadway that has been a major east–west route for centuries. The village of Skaneateles, filled with shops and restaurants, is a 15-minute drive from here. ⊠ 2382 W. Genesee Tpk., Camillus 13031 ☎ 315/672–3022 ⊄ 10 rooms ⬧ Picnic area, some microwaves, refrigerators, cable TV, some pets allowed, no-smoking rooms ⊟ AE, D, MC, V.

Nightlife & the Arts

NIGHTLIFE Since the 1980s, **Armory Square** (⊕ www.armorysquare.com), a once weary factory-warehouse district that includes parts of Jefferson, Harrison, West Fayette, and Clinton streets, has evolved into a vibrant nightlife area. The pub-crawling, dancing, and dining destination encompasses five blocks of redbrick buildings softened by dark-green awnings. On Wednesday evenings from mid-May through August, **Party in the Plaza** (⊠ Clinton St. at Genesee St. ⊕ www.partyintheplaza.com) transforms the James M. Hanley Federal Plaza into a free outdoor party. Bands play from 5 to 8 PM and vendors sell food and drink.

THE ARTS The ornate 1928 **Landmark Theatre** (⊠ 362 S. Salina St. ☎ 315/475–7979
★ or 315/475–7980 ⊕ www.landmarktheatre.org) hosts touring stage shows, dance performances, concerts, stand-up comics, and classic films. LeAnn Rimes, George Carlin, the Moscow Ballet, and the Capitol Steps are among the performers you might see at the 3,000-plus-seat venue. **Syracuse Stage** (⊠ 820 E. Genesee St. ☎ 315/443–3275 or 800/724–3810 ⊕ www.syracusestage.org), a professional regional theater, hosts at least seven productions at its 499-seat theater each year. Productions include musicals, children's programs, dramas, and comedies. The **Syracuse Symphony** (⊠ 411 Montgomery St. ☎ 315/424–8200 or 800/724–3810 ⊕ www.syracusesymphony.org), which has 75 professional members in its orchestra, makes its home in the Mulroy Civic Center in downtown Syracuse, but sometimes performs in other venues.

Sports & the Outdoors

The **Carrier Dome** (✉ 900 Irving Ave. ☎ 315/443–2121 or 888/366–3849, 315/443–4634 tours ⊕ www.carrierdome.syr.edu), a 6½-acre inflated bubble, is Syracuse University's venue for football, basketball, and lacrosse. Tours are available by appointment. The **Syracuse SkyChiefs** (✉ 1 Tex Simone Dr. ☎ 315/474–7833 ⊕ www.skychiefs.com) play other triple-A baseball teams in a stadium on the shore of Onondaga Lake. Scooch, the mascot of this Toronto Blue Jays affiliate, leads the cheering.

Shopping

U.S. chain stores abound at roadside commercial strips and malls in the area, but shops unique to Syracuse give you another way to experience the city. Stores in the five-block area known as **Armory Square** (✉ On sections of Jefferson, Harrison, W. Fayette, and Clinton Sts. ⊕ www.armorysquare.com) feature clothing, jewelry, crafts, antiques, and other wares. The **Hot Shoppe** (✉ 311 S. Clinton St. ☎ 315/424–1010 or 888/468–3287), in the Armory Square district, offers 1,000-plus sassy spice products, including barbecue sauces, marinades, rubs, jams, Cajun and creole goodies, Bloody Mary mixes, and salsas. Crunchy, caramel-coated popcorn in a paper box is the signature walk-around food in downtown Syracuse. **Syracuse's Original Carmelcorn Shoppe** (✉ 116 W. Jefferson St. ☎ 315/475–2390) has been popping on this block in the Armory Square district since 1930. Traditional popcorn, peanuts, fudge, and colorful gummy candies are also sold.

The smell of its bread baking is so good that **Columbus Bakery** (✉ 502 Pearl St. ☎ 315/422–2913) could charge admission. On a side street in Syracuse's Little Italy section, the bakery has just one product and makes it 10 paces from where customers buy it.

SKANEATELES & OWASCO LAKES

Skaneateles and Owasco lakes are in the eastern part of the region, near Syracuse. Of the 11 lakes, these two are medium in size. The village of Skaneateles is mentioned simultaneously with the lake of the same name. Skaneateles, lake and village, set the standard for Finger Lakes hospitality; a number of municipalities attempt to emulate its accent on tourism. Owasco Lake isn't as closely identified with Auburn, several miles from the lake's northern end. But it does feed the Owasco Outlet, which powered Auburn's industrial heritage, and the lake continues to be a huge contributor to the Auburn area's quality of life.

Skaneateles

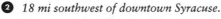 *18 mi southwest of downtown Syracuse.*

On a former stagecoach route, Skaneateles (pronounced *skinny-atlas*) presides over the northern tip of a stunning, 15-mi-long lake with the same name. The village has dodged the so-called urban renewal that destroyed the face of many Finger Lakes communities. Instead, it has treasured most of its Greek-revival and Victorian homes and neat-as-a-pin look. Skaneateles became the highest-profile destination in the Finger Lakes when President Bill Clinton vacationed here with his family in

A HANDLE ON THE LAKES

ROQUOIS LEGEND HOLDS THAT *the Finger Lakes are hand imprints that were left in the soil after the Great Spirit blessed the land. Of the 11 Finger Lakes, 10 do resemble fingers. (Keuka Lake, which is Y-shaped, is the exception.) Geologists say retreating glaciers carved out these north–south lakes. The six that are more than 10 mi long are the major lakes. Their names (all but one Native American), lengths, and depths follow, from east to west:*

Otisco ("Waters Dried Away"): 6 mi long, 66 feet deep.

Skaneateles ("Long Lake"): 15 mi long, 350 feet deep.

Owasco ("Crossing Place"): 11 mi long, 177 feet deep.

Cayuga ("Boat Landing"): 40 mi long, 435 feet deep.

Seneca ("Place of the Stone"): 36 mi long, 632 feet deep.

Keuka ("Canoe Landing"): 22 mi long, 157 feet deep.

Canandaigua ("Chosen Place"): 16 mi long, 262 feet deep.

Honeoye ("Finger Lying"): 5 mi long, 30 feet deep.

Canadice ("Long Lake"): 3 mi long, 91 feet deep.

Hemlock (not named by Native Americans): 8 mi long, 98 feet deep.

Conesus ("Always Beautiful"): 9 mi long, 59 feet deep.

1999. Some shops and restaurants are decidedly upscale: this population-2,660 village is the Beverly Hills of the mostly modest region. Nevertheless, tradition hasn't been forsaken, and you can still treat yourself to plain vanilla ice-cream cones. A cozy graciousness born of prim front porches and subdued commercialism pervades, and community bands perform at the Victorian gazebo at Clift Park, where anybody can feed the ducks.

Creamery Museum. Lake history and local farming take center stage at this 1899 barn-style building where butter bound for New York City was produced. Exhibits here also feature the prickly, cone-shape teasel—a plant used in mills to "tease" the nap of wool. Skaneateles was a teasel-growing center until the 1950s, when synthetic fabrics replaced much of the demand for wool. ⊠ *28 Hannum St.* ☎ *315/685–1360* ⊕ *www.skaneateles.com/historical* 🎫 *Free* ☉ *May–Sept., Thurs.–Sat. 1–4; Oct.–Apr., Fri. 1–4.*

Mid-Lakes Navigation Co. From May through September, the company runs sightseeing, lunch, dinner, and wine-tasting cruises on Skaneateles Lake. Mailboat cruises are another option—the company delivers mail to people living on the lake. Tour narrators deliver who's-who-on-the-lake tidbits. A boat tour also gives you the best look at the region's top collection of Victorian boathouses. Tours begin and end at Clift Park, and take from one to three hours. ⊠ *11 Jordan St.* ☎ *315/685–8500 or 800/545–4318* ⊕ *www.midlakesnav.com* ⊠ *$9–$41* ⊗ *Information booth May–Sept., daily 9–9.*

FESTIVALS & FAIRS **Antique and Classic Boat Show.** The three-day exhibition of restored wooden boats, in and out of the water, has been held each year since 1995 at lakeside Clift Park. A boat parade on the lake is a highlight of the show, which is scheduled for the last weekend of July. ☎ *315/685–0552 Skaneateles Area Chamber of Commerce* ⊕ *www.skaneateles.com.*

Dickens' Christmas. From Thanksgiving weekend through the Sunday before Christmas, Scrooge and other costumed actors stroll the streets of Skaneateles. Streetside caroling and other live music, horse-drawn-carriage rides, and a play are part of the whimsy. ☎ *315/685–0552 Skaneateles Area Chamber of Commerce* ⊕ *www.skaneateles.com.*

Where to Stay & Eat

$$$$ ✕ **The Krebs.** This restaurant dates back to 1899, when Cora and Fred Krebs started serving 50¢ dinners in their home. Today it is known for its seven-course meal, a decades-old Finger Lakes tradition that includes shrimp cocktail, tomato juice, fruit cup, or melon; choice of relishes; broth or cream soup; salad; lobster Newburg, prime rib, pan-fried chicken, sweet and regular potatoes, fresh vegetable, creamed mushrooms, and rolls. Brownies and angel-food cake accompany your choice of homemade desserts. Pared-down dinners, with fewer main dishes, are also available, as is a children's menu. A neon sign out front guides you into the white clapboard house, where fresh flowers and white linens set the mood. ⊠ *53 W. Genesee St.* ☎ *315/685–5714* ⊟ *AE, D, MC, V* ⊗ *Closed Nov.–Apr. No lunch.*

$$–$$$$ ✕ **Rosalie's Cucina.** A sprawling, Tuscan-style space, Rosalie's is upscale but relaxed. No one seems to mind that; unless you read lips, you can forget meaningful conversation on a weekend night. The buzz is about seeing and being seen as well as about the food, served in generous portions. The Italian fare includes appetizers such as carpaccio—ultra-thin slices of raw beef served with mesclun and caper mayonnaise—and main dishes like chicken scaloppine with lemon butter, pancetta, artichoke hearts, and pasta. ⊠ *841 W. Genesee St.* ☎ *315/685–2200* ⌾ *Reservations not accepted* ⊟ *AE, MC, V* ⊗ *No lunch.*

★ ¢–$$ ✕ **Doug's Fish Fry.** Go for the fried fish sandwich and coleslaw, stay for the New England clam chowder and down-home atmosphere at this Skaneateles institution. The menu, posted over the counter where orders are taken, also includes steamed lobster and clams, as well as frankfurters and ice cream. Counter staff shout your name when your order is ready. You can sit in a booth, at the long counter, at an outdoor picnic table, or in a nook in the two-story converted barn adjacent to the cramped main dining-cooking area. ⊠ *8 Jordan St.* ☎ *315/ 685–3288* ⌾ *Reservations not accepted* ⊟ *MC, V* ⊗ *Closed 1–2 wks in early Jan.*

$$–$$$ ✕🏨 **Mirbeau Inn & Spa.** If opulence can also be understated, it is exemplified at this inn and spa. The complex wraps around a water garden à la Monet. An arched wooden walkway and water lilies comple-ment a waterfall that feeds three small ponds in the courtyard of Mir-beau, French for "reflected beauty." The châteaulike building contains the restaurant and guest rooms, all with fireplaces, French-country fur-nishings, down comforters, soaking tubs, and separate showers. The 10,000-square-foot Roman-style spa has the most extensive treatment menu in the region. On Saturday night the restaurant and bistro ($$$) host live jazz. The food is contemporary: radicchio-and-apricot salad with Parmesan cheese, truffle-scented wild-mushroom risotto, Hudson Valley duck breast with cherry sauce, braised lamb canapé over jalapeño polenta, and chocolate souffle with bourbon-pecan ice cream. Four- and five-course tasting menus are available. A shop called Boutique sells everything from negligees to candles to baby items. ⊠ *851 W. Genesse St., 13152* ☎ *315/685–5006 or 877/647–2328* 🖷 *315/685–5150* ⊕ *www.mirbeau.com* 🗇 *32 rooms, 2 suites* ⟡ *Restaurant, in-room data ports, refrigerators, cable TV with movies, in-room DVD play-ers, fitness classes, gym, sauna, spa, steam room, bar, lounge, library, dry cleaning, laundry service, Internet, business services; no smoking* ▭ *AE, D, MC, V* ¶◯¶ *BP.*

★ $ ✕⊡ **Sherwood Inn.** The huge gray building is across the street from Clift Park and Skaneateles Lake. You may book a boat ride, complete with captain, on the inn's 1946 wooden Chris-Craft. Interiors are traditional and tasteful. Guest rooms, individually decorated, have antiques and wire-less Internet access; some have partial or full canopy beds. Some suites have whirlpool tubs and fireplaces. The restaurant serves seasonal Amer-ican fare with contemporary touches, such as lamb with white-truffle risotto, roasted figs, and port-and-shallot demi-glace. An appetizer of seared scallops comes with braised leeks and a puree of sweet English peas folded into heavy cream. The inn's tavern, rustic compared with the country-elegant dining room and guest rooms, is perhaps the best place around to experience Old Skaneateles—"old" as in pre-1980, when the village was more of a cozy bedroom community for Syracuse than a vacation destination. Tavern-menu favorites include traditional pot roast and crab cakes with scallop mousse. Drinks are served from the 1807 inn's original bar. ⊠ *26 W. Genesee St., 13152* ☎ *315/685–3405 or 800/374–3796* ⊕ *www.thesherwoodinn.com* 🗇 *24 rooms, 12 suites* ⟡ *Restaurant, in-room data ports, some in-room hot tubs, cable TV, fishing, bar, library, piano, laundry service, Internet, business ser-vices, meeting rooms; no smoking* ▭ *AE, D, MC, V* ¶◯¶ *CP.*

$-$$$$ ⊡ **Hobbit Hollow Farm Bed and Breakfast.** The large 1848 colonial-re-vival house sits on 300 private acres of woods and meadows across the street from Skaneateles Lake and 1¾ mi south of the village. Interiors are plush but not fussy, with a leather sofa, silk and velvet drapes, Ori-ental rugs, antiques, and a hallway mural. Two bedrooms have fireplaces; most have four-poster beds. Lake views are especially nice from the front and side porches. ⊠ *3061 W. Lake Rd., 13021* ☎ *315/685–2791 or 877/746–2248* 🖷 *315/685–3426* ⊕ *www.hobbithollow.com* 🗇 *5 rooms* ⟡ *Dining room, in-room data ports, some in-room hot tubs, library, Internet, business services, meeting rooms, no-smoking rooms; no room TVs, no kids* ▭ *AE, D, MC, V* ¶◯¶ *BP.*

$$ 🏠 **Arbor House Inn.** Furniture dating from the 1700s and other antiques outfit this 1852 brick inn. Most rooms have a gas or electric fireplace, and several have a whirlpool tub. The dominant feature of the guest-room decor tends to be the bed—a tall four-poster or a bird's-eye maple sleigh bed, perhaps. Hardwood floors are scattered with throw rugs. The inn is a block from Skaneateles Lake and the restaurant and shopping district. ⊠ *41 Fennell St., 13152* ☎ *351/685–8966 or 888/234–4558* 🖷 *315/685–7841* ⊕ *www.arborhouseinn.com* ➫ *8 rooms, 2 suites* ⚘ *Dining room, in-room data ports, some in-room hot tubs, cable TV, in-room VCRs, Internet, business services, no-smoking rooms; no kids under 12* ➯ *AE, D, MC, V* ⦿ *BP.*

¢ 🏠 **The Bird's Nest.** A healthy remnant of the motor court era, which flourished along U.S. 20 into the 1970s, the Bird's Nest is ½ mi east of the village. The Creech family has owned the place since 1976. Room furnishings are straightforward; some rooms have whirlpool tubs. The extensive grounds include a fishing pond and a 1-mi hiking path. Continental breakfast is served in the lobby, where more than 800 books for lending fill built-in shelves. Casual fare—hamburgers, onion rings, soft ice cream—is available next door at the Skan-ellus Drive In restaurant. ⊠ *1601 E. Genesee St., 13152* ☎ *315/685–5641 or 888/447–7417* ⊕ *www.thebirdsnest.net* ➫ *20 rooms, 10 suites, 2 apartments* ⚘ *Picnic area, BBQs, in-room data ports, some in-room safes, some in-room hot tubs, some kitchenettes, microwaves, refrigerators, cable TV, pool, fishing, hiking, cross-country skiing, library, babysitting, laundry facilities, laundry service, Internet, business services, some pets allowed, no-smoking rooms* ➯ *AE, D, MC, V* ⦿ *CP.*

Nightlife & the Arts

★ Chamber music reigns during the monthlong **Skaneateles Festival** (⊠ 97 Genesee St. ☎ 315/685–7418 ⊕ www.skanfest.org), which starts in early August. Grammy Award–winning violinist Hilary Hahn, who made her debut at the event at age 12 in 1992 and has returned annually, has practically grown up at the festival. Pianist Jon Nakamatsu is among the many other acclaimed musicians who have been featured in the program. Performances, about $12–$30, are held in First Presbyterian Church and at the Brook Farm estate.

Sports & the Outdoors

POLO For a thundering change of pace, watch the **Skaneateles Polo Club** (⊠ $2 per car) take on competitors from the Dominican Republican, Boston, Philadelphia, Toronto, and Montréal. Bring a lawn chair and be ready to scoot back if the play comes your way. Home matches begin at 3 on Sunday through July and August at the club's home field, on Andrews Road 4 mi south of the village of Skaneateles.

Shopping

Downtown Skaneateles, encompassing Genessee, Jordan, and Fennell streets, has side-by-side boutique-style shops selling a wide assortment of goods: chocolates, coffees, kitchen items, equestrian clothing, Christmas decorations, antiques and Americana, pet accessories, Dale of Norway sweaters, and sweatshirts. Two-hour parking meters line many downtown streets, and some free spaces are available in an off-street municipal lot behind storefronts. Ample free parking is available just beyond the retail district; the walk over, a few blocks, takes you through charming neighborhoods.

Auburn

❸ *6 mi west of Skaneateles.*

More than 30,000 people live in Auburn, which has an urban feel compared with the rural farmland in surrounding Cayuga County. Nevertheless, Auburn has a number of remarkably intact buildings dating from the early 1800s, and a few are open to the public. The Auburn Correctional Facility, built in 1817 and still used as a maximum-security state prison, subcontracted inmate labor to local businesses until the 1890s. Cheap prison labor combined with water power streaming in from Owasco Lake a few miles to the south and railway transportation routes in every direction conspired to make Auburn one of upstate New York's most important industrial centers in the 19th century.

Cayuga Museum of History and Art. The history and culture of Cayuga County, which stretches from Lake Ontario to outside Ithaca, is carefully curated in exhibits here. Much of the focus is on the Auburn Correctional Facility, which has shaped the area for three centuries; a veritable fortress in the center of Auburn, the state prison is the oldest continually operating prison in the nation. The grand home-turned-museum, on the National Register of Historic Places, is surrounded by an early-19th-century cast-iron fence with a lion's-head motif on the front gate. Behind the museum, in a building now called the Case Research Lab, Theodore W. Case and E. I. Sponable recorded sound on film in 1926—an invention that ended the silent-movie era. ✉ *203 Genesee St.* ☎ *315/253–8051* ⊕ *www.cayuganet.org/cayugamuseum* 🎟 *$3 suggested donation* ☾ *Mar.–Jan., Tues.–Sun. noon–5.*

Emerson Park. The 133-acre park, 3 mi south of downtown Auburn, includes two beaches on Owasco Lake, three boat-launch sites ($5), tables and a pavilion for picnics, grills, a playground, and a snack stand open daily in summer. Lifeguards are on duty July through August, and you can rent canoes and paddleboats. The **Ward W. O'Hara Agricultural Museum** (✉6880 E. Lake Rd. ☎315/253–8051 ⊕www.cayuganet. org/agmuseum 🎟 $2 suggested donation), part of the Cayuga County–owned park complex, is across the street from the main park facilities. The museum includes a blacksmith shop and a circa-1890s general store, kitchen, and veterinarian's office. Kids are encouraged to try out some of the tools. The museum is open Wednesday through Sunday 1–5 from Memorial Day through Labor Day. ✉ *E. Lake Rd./Rte. 38A 2 mi south of Rtes. 5 and 20* ☎ *315/253–5611* ⊕ *www.co.cayuga. ny.us/parks/* 🎟 *Parking $2 (May–Sept.)* ☾ *Daily dawn–dusk.*

★ **Fort Hill Cemetery.** Some of Auburn's most famous residents are buried at Fort Hill, an outstanding example of the parklike burial grounds resulting from the rural-cemetery movement of the early 1800s. At that time Americans turned away from the European tradition of burying the dead in or adjacent to churches and instead harkened to the peaceful idyll of rural life. Funerary art flourished; glorious, symbol-laden tombs and sculptures positioned in English gardens made these cemeteries destinations for 19th-century tourists. Rising over a middle-class residential and commercial neighborhood near downtown, Fort Hill is a great place for a quiet walk under giant trees and for views of the city. Among those buried here are William H. Seward, who served in the cabinets of two U.S. presidents; Harriet Tubman, who liberated hundreds of slaves; and Captain Myles Keogh, who fought (and died) alongside General George Custer at Little Big Horn. The earthen tiers at the cemetery site are believed to be encampment remnants of an early Native American culture. At dusk thousands of crows seeking the city's relative warmth swarm in from the countryside to roost for the night. ⊠ *19 Fort St.* ☎ *315/253–8132* ⊕ *www.cayuganet.org/forthill* ⊡ *Free* ⊙ *Daily dawn–dusk.*

Harriet Tubman Home. The property's simple white clapboard house is where, beginning in 1890, Harriet Tubman tended to elderly African-Americans; the adjacent brick house served as her primary residence. Before Emancipation, Tubman led more than 300 slaves to freedom in the North. At the encouragement of William Seward, an abolitionist who served in two presidential cabinets, she settled in Auburn in the late 1850s. Seward and his family lived on the same road, a mile closer to town. The brick house isn't open to the public, but Tubman's carved wooden bed and her Bible are displayed in the white clapboard building. The site is now run by the African Methodist Episcopal Zion Church, to which Tubman deeded the property before her death in 1913. The church structure where Tubman attended AME Zion services still stands in Auburn, near Fort Hill Cemetery. Tour hours shift, so call ahead. ⊠ *180 South St.* ☎ *315/252–2081* ⊡ *$4* ⊙ *Feb.–Oct., Tues.–Fri. 10–3, Sat. 10–2; Nov.–Jan., by appointment.*

Schweinfurth Memorial Art Center. Many know the art center as the home of a popular quilt show that's been held every winter (usually from early November to early January) since 1982. An annual "Made in New York" juried show is also held here. The center focuses on fine arts, design, and architecture, and hosts many events and arts classes throughout the year. ⊠ *205 Genesee St.* ☎ *315/255–1553* ⊕ *www.cayuganet.org/smac* ⊡ *$5* ⊙ *Tues.–Sat. 10–5, Sun. 1–5.*

★ **Seward House.** William H. Seward (1801–72), a governor of New York, U.S. senator, and secretary of state under Presidents Abraham Lincoln and Andrew Johnson, lived in this distinguished Federal-style home. Seward is perhaps best remembered for arranging the purchase of Alaska from Russia in 1867. The Seward family occupied the house (built in 1816–17) until 1951, and virtually every object here—the furnishings, the library, the tableware—was theirs. ⊠ *33 South St.* ☎ *315/252–1283* ⊕ *www.sewardhouse.org* ⊡ *$5* ⊙ *Feb.–June and mid-Oct.–Dec., Tues.–Sat. 1–4; July–mid-Oct., Tues.–Sat. 10–4, Sun. 1–4.*

Willard Memorial Chapel. Fourteen brilliant stained-glass windows are the centerpiece of the chapel interior, a Louis Comfort Tiffany creation with mosaic-inlay floors and nine leaded-glass chandeliers. It's the only known Tiffany-designed chapel interior still intact. Finished in 1894, the chapel is a remnant of a seminary complex that dated from the early 1800s. Now on the National Register of Historic Places, the chapel was slated to be razed until preservationists stepped in. A weekly lunchtime music series is held here in summer. ⊠ *17 Nelson St.* ☎ *315/252–0339* ⊕ *ci.auburn.ny.us/willardchapel* ⌚ *$3 suggested donation* ⊗ *Tues.–Fri. 10–4, or by appointment.*

FESTIVALS &
FAIRS
Cayuga County Fair. Monster trucks, racing pigs, and 4-H livestock competitions are three traditional favorites at this annual event. Held for five days in July, the fair includes nightly musical entertainment. The fairgrounds—which are 5 mi north of Auburn and include a 4,000-seat grandstand—buzz until midnight with carnival attractions and stock-car races. ⊠ *Cayuga County Fairgrounds, Rte. 34N, Weedsport* ☎ *315/ 834–6606 or 800/499–9615* ⊕ *www.cayugacountyfair.org.*

Sterling Renaissance Festival. Enter Warwickshire, a 1585 English village spread across a wooded hillside, and spend the day as an Elizabethan. Thirty-five costumed improvisational troupe members beckon you to join them for a rollicking round at the dunking pond; courtly dancing; discourse at the village "well"; or cheering at the jousting field, where men astride chunky horses play medieval games. Artisan booths feature Elizabethan-style caps and clothing, handmade musical instruments, jewelry, and many other articles. Foot-long turkey legs eaten out of hand are the traditional festival food, but salads, sandwiches, "steak on a stake," and other options are also available. The festival, in a rural area near Lake Ontario, is open rain or shine for seven summer weekends starting in early July. From Auburn, take Route 38 north to Route 104A; the festival is a 45-minute drive north of Auburn. ⊠ *15385 Farden Rd., Sterling* ☎ *315/947–5783 or 800/879–4446* ⊕ *www.sterlingfestival.com.*

Where to Stay & Eat

★ $-$$$
✕ **Balloons.** Thanks to the prompt service, uncomplicated menu, and warm welcome extended to patrons, the restaurant has been serving since 1934. Having worked here five nights a week since before World War II, one of the waiters celebrated his 86th birthday in 2004. The concrete rear wall of the Auburn Correctional Facility is right across the street, but Balloons is a transporting experience. The original art-deco decor coexists with a clown motif and a U-shape bar, and 1930s and 1940s hits play continuously. Platters heaped with meatballs and spaghetti, surf and turf, and other dependable Italian dishes are accompanied by a simple iceburg salad topped with a somewhat sweet, secret-recipe house dressing that's delicious. ⊠ *65 Washington St.* ☎ *315/252–9761* ▭ *AE, MC, V* ⊗ *Closed Sun. and Mon. No lunch.*

$-$$
✕▥ **Springside Inn.** The red clapboard inn, built in 1851, is best known for its Sunday brunch—always with lobster Newburg and cheese soufflé. The restaurant ($–$$$), open for dinner Thursday through Saturday, serves Continental and American fare, such as Long Island duckling glazed with orange sauce and slow-roasted prime rib. Guest rooms have Victorian antiques and overlook a pond, fountain, and gazebo; some have clawfoot tubs. According to local legend, Harriet Tubman hid runaway slaves in the woods behind the inn. Guests may use the inn's dock, across the street from Owasco Lake. ⊠ *6141 W. Lake Rd./Rte. 38 S,*

13021 ☎ 315/252–7247 🖷 315/252–8096 ⊕ *www.springsideinn.com*
🛌 *5 rooms, 2 suites* ⚒ *Restaurant, room service, in-room data ports,
some in-room hot tubs, some in-room kitchenettes, some microwaves,
some refrigerators, some cable TV, some in-room VCRs, dock, fishing,
hiking, bar, lounge, piano bar, Internet, meeting rooms, no-smoking rooms*
🖹 *AE, MC, V* ⎮◎⎮ *CP.*

$–$$ 🏨 **Holiday Inn.** One of the biggest hotels in the Finger Lakes region, this
five-story business-oriented property has an indoor swimming pool as
its visual centerpiece. The hotel is on Auburn's main north–south axis
and next to its east–west artery; although it's handy for travelers, the
area isn't attractive, so consider a room with a view of the pool courtyard rather than of a parking lot or a gas station. Rooms are spacious,
and range from standard two-bed configurations to two-room whirl-
pool-tub suites. Wireless Internet access is available in the courtyard.
McMurphy's Irish Pub serves Guinness stew, fish-and-chips, and corned
beef and cabbage. ⊠ *75 North St., 13021* ☎ *315/253–4531* 🖷 *315/
252–5843* ⊕ *www.hiauburn.com* 🛌 *163 rooms, 2 suites* ⚒ *2 restaurants, room service, in-room data ports, some in-room hot tubs, some
microwaves, some refrigerators, cable TV with movies, indoor pool, gym,
hair salon, bar, pub, video game room, dry cleaning, laundry facilities,
laundry service, Internet, business services, convention center, some
pets allowed (fee), no-smoking rooms* 🖹 *AE, D, DC, MC, V.*

¢–$ 🏨 **Microtel Inn & Suites.** Overlooking Auburn's busiest roadway, the motel
(built in 1999) has workmanlike furnishings in uncluttered rooms, each
with a window seat. In a commercial-residential neighborhood, it's two
blocks from the center of downtown Auburn and ½ mi from a cluster
of restaurant-shopping strips. ⊠ *12 Seminary Ave., 13021* ☎ *315/253–
5000 or 888/771–7171* 🖷 *315/259–9090* ⊕ *www.microtelinnauburn.
com* 🛌 *79 rooms, 22 suites* ⚒ *Dining room, in-room data ports, some
kitchenettes, some microwaves, some refrigerators, cable TV with
movies, exercise equipment, dry cleaning, laundry facilities, laundry service, Internet, business services, some pets allowed (fee), no-smoking floors*
🖹 *AE, D, MC, V* ⎮◎⎮ *CP.*

Nightlife & the Arts

The **Finger Lakes Drive-In** (⊠ Rte. 5 and U.S. 20 ☎ 315/252–3969
📧 $5), open nightly from May through early fall, is one of the coun-
try's few remaining outdoor-movie venues. The place, 3 mi west of
Auburn, shows many first-run films and is popular with families. The
Merry-Go-Round Playhouse (⊠ Emerson Park, Rte. 38A 2 mi south of
U.S. 20 ☎ 315/255–1785, 800/457–8897 box office ⊕ www.merry-go-
round.com), a professional summer theater, produces up to four classic American musicals every year starting in June and continuing into
August. The theater is in a former merry-go-round building. Tickets are
in the $20-and-up range.

Sports & the Outdoors

BASEBALL The **Auburn Doubledays** (⊠ 103 N. Division St. ☎ 315/255–2489
⊕ www.auburndoubledays.com), a single-A farm team affiliated with
the Toronto Blue Jays, take on sluggers such as the Batavia Muckdogs
and the Mahoning Valley Scrappers. The season runs from mid-June to

early September. Home games start at 7 PM Monday through Saturday and 6 PM Sunday.

Fillmore Glen State Park

4 *17 mi south of Auburn.*

The limestone-and-shale glen and park has five waterfalls and a stream-fed, stone-walled swimming pool. Named for the nation's 13th president, the park also has a replica of the cabin where Millard Fillmore was born. (The actual site is 5 mi east of the glen.) You can fish, hike, snowshoe, and cross-country ski, and more than 50 campsites are available. The park is 1 mi south of the Cayuga County village of Moravia. ⊠ *1686 Rte. 38, Moravia* ☎ *315/497–0130* ⊕ *nysparks.state.ny.us* 🅿 *Parking $6 (May–Sept.)* ☉ *Daily dawn–dusk.*

CAYUGA & SENECA LAKES

Each stretching nearly 40 mi and creating a virtual microclimate, Cayuga and Seneca lakes are the two largest Finger Lakes. Hillsides cup lake warmth, extending the growing season, which is why so many grapes are grown on the sloping shores of Seneca and Cayuga. East–west travel has always been stymied by the length of the lakes. To reach a destination 3 mi across a lake you might have to travel north, then south, for two hours. As a result, glorious swaths of countryside are little touched by visual change. You might drive for an hour without seeing another moving vehicle or losing sight of a magnificent lake.

Aurora

5 *16 mi west of Moravia.*

Stretching nearly a mile along the east shore of Cayuga Lake, Aurora has long been one of the prettiest 19th-century villages in upstate New York. Historically sensitive renovations beginning in 2001 freshened a number of commercial and residential buildings on Main Street, where colonial, Federal, and Victorian structures mix with examples of other architectural styles. A cluster of quality restaurants and one-of-a-kind shops helps make this a worthy destination. Wells College, established in 1868, anchors the south end of town. Built into a hillside overlooking Cayuga Lake, Wells was a women-only institution until trustees decided to admit men (starting in 2005).

MacKenzie-Childs. The design studios and factory of this home-furnishings empire occupy a Victorian farmhouse and other attractive buildings on a bluff overlooking Cayuga Lake. On the 90-minute studio tours you can see artisans creating the company's whimsically painted ceramics, glassware, furniture, and trimmings. Tours of the decked-out farmhouse take 75 minutes. Afternoon tea is served at 3 PM daily from May through Columbus Day; it's $30, which includes finger sandwiches, scones, fruit preserves, double Devonshire cream, lemon curd, and, of course, tea. Reservations are recommended for tea; it's also a good idea to call ahead to confirm farmhouse and studio tour times. The extensive grounds (75 acres)

THE WINE TRAILS

THE REGION'S FOUR WINE TRAILS *are named for the lakes around which the wineries cluster. Admission prices, months of operation, and hours vary by winery.*

Canandaigua Wine Trail. *The trail includes just a few wine-related stops: Casa Larga Vineyards in Fairport, the Finger Lakes Wine Center at Sonnenberg Gardens, Widmer Wine Cellars, and Arbor Hill Grapery and Winery in Naples.* ☎ 877/386–4669 ⊕ www.canandaiguawinetrail.com.

Cayuga Wine Trail. *The organization sponsors events throughout the year and includes 15 wineries on its trail. Honey wine is the featured beverage at Montezuma winery, in Seneca Falls, where you may also buy beeswax candles and other decorative items.* ⌖ Box 123, Fayette 13065 ☎ 800/684–5217 ⊕ www.cayugawinetrail.com.

Keuka Lake Wine Trail. *The trail encompasses nine wineries, including Dr. Konstantin Frank's Vinifera Wine Cellars and Heron Hill in Hammondsport and Hunt Country Vineyards in Branchport. Five of the wineries are on the east side of the lake and all are within 10 mi of one another.* ⌖ 2375 Rte. 14A, Penn Yan 14527 ☎ 800/440–4898 ⊕ www.keukawinetrail.com.

Seneca Lake Wine Trail. *More than 30 wineries encircle Seneca Lake. You may recognize some of the names: Fox Run Vineyards in Penn Yan, Glenora Wine Cellars in Dundee, Castel Grisch Estate Winery in Watkins Glen, Lamoreaux Landing Wine Cellars in Lodi, Red Newt in Hector.* ⌖ Seneca Lake Winery Association, 2 N. Franklin St., Watkins Glen 14891 ☎ 607/535–2223 or 877/536–2717 ⊕ www.senecalakewine.com.

include gardens, trails, and a shop devoted to MacKenzie-Childs wares. At this writing (late 2004), the on-site restaurant is being renovated, and only the area used for afternoon tea is open. ⊠ *3260 Rte. 90* ☎ *315/364–7123* ⊕ *www.mackenzie-childs.com* 🎟 *Studio $10, farmhouse $10* ⊙ *Studio tours May–Columbus Day, weekdays at 9:30 and 1:30; rest of yr, weekdays at 1:15. Farmhouse tours May–Columbus Day, daily at 11 and 2; rest of yr, weekdays at 10:30, weekends at 2.*

Where to Stay & Eat

¢–$ ✕**Dorie's.** The lunch-counter-style spot has five tables, a soup-and-sandwich menu, a case of baked goods, a rack of daily newspapers, darling gifts for children, kitchenware, and a selection of hand-scooped candies sold by the bag. A deck overlooking Cayuga Lake offers choice warm-weather seating. ⊠ *238 Main St.* ☎ *315/364–8818* ▤ *MC, V* ⊙ *No dinner in Jan. and Feb.*

¢–$ ✕**Pizzaurora.** With its sleek, contemporary furnishings—think stainless-steel tables and abstract Italian paintings—and hip industrial vibe, this eatery broke the mold for restaurants in Aurora when it opened in 2003. The fare includes thin-crust pizzas as well as calzones, submarine and wrap sandwiches, and salads. It stays open until 10 on Friday and Saturday nights. ⊠ *382 Main St.* ☎ *315/364–8804* ▤ *MC, V.*

¢ ✕**Fargo Bar & Grill.** A brick building across the street from the Aurora Inn houses this tavern, a once-crusty bar now outfitted with dark wood and hunter-green accents. The food is straightforward tavern fare. The most popular item is the Fargo Burger, topped with cheese, tomato, lettuce, and mayo. Chicken wings and salads are also on the menu. ⊠ *384 Main St.* ☎ *315/364–8005* ▭ *No credit cards* ⊘ *No lunch Sat. No lunch Sun. June–Aug.*

$$$ ✕▥ **Aurora Inn.** Most guest rooms in this 1833 Federal-style brick building have balconies with lake views and rockers; some rooms have fireplaces and whirlpool tubs. The amenities are posh: flat-screen TVs, Bose CD players, high-speed Internet access, Frette linens, terry robes, and marble bathrooms. Floral wallpapers are part of the retro charm. Antiques, paintings, and Oriental rugs outfit the common rooms downstairs. The restaurant ($$–$$$) is well appointed but not overdone—in keeping with Aurora's style. The food is mostly American. Dinner could be pot roast, pan-seared scallops, or rack of lamb. ⊠ *391 Main St., 13026* ☎ *315/364–8888* 🖷 *315/364–8887* ⊕ *www.aurora-inn.com* ⤳ *10 rooms* ⚲ *Restaurant, in-room data ports, some in-room hot tubs, some kitchenettes, some minibars, cable TV, no-smoking rooms* ▭ *AE, MC, V* ⦿ *CP weekdays.*

Nightlife & the Arts

The 200-seat **Morgan Opera House** (⊠ Rte. 90 and Cherry Ave. ☎ 315/364–5437 ⊕ www.auroranewyork.com/moh/), built in 1899, occupies the second floor of the Aurora Free Library, as it has for more than a century. The season runs from April through December, and may include readings, gospel quartets, and other concerts; most performances are free or less than $10 per person.

Shopping

Main Street is the shopping drag in Aurora. **Jane Morgan's Little House** (⊠ 347 Main St. ☎ 315/364–7715) stocks good-quality women's slacks, sweaters, skirts, dresses, and tasteful accessories. The staff is very helpful. The store is in a two-story brick building in the center of Aurora. Fresh flowers, stylish greeting cards, and irresistible gifts with a fresh twist on the traditional are sold at **Posies** (⊠ 381 Main St. ☎ 315/364–8817).

Ithaca

❻ *28 mi south of Aurora.*

Home to both Cornell University and Ithaca College, eclectic Ithaca is the multicultural and intellectual capital of the central Finger Lakes region. The diverse restaurant scene and array of arts venues contribute to Ithaca's urbane air. And the setting, amid steep hills and waterfalls at the southern tip of Cayuga Lake, is spectacularly beautiful.

Buttermilk Falls State Park. Water cascades over 10 falls through a ¾-mi gorge, dropping close to 500 feet, at this park on Ithaca's south end. A swimming hole sits at the base of the falls, and the park also has playing fields, a campground (open mid-May to mid-October), and hiking trails through woodlands and wetlands. Nearly all the trails are closed in winter. ⊠ *Rte. 13* ☎ *607/273–5761 or 607/273–3440, 800/456–2267 camping reservations* ⊕ *nysparks.state.ny.us* 🎫 *Parking $7 late May–early Sept., $6 weekends early Sept.–mid-Oct. and Apr.–late May* ☉ *Daily dawn–dusk.*

Cornell Plantations. The 200 acres of plants and trees adjacent to the Cornell University campus are primarily organized in collections—peonies, rock-garden species, rhododendrons, old-time vegetable and flower gardens, conifers, flowering crabapples, wildflowers. There's even a section for poisonous plants. The winter garden includes evergreens, conifers, and assorted plants with interesting cold-weather colors and textures. The complex's arboretum includes an area with sculptures. Walking and bus tours are available; call ahead for seasonal times. Some tours are free and others are $3. ⊠ *1 Plantations Rd., off Rte. 366* ☎ *607/ 255–2400* ⊕ *www.plantations.cornell.edu* 🎫 *Free* ☉ *Daily dawn–dusk.*

Cornell University. With its historic buildings, weave of natural and man-made spaces, Cayuga Lake views, and two spectacular gorges, the campus of this private university is considered one of the most beautiful in the country. Founded in 1865, Cornell is a mixture of modern structures and ivy-covered 19th-century buildings. Nearly 20,000 students from 120 countries study here. Wear your walking shoes; there is almost no public parking near the campus center. Free 75-minute tours of the campus leave daily from Day Hall, Tower Road, and East Avenue.

Four miles of trails lead through the 220-acre Sapsucker Woods Sanctuary, part of the **Cornell Lab of Ornithology** (⊠ 159 Sapsucker Woods Rd.). Bird artist Louis Agassiz Fuertes named the woods after two yellow-bellied sapsuckers he had spotted in the area. A computer touch screen leads you through interpretive displays. The lab is open weekdays 8–5 (until 4 on Friday), Saturday 9:30–4, and Sunday 11–4.

Cornell University's I. M. Pei–designed **Herbert F. Johnson Museum of Art** (⊠ University Ave. ☎ 607/255–6464 ⊕ www.museum.cornell.edu) houses more than 30,000 works of art, including collections of Asian and modern art. The most stunning sight here, though, may well be one created by Mother Nature: the museum's fifth floor offers an unforgettable view of Cayuga Lake stretching north. The museum is open 10–5 Tuesday through Sunday; entry is free. ⊠ *Central Ave.* ☎ *607/254–2473* ⊕ *www.cornell.edu* ☉ *Tours daily at 9, 11, 1, and 3.*

★ ☾ **Museum of the Earth.** Experience the natural history of New York State through exhibits called "Beneath an Ancient Sea," "Where Dinosaurs Walked," and "A World Carved by Ice." Whale and mastodon skeletons, along with audiovisual theater presentations, help prepare museumgoers for hands-on labs featuring fossils, dinosaurs, and ice. The on-site Paleontological Research Institution runs the museum. ⊠ *1259 Trumansburg Rd./Rte. 96* ☎ *607/273–6623* ⊕ *www.museumoftheearth. org* 🎫 *$8* ☉ *Mon. and Wed.–Sat. 10–5, Sun. noon–4.*

Robert H. Treman State Park. Twelve waterfalls, including Lucifer Falls, which has a 115 foot drop, are the highlight here. Nine miles of hiking trails lace the park, which also offers swimming, fishing, a campground, and a playground. The trails all close for winter in early November. The park is 5 mi south of the city. ✉ *Rte. 327* ☎ *607/273–3440* ⊕ *nysparks. state.ny.us* 🄿 *Parking $7 Memorial Day–Labor Day, $6 rest of season* ⊘ *Daily 8 AM–dusk.*

🐣 **Sciencenter.** A walk-in camera and a two-story kinetic ball sculpture are among the 100-plus exhibits at this hands-on museum catering to youngsters. The Sagan Planetwalk honors scientist Carl Sagan, who taught at Cornell University. Outside there's a wooden playground. ✉ *601 First St.* ☎ *607/272–0600* ⊕ *www.sciencenter.org* 🄿 *$6* ⊘ *Tues.–Sat. 10–5, Sun. noon–5.*

FESTIVALS & FAIRS

Ithaca Festival. Hundreds of poets, dancers, musicians, and other performers and artists entertain tens of thousands of people at this four-day festival in June. A parade is part of the festivities. 🄲 *215 N. Cayuga St., M-1, 14850* ☎ *607/273–3646* ⊕ *www.ithacafestival.org.*

Where to Stay & Eat

$$–$$$$

✕ **John Thomas Steakhouse.** A two-story 1848 farmhouse on the grounds of La Tourelle Country Inn is home to this restaurant that specializes in steak but also serves vegetarian and fish dishes. Filet mignon, prime rib, strip steak, and porterhouse are among the choices. Sides, such as garlic mashed potatoes, are served family style. In summer you may eat outside on the deck. ✉ *1152 Danby Rd./Rte. 96B* ☎ *607/273–3464* ⚶ *Reservations essential* 🝐 *AE, D, MC, V* ⊘ *No lunch.*

$–$$$

✕ **Station Restaurant and Sleeping Cars.** The main dining room occupies the waiting area of an old Lehigh Valley Railroad station, and you may also eat in a railcar. The food is American with Italian touches: broiled lamb chops, prime rib, scampi, fried haddock. Salmon is basted with olive oil and sun-dried tomatoes; manicotti comes with a choice of fillings, including broccoli with mushrooms. Three overnight sleeping "cars" are available by reservation ($). ✉ *800 W. Buffalo St.* ☎ *607/ 272–2609* 🝐 *AE, D, MC, V* ⊘ *Closed Mon. Sept.–June. No lunch.*

$–$$

✕ **The Antlers.** Grilled fare is the specialty at this country inn. Shrimp, chicken, and contemporary pasta dishes are among the many choices. You may order grilled chicken breast with onions, peppers, and Amaretto cream sauce or with apricots, chutney, and orange sauce, for example. Flank steak, coated with creole spices, is charbroiled and served with horseradish barbecue sauce. Sit in front of the fireplace and sip local wine under the watchful gaze of the large deer head mounted above the doorway. ✉ *1159 Dryden Rd.* ☎ *607/273–9725* 🝐 *AE, DC, MC, V* ⊘ *No lunch.*

$–$$

✕ **Moosewood.** Since its founding in 1973, this downtown restaurant has been at the forefront in the field of creative vegetarian cooking, and its cookbooks are known worldwide. The setting is simple and casual. You may also dine outside on a patio. The menu changes daily, and everything is prepared from fresh ingredients. Dishes might include spicy carrot-peanut soup or penne and tomato sauce with Kalamata olives, capers, and cayenne. A vegan option is always available. ✉ *215 N. Cayuga St.* ☎ *607/273–9610* 🝐 *AE, D, MC, V* ⚶ *Reservations not accepted* ⊘ *No lunch Sun.*

¢–$$

✕ **Glenwood Pines.** Three generations of the Hohwald family, which has operated the bilevel restaurant since 1979, work at making this casual place cozy for locals and out-of-towners alike. Two of the three dining rooms have great views of Cayuga Lake; the third shares space with the bar, pinball and arcade games, and a gas-fired stove. Burger meat is ground daily at the Pines. Steaks, fried seafood, pasta dishes, salads, and chicken round out the menu. For lunch, consider the Glenwood Glutton: any combo of ham, roast beef, and turkey on French bread with lettuce, tomato, cheese, and either mayo or Thousand Island dressing. In summer ask to sit at one of the picnic tables lining the lower level, where pine scents from the forested cliff below waft in through the wall of screened windows. ⊠ *1213 Taughannock Blvd.* ☎ *607/273–3909* ▤ *MC, V.*

$$–$$$ ✕🏨 **Statler Hotel at Cornell University.** Cornell's School of Hotel Administration operates this nine-story, on-campus hotel; its full-service restaurant, Banfi's; and two hotel cafeterias. Guests here have access to the university's recreational facilities. Rooms have contemporary furnishings, like those you'd find at an upscale chain property, and give you views of the campus. Suites are spacious and have one full and one half bath. Crab cakes, North Atlantic salmon, and steak are some of the menu choices at Banfi's, where the student staff is refreshingly eager to please. The hotel and dining facilities are closed during the university's Thanksgiving and Christmas recesses. ⊠ *11 East Ave., 14853* ☎ *607/257–2500 or 800/541–2501* 🖷 *607/254–2565 or 800/541–2501* ⊕ *www.hotelschool.cornell.edu/statler/rooms.html* ⬦ *138 rooms, 12 suites* ⟁ *Restaurant, 2 cafeterias, room service, in-room data ports, refrigerators, cable TV with movies, gym, bar, lounge, piano bar, babysitting, laundry service, Internet, business services, meeting rooms, airport shuttle, no-smoking rooms* ▤ *AE, D, DC, MC, V.*

$$–$$$ 🏨 **Holiday Inn Ithaca.** Rooms at this 10-story hotel across from Ithaca Commons are spacious and have large windows. The furniture, made of dark wood, is attractive. Standard rooms have two queen beds. The two suites—huge duplex penthouses—have whirlpool tubs. ⊠ *222 S. Cayuga St., 14850* ☎ *607/272–1000* 🖷 *607/277–1275* ⊕ *www.hiithaca.com* ⬦ *178 rooms, 2 suites* ⟁ *Restaurant, room service, in-room data ports, some microwaves, some refrigerators, some in-room hot tubs, cable TV with movies, indoor pool, gym, bar, laundry service, business services, meeting rooms, airport shuttle, some pets allowed (fee), no-smoking rooms* ▤ *AE, D, MC, V.*

$$–$$$ 🏨 **La Tourelle Country Inn.** The three-story inn sits on 70 acres on a hill 3 mi from downtown and close to Buttermilk Falls State Park. The place has a European aura. The 21 king rooms have swagged windows and light-wood furniture with a feminine feel. The other rooms have a more masculine decor, with furniture of dark Mexican wood. All accommodations are spacious. The well-regarded John Thomas Steakhouse occupies a separate farmhouse on the grounds, which have two ponds. ⊠ *1150 Danby Rd./Rte. 96B, 14850* ☎ *607/273–2734 or 800/765–1492* 🖷 *607/273–4821* ⊕ *www.latourelleinn.com* ⬦ *34 rooms, 1 suite* ⟁ *Restaurant, in-room data ports, in-room safes, some in-room hot tubs, some refrigerators, cable TV, in-room VCRs, 4 tennis courts, fishing, hiking, bar, dry cleaning, laundry service, business services, meeting rooms, some pets allowed; no smoking* ▤ *AE, D, MC, V* ⊙ *CP.*

$–$$$ 🏨 **William Henry Miller Inn.** Rooms at this inn, an 1880 Queen Anne
Fodor'sChoice downtown, are imaginatively decorated to highlight alcoves, built-in
★ shelves, curved walls, window threesomes, and steeple views of the city
center. The decor in one room has a streamlined Scandinavian flavor.
The others have more traditional furnishings: European armoires, cherry-
wood sleigh beds and four-poster beds, swagged window treatments,
wood shutters. Breakfast here is excellent, with treats like fresh orange
juice and fruit platters, pumpkin and lemon-ricotta pancakes, and as-
sorted muffins. Dessert is offered in the evening. ⊠ *303 N. Aurora St.,
14850* 🕾 *607/256–4553, 877/256–4553* ⊕ *www.millerinn.com* 🛏 *9
rooms, 1 suite* 🖒 *Dining room, fans, in-room data ports, some in-room
hot tubs, cable TV, some in-room VCRs, library, piano, dry cleaning,
laundry service, Internet, business services, meeting rooms, no-smok-
ing rooms; no kids under 12* 🍽 *AE, D, DC, MC, V* ⭘ *BP.*

$$ 🏨 **Comfort Inn.** The two-story chain hotel is 2 mi from downtown and
just east of Route 13, which is lined with eateries and other commer-
cial establishments. The staff is efficient and friendly. Rooms include cof-
feemakers, irons, and ironing boards. Some rooms have jet tubs. ⊠ *356
Elmira Rd., 14850* 🕾 *607/272–0100* 🖷 *607/272–2405* 🛏 *79 rooms
🖒 In-room data ports, some in-room hot tubs, some microwaves, some
refrigerators, cable TV with movies, gym, video game room, dry cleaning, laundry service, business services, some pets allowed (fee), no-
smoking rooms* 🍽 *AE, D, DC, MC, V* ⭘ *CP.*

$–$$ 🏨 **Clarion University Hotel.** The three-story hotel and conference center
is on Ithaca's north edge, just south of Route 13. Colorful wall treatments and furnishings give the room decor at this chain property some
oomph. ⊠ *1 Sheraton Dr., 14850* 🕾 *607/257–2000* 🖷 *607/257–3998*
⊕ *www.choicehotels.com* 🛏 *106 rooms* 🖒 *2 restaurants, room service,
in-room data ports, some microwaves, some refrigerators, cable TV, golf
privileges, indoor pool, gym, sauna, bar, business services, meeting
rooms, airport shuttle, some pets allowed (fee), no-smoking rooms*
🍽 *AE, D, MC, V.*

$–$$ 🏨 **Inn on Columbia.** Designed and owned by an architect and a chef,
this B&B is anything but conventional. The house, a Greek revival from
the 1830s, was gutted and renovated in the late 1990s. Contemporary
furniture pieces custom-designed by Kenn Young, the architect, and works
by local artists fill the place, which is quite colorful. Two guest rooms
have gas fireplaces. Breakfast is prepared by Kenn's wife, Madeline, who
has worked in a vegan restaurant. Downtown is four blocks away.
⊠ *228 Columbia St., 14850* 🕾 *607/272–0204* ⊕ *www.columbiabb.com*
🛏 *2 rooms, 1 carriage house* 🖒 *Dining room, some in-room hot tubs,
kitchen, some cable TV with movies, some in-room VCRs, some pets
allowed (fee), no-smoking rooms; no TV in some rooms* ⭘ *BP.*

¢–$$ 🏨 **Grayhaven Motel and Bed and Breakfast.** The combination motel and
lodge is in a suburban spot 3 mi from downtown. Motel rooms are sim-
ple, with no-frills furnishings. Rooms in the separate lodge building have
wood-paneled walls and vaulted ceilings. Picnic tables and Adirondack
chairs, sprawled across the lawn, offer a respite after a long hike at But-
termilk Falls State Park, 1 mi away. ⊠ *657 Elmira Rd., 14850* 🕾 *607/
272–6434* ⊕ *www.grayhavenmotel.com* 🛏 *17 rooms* 🖒 *Cable TV,*

some in-room DVD players, some pets allowed (fee), no-smoking rooms
🖃 *AE, D, MC, V* 🍽 *CP Apr.–Nov.*

Nightlife & the Arts

The **Hangar Theatre** (☎ 607/273–4497 or 800/284–8422 ⊕ www.
hangartheatre.org), some of the best regional theater in the Northeast,
performs at Cass Park from June through Labor Day. Five plays, from
comedies to musicals, are produced each summer, along with five children's productions. The **Kitchen Theatre Co.** (✉ 116 N. Cayuga St.
☎607/273–4497 ⊕www.kitchentheatre.org) features contemporary dramas. Its 73-seat theater is on the Commons.

Shopping

Ithaca Commons (✉ State St. between Cayuga and Aurora Sts. ☎ 607/
277–8679), the historic center of Ithaca, is a pedestrian mall with specialty book and clothing stores as well as dozens of restaurants. Sculptures and gardens give the former motorway some texture and provide
an inviting backdrop for festivals and itinerant musicians. Handmade
scarves, vases, and other choice gifts line the shelves of stores such as
American Crafts by Robbie Dein (158 The Commons). In summer a regional farmer's market is held here each Tuesday (11–2). The open-air
Ithaca Farmer's Market (✉ Steamboat Landing, off Rte. 13, 1 mi north
of downtown ☎ 607/273–7109) is perhaps Ithaca's hottest ticket on a
Saturday morning. Artwork, food, plants, and flowers, all local, fill the
80-plus stalls. It's open until 2 PM weekends from June through October and Saturday from November until Christmas.

Trumansburg

❼ *11 mi north of Ithaca.*

A few miles west of Cayuga Lake, Trumansburg is a self-contained
rural outpost but also something of an Ithaca exurb. The village is
known for its summer music festival and its tidy Victorian homes, as
well as for Taughannock Falls State Park.

Fodor'sChoice **Taughannock Falls State Park.** Stunningly steep shale cliffs and rock sur-
★   round the 215 foot high Taughannock Falls, which are 30 feet higher
than Niagara Falls. A level ¾-mi path takes you from the parking lot
to the falls. Autumn is perhaps the most dramatic time of year to see
the gorge, but the waterway is breathtaking any time of year. And, un-
like many of the rim trails that surround other Finger Lakes gorges, the
trail at the glen's bottom here is open all year. Camping and swimming
are allowed in season. The park, which straddles Route 89, has playgrounds, a boat launch, and picnic grounds. ✉ *Rte. 89, 8 mi north of
Ithaca* ☎ *607/387–6739* ⊕ *nysparks.state.ny.us* 🚗 *Parking $7 late
May–early Sept., $6 weekends early Sept.–Oct.* ☉ *Daily dawn–dusk.*

FESTIVALS &   **Finger Lakes Grassroots Festival.** The music ranges from Cajun and zy-
FAIRS   deco to African and reggae at this four-day festival that raises money
to fight AIDS. The event is held in July on the fairgrounds; four-day passes
cost about $75. Limited tent and vehicle camping is available on-site.
✉ *Trumansburg Fairgrounds, Rte. 96* ☎ *607/387–5098* ⊕ *www.
grassroots.org.*

Where to Stay & Eat

$$–$$$ ✕ **Knapp Winery Restaurant.** The gardens at the restaurant, part of a winery, provide much of the fresh produce used by the kitchen. The food is contemporary. Try fettuccine ladled with roasted garlic, acorn squash, grape tomatoes, and brandy cream sauce, or duck breast in merlot and fig sauce. The outdoor patio overlooking the flower garden is opened for diners when the weather's warm. Lunch and dinner hours vary seasonally, so call ahead. ✉ *2770 Rte. 128/Ernsberger Rd.* ☎ *607/869–9271 or 800/869–9271* ▭ *AE, D, MC, V* ⊘ *Closed Jan.–Mar. No dinner Mon.–Wed.*

$–$$$ ✕▦ **Taughannock Farms Inn.** The property offers a wide variety of accommodations in several buildings. Most rooms here have Cayuga Lake views. You may choose a high-Victorian, no-TV room in the 1873 inn; take one of the homey but deluxe units in the new Edgewood structure; or opt to stay in one of the other three buildings. Two- and three-bedroom units are available. Taughannock Falls State Park surrounds the 12-acre property, giving you easy access to park trails, and the state park lakeshore is across the street. Most of the seating in the restaurant ($$–$$$$) is on a glassed-in porch overlooking Cayuga Lake. The place serves American and Continental dishes, like roast pork loin with apple chutney and whipped sweet potatoes, or roast duck breast with wild rice and orange sauce. ✉ *2030 Gorge Rd./Rte. 89, 14886* ☎ *607/387–7711 or 888/387–7711* ⊕ *www.t-farms.com* ⟿ *19 rooms, 3 guesthouses* ⅙ *Restaurant, in-room data ports, some in-room hot tubs, some kitchenettes, some microwaves, some refrigerators, some cable TV, bar, lounge, Internet, business services; no TV in some rooms, no smoking* ▭ *AE, D, MC, V* ⅋◎⅋ *CP.*

Seneca Falls

❽ *31 mi north of Trumansburg.*

Seneca Falls is a classic upstate village, with loads of history, wide streets lined with century-old homes, 19th-century storefronts, and a sprinkling of small parks. Some celebrate Seneca Falls (population 6,800) as the model for Bedford Falls in the movie *It's a Wonderful Life.* A historic district has helped to retain 19th-century flavor in many neighborhoods.

The falls that powered many factories here in the 1800s were flooded long ago to create Van Cleef Lake and a canal through the village's midsection. In 1848, the village was the site of the first Women's Rights Convention, during which attendees declared that "all men and women are created equal." The convention was organized by reformer Elizabeth Cady Stanton, who raised seven children here.

Cayuga Lake State Park. A swimming beach, bathhouse, boat launch, playground, campground, and trails are the key attractions in this 190-acre park. You can also fish at the park, on the north end of Cayuga Lake and 2 mi from Seneca Falls. ✉ *2678 Lower Lake Rd.* ☎ *315/568–5163* ⊕ *nysparks.state.ny.us* ⊞ *Parking $7 late May–early Sept.; $6 weekends early Sept.–Oct.* ⊘ *Daily dawn–dusk.*

Cayuga-Seneca Canal. The 12-mi-long Cayuga-Seneca Canal links the northern ends of Seneca and Cayuga lakes and connects to the Erie Canal near the Montezuma National Wildlife Refuge. Locks enclose boats in bathtublike mechanisms that fill with water and float the boat to the next level. (Locks are in service daily 8:15 AM–10:15 PM from May to mid-November.) Overnight canalside slips parallel the main downtown drag, so conveniences are steps away. The decorative lamps along the canal near downtown Seneca Falls make this a great place for walkers, night or day. Victorian-style benches provide seating. The **Ludovico Sculpture Trail** stretches along the canal's south bank in Seneca Falls. Access to the canal is also available in nearby Waterloo, at Oak Park, which has fishing, hiking, a boat launch, and a picnic pavilion. ⊠ *9 Seneca St.* ☎ *315/568–5797, 800/422–6254 Canal Corp.* ⊕ *www.nycanal.com.*

★ **Montezuma National Wildlife Refuge.** The area between the Finger Lakes and Lake Ontario was a huge wetlands until settlers began draining the land more than 200 years ago. Montezuma, an 8,000-acre remnant of the giant swamp, is a major stopover for thousands of migrating birds. The numbers peak in mid-April and early October. More than 320 species of birds have been identified at the federally managed site since its establishment in 1937. Look for eagles that raise their young here. You can take a 3½-mi self-guided car tour of the refuge; start at the visitor center, where you pick up a brochure with information about the wildlife you see on the tour. The visitor center has limited winter access; call for seasonal hours. The refuge entrance is 5 mi east of Seneca Falls, at the north end of Cayuga Lake. ⊠ *3395 Rte. 5/U.S. 20* ☎ *315/568–5987* ⊕ *www.fws.gov/r5mnwr* 🎫 *Free* ☉ *Refuge daily dawn–dusk; visitor center Apr.–Oct., weekdays 10–3, weekends 10–4.*

Seneca Falls Historical Society Museum. Elaborate woodwork and Victorian furniture decorate the 1855 Queen Anne mansion on Cayuga Street, which is lined with grand homes. A female ghost is said to wander its 23 rooms. ⊠ *55 Cayuga St.* ☎ *315/568–8412* ⊕ *www.sfhistoricalsociety.org* 🎫 *$3* ☉ *Sept.–June, weekdays 9–4; July and Aug., weekdays 9–4, weekends 1–4.*

Seneca Museum of Waterways and Industry. Why did reform movements flourish in the Finger Lakes? Many of the answers are at this modern museum, where narratives of water power, transportation, industry, and cultural history are interwoven to tell the story of 19th-century Seneca Falls. The museum occupies a former men's clothing shop. "By Hand and by Horse," a permanent exhibit, invites you to experiment with basic tools, and children are urged to ask questions of tour guides. ⊠ *89 Cayuga St.* ☎ *315/568–1510* ⊕ *www.senecamuseum.com* 🎫 *Free* ☉ *Early June–early Sept., Tues.–Sat. 10–4, Sun. noon–4; Jan. and Feb., Thurs.–Sat. 10–4; rest of yr, Tues.–Sat. 10–4.*

★ **Women's Rights National Historical Park.** Exhibits and an orientation film at the park visitor center explore the development of the women's rights movement in the United States. The park encompasses the site of the first Women's Rights Convention as well as three nearby houses where key convention participants lived.

The meticulously restored **Elizabeth Cady Stanton House** (✉ 32 Washington St. ☎ 315/568–2991 ☞ $1) is where one of American feminism's most important leaders shaped social reform as she raised seven children. Stanton's feminist colleague, Susan B. Anthony of Rochester, was a guest in the house. A tour helps you to understand Stanton's charisma and power. The house is open only by tour, by appointment, from March through October; check in first at the park visitor center. The M'Clintock House and the Hunt House are in the village of Waterloo, 3 mi from the Elizabeth Cady Stanton House. Inquire about tour availability for the two Waterloo houses at the park visitor center.

The **Wesleyan Chapel Declaration Park** (✉ 126 Fall St. ☎ 315/568–2991) was the site of the 1848 Women's Rights Convention. The gathering of 300 women and men produced the Declaration of Sentiments, the bedrock document of the modern women's rights movement. It proclaimed—audaciously, at the time—"that all men and women are created equal." The document's words are etched on a 140-foot-long wall between the larger park's visitor center and Declaration Park, which encompasses a steel structure housing remnants of the chapel. ✉ *136 Fall St.* ☎ *315/568–2991* ⊕ *www.nps.gov/wori* ☞ *$3* ⊙ *Daily 9–5.*

FESTIVALS & **Empire Farm Days.** For three days every August the Empire State Potato
FAIRS Growers organization draws tens of thousands of farmers and hobby agriculturalists to a field filled with vendors promoting everything from giant tractors to alpaca fur. Food booths, operated by community not-for-profit groups, sell sausage sandwiches, ice cream, and other fare. ✉ *Rte. 414 near County House Rd., just south of Seneca Falls* ☎ *877/697–7837* ⊕ *www.empirefarmdays.com.*

Where to Eat

¢ ✗ **ZuZu Cafe.** You get free Internet access with the espresso drinks, panini and wrap sandwiches, soups, salads, tortes, pies, and gelato here. The restaurant is named after ZuZu, the daughter of the George Bailey character in the 1946 cinema classic "It's a Wonderful Life." The movie's director, Frank Capra, visited Seneca Falls, and some say the movie's Bedford Falls setting was modeled after the village. ✉ *107 Fall St.* ☎ *315/568–2929* ☐ *AE, MC, V* ⊙ *No dinner Sun.*

¢–$ ✗ **Connie's Diner.** The chrome-trimmed diner, run by the Caratozzolo
★ family, serves tasty comfort food, all of it made in house. Eggplant parmesan, linguine with clam sauce, and liver and onions are popular dishes. The lasagna is made from an old family recipe. The pies—especially the coconut cream and raspberry—are glorious. ✉ *205 E. Main St., Waterloo* ☎ *315/539–9556* ⚏ *Reservations not accepted* ☐ *No credit cards* ⊙ *Closed Mon.*

Shopping

Polo Ralph Lauren, Coach, Calvin Klein, Brooks Brothers, London Fog, J. Crew, Jones New York, Eddie Bauer, Casual Corner, Yankee Candle—you'll recognize most of the names you see at the **Waterloo Premium Outlets** (✉ 655 Rte. 318, Waterloo ☎ 315/539–1100). Laid out in arcs forming a loose circle, the stores have exterior entrances connected by a covered walkway. **Sauder's Store** (✉ 2168 River Rd. ☎ 315/568–2673) is an authentic Mennonite market, with Pennsylvania Dutch meats and cheeses and hundreds of bulk containers brimming with baking supplies, candies, and spices. The eclectic inventory mix includes fresh produce, an array of Bibles, maps, children's books, simple toys, wooden sheds, and swing sets. Young people in traditional Mennonite garb staff the store, which John Sauder's family has run for decades. A farmer's market with 15 or so vendors selling fresh flowers, plants, crafts, produce, and other goods is held Friday 9–7 in and around a barn on the store property.

Geneva

9 *10 mi west of Seneca Falls.*

In the Seneca Lake city of Geneva (population 12,000), wonderful examples of Federal, Victorian Gothic, and Jeffersonian (aka Roman-revival) architecture, among other styles, document two centuries of history. South Main Street row houses dating from the 1820s line Pulteney Park, designed in 1794 as Geneva's original town square. Emancipation celebrations were held here in the 1800s, with Frederick Douglass and Sojourner Truth delivering orations. A bare-breasted sculpture named *Peace* presides over the park, which is not even a block away from the campuses of Hobart and William Smith colleges. A former Finger Lakes steamship port and manufacturing center, Geneva remains an agricultural hub; Cornell University's Agricultural Experiment Station is based here.

Prouty-Chew Museum. The 1829 mansion, run by the Geneva Historical Society, contains period rooms and local history exhibits. It's a good place to orient yourself to Geneva's rich social and cultural history. ✉ *543 S. Main St.* ☎ *315/789–5151* ✆ *Free* ⊙ *Tues.–Fri. 9:30–4:30, Sat. 1:30–4:30, Sun. (July and Aug.) 1:30–4:30.*

Fodor'sChoice ★ **Rose Hill Mansion.** Six huge Ionic columns front this restored 1839 Greek-revival mansion overlooking Seneca Lake. More than 20 rooms are open to the public. They include servants' quarters, the children's playroom, the kitchen, formal dining room, and parlors. Some rooms are outfitted with the Empire-style furnishings that were used from 1850 to 1890 by the prosperous farm family that lived here. Guided tours of the house begin with an introductory film. The grounds include boxwood gardens. A Civil War reenactors' encampment is one of the summer events here. ✉ *Rte. 96A* ☎ *315/789–3848* ⊕ *www.genevahistoricalsociety.com* ✆ *$3* ⊙ *May–Oct., Mon.–Sat. 10–4, Sun. 1–5.*

🅲 **Seneca Lake State Park.** The longest stretch of accessible public lakeshore in the Finger Lakes extends for 2 mi here at the northern tip of Seneca Lake. A children's splash playground with brightly colored water fountains and benches is a popular draw. A tree-lined walking and biking path along the shore leads from the park to downtown Geneva. Other amenities here include picnic tables, a swimming beach, and a marina. The view south from here is spectacular. ✉ *Rte. 5/U.S. 20* ☎ *315/789–2331* ⊕ *nysparks.state.ny.us* ✆ *Parking $7 mid-June–early Sept., $6 early Sept.–late Oct.* ⊙ *Daily dawn–dusk.*

off the beaten path

SAMPSON STATE PARK AND NAVAL MUSEUM – Swim, fish, boat, camp, and walk for miles at this 1,852-acre park. Thousands of U.S. soldiers trained here on the shore of Seneca Lake during World War II, when Sampson was the nation's second-largest naval-training station. A boat launch and 120-plus berths line the marina, next to a gravel swimming beach. More than 240 campsites are nestled among wooded areas. Tennis courts, playgrounds, and a concession stand, open in summer, are also part of the complex. The on-site museum honors the program that brought navy trainees here. ⊠ *Rte. 96A, 13 mi southeast of Geneva* ☎ *315/585–6392 park, 800/357–1814 museum* ⊕ *nysparks.state.ny.us* ⌷ *Parking $7 late June–early Sept.* ☉ *Park daily dawn–dusk; museum Memorial Day–Labor Day, Wed.–Sun. 10–3:30.*

Where to Stay & Eat

$–$$$ ✕ **Pasta Only Cobblestone Restaurant.** Pasta, veal, beef, and fresh-fish dishes are served with contemporary flair at this circa-1820 restaurant, a former stagecoach stop. Dishes might include veal chop stuffed with spinach, smoked mozzarella, and roasted garlic, or pan-seared tuna in soy-ginger sauce with white-bean puree and roasted artichokes. The breads and pastas, as well as the chocolate soufflé, are made on the premises. Fireplaces add to the elegant but cozy ambience. Balcony and porch dining are seasonal alternatives. ⊠ *3610 Pre-Emption Rd./Rte. 5/U.S. 20* ☎ *315/789–8498* ⊟ *AE, D, DC, MC, V* ☉ *Closed Mon.*

¢ ✕ **Water Street Cafe.** Photos of tourists from around the world decorate this casual cash-only eatery. A low-carbohydrate menu mirrors the Atkins diet plan. But the aroma of the home fries makes these carbs hard to resist. The café has counter service, booths, and tables as well as outdoor seating. ⊠ *467 Exchange St.* ☎ *315/789–2560* ⊟ *No credit cards* ☉ *No dinner.*

$$–$$$ ✕ **Belhurst Castle.** The 1889 stone castle (with a 2004 expansion) is
Fodor'sChoice listed on the National Register of Historic Places and has a tower. These
★ are plush digs. Many of the rooms in the original castle structure have four-poster beds, lake-view balconies, beautiful bamboo and maple woodwork, and bronze fireplaces. The newer rooms, in what's called the Vinifera Inn, have king-size beds, gas fireplaces, CD players, two-person showers, and honor bars. Edgar's ($$$–$$$$), the more formal restaurant, features steak and veal dishes. The Stonecutter's Lounge serves sandwiches, potato skins, and other pub fare. The property includes a wine-tasting room and a wine and gift shop. ⊠ *Rte. 14 S, 14456* ☎ *315/781–0201* ⊕ *www.belhurst.com* ⌂ *46 rooms ⌂ Restaurant, in-room data ports, some in-room hot tubs, some minibars, cable TV, in-room DVD players, 2 bars, pub, Internet, business services, no smoking rooms; no TV in some rooms* ⊟ *MC, V* ⑩ *CP.*

★ $$$–$$$$ ⌷ **Geneva on the Lake.** Here's a slice of Europe at the edge of Seneca Lake. Formally manicured grounds and Italian Renaissance architecture are part of the villa flavor. The stunning white manor, built in 1914, has fireplaces of Italian marble and rich upholstery and tapestries. Rooms are furnished with different styles of Stickley furniture. Ten suites have two bedrooms. Studios have living rooms and Murphy beds. Spend a summer afternoon playing lawn games or taking a pontoon boat ride on Seneca Lake. ⊠ *1001 Lochland Rd./Rte. 14, 14456* ☎ *315/789–7190* ☎ *315/789–0322* ⊕ *www.genevaonthelake.com* ⌂ *23 suites, 6 studios ⌂ Restaurant, in-room data ports, kitchenettes, cable TV, in-room DVD players, pool, gym, fishing, badminton, boccie, croquet, lounge,* *piano, babysitting, laundry service, concierge, Internet, business services, meeting rooms, no-smoking rooms* ▭ *AE, D, MC, V* ⑩ *CP.*

$$ ▦ **Ramada Inn Geneva Lakefront.** Geneva has this Ramada, a full-service convention center, as the anchor of its lakeshore. Rooms have a view of either Seneca Lake or the city; first-floor lakeside rooms have patios. The decor varies, with some rooms more traditional and others more contemporary. Only a sweeping wall of glass stands between its Pier House restaurant and Seneca Lake, 100 feet from the dining tables. A 2-mi lakeside walkway and a pier you can walk out on are adjacent to the hotel. ✉ *41 Lakefront Dr., 14456* ☎ *315/789–0400 or 800/990–0907* 🖷 *315/ 789–4351* ⊕ *www.ramadageneva.com* ⇖ *148 rooms, 8 suites* ᗕ *Restaurant, in-room data ports, some in-room hot tubs, some microwaves, some refrigerators, cable TV, pool, lake, exercise equipment, bar, lounge, video game room, dry cleaning, laundry facilities, laundry service, Internet, business services, convention center, some pets allowed (fee), no-smoking floors* ▭ *AE, D, DC, MC, V.*

¢ ▦ **Clark's Motel.** The single-story motel, a local landmark since the 1950s, sits back from busy Route 5/U.S. 20. The current owners took over in 1979. The decor is simple and the technology is late 20th century. Behind the units are 2 acres with tall evergreens, a garden, and a gazebo. Retirees and travelers who prefer byways to highways frequent the place. ✉ *824 Canandaigua Rd./Rte. 5/U.S. 20, 14456* ☎ *315/789– 0780* ⇖ *10 rooms* ᗕ *Cable TV, no-smoking rooms; no room phones* ▭ *MC, V* ☾ *Closed Dec.–Mar.*

¢ ▦ **The Farr Inn.** The Tudor home, on one of Geneva's most handsome
Fodor'sChoice residential streets, opened to guests in 2003. Oriental rugs are scattered
★ throughout the house—even in the bathrooms. Antiques from Sri Lanka—a 400-year-old brass-and-wood chest, a dining-room cupboard, ebony chairs, rosewood tables—help recapture the feel of the turn-of-the-20th-century bungalow in the Ceylonese highlands where the hostess vacationed as a child. Pieces from Mexico, her husband's homeland, add to the multicultural ambience. ✉ *164 Washington St., 14456* ☎ *315/789–7730 or 877/700–3277* ⊕ *www.thefarrinn.com* ⇖ *2 rooms* ᗕ *Dining room, business services, some pets allowed; no room phones, no a/c, no room TVs, no kids under 10, no smoking* ▭ *AE, MC, V* ⑩ *BP.*

Nightlife & the Arts

The 1894 **Smith Opera House** (✉ 82 Seneca St. ☎ 315/781–5483 or 866/ 355–5483 ⊕ www.thesmith.org) presents stage productions, concerts, and films. The exterior of the theater, built by Geneva philanthropist William Smith, is Richardson Romanesque. The interior was gutted in 1930 and redone in art-deco and baroque motifs as an "atmosphere" movie palace with light-up stars on the ceiling. Along with Radio City Music Hall, it's one of the few remaining atmospheric theaters still in use. George M. Cohan, Billy Joel, Bruce Springsteen, and many other famous performers have commanded the stage here. Tours are given by appointment.

Sports & the Outdoors

FISHING Whoever catches the biggest fish at the **National Lake Trout Derby** (✉ Lakeshore Park, 35 Lakefront Dr. ☎ 315/781–2195 or 315/789–

8634), held every Memorial Day weekend, wins $5,000. Also awarded are 45 other cash prizes totaling nearly $30,000.

Watkins Glen

❿ *36 mi south of Geneva.*

Watkins Glen State Park, one of the state's premier natural wonders, is one reason to visit this small village (population 2,500). On the south edge of Seneca Lake, this residential community attracts boaters, who sail from Seneca Harbor. This is also wine and car-racing country. U.S. car racing, which had been halted because of World War II, was revived in Watkins Glen in 1948. Until the current speedway opened in 1956, the competing cars would roar through the center of the village. Area wineries range from large-production operations to intimate family-run vineyards. The Rieslings are among Seneca Lake's most celebrated wines.

Captain Bill's Seneca Lake Cruises. The captain runs meal cruises and 10-mi lake trips from the end of Franklin Street. Cruises range from $8.50 for sightseeing excursions to $33–$38 for dinner cruises. ⊠ *1 N. Franklin St.* ☎ *607/535–4541* ⊕ *www.senecaharborstation.com* ☉ *May–Oct.; call for schedules.*

☺ Farm Sanctuary. A 175-acre working farm and educational center, the sanctuary houses livestock and other animals brought from slaughterhouses and stockyards and nursed back to health. You're encouraged to pet the animals. Tours are given on the hour, 11–3. ⊠ *3100 Aikens Rd.* ☎ *607/583 2225* ⊕ *www.farmsanctuary.org* ⊠ *Visitor center free, tours $2* ☉ *June–Aug., Wed.–Sun. 10–4; May, Sept., and Oct., weekends 10–4.*

Fodor'sChoice ★ **Finger Lakes National Forest.** On a ridge between the southern ends of Cayuga and Seneca lakes, 9 mi north of Watkins Glen, the national forest offers more than 30 mi of easy-to-moderate hiking trails through a variety of terrain. The land was patched together when the federal government purchased about 100 farms between 1938 and 1941. The forest encompasses 16,032 acres, so you might feel like you have the place to yourself—regardless of whether you're camping, cross-country skiing, fishing, or hunting. The forest's altitude is higher than most surrounding points, so great vistas are yours for the hiking. Trail maps are available at some trailheads and at the visitor center. ⊠ *Visitor Center, 5218 Rte. 414, Hector* ☎ *607/546–4470* ⊕ *www.fs.fed.us/r9/gmfl/* ⊠ *Free* ☉ *Daily dawn–dusk; visitor center weekdays 8–4:30, Sat. 10–4:30.*

Watkins Glen International Raceway. "New York's Thunder Road" rumbles from June to September. The season's highlight is the **NASCAR Series,** in mid-August. On a Thunder Road tour ($25), you drive the track in your own vehicle behind a pace car. Call for event schedules and prices. ⊠ *2790 Rte. 16* ☎ *607/535–2481* ⊕ *www.theglen.com* ☉ *May–Oct.*

Fodor'sChoice ★ **Watkins Glen State Park.** The main entrance to this park is in Watkins Glen. Campgrounds are scattered around the beautiful Glen Creek. The waters drop about 500 feet in 2 mi and include 19 waterfalls. The

1½-mi **gorge trail** runs parallel to the creek, and 300-foot cliffs border the water. One bridge spans 165 feet over the water. The park also has an Olympic-size pool. "Timespell," a computerized light-and-sound show, explains the geological development of the gorge. It's screened on the sides of the glen. The gorge isn't accessible in winter. ✉ *Franklin St. near Rte. 17/Old Corning Rd.* ☎ *607/535–4511* ⊕ *nysparks.state. ny.us* 🚗 *Parking $7 late May–early Sept., $6 early Sept.–Oct.* ۞ *Daily dawn–dusk.*

FESTIVALS & FAIRS **Finger Lakes Wine Festival.** More than 70 wineries participate in this three-day festival held annually in July at the Watkins Glen International Raceway. Tastings, seminars, cooking demonstrations, live musical entertainment, and food are part of the event. A one-day ticket costs about $30. ✉ *Watkins Glen International Raceway, 2790 Rte. 16* ☎ *607/535–2481* ⊕ *www.flwinefest.com.*

Grand Prix Festival. In this daylong reenactment held every autumn in Watkins Glen, vintage race cars zoom through village streets, following part of the original 6.6-mi circuit. Inductions into the Drivers' Walk of Fame are made and memorabilia booths are set up in the village, where fireworks and other events honor the area's racing heritage. ☎ *607/535–4300* ⊕ *www.lightlink.com/gpfest/.*

Where to Stay & Eat

$$–$$$ ✕ **Castel Grisch.** Strudel and Swiss fondue highlight the Bavarian deli lunches at this restaurant, part of Castel Grisch winery. German dishes, such as sauerbraten and schnitzels, dominate the dinner menu, but steak and duck preparations also are available. ✉ *3380 Rte. 28* ☎ *607/535–9614* ⊟ *AE, D, MC, V* ۞ *Closed Mon.–Weds. and Jan. No dinner Thurs.*

$–$$$ ✕ **Wildflower Cafe.** The upscale yet casual restaurant occupies a brick-and-wood building near the entrance of Watkins Glen State Park. Oak and brass touches and stained-glass windows accent the interior. Louisiana scampi, jambalaya, ribs, and duck are specialties. ✉ *301 N. Franklin St.* ☎ *607/535–9797* ⊟ *AE, MC, V.*

★ $–$$$ ✕🏨 **Inn at Glenora Wine Cellars.** The deluxe inn, 8 mi north of Watkins Glen, was built in 1999 as an addition to a working winery on the Seneca Lake Wine Trail. Most rooms, furnished with Stickley pieces, overlook the west bank of Seneca Lake; some rooms have fireplaces. Veraisons, the restaurant ($$–$$$), serves contemporary American dishes such as duck breast with pecan-and-maple stuffing and Dijon-marinated rack of lamb. Cathedral ceilings and a stone fireplace grace the dining area. ✉ *5435 Rte. 14, Dundee 14837* ☎ *607/243–9500 or 800/243–5513* ⊕ *www.glenora.com* 🛏 *30 rooms* ♿ *Restaurant, picnic area, some in-room hot tubs, refrigerators, cable TV, business services, no-smoking rooms* ⊟ *AE, D, MC, V* 🍽 *CP weekdays.*

¢–$ 🏨 **Longhouse Lodge Motel and Manor.** You get views of Seneca Lake from the rooms, deck, and gazebo of this motel and adjacent B&B atop a hill off Route 14 just north of Watkins Glen. Rooms have king-size or double beds. Some rooms have VCRs; free movies are available in the lobby. ✉ *3625 Rte. 14, 14891* ☎ *607/535–2565* ⊕ *www.longhouselodge.*

com ⤴ *21 rooms* ⌂ *In-room data ports, 1 kitchenette, some microwaves, some refrigerators, cable TV, some in-room VCRs, pool, Internet, business services, some pets allowed (fee), no-smoking rooms* ▤ *D, MC, V* �|⊙| *CP.*

¢–$ 🏨 **Seneca Lake Watch Bed and Breakfast.** The Queen Anne Victorian has a watch tower and rooms and porches with Seneca Lake views. Accommodations are large and have modern bathrooms; two rooms have private sundecks. The common area has a telephone, fireplace, and piano. Porches wrap around the house, and a lawn gazebo is lighted at night. ⊠ *104 Seneca St., 14891* ☎ *607/535–4490* ⊕ *www.bbhost.com/ senecalakewatchbb/* ⤴ *5 rooms* ⌂ *Dining room, picnic area, piano, no-smoking rooms; no room phones, no room TVs* ▤ *AE, MC, V* ⊙ *BP.*

Sports & the Outdoors

FISHING **Catharine Creek**, famous among anglers for its spring run of rainbow trout, is a premier fishing tributary in the Finger Lakes. Several miles south of Watkins Glen, it flows through a huge wetland and into the southern tip of **Seneca Lake**, which is known for its northern pike, lake trout, salmon, and bass fishing. Pull-offs along Route 14 give you access to Catharine Creek. You can fish the lake from a 300-foot public pier that's just steps from the center of downtown Watkins Glen.

ELMIRA & CORNING

Elmira and Corning anchor the Finger Lakes region in the south, about 10 mi north of the Pennsylvania border. Route 17 links the two, and both are bisected by the Chemung River.

Elmira

⑪ *22 mi south of Watkins Glen.*

Settled in 1788, Elmira was the site of one of the battles of the Sullivan-Clinton expedition of 1779, during which a colonial army routed Native American allied with the British. In the 19th century the city got its industrial start with lumbering and woolen mills. Confederate soldiers were held at a prison camp here during the Civil War; conditions were so bad that thousands of prisoners died.

Elmira's most famous resident, Samuel Clemens (aka Mark Twain), spent more than 20 summers at Quarry Farm, which belonged to his wife's family. The city has also been known as the "soaring capital of America," since it hosted the first national soaring contest in 1930.

Arnot Art Museum. The core collection at this museum came from 19th-century Elmira banker Mathias Arnot, who acquired paintings by Jan Brueghel (the elder), Jean-François Millet, and others. European paintings from the 17th to the 19th century and American paintings from the 19th and 20th century—including works by Thomas Cole, Robert Henri, and Thomas Sully—are also in the collection. The museum is housed in an 1833 mansion with a modern addition. ⊠ *235 Lake St.* ☎ *607/734–3697* ⊕ *www.arnotartmuseum.org* ▨ *$5* ⊙ *Tues.–Sat. 10–5, Sun. 1–5.*

Chemung Valley History Museum. Exhibits about the Seneca Nation, Mark Twain, and Elmira's Civil War prison camp are part of this local downtown museum. ⊠ *415 E. Water St.* ☎ *607/734–4167* ⊕ *www. chemungvalleymuseum.org* 🗺 *$3* ⊙ *Tues.–Sat. 10–5, Sun. 1–5.*

Mark Twain's Study. Twain wrote *The Adventures of Huckleberry Finn* and *The Adventures of Tom Sawyer* in this study built for him by his sister-in-law. The octagonal shape was inspired by a Mississippi riverboat pilothouse. The study was moved to the Elmira College campus in the 1950s and is part of the school's Center for Mark Twain Studies. ⊠ *Elmira College, Park Ave.* ☎ *607/735–1941* ⊕ *www.elmira.edu* 🗺 *Free* ⊙ *Mid-Apr.–Oct., Mon.–Sat. 9–5 and Sun. noon–5, or by appointment.*

★ ℧ **National Soaring Museum.** Dozens of sailplanes and gliders are on display at this museum, part of Harris Hill Park. Movies and exhibits help explain and explore the heritage of gliding. ⊠ *Harris Hill Park, 51 Soaring Hill Dr., off Rte. 17, 15 mi west of downtown Elmira* ☎ *607/734–3128* ⊕ *www.soaringmuseum.org* 🗺 *$6.50* ⊙ *Daily 10–5.*

Woodlawn Cemetery. Mark Twain rests in the Langdon family plot, with his son-in-law, Ossip Gabrilowitsch, at his feet. A 12-foot tall monument marks the spot (12 feet, in river terminology, is 2 fathoms, or "mark twain"). ⊠ *1200 Walnut St.* ☎ *607/732–0151* 🗺 *Free* ⊙ *Daily dawn–dusk.*

Woodlawn National Cemetery. Next to the main Woodlawn Cemetery, this burial ground has the graves of 2,963 Confederate prisoners who died in the prison in Elmira, as well as the graves of 322 Union soldiers. The Elmira Correctional Facility, at Davis Street and Bancroft Road, sits on the site of the city's Civil War prison camp. ⊠ *1825 Davis St.* ☎ *607/732–5411* ⊕ *www.cem.va.gov* 🗺 *Free* ⊙ *Grounds daily dawn–dusk, office weekdays 8–4:30.*

Where to Eat

$$–$$$$ ✕ **Moretti's.** Established in 1917, this family-owned neighborhood restaurant in downtown Elmira serves generous portions of Italian food, steaks, and chops. It is known for its filet mignon. The five dining areas range from comfy, old-fashioned booths to classy cloth-covered tables, and there are two full bars. ⊠ *800 Hatch St.* ☎ *607/734–1535* 🖃 *AE, D, MC, V* ⊙ *No lunch.*

$–$$$ ✕ **Hill Top Inn.** A giant wreath with a shamrock beckons from a hill, making this family-owned restaurant hard to miss. The menu has mostly American fare, with some contemporary and Continental dishes such as braised tenderloin tips with peppers and onions in Cajun cream sauce, or lamb chops dressed with mint jelly. Steak and seafood dishes are popular choices. Open-air dining is an option on the deck and terrace. ⊠ *171 Jerusalem Hill Rd.* ☎ *607/732–6728* 🖃 *AE, D, DC, MC, V* ⊙ *Closed Sun. No lunch.*

$–$$$ ✕ **Pierce's 1894 Restaurant.** The restaurant has several dining areas, including the formal Parlor Room and the clubby, wood-paneled Village Room. The lounge serves casual fare: French onion soup, scampi, crab cakes, individual pizzas. The mostly Continental dining-room menu includes bouillabaisse, roast rack of lamb, and chateaubriand. The bar can make 52 types of martini; regulars can get a card to keep track of how many they've sampled. The restaurant is a 15-minute drive from downtown. ⊠ *228 Oakwood Ave.* ☎ *607/734–2022* ⊟ *AE, D, MC, V.*

¢–$ ✕**Anne's Pancakes.** Home cooking is the star here: country-fried steak, burgers, homemade pies, rice pudding, and the tasty pancakes. On weekends the place closes at noon. ⊠ *114 S. Main St.* ☎ *607/732–9591* ⊟ *No credit cards.*

Corning

⓬ *22 mi west of Elmira.*

One of the world's glass centers, Corning has an appropriate nickname: Crystal City. The Corning Museum of Glass, the big draw here, is one of New York State's major tourist attractions. The town's restored 19th-century Market Street district, Corning's main commercial strip, has interesting storefronts and restaurants and is also worth a visit.

Benjamin Patterson Inn Museum Complex. Guides in period dress take you through this complex of buildings that includes a log cabin, a one-room schoolhouse, a barn, and a blacksmith shop. The centerpiece is a restored 1796 inn. ⊠ *59 W. Pulteney St.* ☎ *607/937–5281* ⊕ *www.corningny. com/bpinn* ⊡ *$4* ⊘ *Mid-Mar.–mid-Dec., weekdays 10–4.*

☾ **Corning Museum of Glass.** About 10,000 of the more than 35,000 glass
Fodor'sChoice objects in the museum's collection are on display at any one time. The
★ works range from contemporary pieces to Frank Lloyd Wright and Louis Comfort Tiffany stained-glass windows to glassware crafted by Egyptians 3,500 years ago. Catch the Hot Glass Show, a live glassmaking demonstration. A workshop encourages you to make your own glass souvenir ($7–$40); even preschoolers may participate. Interactive exhibits show the history, beauty, and creativity of 35 centuries of glasswork. ⊠ *1 Museum Way* ☎ *607/937–53271 or 800/732–6845* ⊕ *www. cmog.org* ⊡ *$12* ⊘ *Early Sept.–June, daily 9–5; July–early Sept., daily 9–8.*

Market Street. Flooded by Hurricane Agnes in 1972, the city's main street was restored to evoke the late 19th century, with brick sidewalks and plenty of trees. It also has more than 20 restaurants and a number of glass-art studios. A shuttle bus leaves the area for the Corning Museum of Glass every 20 minutes. ⊠ *Between Denison Pkwy. and Tioga Ave.* ☎ *No phone.*

Rockwell Museum of Western Art. The museum has the largest collection of Western American art in the East. Art from the 19th and 20th centuries and Native American artifacts and works show the people, places, and ideas of the West. Kids get to use special interactive backpacks as they go through the displays. The museum occupies an 1893 building, the old city hall, in the historic Market Street district. A Southwestern restaurant is on the premises. ⊠ *111 Cedar St.* ☎ *607/937–5386* ⊕ *www.rockwellmuseum.org* ⊡ *$6.50* ⊘ *Early Sept.–June, daily 9–5; July–early Sept., daily 9–8.*

Where to Stay & Eat

$–$$$ ✗ **London Underground Cafe.** The café is named after the London subway, and the British theme carries throughout. Paintings of the Underground adorn the walls, and teapots and British china are on display. The three-level dining room provides plenty of space, and the menu includes fish-and-chips, burgers, and generous salads. Open-air dining is available. A pianist plays on Saturday evening. ⊠ *69 E. Market St.* ☎ *607/ 962–2345* ⊟ *AE, D, DC, MC, V* ☉ *Closed Sun.*

¢–$$$ ✗ **Spencer's Restaurant and Mercantile.** This rustic, family-oriented restaurant is popular with the locals, and has a large and varied menu that includes chicken and biscuits, steak, chops, fish fry, taco salads, seafood, and pasta dishes. ⊠ *359 E. Market St.* ☎ *607/936–9196* ⊟ *AE, D, DC, MC, V.*

$–$$ ✗ **Market Street Brewing Company and Restaurant.** Five beers, two lagers, and red, pale, and dark ales are brewed on-site throughout the year. Each season brings its own specialty brew. The kitchen incorporates Thai, Southwestern, Mexican, Caribbean, and Italian influences, among others, in dishes such as grilled pork medallions with chipotle-maple glaze, jalapeño relish, and fried sweet potatoes, or grilled fresh salmon fillet with cucumber-wasabi sauce, rice, and veggies. Chicken wings and burgers are also available. Beer suggestions accompany entrée descriptions. ⊠ *63–65 W. Market St.* ☎ *607/936–2337* ⊟ *AE, MC, V* ☉ *Closed Sun. and Mon. Nov.–Mar.*

¢–$ ✗ **Old World Cafe & Ice Cream.** Grilled panini, homemade quiche and soup, and imported cheeses are the preludes to dessert at this Victorian ice-cream parlor. Ice cream, of course, finishes the meal, as does old-fashioned candy. ⊠ *W. Market St. and Centerway* ☎ *607/936–1953* ⊟ *D, MC, V* ☉ *Closed Sun. early Sept.–May.*

$–$$ ▥ **Rosewood Inn.** The 1855 home is three blocks from downtown and less than 1 mi from the Corning Museum of Glass. Guest rooms, decked out in Victorian style, have antiques, plush towels, and 300-thread-count sheets. Some have canopy beds. Only the suites, both on the first floor, have phones. One suite has twin beds, and the other has a sitting area with a television. Porch-sitting in summer is replaced by 4 PM tea and cookies by the parlor fireplace in winter. ⊠ *134 E. 1st St., 14830* ☎ *607/962–3253* ⊕ *www.rosewoodinn.com* ⊅ *5 rooms, 2 suites* ⚘ *Dining room, 1 kitchenette; no phones in some rooms, no TV in some rooms, no kids under 12, no smoking* ⊟ *AE, D, DC, MC, V* ▯ *BP.*

¢–$$ ▥ **Comfort Inn.** In a quiet residential neighborhood, this two-story hotel is within walking distance of Market Street, the Rockwell Museum, and the Benjamin Patterson Inn Museum Complex. Rooms are basic but spacious; some have jet tubs. The lobby is large and comfortable. The indoor pool is a plus. ⊠ *66 W. Pulteney St., 14830* ☎ *607/962–1515* ⊟ *607/ 962–1899* ⊕ *www.comfortinn.com* ⊅ *62 rooms* ⚘ *In-room data ports, some in-room hot tubs, some refrigerators, cable TV, indoor pool, gym, laundry service, business services, no-smoking rooms* ⊟ *AE, D, DC, MC, V* ▯ *CP.*

¢–$ ▥ **Days Inn.** The budget chain property, a modern-looking building with interior corridors and elevators, is the closest lodging to Corning's two major attractions, the Corning Glass Museum and Market Street. The rooms are no-frills, but the facilities do include a heated indoor pool.

✉ *23 Riverside Dr., 14830* ☎ *607/936–9370* 🖷 *607/936–0513* ⊕ *www.daysinn.com* ➭ *56 rooms* ♨ *Restaurant, in-room data ports, some refrigerators, cable TV, indoor pool, gym, hot tub, laundry service, business services, no-smoking rooms* ▤ *AE, D, DC, MC, V* 🍴 *CP.*

KEUKA & CANANDAIGUA LAKES

By Kathie Connelly, Anne Johnston

Possibly best known for its sloping vineyards and numerous wineries, the area is rich in history and has scenery that can be enjoyed in any season—whether or not you're interested in wine. Keuka Lake, approximately 18 mi long, is Y-shaped, with the villages of Penn Yan and Branchport at its northern end and Hammondsport—the so-called Cradle of Aviation—at its southern end. Canandaigua Lake, the westernmost of the major Finger Lakes, includes Squaw Island, one of the few islands in the region. Legend has it that many Seneca women and children escaped slaughter by hiding on the island during the 1779 Clinton-Sullivan campaign to drive the tribe out of west-central New York.

Hammondsport

13 *28 mi northwest of Corning.*

Hammondsport, a small village nestled between soft hills at the southern end of Keuka Lake, is considered the heart of the region's wine-making industry. Native son Glenn Curtiss made the world's first preannounced flight here—a 5,090-foot trip aboard the *June Bug* in 1908. Hammondsport has interesting stores, including antiques shops and local crafts purveyors, and there are several small restaurants in town and along the lake.

Bully Hill Vineyards. The views of Keuka Lake from here are spectacular. A tour of the vineyard and winery includes the **Greyton H. Taylor Wine Museum** (☎ 607/868–4814 ☉ Mid-May–Oct., Mon.–Sat. 9–5, Sun. noon–5), which focuses on 18th-century wine-making equipment. Three gift shops are on the property: Seasons I & II, which showcase glassware, antiques, and candles, and the Heritage House, where you may buy posters, T-shirts, and other clothing. Lunch and dinner are available at the Bully Hill Restaurant. ✉ *8843 Greyton H. Taylor Memorial Dr., off Rte. 54A* ☎ *607/868–3226* ⊕ *www.bullyhill.com* 🏷 *Tour free, tasting $1* ☉ *Mon.–Sat. 10–6, Sun. 11–6.*

★ **Dr. Konstantin Frank's Vinifera Wine Cellars.** The winery, overlooking Keuka Lake, was started in the early 1960s and is run by the son and grandson of the founder, Dr. Konstantin Frank. A Ukrainian immigrant, Dr. Frank was a pioneer in growing classic European grapes in the region. Cabernet francs, Rieslings, pinot noirs, and Chardonnays (all European, or vinifera, varietals) are among Dr. Frank's offerings. The Rieslings are excellent, and the pinot noirs are really coming into their own. Also look for *rkatsiteli* (ar-kat-si-*tel*-lee), a spicy wine made from an Eastern European grape. ✉ *9749 Middle Rd., off Rte. 76* ☎ *800/320–0735* ⊕ *www.drfrankwines.com* 🏷 *Free* ☉ *Tasting room Mon.–Sat. 9–5, Sun. noon–5.*

Ⓒ **Glenn H. Curtiss Museum.** The museum, just outside Hammondsport proper, honors Curtiss and his early aviation experiments. The Hammondsport native made the first public preannounced flight when he flew his *June Bug* plane more than 5,000 feet outside the village on July 4, 1908. Exhibits include aircraft, engines, and a collection of antique motorcycles. ✉ *8419 Rte. 54* ☎ *607/569–2160* ⊕ *www.linkny. com/~curtiss/* ☑ *$6* ☉ *May–Oct., Mon.–Sat. 9–5, Sun. 11–5; Nov.–Apr., Mon.–Sat. 10–4, Sun. noon–5.*

Heron Hill Winery. Beautiful Keuka Lake views are one of the draws at this winery built by John and Josephine Ingle in 1977. John Ingle Jr. maintains the winery's Ingle Vineyards, which were planted on the western shore of Canandaigua Lake in 1972 and feature chardonnay, cabernet franc, merlot, Riesling, and pinot noir grapes. Heron Hill's winemaker, Thomas Laszlo, oversees the Heron Hill Vineyards, which were planted here in 1968 and include chardonnay and Riesling grapes. The Blue Heron Café is open from May through October. ✉ *9249 Rte. 76* ☎ *607/868–4241 or 800/441–4241* ⊕ *www.heronhill.com* ☑ *Tastings $1–$5* ☉ *Mon.–Sat. 10–5, Sun. noon–5.*

Keuka Maid. The three-deck boat, which can hold 500 travelers, offers cruises on Keuka Lake, from which you can take in the area's undulating hills and neat vineyards. Two decks have dance floors; all three have bars. Breakfast, lunch, dinner, and Sunday brunch cruises are offered from April to mid-November. ✉ *Rte. 54* ☎ *607/569–2628 or 607/569–3631* ⊕ *www.keukamaid.com.*

Pleasant Valley Wine Co. Established in 1860, this is one of the oldest wineries in the region. It offers various table, dessert, and sparkling wines. One of the highlights of the visitor center is a slide show you watch inside a 35,000-gallon wine tank. The winery is 3 mi south of Hammondsport center. ✉ *8260 Pleasant Valley Rd.* ☎ *607/569–6111* ☑ *Visitor center and tasting free, tour $3* ☉ *Jan.–Mar., Tues.–Sat. 10–4; Apr.–Dec., daily 10–5.*

Where to Stay & Eat

$$–$$$$ ✕ **Three Birds Restaurant.** The crisp, well-trained waitstaff is as impressive as the finely presented contemporary American fare. Specialty dishes include the crab-cake starter, pecan-encrusted pork tenderloin, and roasted New Zealand rack of lamb. Lift your eyes from the plate long enough to take in the view of Keuka Lake. Docking for boats is available. ✉ *144 W. Lake Rd.* ☎ *607/868–7684* ▭ *AE, D, MC, V.*

$–$$$ ✕ **Lakeside Restaurant.** This casual spot occupies an 1880s cottage inn on the west side of Keuka Lake. The food is American: prime rib, fried shrimp, bacon-wrapped beef tenderloin, barbecue chicken, a variety of steaks and chops, and Friday fish fry. Outside, a fire pit and 150 seats overlook the bluff of Keuka Lake. ✉ *800 W. Lake Rd.* ☎ *607/868–3636* ▭ *AE, D, MC, V* ☉ *No dinner Sun.–Thurs. No lunch mid-Oct.–late May.*

$–$$ ✕ **Bully Hill Restaurant.** A spectacular view of Keuka Lake awaits you at this breezy café, part of the Bully Hill Vineyards. The food is eclectic: Maryland crab cakes, buffalo burgers, or chicken or shrimp Florentine. Lunch also includes sandwiches and salads. A complete list of Bully Hill wines is available, too. ✉ *8843 Greyton H. Taylor Memorial Dr.* ☎ *607/ 868–3490* ▤ *AE, D, MC, V* ✪ *Closed Nov.–Apr. No dinner Sun.–Thurs.*

$–$$ 🏠 **Elm Croft Manor Bed & Breakfast.** Stately columns stand guard at the entrance of this 1832 Greek-revival house. Furnishings include antiques, four-poster and wrought-iron beds, and, in some rooms, richly patterned wallpapers. Bathrobes and hair dryers are nice extras. Common areas include a formal parlor and dining room and a screened-in porch with wicker furniture. The B&B has two resident cats. ✉ *8361 Pleasant Valley Rd., 14840* ☎ *607/569–3071 or 800/506–3071* ⊕ *www. elmcroftmanor.com* ↦ *4 rooms* ⚙ *Dining room; no room TVs, no kids, no smoking* ▤ *AE, MC, V* ⦿ *BP.*

$ 🏠 **Amity Rose.** The smell of freshly baked cookies welcomes you to this turn-of-the-20th-century home. Guest-room furnishings are a blend of Victorian and country-romantic styles. Two rooms have whirlpool tubs, two have fireplaces, and one has a private porch. The living room also has a fireplace. ✉ *8264 Main St., 14840* ☎ *607/569–3402 or 800/982– 8818* ⊕ *www.amityroseinn.com* ↦ *3 rooms, 1 suite* ⚙ *Dining room, some in-room hot tubs; no room phones, no room TVs, no kids under 12* ▤ *No credit cards* ✪ *Closed Jan.–Apr.* ⦿ *BP.*

Shopping

The Village Square is where you find most of the shopping in town. The merchandise at **The Cinnamon Stick** (✉ 26 Mechanic St. ☎ 607/569–2278), a gift shop owned by Terry Pennise, includes Christmas ornaments, teddy bears, candles, glassware, jewelry, chimes, and fancy-food items. **Opera House Antiques** (✉ 61–63 Shethar St. ☎ 607/569–3525) is a multi-dealer shop in a 1901 opera house off the Village Square. Furniture, jewelry, silverware, and linens are among the offerings. From January through April it's open only on weekends.

> **en route** Route 54A runs along the west shore of Keuka Lake, between Hammondsport and Penn Yan. On the way, you come to **Bluff Point,** which sits on a headland between the two branches of the wishbone-shape lake and offers breathtaking views of the water. From Bluff Point, detour east through the hamlet of Keuka Park (the home of Keuka College) and take a long, leisurely ride along Skyline Drive, which gives you more spectacular views of the lake.

Penn Yan

🄮 *21 mi north of Hammondsport.*

The small village, which incorporated in 1833 and took its name from its early Pennsylvania and Yankee residents, is at the north end of Keuka Lake. Penn Yan is the seat of Yates County as well as home to Birket Mills, one of the largest producers of buckwheat in the world. Visitors come here mainly for the wineries, spectacular lake views, summer recreational opportunities, and vibrant fall foliage. A drive down the main street, with its shops, restaurants, post office, and Victorian-style houses, is a drive through small-town America. Members of the Mennonite community mix in with the traffic in their horses and buggies.

Oliver House Museum. The museum of the Yates County Historical Society is in an 1852 house that was the residence of the Olivers, a well-known local family of physicians. Guided tours lead you through the Victorian rooms and historical exhibits. Revolving exhibits may cover period furniture, costumes and textiles, carpentry and blacksmithing tools, Native American artifacts, paintings and photographs, and decorative arts. ⊠ *200 Main St.* ☎ *315/536–7318* ⊕ *www.yatespast.com* ⊠ *$5* ☉ *Weekdays 9:30–4:30.*

Viking Spirit Cruise Ship. In season, cruises aboard the *Spirit* leave daily from the Viking Resort. A cruise around Keuka Lake takes an hour, during which you can take in the views of the surrounding shore, hills, and vineyards. ⊠ *680 East Lake Rd./Rte. 54* ☎ *315/536–7061* ⊕ *www.vikingresort.com* ⊠ *$8* ☉ *Mid-May–mid-Oct.; call for schedule.*

FESTIVALS & FAIRS
Yates County Fair. The fair, one of the oldest in the state, is held over five days in early July. Traditional activities include a demolition derby, amusement rides, kids' games, petting farms, 4-H exhibits, and various musical performers. ⊠ *Penn Yan Fairgrounds, Old Rte. 14A* ☎ *800/ 868–9283* ⊕ *www.yatesny.com.*

Where to Stay & Eat

¢–$ ✕ **Essenhaus Restaurant.** With its airy dining space, tall windows, and ceiling fans, the country-style eatery instantly makes you feel welcome and comfortable. Many of the dishes and baked goods served here—like "church supper ham loaf" and shoofly pie—are inspired by the area's Mennonite community. On site is a wonderful bake shop; the loft gift shop carries items crafted by local Mennonites. Benton is a few miles north of Penn Yan. ⊠ *1300 Rte. 14A, Benton* ☎ *315/531–8260* ☰ *MC, V* ☉ *Closed Mon.*

¢–$ ✕ **Penn Yan Diner.** Stepping into this diner in a 1925 E. B. Richardson Galon dining car is like stepping back in time. The eatery offers breakfast, lunch, and dinner menus of diner staples. Delectable homemade pies are what the place is known for, so save room for dessert. ⊠ *131 E. Elm St.* ☎ *315/536–6004* ☰ *No credit cards* ☉ *Closed Sun. and Mon.*

$$$–$$$$ ▦ **Esperanza Mansion.** The stately Greek-revival mansion, built in 1838, sits on a hill overlooking Keuka Lake. Some guest rooms are in the mansion, but most are in the separate two-story inn building. Rooms have four-poster and sleigh beds, armoires, and decorative fireplaces. White-washed furniture and quilted bedspreads give the inn a casual cottage feel. Regardless of which building you're in, the views are spectacular. Linger over a cocktail on the outdoor terrace and drink in the lake, surrounding hills, and farms. The Esperanza is 16 mi north of Hammondsport. ⊠ *3456 Route 54A, Bluff Point 14478* ☎ *315/536–4400* ☐ *315/ 536–4900* ⊕ *www.esperanzamansion.com* ✍ *9 mansion rooms, 21 inn rooms* ☖ *Restaurant, in-room data ports, cable TV, bar, library, business services, meeting rooms; no smoking* ☰ *AE, D, DC, MC, V* ◯| *CP.*

$–$$ ▦ **Merritt Hill Manor.** The 1822 country estate on 12 acres just outside Penn Yan has views of both Keuka and Seneca lakes. You might sit on the front porch in an Adirondack chair or curl up with a book in front of the living-room fireplace. Guest rooms are decorated in charming country style; some have four-poster beds. A hearty country breakfast awaits in the morning. ✉ *2756 Coates Rd., 14527* ☎ *315/536–7682* ⊕ *www. merritthillmanor.com* ⇨ *5 rooms* ⌂ *Dining room, fans; no room phones, no room TVs, no smoking* ➡ *MC, V* ¶⊙¶ *BP.*

★ **$–$$**   ▣ **Trimmer House Bed and Breakfast.** The Queen Anne Victorian, built in 1891 by a wine merchant, has spacious guest rooms with lovely, traditional furnishings. Three rooms have claw-foot tubs. The suite has a fireplace and a private veranda. Common areas include a library with a fireplace. The amenities—terry robes, hair dryers, irons, VCRs and CD players, dual phone lines—are above and beyond the usual B&B facilities. Breakfast includes pancakes and waffles made with locally produced buckwheat. ✉ *145 E. Main St., 14527* ☎ *315/536–8304 or 800/968–8735* ⊕ *www.trimmerhouse.com* ⇨ *4 rooms, 1 suite* ⌂ *Dining room, in-room data ports, some fans, cable TV, in-room VCRs, outdoor hot tub, massage, library, business services, meeting room; no smoking* ➡ *AE, MC, V* ¶⊙¶ *BP.*

Shopping

The small **Belknap Hill Books** (✉ 106 Main St. ☎ 315/536–1186) carries more than 40,000 used, rare, and out-of-print books. Americana, children's books, cookbooks, and murder mysteries are specialties. You never know what's going to be on the block at **Hayes Auction Barn** (✉ 1464 Rte. 14A ☎ 315-536-8818), which holds auctions every Saturday evening. Antiques, tools, furniture, dolls, children's games, sporting items, and many unusual finds have been sold here. Come early enough to enjoy some of the food, find a good seat in the former church pews, and mingle with the crowd. Everyone from local farmers and businesspeople to antiques dealers and members of the Mennonite community come to see what's worth bidding on. **Lown's House of Shops** (✉ 131 Main St. ☎ 315/536–8343) spotlights the wares of 20 vendors. Three floors hold a variety of merchandise that includes Boyd's Bears, candles, candy, collectibles, dried flowers, and women's clothing. Until 1995 the 1890 building was home to Lown's Department Store. When the **Windmill Farm and Market** (✉ Rte. 14A ☎ 315/ 536–3032) opened in 1987 as an outlet for local producers and craftspeople, it had about 100 vendors. Today this farm and crafts market is host to more than 250 vendors and craftspeople, many of them members of the Mennonite community. The 26-acre site houses three main buildings, a street of shops, and a produce shed. Offerings range from farm-fresh produce to on-site chiropractic tune-ups. It's open Saturday 8–4:30 from April through December.

Naples

⑮   *20 mi west of Penn Yan.*

Surrounded by gentle hills, this small but vibrant village sits at the southern end of Canandaigua Lake. It's a haven for artists as well as a favorite with visitors, who appreciate the spectacular scenery, especially in fall when the foliage is bursting with color. The village dates from 1789, and you can see several early landmarks here. These include the Memorial Town Hall, built in 1872 as a tribute to those who fought in the Civil War; a pioneer cemetery with graves of Revolutionary War veterans; and the Old Red Mill, which was put up in 1850 and now houses the town historian's vast collection. Home to Widmer Wine Cellars, the community is famous for its grape pie and prides itself on all things grape. Even the fire hydrants here are painted purple.

Cumming Nature Center. The 900-acre environmental center, owned by the Rochester Museum and Science Center, has 6 mi of nature trails. In winter, 15 mi of trails are groomed for cross-country skiing and snow-shoeing (rentals available). Highlights include the Beaver Trail, on which you can see a variety of habitats on the way to an observation tower overlooking a 35-acre beaver pond, and the Pioneer Trail, with a re-constructed 18th-century homestead and interpretive signage explaining early settlers' lifestyles. A play space called Leap Frog Pond is designed especially for preschoolers. The visitor center has bathrooms and vending machines. The center is 7 mi north of Naples proper. ⊠ *6472 Gulick Rd., South Bristol* ☎ *585/374–6160* ⊕ *www.rmsc. org/cnc* ⊠ *$3 suggested donation* ⊙ *Late Dec.–Oct., weekends 9–5.*

Widmer Wine Cellars. One of the largest wineries on the East Coast, Wid-mer bottles wines under the Widmer, Taylor, Brickstone Cellars, and Man-ischewitz labels. It was founded by a Swiss winemaker in the late 1800s. Tours, which take about 45 minutes, let you see, for example, aging-cellar oak barrels that date from the 1930s and hold at least 10,000 gal-lons of wine; you may also learn about the steps on-site rabbis take to ensure that Manischewitz wines are kosher. The gift shop offers free tast-ings. ⊠ *1 Lake Niagara La.* ☎ *585/374–6311 or 800/836–5253* ⊕ *www. widmerwine.com* ⊠ *Tours $2, tasting free* ⊙ *May–Dec., daily 10–5 (tours at noon, 1, 2, and 3); Jan.–Apr., daily noon–4 (tours at 1, 2, and 3).*

FESTIVALS & FAIRS **Great Naples Flea & Craft Festival.** The event, a fall tradition in Naples for more than two decades, is held in mid-October, usually on Columbus Day weekend. The 100-plus vendors who line Main Street and fill the grounds of the Memorial Town Hall sell crafts, antiques, and flea-mar-ket goods, as well as a wide variety of foods, from homemade candies to venison. ⌂ *Box 157, 14512* ☎ *585/374–2757* ⊕ *www.bvtnaples.org.*

Naples Grape Festival. Juried arts-and-crafts exhibitors, more than two dozen food concessions, and live music from blues to rock are part of the fun at this annual festival held on the fourth full weekend of Septem-ber. The spotlight is on grapes, which means you can try all kinds of grape products. There's a grape-pie competition, and you can take part in grape-stomping contests to raise money for charity. The festival is held at Memorial Town Hall Park, on Main Street, and at Naples High School, on Route 21. ⌂ *Box 70, 14512* ☎ *585/374–2240* ⊕ *www. naplesvalleyny.com.*

Where to Stay & Eat

$–$$$ ✕ **Bob's and Ruth's.** You have a choice of either casual dining in the main room or a more formal setting in the Vineyard Room, which has large windows on three sides and looks out onto the vineyard. In warm-weather months you can eat outside on the patio. The food is mostly American, and the list of daily specials is extensive. The Vineyard Room menu in-cludes scampi and baby-back ribs; the main room has everything from grilled-cheese sandwiches to steak. ⊠ *204 N. Main St.* ☎ *585/374–5122* ☰ *MC, V* ✆ *Closed mid-Nov.–Mar.*

$–$$$ ✗ **Naples Hotel.** The restaurant occupies the first floor of an 1895 Federal-style brick hotel furnished with Victorian antiques. Rich wallpaper, antique light fixtures, and lace curtains outfit the parlorlike dining room, but you don't have to dress up to eat here. The food swings from Continental to contemporary, with such dishes as braised lamb shank and grilled Florida black grouper. Wine suggestions accompany entrée descriptions. In the taproom, also on the first floor, peanut shells crunch underfoot and an elk head peers down from its mount on the wall. Five guest rooms (¢–$) are available upstairs. ⊠ *111 S. Main St.* ☎ *585/374–5630* ☰ *AE, D, MC, V* ✆ *No dinner Mon.*

¢–$$ ✗ **Redwood.** The family-friendly spot, which includes a coffee shop and a dining room, serves home-style fare. In the dining room you might try smoked pork chops, broiled rainbow trout, or New York strip steak. The fare in the coffee shop includes roast-beef sandwiches and salad with marinated chicken breast, peppers, and tomatoes. Fresh-baked pies are also popular with diners here.The coffee shop is open all day, every day; the dining room is closed Monday and scales back in winter, when it offers dinner Friday through Sunday only. ⊠ *6 Cohocton St.* ☎ *585/374–6360* ☰ *MC, V.*

$–$$$ ▦ **Vagabond Inn.** The 7,000-square-foot inn, a blend of rustic elements and contemporary furnishings, sits on a secluded hill overlooking Canandaigua Lake. Tall windows frame the views from the Great Room, where guests congregate by the two large stone fireplaces. Guest rooms have one double bed; suites have queen or king beds and fireplaces. The Lodge Suite, which has its own dining area, is what the owner calls "flamboyantly masculine"; it has stone flooring, wood paneling, and a hand-painted bed. The more traditional Bristol Suite has a canopy bed, a private deck, and art from around the world. The Japanese garden is a serene spot; the in-ground pool, an uncommon amenity in these parts, is a plus. ⊠ *3300 Sliter Rd., 14512* ☎ *585/554–6271* ⊕ *www.thevagabondinn.com* ⟐ *2 rooms, 3 suites* ♿ *Dining room, some in-room hot tubs, cable TV, in-room VCRs, pool* ☰ *MC, V* ⎱◎⎰ *BP.*

$–$$ ▦ **Monier Manor Bed & Breakfast.** The house, built in 1840 by a wealthy local businessman, has views of the Widmer Wine Cellars vineyards from its backyard, and many village attractions are within walking distance from the property. The spacious parlor has a gas fireplace; breakfast is served on china, with sterling silver, in the formal dining room. Guest rooms, all upstairs, have CD players, down comforters, fireplaces, and plush bathrobes; three have four-poster beds. The decor employs bold, rich colors. ⊠ *154 N. Main St., 14512* ☎ *585/374–6719* ⎙ *585/374–9103* ⊕ *www.moniermanor.com* ⟐ *4 rooms* ♿ *Dining room, cable TV, some in-room VCRs, hot tub, massage; no room phones, no smoking* ☰ *MC* ⎱◎⎰ *BP.*

¢–$ ▦ **Cheshire Inn.** The 1830 farmhouse, surrounded by 13 acres of woods and fields 8 mi north of Naples, gives you views of Canandaigua Lake from the terrace and the guest rooms. The country-casual decor incorporates paintings and drawings by innkeeper Laura Moats, whose studio is next door. Rooms have quilt-covered beds, either a queen or two twins, and bathrobes. The Verbena Room has a private porch and a claw-foot tub. ⊠ *6004 Rte. 21, South Bristol 14512* ☏ *585/396–2383* ☏ *585/394–5033* ⊕ *www.cheshireinn.com* ↰ *5 rooms, 4 with bath* ☖ *Dining room, some pets allowed; no room phones, no room TVs, no smoking* ⊟ *AE, MC, V* ☼ *Closed Nov.–early May* ⏍❘ *BP.*

Nightlife & the Arts

Actors, directors, and other professionals from the region and from New York City come to the **Bristol Valley Theater** (⊠ 151 S. Main St. ☏ 585/374–9032 or 585/374–6318 ⊕ www.bvtnaples.org) to stage musicals, dramas, and comedy productions each summer. The theater, housed in a former church with bright purple and green doors, celebrated its 40th year in 2004 and is a draw for theater lovers in the Finger Lakes region.

Sports & the Outdoors

The 6,100 acres of the **Hi Tor Wildlife Management Area** (☏ 585/226–2466 ⊕ www.dec.state.ny.us), just north and east of Naples, are home to steep hills and gullies, eroded cliffs, waterfalls, fields, and marshlands, as well as trails and old logging roads. Depending on the season, users include hikers, anglers, paddlers, bird-watchers, cross-country skiers, hunters, rappelling enthusiasts, and even ice climbers. Fishing enthusiasts head to the West River for its bass and crappies. New York state licenses are required for both fishing and hunting, and rules are posted next to most parking areas. The main entrance to the management area is off Bassett Road (north of Route 53, east of Naples) in the town of Italy, but you find several parking areas around Hi Tor's perimeter, in Naples as well as in Middlesex.

FISHING   Naples Creek, which runs northward into Canandaigua Lake, is known for its rainbow-trout spawning runs. The creek is the site of the local Rotary Club's April 1 **Naples Creek Rainbow Trout Derby** (⊠ Rte. 21 S ☏ 585/374–2608), which draws more than 500 anglers from all over the state. The annual derby has been run since the early 1960s.

Ron Irland, who works as a commercial fisherman in Massachusetts from July through September, has been running charters on the southern end of Canandaigua Lake for almost 30 years. His **Reel Magic Charters** (⊠ 8 Cohocton St. ☏ 585/374–5197) are available from April through June. Those who head out on his 26-foot sportfishing boat may wind up catching lake, rainbow, or brown trout. All equipment is included, but you need a state fishing license.

GOLF   The 6,400-yard, par-71 **Reservoir Creek Golf Course** (⊠ 8613 Rte. 21 ☏ 585/374–8010 ⊕ www.rcgolf.com), a wooded and links-style course in the hills of the Naples valley, has an elevation change of 300 feet. High-season greens fees are $24–$29 for 9 holes and $39–$43 for 18. The complex includes a clubhouse with a bar, restaurant, and patio overlooking the 9th green, as well as a full-service shop. Also on the grounds is the Inn at Reservoir Creek, a turn-of-the-20th-century farmhouse with six rooms ($65–$85 a night).

HIKING   Two large waterfalls and many smaller ones can be found along Grimes Creek in **Grimes Glen** (☏ No phone), which is owned by a local man but open to the public. Trails run along the creek in segments, interrupted by cliffs, so you may have to walk part of the way in the creek. In 1882 a Naples biologist found a fossilized tree—believed to be 350 million years old—in the glen. The tree is now in the state museum in Albany. A parking area and trail access are off Vine Street.

SKI AREA   With a 1,200-foot vertical drop, the **Bristol Mountain Winter Resort** (✉ 5662 Rte. 64, Bristol ☎ 585/374–6000 ⊕ www.bristolmountain.com) is the highest ski area between the Adirondacks and the Rockies. The area has 32 slopes and trails (95% with lighting) and 97% snowmaking. The longest run is 2 mi; about 20% of the runs are for advanced skiers and 35% are for beginners. Skiing and snowboarding lessons are available. The season usually runs from November through mid-March. In fall you can take in the foliage on a chairlift ride; hiking back down is an option. The resort is almost halfway between Naples and Canandaigua.

Shopping
The **Arbor Hill Grapery** (✉ 6461 Rte. 64, Bristol Springs ☎ 585/374–2870, 585/374–2406, 800/554–7553), about 6 mi outside Naples, sells New York State cheeses, grape pie, and other fine foods alongside its wines, which range from Chardonnays to Rieslings. From January through April it's open only on weekends. **Artizanns Gifts** (✉ 23 Mill St. ☎ 585/374–6740) serves as a showcase for more than 150 local artists; articles range from $5 to $3,500. Chimes, candles, jams, and Amish handcrafted furniture and toys are part of the mix at **Timberwood** (✉ 197 N. Main St. ☎ 585/374–5660), which is closed from late December to early April.

Canandaigua

16   *19 mi north of Naples.*

Long a favorite vacation destination for Rochester residents, this small city (population about 11,200) sits at the north end of 16-mi-long Canandaigua Lake. It was here that the 1794 Pickering Treaty was signed, brokering peace between the Iroquois and the U.S. government. Canandaigua's majestic courthouse, which still looms over Main Street, was the site of Susan B. Anthony's trial and conviction—she was found guilty of treason for voting in the 1872 election.

The wide main street with granite curbing is lined with stately Victorians in the north end of town. Heading south you pass through a downtown area with shops before you come to the lake. City Pier, which dates from 1847, is home to an eclectic mix of boathouses. Nearby Kershaw Park is a perfect place for a swim or a stroll.

Canandaigua Lady. You can take a leisurely cruise on Canandaigua Lake in a replica of a 19th-century paddle wheeler. The boat operator offers narrated tours and brunch, lunch, and dinner cruises. Reservations are required. ✉ *Steamboat Landing, 205 Lakeshore Dr.* ☎ *585/396–7350 or 866/926–2467* ⊕ *www.steamboatlandingonline.com* 🎫 *$12–$40* ⊙ *May–late Oct., Tues.–Sun.; call for tour times.*

Captain Gray's Boat Tours. Local history is shared during one-, two-, and three-hour tours offered by Captain Gray, who has been cruising Canandaigua Lake in steel-enclosed boats for more than a quarter century. ☒ *Inn on the Lake, 770 S. Main St.* ☎ *585/394–5270* ⊕ *www. captgrays.com* 🍴 *$8.50–$17.50* ⊙ *Late May–early Oct.; call for tour times.*

Finger Lakes Gaming & Racetrack. Since it opened in 1962, the track has hosted some of the world's top jockeys and Thoroughbreds. The 28,000-square-foot gaming floor has more than 1,000 video-gaming machines. The complex also includes a food court, a sports bar, and a coffeehouse. The track is 8 mi north of Canandaigua. ☒ *5857 Rte. 96, Farmington* ☎ *585/924–3232* ⊕ *www.fingerlakesracetrack.com* 🍴 *Free* ⊙ *Racetrack mid-Apr.–late Nov., Fri.–Tues.; call for race times. Gaming floor daily 10 AM–2 AM.*

Granger Homestead and Carriage Museum. The Federal-style house was completed in 1816 by Gideon Granger, postmaster general for presidents Thomas Jefferson and James Madison. It contains what's known as a flying staircase, and its nine rooms have hand-carved woodwork and many of the original furnishings and paintings. Popular annual events here include a Civil War encampment in September and a Festival of Trees in November and December. Guided tours, offered 1–4 PM, are given on the hour. The carriage house displays 93 horse-drawn vehicles, including an undertaker's hearse. Visit on Sunday afternoon in June through August if you want to take a 10-minute antique-carriage ride ($5) on the 10-acre property. From early January to mid-March, horse-drawn sleigh rides ($20) are an option. From June through September the museum also runs 45-minute narrated carriage tours of Canandaigua (Friday afternoon) or the Woodlawn Cemetery (Thursday afternoon); reservations are required for carriage tours, which cost $20. ☒ *295 N. Main St.* ☎ *585/394–1472* ⊕ *www.grangerhomestead.org* 🍴 *$5* ⊙ *Late May, Sept., and Oct., Tues.–Fri. 1–5; June–Aug., Tues.–Sun. 1–5.*

☺ **Roseland Water Park.** The park has several large waterslides, a water flume, a raft ride with huge inner tubes (for up to five people), a wave pool, and a lake where you can rent canoes and paddleboats. ☒ *250 Eastern Blvd.* ☎ *585/396–2000* ⊕ *www.roselandwaterpark.com* 🍴 *$19.99* ⊙ *June–Sept. Call for days and hrs.*

Fodor's Choice ★ **Sonnenberg Mansion and Gardens.** The grounds at this 52-acre estate are a magnificent example of late-Victorian gardening and design. The rose garden overflows with 4,000 rosebushes; the other themed plantings include Japanese, pansy, blue-and-white, and rock gardens. An early-1900s conservatory houses the orchid collection and other exotic plants. The stunning 1887 Queen Anne mansion was built as a summer home by a wealthy New York City banker and his wife, who became Canandaigua's biggest benefactress. The library, the couple's favorite room, looks out on the Italian garden. The great hall features a massive leaded-glass window and an 1874 Steinway. Walking tours are offered weekdays at 1 and weekends at 10 and 1 from Memorial Day through September. The free **Finger Lakes Wine Center** (☎ 585/394–9016 ⊙ Early May–mid-Oct., daily 11–4), in a separate building near the Sonnenberg Gardens' main parking lot, sells wines and specialty foods from throughout the Finger Lakes region and dispenses information about area wineries. The wines offered for tastings here change regularly.

⊠ *151 Charlotte St.* ☎ *585/394–4922* ⊕ *www.sonnenberg.org* ⊠ *$8.50*
⊙ *Early May–late May and early Sept.–mid-Oct., daily 9:30–4; late May–early Sept., daily 9:30–5:30.*

FESTIVALS & FAIRS
Hill Cumorah Pageant. On each of seven nights in early July this free outdoor production tells the story of the Mormon Church, which was started in Palmyra, a few miles north of Canadaigua. The 75-minute performances involve a cast of more than 600 and assorted high-tech visual and sound effects. The performance area can fit an audience of 9,000. ⊠ *Rte. 21, 2 mi north of I–90 Exit 43, Palmyra* ☎ *315/597–2757 or 315/597–6808* ⊕ *www.hillcumorah.com.*

Historic Downtown Canandaigua Arts Festival. More than 200 arts and crafts vendors line the downtown sidewalks for this annual festival, held on a weekend in mid-July. ⊠ *S. Main St.* ☎ *585/394–7110* ⊕ *www.bardeenenterprises.com.*

Waterfront Art Festival. More than 150 local and national artists display their work on the north shore of Canandaigua Lake as part of this juried show. The event is held the last full weekend in July. ⊠ *Kershaw Park, Lakeshore Dr.* ☎ *585/383–1472* ⊕ *www.waterfrontartfestival.com.*

Where to Stay & Eat

$–$$$ ✕ **Lincoln Hill Inn.** The restaurant, within walking distance of the Finger Lakes Performing Arts Center, is in an 1804 farmhouse. Menus vary seasonally, but always popular is the top-notch prime rib. Lobster-stuffed shrimp, sautéed duck breast, and vegetarian lasagna are among the other selections. Covered decks and porches are used for outdoor dining. ⊠ *3365 E. Lake Rd.* ☎ *585/394–8254* ⊟ *AE, MC, V* ⊙ *Closed Mon. mid-Oct.–mid-Apr.*

$–$$$ ✕ **Steamboat Landing.** Exposed wood beams, two-story windows, and the huge fireplace complement the hunting-lodge theme at this lakeside restaurant, where you may opt to sit on the outside patio. The menu, which changes with the seasons, includes dishes like Louisiana jambalaya, deep-fried coconut shrimp, and roast prime rib. The lobster bisque is a must. ⊠ *205 Lakeshore Dr.* ☎ *585/396–7350* ⊟ *AE, D, MC, V* ⊙ *Closed Mon.–Thurs. in mid-Nov.–mid-Apr.*

$–$$ ✕ **Casa de Pasta.** Tucked away on a side street in downtown Canandaigua, this Italian restaurant offers an intimate setting with burgundy linens and candles on each table. The menu includes scampi, homemade gnocchi, and *braciole* (thin slices of beef rolled with a filling of prosciutto, sliced egg, Parmesan, and onions). ⊠ *125 Bemis St.* ☎ *585/394–3710* ⊟ *MC, V* ⊙ *Closed Mon.*

$–$$ ✕ **Eric's Office.** This casual, friendly restaurant-taproom on the north end of town is a local favorite. The chef shows his creative side with dishes such as tenderloin *au bleu* (with blue cheese). Comfort food, like macaroni and cheese, is served in large portions. Specials change daily. The seafood bisque always sells out. ⊠ *2574 Macedon Rd.* ☎ *585/394–8787* ⊟ *AE, MC, V* ⊙ *Dining room closed Sun.*

$$–$$$ ✕⊡ **Thendara.** The Victorian inn, built in the early 1900s, is 5 mi south of town on a bluff overlooking the east shore of Canandaigua Lake. Some rooms have lake views, which you can also take in from the patio and

the restaurant. Oriental rugs and original antiques are scattered throughout the inn. Three guest rooms have king beds; one has a queen. The Congressman's Room, a corner room, has three windows with wood shutters and water views. The cozy Senator's Room has floral wallpaper and a mahogany bed. The restaurant ($$–$$$; closed January and February) has a formal, candlelit dining room and an enclosed porch, and in warm weather you may eat on the outside porch. The food is upscale American fare: roast pork loin with fruit stuffing, apple cider–cherry sauce, and maple mashed potatoes, or jumbo pan-roasted Rhode Island scallops with pumpkin-and-squash risotto, for example. The Boat House (¢–$; closed late September to mid-May), at the edge of the lake, has a more casual menu that includes sandwiches, salads, and barbecue dishes. ⊠ *4356 E. Lake Rd., 14424* ☎ *585/394–4868* 🖷 *585/396–0804* ⊕ *www.thendarainn.com* ⋈ *4 rooms* ⅃ *2 restaurants, 1 in-room hot tub, cable TV, 9-hole golf course, dock, pub, business services, no-smoking rooms* ☰ *AE, D, MC, V* ⏍ *BP.*

$$ ✕▥ **Canandaigua Inn on the Lake.** The waterfront inn and conference center has spacious grounds and an area where boaters can dock. Rooms have one king or two double beds and tasteful furnishings; suites include living rooms and queen sleeper sofas. The lakefront rooms and suites have private patios or balconies. Wireless Internet access is available throughout the inn. In the restaurant ($$–$$$), large windows give you good views of Canandaigua Lake, Squaw Island, and the nearby city pier. The menu intersperses contemporary and American fare with dishes inspired by other cuisines. Sirloin steak is marinated and grilled, topped with goat-cheese butter, and served with smashed potatoes; ahi tuna is coated with sesame seeds, pan seared, and served with sautéed veggies and seaweed salad. Outdoor dining is an option in warm weather. ⊠ *770 S. Main St., 14424* ☎ *585/394–7800 or 800/228–2801* 🖷 *585/394–5003* ⊕ *www.visitinnonthelake.com* ⋈ *86 rooms, 48 suites* ⅃ *Restaurant, picnic area, room service, some in-room hot tubs, some kitchenettes, some refrigerators, cable TV with movies and video games, 2 pools (1 indoor), lake, gym, beach, lounge, business services, meeting rooms, some pets allowed, no-smoking rooms* ☰ *AE, D, MC, V.*

$–$$ ✕▥ **Bristol Harbour Resort.** Rooms at this lodge-style hotel have balconies with lake views, gas fireplaces, and heated bathroom floors. The rustic decor includes wood paneling and wool blankets; modern conveniences include wireless Internet access in all rooms. The Lodge Restaurant ($–$$$) serves contemporary American and Continental fare, such as pepper-crusted salmon fillet with whipped potatoes and lemon vinaigrette or sautéed chicken breast with basmati rice and vegetables in Chardonnay cream sauce. The menu also includes pastas and grilled dishes, salads, and wrap sandwiches. You may cross-country ski or snowshoe on the grounds in winter, or play the 18-hole championship golf course. ⊠ *5410 Seneca Point Rd., 14424* ☎ *585/396–2200 or 800/288–8248* 🖷 *585/394–9254* ⊕ *www.bristolharbour.com* ⋈ *31 rooms* ⅃ *Restaurant, some kitchens, cable TV, 18-hole golf course, pool, gym, hot tub, cross-country skiing, meeting rooms, no-smoking rooms* ☰ *AE, MC, V.*

$$–$$$ 🖼 **Morgan Samuels Inn.** A long, tree-lined drive leads to this 1810 English-style mansion on 42 country acres. The mansion served as an upstate hideaway for playwright-actor Judson Morgan and was later the home of industrialist and Johnson administration official Howard Samuels. All rooms have fireplaces; three rooms have French doors that open onto balconies. The master suite has French inlaid-wood antiques, a king-size bed, a double jet tub, and floor-to-ceiling windows with window seats. Common areas include a wicker-furnished Victorian porch that has views of the gardens and is popular with guests. ✉ *2920 Smith Rd., 14424* ☎ *585/394–9232* 🖷 *585/394–8044* ⊕ *www.morgansamuelsinn.com* ➼ *5 rooms, 1 suite* ♨ *Some in-room hot tubs, tennis court, library, business services; no room TVs, no kids under 10, no smoking* ⊟ *AE, D, MC, V* ⦿⎮ *BP.*

$–$$$ 🖼 **Acorn Inn.** The late-1700s stagecoach inn has elegant, spacious guest rooms furnished with antiques and a lovely yard with gardens, stone walls, and a hot tub. Most guest rooms have canopy beds; all have down covers and thick robes. The Bristol Room, the biggest of the four, has a soothing cream–and–slate blue color scheme, a sitting area, and a large bathtub. In the Hotchkiss Room, which has a fireplace, French doors lead out to a walled terrace. Libraries throughout the inn contain more than 1,000 books that you are welcome to enjoy. The inn is 10 mi outside the city. ✉ *4508 Rte. 64 S, 14424* ☎ *585/229–2834 or 888/245–4134* ⊕ *www.acorninnbb.com* ➼ *4 rooms* ♨ *Dining room, 1 in-room hot tub, in-room VCRs, outdoor hot tub; no kids under 12, no smoking* ⊟ *AE, MC, V* ⦿⎮ *BP.*

$–$$ 🖼 **1885 Sutherland House.** The Victorian house sits on 5 acres about 1 mi from downtown and the lake. All rooms have wireless Internet access; beds are either king or queen size. Some rooms have gas or electric fireplaces. The red-and-champagne palette in the Parker House Suite makes it the most sophisticated of the rooms. It's also the largest of the rooms, and has a king-size four-poster bed and a whirlpool tub for two. Porches, patios, and a parlor are among the common spaces. ✉ *3179 Rte. 21 S, Bristol St. Extension, 14424* ☎ *585/396–0375 or 800/396–0375* 🖷 *585/396–9281* ⊕ *www.sutherlandhouse.com* ➼ *2 rooms, 3 suites* ♨ *Dining room, fans, some in-room hot tubs, cable TV with movies, in-room VCRs; no kids, no smoking* ⊟ *AE, D, MC, V* ⦿⎮ *BP.*

¢–$ 🖼 **Econo Lodge.** The two-story chain motel is within walking distance of Canandaigua Lake and Roseland Water Park. It's no-frills, but the staff is friendly and accommodating. Complimentary coffee, tea, and hot chocolate are available around the clock. ✉ *170 Eastern Blvd., 14424* ☎ *585/394–9000* 🖷 *585/396–2560* ➼ *64 rooms* ♨ *Some refrigerators, cable TV, laundry facilities, business services, some pets allowed, no-smoking rooms* ⊟ *AE, D, DC, MC, V* ⦿⎮ *CP.*

¢–$ 🖼 **Finger Lakes Inn.** Ten landscaped acres and a family activity center give you plenty of elbow room at this hotel. Rooms are basic, with either one or two doubles or a queen-size bed; family-oriented minisuites include two double beds and a pull-out sofa bed. ✉ *4343 Eastern Blvd., 14424* ☎ *585/394–2800 or 800/727–2775* 🖷 *585/396–3550* ⊕ *www.fingerlakesinn.com* ➼ *124 rooms, 6 suites* ♨ *Picnic area, in-room data* *ports, some kitchenettes, cable TV, pool, basketball, Ping-Pong, volleyball, video game room, meeting rooms, some pets allowed, no-smoking rooms* ⊟ *AE, D, MC, V* ⵈⵔ *CP.*

Nightlife & the Arts

The outdoor amphitheater at the **Finger Lakes Performing Arts Center** (⊠ Rte. 364 and Lincoln Hill Rd. ☎ 585/325–7760 ⊕ ww.rbtl.org), managed by the Rochester Broadway Theatre League, is the summer home of the Rochester Philharmonic Orchestra. It also hosts nationally known rock, blues, jazz, and pop musicians, with seating under what locals call "the shell" and on the grass-covered hillside.

Sports & the Outdoors

FISHING Lake trout as well as rainbows and browns can be found in Canandaigua Lake, which is 262 feet deep and hosts the **Canandaigua Lake Trout Derby** (⊕ www.canandaigua.com) on the first weekend in June. Captain Bill Reeser runs **Happy Hooker Charters** (⊠ City Pier ☎ 315/331–1265) out of Seager Marine Inc. From April through October he takes up to six people out on Canandaigua Lake in his 25-foot boat. You might wind up just as happy as the client who, in 1992, hooked a 22¼-pound lake trout—the biggest on record from the lake. Captain Bill supplies the bait and tackle.

GOLF The highly regarded **Bristol Harbour Resort Golf Course** (⊠ 5410 Seneca Point Rd. ☎ 585/396–2200 ⊕ www.bristolharbour.com), 11 mi from Canandaigua, is a par-72, 6,200-yard Robert Trent Jones course with a pro shop, a golf school, and spectacular lake views. Greens fees are $25–$40 for 9 holes, $46–$65 for 18 holes.

Shopping

South Main Street between Ontario and Saltonstall streets is the heart of the shopping district in downtown Canandaigua. **Nadal Glass** (⊠ 20 Phoenix St. ☎ 585/394–7850), in a former firehouse just off South Main Street, specializes in handblown glass that's also sold in galleries throughout the country.

The **Cheshire Union** (⊠ 4244 Rte. 21 S ☎ 585/394–5530), 5 mi south of Canandaigua, occupies an old schoolhouse with tin ceilings and black-and-white photos of former students on the walls. A deli and grocery store are downstairs; antiques and a wide selection of gifts fill the former classrooms upstairs. The eight antiques stores that make up the **Bloomfield Antique Country Mile** are west of Canandaigua, in East Bloomfield and, in one case, West Bloomfield—along U.S. 20/Route 5, for the most part. Together they represent more than 175 dealers.

GREATER ROCHESTER

By Patti Singer When locals say Rochester, they could just as easily mean Greece, Brighton, Pittsford, or any of the suburbs that make up Greater Rochester. Water is a major feature in the area: the city sprang up along the banks of the Genesee River, and Lake Ontario is 10 mi from downtown. The Erie Canal put Rochester on the map and brought prosperity to communities such as Spencerport and Fairport, which still identify with the waterway.

Rochester

30 mi northwest of Canandaigua, 90 mi west of Syracuse.

A snapshot of Rochester must include the Eastman Kodak Co., the photography giant that for generations was synonymous with the city, where it is headquartered. But the picture is changing. In 2004 Kodak was still Rochester's largest employer, but the company has downsized dramatically, and the city is looking for a new identity.

Reinvention is nothing new to Rochester. First known as the Flour City in the early 1800s, for the mills that were powered by the Genesee River, it became the Flower City when nurseries and seed production replaced the grain industry. Industrialists and entrepreneurs shaped the city at the turn of the 20th century, and photography pioneer George Eastman played a particularly key role.

Pride runs deep in city neighborhoods known for their mix of Federal, Greek-revival, Victorian, and Queen Anne architecture and preservation. Corn Hill, Rochester's first residential neighborhood, is just blocks south of downtown. A mile or so to the east is the Park Avenue area of shops and restaurants, interspersed with tree-lined residential streets. In the South Wedge, an up-and-comer where homes have been restored, people are discovering quirky, personable eateries that range from vegetarian to barbecue. To the north, the waterfront Charlotte (say it like a native: Shar-LOT) neighborhood has taverns, restaurants, and a rock-and-roll bar, but Ontario Beach Park is its point of pride.

Theater, music, and literature flourish, and almost every night there's a performance of some sort. Visual arts—photography, art, and film—are industries as well as avocations. Sports fans get four-season excitement with professional baseball, soccer, and hockey. The locals, tired of hearing jokes about cloudy and snowy days, revel in the dozens of parks and the recreational opportunities offered by Lake Ontario and the Erie Canal. This city of firsts—where the first woman voted (even though Susan B. Anthony's vote didn't count and led to her arrest) and where the fishing reel, mail chute, and fountain pen were invented—celebrates history as it anticipates the future.

20 Center at High Falls. Stand on a bridge over the Genesee River, watch and listen to the High Falls cascading 96 feet, and feel the power that drove Rochester's flour mills in the 19th century. The museum, with interactive exhibits, provides an overview of Rochester history. The Triphammer Forge, a reconstructed waterwheel, is one of the largest in the state. Frontier Field and Eastman Kodak world headquarters are across the street, and pubs and clubs of the High Falls entertainment district serve food and entertainment. ⊠ *60 Brown's Race* ☎ *585/325–2030* ⊕ *www.centerathighfalls.org* 🎫 *Free* ☼ *Tues.–Sat. 10–4, Sun. noon–4.*

Charlotte Genesee Lighthouse Museum. The lighthouse stands about a mile south of Lake Ontario, giving you an idea of how the landscape has changed since the 40-foot-tall stone structure went up in 1822. In the 1960s a group of local high-school students saved the structure—the second-oldest American lighthouse on Lake Ontario—from ru-

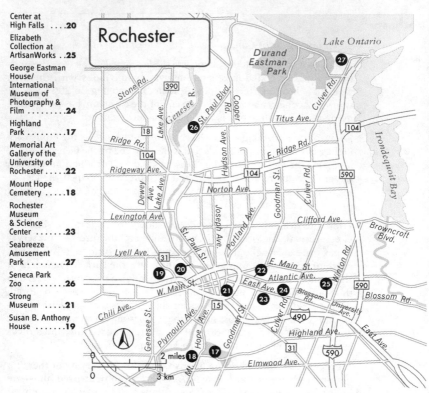

mored demolition. ✉ *70 Lighthouse St.* ☎ *585/621–6179* 💲 *Free* ◷ *May–Oct., weekends 1–5.*

Custom BrewCrafters. If you enjoy a microbrew at a Rochester bar or restaurant, chances are it was brewed here. The 6,000-square-foot brewery makes more than 50 beers (20 kegs at a time), which are served throughout western New York. Tours explain the brewing process, and free samples let you taste brews that have won at the Great American Beer Festival in Denver as well as at other national and local competitions. The drive to the brewery from downtown (Route 31 to Route 65 south) takes you from city to country in about 20 minutes. ✉ *93 Paper Mill St., Honeoye Falls* ☎ *585/624–4386* ⊕ *www.custombrewcrafters.com* 💲 *Free* ◷ *Tours weekends at 1, 2, 3, and 4.*

㉕ The Elizabeth Collection at ArtisanWorks. The image of a locomotive bearing down on you is painted on the entrance to this former cannon factory. Inside, nearly every inch of the 40,000-square-foot structure is filled with art, much of it for sale. Some of the 15,000 pieces have a pedigree: Roy Lichtenstein, Andy Warhol, Frank Lloyd Wright, and Gordon Parks. Displays are set up like individual rooms. A Victorian dining room, table set and ready for guests, is particularly anachronistic; it's like someone rummaged through an attic. You can also watch artists at work here. The rooftop sculpture garden gives you a view of the city skyline. ⊠ *565 Blossom St., Suite L* ☎ *585/288–7170* ⊕ *www.artisanworks. net* ⌨ *$5* ⊗ *Mon.–Sat. 11–6, Sun. noon–5.*

㉔ George Eastman House. The sprawling colonial-revival mansion, once the home of Eastman Kodak's founder, has been restored to its early-1900s appearance. The elephant head on the wall in the conservatory is an eye-catcher, and the rest of the house gives a glimpse into the life and times of the man who brought photography to the masses. Much of the second floor is used as gallery space. House tours are given Tuesday through Saturday at 10:30 and 2 and Sunday at 2. The grounds include a rock garden with scallop-shaped flower beds, a formal terrace garden with more than 90 types of perennials, a cutting garden, a lily pool, and a grape arbor. Garden tours are available May through September, Tuesday through Saturday at 11:30 and 3 and Sunday at 3. The **International Museum of Photography and Film,** behind the mansion, has changing exhibits about the history of photography, film technology, and literature. The collection includes tens of thousands of photos, books, and films as well as photographic equipment. Also here is the **Dryden Theatre,** which shows movies ($6) and hosts film festivals. ⊠ *900 East Ave.* ☎ *585/271–3361* ⊕ *www.eastmanhouse.org* ⌨ *$8* ⊗ *May, daily 10–5 (Thurs. until 8); June–Apr., Tues.–Sat. 10–5, Sun. 1–5.*

⑰ Highland Park. Established in 1888, this was Rochester's first public park. Site of the hugely popular **Lilac Festival,** Highland Park has more than 500 varieties of lilacs. Walking paths crisscross the park and lead to a reservoir that provides an unobstructed view for miles to the south. The **Lamberton Conservatory** (☎ 585/256–5878 ⌨ $1), built in 1911, houses arid desert species and lush tropical vegetation. It's incredibly popular in winter, when Rochesterians crave any sign of their beloved gardens. At the corner of Mt. Hope and Reservoir avenues, a block west of the Lamberton Conservatory, is Warner Castle (☎ 585/473–5130 ⊕ www.rcgc.org), a squat stone structure. Headquarters of the Rochester Civic Garden Center, it has art exhibits and educational materials about gardening. ⊠ *South and Highland Aves.* ☎ *585/256–4950* ⊕ *www. monroecounty.gov* ⌨ *Free* ⊗ *Park daily 6 AM–11 PM, conservatory daily 10–4.*

㉒ Memorial Art Gallery of the University of Rochester. More than 5,000 years of art is contained within the 14 exhibit rooms. Egyptian coffins, medieval tapestries, impressionist paintings, European masters, and African carvings are on permanent display. The collection of American art is strong, and regional artists are represented and compete in juried shows here. ⊠ *500 University Ave.* ☎ *585/473–7720* ⊕ *www.mag. rochester.edu* ⌨ *$7* ⊗ *Wed. and Fri. 10–4, Thurs. 10–9, Sat. 10–5, Sun. noon–5.*

⑱ Mount Hope Cemetery. Formed by a glacier that left undulating terrain upon its retreat, the 196 rolling acres of this cemetery are as much a park as they are the final resting place for more than 370,000 people. Among the more famous laid to rest here are suffragist Susan B. Anthony and anti-slavery leader Frederick Douglass. The cemetery, dedicated in 1838, is one of the nation's oldest. Many headstones retain

Victorian symbols such as the anchor, crown, obelisk, or sheaf of wheat. The city owns the cemetery, but a caretakers group called the Friends of Mount Hope Cemetery offers free tours on Sunday (and some Saturdays) from May through October. ⊠ *791 Mt. Hope Ave.* ☎ *585/428–7999 or 585/461–3494* ⊕ *www.fomh.org* 🖃 *Free* ☉ *Daily dawn–dusk; tours May–Oct., Sun. at 2 and 3.*

Ontario Beach Park. The showcase of the Charlotte neighborhood, the park underwent restorations and improvements in 2004 that recall its days as the Coney Island of the north. Part of this renaissance was spurred by the introduction of high-speed ferry service between Rochester and Toronto, and it included the makeover of old warehouses into a gleaming terminal with shops. The *Spirit of Ontario* ran through the summer of 2004 before suspending operations. At this writing (late 2004), the city has begun studying ways to restore service for 2005.

Swimming is just one attraction at the beach. Concerts are held on Wednesday nights in summer. The 1905 **Dentzel Carousel** ($1) has three rows of animals, not just horses, and is one of only about six such Dentzel menagerie carousels still operating in the country. To get here, take Lake Avenue all the way north until you reach Lake Ontario and the beach. ⊠ *Entrances on Lake and Beach Aves.* ☎ *585/256–4950* ⊕ *www.monroecounty.gov* 🖃 *Free* ☉ *Daily 7 AM–11 PM.*

> **need a break?**
>
> Finish your day at Ontario Beach Park with a true Rochester treat: **Abbott's Frozen Custard** (⊠ Lake Ave. at Ontario Beach Park ☎ 585/663–8770). You can spot this Rochester institution by the line on a hot afternoon. But that's okay; waiting your turn gives you time to decide which flavor to try.

🖐 ㉓ **Rochester Museum & Science Center.** Everyone in the family can play with hands-on exhibits that focus on science and technology, nature, and the area's cultural heritage. Highlights include an exhibit about the Seneca Indian Nation and one about Frederick Douglass, an opened 1873 time capsule, an interactive display about the human body, and the **Strasenburgh Planetarium,** which presents astronomy and laser-light shows and large-format films about space and Earth. ⊠ *657 East Ave.* ☎ *585/271–4320* ⊕ *www.rmsc.org* 🖃 *Museum $7, planetarium $4–$7* ☉ *Mon.–Sat. 9–5, Sun. noon–5.*

Sam Patch. From May through October, the replica packet boat cruises along the Erie Canal and passes through one of the locks. Most cruises last an hour. Lunch and dinner excursions also are available (reservations required). ⊠ *12 Schoen Pl., Pittsford* ☎ *585/262–5661* ⊕ *www.sampatch.org* 🖃 *Lock cruise $10* ☉ *May–Oct. Call for times.*

🖐 ㉗ **Seabreeze Amusement Park.** The Jack Rabbit roller coaster is the most famous ride at this park on the Lake Ontario shore. Sampling all the water rides, the carousel, more coasters, and the midway makes for a very full day. The admission ticket covers unlimited rides. ⊠ *4600 Culver Rd.* ☎ *585/323–1900* ⊕ *www.seabreeze.com* 🖃 *$18.95* ☉ *Mid-June–early Sept., Sun.–Thurs. noon–10, Fri. and Sat. noon–11; late May–mid-June, call for days and hrs.*

🔆 ㉖ **Seneca Park Zoo.** The Rocky Coasts exhibit at this zoo along the Gene-see River gorge provides an underwater look at polar bears, penguins, and sea lions. Above ground, you can spot African elephants and orangutans, among other beasts. There's a barnyard petting zoo and an area where kids can touch turtle shells, snakeskins, antlers, and other animal artifacts. ⊠ *2222 St. Paul St.* ☎ *585/336–7200* ⊕ *www. senecaparkzoo.org* ☞ *$5* ⊙ *Memorial Day–Labor Day, daily 10–5, rest of yr, daily 10–4.*

🔆 ㉑ **Strong Museum.** The second-largest children's museum in the country is
Fodor'sChoice getting bigger and better. In September 2004 a $33 million upgrade began
★ that will add attractions and continue to foster the joy of play. Besides interactive exhibits, must-see attractions (for now, at least) include Sesame Street, TimeLab, a working diner, and an area devoted to all things Jell-O. The doll collection of museum founder Margaret Woodbury Strong is still in residence. ⊠ *1 Manhattan Sq.* ☎ *585/263–2700* ⊕ *www. strongmuseum.org* ☞ *$7* ⊙ *Mon.–Thurs. and Sat. 10–5, Fri. 10–8, Sun. noon–5.*

㉙ **Susan B. Anthony House.** The west-side street where suffragist Susan B. Anthony lived from 1866 until her death in 1906 looks much like it did in her day. The tree out front is bigger, of course, but many of the neigh-boring houses still look the same. You can tour the three-story redbrick Victorian and picture Anthony working to get women the right to vote. The visitor center next door was the home of a sister. A park one block north has a statue of Anthony and friend Frederick Douglass having tea. ⊠ *17 Madison St.* ☎ *585/235–6124* ⊕ *www.susanbanthonyhouse.org* ☞ *$6* ⊙ *Memorial Day Labor Day, Tues.–Sun. 11–5; rest of yr, Wed.–Sun. 11–4.*

**off the
beaten
path**

GENESEE COUNTRY VILLAGE & MUSEUM – The living-history museum has 68 buildings that were moved from throughout the region to re-create 19th-century life in the Genesee Valley. The complex includes the **John L. Wehle Gallery of Wildlife & Sporting Art.** Guided tours of the village, available only during the first two weeks in May and the last two weeks in October, start on the hour from 10 to 3 on weekdays. The 175-acre **Genesee Country Nature Center,** which has exhibits and 5 mi of interpreted hiking trails, is open all year. You may cross-country ski and snowshoe here; rentals are available. Mumford is 20 mi southwest of Rochester. ⊠ *1410 Flint Hill Rd., Mumford* ☎ *585/538–6822* ⊕ *www.gcv.org* ☞ *$12.95 ($3.50 if visiting only nature center)* ⊙ *Museum and village July–early Sept., Tues.–Sun. 10–5; May and June, and early Sept.–Oct., Tues.–Fri. 10–4. Call for nature center days and hrs in Nov.–Apr.*

FESTIVALS & **Corn Hill Arts Festival.** The two-day event, held the weekend after July
FAIRS 4, brings more than 200,000 people to one of Rochester's oldest neigh-borhoods. Artists and crafters create every imaginable design, but some-how shepherd's crooks retain their popularity. ⊠ *Exchange Blvd. and Plymouth Ave.* ☎ *585/262–3142* ⊕ *www.cornhill.org.*

Fodor's Choice **Lilac Festival.** Held the week before and after Mother's Day, the event
★ heralds the start of Rochester's festival season. If the more than 1,200
lilac bushes won't cooperate (Mother Nature is on her own schedule,
after all), you can ogle scores of other flowers. When your eyes and nose
have had their fill, arts and crafts, garden tours, and live entertainment
beckon. ⊠ *Highland Park, South and Highland Aves.* ☎ *585/256–*
4960 ⊕ *www.lilacfestival.com.*

Park Avenue Summer Arts Fest. Rochesterians cannot get enough of arts
and crafts, fried dough, or their neighbors. The two-day Park Avenue
fest, which falls on the first full weekend in August, is the last big
blowout of summer. ⊠ *Park Ave. between Alexander St. and Culver Rd.*
☎ *585/473–4482* ⊕ *www.rochesterevents.com.*

Where to Stay & Eat
The South Wedge/Swillburg neighborhoods and the couple of miles of
Monroe Avenue from the Inner Loop to the I–490 on-ramp in the city
have Asian, Indian, Middle Eastern, and vegetarian restaurants. Chain
restaurants abound near the malls and on major commercial routes such
as Jefferson and West Henrietta roads. To get a true taste of the city,
check out the neighborhood establishments. If you enjoy exploring on
foot, accommodations in the East Avenue area put many restaurants,
attractions, and clubs within blocks.

$–$$$ ✕**Dinosaur Bar-B-Que.** The smoker sits outside, luring passersby with
the aroma. Chicken, beef, and pork are prepared barbecue, Cajun, and
even Cuban style. The downtown building, a 1905 Lehigh Valley Rail-
road station, sits 40 feet above the Genesee River; some tables have a
view of the water. Live blues play nightly. The place stays open until 1
AM Friday and Saturday and until midnight Monday through Thursday.
On Sunday it's open 2–9. ⊠ *99 Court St.* ☎ *585/325–7090* ⚞ *Reser-*
vations not accepted ⊟ *AE, D, MC, V.*

$–$$$ ✕**Hogans Hideaway.** When it opened in 1978, this neighborhood fa-
vorite was in the back of a building behind a grocery store; hence the
hideaway part of the name. These days it's taken over the whole building and spills outside onto a patio in summer. The clientele—from suit-
wearing execs to Teva-shod students—is as varied as the menu. Specials
fill five 4-foot-square blackboards, change daily, and feature many fish
dishes, such as pan-seared salmon fillet with salsa and balsamic vinaigrette. The regular menu includes sandwiches and soups, which make
for a cheap but filling meal. ⊠ *197 Park Ave.* ☎ *585/442–4293* ⚞ *Reser-*
vations not accepted ⊟ *AE, D, MC, V* ⊗ *No lunch Sun.*

$–$$$ ✕**Mr. Dominic's.** The family-run Italian restaurant, a staple in Charlotte
since the mid-1970s, draws a loyal clientele from throughout the city.
Homemade pastas—gnocchi, spinach lasagna, veal and lobster ravioli,
four-cheese manicotti—are a specialty, but then again so are the steaks,
chops, and seafood. It's two blocks from Lake Ontario, which makes
it especially busy in summer. ⊠ *4699 Lake Ave.* ☎ *585/865–4630*
⊟ *AE, D, MC, V* ⊗ *No lunch Sat.–Mon.*

$–$$$ ✕**Tapas 177.** Spanish-style appetizers have been supersized into entrées
for the American appetite. The menu, which changes weekly, highlights
seafood, but includes options for vegetarians as well as carnivores. The

menu might include jumbo bacon-wrapped shrimp with feta cheese stuffing in sherry cream sauce, a salad of grilled quail and goat cheese atop arugula and endive, or potato gnocchi with butternut squash, spinach, and mushrooms. Flavors on the martini menu include chocolate, melon, lemon, and orange. At midnight the casually elegant restaurant turns into a nightclub with an international beat. The candlelit atmosphere turns sexy as the evening and the music heat up. Salsa lessons are given on Thursday night. Parking is by valet on Friday and Saturday nights. ⊠ *177 St. Paul St.* ☎ *585/262–2090* ▤ *AE, D, DC, MC, V* ⊘ *Closed Sun. No lunch.*

$–$$$ ✕ **Tastings.** Going to the grocery store was never like this. The restaurant is adjacent to the 130,000-square-foot Wegmans supermarket in Pittsford, and is run by the Rochester grocery giant. Chefs use the best of the supermarket's fresh, seasonal ingredients, turning out such contemporary fare as pan-seared shrimp with cauliflower puree, braised leeks, and roasted beets or grilled leg of lamb with pumpkin couscous and root vegetables. The open kitchen lets you watch the preparations; two eight-seat chef's tables put you in the front row. Brick walls, polished wood tables, and banquette seats make the large space seem warm and intimate. ⊠ *3195 Monroe Ave., Pittsford* ☎ *585/381–1881* ▤ *AE, D, MC, V* ⊘ *Closed Sun. and Mon.*

¢–$ ✕ **Schaller's Drive-In.** Opened in 1956, the family-owned and -operated, cash-only restaurant has retained a *Happy Days* feel. Place your order and watch the short-order sideshow. The cashier, who appears to be standing in a pit, yells out your request. In the din of all the other orders, yours emerges exactly as you wanted. Burgers topped with Schaller's secret hot sauce are the most popular choice, followed by a Rochester specialty, white hot dogs—aka white hots. These natural-casing dogs have no nitrates and look more like a white sausage than a hot dog. The restaurant, west of Ontario Beach Park in the town of Greece, is particularly popular with the beach crowd. Take out on a sunny day or eat in the bright dining room. ⊠ *965 Edgemere Dr., Greece* ☎ *585/865–3319* ⚏ *Reservations not accepted* ▤ *No credit cards.*

$$ ✕🖾 **Renaissance Del Monte Lodge.** The modern hotel is next to the Erie Canal about 6 mi southeast of downtown Rochester. Rooms have doorbells and are outfitted in soothing, neutral tones and traditional furnishings. Beds have 250-thread-count sheets, specially washed to preserve softness, and down pillows and comforters. Leather recliners and adjustable leather desk chairs provide comfortable seating. The spa offers massages, facials, body wraps, manicures and pedicures, and other beauty treatments. The Erie Grill ($$–$$$$), which overlooks the canal, serves a seasonal American menu that emphasizes game meats in cooler weather. The elegance of the hotel is reflected in the marble floors of the restaurant, and the candlelit ambience invites intimate dinners. ⊠ *41 N. Main St., Pittsford 14534* ☎ *585/381–9900* ▤ *585/381–9825* ⊕ *www.renaissancehotels.com* ⇗ *97 rooms, 2 suites* ⚭ *Restaurant, room service, in-room data ports, in-room safes, minibars, cable TV with movies and video games, indoor pool, hot tub, spa, bar, babysitting, dry cleaning, laundry facilities, Internet, business services, meeting rooms, airport shuttle, free parking* ▤ *AE, D, DC, MC, V.*

$–$$ ✕▣ **The Strathallan Hotel.** All accommodations here are suites, which means you get much more space than in a standard hotel room. The suites, all with high-speed Internet access, look out toward downtown or the East Avenue neighborhood, and some have balconies. In the wood-paneled lobby, leather chairs impart a clubby feel. Furnishings in the suites are fairly standard, however. The highly regarded Grill at Strathallan ($$$) serves mostly contemporary American fare that draws on European and Asian flavors—seared sesame seed–coated tuna with bok choy in *ponzu* sauce, for instance, or pan-roasted veal chop with fettuccine and porcini mushrooms. A vegetarian option, such as veggie-filled cannelloni in goat-cheese fondue, is offered, but seafood and beef take center stage. From here it's a short walk to the Rochester Museum & Science Center and more of a stroll to the George Eastman House, Memorial Art Gallery, and the restaurants and shops of Park Avenue. ✉ *550 East Ave., 14607* ☎ *585/461–5010 or 800/678–7284* 🖷 *585/ 461–3387* ⊕ *www.strathallan.com* ⇨ *156 suites* ⚫ *Restaurant, room service, in-room data ports, in-room safes, some kitchenettes, microwaves, refrigerators, cable TV with movies and video games, gym, piano bar, dry cleaning, laundry facilities, laundry services, concierge, Internet, business services, meeting rooms, airport shuttle, free parking, no-smoking floors* ⊟ *AE, D, MC, V.*

$$–$$$$ ▣ **The Inn on Broadway.** Nightclubs, the Eastman Theater, and dining options from elegant to coffee shop are all within a few blocks of this boutique hotel in the East End cultural district. A private club originally occupied the 1929 building, and refinement lingers in the air here. Rooms, individually appointed, have featherbeds (queen or king), down comforters, and thick towels; some have hardwood floors or gas fireplaces. Suites offer kitchenettes and whirlpool tubs. A sitting area with a small library is a B&B–style touch. ✉ *26 Broadway, 14607* ☎ *585/232–3595 or 877/612–3595* 🖷 *585/546–2164* ⊕ *www.innonbroadway.com* ⇨ *17 rooms, 6 suites* ⚫ *Dining room, in-room data ports, some in-room hot tubs, some kitchenettes, cable TV, in-room VCRs, gym, bar, laundry service, concierge, free parking; no smoking* ⊟ *AE, D, MC, V* ⧀ *CP.*

$–$$ ▣ **Dartmouth House B&B Inn.** A residential setting, large front porch, and cozy backyard give this 1905 Tudor the feel of home. The house, less than a mile from the George Eastman House, contains a small camera collection that includes a model the proprietor used aboard ship during World War II. The decor incorporates floral, striped, and other patterned fabrics and wall coverings. Interior schemes vary from room to room, as do bed configurations. The living room has a beamed ceiling and a working fireplace. Wireless Internet access is available throughout the house. Breakfast, a multicourse affair, is a highlight here. ✉ *215 Dartmouth St., 14607* ☎ *585/271–7872 or 800/724–6298* 🖷 *585/ 473–0778* ⊕ *www.dartmouthhouse.com* ⇨ *3 rooms, 1 suite* ⚫ *Dining room, fans, cable TV, in-room VCRs, piano, Internet, business services, free parking; no kids under 12, no smoking* ⊟ *AE, D, MC, V* ⊘ *Closed Jan. and Feb.* ⧀ *BP.*

$–$$ ▣ **Hampton Inn Rochester South.** The welcoming lobby of this five-story chain hotel has a large-screen TV, a microwave, 24-hour coffee and tea service, and fresh fruit. Rooms have wireless Internet access, fresh carpets and wall coverings, firm beds, and large headboards. King rooms have a pull-out sofa. Radio-alarm buttons are labeled so that you can easily find your favorite type of music. Several restaurants and a small shopping plaza are within walking distance. The University of Rochester is 2 mi away. You have access to a nearby gym. ⊠ *717 E. Henrietta Rd. (off I–390), 14623* ☎ *585/272–7800* ♒ *585/272–1211* ⊕ *www. hamptoninn.com* ↰ *108 rooms, 4 suites* ♣ *Some microwaves, some refrigerators, cable TV with movies and video games, dry cleaning, Internet, business services, meeting rooms, airport shuttle, free parking, no-smoking rooms* ☱ *AE, D, DC, MC, V* ¶◯¶ *CP.*

¢–$$ ☷ **Hyatt Regency Rochester.** Depending on which side of the hotel your room is on, you may look out onto some of the city's finest examples of 19th-century architecture. The downtown location puts you within walking distance of the Blue Cross Arena and Geva Theatre Center. At this writing, the hotel expects to have replaced carpets and added new pillowtop mattresses in all rooms in 2005. The suites have jet tubs. All rooms have wireless Internet access. The easy chairs in the lobby lounge are good people-watching perches. ⊠ *125 E. Main St., 14604* ☎ *585/ 546–1234* ♒ *585/546–6777* ⊕ *www.rochester.hyatt.com* ↰ *319 rooms, 17 suites* ♣ *Restaurant, room service, in-room data ports, some in-room hot tubs, some microwaves, some refrigerators, cable TV with movies, indoor pool, gym, bar, laundry service, concierge, Internet, meeting rooms, airport shuttle, parking (fee), no-smoking rooms* ☱ *AE, D, MC, V.*

$ ☷ **Crowne Plaza Rochester.** Some rooms at this modern, seven-story hotel in downtown open onto the pool deck, which is on the fourth floor. Beds are either kings or queens; all received fresh pillowtop mattresses in 2004 and have hypoallergenic duvets. Adjustable office chairs make working at the desk more comfortable. Wireless Internet access is available. ⊠ *70 State St., 14614* ☎ *585/546–3450* ♒ *585/546–8712* ⊕ *www.rochestercrowne.com* ↰ *354 rooms, 8 suites* ♣ *Restaurant, coffee shop, room service, in-room data ports, some kitchenettes, some microwaves, some refrigerators, cable TV with movies, pool, gym, sauna, pub, dry cleaning, laundry service, concierge, business services, meeting rooms, airport shuttle, parking (fee), no-smoking rooms* ☱ *AE, D, MC, V.*

¢–$ ☷ **Ramada Inn Rochester.** The three-story hotel, on a busy commercial street with many chain restaurants, has small rooms, but they're quiet thanks to sturdy materials that keep the noise out. (The staff frequently hears comments about the intriguing stucco pattern on the room walls.) You have access to a nearby gym. The pub-style restaurant has karaoke and live music on weekends. The hotel is less than 10 mi from downtown. ⊠ *800 Jefferson Rd., Henrietta 14623* ☎ *585/475–9190* ♒ *585/ 424–2138* ⊕ *www.ramadainnrochester.com* ↰ *143 rooms* ♣ *Restaurant, room service, in-room data ports, some microwaves, some refrigerators, cable TV with movies, indoor pool, dry cleaning, laundry facilities, laundry service, business services, meeting room, airport shuttle, free parking, some pets allowed (fee), no-smoking rooms* ☱ *AE, D, DC, MC, V* ¶◯¶ *CP.*

¢   ☷ **EconoLodge Rochester South.** The three-story motel, in the southern suburb of Henrietta, is within walking distance of several chain restaurants and a five-minute drive to a mall. Rooms are tidy and efficiently set up, with sinks outside the bathroom. Interior corridors and elevators connect the rooms. The free shuttle includes the colleges on its travels. ✉ *940 Jefferson Rd., Henrietta 14623* ☎ *585/427–2700* 📠 *585/427–8504* ⊕ *www.choicehotels.com* ⤴ *94 rooms, 2 suites* ⚒ *In-room data ports, some in-room safes, some in-room hot tubs, some microwaves, some refrigerators, cable TV with movies and video games, laundry facilities, Internet, business services, airport shuttle, free parking, some pets allowed, no-smoking rooms* ⊟ *AE, D, DC, MC, V* ℺ *CP.*

Nightlife & the Arts

The performing arts are highly valued in Rochester. The world-renowned **Garth Fagan Dance** (⊕ www.garthfagandance.org), a modern-dance troupe, is based here but spends most of the time touring. Several theaters offer productions many nights of the week. Rock and jazz are favorites in the clubs on Alexander Street and East Avenue in the East End, on Monroe Avenue in the city, and in the St. Paul Quarter downtown. Here are a few places where theater and music are in full bloom.

NIGHTLIFE TVs fill the bar at **Flour City Brewing** (✉ 869 E. Henrietta Rd. ☎ 585/424–4677), but the brewing apparatus is the real eye-catcher. Flour City Pale Ale is one of the most popular brews here, but the Irish-style Black Magic Stout is up there, too. Microbrews from other places also are available. Steaks, chops, and poultry dominate the dinner menu ($–$$). National and local acts play **Milestones** (✉ 170 East Ave. ☎ 585/325–6490 ⊕ www.milestonesmusicroom.com), a fixture of the East End nightlife scene. The music ranges from DJ spins to rock to jazz, and you're as likely to discover a new favorite as to enjoy familiar sounds.

THE ARTS The **Eastman School of Music** (✉ 26 Gibbs St. ☎ 585/274–1100 concert line ⊕ www.rochester.edu) at the University of Rochester includes several performance spaces. The 3,100-seat **Eastman Theatre** (✉ 60 Gibbs St.) was built by George Eastman in 1922 as a center for music, dance, and silent film with orchestral accompaniment. It's the major concert hall for many of the Eastman School of Music orchestras and ensembles. It's also home to the Rochester Philharmonic Orchestra. Many concerts are free at 455-seat **Kilbourn Hall,** an intimate setting with world-famous acoustics.

The **Geva Theatre Center** (✉ 75 Woodbury Blvd. ☎ 585/232–4382 box office ⊕ www.gevatheatre.org), the city's leading professional theater, presents about nine shows a year. Its Nextstage productions are edgier and more experimental.

The 535-seat **Dryden Theatre** (✉ 900 East Ave. ☎ 585/271–3361 ⊕ www.eastman.org ⤴ $6), on the grounds of the George Eastman House, shows classic, art-house, and foreign films most nights at 8 PM, with earlier times on Sunday. It also hosts several film festivals each year. The art-deco **Little Theatre** (✉ 240 East Ave. ☎ 585/258–0444 show times, 585/258–0400 general information ⊕ www.little-theatre.com) shows art-house and foreign films on five screens and also hosts movie festivals. The café is a destination in itself, with jazz and sweets that make you forget about buckets of popcorn.

Sports & the Outdoors

The Erie Canal has shifted from being a transportation route to a recreation area. You can rent a replica packet boat or join a public tour. Joggers and bicyclists enjoy a paved path alongside the waterway. Golfers can choose from nearly 60 area courses, and gardeners can glean ideas from the nearly two dozen parks, many designed by Frederick Law Olmsted. Birders flock to **Braddock Bay** in Greece to watch for hawks and many other species. Rochester takes a big-league interest in its minor-league teams, and even Division III colleges have their followings.

BASEBALL   Some of baseball's greats—Stan Musial and Cal Ripken Jr., to name two from different eras—played for the **Rochester Red Wings** (⊠ 1 Morrie Silver Way ☎ 800/447–2623 box office, 585/454–1001 administrative office ⊕ www.redwingsbaseball.com). The Triple-A International League team's downtown stadium is across from the High Falls entertainment district. Tickets are $5.50–$9.50.

GOLF   The **Greystone Golf Club** (⊠ 1400 Atlantic Ave., Walworth ☎ 800/810–2325 ⊕ www.234golf.com) has a 7,200-yard links-style course that features changes in elevation and undulating greens. The open landing areas belie challenges on the many memorable holes. High-season greens fees for 18 holes (with cart) are $41–$55. *Golf Digest* chose the 7,026-yard course at the **Ravenwood Golf Club** (⊠ 929 Lynaugh Rd., Victor ☎ 585/924–5100 ⊕ www.ravenwoodgolf.com) as one of the best new courses in the country in 2003. The bent-grass fairways help the ball to sit up on the wide fairways. Greens won't play any tricks. High-season greens fees for 18 holes, including a cart, are $59–$69.

ICE HOCKEY   The **Rochester Americans** (⊠ Blue Cross Arena, 1 War Memorial Sq. ☎ 585/454–5335 ⊕ www.amerks.com), an American Hockey League team, are affiliated with the National Hockey League's Buffalo Sabres. The team, nicknamed the Amerks, is a perennial contender and has won several Calder Cup championships. The season runs October to April. Ticket prices are $11–$19.

SOCCER   Soccer may be a foreign sport in much of the rest of the country, but in Rochester it's a fan favorite. The **Rochester Raging Rhinos** (⊠ 333 N. Plymouth Ave. ☎ 585/454–5425 ⊕ www.rhinossoccer.com) play in the A-League, a step below Major League Soccer, although they've defeated MLS teams many times. After sharing Frontier Field with the Red Wings, the team is, at this writing, anticipating a move to soccer-specific PAETEC Park, in 2005. The season runs from May to September. Tickets are $14–$20.

Shopping

Three large malls ring the metropolitan area, but the really interesting stores are in the neighborhoods. Rochester's version of couture can be found on Monroe Avenue in the town of Brighton.

Piercings or pearls (fake ones, anyway), leather or lace can be yours in **Oxford Square** (⊠ Monroe Ave. between Goodman St. and I–490 ramp ☎ No phone ⊕ www.monroeavenue.com), a five-block stretch of bohemia. Secondhand bookstores feed the mind. Mediterranean, vegetarian, and Asian cuisine take care of the body. The upscale eclectic mix at **Parkleigh** (✉ 215 Park Ave. ☎ 585/244–4842) includes everything from greeting cards to freshly ground coffee and Clarks shoes.

In the village of **Pittsford,** about 6 mi southeast of downtown Rochester, the two blocks south of the intersection of Main Street and Monroe Avenue are lined with restaurants, shops, and an overflowing secondhand bookstore. Window shoppers and big-time buyers are drawn to **Schoen Place,** which encompasses a row of jewelry and artisan shops across from the Erie Canal, and the adjacent **Northfield Common,** a mix of crafters, restaurants, and art galleries. A visit to **Bill Wahl's Ice Cream & Yogurt** (✉ 45 Schoen Pl. ☎ 585/248–2080) is perfect for dessert anytime.

THE FINGER LAKES A TO Z

By Mary Bulkot   *To research prices, get advice from other travelers, and book travel arrangements, visit www.fodors.com.*

AIR TRAVEL

The region is served by the Greater Rochester International Airport and Syracuse Hancock International Airport, as well as by the Ithaca Tompkins Regional Airport (ITH) and Elmira-Corning Regional Airport (ELM).

Continental Airlines affiliates fly between Syracuse and Albany, Buffalo, Long Island (Islip), and New York City (Newark Liberty International Airport). They also link Rochester with Albany, the lower Hudson Valley (Westchester County Airport), and New York City (Newark), as well as with the Elmira-Corning airport.

JetBlue Airlines has service between New York City (JFK) and Rochester and Syracuse. Low-cost carrier Independence Air links Syracuse and Rochester with New York City (JFK and Newark) and the Hudson Valley. Northwest flies from Newark to Syracuse and Rochester; it also links Rochester with Albany.

US Airways Express flies between New York City (LaGuardia Airport) and Syracuse, Rochester, and the Ithaca Tompkins airport. Through Philadelphia, the carrier connects Rochester, Syracuse, Elmira-Corning, and Ithaca with Long Island. It also flies between the Hudson Valley and Syracuse, Elmira-Corning, and Ithaca, all via Philadelphia. These connecting flights are still faster than driving.

🛪 Airports **Elmira-Corning Regional Airport** ✉ Sing Sing Rd., Horseheads ☎ 607/795-0402 ⊕ www.elmiracorningairport.com. **Ithaca Tompkins Regional Airport** ✉ Brown Rd., north of Rte. 13, 4½ mi northeast of downtown Ithaca ☎ 607/257-0456 ⊕ www.ithaca-airport.com.

BUS TRAVEL

Although bus travel offers an opportunity to see the countryside, trips can be lengthy, and the cost is sometimes not much less than flying.

Greyhound buses link the Finger Lakes region with the Adirondacks, Albany, the Catskills, the Hudson Valley, New York City, Long Island, and western New York. Stops include Canandaigua, Corning, Elmira, Geneva, Ithaca, Rochester, and Syracuse.

New York Trailways buses link Albany and Buffalo to Syracuse and Rochester; and New York City and Long Island to Ithaca, Syracuse, and Rochester. Stops include Canandaigua, Corning, Elmira, and Geneva.

Shortline's New York City–to–Ithaca run is one of the most heavily traveled of the bus routes, with eight bus trips daily. It also runs three trips daily to Ithaca from Long Island and the lower Hudson Valley (Westchester) and has stops in Corning and Elmira.

🚌 **Greyhound** ☎ 800/231-2222 ⊕ www.greyhound.com. **New York Trailways** ☎ 800/776-7548 or 800/858-8555 ⊕ www.trailwaysny.com. **Shortline Coach USA** ☎ 800/631-8405 ⊕ www.shortlinebus.com.

CAR RENTAL

Avis, Budget, Enterprise, Hertz, and National all serve the Rochester and Syracuse airports. Avis, Hertz, and National serve the Elmira-Corning Regional Airport. Avis and Hertz serve the Ithaca-Tompkins Regional Airport. Enterprise and National are other options in Ithaca. Alamo and Thrifty have offices in Syracuse. *See* Car Rental *in* Smart Travel Tips A to Z for national agencies' contact information.

CAR TRAVEL

Public transportation is limited in upstate New York, even between major cities, and travel between smaller cities and villages is next to impossible without a car. Scenic byways—like routes 14, 54, 54A, 89, and 90, which run along Seneca, Keuka, and Cayuga lakes—make for spectacular driving. The major wine trails follow these routes. The Seaway Trail follows the coastline of Lake Ontario, to the north of the region. In the southern part of the region, be prepared for steep, winding roads.

Traffic is relatively light, even on the New York State Thruway (I–90), except around Syracuse and Rochester. Because the area is still home to some industry, rush hour can start as early as 3 PM but generally is over by 5:30. Rush hour isn't much of an issue outside the major city areas. You may, however, encounter heavy truck traffic on the state routes that serve as conduits between upstate and down. On smaller roads, watch for farm vehicles.

Be alert for deer and other wildlife, especially on lakeside roads. Deer traffic increases in fall, particularly at dawn, dusk, and after dark. Snow can make driving difficult, even for very experienced winter drivers with four-wheel-drive vehicles. Blizzards can hit fast and last long. Strong winds blow snowdrifts across the road, creating a condition called lake effect—a virtual whiteout. Lake effect is especially heavy north of I–90. Town roads tend to be better plowed than county roads or state routes.

EMERGENCIES

In an emergency, dial 911.

🚑 **Emergency Services Crouse Prompt Care** ✉ 739 Irving Ave., Syracuse ☎ 315/470-2951 ⊕ www.crouse.org. **Finger Lakes Medical Care Center** ✉ 303 Grant Ave., Auburn ☎ 315/258-7100. **Urgent Medical Care of Skaneateles** ✉ 803 W. Genesee St./Rte. 20, Skaneateles ☎ 315/685-9355.

🏥 **Hospitals Auburn Memorial Hospital** ✉ 17 Lansing St., Auburn ☎ 315/255-7011 ⊕ www.auburnhospital.com. **Cayuga Medical Center at Ithaca** ✉ 101 Harris B. Dates

Dr., Ithaca ☎ 607/274-4011 ⊕ www.cayugamed.org. **Community General Hospital** ✉ 4900 Broad Rd., Syracuse ☎ 315/492-5011 ⊕ www.cgh.org. **Crouse-Irving Memorial Hospital** ✉ 736 Irving Ave., Syracuse ☎ 315/470-7511 ⊕ www.crouse.org. **Geneva General Hospital** ✉ 196 North St., Geneva ☎ 315/787-4000 ⊕ www.flhealth.org. **Rochester General Hospital** ✉ 1425 Portland Ave., Rochester ☎ 585/922-4000 ⊕ www.viahealth.org. **St. Joseph's Hospital** ✉ 555 E. Market St., Elmira ☎ 607/733-6541 ⊕ www.stjoseph.vwh.net. **Strong Memorial Hospital** ✉ 601 Elmwood Ave., Rochester ☎ 585/275-2100 ⊕ www.stronghealth.com.

LODGING

There are hundreds of bed-and-breakfasts and many quality inns in the region, most with private baths, some with phones and televisions. The Finger Lakes Bed & Breakfast Association has extensive listings.

Because so many locals live or have summer places on the waterfront, vacation rentals on the lakes are harder to find than you might think. Rental Plus Finger Lakes Vacation Rentals has a large selection of rentals—including cabins, cottages, condos, and houses—on Canandaigua, Honeoye, Keuka, and Seneca lakes. Finger Lakes Getaways has rentals, from basic cottages and cabins to plush homes, on Cayuga, Keuka, and Seneca lakes, as well as on smaller lakes. County tourism offices also may have information about vacation rentals.

🚩 **Finger Lakes Bed & Breakfast Association** ☎ 800/695-5590 ⊕ www.flbba.org. **Finger Lakes Cottages** ⊕ www.fingerlakescottages.com. **Finger Lakes Getaways** ✉ 2772 Rte. 54A, Penn Yan ☎ 315/536-4821 or 800/580-4733 ⊕ www. fingerlakesgetawaysinc.com. **Rental Plus Finger Lakes Vacation Rentals** ✉ 142 Lake St., Penn Yan ☎ 315/536-2201 or 888/414-5253 ⊕ www.rentalplus.com ✉ 22 Lakeshore Dr., Canandaigua ☎ 585/393-9280 or 585/393-9281. **Skaneatelesrental.com** ☎ 315/685-4858 ⊕ www.skaneatelesrental.com.

SPORTS & THE OUTDOORS

See Sports & the Outdoors *in* Smart Travel Tips A to Z for additional information.

BIKING The terrain in the region, although flat in many places, especially along the old railbeds that now serve as multipurpose trails, can be quite hilly. The terrain in the south has more hills, with some steep inclines. Roads are well paved, shoulders are wide, and traffic is relatively light.

The Erie Canal Recreational Trail follows the historic waterway. The Ontario Pathways Rail Trail, a former railway, is now a 23-mi multiuse trail. The Keuka Outlet Trail is a 6-mi hiking and biking trail that begins in Penn Yan and snakes between Keuka and Seneca lakes.

The Web site of the Ithaca-based Finger Lakes Cycling Club has information about trails, tours, races, and local bike shops; www.bikeRochester. com is another source for regional biking info. Central Destinations of the Finger Lakes Region offers a biking and hiking booklet with 12 bicycle tours in six counties.

FISHING All the lakes have municipal and/or state launches and private marinas. Keuka, Seneca, and Cayuga have the greatest number of public launches. Some lakes, like Conesus and Honeoye, can be crowded in summer; others, such as Hemlock and Canadice lakes, are practically undeveloped. Boat rental is available at marinas. Charter boats are also available; check with county tourism offices for details.

Fishing licenses and regulations may be obtained at town clerk's offices, fishing-gear retailers, or by phone from the state. For fish and wildlife information, sporting conditions, licenses, and a list of marinas, contact the New York State Department of Environmental Conservation.

GOLF The area has numerous public golf courses that vary in difficulty and amenities. Get information about courses and packages and make reservations via the Finger Lakes Golf Trail. County tourism offices may also be able to provide information.

🚲 Biking BikeRochester.com ⊕ www.bikerochester.com. **Central Destinations of the Finger Lakes Region** ☎ 800/228−2760 ⊕ www.finger-lakes.com. **Finger Lakes Cycling Club** ⊕ www.flcycling.org. **New York State Canal System** 🖂 Box 189, Albany 12201 ☎ 800/422−6254 ⊕ www.canals.state.ny.us. **Ontario Pathways Rail Trail** 🖂 200 Ontario St., Canandaigua ☎ 585/234−7722 ⊕ www.ontariopathways.org.

🚲 Fishing **New York State Department of Environmental Conservation** ☎ 866/933−2257 fishing licenses, 845/256−3000 general information ⊕ www.dec.state.ny.us.

🚲 Golf **Finger Lakes Golf Trail** ☎ 866/969−3548 or 800/288−8248 ⊕ www.fingerlakesgolftrail.com.

TOURS

BOAT TOURS Mid-Lakes Navigation offers seasonal cruises and two-, three-, and four-day excursions on the Erie Canal, which depart from a few points in the Syracuse vicinity. River Otter Boat Tour runs 2½-hour flora-and-fauna trips along the Seneca River and Erie Canal; the cruises pass the towns of Cato, Conquest, and Port Byron.

🚲 Boat Tours **Mid-Lakes Navigation Co.** 🖂 11 Jordan St., Skaneateles ☎ 315/685−8500 or 800/545−4318 ⊕ www.midlakesnav.com. **River Otter Boat Tour** 🖂 9439 Riverforest Rd., Weedsport ☎ 315/252−4171 Ext. 3.

TRAIN TRAVEL

Amtrak's Empire Service connects the Finger Lakes Region with Buffalo and Niagara Falls in the west and the Albany area to the east. It stops in Syracuse and Rochester. To assure a seat, reserve a ticket in advance. Bikes are allowed only as checked baggage, but Amtrak lines that service the Finger Lakes don't usually have baggage cars. Service is often late, and one-hour or longer delays aren't unheard of, especially in bad weather.

🚲 Amtrak ☎ 800/872−7245 ⊕ www.amtrak.com.

TRANSPORTATION AROUND THE FINGER LAKES

Although getting to and from the region by public transportation is fairly easy, getting around it is virtually impossible without a car. Public transportation within the region is limited, and a car is the best way to explore the region's scenic backroads and byways as well as its many natural attractions. If you choose to travel by bus, consider heading to Ithaca, one of the most popular and frequent routes.

VISITOR INFORMATION

🚲 **Cayuga County Office of Tourism** 🖂 131 Genesee St., Auburn 13021 ☎ 315/255−1658 or 800/499−9615 ⊕ www.tourcayuga.com. **Chemung County Chamber of Com-**

merce ✉ 400 E. Church St., Elmira 14901 ☎ 607/734-5137 ⊕ www.chemungchamber. org. **Finger Lakes Tourism Alliance** ✉ 309 Lake St., Penn Yan 14527 ☎ 315/536-7488 or 800/530-7488 ⊕ www.fingerlakes.org. **Greater Rochester Visitors Association** ✉ 45 East Ave., Suite 400, Rochester 14604 ☎ 585/546-3070 or 800/677-7282 ⊕ www. visitrochester.com. **Greater Syracuse/Onondaga County Convention & Visitors Bureau** ✉ 572 S. Salina St., Syracuse 13202 ☎ 315/470-1910 or 800/234-4497 ⊕ www. visitsyracuse.org. **Ithaca/Tompkins County Convention & Visitors Bureau** ✉ 904 E. Shore Dr., Ithaca 14850 ☎ 607/272-1313 or 800/284-8422 ⊕ www.visitithaca.com. **Livingston County Chamber of Commerce** ✉ 4560 Millenium Dr., Geneseo 14454 ☎ 585/243-2222 or 800/538-7365 ⊕ www.fingerlakeswest.com. **Schuyler County Chamber of Commerce** ✉ 100 N. Franklin St., Watkins Glen 14891 ☎ 607/535-4300 or 800/607-4552 ⊕ www.schuylerny.com. **Seneca County Tourism** ✉ 1 DiPronio Dr., Waterloo 13165 ☎ 315/539-1759 or 800/732-1848 ⊕ www.visitsenecany.net. **Steuben County Convention & Visitors Bureau** ✉ 1 W. Market St., Suite 301, Corning 14830 ☎ 866/946-3386 ⊕ www.corningfingerlakes.com. **Wayne County Tourism** ✉ 9 Pearl St., Lyons 14489 ☎ 315/946-5469 or 800/527-6510 ⊕ www.waynecountytourism.org. **Yates County Chamber of Commerce** ✉ 2375 Rte. 14A, Penn Yan 14527 ☎ 315/536-3111 or 800/868-9283 ⊕ www.yatesny.com.

THE NORTH COUNTRY

8

"UPSTATE NEW YORK MAY BE America's best-kept secret," wrote George Meegan, an Englishman who made a seven-year, 19,000-mi trek (ending in 1983) through the Americas, in his account *The Longest Walk*. The "secret" world of the North Country of New York includes everything from refined civility to absolute wilderness. You might cross paths with the rich and famous, or you might cross paths with deer and bear; it just depends on how and where you choose to spend your time in the region.

Much of the region is part of Adirondack Park, which, with 6 million acres—nearly half of which has been declared "forever wild" by New York State—is the largest park expanse in the United States outside of Alaska. Girding it are lakes and rivers, principally Lake George and Lake Champlain to the east, the St. Lawrence River to the north, and Lake Ontario to the west.

The secret character of the North Country came about both through disregard and design. Early American settlers didn't show much interest in the region. The rugged land, inhospitable soil, and often unmerciful winter conditions sent them elsewhere in search of good land to clear for farms. Only the east, from Saratoga Springs, just outside the region's southern rim, to Lake Champlain, saw any significant settlement in the 1700s.

By and large, the Adirondacks were so ignored by early American settlers that it wasn't until 1837 that Ebenezer Emmons, a geologist on assignment from the state legislature to catalog the region, made the first recorded trek to the top of Mt. Marcy, the highest point in New York, in what today is called the High Peaks region. (New Hampshire's Mt. Washington, by comparison, had been climbed almost 200 years earlier, in 1642.)

The extended disinterest in the Adirondacks proved, in the long run, a boon for wilderness lovers. By the 1800s the idea that there was value in the wilderness itself began to gain popular support. Fans as disparate as Ralph Waldo Emerson and Teddy Roosevelt discovered the Adirondack wilds and returned extolling their virtues. After the publication in 1869 of William H. H. Murray's classic *Adventures in the Wilderness*, praising the freshness and purity of the Adirondack air, the area became recognized as a place for recuperation. The famous Trudeau Sanitorium in Saranac Lake was visited by many notables of the late 1880s, among them Robert Louis Stevenson. The North Country became one of the first regions in the United States where tourism was a principal industry. Enormous hotels were built, and the railroads reached as far north as the Thousand Islands area, along the St. Lawrence River.

Wealthy families also discovered the Adirondacks toward the latter part of the 19th century, giving rise to a concept of rustic elegance that became known as the "great camps." These remote lodges were built of native materials—wood and stone—and had a rough-hewn look to them, but were otherwise spacious and luxurious. One of the great camps, Camp Sagamore, was built in 1897 in the village of Racquette Lake; now open for tours, it's a good example of what it means to rough it upper-crust style.

Seasonal closures are a key consideration when planning a trip to this region. It's particularly important to call to confirm open information before settling the details of your North Country trip. The region is best known for its outdoor activities, so these are the focus of many of the itineraries below.

Numbers in the text correspond to numbers in the margin and on The North Country map.

8

If you have
3 days

The North Country is vast, so you should concentrate on one or two areas when planning a short visit. Here are four three-day plans.

The best time to visit ▦ **Lake George ❷** is mid-June through early September, because many places are closed during the rest of the year. Start off in the southern gateway to the Adirondacks, **Glens Falls ❶ ⌐**, where you should make a point of seeing the Hyde Collection before continuing a few miles north to Lake George or ▦ **Bolton Landing ❸**. Make Lake George your base if you're traveling with young children; opt for Bolton Landing if you're sans kiddies. Spend the first two days visiting attractions and water parks, relaxing at a beach, and cruising on the lake. If you're staying at a resort, leave time to take advantage of the recreational amenities. On Day 3, drive north on Route 9N to see the fort at **Ticonderoga ❹** and then continue northward to see the ruins at **Crown Point ❺**, taking in the scenery along the way.

The Thousand Islands area is another good summer destination. Although it's commercial and busy, ▦ **Alexandria Bay ⓰ ⌐** lies in the center of the 50-mi long area and has plenty of lodging options. Attractions include historic Boldt Castle (on Heart Island) and many opportunities to get out on the water and begin counting the islands. The state park on Wellesley Island has a beach and a 600-acre wildlife sanctuary with a museum. Kids also enjoy the Aqua Zoo. In the morning on Day 2, make the short trip to the river city of **Clayton ⓯** to see the wonderful Antique Boat Museum and have lunch in town. After eating, drive another 12 mi or so southwest along Route 12E to the Tibbetts Point Lighthouse in Cape Vincent, where Lake Ontario meets the St. Lawrence River. On Day 3, if you feel up to it, drive south to **Sackets Harbor ⓮** to stroll the battlefield where two engagements of the War of 1812 took place *or* to visit the Seaway Trail Discovery Center. In summer the harbor bustles with cruising activity. In winter the town belongs to hardy cross-country skiers and snowmobilers.

The following two itineraries take you into the mountains. Visit the Hyde Collection in **Glens Falls ❶ ⌐** and then head northwest, via U.S. 9 and Route 28, to North Creek and the ▦ **Gore Mountain Ski Area ⓬**. Warm-weather activities include visiting a garnet mine, taking a scenic railroad trip, mountain biking, hiking, white-water rafting, and canoeing. On either Day 2 or 3 take a side trip to the must-see Adirondack Museum in **Blue Mountain Lake ⓫** and Great Camp Sagamore, in Raquette Lake. Winter options center on snow: downhill and cross-country skiing and snowshoeing.

The ▦ **Lake Placid ❽** area is also sports-focused. In this option you use Lake Placid or the ▦ **Whiteface Mountain Ski Area ❼** in nearby Wilmington as your base for both nights. Take in the Olympic sites on Day 1 and spend the afternoon and evening checking out the shops and restaurants in Lake Placid. Get ready for some action on Day 2. Ice-skating, downhill and cross-country skiing, snowboarding, tobogganing, bobsledding, and snowshoeing are among the winter activities; summer and early-fall diversions include hiking, golf, fly-fishing, mountain biking, and lake cruising. Youngsters might enjoy visiting Santa's Workshop in the village of North Pole. On Day 3 (mid-May to mid-October), follow Route 86 northeast to Route 9N and take that to the spectacular **Ausable Chasm** ⑥.

If you have
6 days

With six days, you can combine elements of and build on the three-day itineraries above.

In summer follow the ▦ **Lake George** ❷ itinerary above, stopping in **Glens Falls** ❶ ⌐ to see the Hyde Collection first. On Day 3 drive north on Route 9N to see the fort at **Ticonderoga** ❹ or, farther north, the ruins at **Crown Point** ❺. Continue north on 9N and then follow it west from Westport toward Keene. You pass through Elizabethtown, home of the quirky Adirondack History Center, which is worth a visit. From Keene take Route 73 into ▦ **Lake Placid** ❽, where you spend the next two nights. Spend Day 4 in the great outdoors— here and in nearby Wilmington and the **Whiteface Mountain Ski Area** ❼— and poke around Lake Placid in the afternoon and evening. Devote Day 5 to seeing the Olympic sites. On Day 6, follow Route 86 northeast to Route 9N and take that to the spectacular **Ausable Chasm** ⑥.

Another way to see the Adirondacks is to start in **Ausable Chasm** ⑥ and then take Route 9N and Route 86 southwest into ▦ **Lake Placid** ❽, where you spend the first three nights. (Or consider overnighting in ▦ **Whiteface Mountain Ski Area** ❼ in nearby Wilmington instead.) Spend Days 2 and 3 checking out the Olympic venues and playing outside. On Day 4 switch to great-camps mode. Pick a lodging in either ▦ **Saranac Lake** ❾ or ▦ **Tupper Lake** ❿ for your fourth and fifth nights. The former is closer to the famed St. Regis Wilderness Canoe Area, which includes part of Upper Saranac Lake and stretches northwest. Devote Day 5 to a canoe trip. If you're not staying at an old camp, schedule a tour of the White Pine Camp in Paul Smiths for Day 4 or Day 6. If you have time and are heading south to go home, detour to the Adirondack Museum, in **Blue Mountain Lake** ⑪. In winter you'll have to skip Ausable Chasm, the canoeing, and the Blue Mountain Lake detour and focus on winter sports.

In the Thousand Islands area, use ▦ **Alexandria Bay** ⑯ ⌐ as your base for three nights. Spend Days 1 and 3 exploring the local attractions. On Day 2 venture northeast to either **Ogdensburg** ⑰, where the main draw is the Frederic Remington Art Museum, or **Massena** ⑱, to see the Moses-Saunders Power Dam and the Dwight D. Eisenhower Lock. On the morning of Day 4 make the short drive to **Clayton** ⑮ and the must-see Antique Boat Museum. Stop for lunch in the city and then go on to the Tibbetts Point Lighthouse in Cape Vincent. Afterward, head south (Route 12E to Route 180 to Route 3) to ▦ **Sackets Harbor** ⑭, where you spend the fourth and fifth nights. On Day 5 stroll the Sackets Harbor Battlefield State Historic Site, visit the Seaway Trail Discovery Center, and take a self-guided walking tour of the historic district with a brochure from the visitor center. On Day 6 bring the kids to Robbins' Farm and Old McDonald's Children's Farm.

In the 1950s the region's popularity declined as summer vacationers began to opt for seaside beach resorts rather than lakes and mountains. Winter travelers seemed to prefer Vermont and the Rockies, where ski resorts were better developed. Farming, mining, and shopping kept economic life ambling along, but tourism played much less of a role. The 1980 Winter Olympics in Lake Placid sparked renewed interest in the Adirondacks, Lake Placid in particular.

The largest city in the North Country is Watertown (population 27,000), which, although in the Thousand Islands area, is not, as its name implies, on the water itself. The 1959 opening of the St. Lawrence Seaway, connecting the Great Lakes and the Atlantic Ocean, prompted modest growth in the smaller cities of Massena and Ogdensburg, and Glens Falls and Plattsburgh were given a push with the opening of the Northway (Interstate 87) in the 1960s. But none of these is a big city in any sense of the word. Besides, cities are not the draw in the North Country. The region is, as it has been historically, a place for escape, a place to retreat from the pressures of city life.

Even during the peak summer period there is little bustle. Sure, there are hives abuzz with tourist activity in Lake George, Lake Placid, and the Thousand Islands. But if you consider the size of the North Country—equal to the states of Massachusetts, Connecticut, and Rhode Island combined—that leaves plenty of quiet, uncrowded space.

It's this lack of civilization that visitors seem to enjoy most about the region. The vast, interconnected waterways and hiking trails of the Adirondacks cover one of the two areas of genuine wilderness left in the Northeast (the other being northern Maine). The abundance of lakes and rivers throughout the region offers plenty of opportunity to hop aboard a canoe or kayak and explore, fish, or just separate yourself from landlocked civilization. In fall, when the leaves change color, the great expanses of forested land make for one of nature's most dramatic spectacles.

Exploring the North Country

The region is bordered by the Mohawk River valley to the south, Lake Ontario and the St. Lawrence River valley to the west and north, and Lake Champlain to the east. The North Country has two interstate highways: I–81 and I–87, both running north south—the former at the region's western edge and the latter near the eastern edge. There are no major east–west highways, although the New York State Thruway (I–90) traverses the state not far from the region's southern rim.

The two main roads through the southern and central Adirondacks are routes 28 and 30. Route 28 forms an east–west arc from Warrensburg, a few miles from Lake George, through Old Forge (and continuing toward Utica). Route 30 reaches north from Amsterdam in the Mohawk River valley, passing through Tupper Lake, Saranac Inn, and Paul Smiths on its way into Canada. The two routes run together for about 11 mi between Indian Lake and Blue Mountain Lake, the approximate geographical center of the Adirondacks. Route 28N makes a northerly swing from Route 28 at North Creek before veering west and joining Route 30 at Long Lake, 11 mi north of Blue Mountain Lake. Route 8, which enters the region in the southwest corner, joins Route 30 in Speculator and is the major road in the southwestern part of Adirondack Park.

The main roadways of the Thousand Islands area are I–81, which runs north from Syracuse through Watertown, and the Seaway Trail, a combination of routes 37, 12, and 12E that follows the St. Lawrence River to the Lake Ontario shore. These two main roadways intersect at the Thousand Islands International Bridge, leading into Canada. An inland road that parallels the Seaway Trail for much of the way is U.S. 11, which runs from northern Lake Champlain through the cities of Malone, Potsdam, and Canton to Watertown.

About the Hotels & Restaurants

The operative words throughout most of the region are "simple" and "rustic" rather than "elegant" and "refined." That is as it should be in a region that makes its statement as a world of retreat and escape. Lodging is generally simple and comfortable, and food is generally simple and good. Room prices and availability vary with the season. Throughout the North Country, expect to pay more in July and August, the fall foliage season, and during the December holidays. The ski centers stay busy into March.

Except for a few places here and there, haute cuisine is essentially nonexistent. Meals at traditional lodges tend to be tied to accommodations, although many establishments accept nonguests for dinner. Indeed, some of the best food in the Adirondacks is being served in resort and inn restaurants. The Olympic region in particular has a number of fine places to eat, primarily in Lake Placid. In the Thousand Islands–Seaway area, you find clusters of good restaurants in Alexandria Bay and Clayton.

WHAT IT COSTS				
	$$$$	$$$	$$	$	¢
RESTAURANTS	over $30	$22–$30	$15–$21	$8–$14	under $8
HOTELS	over $250	$200–$250	$150–$199	$100–$149	under $100

Restaurant prices are for a main course at dinner (or at the most expensive meal served). Hotel prices are for two people in a standard double room in high season.

Timing

The region is very much a seasonal world. Tourism shifts into high gear from June through August, before slowing down in September and October, and slowing considerably thereafter. Active skiing centers, such as Lake Placid and North Creek, continue through the winter, and snowmobilers, cross-country skiers, and ice fishermen throughout the North Country make what they can of the cold winter months. With

8

Canoeing

The vast network of rivers and lakes in the North Country makes canoeing one of the best ways to experience the outdoors here. Trips of 100 mi or more are possible, as are short day trips geared for beginners. One of the best places for canoeing in the Adirondacks is the St. Regis Canoe Area, west of Saranac Lake, where powerboats are prohibited. To the southwest, between Old Forge and Raquette Lake, is the 16-mi Fulton Chain of Lakes, also popular with canoeists. A 1-mi portage links this eight-lake cluster (from Eighth Lake) to Raquette Lake, from which you may paddle north.

Hiking

Hiking is the simplest and one of the best ways to experience the North Country outdoors. Most trails are well maintained and marked by the New York State Department of Environmental Conservation, and many trailheads are along the major routes through the Adirondack area—including Route 28N between North Creek and Long Lake and Route 73 between Lake Placid and Keene.

The most popular—and congested—area for hiking is the High Peaks region, accessible from the Lake Placid area in the north, Keene in the east, and Newcomb in the south. Much ado is made of the so-called Adirondack "46ers"—the people who have ascended the 46 highest peaks in the region. Although the High Peaks area tends to draw the most attention, this is where you find the most rugged hiking. Many less strenuous climbs and hikes offer rewarding views and backwoods experiences, whether for half-day hikes, full-day outings, or multiday backpacking trips. The areas around Schroon Lake, for example, have good hiking with minimal climbing.

Winter Sports

You may see Olympic-caliber athletes in a variety of sports training in and around Lake Placid, which was the site of the 1980 Winter Olympics. National and international competitions in bobsledding and luge are held at Mount Van Hoevenberg, alpine racing and freestyle competition at Whiteface Mountain, and speed skating at the Sheffield Speed Skating Oval in the center of Lake Placid. Hockey and figure-skating competitions are held in the ice arena next door to the Olympic oval. But you don't have to spend all your time on the sidelines. You might strap on some skates and take a spin on the speed-skating oval or the indoor ice arena; shoot down an old ski slide in a toboggan, or hurtle down a bobsled run. Go downhill skiing at Whiteface, the largest alpine resort in the North Country, or cover a few miles on cross-country skis at Mount Van Hoevenberg. Head to the southeastern part of Adirondack Park for the Gore Mountain Ski Center, a Whiteface sibling with a 2,100-foot vertical drop, and the Garnet Hill Cross-Country Ski Center.

---

sizeable winter populations, cities such as Watertown, Glens Falls, and Plattsburgh remain reasonably active during the off-seasons. Generally speaking, though, the North Country itself goes into something of a retreat from November through April.

Black-fly season can start as early as late April, and lasts until early July.

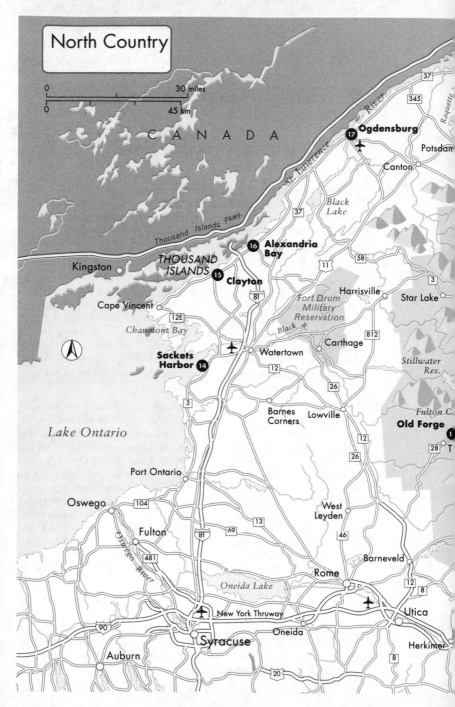

North Country

0 — 30 miles
0 — 45 km

C A N A D A

Ogdensburg **17**

Potsdam

Canton

St. Lawrence River

37

345

Raquette

Black Lake

37

Thousand Islands Pkwy.

Kingston

THOUSAND ISLANDS

16 Alexandria Bay

15 Clayton

11

58

Harrisville

Star Lake

3

Cape Vincent

12E

Chaumont Bay

81

Fort Drum Military Reservation

Black R.

Carthage

812

Stillwater Res.

Sackets Harbor **14**

Watertown

12

26

Lowville

12

Fulton C.

Old Forge **1**

28   T

Lake Ontario

3

Barnes Corners

Port Ontario

West Leyden

26

Oswego

104

Fulton

Oswego River

81

69

13

46

Barneveld

Rome

12

8

481

Oneida Lake

New York Thruway

Utica

90

Syracuse

Oneida

20

Herkimer

8

Auburn

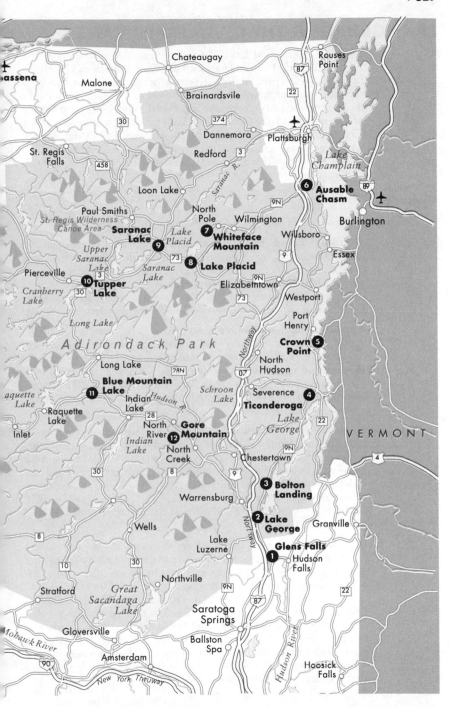

LAKE GEORGE & THE CHAMPLAIN VALLEY

The Lake George and Lake Champlain areas are technically within Adirondack Park. Long and narrow, Lake George stretches 32 mi south to north. Because the local Native Americans considered its waters sacred, Lake George was originally named Lac du Saint Sacrement by the French, who had explored the region in the mid-17th century. A spit of land separates Lake George from Lake Champlain, which is 107 mi long and the sixth-largest lake in North America. The Champlain Valley is largely a farming region that stretches from the north end of Lake George to the border with Canada, west to the Adirondacks, and east into Vermont.

Glens Falls

❶ *194 mi north of New York City, 48 mi north of Albany.*

The road to Lake George begins in Glens Falls, about 10 mi south and east of Adirondack Park's formal boundary. With a population of more than 15,000 in the city and about 25,000 more in surrounding communities (Queensbury and Hudson Falls), Glens Falls is the only really urban area in this part of the state. One good reason to visit is the Hyde Collection of art, which was started by a prominent Glens Falls family.

Adirondack Mountain Club Information Center. The center is run by the Adirondack Mountain Club (ADK), a nonprofit group that aims to protect forest, parkland, and other wilderness areas while supporting responsible recreational use. Information about hiking and other recreational activities available in Adirondack Park is available here. ⊠ *814 Goggins Rd.* ☎ *518/668–4447 or 800/395–8080* ⊕ *www.adk.org* ☞ *Free* ⊙ *Mon.–Sat. 8:30–5.*

Chapman Historical Museum. A visit to the painstakingly restored home of the DeLong family—who lived here from 1860 to 1910—gives you a glimpse of life in the 19th-century Adirondacks. Guided tours of the house are available Tuesday through Friday and Sunday 1–4 and Saturday 10–4. Exhibits showcase regional history, and an extensive photo collection displays the work of Seneca Ray Stoddard (1843–1917). ⊠ *348 Glen St.* ☎ *518/793–2826* ⊕ *www.chapmanmuseum.org* ☞ *$2* ⊙ *Tues.–Sat. 10–4, Sun. noon–4.*

★ Hyde Collection. One of the finest art museums in the northeastern United States, the Hyde Collection encompasses some 2,800 pieces. Included are paintings and works on paper by artists such as Josef Albers, Sandro Botticelli, Georges Braque, Alexander Calder, Paul Cézanne, William Merritt Chase, Leonardo da Vinci, Edgar Degas, Thomas Eakins, El Greco, Childe Hassam, Winslow Homer, Wassily Kandinsky, Pablo Picasso, Rembrandt, and Pierre-Auguste Renoir. Antiques, fine period furniture, and decorative arts are also displayed, as are temporary exhibits. Guided tours are offered in the afternoon. ⊠ *161 Warren St.* ☎ *518/792–1761* ⊕ *www.hydecollection.org* ☞ *Free* ⊙ *Tues.–Sat. 10–5, Sun. noon–5.*

FESTIVALS & **Adirondack Hot Air Balloon Festival.** More than 100 hot-air balloons par-
FAIRS ticipate in this annual four-day event held around the third weekend in
September. There are usually two launches on Saturday and Sunday—
one at sunrise and the other in the early evening—weather permitting,
of course. Smaller launches are held on Thursday and Friday. The event
takes place at Floyd Bennett Memorial Airport, off Route 354 (Quaker
Road) 3 mi northeast of downtown Glens Falls. ⊠ *Floyd Bennett Memorial Airport, 443 Queensbury Ave., Queensbury* ☎ *518/761–6366 Warren County Tourism* ⊕ *www.adirondackballoonfest.org.*

Where to Stay & Eat

$$–$$$ ✕ **Fiddleheads.** Antique collectibles and fresh flowers, grown in the
back, set the tone at this intimate restaurant, where the menu includes
American fare such as herb-encrusted rack of lamb, Maryland crab cakes,
filet mignon, and daily fresh seafood specials. ⊠ *21 Ridge St.* ☎ *518/
793–5789* ▭ *D, MC, V* ⊙ *Closed Sun. and Mon.*

$–$$ ✕ **Davidson Brothers Restaurant and Brewery.** This English-style brewpub
(think brick walls and loads of wood) serves pub fare, like fish-and-chips
and stout-and-cheddar soup; assorted wraps and salads; as well as more
substantial dishes, such as sautéed blackened chicken breast with artichoke hearts, or penne in vodka sauce. Buffalo burgers are made of buffalo. ⊠ *184 Glen St.* ☎ *518/743–9026* ▭ *AE, D, MC, V* ⊙ *Closed Sun.
Oct.–May.*

$–$$ 🏨 **Queensbury Hotel.** Ivy tendrils scale the facade of this five-story red-
brick hotel built in the 1920s. A large fireplace graces the lobby, where
cushy chairs invite lingering. Rooms are traditional, with lace-fringed
windows, soft colors, and dark-wood furniture. The indoor pool, under
a massive skylight, is a nice size. The hotel is across from the city park
in downtown Glens Falls. ⊠ *88 Ridge St.* ☎ *518/792–1121 or 800/554–
4526* 🖷 *518/792–9259* ⊕ *www.queensburyhotel.com* ⊰ *114 rooms,
11 suites* ☖ *Restaurant, café, in-room data ports, some refrigerators,
cable TV, indoor pool, gym, hair salon, hot tub, massage, bar, laundry
service, business services, meeting rooms, no-smoking rooms* ▭ *AE, D,
DC, MC, V.*

Lake George

❷ *10 mi north of Glens Falls.*

The village, in the Adirondack foothills, sits at the southern end of the
lake of the same name. It's a family-focused tourist area, chockablock
with motels, eateries, small outlet malls, and assorted amusements, including theme parks, miniature golf, and a wax museum. In summer,
traffic through the village can crawl along U.S. 9.

Lake George also has historical significance. The area, because of its location on the lake, was inhabited before the European settlers arrived
and later figured prominently in the French and Indian War. It also saw
clashes during the Revolutionary War.

Fort William Henry Museum. The "fort" here is actually a reconstruction
of the 1755 original, which was built by the British, used in the French
and Indian War, and written about in James Fenimore Cooper's *The Last*

of the Mohicans. The complex encompasses barracks, dungeons, and an example of an Iroquois longhouse, as well as artifacts recovered from the original fort site, which is nearby. Tours, led by guides dressed in 18th-century military garb, start on the hour; demonstrations include the firing of muskets and cannons. ⊠ *Canada St.* ☎ *518/668–5471 or 800/234–0267* ⊕ *www.fortwilliamhenry.com* 🖃 *$11.95* ⊙ *May–Oct., daily 10–6.*

Great Escape & Splashwater Kingdom Fun Park. Six roller coasters are among the 125-plus rides at this theme park. The water-park area (open Memorial Day through Labor Day) includes labrythine slides, a 25,000-square-foot wave pool, and a raft ride with waterfalls and water bombs. Shows include a high-dive act. ⊠ *1172 U.S. 9* ☎ *518/792–3500* ⊕ *www.sixflags.com/greatescape* 🖃 *$35.99* ⊙ *Mid-May–Oct.; call for days and hrs.*

House of Frankenstein Wax Museum. More than 50 interactive exhibits of monsters and mayhem are on display here, including such favorites as Dracula and the Wolfman. Kindergartners and younger children may get quite a fright at this haunted-house sight. ⊠ *213 Canada St.* ☎ *518/668–3377* ⊕ *www.frankensteinwaxmuseum.com* 🖃 *$6.50* ⊙ *Apr.–Oct.; call for days and hrs.*

Lake George Battlefield Picnic Area. You may picnic at this park on the southern shore of Lake George. The remains of the original Fort William Henry are here, along with a monument to French missionary Isaac Jogues (1607–46). ⊠ *Beach Rd. off U.S. 9* ☎ *518/668–3352* ⊕ *www.dec.state.ny.us* 🖃 *Parking $6* ⊙ *Early May–mid-June, weekends 9–5; mid-June–Labor Day, daily 9–8.*

Lake George Beach. The popular swimming beach, also known as Million Dollar Beach, has a bathhouse, lifeguards, lockers, picnic facilities, and volleyball nets. ⊠ *Beach Rd., east of U.S. 9* ☎ *518/668–3352* ⊕ *www.dec.state.ny.us* 🖃 *Parking $6* ⊙ *Memorial Day–Labor Day, daily 9–6:30.*

Lake George Steamboat Co. The company offers cruises on its three boats: the *Minne-Ha-Ha,* a steam paddle wheeler; the 1907 *Mohican*; and the 190-foot *Lac du Saint Sacrement.* Cruises, offered daily May through October, include sightseeing excursions ($9.75–$19.75) as well as brunch, lunch, and dinner cruises ($16.75–$35.75). Special themed and holiday cruises are also scheduled throughout the year. ⊠ *Steel Pier, off Beach Rd.* ☎ *518/668–5777 or 800/553–2628* ⊕ *www.lakegeorgesteamboat.com.*

Prospect Mountain Veterans Memorial Highway. The 5-mi corkscrew road takes you most of the way up 2,035-foot Prospect Mountain. From the parking lot it's just 100 feet to the summit, which you may reach via a shuttle. The views can stretch to 100 mi and take in up to five states, along with Lake George and the High Peaks region. You may also hike all the way up from the village. ⊠ *West off U.S. 9* ☎ *518/668–5198* ⊕ *www.dec.state.ny.us* 🖃 *$6* ⊙ *May–late Oct., daily 9–5.*

Water Slide World. The 12-acre park has more than 35 slides, a wave pool, water and sand volleyball, and kiddie pools. Food is available, as are lockers, picnic areas, showers, and life jackets. To get here, take Exit 21 off I–87. ⊠ *U.S. 9 and Rte. 9L* ☏ *518/668–4407* ⊕ *www.adirondack. net/tour/waterslideworld/* ⌂ *$24* ⊙ *Mid-June–Labor Day, daily 9:30–6.*

FESTIVALS & **Americade Motorcycle Tour & Rally.** More than 35,000 motorcycle en-
FAIRS thusiasts flock to the Lake George area for this six-day event held in early June. Activities include an exposition with 200-plus vendors and a huge motorcycle parade. ⊕ *Box 2205, Glens Falls 12801* ☏ *518/798– 7888* ⊕ *www.tourexpo.com.*

Lake George Jazz Weekend. Jazz groups from all over the state converge at the Shepard Park bandstand for an end-of-summer bash, usually on the weekend after Labor Day. ☏ *518/668–2616* ⊕ *www. lakegeorgearts.org.*

Lake George Winter Carnival. Cold-weather activities, such as polar-bear swims, ice sculpting and fishing, snowmobile and dog-pull races, and snowmobile drags are scheduled for weekends throughout February. The carnival also includes a chili cook-off and fireworks. ☏ *518/668–2233* ⊕ *www.lakegeorgewintercarnival.com.*

Where to Stay & Eat

$$–$$$$ ✕ **Log Jam.** The restaurant looks like a refined log cabin, with three stone fireplaces and attractive wood furniture. The place is known for beef, including three cuts of prime rib; onion soup; and barbecued wings. Steak au poivre comes with sautéed mushrooms and shallots in mustard sauce. Fish dishes include surf-and-turf combos as well as more complicated preparations like maple syrup–glazed wild salmon fillet baked in apple-pecan crust. There's also a salad bar ⊠ *1484 U.S. 9* ☏ *518/798–1155* ⊟ *AE, D, DC, MC, V.*

$–$$$ ✕ **East Cove Restaurant.** Cloth-covered tables are a touch of formality in this cozy log-cabin space. The fare is American: prime rib (blackened, if you wish), surf and turf, chicken parmigiana, fettuccine Alfredo. ⊠ *Rte. 9L and Beach Rd.* ☏ *518/668–5265* ⊟ *AE, D, MC, V* ⊙ *No lunch Mon.–Sat. Closed Mon. and Tues. Nov.–Apr.*

¢–$$$ ✕ **Barnsider Smoke House.** Smoked ribs are the specialty, and if you like them you might consider buying the bottled barbecue sauce available to go. This family favorite also serves hearty breakfasts, including all-you-can-eat buttermilk pancakes. In warm weather you may eat on the small deck. There's also a full bar. ⊠ *U.S. 9, just before Waterslide World* ☏ *518/668–5268* ⊟ *AE, D, DC, MC, V* ⊙ *Closed Nov.–Apr.*

¢–$$ ✕ **Shoreline Restaurant.** The waterfront restaurant has loads of outdoor dining, including a large covered deck with lake views. The food is American with an emphasis on seafood. You choose how your fresh fish is prepared: broiled, blackened, grilled, breaded and panfried, or sautéed in one of several sauces. Other entrées include prime rib, grilled pork chops with roasted corn and relish, cheese tortellini in pesto-cream sauce, and crab cakes with roasted red peppers and cayenne cream. Fish-and-chips, hamburgers, and fried chicken tenders are listed as "lite" fare. ⊠ *2 Kurosaka La., off Canada St. at Beach Rd.* ☏ *518/668–4644* ⊟ *AE, D, MC, V* ⊙ *Closed Nov.–Mar.*

¢–$$ ✕🏠 **The Georgian.** The sprawling, family-owned resort has a private beach and a marina. Rooms have views of the lake, the pool, or the courtyard;

some rooms have private balconies or patios. Suites have sitting areas with sleeper sofas. Traditional dark-wood furniture is used throughout. The main dining room ($$–$$$) serves mostly Continental fare: steak au poivre, lobster ravioli, roast rack of lamb, scampi, chateaubriand. From mid-May through October, the Terrace Room hosts dinner theater. ⊠ *384 Canada St., 12845* ☎ *518/668–5401 or 800/525–3436* 🖷 *518/668–5870* ⊕ *www.georgianresort.com* 🛏 *150 rooms, 14 suites* ⟂ *2 restaurants, room service, some in-room hot tubs, some refrigerators, cable TV with movies, pool, beach, marina, bar, lounge, theater, laundry service, business services, meeting rooms, airport shuttle, no-smoking rooms* ▤ *AE, D, DC, MC, V.*

$$–$$$ 🏨 **Fort William Henry Resort Hotel.** The hotel property encompasses a conference center and 18 acres overlooking the southern end of Lake George. Renovations completed in 2004 freshened the decor in many of the rooms, which nevertheless retain a traditional look. Room configurations range from studios with sleeper sofas to huge suites with fireplaces. Some rooms have lake or mountain views. The large outdoor pool looks onto the lake. ⊠ *48 Canada St.* ☎ *518/668–3081 or 800/ 221–9211* 🖷 *518/668–4926* ⊕ *www.fortwilliamhenry.com* 🛏 *99 rooms, 97 suites* ⟂ *3 restaurants, coffee shop, snack bar, in-room data ports, some in-room hot tubs, some microwaves, some refrigerators, cable TV with video games, miniature golf, 2 pools (1 indoor), gym, sauna, bicycles, shuffleboard, volleyball, bar, laundry facilities, laundry service, concierge, business services, meeting rooms, some pets allowed (fee), no-smoking rooms* ▤ *AE, D, DC, MC, V.*

$$–$$$ 🏨 **Holiday Inn Turf.** The two-story hotel is set back 200 feet from the road, on a hill. Rooms, graced with wood furniture and soft earth-tone colors, are attractive and spacious. High-speed Internet access is available. ⊠ *2223 Canada St., 12845* ☎ *518/668–5781* 🖷 *518/668–9213* ⊕ *www.ichotelsgroup.com* 🛏 *104 rooms, 1 suite* ⟂ *Restaurant, room service, in-room data ports, in-room safes, refrigerators, cable TV with movies and video games, miniature golf, 2 pools (1 indoor), wading pool, gym, hot tub, sauna, shuffleboard, bar, video game room, playground, laundry facilities, laundry service, Internet, business services, meeting rooms, no-smoking rooms* ▤ *AE, D, DC, MC, V.*

$$–$$$ 🏨 **Roaring Brook Ranch & Tennis Resort.** The sprawling mountainside property is about 2 mi from the fray of Lake George. The activities, including horseback riding on the property, are a big draw here. A series of small buildings contains the motel-style accommodations. Rooms are spacious, with two double beds. A few rooms are available without the meal plan. ⊠ *Rte. 9N S/Luzerne Rd., 12845* ☎ *518/668–5767 or 800/ 882–7665* 🖷 *518/648–4019* ⊕ *www.roaringbrookranch.com* 🛏 *142 rooms* ⟂ *Restaurant, some kitchenettes, 5 tennis courts, 3 pools (1 indoor), gym, sauna, basketball, horseback riding, shuffleboard, volleyball, 2 bars, children's programs (ages 4–7), playground, laundry facilities, business services, meeting rooms, no-smoking rooms* ▤ *AE, MC, V* ☉ *Closed mid-Oct.–mid-May* ¶⊙¶ *MAP.*

$–$$ 🏨 **Best Western of Lake George.** The two-story, lodge-style chain motel offsets traditional furnishings with Adirondack flair. Some rooms have sloping wood ceilings, and some suites have fireplaces. Lake George beaches are 1 mi away. ⊠ *Rte. 9N off I–87 Exit 21, 12845* ☎ *518/*

668–5701 🖷 518/668–4926 🌐 www.bestwesternlakegeorge.com ⇦ rooms, 8 suites ♨ In-room data ports, some in-room hot tubs, some kitchens, some microwaves, some refrigerators, cable TV, 2 pools (1 indoor), wading pool, hot tub, laundry service, business services, some pets allowed (fee), no-smoking rooms ▭ AE, D, DC, MC, V 🍽 CP.

$–$$ **Still Bay.** The 5-acre property has an expansive patio that overlooks 300 feet of lakefront. Motel-style rooms are paneled in wood and have large windows. A private boathouse provides dock space. ✉ *Lake Shore Dr./Rte. 9N, 12845 ☎ 518/668–2584 or 800/521–7511 🌐 www.stillbay.com ⇦ 19 rooms, 3 suites ♨ Dining room, picnic area, some kitchenettes, cable TV, lake, beach, dock, boating, fishing; no smoking ▭ MC, V ⏲ Closed mid-Oct.–late May 🍽 CP.*

¢–$$ **Howard Johnson Tiki Resort.** The pool at this chain property overlooks Lake George. Rooms have big windows and light-wood furniture. There is a bit of a kitsch factor here, though: Polynesian-themed dinner shows are an option in July and August, and the honeymoon suite has a heart-shaped whirlpool tub. ✉ *2 Canada St., 12845 ☎ 518/668–5744 🖷 518/668–3544 🌐 www.tikiresort.com ⇦ 110 rooms, 20 suites ♨ Restaurant, picnic area, some in-room hot tubs, some kitchenettes, refrigerators, cable TV with movies, 1 indoor and 1 outdoor pool, wading pool, gym, outdoor hot tub, basketball, bar, playground, laundry service, business services, meeting rooms, no-smoking rooms ▭ AE, D, MC, V ⏲ Closed Nov.–May.*

¢–$ **Colonel Williams Motor Inn.** The yellow clock tower rising above this tidy family-oriented motel clearly identifies the 10-acre property. Rooms are uncluttered, with traditional wood furniture and either one or two queen beds or two doubles. Some rooms have decks. The grounds include two playgrounds, one of which has a kiddie-size fire engine, pirate ship, and train. ✉ *U.S. 9 1 mi north of I–87 Exit 20, 12845 ☎ 518/668–5727 or 800/334–5727 🌐 www.colonelwilliamsresort.com ⇦ 30 rooms, 15 suites ♨ Picnic area, some kitchenettes, refrigerators, cable TV, 2 pools (1 indoor), gym, hot tub, sauna, badminton, basketball, volleyball, recreation room, playground, laundry facilities, no-smoking rooms ▭ AE, D, MC, V ⏲ Closed mid-Sept.–May.*

Bolton Landing

❸ *8 mi north of village of Lake George.*

This community of about 2,000 year-round residents hugs the western shore of Lake George, which is dotted with small coves and islands. In the 1800s it became fashionable for the well-heeled to summer in Bolton Landing. Thanks to the waterfront mansions that sprang up here, the area became known as Millionaires Row. Bolton Landing is perhaps best known as the home of the luxurious Sagamore Resort, which occupies its own island. Although the village is quieter and less touristy than the village of Lake George, you can still expect a good deal of summer traffic here.

Marcella Sembrich Opera Museum. Polish soprano Marcella Sembrich (1858–1935), who sang with New York's Metropolitan Opera, used the building housing this museum as a vocal-instruction studio. The studio was part of her summer estate. You can walk along Lake George here and take in the beautiful vista. The museum, on the National Register of Historic Places, includes opera costumes, paintings, and assorted memorabilia. ⊠ *4800 Lake Shore Dr.* ☎ *518/644-9839* ⊕ *www.operamuseum.com* ⊡ *$2* ☉ *Mid-June–mid-Sept., daily 10–12:30 and 2–5.*

Where to Stay & Eat

★ $–$$ ✕ **Cate's Italian Garden.** Excellent gourmet pizza, seafood specialties, pasta dishes, a full wine list, and homemade desserts make it hard to decide what to order at this pleasant spot. With flowers and candles adorning each table and a cherrywood interior, this is a place not to miss. ⊠ *4952 Main St.* ☎ *518/644-2041* ⊟ *AE, D, MC, V* ☉ *Closed Mar.*

$$–$$$ ✕ **Villa Napoli Restaurant.** The restaurant, on the grounds of Melody Manor, specializes in Tuscan dining. Candles and a marble fireplace adorn the quaint wood-paneled dining room, and Pavarotti or Vivaldi plays in the background. A creek runs past the outdoor patio. Osso buco is a specialty. Other dishes include cioppino and grilled swordfish in balsamic vinaigrette. ⊠ *Melody Manor, 4610 Lake Shore Dr.* ☎ *518/644-9750* ⊟ *AE, MC, V* ☉ *Closed mid-Oct.–mid-May. Closed weekdays mid-May–late June and early Sept.–mid-Oct.*

$$$$ ✕📷 **Sagamore Resort.** Occupying a 72-acre island on Lake George, the
Fodor'sChoice Sagamore is an escape to a bygone era. Accommodations in the 1883
★ colonial-revival main house have views of the lake or gardens. The decor, including marble bathrooms and handsome wood furniture, is elegant but not formal. Accommodations in the newer lodge buildings are country-chic. Lodge rooms have garden views; suites have gas fireplaces and a terrace with a lake view. The separate condo units (starting at about $600 a night in season) have two bedrooms, two bathrooms, a kitchen, a living room, a dining area, and two lake-view terraces; leather couches, Adirondack-style furniture, and wood-burning fireplaces contribute to the lodge feel here. The resort offers so many activities and dining options that you don't have to leave the property. The menu at the Club Grill steak house, which overlooks the beautiful championship golf course and is decked out in upscale-lodge fashion, includes dry-aged New York strip steak with braised chanterelle and trumpet mushrooms, or pan-seared scallops with blackberry glaze and bacon-chestnut polenta. Mister Brown's Pub serves contemporary fare amid twiggy furniture and decorative canoes. The acclaimed Trillium restaurant, however, is scheduled for refurbishment starting in May 2005. Other notable facilities here include the spa and the sailing school. ⊠ *110 Sagamore Rd., 12814* ☎ *518/644-9400 or 800/358-3585* 🖷 *518/644-2851* ⊕ *www.thesagamore.com* 🛏 *172 rooms, 178 suites* ᗕ *2 restaurants, snack bar, room service, in-room data ports, some kitchens, some microwaves, cable TV, 18-hole golf course, putting green, 6 tennis courts, pro shop, indoor pool, lake, fitness classes, health club, hair salon, hot tub, spa, beach, dock, windsurfing, boating, parasailing, waterskiing, fishing, hiking, racquetball, cross-country skiing, ice-skating, pub, children's programs (ages 3–12), playground, business services, meeting rooms, no-smoking rooms* ⊟ *AE, D, DC, MC, V.*

$$–$$$$ ⊞ **The Boathouse Bed and Breakfast.** The grand 1917 stone-and-wood boathouse is on Millionaires Row and directly on Lake George. Most of the individually appointed rooms have hardwood floors and a king-size bed. Some rooms have private porches or balconies. The decor mostly relics on floral or quilt bedcoverings. The carriage-house suites, however, are completely different. One suite is decked out in Adirondack style, with a stone fireplace and cedar-post furniture; the other is more refined, with a four-poster bed and boudoir-style upholstered chairs. The two carriage-house suites have gas fireplaces and two-person jet tubs. Breakfast is served in the great room, a lovely space with a timbered ceiling and several large windows. ⊠ *44 Sagamore Rd.* ☎ *518/644–2554* 🖷 *518/644–3065* ⊕ *www.boathousebb.com* ⇆ *4 rooms, 3 suites* ⚒ *Some in-room hot tubs, some microwaves, some refrigerators, cable TV, lake, dock, boating, fishing; no kids under 12, no smoking* ☐ *AE, MC, V* ⊠◎ *BP.*

$$–$$$ ⊞ **Melody Manor.** The 9-acre property encompasses 300 feet of frontage on Lake George, where there's a beach and a dock. Accommodations are in motel-style buildings. The corner rooms are extra-spacious. Some rooms have lake views and balconies or patios. The on-site Villa Napoli restaurant is a local favorite. ⊠ *4610 Lake Shore Dr.* ☎ *518/644–9750* ⊕ *www.melodymanor.com* ⇆ *40 rooms* ⚒ *Restaurant, picnic area, some refrigerators, cable TV, tennis court, pool, beach, dock, boating, badminton, basketball, shuffleboard, bar; no smoking* ☐ *AE, DC, MC, V* ⊗ *Closed late Oct.–Apr.*

Ticonderoga

❹ *30 mi northeast of Bolton's Landing.*

Ticonderoga is an Iroquois term meaning "land of many waters." Ticonderoga is indeed between Lake George and Lake Champlain, and the LaChute River runs through town. The French started building a fort in this strategic location in the mid-18th century. Today Fort Ticonderoga is a key attraction in the area.

Fort Ticonderoga. The fort, built alongside Lake Champlain by the French (in 1755–58), was originally named Fort Carillon. It was captured by the British in 1759 and renamed Fort Ticonderoga. The colonists took over in 1775, but only until 1777, when the British managed to place cannons atop **Mount Defiance**, which overlooks the fort. You may drive up to the summit of Mount Defiance and take in the views of the fort, the valley, and Lake Champlain. The fort presents living-history demonstrations, including cannon drills, musket firings, and fife-and-drum performances (in July and August). Exhibits include weapons and Revolutionary War artifacts. Thirty-minute guided tours with costumed interpreters are available. The grounds also encompass several gardens (open daily 10–4 from June to early October). ⊠ *Rte. 74* ☎ *518/585–2821* ⊕ *www.fort-ticonderoga.org* ⊠ *$12* ⊗ *Early May–late Oct., daily 10–5.*

Hancock House. The Ticonderoga Historical Society resides in this grand Georgian mansion, a replica of the John Hancock home in Boston. The original, built in the mid-1700s, was destroyed in the 19th century. The replica, intended to serve as a museum, was commissioned by Horace Moses, who had built up the Strathmore Paper Company. Works by local artists are shown here, and you may tour the period rooms. ⊠ *6 Moses Circle* ☎ *518/585–7868* ⊕ *www.thehancockhouse.org* ✉ *Free* ⊙ *Wed.–Sat. 10–4.*

Heritage Museum. The brick building that houses this museum served as the main office of the Ticonderoga Pulp and Paper Company in the late 1800s. Exhibits here focus on the industrial history of Ticonderoga, which was known as a center for paper- and pencil-making. ⊠ *Bicentennial Park, Montcalm St.* ☎ *518/585–2696* ✉ *Free* ⊙ *July–early Sept., daily 10–4; Memorial Day–June and early Sept.–Columbus Day, weekends 10–4.*

Where to Eat

$–$$ ✕ **Carillon Restaurant.** The spotlight at this casual restaurant is on steak and seafood. Sautéed scallops, shrimp, and crabmeat are served with vodka sauce and penne; filet mignon, charbroiled, is dressed with peppered cabernet butter. If you'd rather have bird, consider roast duckling with honey-raspberry sauce. ⊠ *872 Rte. 9N* ☎ *518/585–7657* ▭ *AE, D, DC, MC, V* ⊙ *Closed Wed.*

Crown Point

⑤ *8 mi north of Ticonderoga.*

The entire area near Crown Point was once known as Ironville, though that name now belongs to a small hamlet nearby. Crown Point is a quiet town, but the rich bed of iron ore discovered here in the early 1800s once made this an industrial center. The U.S. Navy was particularly eager to use Crown Point's iron ore for its new class of ironclad ships, such as the *Monitor.* Today the main attraction is the Crown Point State Historic Site, a few miles north of the village. The Crown Point Bridge takes you into Vermont.

Crown Point State Historic Site. Since the earliest European explorations of North America, long and narrow Lake Champlain has been considered an important strategic waterway. Both the French and English built forts along its shores. This site includes the ruins of the 1734 French fort, Fort Saint Frederic, and the 1759 British complex, Fort Crown Point. Exhibits at the visitor center give you historical context. ⊠ *739 Bridge Rd., 3 mi north of Crown Point* ☎ *518/597–3666* ⊕ *nysparks. state.ny.us* ✉ *Parking $5 (weekends), visitor center $3, grounds free* ⊙ *Visitor center May–Oct., Wed.–Mon. 9–5.*

Penfield Homestead Museum. Dedicated to preserving the legacy of innovative industrialist Allen Penfield, this museum has exhibits explaining his work using electricity in the process of iron-ore separation. This was the first industrial application of electricity. The museum, 3 mi southwest of Crown Point, also houses many Civil War artifacts and equipment on its 550-acre site. ⊠ *703 Creek Rd.* ☎ *518/597–3804* ⊕ *www. penfieldmuseum.org* ✉ *$4* ⊙ *Early June–Oct., Thurs.–Sun. 11–4, and by appointment.*

Where to Stay

¢–$ 🖼 **Crown Point Bed and Breakfast.** This rambling Victorian-era "painted lady" has a beautiful oak staircase, an oak-paneled dining room, and three parlors with fireplaces. The home was built in 1886 for a banker, but now houses guest rooms filled with period antiques and decorated with floral wallpapers and fabrics. The large Crown Room has an intricate brass-and-alabaster bed. One suite has a fireplace. ⊠ *Main St./Rte. 9N* ☎ *518/597-3651* 🖷 *518/597-4451* ⊕ *www. crownpointbandb.com* 🛏 *4 rooms, 2 suites* ⚭ *Dining room, fans; no a/c, no room phones, no room TVs, no smoking* ➡ *AE, MC, V* ¶O| *CP.*

Ausable Chasm

★ ❻ *50 mi north of Crown Point.*

Over millions of years, the Ausable River carved a seemingly impossible path through deep layers of sandstone, leaving high cliffs (nearly 200 feet in places), waterfalls, and rapids. This 1½-mi-long chasm, in a small Champlain Valley village also called Ausable Chasm, opened to the public in 1870, becoming the country's first natural tourist attraction. (Time hasn't diminished the popularity of this geological spectacle, which is often overrun in summer.)

A deck allows you to view formations such as Elephant Head and Table Rock. The trail around the rim gives you a birds'-eye view. Stone walkways and stairways lead you into the chasm. You may also combine a walk with a kayak, raft, or inner-tube ride on the Ausable River. Two-hour lantern tours ($18.25 per person), which start at dusk, give you another perspective on the 500-million-year-old mass of sculpted stone formations; reservations are required for these guided walks. ⊠ *U.S. 9* ☎ *518/834-7454* ⊕ *www.ausablechasm.com* 🖾 *Walking trails $16* ⊙ *Mid-May–mid-Oct., daily 9:30–4.*

THE ADIRONDACKS

Although most people associate the Adirondacks with high mountains, the southern and central landscape is primarily one of lakes, rivers, and hills. The notable exception is Blue Mountain, which stands high above everything that surrounds it. Its summit lookout tower affords a 360-degree view that includes the chain of lakes stretching west, but the price of this view is a fairly steep scramble of about 1 mi.

For the most part, the tranquillity of the southern and central Adirondacks turns to dormancy in winter. However, because the terrain here is gentler than in the High Peaks region to the north—and nearer the population centers of the south—snowmobiling and cross-country-skiing enthusiasts are drawn to the area. Snowmobilers tend to congregate in Schroon Lake, Speculator, and Old Forge, which is also the center of tourist activity in the southern and central area. Blue Mountain Lake, home of the Adirondack Museum, is the area's cultural center.

In the northern Adirondacks, Lake Placid is unquestionably the hub of activity. To its south is the famed High Peaks area—the 46 highest

CloseUp

ADIRONDACK PARK

ADIRONDACK PARK WAS created by the state in 1892, and two years later a large chunk of the land was designated "forever wild," prohibiting future development. The official park boundaries encompass 6 million acres, almost three times the land area of Yellowstone National Park. There are 1,000 mi of rivers, 30,000 mi of brooks and streams, more than 3,000 lakes and ponds, and 1.3 million acres of forest.

The numbers impress, but they're just by way of introduction to the Adirondacks. Understanding the Adirondacks is a matter of sensory perception rather than number crunching. It's a place that not only has to be seen but also has to be heard and smelled and, during winters that are often harsh, felt as well. From spring through fall, every lake view or mountain vista or walk in the woods comes with the fragrance of hemlock and spruce and musty soil and the sounds of songbirds,

woodpeckers, loons, or any of the 220 species of other birds in the region.

However, this isn't a complete wilderness area; about half the land within park boundaries is privately owned. The checkerboard of public and private lands gives the Adirondacks a different character from most national parks. Motels, lodges, and restaurants are found throughout the park. Canoe rentals, seaplane services, and guide services are all private enterprises. At the same time, most campgrounds, trails, and waterways are maintained on public land by the state, through the Department of Environmental Conservation.

peaks in the Adirondacks, most of them surpassing 4,000 feet. At 5,344 feet, Mt. Marcy is the highest point in New York. On it, at 4,320 feet above sea level, is Lake Tear of the Clouds, which is considered the source of the Hudson River.

Whiteface Mountain Ski Area

❼ Wilmington is 20 mi southwest of Ausable Chasm.

Many people believe that Whiteface Mountain is in Lake Placid, but this well-known ski center is actually in Wilmington, a few miles northeast of Lake Placid. Some of the confusion may stem from the fact that the alpine events of the 1980 Winter Olympics were held here.

Adirondack History Center. An old school houses this center and museum, where the rather eclectic collection includes a bobsled from the 1932 Winter Olympics, antique dolls, artifacts from Fort Crown Point, and, out back, a 58-foot fire tower. The property also includes gardens. ✉ Rte. 9N and Hand Ave., Elizabethtown ☎ 518/873–6466 ⊕ www. adkhistorycenter.org Ꮭ $3.50 ⊘ Late May–Columbus Day, Mon.–Sat. 9–5, Sun. 1–5.

High Falls Gorge. A spectacular 700-foot waterfall and ancient granite cliffs more than a billion years old are highlights of the self-guided tour of this gorge. It was created as the Ausable River cut through the granite base of Whiteface Mountain. In winter you may rent snowshoes here. Nearby are a shop, restaurant, and picnic areas. ⊠ *Rte. 86 at Wilmington Notch, Wilmington* ☎ *518/946–2278* ⊕ *www.highfallsgorge.com* ✍ *$9.95* ☉ *May, June, Sept., and Oct., daily 9–5; July and Aug., daily 9–5:30; Nov.–mid-Dec., weekends 10–4; mid-Dec.–Mar., daily 10–4.*

☺ **Santa's Workshop.** This simple theme park (2 mi northwest of Wilmington) with rides and live reindeer is ideal for small children. Santa and his helpers talk with children, and elves practice their crafts in shops around the park. ⊠ *12946 Whiteface Mountain Memorial Hwy., North Pole* ☎ *800/806–0215* ⊕ *www.northpoleny.com* ✍ *$15.95* ☉ *Late June–early Sept., daily 9:30–4:30; early Sept.–Columbus Day, weekends 9:30–4; mid-Nov.–late Dec., weekends 10–3:30.*

Whiteface Mountain. Though only the fifth highest in the region, Whiteface Mountain is one of the best-known mountains in the Adirondacks. **Veterans Memorial Highway** twists and climbs 8 mi to the top of the mountain. Close to the peak is a lot where you park your car; from here you can ride an elevator or hike the rest of the way up. ⊠ *12997 Veterans Memorial Hwy., Wilmington* ☎ *518/946–2223* ⊕ *www.whiteface. com* ✍ *$9 per car and driver, $4 each additional passenger* ☉ *Late May–early July, daily 9–4; early July–early Sept., daily 8:30–5; rest of Sept., daily 9–4; call for Oct. times.*

FESTIVALS & **Whiteface Mountain Scottish Highland Festival.** Held on a Saturday in
FAIRS early September, the festival features piping, drumming, Highland dancing, Celtic harps, Celtic fiddles, spinning and weaving, a Scottish heavy athletics competition, clan tents, and Scottish imports and food. ⊠ *Whiteface Mountain Ski Center, Rte. 86, Wilmington* ☎ *518/946–2223* ⊕ *www.whiteface.com.*

Where to Stay & Eat

¢–$ ✕🏨 **Hungry Trout Motor Inn & Restaurant.** This refined motor inn is on
Fodor'sChoice the west branch of the Ausable River (bring your fishing gear) and close
★ to Whiteface Mountain Ski Center. Rooms, spacious and comfortable, have handsome wood furniture and large windows with mountain views. The restaurant ($$–$$$) earns high marks for its American fare, served in an attractive dining space with cloth-covered tables, candles, and a wall of windows. A section of the menu is devoted to trout, which may be panfried and served with shallot–Grand Marnier sauce or baked and served with shrimp, scallops, portabello mushrooms, and roasted red peppers. But it's not all about the fish here. Options include broiled venison medallions dressed with port demi-glace and cherry-gooseberry chutney, or roast Long Island duck served with port-berry sauce. The cozy pub serves hamburgers and sandwiches. ⊠ *Rte. 86, Wilmington 12997* ☎ *518/946–2217 or 800/766–9137* 🖷 *518/946–7418* ⊕ *www.hungrytrout.com* ⇋ *20 rooms, 2 suites* ⚅ *Restaurant, some kitchenettes, cable TV, pool, wading pool, boating, fishing, cross-country skiing, pub, playground, some pets allowed (fee); no smoking* ⊟ *AE, D, MC, V* ☉ *Closed Apr. and Nov.*

¢–$ ✕🏨 **Willkommen Hof B&B.** The two-story European-style *Gasthof* (guesthouse), built in 1920 at the foot of Whiteface Mountain, has a large porch and a deck. Some rooms have knotty wood paneling. Fireplaces, skylights, and whirlpool tubs are among the extras in some rooms. The three-room suite includes a sitting room with a TV and a bedroom with bunk beds. Wireless Internet access is available. The dining room is centered on a German *Kachelofen* (tile stove) and features a traditional German *Stammtisch* (corner booth for regulars) and an English-style bristle dartboard. The food doesn't stray from the German theme. Dinner is available Thursday through Saturday in high season; reservations are required. Breakfast for overnight guests includes apple pancakes and blintzes. ⊠ *Rte. 86, Wilmington 12997* ☎ *518/946–7669 or 800/541–9119* ⊕ *www.lakeplacid.net/willkommenhof/* 🛏 *8 rooms, 6 with private bath; 1 suite* ⬧ *Restaurant, some in-room hot tubs, outdoor hot tub, sauna, fishing, hiking, cross-country skiing, business services, some pets allowed (fee); no smoking* ⊟ *MC, V* ⦿| *BP.*

$ 🏨 **Ledge Rock at Whiteface Mountain.** The upscale two-story motel is on a big piece of land across the road from Whiteface Mountain. Rooms are spacious, with seating areas or kitchenettes and either two double beds or one or two queen-size beds. The decor is cheery, with jolts of bright color here and there. Some rooms have mountain views. Common areas include a "great room" with a fireplace, a large-screen TV, a pool table, and assorted board games. In fall and winter, complimentary cookies and hot beverages are served here. During fishing season, guide services are offered. ⊠ *5078 Rte. 86, at Placid Rd., Wilmington 12997* ☎ *518/946–2302 or 800/336–4754* 🖶 *518/946–2379* ⊕ *www.ledgerockatwhiteface.com* 🛏 *18 rooms* ⬧ *Picnic area, BBQs, some kitchenettes, microwaves, refrigerators, cable TV, pool, wading pool, pond, boating, fishing, cross-country skiing, ice-skating, playground, some pets allowed (fee), no-smoking rooms* ⊟ *AE, D, DC, MC, V.*

$ 🏨 **Whiteface Chalet.** Serene woods surround this Swiss chalet–style inn facing Whiteface Mountain. Rooms have two double beds—some also have one or two daybeds. Wood paneling is used in the guest rooms as well as in the common areas, which include a living room and a recreation room. Rates include breakfast and dinner. ⊠ *Springfield Rd./Rte. 12, Wilmington 12997* ☎ *518/946–2207 or 800/932–0859* ⊕ *www.whitefacechalet.com* 🛏 *13 rooms, 3 suites* ⬧ *Dining room, picnic area, cable TV, tennis courts, pool, basketball, billiards, Ping-Pong, shuffleboard, bar, recreation room, playground, airport shuttle; no a/c in some rooms* ⊟ *AE, D, DC, MC, V* ⦿| *MAP.*

Sports & the Outdoors

FISHING The **Adirondack Sport Shop** (⊠ Rte. 86, Wilmington ☎ 518/946–2605
★ ⊕ www.adirondackflyfishing.com), owned for more than four decades by renowned fly-fishing expert Fran Betters, offers instruction, guides, and rentals. A full day of instruction or guide service—10 to 12 hours—is about $200, including lunch. Or pop into the store for a free casting lesson or to pick up one of Betters' many books. The shop Web site also has loads of information about fishing in the area.

SKI AREA The **Whiteface Mountain Ski Center** (⊠ Rte. 86, Wilmington ☎ 518/946–2223, 518/946–7171 snow conditions ⊕ www.whiteface.com), owned

by the state of New York and operated by the Lake Placid Ol
gional Development Authority, is one of the biggest ski centers
East. It has 10 lifts, 75 trails, 95% snowmaking, and a vertical dro
3,430 feet—the largest such drop in the East. Experts have 44% of th
trails, intermediates 36%, and beginners 20%. The views from the top
are unmatched (nearly 100 mi in good visibility). Facilities include a snowboard park, rentals, a school, children's programs, and restaurants.
Day passes are $60–$66. The ski season usually runs late November to
early April. Mountain bikes take over the slopes from mid-June to early
October. Trail passes are $6. Rentals and gondola passes are also avail-
able. Even if you don't plan to bike, you can ride the Cloudsplitter Gon-
dola ($12) to the top of Little Whiteface (3,676 feet), where there's an
observation deck and a picnic area.

Lake Placid

8 *8 mi southwest of Wilmington.*

The village of Lake Placid isn't on Lake Placid; it's on the shore of Mirror Lake, one of the most beautiful of the Adirondack lakes. The village's namesake lake lies just north of the village. Because both the 1932
and 1980 Winter Olympics were held here, Lake Placid is one of the
best-known destinations in the Adirondacks. But it has been popular
since the beginning of the 20th century, when the rich and famous first
discovered the area and came here to participate in winter sports. A tight
cluster of hotels, restaurants, and shops lines Main Street, where traffic often backs up, especially in summer.

Cornell Sugar Maple Research–Uihlein Field Station. The field station, part
of a Cornell University extension program, encompasses more than 200
forested acres, a greenhouse, and orchards. An exhibit here explains how
maple syrup is made. You may buy some syrup to take home with you.
Tours are available by appointment. The station is also sometimes open
on weekends in March and April. ⊠ *157 Bear Cub La.* ☎ *518/523–9337*
⊕ *maple.dnr.cornell.edu* ✉ *Free* ☉ *Weekdays 8–4; and by appointment.*

High Peaks Information Center. The center, 5 mi south of Lake Placid, is
run by the nonprofit Adirondack Mountain Club. It sells camping and
hiking gear as well as regional guides and has information about hiking and other recreational activities in the area. Hours between seasons
fluctuate, so call to confirm before heading over. ⊠ *Box 867, Adirondack Loj Rd., off Rte. 73* ☎ *518/523–3441* ⊕ *www.adk.org* ✉ *Free*
☉ *Early Nov.–Apr., Mon.–Thurs. 8–3, Fri. and Sat. 8–7, Sun. 8–5;
May–early Nov., weekdays 8–5, weekends 8–8.*

John Brown Farm State Historic Site. Abolitionist John Brown lived for a
short time on this 244-acre farm. In October 1859, Brown and his followers attempted to spark a slave revolt by taking over the federal ar-
senal at Harper's Ferry, West Virginia. His two sons and several of his
followers were killed, and Brown was tried and executed. His body was
brought back and buried here. A cross-country ski trail, a nature trail,
and a picnic area are on the grounds, which are open all year. ⊠ *2 John*

m Rd., off Rte. 73 ☎ *518/523–3900* ⊕ *nysparks.state.ny.us* ✉ *$2
ouse May–Oct., Wed.–Mon. 10–5.*

Placid Marina. One-hour narrated cruises on Lake Placid take in
y of the great camps lining the shore. Cruises leave from the Lake
d Marina, and are offered two to four times daily. ⊠ *Mirror Lake
off Rte. 86* ☎ *518/523–9704* ⊕ *www.lpresort.com* ✉ *$7.50
☺ Mid-May–mid-Oct.; call for times.*

★ **Lake Placid Toboggan Chute.** An old 30-foot-tall ski slide right in town
has been converted into a hair-raising toboggan run that spits you out
onto and across iced-over Mirror Lake. The chute usually opens after
Christmas but might open as early as November and as late as February, so call to check conditions. ⊠ *Parkside Dr. next to post office*
☎ *518/523–2591* ⊕ *www.neparkdistrict.com* ✉ *$5* ☺ *Call for hrs.*

MacKenzie-Intervale Ski Jumping Complex. The towers of the 70- and 90-
meter ski jumps here are stark and exposed and seem out of place, but
the view from the top of the taller tower is dramatic. A glass-encased elevator takes you 26 stories to the top, where you get a bird's-eye view of
the lay of the land and the High Peaks around Lake Placid. You also
get a stomach-gripping view of what the jumpers see while preparing to take
flight. During most of the year you may also opt to ride a chairlift up to
the elevator. In summer, freestyle skiers practice twirls and somersaults
into the pool at **Kodak Sports Park.** ⊠ *Rte. 73 2 mi southeast of village
center* ☎ *518/523–2202* ⊕ *www.orda.org* ✉ *$5–$10* ☺ *Daily 9–4.*

Olympic Center. The center was built for the 1932 Olympics and renovated and expanded for the 1980 Games. During the latter, the arena here
was the site of the U.S. ice-hockey team's win over the seemingly unbeatable
Soviets, which led the men to a U.S. gold medal. The victory came to be
known as the "Miracle on Ice." The center also houses other ice rinks,
a museum, and convention space. A stop by the **1932 & 1980 Lake Placid
Winter Olympic Museum** (✉ $4 ☺ Daily 10–5) is a fitting way to begin
your tour of Lake Placid. Displays here, including sports outfits and gear,
explain the history and legacy of the Olympic Games at Lake Placid. A
50-minute audiocassette tour ($5, including museum admission) of the
center is an option. The center hosts hockey and figure-skating tournaments and ice shows as well as other special events. ⊠ *218 Main St.* ☎ *518/
523–1655* ⊕ *www.orda.org* ☺ *Daily 10–5.*

FESTIVALS &
FAIRS
Lake Placid Horse Shows. Hunter and jumper competitions are part of
the back-to-back Lake Placid and I Love New York horse shows, which
start at the end of June and run to early July. Participants include members of the U.S. equestrian team. ☝ *Lake Placid Horse Show Association, 5514 Cascade Rd., 12946* ☎ *518/523–9625* ⊕ *www.
lakeplacidhorseshow.com.*

Where to Stay & Eat

★ **$$–$$$$** ✗ **Averil Conwell Dining Room.** Even if you're not staying at the Mirror
Lake Inn, this restaurant warrants a visit to the resort. Mahogany pan-
eling gleams in the traditional main dining area, which has views of Mir-
ror Lake and the mountains. Another room has two stone fireplaces and
is outfitted in Adirondack style. The food leans toward the contempo-

rary. Venison loin is encrusted with pepper and coffee and
foie gras and a black-currant reduction, for example. Also a
on the menu are so-called spa dishes, which include calorie, fat, an
bohydrate counts in their descriptions. Pan-seared salmon coated in he
and served with a slaw of fennel, orange, and onion weighs in at 395
calories. ⊠ *Mirror Lake Inn, 5 Mirror Lake Dr.* ☎ *518/523–2544*
☐ *AE, D, DC, MC, V* ☾ *No lunch.*

$$–$$$$ ✕ **Great Adirondack Steak & Seafood Company.** The extensive menu at
this casual downtown eatery and microbrewery combines American and
Continental fare. Starters include potato skins topped with bacon, broc-
coli, and cheese but also escargots and mushrooms in puff pastry and
cream sauce. Steak selections include a sirloin sandwich, bacon-wrapped
filet mignon in béarnaise sauce, and New York strip steak au poivre.
Surf-and-turf combos, chicken Parmesan, prime rib, baked or poached
salmon with dill sauce, and linguine with clam sauce also are available.
The place serves breakfast and lunch, too. Beer selections include Bel-
gian-style brews, pale ales, and porters. A patio has umbrella-shaded
tables. ⊠ *34 Main St.* ☎ *518/523–1629* ⌲ *Reservations not accepted*
☐ *AE, D, DC, MC, V.*

★ $$–$$$ ✕ **The Veranda.** The restaurant occupies an old manor on the grounds
of the Lake Placid Resort Hotel & Golf Club. The space is woodsy but
refined, with a big stone fireplace, cloth-covered tables, and twig-style
chairs. Large windows frame lake and mountain views. The menu con-
sists of mostly Continental fare: sautéed duck breast with green-peppercorn
sauce, roasted rack of lamb flavored with Provençal herbs, grilled veal
chops with pancetta in cream sauce. In warm weather, you may dine on
the covered terrace, where you have a lake view. ⊠ *1 Olympic Dr.* ☎ *518/
523–3339* ☐ *AE, D, DC, MC, V* ☾ *Closed Mon. No lunch.*

$$$$ ✕▥ **Lake Placid Lodge.** Accommodations at this posh lakefront retreat,
Fodor'sChoice a member of the Relais & Châteaux group, have stone fireplaces, feath-
★ erbeds, twig and bark furniture—including many one-of-a-kind pieces
created by local artisans—and views of either the woods or Lake Placid.
Some rooms have balconies. Lodge suites ($650 and up) include a sit-
ting room, often with a fireplace of its own; an extra-spacious bathroom
with a large soaking tub; and either a private balcony or patio. Most of
the cabins are one-room units with sitting areas and huge windows. The
restaurant is a draw on its own. The kitchen prepares New American
fare, such as duck prosciutto and roast quail stuffed with pheasant and
black-truffle mousse. Whether you eat on the porch or dine inside by
candlelight, you'll have views of the lake and the High Peaks. ⊠ *White-
face Inn Rd., off Rte. 86, 12946* ☎ *518/523–2700 or 877/523–2700*
🖷 *518/523–1124* ⊕ *www.lakeplacidlodge.com* ⇆ *11 rooms, 4 suites,
19 cabins* ⌂ *Restaurant, picnic area, room service, in-room data ports,
some refrigerators, massage, boating, mountain bikes, hiking, bar, laun-
dry service, concierge, Internet, business services, meeting rooms, some
pets allowed (fee); no a/c in some rooms, no room TVs, no kids under
14, no smoking* ☐ *AE, MC, V* ☾ *Closed mid-March–mid-Apr.* ⦿❘ *BP.*

★ $$–$$$ ✕▥ **Interlaken Inn & Restaurant.** A lovely Victorian houses this classy get-
away with individually appointed rooms and an excellent restaurant.
Some rooms look out onto the Adirondacks and some overlook the In-
terlaken's lush gardens. Interior schemes offset old-fashioned floral and

ed fabrics with neutrals. Rooms have handsome wooden furniture, ding four-poster and sleigh beds, down comforters, and Frette s and towels. A few rooms have private balconies, and third-floor s have sloping ceilings. The smallest, least expensive rooms are sim- ut still attractive. Common areas include a fireplace with wooden scoting and a fireplace. The restaurant ($$$; reservations essential) elegant, intimate space with walnut paneling and a tin ceiling. The food is contemporary but not contrived, with dishes like a starter of gnocchi with pheasant, porcini mushrooms, and Marsala sauce. Entrées range from braised lamb shank atop white-bean puree to chanterelle "dusted" salmon fillet with fennel beurre blanc and potato hash. Desserts are a specialty of the chef, Richard Brosseau, who is well known in the region. Consider warm chocolate-pecan cake, served with wintergreen ice cream, or maple and crème fraîche crème brûlée. ⊠ *39 Interlaken Ave., 12946* ☎ *518/523-3180 or 800/428-4369* 🖷 *518/523-0117* ⊕ *www.theinterlakeninn.com* ⤴ *7 rooms, 2 suites, 1 carriage house* ⟁ *Restaurant, picnic area, cable TV, pub, concierge, business services, some pets allowed (fee); no room phones, no TV in some rooms, no-smoking floors* ⊟ *AE, D, MC, V* ⎮⦿⎮ *BP.*

$$-$$$$ 🏨 **Hilton Lake Placid Resort.** The 7-acre waterfront property has accommodations in three buildings: one is on Main Street in the center of town, another is on the water, and the third (called the Lakeview) is in between. Rooms throughout are attractive, with tasteful wooden furniture. Rooms in the lakeview and waterfront buildings have either a balcony or a patio. Complimentary rowboats and paddleboats are offered to guests. ⊠ *1 Mirror Lake Dr., 12946* ☎ *518/523-4411 or 800/755-5598* 🖷 *518/523-1120* ⊕ *www.lphilton.com* ⤴ *179 rooms* ⟁ *Restaurant, room service, in-room data ports, some kitchenettes, some microwaves, some refrigerators, cable TV with movies, tennis courts, 4 pools (2 outdoor), gym, 2 hot tubs, beach, boating, fishing, bar, video game room, babysitting, dry cleaning, laundry service, business services, meeting rooms, no-smoking rooms* ⊟ *AE, D, DC, MC, V.*

★ $$-$$$$ 🏨 **Mirror Lake Inn Resort & Spa.** The complex is on the small, pristine lake that is its namesake. Most guest rooms here are elegant, with traditional furnishings and large doses of neutral colors. Four-poster beds, fireplaces, private balconies, and couches are available in some rooms. A few have Adirondack-style decor, and the suites tend to be more gussied up and formal than the other rooms. The resort offers a slew of organized activities—sunset cruises, kayak and fishing trips, guided hikes, snowshoe outings, cross-country-skiing lessons, yoga classes—and there's a full-service spa on the property. The Averil Conwell Dining Room earns high marks for its food. ⊠ *5 Mirror Lake Dr., 12946* ☎ *518/523-2544* 🖷 *518/523-2871* ⊕ *www.mirrorlakeinn.com* ⤴ *128 rooms, 11 suites* ⟁ *Restaurant, café, coffee shop, room service, refrigerators, cable TV, some in-room VCRs, tennis court, 2 pools (1 indoor), fitness classes, gym, hair salon, hot tub, sauna, spa, beach, dock, boating, fishing, cross-country skiing, ice-skating, bar, children's programs (ages 3–12), business services, meeting rooms, no-smoking rooms* ⊟ *AE, D, DC, MC, V.*

$–$$$ 🏨 **Lake Placid Resort Hotel & Golf Club.** From its hilltop perch, the four-story hotel takes in the resort's 1,000-plus acres and lovely mountain and lake views. The property encompasses two highly regarded 18-hole golf courses and the well-known Veranda restaurant. It also has a private beach on Lake Placid. Guest-room furnishings are traditional and attractive, with two double beds. Some rooms have jetted tubs and fireplaces. Also on the grounds are chalets and lakeside condominiums. ⊠ *1 Olympic Dr., 12946* ☎ *518/523–2556 or 877/570–5891* 🖷 *518/523–9410* ⊕ *www.lpresort.com* 🛏 *194 rooms, 12 suites* ⚬ *4 restaurants, room service, in-room data ports, some in-room hot tubs, refrigerators, cable TV with movies and video games, 2 18-hole golf courses, 1 9-hole golf course, putting green, 11 tennis courts, indoor pool, gym, hot tub, sauna, beach, bar, library, video game room, playground, dry cleaning, laundry facilities, laundry service, concierge, business services, meeting rooms, some pets allowed (fee), no-smoking rooms* ☰ *AE, D, DC, MC, V.*

★ **$–$$** 🏨 **Best Western Golden Arrow Hotel.** The property sits on the lake side of Main Street, in the heart of the village. Lakefront rooms have private balconies or patios; most rooms that look out onto the village have balconies as well. Standard rooms have either two double beds or a king bed and a sleeper love seat. Accommodations tend to be spacious. Some rooms have gas or wood-burning fireplaces, whirlpool tubs, and upgraded furnishings—a quilt-clad four-poster bed, for instance, or French-country decor. Canoes, rowboats, and paddleboats are available free to guests. ⊠ *150 Main St., 12946* ☎ *518/523–3353 or 800/582–5540* 🖷 *518/523–8063* ⊕ *www.golden-arrow.com* 🛏 *130 rooms, 8 suites* ⚬ *2 restaurants, picnic area, room service, BBQs, some fans, in-room data ports, some in-room safes, some in-room hot tubs, some kitchenettes, refrigerators, cable TV with movies and video games, indoor pool, wading pool, lake, gym, hair salon, hot tub, massage, sauna, beach, dock, boating, Ping-Pong, racquetball, ice-skating, bar, nightclub, recreation room, babysitting, playground, laundry facilities, business services, meeting rooms, airport shuttle, some pets allowed (fee); no smoking* ☰ *AE, D, DC, MC, V.*

$–$$ 🏨 **Mountain View Inn.** Rooms at this family-owned and -operated motor inn, neighbor to the Olympic Center, have balconies and views of the lake, and the mountains. A three-bedroom cottage on the lake is available, too. Guests have beach privileges at a nearby club. ⊠ *140 Main St., 12946* ☎ *518/523–2439 or 800/499–2668* 🖷 *518/523–8974* ⊕ *www.lakeplacidlodging.com* 🛏 *18 rooms, 1 cottage* ⚬ *In-room data ports, some microwaves, refrigerators, cable TV, no-smoking rooms* ☰ *AE, MC, V* ☉ *Closed Apr. and weekdays in Nov.–late Dec.*

¢–$ 🏨 ⚠ **Adirondack Loj.** The lodge, 5 mi south of Lake Placid, was built in 1927 on the shore of Heart Lake. It's run by the nonprofit Adirondack Mountain Club, which also runs the High Peaks Information Center here. The lodge has private rooms, family bunk rooms that sleep four to six ($45 per person), and a coed sleeping area with 18 beds ($34 per person). Two of the private rooms have two twin beds; the other two have a queen each. The main room has a stone fireplace, and the dining room serves homemade breads and soups. You may also order trail lunches here. There's a small beach on the property, and trailheads are steps away.

The lodge has canoes and kayaks, and snowshoe and cross-country-ski rentals are available at the information center. Also on the grounds are 2 cabins, 3 canvas cabins, 36 campsites, and 36 lean-tos. One cabin sleeps 4 ($100 per night); the other, available only from October through April, sleeps 16 ($320 per night). Lean-tos and tent sites are $23–$26 for two people, with discounts in winter; canvas cabins are $32. ⊠ *Adirondack Loj Rd., Box 867, off Rte. 73, 12946* ☎ *518/523–3441* 🖷 *518/523–3518* ⊕ *www.adk.org* ↘ *4 rooms, coed sleeping area with 18 beds, 4 family bunk rooms; all with shared baths* ⚖ *Dining room, picnic area, lake, boating, hiking, cross-country skiing, library; no a/c, no room phones, no room TVs* ⊟ *AE, D, MC, V* ¶⊙¶ *BP for lodge guests.*

¢–$ 🏨 **Art Devlin's Olympic Motor Inn.** The family-owned hotel, named for the famous ski jumper, sits on 2 acres three blocks from the Olympic Center. As of this writing (late 2004), rooms are in the process of being renovated. Wireless Internet access is available throughout the property. Several rooms have already been updated, some getting jetted tubs. ⊠ *350 Main St., 12946* ☎ *518/523–3700* 🖷 *518/523–3893* ⊕ *www. artdevlins.com* ↘ *41 rooms* ⚖ *Some in-room hot tubs, refrigerators, cable TV, pool, wading pool, meeting room, airport shuttle, some pets allowed, no-smoking rooms* ⊟ *AE, D, MC, V* ¶⊙¶ *CP.*

Nightlife & the Arts

NIGHTLIFE The classy **Cottage** (⊠ 5 Mirror Lake Dr. ☎ 518/523–9845), part of the Mirror Lake Inn Resort, serves cocktails late into the night. It overlooks the lake and has a large deck. Sandwiches, salads, and other light bites are on the menu. Upstairs at the **Lake Placid Pub & Brewery** (⊠ 14 Mirror Lake Dr. ☎ 518/523–3813) is a smoke-free zone where you can shoot some pool or have lunch or dinner. Downstairs there's an Irish pub with darts and billiards, and in summer you can sit outside on the deck and bask in the lake views. The beer selection includes the dark-red Ubu Ale, the signature brew here.

THE ARTS The **Lake Placid Center for the Arts** (⊠ 91 Saranac Ave. ☎ 518/523–2512 ⊕ www.lpartscenter.org), the largest arts center in the region, shows classic films and hosts theater, dance, and music performances. Gallery space is used to show works by local artists and changing exhibits.

Sports & the Outdoors

GOLF The **Lake Placid Resort** (⊠ 1 Olympic Dr. ☎ 518/523–4460 ⊕ www. lpresort.com) has two highly rated 18-hole courses: the par-71, 7,0006-yard Links Course, designed in 1909 by Scottish architect Seymour Dunn, and the par-70, 6,156-yard Mountain Course, which was laid out by Alex Findlay in 1910 and remodeled by Alister MacKenzie in 1931. Greens fees, including cart, are $27–$30 on the Links Course and $69 on the Mountain Course. You get stunning mountain views from both. The par-72, 6,490-yard course at the **Whiteface Club & Resort** (⊠ Whiteface Inn Rd. ☎ 518/523–2551 ⊕ www.whitefaceclub.com) opened in 1898. *Golf Digest* gave it 3½ stars in 2004 and cited the well-kept fairways. Greens fees are $40 in high season.

OLYMPIC VENUES National Hockey League training camps are held at the **Olympic Center** (⊠ 218 Main St. ☎ 518/523–1655 ⊕ www.orda.org) during the pre-season, and the women's U.S. national hockey team makes its home here. You might catch ice-hockey tournaments or college games at the arena. From late November to mid-March, you may skate ($5–$6) on the outdoor **Sheffield Speed Skating Oval,** where Eric Heiden won his five Olympic golds during the 1980 games, or at the indoor **1932 Olympic Rink.** From late June to late August, the indoor **Lussi Rink** is open to the public.

During the 1980 Olympics, the **Verizon Sports Complex** (✉ Off Rte. 73 7 mi south of Lake Placid ☎ 518/523–4436 or 518/523–2811), at Mount Van Hoevenberg, was the site of the luge, bobsled, cross-country skiing, and biathlon events. And this is the perfect place to try some of these sports yourself. In winter you might whoosh down the ½-mi bobsled run at close to 60 miles an hour—a professional driver and brakeman accompany you—or steer a modified luge along a serpentine track. From mid-June to early November, the bobsled ride is offered on wheels. Luge and summer bobsled rides are $30 each; the winter bobsled run is $40.

The **Cross Country Center** at the Verizon Sports Complex has 31 mi of groomed cross-country-skiing trails. Full-day trail passes are $14; lessons and rentals are available. You may also rent snowshoes here. From late June to early October, mountain bikers take over the trails ($6).

Shopping

The village is full of shops, many of them with "Adirondack" in their name. The **Adirondack Craft Center** (✉ 93 Saranac Ave. ☎ 518/523–2062) showcases the work of regional but also national artisans. There's a lot to see, and buy, at this 4,000-square-foot store: baskets, twig tables and chairs, fly-fishing ornaments, mica-shaded lamps, quilts and throws, all kinds of jewelry, photographs and prints, wooden bowls, metal sculptures, and stoneware designs. The **Adirondack Store** (✉ 109 Saranac Ave. ☎ 518/523–2646) sells antler chandeliers, bark frames, hand-painted Arts and Crafts–style lanterns, and pine-scented soaps, among many other items sure to remind you of your visit. Book lovers love **With Pipe and Book** (✉ 91 Main St. ☎ 518/523–9096), which sells rare and used books and tobacco items and is often referred to as a "village institution."

Saranac Lake

❾ *10 mi west of Lake Placid.*

The village of Saranac Lake sits on small Flower Lake; the three lakes that go by the name Saranac—Lower Saranac, Middle Saranac, and Upper Saranac—are to the west. Although its population of about 5,000 is nearly double that of Lake Placid's, Saranac Lake is much less touristy than its neighbor to the east. Settled in the early 1800s, it remained a remote community through the 19th century, relying mostly on logging. It also became a center for guiding the occasional intrepid hunter and angler in the Adirondacks. Even today the village is a good base for those who want to pursue the many outdoor recreational opportunities in the area.

In the late 1800s Dr. Edward Livingston Trudeau—having discovered the positive, healthful effects of a prolonged Adirondack vacation himself—established a tuberculosis treatment center here. As the Trudeau Sanitarium became famous, the village suddenly boomed, becoming home to several hotels and a score of what came to be known as "cure cottages," many of which remain in existence. The sanatorium eventually developed into the Trudeau Institute, a biomedical research center.

Adirondack Park Agency Visitors Interpretive Center. The center has natural-history exhibits and hosts lectures and classes on wildlife and other nature-related and outdoorsy subjects. Nature trails here double as cross-country-skiing and snowshoeing trails in winter. From June through Labor Day (daily 10–4), you may observe butterflies in the Butterfly House, a greenhouse-like structure. The center is in Paul Smiths, 12 mi north of Saranac Lake. ☒ *Rte. 30, Paul Smiths* ☎ *518/327–3000* ⊕ *www.northnet.org/adirondackvic* ☒ *Free* ☉ *Center daily 9–5, grounds daily dawn–dusk.*

Robert Louis Stevenson Memorial Cottage. In 1887 the author of *Dr. Jekyll and Mr. Hyde* spent a year here being treated for tuberculosis. Today this quaint farmhouse, with its original furniture, holds a collection of Stevenson memorabilia, including early photographs, personal letters, and his velvet smoking jacket. ☒ *11 Stevenson La.* ☎ *518/891–1462* ⊕ *www.adirondacks.com/robertlstevenson.html* ☒ *$5* ☉ *July–mid-Sept., Tues.–Sun. 9:30–noon and 1–4:30, and by appointment.*

Six Nations Indian Museum. Native American art, crafts, and artifacts are on display at this small museum dedicated to preserving the culture of the Iroquois Confederacy—the Mohawks, Oneida, Onondaga, Cayuga, Seneca, and Tuscarora. It was started in 1954 by Mohawk Ray Fadden and his family, who still run the place. Baskets, canoes, paintings, beadwork, and other items are hung on the walls and from the ceilings. The museum is 14 mi northeast of Saranac Lake. ☒ *Franklin County Rte. 30, Onchiota* ☎ *518/891–2299* ☒ *$2* ☉ *July–Labor Day, Tues.–Sun. 10–6, and by appointment.*

★ **White Pine Camp.** President Calvin Coolidge used this great camp on Lake Osgood as his "summer White House" in 1926. Although built in 1907 and expanded in 1911 by William Massarene and Addison Mizner, the camp is noted for blending rustic architecture with a rather modern sensibility. If you're not staying at one of the guest cabins here, you may see the camp only as part of a guided tour. The tours (1½ to 2 hours) take in the bowling alley, tennis house, dining and great rooms, boathouse, and guest cabins. A Japanese teahouse on a small island is accessed by an arched stone bridge. The camp is 12 mi northwest of Saranac Lake. ☒ *White Pine Rd., off Rte. 86, Paul Smiths* ☎ *518/ 327–3030* ⊕ *www.whitepinecamp.com* ☒ *$9* ☉ *Tours July–Labor Day, Sat. 10 and 1:30.*

FESTIVALS & FAIRS **Saranac Lake Winter Carnival.** The annual festival, held for 10 days starting in early February, is the oldest winter carnival in the country. It includes a lighted ice palace, fireworks, and a costume parade. Inner-tube and ski races, hockey tournaments, and snowshoe-softball games are among the sporting events. The whole town gets into the action, so there are concerts, dinners, and dances at Hotel Saranac; breakfasts at the Masonic temple; and shows at the Pendragon Theatre. ☎ *518/891–1990 or 800/347–1992* ⊕ *www.saranaclake.com.*

Where to Stay & Eat

$–$$$ ✕ **A. P. Smith Restaurant.** Wooden chandeliers hang over candlelit tables, and classical music usually plays in the background at this Hotel Saranac restaurant where hospitality and culinary-arts students from Paul Smith's College train. The food is American: beer-braised beef short ribs, broiled trout fillet with maple-pecan butter, chicken and dumplings. ⊠ *101 Main St.* ☎ *518/891–2200* ▤ *AE, D, DC, MC, V.*

$–$$$ ✕ **Belvedere Restaurant.** Locals come into this casual, family-style restaurant for hearty portions of pasta, veal Parmesan, strip steaks, and a surf-and-turf combo of steak and lobster tails. There's a lounge and pool table. ⊠ *57 Bloomingdale Ave.* ☎ *518/891–9873* ▤ *No credit cards* ⊗ *No lunch. Closed Mon.*

$$$$ ▥ **The Point.** Originally the home of William Avery Rockefeller, this ultra-exclusive retreat evokes the spirit of the great Adirondack camps. The secluded property occupies a forested peninsula on Upper Saranac Lake. Rooms, housed in four buildings, blend rustic furniture with handsome antiques and rich fabrics. Each guest room has a stone fireplace and lake views; some have pine-lined cathedral ceilings or private decks or patios. The Algonquin Room, a cozy book-lined nook, occupies the old library in the main lodge, which also houses the Great Hall (aka dining room) and three other rooms. You may play billiards or darts at the intimate pub, which shares the Eagle's Nest building with three guest rooms. Overlooking the lake is the capacious Boathouse ($2,500 a night; offered from mid-April through October only), a favorite of honeymooners. It has a king bed with a gauzy white canopy, a dining area, and a wraparound deck. Your day starts with Continental breakfast in your room or a hot meal in the dining room. Guests gather for lunch, afternoon tea, and dinner, and menus are set, but you may opt to have a lunch to go or eat in your room. Dinner is rather formal, with jacket and tie upgraded to black tie Wednesday and Saturday evenings. The all-inclusive retreat includes a wealth of recreational opportunities, including use of the canoes, rowboats, kayaks, windsurfer, sailboat, and speedboats. All this comes at a high price. The deposit alone is $500, without which you don't get directions. But that's the point of exclusivity, isn't it? ⌖ *Box 1327, 12983* ☎ *518/891–5674 or 800/255–3530* 📠 *518/891–1152* ⊕ *www.thepointresort.com* ⇆ *11 rooms* ⌂ *Dining room, picnic area, some fans, some refrigerators, golf privileges, lake, beach, boating, waterskiing, windsurfing, fishing, mountain bikes, badminton, croquet, hiking, horseshoes, volleyball, cross-country skiing, ice-skating, pub, library; no room phones, no kids under 18* ▤ *AE, MC, V* ⊗ *Closed mid-Mar.–mid-Apr.* ⫚ *AI.*

$–$$$ ▥ **White Pine Camp.** The camp, built in 1907, has hosted many prominent guests. It was known as the "summer White House" after President Calvin Coolidge vacationed here in 1926. The location, amid majestic pines on 35 acres on Lake Osgood, is a big draw. The property encompasses several cabins, most of them 100 feet away from the water. Cabins vary in size; a few can sleep as many as six or eight people, and some sleep only two. All have kitchens or kitchenettes and fireplaces or woodstoves and are fully furnished. Only six cabins are open all year. From late June through Labor Day, the minimum stay is a week; a two-night minimum is usually required the rest of the year. Because the property is of historic and architectural interest, small tours sometimes come through the camp, including the guest cabins. The management notifies you as early as it can whether a tour might quickly come through during your stay. The camp is 12 mi northwest of Saranac Lake. ⊠ *White Pine Rd., off Rte. 86, Paul Smiths 12970* ☎ *518/327–3030* ⊕ *www.whitepinecamp.com* ⊷ *13 cabins* ⚘ *Picnic area, some kitchens, some kitchenettes, lake, beach, dock, boating, fishing, bowling, hiking, cross-country skiing; no a/c, no room phones, no room TVs, no smoking* ▭ *MC, V.*

¢-$$ ▦ **Hotel Saranac of Paul Smith's College.** The second floor of this 1927 brick hotel in the center of Saranac Lake holds an unexpected space: called the Grand Hall, it's modeled on the foyer of the Davanzati Palace in Florence, Italy. The architect, William Scopes, replaced the Italian coats-of-arms with such regional icons as a snowshoe and a mounted deer. And just like the Italian palazzo, which dates from the 14th century, the ground floor of this hotel was originally an open arcade space. Hotel management students from Paul Smith's College are trained here, working alongside professional staff. Rooms are bright and attractive, with traditional furnishings and matching window treatments. Some have whirlpool tubs. The A. P. Smith Restaurant is part of the hotel. ⊠ *101 Main St., 12983* ☎ *518/891–2200 or 800/937–0211* ☐ *518/591–5664* ⊕ *www.hotelsaranac.com* ⊷ *88 rooms* ⚘ *Restaurant, coffee shop, room service, some fans, in-room data ports, some in-room hot tubs, some refrigerators, cable TV, some in-room VCRs, bar, lounge, laundry service, business services, meeting rooms, some pets allowed (fee), no-smoking rooms* ▭ *AE, D, DC, MC, V.*

¢-$ ▦ **Best Western Mountain Lake Inn.** Wireless Internet access is available throughout this two-story chain property. Interior corridors connect the rooms, which are big and bright and include desks. The heated indoor pool is a plus. ⊠ *148 Lake Flower Ave., 12983* ☎ *518/891–1970* ☐ *518/891–6195* ⊕ *www.bestwestern.com* ⊷ *69 rooms* ⚘ *Restaurant, in-room data ports, cable TV, indoor pool, bar, laundry facilities, business services, meeting rooms, some pets allowed (fee), no-smoking rooms* ⊟ *AE, D, DC, MC, V.*

¢-$ ▦ **Sara-Placid Motor Inn.** The complex offers a variety of accommodations, from standard motel rooms to suites with decks and lakefront cottages with fireplaces. Motel rooms are on the large side and have wood furniture and big windows. One suite has a whirlpool tub. A small park next door has tennis and basketball courts. ⊠ *120 Lake Flower Ave., 12983* ☎ *518/891–2729 or 800/794–2729* ☐ *518/891–5624* ⊕ *www. sara-placid.com* ⊷ *13 rooms, 3 suites, 3 cottages* ⚘ *Picnic area, 1 in-room hot tub, some kitchenettes, cable TV with movies, some in-room VCRs, lake, dock, ice-skating, laundry service; no a/c in some rooms, no smoking* ▭ *AE, D, DC, MC, V.*

Nightlife & the Arts

The monthlong **Adirondack Festival of American Music** (☎ 518/891–1057), held in July at various locations around Saranac Lake, features the Gregg Smith Singers as well as other well-known performers and musicians.

The **Pendragon Theatre** (✉ 15 Brandy Brook Ave. ☎ 518/891–1854 ⊕ www.pendragontheatre.org), a year-round professional company, performs classical and new works. Special events include mystery dinner theater shows.

Sports & the Outdoors

CANOEING ★ Motorboats aren't allowed in the pristine **St. Regis Wilderness Canoe Area**, which includes part of Upper Saranac Lake and stretches northwest. One of the best areas for canoeing in the Northeast, it encompasses nearly 60 ponds and lakes and more than 100 mi of navigable waters connected by portages. Primitive campsites (first-come, first-served) are scattered around the various ponds. One route, called the Seven Carries, takes you about 9 mi from Little Clear Pond to Upper St. Regis Lake. It makes a good day trip, but it's not a loop, so you need to arrange for a way to get back to Saranac Lake. The 11-mi Nine Carries route is more challenging and has tougher portages. To get to Little Clear Pond and other access points from Saranac Lake, take Route 86 north to Route 186 and turn left (west). Local outfitters and the Saranac Lake Area Chamber of Commerce (☎ 518/891–1990 or 800/347–1992 ⊕ saranaclake.com) can provide more information about paddling in the area.

The **Adirondack Foothills Guide Service** (⌂ Box 345, 12983 ☎ 518/359–8194 ⊕ www.adkfoothills.com) runs canoe day trips and overnight camping excursions and can outfit your paddle, whether or not you need a guide. In addition to being able to outfit canoe and camping trips, **Adirondack Lakes and Trails** (✉ 541 Lake Flower Ave. ☎ 800/491–0414 ⊕ www.adirondackoutfitters.com) offers lessons and guided excursions. **St. Regis Canoe Outfitters** (✉ 73 Dorsey St. ☎ 518/891–1838 or 888/775–2925 ⊕ www.stregiscanoeoutfitters.com) has day trips as well as longer excursions into the St. Regis Wilderness Canoe Area, guiding services, and kayak and canoe rentals and instruction. Some canoe trips include mountain hikes. You may also buy camping and other gear here. From April to October, St. Regis runs a Floodwood branch at the Long Pond portage (✉ Floodwood Rd. ☎ 518/891–8040).

GOLF ★ Seymour Dunn, the Scottish architect and professional golfer, designed the **Saranac Inn Golf & Country Club** (✉ 125 Rte. 46 ☎ 518/891–1402 ⊕ www.saranacinn.com), established at the turn of the 20th century. *Golf Digest* magazine gives the par-72, 6,631-yard championship course 4½ stars. Greens fees are $60, including a cart. The complex includes a restaurant as well as a 10-room motel ($) with rooms overlooking the first tee.

Shopping

With everything from camouflage jackets and bathing suits to ice-hockey skates and fishing lures, the **Blue Line Sport Shop** (✉ 82 Main St. 518/891–4680) can outfit you for most outdoor activities **The Ray Brook Frog** (✉ Rte. 86, Ray Brook ☎ 518/891–3333), between Saranac Lake and

Lake Placid, sells twig furniture and cushy leather chairs as well as smaller items, including lamps and lanterns, baskets, and rustic frames and mirrors. The Union Depot, an old train station, is the home of the **Whistle Stop** (✉ 42 Depot St. ☎ 518/891–4759), a showcase for wares made by local artisans and craftspeople. It's open from late May through Columbus Day only.

Tupper Lake

❿ *21 mi southwest of Saranac Lake.*

Once a logging and transportation center, Tupper Lake is today a quiet spot with about 4,000 residents. The village sits on Raquette Pond (the lake named Tupper is just west of it), with smaller bodies of water dotting the area. If you follow Main Street west to where it intersects with the old railroad tracks, you'll come to the part of town known as the Junction. Here you can see well-preserved buildings from Tupper Lake's early days, including the late-19th-century Grand Union Hotel on Depot Street. The Goff-Nelson Memorial Library on Lake Street houses a large collection of photographs and accounts of Tupper Lake's beginnings.

Historic Beth Joseph Synagogue. Jewish peddlers in the Adirondacks built this synagogue in 1905. Listed on the National Register of Historic Places, the synagogue has been restored and contains art exhibits. It also hosts concerts and other activities. ✉ *Mill and Lake Sts.* ☎ *518/359–7229* 💲 *Free* ☾ *July and Aug., weekdays 1–3.*

FESTIVALS & **Woodsmen Days.** Skills and crafts related to the lumber industry are demonFAIRS strated during this colorful two-day event held in July at Tupper Lake Municipal Park. Draft horses pull logs, chain-saw artists sculpt, and modern-day lumberjacks demonstrate chopping and ax throwing. 🖉 *Tupper Lake Woodsmen's Association, Box 759, 12986* ☎ *518/359–9444* ⊕ *www.tupperlakeinfo.com.*

Where to Stay & Eat

$ ✕ **Pine Grove Restaurant.** The restaurant's country-rustic decor is accented by plenty of ponderosa pine, and local wildlife art adorns the walls. The menu includes sandwiches, burgers, steaks, and chops, which you may order at a table or at the bar. ✉ *166 Main St.* ☎ *518/359–3669* 🖃 *AE, D, MC, V* ☾ *Closed Tues. No lunch Mon., Wed., and Thurs.*

$$–$$$$ ✕🏨 **Wawbeek on Upper Saranac Lake.** The turn-of-the-20th-century
Fodor'sChoice lodge, built in 1880 as a great camp, is on 40 wooded acres near the
★ south end of Upper Saranac Lake. Recreational opportunities are plentiful here. You might take a boat out on the lake, pedal around on a mountain bike, stroll the beach, or strap on snowshoes. Guest rooms are housed in three buildings. Accommodations in the Lake House, the newest building, have fireplaces, sitting areas, quilt-clad beds, and decks with lake and mountain views. Two of the three rooms in the Carriage House also have decks. The Mountain House rooms are more rustic, as are the cabins scattered around the property. The Bungabeek cottage has a screened porch, a kitchen, a living room, and three bedrooms. There are also five one-room log cabins with kitchenettes and decks. The restaurant ($$–$$$; reservations essential), which serves seasonal Amer-

ican fare, is popular for its food as well as for its view of Upper Saranac Lake. Indeed, it's so popular that you need to make a reservation even if you're staying here. The menu takes advantage of local products such as venison, rainbow trout, and rabbit. Maple syrup–glazed roast duckling and sautéed veal medallions with caramelized shallots in gin-spiked demi-glace are typical of the dishes prepared here. The North Country cuisine suits the dining-room architecture to a T. Dark-wood paneling, walls of windows, and a stone fireplace with a recessed hearth large enough for two banquettes give the room a backwoods tone. ⊠ *553 Hawk Ridge, 12986* ☎ *518/359–2656 or 800/953–2656* 🖷 *518/359–2475* ⊕ *www. wawbeek.com* ⇔ *17 rooms, 9 cabins, 2 cottages* ♿ *Restaurant, picnic area, some kitchens, some kitchenettes, some microwaves, some refrigerators, golf privileges, 2 tennis courts, lake, beach, boating, fishing, mountain bikes, basketball, billiards, croquet, horseshoes, Ping-Pong, volleyball, cross-country skiing, 2 lounges, laundry facilities, some pets allowed (fee); no a/c, no room phones, no room TVs, no smoking* ▤ *AE, DC, MC, V* ⊘ *Closed Apr. and 3 wks in Nov.* ⦿ *BP.*

¢ 🖼 **Shaheen's Motel.** Most rooms at this two-story motel have knotty wood paneling and forest views; some have two queen beds and a pull-out couch. The location is convenient to canoeing, hiking, and other outdoor activities. ⊠ *314 Park St.,* ☎ *518/359–3384 or 800/474–2445* 🖷 *518/ 359–3384* ⊕ *www.shaheensmotel.com* ⇔ *31 rooms* ♿ *Picnic area, some in-room data ports, refrigerators, cable TV with movies, pool, miniature golf, playground, business services, no-smoking rooms; no a/c in some rooms* ▤ *AE, D, DC, MC, V* ⦿ *CP.*

¢ 🖼 **Tupper Lake Motel.** The single-level motel, a good budget option, has comfortable rooms overlooking the pool. You have a choice of either one or two double or queen-size beds. A supermarket and restaurants are within walking distance. ⊠ *255 Park Ave.,* ☎ *518/359–3381 or 800/ 944–3585* 🖷 *518/359–8549* ⊕ *www.tupperlakemotel.com* ⇔ *18 rooms* ♿ *Picnic area, in-room data ports, refrigerators, cable TV with movies, pool, mountain bikes, business services, no-smoking rooms* ▤ *AE, D, MC, V* ⦿ *CP.*

Sports & the Outdoors

Raquette River Outfitters (⊠ 1754 Rte. 30 ☎ 518/359–3228 ⊕ www. raquetteriveroutfitters.com), a great source for information about canoeing and kayaking in the area, can help you put together a paddling trip. The shuttle service brings your boat to the launch and has your car waiting for you at the end of the route. The store rents and sells canoes, kayaks, and camping equipment. You may also buy fly-fishing gear here.

Blue Mountain Lake

⓫ *31 mi south of Tupper Lake.*

The hamlet, at the edge of Blue Mountain Lake, is home to only a few hundred people. Outdoors lovers come to the area, the geographic heart of Adirondack Park, for the boating, fishing (largemouth bass, lake trout, brook trout, and whitefish), and the excellent hiking trails. Two major attractions, the Adirondack Museum and the Adirondack Lakes Center for the Arts, have made Blue Mountain Lake a regional cultural hub.

Fodor'sChoice
★

Adirondack Museum. More than 100,000 Adirondack artifacts are in the collection of this acclaimed museum that explores the history and culture of the region. The 32-acre complex, on Blue Mountain Lake, encompasses 23 indoor and outdoor exhibit areas that examine nearly every feature of Adirondack life, including resort life, wood crafts, logging and mining, guide boats, and environmental issues. A library, snack bar, and shop are on-site. ⊠ *Rte. 30* ☎ *518/352–7311* ⊕ *www.adkmuseum.org* ⊡ *$14* ☉ *Late May–mid-Oct., daily 10–5.*

Great Camp Sagamore. Sagamore Lodge and the 26 adjoining buildings that make up Great Camp Sagamore were built in the late 1800s by William West Durant, a prominent Adirondack figure. Designed in a Swiss chalet style, the lodge was built with native spruce, cedar, and granite, and its rustic style set a precedent among the well-heeled set with retreats in the area. Bought and expanded by the Vanderbilt family in the early 1900s, Sagamore is now owned and run by a nonprofit organization that sponsors meetings, seminars, and classes, and rents rooms by the night or week. Classes and activities include canoeing, rustic furniture making, mosaic twig decoration, and mountain music and dance. Tours (reservations required) take you to a blacksmith shop, furniture shop, ice house, and livestock buildings, as well as to the main lodge. The camp is about 30 mi southwest of Blue Mountain Lake. ⊠ *Box 40, Rte. 28, Raquette Lake* ☎ *315/354–5311* ⊕ *www.sagamore.org* ⊡ *Tours $12* ☉ *Tours late May–late June weekends at 1:30; late June–early Sept., daily at 10 and 1:30; early Sept.–late Oct., daily at 1:30.*

Raquette Lake Navigation Company. Cruise the waters of Raquette Lake aboard the *W. W. Durant,* a 60-foot double-deck ship that offers lunch, Sunday brunch, dinner, foliage, and moonlight cruises ($7–$45), among other trips. The dining room is enclosed and heated, and there's a bar. Reservations are required for meal cruises. ⊠ *Rte. 28, Raquette Lake* ☎ *315/354–5532* ⊕ *www.raquettelakenavigation.com* ☉ *Call for schedule.*

FESTIVALS & FAIRS

No-Octane Regatta. Only boats without a motor—sailboats, sloops, rowboats, canoes, and guide boats—may participate in this race, sponsored by the Adirondack Museum. The event, held over a weekend in mid-June, includes a grand parade of wooden boats on Blue Mountain Lake, a toy-boat regatta, and boat-building workshops. *Adirondack Museum* ☎ *518/352–7311* ⊕ *www.adkmuseum.org.*

Rustic Furniture Fair. Nearly 100 antiques dealers from throughout the United States and Canada participate in this annual fair, which spotlights rustic furniture and decorative arts. A jury selects the 50 or so rustic-furniture makers showing here; styles include contemporary and traditional pieces. The annual two-day fair is held in early September on the grounds of the Adirondack Museum. *Adirondack Museum* ☎ *518/352–7311* ⊕ *www.adkmuseum.org.*

Where to Stay & Eat

¢ ✕🏠 **Long View Lodge.** The 1929 country inn, on Long Lake, has a covered porch that invites lingering. Guest rooms are homey, with throw rugs scattered across hardwood floors and beds covered with quilts. Furnishings include antique pieces. Two one-bedroom cabins are available from late May through Columbus Day. Smoking isn't allowed in any of the guest rooms. The restaurant ($$–$$$), a warm space with a beamed ceiling, a fireplace, and a lake view, serves interesting American fare, such as grilled lamb chops with roasted potatoes, asparagus, and mint demi-glace, or walnut-crusted chicken on a bed of brie polenta. The menu includes a few vegetarian choices. ⊠ *Rtes. 28N and 30, Long Lake, 12847* ☎ *518/624–2862* ⊕ *www.longviewlodge.com* ⤳ *9 rooms, 4 suites, 2 cottages* ⚭ *Restaurant, some fans, cable TV, some microwaves, some refrigerators, lake, beach, dock, boating, billiards, some pets allowed, no-smoking floor; no a/c* ⊟ *D, MC, V.*

$$–$$$ 🏨 **The Hedges.** This camp, dating from 1880, is where you check in if you want to check out for a while. Forget phones, computers, and TVs—the emphasis here is on the great outdoors. Early-morning views from this property are of mist-covered Blue Mountain Lake and surrounding Adirondack Mountains. You might take a kayak or canoe out on the lake, hit some balls on the tennis court, try to hook a fish, or snuggle up with a book in a cozy nook. Accommodations, outfitted in Adirondack style, are housed in several lodge buildings, three of which are for adults only. Cabins are also available. Some rooms have lake views, and a few have fireplaces. Rates include a full breakfast and dinner. ⊠ *Hedges Rd.* ☎ *518/352–7352* ⊕ *www.thehedges. com* ⤳ *18 rooms, 13 cabins* ⚭ *Dining room, some kitchenettes, tennis court, lake, beach, boating, fishing, Ping-Pong, library, playground; no room phones, no room TVs* ⊟ *No credit cards* ⊗ *Closed late Oct.–late May* ⦿ *MAP.*

¢ 🏨 **Sandy Point Motel.** The small lakefront motel has standard rooms and efficiencies with private screened-in porches and balconies with water views. Some units have kitchenettes. You can rent canoes, rowboats, and paddleboats on the property. ⊠ *Rte. 30* ☎ *518/624–3871* ⊕ *www. sandypointmotel.com* ⤳ *11 rooms* ⚭ *Some kitchenettes, cable TV, lake, sauna, beach, dock, boating, no-smoking rooms; no a/c, no room phones* ⊟ *AE, D, MC, V* ⊗ *Closed Nov.–Apr.*

Nightlife & the Arts

The **Adirondack Lakes Center for the Arts** (⊠ Rte. 28 ☎ 518/352–7715 ⊕ www.adk-arts.org) presents a wide variety of programs, from classical concerts to coffeehouse entertainment, films, plays, exhibits, and workshops. Galleries display regional and national artwork. The center is open weekdays 10–4; in July and August it's also open 10–4 on Saturday and noon–4 on Sunday.

Sports & the Outdoors

HIKING At 3,759 feet above sea level, **Blue Mountain** towers over the waters of Blue Mountain Lake. The well-maintained 2.2-mi Blue Mountain Trail leads to the summit, which offers spectacular views of the surrounding lakes and mountains. The trailhead is on Route 30/28N 1.3 mi north of the hamlet of Blue Mountain Lake. Look for a parking area not far past the Adirondack Museum.

Gore Mountain Ski Area

⑫   *North Creek is 29 mi southeast of Blue Mountain Lake and 21 mi north-west of Lake George.*

Nestled between the mountains and the Hudson River Gorge, the village of North Creek makes a good base for a variety of outdoor activities. Just southwest of the village is Gore Mountain; with a 2,150-foot vertical drop, it's the second-largest ski area (after Whiteface) in the state. Cross-country skiing is an option, too. North Creek is also the white-water hub of the Adirondacks and site of the annual White Water Derby.

☙   **Garnet Mine Tours.** The mine, started in 1878, is one of the largest garnet mines in the world. Guided tours, which include a walk through an open-pit mine, leave from the Gore Mountain Mineral Shop; you follow the guide in your car to the actual mines, at the base of Gore Mountain. ⊠ *Burton Mine Rd., west off Rte. 28, North River* ☎ *518/251–2706* ⊕ *www.garnetminetours.com* ☒ *$9.50* ⊙ *June–mid-Oct., Mon.–Sat. 9:30–5, Sun. 11–5.*

Upper Hudson River Railroad. This scenic railroad offers unparalleled views of the Hudson River. The 2 hour, 17-mi round-trip excursion runs along a section of the old Adirondack Branch of the D&H Railroad. ⊠ *3 Railroad Pl., North Creek* ☎ *518/251–5334* ⊕ *www.upperhudsonriverrr.com* ☒ *$14* ⊙ *Late May–Oct.; call for schedule.*

Where to Stay & Eat

¢–$$ ✕ **Casey's North Restaurant & Tavern.** Sandwiches, nachos, soups, steaks, and salads are on the menu at this casual lodge-style restaurant. Dishes include blackened fresh Atlantic salmon fillet with orange–red pepper sauce, char-grilled New York strip steak, and hamburgers. Friendly servers and reasonable prices make it a preferred destination for families after a day on the slopes. ⊠ *3195 Rte. 28, North Creek* ☎ *518/251–5836* ⊟ *AE, D, MC, V* ⊙ *Closed Mon. and Tues. Sept.–June.*

★ $$$–$$$$ ✕⌂ **Copperfield Inn.** The upscale white-clapboard inn, at the base of Gore Mountain, has a living room with fireplace and other inviting public spaces. Guest rooms have marble bathroom floors, two queen-size beds or one king bed, and sitting areas with pull-out love seats. Suites have marble bathrooms, whirlpool tubs, and spacious living rooms, some with a view of the Hudson River. The decor throughout is tasteful and traditional. Gardens restaurant serves Continental fare in a setting of chandeliers and crystal; the rustic-style Trapper's Tavern serves pub food and, in season, has live music nightly. ⊠ *307 Main St., North Creek 12853* ☎ *518/251–2500 or 800/424–9910* ⊕ *www.copperfieldinn.com* ➳ *24 rooms, 7 suites* ₼ *Restaurant, in-room data ports, some in-room hot tubs, cable TV with movies and video games, in-room VCRs, pool, tennis court, gym, hair salon, outdoor hot tub, massage, sauna, sports bar, laundry service, meeting rooms, no-smoking rooms* ⊟ *AE, D, DC, MC, V* ⎰⎱ *CP.*

¢–$ ⌂ **Garnet Hill Lodge.** Overlooking mountains and a pristine lake 5 mi from Gore Mountain Ski Center, this Adirondack inn was built in the tradition of the great camps. Accommodations are housed in four buildings, including the Log House, which has hewn beams and posts, a wide front porch, and mountain and lake views. Rooms combine paneled walls with contemporary, rustic-style furnishings; some rooms have balconies. Large groups can be accommodated in the few guest rooms at the Birches and the Tea House. The 600-acre complex includes a cross-country-skiing and mountain-biking center. Packages offer lodging, rentals, and instruction. The lodge also has canoes, rowboats, sailboats, and paddleboats. The Saturday buffet dinner is a highlight at the restaurant. ⊠ *13th Lake Rd., North River 12856* ☎ *518/251–2821 or 800/497–4207* 🖷 *518/251–3089* ⊕ *www.garnet-hill.com* ➳ *30 rooms, 3 with shared bath; 1 suite* ♧ *Restaurant, some fans, some in-room hot tubs, 2 tennis courts, sauna, beach, boating, fishing, bicycles, hiking, cross-country skiing, business services, some pets allowed, no-smoking rooms; no a/c in some rooms, no room TVs* ☰ *MC, V* ⦿*I MAP.*

¢ 🖷 **Black Mountain Ski Lodge.** This budget family motel is in a quiet area 5 mi from the Gore Mountain Ski Center. Its dark-wood exterior and the guest rooms' knotty wood-paneled walls give it a rustic chalet look. Rooms are basic but spacious. ⊠ *2999 Rte. 8, North Creek 12853* ☎ *518/251–2800* ⊕ *www.blackmountainskilodge.com* ➳ *23 rooms, 2 efficiencies* ♧ *Dining room, some microwaves, some refrigerators, cable TV, pool, playground, some pets allowed (fee), no-smoking rooms* ☰ *AE, D, MC, V.*

Sports & the Outdoors

RAFTING The real white-water daredevils like to put their kayaks and canoes into the river in spring, after the runoff from the snowmelt has swollen the waters. The most popular runs are along the Indian River from Indian Lake and then on to the Hudson River leading to North Creek. The Hudson River Gorge offers 17 mi of class III and IV white water. From April through October, the well-known **Hudson River Rafting Company** (⊠ 1 Main St., North Creek ☎ 518/251–3215 or 800/888–7238 ⊕ www.hudsonriverrafting.com) runs rafting trips for experts as well as beginners. Trips may include camping behind its Hudson River base.

In early May, the annual **Hudson River White Water Derby** (⌂ Box 84, North Creek 12853 ☎ 518/251–2612 ⊕ www.goremtnregion.org) draws canoeing, kayaking, and camping enthusiasts to the North Creek area. The two-day event includes slalom and downriver races. The Gore Mountain Region Chamber of Commerce has details.

SKI AREAS The **Garnet Hill Ski Lodge and Cross-Country Ski Center** (⊠ 13th Lake Rd., ★ North River ☎ 518/251–2444, 518/251–2821, or 800/497–4207 ⊕ www.garnet-hill.com) has 55 km of groomed cross-country-skiing trails, with 2 km lighted for night schussing. With more than 120 inches of snow a year, the center often has skiing into spring. Lessons, rental equipment, and a ski shop are available; trail passes are $15. The on-property inn has lodge-and-ski packages. In summer, mountain biking becomes the focus ($5 trail pass).

The state-owned **Gore Mountain Ski Center** (⊠ Peaceful Valley Rd., North Creek ☎ 518/251–2411 or 800/342–1234 ⊕ www.goremountain.com), operated by the Olympic Regional Development Authority, has a 2,100-foot vertical drop, 68 alpine trails, 12 snowshoeing/cross-country-skiing trails, and 95% snowmaking coverage. You find some of the longest runs in the East here; the longest stretches 2.9 mi. Intermediate trails account for 60% of the terrain; novices have 10% and advanced skiers have 30%. A ski pass is $48–$57. From August to mid-October you can ride the Northwoods Gondola Skyride ($10) up the mountain, or hit the fairly challenging terrain on a mountain bike ($11 trail passes).

Shopping

Antler light fixtures and lamps are a specialty at the **Rustic Homestead Streamside Gallery** (✉ Rte. 28N, North Creek ☎ 518/251–4038), which also sells rustic birch rockers, cedar beds, bark-framed mirrors, and intricate desks and chests.

Old Forge

⑬ *32 mi west of Blue Mountain Lake.*

The village is at the west end of the Fulton Chain of Lakes, in the southwest corner of Adirondack Park. In years past it was a hub for wealthy travelers who arrived by train and then continued by boat to their Adirondack hotels and summer homes. Today it's kind of touristy, with a water park and souvenir stores, but short side trips take you away from the fray.

Adirondack Scenic Railroad. From July through Labor Day you may take a nature tour by hopping a train bound for Carter Station, northeast of Old Forge. It includes a forest ranger–led walk and a boxed lunch. Or, from late May to late October, you may take a scenic 20-mi train ride south to Otter Lake. Either trip is $12. Trains leave from the station in Thendara, 2 mi southwest of Old Forge. ✉ *Rte. 28, Thendara* ☎ *315/724–0700 or 877/508–6728* ⊕ *www.adirondackrr.com* 🎫 *$12 and up* ⊙ *Early May–late Oct.; call for schedule.*

Arts Center/Old Forge. The arts center sponsors exhibits, performances, artists' receptions, and special events focusing on Adirondack traditions and artists. Classes and workshops for children and adults teach everything from watercolor and basket weaving to poetry. The center also organizes hikes. ✉ *3260 Rte. 28* ☎ *315/369–6411* ⊕ *www.artscenteroldforge.org* 🎫 *Admission varies* ⊙ *Mon.–Sat. 10–4, Sun. noon–4.*

Enchanted Forest/Water Safari. Highlights at this water park include a tidal-wave pool and a multiperson tube ride called the Amazon. The Black River waterslide and the Bombay Blaster chutes have you gliding through darkness. The complex includes traditional amusement rides and themed areas such as Story Book Lane for the younger set; circus shows are offered twice daily. ✉ *Rte. 28N* ☎ *315/369–6145* ⊕ *www.watersafari.com* 🎫 *$23.95* ⊙ *Mid-June–Labor Day, daily; call for hrs.*

★ **Old Forge Lake Cruise.** You can explore the first four lakes of the Fulton Chain on a narrated sightseeing cruise aboard one of two 125-passenger boats. The 22-mi cruises usually take two hours; kids' cruises are 15 mi and take about 90 minutes. Dinner excursions are also available. From June to mid-September you may tag along on the 35-foot *President Harrison* as it delivers mail to lakefront camps and cottages. The mailboat service dates from 1902, and was spurred by Benjamin Harrison, whose family summered on Second Lake. The mailboat can take only 10 passengers, so reservations for this three-hour cruise are a good idea. ⊠*Main St. Dock, Rte. 28* ☎*315/369–6473* ⊕*www.oldforgecruises. com* ⊠ *Sightseeing and mailboat cruises $12–$16.50* ⊙ *Memorial Day–Columbus Day; call for schedule.*

Where to Stay & Eat

$$–$$$ ✕ **Old Mill Restaurant.** Steaks are a specialty at this popular restaurant and bar in a converted mill, but the menu includes plenty of other American fare, such as chicken breast stuffed with spinach and cheese and served with white sauce, or grilled rack of lamb that's been marinaded in wine and onions. Portions are generous. With its stone fireplace and vaulted ceiling, the dining room recalls an Adirondack lodge. Outside is a huge waterwheel. Reservations aren't accepted, so you may face a wait to be seated. ⊠*2888 Rte. 28* ☎*315/369–3662* ⊘*Reservations not accepted* ⊟ *MC, V* ⊙ *Closed Nov.–late Dec. and mid-Mar.–Apr. No lunch.*

¢–$$ ✕▥ **Big Moose Inn.** The large 1903 Adirondack inn on Big Moose Lake has a central fireplace, a cozy lounge, a front porch with rockers, a floating gazebo with checkerboards, and canoes. Accommodations are simple and have brass beds; most rooms have a lake view, and one has a fireplace and a whirlpool tub. Wireless Internet access is available. The restaurant serves American fare ($–$$$) in an attractive space with lake views. A deck with umbrella-shaded tables offers lakeside dining. ⊠ *1510 Big Moose Rd., Eagle Bay 13331* ☎ *315/357–2042* ⊟ *315/ 357–3423* ⊕ *www.bigmooseinn.com* ⇗ *16 rooms, 4 with shared bath* ⚘ *Restaurant, lake, 2 docks, boating, fishing; no a/c in some rooms, no room phones, no TV in some rooms, no smoking* ⊟ *AE, MC, V* ⊙ *Closed Apr.* ⏐⊙⏐ *CP.*

¢ ✕▥ **Van Auken's Inne.** Built in 1891 as a boardinghouse for lumberjacks, this historic country inn is easily identified by its two-story porch with rockers. Guest rooms, all on the second floor, have antiques and quilts; bed configurations vary from a double to two queens or a king. In the restaurant you may order American fare like veal Parmesan, charbroiled Virginia ham with brown-sugar glaze, and pan-seared salmon fillet in a potato crust. The tavern also serves food. ⊠ *108 Forge St., Thendara 13472* ☎ *315/369–3033* ⊕ *www.vanaukensinne.com* ⇗ *12 rooms* ⚘ *Restaurant, cable TV, bar; no a/c, no smoking* ⊟ *MC, V* ⏐⊙⏐ *CP.*

¢–$$$ ▥ **Best Western Sunset Inn.** The chain property has a heated indoor pool with an adjacent outdoor deck. Rooms are simple but spacious. ⊠ *2752 Rte. 28, 13420* ☎*315/369–6836* ⊟*315/369–2607* ⊕*www.bestwestern. com* ⇗ *52 rooms* ⚘ *Picnic area, in-room data ports, refrigerators, cable TV with movies, tennis court, indoor pool, hot tub, sauna, playground, laundry facilities, some pets allowed, no-smoking rooms* ⊟ *AE, D, MC, V.*

¢–$$ ▥ **Water's Edge Inn & Conference Center.** The rustic-style, three-story lodge with modern amenities sits at the edge of a lake in the Fulton Chain. Rooms have balconies, some overlooking the lake, and attractive traditional furnishings. Common areas include a library with cushy chairs, a stone fireplace, and water views conducive to lingering. ⊠ *Rte. 28,*

13420 ☎ *315/369–2484* 📠 *315/369–6782* ⊕ *www.watersedgeinn.*
com 📨 *61 rooms, 8 suites* ⚐ *Restaurant, some refrigerators, cable TV,*
indoor pool, lake, sauna, dock, fishing, bar, library, business services,
meeting rooms, no-smoking rooms ▤ *AE, MC, V.*

¢–$ 🖼 **19th Green Motel.** Tree-lined grounds surround this motel next to the
Thendara Golf Club, and snowmobiling trails are accessible from the
property. Accommodations are roomy and have either one or two queen-
size beds. ⊠ *2761 Rte. 28, 13420* ☎ *315/369–3575* ⊕ *www.19thgreen-*
motel.com 📨 *13 rooms* ⚐ *Picnic area, some microwaves, refrigerators,*
cable TV with movies, pool, no-smoking rooms ▤ *AE, D, DC, MC, V.*

Sports & the Outdoors

CANOEING **Tickner's Canoe Rentals** (⊠ Rte. 28 ☎ 315/369–6286 ⊕ www.
ticknerscanoes.com) has canoe and kayak rentals and organizes paddles,
short and long, on Moose River and in the Fulton Chain of Lakes. Floats
include the kayak or canoe, a life vest, and shuttle service. One package includes return transportation on the Adirondack Scenic Railroad.

The annual **Adirondack Canoe Classic** (☎ 518/891–2744) is a three-day
90-mi canoe race held in early September. The 250 boats participating
make their way from Old Forge through Blue Mountain Lake to the village of Saranac Lake, crossing several portages.

GOLF The 6,435-yard, par-72 course at the **Thendara Golf Club** (⊠ Rte. 28, Then-
dara ☎ 315/369–3136 ⊕ www.thendaragolfclub.com) was designed by
Donald Ross and has a challenging back 9 holes. It rated four stars from
Golf Digest magazine in 2004. Greens fees are $32, excluding carts.

RAFTING In spring, adventurous rafters head for the class III and IV rapids of the
Hudson River and Moose River's 14 mi of class V rapids. If you want
tamer waters, consider summer family rafting and tubing on the Sacan-
daga River. **Adirondack River Outfitters** (⊠ Rte. 9N S ☎ 800/525–7238
⊕ www.aroadventures.com) offers one-day rafting trips on the Hudson,
Black, and Moose rivers and tubing and family rafting on the Sacan-
daga River. Trips include shuttle, equipment, guides, snacks, and drinks.

Shopping

Old Forge Hardware (⊠ 104 Fulton St. ☎ 315/369–6100), an authentic general store, was founded in 1900. The mix of goods is wide ranging, to say the least; maps, canoes, pet food, Woolrich shirts, copper molds,
cast-iron pots and pans, candles, books, yarn, fishing and camping gear,
baskets, snowshoes, and rustic furniture are just some of the things you
can find here.

THE THOUSAND ISLANDS & THE SEAWAY

The name Thousand Islands is less than accurate; there are, in fact, nearly
twice that number of islands, depending on who's doing the counting
and what you consider an island. There is also much more to the region
than the island-studded area of the St. Lawrence River called the Thousand Islands. The name usually refers to an area defined by the Adirondacks to the east, the St. Lawrence River to the north, and Lake Ontario
to the west.

Most of the region is flat or rolling farmland. The St. Lawrence River defines a coastline running for more than 100 mi southwest from Massena to Cape Vincent, where the river meets Lake Ontario. The St. Lawrence is the throat of a waterway that leads through the Great Lakes and which, with the completion of its lock system in 1959, formed the longest navigable inland passage—more than 2,300 mi—in the world.

The region's largest city, Watertown, is more than 30 mi south of the Thousand Islands and is itself something of a misnomer, as it's not on any water itself. Alexandria Bay and Clayton are the focal points for summer visitors to the Thousand Islands. They're the ports from which most of the island owners make their way to their secluded summer homes. Both are good walking towns because they're well away from highway traffic and are fairly compact.

Sackets Harbor

⑭ *80 mi west of Old Forge.*

The Lake Ontario village was settled in 1800, and many of the buildings here are from the early 19th century. The visitor center has a walking-tour brochure you can follow through the historic district. Sackets Harbor was the site of two engagements during the War of 1812, and you may stroll the battlefield where they took place. In summer the harbor tends to bustle with cruising activity. In winter hardy cross-country skiers and snowmobilers take over.

Robbins' Farm and Old McDonald's Children's Farm. Walk up and say hello to cows, camels, and more than 200 other animals. Old McDonald's has been educating children about farm life since 1986. The complex includes a calf-raising facility as part of a 1,200-acre working farm. There's also a miniature golf course. ⌂ *14471 Rte. 145* ☎ *315/ 583–5737* ⊕ *www.oldmcdonaldhasafarm.com* ✉ *General admission $5, dairy tour $2, pony ride $2* ⊙ *Early June–Labor Day, daily 10–6; rest of Sept. and May–early June, Sun.–Thurs. 10–4, Fri. and Sat. 10–6; Oct., Sun.–Thurs. 10–5, Fri. and Sat. 10–6.*

Sackets Harbor Battlefield State Historic Site. During the War of 1812, two battles were fought here between the British and the Americans. The harbor served as headquarters for divisions of the army and navy. Today the site includes a nicely restored commandant's house, which dates from 1850. In summer, guides reenact camp life. ⌂ *505 W. Washington St.* ☎ *315/646–3634* ⊕ *nysparks.state.ny.us* ✉ *$3* ⊙ *Commandant's house late May–early Sept., Tues.–Sat. 10–5, Sun. 11–5; early Sept.–Columbus Day, Fri. and Sat. 10–5, Sun. 11–5.*

Sackets Harbor Heritage Area Visitors Center. Displays focus on the harbor's role in the War of 1812. ⌂ *301 W. Main St.* ☎ *315/646–2321* ⊕ *www.sacketsharborny.com* ✉ *Free* ⊙ *Late May–Columbus Day, daily 10–5.*

Seaway Trail Discovery Center. The Seaway Trail is a 454-mi federally recognized scenic byway along the shores of lakes Erie and Ontario and the St. Lawrence River. Nine rooms in the Discovery Center present interactive exhibits that explain life along the water. Displays include agriculture, history, culture, lighthouses, architecture, and recreation. ⊠ *Ray St. and W. Main St.* ☎ *315/646–1000* ⊕ *www.seawaytrail.com* ⊡ *$4* ☉ *May–Oct., daily 10–5; Nov.–Apr., call for hrs.*

Where to Stay & Eat

$–$$$ ✕ **1812 Steak & Seafood Co.** As the name says, steaks and seafood are specialties at this easygoing restaurant in the village's historic district. You find dishes such as London broil à la 1812—thinly sliced and served with sautéed mushrooms and horseradish sauce—and jumbo shrimp stuffed with lobster meat. The menu also includes surf-and-turf combos and chicken and pasta dishes. ⊠ *212 W. Main St.* ☎ *315/646–2041* ⊟ *AE, D, DC, MC, V.*

★ **$–$$$** ✕ **Tin Pan Galley.** The upstairs dining room, called 110 West Main, begins service at 5:30 PM daily; breakfast and lunch are served downstairs or outside. Salads and sandwiches are popular; try the grilled portobello mushroom sandwich. Alfresco dining is in a New Orleans–style flower garden with wrought-iron gates and a stone archway. ⊠ *110 W. Main St.* ☎ *315/646–3812* ⊟ *AE, D, MC, V.*

¢–$$ 🏨 **Ontario Place Hotel.** Some rooms have views of the harbor at this hotel with a range of accommodations. In addition to standard rooms there are larger minisuites with roll-away beds that can sleep up to five people. Minisuites have refrigerators, microwaves, and in-room hot tubs. ⊠ *103 General Smith Dr., 13685* ☎ *315/646–8000 or 800/564–1812* 🖷 *315/646–2506* ⊕ *www.imcnet.net/ontario_place/hotel.htm* ⊷ *38 rooms, 1 suite, 1 apartment* ⚬ *In-room data ports, some in-room hot tubs, some microwaves, some refrigerators, cable TV, some in-room VCRs, meeting rooms, some pets allowed (fee), no-smoking rooms* ⊟ *AE, D, DC, MC, V.*

¢–$ 🏨 **Candlelight Bed and Breakfast.** Built in 1832, this Georgian redbrick home is next door to the Sackets Harbor Battlefield State Historic Site and a three-minute walk from restaurants, shops, and the Seaway Trail. Rooms have period antiques, four-poster beds, and quilts; two have water views, the third looks out onto the village. ⊠ *501 W. Washington St., 13685* ☎ *315/646–1518 or 800/306–5595* ⊕ *www.imcnet.net/candlelight* ⊷ *3 rooms* ⚬ *Dining room, fans, business services; no room phones, no room TVs, no kids under 18, no smoking* ⊟ *MC, V* ⊙⏐ *BP.*

Clayton

⑮ *20 mi north of Sackets Harbor.*

Clayton, which occupies a promontory jutting into the St. Lawrence River, quietly maintains its riverine heritage. Settled in 1822, it was once a major shipbuilding port and steamship stop. Later in the 19th century, vacationers came here to fish and boat—two activities that still draw people to the area. Otherwise, museums are the main attractions here.

★ ☺   **Antique Boat Museum.** Boats and river memorabilia depict life on the St. Lawrence River. The collection of 205 craft includes an 8-foot canoe and a 65-foot yacht. Landlubbers may appreciate an exhibit that shows the Thousand Islands as a vacation destination; in its heyday, 15 trains arrived daily from New York City and Boston. ☒ *750 Mary St.* ☎ *315/ 686–4104* ⊕ *www.abm.org* ☒ *$8* ⊗ *Early May–mid-Oct., daily 9–5.*

Handweaving Museum & Arts Center. The nonprofit organization aims to preserve and promote traditional arts and handcrafts. Hand-woven, 20th-century fabrics are a focus of the museum, and the center has extensive resources for weavers. A gallery (closed January through March) hosts changing exhibits. ☒ *314 John St.* ☎ *315/686–4123* ⊕ *www.hm-ac. org* ☒ *Free* ⊗ *Weekdays 9–4:30.*

Thousand Islands Museum of Clayton. One special exhibit at this museum in the Town Hall/Opera House is devoted to large muskellunges, a prized local fish. Other displays focus on life at the turn of the 20th century. The museum also has a large collection of decoys. ☒ *312 James St.* ☎ *315/686–5794* ⊕ *www.timuseum.org* ☒ *$2* ⊗ *Mid-May–mid-Oct., daily 10–4.*

Tibbetts Point Lighthouse. One of the oldest lighthouses on the Great Lakes looks out over the outlet of Lake Ontario. The Coast Guard left in 1981, and the building is now used as a youth hostel. It's 12 mi west of Clayton. ☒ *33435 Rte. 6, Cape Vincent* ☎ *315/654–2700* ⊕ *www. capevincent.org/lighthouse/* ☒ *Free* ⊗ *Late May–late June and early Sept.–early Oct., Fri.–Mon. 10–7; late June–early Sept., daily 10–7.*

FESTIVALS & **Antique Boat Show and Auction.** The annual three-day show, held in early FAIRS August, concludes with an antique-boat parade on the St. Lawrence River. Boats are displayed in the water and on land. The Antique Boat Museum hosts some of the activities. ☒ *750 Mary St.* ☎ *315/686–4104* ⊕ *www.abm.org.*

Duck, Decoy and Wildlife Art Show. Artists, carvers, painters, and taxidermists come from all over the country and Canada to show their work at this three-day event in mid-July. ☒ *Recreation Park Arena, East Line Rd.* ☎ *315/686–5794* ⊕ *www.timuseum.org.*

French Festival. The largest festival in the North Country celebrates Cape Vincent's French heritage over a weekend in early July. The fun includes a parade, French music and food, fireworks, band performances, and children's programs. ☎ *315/654–2481* ⊕ *www.capevincent.org.*

Where to Stay & Eat

★ $$–$$$ ✕ **Clipper Inn.** This chef-owned restaurant, a local favorite, serves upscale fare in a casual, comfortable space with cloth-covered tables. The menu emphasizes seafood: shrimp scampi, sautéed or broiled scallops, king crab legs. Filet Oscar is butterflied filet mignon dressed with crabmeat, asparagus, and béarnaise sauce; veal Oscar is similar. The menu also includes chicken Parmesan and other chicken dishes. ☒ *126 State St.* ☎ *315/686–3842* ⊟ *AE, D, DC, MC, V* ⊗ *Closed Nov.–Mar. No lunch.*

★ $–$$$ ✕ **Thousand Islands Inn.** The late-1800s inn, in downtown Clayton, is said to be the first place to have served Thousand Island salad dressing. You can guess what the house dressing is today. The restaurant is known for its game dishes—broiled quail on a bed of wild rice or sautéed venison medallions in demi-glace, for example. But the menu is extensive and includes pasta, fish, pork, lamb, steak, chicken, and veal dishes. The original tin ceiling in the dining room dates from the late 1800s. The second and third floors have guest rooms (¢–$). ⊠ *335 Riverside Dr.* ☎ *315/686–3030* ⊟ *AE, D, DC, MC, V* ⊘ *Closed mid-Sept.–mid-May.*

$–$$ ✕ **Foxy's.** Gaze out at the St. Lawrence River as you tuck into the Italian-American fare at this waterfront restaurant between Clayton and Alexandria Bay. Families like the casual atmosphere, and the kids like the game room. Dishes include four veal preparations, lasagne, eggplant Parmesan, sautéed chicken livers, chicken Parmesan, scampi, fried scallops with citrus sauce, and New York strip steak. Weekend reservations are strongly suggested. ⊠ *18187 Reed Point Rd., Fisher's Landing* ☎ *315/686–3781* ⊟ *D, MC, V* ⊘ *Closed mid-Sept.–mid-Apr.*

$ ⌂ **McKinley House.** The Queen Anne Victorian, built in 1890, is a block from the St. Lawrence River and has a turret and a curved porch. Guest rooms are tasteful, with four-poster or brass queen beds, hardwood floors, large windows, and sitting areas. ⊠ *505 Hugunin St., 13624* ☎ *315/686–3405* ⊕ *www.mckinleyhouse.com* ↪ *3 rooms* ⌂ *Dining room, fans; no room phones, no room TVs, no smoking* ⊟ *No credit cards* ⟋⟍ *BP.*

¢ ⌂ **Bertrand's.** You'll be right in the middle of the village at this 1930s budget motel close to the shore. Exterior corridors connect the rooms, which are simple and have wood-paneled walls. ⊠ *229 James St., 13624* ☎ *315/686–3641 or 800/472–0683* ⊕ *www.thousandislands.com/bertrands/* ↪ *28 rooms* ⌂ *Picnic area, some refrigerators, cable TV, no-smoking rooms* ⊟ *AE, D, MC, V.*

Alexandria Bay

⑯ *12 mi northeast of Clayton.*

The vacation center and heart of the Thousand Islands area, Alexandria Bay sits at the edge of the St. Lawrence River. In the late 1800s the village was a popular vacation spot and steamboat stop, attracting wealthy visitors who built homes on the islands. Today Alexandria Bay caters to visitors who want a quick look at the islands, and restaurants and motels abound. The centerpiece attraction is Boldt Castle, on Heart Island, across from the village. Wellesley Island is home to a couple of state parks and to a cottage community called Thousand Islands Park.

Ⓒ **Aqua Zoo.** The more than 80 exhibits at this aquarium show creatures from lakes, oceans, and rivers around the world. ⊠ *43681 Rte. 12, ¾ mi off Rte. 81* ☎ *315/482–5771* ⊕ *www.abay.com/aquazoo/* ⊞ *$5.50* ⊘ *Memorial Day–Labor Day, daily 10–7.*

★ Ⓒ **Boldt Castle.** George C. Boldt, proprietor of the Waldorf-Astoria Hotel in New York, began building this 120-room Rhineland-style castle on Heart Island for his wife, Louise, in 1900. Four years later, when she died suddenly, he ceased work on the castle. The building remained deserted for 73 years, abused by vandals and weather. Since 1977, millions of dollars have been poured into restoration work. It's worth a trip to the 5-acre island to see the castle. Its fleet of wooden boats is in the Boldt Yacht House, on Wellesley Island. Uncle Sam Boat Tours runs shuttle boats between Alexandria Bay, Heart Island, and Wellesley Island. ⊠ *Heart Island* ☎ *315/482–9724, 315/482–2501, 800/847–5263* ⊕ *www.boldtcastle.com* ≅ *Castle $5.25, yacht house $3* ☉ *Castle May, June, Sept., and Oct., daily 10–6:30; July and Aug., daily 10–7:30. Yacht house mid-May–late Sept., daily 10–6:30.*

Empire Boat Lines. The company runs three-hour narrated sightseeing cruises (including a stop at Singer Castle) as well as dinner cruises from Alexandria Bay. Prices are $15–$27.50; reservations are required for meal cruises. ⊠ *5 Fuller St.* ☎ *315/482–8687 or 888/449–2539* ⊕ *www. empireboat.com* ☉ *Mid-May–Oct.; call for schedule.*

Singer Castle. Guides lead 45-minute tours, up and down many stairs, through this lovely turn-of-the-20th-century castle on Dark Island. The castle, originally known as the Towers, was built as a summer home for Frederick G. Bourne, president of the Singer sewing-machine company. Famed American architect Ernest Flagg modeled the four-story, 28-room structure on a Scottish castle, giving it all sorts of interesting nooks and crannies. To get here, take a boat from Alexandria Bay. Empire Boat Lines and Uncle Sam Boat Tours include Singer Castle in their sightseeing cruises. ⊠ *Dark Island* ☎ *877/327–5475* ⊕ *www.singercastle. com* ≅ *$12* ☉ *Late May–late June, Thurs.–Sun. 10–5; late June–early Sept., daily 10–5.*

Uncle Sam Boat Tours. July and August are the peak months for the 2¼-hour tours that go through the Canadian side of the islands, but fall foliage is also worth catching. Sightseeing cruises take 2¼ hours, with stopovers at Boldt Castle or Singer Castle available. The company also runs frequent 10-minute boat shuttles to the castle. Boats have heated, enclosed lower decks. DInner and lunch cruises are available; reservations for meal cruises are required. Boldt Castle shuttles are $7, and cruises cost up to $35. ⊠ *47 James St.* ☎ *315/482–2611 or 800/253–9229* ⊕ *www.usboattours.com* ☉ *May–Oct.; call for schedule.*

Wellesley Island State Park. The 2,600-acre park is on Wellesley Island. It encompasses a beach, a marina, boat launches, and the largest campground in the Thousand Islands, which offers wilderness sites, tent and trailer sites, and cabins and cottages. A highlight of Wellesley Island State Park is the **Minna Anthony Common Nature Center** (⊠ 44927 Cross Island Rd., Fineview ☎ 315/482–2479 ☉ July and Aug., Mon.–Sat. 8:30–8:30, Sun. 8:30–4:30; Sept.–June, daily 8:30–4:30), a 600-acre wildlife sanctuary with a museum. You may hike, cross-country ski, and snowshoe the 8 mi of trails here (equipment rentals are available). The museum has decoys, live fish and reptiles, and mounted birds, and there's a seasonal butterfly house. To get here by car, take the Thousand Islands International Bridge to the park entrance. ⊠ *Cross Island Rd., Fineview* ☎ *315/482–2722* ⊕ *nysparks.state.ny.us* ≅ *Parking $6* ☉ *Daily dawn–dusk.*

FESTIVALS &
FAIRS

Bill Johnston's Pirate Days. During this 10-day festival in August, pirates invade the village of Alexandria Bay for two weekends, and the mayor hands over the keys to the city to the marauders. Midweek festivities include music and other entertainment throughout downtown. The event is named for an 1830s patriot "pirate." ☎ *800/541–2110* ⊕ *www. alexbay.org.*

Where to Stay & Eat

★ **$$$-$$$$** ✕ **Jacques Cartier Dining Room.** A pianist or harpist adds to the romantic tone of this elegant restaurant where you have views of Boldt Castle and the St. Lawrence River. The kitchen turns out fine American and French fare, all presented with flair. Broiled sea bass, New York–cut prime rib, and veal and lobster dishes are worth trying, as are the flaming desserts. ⊠ *Riveredge Resort Hotel, 17 Holland St.* ☎ *315/482–9917* ⊟ *AE, D, DC, MC, V* ⊗ *No lunch.*

$-$$$ ✕ **Captain's Landing.** The family-oriented restaurant actually floats on the water. (The foundation was once used as a dredge on the New York State Canal System.) The oak-trimmed dining room has antique buffet tables. Try the prime rib (also served Cajun style), seafood pasta, porterhouse steak, or shrimp scampi. The menu also includes plenty of chicken and pasta dishes. The restaurant is part of Captain Thompson's Resort. A deck has open-air dining. ⊠ *49 James St.* ☎ *315/482–7777* ⊟ *AE, D, MC, V* ⊗ *Closed mid-Oct.–early May.*

¢-$$ ✕ **Dockside Pub.** Despite billing itself as the village's "best-kept secret," this sports bar and restaurant near the shore always seems to be hopping. The daily menu includes pizzas, burgers, appetizers, and dinner specials where the chef gets creative with what's in the kitchen. Cheese sauces are common. There's fish on Friday and prime rib on Saturday. ⊠ *17 Market St.* ☎ *315/482–9849* ⊟ *MC, V.*

¢ ✕ **Chez Paris Restaurant.** Run by the same family since 1945, this lunch spot specializes in fresh-pressed hamburgers and homemade peach or blueberry cobblers. Breakfast is available all day. ⊠ *24 Church St.* ☎ *315/482–9825* ⊟ *No credit cards* ⊗ *No dinner.*

★ **$$-$$$$** ▦ **Riveredge Resort Hotel.** This four-story hotel on the St. Lawrence River has views of Boldt Castle and more than 2,000 feet of dock space with power, water, and cable TV hookups. Many rooms have whirlpool tubs, and most rooms have water views. Some are bilevel loft rooms with sitting areas downstairs and sleeping quarters upstairs. Interiors are traditional and incorporate floral patterns. The Jacques Cartier Dining Room is highly acclaimed. ⊠ *17 Holland St., 13607* ☎ *315/482–9917 or 800/365–6987* 🖷 *315/482–5010* ⊕ *www.riveredge.com* ⇨ *88 rooms, 27 suites, 14 loft rooms* ⚇ *2 restaurants, room service, some in-room data ports, some in-room hot tubs, minibars, some refrigerators, cable TV with movies, some in-room VCRs, 2 pools (1 indoor), gym, hot tub, massage, sauna, dock, marina, bar, laundry facilities, concierge floor, business services, meeting rooms, some pets allowed (fee), no-smoking rooms* ⊟ *AE, D, DC, MC, V.*

$-$$$ ▦ **Bonnie Castle Resort.** The contemporary waterfront resort has 68 rooms with hot tubs, a dining room overlooking the St. Lawrence River, a poolside café, and a nightclub that can hold 750 people. The better rooms have balconies and water views. ⊠ *Holland St., 13607* ☎ *315/482–4511 or 800/955–4511* 🖷 *315/482–9600* ⊕ *www.bonniecastle.com* ⇨ *128 rooms, 2 suites* ⚇ *Restaurant, room service, some in-room hot tubs, refrigerators, cable TV, driving range, miniature golf, 2 tennis courts, 2 pools (1 indoor), hot tub, dock, marina, volleyball, sauna, bar, nightclub, business services, meeting rooms, no-smoking rooms* ⊟ *AE, D, DC, MC, V.*

★ **$–$$$** ⌂ **Hart House Inn.** In 1899, this "cottage" was shipped across the frozen St. Lawrence River to Wellesley Island, where it took its place as part of the exclusive Thousand Islands Club. Since that time, the cottage has been restored as a B&B, and today the house overlooks the third hole of the Thousand Islands Golf Course. Accommodations may have four-poster or canopy beds, whirlpool tubs, patios, or fireplaces. The floral prints and flounces used in many of the rooms tend to avoid the saccharine look. The Kashmir Garden Suite, the most expensive accommodation here, is a stunningly handsome space with a fireplace in the bedroom and the bathroom, a private garden patio, a king bed with a tent canopy, and rich-looking faux-leather walls. Common areas include a magnificent, sprawling great room. Afternoon tea is served, and breakfast is a five-course affair. There's also a wedding chapel on the property. ⊠ *21979 Club Rd., Wellesley Island 13640* ☎ *888/481–5683* 🖷 *315/482–5683* ⊕ *www.harthouseinn.com* ⤶ *5 rooms, 3 suites* ♨ *Dining room, some fans, some in-room hot tubs; no TV in some rooms, no smoking* ▭ *AE, D, MC, V* ⎮◎❙ *BP.*

¢ ⌂ **Otter Creek Inn.** Two blocks from downtown, this two-story stone-and-cedar building overlooks the upper bay of the St. Lawrence River. You can make arrangements through the inn to go fishing with a professional guide. ⊠ *2 Crossmon St., 13607* ☎ *315/482–5248* ⤶ *32 rooms* ♨ *Picnic area, some refrigerators, cable TV, dock, fishing, no-smoking rooms* ▭ *D, DC, MC, V* ☾ *Closed Nov.–Mar.*

¢ ⌂ **Rock Ledge Motel.** The 7-acre property has single-story motel buildings as well as cottages and cabins. Rooms are basic, with some wood paneling. Keewaydin State Park and the St. Lawrence River are a short walk away. ⊠ *Rte. 12, 13607* ☎ *315/482–2191 or 800/977–9101* ⊕ *www.rockledgemotel.com* ⤶ *14 rooms, 5 cabins, 5 cottages* ♨ *Picnic area, some kitchens, cable TV, playground; no smoking* ▭ *MC, V* ☾ *Closed Nov.–Apr.* ⎮◎❙ *CP.*

Ogdensburg

🄑 *32 mi northeast of Alexandria Bay.*

Known simply as "the Burg," this industrial city sits at the confluence of the Oswegatchie and St. Lawrence rivers. Across the way is Prescott, Ontario, connected to Ogdensburg via the Ogdensburg-Prescott International Bridge, a suspension bridge. Founded in 1749 as a mission and trading post, Ogdensburg is the oldest settlement in northern New York, and about half the current population is of Canadian origin. Some of Ogdensburg's oldest buildings are in the Library Park Historic District, along Washington and Caroline streets. This architecturally significant collection of 19th-century structures includes the 1810 Parish House, now occupied by the Frederic Remington Art Museum, the city's major attraction. The Greenbelt Park, a downtown walkway along the St. Lawrence River, has numerous historic plaques marking sites from the War of 1812 and the Battle of Ogdensburg.

★ **Frederic Remington Art Museum.** The collection at this museum includes major oil paintings and bronze sculptures by Canton native Frederic Remington (1861–1909), as well as other works by the artist associated with images of the Old West. The museum occupies an 1810 house in which Remington's widow lived for a time; many of the personal possessions and memorabilia here came from her estate. ⊠ *303 Washington St.* ☎ *315/393–2425* ⊕ *www.fredericremington.org* ⊠ *$8* ☉ *May–Oct., Mon.–Sat. 10–5, Sun. 1–5; Nov.–Apr., Wed.–Sat. 11–5, Sun. 1–5.*

Robert C. McEwen U.S. Customs House. The stone structure was built in 1870 to be used as a post office and customs house. During its life, the building housed a federal courtroom, the revenue collector's office, and the special agent of the treasury department. The building is worth a look for history buffs. It was put on the National Register of Historic Places in 1977. ⊠ *127 N. Water St.* ☎ *No phone.*

> **off the beaten path**

TRADITIONAL ARTS IN UPSTATE NEW YORK GALLERY – The gallery is run by a nonprofit organization dedicated to preserving North Country folk arts and traditions—everything from music and crafts to architecture and storytelling. The gallery has audiovisual displays, a photography exhibit, folk-art examples, and changing exhibits. The gift shop is an outlet for local crafts and products, including rustic furniture, baskets, quilts, and maple candy. ⊠ *2 W. Main St., Canton* ☎ *315/386–4289* ⊕ *www.tauny.org* ⊠ *Free* ☉ *Tues.–Sat. 10–4.*

Where to Stay & Eat

$–$$ ✕⬚ **Gran-View Quality Inn.** With wonderful views of the St. Lawrence River, this motel-restaurant facility comes by its name honestly. The riverside property covers 14 acres, with a large outdoor pool and poolside bar, and volleyball courts overlooking the river. Rooms are simple, with traditional furnishings. The restaurant ($–$$$) serves Continental fare, such as chateaubriand, steak au poivre, shrimp scampi, and veal Oscar (sautéed and served with asparagus, crabmeat, and béarnaise sauce). ⊠ *6765 Rte. 37, 13669* ☎ *315/393–4550 or 800/392–4550* ☒ *315/393–3520* ⊕ *www.1000islands.com/granview* ⇨ *44 rooms, 2 suites, 1 cottage* ⬚ *Restaurant, picnic area, in-room data ports, some in-room hot tubs, some microwaves, some refrigerators, cable TV with movies, pool, gym, dock, shuffleboard, volleyball, bar, laundry facilities, meeting rooms, some pets allowed (fee), no-smoking rooms* ☰ *AE, D, DC, MC, V.*

¢–$ ✕⬚ **Stone Fence Resort & Motel.** The 12-acre landscaped property edges up to the St. Lawrence River and offers a variety of accommodations. Hotel rooms are spacious and have balconies with river views. Townhouse units, which sleep up to eight people, have a loft space, a living room, and a kitchen or kitchenette. Motel rooms are also available. The restaurant ($–$$) is a popular destination in its own right. The food is Italian American, and the all-you-can-eat cooked-to-order pasta buffet on Friday night is such a hit with locals that reservations are essential. Choose between the casual but attractive dining room or, in summer, outdoor seating on the patio. ⊠ *7191 Rte. 37, 13669* ☎ *315/393–1545 or 800/253–1545* ☒ *315/393–1749* ⊕ *www.stonefenceresort.com* ⇨ *44 rooms, 6 suites* ⬚ *Restaurant, some in-room hot tubs, some kitchens, some kitchenettes, cable TV with movies, some in-room VCRs, putting* *green, tennis court, pool, gym, beach, dock, boating, basketball, horseshoes, volleyball, playground, meeting rooms, some pets allowed (fee), no-smoking rooms* ▭ *AE, D, MC, V.*

Massena

18 *30 mi northeast of Ogdensburg.*

The small, industrial city of Massena is the northeastern gateway to the Thousand Islands region. When the St. Lawrence Seaway was built in the 1950s, Massena gained fame as the home of the Moses-Saunders Power Dam, the largest power plant along the waterway. Although Massena is in a dairy-farming region, the New York Power Authority is the main economic buoy in the area.

Dwight D. Eisenhower Lock and Visitors Center. Huge cargo vessels pass through the lock on their way to and from the Atlantic and the United States' industrial heartland. At the visitor center, you may view exhibits with cargo samples, photos, President Eisenhower memorabilia, and interactive displays as well as a video about the St. Lawrence Seaway's construction. An observation deck overlooks the lock. To be sure you'll see the lock in action, call ahead to find out when a ship is scheduled to pass through. ✉ *Rte. 131 at Barnhart Island Rd.* ☎ *315/769–2049, 315/769–2422 shipping schedules* 🎟 *Free* ⏲ *Memorial Day–Labor Day, daily 9–9.*

Moses-Saunders Power Dam. The 3,200-foot-wide dam was built and is jointly owned by the New York Power Authority and Ontario Power Generation (previously known as Ontario Hydro). It encompasses two generating plants, one on the Canadian side and one on the U.S. side. At this writing, a new visitor center is in the works and scheduled to open at nearby Hawkins Point in summer 2005. Call for updates. ✉ *Barnhart Island Rd.* ☎ *315/764–0226 Ext. 300* 🌐 *www.stl.nypa.gov* 🎟 *Free* ⏲ *Call for times.*

Robert Moses State Park. To get to the 4,122-acre park—which is partly on the mainland and partly on Barnhart Island—you pass through a tunnel under the Eisenhower Lock. The park has a swimming beach, a marina and boat launch, tennis courts, hiking and cross-country-skiing trails, and a play area. Camping facilities include tent sites and cabins. ✉ *Off Rte. 37 3 mi north of Massena* ☎ *315/769–8663* 🌐 *nysparks.state.ny.us* 🎟 *Parking $6* ⏲ *Daily dawn–dusk.*

Where to Stay

¢ **Econo Lodge Meadow View.** The two-story motel has a U-shape layout with comfortably furnished small rooms. It's 7 mi from the Eisenhower Lock and Robert Moses State Park. The restaurant is closed from November through April. ✉ *15054 Rte. 37, 13662* ☎ *315/764–0246 or 800/553–2666* 📠 *315/764–9615* 🌐 *www.econolodge.com* *52 rooms* *Restaurant, in-room data ports, microwaves, refrigerators, cable TV with movies, some in-room VCRs, gym, bar, laundry service, business services, meeting rooms, no-smoking rooms* ▭ *AE, D, DC, MC, V.*

THE NORTH COUNTRY A TO Z

To research prices, get advice from other travelers, and book travel arrangements, visit www.fodors.com.

AIR TRAVEL

The North Country has two small regional airports: Adirondack Regional Airport (SLK) near Saranac Lake, and Clinton County Airport (PLB) in Plattsburgh. Continental Airlines affiliate CommutAir flies direct from both regional airports to Albany on most days, with connections to New York City (JFK and Newark Liberty international airports), Buffalo, Long Island (Islip), the lower Hudson Valley (Westchester), Rochester, and Syracuse. There are also 20-minute flights between Plattsburgh and Adirondack Regional. Another option is to fly into a peripheral city—Albany, Syracuse, Montréal, or Burlington (Vermont)—and then rent a car and drive the rest of the way. *See* Air Travel *in* Smart Travel Tips A to Z for more information about the major airports and for major airlines' contact information.

🛪 **Airports Adirondack Regional Airport** ⊠ North of Rte. 186, Lake Clear ☎ 518/891-4600 ⊕ www.saranaclake.com/airport/index.html. **Clinton County Airport** ⊠ Rte. 3, Plattsburgh ☎ 518/565-4795 ⊕ www.co.clinton.ny.us.

BUS TRAVEL

Greyhound and Trailways link the North Country with Albany, the Catskills, the Finger Lakes, the Hudson Valley, New York City, Long Island, and western New York. Stops include Canton, Glens Falls, Lake George, Lake Placid, Massena, Plattsburgh, Potsdam, Saranac Lake, and Watertown. Trailways buses also stop in Bolton Landing (summer service) and Ticonderoga.

🛪 **Greyhound** ☎ 800/231-2222 ⊕ www.greyhound.com. **Trailways** ☎ 800/858-8555 or 800/225-6815 ⊕ www.trailwaysny.com.

CAR RENTAL

Hertz serves the Adirondack Regional Airport (on weekday mornings) near Saranac Lake, and the Clinton County Airport in Plattsburgh. Enterprise serves the Adirondack Regional Airport. *See* Car Rental *in* Smart Travel Tips A to Z for national agencies' contact information.

CAR TRAVEL

The main roads through the Adirondacks are well maintained, with 55-mi-per-hour speed limits in many sections. Because the North Country gets considerable snowfall in winter, you should prep your car for snow conditions if traveling here in the cold-weather months. Distances between settlements with lodging and services can be substantial; stretches of 30 mi or more are common, especially in the central and far north Adirondacks, so keep an eye on the gas gauge.

Route 28N between North Creek and Long Lake and Route 73 between Lake Placid and Keene offer some of the best mountain views. For river scenery, routes 86 and 9N from Lake Placid to Keeseville follow the Ausable River and its West Branch much of the way.

EMERGENCIES

In an emergency, dial 911.

7 Hospitals Adirondack Medical Center-Saranac Lake ⊠ 2233 Rte. 86/Lake Colby Dr., Saranac Lake ☎ 518/891-4141 ⊕ www.amccares.org. **Canton-Potsdam Hospital** ⊠ 50 Leroy St., Potsdam ☎ 315/265-3300 ⊕ www.cphospital.org. **Champlain Valley Physicians Hospital Medical Center** ⊠ 75 Beekman St., Plattsburgh ☎ 518/561-2000 ⊕ www.cvph.org. **Claxton-Hepburn Medical Center** ⊠ 214 King St., Ogdensburg ☎ 315/393-3600 ⊕ www.chmed.org. **Glens Falls Hospital** ⊠ 100 Park St., Glens Falls ☎ 518/926-3000 ⊕ www.glensfallshospital.org. **Little Falls Hospital** ⊠ 9 Gibson St, Dolgeville ☎ 315/823-5311 ⊕ www.lfhny.org. **Massena Memorial Hospital** ⊠ 1 Hospital Dr., Massena ☎ 315/769-4237 ⊕ www.massenahospital.org. **Moses-Ludington Hospital** ⊠ 1019 Wicker St., Ticonderoga ☎ 518/585-2831 ⊕ www.mosesludington.com. **Samaritan Medical Center** ⊠ 830 Washington St., Watertown ☎ 315/785-4000 ⊕ www.samaritanhealth.com.

LODGING

The Adirondack Regional Tourism Council and the 1000 Islands International Tourism Council can send you booklets with extensive lodging information. These include town-by-town listings for campgrounds, cottages, cabins, motels, hotels, and B&Bs. Lake & Mountain Properties lists rentals—including cabins, cottages, condominiums, and houses—in the Lake Placid area. The Web site of the Adirondack Bed & Breakfast Association has information about and links to more than 30 inns, lodges, and B&Bs in the Adirondacks. County tourism offices also may have information about vacation rentals and other lodgings.

7 Adirondack Bed & Breakfast Association ⊕ www.adirondackbb.com. **Adirondack Regional Tourism Council** ✍ Box 2149, Plattsburgh 12901 ☎ 518/846-8016 or 800/487-6867 ⊕ www.adk.com. **Lake & Mountain Properties** ▥ 800/220-1940 ⊕ www.lakeandmountain.com. **1000 Islands International Tourism Council** ☎ 800/847-5263 ⊕ www.visit1000islands.com.

SPORTS & THE OUTDOORS

See Sports & the Outdoors *in* Smart Travel Tips A to Z for additional information.

BIKING The North Country has several designated bicycling routes marked by roadside signs. The marked bicycle route on Route 28 covers some pretty mountainous terrain, but the Seaway Trail between Alexandria Bay and Cape Vincent runs through generally flat or rolling farmland. The 10-mi Warren County Bikeway meanders through wooded areas and over a few hills, with glimpses of the mountains, between Lake George and Glens Falls; route maps are available from the Warren County Department of Parks and Recreation.

The centerpiece of Lake Champlain Bikeways, a network of bike routes and loops totaling more than 1,000 mi, is the 363-mi Champlain Bikeway, which circles Lake Champlain and runs north along the Richelieu River into Québec. The Lake Champlain Bikeways Web site has detailed directions and terrain descriptions as well as suggested themed rides; brochures are available.

For mountain biking, consider one of the downhill and cross-country ski centers in the Adirondacks. The Gore Mountain Ski Center, in North

Creek; the Garnet Hill Ski Lodge and Cross-Country Ski Center, in North River; the Whiteface Mountain Ski Center, in Wilmington; and the Cross Country Center at the Verizon Sports Complex at Mt. Van Hoevenberg, near Lake Placid, all have mountain-biking trails in the warm-weather months. The Bike Adirondacks Web site has loads of information about other mountain-bike trails, as well as details about paved routes, multiuse paths, and bike shops, with links to various related organizations and services.

CANOEING   The Web site of the Adirondack Regional Tourism Council has a nifty interactive map detailing canoe and kayak routes in the North Country. The council's free "Adirondack Waterways Guide" includes route descriptions and maps. Franklin County Tourism offers canoe maps that cover the St. Regis area.

Canoe rentals are available at most lakes in the Adirondacks, both on a daily and an extended basis. For extended trips, hiring a guide service is strongly recommended.

FISHING   Fishing is a year-round sport in the North Country. The St. Lawrence River offers some of the best bass fishing in the country. Muskellunges ("muskies" for short) are also a common catch between Ogdensburg and Cape Vincent. Ice-fishing tournaments give Thousand Islanders a little sport on weekends in January and February.

Many lakes, ponds, and streams in the Adirondacks are stocked with trout and salmon. For walleye, the Raquette River and Lake Champlain are the best bets. The Ausable River, near Lake Placid, is known for its fly-fishing. Hiring a guide is highly recommended, especially if you're interested in a backcountry fishing trip. The Adirondack Regional Tourism Council's Web site lists fishing guides and charters; the council also offers a free fishing guide. The 1000 Islands International Tourism Council offers a free fishing-and-hunting booklet that lists fishing guides and charters and state boat-launch sites and describes the types of fish found in the Thousand Islands.

Fishing licenses and regulations may be obtained at town clerk offices, fishing-gear retailers, or by phone from the state. For fish and wildlife information, sporting conditions, licenses, and a list of marinas, contact the New York State Department of Environmental Conservation.

HIKING   The Adirondack Loj, off Route 73 about 7 mi south of Lake Placid, is at the main trailhead to Mt. Marcy, Algonquin, and the rest of the High Peaks core. The lodge is run by the nonprofit Adirondack Mountain Club (aka the ADK), which is a good source for hiking and backcountry information. It publishes a set of regional Adirondack trail guides with topographic maps and trailhead directions. You may buy the guides through the ADK Web site or at its Lake George and High Peaks information centers.

The Adirondack Regional Tourism Council's Web site includes an interactive map that describes some North Country hikes. You may also obtain a copy of the free "Great Walks & Day Hikes" brochure from the council.

OUTDOOR GUIDES The Adirondacks have a rich guiding tradition that dates back to the early 1800s. Whether you're going fishing, hiking, canoeing, or whitewater rafting, a guide can make your trip far more enjoyable, especially if you're making your first trip to the Adirondacks. Guides not only know the best routes and are well versed in the proper safety precautions, but also can make light work of the cumbersome preparations and logistics necessary for any outing. Guides are licensed by the state. You may obtain a list of licensed guides from the New York State Outdoor Guides Association.

🚲 Biking **Bike Adirondacks** ✇ c/o Holmes & Associates, Box 295, Saranac Lake 12983 ☎ No phone ⊕ www.bikeadirondacks.org. **Lake Champlain Bikeways** ✉ Clearinghouse, c/o Local Motion, 1 Steele St., Suite 103, Burlington VT 05401 ☎☎ 802/652-2453 ⊕ www.champlainbikeways.org. **Seaway Trail** ✉ W. Main St., Sackets Harbor 13685 ☎ 315/646-1000 or 800/732-9298 ⊕ www.seawaytrail.com. **Warren County Department of Parks and Recreation** ✉ Fish Hatchery Rd., Warrensburg ☎ 518/623-2877 ⊕ www.warrencountydpw.com/parks-rec/.

🚣 Canoeing **Adirondack Regional Tourism Council** ✇ Box 2149, Plattsburgh 12901 ☎ 518/846-8016 or 800/487-6867 ⊕ www.adk.com. **Franklin County Tourism** ✉ 10 Elm St., Malone 12953 ☎ 518/483-9470 or 800/709-4895 ⊕ www.adirondacklakes.com.

🎣 Fishing **Adirondack Regional Tourism Council** ✇ Box 2149, Plattsburgh 12901 ☎ 518/846-8016 or 800/487-6867 ⊕ www.adk.com. **New York State Department of Environmental Conservation** ☎ 866/933-2257 fishing licenses, 518/897-1200 general information ⊕ www.dec.state.ny.us. **Northern Adirondacks fishing hotline** ☎ 518/891-5413. **Southern Adirondacks fishing hotline** ☎ 518/623-3682. **1000 Islands International Tourism Council** ☎ 800/847-5263 ⊕ www.visit1000islands.com.

🥾 Hiking **Adirondack Mountain Club information centers** ✉ Adirondack Loj Rd., off Rte. 73 ☎ 518/523-3441 ⊕ www.adk.org ✉ 814 Goggins Rd., Lake George ☎ 518/668-4447 or 800/395-8080 ⊕ www.adk.org. **Adirondack Regional Tourism Council** ✇ Box 2149, Plattsburgh 12901 ☎ 518/846-8016 or 800/487-6867 ⊕ www.adk.com.

🧭 Outdoor Guides **New York State Outdoor Guides Association** ✉ 1936 Saranac Ave., Lake Placid 12946 ☎ 866/469-7642 ⊕ www.nysoga.com.

TOURS

AIRPLANE TOURS Adirondack Flying Service offers 20-minute flights over either the High Peaks region or Lake Placid and the Whiteface area. Flights are $25 per person, with a minimum of two passengers required.

ARCHITECTURAL Adirondack Architectural Heritage, a nonprofit historic preservation or-
TOURS ganization, runs tours of Saranac Lake, Bolton Landing, Big Moose Lake, Wilmington and the Whiteface Veterans' Memorial Highway, Camp Santanoni, White Pine Camp, and other camps.

✈ Airplane Tours **Adirondack Flying Service** ✉ Rte. 73, Lake Placid ☎ 518/523-2473 ⊕ flyanywhere.com.

🏛 Architectural Tours **Adirondack Architectural Heritage** ✉ Civic Center, 1790 Main St., Suite 37, Keeseville ☎ 518/834-9328 ⊕ www.aarch.org.

TRAIN TRAVEL

Amtrak connects the North Country with the capital region, the Hudson Valley, and New York City. It stops in Glens Falls, Plattsburgh, and Ticonderoga.

🚆 **Amtrak** ☎ 800/872-7245 ⊕ www.amtrak.com.

TRANSPORTATION AROUND THE NORTH COUNTRY

Public transportation options in the North Country are limited, so getting around the region is virtually impossible without a car. If you're coming from more than 300 mi away, consider taking a plane or train part of the way and then renting a car in a peripheral city and driving the rest of the way.

VISITOR INFORMATION

🚩 **Adirondacks Adirondack North Country Association** ✉ 28 St. Bernard St, Saranac Lake 12983 ☎ 518/891-6200 ⊕ www.adirondack.org. **Adirondack Regional Tourism Council** ✆ Box 2149, Plattsburgh 12901 ☎ 518/846-8016 or 800/487-6867 ⊕ www. adk.com. **Blue Mountain Lake Association** ✆ Box 245, Blue Mountain Lake 12812 ☎ 518/ 352-7659. **Franklin County Tourism** ✉ 10 Elm St., Malone 12953 ☎ 518/483-9470 or 800/709-4895 ⊕ www.adirondacklakes.com. **Hamilton County Tourism** ✉ White Birch La., Indian Lake 12842 ☎ 518/648-5239 or 800/648-5239 ⊕ www.hamiltoncounty. com. **Lake Placid/Essex County Convention & Visitors Bureau** ✉ 216 Main St., Lake Placid 12946 ☎ 518/523-2445 or 800/447-5224 ⊕ www.lakeplacid.com. **St. Lawrence County Chamber of Commerce** ✉ 101 Main St., Canton 13617 ☎ 315/386-4000 or 877/ 228-7810 ⊕ www.northcountryguide.com. **Gore Mountain Region Chamber of Commerce** ✉ 228 Main St., North Creek 12853 ☎ 518/251-2612 or 800/880-4673 ⊕ www. goremtnregion.org. **Indian Lake Chamber of Commerce** ✉ Main St., Indian Lake 12842 ☎ 518/648-5112 or 800/328-5253 ⊕ www.indian-lake.com. **Long Lake Department of Parks, Recreation & Tourism** ✉ Rte. 28N/30, Long Lake 12847 ☎ 518/ 624-3077 ⊕ www.longlake-ny.com. **Saranac Lake Area Chamber of Commerce** ✉ 30 Main St., Saranac Lake 12983 ☎ 518/891-1990 or 800/347-1992 ⊕ www.saranaclake. com. **Town of Webb/Old Forge Tourism Department** ✉ Main St., Old Forge 13420 ☎ 315/ 369-6983 ⊕ www.oldforgeny.com. **Tupper Lake Chamber of Commerce** ✉ 60 Park St., Tupper Lake 12986 ☎ 518/359-3328 or 888/887-5253 ⊕ www.tupperlakeinfo.com. **Whiteface Mountain Regional Visitors Bureau** ✉ Rte. 86, Wilmington 12997 ☎ 518/ 946-2255 or 800/944-8332 ⊕ www.whitefaceregion.com.

🚩 **Lake George & the Champlain Valley Adirondack Information Center** ✉ I-87 between Exits 17 and 18, Glens Falls ☎ 518/792-2730. **Bolton Landing Chamber of Commerce** ✉ 4928 Lakeshore Dr., Bolton Landing 12814 ☎ 518/644-3831 ⊕ www. boltonchamber.com. **Lake Champlain Visitors Center** ✉ 94 Montcalm St., Ticonderoga 12883 ☎ 866/843-5253 ⊕ www.lakechamplainregion.com. **Lake George Regional Chamber of Commerce** ✉ 2176 U.S. 9, Lake George 12845 ☎ 518/668-5755 or 800/ 705-0059 ⊕ www.lakegeorgechamber.com. **Plattsburgh-North Country-Lake Champlain Regional Visitors Center** ✉ 7061 U.S. 9, Plattsburgh 12901 ☎ 518/563-1000 ⊕ www. northcountrychamber.com. **Ticonderoga Area Chamber of Commerce** ✉ 94 Montcalm St., Ticonderoga 12883 ☎ 518/585-6619 ⊕ www.ticonderogany.com. **Warren County Department of Tourism** ✉ 1340 U.S. 9, Lake George 12845 ☎ 518/761-6366 or 800/ 365-1050 ⊕ www.visitlakegeorge.com.

🚩 **Thousand Islands & the Seaway Alexandria Bay Chamber of Commerce** ✉ 11 Market St., Alexandria Bay 13607 ☎ 315/482-9531 or 800/541-2110 ⊕ www.alexbay.org. **Canton Chamber of Commerce** ✆ Box 369, Canton 13617 ☎ 315/386-8255 ⊕ www. cantonnychamber.org. **Clayton Chamber of Commerce** ✉ 510 Riverside Dr., Clayton 13624 ☎ 315/686-3771 or 800/252-9806 ⊕ www.1000islands-clayton.com. **Greater Massena Chamber of Commerce** ✉ 50 Main St., Massena 13662 ☎ 315/769-3525 ⊕ www.massenany.com. **Greater Ogdensburg Chamber of Commerce** ✉ 1020 Park St., Ogdensburg 13669 ☎ 315/393-3620 ⊕ www.ogdensburgny.com. **Oswego County Promotion and Tourism** ✉ 46 E. Bridge St., Oswego 13126 ☎ 315/349-8322 or 800/

248–4386 ⊕ www.oswegocounty.com. **Sackets Harbor Visitor Center** ⊠ 301 W. Main St., Sackets Harbor 13685 ☎ 315/646–2321 ⊕ www.sacketsharborny.com. **St. Lawrence County Chamber of Commerce** ⊠ 101 Main St., Canton 13617 ☎ 315/386–4000 or 877/ 228–7810 ⊕ www.northcountryguide.com. **Seaway Trail** ⊠ W. Main St., Sackets Harbor 13685 ☎ 315/646–1000 or 800/732–9298 ⊕ www.seawaytrail.com. **1000 Islands International Tourism Council** ☎ 800/847–5263 ⊕ www.visit1000islands.com.

8

WESTERN NEW YORK

9

ANCHORED BY the tenacious city of Buffalo and the inescapable Niagara Falls, Western New York is wedged between Lake Erie to the west, Lake Ontario to the north, Rochester and the Finger Lakes to the east, and the Pennsylvania border to the south. In the northwest corner is the Niagara River, which connects lakes Erie and Ontario and is shared by the United States and Canada.

Part of the longest unfortified border in the world, Niagara Falls is actually three cataracts: the American Falls and Bridal Veil Falls, in New York, and the Horseshoe Falls, in Ontario. The cascades spurred the invention of alternating electric current, and they drive one of the world's largest hydroelectric developments. As with many other geographic features, Niagara's origins are glacial. More than 12,000 years ago the glaciers receded, diverting the waters of Lake Erie northward into Lake Ontario. (Before that, they had drained south; such are the fickle ways of nature.) There has been considerable erosion since, more than 7 mi in all, as the soft shale and sandstone of the escarpment have been washed away. Wisely, there have been major water diversions for a generating station (1954) and other developments (1954–63) that have spread the flow more evenly over the entire crestline of Horseshoe Falls. The erosion is now down to as little as one foot every decade. At this rate it will be some 130,000 years before the majestic cascade is reduced to an impressive rapids somewhere near present-day Buffalo, 20 mi to the south.

For many Americans, Buffalo is the blizzard capital of the United States. At least once a year it seems to crop up on television news spots about winter whiteouts and wicked wind-chill factors. The snows are caused in part by the city's location on Lake Erie, but the lake also acts as a giant air conditioner in summer. Days are warm, but not hot.

Though Buffalo is the state's second-largest city, it is definitely "small town" when compared to its glamorous downstate big sister. Still, the city has a distinct style, a product of its rich ethnic, cultural, and architectural history. Elmwood Street, downtown, offers a taste of the city's eclectic mix of shops and restaurants; Chippewa Street (or the Chippewa District), known for its nightclubs and jazz bars, is another lively area in the heart of the city. Friendliness and affordability are also selling points. Distances aren't great, and it's easy to get around.

Chautauqua County, which follows the shores of Lake Erie south of Buffalo to the Pennsylvania border, is a region of soft hills, vineyards and wineries, and fish-filled lakes. For most visitors, however, the main draw is the Chautauqua Institution. The institution offers an unusual mix of arts, education, religion, and recreation during the nine-week summer season. Nine U.S. presidents, from Ulysses S. Grant to Gerald Ford, have delivered addresses here. Other notables have included Leo Tolstoy, William Jennings Bryan, and Amelia Earhart. In 1985 the institution hosted the first in a series of conferences on U.S.-Soviet relations. Two years later more than 200 Soviet citizens came to Chautauqua and lived with American families for a week.

Chautauqua County, which takes its name from its largest lake, is the largest American grape-growing area outside of California; its vineyards produce more Concord grapes than any other area in the country. The

50-mi drive from Silver Creek to Ripley, along the shores of Lake Erie, is known as the Chautauqua Wine Trail. Along the route are wineries, roadside fruit and produce stands, and antiques shops.

Exploring Western New York

Access from the east and south is primarily via Interstate 90, the New York State Thruway. The expressway spur I–190 leads from I–90 at Buffalo across Grand Island to the Robert Moses Parkway into Niagara Falls. The parkway continues north to Lewiston and then Youngstown, where the Niagara River empties into Lake Ontario. On the far east side of the region is another natural wonder, Letchworth State Park, which puts you close to the Finger Lakes region to the east. The scenic New York State Seaway Trail traces the region's perimeter in the north and west, along lakes Ontario and Erie.

About the Hotels & Restaurants

Hotels and motels in the Niagara Falls–Buffalo area fall primarily into two categories: major chains and lower-priced budget properties. In Niagara Falls, high-season rates apply from Memorial Day through Labor Day. Prices are highest in the immediate vicinity of the falls. Most of the area's hotels and motels tend to be moderately priced.

On the Chautauqua Institution grounds you can stay in stately Victorian hotels, guest houses, apartments, modern condominiums, or rooms in denominational houses operated by various religious groups. Some condos are available on a weekly basis, although most apartments are available only during the nine-week season. Because many people return year after year, reservations are essential. At Chautauqua-area restaurants the emphasis is on seafood and American-style menus. Reservations are necessary in summer, especially if you plan a pre-theater meal at the institution.

Fast-food chains are well represented in Niagara, but you do also find numerous respectable restaurants. The ethnic restaurants, particularly the Italian ones, are good. You can also find excellent Continental cuisine. Casual dress is acceptable, and reservations usually aren't necessary.

Buffalo has given the world two classics: Buffalo chicken wings and beef on weck. You'll come across both throughout the region. The former is served mild, medium, or hot, alongside blue-cheese dressing and celery. The latter consists of roast beef, carved on the spot, and heaped on a fresh, flaky kimmelweck roll that has been sprinkled with coarse salt.

WHAT IT COSTS					
	$$$$	$$$	$$	$	¢
RESTAURANTS	over $30	$22–$30	$15–$21	$8–$14	under $8
HOTELS	over $250	$200–$250	$150–$199	$100–$149	under $100

Restaurant prices are for a main course at dinner (or at the most expensive meal served). Hotel prices are for two people in a standard double room in high season, excluding tax.

The following itineraries work best in summer and early fall.

Numbers in the text correspond to numbers in the margin and on Central New York map.

9

If you have 3 days

Start in 🔲 **Niagara Falls** ❶–❿ ⌐ and spend two days taking in the sights, crossing to the Canadian side if you wish. In the afternoon of Day 2, head north of the city to see the Castellani Art Museum, the Niagara Power Project Visitors Center, or one of the state parks. On Day 3, head south to **Buffalo** ❼ via **Grand Island** ⓫. If you have kids in tow, consider a visit to the Buffalo Zoological Gardens or the Buffalo Museum of Science. Otherwise, see the Albright-Knox Art Gallery or the Buffalo and Erie County Botanical Gardens. Frank Lloyd Wright lovers should head straight for the Darwin D. Martin Complex (just be sure to have made a tour reservation).

In summer you might opt to center your trip on 🔲 **Chautauqua** ㉗. Make quick trips around Chautauqua Lake and into **Jamestown** ㉘ if you have time. Otherwise, take advantage of the Chautauqua Institution's rich cultural offerings.

If you have 5 days

Spend Day 1 exploring the magnificent 🔲 **Letchworth State Park** ⓯ ⌐, which is often called the Grand Canyon of the East. On Day 2 drive west to 🔲 **Buffalo** ❼. (See the three-day itinerary above for suggestions about what to do in the city.) On the afternoon of Day 3 head east to **East Aurora**, an attractive village and home of the Roycroft Movement. Consider having dinner at the Roycroft Inn before returning to Buffalo for the night. On the morning of Day 4 make the short trip to 🔲 **Niagara Falls** ❶–❿ via **Grand Island** ⓫. Spend the night here or on the Canadian side. On Day 5 head north to see the Castellani Art Museum, the Niagara Power Project Visitors Center, or one of the state parks.

Timing

Outside the Holiday Valley ski area, high season runs from Memorial Day through Labor Day, when most cultural activities take place and the Niagara Falls boat rides are operating. Consequently, tourists abound and hotel prices are highest. Summer temperatures range from 75°F to 85°F, with occasional light rainfall. The area near Niagara Falls is always misty, a natural refresher in the summertime. Throughout the region, very hot, humid days are infrequent. Winter temperatures create ice-covered tree branches and rocks that sparkle, and the railings and bridges turn almost crystalline.

GREATER NIAGARA

Niagara Falls, on the border of the United States and Canada, is one of the most famous tourist attractions in the world, and certainly one of the most beautiful. There are actually two cities called Niagara Falls—one on the U.S. side and the other in Canada, which is a hop away. North of the falls along the Niagara River is an area rich in orchards and vine-yards. About a 20-minute drive south of the falls is the waterfront city of Buffalo, on Lake Erie. Between lakes Erie and Ontario lie acres of rolling farmland, part of the Great Lakes Plain, which stretches north from the Appalachian Plateau.

Niagara Falls

290 mi west of Albany, 400 mi northwest of New York City.

Nearly everyone who sees Niagara Falls is struck by the wonder of it. Though not among the world's highest waterfalls, Niagara Falls is, for sheer volume of water, unsurpassed at more than 750,000 gallons per second in summer. The falls spurred the invention of alternating electric current, and they run one of the largest hydroelectric developments in the world. And it really is all that water, fueled by four of the Great Lakes—Superior, Michigan, Huron, and Erie—as they flow into the fifth, Ontario, that ranks Niagara as one of the planet's natural wonders.

Niagara Falls has inspired artists for centuries. English painter William H. Bartlett, who visited here in the mid-1830s, noted that "you may dream of Niagara, but words will never describe it to you." And cynics have taken their own stab at Niagara Falls, calling it everything from "water on the rocks" to "the second major disappointment of American married life" (Oscar Wilde). The thundering cascades were dramatically immortalized by Hollywood in 1953, when Marilyn Monroe starred as a steamy siren, luring her jealous husband down to the crashing waters in the film *Niagara*.

The malls, amusement parks, hotels, tacky souvenir shops, and flashy wax museums that surround the falls today attest to the region's maturation into a major tourist attraction. But despite the hordes of visitors jostling unceremoniously for the best photographic vantage point, the astounding beauty of the falls remains undiminished, and unending.

🐾 ❺ **Aquarium of Niagara.** Dive into Niagara's other water wonder. This is a close encounter with more than 1,500 aquatic animals, including sharks, piranhas, sea lions, and moray eels. The aquarium has sea-lion demonstrations and penguin feedings daily, and an outdoor harbor-seal exhibit. ⊠ *701 Whirlpool St.* ☎ *716/285–3575 or 800/500–4609* ⊕ *www.aquariumofniagara.org* ▧ *$7.50* ⊙ *Late May–early Sept., daily 9–7; early Sept.–Oct. and Apr. late May, daily 9–5, Nov.–Mar., daily 9–4.*

❼ **Castellani Art Museum.** The collection at this museum, in a light gray marble–faced building on the Niagara University campus, encompasses nearly 4,000 works—paintings, drawings, photographs, prints, and sculptures—with an emphasis on contemporary art. Charles Burchfield, Alexander Calder, Salvador Dalí, Willem de Kooning, April Gornick, Keith Haring, David Hockney, Marsden Hartley, Amedeo Modigliani, Laszlo Moholy-Nagy, Robert Motherwell, Nam June Paik, Pablo Picasso, and Cindy Sherman are among those represented here. The university is just north of the city. ⊠ *Niagara University, Rte. 104 W* ☎ *716/286–8200* ⊕ *www.niagara.edu/cam/* ▧ *Free* ⊙ *Tues.–Sat. 11–5, Sun. 1–5.*

9

Falling for Niagara

Cynics have had their field day with Niagara Falls, calling it everything from "water on the rocks" to "the second major disappointment of American married life" (Oscar Wilde). Others have been more positive. Missionary and explorer Louis Hennepin, whose books were widely read across Europe, first described the falls in 1678 as "an incredible Cataract or Waterfall which has no equal." Nearly two centuries later, novelist Charles Dickens wrote, "I seemed to be lifted from the earth and to be looking into Heaven. Niagara was at once stamped upon my heart, an image of beauty, to remain there changeless and indelible."

Writer Henry James recorded in 1883 how one stands there "gazing your fill at the most beautiful object in the world." And a half-century later, British author Vita Sackville-West wrote in a letter, "Niagara is really some waterfall! It falls over like a great noisy beard made of cotton-wool, veiled by spray and spanned by rainbows. The rainbows are the most unexpected part of it. They stand across like bridges between America and Canada, and are reproduced in sections along the boiling foam. The spray rises to the height of a skyscraper, shot by sudden iridescence high up in the air."

Understandably, all these rave reviews began to bring out the professional daredevils, as well as the self-destructive amateurs. In 1859 the great French tightrope walker Blondin walked across the Niagara Gorge, from the American to the Canadian side, on a three-inch-thick rope. On his shoulders was his reluctant, terrified manager; on both shores stood some 100,000 spectators. "Thank God it is over," exclaimed the future King Edward VII of England, after the completion of the walk. "Please never attempt it again." But others did. From the early 18th century, dozens went over in boats, rubber balls, and those famous barrels. Not a single one survived—until schoolteacher Annie Taylor did in 1901. Emerging from her barrel, she asked, "Did I go over the falls yet?" The endless stunts were finally outlawed in 1912, but nothing stops the determined: in 1985 two stuntmen survived a plunge, and two years later, someone who had conquered the falls mastered the rapids below the falls.

Besides daredevils, the other thing that springs to mind at the mention of Niagara are honeymoons. The first honeymooners arrived in 1803: Jeromo Bonaparte (brother of Napoléon) and his bride, the daughter of a prosperous Baltimore merchant. On a grand tour of the Northeast, the newlyweds stayed a week, inaugurating a tradition. By the mid-1800s honeymoons at Niagara had become quite the rage and were a definite status symbol for young couples.

---

9 **Earl W. Brydges Artpark State Park.** The 202-acre park, on a bluff overlooking Niagara Gorge, is the only state park dedicated to the performing and visual arts. But you may also fish, hike, picnic, and cross-country ski here. Summer brings a slew of family-oriented events and activities. Lewiston is about 7 mi north of Niagara Falls. ⊠ *450 S. 4th St., Lewis-*

Western New York

Lake Ontario

Youngstown

St. Catharines

Lewiston [104]

QEW

Niagara Falls
1 – **10**
see detail map

North
Tonawanda

QEW

11

Grand Island

[5]

CANADA

Buffalo
17 – **25**
see detail map

Lackawanna

Orchard
Park

Derby

[219]

Lake Erie

[20] [62]

[90]

[39]

Dunkirk **26**

[20]

[39]

Lily
Dale

*Canadaway
Creek*

[60]

Cherry
Creek

[62]

Westfield

[394]

Mayville

[430]

Maple
Springs

Chautauqua **27**

Bemus
Point

Randolph

Salamanca

30

[20]

[86]

*Chautauqua
Lake*

Panama

28 **Jamestown**

[86]

Alleghany River

[90]

*Allegany
Reservoir*

*Allegany
State
Park*

PENNSYLVANIA

[62]

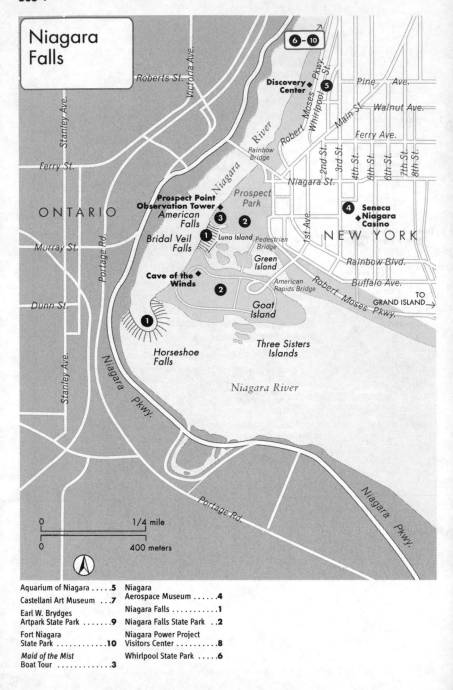

Niagara Falls

Roberts St.

Victoria Ave.

Stanley Ave.

Ferry St.

River

Niagara

ONTARIO

Murray St.

Portage Rd.

Dunn St.

Stanley Ave.

Niagara Pkwy.

6 - 10

Discovery Center ◆ 5

Robert Moses Pkwy.

Whirlpool St.

Pine Ave.

Main St. Walnut Ave.

Ferry Ave.

2nd St. 3rd St. 4th St. 5th St. 6th St. 7th St. 8th St.

Rainbow Bridge

Niagara St.

Prospect Point Observation Tower ◆
American Falls

Prospect Park

1st Ave.

4 ◆ Seneca Niagara Casino

Bridal Veil Falls

3

2

1

Luna Island

Pedestrian Bridge

NEW YORK

Rainbow Blvd.

Cave of the Winds ◆

Green Island

2

American Rapids Bridge

Buffalo Ave.

Goat Island

Robert Moses Pkwy.

TO GRAND ISLAND →

1

Horseshoe Falls

Three Sisters Islands

Niagara River

Niagara Pkwy.

Portage Rd.

Niagara Pkwy.

0   1/4 mile

0   400 meters

ton ☎ *716/754–9000 or 800/659–7275* ⊕ *nysparks.state.ny.us* ✉ *Parking $6 (June–Aug.)* ⊗ *Daily dawn–dusk.*

❿ Fort Niagara State Park. The park is at the edge of the Niagara River where it empties into Lake Ontario. Facilities include picnic tables, swimming pools, hiking trails, tennis courts, fishing access, a boat-launch site, and a playground. In winter you may cross-country ski, snowmobile, or go sledding here. The grounds surround a stone fort complex. **Old Fort Niagara** (☎ 716/745–7611 ⊕ www.oldfortniagara.org) hosts colorful displays of cannon and musket firings, historical reenactments, 18th-century military demonstrations, and archaeological programs. The earliest part of the fort was built as a French castle in 1726, and the complex later played a critical role in the French and Indian War (1754–63). Self-guided tours are available. Youngstown is about 15 mi north of Niagara Falls. ✉ *Robert Moses Pkwy./Rte. 18F, Youngstown* ☎ *716/745–7273* ⊕ *nysparks.state.ny.us* ✉ *Parking $6 (July–early Sept. and weekends), fort $8* ⊗ *Park daily dawn–dusk. Fort Nov.–Mar., daily 9–4:30, Apr. and Oct., daily 9–5:30; May and Sept., weekdays 9–5:30, weekends 9–6:30; June, weekdays 9–6:30, weekends 9–7:30; July and Aug., daily 9–7:30.*

★ ☾ ❸ Maid of the Mist Boat Tour. View the three falls from up close during a spectacular 30-minute ride on this world-famous boat tour. Waterproof clothing is provided. To reach the boat launch on the New York side, take the elevator in the Prospect Point Observation Tower in Niagara Falls State Park down to the base. (Admission includes the $1 tower fee.) Boats depart every 15 minutes. Call for special hours in summer and on holidays. ✉ *Prospect Park, 151 Buffalo Ave.* ☎ *716/284–8897* ⊕ *www.maidofthemist.com* ✉ *$11.50* ⊗ *Apr.–late May and early Sept.–late Oct., weekdays 9:45–4:45, weekends 9:45–5:45; late May–mid-June, daily 9:45–5:45; mid-June–early Sept., daily 9:45–7.*

☾ ❹ Niagara Aerospace Museum. Exhibits and displays here include sailplanes, flight simulators, rare helicopters, experimental craft, and a World War II parachute you can sit under. ✉ *345 3rd St,* ☎ *717/278–0060* ⊕ *www.niagaramuseum.org* ✉ *$7* ⊗ *Tues.–Sat., 10–3.*

❶ Niagara Falls. Native North Americans called it Onguiaahram, or Thun-
Fodor'sChoice dering Waters. For hundreds of years, visitors to Niagara Falls have mar-
★   veled at the sheer immensity of the surging walls of water. Its awe-inspiring views today are enhanced by misty early mornings, sun-streaked rainbows, and grand after-dark illumination with spotlights that penetrate the night sky.

Three cataracts make up the falls: the American Falls and Bridal Veil Falls on the New York side, and the Horseshoe Falls in Ontario. American Falls is the highest, but not by much, and it's about half as wide as the Canadian cascade. Bridal Veil is the smallest of the three. Several small islands dot the river here. Goat Island, part of ⇨ **Niagara Falls State Park,** separates Horseshoe Falls from the U.S. falls and offers spectacular vantage points of both sides. Little Luna Island sits between the two U.S. cascades, between Goat Island and the mainland.

ON THE CANADIAN SIDE

AFTER ENJOYING THE FALLS *from the U.S. side, you may want to walk or drive across Rainbow Bridge to the Canadian side, where you can get a far view of the U.S. falls and a close-up of the Horseshoe Falls. You may park your car for the day in any of several lots on the Canadian side and hop onto one of the People Mover buses, which run continuously to all the sights along the river.*

The amusement parks and tacky souvenir shops that surround the falls attest to the area's history as a major tourist attraction. Most of the gaudiness on the Canadian side is contained on Clifton Hill. Sometimes referred to as Museum Alley, the area includes more wax museums than one usually sees in a lifetime. Here follow some of the more notable attractions in Canada's Niagara Falls.

Students of the **Niagara Parks Botanical Gardens and School of Horticulture** *celebrate the art of horticulture with 100 acres of immaculately maintained gardens. The Niagara Parks Butterfly Conservatory, within the botanical gardens, houses one of North America's largest collections of free-flying butterflies; at least 2,000 are protected in a climate-controlled, rain forest–like conservatory.* ⊠ 2405 N. Niagara Pkwy. ☎ 905/356–8119 or 877/642–7275, ⊕ www.niagaraparks.com/attractions ☜ Gardens free, butterfly conservatory C$10 ☉ Daily 9–6.

At **Journey Behind the Falls,** *your admission ticket includes use of rubber boots and a hooded rain slicker. An elevator takes you to an observation deck that provides a fish's-eye view of the Horseshoe Falls and the Niagara River. From here a walk through three tunnels cut into the rock takes you behind the wall of crashing water.* ⊠ Tours begin at Table Rock House, Queen Victoria Park ☎ 905/371–0254 or 877/642–7275 ⊕ niagaraparks.com ☜ C$10 ☉ Mid-June–early Sept., daily 9 AM–11 PM; early Sept.–mid-June, daily 9–5.

On the site of one of the fiercest battles in the War of 1812 is **Lundy's Lane Historical Museum,** *in a limestone building dating from 1874. There are displays about the lives of settlers during the war period and exhibits of native artifacts and military attire.* ⊠ 5810 Ferry St. ☎ 905/358–5082 ⊕ www.lundyslanemuseum.com ☜ C$2 ☉ May–Nov., daily 9–4; Dec.–Apr., weekdays noon–4.

Rising 775 feet above the falls, the **Skylon Tower** *offers the best view of both the great Niagara Gorge and the entire city. An indoor-outdoor observation deck offers visibility up to 80 mi on clear days. Amusements for children plus a revolving dining room are other reasons to visit. The view from the Revolving Dining Room is breathtaking, and the food is good, too. Traditionally prepared rack of lamb, baked salmon, steak, and chicken make up the list of entrées. (Plan on spending at least C$40 per person to dine here.) The lower level has a gaming arcade, and there's a 3-D/4-D theater within the compound.* ⊠ 5200 Robinson St. ☎ 905/356–2651 or 800/814–9577 ⊕ www.skylon.com ☜ C$10.50 ☉ Mid-June–early Sept., daily 8 AM–midnight; early Sept.–mid June, daily 10–10.

Casino Niagara, *in a setting reminiscent of the 1920s, has slot and video-poker machines and tables for blackjack, roulette, and baccarat, among other games. Within the casino are several lounges and all-you-can-eat buffet restaurants. Also here, and especially notable, is the 21 Club restaurant, which serves high-end steak-house fare and some Italian dishes. Valet parking and shuttle service are available. The place is open around the clock.* ⊠ 5705 Falls Ave.

☎ 905/374–3598 or 888/946–3255
⊕ www.discoverniagara.com.

Marineland, a theme park with a marine show, wildlife displays, and rides, is 1 mi south of the falls. The daily marine show includes performing killer whales, dolphins, harbor seals, and sea lions. Three separate aquariums also house sharks, an ocean reef, and freshwater fish from around the world. Children can pet and feed members of a herd of 500 deer and get nose-to-nose with North American freshwater fish. Among the many rides is Dragon Mountain, the world's largest steel roller coaster. Marineland is signposted from Niagara Parkway or reached from the Queen Elizabeth Way by exiting at McLeod Road (Exit 27). ⊠ 8375 Stanley Ave. ☎ 905/356–9565 ⊕ www.marinelandcanada.com 🖃 C$33.95 ◷ Late June–early Oct., daily 9–6; shows at regular intervals.

The **Whirlpool Aero Car,** in operation since 1916, is a cable car that crosses the Whirlpool Basin in the Niagara Gorge. This trip is not for the fainthearted, but it's one of the few ways to get an aerial view of the gorge, the whirlpool, the rapids, and the hydroelectric plants. ⊠ Niagara Pkwy. 3 mi north of the falls ☎ 905/371–0254 or 877/642–7275 ⊕ www.niagaraparks.com 🖃 C$10 ◷ Mid-June–early Sept., weekdays 10–5, weekends 9–5.

Another way to see the whirlpool is to take a helicopter tour. **Niagara Helicopters** takes you on a nine-minute flight over the giant whirlpool, up the Niagara Gorge, and past the American Falls, then banks around the curve of the Horseshoe Falls. Daily trips run year-round (weather permitting). It costs C$100 per person; family rates are available. ⊠ 3731 Victoria Ave. ☎ 905/357–5672 or 800/281–8034 ⊕ www.niagarahelicopters.com.

If you're here in winter, don't miss the stunning **Winter Festival of Lights** (⊕ www.niagarafallstourism.com/wfol), during which 70 trees are illuminated with 34,000 lights in the parkland near the Rainbow Bridge.

Important note: Citizens and legal residents of the United States don't need a passport or a visa to enter Canada, but proof of citizenship (a birth certificate or valid passport) and some form of photo identification is required. Naturalized U.S. residents should carry their naturalization certificate. Permanent residents who are not citizens should carry their "green card."

② Niagara Falls State Park. The park has two main sections—the one on the mainland, which includes Prospect Point, and Goat Island—and thus surrounds the American Falls and the Bridal Veil Falls. It also encompasses Luna Island and Three Sisters Islands. Established in 1885 to protect the public's access to the land surrounding the falls, this is the oldest state park in the country. It was designed by noted landscape architect Frederick Law Olmsted, who also designed New York City's Central Park.

The mainland sites include a visitor center, an observation tower, and a discovery center. The **Prospect Park Visitor Center** (☜ center free, movie $2 ☉ daily 8–6) is surrounded by gardens and has tourist information, exhibits, and a snack bar. The theater in the visitor center shows the giant-screen "thrill film" *Niagara: A History of the Falls*, which gets your attention with a virtual-reality helicopter simulator ride. The 282-foot-tall

★ **Prospect Point Observation Tower** (☜ $1 ☉ late Mar.–Dec., daily 9–8) offers dramatic views of all three falls. A glass-walled elevator takes you to an observation deck high above the gushing waters. Take the elevator to the base of the tower for the *Maid of the Mist* boat tour. The **Niagara Gorge Discovery Center** (☎ 716/278–1070 ☜ $5) explains, through interactive exhibits and a multiple-screen movie, the natural history of the falls and the Niagara Gorge and their formation.

Goat Island is a wonderful spot for a quiet walk and a close-up view of the rapids. Pedestrian bridges give you access to Luna Island and the Three Sisters Islands. The **Cave of the Winds Trip** (☎ 716/278–1730 ☜ $8 ☉ May–Oct., daily 9–8), on Goat Island, gives you access to the base of Bridal Veil Falls. An elevator takes you down into the gorge, where you follow special walkways to an observation deck near the thundering waters—definitely close enough to get sprayed. Waterproof gear is provided.

There are two main entrances (for cars) to the park, both off Robert Moses Parkway. The south entrance takes you over a bridge to Goat Island; the north entrance puts you near the visitors center. Goat Island has two parking areas, one of which is near the American Falls.

The **Niagara Scenic Trolley** (☜ $5) travels a 3-mi route through the park, picking up and dropping off passengers at six locations. If you plan to visit the majority of the park attractions, the Passport to the Falls coupon booklet ($24) may save you money. It includes the trolley and discount admission to park sights as well as to other local attractions, including the Aquarium of Niagara. The park visitor center has details. Note that hours of operation are seasonal and change frequently. They're usually extended in summer, and bad weather may delay seasonal openings, so it's best to call ahead to make sure your timing is right. ⊠ *Off Robert Moses Pkwy.* ☎ *716/278–1796 or 716/278–1770* ⊕ *nysparks. state.ny.us or www.niagarafallsstatepark.com* ☜ *Parking $10.*

★ ☙ ⑧ **Niagara Power Project Visitors Center.** Niagara Falls generates power at one of the largest hydroelectric plants in the world. The visitor center, 4½ mi north of the falls, has hands-on exhibits, including a working model of a hydropower turbine, computer games, and an explanation of how hydroelectric power is generated. Kids can play with 50 interactive exhibits. A 3-D photo display depicts the construction of the plant. ⊠ *5777 Lewiston Rd./Rte. 104* ☎ *716/286–6661 or 866/697–2386* ⊕*www.nypa. gov* ⊠ *Free* ⊙ *Daily 9–5.*

Seneca Niagara Casino. The Seneca Nation runs this 82,000-square-foot casino. There are more than 3,200 slot machines and 100 table games, including baccarat, craps, roulette, and several styles of poker. The complex includes no-smoking areas. ⊠ *310 4th St.* ☎ *716/299–1100 or 877/873–6322* ⊕ *www.snfgc.com* ⊠ *Free* ⊙ *Daily 24 hrs.*

❻ Whirlpool State Park. From this park 2 mi north of Niagara Falls you get great views of the giant whirlpool that occurs in this part of the Niagara River. A sharp turn in the river is responsible for the swirling waters. Steps and trails lead down 300 feet into the gorge. where you may fish. The park also has a playground and nature trails. ⊠ *Off Robert Moses Pkwy.* ☎ *716/284–4691* ⊕ *nysparks.state.ny.us* ⊠ *Free* ⊙ *Daily dawn–dusk.*

Where to Stay & Eat

★ **$$–$$$** ✕ **Clarkson House.** This local institution occupies an antiques-filled 19th-century building. Cloth-covered tables contrast with hardwood floors and old wood beams. The menu blends contemporary, American, and Continental dishes; steaks—New York strip and Kobe flatiron among them—are a specialty. You have a large choice of starters, such as shrimp cocktail, baked Brie, crab cakes, and teriyaki tenderloin skewers. Reservations are essential on weekends. ⊠ *810 Center St., Lewiston* ☎ *716/ 754–4544* ▤ *AE, MC, V* ⊙ *Closed Mon. No lunch weekends.*

★ **$–$$$** ✕ **Top of the Falls** A panoramic way to dine, this spot, just feet from the brink of Niagara Falls, lives up to its name. The view is awesome, as is the thick New York strip steak. The signature Buffalo chicken wrap (crispy chicken fingers, hot sauce, lettuce, and blue cheese in a flour tortilla) is a good choice for lunch. ⊠ *Niagara Falls State Park, off Robert Moses Pkwy.* ☎ *716/278–0348* ▤ *AE, D, MC, V* ⊙ *Closed Oct.–early May.*

$–$$ ✕ **Como Restaurant.** Since 1927, the Antonacci family has been serving traditional dishes from the south of Italy like veal à la Francesca, chicken cacciatore, and veal Parmesan. The interior evokes Italy with a stone fireplace and faux grapes hanging from the ceiling. ⊠ *2220 Pine Ave./U.S. 62A* ☎ *716/285–9341* ▤ *AE, D, MC, V.*

$–$$ ✕ **John's Flaming Hearth.** Forget the usual men's club steak-house decor: John's serves its New York strip steak and filet mignon in haute surroundings. Enjoy the elegance of red-velvet booths (the Voltaire Room), high-backed chairs surrounded by mirrors and chandeliers (the Gold Room), or a garden atrium (Anna's Room). Try the herb-crusted lamb, salmon with lobster, or daily specials. The pumpkin pie gets raves. ⊠ *1965 Military Rd.* ☎ *716/297–1414* ▤ *AE, D, DC, MC, V.*

★ **¢–$$** ✕ **Buzzy's New York Style Pizza & Buffalo Wings.** Buzzy's, an institution since 1953, serves 30 different pies, calzones, subs, and hoagies. For the adventurous eater, the chicken wings and chicken fingers—fresh, not frozen—come with blue-cheese dip and a choice of 10 sauces, includ-

ing one called Suicide (the warning on the menu says it's "very hot").
⊠ *7617 Niagara Falls Blvd.* ☎ *716/283–5333* ⊟ *AE, MC, V.*

$ ✕ **Goose's Roost.** Casual and homey describe this roost, where the seafood platters are oceanic and the prime beef on weck—actually a salted caraway-seed roll, and a western New York bakery tradition—is a specialty. The place serves three meals a day. ⊠ *343 4th St.* ☎ *716/282–6255* ⊟ *AE, MC, V.*

★ $$$ ✕🛏 **Red Coach Inn.** Established in 1923 and modeled after an old English inn, the sprawling Tudor-style building includes wood-burning fireplaces and a spectacular view of Niagara Falls' upper rapids. Most of the accommodations here are one-room suites; two-room suites also are available and are extra spacious, with two queen beds and a sleeper sofa. Furnishings include antiques, floral prints, and swagged windows; some rooms have canopy beds. Luxurious touches include Frette robes, Bose stereos, and the champagne and cheese tray presented when you arrive. The restaurant is cozy, with plush chairs and a stone fireplace in the main dining area. Dishes, including slow-roasted prime rib and broiled 8-ounce lobster tail with black-pepper fettuccine, are mostly Continental or contemporary. Flowers adorn the patio, where you may dine in summer. ⊠ *2 Buffalo Ave., 14303* ☎ *716/282–1459 or 800/282–1459* 🖷 *716/282–2650* ⊕ *www.redcoach.com* ⌨ *2 rooms, 13 suites* ⚷ *Restaurant, room service, in-room data ports, in-room hot tubs, some kitchenettes, microwaves, refrigerators, cable TV with movies, some in-room VCRs, bar, laundry service, business services, meeting rooms; no smoking* ⊟ *D, MC, V* ⦿*CP.*

$–$$ 🛏 **Howard Johnson Inn Closest to the Falls.** The five-story brick chain property is 1½ blocks from the falls. Rooms are standard but attractive and spacious. ⊠ *454 Main St., 14301* ☎ *716/285–5261 or 800/282–5261* 🖷 *716/285–8536* ⊕ *www.hojoniagarafalls.com* ⌨ *80 rooms* ⚷ *Restaurant, in-room data ports, some in-room hot tubs, some microwaves, some refrigerators, cable TV with movies, indoor pool, sauna, video game room, laundry facilities, laundry service, business services, some pets allowed (fee), no-smoking rooms* ⊟ *AE, D, DC, MC, V* ⦿*CP.*

¢–$$ 🛏 **Best Western Summit Inn.** This comfortable two-story chain property is in a quiet suburban setting 7 mi from the falls. Rooms are contemporary, and there's an Internet café (open May through September) on the premises. ⊠ *9500 Niagara Falls Blvd., 14304* ☎ *716/297–5050* 🖷 *716/297–0802* ⊕ *www.bestwestern.com* ⌨ *88 rooms* ⚷ *Café, in-room data ports, some in-room hot tubs, some microwaves, some refrigerators, cable TV with movies, some in-room VCRs, indoor pool, gym, sauna, bar, laundry facilities, business services, some pets allowed (fee), no-smoking rooms* ⊟ *AE, D, DC, MC, V* ⦿*CP.*

¢–$$ 🛏 **Comfort Inn, The Pointe.** At the entrance to Niagara Falls State Park, this is the closest hotel to the falls in the United States. About half the rooms overlook the Niagara River on its breathtaking tumble. The rooms are standard, but with such scenery about 500 feet away you won't spend much time in them. ⊠ *1 Prospect Pointe, 14303* ☎ *716/284–6835 or 800/284–6835* 🖷 *716/284–5177* ⊕ *www.comfortinnthepointe.com* ⌨ *116 rooms, 2 suites* ⚷ *Restaurant, in-room data ports, some in-room hot tubs, some refrigerators, cable TV with movies and video games,* *exercise equipment, laundry service, business services, meeting rooms, no-smoking rooms ☰ AE, D, DC, MC, V ⑩ CP.*

¢–$$ 🏨 **Ramada Inn at the Falls.** You can hear the rush of the falls from this hotel next door to the Seneca Niagara Casino and within walking distance of key attractions. There's a tour desk in the lobby. Rooms are contemporary, with streamlined furnishings, but have smallish windows. ✉ *219 Fourth St., 14303* ☎ *716/282–1734* 📠 *716/282–1881* ⊕ *www.ramada.com* 🛏 *112 rooms ☾ Restaurant, in-room data ports, some in-room hot tubs, some refrigerators, cable TV, indoor pool, hot tub, bar, laundry facilities, laundry service, business services, meeting rooms, no-smoking rooms ☰ AE, D, DC, MC, V.*

¢–$ 🏨 **Fallsview Travelodge Hotel.** True to Niagara Falls' honeymoon tradition, some rooms in this 11-story brown-brick hotel have king-size beds and red, heart-shaped whirlpool tubs. The building is a block away from the falls, and some units have views of the Niagara River. ✉ *201 Rainbow Blvd., 14303* ☎ *716/285–9321 or 800/876–3297* 📠 *716/285–2539* ⊕ *www.niagarafallstravelodge.com* 🛏 *150 rooms, 44 suites ☾ Restaurant, some in-room hot tubs, some refrigerators, cable TV, bar, lounge, video game room, business services, no-smoking rooms ☰ AE, D, DC, MC, V.*

¢–$ 🏨 **Rainbow House Bed & Breakfast.** Antiques, quilts, hand-painted furniture, and stenciled walls give this turn-of-the-20th-century B&B its folksy charm. Honeymooners love this spot; a wedding chapel on the premises lets them have the ceremony, reception, and honeymoon all in one place. The Honeymoon Suite has white-wicker furnishings and a porch with a swing. Note that there is a cat on the premises. ✉ *423 Rainbow Blvd. S, 14303* ☎ *716/282–1135 or 800/724–3536* 📠 *716/282 1135* ⊕ *www.rainbowhousebb.com* 🛏 *3 rooms, 1 suite ☾ Fans, some refrigerators; no room phones, no room TVs, no kids under 9, no smoking ☰ MC, V ⑩ BP.*

¢ 🏨 **Portage House Motel.** A 10-minute drive north of Niagara Falls and near Artpark, this no-frills motel is a good budget choice. ✉ *280 Portage Rd., Lewiston 14092* ☎ *716/754–8295* 📠 *716/754–1613* ⊕ *www.portagehousemotel.com* 🛏 *21 rooms ☾ Some refrigerators, cable TV, no-smoking rooms; no room phones ☰ AE, D, MC, V.*

Nightlife & the Arts

★ The **Artpark Theater** (✉ 450 S. 4th St., Lewiston ☎ 716/754–4375 or 800/659–7275 ⊕ www.artpark.net), Niagara's premier performing-arts center, hosts reasonably-priced, world-class musical theater, dance peformances, and classical, big-band, pop, and jazz concerts. Peformances are held in a main theater and in an amphitheater, and the center is part of 202-acre state park. The free Tuesday in the Park concert series, held Tuesday evenings from June through August, draws big crowds.

Shopping

Brooks Brothers, J. Crew, Mikasa, Saks Fifth Avenue, Ralph Lauren, Nine West, Bass, and Rockport are some of the names you see at the **Prime Outlets** (✉ 1900 Military Rd. ☎ 716/297–0933), which has more than 150 stores. The **Niagara Arts & Cultural Center** (✉ 1201 Pine Ave. ☎ 716/282–7530 ⊕ www.thenacc.org) houses the studios of more than 70 artists and craftspeople. Their creations are available at the gift shop.

Grand Island

🕚 *12 mi south of Niagara Falls.*

The low and flat Grand Island is the largest of the islands dotting the Niagara River between Buffalo and Niagara Falls. (In fact, it's larger than Manhattan.) Two spectacular high-arching bridges link it to the mainland. Once farmland, much of the island is now residential, and many of its inhabitants commute to Buffalo. Beaver Island State Park is at the southern tip of the island.

🌣 **Grand Lady Cruises.** Two- and three-hour cruises on the upper Niagara River above the falls are offered from May through October. Lunch, dinner, and themed cruises also are available, as are charters. ⊠ *100 Whitehaven Rd.* ☎ *716/774–8594 or 888/824–5239* ⊕ *www.grandlady.com* 🔁 *$16–$45* ☉ *May–Oct.; call for schedule.*

🌣 **Martin's Fantasy Island.** The 80-acre theme park has more then 100 rides, including a wooden roller coaster, and a petting zoo. The water-park area has a wave pool, swirling slides and chutes, and a log-flume ride. ⊠ *2400 Grand Island Blvd.* ☎ *716/773–7591* ⊕ *www.martinsfantasyisland. com* 🔁 *$19* ☉ *May–Sept., daily 11:30–8:30.*

Where to Stay & Eat

¢–$ ✗ **Beach House.** Favorites at this family-style eatery include the fish fries, served Wednesday, Thursday, and Friday. The menu also includes tacos, subs, Italian dishes, and Buffalo wings. ⊠ *5584 E. River Rd., 2 mi north of downtown* ☎ *716/773–7119* ▤ *AE, D, MC, V.*

$ ▦ **Holiday Inn Grand Island Resort.** The sprawling riverfront hotel is adjacent to a golf course and a marina. Traditional furnishings outfit the rooms, which are large and have wireless Internet access. Some have balconies and views of the Niagara River. ⊠ *100 Whitehaven Rd., 14072* ☎ *716/773–1111 or 800/465–4329* ▤ *716/773–1229* ⊕ *www. sixcontinentshotels.com* 🛏 *255 rooms, 8 suites* ♦ *Restaurant, room service, in-room data ports, some in-room hot tubs, some microwaves, some refrigerators, cable TV with movies, some in-room VCRs, 1 indoor and 1 outdoor pool, wading pool, gym, hot tub, massage, sauna, bar, recreation room, dry cleaning, laundry facilities, laundry service, concierge, concierge floor, business services, meeting rooms, some pets allowed (fee), no-smoking rooms* ▤ *AE, D, DC, MC, V.*

Lockport

🕛 *16 mi east of Niagara Falls.*

The city of Lockport has five sets of operating locks along the Eric Canal. The busy lock system still operates in much the same manner as it did nearly a century ago. The historic district downtown surrounds the canal and locks, which you may see in action. Locks 34 and 35 can be viewed from the Big Bridge and Pine Street Bridge. Museums and historic sites trace the heritage of the canal and lock system and the town that grew up around them.

Colonel William M. Bond House. The restored 1824 brick house, on the National Register of Historic Places, has 12 rooms with period furnishings. The Niagara County Historical Society owns the house. ⊠ *143 Ontario St.* ☎ *716/434–7433* ⊕ *www.niagara-county.org* ⊠ *Free* ⊙ *May–Dec., Thurs. and weekends 1–5; and by appointment.*

Kenan Center. The center encompasses several buildings, including a Victorian mansion with gallery space, ornate fireplaces, and formal gardens. Exhibits change about eight times a year and show works by local and nationally known artists. The Taylor Theater, which presents frequent child-friendly productions, is in a converted carriage house behind the mansion. On the other side of the 25-acre property an arena offers sports activities and recreation. The arena also hosts an annual juried crafts exhibit on the weekend after Memorial Day. ⊠ *433 Locust St.* ☎ *716/433–2617* ⊕ *kenancenter.org* ⊠ *Gallery and gardens free* ⊙ *Gallery June–early Sept., weekdays noon–5, Sun. 2–5; early Sept.–May, weekdays noon–5, weekends 2–5.*

Lockport Locks & Erie Canal Cruises. Narrated two-hour sightseeing tours cruise the canal, viewing historic buildings and passing through five locks. ⊠ *210 Market St.* ☎ *716/433–6155 or 800/378–0352* ⊕ *www.lockportlocks.com* ⊠ *$12.50* ⊙ *Early May–late Oct., daily; call for schedule.*

Niagara County Historical Society. A diverse collection of artifacts relating to Niagara County history is housed in five buildings, including a large barn and and 1864 brick house. ⊠ *215 Niagara St.* ☎ *716/434–7433* ⊕ *www.niagara-county.org* ⊠ *Free* ⊙ *Jan.–May, Wed.–Sat. 1–5; June–Aug., Wed.–Sat. 10–5, Sun. 1–5; Sept.–Dec., Thurs.–Sun. 1–5.*

Where to Stay & Eat

$–$$$ ✕ **Garlock's.** Antiques and collectibles set off by tablecloths and wood-paneled walls furnish this restaurant in an 1821 building that was constructed to house canal workers. The food is American; steaks are a specialty, but the menu also includes seafood, chicken, lamb, and pork dishes. Consider filet mignon or extra-thick pork chops. ⊠ *35 S. Transit St.* ☎ *716/433–5595* ▭ *AE, D, MC, V* ⊙ *No lunch.*

$–$$ ✕ **Fieldstone Country Inn.** A stone building with a beamed ceiling and rustic furnishings houses this casual spot, a local favorite. Barbecued ribs, steak, and all other entrées include the soup and salad bar. The fall Harvest Platter features roast turkey, stuffing, and all the trimmings. ⊠ *5986 S. Transit Rd.* ☎ *716/625–6193* ▭ *AE, D, DC, MC, V* ⊙ *No lunch Sat.*

¢–$$ ✕ **Village Eatery.** This casual spot recalls an Italian bistro café. Fresh-baked pizzas, Italian sandwiches, cappuccino, espresso, and a dessert bar are among the offerings here. ⊠ *429 Davison Rd.* ☎ *716/433–0688* ⊜ *Reservations not accepted* ▭ *AE, D, MC, V* ⊙ *Closed Oct.–Apr. No lunch Sun.*

¢–$ ▥ **Comfort Inn.** The tidy two-story chain property is 2 mi from the Erie Canal locks. Some rooms have whirlpool tubs. ⊠ *551 S. Transit Rd., 14094* ☎ *716/434–4411* ☐ *716/434–9649* ⊕ *www.comfortinn.com* ⊅ *50 rooms* ⟳ *In-room data ports, some in-room hot tubs, some microwaves, some refrigerators, cable TV with movies, gym, laundry service, business services, no-smoking rooms* ▭ *AE, D, DC, MC, V* ⊙⏐ *CP.*

Iroquois National Wildlife Refuge

⑬ *16 mi east of Lockport.*

The more than 10,000 acres of wildlife habitat at this refuge—including swamps, freshwater marshes, woodlands, and meadows—attract migratory waterfowl and other birds, as well as resident wildlife. About 60 bird species stay here in winter. There are overlooks and nature trails for biking, photography, and cross-country skiing. The refuge is between Buffalo and Rochester. ⊠ *1101 Casey Rd., off Rte. 63, Alabama* ☎ *585/948–5445* ⊕ *iroquoisnwr.fws.gov* ⊡ *Free* ☉ *Daily dawn–dusk.*

Darien Lakes State Park

⑭ *12 mi south of Alabama.*

The centerpiece of this 1,850-acre park is 12-acre Harlow Lake, which has a sandy beach. Hiking, bridle, and cross-country skiing trails vein the grounds, which are hilly and wooded and include a 158-site campground (open daily from June through September and on weekends the rest of the year) with showers and a comfort station. Fishing, picnicking, snowmobiling, and ice-skating are among the other activities you might pursue here. Some hunting is allowed in season. ⊠ *10289 Harlow Rd., Darien Center* ☎ *585/547–9242 or 585/547–9481* ⊕ *nysparks. state.ny.us* ⊡ *Parking $6* ☉ *Daily dawn–dusk.*

Six Flags Darien Lake. The Superman Ride of Steel will have your heart racing faster than the 70 miles per hour this roller coaster reaches. It's one of five coasters at this theme park, which has more than 100 rides in all. The Viper coaster turns you upside down five times. The water park has a wave pool and twisted chutes and slides. The complex includes a 20,000-seat concert amphitheater, eateries, a hotel, and a mammoth campground (1,200 sites). ⊠ *9993 Allegheny Rd., off Rte. 77, Darien Center* ☎ *716/599–4641* ⊕ *www.sixflags.com* ⊡ *$33.99* ☉ *Early May–Oct.; call for schedule.*

Where to Stay

$–$$$ ⊞ **Six Flags Hotel Lodge on the Lake.** The rustic-style three-story hotel is adjacent to the Six Flags theme park and campground. Rooms are spacious, with two queen-size beds and a queen sleeper sofa. The two suites have wood-paneled walls, a stone fireplace, a dining area, and a soaring ceiling. ⊠ *9993 Allegheny Rd., 14040* ☎ *585/599–2211* ☐ *585/599–5124* ⊕ *www.sixflags.com* ⟿ *160 rooms, 2 suites* ⚑ *Restaurant, café, in-room data ports, some microwaves, refrigerators, cable TV, pool, wading pool; no smoking* ☐ *AE, D, MC, V* ☉ *Closed Nov.–early May.*

Letchworth State Park

⑮ *28 mi southeast of Darien Center.*

Fodor's Choice
★

The Genesee River snakes its way through this 14,350-acre park. The sheer cliff walls of the 17-mi gorge soar nearly 600 feet in some spots, which is why the park is often called the Grand Canyon of the East. The river spills over three large waterfalls—one 107 feet high—and the long and narrow park encompasses awesome rock formations and dense forest. Some 66 mi of trails are used for hiking, biking, horse-back riding, snowmobiling, and cross-country skiing. Many activities here center on water; you may go fishing, white-water rafting, or kayaking, or swim in one of two pools. Ice-skating, snow tubing, and horse-drawn sleigh rides round out the winter options. Park accommodations include tent and trailer campsites (open mid-May to mid-October), winterized cabins, and the Glen Iris Inn. The inn, originally the retreat of park founder William Pryor Letchworth, houses a restaurant. ⊠ *1 Letchworth State Park, off I–390 Exit 7, Castile* ☎ *716/493–3600* ⊕ *nysparks.state.ny. us* ⌫ *Parking $6 daily Apr.–Oct. and weekends Dec.–Feb.* ⊙ *Daily dawn–dusk.*

Where to Stay & Eat

¢ ✕⌂ **Glen Iris Inn.** The country inn, part of Letchworth State Park, overlooks the Genesee River. Park founder William Pryor Letchworth had used the mansion as a retreat. It was turned into an inn in 1914. The interiors are decked out in Victorian style. Standard rooms are on the small side, with one double or two twin beds, but the suites are very spacious. The Cherry Suite has a whirlpool tub, a private porch with great views of the gorge, and striking chevron-patterned hardwood floors. Also available are more modern lodge rooms and two houses. The restaurant ($$–$$$; closed Nov.–late Mar.) serves American and Continental fare, such as baked salmon fillet in port sauce, roast duckling with cherry-brandy glaze, and slow-roasted prime rib with fresh horseradish. ⊠ *7 Letchworth State Park, Castile 14427* ☎ *585/493–2622* ⌨ *585/493–5803* ⊕ *www.glenirisinn.com* ⇔ *12 rooms, 4 suites* ⏚ *Restaurant, some in-room hot tubs, library, no room TVs, no smoking* ⊟ *AE, D, MC, V* ⊙ *Closed Nov.–late Mar.*

East Aurora

⑯ *36 mi west of Castile.*

East Aurora has earned the nickname Toy Town, U.S.A., because it is home to both the headquarters of the Fisher-Price toy company and a unique toy museum. East Aurora is also the locale of two National Historic Landmarks—the honeymoon cottage of President Millard Fillmore and his wife, Abigail, and the Roycroft Campus, an Arts and Crafts movement community founded in 1895 by writer, publisher, and craftsman Elbert Hubbard. You'll want to visit the Roycroft Inn to see the murals painted by Barbizon artist Alex Fournier and for the original examples of Roycroft Mission-style furniture.

Elbert Hubbard-Roycroft Museum. A 1910 Craftsman bungalow contains furniture, glass pieces, books, and other items related to the Roycroft movement and its founder, Elbert Hubbard (1856–1915). A writer and frequent lecturer, Hubbard died along with his wife aboard the *Lusitania*. ⊠ *363 Oakwood Ave.* ☎ *716/652–4735* ⌨ *$5* ⊙ *June–mid-Oct., Wed. and weekends 1–4; tours by appointment.*

☾ **Explore and More Children's Museum.** Designed with youngsters age 10 and under in mind, this museum encourages experimentation, play, and learning in an interactive environment. Children may pick plastic veggies, for instance, and then "sell" them at a play farm market. Budding contractors might work on building a house foundation using faux cement block and bricks, install flooring, and even play at plumbing. ⊠ *300 Gleed Ave.* ☎ *716/655–5131* ⊕ *www.exploreandmore.org* ⊠ *$4* ⊙ *Wed.–Sat. 10–5, Sun. noon–5.*

Millard Fillmore House Museum. In 1826, when Millard Fillmore was just a young lawyer, he built this simple house. The man who was to become the 13th U.S. president lived here for only four years. A National Historic Landmark, the house has been restored and refurnished to reflect life in the early 19th century. ⊠ *24 Shearer Ave.* ☎ *716/ 652–8875* ⊠ *$5* ⊙ *June–mid-Oct., Wed. and weekends 1–4; mid-Oct.–May, by appointment.*

Roycroft Campus. A center for New York's Arts and Crafts movement at the turn of the 20th century, this 14-building community was once home to as many as 500 craftsmen, aka Roycrofters. The community was founded in 1895 by Elbert Hubbard, who had met William Morris during his travels in England. Campus buildings, nine of which are open to the public today, include the Roycroft Inn. The 1905 Blacksmith and Copper Shop is occupied by the Roycroft Shops. The building where Roycroft campus furnishings were made is home to an antiques stores and other shops. ⊠ *Main and Grove Sts.* ☎ *716/652–3333 or 888/769–2738* ⊕ *www.ralaweb.com* ⊠ *Free* ⊙ *Daily 10–5.*

🖰 **Toy Town Museum.** Rare and one-of-a-kind toys are on display at this museum, which also houses a collection of Fisher-Price toys from 1930 through 1970. Children can make toys in the workshop area. Just try dragging Junior out of the gift shop without a souvenir. ⊠ *636 Girard Ave.* ☎ *716/687–5151* ⊕ *www.toytownusa.com* ⊠ *Free* ⊙ *Mon.–Sat. 10–4.*

FESTIVALS &   **Roycroft Festival of Arts and Crafts.** The Roycroft Campus hosts an an-
FAIRS   tiques show, juried art show, and sale with live entertainment twice a year. The two-day festivals are held in late June and early December. ⊞ *Roycrofters at Large Association, 21 S. Grove St., 14052* ☎ *716/ 655–7252* ⊕ *www.ralaweb.com.*

ToyFest. Notable and historic toys from various periods and manufacturers are on display during this three-day festival that also brings a parade, an antique-car show, rides, and other entertainment to the Toy Town Museum. The event is usually held in late August. ⊠ *636 Girard Ave.* ☎ *716/687–5151* ⊕ *www.toytownusa.com.*

Where to Stay & Eat

$$–$$$ ✕ **Old Orchard Inn.** The restaurant, in a 1901 hunting lodge, overlooks a pond and neat lawns on a 25-acre country estate. Traditional dishes like chicken potpie, rack of New Zealand lamb, and filet mignon fill the menu, complemented by pasta and seafood options. In good weather you may dine beneath an awning on a patio. ⊠ *2095 Blakeley Corners Rd.* ☎ *716/652–4664* ▭ *AE, D, DC, MC, V* ⊙ *Closed Mon. No lunch Tues.–Sat. in Jan.–Mar.*

$–$$ ✕▦ **Roycroft Inn.** Original and reproduction Roycroft Arts and Crafts
Fodor'sChoice furnishings fill the rooms at this lovely three-story inn on the old Roy-
★ croft Campus. Most accommodations here are suites, which include sitting areas or rooms. Some have two twin beds or a queen-size bed and
a pullout queen sleeper. Bursts of bright color—in a throw rug or pillow or a bedcovering, for example—play off the straight lines of the fur-
niture and the neutral walls. The restaurant ($$–$$$$), also furnished
with Arts and Crafts pieces, has several cozy rooms with fireplaces. The
fare is American: pecan-crusted prawns with apple cream sauce, grilled
rack of venison *au poivre,* roasted prosciutto-wrapped chicken breast
with sausage stuffing and cranberry sauce. You may dine on a covered
porch in summer. ⊠ *40 S. Grove St., 14052* ☎ *716/652–5552 or 877/
652–5552* ☎ *716/655–5345* ⊕ *www.roycroftinn.com* ➪ *7 rooms, 22
suites* ⚐ *Restaurant, room service, in-room data ports, in-room hot tubs,
cable TV, in-room VCRs, bar, lounge, library, business services; no
smoking* ⊟ *AE, D, DC, MC, V* ⅠⓄⅠ *CP.*

Shopping
Several shops, including Roycroft Antiques and Roycroft Potters, oc-
cupy the **Roycroft Arts and Crafts Building** (⊠ 37 S. Grove St. ☎ no
phone). The **Roycroft Shops** (⊠ 31 S. Grove St. ☎ 716/655–0571) sell
American Arts and Crafts furniture, books, jewelry, and home acces-
sories. Everything you'd expect to find in an old-fashioned five-and-dime—
crafts items, housewares, cards, fabrics, toys—is for sale at **Vidler's 5 and
10 Cent Store** (⊠ 676–694 Main St. ☎ 716/652–0481). Its 15,000
square feet occupy four connected buildings that date from 1890. The
Vidler family opened the place in 1930 and still owns it.

Buffalo

11 mi northwest of East Aurora.

Snow, the Buffalo Bills, and the gateway to Niagara Falls are just some
of the things that come to mind when most people think of Buffalo.
While it is true that the city is hit by at least one to four memorable
snowstorms a year, Buffalo doesn't actually receive a great deal of
snow compared to many other cities in New York. Buffalo is indeed a
great sports town with tough professional teams, but it is also the
home of Buffalo wings, beef on weck (thin-sliced roast beef and fresh
horseradish on a hard roll crusted with salt and caraway seeds), and
sponge candy (a confection with an airy, toffee like center inside a choco-
late shell). The city also boasts world-class architecture, a leading can-
cer-research institute, and one of the four research universities of the
State University of New York.

The city's growth began in the early 1800s, when ships from the Great
Lakes transported millions of bushels of grain from Midwest farms to
Buffalo. The Erie Canal, completed in 1825, connected Buffalo to Al-
bany (and Lake Erie to the Hudson River), allowing the grain to be dis-
tributed along the East Coast, and Buffalo became known as the "Queen
City on the Lake." Railroad tracks laid along the route of the Erie
Canal continued the great migration of products. Laborers were needed
to handle the boats, grain, and, later, the steel mills. The thousands of

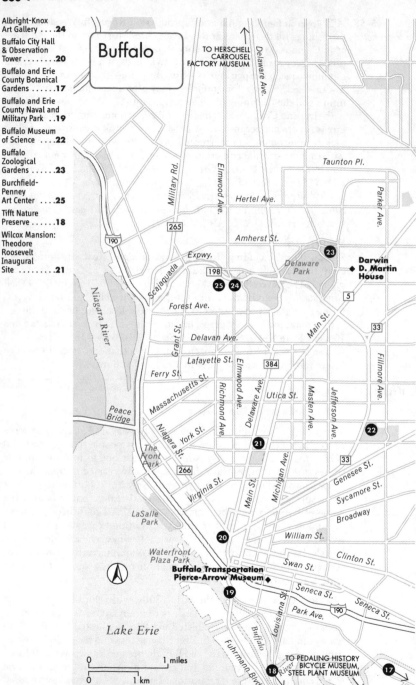

Buffalo

TO HERSCHELL
CARROUSEL
FACTORY MUSEUM

Delaware Ave.

Taunton Pl.

Parker Ave.

Military Rd.

Elmwood Ave.

Hertel Ave.

265

190

Amherst St.

Expwy.

Scajaquada

198

25 24

23

Delaware
Park

Darwin
D. Martin
House

5

Forest Ave.

Grant St.

Delavan Ave.

Main St.

33

Lafayette St.

Fillmore Ave.

Ferry St.

384

Elmwood Ave.

Delaware Ave.

Utica St.

Masten Ave.

Jefferson Ave.

Massachusetts St.

Richmond Ave.

22

Niagara St.

York St.

21

33

Peace
Bridge

Niagara River

The
Front
Park

266

Virginia St.

Main St.

Michigan Ave.

Genesee St.

Sycamore St.

Broadway

LaSalle
Park

20

William St.

Clinton St.

Waterfront
Plaza Park

Swan St.

Seneca St.

Buffalo Transportation
Pierce-Arrow Museum

190

19

Park Ave.

Seneca St.

Louisiana St.

Lake Erie

0   1 miles

0   1 km

Fuhrmann Blvd.

TO PEDALING HISTORY
BICYCLE MUSEUM,
STEEL PLANT MUSEUM

Buffalo River

18

17

immigrants who came to fill those jobs brought rich ethnic diversity to the city.

Buffalo's success as a commercial crossroads resulted in a booming economy at the turn of the 20th century, and majestic mansions sprang up along Delaware Avenue, known as Millionaire Row. (It was in one of these mansions that Theodore Roosevelt was inaugurated after President William McKinley's assassination in 1901.) Many ornate structures went up in downtown during these boom years, including some of the world's first skyscrapers. Among these is the steel-and–terra cotta 1896 Guaranty Building (at 28 Church St.); the 13-story building was designed by Louis H. Sullivan, who also gets credit for several other notable early skyscrapers in the United States.

The cultural scene offers great jazz and theater productions as well as art exhibitions. Resident theater companies put on a broad range of plays in the downtown theater district on Main Street not far from the waterfront. In summer, Delaware Park—one of several Buffalo parks designed by noted landscape architect Frederick Law Olmsted—hosts free outdoor performances of Shakespeare plays.

A stretch of Elmwood Avenue is known for its record shops, boutiques, used-book stores, hip bars, and eateries, all aimed at the twentysomethings who fill Buffalo's six institutions of higher learning. The youthful feel extends along Elmwood from the historic Allentown district, at North Street, to the state college, in the 1300 block on Elmwood. Structures here are mostly two-story redbrick buildings, though there are some Victorian homes too, especially closer to Allentown.

★ ㉔ **Albright-Knox Art Gallery.** Twentieth-century art is well represented here. The gallery's collections are especially rich in postwar American and European art, including Jackson Pollock, Jasper Johns, and Andy Warhol. Works by Pablo Picasso, Vincent van Gogh, Claude Monet, Henri Matisse, and Pierre-Auguste Renoir are here as well. On Sunday afternoons in July and August, free jazz performances are held on the massive front steps. ✉ *1285 Elmwood Ave.* ☎ *716/882–8700* ⊕ *www.albrightknox.org* ▢ *$10* ⊙ *Tues.–Thurs. and weekends 10–5, Fri. 10–10.*

㉐ **Buffalo City Hall & Observation Tower.** The broad-shouldered art-deco architectural masterpiece rises from the heart of downtown. An elevator and three flights of stairs take you to an observation deck with spectacular views of the city and the Lake Erie waterfront. ✉ *65 Niagara Sq.* ☎ *716/851–5891* ▢ *Free* ⊙ *Weekdays 8–4.*

⑰ **Buffalo and Erie County Botanical Gardens.** Even in the middle of winter you can soak in the sights and scents of the tropics under the domes of this Victorian glass conservatory. The greenhouses shelter cacti, fruit trees, palms, and orchids. The American Ivy Association certified the claim of the largest ivy collection of any botanical garden in the world. Formal gardens and a park surround the conservatory. Guided tours are given by reservation. ✉ *2655 S. Park Ave.* ☎ *716/827–1584* ⊕ *www.buffalogardens.com* ▢ *$4* ⊙ *Tues.–Sun. 10–5 (until 7 Thurs.).*

⑲ **Buffalo and Erie County Naval and Military Park.** A guided missile cruiser, destroyer, and a World War II submarine are on display at this 6-acre waterfront site, the largest inland naval park in the nation. ⊠ *1 Naval Park Cove* ☎ *716/847–1773* ⊕ *www.buffalonavalpark.org* ⌧ *$8* ⊙ *Apr.–Oct., daily 10–5; Nov., weekends 10–4.*

㉒ **Buffalo Museum of Science.** Exhibits cover everything from anthropology to zoology. One exhibit uses the stories of three mummies to explore what daily life was like for ordinary citizens in ancient Egypt. ⊠ *1020 Humboldt Pkwy., off Rte. 33* ☎ *716/896–5200* ⊕ *www.sciencebuff.org* ⌧ *$7* ⊙ *Museum Wed.–Sat. 10–5, Sun. noon–5.*

㉓ **Buffalo Zoological Gardens.** Endangered Siberian tigers, Asian elephants, and Indian rhinos are among the nearly 1,000 wild and exotic animals found in this natural setting in Delaware Park. The grounds include an Eco Station, an interactive mock field-research station. ⊠ *300 Parkside Ave.* ☎ *716/837–3900* ⊕ *www.buffalozoo.org* ⌧ *Zoo $7, parking $3* ⊙ *June–early Sept., daily 10–5; early Sept.–May, daily 10–4.*

㉕ **Burchfield-Penney Art Center.** This premier showcase for western New York artists spotlights the works of watercolorist Charles Burchfield (1893–1967) and handcrafted objects from the Roycroft Arts and Crafts community. ⊠ *Buffalo State College, Rockwell Hall, 1300 Elmwood Ave.* ☎ *716/878–6011* ⊕ *www.burchfield-penney.org* ⌧ *$5* ⊙ *Tues.–Sat. 10–5, Sun. 1–5.*

Herschell Carrousel Factory Museum. The old factory contains two operating carousels—one from 1916 and a smaller one from the 1940s—as well as a menagerie of hand-carved carousel animals, some quite elaborate. ⊠ *180 Thompson St., North Tonawanda* ☎ *716/693–1885* ⊕ *www.carrouselmuseum.org* ⌧ *$4* ⊙ *Apr.–June and Sept.–Dec., Wed.–Sun. 1–5; July and Aug., daily 11–5.*

★ **Pedaling History Bicycle Museum.** More than 400 rare and unique bicycles and related antiques and memorabilia are on display at one of the largest bicycle museums in the world. Orchard Park is 12 mi south of Buffalo. ⊠ *3943 N. Buffalo Rd., Orchard Park* ☎ *716/662–3853* ⊕ *www.pedalinghistory.com* ⌧ *$6* ⊙ *Mon.–Sat. 11–5, Sun. 1:30–5.*

Steel Plant Museum. Photos, exhibits, and memorabilia pay tribute to western New York's steel workers and what was once the largest steel plant in the world, Bethlehem Steel. The museum is in the Lackawanna Public Library, 6 mi south of Buffalo. ⊠ *560 Ridge Rd., Lackawanna* ☎ *716/823–0630* ⊕ *www.steelplantmuseum.org* ⌧ *Free* ⊙ *Mon. and Wed. 1–9, Tues. and Thurs.–Sat. 9–5 (closed Sat. in July–early Sept.).*

⑱ **Tifft Nature Preserve.** Five miles of nature trails, boardwalks, and a cattail marsh make this wildlife refuge near the Lake Erie shore an ideal place for hiking, bird-watching, and picnics. The 264-acre preserve is part of the ⇨ **Buffalo Museum of Science.** ⊠ *1200 Fuhrmann Blvd.* ☎ *716/825–6397 or 716/896–5200* ⊕ *www.sciencebuff.org* ⌧ *$2 suggested donation* ⊙ *Grounds daily dawn–dusk. Visitor center May–Oct., Wed.–Sat. 9–4; Nov.–Apr., Thurs.–Sat. 10–4.*

WRIGHT SITES

THE BUFFALO AREA is home to several buildings by renowned architect Frank Lloyd Wright (1867–1959). The Darwin D. Martin House, part of the **Darwin D. Martin House Complex** in Buffalo's Parkside East Historic District, is considered one of the finest examples of a Wright prairie-style structure. The estate was commissioned in 1902 by Darwin Martin, a wealthy Buffalo businessman who would become one of Wright's most loyal patrons. The first Wright house on the property was the George F. Barton House (at 118 Summit Ave.), built in 1903 for Martin's sister and brother-in-law. The final touches weren't applied to Martin's own house until around 1907. At this writing, the complex is undergoing a multiyear renovation; completion is expected in 2006. Part of the ambitious project includes reconstructing Wright's pergola, conservatory, and carriage house, all of which were demolished in the 1960s. During the work, tours of the complex are available on a limited basis; reservations are required. ⊠ 125 Jewett Pkwy., Buffalo ☎ 716/856–3858 ⊕ darwinmartinhouse.org ⌨ $10 ⊘ By appointment.

The Martin estate also included the **Gardener's Cottage** (285 Woodward Ave.). Around the same time, Wright also designed the **Walter V. Davidson House** (57 Tillinghast Pl.) and the **William R. Heath House** (72 Soldier's Pl.), both of which are private residences.

The Martins liked their Buffalo home so much that they also commissioned Wright to design their summer estate. The centerpiece of the 8½-acre **Graycliff** estate is the two-story main house, built circa 1926. Its cantilevered balconies take advantage of its position atop a 70-foot-cliff overlooking Lake Erie. At this writing, the estate is undergoing an extensive multiphase renovation (to continue into fall 2006). Tours are offered infrequently by appointment. The property is about 13 mi south of Buffalo. ⊠ 6472 Old Lake Shore Rd., Derby ☎ 716/947–9217 ⊕ graycliff.bfn.org ⌨ $18 ⊘ By appointment.

In 1928 Darwin Martin commissioned a family mausoleum—a project he dropped after his fortunes were pummeled by the following year's stock-market crash. Today Buffalo's Forest Lawn cemetery is building (near Delavan Avenue) the concrete-and-granite tomb from plans owned by the Frank Lloyd Wright Foundation. And there's another Wright-related project in the works in Buffalo. At this writing, the **Buffalo Transportation/Pierce-Arrow Museum** is building a winged gas station from unfinished Wright plans. A former Wright apprentice is involved with the project, which, once built, won't actually function as a station but will rather complement the museum's collection of cars and automobile memorabilia and artifacts ⊠ 263 Michigan Ave., Buffalo ☎ 716/853–0084 ⊕ www.pierce-arrow.com ⌨ $7 ⊘ Mar.–Dec., Sat. noon–5; and by appointment.

㉑ Wilcox Mansion: Theodore Roosevelt Inaugural National Historical Site. After President William McKinley was assassinated at the Pan-American Exposition in Buffalo in 1901, Theodore Roosevelt was inaugurated as the nation's 26th president in the library of this Greek revival mansion. You can take guided tours and view exhibits and gardens. Architectural walking tours are also available. ⊠ *641 Delaware Ave.* ☎ *716/ 884–0095* ⊕ *www.nps.gov/thri* ☞ *$3* ⊙ *Weekdays 9–5, weekends noon–5.*

FESTIVALS &
FAIRS

Allentown Arts Festival. This nationally acclaimed fine arts–and–crafts show brings nearly 500 exhibitors, food vendors, live music, and outstanding people-watching to the Allentown district for two days in mid-June. ⌂ *Box 1566, Ellicott Station 14205* ☎ *716/881–4269* ⊕ *www. allentownartfestival.com.*

Canal Fest of the Tonawandas. Nautical displays and a midway with rides and games are set up along the Eric Canal for eight days in late July. ⌂ *Box 1243, North Tonawanda 14120* ☎ *716/692–3292* ⊕ *www. canalfest.org.*

Where to Stay & Eat

$$–$$$$ ✕ **Lord Chumley's.** Acres of polished hardwood, soft gold lighting, and linen tablecloths adorn the main dining area of this formal spot in a townhouse setting. The restaurant is a favorite of couples out on the town for a romantic evening. American and Continental dishes are on the menu: lobster bisque, snails, broiled lamb chops, roast quail in cherry sauce, steak *au poivre* over pasta. Jackets are preferred for men but not required. ⊠ *481 Delaware St.* ☎ *716/886–2220* ⊟ *D, DC, MC, V* ⊙ *Closed Sun. No lunch.*

$$$ ✕ **Fiddle Heads.** The casual, experimental cuisine changes seasonally at this restaurant, where you have a choice of two different dining areas. One has an arty watering-hole feel, whereas the other has dim lighting and a more low-key, sedate demeanor. The menu might include steak with sautéed shrimp and horseradish mashed potatoes, chicken with corn and mole sauce, or salmon steak with a teriyaki-like glaze and veggie spring rolls. For lunch, try pesto chicken on homemade focaccia or the pizza of the day. ⊠ *62 Allen St.* ☎ *716/883–4166* ⊟ *D, MC, V* ⊙ *Closed Sun. and Mon.*

★ $$–$$$ ✕ **The Hourglass.** The intimate, family-operated business continues to maintain its reputation as one of greater Buffalo's best restaurants. The menu emphasizes seafood and steaks but also includes pastas, rack of lamb, and other dishes. The kitchen applies contemporary touches, such as balsamic vinegar, to the Continental classics. Regulars love the crème brûlée. ⊠ *981 Kenmore Ave.* ☎ *716/877–8788* ⊟ *AE, MC, V* ⊙ *Closed Sun. and Mon. No lunch.*

$$–$$$ ✕ **Rue Franklin.** French doors open onto a beautiful landscaped courtyard for summer dining. The interior of this sophisticated restaurant, with soft colors and swagged windows, is just as pretty. The changing menu offers French fare as well as contemporary dishes such as braised short ribs with pork dumplings and bok choy or arctic char in soy-citrus broth. ⊠ *341 Franklin St.* ☎ *716/852–4416* ⊟ *AE, DC, MC, V* ⊙ *Closed Sun. and Mon. No lunch.*

$–$$ ✕ **Just Pasta.** Spinach-and-egg spaghetti with prosciutto, peas, and cream, and Gorgonzola ravioli with ricotta and tomato sauce are among the choices at this popular upscale Italian spot housed in a brick building. The menu, which changes often, also includes seafood, steak, lamb, and other fare that has nothing to do with pasta. ✉ *307 Bryant St.* ☎ *716/ 881–1888* ▤ *AE, DC, MC, V* ✪ *Closed Sun.*

★ **¢–$$** ✕ **Anchor Bar & Restaurant.** Anchor claims to have originated Buffalo wings. Some people dispute that, but many come to sample the groundbreaking invention in bar food. Try them "hot" for the full experience. A buffalo's head hanging on the wall is about all the atmosphere you need. ✉ *1047 Main St.* ☎ *716/886–8920* ▤ *AE, D, DC, MC, V.*

¢–$$ ✕ **Coles.** Sandwiches are a specialty of this restaurant, which was established in 1934. Among the mouthwatering favorites is the ham, turkey, and Swiss sandwich with onions and Russian dressing on marble rye. Dinner choices include lobster ravioli in crab-vodka sauce and Gorgonzola-encased New York strip steak with wine sauce. The checkerboard floor, a long bar, and wooden booths are part of the charm of this casual place. ✉ *1104 Elmwood Ave.* ☎ *716/886–1449* ▤ *AE, D, DC, MC, V.*

$–$$ ▦ **Adam's Mark Hotel.** Stay at this nine-story hotel for spacious rooms and suites convenient to downtown activities. Rooms have attractive updated traditional decors; some have whirlpool tubs. The large indoor pool has a sundeck. ✉ *120 Church St., 14202* ☎ *716/845–5100 or 800/ 444–2326* 🖷 *716/845–5377* ⊕ *www.adamsmark.com* ⇖ *479 rooms, 7 suites* ⚭ *Restaurant, in-room data ports, some in-room hot tubs, some microwaves, some refrigerators, cable TV with movies, some in-room VCRs, indoor pool, health club, sauna, lounge, sports bar, laundry facilities, laundry service, business services, meeting rooms, airport shuttle, no-smoking rooms* ▤ *AE, D, DC, MC, V* ❍| *CP.*

$–$$ ▦ **Beau Fleuve.** Each of the rooms at this circa-1881 bed-and-breakfast in the historic Linwood district is furnished to celebrate one of the various nationalities of the people who settled Buffalo. You may choose the French, the Polish, or the Irish room, among others. Rooms have antiques, down comforters, and William Morris wallcoverings. A candlelit breakfast awaits you in the morning. ✉ *242 Linwood Ave.* ☎ *716/ 882–6116 or 800/278–0245* ⊕ *www.beaufleuve.com* ⇖ *5 rooms* ⚭ *Dining room, fans; no room phones, no room TVs, no smoking* ▤ *D, MC, V* ❍| *BP.*

★ **$–$$** ▦ **Hyatt Regency Buffalo.** The elegant 1923 highrise in the theater district and adjacent to the convention center has a glass atrium addition. Rooms are contemporary, with dark streamlined furniture. Some have whirlpool tubs and CD players. Beds have feather pillows and the desks are paired with ergonomic chairs. Guests are allowed to use the health club across the street. The E. B. Green's Steakhouse (named after the architect of the building) earns high marks for its high-quality fare. ✉ *2 Fountain Plaza, 14202* ☎ *716/856–1234* 🖷 *716/852–6157* ⊕ *www.hyatt. com* ⇖ *384 rooms, 11 suites* ⚭ *3 restaurants, room service, in-room data ports, some in-room faxes, some in-room hot tubs, some microwaves, some refrigerators, cable TV with movies, some in-room VCRs, hair salon, laundry service, business services, meeting rooms, no-smoking rooms* ▤ *AE, D, DC, MC, V.*

$–$$ 🏨 **Mansion on Delaware Ave.** The beautiful Buffalo mansion was built
Fodor'sChoice in the 1860s in the Second Empire style. Thoroughly renovated, it
★ houses posh, elegant accommodations and offers the amenities of a much
larger property. The decor is classy yet up to the minute. Beds, mostly
queens, are dressed in down duvets and Frette linens. Some rooms have
fireplaces and whirlpool tubs, and suites include separate parlor areas.
Complimentary cocktails are served in the evening. Also complimentary:
car service to downtown, shoe polishes, and pressings. ⊠ *414 Delaware
Ave., 14202* ☎ *716/866–3300 or 800/448–8355* 🖷 *716/883–3923*
⊕ *www.themansionondelaware.com* ⇨ *25 rooms, 3 suites* ⚭ *Restaurant, in-room data ports, some in-room hot tubs, some refrigerators,
cable TV with movies, exercise equipment, billiards, bar, dry cleaning,
laundry service, business services, meeting rooms; no smoking* ▭ *AE,
D, DC, MC, V* ⏉⏉ *CP.*

¢–$ 🏨 **Holiday Inn–Downtown.** The eight-story chain property is in the his-
toric Allentown neighborhood, across from the Wilcox Mansion, and
near the downtown business district. Rooms have large windows, desks,
and contemporary furnishings. ⊠ *620 Delaware Ave., 14202* ☎ *716/
886–2121 or 800/465–4329* 🖷 *716/886–7942* ⊕ *www.holiday-inn.
com* ⇨ *168 rooms* ⚭ *Restaurant, room service, in-room data ports,
some microwaves, some refrigerators, cable TV with movies, pool, wading pool, bar, laundry facilities, laundry service, business services, meeting rooms, airport shuttle, some pets allowed (fee), no-smoking rooms*
▭ *AE, D, DC, MC, V.*

Nightlife & the Arts

NIGHTLIFE   Elmwood Avenue near the state college and Chippewa Street, downtown,
are dotted with bars and nightclubs. But there are alternatives. The
Lafayette Tap Room (⊠ 391 Washington St. ☎ 716/854–2466 ⊕ www.
lafayettetaproom.com), a blues bar, has a few seating areas, a couple of
bars, and two stages where national and local acts perform. Jazz, blues,
country, and reggae musicians perform at **Nietzsche's** (⊠ 248 Allen St.
☎ 716/886–8539 ⊕ www.nietzsches.com) in Allentown. There's a
show most nights.

THE ARTS   The 18,690-seat **HSBC Arena** (⊠ 1 Seymour Knox III Plaza ☎ 716/855–
4100 ⊕ www.hsbcarena.com) presents family shows and concerts with
★ big-name musicians. It's also a major sports venue. **Shea's Performing
Arts Center** (⊠ 646 Main St. ☎ 716/847–1410 ⊕ www.sheas.org) presents concerts, opera, dance, and touring theater performances in an old
movie palace reminiscent of a European opera house. The **University at
Buffalo Center for the Arts** (⊠ North Campus, 103 Center for the Arts
☎ 716/645–2787 ⊕ www.ubcfa.org) encompasses four theaters, the
largest of which is the 1,744-seat main stage. Operas, concerts, dance
performances, theatrical productions, and musicals are among the events
that take place here.

The **Buffalo Philharmonic Orchestra** (⊠ 71 Symphony Cir. ☎ 716/885–
5000 or 800/699–3168 ⊕ www.bpo.org) plays a variety of classical and
pop concerts throughout the year at **Klienhans Music Hall,** which was
designed by architects Eliel and Eero Saarinen and is renowned for its
excellent acoustics. Bring a picnic basket and a blanket and enjoy the

magic of **Shakespeare in the Park** (⌂ Box 716, 14205 ☎ 716/856–4533 ⊕ www.shakespeareindelawarepark.org), free evening performances of full-length plays. Performances take place behind the Rose Gardens in Delaware Park on most nights from late June through August.

The theater district is at the north end of Main Street, between Chippewa and Tupper streets. **Studio Arena Theatre** (✉ 710 Main St. ☎ 716/856–5650 or 800/777–8243 ⊕ www.studioarena.org), Western New York's premier resident theater, puts on seven main-stage and two second-stage productions annually. The smaller second-stage theater is across the street.

Sports & the Outdoors

The state-of-the-art **HSBC Arena** (✉ 1 Seymour Knox III Plaza ☎ 716/855–4100 ⊕ www.hsbcarena.com), downtown near the waterfront, hosts hockey, basketball, and football games.

The National Football League's **Buffalo Bills** (✉ Ralph Wilson Stadium, 1 Bills Dr., Orchard Park ☎ 716/648–1800 or 877/228–4257 ⊕ www.buffalobills.com) have a strong following. Home games of the National Hockey League's **Buffalo Sabres** (✉ HSBC Arena, 1 Seymour H. Knox III Plaza ☎ 716/855–4444 ext. 82 or 888/223–6000 ⊕ www.sabres.com) are played at HSBC Arena. The **Buffalo Bisons** (✉ Dunn Tire Park, 275 Washington St. ☎ 716/843–4373 ⊕ www.bisons.com), a triple-A affiliate of the Cleveland Indians, play minor-league baseball.

Shopping

Broadway Market (✉ 999 Broadway, off Rte. 62 ☎ 716/893–0705 ⊕ www.broadwaymarket.com), a traditional European indoor marketplace, features more than 40 vendors of ethnic delicacies such as kielbasa, pierogi, and bratwurst. For cool gifts and quirky souvenirs, check out **Positively Main Street** (✉ 773 Elmwood Ave. ☎ 716/882–5858) in the Elmwood shopping district.

CHAUTAUQUA-ALLEGHENY

This area covers the southwestern part of the state, bordered by Pennsylvania on the south, Lake Erie on the west, and the Buffalo and Finger Lakes regions on the north and east, respectively. The region includes the Chautauqua Institution (one of the nation's most respected educational and cultural institutions), the state's largest ski resort, an active and industrious Amish community, the beautiful Allegany State Park, and the expansive Allegany Indian Reservation, which includes the city of Salamanca.

Chautauqua County takes its name from its largest lake, which is 22 mi long. French explorers landed on the Lake Erie shores of the Chautauqua area in 1679. Their quest was for a southward passage to the Ohio and Mississippi rivers, and the route connecting Lake Erie with Chautauqua Lake, known as the Portage Trail, offered an answer. Indeed, the dispute between France and England over possession of this trail led to the French and Indian War.

Dunkirk

26 *36 mi southwest of Buffalo.*

Dunkirk, one of the few harbors along the east coast of Lake Erie, lies in a wine-producing area. Relatively mild winters and glacial soil (left by retreating Ice Age glaciers) make the area south of Buffalo between Silver Creek and the Pennsylvania border perfectly suited for growing grapes. The town was named after Dunquerque in northern France, and was most famous in 1851, when it became the terminus of the longest railroad in the world. Dunkirk's historic lighthouse was built in 1875 and is still operating.

Across I–90 is the pretty village of Fredonia. It's home to Fredonia State University, a four-year college in the State University of New York system and the provider of several cultural opportunities.

ALCO-Brooks Railroad Display. Ring the bell of the No. 444, a steam locomotive built in 1916. A 1907 wood-sided boxcar, a locomotive built in Dunkirk, and a restored 1905 wooden New York Central caboose are also part of this museum's displays, which showcase the railroading history of western New York. ⊠ *Chautauqua County Fairgrounds, 1089 Central Ave.* ☎ *716/366–3797* ⊕ *www.s363.com/dkny/display.html* ⊠ *Free* ⊙ *June–Aug.; call for hrs.*

Dunkirk Historical Lighthouse and Veterans Park Museum. The lighthouse has been a beacon in the dark since 1826, and the staircase from the original is part of the "new" light, built in 1857. The downstairs of the keeper's house is a museum that shows how the keeper and his family would have lived. Upstairs rooms are devoted to exhibits about lighthouses, shipping, and the military. There are Coast Guard boats on display, including a 45-foot buoy tender. You can take a guided tour up to the tower. ⊠ *1 Lighthouse Point, off Rte. 5* ☎ *716/366–5050* ⊕ *www.dunkirklighthouse.com* ⊠ *$5* ⊙ *Apr.–June and Sept.–Oct., Mon., Tues., and Thurs.–Sat. 10–2; July and Aug., Mon., Tues., and Thurs.–Sat. 10–4.*

Lake Erie State Park. On a bluff overlooking Lake Erie, this park has spectacular scenery. You may swim, hike, fish, and picnic here in warm-weather months. A campground (open late April to late October) includes 102 campsites and 10 cabins. In winter there's cross-country skiing and snowmobiling. The park is off Route 5 about 7 mi west of Dunkirk. ⊠ *5905 Lake Rd., Brockton* ☎ *716/792–9214, 800/456–2267 camping reservations* ⊕ *nysparks.state.ny.us* ⊠ *Park $7 (daily late May–early Sept. and weekends early Sept.–Oct.)* ⊙ *Daily dawn–dusk.*

FESTIVALS & FAIRS **Chautauqua County Fair.** A large part of this seven-day fair, held at the end of July, centers on animals: pig and chicken exhibits, horse shows, livestock sales, a petting zoo. Other attractions include kids' tractor pulls, karaoke competitions, a baby crawl, line dancing, magic shows, and amusement rides. ⊠ *Chautauqua County Fairgrounds, 1089 Central Ave.* ☎ *716/366–4752* ⊕ *www.chautauquacountyfair.org.*

Where to Stay & Eat

$ ✕ **Demetri's on the Lake.** Eat Greek or American on a deck overlooking Lake Erie. Entrées such as lamb, chicken souvlaki, prime rib, steak, and seafood go well with the extensive wine list. The Sunday brunch is wonderfully indulgent. ⊠ *6 Lake Shore Dr. W* ☎ *716/366–4187* ▤ *AE, D, MC, V.*

$–$$ ✕▥ **Ramada Inn Dunkirk.** The brick four-story chain hotel overlooks Lake Erie's Chadwick Bay. Rooms are standard, with contemporary furniture; some have in-room whirlpool tubs. In the Windjammer's restaurant, a boat wheel and fish tank create a nautical theme. Menu options include Delmonico steak, salmon, and chicken Alfredo. ⊠ *30 Lake Shore Dr. E, 14048* ☎ *716-366-8350* ⊟ *716-366-8899* ⊕ *www.ramada. com* ➮ *132 rooms* ⚘ *Restaurant, café, in-room data ports, some in-room hot tubs, some refrigerators, cable TV with movies, 1 indoor and 1 outdoor pool, gym, hot tub, sauna, marina, bar, laundry service, meeting rooms, some pets allowed (fee), no-smoking rooms* ▤ *AE, D, MC, V.*

★ **¢–$** ▥ **White Inn.** Parts of this handsome inn date from 1868, when it was a residence owned by the White family. A subsequent owner expanded the building and turned it into an inn in 1919. Victorian antiques and reproduction pieces furnish the rooms, many of which have floral wallcoverings. The suites are very spacious. The Presidential Suite has a king-size bed, a sleeper sofa, a fireplace, and a whirlpool tub. The highly regarded restaurant serves mostly Continental fare that includes specialties such as broiled filet mignon topped with Canadian bacon, Gouda, and Bourbon-mustard demi-glaze, and grilled salmon fillet in a Dijon mustard-and-honey glaze. Prime rib is served Friday through Saturday evenings. ⊠ *52 E. Main St., Fredonia 14063* ☎ *716/672–2103 or 888/ 373–3664* ⊟ *716/672–2107* ⊕ *www.whiteinn.com* ➮ *12 rooms, 11 suites* ⚘ *Restaurant, in-room data ports, some in-room hot tubs, some microwaves, some refrigerators, cable TV, bar, business services, no-smoking rooms* ▤ *AE, D, DC, MC, V* ¶◎¶ *BP.*

Nightlife & the Arts

The **Fredonia Opera House** (⊠ 9–11 Church St., Fredonia ☎ 716/679–1891 ⊕ www.fredopera.org), in a restored 1891 Victorian building downtown, presents concerts, children's theater, films, and other forms of entertainment. It's also the site of a baroque-music festival in June. Guided tours of the opera house are available by appointment. I. M. Pei and Partners designed the **Michael C. Rockefeller Arts Center** (⊠, Fredonia ☎716/673-3217 ⊕www.fredonia.edu/rac), on the State University of New York's Fredonia campus, in 1969. The complex encompasses two theaters, a 1,200-seat concert hall, and two art galleries. The rich schedule includes more than 200 plays and productions each year.

Westfield

16 mi southwest of Dunkirk.

As the home of a Welch's plant, Westfield calls itself the grape-juice capital of the world. Several wineries are nearby, off U.S. 20. Antiques stores and craft shops cluster around the village square, and scattered throughout Westfield are Federal-style mansions. At nearby Cassadaga Lake is the Lily Dale Assembly, a spiritualist center begun in 1879 that still attracts mediums and the psychically curious.

McClurg Mansion. The handsome 14-room Federal-style mansion on the Westfield village green was built in 1820. The Chautauqua County Historical Society runs the house, which is on the National Register of Historic Places and is decorated in high Victorian style. Displays include Civil War documents and American Indian and military artifacts. ⊠ *15 E. Main St.* ☎ *716/326–2977* ⊕ *www.mcclurgmuseum.org* 🖻 *$3* ⊙ *Tues.–Sat., 10–4.*

off the beaten path

LILY DALE ASSEMBLY – This religious colony of Victorian houses was founded on the shores of Lake Cassadaga in 1879, during a period of increased interest in Spiritualism, which believes that the spirits of the dead live on and that some people can communicate with them. Today the world's largest spiritualist community has a 10-week summer season (late June–Labor Day), which offers workshops, medium readings, a research library, lectures, and a variety of recreational activities, including fishing, swimming, and picnicking. Lily Dale has lodging, restaurants, and its own volunteer fire department. You can go for the day or stay overnight, but call ahead for readings with the most popular mediums. Gate passes during the summer season are $5–$10. ⊠ *5 Melrose Park, west of Rte. 60, Lily Dale* ☎ *716/595–8721* ⊕ *www.lilydaleassembly.com.*

Where to Stay & Eat

¢–$ 🏨 **Candlelight Lodge.** Built in 1851, this Italianate brick Victorian mansion is listed on the National Register of Historic Places. The inn has spiral walnut staircases, arched windows, and fireplaces. The owners of the inn also own a large antiques store, and rooms here are furnished with Victorian and other pieces. Some have four-poster beds. The country-casual efficiency is available by the week or month. Common areas include two parlors and a patio. Antiques shops, stores, and restaurants are within walking distance, and the Chautauqua Institute is a 15-minute drive away. Captain Storm's House, a sibling inn, is next door. ⊠ *143 E. Main St./U.S. 20, 14787* ☎ *716/326–2830* ⊕ *www.landmarkacres.com* 🛏 *4 rooms, 2 suites, 1 efficiency* ⚘ *Picnic area, some kitchenettes, cable TV; no room phones* ⊟ *No credit cards (except for deposit)* ⊙ *Closed Jan.–Feb.*

★ $ ✕🏨 **William Seward Inn.** The lovely 1837 Greek revival inn has traditional rooms furnished with period antiques and reproductions, including four-poster and canopy beds. Some rooms are dressed in flirty florals and ruffles, whereas others have a more tailored look. A few have an extra-large whirlpool tub or gas fireplace. The restaurant ($$$$; reservations essential) serves a four-course prix-fixe menu that gives you several appetizers and entrées to choose from. The food is contemporary, with dishes such as mango spring rolls with peanut sauce (a starter), rack of lamb with a honeyed hazelnut crust, and salmon fillet in pinot gris–caper sauce. Note that the owners have cats and a dog. ⊠ *6645 S. Portage Rd., 14787* ☎ *716/326–4151* 🖷 *716/326–4163* ⊕ *www.williamsewardinn.com* 🛏 *12 rooms* ⚘ *Restaurant, some in-room hot tubs; no room phones, no room TVs, no kids under 10, no smoking* ⊟ *AE, D, MC, V* ⊧❘ *BP.*

Shopping

More than 40 vendors participate in the **Cross Roads Farm & Craft Market** (✉ Rte. 21 between Westfield and Sherman ☎ 716/326–6278 or 877/512–7307), open 9–5 Saturday from early May to mid-December. The mix includes hand-crafted furniture, herbs and spices, Amish leather goods, hand-knit sweaters, collectibles, wooden toys, and candles.

Chautauqua

★ ㉗ *10 mi east of Westfield.*

The Victorian splendor of this self-contained 856-acre village and cultural-education center on Chautauqua Lake attracts as many as 180,000 visitors each summer. It all began in 1874, when John Heyl Vincent, a Methodist minister, and Lewis Miller, an industrialist, set up a training center for Sunday-school teachers here. The **Chautauqua Institution** (✉ 1 Ames Ave. ☎ 716/357–6250, 716/357–6200, 800/836–2787 ⊕ www.ciweb.org) rapidly grew into a summer-long cultural encampment. More than 2,000 events take place here from late June through August, including lectures, art exhibitions, outdoor symphonies, theater, dance performances, opera, and open-enrollment classes.

The village has small winding streets lined with gas lights and beautiful Victorian houses, which are often outfitted in bright colors, turrets, multiple gables, and gingerbread trim. The **Miller Bell Tower** is the most recognizable landmark on the lake shore and has become the symbol of the institution; tunes are played three or four times a day, and the Miller Bell is rung manually 15 minutes before amphitheater lectures and evening programs.

Seats for the **Chautauqua Symphony Orchestra** and other large events held at the 6,500-seat Chautauqua Amphitheater are on a first-come, first-served basis. Musicians as diverse as Peter, Paul, and Mary; 10,000 Maniacs; Glenn Miller; and Natalie Cole have performed in the theater, which has a roof and houses an enormous pipe organ. Norton Memorial Hall, a 1,365-seat art-deco building, is where the **Chautauqua Opera Company** presents four English-language operas each season.

The institution's recreational activities complement its cultural opportunities. You may fish, swim, play tennis, golf, or rent sailboats, motorboats, or canoes from the concessions on the lake. The village, a National Historic District, also includes B&Bs, hotels, inns, guest houses, apartments, and condominiums, as well as several restaurants and eateries. You may use a car when dropping off and picking up your luggage, but otherwise car usage is extremely limited here. Lots near the entrance gates offer daily and long-term parking (fee). A free shuttle bus and tram travel through the campus during the season. Another no-no is alcohol, which cannot be purchased or consumed in public here.

Gates passes, required even if you overnight on the grounds, are $7–$39, depending on how long you stay and what you plan to do while you're here. Narrated bus tours of the grounds are available.

Craft Festivals at the Chautauqua Institution. Two annual shows are held in early July and again in mid-August, during the Chautauqua Institution season. More than 60 artists and craftspeople participate, displaying their paintings, jewelry, pottery, carvings, and other works. ✒ *Chautauqua Craft Alliance, Box 89, Mayville 14757* ☎ *716/753–0240 or 716/753–1851* ⊕ *www.chautauquacraftalliance.org.*

Where to Stay & Eat

The Chautauqua Institution publishes an extensive list of on-campus accommodations, including apartments, houses, condominiums, hotels, inns, and other properties. It's available on the institution Web site, or you may request a copy by telephone. Many people who attend the summer program return year after year, so places tend to book up early. If you aren't able to secure lodging in Chautauqua, check in neighboring villages and towns such as Maple Springs, Mayville, Bemus Point, and Jamestown.

$$ ✕ **Giambrone's Seafood House.** This casual, popular lunch spot overlooks Chautauqua Lake. The menu includes fresh shrimp, lobster, scallops, and clams, as well as prime rib, pastas, and sandwiches. ⊠ *7 Water St./Rte. 394, Mayville* ☎ *716/753–2525* ⊟ *MC, V* ⊘ *Closed Mon. and Tues. No dinner.*

$–$$ ✕ **Dick's Harbor House.** The family-style restaurant, 12 mi northeast of Chautauqua, is known for its 8-foot salad bar and Friday fish fry. Prime rib is also popular here. ⊠ *95 W. Lake Rd./Rte. 394, Mayville* ☎ *716/753–2707* ⊟ *AE, D, MC, V.*

$$$$ ✕▥ **Athenaeum Hotel.** The hotel, opened in 1881 on the Chautauqua Institution grounds, frequently hosted Thomas Edison and was one of the first electrified hotels in the country. Modern guests stay for the architectural splendor rather than the technological advances. Rooms are furnished in Victorian and Arts and Crafts styles, and rates include three meals a day. Dinner here is a five-course prix-fixe affair ($$$$; reservations required). The Athenaeum hosts special themed weekends but otherwise is mostly closed from early September to early June. ⊠ *26 S. Lake Dr., 14722* ☎ *800/821–1881* ▤ *716/357–2833* ⊕ *www.athenaeum-hotel.com* ↝ *57 rooms* ♦ *Restaurant, room service, some in-room data ports, cable TV, dry cleaning, laundry service; no smoking* ⊟ *AE, D, MC, V* ⊘ *Closed early Sept.–late June* ⋙ *AI.*

$ ✕▥ **Webb's Lake Resort.** The family-owned and -run complex, near Chautauqua Lake, includes a two-story motel, Webb's Captain's Table restaurant, a candy store, and an 18-hole miniature-golf course. Exterior corridors connect the rooms, which have traditional furnishings. Some rooms have fireplaces, whirlpool tubs, or balconies. The restaurant, which serves American fare with an emphasis on seafood, has a deck overlooking the lake. Dishes include broiled shrimp and scallops, prime rib, chicken and veal Parmesan, and surf-and-turf combos. The menu includes a few vegetarian choices, like veggie lasagna. ⊠ *115 W. Lake Rd., Mayville 14757* ☎ *716/753–2161* ▤ *716/753–1383* ⊕ *www. webbsworld.com* ↝ *53 rooms, 1 suite* ♦ *Restaurant, some in-room hot tubs, cable TV, pool, miniature golf, gym, sauna, laundry facilities; no smoking* ⊟ *AE, D, MC, V.*

$$-$$$ 🖼 **The Spencer.** Rooms at this Victorian hotel are individually decorated and named for great authors. The decor varies considerably from room to room. The Agatha Christie room is decked out with fern-print wallpaper that has a sort of psychedelic effect; the Isabel Allende room has cactus murals on the walls and a desert-hued theme. Some rooms are small and cramped, whereas others are quite capacious. Many have hand-painted murals or faux finishes on the walls or ceilings. Gardens surround the inn, which stays open all year. During the Chautauqua Institution season, the minimum required stay is a week. ✉ *25 Palestine Ave.* ☎ *716/357–3785 or 800/398–1306* 🖨 *716/357–4733* ⊕ *www. thespencer.com* ↪ *21 rooms, 5 suites* ⚲ *Dining room, in-room data ports, some in-room hot tubs, some kitchenettes, cable TV, in-room VCRs, Internet; no smoking* ⊟ *No credit cards* ❑ *CP.*

Bemus Point

14 mi southeast of Chautauqua (traveling clockwise around Chautauqua Lake).

Bemus Point is the largest community on the north shore of Chautauqua Lake. In summer the population swells with vacationers who come from all over New York and Canada to enjoy the lake and the Chautauqua Institution, which is on the opposite shore.

Long Point State Park on Lake Chautauqua. This busy, 320-acre park on Chautauqua Lake has a swimming beach, a bathhouse, a modern boat-launch facility, a marina, and a playground. You may hike, bike, snowmobile, and cross-country ski here, or simply have a picnic. Muskellunge are a draw for fishing enthusiasts, but the lake also has bass, pike, and other fish. In winter you may ice fish. ✉ *4459 Rte. 430* ☎ *716/386–2722* ⊕ *nysparks.state.ny.us* 🚗 *Parking $5* ☉ *Daily dawn–dusk.*

Midway Park. A highlight of this park on Chautauqua Lake is a restored 1946 Herschell carousel, built in western New York's North Tonawanda. Many rides, including a miniature train, are geared for the younger set. You also find bumper boats, go-carts, a roller-skating rink, and a rock-climbing wall. Entry is free; rides are about $1 each. ✉ *4859 Rte. 430, Maple Springs* ☎ *716/386–3165* ⊕ *www.midway-park.com* 🚗 *Free* ☉ *Late May–early Sept.; call for schedule.*

Where to Stay & Eat

$$-$$$ ✕ **Ye Hare 'N' Hounds Inn.** The 1915 English-style country inn has brick fireplaces, cloth-covered tables, and lots of windows overlooking Chautauqua Lake. A porch has open-air dining in season. The menu blends Continental and seafood dishes with contemporary preparations like broiled tenderloin with artichoke hearts, balsamic wild onions, and honey-balsamic glaze, or grilled pork loin paired with sautéed shrimp, roasted asparagus and red peppers, and pepper sauce. Scallops Calvados are crusted with almonds and served with apple brandy cream sauce in a roasted acorn squash. Specialties include rack of lamb. Desserts are made in-house. ✉ *64 Lakeside Dr.* ☎ *716/386–2181* ⊟ *AE, MC, V* ☉ *No lunch.*

$–$$$ ✗ **Italian Fisherman.** Eat indoors or outside on the multilevel covered deck overlooking Chautauqua Lake. (Heat torches warm deck diners up on cool days.) The eatery is known for seafood and Italian dishes—cioppino, large sautéed shrimp with spicy tomato sauce over pasta, grilled catch of the day. The drinks list is extensive, and the place often hosts live music and other entertainment. ✉ *61 Lakeside Dr.* ☎ *716/386–7000* ▤ *AE, D, MC, V* ⊘ *Closed late Sept.–Apr.*

¢–$ ✗ **Bemus Point Inn.** Open until 2 PM, this informal breakfast-and-lunch spot is known for its huge cinnamon rolls. Sandwiches, finger foods, salads, and desserts are also popular. ✉ *4958 Main St.* ☎ *716/386–2221* ▤ *AE, D, MC, V* ⊘ *No dinner.*

$ ▦ **Maple Springs Lake Side Inn.** The gracious Dutch Colonial sits on 11 acres adjacent to Chautauqua Lake and 2 mi from the Chautauqua Institution. The inn has porches and fireplaces, and wireless Internet access is available. Rooms are simply decorated and homey, with traditional furnishings. Three of the suites have kitchenettes and are good family options. There is a cross-country skiing trail near the property. ✉ *4696 Chautauqua Ave., Maple Springs 14756* ☎ *716/386–2500* ⬦ *4 rooms, 4 suites* ➅ *Dining room, some kitchenettes, some cable TV, lake, beach, dock, Internet, no-smoking rooms; no room phones, no TV in some rooms* ▤ *MC, V* ⑩ *BP.*

Jamestown

㉘ *11 mi southeast of Bemus Point.*

Jamestown, founded in 1811, is at the eastern end of Chautauqua Lake. One of Jamestown's claims to fame is that it was the childhood home of Lucille Ball. It was here that Ball first performed her wacky comedy acts, which are now commemorated every year during the Lucille Ball Hometown Celebration. Another well-known Jamestown native was Roger Tory Peterson, who wrote and illustrated the *Peterson Field Guides,* which document the flora and fauna of various U. S. regions.

Fenton History Center. Reuben Fenton, governor of New York from 1865 to 1869, had this brick Italianate mansion built in 1863. It contains Victorian period rooms (some quite ornate) and exhibits showcasing the history of Chautauqua Lake, the life and career of Lucille Ball, and Jamestown's Swedish and Italian communities. Also of interest are the archival and genealogical library and the Civil War exhibits. ✉ *67 Washington St.* ☎ *716/664–6256* ⊕ *www.fentonhistorycenter.org* ▤ *$5* ⊘ *Early Jan.–late Nov., Mon.–Sat. 10–4; late Nov.–early Jan., Mon.–Sat. 10–4, Sun. 1–4.*

Lucy-Desi Museum. A collection of Lucille Ball and Desi Arnaz's personal effects is on display here in exhibits that follow the lives and careers of the two comedy stars. Several of the exhibits are interactive, and there are video presentations. Two annual festivals—Lucy-Desi Days, over Memorial Day weekend, and Lucille Ball's Birthday Celebration, in early August—celebrate the two stars. ✉ *212 Pine St.* ☎ *716/484–0800* ⊕ *www.lucy-desi.com* ▤ *$5* ⊘ *May–Oct., Mon.–Sat. 10–5:30, Sun. 1–5; Nov.–Apr., Sat. 10–5:30, Sun. 1–5.*

Panama Rocks Scenic Park. The rock outcropping here, 14 mi west of downtown Jamestown, is more than 360 million years old and spans 25 acres. The park has caves, 60-foot-high cliffs, and crevices said to have been used by native Americans as shelter and as places to keep meat cool in summer. Outlaws are also said to have used the rocks as hiding places. As you hike along the 1-mi self-guided trail here, you may find rare mosses, wildflowers, ferns, and oddly shaped tree roots. ⊠ *11 Rock Hill Rd., Panama* ☎ *716/782–2845* ⊕ *www.panamarocks.com* ⊠ *$6* ☯ *May–late Oct., daily 10–5.*

Roger Tory Peterson Institute of Natural History. Named for Jamestown native and noted naturalist Roger Tory Peterson (1908–96), this 27-acre center seeks to educate children about nature. You may hike the wooded trails, or explore one of the natural-history exhibits. The gallery shows a selection of works by Peterson and others. ⊠ *311 Curtis St.* ☎ *716/665–2473 or 800/758–6841* ⊕ *www.rtpi.org* ⊠ *$4* ☯ *Center Tues.–Sat. 10–4, Sun. 1–5; grounds daily dawn–dusk.*

Where to Stay & Eat

★ **$$–$$$** ✕ **MacDuff's.** An intimate dining experience awaits you at this eight-table restaurant in an 1873 town house. The elegant furnishings include red linen table cloths, Queen Anne chairs with floral upholstery, and brass chandeliers and sconces. The menu leans to the French side, with entrées like twin tenderloin fillets with port, Stilton cheese, and green-peppercorn sauce, or broiled salmon fillet with pesto hollandaise. Desserts include lavender crème brûlée and homemade orange ice cream that's served in a bittersweet chocolate shell and sprinkled with chocolate bits. ⊠ *317 Pine St.* ☎ *716/664–9414* ⊟ *AE, MC, V* ☯ *Closed Sun. No lunch.*

¢ ✕ **Kaldi's Coffee House.** In addition to great coffee, this low-key java joint serves sandwiches, salads, and homemade soups, including some vegetarian options. ⊠ *106 E. 3rd St.* ☎ *716/484–8904* ⊟ *No credit cards* ☯ *No dinner. Closed Sun.*

$ ▥ **Comfort Inn.** At this two-story chain property at the edge of town, rooms are standard and have small windows. Some units have in-room jetted tubs. Wireless Internet access is a plus. ⊠ *2800 N. Main St.* ☎ *716/664–5920 or 800/453–7155* 🖷 *716/664–3068* ⊕ *www.comfortinn.com* ➷ *101 rooms* ☖ *in-room data ports, some in-room hot tubs, some microwaves, some refrigerators, cable TV with movies and video games, bar, Internet, business services, some pets allowed (fee), no-smoking rooms* ⊟ *AE, D, DC, MC, V* ☷ *CP.*

¢–$ ▥ **Holiday Inn Jamestown.** The eight-story chain hotel is in Jamestown's business district. Rooms have large windows and traditional furnishings in muted color schemes. Rooms have large desks, and high-speed Internet access is available. ⊠ *150 W. 4th St.* ☎ *716/664–3400 or 800/528–8791* 🖷 *716/484–3304* ➷ *144 rooms, 2 suites* ⊕ *www.holiday-inn.com* ☖ *Restaurant, room service, in-room data ports, some microwaves, some refrigerators, cable TV with movies, indoor pool, bar, dry cleaning, laundry facilities, business services, meeting rooms, no-smoking rooms* ⊟ *AE, D, DC, MC, V.*

Nightlife & the Arts

The renovated 1,269-seat **Reg Lenna Civic Center** (⊠ 116 E. 3rd St. ☎ 716/484–7070 ⊕ www.reglenna.com) began life in 1923 as the Palace Theatre, a venue for vaudeville acts and later mostly films. These days it hosts concerts and other live shows as well as movies.

Ellicottville

29 *32 mi northeast of Jamestown.*

Holiday Valley, a popular regional ski resort, is the main draw of the small village of Ellicottville. This is where Buffalo and Rochester area residents go to get in some weekend skiing. Boutiques, restaurants, and nightlife spots line the downtown streets.

★ ☺ **Griffis Sculpture Park.** More than 200 sculptures by prominent local, national, and international artists are displayed in a variety of natural settings at this 400-acre park. Kids enjoy touching and climbing on the pieces, which actually are allowed here. About 10 mi of hiking trails vein the park, which is 1 mi north of Ellicottville. ⊠ *6902 Mill Valley Rd., East Otto* ☎ *716/257–9344* ⊕ *www.griffispark.org* ⊠ *Free* ☉ *May–Oct., daily dawn–dusk.*

Nannen Arboretum. Begun in 1977 as an adjunct to the Cornell Cooperative Extension facility, the arboretum occupies 8 acres with more than 400 unusual trees and shrub. The herb garden has 300-plus species, and there's a popular Japanese meditation garden. ⊠ *28 Parkside Dr.* ☎ *716/699–2377 or 716/945–5200* ⊠ *Free* ☉ *Daily dawn–dusk.*

Where to Stay & Eat

The ski season is the peak season here.

$–$$$ ✕ **Dina's.** In a relaxed space with a long bar and banquette seating, this restaurant offers several interesting pizzas, including one with red-pepper pesto, prosciutto, cappicola, fresh mozzarella, goat cheese, and basil. Spinach ravioli in marinara sauce with a touch of mint, and pork ribs with shallot-and–cheddar cheese mashed potatoes are among the specialties. The menu also includes seafood, steaks, and chicken dishes. ⊠ *15 Washington St.* ☎ *716/699–5330* ▭ *AE, D, MC, V.*

$–$$ ✕ **Ellicottville Brewing Company.** The trendy, rough-hewn microbrewery draws a young crowd. The shepherd's pie is popular, and the menu also includes English-style fish-and-chips and assorted grilled steaks. You may eat outside in the German beer garden, which has a brick patio and vines climbing the walls. Tours of the brewery are available. ⊠ *28A Monroe St.* ☎ *716/699–2537* ▭ *AE, MC, V* ☉ *Closed Mon. in May–June and Sept.–Nov.*

$$–$$$ ▭ **Inn at Holiday Valley.** The inn is at the base of the Holiday Valley ski resort's Sunrise Quad ski lift. In winter a free shuttle brings guests to the main chalet. Most rooms have patios or balconies with mountain views; suites have cathedral ceilings, fireplaces, wet bars, and jet tubs. The decor is traditional but streamlined. ⊠ *Rte. 219, 14731* ☎ *716/699–2345 or 800/323–0020* ⊕ *www.holidayvalley.com* ⇴ *95 rooms, 7 suites* ⌂ *in-room data ports, some in-room hot tubs, some microwaves, some minibars, some refrigerators, cable TV, golf privileges, indoor-out-*

door pool, gym, massage, sauna, bicycles, hiking, cross-country skiing, downhill skiing, library, laundry facilities, meeting rooms, no-smoking rooms ▤ AE, D, DC, MC, V ¶◎¶ CP.

$$ ▦ **Jefferson Inn of Ellicottville.** The Victorian house with a wraparound porch is within walking distance of shops, restaurants, and bars. The B&B rooms are homey, with simple furnishings; the suite has a sitting area with a fireplace. The two self-contained efficiency units are suitable for families with small children or pets. Breakfast is included only in the B&B rooms. ⊠ 3 Jefferson St., 14731 ☎ 716/699–5869 or 800/ 577–8451 🖷 716/699–5758 ⊕ www.thejeffersoninn.com ↩ 4 rooms, 1 suite, 2 efficiencies ⚖ Dining room, in-room data ports, some kitchenettes, some cable TV, some in-room VCRs, outdoor hot tub, some pets allowed; no TV in some rooms, no smoking ▤ AE, D, MC, V ¶◎¶ BP.

Sports & the Outdoors

SKI AREA The **Holiday Valley Resort** (⊠ Rte. 219 ☎ 716/699–2345 ⊕ www. holidayvalley.com) has a 750-foot vertical drop, 53 trails, 95% snow-making coverage, a snowboarding area, three base lodges, 12 lifts, and a skiing and snowboarding school. For night skiing, 36 trails are lit. Trails in the golf-course area may be used by cross-country skiers and snow-shoers. Full-day lift tickets are $38–$44. The resort includes ski-out-your-back-door accommodations. In summer the 18-hole golf course, golf school, tennis courts, three pools, and mountain-biking trails are the main draws.

Salamanca

㉚ 11 mi south of Ellicottville.

Salamanca, on the broad Allegheny River, has the distinction of being the only U.S. city on an American Indian reservation. The region was settled by the Seneca Nation, which leases the land to the government. The small but well executed Seneca Iroquois National Museum is worth a visit. South of Salamanca is the four-season Allegany State Park, which abounds with recreational opportunities.

Allegany State Park. Its 65,000 acres make this the largest park in the state system. More than 85 mi of trails vein the park, which encompasses forest, meadow, lakes and streams, and hills. Hikes here range from short, easy strolls to an 18-mi trek over rugged terrain. The park has sandy swimming areas, bridle trails, boat launches and rentals, fishing, miniature golf, mountain-bike rentals, tennis courts, and picnic areas. Among many other planned activities, the park hosts free summer concerts in the Quaker Beach area. The 90 mi of snowmobiling trails are a big draw in winter. Thanks to the **Art Roscoe Ski Touring Area,** Nordic skiers have access to 25 mi of groomed trails, which are used for mountain biking in warm weather. Campgrounds include tent and trailer sites as well as winterized cabins and cottages. ⊠ 2373 State Park Rte. 1 ☎ 716/ 354–9121 or 716/354–2182, 800/456–2267 camping reservations ⊕ nysparks.state.ny.us ⊟ Parking $6 ◷ Daily dawn–dusk.

Salamanca Rail Museum. A fully restored 1912 passenger depot offers a fascinating look at the history of the Erie Lackawanna Railroad, whose anticipated arrival led to the creation of the city of Salamanca. Exhibits include artifacts, memorabilia, and an extensive collection of vintage photographs. ⊠ *170 Main St.* ☎ *716/945–3133* 🎫 *Free* ☉ *Apr. and Oct.–Dec., Tues.–Sat. 10–5, Sun. noon–5; May–Sept., Mon.–Sat. 10–5, Sun. noon–5.*

Seneca Iroquois National Museum. The history and current culture of the Seneca Nation and of the Iroquois Confederacy is explored at this museum on the Allegany Indian Reservation. Displays include a partially reconstructed longhouse, silver and beadwork, baskets, corn-husk items, and artworks. ⊠ *794–814 Broad St.* ☎ *716/945–1738* ⊕ *www.senecamuseum.org* 🎫 *$4* ☉ *Apr.–mid-Oct., Tues.–Sat. 10–5, Sun. noon–5; mid-Oct.–Dec. and Feb.–Mar., weekdays 9–5.*

Where to Stay

$ 🏨 **Holiday Inn Express.** The decor at this two-story hotel is contemporary. Rooms have desks and high-speed Internet access; some suites have dining areas, kitchenettes, and whirlpool tubs. ⊠ *779 Broad St., 14779* ☎ *716/945–7600* 🖷 *716/945–7200* ⊕ *www.holiday-inn.com* ⇋ *50 rooms, 18 suites* ♿ *In-room data ports, some in-room hot tubs, some kitchenettes, some microwaves, some refrigerators, cable TV, some in-room VCRs, indoor pool, gym, hot tub, dry cleaning, laundry facilities, laundry service, Internet, business services, meeting rooms, car rental, some pets allowed (fee), no-smoking rooms* ☱ *AE, D, DC, MC, V* ¶⊙¶ *CP.*

Olean

③ *18 mi east of Salamanca.*

Olean, founded in 1804, is a community of 16,000 nestled in hills formed by receding glaciers. It's home to St. Bonaventure University, two community colleges, and manufacturers of assorted goods from Cutco knives to Drusser Rand turbines. The old public library, a National Historic Landmark facing the tree-lined town square, has been converted into a restaurant. From Olean you may follow a paved path—on foot, skates, or by bicycle—along the Allegheny River.

Rock City. Perched at the edge of the Allegany Mountains, Rock City is believed to have the largest exposure of quartz conglomerate in the world. Some of the towering prehistoric rock formations are several stories high. Pathways lead you between huge boulders and through the strange terrain. ⊠ *505 Rock City Rd.* ☎ *716/372–7790* 🎫 *$4.50* ☉ *May–June and Sept.–Oct., daily 9–6; July–Aug., daily 9–8.*

Where to Stay & Eat

¢–$ ✗ **Beef 'N' Barrel.** This casual restaurant is known for its generous portions, in-house bakery, and friendly staff. The menu is beef focused, with a special emphasis on roast-beef sandwiches and platters. Juicy roast beef is carved up and served on hard rolls; accompaniments may include German or American potato salad, baked beans, salad, mashed potatoes, fries, or cole slaw. Burgers, salads, and soups round out the menu. ⊠ *146 N. Union St.* ☎ *716/372–2985* ☱ *AE, D, DC, MC, V* ☉ *Closed Sun.*

★ ¢ ✕⌗ **Old Library Restaurant and Bed & Breakfast.** The 1895 Victorian B&B, facing the tree-lined main square, has original oak, mahogany, and maple woodwork, including parquet floors, and stained-glass windows. Guest rooms, most outfitted in a country look, have period antiques; a few have brass beds. The Durkin Suite, which has sitting and dining areas, a queen four-poster bed, and a private entrance, is the most elegant. Next door to the B&B is the restaurant ($–$$$), which occupies a National Historic Landmark that was built as the town library with funds from Andrew Carnegie. Converted to a restaurant in 1983, it retains most of its original architecture. The menu is diverse, with Italian, French, and American dishes. Six-cheese ravioli is served with pesto cream and sautéed spinach; sautéed antelope medallions come with peppercorn sauce; a surf-and-turn combo joins New York strip steak and jumbo scampi. ⌧ *120 S. Union St., 14760* ☎ *716/373–9804* ⊟ *716/373–2462* ⊕ *www.oldlibraryrestaurant.com* ⇝ *6 rooms, 2 suites* ⚘ *Restaurant, room service, in-room data ports, cable TV with movies, business services; no smoking* ⊟ *AE, D, DC, MC, V* ⊘ *BP.*

¢–$$ ⌗ **Hampton Inn Olean.** The three-story chain inn is within 5 mi of Rock City Park and St. Bonaventure University. Wireless Internet access is available in the rooms, which are standard. Some rooms have whirlpool tubs, whereas others may have only showers. ⌧ *101 Main St., 14760* ☎ *716/375–1000* ⊟ *716/375–1279 or 800/426–7866* ⊕ *www.hamptoninn.com* ⇝ *76 rooms* ⚘ *Some in-room hot tubs, some microwaves, some refrigerators, cable TV, some in-room VCRs, indoor pool, gym, laundry facilities, laundry service, meeting rooms; no pets* ⊟ *AE, D, DC, V* ⎀ *CP.*

Shopping

The Cuba area has been known as a cheese center since the late 19th century. Today tourists flock to the **Cuba Cheese Shoppe** (⌧ 53 Genesee St., Cuba ☎ 716/968–3949) to buy locally made cheddar cheese, Old York cheddar spread, or any of the 100-plus varieties of imported and domestic cheeses the store offers. Cuba is 15 mi east of Olean.

WESTERN NEW YORK A TO Z

To research prices, get advice from other travelers, and book travel arrangements, visit www.fodors.com.

AIR TRAVEL

Buffalo Niagara International Airport is the main airport in the region. Continental Airlines affiliates fly direct to and from New York City (Newark Liberty International Airport) and Albany, with connections from the latter to Long Island (Islip), Adirondack Regional Airport, and the Plattsburgh airport. JetBlue Airlines has service between Buffalo and New York City's JFK International Airport, Northwest Airlines flies to Newark, and American Airlines flies into LaGuardia Airport. US Airways flies into Albany and LaGuardia.

Another option, especially if you plan to tour the eastern part of the region, is to fly into the Greater Rochester International Airport, rent a car, and drive the rest of the way. *See* the Finger Lakes A to Z section *in* Chapter 7 for more information about flights to and from Rochester. *See* Air

Travel *in* Smart Travel Tips A to Z for more information about the Buffalo and Rochester airports and for major airlines' contact information.

BUS TRAVEL

Greyhound and Trailways link the region with New York City and much of the rest of the state. Tickets for the two bus lines are interchangeable. Stops include Buffalo, Ellicottville, Niagara Falls, Olean, and Salamanca. Shortline travels between New York City and Olean.

🚌 **Adirondack, Pine Hill, and New York Trailways** ☎ 800/858-8555 or 800/225-6815 ⊕ www.trailwaysny.com. **Greyhound** ☎ 800/231-2222 ⊕ www.greyhound.com. **Shortline Coach USA** ☎ 800/631-8405 ⊕ www.shortlinebus.com.

CAR RENTAL

Alamo, Avis, Budget, Enterprise Rent-a-Car, Hertz, and National Car Rental have counters at Buffalo Niagara International Airport. Budget also has a branch in Niagara Falls. *See* Car Rental *in* Smart Travel Tips A to Z for national agencies' contact information.

CAR TRAVEL

Chautauqua is largely a no-car zone, but there are parking lots near the main gates. You should not have any trouble parking in Niagara Falls or Buffalo.

EMERGENCIES

In an emergency, dial 911.

🚑 **Hospitals Buffalo General Hospital** ✉ 100 High St., Buffalo ☎ 716/859-7100 ⊕ bgh.kaleidahealth.org. **Niagara Falls Memorial Medical Center** ✉ 621 10th St., Niagara Falls ☎ 716/278-4000 ⊕ www.nfmmc.org. **WCA Hospital** ✉ 207 Foote Ave., Jamestown ☎ 716/484-2121 ⊕ www.wcahospital.org. **Westfield Memorial Hospital** ✉ 189 E. Main St., Westfield ☎ 716/326-4921 ⊕ www.wmhinc.org.

LODGING

The Web site of the Inns of Chautauqua County has information about nine lodgings in the area. The Western New York Bed & Breakfast Association represents more than a dozen member B&Bs in Buffalo, Ellicottville, Lewiston, Lockport, Niagara Falls, and Youngstown.

🏨 **Inns of Chautauqua County** ⊕ www.bbonline.com/ny/chautauquainns/. **Western New York Bed & Breakfast Association** ⊕ www.bbwny.com.

SPORTS & THE OUTDOORS

Also *see* Sports & the Outdoors *in* Smart Travel Tips A to Z for information.

SNOWMOBILING Snowmobiling is huge in western New York. Chautauqua County alone has more than 400 mi of groomed trails. You may obtain a trails map from the Chautauqua County Visitors Bureau. Cattaraugus County also has nearly 400 mi of snowmobile trails, not including the 90 mi of trails at Allegany State Park. Cattaraugus County Tourism's Web site lists trail access points. You may also snowmobile in the Darien Lakes, Fort Niagara, Lake Erie, Letchworth, and Long Point state parks.

🏂 **Snowmobiling Cattaraugus County Tourism** ☎ 800/331-0543 ⊕ www.enchantedmountains.info. **Chautauqua County Visitors Bureau** ✉ Chautauqua In-

stitution Welcome Center, Rte. 394, Chautauqua 14722 ☎ 800/242-4569 ⊕ www.
tourchautauqua.com.

TRAIN TRAVEL
Amtrak connects Buffalo and Niagara Falls with the Finger Lakes, central New York, Albany, the Hudson Valley, and New York City. In Albany you may switch to Adirondacks-bound trains.

🚆 **Amtrak** ☎ 800/872-7245 ⊕ www.amtrak.com

TRANSPORTATION AROUND WESTERN NEW YORK
Public transportation is limited in the region, even between cities, and travel between villages is next to impossible without a car. In Niagara Falls most major sites are clustered in a walkable area around the falls. Downtown Buffalo is also a good place to explore on foot; traveling from neighborhood to neighborhood is best by car, however.

VISITOR INFORMATION
🚩 **General Seaway Trail** ✉ W. Main St., Sackets Harbor 13685 ☎ 315/646-1000 or 800/732-9298 ⊕ www.seawaytrail.com.

🚩 **Greater Niagara Buffalo Niagara Convention & Visitors Bureau** ✉ 617 Main St., Suite 200, Buffalo 14203 ☎ 800/283-3256 ⊕ www.buffalocvb.org. **Chamber of Commerce of the Tonawandas** ✉ 15 Webster St., North Tonawanda 14120 ☎ 716/692-5120 ⊕ www.the-tonawandas.com. **Genesee County Chamber of Commerce** ☎ 585/343-7440 or 800/622-2686 ⊕ www.geneseeny.com. **Grand Island Chamber of Commerce** ✉ 1980 Whitehaven Rd., Grand Island 14072 ☎ 716/773-3651 ⊕ www.gichamber.org. **Greater East Aurora Chamber of Commerce** ✉ 431 Main St., East Aurora 14052 ☎ 716/652-8444 or 800/441-2881 ⊕ www.eanycc.com. **Greater Niagara Region of New York State** ⊕ www.greaterniagarausa.com. **Niagara Tourism & Convention Corp.** ⊕ 345 3rd St., Suite 605, Niagara Falls 14303 ☎ 716/282-8992 or 800/338-7890 ⊕ www.niagara-usa.com. **Orleans County Tourism Agency** ☎ 585/589-3198 or 800/724-0314 ⊕ www.orleansny.com/tourism. **Wyoming County Tourist Promotion Agency** ✉ 30 N. Main St., Castile 14427 ☎ 800/839-3919 ⊕ www.wyomingcountyny.com.

🚩 **Chautauqua-Allegheny Cattaraugus County Tourism** ☎ 800/331-0543 ⊕ www.enchantedmountains.info. **Chautauqua County Visitors Bureau** ✉ Chautauqua Institution Welcome Center, Rte. 394, Chautauqua 14722 ☎ 800/242-4569 ⊕ www.tourchautauqua.com. **Chautauqua Wine Trail** ⊕ www.chautauquawinetrail.org. **Discover Southwest NY** ⊕ www.discoversouthwestny.com. **Ellicottville Chamber of Commerce & Visitor Center** ⌂ Box 456, Ellicottville 14731 ☎ 800/349-9099 ⊕ www.ellicottvilleny.com. **Salamanca Area Chamber of Commerce** ✉ 26 Main St., Salamanca 14779 ☎ 716/945-2034 ⊕ www.salamancaofc.homestead.com. **Westfield Chamber of Commerce** ✉ 27 E. Main St., Westfield 14787 ☎ 716/326-4000 ⊕ www2.cecomet.net/chamber/.

UNDERSTANDING
NEW YORK

NEW YORK STATE AT A GLANCE

THE BIG APPLE AND BEYOND

CHRONOLOGY

NEW YORK STATE AT A GLANCE

Fast Facts

Nickname: The Empire State
Capital: Albany
Motto: Excelsior
State song: "I Love New York," words and music by Steve Karmen
State bird: Bluebird
State flower: Rose
State tree: Sugar maple
Administrative divisions: 62 counties
Entered the Union: July 26, 1788
Population: 18.5 million
Population density: 375 per square mi

Median age: 36.5
Infant mortality rate: 6.3 deaths per 1,000 births
Literacy: 24% of adults have some trouble with everyday reading demands
Ethnic groups: White 61%, Hispanic 16%, black 15%, Asian 6%, other 2%
Religion: Catholic 38%, Christian 16% (other than Christian groups listed here), unaffiliated 14%, Baptist 7%, Methodist 6%, other 4%, Jewish 5%, Muslim 2%, Buddhist 1%

Geography & Environment

Land area: 47,224 square mi
Coastline: 358 mi along Atlantic Ocean and Long Island Sound, 8,778 mi total lake shoreline
Terrain: Soft hills and valleys, some with considerable depth and height, and four mountain ranges (with Mt. Marcy, at 5,344 feet, the state's highest point); more than 6,000 ponds, lakes, and reservoirs, and 70,000 mi of rivers and streams. The St. Lawrence River and Lake Ontario are along the north border, Lake Erie is on the west border, and Lake Champlain is on the northeast border. Southeastern edge of the state is coastal and flat, with Long Island and the five boroughs of New York City.
Islands: Fire Island, Long Island, Manhattan, Shelter Island, Staten Island, Thousand Islands
Natural resources: Crushed stone, salt, sand, zinc, dolomite
Natural hazards: Flooding throughout the state caused by slow-moving storms and snowmelt, thunderstorms, and, along the Atlantic coast, hurricanes

Nothing could be more beautiful than our passage down the Hudson . . . The change, the contrast, the ceaseless variety of beauty, as you skim from side to side, the liquid smoothness of the broad mirror which reflects the scene, and most of all, the clear bright air through which you look at it; all this can only be seen and believed by crossing the Atlantic . . . The magnificent boldness of the Jersey shore on the one side, and the luxurious softness of the shady lawns on the other, with the vast silvery stream that flows between them, altogether form a picture which may well excuse a traveller for saying, once and again, that the Hudson River can be surpassed in beauty by none on the outside of Paradise.

–Frances Trollope

Economy

GSP: $826.5 billion
Per capita income: $36,043
Unemployment: 6.9%
Workforce: 9.2 million

Debt: $111 billion
Major industries: Agriculture, apparel, chemicals, computer equipment, electrical equipment, finance, food

products, machinery, manufacturing, optical instruments, paper, services, transportation equipment
Agricultural products: Apples, cherries, dairy, grapes, maple syrup, onions, pears, potatoes, strawberries, wine
Exports: $470 billion

Major export products: Dairy products, feed grains, fruits, industrial machinery and computers, live animals and red meats, primary metal products, scientific and measuring instruments, transportation equipment, vegetables

Did You Know?

• Dairy cows are New York State's biggest agricultural earners. In 2003 they produced 12.2 billion pounds of milk, valued at $1.55 billion—half of the state's agricultural revenue. New York is the third-largest U.S. producer of dairy goods.

• The St. Lawrence Seaway allows ships as large as 730 feet in length to travel from the Atlantic Ocean along the northern border of New York to such inland ports as Chicago, Milwaukee, and Duluth. Iron ore, wheat, and coal are the most common cargoes carried on the Seaway today, which can stay navigable between mid-April and mid-December.

• A cable that stretches across Long Island Sound can transmit enough energy to power 100,000 homes. During New York's blackout in the summer of 2003, a federal order put the cable into operation, with generators in Connecticut powering homes across the water.

• At 641 mi long, the New York State Thruway is the longest toll road in the United States. A drive from one end to the other costs $14.70.

• New York's Genesee, Niagara, and Oswego rivers are on a short list of rivers in the world that flow south to north.

• The first railroad in America spanned the 11 mi between Albany and Schenectady.

• New York was the first state to require that vehicles have license plates.

THE BIG APPLE AND BEYOND

IF THE NAME "NEW YORK" brings to mind images of skyscrapers, Broadway, subways, and round-the-clock activity, what you're really thinking about is New York City, the frenzied tail that wags the statewide dog. With its bright lights and dark corners, this thriving and frantic metropolis reigns as a national and world capital in everything from fashion and food to culture and business, and often seems to eclipse the rest of the state, whose name it shares.

Many say they want to avoid or ignore the city, but 35 million people visit it every year. And many of these visitors and others find, sometimes by accident, that there's plenty more to New York than that fabulous city at the mouth of the Hudson River.

As a whole, New York State embodies some of the best that nature, and humans, have to offer. In addition to Gotham in the south, there's another spectacular tourist attraction to the west: Niagara Falls. These top two sites can give you a thunderous introduction to a state that defies labels but somehow can't escape them. Venture away from the well known and you are likely to make some wonderful discoveries.

The natural spectacles range from the soft-sand beaches of Long Island and the high peaks of the Adirondacks to the sparkling waters of the Finger Lakes and the mysterious hills and valleys of the Catskills.

Sports lovers have the opportunity to see the best, and sometimes the worst, of professional athletics at all levels. Arenas, tracks, and museums throughout the state honor and cater to the best in horse racing, baseball, soccer, fly-fishing, auto racing, and other pastimes.

Arts and literature lovers enjoy the museums and shows of Manhattan, the mansions and gardens of the Hudson River Valley, and the cultural offerings of the Chautauqua Institution, just to name a few.

Thrill seekers can ride one of the tallest roller coasters in the East at Darien Lake, climb into a raft and tumble through the rapids of North Country rivers, and explore caverns and cliffs in the Catskills.

New York's state motto is "Excelsior," meaning "ever upward," and things certainly do seem to go up in New York. Cynics point to the taxes, unemployment, and a general sense of misery based on observations of city sidewalks and rural shacks. They also might argue that "upward" hardly describes the state of manufacturing and farming in New York, since both industries have lost thousands of jobs. Still, agriculturally the state holds its own, as a leading supplier of apples, cherries, grapes, maple syrup, onions, sweet corn, and dairy products. The 37,000 or so farms in New York use about a quarter of the state's land (nearly 7.7 million acres) in the production of food.

Internal contradictions abound. The state has city ponds and churning waterfalls, urban sprawl and virgin wilderness, fabulous wealth and numbing poverty, crystal-clear lakes and murky rivers, rednecks and blue bloods, engineering triumphs and bureaucratic boondoggles. The Empire State boasts both the nation's largest city and the biggest wilderness area east of the Mississippi.

The state's tensions are widely documented. The upstate-downstate rift is the best known, and it's nearly as old as the hills that give upstate New York so much of its character. In the early 19th century New York City politicians scorned a plan to build what was to become the Erie Canal. Little did they know that the project would catapult the city from an also-ran position on the East Coast to the great center of commerce that it became in the 1800s.

Political and racial tensions sometimes eclipse the geographical ones, but conflict seems to be part of the state's history, for better or worse. After all, about 30% of all the battles during the Revolutionary War were fought in New York, which was considered then, as now, a key strategic part of the emerging nation. If you really pay attention, with eyes and ears, you will pick up on the geographical, political, economic, and cultural diversity that makes New York such an engaging place to live in and to visit.

History

About 32 years after Christopher Columbus reached land in the Western Hemisphere, Giovanni da Verrazano slipped into what was to become New York Harbor. He and the droves of Europeans and others who followed were relative latecomers. People had roamed the woodlands, shorelines, and glens for thousands of years. At the time of European exploration, the Algonquins lived in much of the Hudson Valley, on Manhattan, and on Long Island, whereas the Iroquois ruled the west.

Thanks to Henry Hudson's travels and claims in the early 1600s, the Dutch occupied the area and called it New Netherland. In 1626, just over a 100 years after Verrazano spotted New York, Peter Minuit, the first Dutch governor of the colony, purchased the island of Manhattan from the Algonquins for $24 worth of tools and trinkets. Only 38 years later the British acquired the land and changed the name to New York. The Dutch influence lingers in some place-names in the Hudson Valley, such as Kinderhook ("children's corner") and any place whose name ends in "-kill" ("stream").

The colony played a key role in the American Revolution, with nearly a third of the battles fought on New York soil. The area's importance, however, really rose with the development of the Erie Canal in the mid-1800s and New York City's phenomenal growth as a center of commerce. That, in turn, led to its natural place as a port-of-choice for millions of immigrants from Europe and other parts of the world who poured into this country at the end of the 19th century and beginning of the 20th century.

New York City and many areas in the state continue to draw immigrants (legal and illegal) from other nations. Despite economic problems, such as New York City's financial crisis of the 1970s and the Wall Street slump of the 1990s, the city and state continue to play key roles in the nation's life—financially, socially, politically, and artistically.

CHRONOLOGY

1524   Giovanni da Verrazano is the first European to step on New York soil

1570   Mohawk, Oneida, Onondaga, Cayuga, and Seneca nations form the Iroquois League (which the Tuscarora Nation later joins in 1722)

1609   Henry Hudson sails up the river that will bear his name and claims the area for the Dutch

1624   Fort Orange (eventually renamed Albany) is established as the first permanent European settlement in New York

1626   Governor Peter Minuit buys Manhattan Island from the Lenape Indians for the equivalent of about $24

1664   New Amsterdam (Holland) becomes New York (Great Britain)

1777   American colonists defeat the British in the Battle of Saratoga

1779   The military campaign by American generals Clinton and Sullivan in central and western portions of the state disperses Iroquois

1784   While touring the state, George Washington refers to New York as "the seat of the empire," a statement that is believed to have spawned the state's nickname, the Empire State

1788   New York becomes the nation's 11th state

1792   New York Stock Exchange starts with a meeting of two dozen brokers beneath a tree on Wall Street

1802   U.S. Military Academy is built in West Point

1807   The first successful steamship run (Robert Fulton's *Clermont*) ends in Albany

1825   The Erie Canal opens

1826   Joseph Smith meets Angel Moroni in Palmyra, the beginning of Mormonism

1827   Slavery is abolished in New York

1848   The first conference on women's rights is held in Seneca Falls

1872   Chautauqua Institution begins as a vacation school for Sunday-school teachers

1886   New York City hosts its first ticker-tape parade to celebrate the dedication of the Statue of Liberty

1891   Carnegie Hall opens in New York City

1892   Adirondack Park is established

1898   The Bronx, Brooklyn, Manhattan, Queens, and Staten Island become the five boroughs of New York City

1898   Statue of Frederick Douglass goes up in Rochester. It's the first statue in the nation to honor an African American

1900 First subway tunnel built in New York City

1901 President William McKinley is shot dead while attending the Pan-American Exposition in Buffalo

1930 The nation's first supermarket (King Kullen) opens on Long Island

1939 National Baseball Hall of Fame opens in Cooperstown

1947 Levittown, Long Island, is created as the nation's first instant suburb. It contains 17,400 houses

1952 Construction of the United Nations headquarters in New York City is completed

1969 Woodstock Music Festival is held near Bethel

1969 New York City's first automatic bank teller appears

1980 Lake Placid hosts Winter Olympics

1993 Terrorists set off explosions in garage of New York City's World Trade Center. Six people die and more than 1,000 are injured

2000 Playing against the New York Mets and after a win in 1999, the New York Yankees win their 26th World Series. The Yankees make it into the series again in 2001 and 2003, but get beaten both years

2001 On September 11, hijackers steer two commercial jets into the World Trade Center's two towers, setting each ablaze and killing nearly 3,000 people. The towers crumble and five outlying buildings are damaged

2003 In August, a major blackout hits most of the state as well as much of the East Coast

2004 Republican National Convention is held in New York City.

INDEX

NOTES

NOTES

FODOR'S KEY TO THE GUIDES

America's guidebook leader publishes guides for every kind of traveler.
Check out our many series and find your perfect match.

FODOR'S GOLD GUIDES
America's favorite travel-guide series offers the most detailed insider reviews of hotels, restaurants, and attractions in all price ranges, plus great background information, smart tips, and useful maps.

COMPASS AMERICAN GUIDES
Stunning guides from top local writers and photographers, with gorgeous photos, literary excerpts, and colorful anecdotes. A must-have for culture mavens, history buffs, and new residents.

FODOR'S CITYPACKS
Concise city coverage in a guide plus a foldout map. The right choice for urban travelers who want everything under one cover.

FODOR'S EXPLORING GUIDES
Hundreds of color photos bring your destination to life. Lively stories lend insight into the culture, history, and people.

FODOR'S TRAVEL HISTORIC AMERICA
For travelers who want to experience history firsthand, this series gives in-depth coverage of historic sights, plus nearby restaurants and hotels. Themes include the Thirteen Colonies, the Old West, and the Lewis and Clark Trail.

FODOR'S POCKET GUIDES
For travelers who need only the essentials. The best of Fodor's in pocket-size packages for just $9.95.

FODOR'S FLASHMAPS
Every resident's map guide, with dozens of easy-to-follow maps of public transit, restaurants, shopping, museums, and more.

FODOR'S CITYGUIDES
Sourcebooks for living in the city: thousands of in-the-know listings for restaurants, shops, sports, nightlife, and other city resources.

FODOR'S AROUND THE CITY WITH KIDS
Up to 68 great ideas for family days, recommended by resident parents. Perfect for exploring in your own backyard or on the road.

FODOR'S HOW TO GUIDES
Get tips from the pros on planning the perfect trip. Learn how to pack, fly hassle-free, plan a honeymoon or cruise, stay healthy on the road, and travel with your baby.

FODOR'S LANGUAGES FOR TRAVELERS
Practice the local language before you hit the road. Available in phrase books, cassette sets, and CD sets.

KAREN BROWN'S GUIDES
Engaging guides—many with easy-to-follow inn-to-inn itineraries—to the most charming inns and B&Bs in the U.S.A. and Europe.

SEE IT GUIDES
Illustrated guidebooks that include the practical information travelers need, in gorgeous full color. Thousands of photos, hundreds of restaurant and hotel reviews, prices, and ratings for attractions all in one indispensable package. Perfect for travelers who want the best value packed in a fresh, easy-to-use, colorful layout.

OTHER GREAT TITLES FROM FODOR'S
Baseball Vacations, The Complete Guide to the National Parks, Family Vacations, Golf Digest's Places to Play, Great American Drives of the East, Great American Drives of the West, Great American Vacations, Healthy Escapes, National Parks of the West, Skiing USA.

At bookstores everywhere.   www.fodors.com/books